Differential Diagnosis and Treatment in Social Work

Differential Diagnosis and Treatment in Social Work

THIRD EDITION

Edited by **Francis J. Turner**

With a Foreword by
Florence Hollis

THE FREE PRESS
A Division of Macmillan Publishing Co., Inc.
New York

Collier Macmillan Publishers
London

The Free Press
A Division of Macmillan Publishing Co., Inc.
866 Third Avenue, New York, N. Y. 10022

Collier Macmillan Canada, Inc.

Library of Congress Catalog Card Number: 82-48390

Printed in the United States of America

printing number
3 4 5 6 7 8 9 10

Library of Congress Cataloging in Publication Data
Main entry under title:

Differential diagnosis and treatment in social work.

  Includes bibliographical references and index.
   1. Social case work—Addresses, essays, lectures.
2. Psychiatric social work—Addresses, essays, lectures.
3. Medical social work—Addresses, essays, lectures.
I. Turner, Francis Joseph   [DNLM:
1. Diagnosis, Differential. 2. Social work. 3. Social
work, Psychiatric.   WM 58 D569]
HV43.D56 1983   361.3   82-48390
ISBN 0-02-932990-6

To Bert, brother and colleague
JUNE 17, 1935–JUNE 22, 1957

Contents

VASECTOMY

Foreword

How STRANGE it is that not until a half century after the publication of *Social Diagnosis* does a book appear in the social work field addressing itself specifically to the relationship between differential diagnosis and treatment! Over fifty years ago—in 1917—Mary Richmond wrote *Social Diagnosis*, a book dedicated to the then new idea that the social worker, like the physician, must think diagnostically, endeavoring to understand the nature of the disorder with which he is dealing in order to know how to alleviate it. This book so impressed practitioners that for many years it was a text, as if the subject of diagnosis were now understood and social casework could move on to concentrate on problems of treatment methodology. Even in the thirties, when psychoanalytic knowledge was permeating social casework, attention was directed not to diagnostic groupings, but rather to general principles of treatment on the one hand and the specifics of individualization of treatment on the other. It was not until the midforties that attention again turned to diagnosis, and the work started by Miss Richmond moved forward with concentration on the psychological component of diagnosis, often designated the "clinical diagnosis." Diagnosis had not been lost sight of during these intervening years, but the principles of social study and diagnosis presented by Miss Richmond seemed to provide sufficient guidelines for the type of diagnostic thinking upon which treatment was based until the midforties. This was a highly individualized approach with emphasis on idiosyncratic life happenings that could account for the problem under treatment.

With the emergence of the clinical diagnosis, attention began to turn to elements in personality which characterize some people to a greater extent than others, thus distinguishing a group of individuals who might respond in common ways to certain forms of treatment. It began to be recognized that knowledge of such groupings—of types of disorders, that is—could increase the ability of workers to fashion treatment more appropriately to the differentiated need of the individual. Futheremore, once such commonness was seen, knowledge could become cumulative and what was learned from the treatment of one individual could be put to the service of another suffering from a similar disability.

Dr. Turner's compilation is the first book to bring the results of this development to general attention and to provide the social worker a key to the diagnostically oriented articles of the past ten years. Not only is his selection of articles excellent, but the fact that he read virtually everything available in our English literature before making his selection means that this collection provides a reliable guide to the state of our current knowledge of work with differing diagnostic entities. Inevitably any other author would have made a somewhat different selection. I will leave it to the reviewers to comment on the merits of this and that inclusion or exclusion; Dr. Turner's choices seem excellent to me. His organization of the selections into the stages of human development, psychosocial pathology, physical handicaps, and sociocultural factors is logical and should enable the reader to locate easily material that will throw light on the difficulty about which he is seeking information. If no article is included which deals with the specific subject of concern, much may be learned from an article covering treatment of a related disorder.

In addition to Dr. Turner's contribution in making this material available, his Preface and the introductions to all of the major sections add greatly to the value of the book. I am strongly tempted to underscore some of his excellent points about diagnosis and about the education of the profession, but will content myself with urging you to read the Preface and the Part introductions with care. They contain many astute observations.

In the Part introductions Dr. Turner orients the reader to the writings in the area under consideration, briefly brings out important commonalities, and points to uncovered, or scantily covered, diagnostic areas. In the main, however, he allows the selections to speak for themselves. The coverage of the book is not meant to be exhaustive. The bibliographies within the individual selections will lead the reader to further references.

It is an important sign of the times that this book is addressed to group workers as well as to caseworkers and that in many categories material on group treatment is available. The extent to which these two social work methods supplement each other in treatment and the growing tendency for many workers to want to acquire some competence in both methods is one of the very interesting developments of the sixties. This book should contribute to the common knowledge of the two specialties.

A final contribution of the book upon which I should like to comment is its usefulness as a guide to further compilation of knowledge and to publication. As Dr. Turner notes, there is valuable information dealing with many diagnostic categories in agency records and reports which could be brought to light and published. This book can serve as a guide to prospective writers and to editors as to the gaps in our dianostic literature. It can also provide points of comparison against which the practitioner reader's experiences can be studied. Articles based on either similar or different experiences should be written. While controlled experimentation and replication is the ultimate task of knowledge building, practical replication occurs constantly in our day-by-day work. Small groups of similar cases can be studied and reported upon, thus providing cumulative information about different diagnostic groupings.

It is altogether appropriate that *Differential Diagnosis and Treatment in Social Work* should appear so soon after the fiftieth anniversary year of *Social Diagnosis*. Dr. Turner is indeed making a substantial contribution to the teaching and practice of social work.

Florence Hollis

SCHOOL OF SOCIAL WORK
COLUMBIA UNIVERSITY, NEW YORK

Preface to the Third Edition

IT SCARCELY SEEMS POSSIBLE that it is already time to write a preface to the third edition to this book; it is only a short time since the work for the second edition was completed. Yet it was necessary that the book be reedited. In the six years since the last edition much new material has appeared in social work literature. This material is important not just because it is new but because it reflects the dramatic expansion that is taking place in the professional literature in social work; an expansion not just in quantity but in quality, precision, and diversity. New journals have appeared, applications of the wide range of practice theories have been made to various diagnostic categories, new problems have been addressed, and new applications of methodologies have been developed.

The goals of the book remain the same as before. The first is to provide a resource to practitioners that will permit them to obtain some immediate information on the understanding and management of a wide spectrum of presenting situations and conditions met in today's practice. In addition it gives students an entrée to a comprehensive look at the dimensions of current practice.

The organizing concept of the book is that diagnosis remains the heart of practice. Diagnosis is built on knowledge of individual cases, classes of cases, and classes of components of the complexity of the biopsychosocial reality of our clients and the range of problems they bring to us for help.

If one uses the literature of a profession as a reliable reflector of the reality of the practice of that profession, then we can conclude that as our practice is becoming more complex the role of diagnosis is also becoming more important. As we continue to appreciate the necessity and the utility of precision in diagnosis, we are also learning that it is a highly complex process, much more complex than we have ever appreciated.

The long-standing criticism of a too structured approach to diagnosis that relied heavily on efforts to classify clients is rapidly lessening. We are all aware of the potential misuse of uni-category diasnoses but equally aware that one cannot responsibly practice without well-developed and well-tested systems of classification.

An important development in the use and standardization of classifications as an aid to practice is exemplified in the recently published *Diagnostic and Statistical Manual of Mental Disorders: Third Edition.** This book helps bring into focus a component of practice long a part of social work tradition, that is, the need for precision in diagnostic terminology, the need for a multi-axial approach to diagnosis, and the role of psychosocial stressors in understanding persons-in-situations. To what extent this approach to diagnosis will become standardized across professional lines is unclear. Whatever happens in this regard, the goal of that book is very close to the goal of this one.

As before, selection of articles was a difficult problem. In the original review of the literature for this edition several hundred articles were selected for possible inclusion. Narrowing this down to a manageable number was indeed difficult. Because of the richness and diversity of available material a subsequent edition of this book may have to consider the possibility of a separate volume for each of the five major headings.

Keeping the present edition to an acceptable size was a problem. There were so many excellent articles to be included and so many from the first volume that I wanted to retain. Finally the newer articles held preference over the older and diversity of topic over several articles on one topic. In the final selection 26 articles from the second edition were retained and 48 new articles included.

We were pleased to observe that there are many more articles being written from a group intervention perspective that deal with specific aspects of the diagnostic perspective. We were able to include some of these.

The same fivefold classification system has been maintained. The second edition added the category "Presenting Problems," which is included again with an expanded number of topics. As before, further work is needed in developing a classification scheme for presenting problems. Undoubtedly an important component of our assessment needs to be not only who the client is but what his reality is and how we make use of our knowledge of client as a person to deal with the aspect of reality for which help is wanted or indicated.

Few of the articles as yet are built on the formal analysis of data gathered to test hypotheses or to test our approach to treatment. For the most part they remain articles written from a practice wisdom basis, that is, built on the organized disciplined analysis of practice. Although there is a tendency to disparage these types of data, they are still essential to the building of a practice base that will permit us to develop and test the components of practice theory to which we aspire. Hence, even in the practice wisdom articles there is observed a strengthening analytic approach to practice and a disciplined commitment to knowledge building, rather than the arguments from authority that marked earlier articles.

Our writing continues to be uneven, in that some topics become fashionable

---

* *Diagnostic and Statistical Manual of Mental Disorders: Third Edition* (Washington D.C.: American Psychiatric Association, 1980).

at various points in time and get special attention. Deliberate effort was made not to reflect trends in the articles selected but to give as broad a basis to the selections as possible. Even in doing this it was necessary to omit some topics that are a part of practice. As will be noted in the Part introductions, we now have social-work-written articles on several topics which before we had scarcely addressed in the literature even though they were an important part of our practice.

Ours is a dynamic and growing profession, one that is facing with our colleagues in other professions the humbling awareness of the deficiencies in our knowledge and the limits of our interventions. But this very awareness draws us on to increase the precision of our understanding of those persons we serve, an understanding that will ensure that, as effectively as possible, we make available to them the range of knowledge, skills, resources, and services that make up our armamentarium of practice.

Francis J. Turner

SUDBURY, ONTARIO, MARCH 21, 1982

Preface to the Second Edition

IT IS AN INTERESTING EXPERIENCE to write a preface for a new edition of a book, almost ten years after the work on the first edition was carried out. The task appears to divide itself into two components: first, there is the need to explain why the book is being republished, that is, why it is still seen as being a useful contribution to the profession at this time; second, if the book is viewed as still being useful there is the need to explain why it has been altered in the new edition. In the original edition of the book there were 62 articles and in this new one 71, of which 41 are new.

Why the re-edition? I am just as convinced today as before that this type of book provides a necessary aid to the clinical social worker committed to providing efficient and responsible services to clients. Because of the structure of our present delivery system most social workers carry a highly diverse caseload. We have not as yet committed ourselves to a highly structured specialty system. At the same time our periodical literature in clinical practice remains a principal source of new practice ideas and trends. But the periodical literature contained in the better known journals is not easily available to many of our colleagues. Further, with the emergence of several new journals in North America and Europe within the last decade, the question of accessibility becomes even more difficult. Hence the necessity to extract from the literature a series of articles around a common theme. Clearly the question of the utility of collections of articles as compared to independent authorship cannot be ignored. In several of the reviews of the first edition, this question was raised and the emergence of still another collection was decried. In my own view this is not an either/or situation. The present state of practice requires both kinds of books; the collection can present a broad spectrum of current practice issues from a variety of viewpoints, while the single-authorship book presents a longer range, more focused presentation. Both are needed in today's practice.

As before, the underlying unifying concept for the book is the diagnostic component of practice. I am no less convinced of its importance in today's practice even though my perception of its form and content has altered slightly.

Between the time the first edition appeared and the present, we have passed through a period where the whole existence of clinical practice was under attack. As a part of this storm of criticism questions of labeling, classification, and treatment based on diagnosis were severely criticized. Now that this phenomenon appears to be waning, once again we can turn to further efforts at making our work more precise and effective.

I mentioned that my perception of the form and content of the diagnostic component of practice has altered. Let me comment on this. I appreciate more than before that the concept of diagnosis is a much more complex process and activity than has been acknowledged by our field. Although we have often said diagnosis should never, and was never intended to be uni-dimensional, I think we have nevertheless projected a view that it was a more easily manageable phenomenon with rather clear boundaries than in fact it is.

I began to appreciate this misperception about five years ago. At that time, I observed that a common theme was emerging from students I met in many schools and at many levels. In talking with them it was clear that, although professional schools had done a good job in developing the concept of diagnosis and helping them identify with it, what we had not done was to teach them precisely what to do with the concept, that it, the content of a particular diagnosis. It was then that I became less sure that we are as comfortable about the "how" of diagnosis as our literature implied. Thus, I have become convinced there is still much more conceptualizing and experimentation to be done before we can begin to reach some common ground on the operational components of diagnosis in social work intervention.

In no way does this imply that I am less convinced of the need for greater specificity and precision in our practice. As long as we are committed to the value that what we do for, with, and to clients is somehow related to our knowledge about them, we must continue to connect our perceptions of persons and our professional actions with them.

Clearly, the expanding number of thought systems that are influencing current practice and the thrust to a multi-method form of practice have made our search for more precise diagnostic efforts more difficult. When these two developments are taken into account, in conjunction with the already wide array of significant factors in a client's inner and outer life affecting his functioning, the diversity of services we have to offer, and the wide range of clients' requests and expectations, the search for more precise diagnoses appears almost futile.

There is one other way in which I have modified my perception of diagnosis; this concerns its ever changing nature. I think we have always been aware that diagnosis is a fluid concept but nevertheless have somehow conveyed through the literature and to each other that there was a fixed quality to the fact of diagnosis. That is, we have always said we had to alter it as the case developed, but usually I think we meant that any such alterations would be minimal. I am increasingly persuaded by the spiral concept of diagnosis as portrayed by Gordon Hearn in his writings on social systems.*

Nevertheless, difficult as it is, humbly we must continue the search for unifying concepts that will help to bring order to the complexity. But, at the same time, in our search for unifying concepts we must not overlook the knowledge to be gained by focusing on the specifics of our clients and their situations. Thus, for example, there is still much to be learned about how to deal with the suicidal component of some clients. We can all benefit by improving our techniques in dealing with the psychotic aspects of other clients with whom we work even if our overall focus with them is not related to their symptoms. We know we can be more sensitive and responsive to an addicted client when we have the accumulated knowledge, experience and perceptions of our colleagues with similar situations and behaviors.

Thus, in this second edition, as before, I have sought out, from the literature of the last ten years, articles that combined a focus on the understanding of a particular facet of human behavior, healthy or ill, and included related practice-based suggestions aimed at bringing about changes in the identified symptom or problem. Many have found this kind of information helpful in their practice.

As before, I utilized the periodical journals as the principal source of material. In so doing I am aware that there is much unpublished material that exists, although access to it is limited. Again, I found selection difficult. Certainly there was much more material from which to choose. My overall opinion is that the quality of solid clinical articles is improving. One of the new problems in selecting articles this time was the fact that some of our articles are becoming too precise for the goal of this kind of book. Thus, one article might deal with the interconnection between two concepts interrelated in a particular kind of case. Such articles were judged to be beyond the objectives I have for this book and thus, for the most part, were not used.

Once again, I observed that our writings have been uneven with some topics receiving much attention and others very little. I will comment more on this in the introduction to each section. As before, I had hoped to include more articles written from a group focus. A lack of such articles had been one of the criticisms of the first edition. Unfortunately, with the addition of more topics and a new section, I was not able to use all the excellent articles which I located. Some articles written from a one-to-one treatment focus were chosen because the diagnostic component was judged to be stronger, not because of a preference for this modality over groups. Several times, throughout the literature search, I wondered if it might be better to begin to prepare a companion volume that dealt only with group intervention with the same categories of client phenomena, rather than try and mix the two types of treatment.

Family treatment articles presented a different problem. A vast amount of family therapy literature exists, as we all know. Interestingly, much of it dealt

---

* *Social Work Treatment,* Ed. F. J. Turner (New York: Free Press, 1974), p. 350.

with particular aspects of family treatment or very precise components of family functioning too specific for the kinds of general diagnostic clusters I had selected. Thus, there are few specific family therapy articles included.

As before, I retained the same fourfold division of articles with the addition of a fifth section entitled "Presenting Problems." I had resisted including such a section in the first edition, but have since decided it gives a fuller profile of the significant components of diagnosis. Thus in practice, in addition to considering the stage and maturation of the person, his psychological makeup and functioning, his physical health, and his socio-cultural milieu, we are also interested in the kind of situation he or she presents to us. Again, this could not include full coverage but, rather, an overview of some of the prevalent presenting situations we meet in our current practice.

One of the difficulties in deciding about including new articles was the concomitant one of deciding which ones to exclude from the original group. This was difficult. I did not want to assume that more recent articles were better than older ones. Yet it was apparent that in some categories more recent articles did give a richer perspective of interventions and expanded diagnostic thinking. This was not always the case and at times the original older article was retained, even with the availability of many more recent ones.

There was much less difficulty about authorship. In the first edition I apologized for using social work authorship as a criterion of selection. This was not necessary this time; almost invariably the social-work-written articles were the preferred ones from the viewpoint of quality and the book's objectives. Not only has the content of social work clinical writing improved, but so has the format of the articles. For the most part, the new articles have richer footnoes and bibliographies than the earlier articles. These should provide an additional resource to the reader.

Inevitably, our professional writing goes through repeating series of fads and, hence, some topics are very well covered in the literature while others are scarcely mentioned. At times the decision was which article was to be selected from ten or more and in other situations it was difficult to find a single article.

One of the criticisms of the first edition was the extent to which it reflected an ego psychology orientation. Although this did reflect my own primary orientation this is only a partial explanation. This is where the literature was in 1966. But this too has changed. I was pleased to note that the specific diagnostic articles that make up this book are to an increasing extent trying to reflect a multitheory base. This, of course, is good for the profession, but difficult for planning a book such as this, as it introduces a new variable and a new challenge for choice.

As before, my hope is that we are still actively committed to a search for making the diagnostic component of practice more rigorous, our diagnostic categories more precise, the therapeutic implications from them more interdependent, and outcomes more effective and predictable.

Francis J. Turner

WILFRID LAURIER UNIVERSITY,
FACULTY OF SOCIAL WORK

Preface to the First Edition

THE PRIMARY GOAL of this book is to help social work practitioners provide more effective treatment to their clients. Obviously such a goal cannot be attained in a total manner; it requires that one segment of the therapeutic process be selected as a substructure. I have chosen to utilize the diagnostic process as a focal point. This segment was chosen because, on the one hand, it is so crucial to effective treatment and, on the other, it has been a weak point in our practice. The method I have chosen is to bring together in four parts a series of articles from the professional literature, each of which deals with a specific diagnostic variable and the resultant treatment implications.

To say that we are living in an age where quantities of available knowledge are rapidly expanding is already a cliché. Such knowledge expansion, with the accompanying proliferation of writings, creates serious problems for practitioners in all disciplines. Social workers in agencies are well aware that much has been written and is being written of import to their day-to-day practice activities. They are also most aware of the difficulty in maintaining anything more than a fleeting contact or haphazard sampling of what is available. Such sampling is often more anxiety provoking than satisfying, as the little reading and formal studying that is possible clearly alerts them to the quantities of material which perforce are left untouched. Concomitant with the awareness of quantity is the realization that all that is written is not necessarily gold; much valuable time can be wasted in locating and reading material which in fact is not as useful as some other might have been.

Someday in the not too distant future, an agency social worker wishing to know quickly and succinctly what has been written about the treatment of a particular kind of client will turn to the agency data-retrieval unit. This in turn will be electronically connected with a national centralized programed library. In a few minutes he will receive a "print-out" of the requested data. As yet such resources, while theoretically possible, are beyond the scope, structure, and resources of our agencies. For the present, agency practitioners wishing to obtain such data must turn to the literature. This is not an easy task. Rarely is there time available to undertake the required search, presuming there are library resources upon which to call. In the meantime books such as this are required.

Most social practitioners are well acquainted with the major textbooks in individual and group treatment. These have tended to be treatises on treatment in general rather than the specific. Discussions of treatment of specific kinds of problems or diagnostic entities have largely been carried out in individual articles scattered through some 20 to 25 journals and going back 30 to 35 years. Thus, at best, a practitioner can only have a superficial knowledge of the precise type of practice-oriented literature available to him. Because of this, the tendency has been to teach and practice from general rather than specific knowledge and understanding about pepole and how to treat them. This has been effective, and I believe the majority of our clients have been helped to achieve improved psychosocial functioning as a result of the treatment they have received. When practitioners tend to operate from an intuitive and an *ad hoc* framework, it is clear that diagnosis in anything more than a diffuse manner is unnecessary. Effective as is such a general treatment style, a higher level of competence can be achieved when treatment is consciously and selectively based on a detailed diagnosis of the client. It is my conviction that many social workers would greatly improve the quality of their treatment if experience-based observations and discussions of the treatment implications of diagnostic entities found in the literature of the last few years were readily available to them.

The danger of bringing together articles dealing with specific diagnostic entities or variables is that this collection could be misused. There is the possibility of its being seen as a shortcut, as a "How to do it" book. The prospect of having a resource which will lay out a formula of therapy or a prescription of technique for each diagnositic entity is an attractive one. Unfortunately this is not such a book; anyone who tried to use it in this way would only be disappointed. What it does aspire to achieve is to give therapists some anchoring concepts, some experience-based bench marks, some specific analyses of points of theory which will give direction and basic structure to the treatment of clients. The test of the therapist's skill is a dual one: first, to understand how much his client is like other clients of the same type and thus utilize what the profession has said about them; second, to understand how he is different from all other clients thus necessitating a peculiar combination of therapeutic skills most appropriate to him in his individuality. To follow slavishly a prescribed formulation of treatment because the literature suggests it makes the therapist a technician (and a poor one at that) rather than a professional. Whether this latter is a more serious detriment to treatment than working from no diagnosis is a moot point.

The book is designed to serve as a resource to be used in combination with the "practice wisdom" of the practitioner. It is primarily seen as important for the person in the multifunctioned agency who is called upon to serve a wide range of presenting problems and client types; the practitioner in the small agency and the private practitioner, who does not have a well-endowed agency library and readily available colleague consultation; the student and the teacher. It perhaps won't be as useful to persons in more specialized settings. It is presumed that in such settings there would be a concentration of literature appropriate to the field, for example, the treatment of marital problems. The articles chosen for the book on this former topic or on any topic can only be seen as an overview or a viewpoint rather than an exhaustive treatment or the final word. To aid in a broader coverage than one or two articles could give, bibliographies, wherever present, have been included. Thus a person interested in searching for additional information on a particular syndrome or diagnostic variable is given some leads for further reading.

This book contains a predominance of articles on individual treatment. Originally I had hoped to locate an article dealing with the individual treatment of each topic and another dealing with group treatment. This was not always possible. In the literature there have been more individual treatment-based articles than group-based articles. It is hoped that in the future, there will be more written accounts of appropriate group treatment with other client-types. In seeking group articles for each topic there is a presumed implication that every diagnostic variable lends itself to some form of group treatment. This may be incorrect.

Throughout the articles there can be seen a recurring theme. The social work practitioner of today must be a multiskilled person, comfortable in individual, joint, and group treatment, as well as a person skilled in educative and collaborative activities. This does not imply a generic method in the profession, but the necessity of multiskills, and these at a high degree of competence. Truly, this is a formidable challenge.

One of the unfortunate results of the gap between the professional literature and the mainstream of practice has been a tendency to devalue traditional knowledge. It seems fashionable in some segments of current thinking to suggest that much of our traditional theoretical orientation be scrapped and replaced by newer concepts and practice approaches. It is said that our psychodynamic approaches have failed and are unnecessary in understanding clients. Such presumptive thinking is only as valid as the evidence upon which it is based, and laudatory tributes to new approaches do not establish their validity. If the newer approaches to therapy are more effective than those presently used, then we must adopt them. Responsible professional behavior demands this. To make this comparison requires a full understanding and utilization of the old and the new. I raise this point because of a conviction that much of the disappointment in the results of treatment stems not from a fault in our theory and its applications but from a failure to utilize fully the rich amounts of data, knowledge, and skill accumulated over the years. One of the causes of this failure to tap effectively the rich resources of accumulated professional expertise in our profession has been our reliance on oral tradition and the reluctance to set out in an organized useful way what we know, what we do not know, what has been effective, and what has not.

A further purpose in planning this collection was to highlight the necessity of improved diagnostic habits among practitioners. Is not urging the importance of diagnosis to practitioners but a further example of preaching to the converted? In school and agency recent generations of social workers have been assailed with the triad of study, diagnosis, and treatment. Now every student learns early in his professional training that the unity of the therapeutic process is made up of these three elements. Why then emphasize diagnosis? It is because of a growing awareness of the divergence between our value commitment to the importance of diagnosis and the reality of our practice. Time and time again, records of social workers are examined without being able to locate within them a place where a diagnosis was formulated and set out, which the social worker then used to formulate treatment objectives and goals. That some form of diagnosis is made is indisputable; otherwise there could be no way to account for the large numbers of clients whose psychosocial functioning is markedly improved as the result of the therapist's activities and skills. The process of diagnosis evidently is operating, but the fact of diagnosis is lacking. Why should this be of concern? It is because without the availability of a concrete diagnosis there is no way to assess the effectiveness of our treatment except in a globular way. There is no way of correlating the various forms of social work intervention in relation to particular presenting diagnostic variables and assessing their outcome. There is no way of planfully and carefully improving our effectiveness with our clients. Until we can be more precise in declaring how we assess people and what therefore we choose to do with them and for them, our practice efficiency will remain static.

Why this divergence between fact and process? The answers to this are elusive and uncertain. It is easy to utilize the accustomed mutual recriminatory reflex and attribute this omission to a lack of desired professional behavior. This is too simple and obviously incorrect.

Part of the reason seems to be tied up in our strong commitment to the necessity of individualizing the client and maintaining nonjudgmental attitudes toward him. The process of working toward and from a precise, although flexible and evolving, diagnosis seems to evoke in some an emotional response that in some way the client is depersonalized through categorization and judged through opinion. There is also a fear that diagnosis somehow excludes the client. The thinking is as follows: Treatment in social work requires full involvement of the client; diagnosis is a professional assessment made by us not the client; therefore if we emphasize diagnosis we overlook the client. Obviously this is a misunderstanding of the process.

A lack of experience or perhaps of training also seems to be involved in this underemphasis of diagnosis. If there is a value-based reluctance to diagnose among practitioners, then it is to be expected that this is a skill which will not be given first-order priority. It is clear that if this skill is not acquired early in a professional career, it is increasingly difficult later to reorient oneself to it. I want to avoid overgeneralizing here; evidently many practitioners are highly skilled diagnosticians. The selections presented here demonstrate this.

Perhaps the most important explanation of this apparent gap in social work practice stems from the complex conceptual base from which we operate. The number of variables requiring assessment and the multitude of frameworks in which these can be assessed presents a formidable and, at times, seemingly overwhelming task for the practitioner.

Because there is not a single theory of psychosocial behavior which can serve as a unifying principle of practice, it is clear that the process of diagnosis must of necessity be a multifaceted one. Since in the diagnostic phase of treatment the therapist is bringing his professional judgment to bear on the information he has about the client, it is presumed that he has a framework in which he can order the data he has about the client and norms against which he can compare his client. In the complexity of our efforts to study our client in a biopsychosocial context, the process of synthesizing, interrelating, and then formulating a professional judgment about the client is indeed a monumental one. This should not deter us from attempting to do so even though we will never reach a point of complete satisfaction with our assessment of the situations with which we are confronted.

It has been implied at times that there is a danger in forming detailed diagnoses and then operating from them. Such a process, it is said, serves to make treatment too rigid by forming a "mind-set" toward the client. It is therefore better to keep our diagnosis flexible and open and permit the utilization of new understanding and perception of clients. It is true that a diagnosis must not become "locked in" so that we operate from it in an inflexible manner. To do this, of course, is a misuse of the diagnostic concept. Obviously, we are going to shift and clarify and make more precise and enrich our understanding of clients; this in turn will affect the goals and methods of treatment we set for and with them. In no way should this deter us from constantly striving to set out clearly our assessments of them. More treatment efforts are ineffective and more client and therapist time is used uneconomically when a diagnosis is not made than there are gains resulting from nondiagnosing in order to remain, "flexible and open."

No doubt part of the reluctance to diagnose has resulted from misuse to which nominal diagnoses have been put. I am referring especially to the unidimensional type in which a one-word or a one-expression classification is used. Such terms are used to explain the entire client and by implication dictate the format of treatment. For example, Miss R is a defective, Mr. J is schizophrenic, the B's are a multiproblem family.

On the one hand, if a diagnosis consists of only such labels it deserves to be discredited; on the other, these labels or classifications have their place in spite of the current tendency to disparage them. It is one of the principal assumptions of this collection of articles that we have not used them sufficiently, nor appreciated the extent to which they could help us consciously and deliberately to plan our treatment of clients. That they must be used in concert with many other classifications or labels is also a prior assumption. For effective treatment it is essential to understand the significance of the individual variables designated by the "labels" as well as the peculiar and unique combination of them as presented in the life and person of each client.

Classification in any professional activity must not become an end in itself. Whatever other purposes are served, the process should not and must be a pragmatic conceptual tool to assist us in applying the rich and extensive body of knowledge accumulated over the years. Viewing classificatory thinking about clients as a useful tool rather than an absolute helps us achieve some perspective about the classification systems presently available to us. It is clear that we do not have the last word in typologies of clients and the significant variables which must be assessed for effective treatment. Similarly, systems we presently use are far from perfect and complete. It is inevitable that most of them will be replaced as better understanding is achieved and as we become more skilled in integrating the multiple bodies of knowledge from which we draw our understanding of clients.

Our profession does not have a closed body of knowledge. Hence the concepts from which we operate are in constant flux. Theory is formulated in order to be replaced by better theory, better in the sense of helping us more effectively to achieve the treatment goals deemed desirable by the values of the profession. True as this is, we are not thereby excused from utilizing today what we already know.

A further reason for preparing this collection stemmed from a research interest. I was curious to explore the actual situation of the literature. I was aware that articles existed on some categories of clients; for example, we know that there has been a wealth of data on the character-disordered clients in recent years. I did not know how extensive the coverage might be. Have we clearly addressed in our literature the entire range of diagnostic variables customarily considered as being essential to effective treatment? Thus, beyond the wish to produce a book useful to practitioners, I was also interested in locating possible gaps in the literature, to point out strategic areas in which well-thought-out and carefully written articles are required. Some of the gaps which were located will be discussed in the introduction to each Part.

It was further hoped that by bringing together writings which set out our practice, concepts, and thinking in an easily accessible way, practitioners would be given an opportunity to test their "practice wisdom" against the opinions of their colleagues. In this way, we can assess what of our present thinking is still valid, what needs to be replaced with new insights, what can be refined by imaginative experimentation, and lastly, how our traditional understanding of clients can be enriched with new combinations of skills.

There was a further reason underlying this project. From time to time serious concerns have been exhibited as to the extent and diveresity of our knowledge. It is hoped that the breadth of areas addressed in the literature and contained here will help to give a better appreciation of the richness of our practice knowledge. On the basis of this idea, I tended to select articles written by social workers over those written by our colleagues in other disciplines. This was not done exclusively, of course, but presuming the articles were judged to be comparable and relevant to the design of the book, authorship by a social worker was used as a criterion of selection. I realize that this can contribute to professional insularity of which we have suffered more than enough. My own conviction is that we are growing to even greater interprofessional collaboration at all levels. To do this effectively and responsibly necessitates that we know our own field well. It is to aid in this latter task that I have kept the book more social work oriented. I do hope, though, that the collection of readings will be of interest and use to members of other disciplines. Of course, some articles written by members of other disciplines were included. Such articles were selected in which the treatment methods discussed were clearly appropriate for social workers. Thus, for example, an article dealing with the pharmacological treatment of depression would not be considered here, although one discussing some form of treatment utilizing relationship therapy would be. In the same way, it is also hoped that some increased appreciation will be gained as to the complexity of client functioning and responsible therapy. Recent conferences and writings have devoted some attention to the possibility of a generic method of practice to be taught to all aspirants to the profession. Much has been said about the necessity for others without comparable training to be able to do some of the direct work with clients presently assigned to social workers. Obviously there is some merit in examining these ideas. It is known that some understanding of treatment principles can be learned by others. It is also obvious to those directly in contact with clients that *more* rather than *less* specialized knowledge and skill is required to understand, involve, and treat many of the persons who come or are referred to us for treatment. There is a growing need for practitioners of a very high level of competence, who have clear and demonstrated diagnostic and treatment skills.

In searching for articles and in selecting them an effort was made to cover all the professional journals which include articles of import to social work practitioners, as well as standard social work journals. I am aware that a considerable amount of data was missed. For example, frequently papers are given at conferences, speeches given to meetings, and reports made to agencies which do not find their way into the mainstream of professional reading. Many of these are of high calibre and should be more widely available. It is hoped that this book will serve to draw out some of these and to encourage people to make their views more broadly known.

Selecting a framework useful for organizing the wide range of topics located in the literature was difficult. The goal was to utilize articles dealing with a specific diagnostic variable or entity rather than a type of service or problem. Thus adoption, unmarried mothers, deserted wives, separated couples, or other problem or service classifications were not employed. It is not always easy to distinguish between a diagnostic variable with specific treatment implications and a problem classification with a multitude of causes so that little or nothing can be said about generic treatment implications. There are some types of situations which are both a problem for treatment and a variable in diagnosis affecting the method of treatment selected. For example, although treatment of unmarried mothers was not included I did include delinquent youth.

I was particularly interested in finding articles which discussed the therapeutic considerations which result from a precise part of our total assessment of the client. It is assumed that all treatment must be geared to the whole person and not to particular parts of that person. It is also understood that there are dangers in categorizing a segment of a client's total psychosocial functioning and selecting our treatment approach specific to that segment. The danger is the well-known one of stereotyping. It is the extent to which the individual person can be partialized and yet treated as a whole that determines the effectiveness of our treatment methods. It is clear that selective treatment skills are necessary with schizophrenic clients, yet there are no schizophrenic clients as such. There are young, recently married, working class, rural-oriented, dull normal, Irish Catholic schizophrenic clients. Our treatment will be most effective when we can begin to understand the significance of each of these variables and whatever others are important and the peculiar combination of treatment methods most appropriate for different constellations of variables.

The variables which were finally chosen were divided into the traditional biopsychosocial triad based on a framework of human growth and development stages. Obviously it would be much easier for all if a unitary theory of psychosocial functioning could be devised so that clients would only have to be assessed along one dimension. Unfortunately, we are a long way from this and for a long time to come we have to live with the problems arising from the fact that societal man is a most complex creature. To try to understand and explain him in a manner that will permit us to aid him effectively to achieve improved psychosocial functioning will demand a complex conceptual framework. Complex as is our present conceptual basis of human behavior, undoubtedly there are other dimensions whose significance we probably do not realize, such as some genetic, cosmotic, or time-space factors.

No apologies are made for utilizing traditional psychodynamic headings. It is true that there has been recent serious questioning of the utility of classical dynamic interpretations of behavior. No one denies these present difficulties. They require constant critical re-examination in the light of current practice. This doesn't mean that they are to be ignored; for they have supplied and will continue to supply a framework in which people can be understood and, even more importantly, effectively treated. When they are replaced, as is the lot of all theory, it must be done by validated reliable concepts.

In selecting the headings under which topics were gathered there was an additional difficulty that must always be considered in diagnosis. This is the different levels of precision which exist between and among the various diagnostic variables. The presence or the lack of precision affects the degree of exactness with which we can discuss the treatment implications of each variable. For example, our division of clients by socioeconomic classes is a much less precise variable than the distinction between the types of neuroses or between character-disordered and borderline clients.

As our knowledge about these variables grows and more specificity is developed, our precision in formulating treatment goals and methods will grow also. It is hoped that much of what has been written in these pages will be replaced with further experiences, new concepts, and generalizations. It is hoped that the ideas presented in the various articles will be subjected to the keen scrutiny of our colleagues who are secure in their practice and rich in experience. It is hoped that imaginative, responsible experimentation will provide us with new insights and suggest new therapeutic approaches for consideration. In such instances the most useful form of replacement would be by means of scholarly articles building on the past and adding the new. I would hope most seriously that this book would have to be re-edited in a few years, on the basis of new insights, further writing, and an increased acceptance of our responsibility to translate our knowledge into a form readily accessible to our colleagues.

Much remains to be done in improving our diagnostic categories, in clarifying their definitions and descriptions, in specifying commonly accepted indicators, and in developing optimum treatment approaches. In the meantime the practitioner must use the knowledge presently available to him, fully aware of its inherent limitations. It is the purpose of this book to make one segment of this knowledge more accessible to him.

Francis J. Turner

GRADUATE SCHOOL OF SOCIAL WORK
WATERLOO LUTHERAN UNIVERSITY
WATERLOO, ONTARIO, CANADA

Acknowledgments

ONCE AGAIN I am most conscious of the extent to which the editing of a book such as this is dependent on the goodwill, cooperation, and assistance of many people.

As before a considerable part of the work was carried out by secretaries and students. I wish to express my great appreciation to Linda Mainville and Murielle Graff, secretaries, and Cindy Marshall, a senior student in Social Work at Laurentian University, for their loyal and efficient assistance.

I want also to thank the editors of the various journals and the authors of the articles for their promptness and cooperation in granting republishing permission. I appreciate greatly the continuing support of the staff of The Free Press and their encouragement to produce this third edition.

Finally the support of my family was essential in this endeavor. Joanne's collegial support, and Anne-Marie's, Sarah's, and Francis's filial support, were necessary and greatly appreciated. Now that everyone in the house has after-supper homework, it is easier to get to the desk at an early hour, instead of our earlier late night pattern.

Thanks to all.

F.J.T.

Contributors

The contributors are identified by the professional positions they held at the time the articles were first published.

Margaret G. Frank is Program Coordinator, Advanced Social Work Training Program in Teaching and Consultation on Child Treatment, Judge Baker Guidance Center, Boston, Massachusetts.

Leslie Rosenthal, M.S.W. is Chairman of the Group Analysis, Department of Manhattan, Center for Advanced Psychoanalytic Studies in New York.

Jennie Sage Norman is the Assistant Chief Social Worker, Framingham Youth Guidance Center, Framingham, Massachusetts.

Glen Clifford, M.S.W., is a student at the Smith College School of Social Work.

Katharine Odin, M.S.W., is a student at the Smith College School of Social Work.

Eileen M. Brennan is an Assistant Professor, School of Social Welfare, University of Kansas, Lawrence, Kansas.

Ann Weick is an Associate Professor, School of Social Welfare, University of Kansas, Lawrence, Kansas.

Naomi Golan, Ph.D., is an Associate Professor, School of Social Work, University of Haifa, Haifa, Israel.

Marquis Earl Wallace is an Assistant Professor, School of Social Work, University of Southern California, Los Angeles, California.

Richard R. Raubolt, Ph.D., is Staff Psychologist, Pine Rest Christian Hospital, Grand Rapids, Michigan.

Arnold W. Rachman, Ph.D., is in private practice in New York City.

Beverly B. Nichols is a caseworker, Family Counseling Service Region West, Inc., Waltham, Massachusetts.

Phoebe Prosky is a social worker on the staff and faculty at the Ackerman Family Institute in New York and also has a private practice.

Sidney Wasserman is from University of Bradford, School of Applied Social Studies, Bradford, Yorkshire, England.

Abraham Monk, Ph.D., is Brookdale Professor of Gerontology, Columbia University School of Social Work, New York, New York.

Carleton Pilsecker, M.S.S.W., is Social Worker and Chairperson, Hospital Thanatology Committee, Veterans Administration Hospital, Long Beach, California.

Fred R. Volkmar, M.D., is on the staffs of the Department of Psychiatry and Behavioral Sciences, Stanford University School of Medicine, and the Palo Alto Veterans Administration Hospital, Stanford, California.

Sandra Bacon, M.S.W., is on the staffs of the Department of Psychiatry and Behavioral Sciences, Stanford University School of Medicine, and the Palo Alto Veterans Administration Hospital, Stanford, California.

Saad A. Shakir, M.D., is on the staffs of the Department of Psychiatry and Behavioral Sciences, Stanford University School of Medicine, and the Palo Alto Veterans Administration Hospital, Stanford, California.

Adolf Pfefferbaum, M.D., is on the staffs of the Department of Psychiatry and Behavioral Sciences, Stanford University School of Medicine, and the Palo Alto Veterans Administration Hospital, Stanford, California.

Eva Y. Deykin is Co-Director of Research, B.A. Training Program, Simmons School of Social Work and Psychiatric Research Social Worker, Collaborative Depression Study, Boston State Hospital.

Myrna M. Weissman is Chief Social Worker, Yale Clinical Psychopharmacology Unit, and Research Associate, Yale Department of Psychiatry, New Haven, Connecticut.

Gerald L. Klerman is a Professor of Psychiatry, Harvard Medical School, Massachusetts General Hospital, Boston, Massachusetts.

William P. Gilmore is a Caseworker, Southwest Office, Family Service Association of Cleveland.

Jon Weinberg, Ph.D., is Director of Education and Training, Hennepin County Alcoholism and Inebriety Program, Minneapolis, Minnesota.

Arthur D. Moffett, M.S.W., is an Assistant Professor of Social Work and Deputy Chief, Section on Drug and Alcohol Abuse, Medical College of Pennsylvania, Philadelphia, Pennsylvania.

James D. Bruce, M.S., is Coordinator, Chester County Drug and Alcohol Programs, West Chester, Pennsylvania.

Diana Horvitz, B.A., is a Research Assistant, Section on Drug and Alcohol Abuse, Medical College of Pennsylvania.

Kenneth R. Wedel, M.S.W, is a Clinical Social Worker, Clinical Center, National Institutes of Health, Bethesda, Maryland.

Edna Wasser is a consultant and a Professor, School of Social Work, University of Washington, Seattle, Washington.

Monna Zentner is an Assistant Professor, School of Social Work, Renison College, University of Waterloo, Waterloo, Ontario, Canada.

Anne O. Freed is Director of Counselling Services, Family Service Association of Greater Boston, Boston, Massachusetts, and an Adjunct Professor, Boston University School of Social Work, Boston, Massachusetts.

John F. Borriello, Ph.D., is a Clinical Professor of Psychology, George Washington University, Washington, D.C.

Normund Wong, M.D., is Director of the Department of Education at the Menninger School of Psychiatry, The Menninger Foundation, Topeka, Kansas. He is also Adjunct Associate Professor of Psychiatry, Temple University Health Sciences Center, Philadelphia, Pennsylvania.

Steven N. Silver, M.S.W., is Manager, Criminal Justice Project, Eastside Community, Mental Health Center, Bellevue, Washington.

Barton E. Bernstein, J. D., is a partner in the firm of Hochberg, Bernstein and Skor, Dallas, Texas, and Adjunct Assistant Professor of Social Work and Law, Graduate School of Social Work, University of Texas, Arlington, Texas.

Laura Farber is a Psychiatric Social Worker, Hillsdale Hospital, Glen Oaks, New York.

Judith C. Nelsen, D.S.W., is an Assistant Professor, School of Social Work, Hunter College of the City University of New York, New York, N.Y.

Larry L. Smith, D.S.W., is an Assistant Professor, Graduate School of Social Work, University of Utah, Salt Lake City, Utah.

Doreen M. Winkler, M.S.W., is a Social Worker, Lakeshore Psychiatric Hospital, Toronto, Ontario, Canada.

Gene A. Broadland is Senior Outpatient Social Worker, Department of Psychiatry, University of Iowa College of Medicine, Iowa City, Iowa.

N.J.C. Andreasen, M.D., Ph.D., is an Assistant Professor, Department of Psychiatry, University of Iowa, College of Medicine, Iowa City, Iowa.

Elliot C. Brown, Jr., is Supervisor, Baker Social Service Unit, Massachusetts General Hospital, Boston, Massachusetts.

Helen Sloss Luey, M.S., A.C.S.W., L.C.S.W., is the Social Worker at Heaming Society for the Bay Area, Inc., San Francisco, California.

Mary W. Engelmann is a Social Worker, Royal Alexandra Hospital, Edmonton, Alberta, Canada.

Sylvia Schild, D.S.W., is a Professor, School of Social Work, California State University. Sacramento, and Assistant Clinical Professor in Social Work, University of California Medical School, Davis, California.

Alfred H. Katz, D.S.W., is Head of Division of Social Welfare in Medicine and Associate Professor, Social Welfare in Medicine, Department of Preventive Medicine and Public Health, University of California Medical Center, School of Medicine, Los Angeles, California.

Kathleen M. Hickey is Social Worker, Dialysis and Transplant Unit, Social Service Department, University of Minnesota Hospitals, Minneapolis, Minnesota.

Gary John Welch is an Assistant Professor in the Graduate School of Social Work, University of Texas, Arlington, Texas.

Kathleen Steven is Co-director of the Irving Counseling Center, Irving, Texas.

Gladys Lambert is a Social Worker, University of Rochester Medical Center, Rochester, New York.

Kemal Elberlik is an Assistant Professor of Psychiatry and Director, Adult Psychiatric Clinic, Department of Psychiatry, University of Virginia Medical Center, Charlotteville, Virginia.

Alletta Jervey Hudgens, M.S.W., is a graduate student in Family Social Science and a Relationship Counselor in the Student Counseling Bureau at the University of Minnesota, Minneapolis, Minnesota.

Enola K. Proctor is a Research and Teaching Fellow, George Warren Brown School of Social Work, Washington University, St. Louis, Missouri.

Phyllis Laterza, M.S.W., is a full-time Social Worker in the Evening Program at the Young Adult Institute Workshop, Inc., New York, New York.

Shirley Conyard, M.S.W., is a Social Worker at the Jewish Hospital and Medical Center of Brooklyn, New York.

Muthuswamy Krishnamurthy, M.D., is attending Hematologist at the Jewish Hospital and Medical Center of Brooklyn, New York.

Harvey Dosik, M.D., is Chief of Hematology, Jewish Hospital and Medical Center of Brooklyn, New York.

Judith R. Singler is a Clinical Social Worker, Youville Rehabilitation and Chronic Desease Hospital, Cambridge, Massachusetts.

Marie Cohen, M.S.W., is a Social Worker, Oncology Ward, U.C.L.A. Center for the Health Sciences, Los Angeles, California.

Irene Goldenberg, Ed.D., is Director of Psychological Services, Childrens Division, U.C.L.A. Neuropsychiatric Institute, Los Angeles, California.

Herbert Goldenberg, Ph.D., is Professor of Psychology, California State University.

Darielle L. Jones, M.S.W., is a Social Worker, Columbia Presbyterian Medical Center, New York, New York.

Esther Fibush is a Caseworker, Family Service Bureau, Oakland, California.

BeAlva Turnquest is a Caseworker, Family Service Bureau, Oakland, California.

E. Daniel Edwards is an Assistant Professor and Director of the American Indian Social Work Program, Utah.

Margie E. Edwards is a Professor, Graduate School of Social Work, University of Utah, Salt Lake City, Utah.

Man Keung Ho, Ph.D., is an Associate Professor, School of Social Work, University of Oklahoma, Norman, Oklahoma.

Ignacio Aguilar, M.S.W., is Executive Director, El Calvario Community Center, El Monte, California, and Director of Spanish Language Psychiatric Services, Metropolitan State Hospital, Norwalk, California.

Daniel S. Sanders, Ph.D., is Dean and Professor at the University of Hawaii School of Social Work.

Florence Hollis, Ph.D., is Professor of Social Work, Columbia University School of Social Work, New York, New York.

Ben A. Orcutt, D.S.W., is a Professor and Chairperson of the Doctoral Program, School of Social Work, the University of Alabama.

Dennis A. Bagarozzi, Ph.D., is on the staff of the Department of Family and Child Development, Kansas State University, Manhattan, Kansas.

Elizabeth Herman McKamy is a Psychiatric Social Worker, After-Care Services, the C. F. Menninger Memorial Hospital, Topeka, Kansas.

Francis J. Turner, D.W.S., is Dean, Faculty of Social Work, Wilfrid Laurier University, Waterloo, Ontario, Canada.

Lita Linzer Schwartz, Ph.D., is a Professor at Pennsylvania State University, Ogontz Campus, Abington, Pennsylvania.

Florence W. Kaslow, Ph.D., is a Professor at Hahneman Medical College, Department of Mental Health Sciences, Philadelphia, Pennsylvania.

Alice Ullmann is Social Work Supervisor, New York Hospital and Assistant Professor of Social Work, Cornell University Medical College, New York, New York.

Susan J. Wells, M.S.W., is a doctoral candidate, School of Social Work, University of Southern California, Los Angeles, California.

Donald F. Krill, M.S.W., is an Assistant Professor, Graduate School of Social Work, University of Denver, Denver, Colorado.

Leona Grossman, M.P.H., M.S.W., is Director, Social Work Department, Michael Reese Hospital and Medical Center, Chicago, Illinois.

Dory Krongelb Beatrice is a Clinical Social Worker, San Luis Valley Comprehensive Community Mental Health Center, Alamosa, Colorado.

R. T. T. Morgan is a Post-graduate Research Scholar, School of Social Work, University of Leicester, Leicestershire, England.

G. C. Young, M.D., B.Sc., D.P.H., is Deputy Medical Officer of Health for London Borough of Barnet, London, England.

Christine A. Dietz is Site Coordinator, Domestic Violence Prevention Training Project, Empire State College, Buffalo, New York.

John L. Craft is Director, School of Social Work, Research Center, University of Iowa, Iowa City, Iowa.

Kay M. Stevenson, M.S.W. is a doctoral candidate in Social Welfare, School of Social Work, University of Washington, Seattle, Washington.

Ann Wolbert Burgess, D.N.Sc., is an Associate Professor of Nursing, Boston College, Chestnut Hill, Massachusetts.

Lynda Lytle Holmstrom, Ph.D., is an Associate Professor of Sociology, Boston College, Chestnut Hill, Massachusetts.

Elisabeth Lassers, M.D., is an Assistant Professor of Psychiatry and Pediatrics, Abraham Lincoln School of Medicine, University of Illinois, Chicago, Illinois.

Robert Nordan, Ph.D., is an Assistant Professor of Psychology, Abraham Lincoln School of Medicine, University of Illinois, Chicago, Illinois.

Sheila Bladholm, M.S.W., is an Assistant Professor of Medical Social Work, Abraham Lincoln School of Medicine, University of Illinois, Chicago, Illinois.

Harriette C. Johnson, Ph.D., is an Assistant Professor, School of Social Work, Adelphi University, Garden City, New York.

David J. Klugman, M.S.W., is Co-Chief Social Worker, Suicide Prevention Center, Los Angeles, California.

Robert E. Litman, M.D., is Chief Psychiatrist, Suicide Prevention Center, Los Angeles, California.

Carl I. Wold, Ph.D., is Chief Psychologist, Suicide Prevention Center, Los Angeles, California.

Herbert S. Strean, D.S.W., is an Associate Professor, Graduate School of Social Work, Rutgers, The State University, New Brunswick, New Jersey.

Sarah F. Hafemann is a Family Court Marriage Counselor, Milwaukee County Department of Family Conciliation, Milwaukee, Wisconsin.

Catherine S. Chilman, Ph.D., is a Professor and Research Consultant, School of Social Welfare, University of Wisconsin, Milwaukee, Wisconsin.

PART I

Stages of Human Development

Interest in regularities and differences in each stage of development as a critical component of diagnosis has always been important for social workers. Considerable attention to this dimension has been an essential part of our curricula at all levels. Many of our services and specialized practices have been related to developmental stages such as services to children, to youth, to families, or to the aged.

That this differentiating concept is still important was evident from the review of material since the last edition. Obviously we continue to stress that our intervention needs to be as precise as possible and that one aspect of this precision relates to an understanding of stage of development achieved and the roles played therein.

As our interest in more precise knowledge of each developmental stage continues, our writing becomes more focused and more abundant. Indeed, the first selection of articles for this section turned up more than a hundred articles that could have been included. It was difficult to select from the many available, and the final decision was to expand the number of topics from the earlier edition with fewer articles on each topic. To date most of our writings focus on psychosocial development with as yet little attention to the inclusion of biological development, an area where considerable integration is still needed.

We continue to write frequently and perceptively about our work with young children and to advocate the use of diverse approaches that encompass variations of individual work, work with the environment, work with groups and with families. The two articles included in this section reflect this.

Among the child-focused articles the previously noted trend to the addressing of a wide range of topics from varying theoretical perspectives was noted. Several of the articles found dealt with interactions with

1

siblings, even more with the effects of infant deaths in families, and still more with the effects of separation, divorce, and remarriage on young children.

Adolescence as a developmental phase continues to be well covered in the literature. The reduced emphasis on delinquency as being almost coterminous with adolescence continues. Some articles on homicidal acts by delinquents were noted. In this area continued stress is put on the necessity of the therapist's own awareness of his or her ideas and attitudes about this period of maturation. Reference is made to the importance of understanding the period of adolescence in our culture both in sociological and in psychological terms to avoid developing an overly pathological viewpoint.

Although space did not permit their inclusion, an interesting cluster of articles was located that focused on such topics as "the adolescent as student," "the adolescent and the changing sexual mores," and "the overall value conflicts of the adolescent." The predominating theme of much of the current literature is a stress on the need for a reconsideration and a reunderstanding of the adolescent's search for identity and autonomy.

Our literature is now giving more attention to the developmental components of adulthood, reflecting the growing understanding that the maturational process is lifelong. Thus this section includes three articles on adulthood: the young adult, a general discussion of adulthood, and a more specific article by Naomi Golan that looks at transitions in adulthood.

Much excellent writing continues about various approaches to dealing with marital difficulties. The stress is still on marriage problems rather than enhancing healthy marital relationships. Two of the articles selected reflect differing modalities of intervention, different theoretical approaches, and different intensities of problems.

As expected, much material was located on dealing with various aspects of unsuccessful marriages. This material will be addressed in Part Five.

As our writing becomes more sophisticated and precise in the area of human development, we are bringing into focus other aspects of the maturational history of individuals. Thus, along with our rich literature on marriage and family, we have begun to focus on the specific function of parenting as a distinct role with its own problems and interventive implications. Several excellent articles on mothering and, we were pleased to observe, on fathering as well, as distinct adult stages were located. One from each topic is here included.

Much has been written about family therapy in the last two decades. The two articles here give a useful overview of this aspect of treatment as well as some specific discussion of working with multideficit families. Wasserman's article on adulthood looks at a developmental phase frequently alluded to but rarely addressed from a conceptual viewpoint in our literature. It reflects the theme, earlier referred to, that adulthood has its own developmental phases that need to be differently understood.

In our writings we continue to emphasize our interest in and experience with the aged client. In recent years a rich array of articles dealing with both specific and generalized features of this stage of human development has appeared. Our colleagues who write in this area continue to emphasize the extent to which our own feelings and attitudes are an essential part of successful practice with the aged.

In the final article in Part I, dying, the ultimate stage in human earthly existence, is addressed. It is quite remarkable how much this topic, once so denied professionally, has become an acceptable one in the literature. Throughout, the authors stress the necessity of seeing the situation, emotionally laden as it is for all, as a professional responsibility, to be met and dealt with in the same manner as any other and not to be avoided out of our own discomfort or because we misconceived the client's inability or unwillingness to deal with it.

In conclusion, the stages of human development as a diagnostic variable requiring specific therapeutic consideration serve as an important but not exclusive part of the assessment process. Extended practice experience has clearly demonstrated there are commonalities in behavior and problems requiring specific and predictable treatment approaches in the various stages and roles of human life. It is also clear, and each author reminds us, that as knowledge of our client expands and as our interventive plan emerges and is modified, a variety of other variables must be condsidered.

In recent years we have greatly enriched our specific understanding of many aspects of the stages of human development. As our knowledge has become enriched so has our awareness that there are many other aspects of this dimension that as clinicians we have just begun to understand and address.

THE CHILD

CHAPTER 1

Casework with Children: The Experience of Treatment

Margaret G. Frank

Lenny was a thin, gaunt-looking boy, small for his seven years, with an expression in his eyes that reflected the years of misery he had lived. His stance was stiff, on-guard and watchful. Characteristically he "attacked first," kicking, screaming and trying to bite his caseworker. This was his first visit to a placement agency. He knew he was going to be taken from his home.

What he did not know was that by the time he was to leave home he would agree to go and the residence would no longer loom as a house of horrors. Nor had he any idea that four years later he would emerge from the school nervous about leaving, sad to say "good-bye" to Mrs. Lieb, whose legs he had not bruised for some years. He could not envisage that there would ever be a day when he would proudly sport a report card with B's and two A's, or that he would be able to enter a group of age-mates without fear of rejection. Nor could he imagine that there would be a time in his life when hearing the shrill voices of anger didn't send him into a frenzy.

Barbara, an obese, pimple-faced girl of thirteen, defied her caseworker in their first meeting to "do something about me." Little did this young woman know, who was so hell-bent on evoking disgust and anger, busy negating everything her well-to-do, educated family stood for, that during four years she would move steadily toward the bright, able and charming person that she could be. She had no idea that she could ever be trim and pretty, that she could enjoy, albeit anxiously, her first steps into the dating-game, that working well at school would no longer arouse the dilemmas it had, and could carry satisfactions.

Reprinted from *Smith College Studies in Social Work*, Vol. 39 (February, 1969), pp. 127–137, by permission of the journal.

The gratifying development seen in these two children is not unique. Progressive achievement is seen in many children who come to the attention of workers in the children's field. While not unique, neither are such positive outcomes typical. Not all of our work with children is effective. Thus, instances of success, while gratifying, are also disquieting in that they identify unrealized possibilities for effective service by marking off and highlighting our failures.

Mental health practitioners and researchers continually question what happens in treatment, what are the elements that enable or induce a child, stunted and thwarted in ego development, to re-enter the main stream and even to experience pleasure in his new-found ego capacities. This search is crucial to the development of the mental health practice and it has particular relevance to those who would teach others. I say this because, if, as practitioners, we are honest with ourselves we would admit that we are not always planful and aware of what we are doing in treatment and why we do it. We are accountable mainly to ourselves and perhaps to a supervisor or consultant. But those who choose to teach others are faced (happily, I might add) with the constant questioning of "the novice": "How did you know to do or say that?" "What made you choose to be silent?" "How should I handle this?" "What should my attitude be?" "Why?"

From my own experience as a practitioner and teacher I have found it useful to view treatment as comprised of two major elements, cognitive and experiential. While the two are, in fact, highly interrelated and inseparable, we should, for the purposes of study, permit them to be artificially separated.

The purpose of this paper is to examine the experiential elements of treatment. While of great importance, the cognitive element will be defined but not elaborated. I have made this choice because, in my opinion, our training lacks the appropriate study of, and emphasis on, the experiential aspects of treatment.

Cognitive Elements in Treatment

Cognitive work in treatment refers to all those steps taken by the therapist to enable the client to understand aspects of himself, why he feels the way he does, why he behaves as he does, what events have influenced his present being.

Such conscious self-knowledge has proven of great value when the client can use his insight to change or modify his behavior. However, too often it appears that measures are taken to clarify the client's behavior more out of the therapists's needs than the client's. Faced, for example, with the rawness of a child patient's need to be emotionally fed, a therapist may state the meaning of his behavior and the reasons for it prematurely.

The need to make the behavior understood stems from the threat felt by the therapist possibly of being "swallowed up" by the hungry child. The same clarifications might well be made and be of use to the child later, after a "feeding experience."

There is no question, then, of the importance of conscious understanding as a stepping-stone to growth, and yet we know that such understanding is not enough.

Experiential Element of Treatment

In examining the experiential element I am referring to those aspects of treatment which carry a variety of labels: "corrective experience," "treatment relationship," "friendship." I am concerned with therapeutic procedures involving "the use of self, the use of transference, provision of self as an object for identification." Our interest is in all those actions taken in treatment that provide the client with an emotional experience conducive to growth. As noted before I have, only for purposes of study, separated them from those procedures used to bring about conscious comprehension.

Casework with Children

Before we go into the main topic in depth, I want to digress for a moment. You may have noted that no reference has been made thus far to the discipline of casework or to the process called "casework with children." I feel this needs explanation. I confess that I do not differentiate the work done by caseworkers with children from the psychotherapeutic endeavors of the other mental health disciplines. Following from this, I do not see that the knowledge base of caseworkers should be allowed to be less than that of the other mental health disciplines. But I am all too aware of the reality that little specific training in therapeutic work with children is available for our profession. Less than a handful of schools of social work in the United States offer courses in treatment of children. In the few schools whose doors are open to this need, it's still only a crack—one semester, often without concomitant practical field work. Post-graduate training programs are few and far between. In the face of this paucity of training we find that, in fact, caseworkers throughout our nation are seeing and working with a large number of children whose emotional development has been severely crippled. Perhaps the saddest reality of all is that members of the social work profession have allowed their work with children to go on under such labels as "friendly visitor," "companion," "guardian," yes, even "casework with children," all connoting interventions of lesser importance, necessitating less training and knowledge. It seems that we carry the burden of work but do not fight for the knowledge that is vital to that work.

The historical whys of these realities are not germane to this paper, but noting the existence of these realities is crucial. I said earlier that I do not differentiate between the necessary knowledge base and work done by caseworkers with children from the other mental health professions. But I *do* observe a difference in the child client group generally seen in social agencies from those seen in private practice or even many of the child guidance clinics. These are the children who have not only suffered from *early* emotional deprivations that cause stunted ego development, but they usually have also to contend with *continuous*, on-going tumult and disruption in their environments: The "Lennys" seen in child welfare settings, and the "Barbaras" seen in homes for unmarried mothers are the children who need many years of therapeutic work to clear away the blocks in their development. These are the children who can use understanding only after they have experienced something in treatment that develops their capacity to use their comprehension. These are the children whose emotional–environmental conditions need the most knowledgeable and artful interventions. Yet, sadly, it is with these very children that many members of the social work profession deny the importance of their actions by calling their endeavors "friendly visiting" or "supportive casework," What follows from this denial is a contentment to proceed spontaneously, intuitively with little of the rigorous planning, knowledge and thought that is deemed part of the practitioner's responsibility when attempting to bring about change in another human being's life. It is my hope that this paper will stimulate members of the casework profession to seek and utilize the knowledge that is available.

As the dynamics of a child's problems unfold it is not difficult to locate the areas in which we wish him to gain understanding of himself and his circumstances. Neurotic distortions in reasoning are obvious and the goal of clarifying these distortions is clear. It is normal for children, at an early age, to see themselves as the center of their universe. It follows, then, that as "good and evil" befall them, they will perceive all happenings as their own doings. A healthy child will mature cognitively and come to understand that there are forces beyond him that cause events. The daughter of a friend demonstrated this beautifully recently when she asked her mother who was yelling at her, "Are you mad at me, Mommy, or at something else?" We can easily understand that Lenny originally saw the disruption of his home, his parents' divorce, his own placement as punishment for his own badness. It was clear that he had to be helped to understand events differently.

Earlier we said, however, that understanding is not enough to free a child to develop.

It is far less easy for a therapist, as the dynamics of a child's problems unfold, to think out planfully what he wants the child to experience with him and from him which will be therapeutic—conducive to his growth.

Corrective Experience

"Corrective" is the label often given to the experiential part of treatment. By this it is meant that the therapist creates an opportunity for the child to re-experience, to rework, to correct earlier phases of his development, phases that are deemed through diagnostic assessment crucial to his problems. Re-experiencing implies setting up conditions which will encourage the child to "slip back," regress to the troubled phase. If the therapist has deep meaning to the child, his handling, responses, attitudes toward the child's behavior become the corrective forces.

Often I have observed a too literal and overly simplified definition of the corrective experience. It is as if the therapist were saying to himself, "I will correct the wrongs done by the parents. I will offer love, acceptance, warmth, and permissiveness to counter restrictiveness, rivalry, inability to love, et cetera." As important as love, warmth and acceptance are to living and treatment, we have ample proof that they are not enough to bring about growth either in every-day living or in treatment.

One could present another paper on why so many practitioners fill their offices with toys and candies and set about mainly to love and accept their child clients. I want to offer only two thoughts, and briefly, about this kind of practice. One thought has to do with the fact that many people in the mental health profession have not developed a professional self-image which contains the notion that they may be an instrument of pain, even if it is understood intellectually that pain is often a necessary and unavoidable experience in growing. I can recall working with a young girl who had made steady progress. While her mother was gaining in adequacy through her own treatment, I had achieved a strong maternal quality in the transference which had brought about much of her growth. However, the day was coming when she would have to be helped to break her ties to me. The opportunity arose one day when we were observing some animals which were up for adoption. All of her words and actions pointed symbolically to her desire to be taken home by me. Pointing out to her that this was not possible was one of the hardest things I had ever done with a child. First there was the obvious pain of her feelings of being rejected, and then, the uncomfortable for me, ensuing anger, and finally I was also depriving myself of some very pleasurable communications from an appealing child. I remember returning to the clinic later and talking with some colleagues, remarking with only thin humor that no one told me treatment was going to be as painful to do as this. I had never envisaged before that

I would do something purposefully which would cause a client to be angry and pained.

The other thought that I want to offer for brief consideration with regard to a "too loving" style of practice is that many of the people who work with the emotionally disturbed do not understand or use their knowledge of normal growth and development. One can find in normal growth and development an important model for the corrective experience. An example of this can be seen in the following situation. Last year I was supervising a caseworker in her work with a young child who was developing rigid compulsive defenses. The history was dramatically clear in showing the sources of these behaviors, for the mother's discomfort with messing was great indeed. The worker had set about to create a "corrective experience." Permission was being given for the child to mess and little by little the child was accepting the permission. I came on the scene at a point when the worker felt that little progress was being made, despite the corrective atmosphere she was providing.

In our discussions we began to concentrate on how "healthy" children learn to deal with their impulses to mess and the demand that they become trained. We came upon the fact that the healthy mother approaches her child with an expectation that he will master his impulses. She offers love and her pleasure as a reward at the same time that she provides him with a variety of what might be called sublimatory activities. How many children can be observed playing with mud, "washing dishes," slopping in the soapy water at the very period of their lives when they are learning with firmness from their mothers that they must use the toilet. This pursuit became an important guide to the worker. I could not tell her the specific actions she should take with this child, but they were not hard to locate once she had a guide for her direction. Her sessions with the young client began to shift from pure permission to acceptance of the impulse, but with provision of other ways to express it. The boy moved from slopping the office with finger paints to working in more confined areas, to painting with a brush, to working with models where inadvertently his hands always got "messy" from the glue.

Thus far I have discussed the provision of a corrective experience in rather global terms. I have pointed out that it must not be viewed as a simple opposition of parental handling. The practitioner must be comfortable with taking actions which may be experienced as painful by the child (and by himself). I have pointed up the importance of knowledge of the ingredients that go into healthy development to serve as model for corrective experience.

Knowledge and Use of Transference

Somewhat earlier I said that the therapist's responses to the child's behavior have corrective powers *when* the therapist is a meaningful person to the child. Again, we cannot go into the historical reasons behind the fact, but caseworkers have been slow to learn about, understand and utilize the transference phenomena in the treatment relationship. Yet they are there. Sometimes one is lucky, and without awareness treatment can progress because the treatment relationship has room in it for the expression of both love and anger. But all too often practitioners are alert to only the negative. If we know who we are as people, then material from a child of a strongly negative nature: "You're mean. You are not going to approve of this. You are always ready to find fault with me," stands out as obviously stemming from another relationship, and the worker will take steps to diminish the negative qualities. It is not so easy to detect a too positive transference in work with a child. The reason, one can suppose, is that we all find an important positive confirmation of ourselves in the love of a child. If I return to my own experiences with the girl who offered herself up for my adoption, I cannot deny the personal satisfaction that her sentiments brought. There is nothing wrong with experiencing personal satisfaction in work with children, as long as it is also therapeutic for the child. Thus, we must be consciously watchful for the perceptions of us as "the greatest," "the most giving," "the most understanding," no matter how satisfying such expressions may be. What is crucial is that we create room and permission for the expression of both positive and negative feelings.

Our view of transference can be developed further. Time doesn't permit us to go into the history of Lenny's situation, but we can look at an overview of Mrs. Lieb's work. She rode through many months of his need to attack first. She accepted his anger, gave voice to his reasons for having it, acknowledged the legitimacy of it, at the same time that she stopped his biting and kicking with consistent firmness. She continued to see him at regular intervals until he knew firmly inside himself what she had said in words in their first meeting: "Your anger will not drive me away." Eventually he allowed her to feed him with food, attention, interest and some toys. She had taken on the role of the giving mother. Hard won, she turned this role into the giving mother who expected growth and was pleased by it. By this time Lenny treasured her pleasure in him, even though he had not yet developed pleasure in himself. When the time seemed right she began to relate to him less as the little boy who needed affection and encouragement and more as a developing masculine being.

What should be evident in this brief survey of a course of treatment is that there are phases; transference roles shift sometimes in response to the child's development and sometimes to stimulate changes in the child. I recall an early experience I had in working with a borderline girl. She fantasied herself to be a dog; blonde, pretty, petite, she crawled into my office weekly on hands and knees "arfing" away at me. In the months that followed I learned to communicate with her through some dog dolls and we unfolded the story of her disguise through our play. Months later in conference I was stunned when my consultant asked me when we were going to grow up. Perhaps truthful and a bit unkind, his point was that I had to lead the way in shifting our means of communication. I could not wait for her for she would be content to stay where she was. Years later I received a letter from her in which she wrote, "Remember when we used to talk dog talk?"

Shifts in the transference role are not only determined by stages in the child's treatment, but also by his developmental stages. To exemplify this, we can turn to Barbara who was a most thoughtful and self-aware client in her late latency years. I was clearly her mother. As she moved toward adolescence, however, the nature of our relationship changed and I had to change with it. The doors to self-contemplation closed and there was a frenzied entrance into concerns with men, dating, hair styles, et cetera. This was also a time when the doors were closed to mothers, real and transference. To stay in the picture I became a peer or, perhaps better, an older sister, listening, sharing, consulting and occasionally advising on hair-do, dress, manners, et cetera. Through this she was getting permission to know about and learn to be a woman but not from her mother but rather as so often happens in life, from the older girl, the counselor at camp, the girl on the corner who is a few years older.

Object for Identification

The final theme that I want to bring up as part of the experiential element of treatment with children has to do with the therapist's consciously lending himself as an object of identification. One must assume in such a discussion the child's developmental readiness to use the therapist for purposes of identification. Quite often we will observe that a female client fashions her hair style and dress after her worker. Or we can see a young man walking down a corridor with a gait unmistakably similar to his therapist's. These are the baby steps of identification, the early copying the mimicking that is a part of trying something on for size. The process can become more active and fruitful if we are aware of it and encourage it. I refer now to a period in which a child may begin to ask questions about his worker's life, points of view, behavior, et cetera.

Here I must call to our attention the fact that social workers receive a large portion of "do's" and "don'ts" in their training. "Don't talk about yourself; it is inappropriate," is a tenet that concerns me here, for it can interfere with the opportunities to lend oneself to the child as an object for identification. This does not mean that it is always appropriate for a worker to talk about himself. What it does mean is that there must be constant attention to the material with understanding of its meaning. At one phase, it may be clear that the child is simply trying to deflect the attention to the worker as part of a resistance. But the same concerns and questions at another point in treatment may be part of a deep and meaningful search to "be like you." Barbara, in the latter part of her treatment, was highly active in questioning her worker about the worker's schooling, the necessary preparation for becoming a social worker. It would not have been uncommon to see a worker cut off these questions either by saying, "We are here to talk about you, not me," or "I wonder if this is your way of not talking about yourself." Instead she replied simply and directly and these answers followed Barbara's real concerns, her conflict about being feminine and knowledgeable at the same time. Part of her problem was that the two were incompatible.

I am prompted to say that I have become extremely distrustful of any of the "rules" that have been handed down through the years to caseworkers. It makes much greater sense to operate out of a constant quest to understand what the child is dealing with, the meaning of his behavior. Such understanding leads to a flexibility in responding which is far more likely to be therapeutic.

Summary

I have chosen in this paper to divide treatment, albeit artificially, into two parts: procedures designed to bring about conscious self-awareness, and procedures designed to induce growth through the emotionally corrective experience in treatment. I have concentrated on the latter for several reasons: I have observed as a teacher and practitioner that the children seen by caseworkers are in deep need of a corrective experience. Caseworkers often overlook, or do not understand, the importance of the experiential part of treatment. Too often insight and the techniques that produce it have a glamour which overshadows providing a corrective experience where needed. I have observed in much of casework practice with children a laziness, where the search for the meaning of the client's behavior and the purposefulness of the worker's actions seem to be lacking. Too often the work is merely intuitive and spontaneous but not necessarily progressing.

In discussing some of the elements in the corrective experience I have to tried to select the procedures which I see as most therapeutic for the kinds of children caseworkers see in the run of their practice. I have aired some of the misconceptions and misunderstandings that I observe in current practice and have tried to call our attention to the importance not only of knowledge of the child and his problems but also knowledge of the worker. I have noted that the corrective experience must not only offer warmth and acceptance but there must be a readiness to take actions which might be experienced by the child as painful. I have noted that treatment has phases, and that the phases are sometimes determined by the child's own development and growth, but that also the worker must be ready to move both himself and the child in order to stimulate growth. I have suggested that knowledge of the ingredients of normal growth and development is vital as it can serve as a model for the corrective experience.

In short, the therapeutic intervention into the life of a child (or a person of any age) is a serious matter and must be accompanied with a deep sense of responsibility and a wide and deep range of knowledge.

CHAPTER 2

Qualifications and Tasks of the Therapist in Group Therapy with Children

Leslie Rosenthal

A discussion of the tasks of the therapist in group therapy with children is akin to considering the varied responsibilities of a parent in a family. Within the family parental tasks will vary with the age of the children and their physical and emotional capacities at the different stages of development. The parent's life history, cultural, subcultural, and socio-economic affiliations will also shape the formulation and execution of these responsibilities. The assignments the therapist undertakes will be shaped by the age level of the group members and the structure and setting of the specific group modality he is using. The manner in which he carries out these tasks will be conditioned by his background, training, theoretical affiliations, and his life history.

In activity group therapy with latency youngsters, the therapist presents himself as accepting, nonlimiting, and primarily neutral. He seeks to create a group climate which is permissive, tolerant, friendly, and hospitable. With younger children, the therapist, mindful of their lesser controls and greater susceptibility to contagion, would be less permissive and would balance freedom of expression with appropriate restraints. In interview group therapy with young adolescents the therapist orients himself more toward the center of the group's emotional network. Here he becomes, much more than in activity group therapy, an active and engaged participant as he questions, guides, becomes the object of negative transference, interprets, and seeks to facilitate the attainment of insight.

Reprinted from *Clinical Social Work Journal*, Vol. 5, No. 3 (1977), pp. 191–199, by permission of the author and the publisher, Human Sciences Press, 72 Fifth Avenue, New York, New York, 10011.

Obviously, the very important differences in the ego structure of children at different ages makes differential treatment imperative.

There are however certain basic tasks which face the therapist in any group treatment endeavor with children. These are (1) that he know children; (2) that he be an individual therapist; (3) that he be a group therapist, one who can select the right members for the right group and utilize the therapeutic potential of the group setting for the benefit of all the members; and (4) that he know the child in himself.

Knowing Children

The therapist's understanding of children is founded upon the inescapable realities of their physical and psychological incompleteness. He recognizes the child's relatively weak ego organization and the limits of its capacity to mediate between his inner and outer worlds. He is attuned to the primarily narcissistic quality of the child's libidinal functioning with its attendant self-indulgence, impulsivity, and strivings for omnipotence. He is aware of the inadequate protective barriers against excessive stimulation and the weakness of the child's emotional insulation. He sees that the child's capacities for repression are undeveloped as are his abilities to effectively sublimate; hence the more exposed nature of his unconscious. He understands that the child's identifications are labile, fluid, ambivalent, and malleable and that his capacity for change and reintegration is considerably greater than that of adults. The therapist's grasp of the emotionality of children would encompass the child's drive for motoric activity which affords satisfaction of his impelling needs for play and the release of aggression. We may note that each of the children's group therapies devised and conceptualized by Slavson have sought to meet this maturational need for motor activity as a form of release, expression, and communication. Most of all he is related to the child's vulnerability and his urgent need for support and growth, thus enhancing emotional contact with significant others.

When working with adolescents in group therapy our group therapist would have a consistent realization of their deep sense of incompleteness, their exquisite sensitivity to anxiety and emotional discomfort, and their compelling need to defend against feelings of inadequacy and damage. Alert to their emotional volatility and their propensity to swiftly convert impulse into action he sets a high priority on helping group members put into language as early as possible their negative, skeptical, suspicious, and anxious feelings toward the group and himself. He is assured that this expression of negative feeling is the most effective deterrent to precipitous withdrawal from the group. He is alert to adolescents' sensitivities to premature (and too vigorous) attempts to establish contact and closeness or to efforts to help them and know them before they are ready to be helped and to be known. He is therefore prepared to curb his therapeutic zeal; to frustrate his own wishes for greater intimacy with his group members; to curb his impulses to re-enter his own adolescence by seeking emotional proximity to his adolescent patients (and by joining them as a peer in their struggles with authority.

Being an Individual Therapist

Given a basic appreciation by the therapist of the developmental norms of childhood as related to treatment, what then are the tasks and qualifications of the group therapist? The first is that he be an *individual* therapist. Like individual psychotherapy, group therapy has as its *raison d'être* the benefit of the individual. It involves the understanding of individuals concurrent with the understanding and therapeutic exploitation of those forces and emotional currents which emerge when three or more individuals come together in the therapeutic group. The interest in the individual begins necessarily in the selection process where understanding of his dynamics is requisite to an evaluation of suitability for group treatment. Knowledge of the unique dynamics of the individual prior to his entry into the group is also essential to the formulation of a group treatment plan geared to his defensive structure and resistive patterns. If the prospective group member is a withdrawn and guarded child should he be invited by the group therapist to participate and express himself? Would this invitation be gratefully received and enhance his self-image? Or would it be perceived as a demand for achievement or as a destructive maneuver by the adult to expose the child's weakness? If the youngster enters the meeting room silently with averted eyes is he hoping for a warmly inviting greeting from the adult or is he asking that his hostility be accepted and that the therapist forbear from imposing the unwanted burden of his (the therapist's) positive feelings upon him. The indicated therapeutic response resides of course in the child's life history.

The principle of individualization geared to the nuclear dynamics of group members can be illustrated further. One boy, in marked oedipal rivalry with his father, is struggling to saw a long piece of wood. He neither requests nor receives any help from the therapist. Later in the session another member is in a similar situation and the therapist walks over and quietly holds the wood steady for the boy. This second youngster's father left the home when he was two and by his act the group therapist is supplying the maturational ingredient of active paternal interest. It is axiomatic that knowledge of the dynamics of the child's very first group, his family, is of significant predictive value to the group therapist; he knows that the role thrust upon the child in his family by psychologic exigency will be reenacted in the group family. Thus, the group member who was physically or emotionally expelled from his own family will invariably court expulsion from the group (a resistance which unfortunately all too often succeeds). The group therapist forearmed with study and comprehension of each of the individuals who compose his group is less likely to be caught off guard by the profound power of the repetition compulsion.

As a necessary prelude to group therapy the therapist will have had sound experience in treating individuals and thereby encountering the whole spectrum of human feeling within the intense and undiluted confines of the individual therapy setting. He will have developed a respect for defenses and an appreciation of their vital protective function. He will be prepared for the initial resistances of the individual members. He will know that these were initially conceived out of urgent psychological necessity and that these resistances represent the member's attempts to maintain his equilibrium under the stress of family living. He will thus value resistance in that it conveys, in indirect but richly emotional form, the life story of the child. As an individual therapist he will grasp the full import of Freud's statement that in its essense, resistance is nothing more than the character of the child.

Selecting the Group

The next task of the group therapist is to put together a viable group. Appropriate selection presupposes a clear appreciation of the very significant differences between the individual and group treatment arenas and the requirements, advantages, and limitations of each in relation to specific patient etiologies, character formations, and resistive patterns. Proper selection involves choice of those patients who possess that degree of ego strength essential to constructive group membership. Fundamental to this process is the recognition that the group setting involves certain stresses and imposes certain demands that are not inherent aspects of the dyadic treatment relation: the ever-present possibility of exposure to sibling hostility, the unavoidable necessity of sharing therapist, time, and in some settings food with other members, and the much greater degree of emotional stimulation. Thus, basic to the composition of a therapeutic group is the therapist's awareness that the child's capacity to enter and assimilate the world of multiple relations is based upon that which happens or does not happen in that first crucial dyad of child and mother. This embraces careful appraisal of the capacities of those children with marked oral deprivation to endure the built-in frustrations of the group setting. The therapist will also prudently evaluate the ability of impulsive children with minimal inner controls to withstand the permissive setting of activity group therapy where regressive and aggressive impulses can be swiftly mobilized and contagiously intensified throughout the group.

The establishment of group viability is also predicated upon group balance which calls for a therapeutic equilibrium amongst the diverse personalities of the group, particularly with respect to the aggression and withdrawal polarities. Slavson has a clear statement here:

> The ability of any given group to withstand or absorb hostility and aggression has definite limits. Each individual and each aggregate of people has its own capacity to tolerate aggression or hostility density. When these limits are exceeded in groups, tension and anxiety set in which are expressed in hyperactivity or wanton destructiveness. (Slavson, 1948a, p. 318)

Being a Group Therapist

Another task of the clinician who undertakes to simultaneously treat a number of individuals is that he be a *group* therapist. This involves the voluntary surrender of the therapeutic monopoly the therapist holds in individual treatment as the sole object of transference and identification. Being a group therapist embraces a readiness to yield some of his own therapeutic omnipotence as he accepts the concept that maximal therapeutic dividends are attained from the children's contact with each other. In a description of the role of the Activity Group Therapist, Slavson (1948b) stated, "He strives to remain outside the emotional flux of the group so as to allow a maximum interpersonal and intra-group emotional and physical activity" (p. 203). This is no easy task. One group of boys demonstrated their developing feelings of autonomy, competence, and mutual acceptance by busily working together on building a wagon at the far end of the room. The therapist described intense feelings of loneliness and loss in this situation.

Another aspect of being a group therapist is the capacity, usually developed with experience, to recognize and deal with subgroup and group resistances as they emerge. In a mixed group of adolescents, Jennie for several sessions regaled her fellow members with vivid and explicit descriptions of her sexual activity. The group-wide atmosphere of excitement and titillation and the members' overt and implicit encouragement for Jennie to continue labelled this an obvious group resistance on the level of exhibitionism-voyeurism. At the next session the therapist asked the group, "How would you all like Jennie to excite you today?" The anxiety generated by this question raised the developmental level of group functioning from one of perverse behavior to the healthier stage of neurotic functioning. The group members were then able to seriously explore with Jennie the self-damaging ramifications of her behavior.

Another example of successful resolution of a group problem is found in Slavson's first book, *Introduction to Group Therapy* (1943). In a group of thirteen-year-olds, two boys began to fight. Soon the entire membership had paired off in fights. The therapist said, "I think we'll have to get a license from the Boxing Commission for this club." The boys burst into laughter and the fighting stopped at once.

The group-oriented therapist is also aware that certain members can act as spokesmen for the whole group on crucial issues and can epitomize the major group concern with important constellations of feeling. One critical and argumentative member may represent the group's hostility to the therapist. An immature member may voice infantile yearnings for the others. An overstimulated youngster may therapeutically express feelings of sexuality for the more constricted numbers. The value of the group spokesman is reflected in this vignette:

> The therapist of a girls' activity group was impatiently eager to convert the group to an interview group where talk would supplant play. In a session when this plan was being discussed, one girl began to sing a refrain from a popular song, "I don't want to grow up to go with a boy and be his toy." The other members began to hum along with her. The perceptive group therapist understood the message, relaxed her efforts, gave the group more time and subsequently a more successful transition was achieved.

Having formed the group the therapist faces the task of preserving it as a therapeutic entity and protecting the treatment of its members. To accomplish this he assigns highest priority to the resolution of group-destructive and treatment- destructive resistance. When one or more members engage in behavior that threatens continuation of treatment or when a member is exposed to potentially damaging contact, the group therapist becomes active to protect the integrity of the group family. The following illustration of a treatment-threatening resistance is drawn from an activity-interview group of 13- and 14-year-old boys which met in a school setting:

> During a brief silence, Fred turned to John and asked when he is bringing in the dollar. John looked frightened and his voice quivered as he said, "I don't owe you any money," Fred retorted, "We made a bet playing baseball, remember?" Fred then warned John to bring the money tomorrow or he would get him after school, adding "maybe with my knife." John winced, said he was not bringing any money and that he might not come to school for a month.
>
> The therapist asked, "What's going on here? It sounds like blackmail." Fred maintained that the money was owed to him, even if John had not agreed to the bet. The therapist asked Fred how what he was trying to do with John was connected to the purpose of the group. Fred looked embarrassed and said he didn't know. Another member, Kevin, said Fred was trying to con the other members

instead of helping them. Fred turned to John and said he was only kidding anyway. John looked relieved.

In a subsequent session Fred talked about his father always cheating him and never keeping his promises to him. Thus, the therapist protected John's treatment and helped Fred enter treatment.

The participation of a whole group in a treatment-destructive resistance is illustrated in a natural group of predelinquent girls which was referred as a unit by the school. The group was seen on an exploratory basis in meetings with an experienced group therapist. These several sessions were marked by vivid descriptions of acts of sadistic aggression and perverse sexuality. It was then discovered that group members met prior to sessions to plan a contrived agenda designed to shock the therapist. When exploration by the group therapist revealed little interest in understanding themselves or each other and continuing wishes to defeat authority, sessions were terminated by the group therapist. Subsequently several of the girls were able to use individual treatment constructively. In this case the task of the therapist was to evaluate the treatability of the group.

Knowing the Child Within Yourself

As a final task the therapist should know the child within himself and be aware of the ways in which this inner child can interfere with his functioning appropriately as a group therapist. For example, a young therapist, unaware of his own deep fear of groups, in the course of one year rejected as unsuitable every single referral made to his proposed group. One therapist gratified his own unconscious craving for excitement by assembling a group composed exclusively of exhibitionistic and provocative youngsters who kept each other and the therapist in a constant state of titillation. Another reenacted his own sibling hostility as he permitted one very aggressive boy to drive three consecutive new members out of the group. A male therapist of a coed adolescent group paid scant attention as the boys drifted to the periphery of the group and then one by one dropped out in the face of his far greater interest in helping the female members.

The wish for a happy and serene group family is familiar to all of us who have worked with groups. In pursuit of this familial Eden one therapist intervened swiftly to settle any dispute, conflict, or disagreement amongst her group members by a toss of a coin. I recall an incident from my own practice of activity group therapy in the early 1950's. Morris, a withdrawn and suspicious boy, had delayed coming to the table for refreshments and was the last to sit down. I then observed that there was no cake left for Morris. Before he could utter a word I cut my own slice of cake in two and placed half on his plate. Morris accepted the cake silently but left most of it uneaten. Here the therapist's own need to maintain fair play and his overidentification with the youngster impelled him to precipitous intervention which deprived the child and the group of the opportunity to deal with the situation. An additional source of induced feeling in me in this situation was the presence in the observation room of Morris' individual therapist and her supervisor.

Impressed with the intense feelings aroused in myself and in my colleagues by our encounters with activity groups I wrote:

> The group is particularly fertile ground for testing the stability and maturity of the therapist. There is constant probing for his blindspots and the likelihood of reactivation of past traumata in his own familial relations is ever present. Inherent in the structure of activity group therapy are situations which activate and play upon the therapist's own feeling constellations around givingness, frustration, authority, aggression and passivity-activity. (Rosenthal, 1953, p. 440)

In a paper on the qualities of the group therapist, Martin Grotjahn (1971) stated:

> He should consider himself as his own favorite patient, one who has to learn as long as he lives. This thirst for knowledge, for truth and for learning belongs to his basic qualifications. (p. 757)

We are indebted to our groups for propelling us further along the lifelong road toward truth and greater maturity and we are deeply indebted to S. R. Slavson for providing the stage for these encounters—so healing of children and so rewarding to their therapists.

References

GROTJAHN, M. The qualities of the group therapist. In H. Kaplan & B. Sadock (Eds.), *Comprehensive group therapy.* Baltimore: Williams & Wilkins, 1971.

ROSENTHAL, L. Countertransference in activity group therapy. *International Journal of Group Psychotherapy*, 1953, 3, 431–440.

SLAVSON, S. R. *An introduction to group therapy.* New York, Commonwealth Fund, 1943.

SLAVSON, S. R. Play group therapy for young children. *The Nervous Child*, 1948, 7, 318–326.(a)

SLAVSON, S. R. Group therapy in child care and child guidance. *Jewish Social Service Quarterly*, 1948, 25, 203–210.(b)

THE ADOLESCENT

CHAPTER 3

Short-Term Treatment with the Adolescent Client

Jennie Sage Norman

Short-term treatment is a preferred modality for many adolescents. This method of treatment is congruent with the main goals of adolescence—to make an initial separation from the family and to consolidate an identity and value system. There are many therapists who find adolescents "difficult," "impossible," and "untreatable by psychotherapy." Then there are others, like Peter Blos, who state,

> Too little attention has been paid to the fact that adolescence, not only in spite of, but rather because of its emotional turmoil, often affords spontaneous recovery from debilitating childhood influences, and offers the individual an opportunity to modify or rectify childhood exigencies which threaten to impede his progressive development. The regressive processes of adolescence permit the remodeling of defective or incomplete earlier developments, new identifications and counter-identifications play an important part in this.[1]

Where the recovery is not spontaneous or the adjustment for the adolescent is more than the normal struggle, treatment can aid the process. This view is consistent with Mildred Eisenberg, who notes,

> The young person attempting to cope with the sociological and cultural upheaval as it impinges on him in the seventies is developmentally at Erikson's fifth of the eight stages of man, "identity versus role confusion." At this stage anxiety indicates role confusion and a realization that "time is running out,"

---

[1] Peter Blos, *On Adolescence* (New York: Macmillan, 1962), p. 10.

Reprinted from *Social Casework*, Vol. 61 (February, 1980), pp. 74–82, by permission of the author and the Family Service Association of America.

23

that one must terminate, and that binding choices must be made. Therefore, short-term psychotherapy fits the adolescent-postadolescent population.[2]

Time and how it is used make short-term therapy an appealing form of treatment for adolescents, that is, the idea that something can be worked on and a goal achieved in a relatively short period of time. The developmental tasks of adolescence are inherent in the structure of the short-term treatment modality, in its therapeutic process, and in the therapist-patient relationship.

The staff at the Framingham Youth Guidance Center, an outpatient child guidance clinic in a suburb west of Boston, have taken an increasing interest in short-term treatment over the past decade., The short-term treatment program has been in existence since 1972. Due to an increasing number of referrals and to a greater number of staff interested in the program, the program has expanded rapidly, and, in May 1977, a formal short-term treatment team was formed to accommodate this expansion. The team meets weekly, and several senior team members serve as consultants when team time cannot accommodate everyone or when there is a crisis. The team is multidisciplinary, makes dispositions on cases referred, reviews cases for further treatment or treatment problems, provides consultation, and serves as an inservice training program. Group peer supervision and sharing of short-term treatment experiences have increased the quantity and quality of the treatment, making the choice of this modality even more desirable.

Short-Term Treatment: Theoretical Considerations

There continues to be much controversy among mental health professionals regarding the use of brief psychotherapy, or short-term treatment, for any client population. There are those who believe that it is unsuitable for anyone because it is "superficial," "shallow," "antipsychoanalytic," "slick," or, simply, "too short." There are, however, those who have been favorably impressed by its benefits and results, not only from the therapist's assessment, but from the client's as well.

There are many studies of the effectiveness of short-term treatment versus long-term treatment. William Reid and Ann Shyne reported on a four-year field study in which they were trying to determine which methods of casework were most effective in treating family relations. In their sample of 120 families, they found significantly more progress was made by the clients who were in planned short-term treatment than the ones in

[2] Mildred Eisenberg, "Brief Psychotherapy: A Viable Possibility with Adolescents." *Psychotherapy: Theory, Research, and Practice* 12 (Summer 1975): 187.

long-term treatment.[3] Similarly, Patricia Ewalt found that short-term treatment was compatible with psychoanalytic techniques and that the majority of clients felt their treatment was effective.[4] James Mann reports success with time-limited treatment, initially as a response to how to deal with long waiting lists.[5] Leopold Bellak and Leonard Small found that most people came for treatment only when in crisis and stayed for a limited length of time (one to six sessions), and that treatment can be very effective at those times.[6] Many of these authors believe that short-term treatment—the time of which can vary from short to long sessions, of one to twelve sessions— is an effective and practical form of treatment, and, more important, that the clients find it so as well.

A controversial question raised by this modality is: For whom is short-term treatment suitable? There are professionals who make patient selection criteria very narrow. For example, Peter Sifneos selects neurotics with circumscribed symptoms for short-term, anxiety-provoking therapy. His patients must meet four criteria: (1) be of above average intelligence, (2) have had at least one meaningful relationship, (3) have the ability to interact with the evaluator with some affect, and (4) have a specific complaint to work on. They must meet seven motivational critera as well.[7]

Lewis Wolberg focuses on the goal to be achieved for selecting clients. He states three goals as criteria: (1) a rapid restoration of homeostasis in an acute neurotic disorder, (2) a restoration of acute upsets in a chronic personality disorder, and (3) a reconstitution of personality in cases where long-term treatment is not feasible. He also identifies two subgroups: (1) dependent persons who can operate independently, and (2) persons with fragile egos who cannot take more probing.[8]

Mann feels that time-limited treatment is contraindicated for patients who are in an acute state of decompensation or so profoundly depressed that they cannot carry on the work of treatment. He believes that time-limited treatment is indicated for patients, irrespective of diagnosis, who possess enough ego strength to negotiate and tolerate a treatment agreement and schedule.[9]

[3] William Reid and Ann Shyne, *Brief and Extended Casework* (New York: Columbia University Press, 1969).

[4] Patricia Ewalt, "A Psychoanalytically Oriented Child Guidance Setting." in *Task-Centered Practice,* ed. William Reid and Laura Epstein (New York: Columbia University Press, 1977), pp. 25–49.

[5] James Mann, *Time-Limited Psychotherapy* (Cambridge, Mass: Howard University Press, 1973).

[6] Leopold Bellak and Leonard Small, *Emergency and Brief Psychotherapy* (New York: Gruen and Stratton, 1965).

[7] Peter Sifneos, "Short Term Anxiety Provoking Psychotherapy: An Emotional Problem Solving Technique." *Seminars in Psychiatry* 1 (November 1969): 389–98.

[8] Lewis Wolberg. "The Technic of Short-Term Psychotherapy," in *Short-Term Psychotherapy,* ed. Lewis Wolberg (New York: Grune and Stratton, 1965), pp. 127–200. 141–2.

[9] Mann, *Time-Limited Psychotherapy,* p. 17.

Reid and Shyne are even broader in their criteria, stating that brief treatment can include clients who are relatively healthy and well-motivated as well as those whose prognosis for conventional treatment is poor, because of the degree of disturbance, lack of capacity for a relationship, and so on.[10] Little is written on the selection or elimination of clients because of age; authors tend to focus on diagnosis, problem type, or goals in their indications and contraindications for this form of treatment.

Process and Techniques of Short-Term Therapy

What are the processes and techniques that characterize short-term treatment? Wolberg delineates four phases: (1) a supportive phase, during which homeostasis is brought about through the healing influences of the relationship with the therapist, the placebo effect of the therapeutic process, and the decompressive aspect of emotional catharsis; (2) an apperceptive phase, characterized by the ability to understand, even minimally, the meaning of the complaint factor in terms of some operative conflicts and basic personality needs and defenses; (3) an action phase, distinguished by a challenging of certain habitual neurotic patterns, facing them from a different perspective; and (4) an integrative relearning and reconditioning phase, which continues after termination on the basis of the chain reaction started during the treatment.[11]

Mann describes what he calls "the sequence of dynamic events" in the treatment process. The treatment consists of twelve post-evaluation sessions. He believes that knowing the termination date increases the client's anxiety in respect to loss as well as a defense against it. The therapist must keep the focus on the central issue. There is rapid movement in the first three sessions, spurred by a positive transference due to the patient's feeling understood by the therapist's stated understanding of the patient's "chronic and enduring pain." The patient gets angry and/or depressed by the seventh or eighth session, and signs of resistance and negative transference appear. The therapist deals insistently with the patient's reaction (sadness, grief, anger, guilt) to termination in the last three to four sessions. The follow-up appointment is not offered to the patient at termination so as not to interfere with the process of separation; however, the patient is called after six months for an appointment.[12]

Mann's treatment is similar to a condensed analysis or intense psychotherapy that is speeded up. It involves most aspects found in either, except time. Reid uses a more task-oriented approach that includes six ele-

---

[10] Reid and Shyne, *Brief and Extended Casework*, p. 9.

[11] Lewis Wolberg, "Methodology in Short-Term Therapy," in *Brief Therapies*, ed. Harvey Barten (New York: Behavioral Publications, 1971), pp. 62–70.

[12] Mann, *Time-Limited Psychotherapy*, pp. 34–35.

ments: (1) planned brevity, (2) focus, (3) contracts, (4) structure, (5) action emphasis, and (6) empirical orientation. The therapist employs two main strategies: (1) exploration, enhancing client awareness, encouragement, direction, structuring communication to keep on goals; and (2) formulating and carrying out operational tasks.[13]

The process of treatment and techniques may vary somewhat as to client, therapist, and circumstance. However, one similarity throughout the literature is the importance of focus in the work and the activity of the therapist in maintaining that focus. Jacob Schwartz states that the therapist must use all available theoretical knowledge to delimit the area on which to work. The client's symptoms themselves are not necessarily the focus of attention; the focus should be on something potentially progressive rather than regressive, on past and present accomplishments, and on the one which is either/or the most acute or that will provide the most therapeutic leverage. It is also important to choose a focus which is consistent with the client's history, the current problem and the therapeutic goal, and then stay with it. Schwartz also believes that it is important for the therapist to exclude material not pertinent to the focus of the treatment.[14]

Mann emphasizes that the key to successful time-limited therapy is the statement of the central issue gleaned from an understanding of the client's psychodynamics. The central issue is more apt to be of use to the client if it is couched in terms of feelings or maladaptive functions. Finally, a statement is formulated that speaks to the therapist's understanding of the client's coping struggle.[15] The focus varies from very specific behavioral observations or situations to comments on a client's internal life, but it consistently plays a crucial role. Delineating and maintaining the focus calls for the use of therapist's and client's best cognitive functions.

TRANSFERENCE AND COUNTERTRANSFERENCE

Notions about transference and countertransference issues in short-term treatment vary from the opinion that neither are well developed in brief therapy to the feeling that the treatment itself recreates extremely intense feelings in both patient and therapist. Elisabeth Kerns states, "the nature of the client-worker relationship differs in PSTT (planned short-term treatment) from long-term treatment in that the aim is *not* to build a therapeutically dependent relationship with the resulting transference reactions becoming a focal point of treatment. In PSTT the dependency is

---

[13] William Reid. "Task-Centered Treatment and Trends in Clinical Social Work." in *Task-Centered Practice*, ed. Reid and Epstein, pp. 1–26.

[14] Jacob Schwartz, "Time-Limited Brief Psychotherapy," in *Brief Therapies*, ed. Barten, pp. 108–18.

[15] Mann, *Time-Limited Psychotherapy*, pp. 17–18.

not heightened, but rather the relationship takes advantage of the clients' potential for independent problem solving."[16]

Mann emphasizes the importance of an intense positive transference as an integral part of the process and heightened countertransference feelings.[17] It is evident that the intensity depends a great deal not only on goals, tasks, and patient diagnosis, but also on the therapist's orientation, technique, and style.

THERAPIST'S SKILLS

There is general agreement in the literature that short-term therapy requires a great deal of skill on the part of the therapist. Kerns notes the therapist must have emotional readiness, security, refined skills, and flexibility to make assessments and do the work.[18] Veronica Hart, in her study of short-term work in an agency with an orientation toward long-term treatment, found that the workers felt that short-term therapy was a much more demanding modality. The skills and techniques necessary were of a high level and involved a worker's active capacity for eliciting and dealing with client's feelings. She found that these qualities did not relate to the number of interviews or time.[19] Success seems more dependent on the skill of the therapist than factors such as modality, discipline, or orientation. Bellak and Small state:

> Most especially, brief psychotherapy is not easy therapy. The therapist must be acutely alert to every meaningful communication, while rapidly formulating the common denominators, filling in the omitted parts from his vantage point of common sense, and almost simultaneously deciding on the most fruitful intervention, which he balances against his assessment of the patient's ego strengths and real life circumstances and conditions. In brief psychotherapy, the therapist does not have time to wait for insight to develop, he must foster insight. He does not have time to wait for working-through; he must stimulate working-through. And when these basic aspects of the therapeutic process are not following, he must invent alternatives.[20]

Mann discusses similar therapist qualifications, adding that a personal analysis is an enhancement.[21]

---

[16] Elizabeth Kerns, "Planned Short-Term Treatment, A New Service to Adolescents." in *Children and Their Parents in Brief Psychotherapy*, ed. Harvey and Sybil Barten (New York: Behavioral Publications, 1973), p. 84.

[17] Mann, *Time-Limited Psychotherapy*, p. 51.

[18] Kerns, "Planned Short-Term Treatment," pp. 79–91.

[19] Veronica Hart, "Instituting Short-Term Casework in a Long-Term Agency," in *Task-Centered Practice*, ed. Reid and Epstein, pp. 89–99.

[20] Bellak and Small, *Emergency and Brief Psychotherapy*, p. 6.

[21] Mann, *Time-Limited Psychotherapy*, p. 59.

BENEFITS OF SHORT-TERM THERAPY

Benefits of short-term therapy extend from symptom relief to personality change—Hoch emphasizes that resistance is lessened by the modality.[22] Wolberg summarizes the impact:

> Even though change in short-term therapy can only deal with the immediate and manifest, we may ultimately influence the total personality in depth, including the unconscious. Human warmth and feeling experienced by a patient in one session with an empathetic therapist, may achieve more profound alterations than years with a probing detached therapist intent on weaning out resistance. This does not mean that one should be neglectful of the unconscious. For within a short span of therapy, repressed psychic aspects may be elicited and handled.[23]

In summary, those who write about the modality and the short-term clients who have been studied concur in its benefits, both practical and emotional.

Short-Term Therapy with Adolescents

Lovick Miller believes that most adolescent problems can be viewed as a crisis in the maintenance of an ego identity.[24] The short-term therapy goal for adolescents, therefore, is to help achieve integration. Miller identifies four categories of conditions that may hinder an adolescent's development of ego identity; (1) failure to cope with previous developmental problems; (2) exposure to overwhelming tension-producing situations; (3) failures in value systems; and (4) withdrawal from social channels.[25]

Short-term treatment is proposed here as a preferred treatment modality for adolescents for numerous reasons. First, its form deals with the developmental issue of adolescent separation. It recreates that struggle and its resolution. Second, it helps increase autonomy and the ability to do for oneself, so precious to the growing adolescent. Third, it helps lessen the resistance of many adolescents to treatment in general because they know there is an end to the process. It limits the dependency of the adolescent on an adult to "help" and puts the onus on oneself, aided by the support and understanding of the therapist. It helps the therapist and client regulate the intensity of the transference, depending on the nature of the treatment contract. It promotes a healthy identification with an active ther-

---

[22] Paul Hoch, "Short-Term versus Long-Term Therapy," in *Short-Term Psychotherapy*, ed. Wolberg, pp. 51–66.

[23] Wolberg, "Technic of Short-Term Therapy," p. 138.

[24] Lovick Miller, "Short-Term Therapy with Adolescents," in *Crisis Intervention: Selected Readings*, ed. Howard Parad (New York: Family Service of America, 1965), pp. 157–66.

[25] Ibid.

apist who takes well-calculated risks. Most important, short-term treatment helps the adolescent be an active participant, rather than a passive one, in his or her development.

Case Illustrations of Time-limited Planned Short-Term Treatment

The adolescents described in this section were seen by the therapist for twelve post-diagnosis sessions and had an agreed-upon contract for work. Although it is not always feasible, short-term work is enhanced if a transfer can be avoided, so the flow of the work that is in progress through the evaluation period is maintained. As little time as possible should elapse between evaluation and short-term treatment for any client, but especially for teenagers whose ambivalence about treatment and life in general is characteristically high.

At the youth center, all clients in crisis are given an appointment within a week or immediately if need be. Up to four treatment hours can be used to work through the crisis and either terminate or be recommended for some continued treatment. This includes work with parents and/or siblings. All children over twelve years old were assigned as crisis cases. In fact, Ewalt, in her study of the crisis program, found that when adolescents are seen quickly, their dropout rate is much lower and further treatment recommendations more often accepted.[26]

MELANIE

Melanie, fifteen years old, came to the clinic through the crisis intervention program in the fall of 1972. Melanie had been referred by her school guidance counselor. Her parents agreed to come as well, although they were, as they put it, "antipsychiatry." Melanie's difficulties, as seen by all including herself, were: depression, worries over losing control, arguments with her father, minor academic and behavior difficulties in school (cutting, tardiness, not completing work, some backtalk to teachers), and overreacting with anger and hysterics to situations that did not warrant such intense emotions. Although angry at others, Melanie came to understand that these problems were internal, as were the solutions.

Through the crisis contacts her parents saw that they tried too hard to appease Melanie. The placating upset everyone, kept Melanie dependent, and encouraged her hysterics as a method of getting "extras." The parents decided that they needed to set firm but reasonable limits with her, to stick to them, and to control their reactions better. They could see that her histrionics were a method of getting closer to her father in an inappropriate way and that other ways of

[26] Patricia Ewalt, "The Crisis-Treatment Approach in a Child Guidance Clinic." *Social Casework* 54 (July 1973): 406–11.

relating were needed. Further treatment for the parents was not wanted or recommended.

Surprisingly, Melanie agreed that her parents did not need treatment, in contrast to an earlier claim; she felt she was the one who needed the treatment. Melanie agreed to a course of treatment for twelve weekly sessions with two central goals: (1) to attain a better understanding of and control over her behavior and moods, and (2) to promote more independent functioning and to lessen the dependence on her parents. In short, she was to mature by examining and changing the two factors that were getting in the way of that goal.

Melanie felt that short-term treatment would lessen her dependency on adults and increase her self-reliance. Essentially, she was a girl with a lot of strengths who was stuck in a renewed oedipal conflict. The diagnosis was anxiety neurosis or "hysteria." Superficially, she looked less healthy because of her adolescent issues and behavior. Without going into more detail about her psychodynamics, the understanding of which was crucial to the treatment, it is possible to note that she easily accomplished her goals. Treatment dealt directly with her many feelings about growing up and used her ego strengths to the utmost. Although the child side of her was dealt with, her treatment was like that of an adult, forcing her to conceptualize her feelings and behavior, develop insight, and make constructive changes.

The chief complaints were worked on indirectly through direct work on the issues mentioned above. Melanie stopped skipping school, her grades improved markedly, her psychosomatic symptoms stopped, moods improved, her hysterics abated, and her relationships in general became more mutually satisfying. She now wants to be more like her mother (a stable, warm woman) and enjoys a more low-keyed relationship with her father, having given up (or grown out of) the sexualized relationship she previously desired and feared.

Short-term therapy was ideal for Melanie because it used her strengths and undermined maladaptive defenses and behavior. It gave her a model that was consistent with what she needed to achieve—autonomy, and a reasonable degree of emotional separation from her parents.

JACK

Jack, seventeen years old, came to the clinic as part of an evaluation done by the school. The school evaluation was initiated by Jack's father who had been divorced five years and lived with his five children aged twelve to twenty. Jack's mother had deserted the family after numerous psychiatric hospitalizations and visited only sporadically. His father was involved with a woman who also had many children and was dying. Jack was at the clinic because the school told him if he did not go for evaluation, he could not return to class after his current suspension.

Jack was referred to the clinic for chronic school problems for the last two years: underachievement, truancy, disruptions at school. He was involved in semidelinquent activities and was extremely negative toward teachers and peers.

Jack's father felt that he had neglected his children, that Jack had never gotten over the trauma of his mother's desertion, and that Jack identified with his father's lackadaisical attitude. Jack and his father felt the worst problem was that lately Jack was "doing nothing and relating to no one." Both were concerned about Jack's future. Jack was arrogant, surly, hostile, intellectualized, and bitter. He used his large size and intense anger to frighten and intimidate people. He maintained a stance that all the teachers and kids in his school were "scum," and probably everyone else too.

In the evaluation process, however, some pain at his own losses and loneliness was available although well-defended against. Jack was diagnosed as a moderate character disorder who appeared severely passive-aggressive. The therapist believed that this orientation to life masked a healthier obsessive-compulsive personality (but nonetheless, narcissistic character), from clues given during the diagnostic evaluation.

Short-term treatment was recommended to Jack with several stipulations: (1) that he agree to contain his acting out, (2) that he return to school and complete his junior year, and (3) that he complete twelve treatment sessions, like it or not. The school had already readmitted him, so his acceptance of treatment was contingent only on himself. He knew he could break the contract; it was, after all, only a moral one. In short, the treatment asked him to contain his overt current behavior and make use of healthier defenses. The narcissistic side of him was validated by the admission that he had been wounded and rejected (that is, victimized). His high intelligence was acknowledged, but its disuse was also. The short-term modality was recommended for several reasons. Jack's counter-dependent self could not tolerate an open-ended treatment contract or relationship. He needed to feel some control in the therapy. He was also about as ready as one could expect him to be for treatment, and that could fade quickly without intervention. Also, the therapist felt that she could not manage her countertransference (fear) nor could she expect another worker to, in an open- ended situation. In other words, the treatment was tailored not only for the client, but also for the therapist.

The treatment contract with Jack was discussed prior to his acceptance of further treatment. The therapist stated that she felt that because of his earlier real and deep hurts and rejections, that Jack was "getting revenge on others" by rejecting everyone and everything. The therapist said that this, however, was his business, but in her professional judgment she felt that it was self-destructive, not smart, and that he was being unfair to himself. The therapist identified two main problems: (1) extreme hostility toward school personnel and peers which resulted in his not going to school, acting out, and generally withdrawing and constricting his activities, and (2) no relationships, which resulted in loneliness. They discussed tasks, some of which were operational (going to school), but most of which were intrapsychic. Jack accepted treatment sullenly, and although he had been given the opportunity to change therapists if *he* wanted, he said it was, "okay," to stay with this therapist so he did not have to repeat "all the garbage."

Treatment with Jack could best be described as extremely difficult. He was furious with the therapist most of the time, demeaning, castrating, and intimidating. He was outraged that she did not persuade the school to let him out of a year of school "for psychiatric reasons." He was told that he was neither schizophrenic nor retarded, so that a social promotion was against her professional and moral judgment. However, the therapist understood and interpreted his feelings, which had a calming effect on Jack. He came weekly, always on time, and was very verbal and challenging. He rejected support, but the therapist persisted by saying repeatedly that he was capable of feeling better and owed himself good relationships where he could get the love he deserved. The therapist interpreted his displacements, his hostility, and his defenses when he tried to reject them (and her). She told him he was getting what he demanded, her best professional judgment.

The transference and countertransference issues were intense and used in the treatment to demonstrate his problems with relationships, but seductive tactics were avoided. At one point, the therapist told him that she was very angry with him; he had hurt her feelings by calling her a "phony" when she said something genuinely nice about him. He apologized.

The treatment process was very complicated and exhausting. Jack made a great deal of progress, which he tried to hide at first, because he stated, "I wouldn't want to give you credit for any of it." He made some friends at school and work, attended school regularly, and stopped acting out. Near the end of treatment he said, "Okay, I suppose if you have a barrel of apples and have been eating rotten ones, if you keep eating enough some will turn up good. Maybe I just wasn't eating enough apples." Once, when he referred to himself and the therapist's other patients as her "victims," she pointed out that he had her for twelve sessions, not just the other way.

Termination was dealt with fairly perfunctorily and he turned down a follow-up appointment. He acknowledged his progress and said that he felt he would not think about treatment "more than ten minutes a day, if ever." Jack's therapy was a profound experience for the therapist, and maybe for him. This case was included because it added a dimension to the therapist's experience, a treatment tailored to manage the therapist's countertransference. Jack benefitted from the treatment, but so had the therapist.

Short-term treatment was the treatment of choice for this adolescent because of the design of the therapy and the inherent process of promoting autonomy.

Unplanned Short–Term Treatment with Adolescents

Another kind of short-term treatment is short-term because the client decides to terminate early in open-ended treatment. In the cases following, the therapist offered the client trial treatment of a specified number of sessions, but the recommendation was long-term. In the first illustration the hidden agenda had been to keep the client in treatment for at least a year; in the second, no such agenda existed.

DENISE

Denise, fifteen years old, was referred to the crisis program by her school. Denise's mother and the school felt the need for immediate help; Denise did not. Denise had academic and behavior problems in school. She was easily distracted, overwhelmed by her studies, negativistic to an extreme toward herself and others, mistrustful, and critical and resentful of her mother and brother. Her father had died of cancer two years before. Everyone's main concern was Denise's anger and criticism of herself. Denise was furious because she had to go to the clinic, feared that others would see her as crazy, and was paranoid at times. Her reality testing was impaired, she had religious rituals, and she was continually fearful or angry. Her diagnosis was borderline personality, with usable neurotic defenses.

Although long-term treatment seemed indicated, a six-week trial treatment was proposed because Denise was so resistent. The tasks were to help her examine her negative feelings, to deal with peers more realistically, and to gain better control over her behavior and feelings. She was aware that the recommendation was for long-term treatment and that the "trial" was for her benefit. She accepted the trial treatment with great ambivalence but came faithfully, although always protesting. At the completion of six sessions, she recontracted for five more and then terminated. The therapist was disappointed; on the surface, it did not look as if Denise had made much progress. She claimed, however, that she "felt much better." It was questionable that such a severely disturbed girl had benefited much from such as short relationship. The prognosis was poor, but the therapist respected Denise's wish to terminate, emphasizing that she could reapply.

Over the next four years the therapist received a yearly Christmas card and letter from Denise. On two other occasions she also called, wanting "someone she could trust" to talk to, or to seek "advice." She began counseling in her second year at college. The memory of her earlier treatment had prompted her to seek additional counseling because she felt that she "could use it again," although she felt that her "head was on straighter this time." She said that she has thought of the therapist over the past years and what they had talked about; because she recognized that she often got into the same "patterns," this helped "get her out."

Work with Denise might have been enhanced if it had been more specific and time-limited, however, the results were better than had been expected. The therapist learned not to underestimate the impact of a brief therapeutic relationship.

BILL

Bill, sixteen years old, was involved in a treatment contract that was to be short-term, and then transfer to another therapist for long-term work. Bill's chief complaints were severe depression and withdrawal after some scapegoating incidents at school, no friends, recent losses from relatives moving, and extreme criticism and moralizing toward younger brothers. The school psychologist at the technical school he attended was concerned about his depression and worsening school phobia. The school saw him as a severely constricted, sensitive adolescent who did not belong in a vocational school with adolescents who were not as bright or healthy. Two years ago, because of a clash with peers, Bill had transferred from a very good suburban junior high. His parents were good, solid, warm people, but his mother was overprotective. Bill was seen for fourteen sessions, his parents conjointly for four, and the whole family twice. Bill had agreed to work on ventilating his angry feelings and looking at their source, and in the process working through his ambivalence about the significant people in his life—mother, father, and maternal grandmother. He was to re-examine his rigid value system, with the goal of helping him to loosen up, be like other teenagers, and relate to peers.

After several sessions of intense probing and uncovering of unconscious conflicts, Bill transferred to a local high school and became more involved with people in general. He developed a sense of humor and became more assertive. Bill's intelligence, his capacity for insight, the use of healthier adaptive obsessive-compulsive defenses, and a positive transference helped him make rapid progress. He felt ready to terminate at the end of the treatment contract. His parents were pleased with their progress as well as with Bill's. Bill felt his whole life was changed by the therapy; he was doing well in school, had lots of friends, and was actively pursuing a "cute girl" in one of his classes. Bill's progress was confirmed by his guidance counselor.

In retrospect, the therapist underestimated the impact of a short-term contract on this bright and motivated boy who came in a state of acute pain. Later, the therapist realized that the contract could have only been short-term. The format of the therapy demanded greater autonomous functioning on Bill's part, and a very active participation in uncovering, clarifying, interpreting, and working through unconscious conflicts from both Bill and the therapist.

SUMMARY

These illustrations could have been planned short-term contracts; it might have made the treatment less ambiguous. Regardless of the length of treatment planned, the spelling out of short-term goals in the treatment contract with adolescents and a time limit in which to review that contract, and in most cases to terminate, is highly advocated.

Conclusion

Short-term therapy is a preferred treatment modality for adolescents for many reasons. It is economical to the client and the agency. It is a modality that best encompasses the life tasks of the adolescent—separation from parents and the establishment of an ego identity, in a form that is both concrete and symbolic. It presupposes a termination at the onset, just as puberty presupposes the end of childhood. It is not only a modality consistent with the normal process of adolescence, but it is a treatment that is acceptable to most adolescents, even ones who are highly ambivalent about treatment and mental health professionals in general.

Short-term therapy is ideal for adolescents because it is a form that is also ideal for their therapists. It creates a structure that forces the therapist to utilize the most refined skills and understanding and the highest level of mental and physical (verbal) activity. In terms of transference and countertransference issues, it takes some of the edge off the relationship by knowing it will end. It allows for the flow or control of the intensity of feelings in the relationship with which one might be more cautious in a more open-ended alliance. And it enhances the quality of the therapy by making both client and therapist work quickly toward greater autonomy and emotional growth for the client. Therefore, short-term treatment is seen as a preferential form of treatment for most adolescents.

THE YOUNG ADULT

CHAPTER 4

Young Adulthood:
A Developmental Phase

Glen Clifford and Katharine Odin

It is a striking fact that in comparison to the rich body of systematic knowledge concerning child and adolescent development, there exist far fewer studies of normative development in adulthood. Developmental shifts following adolescence, incompletely articulated and understood within the literature, warrant closer and more systematic attention. Since it has already been made clear in psychoanalytic literature that childhood and adolescent behavior may best be understood within a developmental context, (Hartmann, 1958) it becomes necessary to have a clearer understanding of the developmental stages affecting adulthood in order to have a more complete context for interpreting adult behavior.

This study focuses on early adulthood, specifically ages 25 to 35. It is based on the premise that young adulthood may constitute a distinct developmental phase during which phase-specific tasks are negotiated. It also assumes that ego growth and development may extend and continue beyond the earliest years of life. The literature does not provide a coherent view of this period, but only a fragmentary sense that during early adulthood there are significant changes in how the individual views himself. This study is designed to explore the nature of those changes, as well as generate a theoretical framework within which these changes might be understood.

Theoretical Perspectives

Erik Erikson's work on the eight ages of man contains a widely known developmental treatment of adulthood. His two stages of adulthood, the

Reprinted from *Smith College Studies in Social Work*, Vol. 44, No. 2 (February, 1974), pp. 125–142, by permission of the publisher.

stage of Intimacy versus Isolation and the stage of Generativity versus Stagnation are both probably relevant to the age period of this study. Erikson's epigenetic conception advances the view that mastery of the tasks specific to each earlier stage is crucial to the mastery of those in the stages that follow. Thus, the tasks of the stage of Intimacy, the capacity for fusing one's identity with another, for committing oneself to concrete affiliations and for developing the ethical strength to abide by such commitments, require an identiy solid enough to risk such affiliations without overwhelming the ego.

Successful mastery of the tasks of the stage of Intimacy then leads into the stage of Generativity: "The ability to lose one's self in the meeting of bodies and minds leads to a gradual expansion of ego interests and to a libidinal investment in that which is being generated" (Erikson, 1963, 267). This shift requires that the individual create for himself a continuing giving of himself in a creative, caretaking and participatory way that helps him avoid stagnation (Erikson, 1963).

Erikson's description of this particular shift is brief and skeletal, and he provides little in the way of concrete descriptive analysis. What seems implied in his notion of the expansion of ego interests and shift in libidinal investment is a broadening and integration of the individual's self-image, in a way that would incorporate the products of his concrete affiliations, specifically his work and his family and all external representations thereof. If so, the change in self-image would in some way be mirrored in the individual's capacity for and participation in concrete affiliations.

Other clues about adult development derive from research. Gould and his associates, for example, studied a population of 524 adults ranging in age from 16 to over 60. The subjects were asked to rate a series of statements in the order of greatest importance. Curves for each statement were plotted on the basis of the average rank ordering for the 20 subjects of each age.

Findings pertinent to this study are the number changes in the curve around age 30 from a relatively stable baseline at 20 with a return to another stable baseline at 40. Gould characterizes these curves as demonstrative of two major shifts. "There is a gradual peeling away of the magical illusions of omnipotence and omnipotentiality, and there is an identification of the self with the family" (Gould, 1972, 42). Gould's conclusions seem to offer some documentation for Erikson's theoretical notions of the shift from Intimacy to Generativity. Increased identification with the family would seem to support Erikson's notion of the widening sphere of ego interests as a defining characteristic of the stage of Generativity.

Buhler, who has spent a lifetime collecting individual biographies of creative and everyday people, found that the phasic phenomena of the life cycle, as reflected in her biographical studies, could best be described as a three phasic process:

(1) a growth period from birth until the ogranism is fully developed;
(2) a stationary growth period during which the organism's power to maintain itself and develop is equal to the forces of decline and (3) a last period of decline (Buhler, 1968, 13).

She points to age 25 as the age at which phase one shifts to phase two.

This phasic orientation is important to the present study primarily because of the implication that the individual around age 25 experiences a shift from becoming to being, a shift that seems unique to this stage of development. One can infer that such a shift encompasses the loss of a sense of unlimited potential, a sense that had afforded fantasies of omnipotentiality as referred to by Gould, in the face of the encounters with personal and social realities.

Of the literature that focuses on the specific phase of early adulthood, Wittenberg provides the most coherent and detailed examination of the beginning phase of early adulthood: postadolescence. His work, which pertains roughly to ages 20 to 25, provides a backdrop to the period studied in this project.

Wittenberg describes as one characteristic of postadolescence a self-image crisis, during which the individual experiences conflict between superego and ego ideals, which includes the concept of a pseudoideal, "the expression of grandiose and megalomanic strivings" (Wittenberg, 1968, 3). The task involves the striking of a balance between these forces with the ego in full control. He postulates that since the ego is assailed by this and many other conflicts in postadolescence, the ego is usually not in the best position to reach this reasonable compromise and the process of resolution continues beyond postadolescence.

Wittenberg also describes a crisis occasioned by the end of role playing, an activity of adolescence that helps to assimilate anxiety about the mastery of reality. What is demanded of the postadolescent is that he begin to take on a permanent role, to assert the struggle for a persistent experience of sameness and to deal with the superego and ego ideal conflicts. Wittenberg states that some element of mourning accompanies this attempt which involves the holding off of the inevitable recognition of reality limitations. The young adult must take on a permanent role "which is to be his and can no longer be changed without new and often painful anxiety in adult life" (Wittenberg, 1968, 26).

Some of the anxiety experienced by the termination of role playing is related to an emerging awareness of time continuity. This cognition, of the extension of time and the continuity of time into the future, brings about an awareness that the individual determines the way he uses the time ahead of him. According to Wittenberg, this awareness prompts the postadolescent toward long-term commitments (Wittenberg, 1968).

Wittenberg's conceptions seem coherent with Erikson's formulation of the tasks of the stage of Intimacy and could characterize the kinds of crises from which the population in this study were probably beginning to emerge.

The limited developmental literature on adulthood suggests that the late twenties and early thirties is a period during which the individual experiences a change in how he feels about himself and how he defines himself. This project was designed as an exploratory, impressionistic study of the nature and course of such changes. How do these changes relate to age? How are they affected by the individual's capacity for and participation in concrete affiliations, as suggested by Erikson? Is there an experience of mourning in this process as suggested by Wittenberg?

Method

Direct interviews of persons within the 25 to 35 age range were elected as a means for obtaining data. The persons within the age group interviewed were selectively chosen for reasons of availability and capacity for introspection. The sample consisted of thirty psychiatric residents, child fellows and social workers. Other social characteristics of the sample are given in the accompanying table. The findings of this study thus reflect a relatively small and restrictive sample: highly educated, psychologically oriented, professional people.

Utilizing a guide based on the notion derived from the literature that the individual between the ages of 25 and 35 experiences a change in how he feels about and defines himself, the authors structured the interviews to obtain descriptive and affective data on how each individual viewed himself at his present age. The interviews were relatively unstructured, opening with the question, "How does it feel to be your age?" Subjects were encouraged to respond spontaneously and associatively to the question.

During each interview, the authors listened both for the respondent's descriptive feelings about himself as well as the affect accompanying that description. Near the end of the interview each subject over 25 was asked how he would have answered the same question at age 25. This question was asked to provide a perspective on his present view of himself and to elicit data concerning changes since age 25. Each subject under 35 also was asked how he thought he might answer at age 35, so as to obtain information on his ideas about the future and their relation to his present reality. The interviews were approximately one hour long.

The authors jointly interviewed each subject, one having the responsibility for posing questions and following the process of the interview, and the other the responsibility for process notes. This method al-

Selected Characteristics of the Sample

Age	25	26	27	28	29	30	31	32	33	34	35	Total
Number at each age	2	3	4	3	3	2	3	3	2	3	2	30
Number of males	1	3	3	1	2	1	1	2	1	2	1	18
Number of females	1	0	1	2	1	1	2	1	1	1	1	12
Number never married	1	1	1	1	1	1	2	1	1	1	1	12
Number married, no children	1	1	1	1	1	0	1	0	1	1	0	8
Number married, with children	0	1	2	1	1	1	0	2	0	1	1	10
Number social workers	2	0	1	2	1	1	2	2	0	0	1	12
Number psychiatric residents	0	3	3	1	2	1	1	1	2	3	1	18

lowed two perceptions of the same interview in order to provide more objective and reliable observations.

Content analysis was the method used to analyze the data collected. Following the interviews each author individually summarized each interview in terms of predominant tone, content themes and affect. Shifts from past to present, as well as future fantasies were noted. The individual summaries were then compared. Differences in the summaries were found to be primarily due to omission on the part of one of the interviewers. There were 10 such incidents which were readily resolved by discussion, allowing inclusion of omissions in the final joint summaries.

The summaries were initially grouped for analysis according to age. Subsequently, the summaries were also studied when organized according to the sex of the subject, his marital status, parental status and discipline.

Findings

In the analysis of the data that related directly to age, the authors identified some responses to the question, "How does it feel to be your age?" that apparently related directly to the description of the self typically occurring at each age level within the sample. This analysis suggested that it was indeed possible to speak of certain types of self descriptions occurring more frequently during one range of ages than during another. It appeared that the respondents who were twenty-five and twenty-six described themselves differently than the older respondents. Also, it seemed that respondents from 27 to 31 described themselves in a way unique to that group. The respondents from the age of 32 to 35 constituted the final age group. In this report these three age groups will be referred to as early phase, middle phase and late phase.

Age

EARLY PHASE

The predominant tone of the interview of the 25- or 26-year-old was one of intensity and uncertainty. The first association to the question, "How does it feel to be your age?" tended to be a word or phrase like "unsettling," "uncertain," "in transition," or "a little scary." All of these respondents noted that one of their major struggles at this time was in being faced with and forced to grapple with their own limitations in the attempt to actualize adult roles. Within this context they spoke of an earlier tendency to see themselves in rather grandiose terms; two spoke of an earlier expectation that they would be "the new Sigmund Freud." Another described an earlier conviction that she would be a "phenomenal success" by age 25. Although they felt they were moving away from this earlier grandiose view, they expressed uncertainty about what could replace it. As one 25-year-old stated, "I feel I have nothing concrete to show for the past few years. It makes me feel inadequate because of my former fantasies about what I would be doing now." A 26-year-old commented that hearing one of his supervisors describe his interviewing techniques as "typical of a first-year resident" was one of the hardest blows of his first year of residency. In many ways, members of this group experienced confrontation with limitations as a severe blow to self-esteem.

A striking feature of these particular encounters with reality was the amount of sadness and disappointment expressed in regard to the relinquishment of earlier grandiose ideals. "It's sad to have to give up the utopian ideals of college and face the real business of being an adult. It's depressing," The 25-year-old woman mentioned above spoke of the fact that she was not the phenomenal success she had expected to be, as if something promised had been taken away from her. The affect accompanying this statement was a mixture of disappointment and anger. Thus, it appears that the passing of the grandiose inner image is affectively felt as a loss.

The data suggest that the members of this age group are in the process of integrating their private, inner view of themselves with their public, adult roles. In some instances the respondents expressed resentment about having to meet certain adult expectations. "I can't be as outrageous as I used to be. It's no longer age appropriate." One 26-year-old referred to being older and professional as a burden, and another seemed to mourn the loss of membership in a group with stability and cohesion that he had once experienced but no longer found available.

Within these interviews there were also references to new thoughts about the future. The respondents indicated that their former tendency to view the future concretely and in terms of deadlines and milestones was being altered. For many this change was precipitated by an inability to meet real or fantasized deadlines. The validity of deadlines was particularly challenged by the emerging awareness that the deadlines were derived from cultural and parental expectations often not in correspondence to the individual's real experience of life. Parents and their expectations were often referred to by this group. The desire to please their parents was still an issue. One married respondent mentioned that one of the major reasons he and his wife hoped to have children was for the pleasure of their parents.

The respondents over 25 who recalled how they felt about themselves at that age advanced descriptions quite similar to the associations given by respondents who were at that age. In addition, the retrospective data high-lighted certain other aspects of this period. Several referred to a form of playacting of adult roles at that age. Others spoke of a different way of conceptualizing the decision-making process at 25. Decisions made at that age were not perceived as having the effect of closing off future options, although this eventually proved to be the case. This finding underlines the fact that people in this age range tend to view the future as existing outside the same rules of reality to which the present is subject.

MIDDLE PHASE

The respondents between ages 27 and 31 were in general much more confident in themselves and suffered less from feelings of immediate loss than the younger respondents. Instead, they communicated a feeling of transition and discovery which was less charged with the affects of anger and disappointment. Perhaps the tone of these interviews is best sum-marized in the statement of one 29-year-old: "I feel three-fourths through something. Things are beginning to fall into place."

In contrast to the younger group's expressions of inadequacy, most people in this group noted an emerging sense of competence and confi-dence with regard to their profession. They describe a new experience of personal gratification from their work which was becoming less dependent upon external approval and was less generated by external expectations. Several made statements similar to the following: "I feel a growing sense of competence and power. I'm giving up fantasies of power for the real thing. That's a lot tougher than I thought it would be." "I feel more willing to take risks, going out on a limb about what I know. It's getting easier to take criticism." "I now feel like I can still feel competent where I am and also be aware of where I want to go without invalidating the level I'm at." The actual experience of accomplishment by this group seems to have been a compensating factor for the feeling of loss so immediate to the younger group.

Another theme that emerged conspicuously throughout these inter-views was reference to the process of aging. Almost all respondents noted that they were getting older. Often this was acknowledged in relation to their physical condition or to their diminished level of energy. Several ref-erences were made to old age: "Getting old, I mean haggard old, tired old is scary to me." "I wonder how I'll feel when I'm sixty?" A few married respondents queried what life would be like when their children were grown up and gone from home. Several of the unmarried respondents expressed concern about what life would be like in their fifties or sixties if they remained unmarried.

The death or decline of parents was often mentioned by this group and a few made direct remarks about their own mortality within that context: "I feel a little fearful about death. I mean I'm not really over the hump, but I realize the finality of death. My mother's death has affected my thinking." The awareness of mortality seems to be also reflected in this group's emphasis on and strong orientation toward the present. There were several references to the lack of control over events and the relinquishment of "master-plans" in favor of living more in the present. As one respondent stated, "I realize now that you can't make everything come out like a storybook. I don't have as many five-year plans, and I enjoy the present more. I enjoy just seeing how it's all going to come out."

Within this context was also the report that some things in life were becoming more fixed, and that it was becoming increasingly more difficult to change things. While several references were made to the awareness of options narrowing and possibilities limiting, the tone was more one of acceptance than in the younger group. At the same time, however, the past was often recalled in a reminiscent way that related to "the passing of my youth." The most significant amount of affect was expressed with regard to the age 30; apparently the experience of reaching this age stirred up again earlier feelings about the loss of grandiose fantasies. The age was not only anticipated with concern, "I'll really have to give up the things of my youth," but was experienced with some sadness: "At 30, I said to myself, look what Mozart was doing at 30, and look at me."

Within this group were two people whose responses to the initial question differed markedly from the others. One of these was a 31-year-old who impressed the authors as very depressed. He described a crisis around 30 when he realized that certain goals were not going to be reached and became aware that he was destined to lead a very ordinary existence. He felt unsatisfied about his career choices and his unmarried status. He saw parenthood as offering compensation for the loss of his own feelings of potentiality. He looked to age 35 with hopes that he would not be bitter and with the hope that he would find something to devote himself to.

This respondent differed from the others in this age range primarily in his lack of closure on any of the issues of adulthood: career choice, marriage and parenthood. While experiencing the loss of grandiose ideals and omnipotentiality similar to the other respondents, he had no commitments from which to gain self-esteem and enhance his life within a realistic context. This interview seems to highlight the importance of participation in concrete affiliations as a means of mourning or resolving the loss of omnipotentiality.

The other interview was with a 27-year-old married social worker, who having committed herself to both marriage and career, described her present feelings as "intolerable." This respondent reported deriving little satisfaction from her achievements and feeling haunted by the notion that "this isn't enough." Her orientation was continually toward the future and toward further achievement. She stated that she was aware that "what I really need to do is just be what I am."

This respondent impressed the authors as someone whose goals and commitments were highly determined by cultural and parental expectations. The lack of integration between these expectations and personal desires and goals seemed related to her limited capacity for personal satisfaction and self-esteem. This interview suggested some of the pitfalls of premature closure on the basic issues of adulthood, particularly if based largely on external expectations.

LATE PHASE

The interviews with the group between the ages of 32 and 35 were significantly marked by a tone of reflection and calm. One of the most striking features of this group was their tendency to view themselves from a historical perspective. Their first associations to the initial question, in fact, tended to include references to the past. These were statements like, "It's certainly better than 20." "That's an open question. The last ten years have been a big change." "I guess that has to do with where I've been."

In contrast to the expressions of inadequacy and loss advanced by the first group, and of transition and discovery by the second group, this group expressed feelings of integration, clarity and form. Respondents seemed to feel much more defined than the younger respondents and accepting of that definition. As one 34-year-old stated, "I feel more that who I am, I am, and that's not bad." The emergence of structure and form was described by one respondent as somewhat unconscious: "Whether conscious or not, decisions have been made, and you look around and realize you have a structure to your life. It's kind of a relief." Another referred to some of the components of the process that resonated with many of the issues highlighted by the younger groups: "It's been a process of sorting out who I am and what I want to do. You discover what's feasible, you limit and relinquish some of your ambitions—many of which were never real anyway, and you gradually begin to feel more formed."

Another feature of this group was their identification with those who had formerly been parenting figures. One respondent described the sudden realization that those whom she had formerly looked up to were now peers. This new identification seemed to bring to the surface the feeling of having something to offer others. "For awhile, I didn't feel like I belonged to any generation. There seemed to be no compensation for getting older and I had a feeling of loss. I guess I joined the older generation when I realized I had something valuable to offer." Within this context, respondents spoke of success as "a more personal thing," less defined by the environment. Their energy seemed to be focused less on new life plans and more on "making the most of what you've got." For many, this meant a stronger focus on their families and more emphasis on enjoying and ap-preciating life. Those who were unmarried spoke not only of gratification from teaching and supervising others, but of investing energy in activities outside their profession.

While several references were made to the issue of mortality, these were often made within the context of a lifetime perspective: "I see where I've been, but also where I'm going. My age is sort of a middle age. I think more of the end of life as a real possibility." It is this perspective on both past and future which was unique to this group. The frequent use of the word "process" by respondents of this group was also significant. Re-spondents communicated a sense of participation in a process that joined both the past and the future. "Before, I tended to look at the future in concrete terms, but now I feel more carried by and identified with an ev-olutionary process." Perhaps this identification with evolutionary and or-ganic process can be viewed as a way of dealing with mortality.

The responses of younger subjects to the question of how they would feel about their age at 35 indicated that all of the respondents saw them-selves as more settled and secure at 35 than they were now. Many saw this age as a vantage point from which they could evaluate their past per-formance. Those who lacked closure on pressing issues at their present age saw themselves as gaining closure before 35.

Concrete Affiliations

PARENTHOOD

Ten of the 30 people interviewed were parents. One significant finding in analyzing the responses from this group alone was the conspicuous sim-ilarity in their expressions of feelings of form, comfort and clarity. Those with parenting responsibilites often sounded like the 32 to 35 age group regardless of their age. Having a child seems to be an affiliation of unique proportions that accelerates the process of getting in touch with real ca-pacities, real limitations, and a reality based definition of self. Although most parents did not describe why they chose to have children or how the decision was made, parenthood brought with it very unexpected personal revelations. One respondent's comment may sum up the central theme of the experience. "Having a child is a conspicuous definition of who you are." The awareness of the force of that definition for many people pre-cipitated shifts in their marriage and career affiliations.

One female respondent stated that, "having a child said something about myself, made me aware of new capacities...life suddenly had to do with me." It was this new sense of self that prompted her toward a new introspection and examination of her marriage. This experience led ultimately to a divorce several years later. For many the experience brought about within the marriage what is described by one respondent as "a renewed commitment in our marriage, a greater sense of closeness. There was something more final in our relationship then and a feeling that this is really it." One psychiatric resident, who had spent four years in another profession, traced his decision to change professions to the birth of his first child. "Having a child made me question what I was doing with myself. It was almost like being reborn." Another 29-year-old when describing himself stated that he had begun to experience the comfortable feeling of "settling into a groove," of giving up his former adolescent freedoms. When asked when this feeling began, he responded. "About ten minutes after my child was born. It was not there with the decision to have the child."

MARRIAGE

Eighteen of the 30 people interviewed were married; 12 had never been married. The experience of marriage for most of the respondents has also been a reality experience requiring and precipitating struggle and change. Here, as with parenthood, the decision to get married was not well explained. A variety of reasons were expressed: "All my friends were getting married," "I was leaving the city, wanted her with me and felt it was the honorable thing to do," and "I was tired of being alone." It is important to note that all but one of our married respondents made the decision to marry before age 25.

Although many of the more personal marital details were not shared in the interviews, one struggle did emerge as a theme among the married respondents, the struggle with dependence and independence. Many people stated that they found it difficult to acknowledge their own dependency in marriage, to accept their own needs. As one respondent described it, "Accepting that dependency means giving up the notion that I'm superman; I guess that means beginning to accept myself."

Marriage for many brought about a change in relationships with parents. Respondents described a withdrawal on the part of their parents that made them feel more autonomous and responsible. This experience seemed to precipitate what many described as a greater capacity for dealing with the death of parents.

Two of the respondents had been married and divorced. Both were married in their early twenties and divorced after 25. Both described their marriages as relationships built on fantasy and role expectation: "I wanted to be the perfect Good Housekeeping wife." They both described a gradual process of getting in touch with their own true capacities and real potential that made the marriages no longer tenable.

To the respondents who were not married, the issue of marriage was an important one, but attitudes about marriage shifted throughout the age span of our sample. Those in the lower age range did not question whether they would eventually get married, but noted that they were facing new thoughts about it. One 25-year-old described a panicked feeling regarding the deadlines she had set for herself. "I always felt marriage should take place between 25 and 27 and now I'm faced with my deadline. I'm not sure what this means." One 26-year-old stated, "I used to be able to picture myself married, picture my wife and whole family. I can't picture this in my mind's eye anymore. I'm now aware that that has to develop, not just happen. I have a feeling about it now, instead of an image."

As the respondents progressed in age, a shift in thinking occurred away from cultural expectations and pictures of marriage to a more personal evaluation of whether marriage is desirable. Respondents between 28 and 31 spoke less about marriage itself and more about concerns with the quality of a relationship. There appeared a more serious and conscious awareness of the reality and demands of marriage resulting in more thoughtful discriminations about the kind of relationship desired. There also emerged some questioning about how needs could be met without the institution of marriage.

Those at the upper level of our age span, while leaving the question of marriage open, felt that not being married was a state compatible with their self-image. They viewed the unmarried state as a reality with which they had come to terms, a state that entailed a decision-making process as unconscious as that described by those who decided to marry.

CAREER

The most significant finding about the issue of career was that 8 of the 12 social workers in the sample decided to make social work their career and then took decisive steps to actualize their decision around the age of 25. Most traced this decision to a sudden pressure around that age to make a long-term career commitment. As one respondent described it, "I felt that the time had come to get serious about this. Although experimenting around with different jobs had been good for me, I was getting less and less gratification and felt I now wanted something definite."

The finding is significant not only in terms of what appears to be a pressure for closure on the career issue, but also in terms of the contrast to the psychiatric residents, the majority of whom made their career decision at age 21 or younger. What was a period of experimentation with career for one group was a period of intense preparation for career in the other group. The difference between the age at which career commitment is made raised two questions. What is the significance of choosing a career at 21 as opposed to at 25? What is lost or gained in delaying such a commitment until after a period of experimentation?

Discussion

One aim of the present project was to explore the plausibility of viewing early adulthood as a developmental phase. To pursue this aim, it is useful to consider Erikson's criteria for a developmental stage. First of all, Erikson emphasizes that during each stage the person encounters certain phase-specific tasks and that out of these encounters new capabilities are realized (Erikson, 1968). Secondly, as part of this process, the person experiences a crisis because of "the necessity to manage the new encounters within a given time allowance" (Erikson, 1968, 105). Thirdly, he states that the negotiation of a phase has a "proper rate and sequence" (Erikson, 1968, 95). Fourthly, the successful negotiation of a phase will be experienced as, "an increased sense of inner unity, with an increase of good judgment and an increase in the capacity 'to do well' according to his own standards and to the standards of those who are significant to him" (Erikson, 1968, 95).

This study suggests that these four characteristics are present within the time period studied. First of all, the data point toward important shifts in descriptions of the self that begin at 25 and stabilize around 35; in addition, it seems possible to understand these shifts in terms of developmental tasks and emerging capacities. Second, most respondents report a pressure to reach closure on certain issues within a limited time. Third, the shifts in self-description with age could be grouped into three distinct, sequentially related stages, and that the rate of these changes are the result of aging and an interactional effect between aging and the concrete affiliations of parenthood, marriage and career. Fourth, the 31 to 34-year-old respondents and respondents who were parents, the two groups the authors postulate as most likely to have negotiated this developmental stage, describe themselves in terms consonant with Erikson's description.

The two atypical interviews described earlier may be understood as reflecting attempts to avoid the age-specific crisis by either premature or delayed closure on the issues of parenthood, marriage and career. The fact that engagement with the tasks of this stage was found even with these two subjects is further confirmation of the existence of a distinct developmental phase of young adulthood.

Many of the specific themes emerging from the present study seem related to generativity. The expansion of ego interests of these subjects is strongly suggested in the findings. Also, the older respondents begin to view themselves as having certain responsibilities toward the next generation and to prize their roles as parents and as teachers. An important source of self-esteem for those in the latter part of young adulthood came from caring for the next generation. It seems, then, that the stage of young adulthood described in this study corresponds in important ways to Erikson's stage of *Generativity Versus Stagnation.*

A loss of omnipotentiality, that Buhler believed occurs at around 25, was found within our sample. Almost all of our respondents described a progression beyond the level of Wittenberg's postadolescent stage. This progression, which seemed to begin at around 25, included the element of mourning postulated by Wittenberg.

The results of this project can be summarized by a provisioned model of the tasks encountered in early adulthood and the new capacities realized by means of their successful negotiation.

TASKS:

1. Resolution, through mourning, of the loss of the grandiose self-image as the primary organizing element of life goals and self-esteem
2. Gaining closure on commitments to career, marriage, and parenthood
3. Acceptance of the person's ego boundaries in terms of realistic perceptions of one's capabilities, limitations, and the unique position of one's life cycle within history
4. Acceptance of one's self as a person now separate from the preceding and the next generation

NEW CAPACITIES:

1. Capacity to derive satisfaction from one's accomplishments within a realistic context
2. Capacity to value oneself as someone who makes a unique contribution to others
3. Capacity to integrate into the ego the experience accrued in the process of living with choices made in regard to career, marriage, and parenthood
4. Capacity to identify with life as an evolutionary process with a definite end and uncertain course

References

BUHLER, C. 1968. *The Course of Human Life*. New York: Springer Company.

ERIKSON, E. H. 1963. *Childhood and Society*. New York: W. W. Norton, Inc.

GOULD, R. 1959. "The Phases of Adult Life: A Study in Developmental Psychology." *The American Journal of Psychiatry* VII.

HARTMAN, H. 1958. *Ego Psychology and the Problem of Adaptation*. New York: International Universities Press.

WITTENBERG, R. 1968. *Postadolescence*. New York: Grune and Stratton Company.

THE ADULT

CHAPTER 5

Theories of Adult Development: Creating a Context for Practice

Eileen M. Brennan and Ann Weick

Until the 1970s, very little theoretical work underpinned the study of the majority of the human life span—adulthood.[1] Bernice Neugarten offered a fitting metaphor describing developmental theory prior to this decade —that of a circus: The child developmentalists sat too close to the entrance of the circus tent and the gerontologists too close to the exit; both groups missed the center ring (adulthood) and therefore lacked a view of the whole show.[2]

Recent advances in both the empirical description of adulthood and the buidling of developmental theory addressing the social psychology of the adult years have claimed the attention of students of human behavior and of human services practitioners throughout the United States. Signaled by the 1974 publication of *Passages*, Gail Sheehy's best seller that examined adulthood,[3] researchers have reported a series of major studies that investigated the years between adolescence and senescence. George Vaillant, Roger Gould, Daniel Levinson, and several other authors have all recently published works that attempt to describe and explain adult behavior by drawing upon extensive research studies.[4]

[1] Dorothy Rogers, *The Adult Years: An Introduction to Aging* (Englewood Cliffs, N.J.: Prentice-Hall, 1979), p. 4.

[2] Bernice L. Neugarten, "Adult Personality: Toward a Psychology of the Life Cycle," in *Human Life Cycle*, ed. William C. Sze (New York: Jason Aronson, 1975), p. 379.

[3] Gail Sheehy, *Passages: Predictable Crises of Adult Life* (New York: E. P. Dutton, 1974).

[4] George E. Vaillant, *Adaptation to Life* (Boston: Little, Brown, 1977); Roger L. Gould, *Transformations: Growth and Change in Adult Life* (New York: Simon and Schuster, 1978); and Daniel J. Levinson et al., *The Seasons of a Man's Life* (New York: Alfred A. Knopf, 1978). See also Henry S. Maas and Joseph A. Kuypers, *From Thirty to Seventy* (San Francisco: Jossey-Bass, 1975), and Jane Loevinger, *Ego Development: Conceptions and Theories* (San Francisco: Jossey-Bass, 1976).

Reprinted from *Social Casework*, Vol. 62 (January, 1981), pp. 13–19, by permission of the author and the Family Service Association of America.

This article briefly describes the work of the three theorists Vaillant, Gould, and Levinson, addresses the assumptions on which the theory of adult development is based, and proposes a view of social work intervention from a developmental framework.

Adult Life-Cycle Theorists

The three theorists named above acknowledge the pioneering work done by Erik Erikson, whose epigenetic model of the life cycle has often been taught as part of human behavior content in schools of social work.[5] Recently, Erikson has produced an interdisciplinary collection of papers in which he speculated that we may be entering the "century of the adult."[6] In a prior work, *Childhood and Society*, Erikson addressed the psychosocial aspects of developmental change throughout life, and had not confined himself to childhood and adolescence, as was largely true in earlier psychoanalytic and ego psychology formulations.[7]

Erikson postulated that adults go through four critical stages of development during which they struggle to adjust to the demands of the social environment and to master specific developmental tasks. The struggles are expressed in terms of striking a balance between polar qualities specified for each stage: adolescence (identity versus role diffusion), young adulthood (intimacy versus isolation), middle adulthood (generativity versus stagnation), and maturity (ego integrity versus despair).

Klaus Riegel argues that Erikson has built his theory so that it has a potentially dialectical framework, one that acknowledges the mutual influence of the active organism and the changing world in which the organism moves.[8] In Riegel's view of the developmental dialectic, growth comes through crisis and conflict, and every generation develops somewhat differently because of the historical events unique to it.

Each of the following theorists has proposed a view of development that marks out certain stages of the adult life cycle and also acknowledges the dialectic of development that encompasses each adult life.

GEORGE VAILLANT

George Vaillant formulated his theoretical work (*Adaptation to Life*) in conjunction with an in-depth study of ninety-five men who served as sub-

[5] See Sophie Freud Lowenstein, "Preparing Social Work Students for Life-Transition Counseling within the Human Behavior Sequence." *Journal of Education for Social Work* 14 (Spring 1978): 66–73.

[6] Erik H. Erikson, *Adulthood* (New York: W. W. Norton, 1978), p. vii.

[7] Erik H. Erikson, *Childhood and Society*, 2d ed. (New York: W. W. Norton, 1973), pp. 247–74.

[8] Klaus F. Riegel, "History of Psychological Gerontology," in *Handbook of the Psychology of Aging*, ed. James E. Birren and Klaus W. Shaie (New York: Van Nostrand Reinhold, 1977), pp. 70–102.

jects in a study of healthy adult development.[9] The men were investigated continuously from their sophomore year at an Ivy League college until age forty-seven by an interdisciplinary team of psychiatrists, psychologists, anthropologists, and social workers.

Extending the theoretical notions of Norma Haan of Berkeley,[10] Vaillant conceptualized the passage of his subjects through life in terms of the maturation of the ego defenses, which he called adaptation mechanisms. He developed a hierarchy of adaptation mechanisms ranging from primitive (for example, denial and distortion) to fully mature (including sublimation and suppression) and found that as the men got older their ways of coping with reality became more mature. In his view, much behavior that is labeled pathological is actually healing; what appears in cross section to be "mental illness" can in the long run be quite adaptive, given an individual's personal and historical circumstances. Vaillant also found that the isolated traumas of childhood were not as important as predictors of later adaptation as the quality of sustained relationships.

Additionally, the men studied were found to pass through life stages in the sequence hypothesized by Erikson. Vaillant identified six stages of adult development that roughly corresponded to each of the six decades of life from the teen years to the sixties. Adults were successively involved in (1) identity formation, (2) achievement of intimacy, (3) career consolidation, (4) generativity, (5) keeping the meaning through "passing the torch" of culture, and (6) a search of ego integrity. Vaillant cautioned that women may go through a different sequence of stages than men do, especially when they are involved in balancing career consolidation, attaining intimacy, and achieving generativity. He also acknowledged the sociocultural biases of his work that concentrated on an elite population.

ROGER GOULD

Several large scale cross-sectional studies were conducted by Gould in an attempt to get a clear conceptualization of the sequential change that takes place with time in the lives of adults.[11] Gould used the empirical studies together with insights gained from his clinical practice as the basis for *Transformations: Growth and Change in Adult Life*, a book designed for the lay reader.[12]

His first informal study began with his search for patterns in over 125

[9] Vaillant, *Adaptation to Life*, pp. 30–52.

[10] Norma Haan, "Personality Development from Adolescence to Adulthood in the Oakland Growth and Guidance Studies," *Seminars in Psychiatry* 4 (November 1972): 399–414.

[11] Roger L. Gould, "Phases of Adult Life: A Study in Developmental Psychology," *American Journal of Psychiatry* 132 (November 1972): 521–31.

[12] Gould, *Transformations*.

life histories prepared by psychiatric residents. Gould next arranged for direct observation of fourteen therapy groups of outpatients who were assigned to age-homogeneous groups. The groups were observed by a ten-member interdisciplinary team who prepared descriptions of the psychological themes discussed by group members in each of seven age ranges.

In a follow-up study, 524 adult nonpatients completed questionnaires composed of salient statements heard in the age-homogeneous groups. The statements were arranged in sets of sixteen, according to theme (for example, sense of time, relation to parents), and each respondent rank ordered each set as to importance. Gould found similar responses clustered within seven distinct age groups: 16–17, 18–21, 22–28, 29–36, 37–43, 44–50, and 51–60. Recognizing that cross-sectional studies can mask cohort differences, Gould nevertheless concluded that there was evidence that persons changed in their sense of time as they grew older, and that their attitudes toward themselves and others also changed in relation to time.

In *Transformations*, Gould theorized that adulthood is a dynamic time, full of change, in which each person moves away from childhood consciousness toward adulthood consciousness.[13] That is, with each forward movement toward adulthood, unfinished childhood business may intrude, impelling struggle toward further growth. At each stage of life the issues are different, and, as Gould points out, our responses to them are shaped by the social conditions that touch our world.

DANIEL LEVINSON

The most comprehensive theoretical view of adulthood is offered by Levinson in *The Seasons of a Man's Life*.[14] Levinson and his co-workers based their theoretical work on intensive biographical interviewing of forty men, ranging from thirty-five to forty-five years of age. Ten men came from each of four occupational groups: (1) blue and white collar industrial workers, (2) business executives, (3) academic biologists, and (4) novelists.

Levinson traced the course of development of the *life structure*, which he defined as the underlying pattern or design of a person's life at a given time, for each man. The life structure is seen as having two aspects: *external*, referring to the person's pattern of roles, interests, memberships, lifestyle, and long-term goals; and *internal*, consisting of the personal meanings the external aspects have for the individual, as well as inner identities, values, fantasies, and psychodynamic qualities that inform one's engagement in the world.

Levinson pointed out that the life cycle can be divided into four eras, each lasting approximately twenty-five years: childhood and adolescence

---

[13] Ibid.
[14] Levinson, *Seasons of a Man's Life*.

(birth–22 years), early adulthood (17–45 years), middle adulthood (40–65 years), and late adulthood (60 years and over). The eras are conceived of as seasons of life, each with its own distinctive and unifying qualities. As a person moves from era to era, transitions occur during which the outgoing era is terminated and the new era is initiated.

Of special interest to Levinson and his associates were the two middle eras. The eras of early adulthood and middle adulthood were each subdivided into two periods during which the life structure is relatively stable, and each of the two periods is seen as bounded by transitions. The transition is often a time of stress and crisis because the old life structure of the preceding stable period is reevaluated and new choices are often made. Each period and transition is posited as having proper developmental tasks and processes. Levinson's men were seen as passing through eight phases during the eras of interest: early adult transition (17–22), entering the adult world (22–28), age 30 transition (28–33), settling down (33–40), mid-life transition (40–45), entering middle adulthood (45–50), age 50 transition (50–55), and culmination of middle adulthood (55–60).

Using Levinson's theory, Wendy Stewart investigated the life structures of women in early adulthood.[15] She found that Levinson's stage divisions were supported, but that women had greater variability than men in the order in which they completed life tasks. For Stewart's female subjects, formation of a satisfactory, stable life structure was more difficult than for Levinson's men.

Basic Assumptions

It is possible to identify five basic assumptions that are common to the three theorists. The adoption of these assumptions paves the way for a developmental approach to the entire human life cycle and, therefore, to practice.

Assumption 1.   Humans continue to develop throughout life.

The first assumption contradicts the prevailing view as surveyed by Richard M. Lerner and Carol D. Ryff that persons develop rapidly until the end of adolescence, reach a plateau during young adulthood, and then suffer an irreversible deterioration during the second half of the life span.[16] Much of the research done on intellectual development of post-adolescents

---

[15] Wendy Stewart, "A Psychosocial Study of the Formation of Early Adult Life Structure in Women" (Ph.D. diss., Columbia University, 1977).

[16] Richard M. Lerner and Carol D. Ryff, "Implementing the Life-Span View: Attachment," in *Life-Span Development and Behavior*, vol. 1., ed. Paul B. Baltes (New York: Academic Press, 1978), pp. 1–44.

has been based on the irreversible decrement model that draws on the prevailing view. But, recently, researchers have convincingly demonstrated that in one area, cognitive functioning, adults can continue to change positively throughout life.[17] It seems reasonable, given a continual interaction between self and world, to assume that all of the psychosocial aspects of persons (not just intellectual functioning) continue to develop through that interaction.

Assumption 2.   Life unfolds in stages during the course of adulthood.

Erikson, Vaillant, Gould, and Levinson all propose that adult life is best understood in terms of a series of discontinuous stages during which certain dimensions of the person qualitatively differ from stage to stage. Each stage is logically built from the elements of past stages and emerges from those stages in a predictable fashion.

Bernice Neugarten criticized this assumption of adult stage theorists because she believes that evidence points to the recurrence of psychological themes and preoccupations throughout adult life without a single fixed order.[18] A dialectical view of development, however, does not preclude revisiting the issues of earlier stages, and, as Erikson points out, each element of the stages of development exists in some form before its critical time.[19]

Assumption 3.   The stages are divided by transition periods that are sometimes punctuated with crises.

Levinson conceptualizes transitions as critical turning points during which persons are terminating one stage of life and simultaneously initiating the incoming one. When the transition involves, considerable turmoil and disruption—a crisis—may be said to occur. Although a smooth passage from one stage to another may occur for an individual, both Levinson and Vaillant found evidence that crises were by no means rare in their samples of men.

Assumption 4.   Transitions provide opportunities for growth.

In successfully navigating through a transition period, one leaves behind a formerly comfortable way of relating to self and world and seeks new ways to relate. Levinson states that the primary tasks of transitional periods are to question and reappraise one's present life and to explore possibilities for change. Each transition, then, holds out the prospect of grieving and the possibility of growth.

---

[17] See ibid., for a brief review.

[18] Bernice L. Neugarten, "Time, Age, and the Life Cycle," *American Journal of Psychiatry* 136 (July 1979): 887–94.

[19] Erikson, *Childhood and Society*, p. 271.

Assumption 5. Adulthood is to be examined in terms of the underlying health and strength people have to cope with change.

Vaillant addresses the fifth assumption eloquently. He states, "Most of what is called illness in textbooks and in our diagnostic nomenclature...[is] merely outward evidence of inward struggles to adapt to life."[20] In his view then, those in the helping professions should devote much of their effort to identifying and supporting the natural healing processes.

A Developmental Context for Practice

One of the useful functions of behavioral theories is its role as context creator. In the process of linking together pieces of the human puzzle, theory establishes a context for understanding behavior and for applying that understanding to social work practice. Theory becomes an active ingredient in the helping process because the social worker may use it to reframe the client's experience and, thus, create the image of new possibilities and new choices. Clearly, the social worker's theoretical perspective is a significant determinant of the content of the reframing process.

The emergence of life-cycle theory is significant because its assumptions challenge our understanding of the nature of human growth and change and, therefore, radically alter the theoretical context for practice. Because the process of change is a central issue in social work intervention, it is important to examine these assumptions in relation to the change process during adulthood. What the theory says about the process of change may ultimately be its most important contribution to social work practice. Let us examine the assumptions in light of the nature of change and their impact on our current thinking.

PERSISTENCE AND PREDICTABILITY
OF CHANGE

The core assumption of adult life-cycle theory is the persistence of change throughout life. Focus on the adult years brings legitimate recognition to the significant development that continues to take place well beyond the period of childhood and adolescence. After reviewing evidence from life- span research, Lerner and Ryff find the data indicating "that change occurs across the lifespan and takes multidirectional forms."[21]

Adult life-cycle theory also posits as a basic position an appreciation of the normalcy and, indeed, predictability of change. Achieving adulthood does not signal an end stage. Rather, the theory is compatible with

[20] Vaillant, p. 369.
[21] Lerner and Ryff, "Implementing the Life-Span View," p. 5.

the notion that growth is an open-end process. It occurs through the stages and phases beginning to be outlined by adult life-cycle theorists. If achieving one's full potential is a respectable goal of human endeavor, and especially if that endeavor is linked with the needs of the larger human community, then challenge and change must become the accepted vehicles to achieve potential. The commitment of social work to the values of individual and social change makes this a felicitious assumption.

The acceptance of change as a predictable aspect of adult development requires a radical refocusing. In place of a sometimes exclusive preoccupation with the developmental dynamics of childhood, this acceptance requires that we become more finely attuned to the dynamics of change in adulthood. If change is to be seen as the norm, then we must pursue a more sophisticated understanding of the nature of the change process. Adult life-cycle theory, through its focus on change, contributes to that goal.

CRISIS AS A MECHANISM OF CHANGE

Examining change as it occurs in situations of crisis has generated a substantial and useful literature. Because life stages are divided by transition periods that are sometimes laden with stress, crisis literature is a natural resource for extending an understanding of the process of change. One of its fundamental premises is shared by life-cycle theory, namely, its view of crisis as a healthy, rather than a pathological, phenomenon. To the extent that internal developmental changes or external circumstances present challenges that require new behaviors, an individual's familiar patterns of coping are subject to change. The shift from one pattern of behavior to another invariably carries with it some element of crisis. However, it is through such periods of upset that positive growth can occur.[22]

Looking at crisis as a mechanism of change brings us closer to a complicated conceptual issue: whether our understanding of change is best served by the notion of homeostasis or by the notion of adaptation. The issue comes to light when crisis theory and adult life-cycle theory are compared in terms of their implicit positions on the dynamics of change. Crisis theory, as it has developed from Gerald Caplan's early conceptualization, is based on the notion of emotional homeostasis.[23] The perception of and response to crisis is directly related to an individual's habitual problem-

[22] For an extended discussion of this issue see, Lydia Rapoport, "The State of Crisis: Some Theoretical Considerations," in *Crisis Intervention: Selected Readings*, ed. Howard J. Parad (New York: Family Service Association of America, 1965), pp. 22–31; Naomi Golan, *Treatment in Crisis Situations* (New York: Free Press, 1978); Samual L. Dixon, *Working with People in Crisis* (St. Louis, C. V. Mosby, 1979); and Loewenstein, "Preparing Students."

[23] Gerald Caplan, *Principles of Preventive Psychiatry* (New York: Basic Books, 1964).

solving skills. Only when those skills are insufficient to the situation does a crisis arise. The minimal goal of crisis intervention is "psychological resolution of the individual's immediate crisis and restoration to at least the level of functioning that existed before the crisis period."[24]

The notion of a system being in a homeostatic or steady state suggests a negative basis for change. Given this premise, change only occurs when the normative state fails, that is, when an individual's problem-solving skills no longer function. As a result, an individual's failure to cope may in itself be seen as a deficit, even though the failure may be the stimulus for the development of new and better coping skills. It is recognized, of course, that circumstances may be of such severity that even the most capable will experience a crisis- ridden upheaval. The point is that by establishing a homeostatic state as the normative one, the process of change is seen as unnecessarily negative.

In contrast to this, we can consider the state of change as the normative one. This position, as upheld by adult life-cycle theorists, views constant change as a more accurate describer of the human system. The quality and degree of change varies from moment to moment, day to day. The periods we ordinarily think of as change are the visible and demonstrable signs of this ongoing, dynamic state. However, the underlying state is one of continual change.

Drawing from the rich practice history of social group work, Hans S. Falck defines crisis in similar terms. Rather then viewing crisis as an event, he suggests that it could more profitably be viewed as a life-long process.[25] The goal of intervention is not to remediate the crisis but to strengthen coping skills through the ever-present structure of social groups.

If we entertain the notion of change as the norm, the concept that may ultimately prove more useful than homeostasis is adaptation. While homeostasis connotes fairly narrow boundaries within which a system can vary, adaptation suggests a system's ability to move and change in infinitely complex ways within much wider boundaries.[26] Homeostasis perhaps best speaks to very narrow and known conditions that must be present for survival. Adaptation speaks to the unmeasured and unrecognized potential for complex and continuous human change.

LIMITS TO CHANGE

Establishing change as the norm opens up new considerations about the nature of change. At the same time, it presents new puzzles. While

[24] Donna C. Agiulera and Janice M. Messick, *Crisis Intervention: Theory and Methodology* (St. Louis: C. V. Mosby, 1978), p. 21.

[25] Hans S. Falck, "Crisis Theory and Social Group Work," *Social Work in Groups* 1 (Spring 1978): 75–84.

[26] For a comprehensive discussion, see René Dubos, *Man Adapting* (New Haven, Conn.: Yale University Press, 1965).

the notion of continual change and adaptation has an inviting openness, at the same time we must recognize that we have yet to learn the limits of the conditions within which human beings can grow and change. The human system does not have infinite adaptive capacity. The quality, duration, and intensity of change may be subject to some identifiable tolerances that set upper limits on human capacity for change.

The notion that growth is best characterized by a series of successive changes and that adult development—indeed, all development—is characterized by ongoing change shapes a new context for practice. Rather than asserting that equilibrium is desirable and that good coping skills last a lifetime, we must be willing to entertain the converse: that no human system can be expected to remain in persistent equilibrium and that problem-solving skills are time- and situation-linked. Not even a "normal" childhood guarantees the emotional psychological tools that will carry one throughout life.[27] No matter how successfully we have gained skills in our first physical and social interactions with our environment, those skills must be constantly improved and expanded. Facilitation of the change process, based on a more sophisticated knowledge of the related dynamics, becomes the focus of social work practice with adults.

Acceptance of change is a reminder that things do not remain the same, that a steady state is a false promise. Maturity is not a finite fact. One wonders parenthetically whether the reluctance to explore the vast changes of adulthood has been linked to the need to pretend that all the pain and change has been left behind in the turmoil of childhood and adolescence. In fact, the retreat to the skills used at an earlier period only demonstrates even more clearly that we can never return. Our personal and social world has changed, and the only recourse is to develop a view that allows us to break through the pretense.

THE NEED FOR REAPPRAISAL

Exploring the changes occurring in adulthood forces social work practitioners to reexamime their notions about how human beings grow and develop. It is no longer possible to hold smugly to the belief that the quality and direction of all growth is established in the first few years of life and that attention to adults can only be remedial. Nor is it possible to claim an understanding of the dynamics of change in human behavior. The field has been cracked open, and those dynamics are once again subject to investigation.

The advent of this new theory tests practitioner's ability to deal with a reordering of old data. Minimally, it calls for an examination of current conceptualizations about how human beings develop. Potentially, it lays

---

[27] Vaillant, *Adaptation to Life*, p. 369.

the foundation for a new synthesis. It is not that the emphasis on early periods of human development has been misguided or that the wealth of knowledge gained is useless. It is merely that those theories have not been large enough to embrace other important pieces of the puzzle. Now that data has begun to accumulate about the process of adult growth and change, a way must be cleared for incorporating that information into our view of human behavior.

Social work practitioners have a much more practical and immediate investment in this process of synthesis. Because life-cycle theory embraces assumptions about change that posit, in essence, a nonpathological approach to intervention, it provides a new-found compatibility with the philosophical base of social work practice. At the same time, it challenges social workers to reexamine their notions of the change process both at conceptual and practice levels. This act of reexamination in itself is a positive one. By looking more closely at the linkages between a particular theory and its contribution to practice, and at its potential as a helpful guide for practice, the process will at once become more conscious and more open to critical analysis. The accumulating evidence on the adult life cycle deserves this conscious appraisal.

CHAPTER 6

Wife to Widow
to Woman

Naomi Golan

During the past twenty-six years, the phenomenon of early, unanticipated widowhood has become one of the tragic byproducts of Israel's struggle for existence. Since the War of Independence in 1948, some 2,130 women have lost their soldier-husbands.[1] However, until the Six-Day War in 1967, except for the certification and implementation of material benefits, the periodic homage paid to bereaved families in official memorial ceremonies, and the mixed reactions of the rest of the population, little attempt was made to ease the plight of war widows. Since that time, and especially after the 1973 war, there have been numerous efforts undertaken to help these women. And from these efforts much has been learned about the process of widowhood that may be applied to other situations and other countries as well.

Mental health professionals from all disciplines, staffs of social service departments, volunteers from various backgrounds, and interested others have been involved in both organized programs and unorganized efforts. In some situations, a crisis intervention framework, aimed at returning the bereaved family to a precrisis level of equilibrium, has been attempted. In others, bereavement has been assumed to exacerbate previous intrapsychic and interpersonal difficulties and treatment has been geared to a resolution of underlying personality conflicts.

More recently, in response to the publicized cry of widows, "Don't make a case out of me," the extensive use of paraprofessionals and other widows who have successfully passed through the mourning process has been urged, with professionals holding a "watching brief," to use Caplan's term, on the sidelines.[2]

No matter what theoretical approach is used, the professional background of the caregiver and his theoretical frame of reference matter less than his personal involvement during the crucial stages following the husband's death and his willingness to remain in active contact until the various tasks with which the widow and her family are struggling have been resolved. The following framework, a composite of several theoretical stances, is suggested as a workable model to provide direction for helping these women.

Bereavement

The sudden, violent death of a soldier is a crisis-inducing event because no matter how psychologically geared a woman is to the possibility, it still is unexpected and irreversible and is an occurrence with which most survivors, particularly young ones, have had little prior experience. Such a death sets off a series of ever widening reverberations in and among the soldier's wife, children, parents, and siblings, all of whom function within interacting role networks. These reverberations then spread to the interlocking systems of friends, relatives, work companions, army comrades, neighborhood acquaintances, and the general public. Each person reacts to the event according to the significance the death has for himself, his customary patterns of defense and coping, and the resources available to deal with the crisis.[3]

This article deals with the impact of a soldier's death on one particular person—his wife. Not only must the widow struggle with the crushing emotional and physical loss of her husband, but she also must pass through a complex, two-stage transitional process that may take months and even years. That is, from being a wife, she must become a widow, and then a woman ready to engage in future personal involvement with others, including another man.

A transitional crisis is a period in which a person moves from one state of relative certainty to another. It upsets a person's normal equilibrium and creates a shift in his vital roles. It is normal in that it can happen to anyone in similar circumstances. By its nature, it generates a pressure toward reequilibrium and growth of the ego. Each transitional state has its tempo, specific characteristics, and discernible set of instrumental and affective tasks.

Although each person passes through the transitional period in his own fashion, it is possible to discern some common patterns that can provide guidelines for possible intervention. Lindemann, in his seminal study on bereavement, notes that the duration of a grief reaction seems to depend on the success with which the person carries out his grief work: to emancipate himself from his bondage to the deceased, to readjust to the environment in which the deceased is missing, and to be able to form new relationships.[4]

According to Bowlby, the bereavement process consists of three stages: protest and denial, despair and disorganization, and reorganization.[5] During the first stage, Krupp notes, the person makes a desperate effort to recover the deceased in fantasy, which expresses an unconscious denial of the death. Eventually these feelings merge with the second stage in the form of apathy, depression, and withdrawal.[6] In the third stage, the person reorganizes himself and his surroundings and transfers his love and interest from the deceased to a new person or persons.

Silverman uses the disaster framework to talk of impact, recoil, and recovery. Basing her approach on the findings of an extended research project on widowhood at the Laboratory of Community Psychiatry of the Harvard University Medical School, Cambridge, Massachusetts, she sees mourning as a dynamic, changing phenomenon, with each phase having its own demands and tasks.

The initial phase can take from one day to six months or more:

> The bereaved report experiencing a sense of being lost and not knowing what to do. Their sense of being suspended from life, inability to concentrate, indifference to immediate needs, disbelief that the deceased is really gone, and feeling that life can never be worth living again, hinders their ability to arrange for the funeral and make plans for other ongoing life needs.[7]

The second phase, says Silverman, overlaps the first and cannot always be clearly differentiated from it. It can cover from one month after the death to a year or longer. During this stage,

> ...the widowed report experiencing the loss most acutely...because the numbness has lifted and the ability to feel returns. Some report going through a period of trying to do things exactly as the deceased would have liked, as if trying to recapture him in spirit if not in fact. A need to talk about the deceased and to review the facts of his death can become an obsession, to the annoyance of friends and relatives. Sometimes frighteningly irrational feelings about the tricks life has played can come out with great intensity....This is the time when the widowed person experiences acute periods of loneliness....They also report that they begin to move away from their married friends; they resent their sympathy and begin to feel like a "fifth wheel."[8]

The final recovery phase can occur from three months after the death to two years and marks a time of looking at the future. It involves learning to be alone and to find a meaningful social and emotional life in addition to being the head of the household, breadwinner, and combined father and mother. By this time, some widows become aware of their own estrangement and begin to reach out to others in similar situations. They become more independent of their families and tend to find their own modes of accommodation. For people without an extended family who are unaccustomed to reaching out, recovery is marred by isolation and loneliness.[9]

Widowhood, Silverman concludes, does not just "happen" when a spouse dies; the legal status of widowhood does not always coincide with a woman's social and emotional acceptance of the role. Except in those cultures where the role of widow is clearly defined, the first period after the death of a spouse is anomic: the widow does not know what to do, what the death means, what to expect of and for herself.

Gradually she is confronted with the finality of her loss and the truth that her husband is gone permanently. Only then can the period of recovery begin. As she passes through the grief process, she changes her sense of self, and the very nature of her outer world becomes different. She has to adjust to the fact that her life will never be the same, that the past is history and a prologue to the future.[10]

Parkes notes that although grief has no clear ending, it is common for widows to describe one or several events associated with a major revision of their feelings, attitudes, and behavior that both reflect and engender an abandonment of old modes of thinking and living. These events often occur after a special time, such as an anniversary. A memorial service or visit to the cemetery can thus have the significance of a rite of passage, setting the bereaved person free from the dead and allowing him to undertake new commitments.[11]

The Transition

If bereavement is to be considered a normal transitional state for the widow, how can she be helped to pass through this period of disequilibrium more fruitfully? Several years ago, in attempting to work out a model for assisting new immigrants to become integrated into a new society, this author and Gruschka tied Studt's formulation of social tasks involved in problems of social functioning to Kaplan's concept of phase-specific psychological tasks in situations of acute stress.[12] They believed that in situations of acute stress an individual and his family have to accomplish a series of tasks along two parallel and complementary dimensions: "material arrangemental" and psychosocial. (The term "material-arrangemental" refers to the provision of financial assistance and the setting up of substantive arrangements such as housing changes, homemaker services, and substitute child care—services generally grouped under the term "environmental modification.") The model developed seems to be applicable to other types of transitional situations.[13]

On the material-arrangemental level, the person in acute stress must carry out the following activities:

1. Explore available solutions, resources, and possible roles

2. Choose an appropriate solution, resource, and/or role and prepare himself for it
3. Apply formally for the solution or resource, take on the new role
4. Begin to use the new solution or resource, function in the new role
5. Go through a period of adaptation and development of increasing competence until performance rises to acceptable norms

Concurrently, the individual must fulfill the following psychosocial tasks:

1. Cope with the threat to his past security and sense of competence
2. Grapple with the anxieties and frustrations in making decisions or choosing the new solution, resources, or role
3. Handle the stress generated in applying for the solution or resource and in taking on the new role
4. Adjust to the new solution, resource, or role with all it implies in terms of position and status in the family and community
5. Develop new standards of well-being, agree to diminished satisfaction, and be able to delay gratification until he is able to function according to acceptable norms

Obviously, any such model suffers from the limitations of oversimplification. Nevertheless, with some bending and overlapping, it can offer guidelines to where in the transitional process the widow finds herself stuck and with what tasks she needs help. It should be kept in mind that some of these tasks can be carried out by the widow herself and some by others on her behalf.

Bridging the Past

In the initial phase of bereavement, a number of immediate, practical decisions must be made regarding the funeral, burial, financial arrangements, and so forth. The widow may choose to leave such matters in the hands of competent relatives and friends or the physician, clergyman, or funeral director, but she is, at least, usually aware of what is going on. In other areas, she forces herself to take hold: to feed the children, prepare the meals, sign the checks, and carry out all the routine aspects of her other roles as mother, housekeeper, and family manager that serve to give some semblance of normalcy to her shaken world, bring her closer to the present, and act as a bridge to push the transition forward by translating passive grieving into active coping.

In Israel, during and after the Yom Kippur War in 1973, special conditions provided little opportunity for this immediate grappling with the stark reality of death.[14] Because of the difficulties in recovering and identifying bodies, a wife was usually informed of her husband's death several weeks after he had died, was buried, and the survivors dispersed. Sometimes it took weeks and months before a grubby parcel of blood-stained clothing, a burnt-out watch case, or a returned pack of letters marked "died" brought home the first physical encounter with the death. Families were almost unanimous in saying that this lack of certainty, of not knowing and experiencing what had happened, was the hardest aspect of the situation to bear. The tragic situation of the "missing" delayed for many wives even the start of the bereavement process. For some it took a full nine months, until the bodies were reinterred in permanent civilian or military graves in August and September 1974, for death to become a tangible reality.

Ada, 21 years old, widowed after two months of marriage, represents a typical case of the inability to pass through the first stage of bereavement:

> Ada said her husband was first listed as missing and then, when she was finally informed of his death, there were conflicting reports of what had happened. She added that she never believed he was really dead and buried in Sinai. Most of her activities in the first five months were concentrated in trying to verify the facts about his death. Even after the repatriation of the Egyptian prisoners, she clung to the belief that he might still be alive somewhere in Egypt. She closed her apartment and returned to her parents' home, where she is protected from material pressures. She spends much of her time going from office to office and writing letters to army and Ministry of Defense officials.

The primary psychosocial task in the first phase is to loosen the ties with the deceased husband and to take in the fact that he is dead.[15] To do this, the wife must learn to break the thousands of threads of shared experiences with her husband, however poignant this may be, and to transform them into loving memories. This will include such overt acts as learning to use the past tense in talking about him. This phase requires a benign, permissive atmosphere that encourages the overt expression of grief and loss.[16]

Religiously observant widows in Israel found their psychosocial tasks considerably eased in the first phase by the observance of *shi'va*, the week of prescribed ritual mourning.[17] Even though it may have taken place weeks after the actual death occurred, the *shi'va* allowed for an open, shared bereavement; for permitting or even prescribing the recounting of past events in the fallen soldier's life; and for sitting together with childhood friends, fellow soldiers, and relatives, each of whom contributed his share of personal recollections. Through the healing balm of prayers and ordered rituals, the widows gained a measure of comfort and the feeling of continuity.[18]

Women with oriental ethnic backgrounds found relief and comfort by observing the overt mourning rituals and customs sanctioned and followed by their community: tearing their hair and clothes, scratching their cheeks, rocking back and forth rhythmically, and indulging in periodic *crisot* with symptoms of faintness, nausea, and even blackouts. Not only did these rituals serve to demonstrate the intensity of grief, but they enabled the women to slip more easily into their new role of widow. Visits to the cemetery became absorbing and ritualistic in their intensity.

Women from a restrained western background and those who were not religious found it harder to cope with the initial threat to past security. Many reported being given tranquilizers to "ease the pain of suffering" and said it took weeks to take in fully what had happened. In some cases, they confessed they would have liked to weep and wail but felt restricted by well-meaning relatives, who resolutely changed the subject when they tried to talk openly about their husbands or were inhibited by the common *sabra* (native-born Israeli) ethic of denial, stoicism, and inarticulateness.

The widow in the kibbutz, for example, experiences a special problem. In some kibbutzim, although the death of a member is keenly felt and mourned by all members, the absence of meaningful mourning rituals and the tendency to shield the widow from outside contacts or worries usually leaves her roleless and bottled up, unable to find a socially sanctioned way to grieve. She may be relieved of her work and child-caring responsibilities and often spends her time in loneliness or in putting up a facade.

Living with the Present

Once the wife has begun to cut herself off from the past, she must pass on to the second phase in which she turns her attention to the realities of her present role as widow. Again, much of her attention is directed toward material-arrangemental tasks: how to support her family, how to be a single parent to her children, how to manage the household alone. Frequently she has to grapple with such unfamiliar matters as mortgage payments, inheritance taxes, and insurance and survivors' benefits; in some cases she has to enter her husband's business to salvage what she can. She may soon have to face the grim need to provide additional income for her family and must reenter, or enter for the first time, the labor market. This may involve finding out what marketable skills she has to offer, taking vocational retraining, and arranging day care for her children. Silverman reported that some women who previously worked found a return to their jobs a source of comfort and continuity.[19]

At this time many widows become increasingly absorbed in their role as single parent. In addition to their motherly tasks, they must take on such fatherly roles as arbiter of disputes, disciplinarian, captain of outings, and reader of stories at bedtime. They must also deal with the young children's stomachaches, tantrums, regressions, fears, and nightmares that are a reaction not only to the loss of the father, but to the changes the death has wrought in the mother. Even older children, absorbed in their own loss, resort to new behavioral patterns with which the mothers find it hard to cope. Some older children, on the other hand, take over part of the father's role, even to the point of nurturing the mother.

The situation of the war widow in Israel is both easier and harder than elsewhere. Financial assistance is adequately and, in some instances, generously established by law. Among the numerous benefits are these: monthly financial payments; assistance with current debts and mortgages: help in purchasing new housing, furniture, household equipment, and a moderately priced car; cancellation or reduction of purchase taxes and customs duties; and partial telephone, medical, and dental payments. In keeping with its prescribed function of rehabilitation, the social service staff of the Defense Ministry makes a special effort to provide advice and assistance with vocational training programs.

Much of social workers' activities are devoted to filling out the necessary application forms and struggling with departmental red tape to establish eligibility and obtain financial benefits for the widow and her family. On the whole, despite difficulties in breaking through bureaucratic patterns, the occasional oversights and errors caused by confusions in the reporting system, and the sometimes exaggerated expectations of family members, most widows report they have little to complain of in this respect.

However, in the more intangible psychosocial tasks of grappling with anxieties and frustrations, making choices and decisions, and handling the stresses imposed by the shift in their roles, many war widows experienced emotional problems and upsets, particularly after friends, relatives, and well-meaning volunteers returned to their own concerns. At this point, the widows were faced with the essential loneliness of their situation, with feelings of inadequacy and lack of emotional support. As one widow, Ronit, aged 25, said:

> During the day I try to keep myself busy. I go on with my studies, take the children to lessons, am active in the parents' committee at school, polish the pots, and rearrange the furniture. But in the evening, after the children are finally in bed and I can no longer lose myself in television, the loneliness sets in and I feel restless and lost.
>
> What do I do? Fortunately, I have a few friends who still have the patience to listen to me, so I pick up the phone—even at midnight—and we just talk about anything, until I feel tired enough to try to go to sleep.

Another widow, Sara, aged 26, said she found it difficult to adjust to being physically alone. She came from a large, close family and, after her marriage, had never left the house after dark without her husband. She never recalled sleeping alone and, after her husband was killed, her younger sister would come over at night to sleep with her. Sara said she feels strange being alone and has the sensation when she walks on the street that "everyone is looking at me as if something is wrong, something is missing."

During this stage, talking with other widows was sometimes the most helpful means of learning to cope. The Northern Office of the Defense Ministry organized, during the spring and summer of 1974, social interest groups of widows, led jointly by a social worker and a widow who had already passed "successfully" through the mourning process. Small groups met, usually biweekly, at each other's homes and talked about their experiences in fitting into the world without their husbands. Discussions often concentrated on their roles as mothers; at other times the women talked frankly about their lack of companionship and their sexual needs and about their feelings of estrangement from and discomfort in their former social circle of married couples.

Women in these groups developed their own language and grim "in" jokes about their progress in adjusting. They would announce proudly, for example, that they had reached the "red outfit" milestone, when they could put aside their subdued clothes, worn uncaringly all those first months, and purchase a defiantly scarlet suit or dress "with all the accessories."

For some widows, having a volunteer babysit for a few hours a week, provided a welcome respite from the constant pressures and reminders and enabled them to mingle with other people. For others, a car, purchased at nominal cost through the Defense Ministry, was their means of release. "When things got too hard to bear, I'd allow myself the luxury of escaping in the car and driving for hours—anywhere, aimlessly—until I felt ready to come home again."

Still others spent these months crystallizing the memory of their husbands, preparing an album of snapshots of their lives together, and collecting letters and poems and arranging to have them published. Some set up memory corners in the living room, with pictures and mementoes, "so the children shouldn't forget their Daddy."

Paths into the Future

Sometime between the first and the second year, the widow enters the third phase in which she begins to find some measure of adjustment and habituation to her new status. She has learned to function more competently, has become more sure of herself in making decisions, can express herself with great confidence, and feels more adequate in managing the children. At this point she begins to consider her future, not as a widow (although that condition may continue), but as a woman. Observers have noted that a woman at this stage may become more interested in community affairs and active in special interest groups such as Parents Without Partners.[20] Parkes found the turning point often occurs when widows become interested in men and begin to date.[21]

Many of the women widowed during the 1973 Israeli war seem well on their way to adapting to their situation. Some have completed or are in the process of completing retraining courses or obtaining university degrees. Others have become active in parents' groups, joined civil defense units, or begun to press for more rights for themselves and their families.

Because of their youth, remarriage has become a serious issue. In some cases well-meaning friends or relatives have offered to serve as matchmakers. In other cases, the women have taken the initiative in beginning to date and consider a second marriage, often phrased in terms of finding "another father for their children." An interesting complication has arisen in this respect. Because of the benefits obtained, some widows have become more affluent than they were before, and some report that the men they date are interested in their money. One benefit offered by the Defense Ministry is a lump sum of money as a "dowry" to enable the widow to remarry. The monthly allotment, of course, ceases on her remarriage, although child support continues until the last child reaches age 18.

The public nature of the war widows' bereavement, the repeated reminders brought on by the reports in the news media of the return of war prisoners, the search for missing bodies, and the rehashing of the families' reactions to their loss served both to keep emotional wounds open and to help the widows work through their grief reactions. For some women, the continuous chain of memorial services—the Days of Remembrance, the reburial ceremonies, the memorial meetings, the anniversaries of the war, and the religious holidays—was painful. Those who could find comfort in religious services found the *shloshim* (thirty-day service) and *shanah* (first-year memorial) ceremonies marked an end and a beginning.

In other situations, it took well over a year for the widow to begin to come to grips with what had happened and was still happening to her. Some, at this point, began to seek professional help to examine the nature and quality of their relationships with their dead husbands and to consider the maturational effect brought on by their grief. In some cases they were even able to acknowledge that their marriage had not been the idyllic experience they had heretofore maintained it to have been.

The general feeling expressed individually and in the groups is that grieving is not something one "gets over"; one learns to live with it. Perhaps the situation can be summed up in the report of one widow, not from Israel, whose words echo what many widows feel:

> "Widow" is a harsh and hurtful word. It comes from the Sanskrit and it means "empty." I have been empty too long. I do not want to be pigeonholed as a

widow. I am a woman whose husband died, yes. But not a second-class citizen, not a lonely goose. I am a mother and a working woman...and a vital woman. I am a person. I resent what the term widow has come to mean. I am alive. I am part of the world.

.....

Acceptance finally comes. And with it comes peace.

.....

I am stronger, more independent. I have more understanding, more sympathy. A different perspective. I have a quiet love for Martin. I have passionate, poignant memories of him. He will always be a part of me. But—If I were to meet Martin today...? Would I love him?

I ask myself. Startled. What brought the question to my mind? I know. I ask it because I am a different woman.[22]

Notes and References

1. *Report of the State Controller's Office* (Jerusalem: Israel Government Press, 1974).

2. Gerald Caplan. "Crisis Intervention in Time of War." Paper presented at a workshop at the University of Haifa. Haifa, Israel, February 1974.

3. For a discussion of the nature and phases of crises, *see* Naomi Golan, "Crisis Theory," in Francis J. Turner, ed., *Social Work Treatment: Interlocking Theoretical Approaches* (New York: Free Press, 1974), pp. 421-439.

4. Erich Lindemann, "Symptomatology and Management of Acute Grief," *American Journal of Psychiatry*, 101 (September 1944), pp. 1-11.

5. John Bowlby, "Grief and Mourning in Infancy and Early Childhood," *Psychoanalytic Study of the Child*, 15 (New York: International Universities Press, 1960), pp. 9-52.

6. George Krupp, "Maladaptive Reactions to the Death of a Family Member," *Social Casework*, 53 (July 1972), pp. 425-426.

7. Phyllis R. Silverman, "Services to the Widowed: First Steps in a Program of Preventive Intervention," *Community Mental Health Journal*, 3 (Spring 1967), p. 38.

8. Ibid., p. 40.

9. Ibid., pp. 41-42.

10. Phyllis R. Silverman, "Widowhood and Preventive Intervention," *Family Coordinator* (January 1972), pp. 95-102.

11. Colin Murray Parkes, *Bereavement: Studies of Grief in Adult Life* (New York: International Universities Press, 1972), p. 176.

12. Elliot Studt, *A Conceptual Approach to Teaching Materials* (New York: Council on Social Work Education, 1965), pp. 4-18; and David Kaplan, "Observations on Crisis Theory and Practice," *Social Casework*, 49 (March 1968), pp. 151-155.

13. Naomi Golan and Ruth Gruschka, "Integrating the New Immigrant: A Model

for Social Work Practice in Transitional States," *Social Work,* 18 (April 1971), p. 84.

14. The following material is based on the author's experience as a social work consultant for the Rehabilitation Division, Israel Ministry of Defense, Northern District, from November 1973 to June 1974. Illustrations are from case studies.

15. Lorraine D. Siggins, "Mourning: A Critical Review of the Literature," *International Journal of Psychiatry,* 3 (May 1967), p. 423.

16. Stanley B. Goldberg, "Family Tasks and Reactions in the Crisis of Death," *Social Casework,* 54 (July 1973), p. 400.

17. Maurice Lamm, *The Jewish Way in Death and Mourning* (New York: Jonathan David Publishers, 1969), pp. 77–144.

18. For an extensive discussion of the sociocultural aspects of death, *see* Phyllis Palgi, "Death, Mourning, and Bereavement in Israel," *Israel Annals of Psychiatry and Related Disciplines,* 9 (1973).

19. Silverman, "Widowhood and Preventive Intervention," p. 97.

20. Silverman, "Services to the Widowed," p. 42.

21. Parkes, op. cit., pp. 76–77.

22. Lynn Caine, *Widow* (New York: William Morrow & Co., 1974), pp. 221 and 222.

MARRIAGE

CHAPTER 7

A Focal Conflict Model of Marital Disorders

Marquis Earl Wallace

Marital disorders are common and their consequences grave. For people in disordered marriages, the available options are continued misery, spontaneous solutions, divorce, or some kind of professional help. Divorce frequently leads to more misery and to a variety of social ills as well—financial difficulties, mental illness, problems with children such as delinquency, and so forth.

Frequently, social workers attempt to help a troubled marriage, either because of a direct request from a member of the couple or indirectly in response to requests for some other service. However, social workers encounter difficulties in working with troubled marriages and many divorces occur even among those couples that seek professional help. These difficulties may indicate a weakness in the social provisions for dealing with marital problems, but also indicate problems in understanding what causes them and how to help. The purpose of this article is to improve the level of theory used by social workers who work directly with disordered marriages.

Approaches to Practice with Disordered Marriages

Approaches used by social workers in practice with couples in disordered marriages have been of two basic types: the first is work with the individual, either in a one-to-one setting or as a member of a group; the other is

Reprinted from *Social Casework*, Vol. 60, No. 7 (July, 1979), pp. 423–429, by permission of the author and the Family Service Association of America.

work with the marital unit, the husband and wife together, sometimes including other family members as well. There are, of course, many variations of these two basic approaches. Some of the variations are individual work with both partners separately by the same worker, a mixture of individual interviews with conjoint ones, couples' groups, and the use of multiple workers, either in groups or with the marital pair, as in the treatment of sexual dysfunction.

These two basic approaches to practice come from contrasting behavioral science orientations regarding the causes of marital disorder. Work with the individual is based on the idea that the cause of marital disorder is located primarily within the individual(s) in the marriage. The logic here is that each individual's personality constitutes a separate independent variable for which marital disorder is a dependent variable. Work with the individual helps to sort out the extent to which the marital disturbance fills irrational needs, or if indeed the marital choice was primarily determined by irrational forces.

The approach in which the couple is worked with as a unit actually includes a variety of theoretical approaches, which currently are associated with the "family movement." Family theory differs so radically from the individually oriented approach that its adherents believe their approach constitutes a new orientation to behavior.[1] One of the crucial ways in which family therapy differs from the individual approach is in the belief that marital disorder and even psychopathology result from certain kinds of relationship interactions. Although differences in "personality" are acknowledged by family theorists, their influence on marital disorder is rejected, because some individuals who are quite clearly disturbed nonetheless have happy marriages, and some individuals who seem to be functioning quite well as individuals nonetheless have marital disasters. The family-oriented approach then totally reverses the individualistic paradigm: the relationship interaction is the independent variable while personality functioning and marital unhappiness are the dependent variables.

For those who believe that practice should be based on theory and that theory should be internally consistent, this contradiction—disordered personalities caused disordered marital interactions versus marital interactions cause marital and personality disorder—merits further attention. Resolving such contradictions provides opportunities for new theoretical integrations. These can pave the way for improved approaches to practice and greater help for clients. Ignoring such contradictions leaves their implications up to the art of practice rather than the science and therefore to the practitioner. When the practitioner attempts to integrate different con-

[1] Group for the Advancement of Psychiatry, *The Field of Family Therapy*, vol. 7, no. 78 (March 1970): 581–93.

ceptual approaches in practice, inconsistent and even haphazard activities with clients may occur unnecessarily and may be detrimental to treatment.

A Focal Conflict Model of Marital Disorders

The purpose of this article is to integrate the psychoanalytic and family systems perspectives in relation to marital disorders. The concepts of focal conflict theory, a psychosocial approach taken from psychology, will be used in the integration.

The argument follows this format: a description of a point at which psychoanalytic and family systems theory intersect (agree), a description of the elements of focal conflict theory, recent extensions of focal conflict theory to groups, and a description of the focal conflict theory as applied to marriage as a small group. Then, using the focal conflict model, a classification of marital disorders by content and form will be presented. The description of form (interactional type) will be shown to be related to intrapsychic operations and the interpersonal consequences.

AN INTERSECTION OF PSYCHOANALYTIC AND FAMILY SYSTEMS THEORIES

One way to integrate two differing points of view is to examine their areas of agreement. One area of agreement between psychoanalytic and family systems theory concerning marriage is that the marital partners are very similar. Peter Giovacchini defends the traditional approach to marital treatment—that is, treatment of individuals—nonetheless she focuses on their equal need for each other, which he calls symbiosis, and the equivalence of their respective pathologies.[2] The symbiosis may be of a limited type, the "symptom-object relationship" in which there is a need for a specific trait in the other or a "character-object relationship" in which the need is for the whole of the other at many different levels. Although Giovacchini never treats both marital partners, his discussions with colleagues who treat the spouses of his patients led him to conclude that, at least in marriages of long duration, the pathology of the partners is equivalent. The fact that marital partners may appear so different can be attributed to different defenses (he emphasizes the use of projective-introjective mechanisms in the couple), and that the pathology of one can serve to hold off the appearance of pathology in the other. Underneath, however, he

[2] Peter Giovacchini, "Treatment of Marital Disharmonies: The Classical Approach," in *The Psychotherapies of Marital Disharmony*, ed. Bernard L. Green (New York: Free Press, 1965), pp. 39–82; and "Characterological Aspects of Marital Interaction," in *The Psychoanalysis of Character Disorders*, ed. Peter Giovacchini (New York: Jason Aronson, 1975), pp. 253–60.

believes that the points of fixation and regression and the kinds of conflicts are the same.

Similarly, Murray Bowen, one of the early family researchers and the originator of "family systems theory," also conceives of a type of union in marriage which he calls the "common self," an aspect of the "undifferentiated family ego mass."[3] Bowen believes that marital partners are equal in their basic levels of pathology and health, their "level of differentiation of self." He accounts for the apparent differences between spouses in this way: People of equal maturity marry. An automatic battle ensues to see who will get the "ego strength" and become the "functional self" and who will give it up and become the "functional nonself." A typical result is that the "functional self" becomes the "overadequate" partner, functioning at a better level than outside the marriage, and the other partner becomes the "underadequate" one, functioning at a lower level than outside the marriage. The resulting "overadequate- underadequate reciprocity" is a relationship disorder that describes the apparent differences in levels of functioning while the view is maintained that they are basically equal.

BASIC CONCEPTS OF FOCAL CONFLICT THEORY

Thomas French's focal conflict theory is an especially convenient way to examine the integrative function of the ego.[4] Its major elements are these: In response to the environment, an individual may have a wish which for any of a variety of reasons may be unacceptable to the ego. Such an unacceptable wish is called a "disturbing motive." Disturbing motives may proceed from the id, being therefore primarily sexual or aggressive, or may be more distinctly ego wishes, such as a wish for independence, dependence, or mastery. A disturbing motive is disturbing because it elicits other internal fears called "reactive motives." Examples of reactive motives are guilt, fear of being punished, fear of loss of love, shame, fear of being destructive or being destroyed, or the recognition that the wish is unrealistic. The combination of the disturbing and reactive motives constitute the "focal conflict" for the ego. The ego's task is to work out a solution to the focal conflict in relation to and using reality.

Often the focal conflict is beyond the integrative capacity of the ego. The ego may then substitute a problem within its integrative capacity for one beyond it. Hence, a person troubled by a fear of a specific destructive impulse toward a loved one may substitute a worry about whether the car

---

[3] Murray Bowen, *Family Therapy in Clinical Practice* (New York: Jason Aronson, 1978).

[4] Thomas M. French, *Psychoanalytic Interpretations* (Chicago: Quadrangle Books, 1970); see also Thomas M. French and Erika Fromm, *Dream Interpretation: A New Approach* (New York: Basic Books, 1964).

is tuned properly, because getting a tune-up is something that can be coped with much more easily than the feared impulse. This, of course, does not solve the original conflict, but it does facilitate successful ego activity and, therefore, ego integrity.

Substituting one problem for another in this way involves some use of defences, particularly projection. In projection, a drive, an affect, or a thought from the id, ego, or superego can be experienced as originating in someone else, when in fact it is not. The optimal conditions for projection are twofold: first, a situation in which what is self and what is nonself is not clear, and second, projection is best directed where it can be met halfway by reality. As Otto Fenichel states, even the most disturbed paranoid finds a microbe of reality on which to place his projections.[5]

FOCAL CONFLICT THEORY AND SMALL GROUPS

Dorothy Scott Whitaker and Morton A. Lieberman extended French's focal conflict model to formed groups.[6] They believe that the apparent diversity of behavior of members of a group reflects an underlying concern about the here and now situation that can be expressed in focal conflict terminology, that is, consisting of reality, a disturbing motive, a reactive motive, and attempted solutions. They believe that people in groups direct their efforts toward establishing a solution that will reduce their anxiety by alleviating their reactive fears and at the same time satisfy their disturbing wishes as much as possible. Successful solutions are those in which all group members' behavior is consistent with or bound by it. Successful solutions may be restrictive, that is, primarily designed to ward off the reactive motive, or enabling, allowing for greater satisfaction of the disturbing motive.

FOCAL CONFLICT AND MARITAL DISORDERS

The essential elements for developing a focal conflict model of marital disorder presented above will now be applied to marriage and integrated into the model itself.

1. People may respond to reality with conflict: the spouse, marriage itself with its special intensity and structure, and other realities impacting on the marriage can elicit deep conflict.

2. Frequently, a conflict will be beyond the integrative capacity of the ego, and the ego will substitute a problem within its integrative capacity for one beyond it. Although marital disorder causes considerable grief,

---

[5] Otto Fenichel, *The Psychoanalytic Theory of Neurosis* (New York: W. W. Norton, 1945), pp. 146–47.
[6] Dorothy Scott Whitaker and Morton A. Lieberman, *Psychotherapy Through the Group Process* (New York: Atherton Press, 1964).

marital problems may be more desirable from the ego's point of view than experiencing conflict in the self. This may be because somewhat different coping mechanisms can be used in marital trouble—one can blame the other, seek comfort from outsiders, get divorced, and so on.

3. The defence of projection used in such substitute problems works best when the situation of self and nonself is least clear, and when the projection can be met halfway by reality. There is a tendency in marriage toward confusion of self and other (if psychoanalysis and family systems theory are correct) because the partners are so similar and even have identical conflicts. This means projections in the area of conflicts can be met *more* than halfway.

4. Behavior of small groups can be understood as being directed toward the solution of an underlying concern, which can be expressed in focal conflict terms. A marriage is a small group and marital disorder is a part of marital behavior. Marital disorder can, therefore, be understood as directed toward the resolution of an underlying concern, which can be conceptualized in focal conflict terms.

A focal conflict approach to marriage therefore states that *marital disorder can be considered an attempt to solve shared psychological conflict within the context of the marriage.* The shared conflicts are not experienced within the self because they are beyond the integrative capacities of the individual egos. Aspects of the conflicts are instead experienced in the marriage, in the spouse, or in the world as a way to bring them within the integrative capacities of the respective egos. This involves the use of projection, which is made easy by the similarity of the marital partners' conflicts and the confusion of self and other in marriage.

Classification of Marital Disorders

Marital disorders can be categorized by their content and their form. The content, what is actually talked about and acted on, is determined by the level and type of the shared conflict as well as, at times, a shared ego dysfunction. The form is determined by how the projections are managed and the response of the recipient.

THE CONTENT OF MARITAL DISORDERS

The variety of different conflicts that a marital disorder may express is limited only by the kinds of conflicts an individual may have. Some typical conflicts and examples of the kinds of resulting marital disorders are described briefly below. Within each pair, these examples are designated as "more restrictive" or "more enabling" of the disturbing motive.

Aggression versus guilt can be seen (1) in a couple who never disagree and are horrified by couples that do (more restrictive of the disturbing motive of aggression), or (2) in a couple who engage in intense arguments, including physical battles, while accepting mutual verbal and physical abuse (more enabling of the disturbing motive of aggression).

Dependency versus fear of loss of love can be seen (1) in a couple in which one is an alcoholic and the other a nondrinker who threatens divorce (more restrictive of the disturbing motive of dependency), or (2) in a couple who remain on welfare unnecessarily or take drugs, but live in fear of being found out and cut off from welfare (more enabling of disturbing motive of dependency).

Sexual impulses versus fear of punishment can be seen (1) in a couple who refrain from sexual relations (more restrictive of disturbing motive of sexual impulse) or (2) in a couple in which physical abuse is a prelude to sexual relations (more enabling of the disturbing motive of sexual desire).

Ego dysfunctions, either innate or in response to conflict, may also be shared and become part of the content of the marital disorder. A couple who have poor social relations, or are concerned that they do, may fight over who is the socially inadequate one, as if establishing this will make the other more adequate. Or, a couple may have poor judgment, such as a couple always in debt, but may between them attempt to establish one or the other as the cause of this trouble.

FOUR FORMS OF MARITAL DISORDER

More important than the content, for the purpose of integrating focal conflict theory with family systems theory, are the forms that marital disorders may take. Four forms (interactional structures) of marital dysfunction can be discovered from a study of family systems theory.[7] These four interactional patterns are the "overadequate-underadequate" relationship, the "conflictual" relationship, the "distant" relationship, and the "united front" relationship. These are gross categorizations of classes of interpersonal behavior, and, of course, in a marriage more than one type of dysfunctional interaction can occur. From a focal conflict point of view, the form is determined by two factors: to whom the projections are directed and whether the recipient introjects, projects back, or avoids.

Overadequate-Underadequate Relationships. Both Bowen and Giovacchini describe the marital situation in which one person appears disturbed.[8] The symptomatic spouse may have problems with sexual dysfunction, drinking, psychosomatic illness, wife or child beating, anxiety, depression,

[7] Bowen, *Family Therapy in Clinical Practice,* pp. 18–22, 377–79; and Charles Kramer et al., *Beginning Phase of Family Treatment* (Chicago: Family Institute of Chicago, 1968).

[8] Bowen, *Family Therapy in Practice,* pp. 77 and 166; and Giovacchini, "Treatment of Marital Disharmonies," pp. 46–50.

schizophrenia, or a host of other manifest symptoms and disorders. The other spouse appears to have no problems.

It can be argued that in such an overadequate-underadequate relationship, the behavior of one spouse primarily reflects the disturbing motive and the behavior of the other reflects the reactive motive. For example, in a marriage in which one spouse has severe sexual inhibition and the other seems to have no inhibition at all, the person with the inhibition may be expressing the reactive motive through the defense against it and the person with no inhibition, the disturbing motive.

This behavioral outcome appears to result from these intraphysic conditions: The overadequate, or seemingly well-functioning spouse, Spouse A, has a conflict of sex versus guilt that is beyond the integrative capacity of his or her ego. Spouse A defensively assigns (or splits) only the disturbing motive of sexual desire to the self-representation (image of self in ego), while assigning inhibition, a defensive activity associated with guilt, to the object representation (image of spouse in ego), Spouse B. Assignment of the inhibition to the spouse constitutes a projection. Based on this perception, behavior on the part of Spouse A indicates to Spouse B that Spouse B is inhibited about sex (projective identification). Spouse B, who has the same conflict of sex versus guilt, defensively reciprocates by assigning (splitting) the inhibition to the self-representation and the disturbing motive of sexual desire to the object representation of Spouse A. This constitutes a projection of sexual desire to Spouse A. This perception leads to behavior indicating to Spouse A that he or she has sexual desire and is not inhibited or guilty. Each spouse introjects the perception of the projections of the other spouse (introjective identification).

By assigning part of the conflict to the other spouse, each ego has brought the focal conflict of sex versus guilt within its integrative capacity. Now, instead of dealing with the whole conflict in self, each must only deal with part of the conflict in the self. Instead of having to deal intrapsychically with the other half of the conflict, one contends with it in reality by projecting it onto the other spouse. Spouse B's behavior, sexual inhibition, replaces for Spouse A the function of inhibiting his or her own sexuality as a defense against guilt. Spouse A's sexual approaches replace for Spouse B the function of dealing with his or her own disturbing sexual impulses. The type of behavior that is demonstrated by Spouse B presents the appearance of dysfunction, while Spouse A's behavior does not appear to be disturbed. Yet, this superficial perspective ignores the fact they are performing similar mental and behavioral operations (and therefore are equally dysfunctional). Similarly mutual projections and introjections can lead to one spouse who is alcoholic while the other does not drink, or one who is depressed and the spouse happy-go-lucky, and so forth.

Conflictual Relationships. A conflictual relationship involves similar attempts to assign disturbing or reactive motives to the spouse. Assigning whichever motive is desirable to the self-representation and the other to the object-representation (the spouse) is followed by behavioral indications to the spouse as to how to validate these in reality. However, in a conflictual marriage each spouse refuses to introject the projections (refuses introjective identification). Instead, conflictual partners will project back and even organize their behavior so as to disprove the spouse's projections (which may mean intrapsychically there has been some temporary introjection).

A spouse may engage in sexual practices to convince the other that he or she is not inhibited, or give up drinking entirely to prove the absence of a drinking problem. Assignment of the desirable motive to the self-representation and the undesirable one to the object-representation becomes difficult under these conditions, because reality fails to confirm the projections, and the ego is saddled with the full conflict. The ego's choices are to maintain the projections and withdraw from reality, to recognize that the self's problems are in the self (beyond integrative capacity), to try to get others to confirm one's projections, or to decide that the "marriage" is bad (not self or other, just a bad "match"; see "united front" below). Individuals in the conflictual situation, therefore, have considerable difficulty managing themselves and their marriage with accurate reality testing. The conflictual situation then differs from the overadequate-underadequate one in that the projections are refused and no stable intrapsychic condition of having to deal with only one motive is achieved.

Distant Relationships. The distant marriage is characterized by an absence of emotional interaction between the spouses and can be seen as a flight from the anxiety present in a conflictual marriage. It may take the form of having only superficial communication, no communication with the spouse at all, or avoiding the person of the spouse entirely (separation or divorce). The purpose of this avoidance is to keep the focal conflict from being elicited. Projections to the spouse are maintained intrapsychically through avoidance of the reality of the other. Facing the reality of the other would undo the projection and expose the ego to both sides of the conflict and therefore elicit anxiety. The distant marriage, unlike the overadequate-underadequate marriage or even the conflictual marriage, does not produce a sense of closeness between spouses. Frequently, significant involvement with others such as affairs or hyperinvestment in work or social activities —sometimes where projections can be better accepted by others—replaces the marital closeness.

United Front Relationships. Closeness can be achieved within the marriage if a third party is willing to accept one part of the conflict, or at least not refute it. This type of marital dysfunction, the united front marriage, often looks to the outsider like a healthy marriage. It involves an absence of dysfunction in either spouse and the illusion of closeness. However, the united front marriage must have something to unite against—we are to-gether against or for "x." The internal arrangements with regard to the focal conflict appear to be these: The self and object representations of both spouses align with respect to one side of the focal conflict while the other motive is projected (through splitting) to a child, someone in the com-munity, an institution, a life problem, or the past or future which will not project back. Behavior directed toward the person that the motive has been projected to frequently results in the third party, for example, a child, con-firming the projection by developing a problem (introjective identification).

For example, concerns about dependency by parents can successfully be projected to an unborn child without harm. But, continued projection beyond realistic necessity may be introjected leading to distorted devel-opment, such as inability to separate or function in school. Projection of disturbing sexual impulses to an adolescent child, while inhibitions against reactive fears of punishment are assigned to self and object representations of both parents, can result in adolescent promiscuity and severely punitive actions by the parents. Threatening disturbing motives toward indepen-dence can likewise be projected to an adolescent, while reactive fears of abandonment are assigned to the self and object representations of both parents, resulting in a runaway child with parents chasing right after.

The projections of the united front couple can be directed outside of the family as well. A couple may manage aggressive impulses through projection to concerns about United States military involvement overseas while retaining fears of being destructive for themselves. Another example may be a couple accepting disturbing dependency impulses for them-selves, taking drugs and living useless lives while projecting fear of rejec-tion to society.

Summary

Marital disorder, then, is a part of the ego activity of the marital partners. It is a shared attempt to solve shared conflict and is maintained because it protects the partners from suffering the effects of experiencing anxiety. From a focal conflict point of view, at least three independent variables can be presumed to influence the type of marital disorder: (1) the type and level of the shared psychological conflict, (2) the one to whom the projec-tions are directed, and (3) the response of the recipient of the projections.

The point of view that *shared conflicts* are involved helps clients and workers alike protect themselves against the all too easy tendency to find fault or blame in one of the marital partners. This faultfinding often takes the form of benign labeling of one partner as being "sicker" than the other. That the marital disorder is a *shared attempt* to deal with difficulties em-phasizes that both marital partners are involved in a joint effort, albeit a painful one, at precisely those times that they may feel most isolated and cut off from one another, and the social worker can make this point to the couple. The idea that marital disorder is an *attempt to solve* a problem rather than a problem per se opens the possibility of solving the "real" problem in a new way other than marital disorder, an idea that offers hope to the couple being helped. Finally, that the marital dysfunction serves a functional (anxiety reducing) *purpose* should alert the practitioner to the clients' temporary need for the marital problem. In turn, this should help the worker understand in advance that attempts to modify either the psychological level of a marital partner (as is done in individual treatment, for example) or the nature of the marital interactions can have the unintended effect of creating anxiety and other psychological and interpersonal difficulties to both the marital partners and even those in their extended relationship system.

Conclusion

Marital disorders are an important problem. A variety of practice approaches, based on two very different behavioral explanations of the causes of marital disorder, are commonly used. The purpose of this article has been to integrate psychoanalytic and family theories by proposing a focal conflict model of marital disorders.

The focal conflict model presented views marital disorder as an attempt by the marital partners to solve shared psychological conflict(s) in the context of the marriage. The content of marital disorder is seen as influenced by the type and level of the shared psychological conflict while the form—here integrated with four relationship disorders from family systems theory—is influenced by where the projections are directed and the response of the recipient. The relationship dysfunction then is a part of a psychosocial steady state in which conflict, problem solving efforts, and interactional elements have a part. This view casts marital disorder in a more favorable form for work with disordered marriages.

THE PARENT

CHAPTER 8

A Therapeutic Group
Experience for Fathers

Richard R. Raubolt
and Arnold W. Rachman

Psychoanalytic theory has traditionally emphasized the position of the mother in child and adolescent development, while the father is viewed as a secondary agent. With the exception of the development and reso- lution of oedipal conflicts and struggles, fathers are rarely mentioned. Yet the crucial role of the father becomes apparent to any therapist involved in the treatment of adolescent males. There is a need to delineate the role of the father in adolescent development and to develop treatment procedures that recognize, encourage, and support active fathering.

Rachman (1970), recognizing the importance of fathering with delin- quent adolescent males, noted four crucial functions in fostering ego iden- tity formation: (1) final emotional separation from mother and full emotional communion with father; (2) the prime model for masculine iden- tity; (3) emotional support for judicious role experimentation in the areas of sexuality, assertiveness, authority relations, independence, decision- making, social responsibility; (4) encouragement to pursue independent behavior in education, career, recreation, etc. The significant point here is that the father must be available and involved, serving as a bridge from the family to the outside world. Through such involvement the son is as- sisted in developing a firm sense of masculine identity and independence. The father must be willing to engage his son, to share his beliefs, goals, and ideals, in short, to serve as an ego identity role model.

Fathers often, however, are not available to their sons due to their own developmental "mid-life transitions" (Lionells and Mann, 1974). In fact,

Reprinted from *International Journal of Group Psychotherapy*, Vol. 30, No. 2 (April, 1980), pp. 229-239, with permission of the American Group Psychotherapy Association, Inc.

Levi et al. (1972) propose an interlocking crisis of integrity and identity between fathers and sons. Describing the father's integrity crisis, they have written,

> With increasing awareness of declining physical and sexual power and of the imminence of death, the middle-aged father pauses to evaluate both his work and his personal relationships, especially his marriage. He goes through a normative crisis in which he will likely doubt the value of his work efforts and the meaning of his marriage. If the resolution is successful, he will achieve a state of more solid self-esteem basic to integrity. He will perhaps see more clearly the limitations of his marriage and of his work. He must grieve for longtime aspirations, now clearly beyond reach, and reassess the meaning of what seemed success. His ego ideal undergoes a major remodeling toward what is both realistically attainable and relevant in a changed society. Where the man fails to grieve his unattained goals or find value in his achievements, he may indeed strike out on a new course, either in work or in marriage. In our observations of the families of troubled adolescents, however, fathers were unable either to grieve successfully or to find a satisfying new course of action....If the father cannot do this, he may envy and disparage his son or, alternatively, overidentify with his son in trying to relive through him what he feels he has missed [p. 49].

Lesse (1969), approaching the absence of fathering from a different position, has emphasized the effects of our current economic structure.

> A large number of adolescents and young adults seen in psychotherapy today have not had fathers with whom they could develop a strong, positive identification. This appears to be particularly so in families in which fathers work for large organizations, whether it is a large industrial company, the government, or as a member of a large union. This type of father typically comes home and talks in terms of "we" in which he is an integral part of the organization. Too often the child, particularly the male offspring, is unable to identify with a father figure whose feeling of identity is primarily based upon a positive conception of personal worth [p. 381].

Forming the Group: Goals and Structure

An opportunity to translate theoretical concepts into clinical practice was presented when one of the authors (R. R.) became a psychological consultant to an affluent suburban school system. In four adolescent psychotherapy groups, a striking number of father/son conflicts became evident. These conflicts ranged from struggles over academic work, use of drugs and/or alcohol, to use of the family car and hours out in the evening. The connecting theme was that of authority and discipline. This theme was complicated, however, by the fact that the fathers of these boys were seldom home. They worked long hours and their professional positions required a great deal of travel. To all intents and purposes they were "absent fathers."

It became clear that the most meaningful way to help these youngsters was to actively engage their fathers. It was decided to offer, with the support of the school system, a group for fathers. The concept of an "educational group seminar" was developed to suit the needs of the fathers and encourage maximum participation. The rationale for this format included the following considerations:

1. An educational focus would be perceived as more helpful and less threatening than a therapeutic focus.
2. A time-limited format of ten sessions would relate to their busy schedules and frequent need to be out of town.
3. A seminar designation was a familiar, acceptable training experience for both business and professional men.
4. A group conducted in a school setting for the community seemed appropriately advertised as an educational experience.

A news release was sent to the community to announce the availability of an educational group seminar for fathers who wished to improve relationships with their sons. Written invitations and telephone calls were also employed to develop a population of fathers from which to form the group.

The group was initially structured to conform to the prototype of a seminar that business men and professionals had experienced in their work lives. The setting was the guidance suite at the high school. Members were gathered around a small round table. Coffee was served at each meeting. It was expected that as the group coalesced and special techniques were introduced, this table would be removed and a more traditional group format would be adopted.

Group Process and Focus

A group of six fathers was formed as a result of the news release and written invitation. Those who were approached directly by letter were fathers of sons who were seen by the pupil personnel team as having academic problems (defined as truancy, class failures) and social problems (defiant, disruptive behavior, or in one case socially isolated). All six fathers were professional men in their late 40's and early 50's. Five of the six fathers came because they had trouble talking to or understanding their sons. One felt he had a good relationship with his son but wanted to improve it.

These fathers were selected on the basis of interest and time availability. Four fathers were screened out because they could not make a ten-week time commitment and one because his son was pre-adolescent. One also dropped out just prior to the first session, feeling family therapy was more appropriate.

Three of the fathers had sons who were being seen in groups. The problems, as defined by the fathers, varied but centered on two conflicting areas: lack of academic success and poor communication between father and son.

In the first session, after a go-round of introductions and individual expectations, the group was described in the following manner:

"Since I [R.R.] have been in the position of initiating and organizing this seminar, let me build on our stated goals and share the three basic ways I would like to proceed to realize our goals. I conceive this seminar as (1) information-giving, imparting to you some basic information. I have prepared a packet on adolescent development and common problems between boys and their fathers. (2) A second method will be getting in touch emotionally with the problems of adolescents and the problems of being a father. In order to reach our emotional goal, I will ask you to share, as best you can, feelings about yourself and your adolescent youngster, the kinds of joys and hopes and the kinds of conflicts and angers that you have. The more we share, the more comfortable we are going to feel together in recognizing the typical difficulties of adolescent growth. As a special part I would like you to consider sharing what your adolescence was like with your father. This will serve to give a perspective on how your interaction with your father has influenced your son's perspective of you. (3) Once we have discussed the information and shared the experience of being an adolescent and a father, we will have a unique experience here to translate into some direct action. This experience can be created by role-playing. We are going to set up role-playing situations with everyone taking a turn being an adolescent and a father in a basic shared father/son conflict."

We then proceeded over the next few sessions to explore excerpts from Erikson (1968), Josselyn (1952) and Rachman (1970, 1975) on normal adolescent development and the role of fathering. As the group began to talk about the concept of identity conflicts in adolescence, the topic of values became more and more prominent. As the discussion centered on identity questions of: Who am I? What do I believe? and Where am I going? the fathers began to vacillate between being very dogmatic and being unsure about their own values and beliefs.

Initially, the exploration revealed the fathers' need to have their sons adopt their own strict code of values. This code of hard work, academic success, and "pleasure in moderation" (i.e., relaxation, drinking, sports) was initially presented as an unyielding, nonnegotiable demand. Any violation of this code by their sons was to be dealt with harshly. Physical punishment was seen as necessary but as the last resort.

In order to highlight this clash in value codes, a role-playing experience was developed. In this way the group was able to examine the specific flavor of father/son interactions. It soon became apparent that the fathers themselves were often unsure of what to believe in because of their own developmental crises. These professional men were all highly successful in their companies/businesses or in the schools they administrated, but, while they maintained the respect of those above and below them in their professions, they had reached the peak of their careers and did not expect to progress much further. It was a time in their lives when they began to realize that most of their financial dreams had been achieved (oftentimes exceeded). They realized they had success. The question was: now what? This life crisis (and it is important to note these feelings were shared by five of six members) was heightened by their sons' disregard for the code the fathers had lived by all of their professional lives. Since they themselves were unsure of what might lie ahead and did not want to force the "limits of their success" (as one father put it), they reacted severely to their sons' enthusiasm and testing.

This factor became particularly evident in the third session during the following role-play situation: "Your son came home really drunk last night and your wife has been telling you all morning, 'Go talk to him.' When you come down for brunch he is alone in the kitchen. What are you going to say and/or do?" One of the fathers played the son and another the father. The exchange lasted for about twenty minutes, with the father calmly trying to talk to and reason with his son about drinking and the son not giving an inch, answering all questions with a simple "no." Finally, the father, in desperation, stated to his "15-year-old son"..."It's not that I expect you to be a teetotaler, but you have to moderate your drinking." When the role-play ended the other fathers were adamant in their disapproval of this statement. The theme of their responses was, "You were too calm. I would have laid the law down," and "Who is he [the son] to argue with you? It wasn't like that when I grew up. I respected my father, what he said went, there was no discussion about it." In the ensuing discussion, it became evident that the group viewed punishment as necessary to maintain respect and that the trait they could tolerate least from their sons was insolence.

In order to achieve greater clarity and understanding of the issues involved here, we began to focus on Erikson's concepts of "free role experimentation and psychosocial play." The intent of the discussion was on developing an awareness for the fathers of the difference between positive and negative experimentation. Positive examples cited included interest in ecology, civil rights, Eastern thought, and structured risk-taking activities, such as racing and athletics. Negative examples cited included drug abuse, vandalism, and violence. These distinctions became necessary as the fathers, in an attempt to maintain their authority and control, had lost sight of the need for positive guidance. Discipline became synonymous with punishment rather than as a means of providing guidance and direction.

To provide another experience that might assist them in understanding this conceptualization and also to develop a new level of participation and intensity, a meditative experience was suggested. In terms of group process, it had become apparent that the role-playing experience had introduced a more emotional quality to the group that the fathers found helpful. It now became clear that the group format could be restructured along more psychotherapeutic lines. The group interaction was expanded to include a balance between the original cognitive format and a sharing of life experiences.

Fathers Re-Experience Their Adolescence

Using the technique of clinical meditation in groups (Rachman, 1976), the following experience was presented.

> I would like to suggest a positive, meditative experience to help you remember your adolescence. I am going to turn off all but three lights over the bookshelves to reduce all outside stimulation so we can concentrate. I would like all of you to close your eyes and get comfortable in your chairs, relax. I would like you to let your imagination go back to the time when you were fifteen.
>
> Picture in your mind how you looked as a fifteen-year-old. You are getting dressed to go out and meet your friends on the corner. You are putting on your favorite outfit. What does it look like? What kind of shoes are you wearing? What is your hair style? Now you are fully dressed and your way to meet the guys.
>
> Picture yourself saying "Hi." Picture your group of friends. How are they dressed? What do you talk about? After standing on the corner for five or ten minutes, someone says, "Hey, why don't we..." Fill in the blank. It's the kind of crazy notion that excites everyone and you begin planning. Get in touch with what you do to make this happen. Now fully concentrate for a moment on this "crazy experience" so that when we finish you can share it in detail. Take a minute.
>
> Okay, now I'd like everyone to open his eyes and keep alive the experience you had as a fifteen-year-old. Okay, now I'd like to discuss what you have just fantasized. Go around and each person describe to the group how you looked at fifteen, what your group of friends looked like, and what was the crazy experience and who thought of it.

The results of this experience were dramatic. The group shared in an open, direct manner many of the exciting "risky" pranks of their own adolescence. These included stealing from a local fruit stand, staying out all night playing cards and shooting pool when they were thought to be attending a religious retreat, and trying to "gang bang" a girl known for her sexual activity only to "chicken out" when she really showed up. The tone of the group at this point was active, loud, and exciting as the fathers began spontaneously to mention other events of their adolescence.

Before long a most significant theme began to emerge. Many of the group members recalled a very distant relationship with their own fathers. They were all sons of immigrants who were trying to establish businesses and better themselves economically. Consequently, there was little father/son interaction. As one of the fathers noted at the time, "We had to learn how to be fathers by ourselves, trial and error. We had to develop a role we had never experienced for ourselves."

The Loving Fight: Levels of Dialogue and Acceptance Between Fathers and Sons

When the fathers became aware of the discrepancies between their value code and their sons' and its relationship to their own adolescence, they were freer to explore alternative, less conflictive modes of responding to their sons. We then focused on improving father/son communications skills.

In order to assist the group in developing fathering skills, we developed seven necessary communication skills for fathers. They included:

1. *Talking it out:* becoming involved, being present with your son, i.e., "I want to talk with you." "Let's talk this out." "I won't run from you, don't you run from me."
2. *Creating an open dialogue:* allowing your son to say what he feels and thinks; encouraging your son to say anything he wishes, whether you like it or not; being free to say what you feel about him
3. *Developing emotional communion:* identifying true feelings, owning your own feelings, being aware of and taking responsibility for feelings of anger, frustration, fear, inadequacy, failure as well as tenderness, compassion, vulnerability; being emotionally responsive; allowing yourself to be known to your son
4. *Confrontation:* being able to say you don't agree; the art of the loving fight, i.e., "Hey look, you want to do this, but let me tell you how I see it"; giving your son something to bounce off of; taking a stand
5. *Sharing:* being known to your son, i.e., what you believe in and that you hold true to your beliefs, philosophy of life, your values, your identity
6. *Compromising:* being able to give in, i.e., "Well, I really don't agree. I wish you would do it my way, but you have your own life, and I'll just have to sweat it out."
7. *Maintaining the relationship:* giving your son room to breathe, staying with him, i.e., "I will be here with you and for you. I will not ex-

communicate you; I will stand by you as you go your own way. I will not give up on you. Even though we don't agree, I am still connected to you."

This guide created a great deal of discussion, particularly point seven. The idea of *never* giving up on their sons was a hard notion for them to accept.

In order to provide a structure where they might try out these skills we presented a series of videotapes done by the high school drama class. In these videotapes an adolescent boy spoke directly to the camera and expressed rage, confusion, and sadness. The fathers took turns responding to the filmed vignettes. Interaction was greatly enhanced after each response, and the fathers were actively involved in trying out the new skills.

Results and Evaluations

Upon termination of the group, the leader noted a number of significant changes occurring in the sons of the fathers involved. There was a dramatic decrease in school absences, with only one unexcused absence coming to the school's attention during the time the group was meeting. There were also fewer reported incidents of disruptive classroom behavior. Teachers noticed a bettering of academic performance; more work was being turned in with fewer failing grades.

To substantiate these clinical impressions, evaluation measures were developed. A fourteen-point questionnaire was constructed and given to the fathers to elicit their reactions to the group experience. Those questions that measured the father/son relationship before and after the group included:

1. With what problem(s) or concern(s) in your relationship with your son did you want help when you joined the group?
2. Have you changed any of your attitudes, feelings, or behaviors toward your son as a result of this group experience?
3. Did your relationship with your son improve? If so, please cite specific examples of improvement in your relationship with him.
4. Did your son show any changes in his behavior or attitudes, for example, with the school, in his relationships with other family members, or with his friends?
5. Did you find yourself reevaluating any of your beliefs, values, feelings, or ideas as a result of this group experience?

A majority of the fathers (five of six) indicated they joined the group because of communication problems with their sons and a desire for help in this area. According to the results of the questionnaire, this goal was accomplished as all six indicated improved relationships with their sons, with more activities engaged in together, less fighting, and greater academic success cited as examples. In response to the question on perceived changes in the son's behavior, five of the fathers noted there was a change in their attitudes toward the family, with more consideration and friendliness.

All six fathers mentioned that the group encouraged them to reexamine their values and beliefs. This reexamination centered on "life goals and priorities." Three of the fathers felt that they had shortchanged their families and realized now the importance of their involvement. All the fathers, in one way or another, said they now saw the need for greater communicating, sharing, and understanding between father and son.

For all of us concerned, the personal meaning of this group may perhaps be best summed up by the following letter received two months after the completion of the group: "I am sorry I could not get back to you sooner. I have had a chance to reflect on the impact that the sessions had on me and I feel I ought to let you know. When I started I had basically given up. Matt was on his way toward excommunication. I was at the end of my wits. I can say that I have gained a better perspective, and therefore hope. I think I can do something about the situation because I have learned to be more patient and more tolerant. P.S. Matt naturally did not submit his term paper on time, but he did get it in a week late. I hope and pray the English teacher will accept it."

References

ERIKSON, E. (1968), *Identity, Youth and Crisis.* New York: Norton.

JOSSELYN, L. (1952), *The Adolescent and His World.* New York: Family Service Association.

LESSE, S. (1969), Obsolescence in Psychotherapy: A Psychological View. *Psychotherapy,* 23:381–398.

LEVI, S., STIERLIN, H., and SAVARD, R. (1972), Fathers and Sons: The Interlocking Crisis of Integrity and Identity. *Psychiatry,* 35:48–56.

LIONELLS, M., and MANN, C. (1974), *Patterns of Mid-Life in Transition.* New York: William Alanson White Institute.

RACHMAN, A. (1970), Role of the Father in Child Development. Paper delivered at Emanuel Midtown Y.M.C.A. Parents-Teachers Association, New York.

——(1974), The Role of "Fathering" in Group Psychotherapy with Adolescent Delinquent Males. *J. Corrective & Soc. Psychiat.,* 20:11–22.

——(1975), *Identity Group Psychotherapy with Adolescents.* Springfield, Ill.: Charles C Thomas.

——(1976), Clinical Meditation in Groups. (Unpublished paper.)

CHAPTER 9

Motherhood, Mothering, and Casework

Beverly B. Nichols

The redefining and reordering of roles in American family life do not accurately reflect the reality of family life in America. New ideas envision what may come, not what *is*. Role shifts, which may reflect personal dissatisfactions, institutional trepidation, a restructuring or breakdown of the social system, are first tried in *avant-garde* circles. But only very slowly are the resulting processes assimilated by those in the mainstream of society. Change is an ongoing and often painful process, reflecting gaps between ideals and realities, the polarizing and realigning of feelings and attitudes of many divergent individuals and groups.

Motherhood is one of those processes about which there is question and confusion. Motherhood is intrinsic, but the feelings, attitudes, and values regarding it are changing. Most experts in child development agree that the mother provides a crucial first relationship for the infant; that the quality and reciprocity developed in that relationship contribute significantly to the child's achieving his or her optimal potential. That there is conflict between awareness and acceptance of this view with the effort and time necessary to carry it out is evidenced by the numbers of parents who seek help with problems involving parenting their children.

Parent-child relationships comprise one of the major categories of presenting problems in family agencies; marital conflicts affect children; individual problems, focusing on identity issues, self awareness, personal development, and role conflicts, may affect family members; social issues such as child abuse, abortion, day care, and population control remind us constantly that, for many, motherhood is not synonomous with an idealized state of joy and fulfillment.

Reprinted from *Social Casework*, Vol. 58 (January, 1977), pp. 29–35, by permission of the author and the Family Service Association of America.

The social worker is often confronted with questions relating aspects of mothering to specific problems. Experiences of being a mother and of being mothered are inexorably woven together. Understanding the mothering factors and fitting them into a social context facilitates process, contributes to the development of a meaningful exchange, and promotes treatment goals. When the worker is also a mother, an added dimension in terms of identification and empathy exists.

This article will examine some of the theoretical material connecting motherhood and mothering with current casework problems; discuss mothering as a factor in casework treatment relationships; and present some ways in which a knowledge of the mother-child relationship can be used in preventive work.

Theoretical Framework

According to Helen Deutsch, a woman's psyche contains a factor that is lacking in that of the masculine sex—the psychologic world of motherhood. She says that as a result, the human female displays varied behavior and greater complication with regard to the polarity between life and death.[1]

The experience of motherhood is one that is passed from generation to generation, never really beginning, never really ending, described by a "world of events within itself...psychologic processes...the operation of biologic laws of heredity and adjustment, rational processes and seemingly absurd processes, historical and individual psychic elements."[2]

Deutsch distinguishes between the concepts of motherhood and motherliness. She describes motherhood as the relationship of mother to child as a sociologic, physiologic, and emotional entity. By motherliness, she refers to a "definite quality of character that stamps the woman's whole personality and the emotional phenomena that seems to be related to the child's helplessness and need for care."[3]

The quality of motherliness in an individual woman is determined by many factors: religious commitments to procreate; social and economic motives; cultural elements; and personal experience. Beyond these influences, motherhood seems to envelop a mystique of feelings, needs, and destinies, with both positive and negative elements.

Deutsch's Freudian-based concepts of motherhood and mothering have been challenged, particularly by representatives of the Women's Movement. The increased importance of cultural factors; Masters and Johnson's

[1] Helene Deutsch, *The Psychology of Women: Motherhood*, vol. 2: (New York: Grune & Statton, 1945), p. 21.
[2] Ibid., p. 16.
[3] Ibid., p. 17.

studies on human sexuality and new research in endocrinology have relevance to the newer theories. Roles for both sexes are generally described in less rigid terms today. The trying-out of new roles and the increasing opportunities for choice are evident in many segments of society.[4]

Problems Surrounding Parenting

The expanding role options for women have had the effect of allowing negative feelings to surface. These feelings, which previously were usually hidden, are being verbalized more than ever before. Young women question the personal sacrifices necessitated by motherhood.[5] Some women are unsure and apprehensive of their competency to become mothers or of their spouse's maturity regarding parenting. Others find relief, often mixed with guilt, at having the option to reject motherhood. Most women have concerns for the uncertain future. Older mothers, still feeling maternal emotion for grown offspring who no longer need them, question the efforts they have made while waiting in vain for grandchildren. When newspaper columnist Ann Landers conducted a poll of her readers on "Parenthood: If you had a choice, would you do it again?," 70 percent of the respondents said "no."[6] And groups such as the National Organization for Non-Parents support couples who do not plan to have children at all.[7]

Parenting—or sharing the emotional and physical aspects of the total experience of bearing and rearing children—is readily sought after by some young couples. But those who have made a conscious decision to share parenting responsibilities, do not find the process easy. Deutsch says that "the most intuitive and introspective women shy away from observing their own psychic processes during pregnancy,"[8] thus making sharing difficult.

Despite goodwill, expectant fathers often feel isolated and left out. One man expressed his frustration by saying, "I have tried to share her feelings but she is either on cloud nine or she is down in the dumps. I never know whether I am helping or hurting."

Expectant parents face many decisions relative to their lifestyles: If the mother-to-be has been working, should she continue to work after the baby

[4] Elizabeth Janeway, *Between Myth and Morning: Women Awakening* (New York: William Morrow & Co., 1974), pp. 84–92.

[5] Jessie Bernard, *The Future of Motherhood* (New York: Dial Press, 1974), p. 21.

[6] See Albert Rosenfeld's article, Who Says We're a Child-Centered Society?, *Saturday Review*, August 7, 1976, p. 8.

[7] Information on local level non-parent support groups may usually be obtained from Planned Parenthood.

[8] Deutsch, *The Psychology of Women: Motherhood*, p. 105.

is born? If so, who will care for the infant? Couples wonder how they will be able to adjust to the demands of a baby. Problems of space and money are not uncommon. The sex and name of the baby often become major issues.

In fact, parenting proves a more useful concept when children are older. It is still rare that the father participates extensively in the caretaking and primary relationship aspects of the infant's life. In this connection, a father may claim the more rewarding tasks of parenting, leaving the less pleasant ones—changing diapers, formula-making, laundry, and so forth—for the mother. This lack of participation may generate strong feelings of resentment in the mother, while exacerbating her guilt at being critical of the father's efforts.

Because parenting involves redefining and readjusting roles, it is a process which may activate identity problems, stimulate power struggles, and threaten the stability of the marriage itself. Social trends have influenced the size and character of the American family, but rearing even one child is an awesome undertaking.

Of late, more fathers are participating in the actual experience of birth. Increasing interest in natural childbirth and birth in the home are slowly infiltrating our customs. The vast majority of births, however, still occur in a hospital without the father present. Following delivery, many women experience postnatal depression. Difficulties in breast feeding may occur. And soon after the baby is born, the responsibility of caretaking imposes restrictions on the parents' freedom. Most young mothers and their babies quickly find themselves in a relatively isolated social milieu—alone together.

Other concerns regarding motherhood include: a failure to conceive, which becomes an emotionally laden issue—women who experience difficulties in becoming pregnant suffer and so do their husbands; and problems in carrying to term which cause women to know the pain of failing at an experience close to the very heart of femininity.

These concerns continue to emerge despite freer choices, less rigid roles, and more opportunity for personal development. Making the choice to have children is a soul-searching and value-laden process. Such decision-making may endanger a relationship; preclude a going-back; change a person's life; or destroy a dream.

Mothering and the Developing Child

Ego psychologists are credited with recognizing and describing the central importance of the mother's role in child development. Briefly, ego growth permits differentiation of instinctual drives, the development of object relations, and the acquisition of speech.[9] "Indicators" that such development is proceeding depend on the presence of "a good enough mother."[10]

As an outcome of adequate mothering, the infant develops an ability to distinguish between self and others and eventually gains the ability to deal with another person on a reciprocal basis. The libidinal availability of the mother is essential for the optimal development of ego functions; it serves to coordinate maturation and development so that both can coincide.[11]

According to John Bowlby, interruptions and other difficulties in the mother-child dyad are relevant to the development of adult pathology. He reviews the importance of the mother-infant relationship, stating firmly that the warmth, intimacy, continuousness, and reciprocity of that relationship are essential for mental health.[12]

Bowlby believes that adults are often still responding to the trauma of early separations from the mother.[13] expressing their pathology by being demanding and angry, by experiencing chronic anxiety. He considers many pathological situations, tracing their origins directly to anxiety brought on by interruptions in the mother-child relationship which are then carried over in some form to adult life.

The adult client seeks therapy because of some dysfunction in the interpersonal part of his or her life. Dysfunction may range from the mildly disturbing to psychotic behavior. The therapist treats the client according to the dictums of the theoretical framework he embraces. He is limited by agency purpose, practices, time, and also by other factors including those brought by the client, but the individual caseworker influences all other variables. Whether the worker is old, young, experienced, male, or female, will affect the developing relationship in relevant ways.

Mothering attitudes, for example, that are a part of the older female social worker's image will affect treatment regardless of whether they are consciously employed. The motherly qualities of the social worker, openly exhibited, hidden, or unrealistically anticipated by the client color the relationship and, to some degree, set its tone.

Mothering as a Treatment Technique

Mothering, as a treatment technique, is defined as a process by which the caseworker consciously undertakes a nurturing role designed to support,

[9] Rubin and Gertrude Blanck, *Marriage and Personal Development* (New York Columbia University Press, 1968).

[10] Ibid., p. 15.

[11] John Bowlby, Preface, *Attachment and Loss*, vol. 2 (New York: Basic Books, 1973).

[12] Ibid.

[13] Ibid.

encourage, and gratify the client, while, at the same time, conveying, through the medium of the relationship, an appropriate expectation of growth. The female caseworker who is willing to utilize her mothering skills can often provide an atmosphere which will enable the client to share feelings, to ventilate, to discuss options, and to become therapeutically involved. The following case illustrations from a family agency's records, provide examples of when it is helpful to employ mothering as a technique.

> Mrs. C. is a middle-aged, former career woman who had married late and has three children. She is temperamentally ill-equipped to manage a young family. Mr. C's busy career excludes her. Older than the other mothers in her neighborhood, she is isolated from them. She comes to the agency because of a secret drinking problem.

Mrs. C responded to a "mothering" caseworker immediately, sharing her concerns about failing her family, her disappointment with homemaking, the neighborhood's unfriendliness. She expresses a wish for someone to value her as an individual. It is not that being mothered solves Mrs. C's problems simplistically. Rather, it is that the motherly response, with its components of tenderness and understanding, provide space for the client to renew herself.

> Mrs. T has suffered from asthma since childhood. She has had the problems that years of chronic but intermittent dependency bring, along with the passive hostility her constant care evokes in others. Mr. T is weary of her demands. Her children are reacting to her absences. She is depressed.

This client ventilates her hostilities and manipulates in an effort to evoke the rejection which she unconsciously anticipates. The caseworker, aware of the issues, begins by mothering the client. She acknowledges the feelings uncritically and identifies realistic problems. The client's right to her emotionality is accepted. The worker's hopeful outlook, sustained by practical help for Mrs. T, encourages a constructive channeling of energy.

Men, too, are often responsive to mothering techniques:

> Mr. M is thirty-two. He has lived away from his parents since entering the service at age seventeen. Married now for ten years, he and his wife became involved in marriage counseling. Later, he continued in therapy for problems involving chronic irritability, temper tantrums and feelings of isolation.

That Mr. M had requested an "older woman" as a caseworker is indicative of his need to have a "motherly" person with whom to relate. A positive transference was developed through counseling which motivated

Mr. M's growth. His wife was enabled to give up her mothering of Mr. M which had been a source of discord.

> Mrs. D was referred because of abusing both of her children. She is very young, separated from her husband. Her history includes having lost her own mother when she was five; subsequently, poor relations with her father and siblings were constant and there is evidence of much deprivation.

Mrs. D recognized and commented upon her daughterly response to her worker. As the relationship deepened, she began to ask for advice, to offer confidences, and to test the worker's approval of various actions.

If the presenting problem concerns the parent-child relationship, usually the mother is experiencing feelings of responsibility and guilt, even if the problem involves the father-child relationship. These feelings are engendered by the mother's awareness of her importance to the child and complicated by her resentment and anger at being in this role.

Such ambivalence relates to the demands of motherhood pitted against the need for self-expression of a different kind. Fathers rarely experience this phenomenon. They are protected by the social system which grants them greater freedom and does not demand from them the intensity of commitment in the form of service to the young. There are, of course, class differences between families in terms of the father's involvement in child care but when the father is involved, it is always a freer choice for him.

As Deutsch says:

> We find in it, [motherhood], a world of polarities—ego instincts and service to the species, the mother's tendency to preserve her unity with the child and the child's drive to freedom, love, and hostility and a large number of personal, frequently neurotic, conflicts.[14]

When social workers see mothers who present mothering as a problem, the recognition of conflict, latent or active, in the mother is necessary. In today's society, social workers cannot assume that the mother's wish to be a "better" mother, supersedes all her other wishes.

Transference and Countertransference

Unconscious feelings about mothering and being mothered are present in the therapeutic relationship through the process of transference. Transference is defined as the client's unconscious displacement of attitudes, wishes, conceptions, impulses, and ideas from important figures in the

---

[14] Deutsch, *The Psychology of Women: Motherhood*, p. 330.

past onto the person of the therapist, independent of the objective situation, including the therapist's personality.[15]

Generally, important figures from the past refer to the mother and father. Grandparents, older siblings, or other influential persons may contribute to or reinforce patterns of responses which derive from the infant's experiences in having early needs met.

According to psychoanalytic theory, negative and erotic feelings are repressed from consciousness although they retain potency in behavior motivated by the unconscious. Because they are so absolutely incorporated into the basic personality of the individual, there is no awareness of them. Margaret Ferard sums up the importance of transference when she states:

> Relationships an individual establishes with those who had the care of him in his early days are among the most important influences that have shaped his life because they are the pattern or prototype of all subsequent relationships.[16]

Repetitiously, and often inappropriately, in adult life, the individual transfers these early learned responses to persons who are meaningful to him or her. A client can transfer maternal responses to a male therapist or paternal responses to a female therapist. Identifying with a female worker who "reminds me of my mother" is not transference, *per se*. But this kind of identification may enhance or influence transference, perhaps making it more readily accessible in treatment.

In the casework relationship, an understanding of transference provides diagnostic clues to an individual's characteristic patterns of behavior. This understanding can be used in treatment to further psychological growth through correcting unhealthy attitudes and limitations.

Transference is revealed in interview content through associations, timing of material shared, tone, and so forth, and by the affect shown. The relationship itself contains clues to both positive and negative effects of transference.

Because transference reactions are rooted in the unconscious, they are not readily available to discussion, at least not until a strong relationship has been developed. The worker may demonstrate that a difference between the therapist and the parent does indeed exist. Feelings may be examined and connected to behavior, past and present.

Florence Hollis describes this process as a "corrective relationship" which makes use of the transference. She writes:

> By allowing a relationship to develop in which the client regards the worker as a mother figure, it may be possible to counteract the earlier bad mother-

---

[15] Definition given by A. F. Valenstein in a course lecture on "Psycho-therapeutic Principles in Casework," Boston University School of Social Work, 1955–1956, taken from author's notes.
[16] Margaret L. Ferard and Noel K. Hunnybun, *The Caseworker's Use of Relationship* (London: Tavistock Publishers, 1962), p. 13.

daughter experience by enabling the client to see that the characteristics of her own mother which caused her unhappiness are peculiar to her mother and not generally characteristic of all women.[17]

The "corrective relationship" can result in many therapeutic changes for clients, not the least of which is an improved self-image. It is important too for social workers to be aware of countertransference. Motherly feelings toward clients may be inappropriate, overzealous, or sentimental. Deutsch indicates that "excessive motherly feelings can empty real motherliness of its emotional components."[18] Helen Harris Perlman defines countertransference feelings as "impulsive sympathies, impatiences, protectiveness, angers—any of the emotions that certain situations or certain people evoke in us."[19]

Countertransference responses stem from our own early experiences. We seek to recognize and control them; to minimize their influences by the development of self-awareness and through supervision and consultation.

The following is an illustration of some aspects of both transference and countertransference:

> A thirty-five-year-old policeman, hospitalized for alcoholism, broke his hand in an impulsive rage. It was known that he had been a favorite of his mother; that she had indulged him and overprotected him. The client was married, had five children and was separated from his wife. He had been seeing the social worker with whom he was manipulative and evasive.

An interview was focused on helping Mr. S talk about the angry feelings which had led to his rage. During this session, he played the role of a sheepish little boy, inappropriately playing down the behavior, joking, and flirting with the worker. (He did not see her as a professional person, indeed, he cannot see any female in an important role.) Interacting with him, the worker's sympathetic and protective stance was not unlike his mother's habitual way of relating to him. It validated his refusal to accept responsibility for his behavior. The social worker, in fact, unconsciously accepted the client's assumption that she was unable to help him; he does not need help and if he did, a woman would not provide it. This reaction is an example of what Annette Garrett means when she says the client "intuits our response" and thus "directs our treatment."[20]

In this context, it is important for women to feel both confidence and

---

[17] Florence Hollis, *Casework: A Psychosocial Theory* (New York: Random House, 1965), p. 26.

[18] Deutsch, *The Psychology of Women: Motherhood*, p. 21.

[19] Helen Harris Perlman, *Social Casework* (Chicago: University of Chicago Press, 1964), p. 82.

[20] Annette Garrett, The Worker Client Relationship, in *Ego Psychology and Dynamic Casework*, ed. Howard J. Parad (New York: Family Service Association of America, 1958), pp. 53–94.

competence in therapeutic situations. Experiences relative to the functioning and authority of mothers need to be examined. Because mothers have traditionally functioned as family peacemakers and go-betweens, they are often inappropriately assigned to, or assume, this role which offers minimal satisfaction and lacks vitality.

As a professional group, social workers have not dealt with the changing status of women. As individual caseworkers, many are confused and unsure. Because many social workers are mothers too, they need to examine the ways in which their personal beliefs influence their work with families.[21]

Mothering and Preventive Aspects of Casework

The preventive aspects of social work are difficult to measure but they are often confirmed by individual clients, by members of groups, and by those for whom the profession has provided consultation and collaboration. In this area, however, social workers have also been subjected to criticism. For example, Burton White says:

> Social workers become intimately involved in the problems of large numbers of families; as such, the opportunity is there to respond to a request for help by young parents…it is unfortunate that none of the professions (social workers, visiting nurses, homemakers, child study association people) provide very high-caliber training in parent education.[22]

White also criticizes professional training in the early educational development of children, and suggests that *experienced* mothers are better able to help parents than a professional person. He writes:

> I would even suggest that if you are lucky enough to know a wise woman who has raised three or four or more children, and if you are on good enough terms with that person to be able to get the benefit of her advice, you will more often than not find that she will be better able to help you deal with educational concerns in the first years of your child's life than a professional can.[23]

While social workers, as a professional group, can and should challenge this critical view, perhaps those who are mothers too, share a special responsibility to use their experience in helping as wide an audience as possible.

---

[21] Sanford B. Sherman, The Therapist and Changing Sex Roles, SOCIAL CASEWORK, 57:93–96 (February 1976).

[22] Dr. Burton L. White, *The First Three Years of Life* (Englewood Cliffs, N.J.: Prentice-Hall, 1975), p. 247.

[23] Ibid., p. 248.

Through Family Life Education programs, originally developed and fostered by family agencies, many parents can be reached. Focusing on the newer theories of child development presents a challenge that infuses parent groups with interest and vitality.[24]

Educational groups can focus on discussions of social change and how families learn to adapt; how the members feel about adaptation; and what they have lost or gained in this process. Such groups have positive effects in reducing the polarization common to families in conflict. They encourage movement toward the kinds of compromises necessary in today's complex family settings.

Summary

The subject and experience of motherhood has increasingly become the focus of negative thinking. The resulting concerns and questions influence the kinds of problems people have. Social workers, many of whom are mothers themselves, can be helpful in identifying issues and presenting options. Their own feelings and biases, however, must be recognized and handled.

Mothering is important to healthy child development. Inadequate mothering, particularly at an early stage of life, is related to pathology. The appropriate use of mothering, as a technique in casework, can stimulate therapeutic progress. The female social worker clearly has a special and unique opportunity to use her capacity for motherliness constructively.

All therapists can be certain that both they and their clients will unconsciously relate to aspects of mothering, real or imagined. Through self-awareness and understanding, these feelings, and the messages conveyed by them, can be used in effective therapeutic intervention.

---

[24] See, for example, Henry W. Maier, *Three Theories of Child Development* (New York: Harper & Row, 1965).

THE FAMILY

CHAPTER 10

Family Therapy: An Orientation

Phoebe Prosky

Introduction

Despite the fact that Family Therapy is a relative new-comer to the therapies, it has already developed, in its own eclectic fashion, in several directions. This is important because inasmuch as this paper directs itself to the training of professionals new to the family field, it is descriptive of one specific mode of family therapy—that of Nathan Ackerman *et al.*—in an effort to present a clear orientation. Some aspects of the approach set forth here are generic to family work, but others are wide open to variation and contradiction. Contrasting variations of family work are being done by such people as Murray Bowen, Virginia Satir, Fred Duhl, and Ross Speck. It is important to read the literature of these and others to get a picture of the richness and diversity which exists in the field at this time. This paper addresses itself specifically to the gnawing sense of theoretical and technical insecurity a therapist has as he sees his first families and hopefully provides a guideline to hold onto while he flies by the seat of his pants.

Defining the Family Treatment Situation

Who should be seen in family therapy? The answer is everyone—at least for a diagnostic session or two. There is no method of diagnosis that comes

Reprinted from *Clinical Social Work Journal*, Vol. 2, No. 1 (Spring, 1974), pp. 45–56, by permission of the publisher, Human Sciences Press, 72 Fifth Avenue, New York, New York 10011.

close to a family interview for efficiency and completeness. After that, most people who have a family are prime candidates for family therapy.

Family therapy begins at the first moment of the therapist's contact with a family. This is in some sense true, of course, in all therapies. But in family therapy, the therapist is often called on to make a pronounced intervention at as early a time as the initial phone call from the person requesting help. It is in this conversation that the therapist sets the ground rules for a family system approach. The person at the other end of the line will frequently define the problem as being that of one person or a dyad in the family. The family therapist will then want to know who else is in the family. This group, as defined by the caller (and the ''family'' need not be confined to blood members) is the one the therapist must make his bid to see. Sometimes the family refuses to involve one or more of its members. Here the family therapist must be aware of whether he himself is totally, utterly, convinced that the whole family be part of the session. Beginning therapists often have a fear of dealing with so many people, of exposing the children to the affairs of their parents, of handling an explosive marital situation with both partners present. If the therapist is reluctant, it is highly likely that the family will be, too. A beginning family therapist does well simply to maintain as policy that if he is to see the family, they must all be there. Period. This uncompromising approach strengthens his position and is often effective in getting compliance from the reluctant family members. If the therapist gives in to family pressure to start sessions with only part of the family, total involvement will become more difficult, and the treatment will be seriously weakened.

If the therapist is sure of himself and his approach and feels for one reason or another that there is good reason to begin with only part of the family, he may decide to do so, not, however, without making it clear that while he may start in this way, he must gain access to the other family members as he needs it or else the work will be terminated.

This may sound harsh and unreasonable, but there are important reasons for it. First, the greater a part of the patient's environment the family therapist has access to, the more quickly and accurately the therapy will move. Also to leave one person out may be to change the entire picture of the family, and the therapist may work in a useless direction or do harm to the absent member. Later on in the therapy, the therapist may decide to see subgroupings of the family or individuals alone in supplementation to family sessions. But that is after the family orientation is firmly established.

Issues of the First Session

With the phone conversation, the therapy has begun. The work continues when the family arrives at the therapist's office. They often present themselves bits at a time, and even if the last members are quite late in arriving, it is advisable to follow through with the thrust of the telephone intervention and wait to begin the session until all are present. Later on in therapy this same situation will have a variety of meanings in the context of the work, and the decision to start or wait for all members will have to be based on the current meaning. Sometimes on arrival the family confronts the therapist with the information that one member will not be there. Generally at this point the session should take place anyway, but the therapist during the course of the hour should explore thoroughly with the family why the missing member is missing and come to his own conclusions about who present is keeping him out; he will usually do best to assign this member of the family the task of getting the person in for the next session. A chair should be obviously left empty in the circle of seating, and it will become the person in absentia.

Visual data collecting about the family begins as soon as the therapist sets eyes on them. How are they dressed? What are their relative sizes and shapes? How do they hold themselves? What behavior do they display in coming into the situation: do they preen; offer themselves aggressively to the therapist; hang back? How are their handshakes? Is there anything outstanding or peculiar about the way they present themselves? A person who walks into the therapist's office preening is getting ready for courting. A child wearing a button which says something, says something about himself in the wearing. The family will present themselves in a particular configuration when they sit down. It is important to notice who sits next to whom, whether anyone seems off by himself, whether the members seem to close the physical spaces between them or seem rigidly defined and isolated by, or even to enlarge in some way, the distance.

After everyone is seated, the therapist may find himself among a silent, uncomfortable group of people he doesn't know. If luck is with him, the family will begin to talk immediately; but if they present that embarrassed silence which often lies between the greeting and "getting down to work," the therapist's best choice is between remaining silent no matter how uncomfortable it may feel, thereby letting a member of the family begin, and making a comment on something important or striking that has already transpired in the family since they walked in the door. In either case, the therapist is starting with material presented by the family in the situation. "Did you have much trouble getting here?" is rarely a legitimate opener on the part of the therapist. But, "I noticed you told the kids where to sit" (directed to a parent) begins meaningfully by focusing attention on an area of familial behavior which is undoubtedly topical. A question to the family in general about why they've come is also a useful beginning.

An area of exploration which should have a place somewhere early in the initial interview is why the various family members came and what they were told they would find. It is simply incredible how "withdrawn" a child can seem in an interview if the therapist has not bothered to find out that the child obliged his parents in coming only after it was agreed that he did not have to talk. Or how frightened the child is because he fears an injection from the "doctor." Or how reluctant a spouse is to open his mouth because he's sure his partner's purpose is to prove to the therapist that he is insane. Lack of information in this area can throw an entire session out of whack.

In the opening session, the therapist may be required to prove his skill and equanimity by passing a test which the family requires for entrance into its system. The family test is a common phenomenon, though often quite subtle. If the therapist feels unreasonably frustrated or angry at a person or situation in the course of the session, it is important to check over the process as it has occurred so far, because he is probably in the midst of being tested for such qualities as level-headedness and neutrality. On the other hand, if the session seems to be going uncommonly smoothly, and the family appears extremely content and loving without a problem in sight, this is probably a test of the therapist's acuity and eye for prevarication. It is so extremely important to pass these tests as they are presented that it is almost imperative to the life of the therapy. If the therapist cannot quite grasp the nature of the test, he must at least air his uncomfortable feeling of being provoked or placated. If he is sharp enough to at least spot the existence of a game, the family is likely to help him name it.

The bulk of the work of the first session centers around mapping family configurations and patterns of communications. Facts and figures are much less important than the means family members use to communicate with each other in the session, and the overall quality of their interaction.

The work of the first session also includes making beginning interventions into the family patterns. It is how the family uses these interventions which will provide important information on family strengths and coping ability.

Issues of Ongoing Therapy

A vital part of the work of the first several sessions involves the therapist's getting something going between each family member and himself. With some members of a family this may happen quickly, even spontaneously. With others it will take some doing to make the connection, and the therapist may have to woo the family members by whatever means he knows. The value of making a connection with each person relates to a crucial aspect of the family therapist's position—a kind of "staying neutral while taking sides." In individual work it is the accepted rule that the therapist throws himself in line on the side of his patient. In family therapy the whole family is his patient. He must be accepted by the family as having everyone's interest at heart. Yet if he were never to support one person in the face of another, never to take a side, his impact would be severely limited. If each family member feels he has an area of relatedness to the therapist, his tolerance for relatedness between the therapist and others will be sufficiently high to allow the therapist to shift postions and allegiances without disrupting the basic sense of his fairness. This positioning of the therapist I am going to call "pleutrality." Rather than fairness resulting from the absence of alliance anywhere—ordinarily called neutrality—the therapist's fairness lies in the presence of alliances everywhere—or pleutrality. To maintain pleutrality the therapist should see to it that the amount of attention he gives various family members is roughly equal over the span of a few sessions. Another very helpful principle for the therapist in maintaining his own sense of pleutrality vis-à-vis the family is to learn to conceptualize all difficulties raised in the family on the "It Takes Two (or more) to Tango" model. If the therapist becomes accustomed, each time he is confronted with the discomfort of one of the family members, to asking himself two questions—"Who provokes this?" and "Who benefits?"—he will come to see all family problems as interactions among people and will be unlikely to fall into the incapacitating stance of blamer. This is particularly important to bear in mind with families who present one of their members as being "sick" or "the family problem." This is always an indication of the scapegoating of that person in the family, and the family therapist immediately turns his attention to whom the scapegoat is covering in the family, and what the dysfunctional family pattern is that demands that one person bear all the blame.

The first phase of therapy centers around engagement as a whole. This includes pleutrality and the negotiations which take place in testing and wooing. But it also involves the ability of the family or family members to commit themselves. Very often well into the course of therapy the therapist is still aware of a sense of lack of commitment to the work on the part of the family. The clue to this often manifests itself in the therapist's anxiety between sessions that the family may drop out of treatment. The sessions go along with an amount of substance, so that it appears that the major work has begun. But until the hovering sense of uncommittedness disappears, the important therapeutic shifts are not likely to occur. If the family seems uncommitted for long, the therapist, before going any further with his treatment plan, must take up the issue of his contract with them, reviewing with them why they came, what they hope to accomplish in therapy, and securing their commitment to work toward mutually valued goals. It is well to remember that the family came to the therapist out of *their* need, not his, and it is wasted effort for the therapist to continually be prodding them to work. Such prodding prolongs an unnecessary power struggle and in addition is countertherapeutic, since it does not insist that the family be responsible for their own direction and the pursuit of it.

In a family interview the therapist must never let his total attention be captured by the subject matter, no matter how enthralling. He must always monitor what his ears are hearing through the screen of what his eyes are seeing, and his eyes must look everywhere for nonverbal responses of family members to what is being said. His focus is interaction. It is this eye-ear coordination which keeps him from doing one-to-one-therapy-in-the-presence-of-a-group, which is not the same as family therapy. Family therapy takes note of the responses one family member stirs in another. The therapist uses these notations to begin to develop his own picture of how the family functions. Much of his intervention in the session will take the form of his sharing these observations, but which of them he shares and when is a question of his own personal style, intuition, and timing with relevance to the family. These last three qualities are all-important, and unfortunately cannot be generalized or specified. They develop over time as the therapist develops contact with a variety of families and—importantly—with himself.

The initial act of sitting down in a session has nothing final about it, as it might in individual therapy. Everyone in the session, therapist included, should be seen as movable, and it should be kept in mind that physical flexibility stimulates and symbolizes mental flexibility. If two people in a family are separated physically in the room and need to do a piece of work together, it is often catalyzing to move them to seats next to each other. Or if one person seems withdrawn and the therapist is having trouble making contact, he might choose to move next to the person to stimulate interaction.

I want to say something about history-taking, since this takes place in the beginning phase of traditional therapeutic processes. Let me approach it from a more general issue. People often say to me, ''Family therapy may be fine for working on family problems, but I need deeper, individual therapy.'' This illustrates the misconception that family therapy is shallow, while individual therapy is deep. In actuality, if you spread the events of a person's life along a horizontal line in chronological order, you can illustrate the difference in the two approaches by placing traditional individual therapy at the early end of the life spectrum and family therapy at the end representing the present time. (I use ''traditional'' in recognition of the fact that much individual therapy today has departed from that model and often incorporates many of the techniques I have described as used in family work.) Then place arrows from each heading into the continuum. You now have a graphic representation of the distinction between the two processes: traditional individual therapy enters the person's life space through early history and development and works its way through to an understanding of the present; family therapy enters through present interactions and concerns and works its way back to an understanding of the past. Both approaches have as a goal (when practiced at their most extensive) the reintegration of a person's life into a useful, meaningful gestalt. They simply come at it from different ends.

Rather than taking a past-history in the early family sessions, then, the therapist is involved in making a paradigm of the present life-space positions and attitudes of the family members, and this provides the base for his later work, as a history would do for a traditional individual therapist.

The exploration of history takes place at the points at which it breaks through into the present. When a family member says, for instance, "I do this because it got approval in my family," it is probably an appropriate moment to find out about that aspect of his original family's functioning and how it affected his upbringing. In this way, over time, the pieces of his life history emerge and come together in a way that relates each of them to some present issue and brings them alive, and his history comes to co-exist with his present.

Of all a therapist's emotional repertoire, humor is probably the most distinctively important to the family therapist. When the therapist sits with a family, he is outnumbered at the very least two to one. If you conceive of an interviewing room as a kind of emotional echo chamber, it is clear that the intensity of the emotional aura will increase proportionately with the number of people. The classical therapist maintains his own emotional integrity by withholding himself and staying removed. But this stance is not possible for the family therapist. And his task of maintaining his emotional integrity is at least twice as great. This is where humor—a light touch—can help him keep his distance while at the same time allowing him to be actively involved. A light touch is usually extremely helpful to the family as well, providing a sense of hopefulness by the implication that the situation is not so serious as they feared and the therapist is not horrified. When humor is well-timed and appropriate, it is a valuable element in the emotional repertoire with which a therapist approaches a family.

Because of the intensity of the emotional aura, many people voice the fear that to work with more than one person at a time would be hopelessly confusing, complex, draining, and difficult. Sometimes this is the case. But just as often, the therapist finds help and support for his task in the ranks of the family. If there is a deadlock between two family members, he can often call upon a third to provide a useful alternative point of view. If one person distorts something in relating it to the therapist, another will often set him straight, providing the therapist with insight into both the distortion and the fact. The therapist has the unique opportunity to see actual troublesome interactions with his own eyes, rather than relying on a patient's recounting of incidents, and he is in the fortunate position of being able to bring the family to see them on the spot. The advantages of seeing a family together are many for the work of the therapist, and balance the difficulties and complexites.

The therapist must use himself to provide, during the sessions, elements of family functioning that are missing from the family in its state of disease. He may do this through teaching, modeling, or feeding. With a depressed family, the therapist must provide a model for hopefulness and do a great deal of emotional feeding to ease the deprivation. With a disordered family, the therapist must provide a sense of structure. Of course, any time the therapist can draw needed qualities from one or another family member, his most effective use of himself will be to support the quality where he finds it rather than bringing it himself.

As you have been reading these paragraphs, have you been aware of how they are organized, of the use of language, of their general tone, and of what responsive feelings have been stirred in you? Or have you been taking them in on the level of the content alone? Please think about it. It is one essential and common ingredient in all family therapies that the therapist must train his awareness to follow process while listening to content. What does that mean? It means while Johnnie is talking about the fight he had with his father, in addition to listening, the therapist's awareness must be concentrated on such aspects as: What was being talked about before Johnnie started to speak and the relationship between that and what he is saying; changes of posture and expression in other family members as he speaks; previous material from other sessions which contribute to what he is saying; how he's talking about it; the reactions of other family members that follow and the subsequent areas of discussion; the feelings that are stirred in the therapist himself as Johnnie talks. The family therapist must watch spaces between people, nonverbal communications, and the pattern of the progression of events in a session. His observation must be similar to looking through a kaleidoscope where the focus is the changing pattern of the pieces rather than the pieces themselves. And, in addition, he must remain aware of his own emotional responses to the changing patterns.

Because of his own reactions are so important in forming his working diagram of the family (Locke & Prosky, 1971), the therapist has a responsibility to know himself well. This is exceedingly important. For if a therapist doesn't know where his own emotional difficulties lie, he will not only mislead the family with his inappropriate reactions, but he *will not be able to trust and draw upon his appropriate reactions*. Then he will be blind to the processes of therapy.

How long a family session should be is a matter of individual preference. It is generally acknowledged that it should be longer than 50 minutes because of the number of people involved. Anywhere from an hour to an hour and a half are the usual lengths.

How long treatment lasts varies from family to family, therapist to therapist. Some families come into therapy around a crisis, and when the crisis has passed, drop out. Others enter family therapy to do long-term, growth-oriented work.

Special Techniques

What I have talked about so far deals with some of the general principles which guide therapeutic work. There are also some special techniques to be used in the course of therapy.

The Home Visit.   The family therapist should make a home visit to every family he treats. This is not an easy point to sell, given most therapists' resistances to leaving their offices for anything in the line of duty. Yet, how a family makes its home is an important statement about their life together, and the therapist who takes the trouble to look at that statement will be amply rewarded with helpful information.

But it is not for information alone that the therapist makes a home visit. Almost without exception, families look on the therapist's offer of a visit as extremely generous and a gesture of acceptance, and frequently the therapeutic alliance of family and therapist deepens significantly in the course of such a visit. In addition, the therapist has the rare opportunity to see the family in a natural setting, rather than in his office, and is likely to become aware of areas of strength and good functioning that had not previously come to his attention. This is exceedingly important, for the family he sees in his office is wholly concentrated on its areas of stress and tends to appear much more dysfunctional than it actually is. Obviously gains of this kind are well worth the expenditure of a few out-of-office hours.

It is usually useful to make the visit sometime in the early part of the therapy, after the therapist feels comfortable with the family. It is always desirable to make the visit at a family meal time when everyone is present. Sharing a family activity, rather than just sitting and talking, gives the therapist a three-dimensional feeling for family process. He should tell the family ahead of time that he wants to see their home as it is usually, and when he is there, he may ask for a tour. The home visit is counted in the place of an office session, but how much "business as usual" goes on varies from therapist to therapist, family to family. Some therapists structure the talk during the visit along the lines of a session; others follow the drift of the family at home. Whatever the therapist's orientation, the home visit is bound to be an important part of the therapeutic process.

Sculpting.   Before reading further, take a minute to picture your own family. Probably in doing this, a series of people moved across your mind's eye. These were all the people *in* your family. (It's interesting to note whom you included and whom you left out, in discovering what you consider "family" to mean.) Your family, however, is a composite of these individuals and has a shape and life of its own. Picture it again, this time placing the individuals in relation to each other in position, attitude, and size. You should begin to form a visual representation of a family pattern. If so, you have done a mental "sculpture" which, while not as easy to grasp as if you had live people before you, should furnish you with a working diagram of some of the major qualities and content of the relationships among the parts of your family.

Sculpting, as a technique in family therapy, is uniquely useful. When one member sculpts his family, physically placing the actual members with relation to each other and himself as he sees them, an entity emerges with very special features. Most striking is the sensate element: the family has the opportunity to see and feel its characteristic self, rather than dealing in fantasies and abstract, intellectual concepts. Yet it tends to be a relatively nonthreatening way to lead a family to understand itself or some aspect of itself, since the method is experienced as a kind of game, and in the end, everyone's in it together. There is no way to demonstrate the element of time, so that the menacing, misleading aspect of who started a conflict or who is "basically" to blame cannot enter. The family system presents as the process—the gestalt—that it is.

It is possible to have every member sculpt the family as he sees it. It is important for the sculptor to give concrete instructions with respect to detail: What is the expression on a person's face? Where and how does this one touch that one? Or is there no physical contact? After the sculpture is completed, the next step is to ask everyone how they feel in the positions in which they have been placed. Often revelatory truths emerge—aspects of a person's role which were never in awareness before. For instance, a family which sculpts as a cluster, with one punitive member seen as standing off and lecturing threateningly, may for the first time experience the extremely lonely aspect of the dominating figure as it sees him standing separate, unsupported, unprotected. This insight may give a whole new coloring to that position and lead the family to regroup, including the formerly distant member who has become no longer so threatening. Or a family member who is seen as supportive and carrying the entire family may find his physical position in the sculpture untenable and bodily collapse, expressing how untenable and precarious the current family balance is. Dramatic insights such as these speed the process of therapy immensely.

After hearing how each member feels in his position, it is often useful to ask family members to rearrange the family as they would like it to be. Through this rearrangement, people may learn that the family will allow them—even *wants* them—to move out of the family bind into new and more productive positions.

The Use of the Unexpected and Paradoxical Effects.   The use of the unexpected seems to have a peculiarly strong value in family therapy. Sometimes families get stuck and seem to insist on holding onto their dysfunctions. Often one of the best things a therapist can do to shake up this stalemate is something totally unexpected. Some families will react with a healthy start to a simple comment of the therapist, such as "You are driving me crazy" (the idea that the therapist could be crazy is very unsettling). With other families it takes some extreme maneuver (a colleague told me of a family in which the only way he could get a response was finally, in desperation, to stand up, unbuckle his belt, and drop his trousers). There is a variety of things the family therapist can do to do the unexpected which is already a standard, accepted part of the field is the paradoxical effect. In using it, the therapist instructs the family to do the dysfunctional thing they are doing more often and with more gusto. This operates in several ways. It sometimes serves to present the family with the absurdity of their actions and seeing this for the first time, they begin to change. It may enlist the oppositional feelings of the family toward the therapist and cause them to unite in *not* doing what he suggests, which prevents their continuing the dysfunctional pattern. Or the family may drop the behavior in the end from sheer exhaustion!

Involving Young Children.   Involving young children in therapy sessions is often difficult, and many experienced family therapists shy away from it. However, it is worth struggling with, both because the therapist cannot otherwise see how the whole family functions together, and because little kids often say the most candid things. In the case of infants, it is usually adequate to have them brought to occasional sessions in order to keep an eye on their development and position in the family, and on the quality of the parenting they are getting. Toddlers and preschool children ought to be involved more frequently and can be interested in what's being said, if the therapist takes a little trouble toward that end. Children from 6 on up are usually capable of participating quite fully in sessions and ought to be included regularly. Parents will often object that the children don't know the troubles the family is having and will be upset by the session, and therefore should be left home. This is patently untrue. Children always know when something upsetting is afoot, even if they don't know exactly what it is, and the fantasies they build around their feelings of unease have far worse effects than the truth. Children are almost invariably relieved to be let in on the goings-on, and are reassured to see that the therapist is looking after things. Often it will be useful to excuse the children part way through a session, because there are subjects, most remarkably sex, which parents feel uncomfortable about discussing in front of their offspring.

Involving Significant Others.   Family therapy, at its optimum, is a multi-generational approach to corrective family functioning. Unfortunately to-day with the geographical and emotional splitting off of family units, it is a rare family which can or will involve itself as far as the third generation. This usually means grandparents. Where it is at all feasible, the third gen-eration should be included to provide a fuller family picture and greater treatment potential. Sometimes other, lateral, family members are inte-grally involved in a family's functioning and dysfunction. These people should be included in sessions for whatever part of the therapy seems in-dicated. There are situations where significant others are not family mem-bers at all—most classically housekeepers who have stayed with a family for many years, sometimes a friend, neighbor, or lover who is in some way a part of the family's life. Pets also are significant others, and a family may be encouraged to bring a pet to the office, ridiculous as that may seem at first blush; it cannot be denied that very important family business gets carried out around Fido.

Re-Peopling the Family.   Sometimes it becomes apparent that needs within a family are urgent, and that weaknesses either are permanent or will be a long time in the strengthening. In such situations, it is often advisable to make arrangements to re-people the family in some way. This may in-volve hiring a homemaker in a family where the mother is coping margin-ally or absent, or reaching out to an uncle to involve himself more in a family with no father. Or it may mean getting a Big Brother for a boy who is an only child with few friends. Often an environmental manipulation of this sort is the most useful therapeutic intervention, and the family ther-apist should not hesitate to help make it.

Conclusion

The family therapist is an active, involved therapist. He must be emotion-ally lithe and resilient, prepared to deal with, or deal out, the unexpected. His challenge is to learn to use his own impulses and reactions in a way that the family can use to understand themselves better. He makes use also of any people and resources in the family's environment which might be of help to them. There are some basic techniques and orienting prin-ciples available to the family therapist, and it is these which it has been the task of this paper to set forth. Beyond these, the responsibility rests with each family therapist to comprehend himself and his place in his own family, and then to use his creativity to transform what he knows and what he feels into a form which can be used by the families he treats in their development.

Reference

LOCKE, K., and PROSKY, P. Revisions in family therapy terminology. *Voices,* Summer 1971.

MIDDLE AGE

CHAPTER 11

The Middle-Age Separation Crisis and Ego-supportive Casework Treatment

Sidney Wasserman

It has become increasingly apparent in mental health research that the years forty to sixty-five—middle-age—when human beings are at their most responsible, fullest, busiest phase—are the most neglected by theorists and researchers. It is that time of life described as "the crisis point of growth or regression" yet we still know so little as to what determines how individuals caught up in the middle-age crisis grow or regress.

Erik Erikson has conceptualized the normal ego crisis as "generativity versus stagnation," whereby the middle-aged person is primarily interested in establishing and guiding the next generation. On the opposite end of the spectrum, the ego threat is being "unable to generate and guide," to become stagnant and unfulfilled (Erikson, 1959). Many clients who are referred to social agencies are caught in the latter spiral, hopelessly *de-generating*, continuously frustrated and impotent in their ability to guide the next generation—their own adolescent and emerging young adult children. By the time the couple and/or family comes to the attention of a social agency, the marriage and mental health of all members concerned are at serious risk. The adolescent emancipation crisis has ascended in the faces of the 'descending' parents.

This built-in generational paradox gets superimposed on a myriad of conflicts and problems. Middle-aged fathers are often interacting with ad-

Reprinted from *Clinical Social Work Journal*, Vol. 1 (Spring, 1973), pp. 38–47, by permission of the author and publisher, Behavioral Publications, 72 Fifth Avenue, New York, New York 10011. Copyright 1973.

olescent sons at a time when the fathers themselves are most vulnerable regarding loss of role, failure in job promotion and prestige, and the threat of younger men eagerly waiting to take their place. Middle-aged mothers are commonly plagued with psychological anxieties around menopause, fearing loss of sexuality along with the physical reality of loss of fertility. All of this happens while their adolescent daughters are rapidly approaching their prime sexual years.

In our eagerness to rescue the adolescent, social caseworkers frequently convey a sense of helplessness and hopelessness in reaching out to the middle-aged couple who are so unresolved at this time of their life cycle. Aside from the individual dynamics of the mothers (who are often struggling with unrelenting needs to consume and absorb in relationships within their immediate environment) and the fathers (who concomitantly reverse and turn inward overwhelming feelings of aggression), we need also to perceive such clients within a larger context. Frequently, there is a broader theme operating and, as practitioners, we perhaps tend to overlook the obvious. Just why are our caseloads so overloaded with children absorbed by such "grasping" mothers and "self-involved, indifferent" fathers? Why do we so often find that when the adolescent is emerging toward young adulthood and possible independence that the crisis looms so much larger? Exactly what does this mutually opposing time of life mean to the individuals caught in this psychological-social bind? Can this be theoretically explained only along social-economic determinants, or are there psychological components which need to be highlighted and clarified for ourselves?

In studying the past histories of clients, it is not unusual to find that there has been a marked tendency, on the part of the wives and mothers particularly, to be overinvolved with the children—often a son. However, during the adolescence of the child, an increased sense of desperateness is often within the parents. This appears to be primarily related to the fact that the youngster's crisis of adolescence not only sets off the parents' unresolved adolescence but overlaps the parents' crisis of middle age. As Dr. Stanley Cath has said: "As one becomes aware of sexual decline in the self, one's children may be emerging as vibrantly alive and extremely sexual." Thus, he goes on to say: "the parents become most upset when either sons or daughters turn outward and away" (Cath, 1965).

There is growing recognition that the less commitment to the marriage itself, the greater is the stress and difficulty in letting go and separating from the children. Not uncommonly social caseworkers inject into their diagnostic workups the phrase: "poor marital matrimonial relationship" and then appear to proceed as though this assessment had never been made. Inversely, the parental pattern of getting overinvolved with the youngster gets repeated by the social caseworker. In so doing, we lose sight of what the marriage is all about, its ingredients, etc. Perhaps this oversight has a purpose. It enables us to avoid facing up to a pretty de-

pressing fact; that is, that there are millions of marriages which are anything but ideal, and this can be threatening to us as caseworkers. Loveless
marriages were frequently contracted from the start while countless others
"fell out of love" many years ago. Such marriages all too commonly have
sought to gain from the children what the marriage partner has been unable to provide and, most likely, what earlier parental relationships never
provided. What we find is an oft-repeated pattern of a mother-son and or
father-daughter 'hang-up.' And we find these components reflected across
the socio-economic class spectrum.

Middle Age: A Time of Assessment

Though it is vitally important to assess the individual dynamics of each
partner, as well as the marital interaction, we need to gain a clearer assessment of the marriage itself: its past, its present, its potential for further
growth, and how the middle-age separation crisis is being dealt with.

The best of marriages encounter heightened tensions at this time. The
individual partners have to adapt to disillusionment and statistics show
that the highest divorce rate is in the thirties-to-early-forties age group.
According to Dr. H. V. Dicks of Tavistock Clinic, the disillusionment is
"an awakening to the difference between youthful expectation and sober
reality" (Dicks, 1968). After thirty-five, we come to know that we will not
conquer new worlds, or achieve all that we had hoped to. Most of all, we
are confronted, and yes, affronted, by the reality that we really are mortal.
For many, a sense of imprisonment sets in and a feeling of restlessness.
The "old wars" surface again but this time the marital partner becomes
the displaced scapegoat. When this happens, each partner harbors increased disillusioning thoughts regarding going through middle and old
age with such a companion. Each tends to relish phantasies of earlier relationships and affairs, feeling that John Smith or Mary Brown would have
been the 'right' person. The marriage is on trial and each partner is thinking about what it holds for the future, if anything. The climacteric years,
with their physical concomitants, only heighten the realization that "time
is running out."

The weaker the basis of the marriage, the looser the ties, the greater
the ambivalence and the more difficult it is for the partners to cope with
this time of life. In such circumstances, the marriage partner attempts to
ward off this painful assessment process and instead clings desperately to
the emerging adult-child, refusing to give permission for the young person's further development. In surveying a cross section of case recordings
in various settings, clients repetitively tell workers: "He (the child) is all I
have. I love him (her) so much. My life wouldn't be worth living if he (she)
wasn't around." Neither partner feels supported by the other and many
have reached the point of saying: "What's the use of trying?" The wife

will complain that the husband has little affection for the child—"he's jealous"; the husband complains that the wife is "babying" the son. Each are busy sending out all kinds of overt and covert messages to the children about "letting parents down" and leaving them to face old age alone. Guilt-arousal is used consciously, but more often unconsciously, as a mechanism of control. If the children succeed at least in some form of physical emancipation, a number of unrewarding marriages then collapse. Significantly, the youngster going off to a university, or into the armed services, or getting married, or moving into his (or her) own living quarters (particularly, the last child leaving home) often brings the crisis to a head. For some partners the "emptiness" of the marital relationship is too much to bear. The purpose of having "lived together" seems to have disappeared. Such clients have been heard to say: "It was all for the children. As far as I am concerned, I only put up with him (her) because of them." Is it any wonder that so many of the young people caught in such a bind are so ambivalent themselves about leaving their parents to cope with future years of "nothingness"? Some adolescents will actually verbalize the fear that the parents will now divorce, or "do something terrible" to each other. At the same time, the adolescent is usually quite unaware of his own needs to manipulate the situation (e.g., to play one parent against the other) and of his deep-seated desire to remain tied to one or both of the parents. Consciously, he protests for independence and freedom. Unconsciously, he longs to be nurtured and protected from the unknowns of the outside world.

All this does not mean to imply that social, economic, and cultural stresses do not impinge on the stability of the marriage. Of course they do, and we know that the most solid of marriages can undergo acute crisis states—even crumble—under overwhelming external stimuli. However, we also know that the firmer the commitment to the marriage, each partner to the other, the greater is the ability to withstand and cushion various external stresses. When the bonds are weak, the tendency to distort reality increases, sometimes to monstrous proportions. Thus, for example, economic, religious, and racial-cultural differences are often realistic stresses which occasionally get overinvested with all kinds of irrational meanings. The "weak" partner interprets these differences in accordance with his own personal dynamics. As stress increases, so does the need to overproject one's own inadequacies and anxieties onto the partner.

Diagnosis and Prognosis

Perhaps the most disconcerting of efforts is the gaining of recognition and insight into the balance of strengths and weaknesses in the marital interaction at this time in the life cycle. A basic question seems to be: To what extent is the present marital upheaval precipitated by the "normal" crisis of middle-age, reassessment of the marital relationship, and the letting go of the children? Or, to what extent is it a representation of what has smouldered just below the surface (preconscious) for many years, whereby the problems of middle-age, etc., only exacerbate the essentially weak marriage commitment? It is possible to err in either direction in the over-all diagnosis. At times, the worker may tend to underestimate strengths and to assess the present crisis as symbolic of a poor marriage, without clarifying to what degree the marriage is struggling with some reasonably "normal" maturational upheaval. When this happens the worker can easily lose sight of what has been positive in the marriage and where there has been good indication of mutuality.

> Mr. and Mrs. K. had been married thirty-seven years and each were insisting that there was no possible way to save the marriage. The last of three sons was now leaving home to get married and the other two sons had taken over the small family business. Mr. K. had been "pensioned out" by his sons. Each partner, in individual and joint interviews, markedly projected onto the other why the marriage was failing. Mr. K. repeatedly insisted that Mrs. K. no longer cared to provide him with decent, warm meals, as well as other needs of his (physical and sexual). Mrs. K. maintained that Mr. K. only sat around the house complaining, whining, and getting in her way. After a prolonged testing-out period with the caseworker, both Mr. and Mrs. K. cautiously began to talk about their feelings of being let down by their children, of coping with late middle-age and approaching old age. Each spoke of their roles being taken away and each nurtured their own hurts. After several sessions of such verbalization there was a noticeable lessening of projection. Each could begin to bring forth remembrances of the "good years" in raising the children together.

As in all crisis assessments, it is oft times confusing as to where the marital ego strengths lie. From the above situation, one can prognosticate rather hopefully that the partners, encouraged and supported by the caseworker, can now begin to turn to each other for increased gratifications. But what about the innumerable marriages where there has been a pronounced lack of mutuality—at best a pseudo-mutuality? What about those marriages where the sadomasochistic interplay has provided such a weighted amount of negative gratifications?

> Mr. and Mrs. R. spoke of having fallen out of love within the first five years of their marriage. As far as they were concerned they were filling out a "life sentence," living under the same roof and upholding some pretences for "the sake of the children" and community. Earlier years of turbulence and verbal assaults were replaced by months of mutual silence. Any exchange was passed through the children; e.g., "Tell your father (mother), etc." Recently, in honor of their

seventeenth wedding anniversary they took a three-hour auto drive to a large metropolitan city. Within the over-all six-hour trip not a word was exchanged between them. Mrs. R. concentrated on smoking one cigarette after another. Mr. R. focused his eyes on the road and drove the car. Both agreed (in response to the caseworker's question) "We have nothing to say to each other; it's been this way for years."

With such situations, or in marriages where the theme is one of violence, drunkenness, extra-marital relations, child-beating, etc., the temptation to mark off or dismiss the couple is very great. Certainly, the prognosis is usually a very guarded one. However, in many of these marriages there are, in spite of gross negative elements, many interactions which possess latent strengths and underlying degrees of discomfort with the status quo. Each partner is harboring deep-seated feelings of failure and low self-esteem. The challenge of case-work, or any form of therapeutic help, is how to tap into, capitalize on and exploit the discomfort and desire for change. In other words, the question is how to make the demoralizing behavior toward each other as ego-alien as possible. It can be anticipated that those marriages which have been characterized by varying degrees of neurotic interplay will be more likely, with support, to come to grips with the "normal" crisis of middle-age and of separation from children. However, where the acting out within the interaction is of gross proportions, and the behavior is ego-syntonic, the ability to deal with the present crisis is lessened. It is the purpose of this paper to underscore the importance of the middle-age separation crisis and to deal with it in treatment as a means of strengthening the marital partners' egos, individually and collectively. With earlier and clearer recognition of this crisis, the worker increases the possibility of freeing latent strengths which have been disguised or hidden; these may exist even in the most destructive of interactions. Granted, the more destructive the relationship the greater is the likelihood of the need for negative gratification. However, within differential diagnostic thinking, it is important to also assess the individual partner's accessibility to professional intervention, his(her) potential for discomfort with the interaction, and the covert seeking of help.

Treatment

As indicated earlier, it is frequently observed that during the early phase of treatment the marital partner's need to focus on the children, or project onto the partner the present difficulties, is pronounced. It is important, in reaching out, to recognize that this projection is defensive and needs to be respected. Though we have often diagnosed a "poor marital relationship," we have also erred by moving too quickly into the area of the marriage itself, and threatened the desperate defenses of the partners. Many practitioners are somewhat uneasy in "going along" with the defense. However, the anxious, "consuming" mother needs to hear the worker emphasize and verbalize how difficult it is to cope with an adolescent who seems to be wanting things his own way and showing less and less gratitude. Or, that the worker can appreciate the difficulty of feeling unsupported by one's partner. The "up-tight" father needs to hear concern and support as to his distress regarding his needs: i.e., lack of attention, job frustrations, etc. All this must be balanced with what has been identified in the diagnostic workup as the positives in the situation. Not infrequently such mothers put much stress on their immaculate housekeeping standards, their thrifty management of limited economic housekeeping resources, and their rendering of excellent physical care to the children. These need to be supported and held up as indicators of good parenting. So too, the fathers are often reasonably good workers and have established loyal and conscientious work records. Others have had sporadic work records but the desire to have stuck with it has always been there. The reality, as well as the wish, needs to be supported.

It has been stated that destructive interaction needs to be made ego-alien as early as possible. As the partners send out clues related to their interactions: e.g., "all we ever do is fight," or, "we never talk to each other," etc., the worker needs to respond somewhat incredulously. The response should always be based on concern for the individual partner, as well as themselves as a couple. Such remarks as "I know you really do not want to be like this," or, "it concerns me that you do this to yourself, as well as to each other," or, "how upsetting it must be to keep on at each other this way—what do you want to do about it?" are indicated in that they serve as reminders to the individual partners that they are again lowering their own self-esteem.

By attempting to make the destructive interaction ego-alien, we simultaneously move toward formulating the interactional problem for the partners. The worker needs to exaggerate the conflict in order to demonstrate what they are doing to themselves, as well as to each other. By so doing, the worker supports the healthy part of the ego which seeks to gain greater maturity and self-control.

The worker can usually measure the effectiveness of the approach by the degree of response on two levels: (1) the diminishing of the acting out within the marital situation, and (2) the beginning establishment of trust within the therapeutic relationship. As basic trust begins to crystallize, along with the lessening of destructiveness, the worker can gently begin to inject such realities as to the difficulty in raising children for so many years and then having to cope with their beginning to move off on their own. Also, it is important to universalize the fact that all parents have this struggle at this time of life and that this is not an easy time for any of them.

> Mr. A. began to respond to the individual support and attention he was being given by the worker, in that he gradually talked about his fear of having been overlooked in his marriage. He spoke of his feeling that the marriage was never important to his wife; that she wanted it only for the sake of having children. Mr. A. moved on to say that he always felt unimportant to his wife, that she only tolerated him. As far as he was concerned she was giving to the children what rightfully belonged to him. This is why he was feeling a kind of resentment toward the children, especially his son.
>
> Mrs. A. slowly injected remarks about the marriage. She stated that they started raising a family shortly after they were married. She feels that she and her husband "never really got to know each other" and before they knew it, they were "bogged down with the kids." In time, she talked of how she always felt unsure of herself and that her husband wanted too much from her. In fact, she felt let down in that she was wanting him to give her the confidence and affection which she felt she always lacked. Instead, she felt like she had to raise him, along with the children, and she resented having to do so. She was determined that their son was not going to be like the father, but somehow, it had all gone wrong. If anything, she feels her children now resent her.

To reach the above stage in the treatment process takes much patience, time, and perseverance on the part of the worker. It is not meant to imply that there are pat phrases and magical words to get the necessary responses from our clients. However, what is implied is the importance of testing out ways to free clients in order to bring forth some of the above doubts and apprehensions. Doing so reflects a full appreciation for the middle-age separation crisis. Such clients need permission to face up to such feelings. With catharsis, the partners are frequently relieved to hear that each has a right to be *first* in the eyes of the other; that the marriage should have precedence over the children; that it is all right to 'mother' one's husband to varying degrees; and that it is permissible to risk and demonstrate some affection for the other.

With the beginning of this new-found freedom, clients have been heard to express some positives about being middle-aged. Feeling more supported by the other, they talk of "enjoying life at fifty." The wives appear more resigned to the implications of menopause, recognizing the end of their fertility but not necessarily of sexuality; some come to regard it as a time of welcome release from childbearing. In fact, some wives have been somewhat taken back in that "mothering" their husbands a bit more brings a warm response and that motherly affection is what "he has been wanting all along." Having themselves been nurtured and encouraged in the relationship with the worker, each partner feels freer to risk and to test new methods of interacting with the other. Also, having faced up to the fear of being unloved and unlovable appears to make the dreaded reality less threatening, somehow easier to cope with and easier to bear.

It must readily be admitted that there are marital interactions where the characteristic pattern of mutual destruction is so ingrained as to provide minimal opportunity for therapeutic intervention. Knowledge and skill in such instances is, as yet, underdeveloped and undefined as to how to ignite the necessary discomfort and desire for change. Nonetheless, practitioners have not always utilized to the fullest the knowledge and skill available in testing out potential for further growth and development. Not infrequently, practitioners opt for the quickest or easiest avenue (e.g., referrals to other agencies; remaining concentrated on the child; or outright hostility to the parents). Consequently, it is found that the short-cut all too often proves to be ineffective, expensive, and ultimately to perpetuate both acute and chronic crises.

The Practitioner's Dilemma

Earlier it was indicated that the attitude of the worker in identifying and categorizing various "poor marital relationships" is significant. The possibility of one's own inner family struggles being rearoused now requires some elaboration. Helping clients through the middle-age separation crisis means being confronted with: (1) disenchantment regarding the marriage ideal myth and (2) that realistically no one comes from a home where the marriage was "perfect" or "made in heaven." As practitioners, all of us have had earlier life experiences where we felt caught between parental loyalties. Therefore, overidentification with the adolescent can noticeably obstruct one's ability to reach out to the parents.

On the other hand, many workers are today in the "prime" years, with adolescents of their own. A number may understandably be struggling with "letting go," reassessment of their own marriages, and the internal strains of various ambivalent pulls. Dealing with the middle-age couple in crisis means opening up one's own internal conflicts and binds. And so, how much easier it is to keep middle-aged parents at a distance! At least one is protected from any of one's own discomforts.

However, as in all effective means of help, the greater the self-awareness that can be brought to the interaction with clients, the greater is the ability to inject objectivity and thereby increase the opportunity for client growth. We do not come to our clients purified and absolved of all conflicts. Rather, self-knowledge hopefully leads to enhanced tolerance and patience which so often soothes and heals the hurt of others. Most of all, by helping individuals and couples over the middle-age separation hurdle, we provide an opportunity for the persons involved to rediscover each other. For many, it is a chance to discover each other for the *first* time.

References

1. CATH, S. H. "Some Dynamics of the Middle and Later Years." In H. J. Parad, (Ed.), *Crisis Intervention*, N.Y.: F.S.A.A., 1965.
2. DICKS, H. V. "The Seven Ages of Man." In *A New Society Pub.*, Special Edition: (Prime of Life: 30 to 42), London: 1968.
3. ERIKSON, E. "Identity and the Life Cycle." In *Psychological Issues*, Vol. 1, No. 1, N.Y.: International University Press, 1959.

OLD AGE

CHAPTER 12

Social Work with the Aged: Principles of Practice

Abraham Monk

Does social work have a distinctive purpose in regard to the aged? Assuming the answer is affirmative, does this purpose differ in degree rather than substance from social work's purpose vis-à-vis other age groups? At least three positions worthy of mention exist in regard to these questions.

Unique Stage of Life

The first position to be discussed underscores the uniqueness of old age as the phase of life in which individuals have to complete the integration of their experiences and the closure of an existence bordering on death. For social work practitioners, no matter how young, providing services to older people means glimpsing images of and therefore anticipating their own final destiny.

This is a demanding existential enterprise. Younger people tend to view time as an inexhaustible commodity and to see their lives as starting from birth, the point of origin, and then extending infinitely into the future. It is only after "middlescence" that time acquires a peremptory quality and is measured as "life left to live," and the individual takes stock of his or her accomplishments and unfulfilled aspirations. Those who are relatively young, therefore, do not often have the same concerns and perspective on life as those who are aged. Because of this, many social workers may find work with aging clients particularly difficult.

In addition, dealing with older people may be personally threatening to some workers, who may find they would prefer not to deal with the painful feelings and issues that arise for them in work with the aged. When social workers deal with problems such as alcoholism, unwed mother-hood, or renal dialysis, they are attending to critical circumstances or conditions that they may never have to face in their own lives. Becoming an alcoholic is certainly not an intrinsic developmental requirement of their own life "scripts." In contrast, everyone is genetically programmed to grow old, and workers will inevitably experience some of the losses their clients may currently be enduring. Many may wish to avoid confronting the prospect of these losses.

It is not easy to deal with an awareness of the impending losses that are part of life and to establish a thread of continuity with one's past and future ego identity. As suggested earlier, work with the aged seems to be unique because it requires social workers to forge an image of their own old age and to accept the temporality of life and the reality of death. This may be fraught with problems, because it means coming to terms with not being, in a culture that denies death and places it outside the self, as though refusing to accept it as a natural part of living.

According to Butler and Lewis, the Western emphasis on individuality makes the death an insult and a "tremendous affront to man, rather than the logical and necessary process of old life making way for new."[1] Becker alludes to a "morbidly-minded" argument that assumes everyone harbors an unconscious narcissistic urge for immortality and the fear of death is present even when people function normally.[2] Most people can put off this fear and repress it; if they could not, it is doubtful whether the organism could make an effective stand for self-preservation. However, social workers in the field of gerontology cannot afford the luxury of this kind of denial because they constantly witness the existential plight of individuality confronted with its own end. Little in Western secular culture supports the person who is attempting to deal with this plight.

The professional interventions of social workers are exceptional because they ultimately take into account the totality of clients' lives, even when they are designed to search for the last threads of clients' remaining strength amidst tangles of chronic impediments and the overwhelming bombardment of successive losses. When dealing with the aged, workers assist in a process of growth that hardly resembles the development of the preceding stages of life: this growth proceeds through integration rather than expansion and is concerned with the constant imperative to seek out the meaning of life and affirm its value, even in the face of life's impending termination. Butler and Lewis maintain that only older persons develop a personal sense of the life cycle and that younger people do not achieve this understanding of life as a totality with its own rhythm and variability. They maintain that this sense is not the same as "feeling old" but is instead "a deep understanding of what it means to be human."[3]

In essence, this first perspective on social work and the aged argues that only in gerontological practice are social workers confronted with a person's final destiny and with the true meaning of a person's life. Although this confrontation may develop at other points during life, it is frequently ignored or deflected by paying attention to agendas for the future and social, psychological, and functional compensations. With the aged, however, there is no time left for restitution, and there can be no postponement. The agenda is virtually closed.

Is the Practice Worthwhile?

The second perspective on social work with the aged also upholds the premise that older people have a unique status. Paradoxically, however, at the same time it devalues this status and denies altogether the need for intervention, let alone a separate social work purpose, vis-à-vis those who are aging. This perspective relates to Milloy's observation that social workers harbor a conviction, conscious or unconscious, that older people "can progress in only one direction—down. Seeing only death in [the older person's] future, they wonder, What is the use...?[4] Moreover, working with the aged runs contrary to the hero system of this society, which chooses to glamorize youth and achievement. Because the aging—like the poor—bear a stigma that contaminates those who work with them, practice in the area of gerontology is anxiety provoking. However, rather than own up to this anxiety, it is safer to rationalize its rejection on the grounds of cost-effectiveness and to argue that it makes no sense to invest a substantial number of resources in treatment and services for people who have little time left to live.

In addition, the devaluation of social work practice with older people rests on a deeply ingrained therapeutic nihilism that views the aging as rigid and impervious to change. In all fairness, social workers were not the first to reveal a "gerontophobic" state of mind, but they did share the initial pessimism of the mental health professions about the usefulness of therapy for older people. Practitioners of psychiatry and geriatric psychotherapy have not yet fully overcome Freud's skepticism about the treatability of those who are aging, despite the vigorous and at times overoptimistic reactions against this skepticism.

Social work has not been in the forefront of the development of geriatric treatment methods. Instead, many divergent conceptions from allied helping professions have been incorporated into social work practice. No wonder, then, that the ambivalence felt by many social workers concerning the alleged futility of gerontological practice has not yet been resolved. A widespread avoidance of the reality of aging can be observed, even in the face of an apparently sympathetic acceptance. This ambivalence is understandable in light of the fact that most social workers come in contact with the aged who are frail, in times of crisis only, after these individuals have been ravaged by repeated losses.

This is a society that positively sanctions relationships between people of the same age but does not necessarily favor social discourse between those of different generations. Younger social workers, like others their age, have probably seldom had meaningful or lasting relationships with older individuals. Indeed, if interchanges between younger workers and those who are aging have taken place, it is likely that they have been superficial or instrumental exchanges and not prompted by the worker's interest in gaining an understanding of the older person's true self. When undertaking gerontological practice, the worker's sudden encounter with the problems and deficits of old age may reinforce his or her stereotypical beliefs and latent fears about aging, and this may in turn lead to a depersonalization of the older client. Consequently, social work intervention often runs the risk of becoming a process of case dissection that is objectified in an inventory of diagnostic categories.

Social workers who resolve their ambivalence about dealing with older people and decide to engage in gerontological practice still require a change of heart, a sort of a attitudinal "cleansing." However, this is not an affective process only. At the start, it must include a thorough immersion of the individual in the vast knowledge available about aging. For as Hamilton has observed, "learning is an ego function, worked out on the level of conscious processes, even though deeper determinants may be present."[5]

Special Needs Require Special Supports

The third perspective on social work and the aged rests on the recognition of the interdependence of different processes of change that take place over the individual's life span. According to this perspective, aging is not a phase of life in which a cyclic reenactment of previous life events occurs but is instead considered to have its own array of characteristic behaviors and tasks. Moreover, its dynamic variations affect the normative requirements and role definitions that the individual typically encounters during other phases of life.

In addition, the expansion of the number of aging people in the population and the relentless and mind-boggling increase in life expectancy have combined to form a compelling new variable. This may result in a reordering of the patterns of social interaction typical in the course of life and may also lead to variations in developmental outcomes in other stages of the life cycle. In regard to this point, Brody has asserted that "never before in history have there been so many old people numerically and proportionally, nor have they been so old."[6] Given the basic epidemiologic premise that as mortality decreases, morbidity increases, it becomes obvious that as life expectancy increases, the risk of chronic and endemic impairments developing among the aging population is greater. As a consequence of this, the demand for more categorical services grows. The provision of specialized supports for the aged usually takes place through a "reordering of public priorities," a euphemism for a redivision of public resources in a way that is detrimental to other groups of claimants. The swelling number of older people in the population thus affects the allocation of resources for those in other stages of the life cycle, and this is bound to provoke intergenerational confrontations and resentments.

The rationale for a distinctive social work purpose in regard to the aged rests on a seldom alluded to premise, namely, that the individual has the right to complete his or her natural life cycle, with its expectable flow and sense of continuity, without culturally imposed inhibiting restraints. However, problems usually arise in the area of what one generation can expect from the other, owes to the other, and is really capable of doing for the other. Older people often complain that their middle-aged children neglect or ignore them. The latter, in turn, may feel torn between raising their teenage children and attending to their parents. Some end up scapegoating their elders. Relations between individuals and their aging parents may be affected by what Berezin has termed "partial grief," such as when a family must proceed with the institutionalization of an ailing relative.[7] Berezin has characterized the reaction to partial grief in a family as one of guilt and mutual accusation that negatively affects the quality of interaction among family members. In addition, others have discussed various difficulties that are often observable in the interaction between older people and their children. For example, Levin and Kahana have described the process of "fearful withdrawal," in which each episode of resistance to care on the part of the older person provokes a self-defensive withdrawal on the part of his or her younger relative, and Peterson has alluded to "role inversion," an exchange of tasks that occurs when children assume the parental role vis-à-vis their aged parents.[8]

In light of problems such as these, it is the function of social workers to comprehend the chain of generations, unravel the distancing behaviors of family members of different generations, unite these individuals through mutual involvement, and mobilize kin networks so that they take responsibility for those in the family. However, the performance of this function requires an understanding of the limitations and dilemmas that adult children face concerning their parents. It is true that many touching examples can be cited of affectionate and solicitous care extended to older people by their offspring or relatives, but these cases deal with voluntary actions, not efforts demanded by legal constraints or even normative expectations. Instead, the aged and their middle-aged children are becoming more liberated from economic dependence on one another. As Treas has properly stated, "it is unreasonable to assume that family sentiment can insure adequate day-to-day supervision, housekeeping, personal maintenance or nursing of older Americans."[9]

It is also unrealistic to assume that public programs will take over the responsibility of caring for an entire age group. Social work is already being called on to foster greater primary group and family participation in the care of the aged. Moral exhortation will be of little effect in this endeavor unless it is coupled with adequate policy incentives, counseling, information, crisis intervention, and systematic training in the care of the aged who are frail. Sussman, Vanderwyst, and Williams have proposed that direct subsidies in the form of cash allowances, tax reductions, or direct reimbursements be given to members of families or primary networks who are willing to act as care-givers for their aged relatives.[10] New service arrangements will have to be synergistic in nature and foster interconnections among primary and more formalized service systems. An inherent part of social work's purpose is bringing about the proper coordination of these systems to ensure their continuity and monitoring whether they are functioning adequately. How services are actually coordinated and combined, however, depends on both technological and theoretical considerations. Nevertheless, the function of coordinating services for the aged may effectively be carried out through case management. This concept relates to the meaning of independence and the uses of dependence, the unique aspects of assessing older clients and making contracts with them, the use of environmental resources, and the ultimate organization of comprehensive service systems.

The three perspectives that have been reviewed reflect the mainstream of social work thinking vis-à-vis practice with the aging. The first and the third perspectives are not necessarily antithetical, although they stem from different theoretical traditions. The first is more existential, but the third highlights a developmental and interactive dimension. In methodological terms, the argument for case management and case coordination is equally valid from the viewpoint of both perspectives.

Case Management

A case manager is someone acting as a permanent consultant or facilitator in the life of an older person who may still be capable of handling his or her life but who, as described by the Federal Council on Aging,

> needs some help in coping with life's bureaucracies because of the accumulation of vicissitudes of increasing aging, not because of a single physical or mental trauma, or a personal loss or role change.[11]

Case management individualizes the client. The relationship between the case manager and his or her client is a unique and personal one, and the process of case management itself is based on a proactive and holistic view of the elderly client. Although the process is consistent with the concepts of clients' goal-oriented behavior and responsibility for themselves, the risk that the case manager will slip into assuming a paternalistic stance is always present and increases when he or she is dealing with clients who require protective services.

It is true that case managers do not assume a *parens patriae* responsibility, but the line between performing a voluntary function of coordinating and linking services and providing court-ordered protective services is fine. In the latter situation, case management becomes an accessory to intervention that is not initiated at the client's request and is carried out for the most disabled and incompetent clients. When this happens, it may come into conflict with social work's basic belief in client self-determination. Even in those instances in which the provision of services is fully justified because the older person is becoming a nuisance or danger to himself or herself as well as to others, social workers often still experience moral trepidations and concern about the legality of the intervention. They are concerned about the client's civil rights and have a fear of meddling improperly and taking over other people's lives. In addition, reservations about the viability of case management are common, for practitioners often find that the services they are supposed to coordinate for their clients are either nonexistent or unavailable because of eligibility restrictions. They must then become community organizers and policy analysts who bring pressure to bear for governmental review of existing legislation. This kind of activity, however, falls under the category of long-range intervention that does not help satisfy clients' immediate needs.

Finally, there is the question of how directive the practitioner should be when serving a protective or case management function. Some agencies are overprotective and resort more often than necessary to institutionalization and commitment. Others are afraid of legal suits being brought against them for even suggesting judicial action. Resistance on the part of clients is certainly intimidating to the social agency, which is usually concerned with its own reputation and survival. As Wasser has suggested, much of a client's resistance can be a cover-up for pervasive feelings of desperation and a frightening sense of vulnerability that paralyzes his or her will to seek out help.[12] Mistrust may also be a reaction against previous interventions that, no matter how well motivated, were controlling. Wasser concludes that social workers first need to understand the meaning of an older person's resistance, then should establish communication, and, ultimately, can interpose supportive services as natural, and assume that if they are not resisted, they are tacitly accepted. The use of "gentle persuasion" and directive control advocated by her in the case situation highlights the importance of independence as both a social work value and an objective of practice. Complex issues relating to clients' independence such as those just described help explain the difficulty social workers often experience when trying to make contracts with older clients or confront them when they have violated their contracts. Workers frequently report that older clients want services to be performed for them without their having to assume *quid pro quo* commitments. Scherz maintains that contracts are ineffective unless they are preceded by a "therapeutic alliance," or an expression of trust between the helping professional and the client.[13] However, just the opposite is often the case with elderly clients, in whom closeness and mutuality may prompt expectations of freedom from responsibility.

It should be borne in mind in regard to this point that contracting is based on the presumption of the client's potential for autonomy and possession of enough time in which to obtain resources and change his or her life circumstances. However, older people generally feel a sense of urgency about the passage of time. They just cannot wait for long, and some would rather have something done for them now rather than try to do it themselves for the sake of a future they may never experience. In addition, many may doubt they can count on their waning autonomy. They are reticent about contracting and about risking the possibility of having new experiences, unless these undertakings can be carried out immediately and will be limited in scope. Therefore, realistic contracting requires that goals be scaled down to the level of the smallest amount of change that would make a difference in the individual's life. In this context, the importance of partializing problems on a microbehavioral level is obvious.

Assessing clients' psychosocial needs and their capacity to enter into contractual relationships requires expert knowledge of what constitutes typical and expectable behavior in old age. However, baseline determinations of what is characteristic or may be considered normal, even if a decline or deterioration is involved, have not been specified beyond doubt. In addition, many perceived behavioral limitations of older people may not reflect actual physical or psychological deficits. This is the case in the "excess disability" syndrome, which Brody has defined as the development of a discrepancy or gap between an older person's actual functioning and his or her capacity to function.[14] An example of this syndrome can be seen when someone does not leave his or her bed because of an alleged lack of balance or an inability to move but is actually capable of moving around with the help of a cane or walker. Excess disabilities may occur in many areas, such as personal care, mobility, social relations, and family interaction. Although they are susceptible to remediation after treatment, their development is often induced by inexperienced human service professionals—including social workers—who invariably perceive older people as fragile and incapacitated and who consequently foster their dependence by bombarding them with unnecessary services. In such cases, then, excess disability is the consequence of excess or superfluous treatment.

Another aspect of assessing the capabilities of older clients has to do with determining the effect of their morale on their overall behavior and well-being. Methods of assessing clients' morale are never more telling and relevant than when used with older clients. A knowledge of the way in which people perceive themselves in relation to their experiences in life and their sense of satisfaction and accomplishment is essential for understanding them as they strive for closure. Morale, however, is a complex construct. It encompasses an acceptance of life and aging with fortitude and optimism rather than with resignation and defeat, a feeling of having done something good in life, and a generalized sense of adequacy, peace, and well-being. Workers need to be cognizant of this as they evaluate older clients.

Impact of the Environment

The 1958 "Working Definition of Social Work Practice" stated that one of social work's purposes is "to assist individuals and groups to identify and resolve or minimize problems arising out of disequilibrium between themselves and their environment."[15] The imbalance in question tends to be perpetuated and magnified in the urban environments in which most aged people live. No older person is immune to the dullness of hospital-colored nursing homes, the unsanitary conditions and lack of heat of slum dwellings and run-down tenements, the threat of crime in downtown streets, and the difficulty of reaching basic services that are geographically distant. In view of the environmental problems the aged often encounter, social workers are often puzzled about the obstinate resolve of many older people to remain in their stressful environments. They fail to understand that a familiar environment, even if unsafe, contains cues that give the individual a sense of security, whereas sudden relocation may trigger a sense of helplessness and panic. At the least, relocation certainly inhibits the older person's sense of continuity and sameness regarding person-in-situation.

In general, older people must contend with both a macroenvironment, consisting of a maze of support services and social relationships scattered over relatively great geographic distances, and a more immediate microenvironment, usually consisting of their home and its surroundings. Many can no longer negotiate the former, and they become virtual prisoners within the confines of the latter. The "environmental docility" hypothesis suggested by Lawton states that the more disabled the person, the more dependent he or she will be on the immediate environment for basic rewards.[16] Social workers serve a dual purpose in this regard. First, they must facilitate the full use of the macroenvironment by the older individual, given the multiple resources for services found in this environment. They must thus enable the older person to negotiate distances and obstacles to transportation. Second, they should improve the quality of the microenvironment and the stimulation typically found within it. Social planning is consequently usually geared to creating the so-called need fulfilling environment, which in the case of the aged has been conceptualized in terms of "prosthetic" and life-enriching environments.[17] A prosthetic environment is an ecological system scaled down to the level of the older person's coping capacities and set up to compensate for his or her diminished ability to respond. A life-enriching environment is an organized space that activates behavior at three levels: (1) it energizes the person through heightened sensory cues such as bright color schemes, (2) it provides better focal points for mental orientation and social congregation, and (3) it gratifies the need for security and belonging. It becomes a humanizing environment because it eliminates the uniform, depersonalizing drabness one often encounters in institutional settings.

Establishing a prosthetic environment goes beyond providing time-delayed traffic lights and "kneeling" buses whose steps can be lowered to within convenient reach of older people. It involves paying attention to the very design of social services through concepts such as "one-stop" service centers and "enriched housing," in which supportive and personal care services are supplied as part of the living environment.

Objectives of Practice

The preceding discussion points to the need for a specific gerontological perspective that can be used as a kind of corrective lens for viewing the basic social work objectives outlined in this special issue of SOCIAL WORK on conceptual frameworks. The review that follows will in turn highlight the practice guidelines pertinent to this perspective and relating to each objective.

Help people enlarge their competence and increase their problem solving and coping abilities.

1. Social work practice with the aged should be based on a positive attitude toward the intrinsic value of old age and its validity as a distinct state of the life cycle that is endowed with its own meaning and developmental tasks. Practitioners working with older people perceive and encourage the expression of their clients' potential to enrich and contribute to the cycle of generations. Social workers in general seek to understand the meaning of aging, free from the distortions of stereotypical beliefs, through an examination of their own feelings about the process of growing old and a sense of life's value within its inevitable limits.

2. No two older people are exactly alike. The principle of individualization and the concomitant avoidance of age-related biases are the cognitive and ethical foundations of practice. Social work intervention requires

an understanding of each person's lifelong ways of coping. Some individuals may be engaged in nostalgic reminiscences. Others obstinately retain an orientation toward the future. Like individuals of any other age, older people are capable of varying levels of adaptation and self-expression.

3. Social workers identify and assess the extent and quality of an older person's remaining strengths. They strive to help the individual maximize the use of these strengths, even in the face of loss and progressive deterioration.

4. Treatment objectives aimed at enhancing the older person's coping skills must be realistically scaled down to the level of his or her remaining strengths. This should be done on the understanding that even micro-behavioral changes are positive indications of the outcome of the treatment.

5. Although an older individual may never regain his or her waning strength, it is the social worker's task to bolster the person's sense of personal integrity. The dependence that accompanies the receipt of protective services should injure the person's self-esteem as little as possible and should not carry a price tag of moral degradation or infantilization.

Help people obtain resources.

1. Older people are especially intimidated by complex eligibility requirements and the discouraging bureaucratic maze of existing services. In addition, because of value-related conflicts, a sense of pride, or fear of surrendering their personal autonomy, they often refuse services to which they are entitled. Social workers strive to understand the source of such culturally based considerations and personal anxieties that older clients experience regarding the receipt of services. They then attempt to build up the client's trust, facilitate access to services, and make sure that the client knows about and obtains the services to which he or she is entitled.

2. Because most older people have several chronic conditions, they may require services on a continuous basis. In such cases, social workers must focus on case management and coordination with the aim of linking older clients to services, monitoring the delivery of services, reassessing the individual client's condition and needs at regular intervals, and making sure that available services are combined to meet the particular needs of the client.

3. The provision of case coordination on a permanent basis may create overprotectiveness on the part of the worker and increased dependence on the part of the client. Social workers need to make sure that services are provided in a way that restricts rather than promotes the excess disability syndrome. Part of this effort means seeing that primary support networks are involved in concerted action aimed at preserving the older client's life-style and personal options.

Make organizations responsive to people.

1. As the number of aged people grows in this society, social service agencies are experiencing a relentless increase in their gerontological case-

loads. A major task for social workers is to promote an awareness of who these clients are and what their specific service requirements may be. Workers within agencies must develop treatment modalities that take into account the cumulative losses undergone by older clients, the social, mental, and physical limitations that affect an older person's request for help, and the difficulty that many older people experience in making use of services.

2. Social workers must interpret for agencies the need to define service priorities in ways that are congruent with major geriatric needs. For example, services for the aged must be geared to the reduction of stress and the alleviation of the client's sense of helplessness rather than to personality reconstruction. In addition, service systems should include an "early warning" component attuned to the major crises of old age.

3. Workers must also make sure that older people, like competent clients of all ages, remain the masters of their own destiny and are involved in making determinations concerning their own future. Service systems should provide older clients with alternative courses of action from which they can choose. Furthermore, these systems should be coordinated to form comprehensive networks with multiple points of entry and, when possible, "one-stop" stations or centers that provide multiple services.

4. Given the contradictory evidence about whether services are best provided in an age-integrated or age-segregated system, social workers should retain a flexible, open-minded attitude. It is likely that some services obtain better outcomes when they are offered in multigenerational situations but that others may be more effective when delivered to clients of one age group only. In either case, the preferences of clients should be consulted, but when a given course becomes inevitable, such as institutionalization in a long-term care facility, proper counseling and adequate preparation of the client should especially prevail.

Facilitate interaction between individuals and others in their environment.

1. As people grow older, members of their lifelong support systems—spouse, offspring, relatives, and friends—die or move away. Both the onset of widowhood, spelling the probability that loneliness will be a permanent part of life, and the individual's bombardment by repeated losses point to the need for intervention that is geared to the circumstances of bereavement and the client's potential for resocialization. In dealing with bereavement, social workers are called on to provide support to the client and help him or her through the process of grieving resulting from the loss of a spouse, close relatives, or friends.

2. When helping to resocialize the bereaved client, social workers assist in the development of new support systems and facilitate the individual's adjustment and integration to new social contexts, such as self-help groups, multiservice centers, and lifelong learning programs.

3. To the same purpose, social workers facilitate instrumental and ex-

pressive interaction between individuals of different generations. They promote mutual helping efforts that are responsive to the needs of everyone involved.

4. Resocialization is also a challenge for the aging nuclear couple when the last of their offspring leaves home. Social workers facilitate clients' adjustments and their search for meaning in a new family situation that they may never have experienced before.

5. Social workers are increasingly called on to provide relief to those who are middle-aged, most especially when these individuals find they can no longer attend to the needs of aging, ailing parents or grandparents. In such instances, workers facilitate the integration of a family's strengths and resources through formalized personal care services.

6. Ultimately, the activities of social workers enable older people to remain in their familiar environment for as long as possible and thus to retain a sense of competence and continuity in their relationship with the environment. Workers' efforts in this regard may call for enriching the environment with architectural and other supports and ensuring access to services. When it is no longer possible for the older person to remain in his or her home and neighborhood, it is incumbent on the social worker to help the person prepare for the impending transition to institutional care as carefully and smoothly as possible, thus avoiding the trauma of a sudden uprooting.

Influence interactions between organizations and institutions.

The practice guidelines relating to the objective of making organizations responsive to people are applicable to this objective as well.

Influence social and environmental policy.

1. Over two hundred federal programs that benefit the aged directly or indirectly have been generated in the last fifty years, but their apparent abundance is not a valid indication of their adequacy. Social workers must critically examine whether these programs are relevant and appropriate in light of the changing social, economic, and demographic conditions related to the aging.

2. As formulated in the program implementation stage, provisions for eligibility, program restrictions, and determinations of service priorities are at times inconsistent with the intent of legislation. Social workers critically examine whether there is continuity between programs and policies and assist in the improvement of needs assessment and the setting of priorities.

3. Most public funds for the aged are used to provide cash supports, and this overshadows the provision of services. Workers must correct this imbalance by defining the extent and nature of clients' needs related to such areas as housing, nutrition, physical and mental impairment, isolation, transportation, and employment. They may then assist in the formulation of cogent, innovative policies.

4. As indicated earlier, because of the relentless increase in the num-

ber of aging people relative to the rest of the population, neither families nor the public at large can be called on to assume total and exclusive responsibility for those who are aged. Social workers must devise incentives such as tax abatements and exemptions, cash payments, and special demogrants to be given to families and communities for assuming a wider responsibility for older people. In a similar vein, they can design and promote cooperative and communal living arrangements as well as opportunities for work that promote the self-sufficiency of the aging.

Conclusion

Social work practice with the aging is a rich and complex professional domain. Social workers have traditionally been aware of the interrelationship between life deficits and the cumulative effects of loss at the same time that they have focused on the individual's remaining strengths. Overall, social work practice is concerned with the performance of several functions in work with the aging. It strives to enhance the social functioning of the individual through emphasizing the continuity of past roles and the development of substitute and compensatory roles. It provides antidotes to depressive loneliness and overabsorption in the self by exposing the individual to new social environments in which people of common experiences meet. It calls for the aged to exercise control over their own lives through self-help community groups and resident councils in institutional facilities. It plans new prosthetic environments and support systems to compensate for the individual's limitations in functioning and performing the activities of daily life. It fosters discourse and mutual help among those of different generations. Ultimately, it seeks to generate a system of services and resources that is comprehensive, accessible, and capable of providing continuing support to the aging client.

Social work's capacity for ambiguity is taxed to an exceptional degree in the performance of these functions. On one hand, the aged cannot be referred to in the classical terms of social work's purpose and objectives. These statements are couched in language that includes expressions such as "productivity," "effective contributions," "maximum growth potential," and "self-actualization," which do not apply to the aged. On the other hand, some older people have never lost their creative capacities, and not enough is known about the individual's potential for growth during this stage of the life cycle. Although some people in old age feel that their best years are gone forever, others are still endowed with an astonishing and boundless vitality. Many older people reminisce and dwell in their past, but many others consider themselves part of a promising future. The aged remain part of a living web of generations. To ignore them or deny their rightful place in society would profoundly damage the moral quality of life for all. Moreover, it would negatively affect social work's quintessential values. On this matter, then, there is no ambiguity about social work's purpose.

Notes and References

1. Robert N. Butler and Myrna I. Lewis, *Aging and Mental Health* (St. Louis, Mo.: C. V. Mosby Co., 1973), pp. 16–17.

2. Ernest Becker, *The Denial of Death* (New York: Free Press, 1973), p. 15.

3. Butler and Lewis, op. cit., p. 25.

4. Margaret Milloy, "Casework with the Older Person and His Family," *Social Casework*, 45 (October 1964), p. 450.

5. Gordon Hamilton, "Self-Awareness in Professional Education," *Social Casework*, 35 (November 1954), p. 373.

6. Elaine M. Brody, "Social Work Practice with the Aged," *Abstracts for Social Workers*, 7 (Spring 1971), p. 3.

7. Martin A. Berezin, "Partial Grief in Family Members and Others Who Care for the Elderly Patient," *Journal of Geriatric Psychiatry*, 4(1970), pp. 53–64.

8. Sidney Levin and Ralph J. Kahana, eds., *Psychodynamic Studies on Aging: Creativity, Reminiscing, and Dying* (New York: International Universities Press, 1967); and James A. Peterson, "Marital and Family Therapy Involving the Aged," *Gerontologist*, 13 (1973), pp. 27–31.

9. Judith Treas, "Family Support Systems for the Aged: Some Social and Demographic Considerations," *Gerontologist*, 17 (1977), p. 490.

10. Marvin B. Sussman, Donna Vanderwyst, and Gwendolyn K. Williams, "Will You Still Need Me, Will You Still Feed Me, When I'm 64?" Paper presented at the Twenty-ninth Annual Scientific Meeting of the Gerontological Society, October 13–17, 1976.

11. *Public Policy and the Frail Elderly—A Staff Report*, DHEW Publication No. (OHDS) 79-20959 (Washington, D.C.: Federal Council on Aging, 1978).

12. Edna Wasser, "Protective Practice in Serving the Mentally Impaired Aged," *Social Casework*, 52 (October 1971), pp. 510–522.

13. Frances H. Scherz, "Theory and Practice of Family Therapy," in Robert W. Roberts and Robert H. Nee, eds., *Theories of Social Casework* (Chicago: University of Chicago Press, 1970), p. 237.

14. Elaine M. Brody, *Long-Term Care of Older People* (New York: Human Science Press, 1977), pp. 278–280.

15. Subcommittee on the Working Definition of Social Work Practice for the Commission on Social Work Practice, National Association of Social Workers, "Working Definition of Social Work Practice," in Harriett M. Bartlett, "Toward

Clarification and Improvement of Social Work Practice," *Social Work*, 3 (April 1958), p. 6.

16. M. Powell Lawton, "Social Ecology and the Health of Older People," *American Journal of Public Health*, 64 (1974), pp. 257–260.

17. O. R. Lindsley, "Geriatric Behavioral Prosthetics," in Robert Kastenbaum, ed., *New Thoughts on Old Age* (New York: Springer Publishing Co., 1964).

DEATH

CHAPTER 13

Help for the Dying

Carleton Pilsecker

Death is a frequent visitor to hospitals. Yet, in one sense, death is seldom a part of the hospital social worker's experience. Patients usually die when social workers are not around. During the two or more years that the author has worked in a hospital, he was present at the death of only one patient. Even then it was not clear exactly when the patient had died. The cardiac arrest team attended him for over an hour; at first he was responsive, then he was not. After the moving, dramatic, and draining scene, one question remained unanswered. At what point could one say, "Mr. E, who up to now was alive, is now dead"?

During Mr. E's final moments, there was nothing that the social worker could do for him. He was in the hands of physicians, nurses, nurses' aides, inhalation therapists, and an electrocardiograph operator.

In another sense, however, if the hospital social worker is willing, death can be an important part of his experience. With the gradual removal of death from the list of taboo subjects, social workers—along with other members of the hospital staff—are finding numerous opportunities to help patients who are dying and their families.

To a large degree, social work has always been a child of its times. Today, after decades of silence, there is a plethora of books and articles on the subject of death and dying. There are institutes, workshops, classes, seminars—every imaginable vehicle is being used to convey information about the process of dying, its meaning to those involved, and ways in which good emotional and physical care can be given to the dying person. Death is one of the current fads. A psychiatrist has gone so far as to de-

Copyright 1975, National Association of Social Workers, Inc. Reprinted with permission from *Social Work*, Vol. 20, No. 3 (May, 1975), pp. 190–194.

scribe it as a "furor" and to lament the "glamorization of dying and of being dead which is part of a movement toward enjoining people to savor dying and to welcome death."[1]

To find social work caught up in this furor is not surprising, but it is important to recognize that fads are not necessarily bad. The current movement has brought a new, burgeoning awareness that dying people are people with needs that can be attended to and that the process of dying presents some problems that can be solved or ameliorated with the help of the social worker. We need not glamorize death; we need not accept its inevitability by being blasé. But neither do we need to avoid contact with the dying person or to assume that being terminally ill means being outside the reach of social work. Today's climate provides new opportunity for aggressive casework—for reaching out to the dying patient and offering help rather than waiting to be summoned by patient, family, or hospital staff.

If social workers are to reach out, they need to know what it is they have to offer. They have learned and relearned the lesson that, as in all phases of social work, their goodwill is not enough. And so it is in working with the dying patient. In this area it is even more important that the social worker be clear about what help he can provide, because dealing with death can be a frightening, foreboding venture and clarity of purpose can provide some reassurance.

Social work with the terminally ill patient and his family can be conceptualized in terms of five basic categories: planning for living during the terminal process, exploration of feelings about impending death, living with the prospect of death, planning for death, and planning for the family after death. In addition, the social worker may be able to provide support to the family immediately following a patient's death.

Planning for Living

One of the primary functions of a hospital social worker is to help patients and their families deal with such questions as these: How can I and how should I live? Given my physical condition and my prognosis, what alternatives are available to me, what community resources can be brought to bear, what obstacles can be overcome while I am hospitalized, and what sources for help are available when (and if) I leave the hospital? There is no novelty about giving this kind of assistance to any patient. All the social worker need do then is realize that the dying patient is still alive and that the social worker's usual help is, therefore, applicable.

Some aspects of planning for living are essentially unrelated to the fact that the patient is close to death. For example, Mr. M, a 55-year-old patient with lung cancer, was to start a program of chemotherapy that entailed his being an outpatient and reporting to the hospital weekly for tests and treatment. Well aware of what he called his "stygian future," Mr. M's immediate concern was not for his imminent death, but for obtaining sufficient financial resources to enable him to manage when he was discharged from the hospital.

Mr. O, a 56-year-old patient, experienced occasional hallucinations caused by terminal cancer with metastasis to the brain. He needed the opportunity to express his fear engendered by these vivid images; in addition, he used his conversations with the social worker to devise a simple way of coping with his "trips." (The plan entailed checking to see that his usual physical surroundings—the pull-up bar over his head, the bed rails, and the like—were still there, proving that he was still safe in his bed.)

At times the prospect of death will directly influence plans for living. For Mr. C, a patient with an aortic aneurysm, the question was how to arrange matters so that his wife, who worked, would not have to worry about his dying alone after he was discharged from the hospital.

EXPLORATION OF FEELINGS

As is the case with helping the patient and his family plan for living, exploration of feelings is an area in which social workers usually feel comfortable. Indeed, for some hospital social workers, talking about feelings is a pleasant respite from task-oriented duties. However, talking about death and dealing with the emotions it engenders can be a different story. It is not that these feelings are unique. Anger, anxiety, depression, guilt, and fear are all common emotions aroused by many kinds of life situations and encountered daily by social workers. What seems to make them special is their source—the prospect of death.

Social workers are not immune to the general squeamishness that surrounds any discussion of death. This discomfort not only derives from unpleasant experiences with death in their personal lives, but from anxiety about their own forthcoming death. Recognition of this subjective side to the avoidance of the topic is found in the literature on death and dying. The professional is advised to struggle first with the fact of his own mortality and then to offer help to the dying person. Weisman, for example, writes:

> ...until we can accept the personal reality of death as a common legacy of mankind, of mine as well as yours, pertaining to me as well as that other person, we will remain caught in a dense web of artifice and denial....Natural awareness of our mortality will make us less disingenuous, less guilty, and less fearful in the presence of someone else's truth [that he is dying].[2]

Besides his own wariness about death, the social worker may also be concerned about the patient's reaction if he is led or even accompanied into a discussion about dying. Perhaps it will overwhelm the patient, upset him, depress him. Perhaps it will evoke strong and unpleasant feelings that will only make his final days or weeks tumultuous for him, for his family, and for staff members who must attend him. Perhaps, but certainly this is unlikely.

Feifel's research on the subject showed that dying people often appreciate the chance to talk openly about their situation.[3] This theme resounds through the widely read book *On Death and Dying*, in which Kubler-Ross reports that of the more than two hundred terminally ill patients who were asked to participate in interviews at the University of Chicago Billings Hospital, almost all

> ...welcomed the possibility of talking with someone who cared. Most of them tested us first in one way or another, to assure themselves that we were actually willing to talk about the final hours or the final care. The majority of patients...were relieved when they did not have to play a game of superficial conversation when deep down they were so troubled with real or unrealistic fears.[4]

In other settings, terminally ill patients have been brought together in discussion and psychotherapy groups.[5] Again, patients were found to have an "obvious desire and willingness...to communicate their needs" and to speak forthrightly about their dying and their impending death.[6] The overwhelming direction of the evidence is that, given the opportunity, the dying person not only wants to but will talk about his situation and can handle the feelings that such talk will generate.

DENIAL

Of course, at a given moment, some patients may need to deny the seriousness of their condition. Except in unusual circumstances, this denial can be respected. Often it is a temporary, though recurring measure. Weisman notes: "Fluctuation between denial and acceptance takes place throughout the course of illness."[7] He goes on to describe a state

> ...somewhere between open acknowledgement of death and its utter repudiation...an area of uncertain certainty called "middle knowledge."...Patients seem to know and want to know, yet they often talk as if they did not know and did not want to be reminded of what they have been told.[8]

What the social worker must guard against is perpetuating or creating a patient's belief that denial is expected of him.

When Mr. B, a victim of lung cancer, tells the social worker, "My days are numbered," he knows from the response whether he can pursue the topic. The social worker should be able to convey to Mr. B that he is willing to talk openly about the prospect of death and its meaning to the patient. If the two can engage in a "dialogue," Mr. B will let the social worker know, if only by silence or changing the subject, when he no longer wishes to prolong the discussion.

No unique skills or knowledge are needed by the social worker before initiating conversation regarding a patient's feelings about dying. A sensitive awareness of the patient, allowing but not contributing to his denial of reality, inviting and acknowledging the expression of deep feelings—these are common tools of social work. The key to such exploration of feelings appears to be the degree of willingness on the part of the social worker and the extent of his expectation that the patient will want to express rather than to deny his reality.

What has been said about helping the patient explore his feelings applies as well to the patient's family. The death of someone close often evokes many different kinds of feelings, which are related to the history and nature of the relationship and to the prospect of its termination. "We have been married for thirty-three good years." "I don't know how I can cope without him." "It's true we've had some bad times together but things were just getting worked out." "How can he do this to me?" These musings represent a few of the stirrings, conflicts, and ambivalences that may need to be expressed, and the willing social worker can make the opportunity for their expression available to the family.

Living with Death

Intertwined with a patient's feelings about dying are his feelings about life now that its end is near. His life may seem to him to have been long and full or short and painful, meaningful or lacking in meaning, filled with accomplishment or empty of reward. People vary, not only in how they evaluate their life, but also in how explicitly they express their evaluation. Some will spend time and effort converting feeling to cognition, vague and disconnected impressions to concrete and integrated awareness. For some people, comfort or consolation may come from being able to explore or share a review of their life with an interested listener.

At times a patient may want to deal with just one piece of his life. For example, a few weeks before his death, Mr. H lamented the instability of his younger son. He needed to express his longing to see his son settled in a good job—a wish that he knew would not be fulfilled.

Often, living with the prospect of death means deciding how to relate to others. The dying person wonders and worries about what to say and how to interact with family and friends who, in turn, have similar concerns about their interaction with him. On occasion, the basic need of the patient or family member will be simply to voice his discomfort. This was the case with one patient who enjoyed the visits of former golfing partners but, at the same time, grieved silently that his debilitated condition kept him from enjoying this favorite activity. Sometimes patient and family can be helped to clarify how they wish to deal with one another, how openly, for example, they can talk about death.

Pretense and game-playing are frequent devices that family members use with the terminally ill patient—and the patient, no matter how aware of his condition, may feel compelled to participate. Mr. C suffered from an aortic aneurysm that could burst and cause immediate death at any time. When the social worker first visited the patient's bedside, he understood that both Mr. and Mrs. C were fully aware of the gravity of the condition. They had carefully thought about it, discussed it, and together had decided against surgery. After introducing himself, the social worker expressed his understanding that the couple was faced with a serious situation and he wondered if he might be of any help. To his surprise, Mrs. C, seated beside Mr. C's bed, whispered, "I don't want him to know." Mr. C, however, was unwilling to pretend and said, "Now there's no need for whispering. We all know what's happening so let's not whisper about it."

The social worker who ventures to work with the terminally ill patient has to make a basic decision about his goal. Is it to surround the dying patient with as constant an aura of "cheerfulness" as is humanly possible? Or is it instead to encourage openness and sharing even when that means tears and expressions of grief? The social worker cannot force an atmosphere of truthfulness on the client, but he can encourage the patient and members of his family to be open with one another to the limit of their ability.

Mr. W had lung cancer that had metastasized to his brain. At times he was rational, at times confused. Occasionally he felt well enough to go home for a weekend. After one visit, his 22-year-old daughter described to the social worker her consternation when Mr. W spoke of the fact he was dying. "Oh Daddy, don't talk that way," was her usual response. After she was helped to recognize her feelings, she could participate in a discussion of how her reaction probably affected her father. The social worker helped her to consider a different kind of response that did not ask the father to deny reality.

Family members as well as patients can benefit from the opportunity to ventilate their feelings about the difficulty of living with the prospect of the patient's death. Whether relating to the patient with reasonable openness is a particular problem, it can be burdensome to try to carry on the routine of living while a loved one is hospitalized with a terminal illness. All of the following may prove helpful to a family member in handling the situation: recognition of this burden, permission to be ambivalent about the patient's lingering, reassurance that the patient needs to be in the hospital or help in arranging for the patient to be brought home, encouragement to consider one's own well- being in addition to the patient's needs, and exploration of resources for comfort and sustenance.

Planning for Death

Some terminally ill patients have formulated detailed plans for themselves when they die. They have visited a mortuary, purchased a burial plot or made arrangements for cremation, and planned funeral or memorial services. Other patients have wishes but no definite arrangements. And some have no concrete ideas.

If a patient talks at all about his impending death, he will almost certainly be willing to talk about these arrangements. He may welcome the opportunity to review plans, to rethink what he had tentatively decided, or to confirm what had only been a vague idea. Even patients who decline to describe themselves as dying will sometimes want to talk about arrangements for their death.

When a patient initiates a discussion of these plans, the social worker can be helpful by clarifying any uncertainties or by confirming the patient's wisdom. If a patient talks openly about his death but does not speak of any arrangements, it is appropriate for the social worker to take the initiative by asking if his plans are formulated and his family informed.

Patients and family sometimes use the discussion of plans "in case of death" as a way of acknowledging to one another the seriousness of the patient's situation. However, coming to grips with harsh reality can be a frightening prospect. Mrs. B, wife of a cancer patient whose condition had begun to worsen rapidly, spoke of her distress about not knowing Mr. B's wishes at his death. To ask him, she believed, would be upsetting because it would confront him with the imminence of his death. The social worker informed Mrs. B that her husband had often discussed the fact that he was terminally ill, so it was not a secret that needed to be kept from him. With the worker's encouragement she was able to discuss the matter with Mr. B and was relieved to learn his wishes.

When death takes place, even the well-prepared family member may be distraught and unable to think clearly about what needs to be done. The social worker can help minimize confusion by advising family members in advance of the hospital procedures involved. When a member of the family explicitly acknowledges the imminence of the patient's death, such information can be introduced naturally into the conversation. In some cases it may be helpful even before the death to accompany the family member to the office that handles the final arrangements.

Often a patient may be concerned about how the family will fare after his death. Discussion of specific resources available to the family can bring

a considerable sense of relief. Mr. A had become weak from the lung cancer that had metastasized to his brain; the staff expected him to die at any
moment. Sometimes he was lucid and sometimes not. Almost every time
the social worker visited him, Mr. A pleaded with him to make sure his
sons would get the financial benefits they were entitled to, which would
enable his wife to support them adequately. The worker's reassurances
that Mrs. A had completed all the necessary arrangements never seemed
to register. Mrs. A reported the same problem and was becoming frustrated by it. One day when the worker was talking with the couple together, Mr. A repeated his plea. The worker reassured him once more and
Mrs. A stated rather angrily that it was all arranged. For the first time he
seemed to hear and accept this information. A few days later he died.

Patients who speak openly of their dying can be asked if they have
prepared a will and, if so, whether their close relatives know its location.
The patient who has no will can be encouraged to consider having one
drawn up and helped to make the necessary arrangements.

Family members too sometimes find it helpful to review their future
plans with the social worker. Doing this may reassure them about the
soundness of their plans, help them to clarify uncertainties, or provide
them with information about alternatives. Also, they may be comforted by
the fact that, although the patient is the focus of the staff's attention, there
is concern as well for the well-being of the family.

Occasionally the opportunity may present itself for direct service to the
family at the time of the patient's death. For example, the social worker
stayed with Mrs. E for about an hour after her husband's death, helped
her telephone some family members, arranged with a neighbor to be there
when Mrs. E returned home, and escorted Mrs. E to the hospital's Funeral
Details Office. In addition to helping Mrs. E, this allowed the nursing staff
to return to their hospital duties.

This kind of service to patient and family is an appropriate part of the
social work task. The major problem in carrying it out is that the social
worker is frequently unavailable at the time of need. He is usually not on
duty at night and even during the day may be involved elsewhere and
unable to be present at the critical moment. Unless this activitiy is given
priority by the social worker who makes it an explicit part of his job responsibility, it will continue to be handled primarily by other hospital personnel.

Conclusion

This article has focused on the direct service that a social worker may provide to terminally ill patients and their families. It must be recognized,
however, that in a hospital the social worker is a member of a health team

and does not work as an isolated and independent individual. In this area of his work, as in others, he will need to think of how the help he gives is coordinated with that of other staff members. At times the social worker may be performing a unique function for and with the patient and his family. At other times, however, he will be just one of the people who listens carefully, offers comfort, and provides tangible assistance with the problems of dying. Social work input may be an important contribution to such programs. In addition, it may be possible for the social worker to participate in the formal and informal training of other staff members who wish to increase their sensitivity and effectiveness in this area.

Some hospitals have reported successful programs for group discussion for terminally ill patients and their families.[9] It must be realized that these sessions with patients cannot be rigidly scheduled. This is particularly true if patients are in different stages at different times. However, group therapy has been effective with relatives of terminally ill patients who are trying to cope with the same critical illness.[10]

To offer one's skills to help the terminally ill patient and his family, to deal openly and without euphemisms with the hard fact of impending death, to allow the patient's denial of reality without participating in it—these are challenging tasks for the social worker. Practice will not make perfect. Nor will it enable one to be casual or matter of fact about dealing with the dying patient. Death should always command respect and awe. But social workers have learned that it need not terrorize them or cause them to turn away from providing help to dying people. The yearnings of these people are common to all human beings, although some of their needs are peculiar to the fact of their own impending death.

Dying is often accompanied by pain, weakness, and mental confusion, by tubes and catheters and respiration equipment, and by a sense of isolation in the midst of a bustling hospital ward. These are some of the factors that work against the possibility of death with dignity. Social workers cannot eliminate or mitigate all their effects. But in some instances, with some patients and with some families, social work intervention can help capitalize on whatever dignity remains. It is a worthy goal.

Notes and References

1. Alvin I. Goldfarb, "The Preoccupation of Society with Death and Dying," in Symposium No. 12, *The Right to Die: Decision and Decision Makers* (New York: Group for the Advancement of Psychiatry, 1973), pp. 688–690.

2. Avery D. Weisman, *On Dying and Denying* (New York: Behavioral Publications, 1972), p. 18.

3. Herman Feifel, "Attitudes Toward Death in Some Normal and Mentally Ill

Populations," in Feifel, ed., *The Meaning of Death* (New York: McGraw-Hill Book Co., 1959), pp. 114–130.

4. Elisabeth Kubler-Ross, *On Death and Dying* (New York: Macmillan Co., 1970), p. 258.

5. *See* David A. Heyman, "Discussions Meet Needs of Dying Patients," *Hospitals*, 48 (July 16, 1974), pp. 57–62. For a discussion of group psychotherapy, *see* Carleen Copelan, "Comments on a New Study: Psychotherapy and the Dying Patient," *Southern California Psychiatric Society News*, 21 (January 1974), p. 18.

6. Heyman, op. cit., p. 62.

7. Weisman, op. cit., p. 65.

8. Ibid., pp. 65–66.

9. *See* Copelan, op. cit.; and Heyman, op. cit.

10. *See* Kubler-Ross, op. cit., pp. 91–92. *See also* Vrinda S. Knapp and Howard Hanson, "Helping the Parents of Children with Leukemia," *Social Work* 18 (July 1973), pp. 70–75.

PART II

Psychosocial Disorders

Social work continues to play an important role in the provision of psychotherapy to a vast number of clients whose presenting symptomatology covers the total spectrum of psychopathological functioning. As the profession becomes more comfortable and, of greater importance, more knowledgeable and skilled in this area of practice, we are now writing much more on a wider range of topics than when the review was conducted for the second edition. One of the concerns expressed earlier was that our writing about this important aspect of human functioning, so critical in the diagnostic phase, was highly uneven. There were areas of pathology with which we have had considerable experience and about which we have written little; on the other hand, there are topics on which we have written much. The literature review for this edition showed a marked expansion in the range of topics being addressed as well as an increase in sophistication in these articles. There is still, however, considerable unevenness in quality.

In the second edition it was mentioned that selecting a framework by which to order the articles in this section was difficult. This was made much easier on this occasion because of the recently published *D.S.M. III*, which has introduced some significant alterations in terminology and ordering of classifications. The categories listed in *D.S.M. III* were not followed completely in this section, as it had not appeared when most of the articles were written. It was, however, of considerable assistance in ordering the articles selected.

For the first time we have articles in the literature on manic-depressive clients, a type of client we frequently meet but about whom we have written virtually nothing. Obviously depression continues to be a topic of critical importance in practice and as before is one richly addressed in the literature, with more articles than previously focusing on specific aspects of depression in special client groups. Again the wish to include a broader range of topics necessitated stringency in the numbers of articles for each topic.

Alcoholism is obviously still one of our largest societal problems; and the number of articles about it was larger than for all other topics in this section. The one selected emphasizes both the magnitude of the problem in our society and the need for specialized knowledge and skill in the therapeutic intervention with this type of client. The need for careful diagnosis of each client, a carefully defined multifaceted treatment strategy, and a continuing awareness of one's own attitudes and reactions are stressed. In other articles located in the literature about the alcoholic similar themes were observed, including the need for a differential understanding of causality and a multiservice approach to management and control.

Problems with drug abuse are still serious and frequent, and our literature is rich on this topic as well. The article by Moffett and his colleagues stresses the need to develop a broad understanding of the addict's problems and to expand our horizons to include the service network required as well as the personality structure of the client.

One area where material previously was singularly lacking related to the question of dealing with paranoid clients. Persons with paranoid tendencies and mild to moderate forms of paranoid schizophrenia are frequently found in the clientele of our services. Fortunately several articles dealing with some aspects of paranoia have now been published. Monna Zentner's, included here, gives a good understanding of the personality structure and case management material in these presenting situations.

The borderline client continues to be of particular interest to us as we are learning to recognize them and to appreciate the complexities of the classification, and as a body of knowledge about treating them develops. It appears that we were using the very popular character disorder classification to include many persons more precisely diagnosed as borderline.

In the previous edition comments were made about the increased interest in problems in the sphere of sexual functioning, and competence of social workers dealing with them was identified. In particular it was noted that there was a growing acceptance that modification and control in many areas of sexual problems do not require the uncovering and resolution of unconscious materials. Significant gains can be made by means of improved control, changed attitude, and enhanced growth; secondary gains emerge as well, through reduction of the anxiety, fear, and guilt that accompany these problems.

Schizophrenia remains an important topic in the literature, with a rich array of material from which to choose for this section. The literature on this topic continues to stress the broad parameters included in this concept. Treatment must focus on a reality-oriented relationship and must take in the broader system of the client, including, of course, work with the family as well as work with the client in the medium of the group.

CONCLUSION

To aid clients effectively to achieve improved psychosocial behavior it is essential to address their psychodynamic functioning. Although the professional literature indicates that a high degree of attention has been focused on this area, it is clear that coverage has been far from thorough or even. Thus, it requires constant updating and examination for gaps and omissions as well as for discussions of new approaches to treatment using different theoretical viewpoints, modalities, and techniques.

AFFECTIVE DISORDERS

CHAPTER 14

Group Therapy in the Management of Manic-Depressive Illness

Fred R. Volkmar, Sandra Bacon,
Saad A. Shakir, and Adolf Pfefferbaum

Introduction

Patients with bipolar affective illness have been viewed as poor candidates for both individual and group psychotherapy. Before the advent of lithium therapy most psychotherapists viewed manic-depressive patients as resistant to both individual and group psychotherapeutic approaches even during the euthymic phase of the illness. A number of factors seemed to militate against psychotherapy with such patients. Manic-depressive patients were felt to exhibit a facade of conventionality and sociability which, in fact, served as a defense against true intimacy and the anxiety entailed by such intimacy. These patients were thought to exhibit superficial and conventional relationships with strong underlying feelings of dependency, hostility, envy, and competition. The patients' inability to tolerate anxiety or intimacy and their use of massive denial and manipulation were seen as precluding the formation of a treatment alliance even during the euthymic phase of the illness.[1]

Yalom[2] has referred to the presence of a manic-depressive member in a mixed outpatient therapy group as "one of the worst calamities that can befall a therapy group." The recurring nature of the patients' illness and their inability to tolerate closeness and their superficiality present major

Reprinted, with permission, from the *American Journal of Psychotherapy*, Vol. 35, No. 2 (April, 1981), pp. 226–234.

and very significant obstacles to their successful integration into a heterogeneous therapy group.

Many clinicians have, therefore, been discouraged from using psychotherapeutic approaches with these patients and have, instead, relied exclusively on lithium prophylaxis as the major treatment modality for them. The efficacy of such treatment has been shown in over 100 single- and double-blind studies. For example, in one study 50% of patients with bipolar affective illness who were receiving lithium relapsed over a two-year-period as compared to 90% of control patients receiving placebo.[3] With the advent of this effective psyhopharmacological treatment, interest in psychotherapeutic approaches has declined markedly, with but a few exceptions.[4]

Unfortunately, despite its proven efficacy, many patients receiving lithium prophylaxis will relapse, and a significant number of patients will remain chronically ill.[5] The most positive studies of lithium prophylaxis report failure rates of 20–23% with many, if not most, of these failures occurring early in treatment. In a careful follow-up study of 47 bipolar manic-depressive patients, Carlson, et al. report that one-third of their sample remained impaired with moderate-to-severe symptoms which interfered with social and work adjustment.[6] It was their impression that even though lithium could control extreme mood fluctuations and keep patients out of the hospital, it might not control the illness sufficiently to enable many patients to return to former levels of functioning.

In many cases relapse requiring rehospitalization is associated with cessation of lithium use or inadequate maintenance doses of medication, with a subsequent re-emergence of the natural course of the illness. Lack of adherence to lithium maintenance treatment has been related to several factors.[7] Patients' use of denial may lead them to deny the reality of the illness and the need for medication and may lead them to ignore early signs of recurrence. Additionally, patients may miss the euphoria which lithium use sometimes entails. Interpersonal or family problems may also lead to poor compliance, especially in settings which provide little support for the patients' treatment. A further complicating factor may be the patients' attribution of responsibility for the successful management of treatment to the physician.

In their review of the course and outcome of bipolar manic-depressive illness, Welner, et al. concluded that even with lithium treatment the illness has a less favorable outcome than is generally believed and that a substantial minority of patients remain chronically ill.[8] Clearly, despite its proven effectiveness, many patients receiving lithium will relapse; most of those relapsing will do so in situations where their clinical state and perhaps their lithium levels are not being closely monitored, and in which they are receiving little support or encouragement for adhering to long-term lithium maintenance therapy.

In an effort to provide (a) close follow-up for patients on lithium, (b) support for continuing treatment, and (c) the opportunity for psychotherapy, we formed a long-term therapy group composed entirely of patients with a diagnosis of bipolar affective illness. Many of these patients had histories of poor adherence to lithium maintenance treatment. This group is now in its fourth year of existence. A preliminary report based on two years' experience with this group has appeared elsewhere;[9] in this report we shall focus more specifically on the problems and issues raised by patients in a long-term therapy group of this kind.

Group Composition

All members of the group had diagnoses of manic-depressive illness, bipolar type; these diagnoses were established by at least two psychiatrists on the basis of history and mental status examination. Referrals came from inpatient psychiatric wards at the Palo Alto Veterans Administration Hospital. All patients had responded acutely to lithium treatment prior to entering the group. A majority of the patients had histories of poor adherence to lithium maintenance. Patients were screened individually by the two group therapists before they were admitted to the group. During this screening the general purpose and rationale of group psychotherapy and the group format were discussed with the prospective member. When the patients with a primary diagnosis of bipolar affective illness and with a history of responsiveness to lithium were screened, their interest in group treatment was discussed. Only those who expressed at least a tentative interest in group treatment were included in our groups. Many of the patients selected were initially skeptical of the benefits of group therapy; often this was in response to their previous "failure" experiences with heterogeneous therapy groups. Any questions or concerns the prospective member had about the group were addressed as honestly as possible, and the therapists attempted to anticipate problems they thought the prospective member might encounter in the group. At the time of entry patients were generally euthymic; occasionally referrals were made while patients were still hospitalized. Baseline laboratory studies and EKG were obtained on all patients.

To date twenty patients (eighteen male and two female, with a mean age of 41.7 years and a range from 18 to 63 years of age) have participated in the group. The average duration of treatment prior to the patient's entry in the group was 17 months. Four of the members fit the bipolar type II description of Fieve;[10] the other sixteen fit the bipolar type I description. A minority of the patients had histories of episodic alcohol abuse, a majority had family histories suggestive of affective illness.

Group Format

In designing our group, we hoped to provide a weekly meeting that would present the members with the opportunity for interpersonal learning and support as well as providing for close follow-up of medications. The group met for 75 minutes weekly and was conducted with an interactional, interpersonal "here and now" approach as described by Yalom.[2] Thus, the focus of the group was on expression of affect, reality issues, and immediate problems and concerns rather than on past history. The therapists (a psychiatric resident and social worker) attempted to discourage intellectualization, superficiality, and rationalization as much as possible, i.e.,to focus on affect rather than semantics. The group norms that became established encouraged honesty and support with occasional limit-setting by either group members or one of the therapists.

Lithium carbonate was dispensed monthly during a group meeting; lithium levels were maintained in the range of 0.8 to 1.2 mEq./1. Group members were free to discuss concerns or problems with lithium at any time. If a member began to exhibit signs of either mania or depression, other members would discuss this openly in the group and provide support and encouragement, while medications would be adjusted as necessary.

Occasionally patients who were not regular group members were allowed to visit a meeting. Often this was in response to the nonmember's wish to meet other patients receiving lithium.

Course in Group Treatment

Most patients appeared to exhibit substantially the same course during their participation in the group. Initially new members remained somewhat aloof and remote from others in the group.Typically the patient would greatly minimize his or her problems and attempt to relate to other members and the therapists in very superficial ways. The group encouraged new members to focus on affective and reality issues. During this initial period attendance was often somewhat unpredictable. The responsibility for the efficacy of lithium maintenance would generally be attributed to the therapists (especially the psychiatrist), and patients typically gave little indication of more than a passing interest in their lithium levels, etc. The therapists had the impression that this initial period of wariness was more prolonged than that typically associated with a new members' joining a heterogeneous therapy group.

After about ten sessions attendance generally became more regular as the group members became interested in and committed to the group. Increased interest in lithium maintenance and its risks and benefits often seemed to serve as the focus of the member's interest during this period and seemed to indicate the integration of the patient in the group. The new member was often surprised to discover that other members were the source of a great deal of information about lithium use; other group members provided support and reassurance to the new member during this period. The new member would begin to show more interest in his own treatment, e.g., inquiring about blood levels, describing his various side effects, etc. The common interest in lithium served to foster cohesiveness in the group. Other common themes included the patient's sense of loss of the periods of mild-to-moderate euphoria he is less likely to experience when being maintained on lithium.[7] Members often found that they were forced to make changes in their work and social habits as a result of the loss of these periods.

By the sixth month of participation in the group, patients were generally active in the group and committed to it; they served as "culture carriers" for new members. Participants became progressively more open during the course of their time in the group. Common themes during this period included fears of recurrence of mania or depression and the consequent social disruption. Marital and family difficulties often were discussed as well as concerns about feelings of dependency and hostility. Less time was spent discussing medication issues in the group, although there would be a resurgence of interest in lithium-related issues when a group member experienced either a period of depression or euphoria or when a new member joined the group.

During their last months in the group, members expressed increased concerns over the effect of their illness on family members and friends. Representative comments made during this period included statements like: "I feel like I am an introvert trapped in an extravert's body," and "When I'm high I live in the future, when I'm low I live in the past—my problem is learning to live in the present." Patients during this stage of group participation seemed much like other patients in long-term group therapy, i.e., much time was spent in interpersonal learning, instilling of hope, and the experience of mutual sensitivity.

If a member began to exhibit signs of either mania or depression, a considerable portion of the group meeting would be devoted to discussing this. Other members were particularly acute in responding to any indication of an impending manic or depressive episode. Members were especially sensitive to increased need for attention in the group as well as problems of increased activity, unrealistic plans, unexpected hostility, etc. These occasional episodes were less disruptive in this group than they would have been otherwise, since the other members could provide support and encouragement and the sense that they had experienced what the member was experiencing.

Outcome

Members attended an average of 47 sessions during their time in the group. With the exception of three participants who left the group during the first three months of membership, participants typically left the group only after returning to full-time employment. These "graduates" of the group were invited to return periodically for medication follow-up; these members served as models of lithium efficacy to other members.

In the two-year period prior to participation in the group, fourteen of the members had been hospitalized for mania or depression. Only six members were continuously employed during this period. During the two-year period following their entry in the group, four of the participants have been rehospitalized for treatment of affective episodes. The group as a whole has averaged 3.6 weeks per year in the hospital during the period as compared to the average of 16.8 weeks per year in the two-year period prior to their entering the group. In two of these four cases, the rehospitalization occurred some months after the patient had terminated the group and had stopped lithium prophylaxis. The preponderance of group members indicated that they felt a more satisfactory and adequate social and occupational adjustment at the time they ceased full-time participation in the group. While only six members had been continuously employed in the two-year period prior to their participation, in the subsequent two years sixteen members secured continuous full-time employment or full-time student status. Lithium levels in the two-year period prior to group participation averaged 0.62 mEq./1. In the subsequent two-year period mean lithium levels averaged 0.96 mEq./1.

Discussion

Davenport et al.[11,12] have described the use of a couples group in the long-term treatment of manic-depressive patients. The patients followed in couples group therapy generally had more benign hospital courses than those who received the usual medication follow-up. Rosen[13] has reported on two and a half years of experience with monthly "lithium group" meetings aimed primarily at promoting lithium compliance. The patients in that group were homogeneous only in that they were receiving lithium therapy and were not uniformly bipolar patients. In that group a majority of the patients at follow-up were managed successfully in the group.

Although some investigators[14] have recently questioned the existence of character pathology in the euthymic phase of this illness, the consensus of psychotherapeutic opinion has tended to support the notion that these patients have character pathology that makes psychotherapy difficult, at best. These patients have been generally thought to have problems with dependency, hostility, impulsivity and the frequent use of denial as a defense. They have been viewed as being capable of forming only the most superficial of relationships.[1] Characteristic interpersonal patterns have been found to occur in acutely manic patients, e.g., projection of responsibility, sensitivity to others' vulnerabilities, etc.[15] Our experience has been that many of these patterns are also present, at least initially, during the course of a patient's participation in a homogeneous group of this kind.

We found that even though such problems may arise, they are not insurmountable obstacles to group treatment. The attempts of the patient to project responsibility on the therapists and to avoid focusing on a sometimes painful reality are readily dealt with in a group setting. The advantages of such an approach are numerous. The use of lithium is demystified, and patients are forced by other members to accept responsibility for lithium maintenance; indeed, in this setting their "conventionality" encourages compliance. Close follow-up is obtained with both the patient's clinical state and lithium levels being regularly monitored. The occasional episode of euphoria or depression can be handled in a much more supportive and empathic fashion than would be the case in a mixed therapy group. Finally, the patient is unable to say, "You can't understand what I'm going through" since the other members have experienced the same problems and feelings.

Davenport, et al.[11] remind us that even though lithium can stabilize mood swings, the patient's interpersonal difficulties can remain and interfere with successful lithium prophylaxis; lithium use does not solve all the patient's problems. Our experience is that cessation of lithium use seems more often to result from denial of illness and lack of information about lithium and lack of support from family members or friends, rather than from a conscious desire to precipitate a manic episode.

Despite our patients' histories of poor adherence to lithium maintenance, the relapse rates we report compare favorably to those reported in other studies of lithium maintenance.[8] It is not clear whether the high rate of compliance is secondary to the effects of group therapy as such or to the close follow-up patients received or to the interaction between the two; such interactions have been reported between antidepressant medications and psychotherapy.[16] Certainly the modeling of lithium compliance and effectiveness provided by the attendance of "graduates" of the group encouraged compliance, as did the support they received each week from other group members.

Contrary to expectation, we found that these patients worked well in a homogeneous therapy group of this kind. The common experience of manic-depressive illness made the episodes of hypomania or depression much less disruptive than would have been the case in a heterogeneous therapy group. The same therapeutic factors are presumably at work in groups of this kind as in other groups, e.g., instillation of hope, interpersonal learning, support, mutual sensitivity, universality, and imparting information.[2] The benefits of this kind of psychotherapeutic approach included the demystification of lithium treatment with a consequent lessening of the patient's unrealistic expectations as well as the involvement of the patient in the treatment process and an increase in the patient's sense of control over his illness. Groups of this kind may serve as a simple, efficient, and cost-effective adjunct to lithium maintenance therapy, especially for patients with a history of poor adherence to lithium prophylaxis. They may also offer a way of providing the benefits of psychotherapy to a group of patients generally seen as poor candidates for such treatment.

Summary

Because patients with bipolar affective illness have generally been viewed as poor candidates for psychotherapy, many clinicians have relied on lithium prophylaxis as the major treatment modality. However, even with lithium prophylaxis many patients still relapse, often in settings providing little support for maintenance treatment. This report presents the results of a long-term therapy group composed exclusively of bipolar manic-depressive patients, many of whom had histories of poor adherence to lithium maintenance. The group met weekly and was conducted with an interpersonal, interactional "here and now" format. Patients attended an average of 47 sessions. Members were initially somewhat aloof and remote and minimized their problems. Over the course of their participation, members became more open and began to discuss their concerns about their illness and lithium maintenance treatment; during this time they functioned much as members in any long-term psychotherapy group. In the two-year period prior to entering the group, patients averaged 16.8 weeks of hospitalization; in the subsequent two-year period they averaged 3.6 weeks of hospitalization. Groups of this kind may offer a simple, cost-effective adjunct to lithium maintenance treatment and may provide the advantages and opportunities of psychotherapy to a group of patients generally seen as resistant to such approaches.

References

1. COHEN, M., BAKER, C., FROOM-REICHMANN, F., et al. An Intensive Study of 12 Cases of Manic-depressive Psychosis. *Psychiatry* 11:103, 1954.
2. YALOM, I. D. *The Theory and Practice of Group Psychotherapy*. Basic Books, New York, 1975.
3. STALLONE, F., SHELLEY, E., MENLEWICZ, J., et al. The Use of Lithium in Affective Disorders: III. A Double-blind Study of Prophylaxis in Bipolar Illness. *Am. J. Psychiatry*, 130:1006, 1973.

4. BENSON, R. The Forgotten Treatment Modality in Bipolar Illness: Psychotherapy. *Dis Nerv. System* 36:634, 1975.

5. CLAYTON, P. J. Bipolar Affective Disorder—Techniques and Results of Treatment. *Am. J. Psychother.* 32:81, 1978.

6. CARLSON, G. A., KOTIN, J., DAVENPORT, Y. B., ADLAND, M. Follow-up of 53 Bipolar Manic-depressive Patients. *Br. J. Psychiatry,* 124:134, 1974.

7. VAN PUTTEN, T. Why Do Patients with Manic-depressive Illness Stop Their Lithium? *Comp. Psychiatry,* 16:179, 1975.

8. WELNER, A., WELNER, Z., and LEONARD, M. Bipolar Manic-depressive Disorder: a Reassessment of Course and Outcome. *Comp. Psychiatry,* 18:327, 1977.

9. SHAKIR, S., VOLKMAR, F., BACON, S., PFERRERBAUM, A. Group Psychotherapy as an Adjunct to Lithium Maintenance. *Am. J. Psychiatry,* 136:455, 1979.

10. FIEVE, R., KUMBARCI, T., and DUNNER, D. Lithium Prophylaxis of Depression in Bipolar I, Bipolar II, and Unipolar Patients. *Am. J. Psychiatry,* 133:925, 1976.

11. DAVENPORT, Y., EBERT, M., ADLAND, M., et al. Couples Group Therapy as an Adjunct to Lithium Maintenance of the Manic Patient. *Am. J. Psychiatry,* 47:495, 1977.

12. ABLON, S., DAVENPORT, Y., GERSHON, E., et al. The Married Manic. *Am. J. Orthopsychiatry,* 45:854, 1975.

13. ROSEN, A. M. Group Management of Lithium Prophylaxis. Paper presented at the 133rd annual meeting of the American Psychiatric Association, San Francisco, CA., May 6, 1980 (mimeo).

14. MACVANE, J., LANGE, K., BROWN, M., et al. Psychological Function of Bipolar Manic-depressives in Remission. *Arch. Gen. Psychiatry,* 35:1351,1978.

15. JANOWSKY, D., EL-YOUSEF, M., and DAVIS, J. Interpersonal Maneuvers of Manic Patients. *Am. J. Psychiatry,* 131:250, 1974.

16. KIERMAN, G., DiMASCIO, A., WEISSMAN, J., et al. Treatment of Depression by Drugs and Psychotherapy. *Am. J. Psychiatry,* 131:186, 1974.

DEPRESSION

CHAPTER 15

Treatment of Depressed Women

Eva Y. Deykin, Myrna M. Weissman, and Gerald L. Klerman

Introduction

Depressions are among the most common forms of mental illnesses.[2] The exact incidence is difficult to determine as the availability of tranquilizers and effective anti-depressant drugs often facilitates the remission of depressive symptomatology without psychiatric intervention. Although a large proportion of depressed patients are treated by their family physicians, a great many others apply for psychiatric help. Psychiatrists in private practice have estimated that between 60 percent and 75 percent of their private patients are suffering from some degree of depression.[1,11]

While the term depression has been used to describe reactions as varied as mild emotional malaise to the severe forms of psychotic melancholia, in this paper depression refers to the clinical syndrome consisting of a number of symptoms sometimes appearing singly and sometimes concomitantly in the same patient.[5] These symptoms include painful subjective feelings of hopelessness, despair, helplessness, worthlessness, guilt, and emptiness; somatic symptomatology such as headaches, gastro-intestinal discomfort, chest tightness, difficulty in breathing and urinary problems. Insomnia, fatigue, appetite loss, weepiness, retarded speech, and anxiety are also features of the depressed state.

The onset of depression can be either rapid or gradual. While it is not always possible to delineate the exact time of onset or a precipitating event, the patient and family generally agree that the patient's current state marks

Reprinted from *British Journal of Social Work*, Vol. 1 (Fall, 1971), pp. 277–291, by permission of the authors and the Association.

a radical departure from his normal mood and behavior. Families of depressed patients will often describe the patients as particularly strong individuals to whom others could turn in times of crisis. In this respect, depressed patients differ from other mental patients, especially schizophrenic patients, who even in periods of remission often lead marginal lives requiring significant societal supports.

In recent years, there has been an increase in the number of depressed patients seeking psychiatric help. It is not clear whether this rise represents greater incidence, a growing sophistication in the medical and lay population about mental illness, or an increase in the availability of local community mental health centers. Psychiatric facilities are seeing more depressed patients, and frequently at an earlier stage of illness. While there probably always will be patients who postpone psychiatric treatment until their symptomatology becomes intolerable, an increasing proportion of depressed patients now seek help while only mildly or moderately ill and can be treated as outpatients.

This paper discusses casework techniques useful in treating depressed patients whether in the hospital or in outpatient clinics. Our experience is derived mainly from adult females who were generally married. The focus of casework has been on the patient and her immediate family. In spite of the homogeneity of this group, it is suggested that the casework techniques discussed here have relevance to other groups of depressed patients, including males and unmarried females.

Since caseworkers perform different roles depending on the institutional setting, this paper integrates experience of caseworkers in hospitals and outpatient clinics. In the hospital setting, the caseworker's role was a collaborative one with the physician. The primary focus of work was with the patient's family and occasionally participating with the psychiatrist in conjoint family-patient therapy. Conversely, in the outpatient clinic, the caseworker's major function was direct work with patients. In this instance, the caseworker was an important liaison between the patient and psychiatrist who saw the patient only briefly to regulate anit-depressant medication.

Given these differences, the paper addresses itself to the various issues arising from the casework treatment of hospitalized and outpatient depressed women; the role casework plays in their drug treatment; and the influence of casework on their recovery phase and aftercare. The hospitalized patient is permitted to assume the sick role;[13,7] legal responsibility for the patient is assumed by the hospital and clearly understood by its staff, the patient and her family; and the hospital constitutes a structured environment where life influences on the patient are somewhat controlled and observable. In contrast, the outpatient is not usually viewed as sick but rather as a person with a problem. This perception frequently causes the patient's family to have a lower tolerance for a diminution of the patient's usual social functioning.[16]Since outpatient treatment occupies only one or two hours a week, the patient's major involvement is still with her family thus reducing institutional dependency, and maximizing early re-establishment of normal functioning.

The Hospitalized Depressed Patient

Hospitalization almost always produces major stresses for both the patient and family. The separation of the patient from her family generates difficult role readjustments. Hospital admission initiates a definite change in a depressed person's status and added responsibilities for the family. For the depressed patient, a change in status may be difficult to accept, often it is interpreted as a loss and tends to intensify and confirm a patient's feelings of worthlessness. Many patients relate their self-esteem to performance of their role; thus a patient may wonder whether she is still a good wife and mother when she is unable to perform the usual wifely and motherly functions.

The newly hospitalized depressed patient may experience feelings of abject dejection. Occasionally, these feelings are so intense that the patient maybe unable to convey her psychic discomfort and can only make statements like 'you don't know how badly I feel' or 'no one who feels like I do can ever feel well again'. In the face of this overwhelming pessimism it is useful for the caseworker to maintain a stance of strong hope and qualified reassurance. This is justified because most depressive episodes are time limited, and even without treatment the majority of severely depressed patients will improve if they can be prevented from committing suicide during the acute illness.

Working with such pessimistic patients can be extremely trying. The patient's unremitting expressions of hopelessness to the exclusion of any other sentiments appears to provide no basis for a therapeutic alliance. It is not unusual for the caseworker to begin to feel angry and impotent. During the initial phase, support and reassurance should be maintained, but the words carefully measured so as not to challenge the patient into becoming sicker. It is often therapeutic for the caseworker to agree that he cannot fully feel the patient's pain but that he has seen patients who have expressed similar despair and who, in time, have recovered. It is essential for the caseworker to be aware of the possibility of a negative counter-transference, and to acknowledge to himself his own feelings of anger and frustration. The awareness and control of such feelings is important since anger, frustration, or veiled impatience are frequently perceived by the patient as rejection or loss of control on the part of the caseworker. This situation may be particularly threatening to patients with strong dependency needs and whose own control of impulsivity is shaky.

The Impact of Depression and Hospitalization on the Patient's Family

Even before hospitalization, many families have to deal with the discrepancy between the patient's former functioning and her depressed state. Some relatives are unprepared to cope with role reversals and may themselves become discouraged when their emotional needs are unfulfilled. While this reaction can be seen in any relatives, it is most evident in the patient's spouse. Many husbands develop symptoms similar to those of the patients, especially somatization. In such marriages, it appeared that both the patient and spouse were vying for the position of the 'sick' person. Therefore, in initiating casework with such a family, the caseworker should anticipate this pathologic competition.

A spouse who has had to assume many household responsibilities may feel overwhelmed and resentful. Concentrated attention to the patient without any exploration or acknowledgement of the husband's position tends to entrench the spouse's feelings of burden and to diminish his ability to cope with these responsibilities. A simple acknowledgement of the spouse's difficulties may suffice to support him over this trying period. Occasionally, the caseworker has to initiate intensive work which may include helping the spouse to modify his existing living patterns.

The interruption of the characteristic interpersonal family balance, whether it be between spouse and patient or between the patient and other relatives, may have repercussions on all other family relationships. The nature of the relationship between the patient and her significant relatives, such as children, parents, or siblings, is sometimes expressed in the content of her symptoms. For example, some patients present symptoms which have a decidedly sado-masochistic flavor, and the intensity of these symptoms has been noted to vary according to who is with the patient at any given time. Patients with somatic symptoms frequently suffer an exacerbation of symptoms when they are visited by certain relatives, but verbalize considerably less somatic discomfort when alone with the therapist. Chasin and Semrad[4] have commented on this phenomenon, and make the point that hypochondriacal symptoms serve both to arouse guilt in family members and as safeguards or defenses for the patient against the open expression of hostility. Careful observation of the content of the patient's symptomatology and the method of expressing it may serve as a useful tool in determining where the patient's interpersonal impasses lie.

Casework with the Patient and Family

The patient's difficulty in communicating is a major source of her interpersonal difficulty. The depressed patient may have lost the capacity for the traditional and accepted forms of direct expression, and compensates for this by disguised communication through symptoms or other primitive symbolic and non-verbal communications. As one recovered patient eloquently described it, 'I felt as if I were at the bottom of a well calling for someone to help me, but all that came up were muffled sounds'. Like others who have worked with depressed patients,[17] we have noted that as the patient's capacity for appropriate verbal communication increased, somatic and depressive symptoms diminished.

The caseworker can be of significant help in reinstituting meaningful communication between the patient and family. One possible technique for re-establishing communication is a family conference in which the patient and family members are given the opportunity to express their perceptions of illness, their expectations of treatment and hopes for the future. A family interview held either at admission or shortly thereafter can serve as an important diagnostic aid allowing the caseworker to observe existing interaction and provides a psychologically protected setting in which difficult or painful subjects can be discussed.

It is not surprising to find that communication between patient and family is frequently inadequate and distorted when one considers that hospitalization represents a last resort to a problem for which no solution has been found. A careful history of the events leading to hospitalization will usually reveal unsuccessful adaptive measures undertaken by both patient and family to avoid or postpone hospitalization. Frequently the unsuccessful measures involved the change or modification of role performances among family members.[15] The failure of such role modification usually provokes anger, and a growing impatience with the patient's limited functioning. Maladaptive communication can be viewed as the by-product of the frustration, guilt and anger felt on all sides.

The patient's relatives may indicate their anger covertly, through messages with ambiguous or contradictory meanings. For example, some families try to 'cheer up' the newly admitted patient by pointing to the misfortunes of others. The hidden message is 'maybe you are not trying hard enough'. The caseworker may be able to modify this interaction by pointing out the correct message thereby appealing to the family's conscious wishes for the patient's recovery. It is at times advisable to point out the latent hostility in such a message. Once the family is able to recognize its hostility, it can usually express it in more appropriate ways, thereby lessening the ambiguity of communication.

A more serious form of distorted communication is seen in the families who wish to exclude the patient from information they share with the caseworker. These families characteristically contribute little during a joint interview or will totally agree with the patient, but will then indicate to the caseworker that there are other facts which they will disclose later. Allowing oneself to become a party to this type of secret sharing is not only harmful to the patient but damaging to the success of any casework subsequently undertaken with the relatives.

A variant of this pattern occurs in families who wish to withhold any 'bad news' from the patient on grounds that it would aggravate the patient's condition. The caseworker should encourage families to share all significant happenings—good and bad—pointing out that should the patient react badly, the family and the treatment staff would be available for help. On the other hand, exclusion of the patient from knowledge shared by other family members would deny the patient her adult status and thus increase feelings of alienation and worthlessness. Families who find it particularly difficult to discuss what they feel to be traumatic news can be helped to do so in the setting of a joint family-patient interview. Many families have been surprised to find that the patient was able to tolerate and deal with the news in a mature way.

There is a number of families whose interaction with the patient is so poor, that lying and conscious distortion of reality constitute the dominant form of communication. While this group is not a large group, it does present a serious challenge for casework treatment in that these families' wishes for the patient's recovery are markedly ambivalent. While it is possible to help these families work through their ambivalence towards the patient, occasionally it is necessary to intervene in order to protect the patient by limiting direct visits.

Sometimes the poor communication between family and patient is due not so much to their inability to verbalize but rather to a fear that their shared meaningful interaction would lead to a discussion of intolerable or taboo topics. Foremost among intolerable topics is suicide. A depressed patient who is sick enough to be hospitalized is often also potentially suicidal. For this reason, it is important to establish whether the patient is suicidal and if so, to what degree. A forthright discussion of suicide potential between patient, family and clinician accomplishes several goals. First of all, if a patient has suicidal thoughts it is essential that the hospital staff responsible for the patient know it, and it is equally important that the family know it, especially when the patient makes weekend visits home. Secondly, in asking about suicide, the clinician conveys to the patient that her distress is taken seriously. This often helps establish a basis for a working relationship. Lastly, the honest exploration of what many people consider a 'taboo' subject opens the way for the discussion of other forbidden topics especially those which have to do with unacceptable hostility and aggression. A striking example of this was one newly admitted patient who when asked about suicidal thoughts, blurted out with obvious relief, 'I've never thought of killing myself, but I have had thoughts of killing my mother'. Contrary to the belief of some families, an exploration of suicidal potential does not 'put ideas into the patient's head'. Patients are usually quite frank in their talk of suicide if given the opportunity, and are grateful for the chance. It is particularly important, for patients who are worried about their impulses, to verbalize suicidal fantasies with someone who takes them seriously. This lessens a burden which otherwise the patient would have to bear alone.

Initiating Casework with the Acutely Depressed Outpatient

In contrast to hospitalization, the patient maintains her status within the family in outpatient treatment. The important consequences of this difference need be stressed. While certain aspects of the patient's roles may have to be performed temporarily by others in the family, the basic family role structure is not as radically altered as in hospitalization. This facilitates the gradual resumption of usual duties as the patient recovers. Patients who can be treated in outpatient settings are either those who have significant familial supports or those who have less florid symptomatology than their hospitalized counterparts.

In the acute phase of illness the performance of ordinary tasks requires considerable effort for the depressed patient. The patient frequently expresses a strong desire to rest and be nurtured. In this situation, casework therapy has three tasks: (1) the reduction of symptoms, (2) the restoration of the patient's social functioning, and (3) the initial exploration of the patient's maladaptive patterns of behavior. Before the caseworker begins to explore the patient's maladaptive patterns of interaction, it it important that at least a small degree of her usual social functioning be restored. Premature exploration can add to the patient's feelings of despair.

Casework during this early phase is predominantly supportive in nature. Specific techniques include advice, encouragement, reassurance, reduction of guilt, ventilation, and direct help to modify the environment.[9] Since many patients deny deeper problems when they are recovered, the casework relationship established during this early phase may provide a more enduring bond for deeper treatment.

Unlike the hospital setting where the patient has twenty-four-hour attention, outpatient therapy occupies only a few hours a week. Family demands on the patient continue the rest of the week. Although considered a patient by the treating staff, she is still 'Ma' to a family who is both disturbed and perplexed by her decreased performance and lessened capacity of affection. The family's anger and confusion are reinforced when mother, who used to bake her own bread and noodles, can't make the morning coffee.

Casework undertaken during the acute phase of depression must deal with the patient's conflict and ambivalence over her wish for regression. A supportive relationship should allow the patient to feel accepted despite her symptoms, but not because of them. Although symptoms are acknowledged, focus is not maintained on them and the patient is encouraged to discuss herself and her feelings. A useful technique is to explore the daily demands made on the patient and to reassure her that inability to meet these demands is part of the illness and will improve. This serves to decrease any unrealistic expectation the patient has for herself. At the same time, the few non-expendable household tasks are identified, allowing the patient a degree of mastery.

Many patients treated on an outpatient basis spend long, unstructured days at home alone doing very little. Some of these patients are ashamed to discuss their daily routine as they tend to view inactivity as a personal failing rather than as a symptom of illness. One formerly active and conscientious mother of six, persistently avoided discussing her household routine with the caseworker while remaining preoccupied with her somatic symptoms. Weepiness and constipation, she finally admitted, were less of a disgrace than her inability to take care of her house and children. These discussions were useful in decreasing the patient's feeling of guilt and isolation and served to relieve the immediate distress.

Because of the disorganized nature of many depressed patients' lives, it is both useful and therapeutic for the caseworker to provide a measure of structure. Appointments at regular and specified times once or twice a week help to accomplish this. The importance of keeping these appointments should be emphasized. Appointments on an irregular schedule are not recommended during the early phase. A regular, externally imposed appointment schedule makes it easier for a patient to work out her plans and, conversely, this structure has a beneficial effect on symptoms. Other patients who have an enormous need to please the social worker may attempt to cancel appointments when they cannot report improvement in their clinical condition. The caseworker should interpret setbacks as part of the normal and temporary course of the illness and not necessarily related to a lack of progress.[12] The value of seeing a patient at her best as well as at her worst should be stressed. Missed appointments can be followed up by a telephone call, and at times, a home visit.

Family Involvement in Outpatient Treatment

Despite the obvious need for involvement, the family of an outpatient can more easily exclude itself from treatment. In a hospital setting, the patient's family is almost always involved at intake when it provides historical information and later on when it visits the patient. An outpatient, on the other hand, is frequently self-referred and provides her own history.[14] Often she seeks treatment without her family's knowledge. Unlike the hospitalized patient who may blame the family for placing her in the hospital, the outpatient is more likely to express guilt for her diminished performance within the family unit.

The frequent intricate balance between the depressed patient's clinical symptoms and family relationships has been well documented.[6,10,15] Often the successful treatment of a depressed outpatient is dependent upon the quality of the family's involvement. The outpatient living at home is constantly subject to familial pressures and irritants. Unless the patient has made a dramatic suicide gesture or exhibits psychotic symptomatology, the family may not perceive her condition as an illness. Furthermore, as outpatient therapy does not initially produce immediate impact on the patient's life, the family often has difficulty in perceiving the patient as sick. The family's reactions to the patient's decreased activity may range from direct accusations—'Why don't you get off your behind and do something', to more subtle messages such as, 'You ought to get a new job, take a course, get a hobby'. In either case, the family's frustration and misinterpretation of the illness is conveyed. To some families, the hours spent at the clinic may loom as a mystery, an intrusion of privacy and a source of anxiety. One husband suspiciously asked his wife, 'When you go there, do you blame everything on me?''

Although families of outpatients are tolerant, to a degree, of the patient's decrease in performance, diminished communication and hopeless affect, this tolerance is not endless and comes with a price. Daily confrontation with the patient's gloomy affect as well as the necessity for the family to assume some of the caretaking may foment additional conflicts. For example, the daughter of one patient became withdrawn during her mother's depression. It was gradually learned that this child feared that any misbehavior on her part would result in her mother's suicide.

In contrast to families of hospitalized patients who have little or no difficulty in perceiving the patient's symptoms as part of an illness, the families of outpatients frequently are amazed to learn that the clinic staff considers the patient a sick person in need of professional help and medication. This difference in perception has implications for the family's willingness and ability to involve itself therapeutically. Family conferences, as with inpatients, geared to eliciting the family's perception of the illness are generally non-threatening to families who deny problems. In addition, these conferences serve to define the patient's illness as well as to give recognition to the added burden the family bears, thereby laying the groundwork for the family's more intensive involvement.

Casework and Drug Therapy

Pharmacotherapy is widely used in the treatment of depressed patients. While the physician is ultimately responsible for the prescription and regulation of drug therapy, the social worker is often instrumental in the interpretation of this therapy to both patient and family and in dealing with the hopes and anxieties arising out of drug treatment. Here, the caseworker has a dual function: to help the patient and family accept drug therapy and to relate to the physician possible problems which the patient reports in the taking of the medication. It is necessary for the caseworker to have a working knowledge of the action of the drugs used, their effectiveness, common side effects, toxicity, and the time needed before drug effects can be expected.

The function of the caseworker in relation to medication is diminished in the hospital where drugs are dispensed by nurses who remain with the patient until the medication is swallowed. In the hospital, therefore, the caseworker's primary function is to interpret drug treatment to the family, and to allay their anxiety if they do not see immediate improvement. The most common questions and anxieties families express regarding medication refer to the possible addictive qualities of the drugs used, and to whether the patient will have to take the medication for the rest of her life. At times, the hospital social worker may have to stress to the family the patient's need to continue taking medication while on home visits and after hospital discharge, even when improvement is clearly evident. In cases of potentially suicidal patients who go home on visits, the social worker should call the family's attention to the fact that the patient has medication with her and if necessary, ask a responsible relative to dispense the drug. Occasionally, a patient may be taking an anti-depressant drug which can prove toxic if taken in combination with a variety of common foods. If this is the case, the social worker should instruct the family as to the patient's diet while on home visit, and explain the need for the elimination of certain foods.

In an outpatient clinic, the role of the caseworker in pharmacotherapy becomes much more important since medication cannot be as well controlled as in the hospital. In outpatient settings, it is crucial for the caseworker to gain the patient's and family's confidence and co-operation. It is not unusual for the patient and her family to become discouraged by the lack of immediate improvement which is often interpreted by the patient as further proof that she is 'hopeless'. Conversely, when the improvement does occur, the patient and family may assume that the depression has been cured and may have considerable conflict about continuing medication fearing a possible dependency on it.[18] In either case, the social worker is in a strategic position to interpret the expected sequence of events, to reassure the family and patient about the delayed effects of the drug and to encourage them to continue.

Equally important is the social worker's communication with the physician who is prescribing and regulating anti-depressant medication. In treating the outpatient, the social worker is usually the first, and sometimes the only person, to hear of unusual or persistent side effects. In addition, the social worker should mention to the physician any indication of increased alcohol intake, impulsivity, or suicidal ideation in the patient, as a month's supply of medication in the hands of an impulsive, suicidal patient can be disastrous.

The caseworker's professional relationship with the doctor is an important accompaniment of combined drug and casework treatment. The ideal patient says, 'drugs help, but not with everything'. The caseworker helps with the other issues, predominantly in the realm of interpersonal relationships.The area of therapeutic responsibility and eventual credit for patient improvement are well mapped out. More often, one or all of the following problems arise. The patient uses the medication and doctor to reject the caseworker and make him feel unneeded. The patient attributes magical powers to the pill, and may reject looking for antecedents to the depression. As one patient told the caseworker, 'If anyone knew what caused my depression, they'd get the Nobel prize. At least, the pills make me feel better.'

If casework is initiated after the patient has improved symptomatically as a result of medication, the caseworker may feel like 'Johnny-come-lately'. Fantasies of rescuing the patient are thwarted and can lead to a negative counter-transference. In addition, the patient may be angry about being treated by a 'lesser' person, and may wonder if she is less interesting now that she is less symptomatic. Casework becomes interspersed with the patient's memories of 'the good doctor'. The patient, after many months of combined drug and casework therapy, ends by attributing improvement to her medication. Even the most disciplined caseworker will have some negative reactions.

Casework with the Recovering Patient

Most depressed patients, whether they were treated in a hospital or as outpatients, begin to show significant improvement within a few weeks of starting on anti-depressant medication. Feelings of helplessness, hopelessness, insomnia and diminished appetite are relieved although some residual sadness may continue. At this point, the hospitalized patient begins to show more interest in the outside world. She wants to know what her family is doing, how they have coped during her absence and may even begin to resume part of her usual role by giving advice to her family and participating in decision making. At the same point of recovery, the outpatient, on the other hand, may be far more advanced in her social functioning, since she was never removed from her family.

It has been suggested that with symptomatic improvement the patient is more able to focus her energies on understanding the causes of the depression. This is only partially true; two groups of recovering patients can be identified: those who feel so well that they find looking to psychological antecedents runs counter to the positive effects of medication and those who do, in fact, have renewed energy and willingness to explore their intrapsychic and interpersonal difficulties.

The first group tends to lose interest in casework as the depression lifts. When they do attend, they are not interested in engaging in reflective consideration of their problems or in historical material. They continue to dwell on routine daily activities, in order to show how well they are doing. In one study, the common characteristic of this group was found to be their good marital relationships and stable social situations. Family conflicts which existed were covert, and the illness served to gain additional attention from family and friends. Their usual daily functioning, when well, was good, and they had no critical social problems.[15] Often they had some concurrent medical problem, which they believed brought on the depression—e.g. hormone shots or an operation. They tended to over-evaluate the drug effects and the doctor who treated them. They denied the extent of their illness as soon as they recovered. It was difficult for the caseworker not to partake of this denial as the patients seemed to be bubbling over with good health and activities. Casework with this group was similar to that described for the depressed 'latent conflict patients' of Deykin et al.[6] Such casework was geared to the reestablishment of interest in activities, work, and friends rather than to a confrontation of underlying conflicts. Insight development was minimized, and the reinforcement of successful adaptation, prior to illness, stressed.

The following case is an example of the patient who was uninterested in ongoing casework when recovering:

Mrs. S. was a fifty-year-old married housewife with one previous depression. Her current illness was attributed by her to hormone shots for menopausal symptoms. A number of family stresses in addition to the patient's menopause could have contributed to the precipitants of the depression. Her only son, to whom she was devoted, married. She and her husband had purchased a smaller home and were unsuccessful in the sale of their first home, increasing their financial burdens. The maintenance of two houses stressed the patient's excessively high standards of cleanliness. Her husband had taken a second job to ease their finances, which left her alone at night. Therefore, she had lost the company of her husband and son at the same time. After a six-week course of antidepressants, the patient's acute symptoms subsided. During the acute phase of her illness, her husband gave up his second job and the family rallied around, giving her much help and attention. While the patient was recovering, she quickly resumed her pattern of 'over-doing'. Casework interviews consisted of detailed reports of her activities to show how well she was doing. These included new recipes, square dancing with her husband, etc. She hardly could recall that she had been ill. Casework supported and encouraged her new interests, and the patient, after a few months, could see no need for continuing interviews as she was doing so well. Her obsessive compulsive adjustment remained intact and eight months after her illness she reported feeling better than she ever had.

A second group of patients consists of those who were quite interested in continuing casework once they recovered from the acute illness. They saw casework as an opportunity to understand antecedents and often said, 'Now that I feel better I can really look at what was bothering me'. These patients did not separate the depressive illness from social and personal problems, and feared that failure to relieve these problems could result in relapse. They saw the depression as an inability to cope with accumulating stress. The most common stress was overt marital conflict. The illness served to further alienate the spouse rather than win his sympathy. The frustrated need for object relations and interpersonal gratification because of the poor marriage served to motivate these patients into a therapy situation which would meet some of these basic needs. They were usually eager to engage in long-term casework, and came at least once and often twice per week for interviews. Continued family conferences, in which expectations and conflicts between the patient and other family members could be explored, were found extremely useful. Like the depressed 'overt conflict' patients described by Deykin et al., therapy was geared to helping the patient view family conflict in a more appropriate way and to seek constructive means of dealing with reality.[6] The patient in individual sessions was helped to identify precipitants to depression.

This woman is an example of a patient motivated for continued casework while recovering from a depressive illness:

Mrs. E. was a forty-year-old housewife with four children and no history of depressive illness. Although her marriage had always been stormy, the family stayed together. About one year prior to her depression, a number of changes resulted in increased family disintegration. Mr. E. lost his job and moved the family over 1,500 miles away. Mr. E. could not find employment, and his wife took a job to support the family. Their two teenagers left school and went to live with relatives. Mrs. E. had an extra-marital affair and contemplated divorce, which was against her religious belief and caused her tremendous guilt. She became acutely depressed when she and the family finally did return home. She felt she had lost self-respect, and withdrew from her family, spending days on end without speaking to them. They in turn, angered by her withdrawal, retaliated by doing whatever they felt would displease her.

Summary

This paper has focused on some issues in the casework therapy of hospitalized and outpatient depressed women. While the clinical symptomatology presented by both groups of patients may be very similar with the exception that outpatients, in general, have less bizarre or florid symptoms, the difference between the twenty-four-hour hospital and the outpatient clinic produces separate kinds of problems and necessitates specific casework techniques.

The hospitalization of a depressed patient causes a certain degree of alienation of the patient from her family. Treatment should address itself to the restoration of appropriate communication and interaction between the patient and family. The cloistered nature of the hospital is useful in that it allows for the direct observation of the methods which families and patients employ to communicate with one another and thus provides the caseworker with valuable information into the nature of interpersonal conflicts as well as to possible ways of resolving them. Joint family-patient interviews, at least in the phase of casework, have proved to be valuable both as a diagnostic aid and as a means of fostering open and free communication between patient and family.

In treating an outpatient, on the other hand, one is faced with the problem of preventing the alienation of the patient by the family; of encouraging both the patient and family to allow the patient to maintain her status in the family unit while at the same time relieving her of some of her usual duties. In working with the depressed outpatient one should be cognizant of the patient's need for rest and recovery and at the same time, the family's demand for her continued role performance within the home.

The initial goal of casework should be the restoration of the outpatient's personal and environmental mastery rather than the exploration of maladaptive patterns. Early family involvement in the patient's treatment is particularly important because the family has to assume the burden of caring for a depressed patient at home.

In addition, the caseworker treating outpatients has a special responsibility regarding the patient's drug treatment. This often calls for the early detection and reporting of negative side effects and for dealing with the family's and patient's ambivalent feelings towards the continuation of medication. Potential professional rivalries between caseworker and physician have been identified.

During the recovery phase, the outpatient's motivation for intensive casework is related to the degree of her ongoing social and marital stresses.

Those patients with few overt social problems may not be interested in casework as a means of insight into the underlying causes of their depression, but rather choose to use the relationship with the caseworker as a means of support, while they are re-establishing their relationships and activities disrupted by the illness.

Acknowledgments

The authors are indebted to, and would like to express their appreciation to, Ruth Bullock, Effie Geanakoplos and Shirley Jacobson, Clinical Caseworkers, for their discussion of their cases in hospital and outpatient settings.

References

1. AVNET, HELEN H., 1962. *Psychiatric Insurance.* New York: Group Health Insurance.

2. AYD, FRANK J., 1969. *Recognizing the Depressed Patient.* Grune & Stratton (New York).

3. BURKE, LEE, DEYKIN, EVA, JACOBSON, SHIRLEY, and HALEY, SARAH, May 1967. "The Depressed Woman Returns." *Archives of General Psychiatry,* 16.

4. CHASIN, R. M. and SEMRAD, E. V., October 1966. "Interviewing the Depressed Patient." *Hospital and Community Psychiatry,* 17:283-6.

5. COMMER, LEONARD, 1969. *Up from Depression.* Simon & Schuster (New York).

6. DEYKIN, EVA, JACOBSON, SHIRLEY, KLERMAN, GERALD, and SOLOMON, MAIDA, June 1966. "The Empty Nest: Psychosocial Aspects of Conflict Between Depressed Women and Their Grown Children." *American Journal of Psychiatry,* 122, No. 12.

7. FREEMAN, H., LEVINE, S., and REEDER, L. G., 1963. *The Handbook of Medical Sociology.* Prentice-Hall (Englewood Cliffs, New Jersey), pp. 111-19.

8. HANKOFF, L. D., and GALVIN, JOHN W., July 1968. "Psychopharmacological Treatment and Its Implication for Social Work." *Social Work,* 13, No. 3.

9. HOLLIS, FLORENCE, 1966. *Casework: A Psychosocial Therapy.* Columbia University School of Social Work (Random House, New York).

10. JACOBSON, SHIRLEY, and KLERMAN, GERALD L., February 1966. "Interpersonal Dynamical of Hospitalized Depressed Patients' Home Visits." *Journal of Marriage and the Family.*

11. KLINE, N. S., 1964. "The Practical Management of Depression." *Journal of the American Medical Association,* 190:732-40.

12. LEVIN, SIDNEY, January 1965. "Some Suggestions for Treating the Depressed Patient." *Psychoanalytic Quarterly,* 34:48.

13. PARSONS, T., 1951. *The Social System*. The Free Press of Glencoe, Inc. (New York).

14. PAYKEL, EUGENE S., KLERMAN, GERALD L., and PRUSOFF, BRIGITTE A., 1970. "Treatment Setting and Clinical Depression." *Archives of General Psychiatry*, 22.

15. SPIEGEL, JOHN P., 1957. "The Resolution of Role Conflict Within the Family." *Psychiatry*, 20.

16. SPIEGEL, J., and BELL, N. W., 1959. "The Family of the Psychiatric Patient." in *American Handbook of Psychiatry*, edited by S. Arieti, Vol. 1, pp.114–49. Basic Books (New York).

17. STUART, RICHARD, April 1967. "Casework Treatment of Depression Viewed as an Interpersonal Disturbance." *Social Work*, 12:No. 2.

18. UHLENHUTH, E. H., LIPMAN, R., and COVI, L., 1969. "Combined Pharmacotherapy and Psychotherapy." *Journal of Nervous and Mental Disease*, 148, No. 1.

19. WALZER, HANK, December 1961. "Casework Treatment of the Depressed Parent." *Social Casework*, 42, No. 10.

ANXIETY DISORDERS

CHAPTER **16**

Diagnostic and Treatment Considerations with Phobic Symptomed Clients

William P. Gilmore

Introduction

It seems to me that we, from family service and community mental health agencies, who deal with maturational and emotional problems in individuals and families, need to take another look at the way we think about and sometimes deal with phobic symptomed clients.

Phobias and phobic symptoms need to be regarded as ways of dealing with anxiety, rather than as independent pathological processes per se. We have no less an authority than Dr. Sigmund Freud for this.[1]

Phobic symptoms, which I at one time associated with genital (neurotic) functioning are to the best of my understanding, much more commonly found today in people functioning on pregenital levels of development. One can deduce from this that the phobic symptoms we see in these clients are not operating so much to handle genital (neurotic) level feelings but rather to handle earlier, pregenital (character disordered) level feelings.

[1] James Strachey and Anna Freud (1909). *Standard Edition of the Complete Psychological Works of Sigmund Freud*. Vol. X, 115...in his discussion of the "Little Hans" case Freud states: "In the classificatory system of the neuroses no definite position has hitherto been assigned to 'phobias.' It seems certain that they should only be regarded as syndromes which may form part of various neuroses and that we not rank them as an independent pathological process."

Reprinted from *Smith College Studies in Social Work*, Vol. 41 (1971), pp. 93–102, by permission of the publisher.

This paper is a reflection of my own struggle to adapt the psychoanalytic theory I learned in school, through agency in-service training and consultation, and through my own reading, to the differential diagnosis and treatment of clients with phobic symptoms. For the past ten years, I have been interested in phobic symptoms and the people who suffer from these intriguing, but nonetheless painful and restricting psychic entities. This paper is likewise a further attempt to share with other practitioners some of the helpful insights I have gained from consultations with Dr. Murray Goldstone, one of our agency consultants on adult problems.[2] I am also indebted to the work of Dr. Eduardo Weiss on agoraphobia which has served as a stimulus for this paper.[3,4]

The learning of technical psychiatric theory and its application in practice is a difficult, time and energy consuming process for social work practitioners. This learning makes heavy demands on our cognitive and emotional faculties as the material itself is highly technical and heavily laced with emotional content. As in all learning and as in all application of theory to practice, it comes unevenly in fits and starts, as the learner is able to accept it and make it a part of himself. Such an integration of theory by the worker must come before he can really make it a part of his practice. Another complication arises from the fact that our traditional psychoanalytic theory of human growth and development is based on the theory of neurosis. In our current practice (as mentioned above) we see fewer and fewer people functioning on the neurotic level. We do see more and more people functioning on character disordered levels, hence the need to broaden and adapt our traditional psychoanalytic theory to the differential diagnosis and treatment of people functioning on these pregenital levels of development. This is why we are so indebted to the growing number of casework and psychiatric writers who have been able to adapt psychoanalytic knowledge in an understandable, step by step, practical way to the needs of the clients we serve—a preponderantly large number of clients functioning on pregenital levels of development—and to the needs of the practitioners who serve them.[5,6,7]

[2] William P. Gilmore, *Notes from Consultation with Dr. Goldstone(8-2-68)*. Family Service Association of Cleveland—12/4/68 (Mimeographed).

[3] Eduardo Weiss, M.D. "The Psychodynamic Formulation of Agoraphobia," in *Psychoanalytic Forum*, Vol. II, Winter 1966, 378–398.

[4] Eduardo Weiss, M.D. *Agoraphobia in the Light of Ego Psychology* (New York and London: Grune and Stratton, 1964).

[5] Effie Warren, "Treatment of Marriage Partners with Character Disorders," *Journal of Social Casework*, Vol. XXXVIII, No. 3 (1957),118–125.

[6] Beatrice Simcox Reiner and Irving Kaufman, M.D. (1959),*Character Disorders in Parents of Delinquents*. (New York: Family Service Association of America, 1959).

[7] Irving Kaufman, "Helping People who Cannot Manage their Lives," *Children*, Vol. 13, No. 3, (May–June, 1966).

Definition of Terms

Character disordered people are "those persons fixated at pregenital levels of development and who express their conflicts primarily by behaviorial manifestations that are based on characteristics associated with the oral, anal, and phallic-urethral levels of development....They are constantly threatened by the anxiety stemming from an unresolved depression. Much of their activity is designed to ward off the anxiety. They attempt to deal with it "behaviorally" or by developing physical symptoms."[8]

Phobia or phobic reaction. "The anxiety of these patients becomes detached from a specific idea, object, or situation in daily life and is displaced to some symbolic idea or situation in the form of a specific neurotic fear...the patient attempts to control his anxiety by avoiding the phobic object or situation."[9]

Agoraphobia. In psychiatric literature the term agoraphobia was extended from its original meaning of fear of open places, or fear of crossing open places, to designate "all anxiety reactions to abandoning a fixed point of support, e.g., the anxiety reaction to venturing some distance from home."[10]

In this paper the term *phobic symptom* is used to designate both phobic and agoraphobic type thoughts, feelings and resulting behavior.

Diagnostic and Treatment Considerations

A great many of the phobic symptomed clients now seen, in addition to their phobic symptoms, show depression and often somatic complaints which point to oral, early pregenital problems in ego development and functioning. The similarity of phobic symptoms in these character disordered people and their neurotic level brothers and sisters can be misleading. Needless to say, if we attempt to treat a client with phobic symptoms operating on a character disordered level of development, we and the client are in trouble. It would be similar to an orthopedic specialist treating a patient for leg bruises when in fact he is suffering from a broken leg.

There are, however, certain differences in the phobic *object* and *content* which can be helpful in differential diagnosis and treatment. As we know, the phobic symptom in a neurotic level client is a displacement of feelings from the person to whom the feelings originally were directed onto another object, person. This phobia is usually an *object* phobia i.e., relating to a person or thing (animal). A classic example is Freud's "Little Hans"

[8] Reiner and Kaufman, *loc. cit.* 7–8.

[9] "Diagnostic and Statistical Manual of Mental Disorders," (Washington, D.C.: American Psychiatric Association, 1952), 33.

[10] Weiss, *The Psychodynamic Formulation of Agoraphobia,* 378.

case. The phobic symptom in a character disordered client is likewise a displacement but on a lower level of differentiation of the self. In this instance, the feelings are related to the *self* in a *situation*. This type of phobia is called *agoraphobia* or situation phobia, e.g., a person is afraid to leave the house, or is fearful of open places, crowds, etc.

The differences in *content* of the phobic thought are also generally an indication of the nature and level of anxiety the client experiences and hence can be an important clue as to the predominant level of development at which the individual is functioning. Object phobias, having to do with specific people or things (such as animals) are a representation of the predominantly sexual anxiety the genital (neurotic) client is struggling with. The danger as percevied by the neurotic client has to do with *external* dangers impinging on the "I" (the ego). Agoraphobic type phobias, dealing as they do with situations, circumstances, environmental factors the client feels incapable of handling adequately, point up the anxiety around early separation and loss of the inconsistent mother figure the client has experienced. His feelings of inadequacy stem from *within* the self (the ego) in a situation, not from a differentiated object (person, thing) outside the self.[11]

The anxiety with which the character disordered client is struggling is predominantly around handling his own and others' aggression. In the character disordered client the unsatisfactory, primary relationship with mother has, in effect, conditioned subsequent ways of relating to others in a more severely incapacitating manner than in the neurotic client. The frustration, deprivation, primitive anger and discomfort in the primary relationship has left the character disordered individuals terribly vulnerable to their own anger and to the anger, slights, rejections of others. Hence they experience very great and pervasive problems in human relationships, lacking ego strengths and inner resources to sublimate their own basic drives and to cope with the demands of others and their environment.

In treating a neurotic client we would hope to help primarily with the struggle around *sexuality* (related to oedipal, castration anxiety). In treating

---

[11] *Ibid.*, 379. Dr. Weiss delineates agoraphobia thus: "All cases which should be called agoraphobia are characterized by two factors: a) an anxiety reaction to a danger which is consciously sensed as an internal one; b) the situation from which it ensues, namely by the patients leaving home and venturing some distance from it. This feeling of insecurity can, of course, also be experienced in other situations, but it is always provoked by the patients leaving a place of support and venturing some distance from it. All types of real agoraphobia are characterized by such a depletion of ego energy and/or the confidence in the ability to function in an adequate manner."

To further differentiate simple phobia from agoraphobia he states "Patients who have a phobic fear of dogs, of being struck by lightning, or of being run over, fear an *external* danger to an exaggerated and irrational degree whereas agoraphobic patients are actually exposed to a danger which is consciously perceived as an *internal* one. They fear to be trapped by a feeling of ill being which incapacitates them from functioning in a rational and integrated manner."

a character disordered client we would hope to help primarily with the struggle around *aggression, anger* (related to early mother object loss—early separation anxiety).

We all recognize that, just as there is a mixture and/or overlapping in levels of maturity and levels of functioning in human beings, so too we find a mixture, an overlapping of phobic symptoms (like all other symptoms) in people functioning on different levels of development. We do at times find agoraphobic (situation) phobias which have genital (neurotic) aspects to them. Also, although less often perhaps, we find object phobias which have pregenital aspects to them. We at times see, in the common night phobias and irrational daytime fears of young children admixtures of early separation anxiety, phallic symbols and elements of oedipal, castration (neurotic) anxiety. Much of this is age related and dependent on the amount of ego involved in manufacturing the symptoms. Anna Freud explains that the archaic fears of very young children which appear phobic-like are not true phobias, since they are not based on regression, conflict or displacement as are actual phobias.[12]

Case Examples

Three examples of casework treatment of agoraphobic (character disordered) clients follow:

Mrs. Lamb, a widowed 34-year-old mother of two latency-age children came to the agency several years ago. She was afraid to venture from her own home for fear of "losing control of myself." This lady had been chronically depressed since the death of her husband from cancer several years before. She suffered from what her physician described as spastic colitis. She experienced severe stomach cramps and frequent loose bowel movements, particularly in the morning when thinking of what life demands might be expected from her that day. Mrs. Lamb shared her parent's home with her alcoholic father and depressed, victimized

---

[12] Anna Freud (1965) *Normality and Pathology in Childhood,*161. "Before children develop the anxieties which are coordinate with the increasing structuralization of their personality, they pass through an earlier phase of anxiety which is distressing not only to them but also to the onlooker, due to its intensity. These anxieties are often called 'archaic' since their origin cannot be traced to any previous frightening experience but seems to be included in the innate disposition. Descriptively, they are fears of darkness, of loneliness, of strangers, of new and unaccustomed sights and situations, of thunder, sometimes of the wind, etc. Metapsychologically, they are not phobias since, unlike the phobias of the phallic phase, they are not based on regression or conflict or displacement. Instead they seem to express the immature ego's weakness and panic-like disorientation when faced with unknown impressions which cannot be mastered and assimilated. The archaic fears disappear in proportion to the developmental increase in the various ego functions such as memory, reality testing, secondary process functioning, intelligence, logic, etc., and especially with the decrease of projection and magical thinking."

mother, with whom Mrs. Lamb had a very dependent relationship. She was not able to tolerate the mother's leaving her to go to work and required mother to accompany her to agency appointments.

Mrs. Lamb complained of having "no self-confidence whatsoever." She was propelled into casework treatment by her morbid fears of "losing control"and doing harm to her children, plus the realization that when her children became of age and social security benefits stopped, she would have to leave home and work to support herself.

Mrs. Lamb at first could not admit to having negative feelings toward anyone except herself. Slowly she developed a trusting relationship to me, began to talk of irritations with others, feelings of slights and rejections from others, and later the feeling of not being wanted or loved by her parents as a child. Slowly in treatment, as she dealt with her angry feelings and her current everyday life, she began to venture out into the neighborhood, then further from home. She bought another home, although her parents continued to live with her; she also established firm friendships with several neighbor women, and finally took a part-time clerical job. Subsequently she accepted full-time employment, where she often worked in the office alone. Mrs. Lamb even bought her own car, took driving lessons and admitted that she was "beginning to have a little self-confidence." She became much less dependent on her mother. In fact, her relatives began to turn to Mrs. Lamb in times of trouble. She could allow her two children to grow up more independently and lead their own lives. What apparently helped Mrs. Lamb most in counseling was the working on her angry feelings in current day-to-day living. At one time this lady's dream was to "have a trailer and travel where I can take my home along wherever I go." She has settled for a more conventional way of life, using her abilities to support herself and get more gratification from her life with a marked diminution of her agoraphobic anxieties; she became almost free of physical symptoms, was much less depressed, and looked to the future with hope.

Mr. and Mrs. Taylor, parents of four latency- and adolescent-age children, in their early forties, were referred to the agency by a private psychiatrist as he believed that theirs was a family problem rather than a psychiatric problem. In addition, they realistically could not afford private treatment. When first seen they could admit to "no problems between us, no anger, we get along just fine." They said that all of their trouble was around management of their eldest,17-year-old daughter who had a serious identity problem and severe school phobia. However, the anger in their voices when speaking with, and of each other, the bitter tone and caustic comments they accepted as common conversation, demonstrated long-standing, unresolved conflict.

Mrs. Taylor had had several psychiatric hospitalizations for "depressive reaction." She had numerous psychosomatic complaints, chiefly hypertension and bronchial trouble. In the initial stage of treatment I saw the total family for six interviews at which point Mrs. Taylor became very anxious, had trouble getting to the office and her long-standing fears under stress of leaving the house, anxiety attacks when attending church, fears about mixing with friends and relatives came to the fore.

I switched from family interviews to joint interviews with the parents and focused on their reciprocal anger, disappointments and hurt with each other. Mrs. Taylor later admitted she got upset with the family interviews because she believed that her husband and children would soon be getting around to talking about her, telling about how "sick and complaining I am." Prior to this the children and Mrs. Taylor had all focused their complaints on the rigid, anally-oriented father who inconsistently provided whatever limits and controls the family had.

Mr. and Mrs. Taylor were able to talk with each other about deeply ingrained, ambivalent feelings they had toward each other prior to marriage. They also concluded that Mrs. Taylor's pregnancy with their "problem child" when they married may have something to do with their difficulties in managing this adolescent.

Now whenever Mrs. Taylor has a recurrence of her agoraphobic fears we talk about *what she has been angry about and with whom currently.* This way of dealing with her current anger at the resurgence of her fears invariably diminishes the agoraphobic anxiety and allows Mrs. Taylor and her husband to continue working on their feelings and considering how better to manage themselves and their children.

Mrs. Ford, a 39-year-old mother of four children ages 6 through 18, came to the agency with her husband because of their concern over 7-year-old daughter's trouble in getting to school. This couple readily admitted both had similar trouble in leaving home for school as children. After several joint appointments, Mr. Ford bowed out of counseling on the pretext of his job commitments. I believed that he simply could not tolerate looking at or working on problems in his children or in himself. Since he was functioning better in getting to work than he had at times in the past, I decided to accept this arrangement.

Mrs. Ford then brought the problemed 7-year-old and a middle adolescent daughter in with her for several appointments. After several of these partial family interviews, the communication problems quickly improved between mother and these two children. Mrs. Ford realized that she did not have to have all the answers for everything her children might bring to her. Previously, out of her anxiety she would say, "don't worry," or attempt to answer their questions, some of which were simply unanswerable. She realized that the children did not so much want answers, but rather wanted their mother's understanding and acceptance of their feelings and concerns as individuals.

As Mrs. Ford talked about her long-term depression which started before the 7-year-old was conceived, as she revealed her tremendously ambivalent relationship with her alcoholic mother and her feelings of disappointment and anger with husband for his inability to give, subsequently she was able to set more reasonable limits with and convey more realistic expectations toward her husband instead of accepting his utter dependence and lack of responsibility. In the subsequent school year the 7-year-old daughter showed no ambivalence about going to school; the undifferentiated ego tie between this daughter and Mrs. Ford diminished greatly. Mother's anxieties about her own inadequacy, her former isolation at home and retiring to bed with somatic complaints when upset decreased. After a two-month break in casework treatment, Mrs. Ford returned to the agency, and I believe is about to enter a new stage and level in treatment. She now wants to work on her own problems; previously she always presented the problems of others. Mrs. Ford wants to consider how she can deal with "a feeling of unfulfillment, of emptiness within me." Presently, she states a two-fold problem: (a) how I can effect more mature, adult social relationships and share them with my husband; (b) how I can modify a problem of lack of sexual enjoyment which relates in part to resentment toward my husband.

Common Pitfalls in Treatment

I would like to mention two common pitfalls in treatment of phobic symptomed clients. These pitfalls are by no means limited to the treatment of only this category of client, but are perhaps more salient because clients with phobic symptoms often appear more genital, better put together than they really are.

1. If the worker mistakenly treats these clients as operating on the neurotic level of development, he may be tempted to move too quickly into areas of great anxiety. The worker may move precipitously into the matter of their angry feelings or their conflicts about sexuality. The result of this commonly is that the clients break contact. They simply do not possess the ego strengths to deal with such material and their related feelings until a strong, viable relationship with the worker has been established and considerable ego strengthening has already taken place.

2. Some clients, sensing that the worker wants to hear about certain aspects of their lives, e.g., genital problems, will "play the psychiatry game." In other words, the clients will talk endlessly of their difficulties, not really working in a manner to modify or resolve these conflicts but rather to give the worker what they think he wants to hear, to please the worker and keep the relationship with the worker. This so-called "treatment" plays into the dependency needs of the client and is of little value to the client for improving his life.

Summary

To the extent that we can adapt our psychoanalytic knowledge of human growth and development to accurate, differential diagnosis and treatment of pregenital (character disordered) clients, we will meet one of the greatest challenges we face today—the effective treatment of character disordered individuals and families. On the basis of my experience at the Cleveland Family Service, a number of such clients present agoraphobic symptoms. In spite of the neurotic flavor of their symptoms, these clients for the most part are functioning on pregenital (character disordered) levels rather than on a genital (neurotic) level of development. I believe that the phobic *object* and *content,* considered in the context of the clients' overall functioning, can provide very helpful clues as to the level of their problem and hence can offer direction for the focus, level, techniques, and goals of their casework treatment.

DRUG USE DISORDERS

CHAPTER 17

Counseling Recovering Alcoholics

Jon Weinberg

The magnitude of the problem of alcoholism—which afflicts about 5 percent of the population over 15 years of age—is gradually coming to the attention of the public. In general, those in the helping professions have contributed relatively little toward effective intervention in the problem, primarily because their training has not provided a basic understanding of alcoholism.

This article focuses on treating recovering alcoholics—those who recognize their illness, have stopped drinking because they realized the central role it was playing in their difficulties, are currently sober, and intend to maintain sobriety. The term "recovering" is used instead of the more typical "recovered" to stress the chronic nature of the disorder and the patient's eternal susceptibility to relapse.

Many sober alcoholics do not seek counseling because, when their illness is arrested, they return to their premorbid level of adjustment, in which they were reasonably healthy. Others do not seek it because they are successfully following a program of recovery such as Alcoholics Anonymous (AA), which has a strong mental health component. Some who need counseling avoid it. They believe—often with considerable justification—that their potential counselor might not be knowledgeable about alcoholism and might even do them more harm than good.

However, a considerable number of alcoholics do seek counseling after attaining sobriety, and some stop drinking during treatment. The suggestions for counseling given in this article are designed to make professional

Reprinted from *Social Work*, Vol. 18, No. 4 (July, 1973), pp.84–93, with permission from the author and the National Association of Social Workers.

social workers more aware of the special problems of the recovering alcoholic, to help them avoid common pitfalls (such as identifying alcoholism as secondary or symptomatic, rather than the primary disorder), and to point out techniques and attitudes that have proved effective.

Family Involvement

Alcoholism has usually been described as a family illness. This does not imply, as many believe, that the spouse is in some way responsible for the alcoholism. Rather, it means that other family members, especially the wife or husband, are caught up in the pathological processes of the alcoholic's illness in such a way as to develop parallel emotional and/or behavioral problems. Successful treatment for the recovering alcoholic often hinges on involving the spouse effectively in the counseling process.[1]

It is obviously preferable to involve the spouse directly—through joint counseling interviews, for example—but this is not always possible.When it is not, the counselor, with the client's knowledge, is strongly advised to maintain at least occasional telephone contact with the spouse. Self-delusion, or at least marked rationalization, which develops along with the more visible aspects of the illness, is a cardinal feature of alcoholism. Thus it is virtually imperative for the counselor to have an independent source of information about the client's behavior outside the interview situation. The client may be reporting sobriety when he has been drinking; or he may indicate that everything is rosy at home when he has actually been moody and irritable, perhaps getting close to a slip. Without independent information, the counselor may be falsely lulled into a feeling of optimism, which would be followed by resentment ("I was conned") if ultimately disastrous events occurred as a complete surprise. Counselors whose values make them rankle at such "prying" into the client's life beyond the interview may be more successful with nonalcoholics.

One problem frequently encountered in the early phases of recovery is the disappointment or resentment stemming from unrealistic expectations. The alcoholic often expects the family to greet his sobriety with the utmost enthusiasm and gratitude. Unfortunately, the family has been previously conditioned by a thousand broken promises, and may be skeptical or distrustful rather than thrilled. The alcoholic in turn feels let down or angry. Similarly, the family may expect the sober alcoholic to begin functioning at full capacity, to "make up for lost time"; the reality often is a gradual recovery from the physical and psychological ravages of the illness. The alcoholic is taught in recovery programs such as AA to put sobriety ahead of everything, including his family. This may necessitate

---

[1] *See* John F. Mueller, "Casework with the Family of the Alcoholic," *Social Work,* 17 (September 1972), pp. 79–84.

frequent attendance at AA meetings, avoidance of overwork, and other therapeutic measures. The family may not believe that these activities are vital to recovery. The counselor's role is to help the alcoholic and his family understand and accept the feelings each has, and educate them regarding appropriate expectations, always emphasizing the patience both sides must have to deal with a serious illness that was years in the making.

A special caveat is in order with respect to women alcoholics who are married. Many husbands of recovering alcoholics deal with the problem of alcoholism largely by denial, unlike most wives of alcoholics, who more typically try sincerely to be cooperative and understanding. Although the husbands may acknowledge the improved behavioral functioning in their wives, they often resist the use of the alcoholic label or only pay lip service to it. A man may consider his wife's alcoholism a blow to his pride, and if he is a heavy drinker, her abstinence may be a threat. The increasing self-confidence and independence that is likely to accompany her lengthening sobriety often poses an additional threat.

The counselor should attend closely to such factors, working directly with the husband when possible. Since the husband of an alcoholic seldom makes himself available to the counselor, the wife should be helped, as far as possible, to avoid feeling discouraged or sabotaged by the lack of understanding and support. She is more likely to have to depend on herself and other sober alcoholics for the reinforcement needed to maintain recovery.

The Fallacy of Reasons

Both the genesis of alcoholism and its optimal solution are extremely controversial issues. Most people in the helping professions (and the public at large) have a strong bias toward the view that alcoholism is psychogenic and that its solution primarily involves unraveling the presumed psychological roots of the disease.

The author's position, by contrast, is that intrapsychic factors alone do not account for alcoholism and that the search for its psychological origins cannot provide an appropriate or effective solution. Further, he believes that, with some exceptions, alcoholics have a genuine illness with biological and cultural as well as psychological factors in the etiology. An enormous amount of evidence has accumulated from research, which unequivocally contradicts the notion of an "alcoholic personality," but many mental health professionals cling tenaciously to this myth.[2]

The view that alcoholism is a complex, chronic disorder without an

---

[2] *See,* for example, Edwin H. Sutherland et al., "Personality Traits and the Alcoholic: A Critique of Existing Studies," *Quarterly Journal of Studies on Alcohol,* 11 (1950), pp. 547–561; and L. Syme, "Personality Characteristics and the Alcoholic: A Critique of Present Studies," *Quarterly Journal of Studies on Alcohol,* 18 (1957), pp. 288–302.

established etiology has several implications. The counselor should remember that a great many disorders are successfully treated even though the etiology is obscure. What does successful treatment involve? What are the priorities? Sobriety—not simply healthy psychological functioning—must be given primary consideration because it seems that an abnormal reaction to alcohol is a life time proposition for the vast majority of alcoholics. The evidence at present suggests that no matter how well psychologically alcoholics may become, few can ever return to social drinking.[3]

Although the causes of alcoholism have not been established, the counselor can profitably examine the reasons for drinking, about which more is known. The reasons for drinking are not equivalent to the reasons for alcoholism; they do not explain alcoholism, nor are they necessarily abnormal in any way. In fact, virtually all the reasons why alcoholics drink are the same as the reasons why many nonalcoholics drink at times.

The counselor should become familiar with these reasons so that he can help the recovering alcoholic be on guard for the stimulus cues that are likely to precipitate a response of alcohol or other drug use. In other words, the counselor can forewarn the recovering alcoholic of what he can anticipate and can point out alternative responses and guide him toward them, thus offering constructive help in avoiding relapses. For example, both alcoholics and nonalcoholics may drink to become more relaxed and voluble at a large social function. In recovery, the counselor can help the alcoholic by teaching him how to be socially comfortable at a party without using chemical aids. Similarly, having a few drinks to relieve tension after a hard day at work is a habit the culture generally condones, but alcoholics in recovery must learn other strategies for unwinding.

It is important to note that, as the examples demonstrate, the recovering alcoholic must strive for superior, not average, emotional adjustment because in our society the average person at times uses alcohol and other drugs instead of internal coping mechanisms. This is a luxury the sober alcoholic cannot afford.

Alibis and Antabuse

A cardinal feature of alcoholism is the alibi system that the alcoholic must develop to maintain the addiction. That is, a person must become delusional in the sense of denying reality and blaming factors outside himself for the terrible problems actually produced by the drinking; otherwise, he

[3] *See*, for example, R. E. Reinert and W. T. Bowen, "Social Drinking Following Treatment for Alcoholism," *Menninger Clinic Bulletin*, 32 (1968), pp. 280–290.

would be forced to give up the chemical—hardly the solution an alcoholic prefers. However, the alibi system does not automatically fade away with sobriety. Since most alcoholics stop drinking under great pressure by their families, their employers, or the courts, or under the duress of some situation that has precipitated a crisis, they may still fail to perceive reality and instead blame their problem on their "rotten spouse," their "bigoted boss," or the unfair judicial system.

A person with such delusions, although reluctantly sober, is not yet a recovering alcoholic because he has not recognized his illness as the source of his difficulties. The counselor should treat such a person essentially the same as he treats a practicing alcoholic—that is, teach him about the illness and help him to see reality in terms of the harmful consequences of his drinking.

The alibi problem also occurs with those who are in recovery and even with those who have long been sober. This is called "stinking thinking" in AA terms, and counselors should be aware of some of the many forms it may take. These include:

1. Minimizing retrospectively the harmful consequences of drinking: "I was never that bad."
2. Attributing alcoholism to factors no longer present, thus implying that the illness may have waned: "That job I had would make anybody an alcoholic."
3. Suggesting that a beverage with a lower alcoholic content will be safe: "A little wine with dinner won't hurt me, and besides my husband will be happier if I join him."
4. Showing self-pity: "Nobody understands how rough it is for me."
5. Clinging to resentments or blaming others: "Those kids of mine had just better straighten out, and my wife too."
6. Disparaging or avoiding his AA group: "Those people at AA are really hypocrites. Anyhow, I can't go Monday nights during football season."

These examples of the resurgence of the alibi system are a signal that relapse may be lurking around the corner. It is critically important that the counselor not only avoid reinforcing these often seductively plausible rationalizations, but also make a direct, persistent attempt to bring the person's thinking back to reality. This may require a combination of forceful confrontation and diplomatic delicacy that will tax the counselor's ingenuity. The counselor must remind the client of the nature of his illness and show him that his thinking in alibis is preparing him for drinking again. At the same time, the counselor has to maintain an atmosphere of acceptance that will encourage the client to continue the counseling process.

A special word is in order about clients who are on Antabuse (disulfiram), an inexpensive deterrent drug taken daily that causes an extremely unpleasant physical effect when any alcohol is ingested. In general, the counselor should consider highly suspect any decision that the client makes on his own to discontinue this medication. The client may give an extremely plausible reason—such as ''I am doing so well now, I just don't need it''—but in most cases he is planning to drink even though he is not aware of it.

The counselor should try to persuade the client to delay his action for an arbitrary period, perhaps two or three months, and then the decision can be jointly reconsidered. If he insists on discontinuing the drug, the counselor can explain the dangers of the unconscious alibi system, but should not be surprised if the client relapses before the next counseling session.

Routine and Rest

The collective experiences of alcoholics—and of those who work with them regularly—have yielded a number of commonsense conclusions that few professional counselors are aware of.[4] These may sound trivial, but they often spell the difference between maintaining sobriety and relapsing, especially in the first year or two of recovery, and for many even far beyond that.

A primary point is related to changes of routine. It is best for the recovering alcoholic to develop a stabilized life routine, and most do so. A drinking problem arises when something unusual or different occurs. Two important examples are business trips out of town and any type of vacation, from a weekend at a nearby resort to two or more weeks far away.

Frequently environmental changes seem to awaken a desire for drinking, and the counselor should discuss the risks in advance with the client. Similarly, the client should be prepared for an inclination to drink whenever a change in job, a move to a different neighborhood or town, or some other important shift in scenery or routine is impending. The counselor should make certain that clients who are in AA are informed about meetings in places they will be visiting while away from home, and attendance should be strongly encouraged.

Another important caution involves rest. It is fairly typical for the recovering alcoholic to be an unusually hard worker. In some instances, in his zeal to make up for lost time, he tackles more than he is physically capable of, with resultant fatigue and a greatly increased risk of relapse. The counselor should generally advise a client to forget trying to do two taxing jobs even if he is debt ridden. He can instead pay off the creditors

---

[4] See, for example, Elizabeth D. Whitney, *Living with Alcoholism* (Boston: Beacon Press, 1968).

more slowly. Or the housewife and mother of five might well be counseled to leave the kitchen floor for another day instead of laboring until midnight. Naturally, the rest of the family should be helped to understand the necessity for putting the alcoholic's sobriety first.

Flare-ups and Flashbacks

The early phases of recovery from alcoholism involve a complex physiological readjustment of the organism to an unaccustomed state—a state of complete freedom from ethyl alcohol. A variety of medically significant laboratory findings are typically noted immediately after withdrawal, but within several weeks such conditions generally return to normal. Clinical observation suggests that a physiological rather than an environmental hypothesis better accounts for sporadic abnormalities in psychological state that some alcoholics experience during recovery.[5] These abnormal states, which may be called flare-ups, typically include general irritability, tension, and/or depression. Their cardinal characteristic is a complete lack of any reasonable psychological explanation. On the contrary, they occur with fairly sudden onset in spite of the most favorable environmental circumstances.

A further diagnostic clue—which favors a physiological etiology—is the tendency for such states to occur for most people at specific time spans during recovery. Flare-ups most frequently occur from the fifth to the seventh week, from the fifth to the seventh month, and from the eleventh to the thirteenth month of the recovery period, but there are wide individual variations. They usually pass within a few days.

The counselor should be aware of this phenomenon in order to warn clients and reassure them by stressing the transitory nature of flare-ups. Clients will otherwise feel bewildered and discouraged, since their efforts to recover seem to be sabotaged, and relapse is a threat. The wise counselor will not only avoid compounding the problem by insisting on a search for psychogenic explanations, but will explain the flare-ups before they arise.

Recovering alcoholics often have anxiety dreams in which they are drinking. Or, despite not drinking, they may wake up with a hangover feeling, especially after a party. Or they may experience in other episodes the kinds of feelings formerly elicited by drinking. All these phenomena may be conveniently labeled flashbacks. Again, the counselor needs to reassure the client about the normality of the occurrence, carefully avoiding psychodynamic speculations.

[5] *See,* for example, J. Milam, *The Emergent Comprehensive Concept of Alcoholism* (Seattle, Wash.: Alcoholism Center Associates Press, 1972).

Humility

A pervasive goal in most psychological counseling is enhancing the client's self-esteem, which is nearly always low—and alcoholics are certainly no exception. Counseling the recovering alcoholic-dependent person does, however, introduce an apparent paradox with regard to ego-building. For successful recovery, both self-confidence and humility must be sought. A comprehensive understanding of alcoholism is needed to appreciate fully the critical importance of humility, but a brief rationale may be helpful.

In his illness the addicted person becomes completely self-centered and even grandiose. He believes he can manage his life if others do not interfere. Usually recovery can begin only after his life has begun to crumble in one or more ways and he has finally abandoned the delusion that he can manage everything. Once in recovery, he must continue to acknowledge that a host of people, events, and conditions influence what happens in his life.

Failure to attain and retain this humble perspective of his power to control his own life usually leads to a return to what AA calls "the big I," or the grandiose idea that one has total control. This is quickly generalized to the use of alcohol or other drugs—which of course "I" can manage—and the result is relapse. Although some alcoholics, by single-minded involvement with AA, do seem to combine grandiosity and sobriety successfully, this is unlikely to occur among clients who seek counseling.

In practice, the counselor should have little difficulty in directing the alcoholic client toward both self-esteem and humility. He works to build self-esteem by helping the client to accept himself as a worthwhile person, recognize his assets, set reasonable goals.

The counselor works to develop humility by emphasizing recognition of reality. He may point out examples illustrating that people do not fully control outcomes in their lives:

1. An executive intends to be on time for an appointment but a traffic snarl makes him an hour late.
2. A father means to take his family on a picnic but thunderstorms upset the plan.
3. A student studies hard for a test but an attack of flu impairs her performance.

Above all, the alcoholic cannot control the outcome of his drinking. His illness renders him as powerless over the effects of alcohol as the diabetic is over the effects of excess sugar.

Morality

Counselors are usually well aware that their own values and attitudes influence the way they interact with their clients. Experiences derived from counseling alcoholics suggest that moral values are especially significant to this population. The great majority of sober alcoholics seem to have traditional, often somewhat rigid, moral values, even though the active stages of the illness have brought about the temporary deterioration of such values.

The most effective counseling strategy for alcoholics is to reinforce behavior consistent with their conventional values, unless these are demonstrably self-defeating and therefore desirable to modify. The counselor should recommend that they avoid behavior contrary to their values because it is highly probable that even relatively low levels of guilt may precipitate a relapse into drinking. While other types of clients may be quite willing to suffer mild or moderate degrees of guilt in order to reap the benefits of "immoral" behavior—and may occasionally drink to relieve guilt without getting into serious trouble—the recovering alcoholic should be encouraged to live up to his own values scrupulously.

The two most common problem areas are honesty and sex. Dishonesty or cheating, whether in job applications, income taxes, interpersonal behavior, or other aspects of life, poses a real hazard to recovery. Even when signs of guilt are not immediately evident, guilt feelings, often unrecognized, tend to grow and eventually erupt in the form of relapse. With regard to sex, the counselor should adopt a highly conservative stance. Any nonmarital sex relations contrary to the values of recovering alcoholics carry an enormous risk. If both partners in a relationship that is counter to their values are chemically dependent, a joint relapse is a near certainty.

In addition to the guilt component, many alcoholics (especially women and homosexuals) have developed a strong association between "illicit" sex and a state of intoxication. Engaging in the former will be likely to awaken a craving for the latter, with disastrous results. Although he may have a long-range counseling goal of helping the client adopt new values or of breaking up old behavioral associations, the counselor must focus primarily on steering the alcoholic toward keeping sober. This means the client has to move with the utmost caution in the area of morality.

Relapses

Because alcoholism is a chronic disease, its victims are subject to relapse throughout their lives. Some counselors may believe that a cure is possible, but the majority accept the fact that sobriety for any length of time is no insurance against a return to the destructive consequences of drinking. Most alcoholics do in fact experience one or more relapses during the recovery process, especially in the first two years. Disastrous slips after twenty years or more of sobriety are by no means unknown.

The attitudes and actions of the counselor may be critically important when his alcoholic client has a relapse. A major hazard is that the counselor may reject the client, overtly or covertly. Since most social workers intellectually accept the chronic nature of the disorder, rejection probably originates in latent moralistic attitudes toward alcoholism. Or a counselor's rejection of an alcoholic may be derived, at least in part, from a sense of inadequacy because of the client's apparent failure to benefit from counseling.

To ascertain his real feelings about alcoholics, the social worker might ask himself the following questions:

- How do I react when clients with other types of chronic problems take a turn for the worse?
- Do I get angry, for example, at a chronic schizophrenic who stops his medication and must be rehospitalized?
- Do I condemn the obese client who departs from his prescribed diet?
- Do I denounce the borderline student who fails to adhere to the agreed-upon study schedule?

If the answer to these questions is yes, then the counselor should look at his own self-concept in relation to his professional role. If, however, he does not feel angry and rejecting toward some types of clients, but does toward the relapsing alcoholic, he has yielded to the entrenched cultural attitude of judging his client as morally inferior and thus unworthy or unmotivated.

It is worth remembering that our society generally stacks the deck in favor of relapse. Although the alcoholic's sobriety initially delights the family and most other people important in his life, they tend after a time to assume that the problem has ended, that the person is cured. Sooner or later well-intentioned but uninformed friends and relatives will encourage or even pressure recovering alcoholics to try drinking "like gentlemen or ladies" now that they have "reformed." The power of social conformity may jeopardize recovery as much or more than the internal psychological stresses on which most counselors focus.

The counselor's role when relapse occurs is to help interrupt the drinking if he has an opportunity to do so. He may assist by advising the family to take forcible action, since the client is not likely to be available to him. He should also avoid condemnatory judgments when the client returns and help the client examine the probable causes of the relapse with an eye toward future prevention.

Alcoholics Anonymous

Professionals typically have mixed feelings about AA. On the one hand, nearly everyone acknowledges the superior effectiveness of AA in comparison with professional mental health treatment for alcoholics.[6] On the other hand, for varying reasons, counselors tend to have negative feelings or at least serious reservations about the AA approach. Some feel it is too religious. Some suggest that it involves too much dependence or rigidity. Others object to the zealous or smug attitudes of some AA members.

The author believes that AA offers an outstanding program, both for recovery from alcoholism and for general emotional adjustment which those counseling the alcoholic should strongly endorse. Careful study of the Twelve Steps of AA reveals the following major components, telescoped and grouped for the sake of brevity.[7] In the first three steps, the alcoholic acknowledges the crux of his problem and commits himself to the necessary solution. In the next four steps, he takes an honest look at himself, shares this information with a special person, and works to modify his behavioral deficiencies. Through the succeeding four steps, he continues to scrutinize himself honestly and humbly, trying to follow a virtuous path—that is, behaving sensibly toward his fellow man. Finally, in the last step, he assists others by teaching them what he has learned.

Individuals rigorously applying these principles may reap rich benefits, not only in sobriety, but in a highly satisfying emotional life and rewarding relationships with others. Al-Anon and Neurotics Anonymous are self-help organizations for those who are not chemically dependent on alcohol. They utilize the identical program because of its established effectiveness.

In addition to the twelve-step program, AA provides for the alcoholic a fellowship that offers immediate and complete empathic acceptance to individuals who have been widely rejected and who have come to despise themselves. This is of critical importance to many in the initial phases of recovery. Furthermore, AA groups represent virtually the only social subculture that assures permanent positive reinforcement of lifetime abstinence, and they are immediately available to replace the former "drinking buddies."

As for the common objection that AA is too religious, it should be noted that the program is spiritual but not religious in the sense of being tied to organized religion or the tenets of any particular faith. Agnostics and atheists are free to interpret the program in ways acceptable to their values.

Then there is the criticism that AA is too restrictive and rigid. AA has no eligibility requirement except a sincere desire to be sober. However, those trying to follow the program should adhere to it closely for the same

[6] *See,* for example, James C. Coleman, *Abnormal Psychology and Modern Life* (Glenview, Ill.: Scott Foresman & Co., 1972), p. 421.

[7] For a fuller explanation of the AA program and the common objections to it, *see* Jon R. Weinberg, "Alcoholics Anonymous: An Interpretation for the Professional." (Mimeographed by the author, 1972.)

reason a diabetic should scrupulously follow his diet-insulin regime. If that is rigidity,the author endorses it.

Smugness? Some individual AA members may be smug, just as some ex-smokers are. And some are zealous, just as some Democrats, abortion advocates, and ecology enthusiasts are. People tend to take notice of the vocal minority—in AA as in any group—and forget that most of the half million AA members are living as productively and unobtrusively as anyone else.

The author believes the principal points about AA that the counselor should consider are the following:

1. The AA program should routinely be recommended even if the counselor does not fully understand it, simply because of its effectiveness. The client frequently resists, offers alibis, or otherwise tries to avoid becoming involved. As a rule, counselors should patiently persist in the advocacy rather than accept the alibis. Of course, it would not be necessary to advocate AA for someone who had never been in it, but had long been sober.

2. A referral to AA should be personal rather than general. Ideally the counselor should contact AA and arrange for the initial visit, rather than simply telling the client "Go to AA."

3. Clients should be asked to refrain from making a judgment about the program until after they have attended regularly for at least three months. Objections to a specific AA group may be valid and one change of group is often legitimate. After that, the counselor can assume that the client is resisting the program, and his alibi should not be supported.

4. If the client is already established in AA, the counselor should be wary of declining attendance and any other sign that the alcoholic is avoiding AA, since such avoidance is often a forerunner of relapse.

Other Psychoactive Drugs

The use of psychoactive medication for recovering alcoholics is an extremely controversial issue. The author's position is definitely a conservative one, based on the disastrous experiences of a great many recovering alcoholics. No doubt, some alcoholics have been able to use such drugs without harm. However, since what will happen in the individual case cannot be predicted, one must be thoroughly persuaded that the potential benefits outweigh the known risks.

Prescribing such drugs is obviously a medical decision, but counselors may need to take responsibility for advising alcoholic clients in regard to seeking or using certain kinds of drugs, because most physicians have had no relevant training in drug dependence and may have been misled by pharmaceutical houses about the risks of most of these medications.

The drugs of greatest risk are those chemically related to alcohol in that they act primarily as a depressant of the central nervous system. These drugs, which produce both physical and psychological cross-dependence, include all hypnotics and sedatives and nearly all minor tranquilizers.

Thus any sleeping pill and all the popular minor tranquilizers—regardless of the alleged safety from dependence promised by the manufacturer—pose a twofold hazard to the recovering alcoholic. Besides the obvious risk of substituting one chemical for another in a harmful fashion, a danger that is probably greater is often observed. Because the prescribed drug creates in the brain a state sufficiently similar to the state created by alcohol, it strongly awakens a desire for the drug of first choice, alcohol. Many alcoholics with years of sobriety have been innocently sentenced to instant relapse by a simple prescription.

In addition to the drugs chemically related to alcohol, all narcotic analgesics—including allegedly safe synthetic narcotics—should be avoided unless medically imperative. Over-the-counter medications intended to sedate or tranquilize are also risky, as are antihistamines and other cold medicines. For example, one of the most familiar nighttime cold medicines is 25 percent alcohol. Even trips to the dentist have been known to cause a relapse for alcoholics who were given a form of pain killer that resulted in a "high" feeling. The general rule of thumb to keep in mind is that drugs arousing strong pleasurable feelings or those paralleling the effect of alcohol should be taboo. It is irrelevant that the manufacturer or the prescribing physician may have given the client assurance that the drug is not hazardous; they do not fully understand chemical dependence.

Psychoactive medications that do not ordinarily generate problems for an alcoholic include all major tranquilizers and the antidepressants (excluding amphetamines and other pure stimulants). In some cases when counseling alone does not dispel marked symptomatic anxiety, it may be advisable to suggest that the client request small doeses of a major tranquilizer rather than the ubiquitous minor tranquilizers. If alcoholic clients who are using any of the foregoing drugs described as hazardous report no problems with them, the counselor should accept this as accurate only when counseling is manifesting satisfactory progress and when a knowledgeable person can certify the client's statement about his drug use and general progress.

Role of the Social Worker

The most important potential contribution that social workers might make in the treatment of alcoholism would be to move from intellectual recognition that alcoholism is a prevalent problem to direct application of appropriate helping strategies in clinical practice. First and foremost, social workers should systematically screen all adult clients, prior to launching into treatment of the presenting problem, to see whether they can rule out a diagnosis of alcoholism. The alcoholic will derive little or no benefit and much time will be wasted if his treatment focuses on secondary or interdependent individual, family, or marital problems.

When alcoholism is identified, the next task is to deal directly with it. This includes educating the client and his family about the illness, working toward an acceptance of the problem, and obtaining a commitment to helpful action.

The third task is to guide the client toward whatever action seems most appropriate. This may involve referral to a specialized treatment agency or self-help group, but generally counseling with the social worker should continue

Unhappily, social workers, like other professionals, are seldom trained to perform effectively the three tasks described. This deficiency can best be remedied by seeking competent remedial training from professionals and/or paraprofessionals who have the specialized knowledge required.

The author has conducted many such training sessions and has found that, in general, social workers are highly receptive to learning more about strategies for identifying and dealing with alcoholics. Gaining such practical knowledge should help break the vicious cycle that the professional untrained in this specialized field may experience: first, he feels inadequate to deal with alcoholism and is unreasonably pessimistic about it; then, he avoids or minimizes the problem when counseling the alcoholic; subsequently, he verifies his initial feelings (a self-fulfilling prophecy) as the treatment fails to help.

This paper has dealt mainly with the social worker's fourth task in treating the alcoholic: to understand the complexities of the recovery process in such a way as to enhance the effectiveness of psychotherapy for the sober alcoholic. As the social work profession begins to carry out the first three tasks more effectively, vastly increased opportunities will be presented for dealing with the fourth task. Ultimately, social workers may be pleasantly surprised to learn that treatment of the alcoholic, rather than being the one massive disappointment that many have supposed or found it to be, is actually one of the more gratifying social work experiences.

CHAPTER 18

New Ways of
Treating Addicts

Arthur D. Moffett, James D. Bruce,
and Diana Horvitz

"...One thing is certain. Without the willing cooperation of the addicts themselves in the treatment leading to a cure, you will get nowhere."[1]

Many social workers are not prepared for the responsibilities they are having to assume in the treatment of drug addiction. Senior social workers (those with a graduate degree in social work who have specialized training and experience) as well as junior social work counselors are performing most of the administrative functions and providing much of the treatment for drug-dependent persons. They are directing drug treatment programs, treating patients, and initiating research.

All this has come about because the focus of the addiction sciences has shifted from the field of criminal justice to that of mental health. This shift has led social workers, along with other mental health professionals and nonprofessionals, to become increasingly involved in the treatment of drug addicts.

In a recent statewide survey of all drug treatment facilities in Pennsylvania, the authors found that most of the personnel did not have the training and the experience to enable them to cope with the enormous tasks confronting them.[2] The ex-addict leadership was an exception to this—and this group, despite its importance in treatment, has its own particular problems caused by a lack of professionalism and sophistication.

Directors who had previously worked in other areas of social service were unfamiliar with the problems of treating the addict; they had to learn through on-the-job experience and, in many cases, were insecure and anxious. It is not surprising that social workers, in spite of direct experience and skill in handling a myriad of individual and social pathologies, are similarly handicapped in the treatment of drug addicts.

What was the educational background of the personnel in these facilities? The study revealed that 13 percent of the directors and 33 percent of the staff had a bachelor's degree in social work and considered themselves social work counselors. Other treatment and administrative personnel who share the responsibility for Pennsylvania's drug programs are drawn from medicine, psychiatry, psychology, education, the clergy, business, the community, and a large pool of ex-addicts.

Either from inability or a lack of interest schools of social work, along with medical schools and until recently law schools, have not provided courses that focus on the realities of dealing with addicts. Social work methods have lagged in developing techniques for working with drug-dependent patients. Casework, which relies on a traditional psychodynamic approach, is too often an inappropriate method for the drug user, who usually sees himself as a person with a drug problem but not a psychosocial problem. It would appear that most schools of social work are caught in the cross fire of conflicting social, medical, and legal definitions of the addiction problem and do not as yet know how to train students to be specialists in addiction. Such ambivalence is intensified by the constant emergence of new patterns of addiction that depart from the traditional criminal model of heroin addiction.[3]

Clearly there needs to be a redefinition of social work goals, particularly those of casework, and a few practical guidelines regarding the profession's dealings with addiction. Further, during the last several years, while addiction problems and the need for treatment have mushroomed, the professional social work literature has conspicuously lacked reports of experiences in treating drug addiction. Surely social workers are coming into contact with the addicted, but most are not writing about it. Why?

A Misdirected Skill?

It is likely that one reason why social workers are uneasy about communicating their experiences is that casework, which is the professional tool most often used with addicts, is inadequate to the task. Is it enough, as Richmond indicates, to consider the treatment of the drug addict only in terms of personality development, the approach to the individual, and the individual's relationship to his environment?[4] Professional concerns with the processes of adaptation, dynamic interaction, and the mediating functions of social workers in relating to individuals, groups, and the environment have created an overemphasis on psychotherapy. As Briar noted, "the image of the modern caseworker...is above all that of a therapist, which is to say that for the most part he performs only a therapeutic function."[5] Thus the caseworker, in his overemphasis on process to the neglect of problems, gives low priority to drugs and their use as the focal point of the abuser's life—the reason for which he seeks treatment and the thing he wants to talk about.

It may well be that the use of drugs is a symptom of life's crises and not the problem itself, that the drug culture represents an escape or protective mechanism, and that indeed drug abuse today is a leading manifestation of psychopathology, much as hysteria or alcoholism have frequently been indexes of emotional illness.[6] However, social workers should not equate the drug experience with a "way of running away from...painful feelings and...inability to cope adequately with life." Nor should they assume that the stimulation of dialogue about life, relationships, and significant issues can replace "the euphoria of drug use in...social encounters."[7] Nor will social workers find the answers to the problem of drug abuse by doing content analyses on the dreams of heroin addicts.[8] All these reactions and approaches to addiction—because they are not based on reality—might be called part of the game that is played by both social caseworkers and white middle-class well-educated abusers, who are motivated to give up drugs and hence tolerate some psychic probing.

On the other hand, many hard-core addicts and users will not be pushed into this therapeutic mold, because they are not motivated to stop their use of drugs. They derive great pleasure in the release from psychic tension that drugs provide. For them this seems to outweigh the negative consequences of drug use. It has been suggested that an addict's willingness or unwillingness to give up drugs is related to the presence or absence of satisfactions in his life.[9] But often addicts do not really want to discuss in depth *why* they want or need drugs. Instead, as the following paragraphs indicate, they show a need to talk about the experience itself and their highs and lows.

> One young addict reported that after experiencing his first heroin high he had exclaimed to himself: "Why didn't they tell me such wonderful feelings existed?" The addict can conceive of nothing in the real world that could produce a comparable feeling in him. A significant number of heroin addicts made the statement that unless the world could provide them with a feeling to compensate for the loss of the high, they would never be able to give up heroin. For this reason an addict usually scoffs when it is suggested that he search for substitute satisfactions.
>
> One explained: "The only time I feel normal is when I'm on drugs; I didn't realize how tense and depressed I was until I started using drugs." Another patient, struggling through his fifty-third straight day of barbiturate abstinence, telephoned his counselor to pour out the anguish and torment he felt in having to cope with his employer, his mother-in-law, and his wife. "I can't stand it," he complained. "I didn't realize what these pills meant to me. I'm holding the pills in my hand now and I feel I could kiss them." The addict is caught in a mammoth struggle. For the majority, escape from painful feelings was the most frequent motivating factor in drug dependency.[10]

Ten years ago, Brill warned that social workers in the area of drugs would have to relearn methods, develop a less intense casework, and sacrifice the role of psychotherapist for one of a strong helping figure.[11] In making these suggestions, Brill realized how important drugs are to the user. He believed that users may want to give up drugs at the same time that they cling to old patterns of escape.

Brill recognized that often there are psychodynamic explanations for drug abuse and that addicts tend to be immature, not socially oriented, and, in fact, in need of the casework approach. He cautioned that the traditional concept of casework should not be abandoned, but neither should it be adhered to too closely. "Frail egos" must be strengthened and "positive strivings created" without exposing the deeply rooted conflicts that addicts are often not prepared to face.[12] In particular, the worker must take into consideration the overwhelmingly powerful allure of drugs and realize that the resolution of inner conflicts does not necessarily free an addict from compulsion to take drugs. It is possible that the drug abuser, particularly the addict, does not seek treatment to curtail his commitment to drugs.

Perceptual Gap

The apparent gap between traditional treatment and the needs of addicts themselves is not limited to the social work profession. The precedent for this dichotomy was set by others in the helping professions, particularly in the field of medicine.

The theory that most addicts are not in treatment for their addiction is related to the observation that addicts generally seek treatment only when they are "down and out," i.e., when they are in financial distress, their drug supply is short, and their health has deteriorated. It has been said that addicts have applied to a treatment agency either because they have "hit bottom," are worn out from being on the run or from hustling money for drugs, have watched a close friend die of an overdose, or are in some other way in disequilibrium. Or else they have been caught by the law and have been offered an opportunity to come to the treatment agency as an alternative to going to jail.[13]

Inquiry into the nature of treatment, the attitudes of physicians, and the values and expectations of the addicts themselves points to perceptual differences regarding the nature of the problem and its treatment. Addicts, for whom imprisonment is often one of many routine experiences throughout life, have expectations that deviate from the reality of their experience. Physicians often view them as physically or mentally ill, while they see themselves as having one specific problem—drugs—and may even look to the physician as a source of supply rather than a source of cure. Professionals concerned with treatment may also have unrealistic expectations about the addict's ability to change his life-style. By projecting their middle-class values on the addict, they blot out the perceptual differences instead of using them to achieve a cure.

Unfortunately, little systematic research has been done to discover the attitudes of addicts toward the treatment process. Little has been done even to investigate the lifestyles, values, and moral precepts of the drug subculture to gather data that might be used as predictive measures of outcome. Grupp has stressed this relationship:

> ...the effectiveness of any narcotic control program demands that consideration be given to the experiences, characteristics and attitudes of those drug users whom the respective measures attempt to control or treat....The underlying rationale of all proposals for handling addicts is the assumption that we are manipulating or facilitating the manipulation of certain personal-social attributes as well as patterns of drug use. Of crucial importance to this process and the success of control-treatment procedures is the orientation—the attitudes toward the procedures—of persons subjected to them.[14]

Recent research to coordinate the thinking of addicts and professionals is of interest and deserves mention. Toll's study investigated the attitudes of fifty Swedish addicts who attempted to cure themselves of the use of drugs, analyzing their reasons for and the extent of their desire to be cured, their view of the future, their desire for further rehabilitation, and their observations about the drug scene.[15] Although she established no direct relationship between positive or negative attitudes and outcome, she found that the patient's replies were influenced by the severity of their addiction. It is interesting that the uncorrelated findings of this work indicate a high degree of posttreatment relapse (94 percent) and of drug use during the treatment period (almost 50 percent) as well as a less-than-enthusiastic response toward treatment and complaints of boredom.

Grupp used attitudes toward the narcotic control Nalline (an opiate antagonist used to detect the surreptitious use of drugs) as a means of identifying addicts most likely to benefit from traditional treatment.[16] The use of drugs later in life and the use of fewer drugs with no particular preference is related to a more receptive Nalline attitude, as are age, race, higher degrees of socialization, self-control, a good self-image, and the status of parolee rather than probationer. Conversely, Richman and Richman found that a positive attitude toward methadone maintenance treatment is related to a history of prior treatment, rather than to factors of age, sex, or race.[17] According to Stewart and Wadell, a high regard for traditional mores is characteristic of heroin addicts and patients on methadone; however, they have been unable to predict a profile of addict attitudes or make any clear prognosis from data other than psychological profiles.[18]

An analysis of attitudinal differences between the staff and the addict

population of one methadone maintenance program revealed greatly conflicting views.[19] The professional looks on the addict as an individual who
is mentally, and to a lesser degree, physically ill. He orients psychotherapeutic treatment to changing the addict's life-style and removing him from
the environment of the drug subculture. This view is at loggerheads with
the addict's notion that drugs, drug-craving, drug-getting, and battling
against relapse are his major preoccupations in life. Sixty-four percent of
the staff said that the molding of productive individuals was the primary
goal of the program. Less than half the patients (44 percent) expected to
"get off drugs" as a result of their treatment: others were there to "keep
from being sick," to "straighten out their lives," as a response to legal
pressure, or to obtain other help. In fact, 16 percent of the patients indicated a desire for the unrestricted use of drugs and many were taking tranquilizers and sedatives along with methadone. Perhaps it is naïve of
professionals to be aghast at the drug dependence of addicts in treatment
because, after all, methadone is an addictive drug and the treatment center
might be regarded as a drug subculture. One could argue that methadone
maintenance is a form of treatment which, by its very nature, perpetuates
a commitment to drugs.

Although both addicts and professionals liked methadone as a drug
and liked the treatment program, the dichotomy points to further need to
pinpoint perceptual differences as well as to find the similarities. For example, one of the findings of this study was that addicts, although they
did not perceive themselves as mentally ill to begin with, admitted to having gained self-knowledge and insight through their exposure to the psychiatric setting.[20]

Several other studies have attempted to identify significant interactions and attitudinal changes concerning the treatment process. Inquiry
into the values, attitudes, and opinions of the users of psychedelic drugs,
as opposed to the hard-core heroin subculture, has promoted the conclusion that physicians must reexamine their outdated convictions.[21] Crowther
and Pantleo have investigated the relationship between positive experiences in encounter groups and attitudes toward treatment programs and
staff members.[22] Glatt invited the opinions of the new wave of younger
cocaine and heroine addicts concerning their sharing common wards with
middle-aged barbiturate addicts and alcoholics.[23] Such questions as "Is it
preferable to treat addicts singly or in groups?" or "Is there danger in
treating pill-takers, 'smokers' and 'junkies' together?" were asked in an
effort to enlist the cooperation of young addicts.

The Medical Addict

In the past, the task of dealing with the true concerns of addicts has been
all but ignored in the effort to resocialize and treat them. In some cases,

the result has even been to feed their addictions. A case in point is the experience of Chinese opium addicts who were admitted to the U.S. Public Health Service Hospital in Lexington, Kentucky. These patients had histories of addiction related to their cultural milieu and their long-standing association with opiates. Their addiction, itself, was not a reason to visit the physician. If anything, the physician was a source of more drugs. Rather than a desire for detoxification, what led them to treatment was poor health or a lack of funds.[24]

Traditionally the physician has been an agent of addiction, providing and replenishing the patient's initial source of feeding an existing medical habit with one prescription after another. Thus the concept of the medical addict is well founded.[25] This may have been done for mercenary reasons, out of compassion for the addict, or, in times gone by, out of ignorance of the harmful effects of certain opiates or because of the absence of non-addictive pain-killing synthetics. The decrease in the availability of prescribed narcotics has shifted the addict-physician relationship to one of conflict and "mutually derogatory opinion."[26]

The pattern of addiction, characterized by middle-class middle-aged white medical addicts in nonurban areas, has certainly not disappeared. But it has been upstaged. In recent years there has emerged a criminal drug subculture made up of minority populations from urban slum areas. This phenomenon has further removed the physician from legal or quasi-legal drug involvement.[27] The criminal subculture in combination with "the cult of the needle" have taken on many of the functions once performed by the physician. They now provide the drug, administer it, and give verbal support to its use. Further, the addict subculture now transmits criminal skills and values, all geared to the illegal acquisition of "the stuff." Most recently, the psychedelic cult—a subculture of the subculture—has taken over these functions for those who choose the "softer" approach to addiction.

Nowhere is the division of attitude more obvious than in its echoes through the philosophies and goals of contemporary treatment. The "all I've got going for me is my addiction" rationalization of the addict or ex-addict is challenged by programs that seek to invalidate the old foundation, build a new one with a new life-style, and remove the addict from his old frame of reference.[28] Methadone maintenance programs represent a modification of this goal, since they attempt social rehabilitation without necessarily eliminating the addiction. Various approaches to treatment see their goal in terms of correcting individual character disorders that are aggravated by a detrimental environment, faulty socialization, and the availability of drugs. Another approach to treatment sees addiction as a social process that involves the individual who must free himself from it. Essentially, all types share the goal of trading a liability for an asset to the community.

Contributing to the mutual misunderstanding between addicts and treatment staff is the stereotype held by the general public about the chronically ill, physically wrecked addict and the disease and death that invariably result from drug overdose or withdrawal. To be sure, addicts die from a broader spectrum of diseases than do nonaddicted patients. The range, which includes overdose, infection, and malignancies, is well documented in the literature. Addicts and drug users seek the services of physicians to get drugs to alleviate physical conditions if not to get a cure. It is certainly true that the injection of a foreign substance into the body and the use of barbiturates, amphetamines, or hallucinogenic drugs may have an immediately debilitating effect on the patient.[29] However, death from withdrawal itself is a rare occurrence, and there is evidence that despite the high death rate of addicts, some do remain in good health. There is no evidence pointing to any major medical problem or syndrome associated with long-term use of opiates.[30]

Conclusions

The communication gap exists both in the medical and social work professions and indeed in all mental health professions. The following conclusions are directed toward social workers, but can be applied to all who deal with drug abusers.

The attempts to "change the man" or treat the addict as a sick individual are not bad in and of themselves because the profession must offer a more productive way to help the downtrodden and to comfort the sick. But first one must be sure that the man really is downtrodden and sick, even though he may not realize it. If one can determine how the addicts see themselves and attempt to deal with them through channels in which the perceptual gap is lessened, they may begin to seek treatment of their own volition.

For social workers—especially caseworkers—a first step may be to relinquish the notion that rehabilitation is synonymous with total abstinence from drugs and that the reliance on a chemical is incompatible with progress. The use of methadone maintenance and new forms of chemotherapy lend credence to this approach.

In working with the addict, limited goals seem to be the only feasible ones. It is important to view addiction as a chronic illness in which periodic abstinence, even for a few weeks or months, is considered a boon to a patient, family, and community. For most patients, total abstinence for extended periods may be a goal beyond realization.

Even if abstinence from drugs is established as a primary goal, it can rarely be achieved directly. If it occurs at all, it will come about through a series of stops and starts and allowances made for an indefinite number of relapses. One must recognize that addicts continually fall back on drugs in an effort to achieve some balance in their lives and to bolster their strength for meeting the strains of living and coping with social situations.[31]

In dealing with addicts, social workers might do well to part with some previously held stereotypes of the ideal client and the ideal client-worker relationship. These were based on assumptions that the client will be responsive, open, and agreeable and will keep his appointments. What is more than likely is that the drug user, to the chagrin of the workers, will not be or do any of these things.

The concept of modifying one's expectations and reaching out to the community and culture of the addict to minimize the gap in life-styles has a close parallel in the profession's current awareness of the need to lessen the racial gap.[32] The following description of differences between workers and clients because of race might just as well apply to drug use:

> Thus separated by race, money, education, social position, power, and lack of real knowledge of and feeling for the other's life experience, the white professional and black client come together. They face each other and are confronted with the necessity of doing something together. The reactions they may have to each other and to the situation in which they find themselves are the dynamics of the encounter with which they must cope in order to work together. In essence, both professionals and clients are what they are, based upon their past experiences and the society in which they live and interact. They do not know each other; they do not trust each other. Indeed, they most probably have many feelings about each other, themselves, and their respective positions which in reality impede the development of trust and concomitant mutual honesty.[33]

Another hint to be taken from the campaign to lessen racial obstacles is the need to minimize the psychiatric orientation that a large group of addicts are sick, have character disorders, or are at pregenital levels of development. If there is any truth to the statement that "the diagnosis of character disorder has become a new catchall term of opprobrium to be used along with other epithets as a weapon against the lower classes," social workers need not be among the guilty.[34]

Schools of social work, and indeed all professional schools, need to rethink the content of their training programs. Professional energies should be redirected from a preoccupation with the psyche to a consideration of tangible services that are grounded in sociocultural and epidemiological inquiry. Casework, group work, community organization, administration, and research all have a place in a new body of addiction specialists drawn from a multiplicity of disciplines. In this effort, social work will have to cooperate and ally itself with clinicians in medicine and psychology as well as ex-addict personnel with their unequaled expertise. Schools of social work and other training institutions will have to prepare their graduates to work with the nonprofessional and the ex-addict. Schools should also offer certification programs for the ex-addict who, with some professional coaching, is often an excellent worker. In addition to providing information about the epidemiology of drug abuse, community resources, and in-service training, schools of social work will have to train students to understand the dynamics of the addict's emotional and social behavior and certain facts about the use of chemical agents and their physiological effects. This must be done without allowing the social worker to drown his client in the depths of his psyche. There is much work to be done.

Notes and References

1. Anna-Ma Toll, "Case Study on the Attitudes of Drug Addicts to Treatment," *British Journal of Addiction*, 65 (August 1970), p. 158.
2. Freda Adler, Arthur Moffett, Frederick Glaser, John Ball, and Diana Horvitz, *The Treatment of Drug Abuse in Pennsylvania*. Report to the Department of Public Welfare, Commonwealth of Pennsylvania, October 1972. This study was one of the first of its kind in mental health research and involved actual site visits by a team of professionals to every drug treatment facility in Pennsylvania.
3. *See* Arthur D. Moffett and Carl D. Chambers, "The Hidden Addiction," *Social Work*, 15 (July 1970), pp. 54–59.
4. *See* Mary E. Richmond, *What Is Social Casework? An Introductory Description* (New York: Russell Sage Foundation, 1922), pp. 98–99.
5. Scott Briar, "The Casework Predicament," *Social Work*, 13 (January 1968), p. 7.
6. Leon Wurmser, "Discussion: Casework with a Troubled Teen-ager and Drug Abuser," *Social Casework*, 52 (November 1971), pp. 558–561.
7. Martha J. McLaney, "Casework with a Troubled Teen-ager and Drug Abuser," *Social Casework*, 52 (November 1971), pp. 553–558.
8. Maryanne Looney, "The Dreams of Heroin Addicts," *Social Work*, 17 (November 1972), pp. 23–28.
9. C. Andre St. Pierre, "Motivating the Drug Addict in Treatment," *Social Work*, 16 (January 1971), pp. 80–87.
10. Ibid., pp. 82–83.
11. "Rehabilitation in Drug Addiction: A Report of a Five-Year Community Experiment of the New York Demonstration Center," *Public Health Service Pamphlet* No. 13 (Washington, D.C.: U.S. Department of Health, Education & Welfare, 1964), pp. 8–30.
12. Ibid., p. 21.
13. Raymond Glasscote et al., *The Treatment of Drug Abuse: Programs, Problems, Prospects* (Washington, D.C.: Joint Information Service of the American Psychiatric Association and the National Association for Mental Health, 1972), p. 5.

14. Stanley E. Grupp, "Drug Users' Attitudes Toward the Nalline Test," *International Journal of Addiction*, 5 (December 1970), pp. 661–662.

15. Toll, op. cit.

16. Grupp, op. cit.

17. Edward L. Richman and Alex Richman, "Preference for Methadone Maintenance Among Applicants for Short-Term Detoxification Who Completed a Discharge Plan Questionnaire," in *Proceedings of the Fourth National Conference on Methadone Treatment* (New York: National Association for the Prevention of Addiction to Narcotics, 1972), pp. 137–139.

18. Gordon T. Stewart and Kathleen Wadell, "Attitudes and Behavior of Heroin Addicts and Patients on Methadone," in *Proceedings of the Fourth National Conference on Methadone Treatment*, 1972, pp. 141–144.

19. Arthur Moffett, Freda Adler, Frederick Glaser, and Diana Horvitz,"Methadone Maintenance," in William White, Jr., *North American Symposium on Drugs and Drug Abuse* (Philadelphia, Pa.: North American Publishing Co., 1974), pp. 160–171.

20. Ibid.

21. Victor Gioscia, "LSD Subculture Acidoxy vs. Orthodoxy," *American Journal of Orthopsychiatry*, 39 (April 1969), pp. 428–436.

22. Betty Crowther and Paul M. Pantleo, "Marathon Therapy and Changes in Attitude Toward Treatment and Behavior Ratings," *Mental Hygiene*, 55 (April 1971), pp. 165–170.

23. M. M. Glatt, "Group Therapy with Young Drug Addicts," *Nursing Times* (April 21, 1966), pp. 519–520.

24. John C. Ball and M. P. Lau, "The Chinese Opiate Narcotic Addict in the United States," *Social Forces*, 45 (September 1966), pp. 68–72.

25. John C. O'Donnell, *Narcotic Addicts in Kentucky*, Public Health Service Publication No. 1881 (Washington, D.C.: U.S. Department of Health, Education & Welfare, 1969).

26. John C. Ball, "Two Patterns of Narcotic Addiction in the United States," *Journal of Criminal Law, Criminology and Police Science*, 56 (June 1965), pp. 203–211.

27. O'Donnell, op. cit.

28. Glasscote et al., op. cit., p. 56.

29. Frederick B. Glaser, "Shazam! or the Medical Management of Complications of Non-Opiate Drug Abuse," *Pennsylvania Medicine*, 74 (March 1971), pp. 51–58.

30. John D. Sapira, Harry Penn, and John C. Ball, "Causes of Death Among Institutionalized Narcotic Addicts," John C. Ball and Carl D. Chambers, eds., *The Epidemiology of Opiate Addiction in the United States* (Springfield,Ill.: Charles C Thomas, 1970), pp. 251–262.

31. "Rehabilitation in Drug Addiction," p. 9.

32. *See* Leon Brill, "Three Approaches to the Casework Treatment of Narcotic Addicts," *Social Work*, 14 (April 1968), pp. 25–35; Alex Gitterman and Alice Shaeffer, "The White Professional and the Black Client," *Social Casework*, 53 (May

1972), pp. 280–291; and Evelyn Stiles, Susan Donner, Jean Giovannone, Elizabeth Lochte, and Rebecca Reetz, "Hear it Like it Is," *Social Casework*, 53 (May 1972), pp. 292–299.

33. Gitterman and Shaeffer, op. cit., pp. 281–282.

34. Brill, op. cit.

FACTITIOUS ILLNESS

CHAPTER 19

A Therapeutic Confrontation Approach to Treating Patients with Factitious Illness

Kenneth R. Wedel

Factitious illness has received attention in the medical literature for a number of years. Broadly defined, this diagnosis includes patients who, for a variety of little-understood reasons, simulate real patterns of illness and/or symptomatology suggesting real illness. The illness ranges in severity from the so-called "Munchausen's syndrome," a term applied to patients who chronically wander from hospital to hospital seeking admission by distorting their medical histories, to self-induced simulated disease or common malingering.

Petersdorf and Bennett have described the most commonly used methods of creating factitious fevers.[1] Patients may hold the thermometer next to a hot water bottle, steam pipe, light bulb, flame, and the like; shake it; or produce a higher reading by rubbing the teeth, gums, or anal sphincter. Another method is to substitute the thermometer offered by the nurse with one from a cache of thermometers that the patient has set at various readings. Patients have also been known to inject themselves with vaccines, toxoids, and pyrogenic substances to produce a real fever.

A comprehensive review of the literature on factitious illness has been made by Spiro, who found the psychiatric literature contained only three

---

[1] Robert G. Petersdorf and Ivan L. Bennett, "Factitious Fever," *Annals of Internal Medicine*, Vol. 46, No. 6 (June 1957), pp. 1039–1062.

Reprinted with permission of the National Association of Social Workers, from *Social Work*, Vol. 16, No. 2 (April 1971), pp. 69–73.

reports of factitious illness.[2] The medical literature, however, described thirty-eight cases with various presenting symptomatology. The behavior of these patients in the hospital was characterized by uncooperativeness and hostility. Following diagnosis of factitious illness, their most common reaction was to sign out of the hospital against advice. Only sixteen of the thirty-eight patients were seen by a psychiatrist, and generally the motivating factors for the illness were not discussed.

A central theme in the literature is the hostility of hospital staff toward the patient that is common when factitious illness is diagnosed, with immediate hospital discharge prompted by either the patient or the physician as the result. One approach to the control of serious factitious illness is the "blackbook"—a list of names kept in hospital emergency rooms to identify patients who chronically wander from hospital to hospital. English physicians have sometimes initiated legal action when all other methods have failed.[3] In general, the literature emphasizes both the waste of valuable medical resources and the human and economic loss to such patients and their families.[4]

The Study

Ten patients took part in the clinical study of fever of unknown origin conducted at the Clinical Center, National Institute of Allergy and Infectious Diseases, National Institutes of Health.[5] Seven of the patients were female and ranged in age from 16 to 41 years. The three male patients were much younger: two were 11 years old and the other was 13. Five of the patients worked in medically oriented occupations: three were registered nurses, one was a pharmacist, and one was a medical laboratory technician. Psychiatric diagnoses and social histories did not reveal any common characteristics among the patients, but five of them had recently experienced a death, tragic accident, or severe illness in the family. Follow-up data were available for five patients; of that group, four made a satisfactory readjustment, as measured by completion of recommended psychotherapy and freedom from factitious illness, and one patient refused to be seen by the consulting psychiatrist and left the hospital against medical advice when her factitious illness was verified. She later died under circumstances that suggested suicide.

[2] Herzl R. Spiro, "Chronic Factitious Illness," *Archives of General Psychiatry*, Vol. 18, No. 5 (May 1968), pp. 569–579.

[3] P. Blackwell, "Munchausen at Guy's," *Guy's Hospital Report*, Vol.114, No. 3 (1965), pp. 257–277.

[4] Joseph J. Bunim et al., "Factitious Diseases: Clinical Staff Conference at the National Institutes of Health," *Annals of Internal Medicine*, Vol. 48, No. 6 (June 1958), pp. 1328–1341; and Spiro, op. cit.

[5] The study began in 1960, and of the 175 patients seen to date, ten were found to have factitious illness.

At the Clinical Center it has been found that a multidisciplinary approach involving medicine, nursing, social work, and psychiatry is most successful in working with patients exhibiting factitious illness. Central to the approach is the recognition that factitious illness represents the patient's attempt to cope with emotional problems. Although the patient may not acknowledge or recognize that his problems are emotional, he has managed to convey his desperate need for help by placing himself in the hands of physicians and other hospital staff. An understanding response by the staff makes it possible for this disguised request to become more direct and opens the door to treatment planning.

Confrontation Process

The first step in the confrontation process is the search for organic disease. As organic causes for fever are ruled out, suspicion grows that the illness may be factitious. Clues that signal the possibility of factitious fever to the ward physician are the absence of laboratory data to substantiate fever and an unusual fever pattern. To determine whether the patient may be switching thermometers or manipulating them in order to produce a high reading, the nurse remains with the patient while his temperature is being taken. The serial numbers of thermometers also may be checked. A room search by the ward physician and head nurse has revealed substitute thermometers, unauthorized drugs and chemicals, and needles and syringes in some cases.

Following the verification of factitious illness, the ward physician requests a psychiatric evaluation. The psychiatrist is asked for (1) an analysis of the patient's personality dynamics together with a diagnostic impression, and (2) advice and assistance when the patient is confronted with his factitious illness. Particular attention is paid to any contraindications to confrontation, such as the risk of suicidal or psychotic behavior.

After the psychiatric evaluation is completed, a meeting of the patient, senior staff physician, ward physician, head nurse, social worker, and psychiatrist is held so that the senior staff physician (who has primary responsibility for the patient) can confront the patient with the factitious nature of his illness. The patient is given an opportunity to react after the confrontation. Frequently his reaction will be one of defensive anger, which is usually directed at the confronter, i.e., the senior staff physician, who serves as a lightning rod for the patient's emotions. Because the patient's intense initial need to storm and protest is accepted, he usually will not need to vent his angry feelings later on staff members who must give him day-to-day care. As a result, they are able to offer support to the patient as he goes through the difficult period of readjustment. At the conclusion of the meeting, the patient is reassured that he will have time to come to terms with the experience and plan for his return home.

During the confrontation a redefinition of the illness takes place for both patient and staff. Prior to this, the major goal was to diagnose an organic cause for the fever. Following confrontation, the goal of medical care is to interrupt effectively the patient's maladaptive behavior pattern. To be successful in this, the confrontation process must be firm, but gentle and nonpunitive. The patient must be helped to remain in the hospital long enough to work through the worst of his feelings of rage and shame, to begin reconstructing his shattered self-image, and to experience the staff's continued acceptance of him as a person who is worthy of concern and has not wholly forfeited the staff's trust.

Social Work Practice

Social work services are provided for all patients admitted to the study. Contacts early in the patient's hospitalization are valuable because (1) the broad diagnostic category "fever of unknown origin" may encompass a number of serious illnesses or it may mask emotional problems, (2) a final diagnosis of factitious illness is a possibility, and (3) the exhaustive medical workup may in itself be a source of anxiety and stress. The casework relationship is an important tool in cases of fever of unknown origin, but the worker recognizes that most of these patients are unable to form mature and trusting interpersonal relationships and they will relate in different ways—some will be guarded and defensive, while others will reach out for understanding and sympathy. The worker also avoids probing to uncover the patient's underlying feelings in order to minimize disruption of emotional defenses essential to the patient's functioning. Attacking these defenses would only increase the patient's resistance and blunt the relationship. Thus the initial treatment goal is to support the patient through the medical diagnostic workup, to convey the worker's commitment to him as a person, and to develop a contact with enough meaning to the patient so that the worker can help him when his defenses are breached by the confrontation procedure.

If the social worker has succeeded in developing a firm supportive relationship with the patient, it is helpful for him to be present at the actual confrontation. His presence can be regarded as a commitment to be with the patient during a difficult time. The worker has heretofore been accepting of the patient's emotional defenses and is not an active participant in the confrontation, but his presence symbolizes his alliance with the goal of medical treatment—the interruption of maladaptive behavior patterns. As a witness, he is better able to handle the patient's subsequent need to distort the intent of the confrontation.

Once the confrontation has taken place, the social worker shares with the rest of the staff a number of therapeutic tasks, all of them carried out in a spirit of acceptance and continuing concern. The patient feels stripped and may be tearful, anxious, or storming. He may cloak his sense of shame and helplessness in attacking or defensive behavior, or he may withdraw; however, his feelings of being worthless and untrustworthy nevertheless come through. The social worker and other staff members can help the patient handle his sharp and conflicting feelings about the confrontation. He will need a "winding down" period for self-reassessment and for consideration of the treatment recommendations, and his heightened anxiety often can be used constructively to help him accept psychotherapy—a concrete step in relinquishing old patterns. Arrangements for psychotherapy after discharge are usually made by the patient and the local referring physician. In some cases the social worker may assist with these referral arrangements, but his most important function is to be a source of support and encouragement to the patient. He may also be called on to help the patient's family understand the patient's illness in terms of his emotional needs and problems.

Illustrative Case

The case of Mrs. A, a 39-year-old registered nurse admitted for fever of unknown origin, illustrates the confrontation approach to treatment. Her medical history revealed numerous hospitalizations in the past for excision of a benign cyst of the breast, hysterectomy, suture granuloma of the colon, hiatal hernia, cystitis, gastritis, and fever of unknown origin. During the year prior to her most recent admission, the patient suffered from fever with associated aches and pains and had been unable to work.

Social work contacts with Mrs. A began at the time of admission. In early interviews she was friendly but guarded when talking about her life situation. As the casework relationship developed, she expressed concern that even the experts would not find the source of her illness. She also disclosed that she had not advanced professionally to her satisfaction because she was unable to get along with superiors. However, she was quick to deny that her medical or employment history indicated any adjustment problems. Despite the system of denial and superficiality maintained by the patient, she seemed to regard the social worker as a safe person with whom she could share negative feelings about the unpleasant aspects of hospitalization.

Shortly after admission, the nursing staff discovered that Mrs. A was substituting thermometers each time her temperature was taken. In order to confirm this, the serial numbers of thermometers given to the patient were compared with those on the thermometers handed back. This documented information was kept in the patient's medical record.

The diagnostic medical evaluation revealed no organic basis for the patient's fever. The psychiatric evaluation described her as a fairly rigid individual with many dependency needs and a strong defense of denial concerning her psychosomatic illness. No evidence of psychotic or prepsychotic behavior was found.

In a meeting with the senior staff physician, ward physician, head nurse, and social worker, the patient was confronted with the fact that she had been switching thermometers. A nonaccusatorial, understanding, straightforward approach was used by the senior staff physician to describe the staff's concern about her. The patient was told that there were no physiological findings to explain her illness and her behavior indicated she needed therapy for her emotional problems. Furthermore, she would be given ample time to consider the recommendation for therapy and to make plans for her return home.

During the confrontation the patient maintained her composure and insisted that she did not understand the matter of differing serial numbers because she had not switched thermometers. She was not questioned further about this and was allowed to save face when the senior staff physician indicated that several laboratory tests would be repeated to confirm past findings.

Following the confrontation, Mrs. A became markedly anxious, began weeping, and remained in her room. After she had regained her composure somewhat, she verbalized to the social worker her anger toward the senior staff physician for saying that she had switched thermometers. She continued to deny that she had switched them and wondered how anyone could now believe her. How could she face the nurses who would soon arrive for the evening shift? Several hours after the confrontation, however, she confided individually to the head nurse, senior staff physician, and social worker that she actually had switched thermometers because she believed she must have a fever if her physical ailments were to be given sincere consideration.

Following the confrontation, hospital care was continued for several days so that Mrs. A could prepare for her return home and make preliminary plans for the future. She was able to make constructive use of the casework relationship by discussing her fears and misconceptions concerning psychotherapy, which helped to reduce her ambivalence about accepting the recommended treatment. She was doubtful that her former supervisors would approve of her undertaking psychiatric treatment and felt her future employability would be jeopardized if she did so. With encouragement, however, she contacted her own physician, who assured her he would not divulge the factitious nature of her illness to her former employer and would arrange for her to obtain therapy in her own community.

Conclusion

Factitious illness is an expression of a complex network of psychosocial and physiological factors that are not clearly understood. It is clear, however, that this illness is not merely a malicious hoax perpetrated by the patient; it is the desperate plea for help of a person who has been unable to devise a better solution for his emotional problems.

A hospital team that understands the message of the patient's behavior and has a treatment plan geared to his emotional needs will not react with hostility toward the patient or punish him through premature discharge. The primary social work contribution to treatment is to develop a relationship with the patient that will help carry him through the difficult period of confrontation with the factitious nature of his illness. Following confrontation, this sympathetic but reality-based support sustains the patient as he struggles to abandon modes of behavior that have been so damaging to him.

ORGANIC MENTAL DISORDERS

CHAPTER 20

Protective Practice in Serving the Mentally Impaired Aged

Edna Wasser

The problem of the aged person requiring protective services usually surfaces when his way of living and his incapacities arouse a mixture of concern and revulsion in others in his surroundings. Attempts to help and otherwise deal with the problem by many in the community—social agencies, police, church, health services, landlords, relatives—usually culminate in a stalemate. Individual situations are found to be highly complex and thwarting to solve. The aged person is usually fearful and wishes to avoid the entry of others into his life lest they disturb whatever equilibrium he has achieved despite his limitations.

Referral Data

Source: visiting nurse association. Seventy-four-year-old woman, never married, living in vermin-infested unsafe house, refuses to leave, begs food, had a fire, acts paranoid, is diabetic, forgets medication, refuses treatment for ulcers. Visiting nurse, minister, health center, housing and sanitation departments are involved.

Source: health center. Eighty-six-year-old woman and sixty-two-year-old unmarried son, both shaky physically and mentally. Son cares for mother, gives her

Reprinted from *Social Casework,* Vol. 52, No. 8 (October, 1971), pp. 510–522, by permission of the author and the Family Service Association of America.

animal medicines, works sporadically, claims he carries a gun, frightens away neighbors.

Source: family service agency. Eighty-year-old man, unmarried, blind, suspicious, demanding, evicted from hotel because of homosexual activity. Unacceptable in various settings—residences, shelter, rest home, home for aged—all attempted through efforts of referring agency.

Source: housing authority. Eighty-four-year-old man and eighty-three-year-old wife, formerly refined couple, deteriorating last two years in appearance, housekeeping. Use newspapers for curtains, confused, living on milk and ice cream. Have marginal income from Social Security and work pension. Refuse nursing home care.

This article reports the essentials of a direct protective service practice in social work with mentally impaired older people who are not institutionalized but are considered, primarily by others, to constitute a high-risk population because of their seriously limited level of functioning and inability to manage alone.[1] The article will also deal with considerations and concepts that have special applicability in work with such older individuals. Comments will be made in reaction to research findings in the study that are of special significance to practitioners and other providers of service.

Because the disorder of the aged person is manifested in his deteriorated social functioning and self-management, social work has been regarded as a logical, although not always welcoming, primary resource in the provision of protective service. Since the aged person is an individual whose needs require that he be dealt with directly in relation to his lessened coping capacity and his disturbed and disturbing relationship with his environment, casework has been regarded as a responsible, indeed, desirable modus operandi. In this report, the practitioner operates as change agent primarily in relation to the client system.

Background

Protective service has developed as part of the broad range of social services to older persons. Although most of the aged manage in a relatively independent way, largely connected with family or other associates, many need help. The aged clientele served by social work represents a contin-

---

[1] The direct practice was developed by the casework and ancillary service staff of the Benjamin Rose Institute, Cleveland, Ohio, who were involved in the protective service project. This article is based on the practice of Helen Cole, Helen Beggs, Jane Lenahan, and Margaret McGuire, caseworkers on the project. A more inclusive document on this practice is contained in the full report of the study.

uum of those who are relatively healthy and well functioning but have some difficulties ultimately to the mentally impaired whose functional incapacities result in inability to care for themselves, who lack responsible, responsive relatives or friends, and who are highly vulnerable to exploitation.

Protective service for the aged represents society's way of caring for those of its aging members who have become limited in their capacity to care for themselves and who lack the personal associates who would usually provide care. The service can be viewed also as society's efforts to deal with what it may construe as deviant behavior.

The burgeoning interest in protective services for the aged, heightened during the past fifteen years, has yielded well-intentioned, sporadic, partly interrelated attempts to deal with a grave social problem. Efforts have been on an individual and on a community basis, within the voluntary and public welfare systems and on local, state, and federal levels. They have cut across such disciplines as social work, medicine (including psychiatry), law, and nursing. The literature on protective services reflects much more the concern with the nature of the problem, the person, and various individualized and organizational activities[2] than with a delineation of the casework practice in a direct service.[3] Literature about work with the mentally

---

[2] See, for example, Edna Wasser, Responsibility, Self-Determination, and Authority in Casework Protection of Older Persons, SOCIAL CASEWORK 42:258–66 (May–June 1961), reprinted in *Authority and Social Work: Concept and Use*, ed. Shankar A. Yelaja (Toronto: University of Toronto Press, 1971), pp. 182–95; Virginia Lehmann and Geneva Mathiasen, eds., *Guardianship and Protective Services for Older People* (Albany, N.Y.: National Council on the Aging Press, 1963); Rebecca Eckstein and Ella Lindey, eds., *Seminar on Protective Services for Older People: Proceedings of a Seminar Held at Arden House, Harriman, New York, March 10–15, 1963* (New York: National Council on the Aging, 1964); Louis L. Bennett, Adult Protective Services and Law: Some Relevant Socio-Legal Considerations (Paper presented at the meeting on Protective Services for the Aging, American Public Welfare Association Northeast Regional Conference, New York, N.Y., September 13, 1965); Gertrude H. Hall and Geneva Mathiasen, eds., *Overcoming Barriers to Protective Services for the Aged: Report of a National Institute on Protective Services, Savoy Field Hotel, Houston, Texas, January 16–18, 1968* (New York: National Council on the Aging, 1968); U.S., Department of Health, Education, and Welfare, *Project on Protective Services Interim Report*, prepared for the Social and Rehabilitation Service by James J. Burr (Washington, D.C.: U.S. Department of Health, Education, and Welfare, 1970); and John B. Martin, Protective Services (Position paper, Administration on Aging of U.S. Department of Health, Education, and Welfare presented at the Conference on Protective Services, San Diego, Calif., April 29–May 1, 1970).

[3] See, for example, Beverly Diamond et al., Casework with the Aging: Proceedings of a Seminar at Arden House, Harriman Campus of Columbia University, October 30–November 4, 1960, SOCIAL CASEWORK, 42:217–90 (May–June 1961); Mary L. Hemmy and Marcella S. Farrar, Protective Services for Older People, SOCIAL CASEWORK, 42:16–20 (January 1961); Helen Turner, Personality Functioning in Later Life: Implications for Practice, in *Planning Welfare Services for Older People: Papers Presented at the Training Institute for Public Welfare Specialists on Aging, Cleveland, Ohio, June 13–24, 1965* (Washington, D.C.: U.S. Department of Health, Education, and Welfare, Welfare Administration, Bureau of Family Services, 1966), pp. 59–65; Edna Wasser, *Creative Approaches in Casework with the Aging* (New York: Family Service Association of America, 1966); and Edna Wasser, *Casebook on Work with the Aging* (New York: Family Service Association of America, 1966).

impaired aged person tends to deal with him as a patient or resident in an institution.[4]

The fact that there are twenty million persons over sixty-five years of age in the United States and that 4 to 5 percent of them are institutionalized is well known. Less well known is the reasonably developed, but still to be definitively ascertained, conjecture that there is an additional 7 to 10 percent of older urban population who are mentally impaired and in probable need of some form of protection.[5]

A central problem of the local community in providing help to aged protective persons is the organization—or lack of organization—and lack of services to meet their needs. The locus for a service, a source that will assume responsibility for carrying through until some reasonable solution is achieved, is troublesome to secure and a function resisted by many established agencies. A limited number of communities are experimenting with different forms of organizational responses. Illustrative solutions include experimenting with geriatric screening units,[6] setting up an office of public guardian,[7] developing emergency care facilities,[8] creating "foster home" programs that can serve the elderly,[9] and casework services within the court structure.[10]

The concerns on the federal and state levels have to do with the development of policy, legislation, funding, and the promotion of sound relationships with communities and practices in organization and delivery of services. The numerous endeavors within social work about protective

[4] Elaine M. Brody et al., Excess Disabilities of Mentally Impaired Aged: Impact of Individualized Treatment, The Gerontologist, II:124–33, Part I (Summer 1971); Morton H. Kleban, Elaine M. Brody, and M. Powell Lawton, Personality Traits in the Mentally Impaired Aged and Their Relationship to Improvements in Current Functioning, ibid., 134–40; Marcia Bok, Some Problems in Milieu Treatment of the Chronic Older Mental Patient, ibid., 141–47.

[5] Margaret Blenkner, Martin Bloom, and Margaret Nielsen, A Research and Demonstration Project of Protective Services, SOCIAL CASEWORK, 52:483–99 (October 1971).

[6] Richard J. Levy, Dorothy M. Asbury, and Gerald Lutovich, Inpatient and Emergency Services, in Handbook of Community Health Practice: The San Mateo Experience, ed. H. Richard Lamb, Don Healy, and Joseph D. Downing (San Francisco: Jossey-Bass, 1969), pp. 82–116; and Russel F. Rypins and Mary Lou Clark, A Screening Project for the Geriatric Mentally Ill, California Medicine, 109:273–78 (October 1968). The Baltimore Geriatric Evaluation Service of the Baltimore City Department of Health, Baltimore, Md., Lee Muth, director has also conducted experiments in geriatric screening.

[7] Tri-County Community Council, Proposal for a Public Guardianship Project in Multnomah County (Portland, Oreg.: Tri-County Community Council, 1970).

[8] National Council on the Aging, Progress Report on Project for Developing an Emergency Care Facility for Older Persons in Need of Protection, mimeographed (New York: National Council on the Aging, 1970).

[9] State of Washington, Department of Social and Health Services, Division of Public Assistance, Foster Family Homes for Adults (Progress Report 1115, Project no. II–P–57021/0–03, December 31, 1970).

[10] University of Washington, School of Social Work, Education and Development in Gerontological Service (Proposal for Grant no.94–P–50072–9–01, Administration on Aging, U.S. Department of Health, Education, and Welfare).

services may suggest erroneously that definitive answers have been found concerning their provision. Rather, the range and intensity of activity may be considered a reflection of the complexity of the social problem it attempts to meet.

Casework with Aged Protective Clients

Why is protective service practice with an aged person different from direct practice with one who is not considered to have a protective problem? Who is this person? What are the essential conceptual considerations in providing service? What is intrinsic to such practice? What are the ways of delivering services? What is the process in helping?

The caseworker who serves the older person having a protective problem derives his practice from what has been developed as sound casework with older persons.[11] He then clarifies additional aspects that are specific to this problem.

NATURE OF THE CLIENTELE

Underlying all practice considerations is the nature of the clientele being served. The person with a protective problem has been clearly described and defined, with some variations.[12]

The finding that a person has a protective problem is based on the social judgment that he is suffering from a grave incapacity in social functioning manifested by his disorganized behavior and social disorientation. Such a condition can be caused not only by a person's mental incapability, but also interactionally by many social and environmental factors. Mental incapability in association with inadequacy for self-care, lack or inadequacy of others to help, and lack of situational control are focal. Not every person who has a mental disorder has a protective problem.

In the literature, frequent references are made to the person who is dependent and in need of care because of incapacitating physical illness. Many services, particularly medical and nursing, have been developed and

[11] See Diamond et al., Casework with the Aging; Turner, Personality Functioning; and Wasser, *Creative Approaches.*

[12] Ruth E. Weber, Older Persons in Need of Protective Service Encountered by Thirteen Selected Cleveland Agencies in March, 1964: A Survey, mimeographed (Cleveland, Ohio: Benjamin Rose Institute Protective Service Project Progress Report on Planning Phase, Supporting Document no. 3, September 1964). Definition: "A non-institutionalized person sixty years of age or older, whose behavior indicates that he is mentally incapable of adequately caring for himself and his interests without serious consequences to himself or others; and has no relative or other private individual able and willing to assume the kind and degree of support and supervision required to control the situation." See also Hall and Mathiasen, *Overcoming Barriers,* pp.13–18.

generally are accessible to him. These services, however, are generally not accessible to the individual who is mentally incapable and seldom reaches out for care. A thin line separates these two kinds of persons. One who is severely ill organically and who is also unable to negotiate for himself is likely to need protective service. A person's mental capacities are inextricably interwoven with his physical limitations—a condition that results in varying degrees of physical, behavioral, and social dysfunctioning.

The caseworker's practice is bound to be affected by the way in which he understands and deals with behavior. Cognitive processes in aging have been coming under increasing scrutiny.[13] Traditional methods of assessing a client's personality and ability to function based solely on theories from psychoanalysis and ego psychology limit the practitioner in understanding and working with the aged client who is suffering from thinking deficits that are so largely derived from organic changes and associated with the aging process. When disintegration of the person becomes evident, it is manifested not only by personality changes but also by a breakdown in mentation (memory, orientation, perception, and judgment), which is central to his behavior and inability to perform.

The nature of this older person's pathology is such that an expectation about client motivation for service requires revision. If the client has such serious need, why is there no reaching out for help or effort expended by him to take or use help even when offered?

First, the level of energy available to such a client is very low, and organic failures are likely to drain and limit him. In addition, the caseworker is confronted with ravages in client ego functions, most particularly in the person's mentation and problem-solving processes. Ordinarily a caseworker can assume that a nonpsychotic, nonprotective client who is reacting emotionally to stress, nevertheless has thinking abilities at least potentially in good working order. An aged person also reacts emotionally to his situation, but his thinking processes are likely to be intrinsically affected. How can a person who is drained of energy and is no longer capable of a good level of thought think through the moves to solve a problem in some consistent way? Failure by an aged client to keep appointments or to take his medications may be due not to emotional resistance or lack of wish, but to sheer inability to recall. A lack of impulse control can result not only from lack of control of emotions or a breakthrough of primitive id forces, but from organic senile changes. For diagnosis and treatment, therefore, a reorientation is required to identify specifically the cognitive capacities and limitations that have an overriding effect upon behavior and personality.

The concept of motivation in regard to casework can be reviewed con-

---

[13] Jack Botwinick, *Cognitive Processes in Maturity and Old Age* (New York: Springer Publishing Company, 1967).

cerning whose responsibility it is to instigate service and under what circumstances. Must the client always be motivated to seek service, or are there times when the worker should provide service so that the client—motivated or not—is cared for and comes to use the service because his need for it is great?

The aged person's failure to seek help or his refusal of help as an intrusion does not represent a measure of his need. Rather, it may cover up his underlying desperation. His will to seek help may have become paralyzed, and his judgment and perception about the very deteriorated conditions in which he lives have diminished along with his strength. Although he cannot reach out for help, his relief can be enormous if a helper succeeds in breaking through these barriers that are defended by his mistrust. Mistrust can be a reaction to previous efforts by others, however well meaning, who try to direct and control him. Mistrust can also be caused by his own increasing sense of vulnerability and diminishing grasp on his selfhood.

Those who would help may be inclined to withdraw from the aged person's mistrust, considering it a refusal. Yet behind a manifest resistance is likely to lie a latent wish to be cared for, protected, and helped. The aged person's anxiety that the refusal represents emphasizes the fear of loss of control and identity.

INTERVENTION AND THE VOLUNTARY
AND INVOLUNTARY CLIENT

Intervention has become an increasingly familiar concept to social workers.[14] Protective intervention is a dominant component of protective casework practice. It is justified, insofar as intervention in the life of any individual can be justified, by the assumption that self-destructive and dangerous behavior of the aged adult comes not from his free choice but from deteriorating organic and personality changes and that failure to intervene constitutes social neglect.

Aged protective persons who are living alone are, at least to start with, not voluntary but involuntary clients who seldom if ever seek service. If the caseworker is to gain access, to maintain contact, and some control of the individual problem is to be achieved, a central characteristic of the practice is the use of professional authority as expressed in intervention.[15] In-

[14] See Harriett H. Bartlett, *The Common Base of Social Work Practice* (New York: National Association of Social Workers, 1970), pp.76–80, 161–90; and Scott Briar, Family Services and Casework, in *Research in the Social Services: A Five-Year Review*, ed. Henry S. Maas (New York: National Association of Social Workers, 1971), pp. 108–29.

[15] For application to the aged, see Wasser, Responsibility, Self-Determination, and Authority; and Saul Bernstein, Self-determination: King or Citizen in the Realm of Values, in *Authority and Social Work*, ed. Yelaja, pp. 229–42.

tervention may range all the way from the simple entry of a caseworker into the situation to decision making and decisive action undertaken on behalf of a client. The intervention per se, however narrowly or broadly conceived, is essential to the agency's treatment. Protective intervention with the aged is socially and professionally based. Conceivably, it could become legally based, as in the child protective agency or mental hospital. It can always proceed beyond its own limits to call on legal intervention or genuine power to act.

These elements are different from casework practice with the adult who voluntarily seeks service and does not suffer from such extreme social and mental pathology. When a person ordinarily applies for help, he gives implicit consent for the procedures to follow. He is encouraged to participate in the interactional helping process and to initiate his own planning. The emphasis is on the voluntary agreement of the client even though he is affected and influenced by the contact. In the protective service situation, the agency and worker move away from the relative safety of serving the applying, motivated, voluntary client, to the converse, the nonmotivated and apparently nonvoluntary client.

An important insight from protective practice is that once responsibility is taken for entering into the home and situation and for responding to the obvious need of the client rather than to his inability to ask for help or refusal through fear, the worker is likely to find voluntary clients in many apparently uninterested, unmotivated aged persons. Hence, the first step is to help the aged person become a voluntary client and accept those services that are offered and instituted, regardless of whether he asks for them. When he agrees with or can be influenced to accept the caseworker's judgment about necessary care, he has in essence become a voluntary client whose wishes can guide needed changes. It is possible to work on a voluntary basis with most clients having protective problems.

Nevertheless, a client may continue to resist help. His unwillingness may be only partial and related to one or another aspect of his situation and behavior. He may refuse to accept lifesaving medical advice or attention or to stop eating foods that are harmful, or he may be incapable of doing so. An intervention that is introduced may appear superficially helpful, and yet it may turn out to be intolerable. The worker needs to understand and evaluate the basis for the person's resistive behavior. For example, an elderly blind man with a history of homosexuality is known to have made it unbearable for a series of women home aides, or an ill woman who needs to be helped desperately and who resists a placement plan, nevertheless cannot yield control in any way and accept a home aide. Compromises to enable a client to pursue his wishes often become necessary with a yielding of the seemingly desirable course.

Infrequently, for some aged persons the most critical point may be reached when a decision must be made that the risks and dangers have become too great in following their inclinations and that a step must be taken toward placement against their wishes. It is with such involuntary clients that legal authority is called on, and, for example, guardianship or commitment proceedings are instituted through court procedures.

An older person may at times accept the idea of guardianship quite voluntarily when he has experienced some positive relationship with and trust in the worker, and such an arrangement may be made while the client is enabled to remain at home. Another older person—even one having a fairly good relationship with the agency staff—may take the step to which he has the right and resist the court action. A legal requirement that incompetency be established for guardianship can have devastating impact in humiliation and loss of civil rights, and any ameliorating steps that can help a person retain his sense of control over his own destiny are desirable. Adaptations of the existing system of guardianship have been reviewed considerably.[16]

The securing of guardianship in relation to an involuntary client, however, in no way lessens the difficulty of enforcing legal decisions even though these have been deemed essential for the client's survival. There is no magic in guardianship. How does one proceed to get a completely negativistic, ill, frightened, and helpless person to leave a foul setting that he prefers, although he cannot be cared for adequately there? After all, if the purpose of moving a recalcitrant human being to another setting—even a hospital—is to help him survive, the caseworker must be acutely aware that the client not be destroyed in the process.

THE SERVICE

The model for the delivery of service that is being reported here uses casework as the core service, complemented by extensive ancillary services, within the structure of a voluntary social agency. The reinforcements provide financial aid, home aide service, medical care, psychiatric consultation and examination, legal consultation and service, fiduciary and guardianship service, and placement service.

The caseworker represents the fulcrum of the service to the individual client, drawing heavily on ancillary services as needs are perceived. The worker carries primary responsibility for serving the client and directing the course of activities with him and with community resources. Values are those that are rooted in individual worth and building trust, that maximize the client's decision-making capacities and sense of mastery, and that are well contained by a circumscribed use of influence. Efforts are

[16] For discussion of the idea of a "social guardian," see HelenTurner, Personality Functioning in Later Life. See also John B. Martin, Protective Services, on the need for surrogate and conservator services and recognition of the activities of the Office of Economic Opportunity and the American Bar Association in bringing aboaut more desirable laws.

strongly directed to enable the client to remain in his familiar surroundings if at all possible and to engage the concern and support of relatives and friends on a disinterested nonexploiting basis. The central dictum is that the caseworker is prepared to do or to get others to do whatever is necessary to meet the demands of the situation.

General service goals and areas of sought-for improvement can be considered in relation to the client's welfare, survival, contentment, behavioral or affective signs and symptoms, functional competence, environmental protection, and collateral stress.[17] Although upward change is sought, arrest of deterioration and relief of suffering and stress are valued.[18] Although the central emphasis is on direct service to the aged person and treatment of individual situations, inevitably the worker becomes engaged in lesser measure with other persons and institutional structures in the community impinging on or being impinged upon by the client.

The phases in protective intervention and control can be identified as follows:

1. Entering into the situation, whether invited or acceded to by the client. This action means gaining and holding access. The caseworker determines if the client is willing to be helped once he becomes reassured and acquainted with the possibility of assistance. If he is unwilling, the worker attempts to turn the resistive, involuntary client into a voluntary client and helps him to accept assistance. This process entails reaching out to the client, if necessary persistently and repeatedly with tact and understanding of his fears; it means relating, communicating, interacting with, and influencing him.

2. Interposing a variety of supports and services. The worker does not wait to be asked, but deftly introduces what is needed, assuming agreement unless there is marked rejection. The worker presumes that the client develops a taste for service by tasting it.

3. Developing a stand-by plan when unable to effect change. When the situation seems frozen and unchangeable, the worker takes steps deliberately to stand by with a plan in the event of a crisis, which may provide a point of entry for resolution.

4. Determining the advisability of securing legal control if unable to resolve a grave situation. Control over the client's affairs and way of living in some or many aspects may be indicated when such a

---

[17] These items represent the variables under study in the Benjamin Rose Institute Project on Protective Services.

[18] Bernice K. Simon, Social Casework Theory: An Overview, in Robert W. Roberts and Robert H. Nee, eds., (Chicago: The University of Chicago Press, 1970), p. 392. Simon states, "Inherent in the discussion of change permeation is a notion of prevention. And a kind of prevention—arrest or deterrence of continuing deterioration or disability development—has been implicit in the caseworker's general goals of treatment throughout our history."

procedure offers the sole potential for a solution and suitable safe-guards and accountability are set up.

Diagnostically, in relation to the specifics for each person, the case-worker arrives at an understanding of the nature of his mental and phy-sical condition, at a working social diagnosis about the need for intervention and supports, and the possibility of stabilizing the situation and effecting some balance in his relationship with his environment. The worker con-centrates, usually under community pressure and his own impulses to bring rapid relief, on a functional rather than on an etiological concept,[19] that is, the capacity of the individual to function[20] rather than on the origins of his condition. Acute diagnostic acumen is required for differentiation about what aspects of the client's mental and psychological processes are still relatively intact. These aspects then suggest the areas of functioning and decision making in which the person is still capable and which may be supported and enhanced. Medical evaluation is of overriding impor-tance.

The practitioner's assessment is based on a sound comprehension of the health of the client, his ailments, and his positive physical attributes as they affect his physical and mental functioning; his cognitive capacities and deficiencies; his ego capacities and functioning; his quality as an in-dividual and what he appears to have valued most in his way of living; what meaning his behavior conveys as well as what he can convey orally; the type and nature of his personality structure to the extent it is revealed by his behavior; his libidinal needs and manifestations; the severity and possible reversibility of some aspects of the pathology; his adaptability and in what areas of functioning it appears; the quality of any underlying wish to be helped—even if unexpressed—in juxtaposition with fears of losing control of the directing of his life; his vulnerability to exploitation or his harmful exploitation of others; his possible resistance to intervention; and the sources of deprivation and stress in his environment.

The disorganized person, his way of living, and frequently the great differences in cultural values can have a marked impact on the worker. Dealing with his own reacting negative feelings makes for additional heavy demands on the worker.

Often the severity and critical character of the problems force the

[19] Warren G. Bennis, Kenneth D. Benne, and Robert Chin, eds., *The Planning of Change: Read-ing in the Applied Behavioral Sciences* (New York: Holt, Rinehart and Winston, 1966), pp. 196–97. The editors draw particular attention to the etiological pitfall in which practitioners may become entrapped in searching for causes and a consequent effort to remedy the original causes. They suggest, "One way of avoiding this pitfall of extreme dependence upon 'etiol-ogy' is for the change-agent to start with scientific formulations of a strategy of action and intervention and then test the relevance of the diagnosis of origins or causes against the proposed plan."

[20] Charles M. Gaitz and Paul E. Baer, Diagnostic Assessment of the Elderly: A Multifunctional Model, *The Gerontologist*, Part I, 10:47–52 (Spring 1970). The article deals with assessment based on functional capacity.

worker into making rapid judgments as a basis for quick actions. Crisis theory and concepts offer leads for adaptation in work with aged clientele.[21] The client's personal and social pathology create unusual predicaments and enormous need for help from some source. An interacting stressful impact between the older person and his environment cause a downward spiral, and a crisis or a series of crises tends to occur. The crisis may occur not only at the inception of the casework contact but also in the course of providing service.

Because information about the life history of the client frequently is not obtainable or is accumulated slowly and because casework judgments keep developing along with client reactions to the testing-out techniques used by the worker, the diagnostic process is a dynamically evolving one. In view of the character of the behavior and dysfunctioning of the older person, the diagnostic comprehension of the worker is likely to depend heavily on observations and judgments from ancillary disciplines and service personnel and collaterals. Because of the memory and verbal communication limitations in the client, the worker seeks other sources in the client's milieu for confirmation of data and his own intuitive judgments while he maintains confidentiality.

Simply stated, the caseworker makes an assessment of the activities necessary for the daily living of the client. He also determines whether his mental processes function well enough for him to continue in at least a quasi-independent way in the community if supports are introduced and some health improvement can be achieved.

Ordinarily, a caseworker assumes that a client is able to get to bed at night and arouse himself in the morning; toilet and cleanse himself; obtain, prepare, and eat some foods, however simple; take necessary medications; care for a home in some elementary fashion; and keep track of and spend his money, however little. Many aged persons, however, who have an intense will to remain in their own settings are incapable of carrying out one of many of these functions even unsatisfactorily. The caseworker is faced with determining the specific lacks and whether it is at all possible to create a prosthetic-like or even therapeutic environment within the home.[22] Practical devices and supports of various kinds, such as home aide

[21] See Lydia Rapoport, Crisis Intervention as a Mode of Brief Treatment, in Roberts and Nee, *Theories of Social Casework*, p. 304. Rapoport discriminates between client groups for whom crisis intervention as defined by her may or may not be deemed effective. In responding to her own question—"When is a 'crisis' not a crisis?"—she alludes to those "...who live in a chronic state of crisis. For them, being in a state of crisis is a life style." For these people, emergency and first aid help is often needed. See also Muriel Oberleder, Crisis Therapy in Mental Breakdown of the Aging, *The Gerontologist*, 10:111–14 (Summer 1970).

[22] Ogden R. Lindsley, Geriatric Behavioral Prosthetics, in *New Thoughts on Old Age*, ed. Robert Kastenbaum (New York: Springer Publishing Company, 1964), p. 46. Lindsley explains that the prosthetic environment compensates for the specific behavior deficit of the aged person so that the deficits are less debilitating. In contrast he says, "Therapeutic environments are essentially training or retraining centers for the generation of behavioral skills which maintain themselves once the patient has left the therapeutic environment."

service, visiting nurse service, and medical and paramedical services, can be introduced. It is intended that they lessen stress and stimulate the older person to keep whatever sense of wholeness his usual setting may provide, improve his self-image, and feel less depressed.

The treatment process is carried out with a full comprehension by the worker that a person's psychic (and perhaps physical) survival is likely to depend as much on retention of his sense of self, of which his will is central, as on the amelioration of the deteriorating forces in his person and social situation. It is particularly necessary to balance interventions intended for the very survival of the client against the negative impact that these can have on the client's sense of self, will, and control of his own life.

The purposes of treatment steps are the alleviation of the suffering of the client, the amelioration of the conditions under which he is living up to a minimum level of human decency, the improvement of his physical and mental health and sense of well-being, and the deterrence of further deterioration.To this end, the worker supplements client resources with agency funds and the ancillary resources. These add to what the worker is able to bring to the relationship with the client through supportive encouragement, persuasion, and the strength of his own ego—which, it may be said, needs to be strong indeed.

The referring individual may prepare the client for the worker's visit, although many clients may not comprehend explanations. The referrent may accompany the caseworker on the first visit to lessen client fears about a new person. The client may be asked to tell what is bothering and troublesome to him. Concern is shown by demonstration. For a person who has not eaten, is without food, or is unable to cook, food may be purchased and cooked on an emergency basis. An immediate action for hospitalization and medical care may be taken, or a rapid appraisal of the person may cause the worker to revisit, observe, evaluate slowly, gather knowledge about him, and test out what he can and may wish to do. Momentum is sustained by frequent visiting and continuing assessment as the client is given the opportunity to learn about the benign and helping intent of the worker.

The caseworker with good humor and a gentle, light touch suggests, persuades, and enables the client to act in his own home so that he may gradually achieve and maintain basic decent standards of self-care. Faced with varying degrees and kinds of resistance, the worker facilitates planning regarding problems of health, housing, money, basic conduct in daily living, relatives, and other persons.

Social treatment commences as judgments are made, often immediately. Imperceptible relational experiences introduced by the professional person set subtle forces of influence into motion. At times, even larger quite perceptible interventive actions may win client accord.

The caseworker frequently intervenes in the client's behalf with such outside environmental forces as neighbors, landlord, or other offended community representatives in order to lessen the impact and stress on the client and win them over to helpfulness. The caseworker may intervene by stimulating outside authorities, such as the health, fire, and police departments, to present realistic requirements to the client that he meet community standards. The aged person who gathers rubbish or collects wood but is careless about fire can seriously endanger himself and others. By using outside authorities, the caseworker can structure reality requirements, becoming not the enforcer but the assistant to the client in meeting standards.

Decision making weighs heavily on the caseworker as it looms larger than is usual in casework practice. Decisions must be made about when, how, to what degree, and, indeed, whether to act. The worker is constantly weighing alternatives and evaluating likely outcomes. How much risk should be tolerated for the sake of the client if the risk involves the opposing interests of others? Do the risks of remaining in his setting overbalance the gratifications for the client? At what point and on what basis is a decision made to help the client remain in his own setting or to influence him to change to a new one—most usually to a nursing home? If the client is unwilling, should legal recourse be sought and guardianship obtained? Is commitment indicated?

To the extent possible, the client can be encouraged to make decisions and act on his own, even if the choices are relatively simple, such as selecting his clothing, choosing his foods, or arranging his household. Acceptance of these choices conveys the worker's regard for him.

That an intervention may be great or of critical importance may not be felt by the client. Much depends on the way the intervention is handled by the worker. When the incapacity is crucial to life or safety and the person himself does nothing about it, the greater is the need for intervention. When a person needs to be persuaded or induced to stop some behavior, the simplest way is found. The worker acts himself or gets other to act.

For example, Mrs. B is a diabetic who can be impelled into a diabetic coma by her lack of self-control in eating sweets. The caseworker simply removes the sweets and encourages other sources of gratification. Mr. K lives in a third-rate hotel. His poor judgment in disregarding medical recommendations, medications, and diet are leading him to congestive heart failure. ''How can eating ham hurt?'' He cannot grasp the possible harmful results of salted foods. When he becomes gravely ill, it takes the combined activity of the caseworker and the visiting nurse to persuade the hotel manager, who is not eager to lose a paying customer but who has some influence with Mr. K, to take him to the hospital.

With the caseworker acting as a central regulator, ancillary services all play indispensable collaborative parts in varying degrees in the seeking of solutions and the meeting of needs. It is difficult for the caseworker to make quick decisions if no emergency funds are available. Collaboration with a particular member of a different profession is useful not only in the individual case but on pertinent broader issues affecting the larger social problem of protective services in the community.

Home aides are invaluable in the everyday living of the client and in the planning for his care. They can provide home care, cooking, shopping, companionship, personal care, and some simple nursing procedures. The introduction, continuance, and discontinuance of the service is integral to the casework planning. A preliminary evaluation of the kind and amount of service is made. Training and supervision of home aides make their service effective. In most instances, part-time service is sufficient.

Practical supportive devices can help. Memory aids can be built into a client's way of living, such as putting a sign on the kitchen counter that reminds him to take his pills or placing his medication in a familiar place. The worker's visit or a medical examination can be flagged by a telephone call the previous day. Since isolation may play into memory loss through sensory deprivation, it is useful to introduce the stimulation of other persons, such as a home aide, or to take the person out-of-doors to expose him to others.

Can the aged person's self-awareness about his limitations be used to build in protections? Do these limitations interfere with his well-being? How anxious is he? Is the client's memory poor? After all, defect of memory does not mean that a person is not able to eat, dress, or sleep. The nature of the client's incapacity is a clue to what needs to be built in or what substitutions have to be made.

Although improved nutrition, physical care, understanding, and stabilization of a situation may make for some improvement in behavior, it is difficult to judge if the pathological processes have been reversed or if that which is latently present thereby becomes more usable by the individual. The emotional support received from the concern and attention are bound to have a benign effect on the ego functions of many persons.

Frequently other individuals can be found who have some significant, if not always healthy, association with the client. Such persons may represent either substitute familial supports or drains upon the aged person and need to be included in the diagnostic assessment and planning. The involvement of the agency offers relief to many collaterals who may be finding the aged person an insoluble burden.

The beginning phase of treatment is likely to make the greatest demands on the time, planning, and activity of the caseworker. By its nature, care of the mentally impaired person is potentially long term, but once a situation is brought into some balance, the caseworker may be needed relatively little except at points of stress or change. Paraprofessional workers or home aides are able to meet client needs on a continuing basis.[23]

If improvement or stabilization is not achieved, nursing home placement or mental hospital commitment are ultimate next steps. A basic principle in protective service is that when a crucial issue in the life of the client allows for no other solution and when all conceivable courses have been attempted, the most drastic step of calling in legal intervention be readily undertaken. When a legally based form of intervention and control is resorted to, the manisfestations leading to it are (1) a medical problem of unusual gravity about which a client cannot, and will not, or fails to take the necessary steps for the treatment that is essential for life; (2) an emergency or direct threat to a client's life; and (3) the client's inability to make a decision on his own behalf in an aspect that is crucial to his life. Important is the fact that the person nevertheless may be able to be self-determining in some other aspects of his functioning.

But what will be the effect on the client who yields to persuasion to accept a change to a nursing home or a mental hospital? Will enforced placement create more trauma than continuance in a risky home setting? Does the fact that the worker, neighbors, relatives, or community agencies find an individual's way of living intolerable or unbearably risky mean that the changing must be solely by the aged person? Will the person do better if he must be moved by force to a sanitary, new place of good quality that may nevertheless have a disintegrating effect upon him? Whose needs is the move serving? It is most important to evaluate the danger of "transplantation shock" that may result from placement.

Perspectives on Practice and Research Findings

The research finding of a higher death rate among those who received service in the project and of its possible link to institutionalization challenges review of the use of the institution, particularly the nursing home, in work with the aged protective client. In social welfare, the institutional solution for social problems has undergone reexamination and revision in one field of service after another—in child welfare for quite a time, in progressive corrections, and in mental health with its newer emphasis on community-based services. In each, the institution has come to be conceived less to serve the dilemma of society in its efforts to rid itself physically of

[23] Marcella Farrar and Mary L. Hemmy, Use of Nonprofessional Staff in Work with the Aged, Social Work, 8:44–50 (July 1963); and Family Service Association of America, Social Work Team with Aging Family Service Clients: Third Summary Progress Report, submitted to the National Institute of Mental Health, mimeographed (New York: Family Service Association of America, August 31, 1969).

the one who is disturbing and more to serve the needs of the troubled individual. For the aged protective individual and perhaps for the aged generally, the time has come for a reevaluation of whose purposes are served by the institutional solution.

It is especially noteworthy in a professional protective program so highly oriented toward noninstitutional solutions and rich in the many supporting services ordinarily not available, that service should nevertheless be associated with the likelihood of institutionalization at a rate higher than would occur even in the ordinary course of events. In another article in this issue, the authors suggest a societal and a practice ambivalence that treats the aged protective client as borderline between social deviance and social disorganization.[24]

When the protective client is viewed by the society in which he lives as a social deviant, albeit one who may be unable to control his conduct without outside help, if at all, a practitioner, however well trained professionally, inevitably carries within himself as a member of this society some germ of such an attitude. Ambivalence is supported by the fact that the practitioner functions with a dual stream of opposing incentives, that of dealing with a protective client as a self-determining adult and, simultaneously, as one for whom serious interventions are required if he is to be helped to bring his disturbed and disturbing behaviors under control.

It is possible that even trained practitioners are unable to tolerate taking the risks involved in leaving alone many elderly people who prefer to continue in their unwholesome, marginal way of life. The frightening spectre remains of the occasional protective person who is consumed by fire in his own home or attacked by his starving animals. Yet interventions, especially institutionalization, may be felt deeply by an aged person to be contraventions of his will and his most cherished desires rather than care and protection. A throttling of his life force may occur and diminish his impulse to survive. This effect is likely to be as true for a mentally impaired person as for one considered normal. The impact may be magnified by the helplessness of the debilitated aged person to resist.

Removal from society is usually construed as a punitive action, even though the deviant behavior or conditions may not be within the individual's control. The aged person with a protective problem—like the carrier of contagious disease—has lived in society, absorbed the meanings of its constraints, and regards removal as punishment. The worker who often expends innumerable efforts unsuccessfully to avoid the institutionalization route may also consider it as punishment.

From another stance, survival may be reevaluated as a measure of treatment success. Is it the fact alone of survival or is it also the quality of survival that is important? The how of living and the meaning of dying

[24] Blenkner, Bloom, and Nielsen, Research and Demonstration Project.

and death raise important philosophical and ethical problems and are coming under increasingly intensive study.[25] Is total death always associated with unfavorable status? With those who are in terminal decline, are there times when cessation of life may be considered favorable? If so, at what specific time in an individual's decline would it be? Theorists have conceptualized various aspects of death—psychological death, social death, physical death. Even the exact time that death is considered to occur physiologically is under medical scrutiny.

In addition to the results on survival, some notice should be taken of several other suggestive research findings significant to the practitioner. First, although the data were not as complete as desired for definitive conclusions, the reaction to the helpfulness of agency service by participant, collateral, and referring agency was highly favorable.[26] Further, although the number of collaterals was limited by the nature of the sample under study, service was found to have the effect of relieving collateral stress. The implication is clear for the value of service to relatives and other associates who are under stress because of the aged person's problems.

In addition to that which appears pragmatically sound in the direct practice approach described herein, some leads are implicit for ongoing practice. The caseworker, whose roles are expanding in current practice reconceptualizations,[27] emerges here as a kind of regulator, case manager or balance wheel in the intermeshing of the needed disciplines, or supporter of client strengths along with that of interviewer and decision maker, and of provider of services. The emphasis on behavior, on the cognitive as well as on the social functioning of the protective client, and on the provision of supportive means within the home setting suggests inquiry into use of behavior modification techniques.[28] Moreover, the way is open for adaptations of what is clearly an unusually expensive form of service if highly trained professional caseworkers are used exclusively. Instead, centralizing responsibility for leadership in a case situation and identifying the crucial points when expertise is required in the social planning can make it possible to provide sustaining adequate paraprofessional services in a much more extensive way so that many more needy aged can be reached.

[25] Elizabeth Kübler-Ross, *On Death and Dying* (London: The Macmillan Co., 1969); Avery D. Weisman and Robert Kastenbaum,The Psychological Autopsy: A Study of the Terminal Phase of Life, *Community Mental Health Journal*, Monograph Series, no. 4 (New York: Behavioral Publications, 1964); and Leonard Pearson, ed., *Death and Dying: Current Issues in the Treatment of the Dying Person* (Cleveland: The Press of Case Western Reserve, 1969).

[26] Margaret Blenkner et al., Protective Service for Older People: Final Report (in process).

[27] Scott Briar, The Current Crisis in Social Casework, in *Social Work Practice, 1967: Selected Papers, 94th Annual Forum, National Conference on Social Welfare, Dallas, Texas, May 21–26, 1967* (New York: Columbia University Press, 1967), pp. 19–33.

[28] Edwin J. Thomas, Behavioral Modification and Casework, in Roberts and Nee, *Theories of Social Casework*, pp. 181–218.

In this article, the emphasis has been on the practitioner as change agent and intervenor in the client system. A more comprehensive community-wide systems approach to the social problem of protective services for the aging adult may well incorporate those direct service practices found to be desirable.[29]

The kinds of needed community-based services to provide protection are fairly clearly known and require expansion. Institutional care that serves the needs of others than the aged protective client is far too costly in human values as well as in economics. Although institutional facilities that truly serve the genuine needs of the aged protective client are essential in the continuum of care, these could well be far less necessary if adequate community-based services are available and sensitively delivered.

Finally, as the protective syndrome in social welfare has been increasingly comprehended in mental health and public health terms, thoughts about prevention arise. In relation to the public health framework, the protective service described here represents the tertiary level in its efforts at disability limitation and rehabilitation. Prevention at earlier levels may be sought at critical points sooner in the lives of aging people when interventions and services may lessen the numbers and extreme conditions of the aged who develop problems that require protective services.

---

[29] For potentials of a broader systems approach to protective service, see Margaret Purvine and Andrew Billingsley, Protective Service as a Social System, *Journal of Public Social Services,* 1:34–45 (March, 1970); and Allen Pincus and Anne Minahan, Toward a Model for Teaching a Basic First-Year Course in Methods of Social Work Practice, in *Innovations in Teaching Social Work Practice,* ed. Lilian Ripple (New York: Council on Social Work Education, 1970), pp. 34–57.

PARANOID DISORDERS

CHAPTER 21

The Paranoid Client

Monna Zentner

Considered in its more extreme form, paranoia involves a drastic loss of reality. In many respects it may involve an especially serious deviation from normal functioning. However, it is not necessarily psychotic or even near-psychotic behavior. The influence of suspiciousness on a client's style of functioning, affective experiences, style of thinking, and so on, appears along a scale of severity and is helped or hindered in a great many ways by other factors. If we wish to categorize those who are paranoid, we might group them into clients who appear to be rather open about their suspicions, filled with a sense of their own omnipotence, and often rigidly contemptuous of others, or we might have a group that could fairly be described as being very constricted, fearful, and protectively secretive of their own suspicious attitudes.[1] Generally, however, in one's caseload one finds representatives of a great range of severity and representatives whose character distortions do not fit them neatly into either classification exclusively.

Classifying Paranoid Behavior

This article will address itself primarily to those clients who may be described as nonpsychotic, clients who have long-standing and pervasive traits, such as suspiciousness, that are classically associated with paranoia.

Some writers have established frameworks for consideration of style, for example, Sibylle K. Escalona and Grace Heider referred to a general

[1] David Shapiro, *Neurotic Styles* (New York: Basic Books, 1965), p. 54.

Reprinted from *Social Casework*, Vol. 61 (March, 1980), pp. 138–145, by permission of the author and the Family Service Association of America.

"inherent continuity of behavioral style" in their developmental study; Wilhelm Reich suggested that character forms, the crystallization of functioning modes, gave people their uniqueness; Heinz Hartmann supplied an angle of focus for character development and modes of functioning; Erik H. Erikson described patterns of direction, of approach, of seeking relationships; David Shapiro supplied a carefully developed groundwork for understanding styles or modes of functioning.[2]

When we identify clients as being paranoid, or when we believe that clients are apprehensive and that reality does not support their lack of trust, we are often referring specifically to the content of their thoughts. We usually note fears that do not seem warranted, a continual expectation of being fooled, or certain ideas that the client may have that suggest that he or she anticipates danger from others. In other words, we generally address ourselves to the content of the concern. But, in practice, paranoia, particularly when it is not a single instance, very aptly describes a process, a way of thinking, and a particular direction of attention.

Paranoid clients are individuals who may have an axe to grind, an idea to be supported, persons whose interest in that idea so seems to consume them that they are not open to data other than those that will support their ideas. Caseworkers have learned, often through bitter experience, that if they attempt to persuade their clients to abandon their paranoia not only is the original idea retained, but often the caseworker becomes a target for suspicion.

CASE EXAMPLE

The following occurred with Jane, a twenty-six-year-old social work graduate student:

JANE: I don't care if Dr. Smith doesn't want to take me. I am going to the office, and he's going to examine me.

WORKER: But his secretary did offer you an appointment for next week. I thought she said that he couldn't see anybody except on an emergency basis for the next few days.

JANE: He just doesn't want to see me because I am a feminist.

WORKER: I don't know if he likes feminists, but you were offered an appointment there. Are you feeling that it's an emergency that you see him?

JANE: It doesn't matter if it is an emergency or not. I know damn well why he doesn't want to see me. You are just defending him because you don't like me being a feminist either.

[2] Sibylle K. Escalona and Grace Heider, *Prediction and Outcome* (New York: Basic Books, 1959), p. 9; Wilhelm Reich. *Character Analysis* (New York: Orgone Institute Press, 1949); Heinz Hartmann, *Ego Psychology and the Problem of Adaptation* (New York: International Universities Press, 1958); Erik H. Erikson, *Childhood and Society* (New York: W. W. Norton, 1950); and Shapiro, *Neurotic Styles.*

It becomes apparent through looking at this process that the client does not seem to be able to be attentive to data that do not support her idea; ostensibly, she believes that the physician does not wish to see her because she is a feminist. The fact that she has been offered an appointment, although not at the time she preferred, does not seem to influence her at all. It is important to note that Jane does not deny that the doctor might have been too busy to see her, nor does she insist that it was an emergency and that perhaps he was, therefore, treating her unfairly. She simply seems to dismiss the facts and to be interested only in any aspect or feature that would lend support to her original idea. Further, when the social worker addresses herself to the data she becomes included as somebody to confirm the original idea of some kind of danger from others.

The above process seems to support the thesis that paranoid clients view information with great bias. They certainly don't ignore any piece of information; indeed, they seem to be acute examiners of it. The problem seems to be that if what they examine does not support their original supposition they simply disregard or dismiss it. This is a fairly typical interaction between a paranoid client and a caseworker. Such clients seem to operate with the belief that that which does not confirm their own idea is really only a sham. They will rationalize conflicting or new information by pointing out that it is simply a superficial aspect, that they want to get to the core of the matter, and that the data do not represent the underlying truth but only an appearance of it. What paranoid clients finally term to be the truth is that which seems to justify their own suspicions.

Symptoms of Intensity and Rigidity

Paranoid people may be difficult to work with because their observations, although frequently biased, contain aspects of reality. In truth, they often make brilliant observations and may have great success in attending to that which bypasses most individuals. Their scanning is not only very intense, but also extremely active. Many social workers have had the experience of having a client notice that a pencil case, for example, has been moved from the right side of the desk to the left, when the worker may not have noticed it. Most workers have also had the experience of having certain clients notice something different about their own appearance, to which they themselves may not have been particularly attentive at all. At first glance, one might believe that the passionate scrutiny of the suspicious client is only a time-limited response to threat: that is, from his or her point of view, danger exists, and anybody will be much more careful and much more observant in the face of danger. Of course, the social worker must carefully examine the premise held by the suspicious client that there is a threat of danger. But, even if the person were in some potentially threatening position, not all clients respond by such intense observation and by such intense attention.

In long-term treatment, it becomes clear that careful scrutiny and well-directed attention are not simply occasioned by a specific danger, but seem to be a fundamental part of a *modus operandi*. It is not just a specific suggestion of danger that brings forth such careful observation and scrutiny; even when a paranoid client applies attention to problems in mathematics, statistics, or some kind of language abstraction he or she seems to apply the same kind of intensity. Such clients are ever vigilant, and no matter what the external circumstances they do not seem capable of ever being passive or casual. They always seem to be searching, always intensely attentive, always looking for something, as if they always have a very specific aim and purpose.

Certainly, paranoid thinking is only unrealistic in some ways and in many other ways is sharply perceptive. But, perceptive as it may be, it seems to be so biased and so narrow that it does not serve the client well. Helen Merrell Lynd, in discussing Rorschach, pointed out that "underlying his whole method is the conception that style and organization are more basic than the specific content ... of experience. He regarded the process of arriving at a particular perception as more significant than the end result." In the same discussion, Lynd mentions Schachtel who "elaborated the view of perception ... as an expression of the whole personality."[3] In essence, for each of us, at any given time or place, there are myriad stimuli, but we perceive only a relatively small number. We are influenced by what we have perceived in the past, as well as by our fears and desires to perceive certain stimuli.

DISTORTIONS OF PERSPECTIVE AND REALITY

Most of us observe our world with ideas that guide us, with beliefs and values that bias our observations, with preconceived notions of that about which we are ignorant, and, it is hoped, our ideas then become influenced by what we do observe. Others view the world from a much less firm stance, with a vague viewpoint, and may become easily impressed in their observations by whatever dramatic proclamations they happen to hear. But paranoid clients view the world from such a rigid interest, with such a narrow focus, that rather than allow their perspective to be modified by fact, they seem to impose their own convictions on whatever data they may observe.

Paranoid clients seem bent on confirming their anticipations. Because these anticipations are based on an idea that seems to be all inclusive of

[3] Helen Merrell Lynd, *On Shame and the Search for Identity* (New York: Science Editions, 1961), pp. 138, 139.

their interests they operate as if they are inattentive either to contradiction or to new information that does not support their anticipations. The not inconsiderable capacity for intellect and the astuteness of some paranoid clients do not become tools to help them to recognize and adjust to reality, but rather are used to mold reality to fit their own prejudices. It is as if paranoid clients are in a very narrow tunnel, and although they may perceive brilliantly within that tunnel, their perceptions are always open to question because they cannot see past the walls of their own trap. For instance, a paranoid client may be the only person to observe that there is a speck of blue on a red canvas. The difficulty is that this talent for intense and direct observation may lead him or her to contend that the only significant color in the painting is blue.

ATTITUDES TOWARD THE UNEXPECTED

Often a paranoid client seems to have a particular problem in dealing with the unexpected. In fact, for all of us, dealing with that which has not been anticipated or that which is outside of the normal demands that we tolerate uncertainty. Paranoid clients seem extraordinarily aware of and sensitive to that which is unusual. The appearance of something unanticipated seems immediately to invite their searching and intense scrutiny. It is as if they must bring it under their control, into their own framework. And the unexpected is observed very closely—again, as if the client must actively master the phenomenon. It does not seem to be merely that they are afraid that that which is new will be of danger to them, although that may be a concern. But whether that which is new is seen to be a danger or not, it is as if the threat exists not merely by virtue of the particular stimulus but by virtue of its newness, by virtue of the fact that the paranoid client did not expect it. Shapiro concludes that this cognition is characterized "by directedness that is maintained in a state of such extreme tension that it resembles a muscle so tense it springs to the touch."[4] In other words, alertness is so finely drawn that a mere touch—from a benign or a dangerous stimulus—causes it to quiver and respond.

We have seen that nonpsychotic, paranoid clients have distortions of reality that are certainly not all encompassing. Further, as reflected above, many of their perceptions may be quite accurate. The difficulty for paranoid clients seems to be that they lose sight of the context of their perceptions, and they have a collection of perceptions attended to and based on biases. Although suspicious clients often observe accurately that which is missed by most people, unfortunately they lose their sense of the factual world. Clients will explain this by saying, in essence, that they disdain the

[4] Shapiro, *Neurotic Styles*, p. 63.

superficial, that they want to get beyond the trivial, inside the core of the problem.

CASE EXAMPLE

Tom hated and feared women. Finally, he told the social worker and defended his argument by saying that most women have a capacity for great rage and anger. He thought this was specifically true for mothers of young children and believed that most of them would secretly like to hit their children at times. From this, he seemed to conclude that there was something dangerous and something to be feared about the mothers of young children.

In fact, some of Tom's perceptions may have been based on truth. Some mothers of young children may, at one time or another, feel like hitting or beating their children. However, most mothers of young children neither give in to such wishes nor feel them in isolation. They may wish to hit their child; at the same time they may be feeling dissatisfied with themselves, and may be feeling tenderness, pity, and guilt and so on toward that child. But Tom, as is the situation with so many paranoid clients, could not see the forest for the trees. When this was pointed out to him he observed that, indeed, mothers may have feelings other than angry ones; he could not, however, attend to this, and seemed only to be able to focus on the potential violence of maternal figures.

Projection

Projection, or the attribution to external objects of feelings, motives, and impulses unacceptable to one's self seems to be characteristic of those who are paranoid. Projection does, of course, occur in many people who would not be characterized as being paranoid. The tendency to see the world with subjective blinders dictated by personal values and natures leads to the use of projection as a mechanism in most of us. It is, however, a particular feature of paranoid clients, whereas for most of the rest of the world it is not a basic characteristic.[5] The use of projection by paranoid clients is particularly of interest because they bring such scrupulous attention and intense scrutiny to the object of their projection. And, they seem to come up with observations of that which is really there as well as observations having to do with that which is not there. In other words, they attend to the external world with the conviction that they must understand the hidden intent of that scrutinized object. They are already observing with a bias, one that supports the idea that there is a hidden intent—and that, quite possibly, this hidden intent may be threatening.

[5] Gordon R. Lowe, *The Growth of Personality* (London: Pelican, 1972), pp. 34–36.

Because of the biases that attend the scrutiny of paranoid clients there seems to always be a distortion of the meaning of perception. That which clients are already searching for, some affirmation that their fear of the object of projection is well founded, is, of course, always understood according to their prejudice or expectancy. For example, the paranoid client may closely observe the body posture of the social worker. Should the social worker's body unexpectedly stiffen, the client may interpret that stiffness as a sign that the social worker is expressing anger. The client may not have been consciously aware of looking for such a sign, but the change of body posture by the social worker will affirm and often crystallize the expectancy that the social worker is angry. It is possible that sometimes the paranoid client is quite correct that the social worker's body may stiffen because the social worker is angry at the client. But the stiffening of the body is seized on by the client only because it matches his or her already preconceived expectation. Most of us have enough flexibility to test out a bias, to at least consider alternative explanations for a change in body posture, for instance. But the client who has such a narrow focus and who needs support for his or her anticipation will not be able to entertain alternative explanations for the change in posture.

CASE EXAMPLE

The following process demonstrates this. A young psychiatrist, Bill, who had been in treatment for a few months brought in a letter he had received from his supervisor. The psychiatrist's probationary period at work was almost over, and the supervisor had reminded him in the letter that he had not yet begun the research project he had agreed to do when hired. The supervisor had gone on to suggest that Bill not start treatment with a new group of patients; instead he should devote part of his time to setting up the research project.

BILL: Well, how do you like this? I can recognize a set up when I see one (referring to the letter).

WORKER: Why do you think it's a set up?

BILL: C'mon. What else would it be? He wrote this so I could be fired at my probationary review.

WORKER: Why would he want you to be fired?

BILL: I don't know. Maybe because I don't suck up to him.

WORKER: I thought you had the impression that he likes you.

BILL: Yeah, but obviously he doesn't.

WORKER: Why do you think the letter is a set up?

BILL: Well, now if I don't start the research, he can say he warned me but I didn't listen.

WORKER: But you were hired with the understanding that you would set up the research project.

BILL: Yeah, but maybe he's jealous because I do well with patients.
WORKER: The letter sounds as if he's trying to help you to keep your job.
BILL: I just knew he'd get me. I've wondered all along if he's jealous.

The client was unable to shift focus for a few weeks. Finally, after he set up the research in time to save his job, he was able to explore alternative explanations.

Shapiro posits that it is "tension and threat that are invariably and essentially transferred and externalized in projection; they achieve a substitute form in the experience of the projective object but not necessarily by the reproduction of their contents in the attributes of that object." In his view, "the internal tension achieves externalized form, first by transformation into defensive tension, and then, by projective reconstruction."[6]

Control and Problems of Autonomy

It often appears that paranoid clients are in a constant state of anticipation for crisis. That is what is so noticeable in their concentrated observation. Sometimes paranoid people seem to be extremely controlled, sometimes irritable and ready to attack. Very paranoid clients certainly seem to lack spontaneity; they observe themselves as well as others very carefully. It is as if all of their behavior must be under constant control. Even certain social behaviors that are automatic in most people seem to be consciously controlled in suspicious clients. And, of course, most paranoid clients attribute to others the same source of intentionality in their behavior. Paranoid clients are often so guarded, their behavior so purposive, their energy so highly mobilized in the event of a feared attack, that it is no wonder that they often seem fearful of feelings that might soften such vigilance. Feelings of concern or tenderness are regarded by paranoid clients with contempt if they appear in someone else; if the paranoid client feels them internally then they seem to be regarded as a sign of weakness. Sensuality seems to be held in constraint, and perhaps understandably so, for how can one open oneself to pleasure if one must be on guard?

The underlying concern of such a constricted mode of functioning seems to be one in the area of autonomy. All of us are probably capable of the intense and narrowed scrutiny of the paranoid client, but we are also able to accept the unanticipated, to be passive in our attention, and to welcome that for which we had not planned. All of us are able to be purposive and directed like the suspicious client, but we are also capable of spontaneity, of letting go, of being playful. It is as if paranoid clients

[6] Shapiro, *Neurotic Styles*, pp. 95–96.

can guard self-mastery or self-authority only in direct proportion to the rigidity with which they direct themselves, and with which they turn their scrutiny to others.

We would assume that a sense of internal mastery allows one to feel some freedom in his or her choice of behavior, and also allows one to feel able or competent to behave in various ways.[7] In contrast, very paranoid clients seem to feel neither able nor free, but rather appear to be arrogant, secretive, and almost always ashamed. They seem to feel a general sense of self-contempt and a particular fear of vulnerability to others, as if their control over themselves and over the events and their environment will disappear at a touch. Lynd points out that "even more than the uncovering of weakness or ineptness, exposure of misplaced confidence can be shameful—happiness, love, anticipation of a response that is not there, something personally momentous received as inconsequential. The greater the expectation, the more acute the shame."[8]

For a person to have a sure sense of self and place vis-à-vis others, both sense of self and sense of the outside world must have "coherence, continuity and dependability." In order for an adult to have a clear and consistent sense of self, he or she would successfully have had to test the world outside for coherence. "Shattering of trust in the dependability of one's immediate world means loss of trust in other persons...."[9] Because the development of a clear sense of self would have to depend on a clear sense of the external world, it is no wonder that the person with a brittle sense of autonomy might use a paranoid mode of functioning, and might be afraid of self-betrayal. If the person has an overwhelming sense of shame, he or she would have learned not only that trust in others is not warranted, but trust in self—a self free with feelings, with yearnings and need for contact—is equally dangerous.

ATTITUDES TOWARD POWER AND MASTERY

Paranoid clients seem always concerned with a fear of being subjugated. The person with a sense of self-mastery can act with abandon, behave nonpurposively, and, within certain parameters, relax enough to be able to comply with the wishes or authority of others. This can be achieved without feeling undue stress and without feeling subjugated. In other words, the paranoid client's lack of spontaneity, rigid directiveness, purposefulness of behavior, and fear of being subjugated by others are two sides of the same coin. It is as if the feeling or wish for self-mastery will be attacked internally as well as from the outside world. Paranoid clients

---

[7] Erik H. Erikson, *Identity: Youth and Crisis* (New York: W. W. Norton, 1968).

[8] Lynd, *Shame and Identity*, pp. 43, 44.

[9] Ibid., p. 45–47.

often seem preoccupied with their fear that somebody will force them to submit to his or her power, someone will trick them into giving over some part of themselves that should be under their own control, someone will force them to have their freedom limited by use of some regulation.

These clients seem to be extremely cognizant of authority and of power: who has the higher rank, who is under whom and who is over whom, who is the chief and who is the lackey, who has the most power to endanger others. When they are with others, part of their narrow focus seems to be on the sense of authority or the position of authority that the other person is in. Their attitude toward authority and power may be one of great anger and resentment, but that is not the important issue: it is most important to recognize their often deep-seated feeling that the one with power, no matter how resented he or she is, is to be understood as a person of more value than paranoid clients can attribute to themselves.[10]

Paranoid clients are extremely fearful of any kind of rejection from those in power. In fact, it often occurs that the simple process of having the social worker attentive to the client may awaken in him or her a sense of humiliation, "a sense of being visible and not yet ready to be visible."[11] One great difficulty for suspicious clients is an internal sense of vulnerability. The sense that they have made themselves vulnerable often results in more rigidly sustained suspiciousness.

CASE EXAMPLES

Mrs. S had experienced very intense negative feelings toward her caseworker for several months. She spent most of her sessions complaining bitterly that the caseworker was ruining her life, hated her, and was against her. Despite this, she couldn't help but note that life in general seemed to be improving. During one session she was able to tell the caseworker very hesitantly that perhaps the caseworker was being of some positive use to her and, even more daring for Mrs. S, that she was beginning to have some positive feelings toward the caseworker.

Soon after she was able to express these positive feelings, her obsessive worry about what the caseworker "really thought" of her became intensified; accompanying that worry was her fear that now that she had "opened" herself to the caseworker, the caseworker would take advantage of her "weakness." Although she continued to do well outside the therapy hours, the next several sessions after her declaration of positive feelings were marked by a tunnel vision that focused only on whether the caseworker was rejecting her, making fun of her, or trying to hurt her in some way.

Apparently, Mrs. S experienced her affection for the caseworker and

[10] Shapiro, *Neurotic Styles,* pp. 82–86.
[11] Erikson, *Identity,* p. 110.

her declaration of it as a probable self-destructive act, an exposure to shame, and an invitation to invade and hurt. It is as if she were giving up a certain amount of autonomy or inviting the social worker to step in for her.

A nurse, who had always been concerned that taking orders from her superiors might put her in a humiliating position, had a new supervisor whom she admired. The new supervisor was well thought of in hospital circles, and the nurse wished to impress her. She was very careful to make clear to the supervisor that she would follow her orders, simply because she liked her and she wanted to, rather than as an "underling."

Although the supervisor seemed to have positive feelings for the nurse, she obviously did not single her out over anyone else; despite the nurse's wishes, it was clear that she was not a special favorite. At this point, the nurse began to get very concerned that perhaps the supervisor might be taking advantage of what she considered her "complacency" in following orders. She not only began to look for signs that the supervisor was taking advantage of her and did not care for her, but began to anticipate such symbols.

Within a relatively short time the client changed from simply longing for the supervisor's approval into being suspicious of her. The nurse became angrier and angrier. Instead of complying with routine assignments, she began to refuse them, feeling that she now had proof that the supervisor was trying to "reduce" her in some way. In a relatively short time the supervisor had gone from a person to be admired and a person from whom one would seek approval to a potential enemy.

As the once-admired person becomes the dangerous person, the behavior of the client may evoke such negative responses that the original suspiciousness, arising from a sense of vulnerability that seemed to have no base in reality, will now be sustained by repercussions from negative behavior toward the suspected enemy. In the beginning of the process described above, the nurse had responded to her own affection for the supervisor in a somewhat paranoid manner, as if a positive feeling for someone would weaken the nurse, might be a sign that her self-mastery was less under control than it should be, or might be a sign that the nurse had something weak or soft inside of her.

The process example reflects how the same concern is now externalized. The nurse examines and has the same intense scrutiny toward the supervisor she once had toward herself, but it is now the supervisor who is the enemy and not some part of the self that might open one to other people in a dangerous way. It is not just that the supervisor is now seen as potentially dangerous, a person who will take advantage of those who comply with her wishes, she is seen as personally, directly, and specifically dangerous to the nurse. In other words, it is not just a specific content that may be attributed to the superior, but a specific process or style—the superior is seen or suspected as bent on the destruction and humiliation of the nurse.

These case examples simply dramatize a constant subjective experience for the paranoid client. For the most part they are continually alert, as if they must never let down their guard. It is as if they may never stop taking precautions for, if they relax, what defenses will they have against an anticipated threat? It has been mentioned that change or surprise is very difficult for the paranoid person. Thus, their ever-ready state of being on guard protects them from being taken unaware by danger, protects them from feeling surprised by the unexpected, and prepares them to be ready for action rather than passivity in response to the unexpected.[12] It is as if they are always open to the possibility of threat.

To express positive feelings for someone, as in the example of the client who expressed affection for the social worker or the nurse who admired her superior, is subjectively experienced as a dangerous letting down of the guard. The subsequent feeling of vulnerability is then critically and negatively evaluated: to like the caseworker is to give in to the caseworker; to admire the supervisor is to be infantile and passive.

Summary

In summary, paranoid clients might be said to interpret certain subjective feelings—tenderness, admiration, and so on—as a threat to their sense of autonomy. They seem to question themselves and examine their own motivations and feelings with close scrutiny, as if the feelings were in some way a dangerous betrayal of self-mastery. They may then become more paranoid, and with their particular tunnel vision search for proof that their original suspicious ideas are correct and can be confirmed. Paranoid clients tend to ignore the content that most people see and dismiss it as superficial or not the real thing. In other words, that which is substantially real is disdained. Generally, the narrow scrutiny persists until the suspiciousness that seems to have as its origin a fear of the loss of autonomy is confirmed. Even when there is no particular threat to paranoid clients they live in a state of guardedness, ever ready to defend against the unexpected.

This particular angle of vision suggests further areas of exploration for our understanding beyond the scope of this article. The concept of narcissism reviewed by Sophie Loewenstein[13] should be examined with specific focus on difficulties involving autonomy, vulnerability, and suspiciousness. Otto Kernberg's contributions in this field, particularly his theori-

---

[12] Shapiro, *Neurotic Styles*, pp. 54–108, 176–201.

[13] Sophie Loewenstein, "An Overview of the Concept of Narcissism," *Social Casework* 58 (March 1977): 136–42.

zations based on experiences with nonpsychotic clients, offer a firm foundation on which to build. Erich Fromm adds valuable perceptions, but a more thorough investigation of the relationship between narcissism and paranoid styles promises to be quite useful.[14] In addition, a more thorough understanding of the development of trust and autonomy as related to paranoid modes of functioning, with their correlates of hope and omnipotence, would appear to greatly bolster an understanding of suspicious clients. Most important, from these studies must emerge a clearly delineated treatment framework for paranoid clients.

---

[14] See Otto Kernberg, *Borderline Conditions and Pathological Narcissism* (New York: Jason Aronson, 1975): and Erich Fromm, *The Anatomy of Human Destructiveness* (New York: Holt, Rinehart and Winston, 1973).

PERSONALITY DISORDERS

CHAPTER 22

The Borderline Personality

Anne O. Freed

The recent proliferation of books, articles, institutes, seminars, and work-shops on the borderline and narcissistic personality disorders makes it evident that all of us in the mental health field are searching and striving to understand the angry, depressed, demanding, and disturbing clients who constantly challenge us. Beatrice Simcox-Reiner observed that depression is the most prevalent emotional problem we confront, that more persons being seen by psychiatrists (and social workers) have character disorders, and that "more patients seem at times dissociated from reality and are described as 'borderline personalities'."[1]

Social workers have always worked toward understanding what is responsible for the anger, rage, rejection, ambivalence, instant requests and demands, and fear of closeness yet insistence on dependence that characterize such clients. Now that it appears that these clients are labeled "borderline," social workers are asking what exactly is a borderline disorder? What is its etiology? What are its dynamics? How does one treat borderline clients? What is their prognosis? How can the pathology be prevented? The current literature contains a new language, new meanings of familiar words, and new elaborations of old concepts like narcissism, pseudoneurosis, mirror transference, object relations, self-object representations, introjects, separation- individuation, rapprochement, whole and part objects, and transitional objects and phenomenon, to name only a few.

The purpose of this article is to define the syndrome called "border-

[1] Beatrice Simcox-Reiner, "A Feeling of Irrelevance: The Effects of a Nonsupportive Society." *Social Casework: The Journal of Contemporary Social Work* 60 (January 1979): 4.

Reprinted from *Social Casework*, Vol. 61 (November, 1980), pp. 548–558, by permission of the author and the Family Service Association of America.

line'' and to sort out some of the theories on borderline personality in order to understand them and decide which are most helpful to social workers. In addition, it will describe the developmental issues on which these theories are based, raise questions concerning social origins of borderline theories in addition to the intrapsychic, clarify some of the psychodynamics involved, and suggest treatment, goals, and methods based on a psychosocial diagnosis.

Defining the Borderline Personality

Borderline personalities have been known by many descriptive titles representing a wide range of characterological pathologies. For example, they have been designated as pseudoneurotic, schizoid-inadequate, narcissistic, infantile, paranoid, impulse-ridden, polymorphous-perverse, alloplastic, ''as-if,'' sociopathic, and cyclothymic personalities. Symptoms, behavior, and affects of borderline personalities range from rage, emptiness, depression, persistent narcissistic demands, infantile pleasure-seeking, projective identification, object splitting in relationships with people, primitive idealizations, vulnerable reality testing, and identity diffusion. They are described as feeling bad and worthless, but at the same time, as asserting feelings of omnipotence and magically trying to control their environment.

For some time, the group of people referred to as borderline were limited to those identified as being *on the border of shizophrenia*. These clients were not overly psychotic, had a number of defenses that appeared to maintain them, and parts of their egos were functioning reasonably well. Yet, they constantly appeared to be on the brink of disaster. They were also described as pseudoneurotics, who were really schizophrenics masked by multiple neurotic symptoms and pananxiety.[2] Others considered them to be on the continuum of character pathologies between neuroses and psychoses.[3] Helene Deutsch added considerably to these observations by her description of the ''as-if'' personality, people with no identity of their own, chameleon-like as they assumed and reflected the personalities of those with whom they associated. She pointed to their lack of emotional attachments and morals and their narcissistic level of functioning. She thought they had a schizoid core and features.[4]

[2] Paul Hoch and Phillip Polatin, ''Pseudoneurotic Forms of Schizophrenia,'' *Psychoanalytic Quarterly* 23 (April 1949): 248–76.

[3] Robert Knight, ''Borderline States,'' in *Psychoanalytic Psychiatry and Psychology*, ed. Robert Knight and Cyrus Friedman (New York: International Universities Press, 1962), pp. 97–109.

[4] Helene Deutsch, ''Some Forms of Emotional Disturbance and Their Relationship to Schizophrenia,'' in *Neurosis and Character Types* (New York: International Universities Press, 1965), pp. 262–81.

A growing number have disagreed with the concept of *on the border of schizophrenia*, preferring to see this group as unique, with certain capacities for adaptive functioning, while, at the same time, having very serious interpersonal problems. They have commented that the syndrome was stable and predictable in its instability. As early as 1938, A. Stern observed a group of patients who had narcissistic character neuroses and flat affects, living and behaving as if they were still in their childhood world and suffering from a developmental injury caused by insufficient maternal affection. He wrote that they required "a corrective emotional experience" in treatment if they were to change.[5] They were shallow, inconsistent, highly ambivalent, and overanxious.

More recently, others have agreed with Stern and, in studying the borderline syndrome, concluded it contained a variety of types of people, not psychotic but with severe emotional disturbances rooted in a developmental arrest. Affects were seen to range in intensity from close to psychotic to more neurotic expressions.[6] Roy Grinker and associates observed four major characteristics: anger, defect in affectional relationships, poor self-identity, and depressive loneliness. Despite their common attributes, four classifications distinct from schizophrenia were suggested on a continuum of severity:

1. The psychotic borderline—hostile, negative, close to psychotic disintegration
2. The core borderline—acting out behavior and shifting involvements with people
3. The adaptive, affectless, defended, "as-if" person—characterized by blandness, no self-identity, schizoid withdrawal, and intellectualization
4. The neurotic borderline—always anxious, depressed, narcissistic, and clinging[7]

Elizabeth Zetzel[8] also saw borderline clients as regressed but not psychotic, fixated at a higher level, but with a weak, impaired ego and utilizing primitive mechanisms of aggression, destruction, and hostility in their core. She was impressed with the splitting she observed as clients carefully divided good and bad feelings defensively.

Later, John Gunderson and Margaret T. Singer were impressed with

---

[5] A. Stern, "Psychoanalytic Investigation of and Therapy in a Borderline Group of Neuroses," *Psychoanalytic Quarterly* 7 (1938): 467–89.

[6] Richard Chessick, *Intensive Psychotherapy of the Borderline Patient* (New York: Jason Aronson, 1977). pp. 43–51.

[7] Roy Grinker, Beatrice Werble, and Robert Drye. *The Borderline Syndrome* (New York: Basic Books, 1968).

[8] Elizabeth Zetzel, "A Developmental Approach to the Borderline Patient," *American Journal of Psychiatry* 127 (January 1971): 867–71.

the considerable social adaptiveness borderline personalities achieve, but they found prominent hostile and depressive features, fear and anxiety, problems with impulse control, and, from time to time, evidence of primitive, illogical, and occasionally bizarre manifestations beneath this facade. They believed that there is enough evidence to support the idea that a borderline personality disorder is a nosological entity of its own.[9]

Theories and Theoreticians

An important group of investigators of the borderline personality identify themselves as object relations theorists stemming from psychoanalytic ego psychologists and, to some extent, those followers of the controversial Melanie Klein. In the 1940s and 1950s, the most important of these were Ronald Fairbairn, Harry Guntrip, and Donald Winnicott, all of England. They were interested in how people develop the capacity for object relations and referred to Melanie Klein's studies of beginning ego and object development in the mother-child dyad.[10] Fairbairn, building on Klein, saw the roots of schizophrenia in the person who could not resolve object and ego splitting.[11] Donald Winnicott agreed with him and stressed that the "good enough mother" is crucial to the child's development of the capacity to form adequate object relations as it grows. The child may even assume a "false self" if the mother is "not good enough," is inflexible, unresponsive, overdemanding of conformity, and does not allow individuation to take place. The child, unable to resolve ambivalence and control its aggression and impulses, cannot develop trust and continues the splitting and the projection-introjection process defensively because of its angry, frustrated, disappointed, and hostile feelings. Low self-esteem and a poor self- image result.

   In the United States, Otto Kernberg is probably the most quoted and most prolific writer among American object relations theorists. He sees the borderline personality in persons having problems with interpersonal relationships; they are in a state of "stable disorder," having ego defects and pathology as a result of a developmental arrest in the mother-child dyadic period originating at the end of the first year of life. The continuum theory is rejected, but he divides symptoms into high-level and lower-level functioning.[12]

[9] John Gunderson and Margaret T. Singer. "Defining Borderline Patients: An Overview," *American Journal of Psychiatry* 132 (January 1975): 1–10.

[10] For detailed discussion of Melanie Klein's theories, see Harry Guntrip, *Psychoanalytic Theory, Therapy and the Self* (New York: Basic Books, 1971).

[11] Ronald Fairbairn, *Psychoanalytic Studies of the Personality* (London: Routledge and Kegan Paul, 1952).

[12] Otto Kernberg, *Borderline Conditions and Pathological Narcissism* (New York: Jason Aronson, 1975), pp. 3–49.

In describing the numerous symptoms and combinations of borderline personalities, Kernberg notes they lack the ability to internalize good interpersonal relations—he refers to this as taking in "object-representations" and reminds us that self-image, self-concept, ideal-self, and attitudes about the self grow and evolve within the individual only as a result of early good interpersonal relationships. The child introjects attitudes and feelings from its relationship with the parents, who are its first ego ideals and later contribute to the formation of the superego. If these relationships have defects that originated in the latter part of the first year of life, the foundation for the borderline personality is established. Thus, he says, while some reality testing is present, the synthesis of the good and bad introjects and identifications from the parents do not take place, the split persists, and future interpersonal relationships do not develop well.[13] Selma Fraiberg refers to this as "disease of the ego" or "disease of nonattachment."[14] Without the ability to form meaningful, lasting interpersonal relationships based on trust, love, and reciprocal gratifications, life is unfulfilled, empty, hopeless, lonely, and depressing.

Given the importance of this early internalization process, Kernberg proposes that there are four stages of early ego development, with the fixation of borderline character occurring in the third stage, in the latter part of the first year of life, when the child and the internal good mother image are still split from the aggressive self and bad mother image, but, because of poor mothering and other traumas, the integration of the good and bad does not occur. Thus, an integrated self-concept fails to develop. The child remains chronically dependent on outside people, develops contradictory traits, and eventually inconsistent and chaotic interpersonal relationships. A unified sense of self, superego, and ego ideal cannot be accomplished. Instead, extreme idealized images and an excessive sadistic superego develop that punish the bad self-image. To counteract the bad self-image, praise and assurance from others is sought, but rarely is it sufficient for satisfaction and self-assurance. With effort going to controlling the good-bad conflict as well as the anxiety and frustrations, there is insufficient energy to develop healthy coping mechanisms and channels of creative enjoyment of life. Although these etiological factors are described in detail by Kernberg, he does not rule out such constitutional factors as inborn excessive oral aggression, poor capacity for neutralizing aggression, and inborn lack of anxiety tolerance.[15]

Kernberg accounts for variations of development, saying there is a primitive low-level borderline, where internalized object relationships are

[13] Otto Kernberg, *Object Relations Theory and Clinical Psychoanalysis* (New York: Jason Aronson, 1976), pp. 19–55.

[14] Selma Fraiberg, *Every Child's Birthright: In Defense of Mothering* (New York: Basic Books, 1977).

[15] Kernberg, *Borderline Conditions and Narcissism*, pp. 24–39.

poorly formed, a somewhat higher level, where some integration of self-images and those from outside have taken place, and, finally, a high level, where one finds the fixation of the narcissistic personality structure. In this third level, there is an integrated self, but also a grandiose "special child" syndrome, with an ideal-self fantasying power and wealth. This behavior serves as a defensive reaction against the rage the child feels about the reality that the mother is not ever-loving and ever-giving and, in addition, threatens either abandonment or engulfment.[16]

Projective identification is another mechanism common in borderline experiences. In order to feel less anxious, the borderline personality projects and externalizes the bad aggressive mother-image. Although appearing to fear the external object, it is, in reality, the danger and badness within that is feared and projected onto an external object. At the same time, the borderline character identifies with that object, seeing it as having its own characteristics, qualities, and aggression. Its efforts go both into controlling and attacking the object to prevent being attacked by it. Thus, projective identification indicates a lack of differentiation between the self and the external object.[17]

James Masterson agreed with Kernberg that the borderline personality structure is fixated at an early developmental point, but suggested its origins are in the rapprochement period (from the sixteen to seventeen months to twenty-five months) identified by Margaret Mahler as part of the separation-individuation process. Rapprochement, part of the separation-individuation process, occurs after the child has practiced separating and is now psychologically ready to return to the mother, having asserted itself and begun its individuation.[18]

PROBLEMS OF THE MOTHER–CHILD DYAD

Masterson states that during the rapprochement period problems may occur in the mother-child relationship leading to borderline personality formation. The child may be given messages that it may not be a separate being, that it may not be an individual in its own right. It may be so rejected that it feels worthless and useless and must beg for what it wants. It may learn it must always conform to receive any approval. On the other hand, it may be given such confused messages that both symbiotic demands and rejections are communicated.

[16] Ibid., pp. 277–313.

[17] Otto Kernberg has written many articles and books on this subject. Suggested reading are *Borderline Conditions and Pathological Narcissism;* and *Object Relations Theory and Clinical Psychoanalysis.*

[18] James Masterson, *Psychotherapy of the Borderline Adult* (New York: Brunner/Mazel, 1976), pp. 23–45; and Margaret Mahler, Fred Pine, and Anni Bergman, *The Psychological Birth of the Child* (New York: International Universities Press, 1975).

Further, Masterson found that mothers of borderline patients usually suffer from a borderline syndrome themselves and could not separate from their own mothers. They foster a symbiotic union and cannot perceive the child as an individual, seeing it instead as an object to help them defend against their own fears of loneliness and abandonment. The child is forced to give up his budding individuation to preserve the mother's sense of self and to get her approval. As the child grows older, he begins to sense the psychological abandonment and drain, feels anger, rage, depression, guilt, fear, helplessness, passivity, and emptiness. With rapprochement never adequately negotiated, the child never achieves the last step of Mahler's developmental sequence, object constancy.[19]

Masterson also points to the father in the borderline child's life, finding many have pathologies of borderline, narcissistic, or schizophrenic proportions. The father is unavailable to the child during the formation of the child's individuation and identity. He may be unconsciously reinforcing the mother's clinging relationship to the child, either by his absence or by acquiescing passively to the mother's wishes. He may be symbiotically tied to the dominant mother or more involved with his work than with his family.[20]

In recent years, Heinz Kohut has become widely known for his writings on the self and the narcissistic personality disorder. He describes two parallel lines of normal narcissistic development. In one line, after the infantile narcissistic stage, the child develops a grandiose self that has highly omnipotent features. Only as the ego develops and the child becomes aware of reality and has satisfactory object relations does it move from its grandiose stance, slowly transforming that narcissism into a sense of self-esteem, self-confidence, ambition, enjoyment of activities, and object love. At the same time, following the early infantile period, the child moves toward a strong identification with parents who are idealized, in fact the first ego ideals. Only after the ego and object relations maturational processes take place is the idealized parental image viewed more realistically and changed, ultimately, into a set of internalized ideals and an adult superego. This total process is called transmuting internalization.[21]

Narcissistic injuries in the grandiose self or the idealized parental image stages caused by traumas or unempathic, rejecting, disappointing parents may result in a developmental arrest. These persons then spend a lifetime seeking objects to replace the disappointing, rejecting parents, or continuing to assert their grandiosity unrealistically to convince themselves of their self-worth. They repeatedly display a narcissistic rage. Di-

[19] Masterson, *Psychotherapy of Borderline Adults*, p. 3–89.

[20] Ibid.; and James Masterson, ed., *New Perspectives on the Psychotherapy of the Borderline Adult* (New York: Brunner/Mazel, 1978).

[21] Heinz Kohut, *The Analysis of the Self: A Systematic Approach to the Psychoanalytic Treatment of Narcissistic Personality Disorders* (New York: International Universities Press, 1971).

agnosis of pathological narcissistic character structures is, according to Kohut, confirmed through analysis of the transference. If the therapist is overidealized, fixation is at the idealized parental image-narcissistic stage. If the client demands merger, twinship, or mirroring with the therapist, a diagnosis of grandiose stage narcissism is established.[22]

THE SOCIETAL CONTEXT

Up to this point, the literature concentrates on intrapsychic conflicts arising from interpersonal relationships originating in the problems of the mother-child dyad, which then lead to borderline personality formations. It is only as we turn to explorations of "new narcissism," discussed by Reiner, that the societal context is added to the other etiological considerations. She states that a sense of irrelevance in society, alienation, narcissistic "deification of the isolated self," "lifeboat ethics," social pressures and stresses, massive traumas (as the violence of the Holocaust, widespread terrorism, the Vietnam War, nuclear war, as well as the spread of violence in families), inhuman environments in which people live, and wide discrepancies between values and beliefs contribute to problems in interpersonal relationships[23]—and that is what the borderline and narcissistic personalities are all about. Christopher Lasch reinforces the contributions of Reiner in describing the social structure and values today as a "social invasion of the self". He sees the emergence of the narcissistic personality as part of the human condition of our age.[24]

Treatment Issues and Suggestions

Theories of the origin and etiology of the borderline personality and descriptions of borderline behavior without realistic suggestions on treatment planning leave social workers in a state of frustration. Recommendations for long-term psychoanalysis or even psychotherapy are not practical or feasible for social workers. Limitations of time and staff, treatment methods, and the client's frequent lack of motivation contribute to the despair of the social agencies in treating these people. Many of these clients come for help only in crises. Many come because the courts or other sources of authority demand it. For most, the goals are not personality change (they do not see the need) but immediate relief from discomfort, inner conflicts, tangled interpersonal problems, depression, and loneliness. They frequently come for help with a concrete problem (like the loss of a job) or

---

[22] Ibid.

[23] Reiner, "Feeling of Irrelevance," p. 3–10.

[24] Christopher Lasch, *The Culture of Narcissism* (New York: W. W. Norton, 1978).

general feelings of discontent. They are vague and indecisive in defining their problems.

SPECIAL AGENCY CONSIDERATIONS

Given the difficulties in engaging these clients, determining their problems, and contracting to help them, the kinds of issues social workers and agencies must take into account are multiple and complex and relate to clinical questions, social workers' capacities, and agency policies.

Some of these considerations are:

1. The level of functioning and the ego development of the client
2. How long the client is really prepared to engage in treatment
3. How long the worker and the agency are prepared to engage in the treatment and the level and intensity of treatment to be expected and needed
4. Whether the client's problems can be partialized into a series of short-term contracts and limited goals that are attainable
5. What the social and reality pressures are, for example, child abuse, family violence, legal pressures, unemployment, poor housing, and the degree of seriousness of the situation
6. Whether the worker is prepared to handle the extremely negative transference, even psychotic transference, that Kernberg states occurs in work with borderline clients. Also, the worker's flexibility, creativity, tolerance, and ability to handle countertransference reactions need to be assessed
7. The type of agency, its functions, and its staff capacity to respond to these clients' needs and demands
8. The modalities available in the agency, the workers' skills in these modalities, supervision, staff development, and consultation
9. The workers' capacity to effect family interventions and to address interpersonal relationships, particularly their destructive, violent aspects

CHARACTERISTICS OF SOCIAL WORKERS

Because object relations and the establishment of a corrective emotional experience are the core of treatment for borderline personalities, the following capacities are necessary within the social worker:

1. A worker who can *reach out* to form a therapeutic relationship, who can offer the support, empathy, and understanding that was missing in the client's early primary relationships
2. A worker who can help the client become a separate being with his or her own unique identity

3. A worker who will not be passive and will establish him or herself as a *real person* and reduce fantasies and negative transference
4. A worker who will focus on reality issues and problem solving to help the client achieve a sense of success and a better self-image
5. A worker who can establish an attitude of mutual respect and have expectations of achieving successful results. This is the only way clients can develop improved self-esteem and self-confidence.
6. A worker capable of establishing ground rules and a contract with the client not to act out impulsively and precipitously and who can harness these acting-out pressures for the casework hour so that they may be talked about and worked on step by step
7. A worker who agrees to assume a caring, nurturing role and makes this evident early in the contract
8. A worker who is able to use his or her own ego in the relationship, acting as an observing and auxiliary ego for the client
9. A worker who can help the individual client and, at the same time, engage the family in the therapeutic process because, where possible, *a family approach is essential*
10. A worker who not only focuses on the personality of the client, but also provides concrete services, using them as a means of reaching the client

Long-Term Treatment Goals

Treatment needs to be both individual and family-oriented and to be either supportive or restitutive. Goals need to be feasible and realistic. The immediate social situation must be part of the treatment plan. If long-term treatment is agreed to by the client and worker, they may articulate three phases: (1) the testing phase, in which establishment of a working alliance and trust takes place; (2) the working-through phase (by far the longest), which includes especially resolution of the underlying depression; and (3) the separation and establishment of a constructive life direction. These long-term goals are readily definable, but not so readily achievable given the propensity for these clients to flee from treatment because of their long-term self-defeating behavior, their pain in experiencing their depression, and their narcissistic rage. If the client is capable of being engaged over a period of time, the theories described in this article indicate that the goals should be:

1. To help bring about an integration and coalescence of good and bad splits, thus eliminating the splitting mechanisms and patterns
2. To accept the primary ambivalence rather than fight it
3. To bring the primitive idealizations and projective identifications within reality contexts and develop normal repression

4. To develop mature dependence[25] through the therapeutic relationship instead of infantile, immature dependence
5. To establish efforts at mastery, control of impulses, and frustration tolerance
6. To engage the ego in realistic planning and healthy coping behavior through the problem-solving process
7. To bring about better feelings about the self, acceptance of these good feelings, and achievement of an improved self-image through reduction of self-defeating behavior and through recognition of achievements
8. To bring about acceptance of one's separateness and wholeness
9. To establish the client's capacity to relate to others and others to relate to him or her through the therapeutic relationship of trust and warmth. To permit closeness without fusion, separateness without abandonment, and individuality within the social and family context
10. To help the client meet concrete needs and use this experience as part of relationship and trust building

General Treatment Considerations

Treatment for the borderline client requires an imaginative, creative, flexible, patient worker with awareness of the vicissitudes inherent in the client's behavioral patterns in order to be adaptive to the client. To offer a corrective experience when the client is full of rage or feels completely empty requires careful ongoing assessment, a slow building of relationship, and a capacity on the part of the worker to tolerate rejection and, at the same time, to feel empathy toward the client. Just as important, because these clients are crisis-ridden, the worker needs to be immediately available to neutralize conflict, defuse rage, and offer an auxiliary ego to help master the situation and solve immediate problems.

The worker must be able to tolerate the tenacity and demands of the client and help bring these into realistic focus. The worker also has to know when to move in with closeness and caring and when to maintain a respectful distance because the client cannot tolerate closeness. The worker who can, in a benign way, set limits and expectations, be available, and maintain a reality orientation while, at the same time, become a positive model for the client to internalize is the ideal person to work with borderline clients.

Because many borderline clients tend to somatize their stresses, hypochondriasis, particularly in adults, is a common response. Thus, it may

---

[25] Fairbairn, *Psychoanalytic Studies of the Personality,* pp. 42, 163.

be necessary to have all symptoms medically examined so that organic disease can be clearly ruled out. Showing concern and acceptance is vital, especially because so many clients convert bad feelings about themselves into bad physical symptoms.

Among the activities expected on the part of the worker, outreach is especially urgent as a technique, because these clients need to be pursued if they are to be engaged in treatment. Either they are distancers, or their clinging may make the worker turn into a distancer. Once an alliance is achieved, the possible transference reactions need to be actively handled by the worker, who now anticipates clients' fears and vacillations. Further, because these clients tend to act out feelings rather than engage in a thinking-through process, the worker is forced to assume a strong role to bring about control of impulsivity. When a relationship is well underway, confrontation and interpretation are used repeatedly regarding destructive patterns, in an effort to help the client protect him or herself. To turn around the client's low self-esteem requires a strong casework relationship and a quick response by the worker whenever problem solving is required. Repetition and reinforcement of successful decisions and experiences are essential.

Short-Term Treatment

Many of the techniques, concepts, and processes of long-term treatment, may also be used in briefer treatment. Short-term, well-planned goals are frequently the only approach possible with borderline clients. This should not be frowned on or scoffed at as inadequate. This modality may be the most practical when agencies are confronted with large numbers of such clients, and when it is evident the clients, cannot or will not engage in sustained long-term therapeutic plans. Crisis intervention is a type of short-term treatment that may at least bring about a temporary homeostasis. Planned short-term treatment, with its focus on smaller, immediate, manageable issues, does not foster an intensive relationship (which the borderline client may not be prepared to engage in for some time), and a built-in separation plan may be better tolerated by the client, making him or her feel safe. If the brief treatment is successful and goals are achieved, the client will feel better about him or herself and be more ready to engage in further treatments at a later date.

An invitation to return to the agency and the offer of the possibilities of a series of planned short-term treatments, intersected by periods away from treatment, may be more feasible and acceptable to some clients. Some therapists maintain that telephone contact in between periods of treatment is desirable, because it maintains the ties of the relationship on a level tolerable to the client. More often than not, these agency clients have families and, out of concern for other family members, it may be decided to maintain such protective contacts.

Treatment Techniques

Once a therapeutic relationship is established with borderline personalities, the treatment techniques used in any character disorder case may be appropriately attempted. Confrontation, insight, interpretation, supportiveness, availability, crisis intervention, and transference are among the techniques available. Work on losses, depression, ego and object splits, neutralization of aggression, reduction of projective identification and primitive idealization are treatment issues. Often, it is not possible to undertake all of these techniques, but it is essential not to underestimate the importance to such disturbed people of worker and agency availability, caring, and active intervention. Eventually, this may become internalized and, through such help, the client will learn to think through problems instead of acting precipitously, just as the client will learn that there are people who *are* concerned.[26]

CASE EXAMPLE

Mrs. P, a forty-five-year-old childless divorcee who had been married several times, was treated for a number of years, at first weekly and, during crises, twice weekly; later, she was treated once every two or three months, and eventually only a few times a year. The social worker was always available for telephone interviews as needed and occasionally called her just to keep in touch. At first, Mrs. P was immobilized when confronted with any conflict situation. She came for treatment because she hated her boss and wanted to quit her job and move elsewhere, but couldn't do anything about it; she could make no decisions. Her anxiety when confronting an authority figure paralyzed her because she saw all authorities as critical of her. She was an angry, depressed woman, unable to verbalize her feelings fully. She would sit for long periods saying nothing to the worker. She hated herself, drank too much, and considered herself on the verge of psychosis, but also thought herself intellectually superior to most of the people with whom she associated. After a considerable period in treatment, when she finally felt accepted and supported, she began to talk at great length about her hurts. Her parents did not protect her from the excessive abuse of an older brother and she never felt able to get close to her aloof, proper mother and her hypercritical father, whom she could never please however hard she tried. As an adult, she doubted

[26] For discussions of treatment issues and techniques the following books are recommended: Arlene Wohlberg, *The Borderline Patient* (New York: Intercontinental Medical Book, 1973); Chessick, *Intensive Psychotherapy of the Borderline Patient*; and Peter Hartocollis, ed., *Borderline Personality Disorders* (New York: International Universities Press, 1977).

her abilities, belittled herself, avoided closeness, and yearned to be a "free agent." She could not, however, even bring herself to move from her parental home, where by this time she lived alone.

When Mrs. P did speak up to authority figures, it was with rage and sarcasm and this behavior generally resulted in hurt to herself, leaving her fearful and shaken. In addition, she overidentified with people she perceived as weak, hopeless victims, often rather impulsively offering to help them by giving loans of money or other tangible items, only to find herself repeatedly victimized because she had not perceived how disturbed they were. These actions provide vivid examples of projective identification. Over the years in treatment, she experienced the worker's concern, deep interest, caring, active support, tenacity, crisis interventions, and efforts to help her control her acting out. She began to talk about her feelings instead of acting impulsively, to plan ahead, and to think through consequences of possible actions. Slowly, both worker and client observed fewer self-destructive experiences. Mrs. P could make connections between her early childhood hurts and her current relationships (including the husbands she rejected), and she could start individualizing people she interacted with, ceasing to identify them unconsciously with people from her distant past. She began to acknowledge the "good" and the "bad" in her siblings and parents and her rage against her parents reduced as the splitting became less pronounced. This led to less acting out with authority figures, and she finally started living in the present and assessing and planning for her future. She was able to go on several extended trips, earn an advanced degree, and seek a job in another community while holding on to the one she had until she found another. She ceased referring to herself as a "kook," accepted that she had talent and intelligence, and that people could like her. Although she was constantly subject to regressions and depression when confronted with important decisions, her range and level of functioning broadened and she had more periods of satisfactions. She still calls the worker from time to time when making an important decision, or just to say hello. She may never be a happy person, but she is leading a less anxiety-ridden existence and maintains good relationships with a number of people.

Group Therapy

In working with borderline clients, serious consideration should be given to group therapy when significant weaknesses in ego functioning and in object relations development are presented. Group treatment is recommended by numerous therapists as offering the kind of support and mutual control many of these clients require. Leonard Horwitz reported successes in use of confrontation in a group to help them overcome "egocentric and abrasive character traits"[27] through being accepted in a group.

[27] Leonard Horwitz, "Group Psychotherapy of the Borderline Patient," in *Borderline Personality Disorders*, ed. Hartocollis, pp. 399–422.

Group therapy helps clients learn to listen, explore, and understand each other's communications. Reality testing and a corrective emotional experience without the forced closeness of one-to-one therapy may be achieved. The group offers safeguards, can regulate the intensity of reactions, and clients need not feel narcissistically devastated by criticism when several in the group are simultaneously hearing similar comments about themselves.[28] Wilfred Bion reports projective identification and splits of good and bad are ideally handled in the group.[29] Although resolving the basic separation-individuation issues in the borderline personality remains an individual therapy goal, the group can be used for ameliorating maladaptive behavior.[30] For many social work agency clients, this goal is more urgent than the more ambitious one of working through early life issues. Other therapists'[31] experiences in leading groups for borderline clients over a considerable period report that this therapy has led to formation of trust and closeness, fostered relationships, created a sense of support and family, and permitted individuation. This is a slow process, but worth the time and effort.

TREATMENT EXAMPLE

An open-end therapy group at Family Service Association of Greater Boston is made up of seven middle-aged borderline women who range from very well educated and high socioeconomic backgrounds to uneducated and poor, from those whose psychotic core is evident to those with somewhat better defenses, from those with jobs to others fearful of working or on public assistance, from age forty-five to sixty-four. The members are:

1. Mrs. W, aged sixty, a college graduate and a secretary, three times divorced, who was phobic and depressed five years ago when she joined the group. She thought of herself as "a nothing," and deserving of her job, in which she was pushed around. The group has helped her to see herself as a valued person, supported her to find a better job, and successfully pressed her to budget more carefully to pay off her debts. Whenever her paranoia was expressed they patiently pointed out and clarified her distortions, misperceptions, and misinterpretations.

2. Mrs. P, aged sixty, who has spent five years in the group, is a recovered alcholic. She is phobic, had never worked, and blamed her husband for all her woes. She joined the group following individual treatment. The group has helped her plan to shop for herself, to go to meetings, and eventually even to travel by air. When her husband refused to pay for group treatment, they urged her to get

[28] Ibid.

[29] Wilfred R. Bion, *Experiences in Groups* (New York: Basic Books, 1971).

[30] Horwitz, "Group Psychotherapy," pp. 399–422.

[31] Irving D. Yalom, *Theory and Practice of Group Psychotherapy* (New York: Basic Books, 1975).

a job to pay her own way. They sympathized with her struggles until she found a job. They also cut through her paranoia, and she now is less blaming of her husband.

3. Mrs. T, aged sixty-four, a very bright college graduate, who has been in the group for three years had never asserted herself and masochistically described herself as her husband's "slave." When he separated from her, the group helped her think through legal action and to assert herself. She now has a good job.

4. Mrs. L, forty-six, is a high school graduate who was referred to the group by a shelter two years ago. She had a drinking problem and had experienced several psychotic episodes. She grew up terrified by her mother's psychotic episodes. The group members helped her to make a decision to get a divorce, to organize herself to find a job, and to control her drinking. She now manages well, has a nice apartment, and never misses a group meeting.

5. Mrs. B, one year in the group, is aged fifty-three. She had a pathological grief reaction after her divorce, cried constantly, and was so dependent that she could not live alone. The group encouraged her with her grief work and urged her to explore going out to work. She is now job hunting and functioning much better.

6. Mrs. C, aged forty-seven, is divorced from a man who is an alcoholic and beat her. She had a waitress job, dressed poorly, and appeared unaware of reality. Mrs. C has been in the group one year. The group urged her to set higher sights for herself, to find a better job, to continue to attend Al-Anon meetings, and to dress better. She now has a boyfriend who is loving and giving to her.

7. Mrs. I, aged forty-five, is studying for a doctorate degree. She joined the group one year ago. She was phobic and depressed, felt she never met either her adoptive parents' or her husband's expectations, and saw herself as a failure. When her husband was discovered to be sexually involved with another woman, she pulled herself together and, with the group's help, left him and concentrated on her studies. She is now looking and feeling better about herself.

The group members have been supportive of one another, set goals for one another, confronted each other about destructive behavior, cheered each other's successes, empathized with failures, and expected efforts at mastery. Each woman has demanded of others what she found difficult to achieve in herself. Splitting and projective identification seen in individual dynamics has been challenged in the group and not allowed to persist. It has been easier to acknowledge other women's realities and the group has confronted each individual with her own realities. Although personal growth and change are slow, members are excited as they see them take place. Self-esteem, phobias, paranoia, alcoholism, work problems, decisions to work, grief, and depression are among the issues that have been worked on and changes have occurred.

Because social and environmental issues should not be ignored as factors creating an unhealthy milieu that has the possibility of contributing to borderline personality formation, social workers must offer assistance in these areas at all times. Unfortunately, these conditions are frequently frustrating both for the worker and the client, because, the social and cultural milieu require massive efforts if these are to be changed substantially. Advocacy is part of the treatment of the borderline personality in the long run.

Conclusion

This article has been written to summarize, however briefly, the current thinking in the vast new literature on borderline personalities, a group of clients known more to social agencies over the years than to psychiatrists, who have now joined the social workers in their struggle to understand the dynamics of the borderline personality and to find new ways to treat them. Inventiveness, creativity, advocacy, empathy, and the ability to "hang in" are essential elements in treatment.

CHAPTER 23

Group Psychotherapy with Acting-out Patients: Specific Problems and Technique

John F. Borriello

In this paper I describe some of the problems and technique I have come to find very useful in my psychotherapy with acting-out patients. The paper's title specificies group psychotherapy rather than individual. This preference is based upon a careful review of my work with these patients in both modalities.[1] I obtain optimal results with the group, as a matter of fact, my success rate is 80 percent. Why? Because as these patients have reported over and over: "I can game in the individual and con the therapist but its tough to do in the group and get away with it; other patients pick it up immediately."

The acting-out patient characteristically handles life problems through action. Today, such patients are being seen in greater numbers than ever before. Many professionals label such patients as aggressive psychopaths, delinquents, antisocial personalities, sociopaths, impulse-ridden neurotics;[2] I prefer calling them patients with acting-out character disorders.[3] It is not my intention to argue the label, but rather to delineate how such patients can be helped by the psychotherapeutic process if, in the course of the treatment, attention is paid to their unique characteristics.

Ground Rules

It has been my experience that such patients generally seek therapy only when in severe crisis. The crisis can be, for example, trouble with the law,

Reprinted with the permission of the *American Journal of Psychotherapy*, Vol. 33, No. 4 (October 1979), pp. 521–530.

family conflicts, or loss of a loved one through separation, divorce, or death. It has also been my experience that while in crisis these patients attend psychotherapy regularly. Dependent upon the severity of the crisis, some demand daily sessions. At this time my experience indicates that they are not interested in self-investigative work, but rather in having the therapist rid them of their severe discomfort. I use this time period to activate self-thinking and self-curiosity. I educate them regarding the psychotherapeutic process and the roles of the patient and the therapist. I find that this provides the opportunity to lay the ground rules for psychotherapy. Because of subjective distress, the patient is in a state of readiness to listen and to apply. Activation of self-thinking and self-curiosity and education about psychotherapy serve two purposes. First is the minimization of irregular attendance or termination which are customary for these patients when their crises decline with the passage of time. Second is the reinforcement of patient motivation to want to change. In my opinion, this is the most crucial period in the treatment process if change is to occur.

During this period, as stated above, my focus is to: (1) get the patient to think about himself, (2) be curious about what has happened to him, (3) do an inventory of his life experiences, and (4) go into detail regarding the X number of times he has experienced similar crises. I strive to get the patient to realistically confront himself. My goal is to have him internalize the realization that the crisis of the present is the crisis of the past and will be the crisis of the future unless he starts doing something about himself. The doing does not mean presenting himself to the therapist and to the group as a passive recipient of their ministrations, but as an active, searching self-investigator. This involves, at times, experiencing periods that are very painful and scary. What is emphasized is that in the long run these experiences of pain and fear are well worth the effort. They lead to effective self-understanding. They insure that future crises will not be experienced as hopelessly debilitating and will not be reacted to with devastating life history recapitulation. As one patient stated, "Work in therapy is like putting money in the bank to have for hard times."

CASE 1

Jim called for an appointment. He stated it was urgent. He was in a state of panic and despair. He said that his girl walked out on him. He felt that he was "going to go crazy." An appointment was scheduled for later that day. He came to the office two hours early. During the first ten minutes he described what had happened. I empathically listened and then posed several questions. He stated that he did not understand why all the questions. He came for the doctor to make him feel better. At this point, the psychotherapy education process was introduced. A clear, concise description of the tasks of psychotherapy, psychotherapist, and patient were given. Jim was asked to describe in detail his present crisis. He was questioned about other times in his life similar crises had occurred. I focused on the misery that he was experiencing and had experienced. I told him that I understood his desperation and his desire to do something about his misery. I added that his predicament appeared to me to be tragic and that it sounded as if he saw himself as a prisoner to such crises in his life. I strongly reinforced the linkage of the past, present, and future.

During a period of silence, I asked him what he was thinking. He responded, "my mind is a blank," the typical response of the acting-out patient. I told him that he could benefit from spending short periods each day thinking. I warned him that this would be very difficult at first. With practice and time it would become easier and easier. He was asked to speculate regarding the reasons for his present crisis. He saw himself as not responsible for what happened. All reasons related to external events, places, or other persons. These made him do what he did. His girl left him. He did not know why. He was asked to delineate between the present girlfriend situation and other past girlfriend situations. He stated that he never compared his situation with women before, but in so doing, he was now beginning to see nothing but disaster. He was told that group psychotherapy could provide him with opportunities to (1) reflect upon these disasters; (2) affectively understand his contributions; and (3) minimize their repetition in the future. He stated that he would give it a try but why group?

Another interview was scheduled for two days later. He was instructed to think about what had gone on today with the therapist; to jot down any thoughts, dreams or recall he had regarding the interview, therapist, and group psychotherapy that he ambivalently had agreed to try. Instructing the patient from the beginning to reflect upon the interview during the interval between interviews, I see as a necessity, since it helps to activate the patient's self-thinking process.

Another important factor to consider at this time is the out of sight out of mind phenomenon—one of the major characteristics of the acting out patient. When Jim was questioned regarding this phenomenon, he smiled knowingly. He was told that he would have to watch for this. If he did not, he would experience no change from his psychotherapy. He was informed that he was going to have to fight the tendency to want to forget about what had been discussed and learned in the therapy session. What happens generally with the character disorder is that as he steps over the threshold of the therapist's office to the outside world, he immediately wipes out of mind what has transpired. I instruct these patients that this is a misfortune. They will have to struggle to keep in mind what had transpired in the session. I tell them that this will not be easy. They will experience considerable discomfort. This is what psychotherapy is all about. An indication that the change is in motion.

When Jim returned for his next appointment, he was asked to speak about his thoughts and reactions to the last session and about what had happened in the interval. He did as most of these patients do—rather than describe his thoughts and reactions he began an intellectual explanation of whys and wherefore of his behavior. He used the jargon of the standard abnormal psychology textbooks. During this explanation, he was forthright. With charm and earnestness, he vehementally applied himself. When finished, he proudly looked at me. He asked if I had ever had a better job done from any of my patients. I answered that it was an excellent explanation, but that his task in psychotherapy was not to explain his behavior, but to attempt to affectively understand it. I asked him what he made of this. He seemed puzzled. I asked him if he had any thoughts to share. He stated that he thought that I was disappointed in him. He did not understand what he was supposed to do.

I asked him to talk about his experience of the last interview. What happened in the interim. He stated that he was very uptight. He could not sit alone in his apartment at night. He felt lousy. He avoided thinking about the interview because he did not want to face the thought that maybe I could not help him. He phoned several acquaintances. He bragged to them that he had kicked his girl out of the apartment. She was becoming a drag, cramping his style. She demanded too much of him. I mentioned that during the initial interview he reported the opposite, that she left him. He responded that I had a good memory. He did not like the idea though, that maybe I wasn't going to let him get away with anything. He stated "you know doc it's important to have a nice beautiful house with a locked front door for people to admire, but you also need an unlocked back door for quick exit when the heats on." He was hoping that psychotherapy would teach him how to exit without getting burned. I responded that if it was in his best interest psychotherapy would, if it was not, psychotherapy would not.

Next he reported that he had visited several singles bars. He picked up two women and had sexual intercourse. He stated sex was in his best interest. It made him forget all of his misery. I asked, "forget all?" He responded at least for a couple of hours. He stated that he did not want group. He wanted individual psychotherapy. I responded that he would have to go elsewhere since my recommendation was that group was in his best interest. I also told him that his work in group was to: (1) focus upon himself, (2) be curious about why he did what he did and (3) note his reactions to others and to the therapist. He was told to consider himself the single most important person to understand in the group. He reluctantly agreed, but added "I don't see how a bunch of nuts are going to help me, I come to see you doc not a bunch of nuts."

Another appointment was scheduled with Jim, again within two days in order to maintain close continuity with and to reinforce what had been accomplished in the two earlier sessions. This time Jim came ten minutes late. When questioned he stated that he had several errands to do. He had lost track of time. He was questioned further and asked if possibly he did not want to come. He smiled knowingly. He said that he really did not see any purpose in coming. Things were going too slowly. He was still feeling lousy. He said that when he thought about what had been going on, especially my trying to get him to think of his past in relation to the present, he felt panic and resentment. He was convinced that I was using his experiences against him. He stated "the past is the past and the present is the present." Couldn't I speed up helping him by just dealing with the present. I asked him to elaborate further. He responded that he had begun an inventory of his life. As we had done in our sessions, he linked different events together for their similarity. This activity made him feel miserable and he was not beginning to understand the word tragic in relation to his life.

He went on to say that he always prided himself on having the freedom to do what he wanted. My use of the word prisoner set him into a tail spin. Prisoners have little freedom. He did not want to think that he had little freedom. I responded that that was a concern that he should investigate in the group. I told him that he would frequently experience (1) a part of himself that would not want to come, that would want to withdraw from the group; and (2) another part of himself that would want to come to work in the group. These two parts would seesaw throughout most of his life in therapy. If he wanted to change he would have to force himself to come when that part of himself that wanted to not come and to quit was in ascendence. I congratulated him for telling me about what he had experienced away from the group. I reiterated that this and regular attendance were two of the must conditions if he wished to continue in treatment. Saying one thing in therapy and doing another outside was wasting his time, my time and the group's. He was told that change does not occur with this type of behavior. Next he was informed that he could join the group next week. He was asked if he had any thoughts about the group. He said no except "the sooner the better, I join this damn group, so that I can get better." He hoped, however, that the group had men and women members. I asked why? He responded that it would be more interesting than with just men. I said maybe easier to con? He looked surprised and said "In this place my con doesn't work."

One year later in group Jim referred back to his initial individual interviews. He spoke of his strong need to impress the therapist at that time. He wanted me to say that he was extra special and that because of this he would get individual therapy. He remembered the two women he picked up the night prior to his second interview. He wanted to impress them that he was a cool strong person whom everyone admired and wanted to be like. He stated that he thought after the first interview that psychotherapy was going to destroy him, make him blow his cool, get him to admit that the others affected him and that he was weak and ineffectual. These came to mind while Bernie who had been in the group for two years, reported on his encounter with Susan, a new employee at work. Bernie decided that he was not going to try to impress Susan. He was not going to say things that would make her think he was the greatest. He would try to speak honestly about himself. As he said this, he sighed relief and shouted "no more lies to keep track of! Maybe now he hoped that he could establish a freer relaxed relationship with a woman.

Features of Maladaptive Behavior

Up to now I have described what I have found to be effective in arousing interest and motivation for psychotherapy the acting-out patient. Throught their interaction with me and through the material they present, I demonstrate what is and is not expected of them. This education process is crucial for success. They have to know the tasks of the psychotherapy, and the psychotherapist and the patient. Some important factors of their maladaptive behavior—on which I have only touched before—but that I stress in initial contracts are:

1. Action handling of life problems
2. Demand for psychotherapy only during crises
3. Lack of self-thinking
4. Poor self-curiosity
5. Conning behavior
6. Out-of-sight-out-of-mind usage
7. Saying one thing in therapy and doing another outside
8. Strong pull to not link the past, present and future
9. Poor frustration tolerance level
10. Strong tendency to externalize and deny
11. Self-destructiveness of acting-out behavior
12. Intellectual explanation of behavior to avoid conscious experience of affect
13. Image maintenance of strength and admiration
14. Irregular attendance
15. Premature termination

As mentioned, a period of time for education with a focus on the factors listed above is critical. Without such I have found that these patients do not remain in therapy for long. Again, they have to know what psychotherapy is all about, the role of the therapist, and what is required of them. In other words, what they are getting themselves into.

Mores of the Group

Now what about the group psychotherapy? The outpatient groups these patients join are heterogeneous in age, sex, race, soci-economic status, and education. I do avoid, however, extremes in any of the above dimensions. The group psychotherapy is analytic[4] and deals with, among other things, the characteristics highlighted in the preparatory sessions. With inpatient groups, heterogeneity is not always possible. Even so, my technique is similar. I encourage and acknowledge a culture that reinforces certain mores some of which have been touched upon in the initial contacts. These mores are: (1) continuous attendance; (2) confidentiality; (3) honesty and futility of self-deception; (4) self-investigation; (5) how do I bring about that which I experience; (6) responsibility for behavior; (7) past-present-future linkage of experience; (8) therapy task diligence; (9) tolerance for uncomfortableness; (10) immediacy of affective expression; (11) self-destructiveness of acting-out behavior; (12) consequences of acting-out behavior; (13) futility of manipulation; (14) control of impulses and choice involved.

Each of the mores is introduced only when therapy material appropriate to its advancement emerges. For example, in the beginning stages of a new group, the honesty, confidentiality, continuous attendance, and self-investigation mores are put forth. In later stages, when relevant, each of the other mores is likewise put forth. With the introduction of each, the patients are told that they must adhere to them if they are to continue in therapy. As new patients are added, the old ones take on the task of introducing each of the mores, but again, only when relevant to the therapeutic material at hand. The rationale for adherence to mores is that the patients do themselves a disservice if they continue in therapy while unwillingly to do what is required for change to occur. They are also told that this decision rests with them. They have a choice, either to work for change and freedom or to remain static and enslaved to their acting-out behavior.

CASE 2

Thirty-five-year-old Earl joined an ongoing group after having had two years of psychoanalysis. At the time of entry, he was in severe crisis. His wife had left him. She had taken the children. She wanted a divorce. She worked and supported the family, while Earl involved himself in a series of questionable business deals. All were supposed to net the family a million dollars. None did. Now Earl was confronted with a possible legal charge of fraud. Over a period of two months, he was introduced to the group mores. The honesty and futility of self-deception more effected him most. He stated: "I am very glad to hear this. Before when I was in analysis, I used to lie on the couch and have a ball talking about everything that came to mind except for what I was really doing outside. I am beginning to realize that I was deceiving myself and not being honest in my analysis. I would say things to impress my analyst. I wanted him to admire me. All of this has backfired. I believe now that if I spoke of what I was doing inside and outside of my analysis I would not be in my present predicament. What a fool I have been. It is as if I was making believe that nothing was wrong. As long as I did not talk about what I was doing then it was not a problem. As I am talking I see myself on the couch. Now I am off it standing close by watching myself talk. I am very angry at myself."

Importance of Effective Expression

If the self-investigative task of the therapeutic experience is to be meaningful, immediacy of affective expression through words must predominate. Without it, the group therapeutic experience becomes a monologue achieving little, if any, effective behavior change. Immediacy of affective expression is extremely crucial for the "actor-outer." In my experience, the acting-out patient can eloquently and comfortably involve himself in an intellectual discussion of dynamics, the whys and wherefores of his behavior, genetic factors, and so forth, and continue in self-destructive behavior. But if the discussion also deals with accompanied affect, the self-destructive behavior diminishes. It is this aspect that is related to the major problem, that is, the avoidance of the conscious experience of feeling.

It must be remembered that for some of the patients the acting-out behavior can be very self-destructive. What do I mean by very self-destructive? Besides the possibility of loss of freedom and even loss of life, these patients lack the capacity for mutual meaning and permanence in human relationships. In therapy, the point is repeatedly made that if feeling is expressed through words, need for acting out decreases. The difficulty that has to be wrestled with initially is that there is little, if any, understanding of this point, since acting out has become very pervasive and entrenched as a coping mechanism. It has become the life style, with minimal, if any, awareness of internal tension, anxiety, or thought accompanying it.

Here-and-Now Situation

As therapy progresses, this difficulty can be dealt with through an increasing focus in the group sessions on the here-and-now.[5,6] Group content, interactions, emotional relationships, and the significance of these to outside living, both present and past, are explored. Particular attention is paid to an exploration of stress situations handled through action. Emphasis is placed upon the development of awareness of what was happening and subjectively being experienced prior to and during the action, and what internal sensations are felt, if any. Later, when the preceding has been psychologically and therapeutically accomplished, thoughts and fantasies accompanying the internal sensations and actions are sought. Once the pattern is established then linkage of the similarity of what is felt, thought, and fantasied in the here-and-now of the group to other experienced situations, both present and past, becomes the rule. In effect, this is the essence of the group psychotherapy. The patient is provided with the opportunity to get in touch with his anxiety and to build a higher tolerance threshold. This in turn, allows for the emergence of feeling. Feeling, then, both in its present and past relations to experience is analyzed.

CASE 3

It was noted that Bill, in and out of trouble and school for years, and the oldest and only son of a university professor responded with silence, slumping in his chair, tense facial expression, and fingernail picking, when Brenda, a law student was added to his group. When questioned regarding what this was all about, what if anything, he was internally experiencing, he could not answer. Initially, he stated, "my mind is a blank to these questions" and added, "probably I am behaving this way because I may be tired. I don't know why." Another time when questioned regarding whether the addition of Brenda had anything to do with his present behavior he flatly stated "no." When questioned further about other situations in which he may have found himself behaving in a similar manner he stated, "as far as I am concerned, what I am doing this evening is not unusual, everybody does what I do sometimes. I see nothing unusual about being quiet or slumping in my chair or picking my fingernails." Another member added, "What about the expression on your face." Bill snapped back, "Now that I don't know about, I will look in the mirror after the session and give it some thought."

Two months later, Ann, a computer specialist, was added and the same silent slumping in the chair fingernail picking behavior was observed. When questioned Bill stated that he did not know what was bothering him, but something was. He would give it some thought. At the next session he reported that he had a dream. He was sitting on the porch of the house in which he was reared. He was watching his father play with his three sisters. He was feeling sad. He felt that his father preferred them to him because they were much smarter than he. They would get excellent grades in school and he did not.

Four sessions later, Rita, a nurse joined the group. During this session Bill became very talkative. He stated that he was thinking about his sisters and father. He was recalling many experiences with them. It was scary. He was encouraged to talk more. He stated that the women in the group reminded him of his sisters. He was very angry at them and the therapist. He felt that the therapist preferred them as he had felt as a child that his father preferred his sisters. It was scary for him today. He was very angry. He did not realize that he was capable of so much anger. Work on these areas during the next six months resulted in Bill coming to the group one evening and announcing that his relationship with his girl had improved. He was not as uptight around her. He did not feel as inferior. He seemed to have lost his drive to impress her with his intelligence, wit and charm. She mentioned that he was kinder, more considerate and loving.

Certain salient features of the actor-outer are described in the literature.[7] Among them are poor frustration tolerance, manipulation, externalization, minimal capacity for empathy, and utilization of acting out from triumph and revenge. In the course of treatment, these factors appear repeatedly. The defeat and despair of the therapist to these features only reinforces the actor-outers' strong need for maintenance. Active firm interpretation, however, done over and over at the moment of their appearance results in their extinction. I want to emphasize my active firm interpretative style. My experience supports a firm, persistent active-caring approach with these patients. The more traditional passive-caring approach intensifies resistance and frequently leads to hostile dependent, stubborn behavior.

CASE 4

Jim, twenty-seven years old, fought desperately to have individual psychotherapy rather than group psychotherapy. He rationalized, "the group is doing me no good, I need individual." Attempts to learn why only resulted in strong denial and contempt, with considerable hostility. Finally, when attempts proved unsuccessful, he left the group; but a month later he wrote a letter asking to return. When he rejoined the group, he spoke about his amazement that the therapist had not tried to induce him to return to therapy. When one of the group members asked him if he would have returned if the therapist had called him, he responded, "No, but I would have achieved what I wanted." Another group member asked him what that was. He retorted, "To make the therapist feel guilty, that it was his fault for my quitting, because he did not give me my way," to which the therapist responded, "What's that all about?" and the self-investigative task started again with no more dropping out.

A word about the acting-out patient leaving therapy prematurely. In my experience, unless a positive relationship has been developed with the therapist, the patient rarely returns if the therapy is individual. However, with group psychotherapy, there does not necessarily have to be this positive therapist relationship. It could be with any or all of the group members.

Interpersonal Style

Of crucial importance to remember is that the acter-outer does not behave in interpersonal relationships the way he really wants to, but rather as he believes those with whom he is interacting expect him to behave. Getting these patients to talk about this behavior will reveal that they want human contact, affection, and intimacy as everyone else does, but feel their maladaptive way is the only way they can get it. Unfortunately, the end result of their maladaptive style is severe hostile resentment which they often express in such behavior as avoidance of others, stubborness, passive obstructionism, belligerence, and aggressive outburst. Eventually, as the hostile resentment mounts, their controls weaken because of the strain involved and tragic antisocial acting out occurs. A final comment. My experience suggests that keeping the foregoing in mind can help the therapist to maintain empathy and motivation to work with these patients.

Summary

Effective psychotherapy with acting-out patients focuses on their uniqueness. Initially the therapist educates them about what psychotherapy is. The tasks of the psychotherapy, of the patient, and of the psychotherapist are clarified. Fifteen critical factors, typical for the behavior profile of those patients, are taken into consideration. These factors are considered within the context of appropriate psychotherapy material. One of the major goals is to have the patient listen and internalize.

Group therapy is the treatment of choice. Groups are open-ended, heterogeneous, and analytic. Manipulation by patients proves less successful in this modality. A group psychotherapy culture based on mores that reinforces the awareness of the futility of acting-out behavior and aims to lessen the patient's reliance on acting out is encouraged and acknowledged. Case material is cited.

References

1. BORRIELLO, J. F. Patients with Acting-Out Character Disorders. *Am. J. Psychother.* 27:4, 1973.
2. ABT. L. E., and WEISSMAN, S. L. *Acting Out.* Second edition. Jason Aronson, New York, 1976.
3. GIOVACCHINI, P. *Psychoanalysis of Character Disorders.* Jason Aronson, New York, 1975.
4. LOCKE, N. *Group Psychoanalysis.* New York University Press, New York, 1961.
5. BORRIELLO, J. F. Leadership in the Therapist-Centered Group-As-A-Whole Psychotherapy Approach. *Int. J. Group Psychother.* 26:149, 1976.
6. BORRIELLO, J. F. Intervention Foci in Group Psychotherapy. In *Group Therapy 1979*, 6:52, Intercontinental Medical Books, New York, 1979.
7. KANZER, M. Acting Out and Its Relation to Impulse Disorders, Panel Discussion. *J. Am. Psychoanal. Assn.*, 5:136, 1957.

CHAPTER 24

Clinical Considerations in Group Treatment of Narcissistic Disorders

Normund Wong

Interest in the subject of narcissism seems timeless and ever applicable to the current scene. In 1971, Malcolm, the author of a popular book entitled *Generation of Narcissus,* made the point that because the younger generation of today sees the adult world as fragmented, competitive, and powerless to affect its own destiny, they continue to live out the narcissistic experiences of their childhood. A *Time* magazine essay called the 70's the "Age of the New Narcissism." The January 30, 1978, issue of *Newsweek* launched into a thoughtful review of recent works which address the pervasiveness of narcissism in contemporary society. In the first edition of *The Theory and Practice of Group Psychotherapy,* Yalom (1970) did not discuss the narcissistic patient, but in his second edition (Yalom, 1975) he devoted four pages to this topic. Despite the fact that therapists have treated narcissistic patients in group therapy for many years, only three articles on this subject (Fried, 1955; Glatzer, 1962; Stone and Whitman, 1977) have been published in the *International Journal of Group Psychotherapy* over a twenty-year period. I believe that the sporadic contributions to the group literature on this subject can be attributed to a large extent to the lack of clarity surrounding the term and the concept of narcissism. Jones (1955) reports that in a letter to Abraham, Freud himself stated misgivings over his exposition of narcissism: "I have a very strong feeling of vexation at its inadequacy." In his 1914 work entitled, *On Narcissism,* Freud arrived at his final conclusions, stating that narcissism referred to a phase in libidinal development, a type of object choice, a mode of object relationship, and self-esteem. From their

Reprinted from *International Journal of Group Psychotherapy,* Vol. 29, No. 3 (July 1979), pp. 325–346, with permission of the American Group Psychotherapy Association, Inc.

experience clinicians were quick to appreciate the significance of Freud's contributions while recognizing that further refinements were needed. It is not surprising, therefore, to hear therapists talk about the narcissistic personality although this classification is not found in the APA *Diagnostic and Statistical Manual II*. To the majority of clinicians, the term is a useful signal alerting us to particular theoretical and treatment constructs.

Since Freud's time, a number of investigators have attempted to re-define the understanding and usage of the concept, with Kohut (1966, 1968, 1971, 1977) and Kernberg (1974, 1975), in particular, rekindling interest in this subject. However, group therapists must realize that the writings of Kohut and Kernberg are based on the individual treatment of patients in psychotherapy or analysis; to assume that their contributions can be applied in unmodified fashion to the treatment of patients in group therapy is a mistake. In this clinical paper, I intend to focus on a few ideas expressed by Kohut and Kernberg and to illustrate via a detailed case how their contributions can be applied in the group setting. It is not my intent to undertake a systematic examination of all the issues involved in comparing the theoretical positions taken by these two authors. I shall also present some of my observations in order to elaborate further a theoretical basis for a group approach and to emphasize the role of the group as a transitional object in the overall treatment of narcissistic personalities.

Definition of Narcissistic Personality

Both Kernberg and Kohut make the diagnosis of narcissistic personality largely on the basis of the transference manifestations. Kernberg sees the denial of the existence of the therapist as an independent autonomous human being as one of the major characteristics of the narcissistic personality. It is Kernberg's contention that the narcissistic personality structure he describes should be strictly reserved for those patients exhibiting an unusual degree of self-reference in their interactions with others, a great need to be loved and admired, and an apparent contradiction between an inflated concept of themselves and an inordinate need for attention from others. He further feels that these individuals have a shallow emotional life, experience little empathy for the feelings of others, seem to derive little enjoyment from life other than from tributes received from others, and, in general, feel restless and bored when the external glitter wears off and no new sources feed their self-regard. Kernberg mentions their intense envy of others, their tendency to idealize persons from whom they expect narcissistic supplies, and their depreciation and contempt for those from whom they expect little (Kernberg, 1975). He regards most of these patients as suffering from an underlying borderline personality organization for they share the same defensive organization as the borderline patient with only a particular difference: there is predominance of mechanisms of splitting which are maintained and reinforced by projective identification, primitive and pathological idealization, omnipotent control, and narcissistic withdrawal and devaluation.

Kohut feels that the diagnosis of narcissistic personality is made when specific resistances in the transference neurosis allow the discernment of one of two transference or transference-like responses, namely, the idealizing transference and the mirror transference. The patients tend to have ill-defined symptomatology and may present with disturbances in the sexual sphere such as perverse activities, fantasies, or lack of interest; social difficulties such as inability to form and maintain significant relationships, work inhibitions, disruptive personality features such as lack of empathy and feeling for people's needs, humorlessness, pathological lying, attacks of rage; and hypochondriacal preoccupations. There is a loss of self-esteem, hypersensitivity to slights, and feelings of emptiness (Kohut, 1971, p. 23). Kohut, in contrast to Kernberg, has addressed himself to the study of those individuals with a narcissistic personality disorder who nevertheless are "socially comparatively well-adjusted and reasonably well-functioning people ..." (Kohut, 1971, p. 1). Thus, these authors are writing about two different populations although narcissistic concerns are present in both.

Development of Pathological Narcissism

Kernberg believes that pathologic narcissism represents libidinal investment in a pathologic self-structure which "has defensive functions against the underlying investment in both libidinally determined and aggressively determined primitive self and object images in the context of intense, predominantly pregenital conflicts around both love and aggression" (Kernberg, 1974, p. 258). He sees the narcissistic personality as having a specific pathologic sort of infantile narcissism and the resistance as representing a rigid defense against primitive pathological self- and object-relations. He feels that there is no separate development of the representations of the self and objects. Furthermore, he feels that such patients do not suffer from an absence of structures in the ego and superego but, rather, that they maintain the presence of pathologic primitive structures.

It is Kohut's contention that narcissism and object love have a side-by-side existence and development wherein there is a separate development of narcissism with a separate kind of libido differentiated from object libido which apparently is not convertible. Thus, two independent developmental lines exist; one leads from autoerotism via narcissism to higher forms and transformations of narcissism, while the other leads from autoerotism via narcissism to object love (Kohut, 1971, p. 220). Mature self-esteem or narcissism occurs when the exhibitionism and grandiosity of the archaic grandiose self are gradually tamed, allowing the self-structure to become integrated into the adult personality and to fuel normal ego-syntonic endeavors. Under favorable circumstances the idealized parent imago becomes introjected as the idealized superego. With severe narcissistic traumas the grandiose self may retain its unaltered form and continue to strive for fulfillment of its archaic aims. Similarly, disappointments with the admired adult may result in the retention of the idealized parent imago, which remains an archaic, transitional self-object which is not transformed into a tension-regulating psychic structure. Clearly, with such different theoretical contructs the authors must, of necessity, differ in their treatment approaches.

Treatment

In many respects Kernberg's analytic treatment of a narcissistic personality follows his principles for the treatment of patients with borderline personality disorders. He emphasizes the need to focus on both the positive and negative transference, interpret systematically the primitive idealization, omnipotent control, and devaluation of the therapist in order to protect against the reactivation of underlying oral rage and envy and the related fear of retaliation from the therapist. Kernberg feels that the narcissistic transference activates past defenses against deeper relationship with the parents and only then the real relationship with them.

In the early stages of treatment, Kernberg regards the idealizing of the therapist as defensive and more apparent than real. It is to be understood as hostile in nature with the intent of extracting. The idealizing transference corresponds to the activation of the grandiose self. The treatment should center on allowing the grandiose self to emerge, but Kernberg feels that the vicissitudes of aggression must be systematically interpreted. The oral rage and envy aroused should culminate in depression and guilt which, if resolved, allow for the merger of the loved and hated internal object. To avoid almost exclusive attention to the negative transference, he recommends focusing on the remnants of the patient's capacity for love and object investment.

Basically, Kohut's treatment represents a traditional analytic approach where there is recognition of the resistance or defense, a "correct understanding" of it in order to avoid premature and intellectualized interpretations, the understanding and mastery of countertransference, and the allowing of the transference neurosis to develop. One then gradually maneuvers to allow its resolution. There is no undue emphasis on the interpretation of aggression. It is in the nature of the understanding and "correct interpretation" that Kohut's approach varies from the traditional approach in that he refrains from seeing the need for narcissistic objects as libidinal strivings or as regressions from oedipal issues. He emphasizes the role of the analyst as an object to be experienced as part of the patient's self. In repairing the narcissistic pathology the analyst should empathetically allow the transference to develop without undue interpretations or disruption.

Group Applications

It becomes obvious to us at this point that when Kernberg and Kohut talk about the narcissistic personality, they are referring to a different patient population, adhere to a different developmental model, and advise a different treatment approach. Yet each author has contributed significantly to the further understanding of narcissistic pathology. Acknowledging these differences, how then to apply their work to the area of group psychotherapy?

Treatment parameters must be added to utilize their contributions in the group field. From what little has been written about the treatment of narcissistic patients with group psychotherapy, we know that such patients have generally not fared well. If, in addition to the manifest narcissistic pathology in a patient, we diagnose an underlying borderline personality organization, as is the case of the narcissistic patient which Kernberg describes, we should consider the combined individual and group approach recommended by many authors (Greenbaum, 1957; Horwitz, 1977; Slavson, 1964; Spotnitz, 1957). I feel that a period of preparatory individual therapy must be undertaken before such a patient is brought into the group and that, ideally, the therapist doing the individual and group treatment should be the same person (Wong, 1977).

In the longitudinal case which follows, I shall illustrate how I have attempted to apply the contributions of Kernberg and Kohut to the successful treatment of a narcissistic personality with a borderline personality organization over a seven-year period.

THE CASE OF ALICE

Alice was referred to me for treatment after having been in individual therapy with five different therapists over the previous two years. Her treatment experiences were short-lived, and while she devalued the therapy and therapists, she was despondent, feeling that she had personally failed. She continued to pursue therapy believing she would eventually find the perfect therapist who would transform her.

A glamorous woman in her early twenties, intelligent and well-educated, Alice had been her grandmother's darling until age seven, when grandmother became senile and had to be institutionalized. The patient was the oldest of three children born to a middle-class Jewish family. Her parents worked long hours to develop a prospering business and spent little time with Alice. Aside from the grandmother, whom she saw several times weekly, Alice spent most of her early years with housekeepers and maids who changed frequently. Possessing a creative imagination, Alice passed many lonely hours engaging in a fantasy where she was a lost princess awaiting discovery by her royal parents and a prince charming. In fact, her grandmother had called Alice "my little princess" and had made sure that Alice was always dressed in the finest clothing.

When Alice was three, a brother was born, and when she was five, a younger sister arrived, giving Alice even less time with her parents. As the family business became more successful, her parents attempted to lavish time on the children, but Alice always felt that they could not replace grandmother. Although Alice did well in school, she was outstripped by her siblings who excelled academically with little effort. Her brother was not only intellectually talented but also handsome and athletic. Alice grew increasingly resentful and envious of her siblings, feeling overlooked and neglected.

Upon graduation from high school, Alice went to college in another city where her attractiveness and intelligence got her into the sorority of her choice and won her the attention of the most popular men. In order to curry favor with Alice, her sorority sisters often wrote her term papers, and one even took a final examination for her. There was no paucity of dates. Calamity occurred when Alice became physically ill while abroad in Europe. She made a slow recovery, losing much of her physical attractiveness. Shortly thereafter, she contracted an endocrine disorder, becoming hirsute and developing acne. After six months of convalescence, she returned to college. However, she was a ghastly caricature of her former self. No longer was she the belle of the campus. She spent most of her senior year feeling abandoned and alone. Haughty and arrogant with her peers in the past, Alice now found herself devalued and overlooked. She became increasingly depressed and withdrawn and sought solace in her childhood fantasies. She was frightened by transient lapses of reality testing. At the urging of school administrators, she underwent psychiatric care and was able to graduate with her class. She returned home to her family where she lived for the next five years. To her family, Alice appeared greatly changed, manifesting a great deal of self-pity and helplessness. Although she remained under psychiatric care, she was never satisfied with any of her therapists. She remained a recluse, was morose and bitter, and dressed in dark, drab attire which dramatized her plight in life. Her appearance and personal habits continued to deteriorate. Relationships with her family became more detached and attempts to reach out to her were met with disdain and anger. Over a two-year period, Alice was unable to form a significant relationship with any of her therapists. To dramatize her demands for a new therapist, Alice would overdose on medications and refuse to keep appointments. After two sessions on the couch with a well-known analyst, she ingested a large number of sleeping pills, complaining that the therapist did not understand her and had ignored her. She was hospitalized several times and received shock treatment.

At the request of a family friend who was a psychiatrist, I agreed to see her. It was apparent that Alice possessed a borderline personality organization. Her narcissistic pathology was also obvious but the state of her ego integration was so precarious that this area could not be immediately addressed. For two and a half years, I treated her on an individual basis before starting her in combined group and individual therapy.

Alice seemed to fit Kernberg's description of the narcissistic personality. She showed a high degree of self-reference in her interactions with others, a great need to be admired and loved, and a curious contradiction between a very inflated concept of herself and an inordinate need for tribute. She experienced little empathy for the feelings of others. She envied and idealized many from whom she expected narcissistic supplies and depreciated and treated with contempt those from whom she expected nothing. Her haughty, grandiose, and controlling behavior was used as a defense against paranoid traits related to the projection of her oral rage. In keeping with the defensive organization of her borderline personality make-up, she exhibited primitive defense mechanisms such as splitting, denial, projective identification, omnipotence, and primitive idealization. Frequently she viewed the outside world, even her family, as denying and threatening.

Alice's individual therapy was initially aimed at reinforcing her grasp of reality and this was accomplished through some family sessions which established the treatment parameters. Within a few months, her regressive slide into chaos accompanied by further shame and guilt was successfully checked. With the cooperation of her parents, Alice and I agreed that they were to dispense any medications under my directions, taking into consideration her expressed needs. I helped construct a daily routine for her. She was no longer permitted to stay in bed all day as had been the case. I would be available to her at all times for real emergencies and during the first few months would see her as often as three times daily, seven days a week, albeit for a few minutes. It was usually with the understanding that she would have to make the arrangements to come down to my office. Much of the first year in individual therapy was used to allow her to develop an idealizing transference which contained elements of the idyllic situation with grandmother. This was fostered by my reasonable availability to her during periods of great anxiety and my attempts to empathize with her over the slightest narcissistic insults which occurred frequently throughout the day. This "good-enough mothering" (Winnicott, 1965) approach also allowed us to develop a therapeutic alliance which had been lacking with her previous therapists.

During the second year, the idealizing transference began to blend into a mirror transference at which time both her grandiose self and her borderline personality organization emerged in full bloom. Fears of merger and loss of her own identity were manifested through splitting and projective identification. The deprivations of reality, in contrast to the expectations of her grandiose self, and the mirror reactions (Foulkes, 1964) which revealed the bad and punitive parts of herself as well as the reflection of the grandiose self were manifested by abrupt shifts in which I was now depreciated and she was overvalued. Such shifts were usually accompanied by massive outpourings of intense oral rage and loathing accompanied by the feeling that she was locked into treatment. While depreciating me, she lamented the lack of fulfillment of her own grandiose destiny. Alice's feelings were ambivalent for, while loathing me, she desperately needed me. Following an outburst, she would appear for the next session apologetic and ashamed. At such times, she would feel panicky and experience dissociation phenomena. The all-bad, all-good splitting in which she saw most of the world and its inhabitants as persecutors and the therapist as the "good mother" now changed. She began to accept others as purveyors of good supplies and alternately depreciated and overidealized me in accordance with her failures and successes outside of treatment. In noncritical fashion, I attempted systematically to clarify, confront, and interpret to her in the "here and now" the disappointment, rage, and anger directed toward me manifested in the negative transference. Exploration of the negative transference as it emerged diminished the idealizing transference only slightly. It helped improve her reality testing in separating out parts of herself from me, reduced her acting out and splitting behavior on the outside, and lowered her intense anxiety following recriminations levied at me. During the all too rare "good" hours in therapy she would thank me for my tolerance and understanding in "taking all the shit I throw at you" and the "courage to call a spade a spade." Such self-revelations did not hinder her during subsequent fits of passion from labeling the same behavior on my part as "disdainful aloofness, arrogance, and Asian pomposity." During the second year in treatment she underwent cosmetic surgery and her physical appearance was greatly improved.

Typical alternating reactions during the third year of treatment are as follows. For a time, the theme of idealization would prevail: "You are so strong and smart; you understand me; you're what I would want to be like." The next phase of narcissistic rage, envy, and devaluation which lasted a few months would be characterized by such statements as: "You are so arrogant and cocky; you seem to have all the control over me. I see you as the warden and I feel like a prisoner. You prevent me from accomplishing anything." This would be followed by the message, "If you leave me, I will perish," in which the desperate longing for a loving relationship able to withstand her rage would emerge. As her negative feelings were accepted, worked through, and interpreted, she was able, with some humor, to arrive at the point of stating: "If I think you're so great, how come I'm not better by now?" Her attenuated aggression could appear in the guise of, "Who needs you anyhow? All you care about is my money," only to be quickly followed by, "You seem so dangerous and angry with me today. I guess I'm still so confused, I don't know which is you and which is me."

At this time, I advised her to enter a beginning group to be in concomitant group and individual therapy with me. There were sound reasons for placing her in a group. The symbiotic tie in our relationship was intense and often frightening to her. Although she was now capable of venturing forth and was less regressed in social relationships, she was getting into frequent difficulties, being fired from several jobs and engaging in disastrous relationships with men. The group might dilute or lessen the negative transference which was contributing to her acting out, afford her opportunities to experience in vivo in a safe environment the self-destructiveness of her pathologic ego, and facilitate healthy identification processes with others. It would also decrease her fears of engulfment by me as I would be viewed more realistically interacting with others, diminish her primitive idealization of me, and mitigate the fear of destroying me and the need to control me. A beginning group was chosen to decrease the anticipated narcissistic mortification which she might experience in an established group and to lessen the shock upon realizing that she was not my only patient as manifested in her grandiose fantasies.

Initially, she helped get the group started because she idealized the membership, seeing them as more people to fulfill her oral narcissistic and exhibitionistic needs. A monopolizer and an engaging speaker, she easily captured the attention of the men in the group. However, when other women in the group began to steal the limelight from her, Alice became irritated and annoyed. No matter what topic was being discussed in the group, Alice had a propensity for finding a connection to events in her own life and would dominate the floor.

Her insensitivities did not go unnoticed. Once, when she arrived late for a session, a depressed and usually silent member had been talking of her husband's impending death from heart disease. Alice rushed into the room and immediately began to tell how she had been slighted the previous night by a boyfriend. Oblivious to the focus of the group, Alice was shocked by the sudden outburst from the member who pointed out Alice's insensitivities and obtuseness. Stunned, Alice remained silent for the rest of the session and did not show up for the group for the next two weeks. Following her reentry into the group three weeks later, she explained that she had taken time off to shop to prepare for a vacation and that the only opportunity available for such activities was on the morning of the group meeting. The group attacked her for her lack of commitment to the group and her self-centeredness. Although not the first such episode to occur in the group, this event was probably the most memorable for Alice and to the group.

Alice began to show a twinship reaction to Janet, another narcissistic member of the group, and her resulting fear of loss of identity and the unanchoring phenomena occupied her in concomitant group and individual treatment sessions. To a great extent, I regarded her experience in this group as educational. Alice could internalize some of the group norms in response to group confrontations with Janet, but still reacted with narcissistic mortification whenever the group confronted her for her lack of empathy and her need to monopolize. After two years, Alice left the group with the excuse that now she had been accepted into law school and was no longer able to spend much time in therapy. She felt torn between individual and group therapy and opted for the former. In contrast to the usual neurotic patient, Alice exhibited little mourning for the group; in keeping with her narcissistic pathology, she felt rage at being "denied" membership in the group and envy for those members who continued group therapy.

In individual therapy, Alice continued to wrestle with the negative transference alternating with an idealizing transference. However, these were being worked through. She had derived benefits by being in the group, which had directly confronted her narcissistic acting out and splitting. In addition, she had gained some insight into herself by identifying with Janet and seeing the pitfalls in her behavior. A rise in her self-esteem was apparent. This had been brought about through therapy and realistic achievements in law school and her social life. In general, she appeared to be a less needy person. There was increased capacity to tolerate anxiety and the glimmering of a more stable, integrated self. However, she never ceased to bring up the group experience in which she now felt that she had failed and suffered an unfair rebuff. She reached a point in therapy where she could appreciate that her relationships at school were less than satisfactory and that many of the problems she had experienced with the group members were similar. In typical manner, she first demanded and then debated with me for an opportunity to join another group. Nine months after her departure from the first group, I placed Alice in an ongoing established group whose members functioned on a level comparable to that of people in her life.

In this group she was able to work through feelings of abandonment and rejection and separation and individuation issues which had been emerging in her individual therapy. She moved out of her parents' home and gradually reduced her individual sessions to once weekly. She seemed more sensitive to the needs of others and even to demonstrate some real empathetic understanding. Alice's transmuting internalization (Kohut, 1971) of idealized parts of the group manifested itself through the behavior of an "as-if personality," trying on different personalities in the group until she eventually shifted into the role of the "doctor's assistant." It was evident that her primitive grandiose and exhibitionistic needs were more under control and that she was internalizing the caretaking role of the therapist.

She remained in this group for two years, ending all treatment when the group terminated. Aside from brief flurries of unmasked grandiosity and flagrant exhibitionism during examination periods, she behaved in this group like a typical high-level neurotic patient struggling with manifest oedipal issues which camouflaged the separation-individuation problems. In summary, I am happy to report that after seven years of our working together, Alice graduated from law school and passed her bar exam. During this seven-year period, she required only one brief hospitalization, which followed a suicide attempt in the second year of therapy.

Discussion

From the course of Alice's therapy, the conclusion can be drawn that in order to employ Kernberg's treatment approach for the narcissistic patient with overt borderline features, it is helpful in the beginning to follow Kohut's recommendations. However, it must be kept in mind that Kohut's writings are addressed primarily to individuals who function on a higher level than borderline patients. Therefore, it is necessary to adopt the following modifications.

In Alice's case it was well known that the traditional psychoanalytically oriented approaches had been unsuccessful in her treatment. The contribution that Kohut added to the therapy was to allow and to accept the emergence of the idealizing and mirroring transference, particularly in individual therapy. This was made possible by adopting an empathetic stance and in the beginning not systematically interpreting the negative and positive transference.

Once the patient felt secure in the treatment setting, it became possible gradually and consistently to interpret the pathologic defenses in an intrusive although neutral manner. Clarification, confrontation, and interpretation in the "here and now," as recommended by Kernberg, took precedence over Kohut's more passive approach at this juncture. Such a change in the therapist's stance served to ferret out the oral rage and envy intrinsic to the archaic, grandiose self and also highlighted fears of engulfment and retaliation from the therapist. When Alice's primitive fears and anxieties became too intense, I placed her in combined individual and group therapy to provide her sufficient distance and space to maintain the working alliance. In addition, using Mahler's developmental model (Mahler et al., 1975) and Kosseff's notion of "the group as a transitional object" (Kosseff, 1975), I hoped to provide Alice with the opportunity to differentiate and to practice in the group setting. When these goals were accomplished, she returned to individual therapy to begin work on her rapprochement problems, and in the second group, she started on her way to libidinal object constancy. In this group she also worked through the issues of abandonment and separation.

The application of Kernberg's more intrusive and systematic, interpretive approach to Alice's rage and hostility in the transference did not seem to unduly impede the blossoming of the archaic, grandiose self and idealizing parent imago nor did it prevent the subsequent transmuting internalizations from occurring. Perhaps my interpretations were sufficiently "correct" and empathetic. However, it bears repeating that a concomitant individual and group approach should be employed where one intends to do reconstructive therapy with a narcissistic patient with an underlying borderline personality organization.

I now wish to address three particular areas in which treatment might ordinarily fail unless the combined individual and group approach is used. They are, one, the treatment benefits for the group and the patient; two, the countertransference problems; and, three, the manifestations of change in the narcissistic patient.

First, not all group therapists would agree that the narcissistic patient is best treated in the group setting or that such a patient is good for the group. Yalom (1975) states that "the narcissistic patient generally has a stormier time of it in group therapy than in individual therapy." In his book (pp. 342–351), he describes in detail the relationship between Bill and Jan, emphasizing the narcissistic features of Bill's interactions with the group. He points out that the price paid by the group was enormous; that other members were neglected and many important issues were left untouched. Horner (1975) has found in her experience that the narcissistic personality disorder as delineated by Kohut has not responded well to group treatment. She believes that "the group has been nonproductive for the patient at best, and destructive for both the patient and the group at worst." Other group therapists contend that, although group therapy may be effective in confronting a patient with the pathologic aspects of his narcissism, the group does not provide the opportunity to allow the narcissistic patient a good enough one-to-one relationship with the therapist. Without such a relationship, the patient is unable to progress from the position of narcissistic fixation and entitlement. In addition, through his behavior, the narcissistic patient is likely to become the focus of negative transferences from other group members, be scapegoated, and eventually be extruded from the group.

Some therapists would place patients exhibiting excessive narcissistic manifestations in the same category as paranoid, sociopathic, or acutely depressed patients, regarding them as unsuitable for the group on the basis that they are too disruptive, intefere with culture building, and prevent group cohesion. Group therapists who adhere to the "group as a whole" approach often voice this opinion, recognizing that the narcissistic patient does not respond well to situations in which he is afforded little opportunity for recognition of his uniqueness. In such cases, he may attempt to overidealize the leader but frequently becomes enraged and withdraws from the group.

The combined individual and group approach can overcome the aforementioned difficulties. In individual therapy, the transference reactions are allowed to develop without intrusion. Here the therapist can convey to the patient a sense of constancy, empathetic awareness, and security—the very feelings the narcissistic patient has lacked in his life. It is a rare group, indeed, which early in its life can give the patient the feeling of acceptance and stability and, later, the adaptability necessary to satiate his immense oral needs. No doubt, in the beginning the narcissistic patient is readily welcomed in order to drain off the primitive anxieties for the group. To the inexperienced group leader, the narcissistic patient is seen as the initiator of self-disclosure, catharsis, and universality. It is usually in the second stage of group formation, described by Yalom (1975), that the group and the narcissistic patient come to grief. This stage is characterized by conflict, dominance, and rebellion. If the group leader does not properly understand and handle the narcissistic patient, he may bolt and the group may remain in chaos or it may dissolve.

In Alice's case with the first group, there was no doubt that she gained more by being in the group than the group gained by her membership. Once she left the group, it made more progress. In the group, she had an opportunity to work through problems centering around her grandiose self and to vent her aggression in a safe environment, while her individual sessions buffered her from undue narcissistic mortification and provided her with breathing space to call upon her observing ego. Dilution via the group of the negative transference as well as the idealizing transference generated in individual therapy afforded her an opportunity for reality testing and consensual validation of my interpretations and strengthened the therapeutic alliance. By the time Alice entered the second group, many of her liabilities as a group member had been resolved and she would have been considered an acceptable candidate for most groups.

Second, countertransference problems invariably arise when treating narcissistic patients. Kohut (1971) states that the analyst who works with narcissistic patients "must, furthermore, be aware of the potential interference of his own narcissistic demands which rebel against a chronic situation in which he is neither experienced as himself by the patient nor even confused with an object of the patient's past. And finally, in specific instances, the analyst must be free of the active interference by archaic fears of dissolution through merger." When a therapist is aware that his countertransference reaction is becoming too intense, placing the patient in concurrent group and individual treatment is of mutual benefit. This is especially true if the narcissistic character possesses an underlying borderline personality organization.

Much is demanded of the therapist and group members in terms of understanding the potential countertransference reaction which may be induced by the patient's narcissistic transferences. Frequently the narcissistic needs, both normal and pathological, are rekindled in group members by the narcissistic patient's blatant primitive grandiosity and exhibitionism. By asking the members of the group to focus upon the narcissistic patient's need to be recognized, rather than to respond to the content solely, the group therapist can circumvent the negative reactions which typically occur to the detriment of the group and to the patient. Eliciting an empathetic response from the group members in this manner need not reduce the confrontational impact of the narcissistic patient's behavior but takes into account meaningful involvement of the other members, who otherwise would respond with anger as a denial of their own unacceptable narcissistic wishes or would attempt to isolate the patient. The therapist must be active in heading off prolonged, unproductive confrontations made to the narcissistic patient in the group. Where this occurs frequently and with great intensity and relative inactivity on the part of the therapist, he must consider the possibility that his countertransference feelings toward the patient are being acted upon by the group.

As the third and last point, I wish to stress that over a long period of intensive therapy, the narcissistic character may frequently assume a number of different roles in the group. In Alice's case, she initially served as the group "monopolizer," and when the group succeeded in stifling her, she resorted to the use of a mirror transference. In the second group, she appeared as an "as-if personality" before settling on the role of "doctor's assistant." At times when she was the "silent member" of the group, usually in response to a narcissistic insult, she engaged in the fantasy of withholding something of value to the group. In her fantasy she would possess something of vital importance to the group; she would only plunge into the breech at the last moment to save the group when they repented and recognized her greatness. Her changing postures could be understood in accord with Kernberg's theory as manifestations of the reshaping of pathologic, primitive, intrapsychic structures or, as postulated by Kohut, as manifestations of new psychic structures in the process of formation. Once again, the combined individual and group approach is invaluable in helping both therapist and patient understand and appreciate the changes occurring. During these changes, the therapist can function as the stabilizer, integrator, and anchor upon whom the patient can depend. Both healthy and unhealthy identifications in the group setting may be expected to occur and there will be excessive swings as the patient struggles to evolve a whole and constant self. The therapist who can observe the patient individually and in the group setting is at an advantage in understanding and dealing with the evolving facets of the patient's emerging identity.

It may be helpful at this time to note how others classify and attempt to handle what we now see as probable manifestations of the narcissistic patient. In discussing the treatment approach to the "monopolizer," several authors (Spotnitz and Meadow, 1976; Stone and Whitman, 1977; Yalom, 1975) recommend that the patient be allowed to say more about himself rather than less. A similar tactic has been applied with success to the "help-rejecting-complainer" (Berger and Rosenbaum, 1967), the "doctor's assistant," and in some instances, the "silent member." Based on our newer understanding of the treatment of the narcissistic character, which advocates the drawing out of the grandiose self and fostering the development of idealizing and mirror transferences, and accepting, encouraging approach, when successful for these categories of patients, confirms the presence of pathological narcissism. The positive, accepting approach is indicated in lieu of the customary pejorative, negative, confrontational tactic which results in mutually unsatisfactory results for the patient and the group.

To return to Alice, because of the work performed in treament, she was able to resolve much of her primitive infantile narcissism and to sublimate her grandiose and exhibitionistic needs through healthy channels by working as a trial lawyer and eventually marrying someone who delighted in indulging her. The argument that she did achieve intrapsychic change rather than being cured through a flight into health or via gratification of her grandiose fantasies may be supported by her newly found resort to wit, humor, and wisdom, usually indicative of stable internal structures, and in maintaining a reasonable career and marriage. Now she can lose a case in court without resorting to a drug overdose or feeling that her world has collapsed around her.

Summary

The positions taken be Kernberg and Kohut in regard to the definition of a narcissistic personality, development of pathological narcissism, and treatment have been compared. The combined individual and group therapy of a narcissistic patient with a borderline personality organization has been presented, acknowledging the contributions from both authors. In order to do reconstructive treatment with this type of patient in a group setting, the writer feels that it is necessary to employ individual therapy to prepare the patient for a group and to foster a therapeutic alliance by adhering to Kohut's recommendation that the idealizing and mirroring transferences be allowed to develop unimpeded. Only then can Kernberg's intrusive, systematic, interpretive approach of the negative and positive transferences be undertaken. In combined treatment the group serves as a transitional object to reduce the fears of engulfment and retaliation projected onto the therapist and allows the subphases of the separation-individuation stage to progress once more. The group is especially valuable in, first of all, helping work through grandiose and aggressive issues and in easing the therapist's countertransference burden, and later in providing a variety of role models and possibilities "to try on for size" as the patient works through feelings of separation and abandonment en route to the establishment of a mature, integrated self.

References

BERGER, M. M., and ROSENBAUM, M. (1967), Notes on the Help-Rejecting Complainer, *This Journal*, 17:357–370.

FOULKES, S. H. (1964), *Therapeutic Group Analysis*. New York: International Universities Press.

FREUD, S. (1914), On Narcissism. *Standard Edition*, 14:69–102. London: Hogarth Press, 1957.

FRIED, E. (1955), Combined Group and Individual Therapy with Passive Narcissistic Patients. *This Journal*, 5:194–203.

GLATZER, H. I. (1962), Handling Narcissistic Problems in Group Psychotherapy. *This Journal*, 12:448–455.

GREENBAUM, H. (1957), Combined Psychoanalytic Therapy with Negative Therapeutic Reactions. In: *Schizophrenia in Psychoanalytic Office Practice*, ed. A. H. Rifkin. New York: Grune and Stratton, pp. 56–65.

HORNER, A. J. (1975), A Characterological Contraindication for Group Psychotherapy. *J. Amer. Acad. Psychoanal.*, 3:301–305.

HORWITZ, L. (1977), Group Psychotherapy of the Borderline Patient. In: *Borderline Personality Disorders*, ed. P. Hartocollis. New York: International Universities Press, pp. 399–422.

JONES, E. (1955), *The Life and Work of Sigmund Freud*, Vol. 2. New York: Basic Books.

KERNBERG, O. (1974), Contrasting Viewpoints Regarding the Nature and Psychoanalytic Treatment of Narcissistic Personalities: A Preliminary Communication. *J. Amer. Psychoanal. Assn.*, 22:255–267.

——(1975), *Borderline Conditions and Pathological Narcissism*. New York: Jason Aronson.

KOHUT, H. (1966), Forms and Transformations of Narcissism. *J. Amer. Psychoanal. Assn.*, 14:243–272.

——(1968), The Psychoanalytic Treatment of Narcissistic Personality Disorders. *The Psychoanalytic Study of the Child*, 23:86–113. New York: International Universities Press.

——(1971), *The Analysis of the Self*. New York: International Universities Press.

——(1977), *The Restoration of the Self*. New York: International Universities Press.

KOSSEFF, J. W. (1975), The Leader Using Object-Relations Theory. In: *The Leader in the Group*, ed. Z. A. Liff. New York: Jason Aronson, pp. 212–242.

MAHLER, M. S., PINE, F., and BERGMAN, A. (1975), *The Psychological Birth of the Human Infant*. New York: Basic Books.

MALCOLM, H., (1971), *Generation of Narcissus*. Boston: Little, Brown.

SLAVSON, S. R. (1964), *A Textbook in Analytic Group Psychotherapy*. New York: International Universities Press.

SPOTNITZ, H. (1957), The Borderline Schizophrenic in Group Psychotherapy: The Importance of Individuation. *This Journal*, 7:155–174.

——and MEADOW, P. W. (1976), *Treatment of the Narcissistic Neuroses*. New York: Manhattan Center for Advanced Psychoanalytic Studies.

STONE, W. N., and WHITMAN, R. M. (1977), Contributions of the Psychology of the Self to Group Process and Group Therapy. *This Journal*, 27:343–359.

WINNICOTT, D. W. (1965), *The Maturational Process and the Facilitating Environment*. New York: International Universities Press.

WONG, N. (1977), The Treatment of the Borderline Patient: A Case for Concomitant Individual and Group Therapy. Paper presented to Sixth International Congress of Group Psychotherapy, Philadelphia, Pa., Aug. 1.

WOODWARD, K. L., and MARK, R. (1978), The New Narcissism. *Newsweek*, 91(5):70–72.

YALOM, I. D. (1970), *The Theory and Practice of Group Psychotherapy*. New York: Basic Books.

——(1975), *The Theory and Practice of Group Psychotherapy*, 2nd ed. New York: Basic Books.

PSYCHOSEXUAL DISORDERS

CHAPTER 25

Outpatient Treatment for Sexual Offenders

Steven N. Silver

Studies concerned with the etiology and treatment of sexual deviance are usually based on programs administered in correctional and psychiatric institutions.[1] Certainly, there are individuals who require total institutional care so that interpersonal behavior can be monitored and controlled. However, this institutionalization frequently fosters the development of dependent and manipulative behaviors, provides inadequate social experience, weakens self-esteem, and generally increases the probability that the client will become an offender again following discharge.[2]

Sexual deviance is conceptualized in this article as a collection of learned behaviors that can be unlearned frequently in an outpatient setting. The author will describe the structure and process of an experimental, community-based program for the treatment of sexual offenders built primarily on principles of guided group interaction and behavioral engineering.[3] The relationship of the law enforcement and judicial systems to the treatment agency will be discussed as well.

The Sexual Deviance Program (SDP) described in this article was developed in the outpatient facility of a comprehensive community mental health center in Bellevue, Washington. Although there is an urgent need for outpatient treatment programs for sexual offenders, this center's SDP is the only one of its kind in King and neighboring counties. It is hoped that a description of this program will give visibility to an effective treat-

Copyright 1976, National Association of Social Workers, Inc. Reprinted, with permission, from *Social Work*, Vol. 21, No. 2 (March, 1976), pp. 134–140.

ment approach, thus encouraging other service centers to develop programs for similar populations.

The outpatient clinic that houses the program provides diagnostic, treatment, consultative, and training services to agencies and individuals in a catchment area covering 1,400 square miles and 212,000 people. The treatment staff is multidisciplinary and includes clinical social workers, psychiatrists, psychologists, nurses, and students. The theoretical orientation of the clinic is mildly psychoanalytic. The author, though eclectic, tends to rely on a learning theory and behavioral approach in treating sexual offenders because he has found traditional psychotherapeutic approaches to be ineffective and inefficient with such clients.

Admissions Procedure

Table 25-1 shows that only 33 percent of the clients at SDP are voluntary; the remainder have been referred by the law enforcement and judicial systems. Preceding the initial interview with the cotherapy team, which consists of one male and one female, the applicant is asked to authorize the release of information that would enable the team to consult with previous therapists or court officers on matters relevant to his treatment. During this initial evaluation, the cotherapy team obtains a psychosocial history of the client and assesses his mental status, paying particular attention to motivation, psychological sophistication, legal history, "dangerousness," and, of course, the individual's sexually deviant behavior or "outlet." The therapists are especially interested in the client's attitude toward his offending behavior, his awareness of environmental cues that might trigger deviant impulses, and his pattern of procedure. Of interest as well is the client's perception of the origin, chronicity, harmfulness, and objective of his outlet.

To be admitted into the program, a potential client must be at least 16 years of age and be considered "safe to be at large," predisposed to repeat the antisocial behavior, and amenable to treatment. Because the program expects participants to be cohesive, to conform to rules, and to be able to make decisions and accept responsibility, chronic drug abusers, persons suffering from organic conditions that might hinder relearning, and those

TABLE 25-1.   Referral Source for Offenders and Disposition ($n = 30$)

SOURCE	NUMBER	PERCENTAGE	IN GROUP	PREMATURE TERMINATION	GRADUATION
Court	15	50	5	4	6
Voluntary	10	33	2	5	3
Law enforcement	5	17	2	2	1

manifesting below-normal intelligence or disorders in the thought process are excluded from group membership. A client gains admission to the program if the group, during his first session, votes unanimously to include him. However, the therapy team retains final authority on group composition and on all other clinical issues.

Once admitted, the client receives the Minnesota Multiphasic Personality Inventory (MMPI) and the Adjective Check List; both tests are administered again during the termination and follow-up stages of the program. The client is required to attend a minimum of twelve weekly sessions of ninety minutes each and to write an autobiography with an emphasis on his sexual and legal history to be distributed among the group members. The task of the therapy team, which is assisted by a graduate of the program, is (1) to provide group structure and maintenance, (2) to help the client control and understand his deviant sexual behavior, (3) to assist the client to learn socially acceptable ways of relating to his environment, and (4) to help meet the client's needs for recognition and approval.

Personal Characteristics

Swenson and Gaines have described the personality characteristics of the sexual offender.[4] For the most part, the offender in SDP is emotionally immature, has marginal social development, is passively dependent, and has low self-esteem. Psychosexually, these men are believed to have been "fixated" between the ages of 2 and 6 years. The typical offender comes from a broken home or reconstituted family and has moved many times before reaching adolescence. He remembers his mother as unaffectionate, demanding, intrusive, and belittling; his father as emotionally distant, indifferent, and uninvolved in family functions. Both parents are described as having been hypocritical in their use of religious principles. If urged to think about it, the offender may recall colluding with his parents to limit socialization outside the home. There are also memories of sharing a bed with his mother or siblings before the onset of puberty. When the presenting problem includes homosexuality, it is common to find that the client's older brother initiated this form of sexual behavior. There is a history of loneliness, school phobia, infantilization of intelligence, and antisocial or nonsocial behavior used "to attract attention."

The client's outlet is usually incongruent with the rest of his personality structure. In fact, the client often dissociates himself from his behavior—"It was like watching a movie. I must have been drunk to do that." In addition, the offender is frequently unrealistic about his ability to control his outlet.

Looking at Table 25-2, one can see that crimes which include physical contact are generally perpetrated by older offenders. Further research indicates that there is a progression of offenses; that is, the rapists have gone through previous periods of peeping, exposing, and soliciting. The men who have solicited minors for sexually immoral purposes have graduated from voyeurism, exhibitionism, and so on. This knowledge can be alarming for the group participant who is concerned about his occasional nonviolent sexual deviance.

Clients in SDP have reported that their sexual offenses are frequently preceded by warning masturbatory fantasies that predict the occurrence of the outlet. It is possible that the offender's recognition, unconscious or otherwise, of the connection between masturbatory fantasy and future sexual misconduct enables him to plan outlet strategies in such a way as to increase the likelihood of apprehension by the authorities. This apprehension then acts to alleviate the offender's sense of shame and guilt.

With the exception of the exhibitionist, the offender generally selects victims who are younger than himself. Some of the explanatory phrases associated with this preference are as follows: "more easily impressed," "more ready to give affection," "fewer comparisons," and "I wanted someone to care for me when I was that age." Frequently the offender shows his identification with the victim: "I wish I was a kid again" or "If I was a girl I wouldn't have to be the aggressor." In approximately one-third of the cases at SDP, the victim was known to the offender.

Sexually deviant behavior is often the offender's defense against anxiety and a more clearly overt aggressiveness. To protect himself, the offender will most often use denial, rationalization, and projection. Examples of such justification of deviant behavior include these: "We've all got it in for the broads," "I wanted her to expose herself," "I've got too much sexual energy," "My wife holds out on me," "There were no other women around," and "I drank too much and didn't know what I was doing." For many offenders, the act of doing something that is forbidden, along with

TABLE 25-2.   Age Distribution of Offenders for Each Offense ($n = 30$)[a]

Primary Offense	Number of Clients	Age at Beginning of Treatment[b]	Median Age
Obscene phone calls	4	15(2), 16, 30	19
Indecent exposure	9	16(4), 17, 22, 24(2), 31	20.2
Solicitation of minor females	6	24, 25(2), 26, 28, 33	26.8
Child molestation	4	23, 24, 28, 36	27.7
Rape	2	26, 34	30
Homosexual activity	5	17, 21, 23, 26, 34	24.2

[a] Median ages are slightly lower than law enforcement statistics might suggest for this catchment area. This is probably due to the process of selection. No offender who has spent more than two years in either a psychiatric or correctional institution is accepted into the program.
[b] Number in parentheses indicates the number of offenders at that age.

the attendant physiological response, is a means of proving to themselves and to others that they are alive and important. These clients are usually motivated by a need for recognition, approval, and power. The sexually deviant outlet is obviously a substitute for other expressions of feeling.

Group Approach

Treatment at SDP takes place in a staff-guided, client-led group. Each member is held personally responsible for working toward his own behavioral change while helping his fellow group members to do the same. Group membership breaks the loneliness and solitude that these men have known throughout their lives. In many instances, SDP is the first stable community men as these have known, the first place where they are asked to share feelings and fears. Revealing sexually deviant experiences to sympathetic, empathic listeners often lessens the impulse and weakens the client's defensiveness. In the group sessions the men reenact and then alter their dysfunctional interpersonal patterns. Feedback on this interpersonal style is constructive rather than belittling, and there is little moralizing because this would only contribute to feelings of sexual guilt and inferiority. A sense of belonging fosters client-to-client identification, so that each man can share in the success of the other members.

This group approach, from the model used by Alcoholics Anonymous, was chosen because of the belief the offender would be more adept than staff members at recognizing devious and deceitful thinking and behavior on the part of his associates. This was in fact the case. Group therapy also offers the participants an opportunity to learn that emotional and behavioral problems are universal and that even sexually deviant thoughts are within all of us at one time or another. Group therapy can be an effective way of changing attitudes as well as a means of encouraging social responsibility.

Broadly defined, the goal of this program is neither "cure" nor profound personality change, it is the control and understanding of deviant sexual behavior. Secondary objectives are numerous and include the following: (1) learning to accept responsibility for behavior ("Why did you choose your particular outlet?" "What do you do to make people treat you unfairly?" "How are you harmful or self-destructive?"), (2) enhancing self-esteem or self-assertion and building social skills, (3) expanding sexual knowledge while dispelling sexual myths, and (4) increasing awareness of the "here and now."

Initially, the offender displays little insight into the role that environmental cues and emotional factors play in signaling his outlet. To increase this awareness, the men are asked to keep daily logs during the first month of treatment giving special attention to their deviant impulses and behaviors. Each man notes and summarizes for the group his emotional state at the time of the outlet, as well as where he went, whom he saw, what he did, and the style of disengagement. Each searches for outlet patterns in the behavior of other members. These deviant patterns usually indicate that getting caught is part of one's system.

To some extent, the development of self-regulatory functions is the goal of all treatment in this program. Many of the group's rules and norms are concerned with enhancing self-control. Group rules include no smoking, no returning to the sessions after early departure, no socializing outside the group, no lateness, and no unexcused absence.

Control over one's outlet is a difficult task and one that the client usually approaches with ambivalence. Frequently, his outlet is the only stable identity that the offender owns or can acknowledge. There is an element of grandiosity here—"No other guy would do that!" For many offenders, freedom, autonomy, and identity are found only in the unconventional and offensive. Furthermore, the outlet is certainly sexually pleasurable, regardless of possible consequences. The performance of deviant sexual behavior also directs the person's attention away from stress-provoking events. Even this temporary shift in attention may produce a substantial reduction in anxiety. The problem of controlling one's outlet is further exacerbated by the client's belief that control is not possible to attain. The outlet is often his only means of establishing relationships with females. The offender's ambivalence is also fed by his attitude toward women in general and is manifested in a general blurring of sexual and aggressive impulses.

Treatment

The mode of treatment is guided group interaction, with the primary focus on the client's current interpersonal behavior. Diagnosis and group discussion do contain elements of traditional psychodynamics. That is, some attention is given to dreams (especially if they include other group members or themes of castration anxiety), childhood memories and experiences, and analysis of the treatment relationship. However, most of the group's energy is invested in the "here and now," and treatment is for the most part behavioral.

COGNITIVE INTERFERENCE

Most of the men in the program show poor impulse control in that they give little attention to the period of time that occurs between impulse and behavior. The element of risk is not a primary conscious concern. Therefore, one way of teaching control is to help the client search for the most aversive consequences that could befall him. The client then constructs a photographic scene embodying these noxious elements. For example, he envisions getting caught, being sentenced to prison in a courtroom of family and friends, and, finally, being homosexually assaulted by other inmates in a correctional facility. Eventually, the client may be able to interrupt his outlet by saying a cue word that represents the aversive stimulus.

Successful interference should include evidence of physiologial change, such as trembling and nausea, that are incompatible with the offending behavior. For this exercise, a client might be asked to recall a situation in which he actually did become nauseous, and he would practice pairing this recollection with his deviant impulse until control was attained. During particularly stressful times, practice pairing could be increased. To prevent generalization, however, it is important to intersperse images of appropriate sexual behavior without the addition of noxious consequences.

BEHAVIOR CHAIN

Mood, location, age and appearance of victim, time of day, approach, outlet, and disengagement are usually consistent and form the offender's behavior chain until he moves to different outlet. However, the client is frequently unaware of cues that precede his antisocial act and responds to his impulse as if it occurred in a vacuum. By keeping a daily log, a client can learn a great deal about the emotional and environmental elements that signal his outlet. The earlier the break in the behavior chain, the easier it will be to terminate it.

Because it tends to reinforce the deviant fantasy, masturbation is not used as a control for outlet behavior. McGuire and associates write:

> Deviant sexuality often develops through masturbatory conditioning in which aberrant sexual fantasies are endowed with strong erotic value through repeated association with pleasurable experiences from masturbation.[5]

If the offender will not substitute a "normal" masturbatory fantasy, he is asked to terminate masturbation. In addition, the offender may be asked to discard erotic material from his car, seek marital therapy, or change professions if his employment, teaching or bartending for example, brings him too close to his outlet environment.

ENHANCING SELF-ESTEEM

With the many clients who initially describe themselves as "criminals," "perverts," and "crazy," rebuilding self-esteem is no easy task. Group leaders describe themselves as teachers, the men as students, and the group as a class in sexual deviance. During the first twenty minutes of each session, one member is asked to direct the group. In addition, although the therapy team does not relinquish its power, such decisions as admission of new members, invitations to professional visitors, and where to go for a community outing must be unanimous.

Self-esteem is also bolstered as the men learn to question self-defeating assumptions.[6] For example, "Where is it written that you must always have to be an excellent sexual performer, must always be socially skilled and comfortable, must have all the women crazy about you?" In addition, group members provide feedback on one another's personal strengths, potentials, and limitations. The men also learn that sexually deviant impulses are universal and that many people experience behaviors that are ego-alien and even compulsive. Group leaders explain to the client psychodynamic interpretations about his outlet, which helps the group member feel intellectually capable and worthy of consideration. The men are also encouraged to explore alternative identities—as employees, family members, participants in organizations, and hobbyists—as opposed to the sexual-genital identity that they have previously assumed.

BUILDING SOCIAL SKILLS

Periodically, female staff members and well-screened volunteers are invited to the weekly meetings or join the men for gatherings. Not only does this provide socialization but it serves as a testing ground for new interpersonal behaviors. The women are introduced to the group not as therapists but as caring people who can help provide an opportunity for the development of more effective social functioning. The "party" is held in a large conference room at the center, and women generally outnumber the men two to one. Cards, checkers, and other games are available, and refreshments are served.

The meeting following the party begins with a discussion of the previous encounter. Written statements concerning feelings and perceptions, which the women are asked to prepare, are read to the group at this time. Occasionally, the female staff and volunteers work with the offenders in role-playing situations that might be anxiety-producing. Such situations include being interviewed for a job, asking for a date, approaching intimacy, and assuming the role of victim. This psychodrama can be accompanied by relaxation exercises.[7]

With the consent of the group, community professionals are invited to occasional meetings to discuss topics of mutual concern, and this provides a further opportunity for the men to develop social skills. Members of the clergy, law enforcement and judicial personnel, and professionals who work with victims of sexual crimes are among those who have attended the program.

SIDETRACKING AND REWARD

For this exercise the client is asked to note the environmental conditions and mood that exist when his deviant impulse surfaces. Frequency of outlet (or impulse, if the outlet has been controlled) is plotted on a graph, and this chart is discussed during the weekly meeting. The purpose of this exercise is threefold: (1) it increases the client's awareness of cues that signal the onset of his deviant behavior, thus enabling him to avoid it, (2) it provides an intermediate step between impulse and behavior, and (3) the counting and charting frequently sidetracks the client from resorting to his outlet. If the client chooses, he can call the agency crisis clinic or therapy team and be "talked down" by discussing the catalyst that may have brought about the impulse. Eventually, the client's own friends and relatives can be substituted for professional caretakers. In conjunction with sidetracking, the client may be asked to prepare a "reinforcement menu," rewarding himself according to the length of time since a previous fantasy or outlet.

ASSERTIVENESS TRAINING

Early progress in treatment occurs when a client learns to drop his defenses and understand and control his outlet by viewing it as a form of assertive behavior aimed at reaching out to other persons—"I did it for myself!" Although the outlet is essentially a selfish, harmful act, therapy is facilitated by viewing it first in a more positive light.

Many of the offenders attending SDP present themselves as socially inept, withdrawn, passive, and deferent. Furthermore, some clients mistakenly equate passiveness with femininity, which occasionally leads to a "pseudohomosexual panic."[8] This panic might arise during an emotional crisis or when an individual is feeling unprepared to deal with a major decision, such as career planning.

Assertiveness is defined as honest self-expression without undue anxiety and without denying the rights of others. This quality is closely linked to self-confidence and social functioning, and, for this reason, assertiveness training is an important aspect of this treatment program.[9] During the session, group members may be asked to construct individual hierarchies of assertive behavior, such as learning to turn down requests, expressing personal strengths, rehearsing requests for raises, initiating social contacts, learning to give and receive criticism, and handling disagreements. Devices used to help clients become more assertive and self-reliant include counterconditioning, self-praise, token systems, prompting, and modeling.[10] A repertoire of assertive behaviors can replace sexual deviance as a means toward the gratification of needs.

DIDACTIC APPROACH

Relevant readings are assigned to individual group members who summarize them for the benefit of others.[11] These are then discussed, and examinations are given as a means of assessing comprehension. In addition, open-ended questionnaires are given to the men to assist the therapy team develop their plans for individual treatment. Questions on these are, for example: Why did you choose your outlet? How would your life be different if you stopped going to your outlet? In what ways are you harmful or self-destructive? What can a victim do to terminate your outlet or to enrage you? What is it like to be your victim? What rationalizations do you give to yourself or others for your behavior? How has your outlet pattern changed over time? What are your personal strengths or weaknesses?

Termination

During the termination period the emphasis is on the development of self-regulatory functioning. This is done to lessen the likelihood that the offender will return to his outlet following discharge. Several procedures are used in developing self-regulatory behaviors, one of which might be to transfer gradually evaluative and reinforcing functions from the counselors to the individual himself. Rewards are not only contingent on the occurrence of desirable behavior or the control of undesirable behavior, but also on the individual's accurate evaluation of his own performance. Another method is to utilize the graduating client as a role model or third therapist. In addition, the graduate is expected to practice from time to time cognitive interference and other behavior techniques that he has learned while in treatment. If they are willing to take part, relatives and friends can be taught to help the offender by altering whatever of their own behavior may trigger his outlet. If these and other procedures are insufficient, the client can call the center's crisis clinic or return for additional treatment.

It is essential for the therapist to share his attitude about the deviant behavior and to separate this from the personality of the client without rationalizing his feelings. Not only might the client be unmotivated for treatment; there is also the possibility that the unmotivated therapist will guarantee that the offender will not succeed. In addition, the moral beliefs of the therapist should be labeled as such. If treatment is not successful, there is also the danger of the therapist's feeling responsible for the client's continued probationary status. The co-therapy team may need to exercise caution and to monitor one another so that they do not unintentionally reinforce deviance by providing nonverbal cues that indicate their sanction of the problem behavior. Halleck writes:

> Though few sexual offenders are thus psychopaths, many do exhibit some psychopathic traits. The charm of the psychopath, his bewildering comfort in

stressful situations and the observation that we at times envy, admire or even hate him are clarified if we consider his behavior in the light of a search for freedom ... people will be attracted to the psychopath because he holds out the possibility of sharing his freedom. Women are especially fascinated by his straightforwardness and apparent lack of dependency.... We can argue that this is an immoral freedom, that it is an unsatisfying freedom or that it is basically an inhuman freedom. It is still a commodity so often lacking in the lives of most of us that it is highly coveted.... Approaching the problem from this frame of reference may explain the defensive urgency of many groups to consider psychopathy as a mental illness.[12]

Legal Involvement

Sixty-seven percent of the clients are referred to SDP by court or law enforcement personnel. Although this can spare those referred by law enforcement personnel the emotional and financial hardship of dealing with court proceedings, it also leaves him without due process and at the mercy of a vaguely defined statute of limitations. If the need for treatment seems indicated, the case against the offender is put on continuance, and time-limited treatment is specified and agreed on by the patient, law enforcement personnel, and the therapy team.

The client referred by the judicial system has usually been directed to obtain counseling as part of his probation or parole. During the initial interview, it is made clear to the offender that treatment team plays only a minor role in determining whether he is a sexual psychopath, whether he can be placed on conditional release, and whether he is safe to be at large. These are legal dispositions and as such are determined by the appropriate referring agency. Before a contract for services is initiated, the team and the mental health center are released from responsibility in the event of subsequent offense.

The literature that questions whether dangerousness can be defined or predicted is inconclusive.[13] Equally important are the ethical issues involved in depriving a person of his freedom because he may later become a danger to himself or others. The writer has developed a weighted "danger potential list" to assist him in determining the dangerousness of a client. A partial list of these criteria include the following questions:

During his childhood, was the client prone to temper tantrums, setting fires, or cruelty to animals?

Was he enuretic?

Did he have either social or academic problems in school?

Has there been early contact with violent role models?

Does the client have a history of using force to resolve conflicts?

Does he blame others for his problems?

Are there disorders in thought processes?

Is the client severely depressed?

Does the offense leading to referral include the threat or use of force against another person?

Is he abusing alcohol or drugs?

Does he express doubts about his masculinity?

Does he avoid close interpersonal ties and express extreme dissatisfaction with family and social life?

Ultimately, a client's potential for danger or likelihood of reoffense depends on the immediate situation. When a client is referred to SDP, monthly communications are arranged between the referring source and the therapy team. This transaction includes a general statement of attendance and progress. If during group meetings the client threatens the safety of another individual and if the team believes that there is serious possibility of physical harm, the team instructs the client to notify the referring agency and the appropriate police department within two hours. Appropriate notification is confirmed by the counselors. Protecting the community from an individual who is predisposed to behave in a predatory and hurtful manner is as important as an offender's right to confidentiality.

In addition to referring offenders, probation and parole officers are used as "network therapists." The role of the court officer in treating the sexual offender is threefold:

1. He can facilitate the referral to the mental health center. Because probation or parole may be contingent on outpatient treatment, the court officer and his agencies obviously motivate the client to seek help. Not only that, the corrections officer can alleviate some of the client's anxiety by talking with him about the center's structure and purpose and by explaining the dynamics of SDP.

2. Under the supervision of the therapy team, he can serve as a secondary therapist. By talking to the client's employer and visiting the family, he can assess individual needs and progress. In addition, the court worker is a valuable assistant during the follow-up period as he usually maintains relationships with individuals who are in a position to assess the client's interpersonal performance.

3. He can also act as broker and advocate for his client by helping him obtain employment or vocational training, budget counseling, welfare funds, public housing, out-of-state passes, and less stringent monitoring of his behavior. Of course, these "favors" can be used as well to encourage the client's continued participation in the treatment process.

Evaluation

Criteria for evaluating the effectiveness of the program are both objective and subjective. Some of the objective criteria include a client's legal record of complaints or arrests, pre- and post-therapy test profiles determined by MMPI and the Adjective Check List, time-frequency charting of outlet fantasy and behavior, examination results on didactic material, progress in education or employment advancement, and membership in organizations. More subjective standards of improvement include physical appearance, increase in self-assertion and curiosity, decrease in verbal defenses, and improvement in the quality of significant relationships. Client input, which is ascertained by the group charts plotted by clients and therapists, is considered in the evaluation. Assessment takes place at the evaluation, termination, and follow-up period of treatment.

The Sexual Deviance Program has been in operation for approximately one year. During this time fourteen individuals have been evaluated and deemed unacceptable for the program because of "dangerousness," likelihood (or unlikelihood) of reoffense, age, difficulty in thought processes, drug or alcohol abuse, and unstable living situations. The lack of agency resources precluded an additional thirty-eight applicants from receiving treatment although they were found appropriate.

An element of coercion is frequently necessary to insure continued involvement in the therapy program. This may be due to the demanding and confrontive nature of group process, the offender's ambivalent attitude towad giving up his outlet, or the resistance to change displayed by family members ("covert offenders"). In general, SDP therapists were unsuccessful in enlisting the ongoing participation of significant others in the program.

After the initial twelve-week evaluation, the duration of treatment depends primarily on the chronic nature of the outlet, motivation, psychological sophistication, and the degree of family involvement. The average length of treatment has been thirty sessions. In general, this period was slightly shorter for the offender whose sexual deviance included physical contact, because this offender seemed to have a less difficult time developing empathy and learning to care about his victim.

Sexual deviance is often habitual if not compulsive and, by the time the client enters treatment, is self-reinforcing. Therefore, it would be unrealistic to expect total abstinence once treatment is initiated. Some men do become offenders again, particularly during the early stages of therapy, and this information is communicated by the client and the therapy team to the referring agency. As yet, no client has been removed from the program for resorting to his outlet. This may be attributed to the relationship between the program and the legal systems and to the fact that there has not been a reoffense by a client whose outlet involved excessive physical contact.

On the basis of SDP's experience in the assessment and treatment of sexual offenders, it is apparent that a program like SDP offers a viable and necessary alternative to traditional psychotherapeutic techniques and, in some cases, to total institutional care. SDP, which is based largely on the

principles of guided group interaction and behavior modification, appears
to be a viable approach to the outpatient treatment of the sexual offender.

Notes and References

1. *See* Seymour Halleck, *Psychiatry and the Dilemmas of Crime* (Berkeley: University
   of California Press, 1971); and George MacDonald, *The Washington State Sexual
   Psychopath Law: A Review of Twenty Years Experience* (Fort Steilacoom, Wash.:
   State of Washington Department of Social and Health Services, 1971).
2. Nicholas N. Kittrie, *The Right to be Different: Deviance and Enforced Therapy* (Baltimore, Md.: Penguin Books, 1973).
3. Irvin D. Yalom, *The Theory and Practice of Group Psychotherapy* (New York: Basic
   Books, 1970); and Albert Bandura, *Principles of Behavior Modification* (New York:
   Holt, Rinehart & Winston, 1969).
4. William Swenson and Barbara Gaines, "Characteristics of Sex Offenders Admitted to a Minnesota State Hospital for Pre-sentence Psychiatric Investigation." Paper presented at the Annual Meeting of the American Psychological
   Association, San Diego, Calif., May 1956.
5. Robert McGuire, Jay Carlisle, and Barbara Young, "Sexual Deviations as Conditional Behavior: A Hypothesis," in Bandura, ed., op. cit., p. 513.
6. Albert Ellis, *Reason and Emotion in Psychotherapy* (Secaucus, N.J.: Lyle Stuart,
   1962).
7. Joseph Wolpe, *Psychotherapy by Reciprocal Inhibition* (Stanford, Calif.: Stanford
   University Press, 1958).
8. Lionel Ovesey, *Homosexuality and Pseudohomosexuality* (New York: Science
   House, 1969).
9. Robert Alberti and Michael Emmons, *Your Perfect Right* (San Luis Obispo, Calif.:
   Impact, 1974).
10. Robert Hogan, "Implosive Therapy in the Short-Term Treatment of Psychot-
    ics," in Harold Greenwald, ed., *Active Psychotherapy* (New York: Jason Aron-
    son, 1974), pp. 281–294; and J. Krumboltz and C. Thoresen, *Behavioral
    Counseling: Cases and Techniques* (New York: Holt, Rinehart & Winston, 1969).
11. Anthony Storr, *Sexual Deviation* (Baltimore, Md.: Penguin Books, 1965); and
    James McCory, *Sexual Myths and Fallacies* (New York: Schocken Books, 1973).
12. Halleck, op. cit.
13. Henry Steadman, *The Prediction of Dangerousness* (Albany: Mental Health Re-
    search Unit, New York State Department of Mental Hygiene, 1973); and Stead-
    man, *The Determination of Dangerousness* (Albany: Mental Health Research Unit,
    New York State Department of Mental Hygiene, 1973).

CHAPTER 26

Legal and Social Interface in Counseling Homosexual Clients

Barton E. Bernstein

A recent panel of members of the local gay organization consisted of five homosexuals. Dan was a twenty-seven-year-old doctoral candidate, majoring in psychology. He had just found a lover, and was being teased about it. His co-panelists kidded him mercilessly about his new emotional entanglement. Susan, thirty, and Jan, twenty-seven, were "married" by a Unitarian minister five years ago, and they share a home where they rear Susan's three children by her prior marriage. Both are secretaries, gainfully employed, and both attend school in the evening. Jack, thirty-seven, who owns his own business, and Ed, twenty-six, a corporate employee, have shared an apartment for about a year. They acknowledged that their relationship might be permanent, but further acknowledged that their friendship, like any friendship, could be terminated.

All five had a meaningful relationship with a person of the same sex, and now live openly as homosexuals in the community. They have begun to accumulate property, both real and personal, in the form of a home, appliances and furniture, bank accounts, and retirement provisions. All had at one time or another consulted a "helping professional," including a social worker, concerning their feelings and relationships. Yet, *at no time were any of them advised that their legal status was about to change, or had changed, and their future, whether together or separately, would, of its nature, require certain legal planning.*

The status and concept of the homosexual "marriage," being relatively new in law, has no precedents. Although children are not a factor, almost

Reprinted from *Social Casework*, Vol. 58 (January, 1977), pp. 36–40, by permission of the author and the Family Service Association of America.

317

every other problem that faces a married couple must be considered by a homosexual couple when they live and share together.

The social worker and other professionals consulted had discussed with the clients the deep personal feelings, emotions, possible public intimidation and harassment, and the place of the homosexual in the "gay" and "straight" communities. Never did it occur to any of the professionals, however, that these areas are but the tip of the iceberg, and that below the surface were profoundly affected legal rights, duties, and obligations. An interdisciplinary team approach, however, would have been beneficial, and proper and effective planning would have benefitted the client as well as the counselor, with the social worker exploring with the client his areas of professional competence and the lawyer explaining the gradual shift in legal rights and the methods in handling them. In this manner the client would be truly served, and he would be made aware of all the basic concepts, legal and social, which affect his existence.

In a heterosexual marriage, the legal rules are more easily defined. Cases, precedents, texts, and family codes of the various states abound will all the ground rules, both substantive and procedural. Special courts and special judges are available. The attitudes of judges, lawyers, and juries are reasonably predictable regarding the outcome of any particular conflict, even complex litigation. There is a history of family law with known patterns which is available in any given situation. Thus, in the traditional marriage the inception and the termination are governed by known quantities, and even without personal planning, there is the state, planning as to the rights, duties and obligations of each party to the other, and both to children and family.

The homosexual marriage has no such tradition or identifiable body of law and for this reason requires more planning in its inception and provisions for termination. Because the governing law may vary, a contractual arrangement should be established to provide for ease in the ongoing day-to-day accumulations, as well as in the event of a sudden or gradual termination. Not one professional consultant directed any of the five homosexuals to an attorney in order to engage in this preplanning.

If a homosexual "marriage" follows the pattern of complete sharing, there is a true community of interest, and the parties are tenants in common of any property so acquired. Usually both parties have gainful employment. If, however, one works and contributes financially and the other contributes homemaker services, a more difficult problem evolves. Each makes a contribution. Each must be compensated. Each must be protected where there is a common bank account, joint savings account, a regular accumulation of personal property, or any other items which the parties acquire.

The Homestead

The title to a homestead is record evidence of ownership, and third parties or mortgage companies will loan money to single people on the basis of income as well as the value of the security. A peaceful parting would not cloud the title, as the recorded deed would govern. Suppose, however, the parties purchased a house in a rapidly appreciating area, and the $30,000 home is now a $50,000 home, or the $5,000 shack on the lake becomes a $50,000 resort property. In the event of a termination of the relationship, is it fair for the record owner to realize all of this unforeseen gain? Is there some other equity which should prevail? Needless to say, the non-record owner would truly feel cheated and if sufficiently agitated would consult an attorney who would endeavor to impress either a partnership interest, a constructive or resulting trust, or some other type of equitable ownership in the property. Litigation, with all its bitterness, invective, and expense, would surely result. Some arrangement must be made to provide a release and clear deed for either party in the event the relationship terminates.

Personal Property

All couples accumulate jewelry, clothing, appliances, furniture, automobiles, retirement plans, and, perhaps, if the parties are planning for the future, even stocks and bonds and other securities. Automobiles have a record owner in all states, and the title certificate would govern. Similarly, securities are issued on one or both parties' names, and the person in whose name the security was issued would be the record owner. Some other items are handled differently. Personal items are sold, bought, replaced, exchanged, traded, and altered. The tracing of household goods after a few years of accumulation is virtually impossible. A division in kind is possible, but it takes a genuine sense of fair play which may not be present should the division be hostile.

A suggestion in this area would be to have a "yours" and "mine" list. Thus, as substantial items were purchased and placed into common use, they would be inserted on a list. Each list would indicate that the owner of the property on the list was one or the other, although both parties could share in the use of these items so long as they resided together.

Another method might be a clear understanding that various items would be purchased and receipts or bills of sale received in the name of one party or the other. In the event of a division, each party would receive that item for which he had a written bill of sale. Other techniques might be available the same as a dissolution of a partnership. Whatever the technique, it must be reduced to writing, signed, and available for use in a courtroom in the event the division cannot be effected peaceably.

Insurance

Few homosexual couples have considered or taken out insurance on themselves or the other party. Still, the problems are the same. A lasting relationship requires the parties to consider insurance possibilities and probabilities and purchase appropriate policies which reflect the relationship. Not all parties are covered by their employers for insurance, and major medical insurance will cover a "spouse" only. Genuine care must be exercised in procuring insurance. The agent must guarantee that the surviving beneficiary has an insurable interest, and that the insurance contract is not subject to contest by a former spouse, children of a former spouse, parents, or other family members. All parties should explore the usual major medical, income disability, retirement, and life insurance plans. Certainly, if the survivor of a short-term homosexual relationship becomes the beneficiary of a substantial death policy, one can be almost sure that the family of the deceased would seek some theory, in law or in equity, which would enable the family to share in the insurance bonanza, especially if there are children of a former heterosexual marriage. Such a case is the potential situation with Jan and Susan. In a homosexual relationship the surviving person will have all the problems of a surviving spouse without any legal protection; a carefully planned insurance estate is critical.

Wills

A will may be drawn by hand. Many wills have been admitted to probate which are holographic, or which have been prepared by the deceased personally, in his own handwriting. Probably, if the amount is small, there will be little problem. The incidence of will contest probability increases with the value of the total estate. If two people of means care for each other they must have a professionally prepared will, disposing of the joint and separate assets in a way that takes into consideration the relationship of the parties as well as relatives, and, perhaps, children. With a professionally drafted and executed will, the details are neatly put into place as the beneficiaries receive what the testator intended, in accordance with local law. A poorly drafted will, however, will surely give rise to a contest. And although the incidence of successful will contests is relatively small, if only the slightest loophole exists, the survivor of a homosexual relationship, depending on the community, can rarely count on a sympathetic or understanding jury or judge.

Custody

A recent Dallas case indicated the peril of homosexuals living openly in an admitted lesbian relationship.[1] In this case, the evidence indicated that two women were living together as a family unit, each having the possession and custody of a child by a former heterosexual marriage. There was no problem concerning the eleven-year-old daughter of one of the women. The case revolved around the father's application for a change of custody concerning a nine-year-old boy living with his mother.

The testimony on behalf of the father indicated a well-rounded home. The social worker appointed by the court to make a case study favored the father, as did the psychologist appointed by the court. An independent family counselor hired by the father also favored him. Testifying for the mother was a psychologist in private practice, a professor of psychology, a psychiatrist in private practice, and an Episcopal chaplain at the hospital where the woman was employed. Testimony indicated that the child was not aware of his mother's lesbian tendencies, and further that the mother's home was basically a good one. The foreman of the jury indicated what when the jury was first polled, the vote was nine to three in favor of the man. After approximately five hours of deliberation, the jury voted ten to two in favor of the father, and decided that the best interests of the child would be served by modifying custody and by making the father the managing conservator (with custody) and making the mother possessory conservator (with right of visitation).

The National Organization for Women has passed a resolution supporting the two women. Funds are now being raised to assist the mother through the appeal process.

This case dramatically indicated that homosexual individuals face an uphill fight to retain the custody of their children by their former marriages. Apparently, in Dallas, and conceivably elsewhere, contemporary community standards have not evolved to the point where a homosexual lifestyle is accepted for purposes of rearing children.

Regardless of one's personal persuasion, homosexual individuals in counseling should be made acutely aware that the custody of children of former heterosexual marriages can be placed in jeopardy by living in an

---

[1] For a complete discussion of the lesbian mother, see Marilyn Riley, The Avowed Lesbian Mother and Her Right to Child Custody. A Constitutional Challenge that can no longer be denied, *San Diego Law Review*, 12:799 (June, 1975).

open homosexual relationship and fitting into a homosexual lifestyle. Judges, as well as juries may differ. A homosexual faces the danger of losing the custody of his or her children, not withstanding the many years of devoted and effective parenting.

The Interdisciplinary Team Approach

Lawyers and social workers often function as an interdisciplinary team. They consult concerning common clients and are a referral source, one to the other. The social worker is held in high regard by attorneys and courts in areas of adoption, and also when the custody of childen is an issue and the court or jury has to decide what is in the best interest of a child or children. After each is aware that he has helped the client as much as possible and has reached the outer limits of professional and educational competence, the other profession is often consulted in order to handle all the involved feelings and rights. Clearly, in the area of homosexuals' rights, social worker and lawyer should be aware of all possibilities, and should a homosexual consult with either, the other should be consulted. The considerations listed below should be explored by the social worker and the lawyer, both individually and, perhaps, jointly, and the problems discussed should be solved in the most effective manner.

1. Documents should be prepared on methods to divide personal property in the event of a separation or death.

2. Recordable documents, should be signed, sworn to, and filed, which determine the interests of each party in and to any realty accumulated.

3. The parties should execute a professionally drafted will which acknowledges the relationship and devises the accumulated property in a way that effectuates the wishes of the parties.

4. The parties should periodically review all insurance programs so that the owners and beneficiaries are protected.

5. When children of a former marriage are involved the parties should take proper steps to protect one's custody by insuring that no errors of judgment are committed which might give rise to a change of custody suit. The elements necessarily change from jurisdiction to jurisdiction. In this important area especially, a lawyer familiar with custody problems should be consulted so that the life-style of the homosexual couple can be protected and the right of privacy insured.

Once these problem areas have been considered and handled, the social worker and lawyer are secure in the knowledge that the package of rights and obligations are neatly wrapped in a bundle, and that the couple can continue their relationship with most contingencies professionally handled.

Conclusion

While law concerning the traditional marriage is well settled, the law concerning the homosexual "marriage" or relationship is less clearly defined. Dan and his lover, Susan and Jan, Jack and Ed, have all entered into a relationship by which they are beginning the same pattern as a heterosexual marriage. They will accumulate, they will buy, they will sell, they will rear and visit children by former marriages, they ultimately will hope to live comfortably in retirement on the estate they have garnered during their life together.

Contract, partnership, and family law apply to parts of the arrangement, but there is no consolidated body of law, nor is there likely to be, such as a family code governing homosexuals. Therefore, when a social worker consults with an admitted homosexual or a party with homosexual tendencies, he must explore or at least make his client aware of present and future legal perils. Custody is the most likely and traumatic potential.

If the client is a heterosexual and seeks custody from a former spouse, a homosexual, the social worker should inform his client and make him aware of the law, legal procedures, and community thinking concerning a change of custody on the basis of the former spouse now living in a homosexual lifestyle, and should suggest ways to protect the present status quo. Conceivably, the change from heterosexual to homosexual would be reason enough for a custody change.

The client should be informed of the changing legal status of personal and real property as it is accumulated, and as values change. The client should further understand that as the natural object of his bounty changes, his wishes concerning his estate should be set forth in a will.

Legal problems begin as soon as the parties acquire real estate, household goods, and insurance with the proceeds of both salaries. The problems continue through the disposition of the accumulation on the death of either party. A widow has rights intestacy, a homosexual partner has none. Only a carefully drafted will insures that the intention of the deceased be carried out and that the survivor can enforce the rights of survivorship.

Social workers are not encouraged to practice law. The purpose of this article is to encourage "helping professionals" to recognize the actual and potential legal problems and refer these problems to an attorney for solution.

Where children are involved, as in Susan's situation, the client should be made specifically and realistically aware that her former spouse may file a motion to change custody. She should also be made aware that the homosexual relationship, if either proved or admitted, would place her in a clear and present danger of losing her children. Discretion and precaution are of paramount importance.

Lawyers and social workers interface in their endeavors to represent clients. Each is responsible to recognize when the other professional could contribute to the well-being of the individual or couple with a problem. Homosexual problems are unique not only because of the history but also because of changing diagnosis and treatment. For this reason the problems must be considered and solved by co-professionals with the client's best interest in mind. Therapy as offered by a social worker relates to the mental health of all the people concerned. When one's legal rights are affected, social worker and lawyer should associate as an interdisciplinary team for the best long-range solution for all concerned.

SCHIZOPHRENIA

CHAPTER 27

Casework Treatment of Ambulatory Schizophrenics

Laura Farber

This paper deals with some theoretical aspects of casework with ambulatory schizophrenics, and with a number of specific treatment techniques that are particularly applicable to work with these persons, although they are also used with other diagnostic groupings. The discussion is focused on one aspect of casework with the schizophrenic person—direct treatment in which the objective is improvement in his social functioning. The techniques described are based on the understanding of ego functioning. Since this presentation is drawn from the writer's experiences as a caseworker in both the in-patient and out-patient services of Hillside Hospital, the word "patient" will be used throughout.

Because the number of schizophrenics living in the community seems to be increasing, their treatment is a problem that confronts not only caseworkers in psychiatric clinics, but also caseworkers in many other settings. Clients with similar, if not identical, problems come to the attention of all community social agencies. If caseworkers are to be effective in their work with schizophrenics and are to be dealing with more and more of them, it is imperative that they have adequate clinical knowledge of the nature of the personality disturbance called "schizophrenia." Such knowledge will influence the way in which cases are handled since it will enable the caseworker to know in advance the problems he is most likely to encounter.

The term "schizophrenia" has not been clearly defined. It holds dif-

Reprinted from *Social Casework*, Vol. 39 (January, 1958), pp. 9-17, by permission of the author and the Family Service Association of America.

ferent meanings for different people; there are wide areas of disagreement about it and no single treatment approach can be proposed. Although there are characteristic modes of schizophrenic functioning, and schizophrenic patients resemble one another to some degree, they can actually be distinguished from one another in respect to the degree of their affective thinking, and behavioral disturbances.

We are primarily concerned with what is generally called ambulatory schizophrenia. The term as used in this paper includes individuals whose ego functions are not so markedly impaired that they cannot maintain themselves with some measure of effectiveness in the community. A large number of patients known to the Out-Patient Clinic of Hillside Hospital fall within this group. For the most part they show none of the dramatic symptoms, such as hallucinations, delusions, and bizarre behavior, which commonly are diagnostic indicators of schizophrenia. However impressive, these are but accessory symptoms, characteristic only of the more advanced stages of illness, and they may be altogether lacking in the ambulatory patient.

Characteristic Symptoms

The characteristic symptoms of the ambulatory schizophrenic patient are those that are fundamental to schizophrenia, in that they are always present but in varying degrees. As outlined by Bleuler, these symptoms are: disturbances of association, disturbances of affectivity, the predilection for fantasy as against reality, and the inclination to divorce onself from reality.[1] These disturbances constitute failures in acquired ego functions. In the later stages of schizophrenia these symptoms may be readily discernible, but their manifestations are more subtle in the ambulatory patient and often not immediately recognizable. For example, after several interviews, it becomes apparent that many of the patient's verbal communications, regardless of specific content, consistently lack a certain vital clarity. Or, while listening to a patient, one may suddenly realize that a sentence or two, flowing smoothly along with everything else that he has said, is inappropriate to the context.

It is important to note the extent of impairment in the ego functions of the ambulatory schizophrenic; specifically, impairment in the areas of judgment, perception, organization, self-preservation, synthesizing of experience, and reality testing. Not all these functions may be uniformly affected in any one patient. Since a failing ego has but limited "coping"

---

[1] Eugen Bleuler, *Dementia Praecox; or, The Group of Schizophrenias*, translated by Joseph Zinkin, International Universities Press, New York, 1950.

energy, defenses are created in order that some degree of cohesiveness may be maintained and disintegration avoided.

A schizophrenic may thus be viewed in part as a person who is to some degree regressed and who, like the infant whose boundaries between himself and others are vague, has intense needs, lacks control, and is sensitive to slight indications of psychic danger. In reality, however, he is not the infant who is moving ahead on the road and who has not yet learned to differentiate himself from the environment. He is, instead, the adult on the path back, having undergone life experiences, many of which have created anxiety so painful that he has had to withdraw into himself from the world about him. His disorder is thus an ego-defensive function.

The ambulatory schizophrenic's tolerance for pressure may be decreasing as he struggles with unconscious impulses threatening expression. Because his feelings are so easily stimulated, getting close to external objects is a risky business, and the patient maneuvers to maintain distance. Such patients often complain, during initial interviews, that the world seems cold, empty, strange, and alien. Other parts of the schizophrenic's personality may be intact, however, and in a number of respects he is like others rather than different from them. The caseworker should relate to and thus strengthen these stable parts of the patient's personality. At the same time the caseworker should be respectful and accepting, although not encouraging, of the existing impairments since these are also part of the patient's unique differences and individuality. It may be necessary first to meet the patient's infantile needs to some degree in order later to strengthen his more mature drives.

Preserving Ego Defenses

The casework process is primarily one of reorienting the patient to his present social reality, rather than one of attempting to help him resolve internal psychological conflicts. Although casework treatment with schizophrenics may frequently be geared toward the maintenance of present levels of functioning, in order to prevent further deterioration, it need not exclude the possibility that some degree of modification in adaptive behavior may be achieved. Treatment goals as well as treatment techniques should be flexible. The basic casework approach to schizophrenic patients rests, however, upon attempts to nurture carefully and to preserve their ego boundaries and defenses. The worker's efforts are directed toward massive support of ego defenses and reinstatement of ego functions with particular emphasis on reality testing if this is failing. The degree to which these efforts are successful depends upon the establishment of the worker-patient relationship. Casework with schizophrenics is based upon the traditional broad techniques of support and clarification, and within these wide categories a variety of specific approaches may be used. Caseworkers achieve good treatment results with these patients even though the techniques employed may vary from worker to worker. Choice of specific techniques frequently grows out of the uniquely personal manner in which a particular caseworker relates to an individual patient, and it was from individual experience that the writer arrived at some of the following formulations.

The formerly warranted prudence of many caseworkers in attempting to work with schizophrenics—a prudence that resulted from the potential dangers and unpredictable nature of casework treatment of them—has blossomed into anxious caution which may be limiting and incapacitating. Although schizophrenics make challenging patients, they also inspire pessimism, precisely because they are difficult to treat. A pessimistic attitude in itself may handicap a caseworker in attempting to achieve results that are realistically possible. If the casework goals set are flexible and considerate of the patient's limitations, the worker can afford to be optimistic. Because the treatment course with the schizophrenic is often stormy and, by our usual standards, the gains are relatively small, caseworkers are often ready to call the patient "untreatable" or "unreachable." Although this may be true at times, it is preferable in the beginning for the caseworker to be as flexible as possible in relation both to treatment processes and to goals, rather than for him to begin with the assumption that the patient is beyond help.

Reality-oriented Treatment Approach

Some caseworkers treat many patients, including ambulatory schizophrenics, by means of what may be called the laboratory method. They are advocates of "objectivity" and "neutrality," who seem to regard their function as that of providing a screen for the patient on which he may safely project a wide range of thoughts and emotions, which the caseworker then "interprets." The development of this method may in part be attributed to the early development of casework in analytically oriented settings where caseworkers were brought into close contact with the ideas of classical analysis, some of which were then modified for casework purposes. Although this approach is desirable and effective with some patients, it may be not only useless but even harmful with schizophrenics, since it may foster an impersonal and passive attitude on the part of the caseworker.

A passive casework approach may encourage both regressive withdrawal and anxiety. The atmosphere of remoteness which it creates serves perfectly as a setting for the silent patient, or for the patient who is introspective. The schizophrenic patient, on the other hand, needs actual direction in turning his attention toward externalities. The simple fact of the caseworker's "being there" is of particular benefit to the schizophrenic, but it may not be sufficient in itself. The necessary atmosphere of mutuality resulting from the interaction of two human beings will not be achieved if the caseworker's contribution and participation are limited to his merely being present or occasionally punctuating silent listening with a few words. The caseworker cannot establish the effective relationship through which all treatment gains are achieved if he sits in remoteness from the human struggles confronting the schizophrenic patient.

In working with the schizophrenic patient, the caseworker should utilize an active, reaching-out, reality-oriented approach in which he establishes what can be called a "controlled" involvement—controlled, that is, by the realistic limits of the worker-patient relationship of which he never loses sight. An active casework approach will furnish the schizophrenic—a person whose perception of the external world is blurred as a result of his anxiety and whose ego boundaries are ill defined—with what he needs, the opportunity of relating himself to a real person from whom he can gain a clear and dependable image. The nature of the schizophrenic's problems demands that the caseworker represent a segment of reality, and thus the worker must allow his own feelings to be acknowledged in order to enter into his relationship with this patient.

The caseworker's genuine emotional responsiveness to the feelings of the schizophrenic may evoke in the patient a variety of personal feelings toward the worker from which he may build a fantasied relationship which transcends professional limits. Problems may arise if these feelings exceed the level of moderate strength. It is usually desirable for the patient, although he is characteristically ambivalent, to have predominantly positive feelings for the caseworker, since there is less danger of serious difficulties resulting from overpositive than overnegative feelings. If a patient reveals strong feelings of affection for the caseworker as a person, it is extremely important that such expressions be graciously and respectfully accepted. To the schizophrenic patient these may be represented by a cautious offering of a precious gift. Interpreting them as "transference" feelings, truly meant for another person, as might be done with non-schizophrenics, can be devastating to this vulnerable person and may be experienced by him as harsh rejection.

It is often difficult, yet necessary, to discover ways in which it is possible to reject the feelings but not the patient. It is possible to accept expressions of positive feeling and then to translate them into broader terms. For example, a man in his twenties expressed affectionate feelings for a female caseworker and made references to being sexually attracted to her. The caseworker accepted his feelings as meant for her, and since she knew him to be a shy person with strong feelings of isolation, commented that he seemed to be really telling her that he was beginning to feel some closeness toward other people, which was a healthy gain. She added that she was pleased to hear this and that, although he seemed to feel attracted to her as a woman, she felt that he needed her most, and that she could help him best, as his caseworker. In doing this, the caseworker refused the role of girl-friend, yet she did not reject the patient since she made clear to him her desire to continue to relate to him in her professional role.

On the other hand, strong negative feelings toward the caseworker can create serious problems as they can disrupt the treatment relationship. In his active role the caseworker is bound to display some of his own individual personality characteristics, some of which the patient may dislike and respond to with anger. These negative feelings must first be listened to and accepted; but it then is helpful for the caseworker to initiate discussion of the circumstances relevant to their being expressed—why the patient is preoccupied with his dislike for the worker at this particular time. His preoccupation may be a reaction to something the worker has unwittingly said or it may simply be a means by which the patient can avoid talking about himself. Generally speaking, in order to assist the patient in identifying the reason for his feelings, and in order to reduce the possibility of distortion, the caseworker has to be free enough to disclose his own feelings and the meaning of his actions so that they may be objectively examined. The frequently used casework technique of responding to questions with questions—for example, asking "why" when the patient asks a somewhat personal question—must frequently be discarded with the schizophrenic, particularly if negative feelings are to be kept within reasonable limits.

The Patient–Worker Relationship

It is important that the beginning phases of treatment be concerned primarily with the establishment of the vital patient-worker relationship, particularly since the schizophrenic is often unusually resourceful in defending himself against interpersonal involvements. The manner in which the early interviews are handled may either greatly facilitate the development of the relationship or make it practically unattainable. It may be added that the schizophrenic patient who has established any degree of relationship will repeatedly test the caseworker's ability to remain constant, the extent of his interest, and his capacities to tolerate the patient. The relationship, once established, is, in any event, but precariously maintained. During the early stages of contact, the ways in which the patient tests may often be subtle. His attitude may be one of quiet scrutiny. If, so to speak, the caseworker passes the first tests and the relationship moves forward, the testing becomes more direct and piercing, and may produce in the caseworker anger, helplessness, or anxiety, none of which are comfortable feelings. Although it is distressing to witness the schizophrenic's need to confirm the caseworker's reliability over and over again, it is also painful at times for the caseworker to be in the position of test target.

Where the work setting offers a time-limited period of treatment, it is even more necessary for the caseworker to provide the stimulus and assume the initial responsibility for establishing the relationship, as this cannot be left to chance nor delayed until the patient makes a move. Each caseworker must make continuous efforts in his own individual manner to emerge as a solid object on which the patient can focus and to which he can also cling at times if necessary. Fundamental attitudes such as empathy, warmth, and respect are often insufficient, particularly with those patients who are constricted or detached. These attitudes must be accompanied by energetic efforts to induce the patient to direct his attention away from himself and toward the external world in the person of the caseworker. In addition to the highly important non-verbal communications such as glance, gesture, and posture, these efforts include verbal communication in which it is not only what the caseworker says that matters, but, equally important, how it is said.

The effectiveness of speech very much depends upon the tone of voice and the feeling qualities that accompany the words. The caseworker, on certain occasions, should have a suggestion of conviction, firmness, or insistence in his voice. Language is a potent means of communication and may be used freely, although not as the sole means. Not only should the caseworker be actively inquiring by continuing to ask questions despite sparse answers, but also he must be active in responding by commenting frequently upon the patient's remarks so that the patient at least knows that he is being heard. Although schizophrenics are persons for whom nonverbal communication assumes special significance, they frequently need to have the worker's support, interest, and attention demonstrated in words.

Exploring the Patient's Problems

Casework usually starts with an exploratory phase during which the nature and scope of the problems confronting the patient are determined. Casework with the ambulatory schizophrenic places emphasis on the problems the patient is encountering in his handling of current reality situations; thus the initial focus should be on the facts and feelings surrounding the circumstances of the patient's coming for help. Although these facts and feelings may seem obvious, the obvious can often be obscure. The caseworker cannot assume that these are at all clear to the schizophrenic patient, but rather should assume that they need to be both established and clarified. Thus, it is often valuable for the caseworker to put what appears to be the obvious into words. Many schizophrenics are unable to verbalize concretely their need for help, and the caseworker must often do this for them. The caseworker takes his cues in doing this from what the patient has thus far said and from his non-verbal attitude, and thereby attempts to convey some understanding of the patient's feelings.

It is possible to anticipate the patient's probable attitudes toward seeking to help because his fears, doubts, confusions, and expectations are not basically different from those of other patients although they certainly may be more intense. Many of these patients cannot be expected to focus on, or even to identify, their problems. The caseworker may have to identify the patient's unexpressed concerns and, at times, emphatically state them. During this process the caseworker does not depend solely upon verbal explanations; he acts out his function, thereby demonstrating to the patient how casework operates. He conveys something of what his help involves, and what he and the patient may attempt to do together, so that the patient's expectations of him will not get so far out of touch with what is actually possible of achievement in the situation that the patient becomes angrier and more frustrated.

As a result of the caseworker's verbalizing for the patient and bringing some of his feelings into the open, the patient may visibly experience relief of tension. It seems to be enormously encouraging to the schizophrenic to feel that another person has managed to understand at least a part of what he is feeling and has shown respect for him by communicating this to him. The fact that he can be understood implies further to him that his feelings are not unusual nor are they beyond the pale of human understanding. In addition, the schizophrenic is very concerned about whether the caseworker is a competent person. For example, during an initial interview a patient, in a challenging manner, said to the caseworker: "If I tell you my problems, what more can you do for me besides giving me empathy?" This attitude of infantile defiance is not uncommon, and it may be wiser for the caseworker to answer such questions directly as they arise than to postpone or avoid answering them.

Encouraging Verbalization

One technique that may be used to encourage the schizophrenic patient to verbalize involves the caseworker's giving him something specific to which to relate. For example, a patient reported that he attended a family social function which he did not enjoy. He could not on his own say why it was so unpleasant, nor could he answer the caseworker's questions. The caseworker then made use of his knowledge of this man's characteristic difficulties and suggested a possible reason why he had failed to have a good time. The worker suggested that the patient did not feel comfortable because he felt obliged, as he usually did when his mother was present, to limit his freedom of action for fear of evoking criticism from her. As a result of the caseworker's stating this one possibility, the patient had a specific factor on which to focus and to which he could respond. He then said that he had actually been made uncomfortable by something else—the presence of a fellow employee whom he had not expected to be present. This comment was pursued and led into a discussion of the patient's interpersonal relationships on his job—an important area of functioning which it had not previously been possible to discuss.

Something may be gained, also, from the worker's venturing an opinion regardless of whether it eventually proves correct. A need on the part of the worker to be correct most of the time hinders vital spontaneity and defeats the objective of bringing the patient's thoughts, feelings, and attitudes into the open where they may be realistically appraised. A possible error or what may actually be a difference of opinion helps the schizophrenic to separate his attitude from his total self as he considers the different ways in which a situation can be viewed and described. If the caseworker can acknowledge being wrong without being defensive, the patient is provided with the opportunity of seeing the worker more accurately and realistically as another fallible human being. As a result he may not need to regard his own mistakes as unique or devastating, and may be freed from some feelings of inadequacy. For example, a patient in her early thirties was involved in a chaotic marital relationship and vehemently denied that she in any way contributed to the violent battles that took place regularly. She projected the entire responsibility for these scenes onto her husband, thereby stabilizing her own rage toward him. For many months, while viciously criticizing neighbors whom she felt were pitying her, she nevertheless presented herself to everyone as the victim of her husband's abusiveness.

At the beginning of the contact there were but few attempts made to discuss these projections with her since the casework relationship was tenuous. As the relationship developed, so did an identification with the worker, and the patient gradually revealed more specific information as to how these arguments arose. During one particular interview, the caseworker managed to elicit details that indirectly revealed that the disagreement under discussion had resulted from her insisting to her husband that she had been right in her evaluation of a particular situation when she had actually not been. She was able to examine realistically the circumstances under which this argument had arisen when she was reminded of some of the mistakes the caseworker had made during the contact and was then asked why she found it so hard to admit the possibility of human mistake in herself.

Holding the Patient to Reality

Since certain schizophrenics are vague and confused in their thinking, it is important for the caseworker to consider ways in which the patient may be held to discussion of important realities so that the interviews do not become "much ado about nothing." These patients readily escape into irrelevancies and generalities, avoiding topics of significance by all sorts of circuitous means, and some become more anxious as they become more confused. The caseworker must listen intently to the patient who rambles, or the one who talks compulsively, in order to understand what he is trying to convey and in the hope of picking up at least one significant statement which then may be pursued. If a patient dwells on a circumstantial narrative about a situation that is irrelevant to his difficulties, it is the caseworker's responsibility to direct his interest elsewhere. This may be accomplished by referring back to an area discussed previously, bringing it to the patient's awareness in a general way so that the topic does not appear to be abruptly changed. Once it is in front of the patient it may be followed by a question that requires a more specific answer. Sometimes a patient resents the worker's firm attitudes in interrupting his verbal wanderings, and he feels thwarted and angry. Since such feelings may hinder further communications, the caseworker should help the patient realize that his anger is related to the worker's activity and that this reaction is understandable.

Dealing with Anger

Most schizophrenics suffer from pervasive or chronic feelings of rage to which the term "unassuageable anger" has been applied.[2] In his struggles with rage, the schizophrenic will feel more secure from his own impulses if the caseworker's strength or control serves to reinforce his own impaired ego. Although the caseworker may feel more comfortable in being permissive, he must often be firm and even demanding since the patient needs external controls. The caseworker must set limits, but not arbitrarily, and these limits may be more acceptable to the patient if he is given reasons as to why they are necessary. A 20-year-old patient, whose grandiose schemes revealed poor reality testing, frequently expressed anger toward the caseworker. One day, during a period when she was particularly distressed, she became furious with the caseworker when the latter refused to comply with a request to write a letter to the patient's sister in her behalf since the worker felt that the patient was capable of handling this on her

[2] Karl Menninger, M.D., "The Diagnosis and Treatment of Schizophrenia," *Bulletin of the Menninger Clinic*, Vol. XII, No. 3 (1948), pp. 96–106.

own. Feeling helplessly angry, the patient grabbed a small ash-tray from the caseworker's desk. The caseworker did not wait for the minute to pass during which the patient might have returned it to its place, but instead ordered her to put it down and gave as the reason the fact that she would not allow the patient to hurt either one of them. When the patient did not respond even after the caseworker repeated this, the caseworker reached over and removed the object from the patient's hand. The patient was shown that the caseworker possessed the control the patient lacked.

The schizophrenic is caught up in a circle of anger; the original anger, after being expressed, brings guilt, which in turn creates additional anger. Whether the verbal expression of hostility is subtle or blatant, it is wise to clarify it at once since otherwise the patient may be left with discomforting guilt. This unmitigated anger of the schizophrenic may be a further problem in treatment since he may project a good deal of it onto the caseworker and thus may readily feel that the worker is attacking or rejecting him. In addition, by verbally attacking the caseworker and attempting to disparage him or to prove him worthless, the schizophrenic attempts to prove that he in no way needs the worker, and thus he increases his provocative testing as the relationship assumes importance and his anxiety mounts.

Dealing with Paranoid Ideas

A large number of schizophrenics, particularly when under stress, develop paranoid ideas which serve to ward off anxiety but in many instances create social difficulties. Since new experiences are frequently terrifying to the schizophrenic, he may develop suspicions regarding the intentions of others. Whether the expression of the paranoid idea is directed toward the caseworker or toward another person in the patient's environment, immediate handling is nevertheless called for lest the distortion become more involved. The caseworker neither agrees nor disagrees with such ideas, but accepts them as what the patient is experiencing. If the caseworker disagrees with a distortion, the patient may become more cautious or may be forced to elaborate.

One way in which the caseworker may deal with paranoid distortions is illustrated by the following brief case excerpt. A 20-year-old man was being seen regularly with particular focus on his problems in employment and residence. A few weeks after beginning a new job that was potentially promising, he told the caseworker about his idea that co-workers were laughing at him as he passed their desks; hearing the murmur of their voices as he reached the other end of the office led him to believe that they were also talking about him. The caseworker first approached the patient's reactions to what he perceived, which were feelings of fear, anger, and rejection. With persistence she then attempted to elicit factual material about the circumstances under which his ideas had arisen. She asked questions about the office situation in general, about particular people of whom the patient was suspicious, and inquired as to whether the patient had ever felt this way before in any other situation. At the same time she attempted to create some doubts in the patient's mind and to have him consider alternative meanings, through questions such as, "What other explanations might there possibly be for their laughing?" She did not deny the validity of the patient's feelings, but indicated that she was dubious about the validity of his perception.

In order to strengthen the patient's reality-testing ability, the caseworker should elicit details of the reported situation. With these details the caseworker can then review the relevant circumstances step by step, trying to pull them together into some sort of objective sequence of events, so that the patient can become aware of the relationship between the actual situation and his feelings about it. In this case, the patient was helped to relate his own feelings of humiliation resulting from a public criticism by his supervisor, to his later feeling of being laughed at by others. Since effective reality testing depends to some degree on the identifications supporting it, it may be advisable for the caseworker to assume a position of critically examining the patient's attitudes toward the worker himself so that the patient may then assume a similarly critical attitude in relation to his own actions and those of others. The caseworker should be explicit, frank, and detailed in his discussions with the suspicious patient in order to prevent some, although certainly not all, of his potential misinterpretations. There should be no tacit understandings with these patients, and absence of comment regarding a distortion may mean to the patient that the worker is tacitly giving consent.

Conclusion

The casework approach outlined in this paper can best be called "directive." Some of the difficulties that frequently arise during casework treatment of the schizophrenic patient have been described, and techniques for handling them have been suggested. It is recognized that this is a complex area of treatment in which further exploration and experimentation are needed. Although one cannot suggest final answers to many of the questions posed, caseworkers should be willing to be flexible in experimenting with various, and possibly new, treatment techniques.

CHAPTER 28

Treatment Issues in Schizophrenia

Judith C. Nelsen

In an earlier article on planning social work treatment for schizophrenia, the writer asserted that to help this client group a social work professional must assess and deal with systems balance over space and time. In this article, core issues in the actual treatment process are discussed. The individuals and families under consideration are primarily those in whom schizophrenic symptoms occur intermittently or in recurring cycles; clinical diagnosis of the identified patient is usually ambulatory schizophrenia or schizophrenia in partial remission. The discussion here is based on material from ego psychology and the systems-communications theorists, as well as on the writer's experience with direct treatment, supervision, and consultation in the area of schizophrenia.

Three major issues will be discussed that are basic to effective treatment and often problematic for social workers. They are the management of relationship factors in individual and group treatment, the dynamic enhancement of ego coping in individual and group treatment, and the reorientation to process factors in family work.

Management of Relationship Factors

In individual and group treatment of schizophrenic clients, there is a surfacing of relationship issues which must be handled if treatment is to progress. The initial process of relationship-building is often a painstaking one. Sessions may be characterized by frequent silences which the worker must

Reprinted from *Social Casework*, Vol. 56 (March, 1975), pp. 145–152, by permission of the author and the Family Service Association of America.

fill, monosyllabic answers to questions, awkwardness, apparent disinterest in proceeding with treatment, or highly inappropriate discussion. Clients may relate too openly at the outset, spilling innermost thoughts or content apparently straight from the unconscious. Most schizophrenic clients who continue therapy become dependent on the worker, whether or not they can express this emotion.

Almost inevitable problems come with such dependency. Even gentle, supportive workers who are clear about the limitations of their professional role may see clients who show unrealistic expectations about treatment and then flee, via broken appointments or paranoid ideation, with the accusation that the worker has taken over. These typical schizophrenic relationship distortions, or psychotic transference, must be understood and handled.

Theories about early or continuing patterns in the family of orientation can help clarify such distortions. These theories suggest that the parents, for various reasons, have not allowed the schizophrenic offspring to separate from them as he must to establish independent means of dealing with his affects and of evaluating reality. Implicitly, they promise that if he remains with them and represses all negative feelings, they will meet all his needs. Messages about sexuality are conflicting; parents may be subtly seductive while demanding abstinence. Either because the family continues its influence or because the schizophrenic individual has not learned to assess new relationships differently, both positive and negative expectations of parent figures will be transferred onto the treating person.[1]

As the client moves toward the worker emotionally, he will expect the worker to meet all his needs. Inappropriate sexuality and dependency may be made explicit: The client claims that he loves the worker, wants to marry the worker, or wants to go to live as the worker's child. There are sometimes positive expressions about merger; one client told a worker, "We will marry and become one person." Covert signs may include a client's showing up at unscheduled hours with an adoring smile, touching the worker, making overly enthusiastic comments on the benefits of treatment, or showing possessive jealousy in the presence of other group members.

The client usually tries to keep his part of the presumed bargain during this time by repressing or suppressing any negative feelings toward the worker. However, frustration builds because the worker, like the parents, can not meet all his needs. Failures on the worker's part are seen as a lack

---

[1] Thomas Freeman, John Cameron, and Andrew McGhie, *Studies on Psychosis* (New York: International Universities Press, 1966), pp. 15–37; and Theodore Lidz, Stephen Fleck, and Alice Cornelison, Therapeutic Considerations Arising from the Intense Symbiotic Needs of Schizophrenic Patients, in *Schizophrenia and the Family*, ed. Lidz, Fleck, and Cornelison (New York: International Universities Press, 1965), pp. 61–71.

of concern rather than a limited ability to help, because the worker's omnipotence is taken for granted. At some point, anger will be shown, obviously or subtly, perhaps symbolically by heated complaints about other authority figures. If not handled, increasing levels of rage can cause clients to leave treatment.

Clients who receive no comment from the worker about sexual fantasies which have surfaced in some form may also discontinue treatment because of fears that a sexual relationship will actually take place. The heavy incestual component of their sexual feelings makes this fantasy a terrifying prospect. Clients who express a strong wish for merger are often frightened that the worker will take them over eliminating their very existence as separate human beings.

To deal with these various disturbed relationship elements, a social worker must not send mixed messages related to self-feelings of omnipotence, fear of aggression, or special interest in sexuality. A worker's distress about handling such material may blind him or her to the veiled manifestations of relationship distortions that do exist. The writer is convinced that relationship factors must be anticipated, that the worker's stance must be made explicit before or as soon as such issues arise, and that the client's difficulties in accepting such messages must be discussed at times.

Generally, the first factor to arise is the client's belief in the worker's omnipotence. It can be anticipated by the worker's spelling out how he or she will try to help, the limits of such help, and what the client will need to attempt for himself. Many clients will not fully hear these comments. The worker must notice when clients seem to hold unrealistic expectations or to attribute change magically to the worker and must gently expose the realities involved. If the worker's attitude is that misunderstandings do occur in relationships but that it is helpful to look at them, he or she may help clients make their unrealistic expectations a matter for ego awareness and further discussion. A schizophrenic individual can examine and seek to control his conscious ideas about relationships, such as his understandable wish for complete help, without having to consider why he is this way. Finally, prior work in the area of unrealistic hopes will lead to discussion of client disappointments when hopes are not met. Disappointments will be smaller and easier to consider when this groundwork has been laid. The worker must be careful to verbalize disappointments which a client only hints at and to express empathy about them. By means of such discussion, a client may have his first real experience that negative feelings can be expressed and understood in a close relationship.

Wishes for and fears of merger can be handled similarly. The worker may establish himself or herself as a separate individual by some limited revelation of personal material, although this disclosure should not be extensive or it may have the opposite effect of implying that a close personal and, to the client, sexualized relationship will develop. The worker must also empathically examine the client's subtle wishes and fears when they arise and clarify that both worker and client are and will remain separate individuals. Client expressions of love and sexual feelings, especially if made nonverbally by touching, are often difficult for workers to react to because they do not wish to indicate rejection. One may show understanding of the feeling while noting that it can not be appropriately expressed in this relationship. The momentary sense of rejection which the client may feel is preferable to increasingly frightening fantasies or greater feelings of rejection at a later time.

In group treatment, member relationships may dilute the relationship with the worker. However, the above distortions can arise between members as well as between individual members and a group leader. Explicit handling by the worker is necessary in such situations. Although it may be more difficult to notice individual covert reactions in a group, group members often move along together in their expectations, hopes, and fears. Also, in a group, members can learn to help each other find and manage relationship distortions.

There is one other facet of handling relationship material with schizophrenic clients. Frequently, a client will not openly acknowledge feelings that he expresses nonverbally, no matter how nonjudgmentally the worker comments on them. The worker's benign comments are usually received without arousing great anxiety. Sometimes feelings can be acknowledged by a client at a later time; in any case, they do not seem to build up as they do otherwise. It is also true that the worker's clarifications, whether heard or not, do not usually prevent a continuation of some distortions. The difference is that part of the client's ego is now on the side of realistic handling, or at least the client is reassured that the worker will not succumb, for example, to a sexual relationship, even though the client may continue to talk of such a possibility.

Dynamic Enhancement of Ego Coping

After experiences in which psychoanalytic-style probing led to an increase of symptoms, social workers doing individual or group treatment with schizophrenic clients have often avoided discussion of feelings and have talked only about reality events in clients' lives. Help with reality-testing is important, including the clarification of distortions in client-worker and group member relationships, but a dynamic approach to the enhancement of other ego coping is also necessary.

As a foundation, the worker must gain extensive awareness of each client's coping capacities and personality style from observing him during treatment sessions and in interaction with other people, from hearing how the client is handling life situations, from considering recent historical information, and sometimes from working with collateral persons. Strengths must be found even in situations of considerable pathology. Perhaps the client's intelligence, his physical stamina or ability to discharge stress through physical activities, an appealing manner which makes others more willing to help him, or an extraordinary will to survive his difficulties can be determined. Limitations must be identified, not in the static sense of a symptom picture, but by understanding what causes anxiety or an increase in symptoms.

The worker must determine how the client maintains balance in his life. To whom does he look for positive regard and emotional security? What does he do with affects? If the client does not show anger or sexuality in situations where these would normally be aroused, what defenses are employed to maintain repressions? Workers often must combine knowledge of life happenings and of indirect reactions because clients may be unaware of feelings or their source. How do clients show anxiety or deal with anxiety to avoid showing it? In interviews, decreasing anxiety levels are a sign that current treatment is helpful or inoffensive to the ego; escalating upset indicates that discussion is moving too quickly.

Clients can participate in getting to know themselves, their appearance to others, the areas of functioning that are difficult for them, and their areas of strength. Everyone has personal characteristics, strengths, and limitations; understanding of these factors over a period of time can help an individual anticipate feedback, utilize strengths, and marshal resources to cope with difficulties. For example, a rigid but reliable group member who finds than other members slowly grow to like him can expect something similar to occur in a sheltered workshop situation. Another client may be able to use his intelligence to categorize situations and later devise means of dealing with those that upset him. Awareness of problem areas becomes a strength in itself because clients can help the worker see where assistance is needed. The presumption is that as confidence grows and as mastery and control can be felt in some areas, there is a greater capacity to try to change in other areas.

The most important area with which schizophrenic clients have difficulty is the management of affects. Normal feelings and primitive impulse material are uneasily repressed; they are often clear to the observer in symbolic content. Elaborate ego defenses against frightening affects may be buttressed by unreasonably strong superego prohibitions. Even when conscious feelings are misdirected—for example, when a client fixes on one sibling as the source of all his troubles or shows paranoid anger toward a neighbor—the ego may be defending against an affect, such as rage, which would erupt dangerously if its true object were known. Although social workers know that schizophrenic defenses and inappropriate behavior should not be attacked, they often try unsuccessfully to talk clients out of such incidents. An approach based on dynamic understanding is more likely to facilitate positive change.

The worker must have a sense of when primitive forces are theatening to engulf a client's ego and must actively ally with the ego to maintain repressions at these times. The client who anxiously tells about a hallucination or homosexual feeling does not need implicit encouragement of expression through treatises on the beauty of mind-expanding experiences or the normality of bisexual inclinations. If a client expresses inappropriately directed feelings like paranoid rage, the worker can neither ignore the affects nor in most situations interpret what has actually aroused them. A client usually expresses such content in a safe environment where he knows he will not be condemned and will be helped to regain control. Workers can sometimes listen to inappropriate feelings and then veto their being expressed elsewhere on the grounds that this act can cause trouble for the client. Occasionally, what clients need to discuss regarding such feelings or psychotic material is the fear of losing control.

Additional help may be given by considering with the client how to extricate himself from reality situations which seem to spur the experiences, by talking about medication, by assuring the client that the worker may be telephoned to help with control, and so on. Client strengths in dealing with feelings effectively may be supported—for example, by encouraging the sublimation of aggression through physical activity. The worker who knows his client well may offer another defense to help with a slipping one. Thus, for an intellectualized individual whose envy of a friend is turning into delusional thinking, the social worker may suggest a rationalization about why the friend received what the client did not.

When clients find the worker helpful in repressing primitive material, they are more ready to allow normal affects into consciousness because the worker is sensed as a reinforcement to the ego in case of need. The worker who knows what is going on in clients' lives or in group process can help individuals to identify sources of less primitive feelings and what the feelings are. Even the worker's clarification of what is a normal response can be enlightening. Clients may have been aware of, and concerned about, feelings or they may have been experiencing general distress without knowing why. Discussion of anger toward the bus driver, of jealousy of a friend, or of empathy with other group members may be reassuring. Sometimes normal affects are expressed symbolically. A client whose worker has arrived late may describe with concern how his uncle did not keep a promise to him as a child. In the writer's experience, clients will not be made anxious by a mild inquiry as to whether they are annoyed or by a statement by the worker that any possible annoyance will not upset the worker. Other ego teaching may occur—for example, that talking about feelings with the worker or in a group need not lead to other expression or action unless the individual so chooses. The effort is to help clients experience small amounts of affect in a structured situation where they can be given help. When blanket repression of feelings is no longer necessary, some ego energy should be freed for healthier overall functioning.

In eliciting normal feelings, one caution must be noted. Workers should proceed extremely slowly in the area of a client's feelings about family members. Even when such affects are within a normal range, justified, and perhaps volunteered by clients, the worker's encouragement of expression rather than a neutral stance may upset a balance. Possibly, this result occurs because evern normal affects toward family members are very close to, if not mingled with, such primitive feelings as rage toward them for not meeting symbiotic needs.

If clients learn to have needs met in less conflicted relationships than are possible with family members, some force of rage owing to unmet needs is reduced and, thus, the pressure on the ego is lessened. A client will be readier to relate to nonrelatives for need satisfaction if and when he can achieve some separation from parental family or feel less helplessly dependent on his spouse. One means of facilitating individuation is through family work. Workers must also help to reduce fears and distortions which could curtail or prohibit outside relationships. Schizophrenic individuals may meet some needs for emotional security, positive regard, and expression of aggression in client-worker and group member relationships, if psychotic transference is kept to a minimum. Continued work on reality-testing and management of normal affects may allow clients to relate more easily to other persons as well. Even if fully mature object relationships are not possible, a capacity for friendships, job functioning, or relative ease in handling day-to-day living can improve clients' need-satisfaction balance.

In all enhancement of ego coping, clients must move at their own pace, whether they are seen individually or in groups. If workers understand clients' dynamic functioning, are willing to teach them much of what they know, and can time their support appropriately, growth can be seen in many situations.

Process Factors in Family Work

Communications theorists assert that the question in schizophrenia "is not *whether* the members of a patient's family are to be dealt with, but *how*."[2] The writer's earlier article[3] suggested that work with the parental family

[2] Don D. Jackson and John H. Weakland, Conjoint Family Therapy: Some Considerations on Theory, Technique, and Results, in *Therapy, Communication, and Change*, ed. Jackson (Palo Alto, Calif.: Science and Behavior Books, 1968), p. 224.

[3] Judith C. Nelsen, Treatment-Planning in Schizophrenia, SOCIAL CASEWORK, 56:67–73 (February 1975).

is imperative in the treatment of a young schizophrenic client who has never functioned in independent living arrangements. Possibilities for seeing families of procreation were also discussed. The systems-communications literature on treatment techniques with parental families is impressive.[4] However, in the writer's experience, many social workers have difficulty with the necessary reorientation to process factors in family work.

According to systems-communications theorists, schizophrenic behavior of an identified patient living with his parents is in some way appropriate to or required by current family interaction patterns. This assertion may seem similar to the traditional assumption that parents, possibly in interaction with genetic factors, have influenced the individual in childhood toward a pathological development, but the two points of view are divergent in some of their treatment implications. Don D. Jackson, Jay Haley, Murray Bowen, Ivan Boszormenyi-Nagy and others believe that all family members, including the identified patient, are locked into presently dysfunctional family interaction patterns, whatever their original source. All are at some level suffering from the characteristic mixed communication, enforced closeness, and inability to escape the system.[5] If this concept is valid, the family as a whole is truly the client, and all members must equally receive the attention, scrutiny, empathy, and interventive help of the social worker. All persons should be treated, sometimes together, sometimes separately.

Social workers may betray their misunderstanding of this position—thus suffering subsequent difficulties in reorienting to the family as a system—in several ways. These include subtle rejection of parents because of what they have done to the identified patient, expressions of surprise when parents demonstrate disturbed functioning, or interpretations showing parents how they are hurting the identified patient rather than commenting to all on their joint responsibility for family functioning. A

[4] See Don D. Jackson, Family Interaction, Family Homeostasis and Some Implications for Conjoint Family Psychotherapy, and idem, Family Therapy in the Family of the Schizophrenic, in *Therapy, Communication, and Change*, ed. Jackson, pp. 185–221; Jackson and Weakland, Conjoint Family Therapy, in *Therapy, Communication, and Change*, ed. Jackson, pp. 222–48; Don D. Jackson and Virginia Satir, A Review of Psychiatric Developments in Family Diagnosis and Family Therapy, in *Therapy, Communication, and Change*, ed. Jackson pp. 249–70; and Ivan Boszormenyi- Nagy and James L. Framo, eds., *Intensive Family Therapy* (New York: Harper & Row, 1965).

[5] See Gregory Bateson et al., Toward a Theroy of Schizophrenia, and idem, A Note on the Double Bind—1962, in *Communication, Family, and Marriage*, ed. Don D. Jackson (Palo Alto, Calif.: Science and Behavior Books, 1968), pp. 31–62; Murray Bowen, Family Psychotherapy with Schizophrenia in the Hospital and in Private Practice, in *Intensive Family Therapy*, ed. Boszormenyi-Nagy and Framo, pp. 213–43: and Ivan Boszormenyi-Nagy, A Theory of Relationships: Experience and Transaction, and idem, Intensive Family Therapy as Process, in *Intensive Family Therapy*, ed. Boszormenyi-Nagy and Framo, pp. 33–142.

more insidious manifestation involves workers' exhorting family members to find outside activities or single parents to date or remarry without realizing that total family fears of separation and individuation must be handled first.

Another difficulty, particularly for those professionals trained in casework, is maintaining an awareness of process as well as of discussion content. In family work, particularly with families with a schizophrenic member where discussion may initially obscure more than it clarifies, close attention to process factors is necessary. They include who is taking over, who is contradicting by bodily movement or facial expression what he is verbalizing, who is assuming responsibility for distracting behavior as someone else is forming a coalition, and so on. It can be productive to view family videotapes with no sound to gain awareness of these matters. How the social worker is entering the dynamic balance must also be considered. A comment can be destructive even if it is accurate and empathically given—for example, if it interprets behavior of the identified patient so as to imply that the worker and the parents must align to treat him.

In work with families in which the schizophrenic individual is one of the parents, a systems-communications orientation may seem very unnatural, for the spouse and the children clearly did not cause the schizophrenia. Such thinking suggests failure to grasp the full implications of the theory. No matter how family patterns start, they are assumed to influence the present behavior of all family members. Overt schizophrenic symptomatology may be facilitated or required because family balance both incorporates and perpetuates the pathology. In seeing families of procreation, workers must take care to view identified patient, spouse, and children as fellow sufferers and unwitting co-conspirators of the status quo, not as villains or victims.

Even when parents or spouses are not available for total family work, a systems communications orientation can guide whatever contacts are made with family members. In one situation known to the writer, a schizophrenic client being seen individually developed some delusional thinking about a relative staying in the home on a brief visit. The parents, who were in their seventies and not interested in psychotherapeutic help, had been seen twice by the worker during several years of treatment. However, based on the assumption that the distress shown by the client might exist in other family members, a telephone contact was made. The parents had considered rehospitalizing the client out of their own distress over the relative's visit, on the mistaken assumption that the client was having another breakdown. When the worker offered sympathy and took responsibility for suggesting that they avoid action until the relative left, they agreed. The client's functioning improved and the parents subsequently used telephone help to deal with another emergency.

Conclusion

Ego psychology and the systems-communications approaches to under-standing schizophrenia can clarify overall treatment-planning and core treatment issues with this client group. Social workers offering service must routinely assess and consider intervention, not only with the identified schizophrenic individual but also with family and impinging social systems. Timing of intervention efforts can be geared to an awareness of cyclical dynamics in chronic schizophrenia. And to treat clients effectively, social workers must deal with schizophrenic relationship distortions, ego functioning especially in the management of affects, and family process.

PART III

Physical Disorders

The physical condition and health of a client constitute one of the important areas of the total situation that the social worker must consider in diagnosing and planning treatment. This is not to suggest that a medical assessment of the client is the social worker's responsibility. Rather, the task is to consider the extent to which the life patterns, problems, and potential for psychosocial functioning as presented by the client are affected by his physical condition. This is an area in which we have long been interested but frequently only in a peripheral way. We have been psychosocially oriented rather than biopsychosocial.

This responsibility rests both in the assessment phase and in the selection of treatment goals and methods. It presumes therefore some knowledge of physical functioning and its impact on personality, the client's attitude toward his health, and societal views on particular illnesses and disabilities. In every case the necessity to individualize must be kept in mind; the therapist would seriously err if all clients with particular handicaps or disease entities were to be treated the same. However, the necessity to individualize does not imply that we cannot acquire some understanding of clients by considering the common factors of their physical condition. For example, only when we understand how much a particular blind client is like other blind clients can we understand how he or she is unique and different.

There is a further reason for understanding physical functioning. Frequently, our work with people will involve helping them understand, accept, and cope with various physical problems of other family members. As well as assisting in this recognition and the working through of feelings, we will also aim at helping them to cooperate with, and at times participate in, the treatment of the afflicted family member. As suggested in the articles of this section, there may be considerable resistance and denial on the part of the family, loath to accept such a diagnosis. This in turn frequently limits the potential of the client to mature and progress.

The appropriate involvement of other significant persons in treatment requires that the social worker understand the nature of the physical condition, its manifestations and effects on patients and others. Also we must have the same understanding of various medical procedures related to a condition as well as the sociology of health institutions and systems.

There are several difficulties that can arise from a failure to understand these factors. For example, social workers have been known to support the patient's denial of a diagnosis, to overlook manifestations of illness, to miss seeing changes in a situation, to avoid supporting and encouraging cooperation in medical treatment, or to fail to recognize counterproductive aspects of the health system.

Although it is not our primary task, we do have a responsibility to recognize obvious physical problems. Certainly we should not be diagnosing medical conditions. Nevertheless, we do need to be aware of some of the possible physical conditions and their manifestations that clients tend to deny or not recognize. We can use the example of a mildly brain-damaged child. It would be tragic if, through lack of awareness of easily recognized patterns, such a child were treated as a reactive type of problem to a family situation instead of a child with a physical handicap. In multiprofessional settings the cooperation and amalgam of several disciplines assist in this regard, and social workers are more attuned to these areas. It is much more difficult and yet much more crucial for social workers in nonmedical settings to be equally attuned to physical factors in our clients.

With the growing importance of social workers in health fields, as well as an increased psychosocial orientation in psychiatry and medicine, it is evident that social workers are going to be involved much more with persons suffering from, or recovering from, various physical illnesses. The increase of shorter hospital stays, home care for patients, widespread rehabilitation programs, retraining programs, and publicly supported insurance programs will all demand that social workers be even more physically oriented than has been the case in recent years. This obviously has implications for our schools of social work as well.

The selection of articles presented in this section is not all-inclusive. It does represent a sampling of the range and focus of articles relevant to this area as found in recent literature. It is evident and understandable that the topics addressed in the literature reflect trends in medical interest. Many of the articles located for consideration in this section were, as before, a "one-of-a- kind" category, that is, they were not selected from a large group of several articles dealing with the same topic. This is mentioned to emphasize the irregular and almost haphazard pattern of writing in this area of our literature. In the last edition, comment was made that social workers had not contributed extensively to medical journals. This is now beginning to change. In addition there are now several new journals in social work literature specifically focused on health issues such as *Health and Social Work* and *Social Work and Health Care*. Undoubtedly this development has enriched and will continue to enrich this aspect of the literature.

There are some observable patterns to the writings in this field, that is, areas where we have been more prolific than in others. Certainly we have written more on the topic of retardation than on any other. Other areas of emphasis have been in the visually handicapped and long-term geriatric illness, situations where little change in the condition can be expected and long-term domiciliary or institutional care is required, involving heavy use of services.

Several articles included in this section deal with various forms of cerebral dysfunctioning. A common trend can be observed throughout these: (1) the necessity of understanding the nature of the handicap, (2) its effect on the psychosocial development of the person, and (3) its effect on the significant others in the client's life. The authors all emphasize the relationship capabilities in these types of clients and the frequency with which we underestimate their potential for improved functioning.

As mentioned above, social work treatment of retarded clients and their families has been given heavy emphasis in the literature. Separate approaches to the many problems presented by these clients and their families are discussed in the articles included here. The theme of individualizing and building our treatment on diagnosed strengths rather than presumed limitations is highlighted.

One interesting trend noted in this most recent review of the literature is that we have now begun to give almost equal emphasis to clients of all ages and stages of development, unlike earlier days when we directed much of our attention to child patients.

The articles in this section are listed in alphabetical order rather than grouped by related conditions since the social work literature has been uneven with regard to specific physical and medical problems. The format of the articles in this division is varied: some contain a detailed analysis of the particular symptom and a consideration of the treatment implications; others discuss the analysis of a particular approach to treatment; others outline a program of service; still others offer the analysis of one or a few cases. Many stress the intrafamilial impact of physical handicaps on families and significant others. As a totality they represent a rich overview of social work treatment of physically handicapped persons.

Although the focus of most of the articles in this section is specific, it is clear that there are diagnostic and treatment concepts with import for other forms of illness and handicap. Thus the concept of adjustment to the crisis of blindness and the analysis of the adjustment process can be applied to similar crises resulting from the onset of illness or disease. The themes of denial of the illness and damage to the concept of body image and adequacy are important ones that appear in several articles.

Even though much of the material has been written from a particularistic point, sufficient experience and sufficient material now exist to begin a general theory of working with physically ill or handicapped people. There are some indications that this is happening. Some articles located did contain such a generalized focus as, for example, those that discussed work with the chronically ill patient, the handicapped patient, or the fatally ill patient. It is hoped that such synthesizing and generalizing will continue.

Throughout the articles there is a common theme of the necessity to incorporate into our practice with physically ill or handicapped patients generalized knowledge and skills about their conditions but then to apply them individually adjusted to the need of each client or group of clients.

One theme related to the physical handicapped, addressed only in an indirect way, is the need for highly specialized skills, especially communications skills for social workers. So much of our work with clients requires highly developed communication skills, yet our repertoire of communications skills is limited. Learning sign language for the deaf is an example of this. It is critically important that more intensive work be done in developing and teaching specific communication skills to people as an aid to dealing with all forms of communication limitations rather than rely on traditional skills; most of which presume adequacy of functioning by the client. The challenge of conducting a group with some wheelchaired deaf clients brings this point into focus.

CONCLUSION

This group of articles is interesting, important, and useful. Additional knowledge about working with clients with physical handicaps exists. This material should be made more widely available to help all practitioners to expand their knowledge of persons from the viewpoint of their physical potential.

ARTHRITIS

CHAPTER 29

Helping to Manage
the Emotional Effects
of Arthritis

Larry L. Smith

There are at least 50 million Americans with some type of arthritis. The Arthritis Foundation reports that 20 million of these people have arthritis severe enough to require medical care.[1] Although many Americans recognize the physical problems that may result from arthritis, especially the swollen and inflamed joints, few people understand the social and emotional concerns of arthritic patients. Despite the physical and psychosocial problems faced by arthritic patients, however, social workers, psychologists, and other therapists can help these patients and their families cope with the disease and live more productive lives.

Description of the Disease

There are many myths about arthritis. In order to dispel these myths and help patients gain a clearer understanding of the disease, social workers themselves must know something about it. According to the Arthritis Foundation, the term arthritis "is widely used to cover close to 100 different conditions which cause aching and pain in joints and connective tissues throughout the body, not all of them necessarily involving inflammation."[2] The five most common kinds of arthritis are (1) rheumatoid arthritis, (2) osteoarthritis, (3) ankylosing spondylitis, (4) systemic lupus erythematosus, and (5) gout.

Rheumatoid arthritis "is a systemic disorder of unknown cause in which symptoms and inflammatory change predominate in articular and related structures. The disease tends to be chronic and to produce characteristic, crippling deformities."[3] Rheumatoid arthritis is the most serious form of arthritis because it can result in crippling. Even though it attacks the joints primarily, it can also affect the heart, lungs, spleen, and muscles. The disease may subside and then flare up unpredictably, and it affects women three times more often than men. When it occurs in children, it is called juvenile rheumatoid arthritis and is extremely serious. Approximately 5 million Americans have rheumatoid arthritis.[4]

Osteoarthritis is a chronic disorder characterized pathologically by degeneration of articular cartilage and clinically by pain that appears with activity and subsides with rest.[5] It is primarily a wear-and-tear disease of the joints that comes with getting older. Although osteoarthritis is usually mild and not generally inflammatory, it is often painful and can cause mild to severe disability. Osteoarthritis does not affect parts of the body other than joints. It is estimated that over 12 million Americans have osteoarthritis.[6]

Ankylosing spondylitis is a chronic progressive disease of the small joints of the spine, which often begins in the teens or early twenties. Immobility of the spine ensues with the disease, and flattening of the lumbar curve is common. Studies indicate that 90 percent of those afflicted are men. The most important diagnostic indicator is radiologic evidence of spinal erosion and sclerosis of the sacroiliac joints.[7]

Systemic lupus erythematosus, called "SLE" or "lupus" or "lupus arthritis," is an acute systemic disease without a known cause.[8] It can damage and inflame joints and organs throughout the body, including the heart, lungs, kidneys, and brain. Females are affected more frequently than males, and the age of incidence is 20 to 40 years. It is often difficult to make a clinical diagnosis of SLE because its symptoms often are confused with those of other diseases such as rheumatic fever, viral pneumonia, and various disorders of the skin.[9]

Gout is an inherited metabolic disorder manifested by recurrent attacks of acute arthritis. It can inflame any of the joints of the body. Most victims are men, and the disease is extremely painful. The likelihood that gout will be inherited from one generation to another is often reported at 6 to 18 percent in the United States, although it may be higher. For example, studies in England suggest familial inheritance figures for gout as high as 75 percent.[10] When gout becomes clinically manifest, it often appears as arthritis of a peripheral joint, most often the big toe.

Treatment

Although there is no known cure for rheumatoid arthritis, effective treatment can control the disease and prevent deformities and crippling. The treatment for rheumatoid arthritis, as well as other forms of arthritis, may include all the following measures: (1) medication, (2) rest, (3) exercise, (4) splints, (5) walking aids, (6) heat, (7) surgery, (8) rehabilitation, and (9) rules of posture.[11] Anti-inflammatory drugs such as aspirin, ibuprofen, indomethacin, and phenylbutazone are often effective in treating rheumatoid arthritis because they reduce inflammation and the pain and swelling. Other drugs including corticosteroids, gold salts, and antimalarials also give relief to patients. Rest can also help reduce inflammation; yet moderate exercise can prevent stiffening of the joints.

There are also no known causes or cures for osteoarthritis. Although inflammation does not occur, considerable pain may exist around joints, and the patient often loses the ability to move the joints easily. Osteoarthritic joints should be protected from undue stress and strain. Any activity that leads to pain in an arthritic joint should be avoided, and overweight patients are encouraged to diet. Artificial hip joints have successfully relieved pain and restored movement in advanced cases of osteoarthritis of the hip. Because osteoarthritis is a chronic disease, treatment often continues throughout a patient's life.

Ankylosing spondylitis, which causes inflammation and deformities in the spine, has no known cause or cure. Medication, exercise, and methods to correct posture can help minimize the pain and control deformities. With prompt and proper treatment, most patients continue to lead productive lives. If the disease is not treated, curvature of the spine may develop, and the patient may be forced into a stooped posture.

Systemic lupus erythematosus affects the skin, joints, and internal organs and usually results in painful arthritis. Like rheumatoid arthritis, SLE follows an irregular course with painful flare-ups as well as periods of remission. Treatment varies considerably but usually includes rest and medication to control the pain and inflammation. If the disease is not treated, the patient can experience fever, skin rash, loss of weight, anemia, and kidney problems.[12]

Although gout is extremely painful, treatment exists to control it effectively. This represents the first victory of medical science over a major form of rheumatic disease.[13] The treatment is designed to reduce the uric acid in the patient's system to tolerable levels, thereby preventing further painful attacks. Drugs and a special diet with moderate protein and little fat are used for this purpose, and they control rather than cure the disease for as long as the patient continues medication.

Emotional Impact

It is frustrating for a person to have a disease that can last a lifetime and has no known cause or cure. Arthritic patients struggle with a disease that can inflict excruciating pain one week and unexpectedly leave them free of pain the next. Arthritis often follows this roller-coaster course, which makes it difficult for a patient to plan ahead. A patient is often unable to follow through on plans because of the sudden onset of a painful flare-up. Living with such a disease may make a person temperamental, despondent, and angry.

One of the greatest frustrations arthritic patients encounter is with the physical restrictions forced on them by their disease. The author has spoken with many men and women who bitterly resent these restrictions. Men who once fished and hunted, played golf or bowled cannot now continue with these leisure activities. Other men who operated heavy equipment or worked as machinists have been unable to continue working and have had to find other employment. Women who painted, crocheted, and knitted often find it impossible to continue. These same men and women are sometimes severely hampered in the activities they can enjoy with their children and grandchildren. Children with juvenile rheumatoid arthritis, struggle with these same restrictions, which may isolate them from other children and make their lives miserable.

These frustrations are sometimes too much for arthritic patients to endure. The author remembers one 50-year-old man who had not been able to fish for five years because of his arthritis. One summer he ignored his physician's warning and hiked out to some remote lakes in northern Utah for a week of fishing with some friends. The first three days were not too painful, but on the evening of the fourth day the pain became unbearable, and his companions had to bring him back to a Salt Lake City hospital on a stretcher. Mr. H still looks back fondly on that experience; he says he did it "to feel alive again." Mrs. P had a similar experience. Although crippled with rheumatoid arthritis in her knees, she spent four hours kneeling one afternoon planting roses in her garden. She knew she would suffer pain the next day, but she did not care. It was her way of striking back at a disease that had plagued her for ten years.

Social workers who work with arthritic patients should encourage them to verbalize their frustrations and speak frankly about their feelings. This expression of frustration and anger often benefits the patient and may be a step toward helping the person cope with the disease. Patients also need to review what they can and cannot do because of their arthritis. Patients who can no longer hike, for example, need not give up the outdoors altogether. Scenic automobile rides in the country can help compensate for their lost activity. Arthritic patients who can no longer camp out with their families can still enjoy leisurely picnics in the park. Sometimes new interests can be substituted for old ones. One woman who could no longer knit because of her arthritis told the author that she became an avid reader on American Indians and started collecting Indian artifacts. She speaks to church and civic groups about her research and feels important and worthwhile once again. A sense of self-worth is difficult to maintain when many of the activities a person enjoys are suddenly taken away because of crippling arthritis. Social workers need to help arthritic patients in their quest for continued self-respect.

Pain

Most people are unaware of the pain arthritic patients suffer each day. Many patients have told the author that their families and friends cannot understand how someone with arthritis "can look so well and still be in pain." Some patients have halfheartedly suggested that if they wore older clothes and appeared disheveled, people would be more compassionate. If social workers are to understand and help the arthritic patient, they must know something about the pain experienced. Some patients have described arthritic pain as a throbbing toothache that never goes away. Others have said that the pain comes unexpectedly and feels like "a thousand hot pins twisting in your shoulder." Still others describe a dull throb that is always there, morning, noon, and night. With some arthritics, the pain in their crippled and inflamed hands and knees is almost visible.

Some arthritic patients find it almost impossible to do even simple tasks without experiencing considerable pain. The author spoke with one woman who could not take the lid off a bottle of pickles without pain. This same woman had difficulty walking up a flight of stairs because of her inflamed knee joints. Another woman reported that she could not lift her arms above her shoulders. She found it impossible to comb her hair or give herself a permanent and said she was angry at her husband for needling her about her hair. Arthritic men have similar problems. One man confided how painful it was for him to shake hands with his business clients and friends. He had developed the habit of keeping his right hand in his pocket in self-defense. Another man mentioned how difficult it was to turn doorknobs or walk through revolving doors that sometimes slammed against his shoulders and arms. This same man also found it difficult to lift his beloved grandchildren.

The author encourages the arthritic patients he works with to let their families and friends know of their arthritis and that sometimes they have sudden painful attacks. The author is not suggesting that patients dwell on their illness. He is suggesting that arthritic patients be honest about their feelings. If shaking hands with other people gives a patient pain, he or she should let this be known so people do not interpret a reluctance or refusal as unfriendly or haughty behavior. If a father or mother cannot play with his or her children because of arthritic pain, the children should be told why and assured that the parent still loves them. Planning less painful activities with the children can help solve this problem.

Physicians

In helping the arthritic patient cope with pain, the social worker should encourage the patient to see a rheumatologist—a physician trained in managing arthritis—on a regular basis. If a rheumatologist is not available, the patient can be seen by an internist, family physician, or general practitioner who has experience in treating arthritic patients. Competent medical care is essential in helping the arthritic patient make the best possible adjustment to his or her illness.

After working with arthritic patients for three years, the author is convinced that many of them are not receiving the medical care they need. Some patients claim that their physicians are too busy to spend time with them. Others report how difficult it is to find a physician who is willing to add an arthritic patient to an already crowded work load. Still others criticize physicians because they cannot cure arthritis and only suggest ways to minimize rather than eliminate the pain. Some of these criticisms are justified; others are reactions that many patients with chronic illnesses voice against physicians.

Arthritic patients must become knowledgeable consumers of medical care if they are to work effectively with their physicians. Few Americans expect the same treatment from a physician that they do of other professionals, such as dentists, accountants, and lawyers, who dispense services. Arthritic patients are paying large sums of money for medical care and are entitled to certain services. Patients are entitled to the full attention of their physician during an office visit. It is not unreasonable to expect that a physician should spend fifteen minutes or more with a patient answering questions related to arthritis. The author even suggests to patients that they compile a list of questions prior to speaking with their physicians so they will not forget what questions they want to ask. The author has found that most physicians appreciate the patient's interest. If arthritic patients believe their physicians are not responsive to their needs, they should have a frank discussion with them. If the situation does not improve, the patients should consider changing physicians.

Families

The arthritic patient and his or her family do not always understand each other either. The author has listened to many patients who complain about the lack of concern shown to them by their family. One feisty patient even wished that his family could have arthritis for one day; they would then appreciate what he had been struggling with for fifteen years. Family members are equally frustrated with the arthritic patient. They want to help, but often everything they do seems to upset the patient and makes the problem worse.

The author believes a family must first know something about arthritis before they can begin to understand an arthritic family member. A family must understand that arthritis is a chronic disease with no known cause or cure that can cause great pain and crippling. Even though arthritis may begin with minor aches and pains, it is a serious illness that can lead to deformities of the hands, wrists, hips, knees, and feet. Family members also need to know that arthritis is not an old people's disease. Even though a brother or sister or parents may be less than 40 years of age, they may still suffer from arthritis. Arthritis can strike very early, and often first appears during the prime years of a person's life. Another myth that family members should recognize is the belief that nothing can be done for arthritis. With proper medication, much can be done for arthritic patients, especially in preventing further crippling and reducing pain.

As family members learn more about arthritis, they should be encouraged to discuss it with the patient. Family members should also ask the patient how they can be most helpful. One family resolved many of their problems when the patient finally agreed to let the family know when his arthritis was flaring up. This was a signal to the family that their father was in pain and could not be as helpful to them as he wanted. When the pain passed, the father said so, and they all went back to their regular routine. This example of open and honest communication should be seriously considered by all arthritic patients and their families.

Sex and Arthritis

Little has been written about the sexual problems arthritic patients encounter. Patients are reluctant to discuss the subject openly, but, based on private conversations with patients, the author knows it can be a serious problem: In "Sex and Arthritis and Women," Lachniet and Onder discuss this problem as it affects women. They believe open communication is one of the key ingredients in resolving sexual problems:

Problems of mobility and flexibility caused by arthritis make it extremely important that the arthritic and her partner talk together. Whether the situation is a new sexual partner or is the onset of arthritis with an established sexual partner, the relationship will be strengthened if possible limitations in sex are discussed and interest indicated. For a woman to say, "Let's experiment and find out what we can do!" tells a man she is interested in sex and him. This is much more encouraging than saying, "I can't do much. I have arthritis."[14]

Lachniet and Onder believe a woman who wants to have sexual relations with a man must de-emphasize her reaction to arthritic pain. They offer the following suggestions:

If a man feels he is hurting you every time he touches you (either in hugging, kissing, caressing, as well as intercourse), the fear of hurting you may keep him from having an erection and even from approaching you sexually or affectionately. If you think you may be unable to avoid saying "Oh!" or "Ouch!" when having sexual relations, it might be a good idea to tell the man something like this ahead of time: "Please don't worry if I say 'ouch!' I know you don't mean to hurt me. It sometimes gets to be a habit to say 'ouch' when I am touched. I don't want you to stop what you are doing."[15]

Quackery in Treatment

This article would not be complete without discussing the problem of quackery in the treatment of arthritis. According to the Arthritis Foundation, "Arthritis sufferers are the most exploited of all victims of disease in the country today. They spend an estimated $485 million a year on worthless remedies, treatments, devices, and gimmicks. These fall into four general categories: (1) drugs and other medication; (2) devices; (3) dietary supplements; (4) advertised clinics."[16] Many of these products and treatments are harmful and even dangerous, while others only waste the patient's money. Even so, all worthless remedies are dangerous if they keep the arthritic person from seeking a qualified physician.

Why are arthritic patients so vulnerable to quackery? Many explanations probably exist, but the chronicity of the disease, the lack of knowledge about its cause or cure, and its infliction of great pain are certainly important factors. Very few people enjoy pain; most try to avoid it. The arthritic patient is no different and will try almost anything to stop the pain, including mysterious "cures." In addition, arthritis is an illness with periods of remission that follow periods of painful flare-up. If the arthritic patient happens to be wearing a copper bracelet or drinking vinegar and honey or following a special diet when a remission occurs, it is not difficult to understand why the patient might continue wearing the bracelet or drinking the mixture or following the diet, or why he or she might tell others the treatment "cured," his or her arthritis. Social workers need to be aware of the dangers of quackery and should encourage patients always to seek qualified medical help.

Notes and References

1. *Arthritis: The Basic Facts* (New York: Arthritis Foundation, 1976), p. 2.
2. Ibid., p. 3.
3. Maxwell M. Wintrobe, ed. *Principles of Internal Medicine* (6th ed.; New York: McGraw-Hill Book Co., 1970), p. 1944.
4. *Arthritis: The Basic Facts*, p. 2.
5. Wintrobe, op. cit., p. 1949.
6. *Arthritis: The Basic Facts*, p. 2.
7. David N. Holvey, ed., *Merck Manual of Diagnosis and Therapy* (12th ed.; Rahway, N.J.: Merck Sharp & Dohme Research Laboratories, 1972), p. 1218.
8. *Arthritis: The Basic Facts*, p. 4.
9. Wintrobe, op. cit., p. 1965.
10. Ibid., p. 597.
11. *Arthritis: The Basic Facts*. p. 9.
12. Ibid., p. 18.
13. Ibid., p. 17.
14. Donna Lachniet and Jan Onder, "Sex and Arthritis and Women." Unpublished presentation, University of Michigan Medical Center, June 1973.
15. Ibid., p. 1.
16. *Arthritis: The Basic Facts*, p. 24.

BLINDNESS

CHAPTER 30

The Blind: Psychological and Emotional Needs

Doreen M. Winkler

Since formalized work with the blind began in North America about 1828, a good deal has been thought, written and said about their physical needs and how best to meet them. Much less attention has been paid to the psychological and emotional needs of blind individuals and their families. Perhaps this is because much less is known about these needs. Or, there may be a reluctance on the part of both blind and sighted people to become involved in discussions of them. The psychological needs created by blindness are important not only to blind people themselves but to all those who attempt to assist them.

This paper explores some of the psychological needs blind people and their families have: what they are, why they exist, and why they are often unmet. There are three major needs.

First, a person who is congenitally or adventitiously blind needs to know as honestly and objectively as possible the facts about his condition. The individual must be given accurate data and emotional help to accept and adjust. Second, a blind person needs to be rehabilitated according to the individual requirements of his personality and circumstances. He cannot be reconstructed according to a mold his rehabilitators have made for him. Third, in so far as possible, a blind person needs to have some control and power to shape his own destiny.

To achieve this third goal, he needs skilled intervention of an objective, knowledgeable worker to help him consider possible alternatives, to make

Reprinted from *Social Worker*, Vol. 40, No. 4 (December, 1972), pp. 262–269, by permission of the publisher.

realistic decisions for himself, and to attempt goals that are within his capabilities.

In part, all people have these needs. But with the advent of blindness, such psychological needs become intensified, urgent, and all-encompassing.

My observations and impressions have come from my personal experiences as a congenitally, totally blind person; and from my professional experiences as a social worker variously employed in a family service centre, a child guidance clinic, a medical clinic of a general hospital, a treatment ward in a psychiatric hospital, and, briefly, in the Social Service Department of the Canadian National Institute for the Blind in Toronto.

The Need to Know

Dr. Louis Cholden, in his writings, argues that blind people need to know as quickly and as realistically as possible the unvarnished truth about their condition, and to adjust and accept that as a prerequisite to rehabilitation.[1] Secrecy is harmful to all concerned because it leads to distortions of reality.[2] Some sightless people begin and even successfully complete their education and training without accurate knowledge about their condition and without help in dealing with it emotionally. They do this, however, at great uncounted cost to themselves and, in some instances, to their families as well.

Parents of blind children are in need of special help. Their burden of anxiety and remorse is usually clearly evident. Because feelings are often irrational, most parents will inevitably blame themselves for what has happened to their child. If the marriage is not a strong one they will invariably blame one another for the occurrence. Such parents need a skilled counsellor to give factual information about their child's condition, and emotional support to sustain them in the crisis. Some form of marital or family therapy should always be made available to these parents for short periods of time.

Certain psychological factors account for information being witheld from the sightless and their families. Dr. Cholden suggests it may be partly due to society's concerted efforts to prevent such persons from accepting their blindness as a fact.[3] Such efforts may begin specifically with the attitude of the ophthalmologist. This physician has devoted his life to the

---

[1] Louis S. Cholden, M.D., *A Psychiatrist Works With Blindness*, American Foundation For The Blind, New York, 1958, p. 23.

[2] *Ibid.*, p. 16.

[3] *Ibid.*, pp. 76–77.

conservation and preservation of sight.[4] Its loss in one of his patients may cause him to react emotionally rather than clinically.

Blindness in one of his patients may mean loss of self-esteem, loss of prestige among his colleagues, or injury to his reputation. His patient may no longer believe in his ability to treat him or he may hold him responsible for his blindness.[5]

Out of his own discomfort with blindness, or out of his need to spare the patient the pain he himself feels, he may distort or minimize information.[6] In fact, he may choose an even less desirable alternative and avoid the patient and his family altogether, assigning the task of information-giving to someone less qualified. If he does discuss the patient's condition at all the doctor's attitude will be conveyed by what he says, and the manner in which he says it.[7]

If the doctor holds out hope that his patient may live a full and productive life as a blind person that patient may be able to begin to think of his condition in a rather more positive light. If, on the other hand, he views blindness as a tragedy or as something akin to death, his patient will tend to reflect that attitude. If the experience of being informed is a negative one, the blind person may direct all the hostility he feels to the ophthalmologist and refuse further treatment which he may urgently need.[8] By being misinformed or misguided about his blindness, his family may have their worst fears confirmed and either blame themselves for what they do not know, or embark on an endless and painful search for miraculous cures.

If false hopes are repeatedly offered to the patient he may be prevented from coming to terms with his blindness and this will invariably hinder his adjustment to it.

Reluctance to Disclose Condition

Some ophthalmologists may be reluctant to disclose information to a blind person because of what happens when he is told of his condition. Dr. Cholden described his initial emotional shock as a state of being "frozen," immobilized, unable to think or feel.[9] This is disturbing to the observer. Yet it is Dr. Cholden's belief that such a reaction on the part of a blind person is natural and essential, and must neither be prevented nor blocked. Time is needed by the blind person to recognize his inner strength to deal

[4] *Ibid.*, p. 22.
[5] *Ibid.*, p. 23.
[6] *Ibid.*
[7] *Ibid.*, p. 25.
[8] *Ibid.*, p. 22.
[9] *Ibid.*, pp. 25, 73–75.

with the next phase of his adjustment. When his emotions return the first thing he feels is loss, the loss of his sight. Dr. Cholden describes the experience of a blind person that follows his initial shock as one of normal, reactive depression. His symptoms are those common to all reactive depressions: self-recrimination, feelings of hopelessness, self-pity, lack of confidence, suicidal thoughts, and psychomotor retardation. For a few days he may not want to get out of bed and he may have trouble eating and sleeping. In parents of blind children who experience this depression some genocidal fantasies may be present.

When this "expression of grief over the lost sense"[10] has run its natural course and the blind person begins to do some minor activities on his own he will be able, with skilled assistance from a counsellor or therapist, to start working on adjusting to his handicap.

At some time in his life the congenitally blind person must experience a process of mourning for his *lack* rather than his *loss* of sight.

In the initial stages of blindness a person will find contact with other sightless people very helpful to him. Dr. Cholden conducted group therapy with newly-blinded residents at the Kansas Rehabilitation Centre for the Adult Blind. He was impressed by the recurring themes around which discussions revolved. He found, for example, that many blind people felt their fears, anxieties, and emotional problems, were peculiar to themselves. He observed that "It is amazing to a blind person sometimes to know another feels uncomfortable in a silence, or that his blind friend is fearful when he is lost."[11]

A blind counsellor who has made a good adjustment to his own handicap is often better qualified emotionally and has greater depth of intellectual understanding of his newly or congenitally blind client than do his sighted colleagues. An early visit by a well-qualified blind worker to parents of a blind child is likely to give them more hope for their child's future than any number of visits by a sighted worker.

Dr. Cholden suggests that, in most cases, the blind person should be isolated from his family during his initial stage of depression as well-meaning members will tend to interfere with or try to prevent the mourning process.[12] The author is inclined, however, to share the opinion of Dr. Robert Scott that "a family crisis precipitated by the onset of blindness in one of its members is a family problem and not generic to blindness".[13] Experience in working with many families in crisis has been that whenever one member is suffering pain or loss all members feel that pain or loss in

[10] *Ibid.*, p. 20.

[11] *Ibid.*, p. 37.

[12] *Ibid.*, p. 27.

[13] Robert A. Scott, *The Making Of Blind Men*, Russell Sage Foundation, New York, 1969, p. 76.

some way. The mourning process so necessary to a blind person's acceptance of his handicap is equally necessary to his family's acceptance of it.

Forces Blocking Acceptance of Blindness

Even though adequate information has been given to blind persons and their families and they have received help in working through the first stages of shock and grief, many of them continue to have difficulty accepting and adjusting to blindness. Many external and internal forces thwart their efforts to do so.[14]

1. There is resistance to change in the human personality that makes it hard for everyone to accept a new self-concept. The sightless individual may feel that he will never be fully accepted by society. And he may see little need to reorganize himself in another, perhaps more painful way.

2. This observation underscores Dr. Cholden who writes that, according to his personality make-up, every individual will have his own individual reaction to blindness. Some reactions though are common to many. For instance, people who have always depended on others will react in an even more dependent way to being blind. Blindness may be used by them to rationalize the gratification of those needs. They may try to prolong the period of regression that often accompanies the onset of blindness because they enjoy the attention and extra affection their family and friends have shown them because of it.[15]

Another person may see his blindness as a new way to controlling family members, or as a means of absolving him from family responsibilities. Some may use their blindness to punish themselves or their families in some way, or force sacrifices to be made on their behalf because of it. Still others may use their blindness to justify their recriminations against the world.

Sometimes a blind person who is enjoying his dependent role is encouraged in it by members of his family.[16] Many families sabotage a blind member's efforts to make a satisfactory adjustment.[17]

3. A blind person's adjustment may be hampered by the stereotypes he and others around him may believe concerning "the blind".[18] Some of the more common stereotypes are: (a) that of the blind beggar, completely

[14] Cholden, pp. 76-77.

[15] Ibid., p. 19.

[16] Ibid.

[17] Ibid., pp. 68-69.

[18] Ibid., p. 21.

dependent, constantly demanding charity in an inferior role;[19] (b) that of the blind genius, able to overcome all odds at great cost to himself, and magically able to do things no one else can;[20] (c) the notion that the blind have extra perceptions by which they can be guided, which the sighted do not have;[21] (d) the idea that the blind live in a "world apart", with spiritual qualities, aesthetic preoccupations and inner thoughts others cannot have;[22] (e) the assumption that blind people live in a "world of darkness" and that most of them are docile, melancholy, helpless and dependent.[23]

4. Closely linked with stereotype beliefs are what Dr. Cholden refers to as "the irrational feelings concerning blindness and its sexual meanings and historical connotation as punishment for sin."[24] Psychoanalysts' investigations have furnished proof of the close, unconscious connection between the eyes, vision, and sexual activity.[25] Child psychiatrists have often observed children in play therapy to expect punishment by blindness for masturbation or sexual curiosity. These unconscious connections often cause exaggerated, irrational responses by the sighted, and greatly affect the blind person's image of himself.

Out of these fears and irrational feelings the notion may arise that blindness is a stigmatized condition which causes the sighted to regard the sightless as their physical, moral and emotional inferiors, or, as somehow contaminating with the power to inflict physical or psychic damage.[26] Dr. Scott emphasizes that few blind people can ignore the stereotype beliefs of the sighted. Some actually come to believe in them themselves and so internalize them. Others try to insulate themselves against them or reject them as false. In either case, Scott's argument maintains that "these beliefs are a fact of life for the people who are blind". They must be reckoned with in some way.[27]

5. A blind person may be psychologically blocked in his adjustment by his knowledge that his blindness makes him part of a minority group which may represent to him a lowered social status and reduced self-worth.[28] It certainly means that he is different, and his encounters with the sighted are likely to confirm his feeling.[29]

More could be said about the obstacles to adjustment blind people en-

[19] *Ibid.*
[20] *Ibid.*
[21] *Ibid.*
[22] Scott, pp. 21–22.
[23] Cholden, p. 77.
[24] *Ibid.*, p. 20.
[25] Scott, pp. 18, 24.
[26] *Ibid.*, p. 117.
[27] *Ibid.*, p. 77.
[28] *Ibid.*, p. 30.
[29] *Ibid.*

counter. The author's experience supports Gloria Sewell's conclusion, drawn from the findings of her study, that "every sightless person could benefit from professional help to build a sufficiently strong self-image to cope with community attitudes and his own feelings of difference" and to assist him in his integration into the sighted world.[30]

Rehabilitation Is Not Always Successful

However, as Dr. Cholden suggests, a person who has been independent and mature, and accepts and adjusts to blindness, is not always successfully rehabilitated.[31] I share the view of Dr. Cholden that all blind persons are motivated to adjust to blindness, and to be rehabilitated, but there are many blocks that hinder the utilization of their motivation. As was indicated at the beginning of this paper, much is known about the physical needs of the blind. Much is known about their physical rehabilitation—how to teach braille and mobility skills, and so on. But, as Dr. Cholden has pointed out, much less is known about "making a frightened handicapped person courageous or a dependent client desirous of independence."[32]

Dr. Scott's sociological study vividly documented in his book, *The Making of Blind Men*, dramatically reveals that many sighted persons and workers in organizations for the blind clearly do not want to know the answers.

The thesis advanced by Scott is "that blindness is a learned social role. People whose vision fails will learn the attitudes and behavior patterns that the blind are supposed to have in their relationships with those with normal vision and in the organizations that exist to serve and to help blind people."[33] Further, "the needs of the blind are not determined from scientific studies of the impact of blindness on the functioning of the human organism. They are invented to justify the creation of programs and institutional arrangements required to palliate community reactions and fears about blindness."[34] Since the blind person must rely on the sighted for assistance in the most ordinary situations he finds himself automatically placed in the sighted person's debt and he may be restricted in his ability to reciprocate.[35] Therefore, as Scott emphasizes: "The blind person, by virtue of his dependency, is the subordinate in a power relationship."[36]

[30] Gloria Sewell, *The Adventitiously And Congenitally Blind*, School of Social Work, University of Toronto, unpublished master's thesis, Toronto, 1964, p. 98.

[31] Cholden, pp. 20, 67.

[32] *Ibid.*, p. 64.

[33] Scott, p. 71.

[34] *Ibid.*, 91.

[35] *Ibid.*, p. 36

[36] *Ibid.*, pp. 118–19.

Within organizations for the blind there are also factors which prevent many blind people from receiving much-needed assistance. The findings of Scott's study indicate that, although there are many blindness agencies in the United States, only about one-quarter of the blind population is helped by them.[37] They are mainly blind children who can be educated and blind adults who can be employed. For the most part, the elderly, unemployable, uneducable, and multiple-handicapped blind are excluded or minimally served.

Traditionally, blindness has meant or at least implied total absence of vision so that most of the programs of blindness agencies have been geared to the needs of the totally blind.[38] For example, in many agencies braille is taught to some who, with the aid of special lenses, can read enlarged or ordinary inkprint. People with partial vision are frequently trained to do jobs devised for totally blind people when, with a few minor adjustments, they might be able to continue in the jobs they held before their vision began to fail.

Scott's study also shows that when a person is legally "blind," he ceases to be "a sighted person with visual difficulty" and becomes "a blind person with residual vision".[39] His problems are seen not so much as medical ones but more as sociological ones pertaining to his adjustments to his disability, whether or not this is the case. Once accepted by the blindness agency, Scott's theory maintains, the person who has difficulty seeing is taught how to behave like a blind person.[40]

Two Approaches to Rehabilitation

Dr. Scott outlines two approaches adopted by blindness workers in rehabilitation agencies for the blind. The premise of the first is that blind people can be restored to a high level of independence enabling them to lead a reasonably normal life but this is only possible after they have come to fully accept the fact that they are blind, with the implication that this is a permanent role they must assume.[41] The second approach acknowledges that the first is noble but impractical for most blind people. It holds that blindness creates enormous obstacles to independence which can be overcome only by a few, highly-talented blind people through great personal effort. A more realistic objective is to provide an environment to which blind people can accomodate easily.[42] This "accommodative" approach as-

[37] *Ibid.*, p. 73.
[38] *Ibid.*
[39] *Ibid.*, p. 74.
[40] *Ibid.*, pp. 76–80.
[41] *Ibid.*, pp. 80–84.
[42] *Ibid.*, 84–89.

sumes that most blind people are incapable of true independence, that most blind people prefer their own company, and that most blind people need to perform special kinds of work because of their disability.[43]

Scott's investigation shows that, as recently as 1968, although most agencies in America theoretically accept the "restorative" approach, most practise the "accommodative".[44] There are economic, political and sociological pressures which make this necessary.

When a sightless person comes for help with his blindness he has some definite ideas about his needs or about what problems he has that must be dealt with before he can cope with his situation. The place to which the blind person comes for help, and the means by which he is sent there, has significance in relation to his knowledge about it as well as how he is received. If his need for self-determination in planning his program of rehabilitation is ignored, he will react in a number of ways. His anxiety may cause him to present himself inappropriately as resistant or acquiescent. His views about his blindness are essential to an understanding of how best to help him with it. If, as so often happens, he is listened to very nicely and later finds his opinions have been discredited or dismissed as inaccurate or superficial, he may react with so much anger that he will leave the agency feeling more confused, frightened and frustrated than when he came to it. Thus he may fail to avail himself of the agency's services he needs, wants, must have, and indeed, to which he is entitled.

In the rehabilitation process, Scott discovered, "the blind person is rewarded for adopting a view of himself that is consistent with that of his rehabilitator's view of him, and punished for clinging to other self-conceptions. He is told that he is insightful when he comes to describe his feelings and personality as his rehabilitators view them and he is said to be blocking or resistant when he does not."[45]

Many clever blind people learn to behave as they are expected to and demonstrate "insightfulness" in order to receive tangible services or proceed through the agency's course of rehabilitation to make use of its programs. Such a person learns to play the rehabilitation game in much the same fashion as the prisoner learns to walk the straight line in order to be paroled, or the psychiatric patient learns to recite all the right responses in his therapeutic sessions in order to procure his discharge from hospital.

Summary

This paper has identified three basic psychological needs I believe to be common to all unsighted or partially-sighted persons. The need to be in-

[43] Ibid., p. 93.
[44] Ibid., p. 90.
[45] Ibid., p. 119.

formed as quickly and honestly as possible the facts of his condition and to receive professional help in accepting and adjusting to it. The need to be given rehabilitation assistance as an individual and not sociological reconstruction as a blind person having thoughts, feelings and abilities that sighted and many blindness workers believe he must have because he is blind. The need to be a partner with his rehabilitators in planning for a future as a sightless person and to be allowed some psychological autonomy in shaping his own destiny according to his personal preferences and desires.

Obstacles that hinder many blind people in their adjustment have been explored. The difficulties many blind people and their families encounter in meeting psychological needs have been examined primarily in the light of observations and research of Doctors Cholden and Scott.

Workers in rehabilitation agencies and educational institutions for the blind must employ great flexibility and imagination in their work with blind people. They use techniques and skills based on scientific knowledge of human behavior rather than on subjective experience with blindness and the unsighted. They must listen well to what each individual has to say about his problems with blindness as well as his feelings about being blind. The simple fact is that those who have difficulty seeing or who cannot see at all are, after all, individual persons who happen also to be blind persons. From this very simple fact comes the conviction that if a person's needs as an individual are not accounted for or met satisfactorily, his needs as a blind person will never be understood and total life adjustment will never be complete and happy.

BURN PATIENTS

CHAPTER 31

Adjustment Problems of the Family of the Burn Patient

*Gene A. Brodland
and N. J. C. Andreasen*

Patients who have been severely burned experience an intense and varied trauma involving catastrophic injury, severe pain, possible cosmetic or functional deformities, and a threat to their sense of identity and worth. Hospitalization is usually prolonged. During this time, the family of the burn patient often remains with him to comfort and console him. Because most of the attention of the medical staff is focused on the suffering patient, the family members remain in the background and few people are aware of their suffering and emotional needs. Yet, just as the patient himself must adjust to his injury, so the family must go through a complicated process of understanding, accepting, and adjusting to the illness and distress of the loved one.

The adjustment problems of the adult burn patient have been the subject of only a few studies, and the problems of his family have drawn still less attention.[1] Studies done in England have examined the grief reactions

[1] N. J. C. Andreasen, Russell Noyes, C. E. Hartford, Gene A. Brodland, and Shirlee Proctor, Management of Emotional Problems in Seriously Burned Adults, *New England Journal of Medicine,* 286: 65–69. (January 13, 1972); David A. Hamburg, Curtis P. Artz, Eric Reiss, William H. Amspacher, and Rawley E. Chambers, Clinical Importance of Emotional Problems in the Care of Patients with Burns, *New England Journal of Medicine,* 248: 355–59 (February 26, 1953); and David A. Hamburg, Beatrix Hamburg, and Sydney DeGoze, Adaptive Problems and Mechanisms in Severely Burned Patients, *Psychiatry,* 16:1–20 (February 1953).

Reprinted from *Social Casework,* Vol. 55 (January, 1974), pp. 13–18, by permission of the authors and the Family Service Association of America.

of parents of fatally burned children and pathology in the parents which may have contributed to behavioral problems in surviving children.[2] One follow-up study of ten children and their parents, an average of four and a half years after injury, discovered recognizable psychological disturbance (usually depression) in eight of the mothers and none of the children.[3] This morbidity is high, and it suggests that further examination of the reactions of families is needed.

The observations presented in this article are based on a study done over a period of approximately one year on the burn unit at the University Hospitals in Iowa City. A total of thirty-two adults and their families were evaluated psychiatrically on admission and were interviewed daily thereafter until the time of discharge. Initial evaluation was based on complete psychiatric and social histories and mental status examinations. The patients ranged in age from twenty to fifty-nine with a mean of thirty-six, in total body surface burn from 8 percent to 60 percent with a mean of 29 percent, and in duration of hospitalization from two and one-half weeks to three months with a mean of one month. Patients outside the age range of eighteen through sixty or with severe mental retardation were excluded.

The relatives of the burn patient appeared to go through an adjustment process, similar to that of the patients, involving two stages. The first stage was one of acute shock and grief analogous to the acute physical and emotional trauma experienced by the patient himself. In the second or convalescent stage, the relatives had overcome shock and disbelief; they rationalized and accepted the fact of the injury and its accompaniments and began to assist the patient in the process of recovery.

Initial Reactions of Relatives

The family's first reaction on arriving at the hospital is usually relief that the patient has not died or been burned more severely. Rationalizations that "it could have been worse" provide an affirmative basis from which to begin coping with the stress that they face. In this first stage, the relatives express little concern about the potential scarring that might take place. Their primary concern is for the recovery of the patient, no matter what his appearance on recovery. The following case history illustrates the initial reaction of many families in the first stage of hospitalization.

[2] Helen L. Martin, J. H. Lawrie, and A. W. Wilkinson, The Family of the Fatally Burned Child, *Lancet*, 295:628–29 (September 14, 1968); Helen L. Martin, Antecedents of Burns and Scalds in Children, *British Journal of Medical Psychology* 43:39–47 (March 1970); and Helen L. Martin, Parents' and Children's Reactions to Burns and Scalds in Children, *British Journal of Medical Psychology*, 43:183–91 (June 1970).

[3] Aldo Vigliano, L. Wayne Hart, and Frances Singer, Psychiatric Sequelae of Old Burns in Children and Their Parents, *American Journal of Orthopsychiatry*, 34:753–61 (July 1964).

Mr. S, aged twenty-three, was severely burned in a car-truck accident. Having been pinned in the truck cab which caught fire, he sustained third-degree burns over 45 percent of his body. He was transferred to the burn unit two and one-half weeks after being burned and remained hospitalized for two and one-half months. His wife, who visited him daily, expressed her feeling that the scarring which might result was not important. She said she "would be happy if he could get well no matter what his condition is, so the kids will have a father." She demonstrated a considerable amount of quiet desperation; tears were often evident when she expressed her feelings.

Despite expressions of relief that the patient has not died, the fear that the injury might ultimately prove fatal lingers with many relatives. Sometimes this fear is expressed overtly. Interwoven with these feelings is a well-repressed wish by some relatives that the patient would die and thereby avoid the pain and frustration that lie ahead of him. Relatives of patients who die as a result of burns support this idea; when informed that a loved one has died, they often comment, "It is probably a blessing for he won't have to suffer any more now." Such feelings are usually suppressed because of the guilt they could arouse. The case of Mrs. K illustrates this reaction.

Mrs. K, aged twenty-four, was burned in a natural gas explosion in her home. Her husband suffered more severe burns and subsequently died. Her comments following his death indicate a degree of relief. She said, "I will miss him and it will be hard without him. He won't have to suffer for months and months. I'm glad God took him soon. I know he wouldn't want to live being terribly burned as he was. His death was a blessing." Mrs. K probably would not have said this before his death but as she rationalized in an attempt to face reality, these feelings were allowed to come to the surface.

During this early period, the relatives and the patients form feelings of trust or mistrust toward the medical staff. When a patient suffers from pain and fear, he and his relatives have to decide whether everything is being done medically to insure his comfort and recovery. Occasionally, patients and relatives question the competence of the staff and feel that the patient is the object of experimentation. The extended waiting period prior to skin grafting is often seen as abandonment and may lead to feelings of mistrust. Such feelings were expressed to the psychiatric social worker more often than to the medical staff. Relatives were concerned that by expressing angry feelings toward the staff they might jeopardize the patient's relationship with the staff.

Mr. L. sustained a steam burn while working on a construction job. After skin grafting failed to take, the patient became suspicious and remarked that the resident doctor was practicing on him as if he were a "guinea pig." He requested that the social worker arrange for a transfer to a private doctor or to another hospital. He did not want to talk to the nurses or the staff doctor about this change, because it might cause hard feelings. It was determined later that his problem centered on the lack of communication between the resident and the patient. The problem was resolved when the resident made conscientious efforts to explain the treatment procedures more fully to the patient.

Soon after admission, a number of extensively burned patients experience confusion and disorientation as a result of an acute brain syndrome that often accompanies burn trauma. Many relatives found this reaction stressful. Sometimes a patient was verbally abusive or assaultive, and relatives had a difficult time in deciding whether this behavior represented his true feelings or whether it was the result of delirium. Relatives were frightened by this sudden "mental illness" and needed reassurance that delirium is a common occurrence in burn patients and that once the burn begins to heal, the delirium passes.

Mr. R, a twenty-eight-year-old farm hand, was burned over 60 percent of his body in a natural gas explosion. About a week and a half after admission to the burn unit, he became delirious. During his periods of confusion, he thought of a period during his second year of marriage when his wife had had an extramarital affair. Mr. R angrily expressed the belief that this affair was still going on. His bewildered wife thought that this problem had been resolved eight years before. Mrs. R needed reassurance that his accusations were a result of his delirium. After Mr. R recovered, he denied any feelings of suspicion toward his wife.

Another source of difficulty for relatives is the psychological regression that is often observed among the burn patients. Patients who have been quite self-sufficient in the conduct of their daily lives before being hospitalized often become complaining, demanding, and dependent during hospitalization. The family, unaccustomed to this behavior, becomes alternately confused and angry. They want to respond to the patient's needs but are confused by demands that seem out of character. Relatives become angry when the patients do not give them credit for their efforts and continue with their childlike behavior.

Reactions After Initial Crisis

During the second phase of adjustment, the family is assured that the patient will survive and begins to consider the process of getting well. The family members begin to recognize that they and the patient still have many weeks in the hospital ahead of them. The patient and his relatives usually have no prior knowledge of the treatment and procedures required for recovery; now they begin to ask questions of physicians and nurses about the process of healing, dressing changes, grafting procedures, and so on. Often relatives of other patients on the ward are important sources of information, just as they are sources of reassurance. The family of the patient must prepare themselves psychologically for an extended stay in the hospital. From a practical standpoint, family members must make arrangement for their own physical well-being during this period and establish ''a home away from home.'' This often involves spending days at the hospital and nights in a nearby motel.

The pain the patient suffers is a primary problem at this time, and it often results in a sense of helpless frustration in the relatives. The patient seems to become increasingly cognizant of his pain once the threat of death has passed. He then begins to verbalize the pain, at times in tones of desperation. The helplessness which relatives feel in handling this pain produces conflict. On the one hand, they try to do everything within their power to aid the patient by making him physically comfortable and providing emotional support. On the other hand, relatives sometimes feel the staff could relieve pain more adequately by the administration of analgesic medication. The relative often is in a precarious position, trying to maintain a good relationship both with the patient and with the medical staff. Few persons understand fully the principles followed in the use of pain medication. The following example illustrates the development in one relative of mistrust of the staff.

> Mrs. B was burned when she and her family were trapped upstairs in their burning home. She broke her arm when she jumped from a second-story window to escape the flames. Because of the burns, the staff were unable to put her arm in the correct cast. The arm was very painful. Because of her complaints of pain and her mother's frustration in attempting to alleviate the pain, the mother confronted the nurse with the accusation that the staff was neglecting her daughter by not giving her enough pain medication. Once the problems inherent in using potent analgesics for long periods of time were explained in detail, the patient's mother was much relieved and could again be supportive to the patient.

Another source of pain occurring during this period is the process of autografting. The donor site, from which the skin for grafting is taken, often is more painful than the burn site itself, causing great distress to the patient. Further, the patient must lie quietly after the grafts have been placed, increasing the sense of helplessness felt by both patient and relatives. The fear of doing something that might disturb the graft is a significant cause of anxiety.

The frequent trips to the operating room for skin grafting are yet another source of anxiety. The fear of anesthesia must be faced each time the operative procedure approaches; the patient is anxious about being put to sleep and having to relinquish control. This anxiety is often sensed by the relatives.

Reactions During Recovery

Still later in the recovery period, the problem of pain is supplanted by one of itching, which creates a problem for the relatives who try to help the patient to tolerate each new stress. It often seems that total recovery will never arrive and that one discomfort is simply succeeded by another.

Another major problem faced during the recovery phase is fear of deformity. Most families initially expect grafting to restore fairly normal appearance. What medical personnel consider an excellent job of skin reconstruction is often viewed by the lay person as almost grotesque. Thus, patient and family tend to be disappointed by the results of grafting and to find a gap between their expectations and those of medical personnel. During this stage of recovery, the patient begins to prepare himself for facing the outside world by realizing that scarring and deformity may have made him unattractive and unacceptable to others with whom he has previously associated. He becomes hypersensitive to initial reactions and wonders what reactions he will find himself meeting the rest of his life. Relatives have similar fears.

The relatives' reactions are the first ones that the patient observes, and his distress is increased when he sees revulsion. A fairly typical case of family reaction was noted in a follow-up study of burn patients.[4] A young mother who had been hospitalized for three months eagerly anticipated seeing her children. She was greeted by her five-year-old with "Yuk, Mommie, you look awful." Adult family members, on the other hand, tend to recognize intuitively that they need to be supportive and to help the patient establish a denial system. Yet, providing a reassurance that they do not always sincerely feel is often quite stressful for them. Only with time and thoughtful support on the part of doctors, nurses, and relatives can the patient resolve his feelings about disfigurement and come to realize that angry red scars eventually fade and that his appearance will gradually improve.

Sometimes relatives carry an additional burden because of their feeling that they have contributed to or caused the accident in which the patient was injured. Even when the relatives have had nothing to do with the injury, some feel guilty; they explain this feeling on the basis of not having foreseen the possibility of the accident and not having taken steps to pre-

---

[4] N. J. C. Andreasen, A. S. Norris, and C. E. Hartford, Incidence of Long-Term Psychiatric Complications in Severely Burned Adults, *Annals of Surgery*, 174:785–93 (November 1971).

vent it. Eventually, the relative resolves his guilt feelings and achieves a rationalization that relieves him of full responsibility for the accident—for example, that the accident happened because it was God's will, because it would draw the family together, or because of the carelessness of others.

Notable throughout the recovery period is the difficulty that relatives have in dealing with the patient's need to express his feelings. They find it difficult to strike a balance between letting the patient describe his feelings about being burned and possibly handicapped and providing adequate emotional support. Sometimes relatives attempt to discourage the patient from expressing feelings of grief or fear and try to be constantly supportive and optimistic. In preserving their own comfort, they sometimes unwittingly deprive the patient of a necessary safety valve.

There are also relatives who become overwhelmed by the emotional stress of sitting at the bedside of a loved one and sharing his suffering. Many are reluctant to leave the bedside in the early stages of recovery, fearing that something might happen while they are gone. Occasionally, relatives become too depressed or anxious and must be asked to leave the ward temporarily to regain their emotional equilibrium. Remaining at the bedside of a burned patient is an unusually draining experience for his relatives. Much like a young child, the burn patient tends to focus only on himself and provides little support in return, leaving little opportunity for relatives to converse or receive support from others.

Recommendations from This Study

A burn injury is a traumatic experience for the uninjured relatives, as well as the patient himself. The families of the burn patients face multiple stresses and adjustment problems. They go through essentially the same phases of adaptation as the patients, for they must cope with anxiety about death, communication difficulties with the medical staff, fear of deformity, and the boredom of a prolonged hospital stay, as well as enduring the trauma of watching a loved one suffer. In some respects, their suffering may be greater than that of the patient. Although they do not suffer pain directly, they must stand by in helpless frustration, their guilt over the fact that the injury occurred at all further enhanced by their guilt about the anger which they must inevitably feel sometimes. Although they do not fear death or deformity for themselves directly, the must face these threats more immediately than the patient. Few patients are informed of their prognosis soon after admission and, if they were, their minds would be too clouded by trauma to comprehend it fully; however, relatives can not be shielded from this information, and they must receive it when their minds are usually in a state of heightened sensitivity and alertness.

Relatives may provide valuable assistance on wards by helping to feed the patient, by providing companionship for him, and often by encouraging and assisting him with exercise and physical therapy. Nevertheless, nurses and physicians provide primary care, and the role of relatives must inevitably be simply a supportive one. This role is a difficult one to fulfill in such an emotionally draining situation unless the person providing the support receives support from others for himself. On the burn unit, this need was often met by the relatives of other patients. Although there was no formal effort by the staff to enhance such relationships, relatives often pooled their information about treatment methods, compared notes on the condition of the patients, and consoled one another when things were going badly.

Hospital burn units could learn a lesson from this phenomenon and formalize it in several ways. Relatives could be helped greatly if hospitals prepared a simple pamphlet to be given to them on arrival, explaining simple facts about injuries from burns and the operation of the unit. It should state the visiting hours established and describe the daily routine, the purpose of unfamiliar treatment methods such as the use of silver nitrate and sulfamylon, the rationale behind the use of milder and preferably oral analgesics, the usual course of recovery from a burn injury, the nature of the grafting procedures usually done, and so forth. A glossary of unfamiliar terms—*autograft, zenograft, debridement,* for example—should be included. Because of the complex nature of this type of injury, burn treatment units are often run quite differently from other hospital facilities, and relatives can not carry over any prior hospital experience. For example, they find it difficult to understand the infrequent use of potent analgesics, although this practice usually becomes acceptable when they realize that the long-term use required in a burn injury might lead to dependence or addiction. On the affirmative side, on some burn units, rules about visiting hours are flexible and most relatives are permitted to remain with the patient as long as they wish.

A second way of providing communication and understanding among relatives would be the establishment of group support meetings. A group composed of family members or close friends of patients currently on the burn unit could meet at a regularly scheduled time once or twice weekly. The group would remain in existence, although the membership changed as the patient population changed. Ideally, this group would be conducted by a pair of group leaders—a psychiatric social worker and a nurse or physician who are members of the burn unit treatment team. A physical therapist, a dietitian active on the burn unit, and a psychiatrist familiar with the problems of adjustment to chronic illness would be other potential members or guest visitors.

The establishment of such a group would serve several purposes. It would demonstrate to the beleaguered relatives the interest and concern of the hospital staff, sometimes prone to leave relatives out of the picture because of their concern for primary patient care; regular group meetings would make efficient use of the professionals' time and experience. The meetings would also serve to educate relatives about problems of burn trauma, particularly when discharge draws near. Family members often take on primary responsibility for the patient at discharge and they greatly need adequate information about wound care, the need for continuing physical therapy, and the problems of emotional and social adjustment. The group discussions would provide relatives with an open forum for raising questions and for airing complaints. They would provide emotional support by strengthening the bonds formed between family members and alleviate some feelings of fear, frustration, futility, and boredom. Such a group would not be designed as therapy, but as a means of sharing strength and information. Limited experience with such group meetings on burn units indicates, however, that often staff members also receive information and support from them.

A final way for social work staff to be effective on a burn unit is perhaps the most obvious. Families of patients often suffer significant financial expenses, and even after the patient is discharged the period of rehabilitation is prolonged. Family members and patients need to receive information about funds available to assist in the high cost of hospitalization, funds for care of dependents, and opportunities for vocational rehabilitation. An experienced and sensitive social worker can often provide subtle emotional support by demonstrating his concerned involvement as he offers his resources of information and interest to the family.

CANCER

CHAPTER 32

Terminal Cancer: A Challenge for Social Work

Carleton Pilsecker

"Advances in cancer control ... have nearly doubled the survival of American cancer patients over the last four decades. One and a half million who have had cancer are alive and well." (American Cancer Society, 1975.) Surgery, radiation therapy, chemotherapy, and immunotherapy are contributing significantly to effective treatment of cancer. Great energy and sums of money are being devoted to research which promises one day to cure and even to eradicate this dread disease. Thus there is hope.

Hopefulness, however, is not usually associated with cancer. The initial reaction to a diagnosis of cancer is to be "scared to death", i.e., scared of death. There are two good reasons for such a reaction: (1) in spite of the "advances in cancer control", cancer remains the second-leading killer in this country and the death rate from cancer continues to rise (American Cancer Society, 1977), and (2) death by cancer is viewed as an ugly end to life.

If you could choose your way of dying, would your choice be cancer? Probably not, for cancer is seen as an insidious, debilitating, painful, drawn-out process. Most people want to die one of two ways: either suddenly and with as little prior trauma as possible (e.g., heart attack while at home, in bed, asleep) or peacefully and painlessly over a two to three month period in which life's business can be put in order, goodbyes can be said, and a dignified withdrawal from living can be made (Schneidman,

Reprinted from *Social Work in Health Care*, Vol. 4, No. 4 (1979), pp. 369–380, with permission of the Haworth Press.

1971). Cancer, by contrast, threatens to hurt, to lay waste, to lead to physical dependence, to spread indecently so that, at last, one may even lose
control of the execretory functions whose conquest first starts us on the
way to becoming civilized and of the mental abilities which give *homo sa-
piens* its glory and its name.

The wishes of human beings seem often to have little influence on the
operations of nature, so over and over again people are seized by cancer.
Though less often than in the past, frequently the medical armamentarium
developed to combat cancer fails. The dying that few would choose takes
place. And in that dying time there may well be opportunity for the social
worker to provide important help for there are crucial tasks which are amenable to social work intervention.

Before addressing those tasks, however, the social worker first needs
to struggle with some basic questions.

PERSONAL REACTIONS TO DEATH

How do I react to dying and to death? For many people, including
health professionals, these are morbid, frightening events. Hospital staff
have been known to shy away from terminally ill patients, to attend to
them quickly and perfunctorily when unable to avoid them, to refrain
from significant conversation with them. The past decade has seen a considerable breakthrough in awareness of the needs of dying people and their
significant others and some noble efforts to meet those needs. But death
remains awesome and foreboding to many; to be in close proximity to it
produces anxiety; to be starkly reminded that mortality afflicts us all is
disquieting; to have previously experienced feelings about the deaths of
significant others resurrected is painful. Can I manage my fear and anxiety
in the presence of death while retaining my respect for the person who
moves ever closer to it?

PERSONAL REACTIONS TO CANCER

What are my feelings about encountering the special sights and smells
and sometimes twisted sounds emanating from the patient dying of cancer? Cancer and/or its treatments have a peculiar ability to produce results
which are discomfiting to the senses. How do I feel knowing that I, as a
social worker, cannot change those sights and smells and sounds—perhaps
no one can—and that they are the products of a process which I do not
like, which I dread, which I do not want to touch me or those I love?

When the cancer invades the brain and alters mental functioning, am
I willing to try to sift through the confusion of words and phrases to find

the patient's meaning? And am I able to forgive myself when the confusion overwhelms me and I stay away for longer and longer periods of time?

ABILITY TO TOLERATE UNCERTAINTY

How well can I tolerate uncertainty and ambiguity? Certainly they are part of the daily experience of every social worker, but the situation of the terminally ill cancer patient seems to conjure up an extra measure of each. First, there is often much uncertainty about the course of the affliction. Mr. W, mid 40's, had bronchogenic cancer which had widely metastisized. For weeks he hung on to a thread of life while the hospital staff wondered what kept him alive. On the other hand, Mr. S, early 50's, had battled cancer of the face and neck for over two years, submitting to a series of disfiguring surgeries, maintaining hope in the midst of pain and isolation. But, though in relatively good physical condition, when he learned that the new lump in his chest was malignant, he died within two days.

Then there is the ambiguity of the patient's emotional state. Much effort has gone into the creating of conceptual schemes which ostensibly eliminate this ambiguity and make the patient's overall course as well as his feeling state of the moment predictable. Kübler-Ross' five stages of dying (denial, anger, bargaining, depression, acceptance) (Kübler-Ross, 1969) is the most notable example. But patients have a knack for disrupting any schema, flitting from one emotion to another, challenging us to dare to discard our neat conceptualizations and find out what their feelings really are.

Underlying the ambiguity is the fundamental fact that one reacts ambivalently to imminent death. Mr. O was a living illustration. At age 56 he was hospitalized with a cancer which had begun in his bladder and then spread throughout his body. He was well aware of his terminal condition. The loss of control of many bodily functions, the distress at being unable to engage in the work and play which had once given him considerable pleasure, and the necessary distortion of his family relationships caused by the disease had prompted him to extract a promise from his physician that nothing would be done simply to prolong his life. One day when I entered his room, he pointed to the intravenous tube in his arm and expressed his anger at his physician for having it inserted during the night while he slept. The tube represented a breaking of the promise that no barriers would be erected to his dying. Immediately upon telling me this, he looked at the apparatus and noted that it was not working properly. His reaction was a quick: "Call the nurse," and as soon as the nurse arrived he informed her of the malfunction and relaxed only when it had been corrected. In those few minutes, Mr. O had dramatically expressed his ambivalence: I wish to die; I do not wish to die. He provides an important lesson.

SOCIAL WORK GOALS

Having decided that the anxiety and ambiguity, which cancer and dying evoke are tolerable and that the cancer process is not necessarily one of ugliness and agony, what, then, are appropriate social work goals? Should a goal be, for example, to contribute to keeping the patient and his family as calm and outwardly peaceful as possible? Or, in contrast, should a goal be to facilitate the expression and exploration of strong feelings, feelings such as fear, anger, frustration, depression, which some people call "negative"?

Social workers seem to have less problem choosing the latter course than some other health professionals. Social work tends to attract people fascinated by tumultuous feelings; within social work the mental health world view is pervasive and offers continual encouragement to the ferreting out of such feelings. Yet even the social worker can be frightened by the depth of feeling which surrounds death, both within the patient and family and within herself. It may take several conversations with clients, proving that client and social worker can survive expression of these feelings, before the anxiety begins to abate.

Not all social workers will agree, however, that the solicitation of the patient's feelings about dying is appropriate. Ruth Abrams writes: "(As a result of) my study of the cancer patient at the terminal stage ... I am convinced that the patient ... should be permitted ... to control his dying himself—to speak of it or not, as he wishes, without prompting ... his caregivers must realize that perhaps it is they who wish to talk of death, even though the patient wishes to maintain silence." (Abrams, 1974, p. 77)

The inflicting upon the patient of what are needs for oneself is a primary hazard for any helping professional. In any given situation a discussion of death between patient and social worker may spring primarily from the social worker's inner demands. There is, however, strong reason for believing that, in this area, silence is more suspect than talk for the rule of our culture in general and of the health care system in particular is still that death is not to be discussed. Silence, then, may well reflect the patient's bowing to what he believes is expected of him and, if this is the case, "prompting" may be necessary to help him realize that the rule need only apply if he himself so desires.

Another question about goals is whether or not the social worker should help the patient and his significant others move in the direction of accepting the patient's unhappy fate. A strong implication of Kübler-Ross' stages of dying, for example, is that acceptance is the natural, appropriate goal. The helper will recognize that some patients, perhaps many, will not get there, but this will be a falling short, a less than optimum result. If, however, you believe that one should "rage, rage against the dying of the light'', (Thomas, 1973, p. 911) then your goal will be different: to permit the expression, in word and behavior, of that rage as long as there is energy to fuel it and you will see acceptance as a deviant maneuver.

Social workers tend to be glib in response to this kind of issue. "Whatever the patient wants is all right with me. If he seeks to move toward acceptance, fine. If he wants to persist in being angry, that's fine, too." What this overlooks is that one's own priorities always influence the approach one takes to helping clients. (Hardman, 1975). The only way to minimize this influence is to recognize what those priorities are. If, for example, you believe that an attitude of acceptance is the appropriate frame of mind with which to approach death, that belief will give some direction to your efforts no matter how eloquently you speak of client self-determination unless you bring the belief clearly into view and consciously root it out of what goes on between you and the client.

A similar commentary can be made about the matter of whether or not we expect the patient to maintain hope for survival until the very end. There is a widely held belief that such hope is both ubiquitous and essential to a terminally ill person's emotional well-being. Kübler-Ross writes: ''... all our patients maintained a little bit of it (hope for survival) and were nourished by it in especially difficult times.'' (Kübler-Ross, 1969, p. 123) For the cancer patient this hope presumably is formulated in terms of a cure that will surface just in the nick of time or an unfathomable natural process that will cause the hated tumor to disappear.

Another point of view, however, is that such "hope" is really an illusion which patients do not need nearly as much as those who deal with the patient. Perhaps it is the helper's discomfort with the reality and finality of the impending death that creates the idea that a patient must continue to hope. Or its source may be the professional person's need to keep death at a distance from herself.

The decision you make about the naturalness and/or necessity of hope will influence your action. Holding the first view, you will look for hope, encourage it, perhaps even try to plant some seeds if it seems missing. The other view will more likely lead you to try to learn if an expression of hope belongs to the real feelings of the patient (or family) or is his way of being nice to you, that is, by offering a commentary that he feels is expected of him.

Social Work Tasks

Having begun to struggle with these basic questions, it is then timely to consider the social work tasks appropriate to the helping of terminal cancer patients and their families. In essence they are the same as those which pervade all of social work, regardless of the kind of client served or the auspices under which the services are rendered; that is, people are helped to make contact with whatever will enable them to more fully and more effectively carry out one or more of their assignments. Specifically these tasks are: (1) Helping patients and their significant others to get in touch with their feelings and to recognize their behavioral options. (2) Assisting patients and their significant others to develop and/or maintain meaningful communication with one another. (3) Aiding patients and their significant others in locating and linking up with resources beyond themselves. (4) Helping health professionals, whose activities impinge upon the patient and his significant others, to acknowledge their own feelings, to understand the feelings and needs of those being served, and to learn effective and sensitive ways of meeting the recognized needs.

GETTING IN TOUCH WITH ONESELF

Once the social worker, in considering her goals, decides that it is worthwhile for the patient and those important to him to be given full opportunity to express and explore their feelings about the terminal cancer, one part of this task automatically follows. There is nothing automatic, however, about either the way it is to be carried out or the results which can be expected.

Some patients and families effectively avoid taking notice of their feelings by denying the terminal nature of the patient's cancer. In most cases the social worker will not want to challenge this denial but will want to be careful not to participate in it. There are few clients, however, who massively and continuously deny the illness and its attendant emotional turmoil. Most people, at least at times, admit to themselves what is going on within their body and their feelings (Weisman, 1972; Glaser and Strauss, 1965) but are selective about whom they will share these realities with. A patient's silence, therefore, may not reflect denial as much as politeness or conformity to the taboo against speaking of death and dying, or his belief that the social worker could not possibly be interested in his struggles.

To be most useful to the client, the social worker will do well to operate on three premises:

1. The client has a right to conceal or reveal whatever he chooses;
2. The client has a right to choose the person(s) to whom he will reveal himself (and being empathic will not guarantee the social worker that she will be one of those chosen);
3. A clear invitation by the social worker will likely be important to the client's decision to express himself freely to her. This invitation can be issued by (a) listening carefully to the client, (b) responding to the feelings

and hints about feelings that come forth, (c) offering comments which explicitly state the expectation that strong feelings accompany serious illness; e.g., "Having a cancer like yours can be pretty scary."

This last technique seems to be the kind of "prompting" that Abrams inveighs against (Abrams, 1974, p. 77), but it is often necessary to combat the broad cultural expectation of silence, the health-care system's message that positive thinking and speaking are required of "good patients", and the caricature of the social worker as someone interested only in providing tangible services.

When does such "prompting" become the social worker's projection of her own needs onto the client? The answer to this question is only available in interaction with the patient or family member. As a general guideline, I usually allow myself two sequential promptings before deciding the patient is not interested in sharing his feelings with me.

> PATIENT: I guess you know that my cancer is pretty far along.
> SOCIAL WORKER: Yes and I can imagine that's frightening to you. (Prompting #1)
> PATIENT: Oh, I'm not scared.
> SOCIAL WORKER: My guess is that most people in your situation would be. (Prompting #2)

If that does not call forth a response describing emotions of some kind, then the usual conclusion is that the client is not willing to open up at this time.

Part of the value of discussing feelings, particularly tumultuous ones, is the opportunity it provides to discover within oneself the ability to struggle with and obtain some measure of control over those feelings. "Though the cancer may kill me, the feelings won't." Alternative ways of thinking about one's situation as well as more comfort-producing behaviors may also evolve from conversations about feelings. When Mr. C's cancer finally metastisized to his brain, he occasionally had hallucinations in which he saw himself in places he had frequented when healthy. He could talk about how frightening these experiences were and, through the conversation, decided he could assure himself of being safely in his hospital bed when these hallucinations occurred by focusing on some specific pieces of the familiar hospital equipment which surrounded him.

As in Mr. C's situation, explorations of feelings and behavioral options are often intertwined. At times behavior in itself is a useful topic for discussion, enabling the patient to consider (1) how he wants to respond to his physical limitations, (2) means by which he can continue to exercise control over his life, (3) what treatment options are acceptable to him, and (4) the most comfortable ways for him to relate to his significant others and to health-care personnel. For family members, discussion of their options after the patient's death can be an important preparation for the difficult time ahead.

COMMUNICATING WITH OTHERS

Estrangement from others is a frequent concomitant of terminal cancer. The changes in the way the patient's body functions, the alterations in his appearance, and the aura of dread which cancer evokes can create severe obstacles to the maintenance of consistent and meaningful contact between patient and significant others. It can be an important social work task, therefore, to help those involved to maximize beneficial interaction while accepting their own and the other person's limitations.

When the cancer has reached the terminal stage, the patient may have limited endurance and be able to tolerate only carefully restricted visitation. Emotional limitations may exist as well. Mr. A, for example, needed to decide whether or not he wished further visits from his former golfing partners. Although it felt good to him to be remembered by them, their presence evoked in Mr. A very painful feelings about never again being able to engage in his once favorite pastime. Family members at times need recognition that they have a life apart from the patient, especially when he is being cared for at home, which needs their time and guilt-free attention.

Time spent together, however, is not usually the primary problem between the terminally ill patient and others. Rather, it is the kind of contact which they permit themselves that creates or reflects difficulties. "Let's pretend," is a common theme. "Let's pretend that you are not going to die." "Let's pretend that I, the patient, don't know about the deadly force which holds me; after all, the doctor hasn't really said there's no hope." "Let's pretend that by smiling and talking positively and saying what good care the health-care professionals provide and taking note of all the flowers and get-well cards and not mentioning cancer and definitely not talking about death, all of us will come through our meetings together unscathed."

The personality, life-style, and past relationship of patient and family members may make such pretending the only way they can deal with one another while the patient is dying. Then the social worker need not set herself to undo a lifetime of fixed behaviors. Frequently, though, patients and their family secretly wish to be able to share with one another their hurts and hopes, their frustrations and fears, their wishes and wonderings, but are blocked by a need to protect the other person as well as a concern that they themselves will be overwhelmed if they once open the door on the feelings and questions that surge within. In such situations the social worker may be able to help her clients express the wish they harbor and support them as they then, with trepidation, begin to talk and plan candidly with one another. Occasionally a very small amount of social work input can contribute to a considerable change in the way a patient and his significant others interact. Mrs. B, for example, told the social worker that she well knew that death was imminent for her husband who was hospitalized with lung cancer. Her distress was compounded by the fact that she had no idea what kind of funeral or burial arrangements he wished, "Of course," she said, "I can't talk with him about this because then he will know that he is dying." The social worker's brief comment that he and Mr. B had frequently talked together about Mr. B's dying was a revelation to Mrs. B which enabled her to talk openly with her husband about the situation they faced, to the relief of both.

RESOURCES

Connecting clients with community resources is a well-recognized social work task. It can be carried out to the benefit of patient and family whether or not they allow the social worker to help with their feelings, behaviors, and relationships. Home-health agencies, American Cancer Society programs, self-help groups, financial assistances, and whatever other supplies and services the local community have available can be important means for maximizing the well-being of patient and family.

Another kind of resource for some patients is the formal opportunity for expressing wishes about the prolongation of their lives. California, for example, in 1976 became the first state in the nation to enact a law giving a terminally ill person a means by which he could direct his physician to refrain from using life-sustaining procedures when they "would serve only to artificially prolong the moment of my death and where my physician determines that my death is imminent whether or not life-sustaining procedures were utilized ..." (California Health and Safety Code, paragraph 7188). Subsequently a number of other states have passed similar legislation (Friedman, 1978). Where such legislation has not been passed, a document such as the Living Will (Euthanasia Educational Council, 1974), although generally considered not legally binding, has the potential for guiding a physician, where he has discretion, to minister to the patient in a way compatible with the patient's desires when the patient can no longer express those desires.

For some patients, putting them in touch with religious resources meaningful to them can be a useful service. Calling the local minister or the hospital chaplain is an appropriate action for the social worker when it springs from the wishes of the patient. Wary of inflicting a religiously oriented visit upon an unreceptive person, social workers sometimes miss seeing that such a visit may provide considerable solace and support. Along with other resources, it is one that needs to be kept in mind and offered as an option to the patient.

Occasionally, however, a social worker will make a too quick referral to the clergy. The fact that a patient raises crucial existential questions such as: "Why is this cancer being visited upon me?" or "How can such a terrible affliction fit into a good God's plan?", does not necessarily mean that calling in a religious professional is indicated. Such questions may reflect a need to ventilate some of the feelings that accompany the patient's dire circumstances or a need to struggle through to his own answers or his own recognition that for him there are no answers. In either case the task is one that well fits within the purview of social work provided the social worker is clear that it is not her responsibility to provide answers. When the feelings have been expressed and the questions wrestled with, if the patient then wishes to hear the answers contained within a particular religious framework, the appropriate clergyperson can be sought.

HEALTH PROFESSIONALS

An increasing number of health professionals are finding themselves having significant contact with terminally ill patients and their families as health services are more and more provided to seriously ill people in their homes and as dying is transferred from the home to the hospital or nursing home. That many health-care personnel have a strong interest in learning about what was once a "taboo topic" (Faberow, 1963), is evidenced by the proliferation of workshops, courses, and writings on death and dying. Social workers have both informal and formal opportunities to contribute to their co-workers from other disciplines becoming more aware of their feelings in this area and knowledgeable about sensitive ways of meeting the needs of patients and families. Impromptu conversations, ward rounds, staff meetings, and educational programs can be vehicles for social work input. With social work leadership, some hospitals have developed a Thanatology Committee of multi-disciplinary membership, one of whose charges may be to provide education for the staff. The imaginative social worker, then, can find a variety of ways to contribute to the growth of her co-professionals.

There is a danger in assuming these several tasks: that continued immersion in the tragedy of terminal cancer may exact a heavy emotional toll from the social worker. The specter of possible burnout is ever present. The courage of patients and families and the love and concern shared by them will help diminish the drain on the social worker, but she will still need to be well aware of her own limits and of her own personal resources for renewal.

For many people cancer proves to be a deadly enemy. The social worker who is willing to work with patients engaged in this final struggle, and with their families, has some important questions to begin to answer, some difficult self-assessments to make, and some vital tasks to perform.

References

1. ABRAMS, RUTH, *Not Alone with Cancer*, Springfield, Ill.: Charles C. Thomas, 1974.
2. American Cancer Society, "Cancer Research: Increasing Survival" (pamphlet), 1975.
3. American Cancer Society, *1978 Cancer Facts and Figures*, 1977.
4. California Health and Safety Code, Division 7, Part I, Chapter 3.9 (Natural Death Act).
5. Euthanasia Educational Council, "A Living Will". New York, 1974.
6. FABEROW, NORMAN L., editor, *Taboo Topics*. New York: Atherton Press, 1963.
7. FRIEDMAN, EMILY, "'Natural Death' Laws Cause Hospitals Few Problems", *Hospitals*, May 16, 1978, Vol. 52, pp. 124–130.
8. GLASER, BARNEY AND STRAUSS, ANSELM, *Awareness of Dying*. Chicago: Aldine Publishing Co., 1965.
9. HARDMAN, DALE G., "Not with My Daughter, You Don't!", *Social Work*, July 1975, Vol. 20, No. 4, pp. 278–285.
10. KÜBLER-ROSS, ELIZABETH, *On Death and Dying*. New York: The Macmillan Company, 1969.
11. SCHNEIDMAN, EDWUB S., "You and Death", *Psychology Today*, June 1971, Vol. 5, No. 1, pp. 43–45.
12. THOMAS, DYLAN, "Do Not Go Gentle Into That Good Night", in Ellman, Richard and O'Clair, Robert, editors, *The Norton Anthology of Modern Poetry*, New York: W. W. Norton and Co., 1973.
13. WEISMAN, AVERY D., *Dying and Denying*. New York: Behavioral Publications, 1972.

CARDIAC DISORDERS

CHAPTER 33

Casework with Patients Undergoing Cardiac Surgery

Elliot C. Brown, Jr.

Recent developments in cardiac surgery, including the cardio-pulmonary by-pass machine, synthetic material prostheses for valve replacement, and surgical approaches to the relief of coronary artery disease, are presenting new opportunities and challenges to patients with heart disease. Those for whom there was no recourse twenty years ago may now have surgery that will at least enable them to survive. Others, for whom the prospect was one of stable existence, but with severe limitation, may achieve or regain a full, active life. Surgeons are addressing themselves to the amelioration of a broadening range of heart ailments. Vastly increasing numbers of patients are undergoing the various procedures. In 1970 at Massachusetts General Hospital, 530 cardiac surgery procedures were carried out. This number represented an increase of ninety-seven cases over the preceding year, and in each of the several years before that, there were somewhat smaller increases in the total number of procedures. In the first year's experience with a new surgical treatment for certain kinds of coronary artery disease, approximately twenty-five patients received the operation; in the second year of its use, approximately one hundred and fifteen patients underwent surgery.

The risks, expressed statistically in percentages and mortality rates, continue to decline. The challenge to each individual patient remains the same: to dare to undergo what is ironically at the same time a life-threatening, life-saving, and usually elective operation and to agree to incur al

Reprinted from *Social Casework*, Vol. 52 (December, 1971), pp. 611–616, by permission of the author and the Family Service Association of America.

most inconceivable amounts of acute anxiety and physical and chemical assault on the organism.

The challenge to caseworkers in this exciting field also remains the same, but the number of patients involved has trebled and quadrupled. We are challenged to develop greater skill in assessing the psychosocial history and functioning of people coming to surgery, especially in appraising ego strength and capacities for coping with anxiety. There are seemingly infinite demands to be placed on clearly finite and often overextended manpower resources. We must further the application of sound generic concepts to the special setting of the cardiac surgical service.

We are challenged to develop the skill to enable patients with a wide variety of personality structures and from various social environments to cope with the acute stresses of the surgery period itself, so that they can take full advantage of the objective improvement surgery gives them. Casework in this field draws on the main body of personality theory and on the special insights of crisis theory. It requires skill at initiating a supportive relationship where the concerns, perhaps because they are so extensive, are often either vaguely formulated or displaced to the most distant, concrete issues. The caseworker must also learn to be comfortable with all the paraphernalia of a modern hospital's surgical service, offering a relationship that transcends the particular awe-inspiring, intimidating instruments of modern medical technology.

The Literature

The plight of the patient facing heart surgery has received increasing attention in recent years. Drawing on the earlier works of Erich Lindemann, Helene Deutsch, William Bainbridge, and others, investigators have focused on the cataclysmic, life-threatening, or traumatic aspects of the surgical experience.[1] They describe the psychologic stress and delineate common coping mechanisms. The studies of the newly developed coronary care units (CCU's) by Thomas Hackett, Julia Ezra, and others have infused an awareness of the peculiar stresses of that setting.[2] Donald Kornfeld and others have suggested that the environment of the recovery room,

---

[1] Erich Lindemann, Observations on Psychiatric Sequelae to Surgical Operations in Women, *American Journal of Psychiatry*, 98:132–39 (July 1941); Helene Deutsch, Some Psychoanalytic Observations in Surgery, *Psychosomatic Medicine*, 4:105–15 (1942); and William Seaman Bainbridge, Consideration of Psychic Factors in Surgical Diagnosis and Procedure, *Psychiatric Quarterly*, 4:414–24 (1930).

[2] Thomas P. Hackett, N. H. Cassem, and Howard A. Wishnie, The Coronary-Care Unit: An Appraisal of its Psychologic Hazards, *New England Journal of Medicine*, 279:1365–70 (December 19, 1968); and Julia Ezra, Casework in a Coronary Care Unit, *Social Casework*, 50:276–81 (May 1969).

with its exotic equipment, eerie science-fiction atmosphere, hypnotically monotonous and repetitive sounds, and disruption of usual sleep-wake patterns, explains why 38 percent of the patients in their sample had episodes of acute delirium.[3] Another sizable group of investigators believes that the disruption and alterations of normal biochemical variables account for the changes in ego functioning that many patients experience.[4]

Much of the psychiatric literature, especially the recent literature, is focused on the etiology of postcardiotomy delirium. That phenomenon is interesting, but it is, after all, apparently a self-limiting condition, whatever its etiology, and it may be occurring less frequently than in the earlier days of open-heart surgery.[5] This material is of limited usefulness to social workers primarily concerned with the long-range readjustment of patients following surgery.

Many investigators report undertaking successful therapeutic interventions to limit disorientation and hasten successful ego adaptation to the stresses of the surgery.[6] The time perspective in which most of these studies have been carried out is limited to the "perioperative" period itself, a few days on either side of the surgery. Thus, any appraisal of the patient's psychological makeup is handicapped by the pressure of time, the anxieties of the present crisis, and the limitation of an often hasty, frequently a historic, retrospective evaluation.

Casework Evaluation

For the social worker to help patients endure and recover from the experience of cardiac surgery, it is necessary to carry out a thorough psychosocial evaluation of patients coming into cardiac surgery. If it is done well in advance of the surgery itself, such an evaluation can be the basis for deciding the nature of the casework help offered each patient and the kind of consultative help the caseworker can provide to nursing and other personnel caring for the patient during the actual admission. It is this approach that is used at Massachusetts General Hospital and that will now be described in greater detail.

The psychosocial evaluation seems the best procedure for gathering important information about the patient. Properly done, it provides a historical perspective to the description of the patient in his current predic-

[3] Donald S. Kornfeld, Sheldon Zimberg, and James R. Malm, Psychiatric Complications of Open-Heart Surgery, *New England Journal of Medicine*, 273:287–92 (August 5, 1965).

[4] S. J. Hazan, Psychiatric Complications Following Cardiac Surgery: Part I, A review article, *The Journal of Thoracic and Cardiovascular Surgery*, 51:307–19 (March 1966).

[5] Stanley S. Heller, et al., Psychiatric Complications of Open-Heart Surgery: A Re-examination, *New England Journal of Medicine*, 283:1015–20 (November 5, 1970).

[6] Janet A. Kennedy and Hyman Bakst, The Influence of Emotions on the Outcome of Cardiac Surgery: A Predictive Study, *Bulletin of the New York Academy of Medicine*, 42:811–49 (October 1966).

ament, and it inventories those personal and social supports available to the patient through this crisis period. This assessment is the key to determining what sort of casework supportive relationship to offer and to providing accurate information useful to the many people who will work with the patient. The systematic appraisal goes far beyond merely affording each patient the opportunity to ventilate his fears about the surgery itself. Indeed, in some instances, this material should not be uncovered.

We try to determine the general level of functioning of each patient. How well has he or she done in the role of husband or wife, breadwinner or housekeeper, parent, employee? Further, we try to gain a full understanding of what the heart disease means to the patient and of the effects the manifestations of the illness have had on the patient's life. Has the patient found ways to cope with these successfully, or has he yielded and retreated to a more limited life than seems medically necessary? Have there been important secondary gains to the patient, extra attention from an otherwise not-too-attentive spouse, for example? Or has the illness been used to avoid certain stressful roles and situations, to gain exemption from important obligations? If so, does it seem that modifications in the patient's psychic economy can take place which will enable him to give up the prop of his illness? This aspect can often be gauged by learning what the patient's expectations are for after surgery. Those patients who may not be able to relinquish the illness often have exceedingly modest hopes for improvement and seem unable even to have the fantasy of being really well.

To what extent is coming to surgery an unexpected crisis? Patients with rheumatic heart disease have, in a very real sense, been chronically ill for some period of time previous to surgery. If the proposal of surgery is received as an unexpected blow, denial must certainly have been a principal coping mechanism.

What are the patient's usual methods of coping with anxiety? Are there any analogous situations to the present one that might provide clues?

What is the history of recent and remote losses? The threat of death or of the loss of some important function during the impending surgery usually evokes a reexperiencing of such losses. Many patients appear to work over previous losses, and the urgency of these feelings often puzzles and frightens them.

Finally, what is the social setting in which the patient will come to surgery? Can he count on the support of important family members, or will quiescent tensions be aroused that will prevent others in the family from communicating emotional support to the patient?

Treatment Plan

From the evaluation, a casework treatment plan is formulated. This plan provides for a series of judgments and decisions based on the worker's understanding of the patient and his situation. These decisions determine the nature and intensity of the relationship, the frequency of visits, and the kind of transference the worker hopes to encourage.

Some patients require frequent visits for reassurance. Under these circumstances, the worker may be cast in something of a parental role. He likely will have to be active and giving in a parental way, finding things out, giving information, and paving the way for the patient. He should convey his readiness to step in and help sort things out if the stress becomes too much for the patient.

Other patients would interpret such activity as a sign that the caseworker considered them not strong enough to endure the tensions of the situation. To communicate such an idea would clearly be nonsupportive, and for these patients something quite different is indicated. One would hope to nurture a peerlike relationship—casual, measured, and carefully respectful of the patient's independent competence. If the worker is too active, he may undermine the patient's confidence in his own ability to negotiate a difficult road. Patients in this group may need to mask their need for support with specific requests and concrete concerns. The worker should answer the specific request, hoping to discover other acceptable ways to respond to the unstated wish for help.

Some patients ask for help in dealing with the mysteries and intricacies of the surgical experience itself. They want information about what will happen to them, what the machines are, who the various technicians are, and what the tests are for. These are usually people who use intellectual techniques to gain a feeling of mastery over their situations. Providing full and complete information helps because it gives them the tools they use best to cope with frightening situations.

Other patients ask, in one way or another, to be spared the details of what awaits them. Directly or indirectly, these patients usually seek a general reassurance that the hospital staff is concerned about their well-being and stands ready to lend a comforting presence to the proceedings. Although other patients may be primarily concerned with the technical competence of their physicians and surgeons, patients in this group seem most responsive to the charisma of their physicians.

From the foregoing descriptions, it is clear that there are wide variations in how patients respond to the crisis of the cardiac surgery experience.[7] Fortunately, caseworkers have a wide variety of tools and skills available to help each individual patient.

Our expertise at focusing on ego strengths and undergirding defenses helps patients cope with the acute anxieties of the surgical period. Our skill at using concrete services—finding funds to pay for surgery, making blood

---

[7] For an excellent typology, see Chase Patterson Kimball, Psychological Responses to the Experience of Open Heart Surgery: I, *American Journal of Psychiatry*, 126:348–59 (September 1969).

bank arrangements, helping families cope with financial crises during the surgical period, and making discharge and follow-up plans—meets real needs. It is also opens the way to helping patients with their emotional responses to their illness without labeling them "needy" or "dependent." Finally, the caseworker is the member of the team best equipped to develop and disseminate a clear awareness of the interpersonal setting in which illness and recovery take place.

Illustrations

Mr. B was an example of someone who used a request for concrete help as a way of asking for assistance in mastering his fears concerning the illness and surgery. The family sought social service help just after Mr. B was admitted for aortic valve replacement. They wanted aid in preparing and pursuing an application for public assistance for the period of time Mr. B would be out of work because of the surgery. They appeared worried about a weekly income, although Mr. B still had extensive sick-time benefits. They seemed immobilized by anxiety and had made almost no preparations during the two months they had known about the impending surgery. Seen together at Mr. B's bedside for the initial interview, they were smiling and jovial, but there were undercurrents of inarticulated, massively denied fears relative to Mr. B's situation. The financial concerns were the only specific focus for these fears.

At an interview alone shortly thereafter, Mr. B was more open about his fears. He cried several times while the worker was taking a fuller history and as the special meaning of the illness and the need for surgery became clear.

There had been major deprivations in Mr. B's early years. Mr. B's father had spent nearly all of those years in a mental hospital suffering an organic, deteriorating brain disease. Mr. B had been reared by his mother and there had been no adequately functioning men to serve as models for him.

The three years leading up to Mr. B's admission had been ones in which the B family, and Mr. B in particular, had suffered several reverses or disappointments. At great expenditure of energy and entirely on his own, Mr. B had put himself through school, but shortly after moving into his third professional position, he had been "furloughed," when a recession in the industry led to major economy moves by the company. Mr. B sought the security of a clerk's job in a government agency—a safe job, but one considerably below his potential.

Shortly thereafter, the older child, an eighteen-year-old girl, announced that she was pregnant and subsequently married the father of the child. In addition to his feelings about his daughter's pregnancy, Mr. B also had to adjust to the fact that his new son-in-law was of a different ethnic and religious background. Mr. B said he wished his daughter had "given him time" to get his affairs in order so that he could give her away properly, but it seemed clear that he felt he had failed as a father and somehow forced his daughter into her course of action.

In this context, and from remarks in the interview, it seemed clear that Mr. B considered the surgery one more reverse, another thing to contend with, a crisis that he had somehow brought on himself or a cruel fate had visited upon him, and from which it was unlikely he would emerge unscathed. His confidence in his own competence had been severely sapped by his other losses and reverses. His guilt and disappointment led him to expect the worst.

The caseworker's tasks were clear. The financial situation was quickly clarified and the B family was reassured. Then, in the few days between the referral and the surgery, the caseworker helped Mr. B to see the illness and surgery as a medical event being competently handled, diluting as much as possible Mr. B's association of it to other reverses. By generalizing Mr. B's feelings and pointing out his good judgment and good functioning, the caseworker sought to decrease Mr. B's guilt over various past events, strengthening his picture of himself as a competent person deserving another chance at good health, important to his family, and potentially to his profession.

Mr. B's surgery went smoothly, and after a suitable convalescence he returned to the security of his clerk's job. Six months later, he was able to return to employment in his chosen field. Mr. B had been restored to the good level of functioning he had shown prior to the reversals.

Patients who have major problems with dependency present special difficulties to the caseworker and to all those caring for them. It is usually hard to assess the extent of their need for support. They often adopt a counter-dependent, cold, or aggressive way of relating that alienates the staff and heightens the chances that the patient will undergo surgery without sufficient preparation.

Miss C worked as an occupational therapy aide at a regional center for crippled children, but she sheepishly said she really "couldn't stand" sick children. Being a patient was very difficult for her. She disliked the "implied dependency"; she wanted to be left alone when she felt sick rather than be comforted, and she kept most of her feelings to herself. She said that occasionally when was alone, she might "break down" in response to anxiety, but it was important to her to be in perfect control when she was with people. It was difficult to know for certain where this feeling originated, except that all five girls in her family had apparently been forced to become self-reliant prematurely, when the patient's father deserted the family and her mother became more withdrawn. Even during Miss C's admission, the mother seemed preoccupied with her own health and only secondarily concerned about Miss C. The mother regarded the surgery as something her daughter was being given, and thus something she, the mother, was being deprived of. It seemed unlikely that the mother would be much support, but Miss C had erected barriers against acknowledging that she wanted or needed such encouragement.

Through the preoperative period, Miss C maintained the most abrasive facade regarding anxieties about the surgery. Although she appeared tense and concerned about what it was going to be like, she made a point of not giving in and admitting how upset she really was. When the caseworker tried gently to speculate about how Miss C must be feeling and the kinds of questions she must have, she berated him for not being able to read the clues in her rather immobile face. After all, he was the social worker!

A social service note in the medical record suggested that preoperative teaching and preparation of this patient should be casual and matter of fact, and that it should be carried out even if there were no indication from the patient that it helped. It was necessary in working with Miss C to avoid the connotation that such preparation was to make the experience comfortable, to relieve anxiety, or in any other sense to coddle the patient.

Concerns about death and dying are often denied, displaced, or projected. When such concerns are expressed more directly, the patient will usually have discovered some way of partially neutralizing his feelings. Frequently, this fact is clear from what the patient says.

Mr. R was a thirty-six-year-old man, the father of seven children. He had rheumatic heart disease with severe aortic stenosis. Of special significance was the fact that Mr. R's mother had died in the operating room having open-heart surgery six years prior to Mr. R's admission.

Preoperatively, Mr. R was able to talk about his misgivings about the surgery, relating it directly to the loss of his mother. Fortunately, he saw the hospital as having made a valiant attempt to save her. He saw himself as in quite a different position: younger, without other major diseases (his mother was diabetic), and benefiting from medical advances in the intervening years.

When the concerns are expressed directly and no adequate way to defuse them has been found, the patients present a striking picture. They seem globally anxious, distraught, panic striken, with agitation and tears never far away. They grasp at straws of reassurance from whatever source, but nothing comforts them for long. Ironically, they often hide their distress from the physician, usually out of a wish not to seem childish or weak. These patients present management problems post-operatively if they are not helped to develop better ways of coping.

Mrs. F was such a patient. Lying there, frightened before her surgery, searching every visitor's face for some clue as to how they thought she would do, clinging, weeping and wordless, to each of her children in turn, she seemed strikingly different from the competent, controlled person the caseworker had interviewed several months before. During the intervening time, Mrs. F had suffered a stroke which was probably caused by her heart lesion. She had recovered fully, but that emergency evidently heightened her awareness of the risk of death from the surgery. She had apparently no way to come to terms with this threat.

The caseworker knew her early history in detail from the initial interview. Mrs. F's life was a chronicle of ultimately successful struggles against great odds: a poor, unassimilated, old-world Italian family, a difficult marriage to an immature man, and chronic economic problems which interfered with her attempts to educate her several bright children. In ruminating about her life, Mrs. F seemed certain she had never made a correct decision, although evidence of her good judgment was all around her.

The caseworker began the discussion by observing that Mrs. F held on to her children "as if she thought she'd never see them again." Mrs. F seemed relieved to be able to share her fears about dying. She confided that what particularly distressed her was her fear that more would be demanded of her, in relation to courage, stamina, and emotional fortitude, than she could muster.

Once these issues were clarified, the caseworker was able to help Mrs. F come to terms with her situation and make peace with the people she might not see again. More important, she was helped to apply her "when the going gets tough, the tough get going" philosophy. As Mrs. F began to tell the caseworker of other difficult situations and how she had been able to handle them, she became much less distraught and much more actively involved in her own preoperative preparation.

After the surgery, she had to spend more than twice the average time in the surgical intensive care unit, perhaps because she had been so ill preoperatively. Yet, despite a day or so of being disoriented about place and time, she emerged intact and has begun what promises to be a complete recovery.

Summary

A method of providing ego supportive casework treatment to patients undergoing cardiac surgery has been described. The treatment begins with the recognition of the particular stresses of this kind of illness and of the setting in which surgery and initial recovery take place. The content of a casework evaluation for these patients is suggested, as well as the development of a casework treatment plan based on diagnostic understanding. The case illustrations show something of the range of responses to the cardiac surgery situation which patients demonstrate and the casework activity involved.

DEAFNESS

CHAPTER 34

Between Worlds:
The Problems of
Deafened Adults

Helen Sloss Luey

Deafness directly affects the interaction between an individual and his environment. By its very nature, then, this disability should hold special interest for social workers. Yet the whole field has been largely ignored in the professional literature.

Social workers may be called upon to help deaf people in a variety of situations. Sometimes people seek social work help to cope specifically with the impact of deafness. Deaf people, of course, are also vulnerable to all social and emotional problems, and they may seek help from a social worker in any area of practice. It is important, then, that all social workers have some understanding of the ramifications of deafness.

From the limited social work literature available, one might get the impression that deafness occurs primarily at birth or in infancy, and that most deaf people suffer the problems in language acquisition which stem from an early sensory loss. The few existing articles about deafness and social work deal almost exclusively with prelingually deaf people, or with individuals who lost their hearing before they had learned language (Chough, 1976; Hurwitz, 1969; Newbold, 1979; Silver, 1963). To be effective with this group of clients, a social worker must obtain highly specialized knowledge and an advanced level of sign language skill. The vast majority of deaf people, however, are not prelingually deaf. According to recent statistics, there are 1.8 million deaf people in the United States, of

Reprinted from *Social Work in Health Care*, Vol. 5, No. 3 (1980), pp. 253–266, with permission of the Haworth Press.

whom only 0.4 million lost their hearing before the age of nineteen (Schein, 1974, p. 4). In other words, 78% of all deaf people in the United States lost their hearing after having reached adulthood, long after having learned speech and language, and in most cases after having established a firm identity as a hearing adult. These people have a distinct set of problems and experiences which social workers have not addressed.

For purposes of this discussion, the following definition of deafened adult will be used: "those individuals who at one time possessed enough hearing to learn language and oral communication through hearing, but who suffer with a loss of hearing so severe that audition is useless for purposes of receiving oral communication" (Krug, 1969, p. 99). The people discussed in this paper are those who would qualify as deafened by this definition, even when using the best amplification. This paper does not deal with prelingually deaf people, nor does it discuss hard of hearing people, i.e., people who have lost some ability to hear and understand speech but who, with proper amplification, good communication skills, and moderate adjustments in their social lives can reasonably be expected to participate in familiar pursuits. Because of their previous life experience, deafened people are quite unlike prelingually deaf people. Because of the severity of their hearing loss, they are also unlike hard of hearing people. They are between worlds.

Some Problems for the Social Worker

In his first encounter with a deafened client, the social worker quickly perceives that his usual methods of communicating and of establishing relationship are ineffective. When he speaks at his normal rate and in his usual manner, the client understands virtually nothing. The client may aggressively demand repetition, may simply look pained and frustrated, or may nod politely and then reveal his lack of understanding with inappropriate responses. The social worker may not understand the reasons for these difficulties. He may think the client is inattentive, stupid, or hostile. Mutual frustration is inevitable.

A social worker in such a situation is likely to feel helpless, and helplessness may provoke anger at the client or guilt over one's own poor performance. Rejection is likely, and is damaging to the client, even when disguised by a conscientious effort to find some "more appropriate" agency.

If the social worker gets past the initial communication barrier, he may encounter deeper problems in diagnosis or countertransference. The client may be experiencing intense feelings related to his deafness. His social functioning may seem limited or inappropriate. Without specific knowledge about the impact of deafness in adult life and normal responses to this crisis, a social worker is unable to separate problems in adaptation to deafness from other issues in the client's situation, background, or personality.

A hearing social worker may also feel personally threatened by a deafened client. Unlike prelingually deaf people, the deafened person has grown up in a hearing world, and his life experience and cultural orientation may be similar to that of hearing people, perhaps that of the worker. The disability does not show in the person's appearance, nor is it necessarily obvious from his speech. The significance of the disability becomes apparent slowly, as the worker listens to the client's feelings. At that point, the worker has to face the fact that deafness can happen to anyone, and that he too is vulnerable to this devastating experience and to all of its permanent deprivations. Whether he expresses these feelings by outright rejection or compensates with overly solicitous behavior or over-protection, his personal discomfort will interfere with the quality and effectiveness of his service.

With some special knowledge, social workers can overcome the difficulties outlined above. This article will present information about deafness and its psycho-social ramifications. It will conclude with some practical suggestions for social workers.

Levels of Hearing

In order to understand the impact of deafness in adult life, it is essential to understand the role of hearing in the person's previous life and, indeed, in all of our lives. Hearing has been divided into three levels, and a description of each level clarifies the different dimensions of sound in everyday life.

The symbolic level encompasses the part of hearing used to understand speech. In using language, we agree to accept certain sounds as symbolic of certain things or ideas. Conversation in the usual mode is dependent on hearing at the symbolic level (Ramsdell, 1970). Many aesthetic or inspirational experiences might also be considered part of hearing at this level. Music, the sounds of nature, and many religious experiences must be heard to be appreciated.

Contrary to popular opinion, lipreading skill can compensate for hearing at this level only to a limited degree. It is not possible to lipread all of the sounds of spoken language accurately. In fact, audiologists and lipreading teachers estimate that only one third of the sounds of English are clearly visible on the lips.

> Speechreading, whenever possible, must always be subordinated to hearing. It can supplement hearing, but it is no substitute for hearing. Most of the motor (muscular) movements involved in sound formation occur within the mouth and cannot be detected by the eye. The lip movements play a relatively minor part in the formation of sound.... Under usual viewing conditions, it is estimated that approximately 60% of the speech sounds are either obscure or invisible (Jeffers, 1974, pp. 14–17).

The lipreader learns to recognize some sounds from watching the speaker's lips, but he must guess the rest of the communication from the context and from visual clues. Lipreading is a skill which requires good vision, good knowledge of language, an ability to concentrate, and a certain mental agility and flexibility. Intelligence seems to be necessary, but it is not sufficient. Some people have a talent for lipreading; others do not. Even those people with good lipreading skill are limited to communication which is directed specifically to them. They must be able to see the speaker clearly. The light must be good. The speaker may need to talk more slowly than usual, to give the lipreader time to make the necessary guesses. In a group situation, the deafened person has difficulty knowing where to look, and he misses the rapid movement of the conversation. Lipreading itself is fatiguing, so the deafened person cannot converse for long periods of time. In all conversations, he misses the vital information transmitted through the tone of the speaker's voice. For those deafened people who are able to lipread, then, the skill helps to a degree, in some listening situations, for some of the time.

In addition to these significant deprivations from loss of hearing at the symbolic level, deafness involves losses in other dimensions. The warning or environmental level of hearing refers to the noises which alert us to circumstances in the environment. Hearing is the one sense which enables us to scan our environment. from all directions at once, regardless of our specific attention, of light, of obstacles between us and the source of sound, and even of whether we are asleep or awake. Hearing at this level enables us to anticipate changes in our environment, such as the approach of another person. The absence of unusual noise gives us constant reassurance that all is well.

The primitive level of hearing refers to the subtle, constant, connection with the rhythm of life which sound provides. Hearing at this level gives us a sense of being part of the environment and of other living things. It is impossible for a hearing person to simulate the absence of hearing at this level. But hearing at the primitive level gives us much of our sense of being alive (Ramsdell, 1970).

Psycho-Social Impact of Deafness

COMMUNICATION PROBLEMS

When deafness interferes with communication, all human relationships are affected, and the person feels an overwhelming sense of isolation. He can see other people, but he feels as if he is locked behind a glass wall. He may be able to obtain some information by lipreading, or by persuading people to write. But lipreading requires great concentration and energy and, even with the greatest skill and the utmost attention, a great deal of misunderstanding will occur. Whenever the person is tired or preoccupied, his lipreading skill decreases. The sharing of ideas or experiences becomes a labored and sometimes impossible process. Easy, social intimate conversations become awkward. Casual interchanges with strangers are lost completely. The person is alone.

For many people, a sense of adequacy is connected with making appropriate responses to verbal information or to a social situation. When a person cannot understand what others have said, he is at a loss as to what to do. He feels awkward, stupid, and useless.

Much of the emotional content of conversation is transmitted by subtle changes in one's tone of voice, or in words which are deliberately said under one's breath. Humor, particularly, is often expressed in low tones, or while people are smiling, and thus hard to lipread. The deafened person misses many of the lighter moments, which are important in communication, and he also misses the discharge of tension and the feeling of closeness which shared laughter can bring.

All deafened people live with the reality that they misunderstand a great deal of what is said to them or around them. They often feel embarrassed by their mistakes, and terrified that others will label them as stupid. Hearing people often become impatient with the deafened person, and they sometimes react by excluding him from discussions and from decision-making processes. Some people actually take advantage of the person's deafness, by laughing at his misunderstanding, by talking about him in his presence, or by withholding information from him. One popular characterization of deaf people is that they are suspicious. Studies of the personalities of deafened people show that the incidence of paranoia is no higher in the hearing-impaired population than in the population at large. The suspicion shown by deafened people seems appropriate in view of the real responses they encounter from the public (Knapp, 1948; Levine, 1962).

The deafened person knows that other people have to go to some trouble to enable him to understand. Many people refuse to make the necessary accommodations, and the deafened person becomes angry at those individuals, and sometimes at society in general. Then, when people are willing to make the effort, the deafened person's sense of inadequacy is intensified by his awareness that others are going to some trouble for him.

> I took a cup of tea to a table to join four friends. When one of them asked me a question which I could not understand, the other repeated it for me, but I was still unable to lipread it. They paused while one of them wrote it down and I was aware that the easy-going conversation they had been enjoying before my arrival was now disrupted ... within a few minutes two of them left and after a brief pause the others explained that they had to go because of pressing engagements. They were genuinely sorry and I understood, but it was small solace as I sat alone drinking my tea (Ashley, 1973, p. 149).

The deafened person almost inevitably loses some of his friends along with his hearing. Almost every individual's social group includes at least some people who are unwilling to accept the slow and labored communication of a newly deaf person. Other people are threatened or repelled by the sheer intensity of the deafened person's feelings. Also, the deafened person's style of socializing is limited. He can no longer enjoy his friends in large groups, or in noisy or visually distracting surroundings. He cannot converse socially for more than an hour or two at a time. His whole social life is altered. His loss in this area ranges from moderate to enormous, depending on the quality of his friendships and on his previous social habits.

ALIENATION FROM SELF AND ENVIRONMENT

In addition to the problems caused by difficulties in communication, deafened people suffer from alienation from their environment. Events are no longer announced for them in advance, by the sounds of footsteps approaching, brakes squeaking, or a door opening. A deafened person is forever being surprised, and is therefore in continual expectation of being caught unprepared. Nervousness, anxiety, and fear are common experiences. People who had been comfortable living alone can become fearful of their own safety. The sense of loss of control over the environment brings stress into all aspects of daily life.

Objects in the environment seem to lose their identities when they lose their characteristic sounds. When one cannot hear the sounds of one's own body, a person can feel detached even from himself. Breathing, coughing, walking, or turning over in bed become disorienting experiences when they are unaccompanied by sound. A deafened person may feel suddenly alienated from the world and from himself (Levine, 1962).

The deafened person not only misses sounds which are really in the environment, but often "hears" sounds which are not from outside, but which come from his own inner ear. Deafened people frequently suffer from tinnitus, or head noises. A truly deaf person may "hear" sounds which, to him, may be as soft as a distant hum, or as loud and intrusive as a clanging or roaring sound. Strong emotion may intensify the experience, but it is a physical phenomenon, caused by damage in the nerves within the ear. The deafened person, then, has lost the comforts of both sound and silence.

Some deafened people retain a small amount of residual hearing. Although useless for understanding words or perceiving warning sounds, this degree of hearing helps the person to feel alive. If that last shred of hearing is lost, a depression results which seems greater than even the losses outlined above can fully explain (Ramsdell, 1970). "That fragile wisp of hearing had maintained for me a slender contact with the ordinary world; it had given some sense of reality, a hint of that background of sound, which, to a normal person, is so familiar as to be unnoticed. Without it, life was eerie (Ashley, 1973, p. 136)."

IDENTITY CRISIS

Implicit in the above discussion is a recognition that a deafened person has great difficulty functioning comfortably and competently with hearing people. His previous life style is drastically altered, and new skills, new social habits, and, in some cases, a new vocation must be found. A common misconception is that a deafened person is now like other deaf people, and able to find a satisfactory new sense of community in a society of prelingually deaf people. The first barrier to integration into the deaf community is language. Even after considerable effort to learn sign language, a deafened person may not have developed fluency in American Sign Language and his first encounter with a prelingually deaf person can be a frustrating and distressing experience. In addition to language problems, there are cultural differences. People deaf since birth have had a very different life experience from hearing people, and have developed attitudes and a culture of their own. Hearing people and deafened people can learn about the language and culture of deafness, but only with a great deal of time and careful attention. By the same token, many prelingually deaf people are understandably suspicious of hearing people, and a deafened person, after all, is essentially a hearing person who can no longer hear. A deafened person can encounter as much misunderstanding and suspicion from the deaf community as from many hearing people. Holly Elliott (1978), a professional counselor who is, herself, deafened, described the problem clearly:

> Even now I find myself wondering from time to time who I really am. Hearing people often think I am hearing because my speech is good; deaf people often think I am hearing because my signs are bad ... Hearing people have their culture based on spoken language and deaf people have their culture based on sign language and we are caught between incomprehensible speech on the one hand and incomprehensible signs on the other. If only those hearies would

talk more clearly! If only those deafies would sign more slowly! Who's taking care of us?

Crisis

Along with these powerful and disturbing feelings, many of which will persist throughout his life, the deafened person at some point undergoes a crisis, and experiences all of the stages of adjustment which have been noted for people going through a catastrophic change (Kübler-Ross, 1969). The literature on reactions to crisis is enormous and there is no need to summarize it here. It is important, however, to examine the ways in which a deafened person experiences each stage.

Deafened people vary tremendously in the time they need to go through the stages of reaction to crisis. Some people remain in one stage for many years. There are some special reasons for the variation in time. Deafness is an invisible handicap and many uninformed people under-estimate its significance. Deafened people are frequently reinforced by others for remaining in the stage of denial. Services for deafened people are scattered and inadequate, so many people are not offered the help they need to experience and cope with the various stages of adaptation. Also, even after achieving a high level of adaptation to deafness, an individual may at any time encounter a new experience which threatens his adjust-ment and plummets him into a stage he had long since mastered. For these reasons, it is impossible to predict what stage an individual might be in on the basis of the length of time he has been deaf.

The stage of denial is reflected in many people in feelings that there is a doctor or medical procedure somewhere which will make him hear again. Many people go from one doctor to another, then into acupuncture or other methods, all in the desperate hope of finding a cure. Sometimes people shop for the perfect hearing aid with the same desperation. Occasionally, as a person learns lipreading skills, he imagines how words sound, and he feels as if he is hearing again. His communication skills are likely to be uneven, and he may use his better moments to convince himself that the disability is not really significant. A sad by-product of the stage of denial is a refusal to learn useful skills, such as lipreading and sign language, and also a refusal to meet other deafened people. When a person remains in this stage, he can be immobilized for long periods of time, with devastating consequences to his rehabilitation.

The anger of a deafened person has many natural targets. First, there are doctors who have failed to restore hearing. Then there are audiologists and social workers, whose skills are never adequate to relieve the person's all-consuming pain and panic. And of course the general public knows all too little about deafness. The deafened person meets countless individuals who insist on talking with their backs turned, or with their mouths covered, who mumble, or who have the audacity to sport a mustache. There are still far too many people who think of deaf people as "deaf and dumb," and who associate deafness with stupidity or senility. Other people are convinced that, if a person can speak he can hear, and they act as if the deafened person is lying or malingering. These realities give the deafened person a legitimate basis for feeling that other people are to blame for his problems, and they make it difficult for him to move beyond this necessary phase of his adjustment.

Bargaining is occasionally expressed directly. One man said, "If only my ears hurt. I'd gladly stand the pain, if I could just have my hearing back."

Guilt is sometimes evident in a person's concern about the difficulties his deafness causes others. If the deafness was caused by an accident, some people view their deafness as fitting punishment for their carelessness. If the condition is hereditary, the person may feel responsible for passing the problems on to another generation. Until these feelings are worked through, rehabilitation is impossible.

The many reasons for a deafened person to be depressed have been given above. Another important dimension to depression for a deafened person is that it also interferes with learning and using communication skills. The depression, in itself, can block communication and intensify a person's sense of isolation.

> There is a great difference between grief and depression. Deafness is a frightening loss and grief is a natural response to loss, an active process that must be experienced to be resolved. Depression is a giving-up process, a long term withdrawal. The feeling of being 'left-out'—and not doing anything about it—is a feeling of depression. I have a hunch that depression interferes with communication more than deafness. The combination of deafness and depression makes communication very difficult (Elliott, 1978).

After the person acknowledges his loss as reality and experiences all of the feelings the loss inspires, he is able to adapt constructively to his deafness. He actively learns all appropriate communication skills. He starts to convey an interest in other people, a desire to communicate, and a sense of humor about his misunderstanding. As he learns to help other people feel comfortable with him, his social world expands considerably. He may be able to find compensations for the recreational and aesthetic experiences he misses. Holly Elliott (1978) for example, used to be a choral conductor; she now directs a sign language choir in her church. Joann Bartley (1978) also has found compensations which help her: "True, I can't hear music but I can still dance and watch someone sign a song. I can still go to parties and play sports. True, I can't hear, but I can still listen. Many people who can hear can't listen." Good adaptive skills enable a deafened person to have many satisfying experiences, and to feel some justifiable pride in the strengths he has found within himself.

When people talk about crisis, however, they often end with a discussion of acceptance, as if this is the goal the individual and his social worker should seek.

> We on the outside talk pretty glibly of 'accepting disability.' To accept sudden severe deafness is to accept the abrupt transition from pulsating life to the isolation, unreality, and flatness of a soundless world while at the same time straining to keep up with the demands of a hearing one (Levine, 1962, p. 304).

To ask another human being to accept such a global disruption to his whole existence seems arrogant indeed. A deafened person is never going to forget what his life was like when he could hear, and he will always miss many parts of his former world. One woman, who has become very successful personally and professionally in a community of hearing and deafened people, still gets tears in her eyes when she allows herself to think about music. Another person has maintained a continually positive attitude in recent years, and has found many activities which are fulfilling for her. But when playing happily with her new grandchild, she suddenly became deeply pained as she realized that she would never hear the child's voice. Acceptance, then, is never so complete that it cannot be shattered by some reminder of the past or an inadvertent expectation of an unimpaired future.

Clues for Assessment

There is no real psychology of the deafened. Deafness has a particular set of difficulties which each person handles in his own way (Knapp, 1948, p. 208). To understand the meaning of deafness in the life of an individual, it is necessary to do a thorough assessment of that person's personality, his history, and his strengths. The social worker might well consider the same questions and issues as in any psychosocial assessment. Some additional questions might be raised, however:

- —What is the history of this person's deafness? Was the loss gradual or sudden? How long has the person been deaf? What rehabilitation has been attempted?
- —How has this person coped with other losses and crises? What are his defenses? What are his strengths?
- —What are his social supports? Does he have close friends or relatives who will stay with him as he handles his problems?
- —Which of the feelings associated with deafness are particularly threatening to him? Is he prone to anger and projection? Is it hard for him to ask other people to accommodate themselves to him?

Is he generally insecure, especially sensitive to feelings of social inadequacy? Is he fearful? Is being alone hard for him?
—What was his style for socializing? Did he enjoy being with one or two people at a time, or was his social life primarily in large groups?
—Is his work dependent on his hearing? If so, can adaptations be made in his job responsibility, or will he have to find a new career?
—What is his aptitude for learning compensatory skills? How is his vision? How well does he know English, or his native language? Is he flexible enough to tolerate the imperfection of lipreading? Does he have the manual dexterity necessary for sign language? Does he enjoy learning?
—Does he have interests or hobbies which are not dependent on hearing? What meaning did music have in his life?
—Does he have a sense of humor? Is he able to laugh at some of his misunderstanding?
—What is his philosophical or spiritual perspective? Does he have the capacity to care about issues larger than himself? Is he able to appreciate positive experiences, beautiful sights, or moments of shared understanding, even in the midst of deprivation?

Rehabilitation

If a social worker is to help a deafened person cope with his disability, he must have a general idea about the different rehabilitative options available. The benefits and limits of lipreading have been discussed above. Some deafened people may be able to benefit from lipreading classes, or from individual instruction.

Most deafened people resist the idea of learning sign language at first, largely because their relatives, friends, and colleagues do not use it. If the person overcomes that mental barrier, he often finds that sign language gives him the opportunity for full, easy communication at least with the few other people he knows who use it. The social support available from other people who are learning the new language can be very valuable. One difficulty is that there are different forms of sign language. Deafened people tend to be most comfortable with Siglish (Signed English) or some form of sign language which follows the syntax and linguistic structure of English. Anyone with a solid knowledge of English finds such kinds of sign language easier to learn than the native language of deaf people, which is Ameslan (American Sign Language). Ameslan uses many of the same hand positions as Siglish, but grammar and word order are quite different. Also, Ameslan requires some use of facial expression and spacial relationships (Fant, 1977). A deafened person who learns Siglish may find himself unable to communicate with a prelingually deaf person, whose first language is Ameslan. If the deafened person can be assisted in clarifying his goals for the use of sign language, he can then be referred to the most appropriate program.

Deafened people, of course, cannot use a regular telephone, but there is special equipment which can provide some telephone communication. Teletype Devices for the Deaf (TDD's) are machines which enable a person to type messages through telephone lines. The equipment is expensive, and it enables the person to communicate directly only with other people who have compatible machinery. In some communities, there are TDD answering services, through which a deaf person can make telephone contact with people using voice phones only.

With a small amount of electrical work, homes can be wired for sound. Lights can be hooked up so that they flash when a doorbell rings or when a baby cries. There are alarm clocks which awaken a person with a flashing light, or with a vibrator placed under the pillow or in the bed frame. The American Humane Association is currently training "Signal Dogs," dogs who regularly alert their deaf owners to sounds in the environment.

Suggestions for the Hearing Social Worker

A social worker's first job is to establish communication with his client. Once this is accomplished, he is able to use all of his clinical and practical skills normally at his disposal. He no longer feels helpless. Many deafened people lipread to some extent, so clear, slow speech, in good visual contact with the client, may help a great deal. Minimizing background noise and visual distraction will help. If the client knows the subject under discussion, he has a better opportunity to lipread, so the worker might first establish the general subject, maybe by writing one or two words, or by restating that part of the communication until assured that the client understands. Some clients appreciate it if the worker writes at least some of the communication. Some clients prefer to use sign language, and would welcome a sign language interpreter. The only way for the social worker to know what is appropriate is to ask the client. Not only does the direct question yield essential information, it also opens up the whole area of communication style for frank discussion.

The lives of many deafened people are more limited than necessary, because of ignorance about the rehabilitative options discussed above. By its very nature, deafness limits a person's access to information, so special efforts are often necessary to keep the person informed. A social worker can be of tremendous help to a deafened client simply by obtaining accurate information about all available resources, their merits, and their limitations.

Social workers are accustomed to working at a certain pace. Communication with a deafened person is significantly slower than with a hearing client. It is also slower than working in sign language when the client and worker are fluent in manual communication. It is easy for a social worker to become impatient. The only answer to this problem is to accept a slower pace as a necessity, to budget time accordingly, and to remember that the deafened client is at least as impatient as the worker.

The social worker inevitably recognizes that deafness imposes real limitations upon the deafened person's functioning. It may be necessary and appropriate for the worker to engage in activities which he would normally expect his client to handle by himself. Because the worker can use the telephone and the client cannot, for example, the worker may need to make some phone calls for the client. Once involved in a client's personal phone call, however, it is all too easy for the worker to become active in areas of the client's life which do not warrant his intervention. The worker needs to be flexible, willing to go beyond the usual confines of a clinical role, when such activity is appropriate. But he must also remember that the client's inability to hear does not in itself interfere with his ability to make his own decisions. The worker's challenge, essentially, is to remain sensitive to the nature and scope of the problem of deafness and, at the same time, to maintain confidence in the client's capacity to manage his disability and his life.

There are few disabilities which affect a person's life as broadly and profoundly as deafness. Work with deafened clients is difficult, presenting a real test of a worker's flexibility of style, depth of understanding, and tolerance for pain. At the same time, deafened clients offer a social worker a rare opportunity when they allow him to share their intense experiences and participate in their struggle for a satisfying life in an altered world.

References

ASHLEY, J. M. P. *Journey into silence.* London: The Bodley Head Ltd. 1973.

BARTLEY, J. Unpublished Speech, San Francisco, 1978.

CHOUGH, S. K. Casework with the deaf; a problem in communication. In Francis J. Turner (Ed.), *Differential diagnosis and treatment in social work,* Second edition. New York: Free Press, 1976.

ELLIOTT, H. Acquired deafness: Shifting gears. Unpublished Speech, San Francisco, 1978.

FANT, L. J. *Ameslan, an introduction to american sign language.* Northridge, California: Joyce Motion Picture Company, 1977.

HURWITZ, S. N. The contributions of social work practice to the mental health of the hearing impaired. In Kenneth Z. Altshuler and John D. Rainer (Eds.), *Mental health and the deaf: Approaches and prospects.* U.S. Department of Health, Education, and Welfare, 1969.

JEFFERS, J. and BARLEY, M. *Speechreading (lipreading)*. Springfield, Illinois: Charles C. Thomas, 1974.

KNAPP, P. H. Emotional aspects of hearing loss. *Psychosomatic Medicine*, 1948, 10, 203–222.

KRUG, R. F. The relevance of audiologic data in planning mental health services for the acoustically impaired. In Kenneth Z. Altshuler and John D. Rainer (Eds.), *Mental health and the deaf: Approaches and prospects*. U. S. Department of Health, Education, and Welfare, 1969.

KÜBLER-ROSS, E. *On death and dying*. London: Macmillan, 1969.

LEVINE, E. S. Auditory disability. In James F. Garrett and Edna S. Levine (Eds.), *Psychological practice with the physically disabled*. New York: Columbia University Press, 1962.

NEWBOLD, H. S. L. Social work with the deaf: A model, *Social Work*, 24(2), March, 1979, 153–156.

RAMSDELL, D. A. The psychology of the hard of hearing and the deafened adult. In Hallowell Davis and Richard S. Silverman (Eds.). *Hearing and deafness*, third edition. New York: Holt, Rinehart, and Winston, 1970.

SCHEIN, J. D. and DELK, M. T. *The deaf population of the united states*. Silver Spring, Maryland: National Association of the Deaf, 1974.

SILVER, M. K. Casework with deaf clients. In U.S. Department of Health, Education, and Welfare, *Orientation of social workers to the problems of deaf persons*. Berkeley, California: University of California, 1963.

DIABETES

CHAPTER 35

The Diabetic Client

Mary W. Engelmann

Diabetes Mellitus is a common disease in North America. In Canada alone there are approximately 200,000 known diabetics. This figure will undoubtedly increase as detection methods improve, and as greater medical knowledge enables diabetics to enjoy longer and healthier lives. Social workers in both medical settings and community agencies can expect to see more individuals with this chronic condition in the future.

At first glance it would not seem that this handicap is particularly serious. Diabetes does not have a marked effect on the victim's appearance and no stigma is attached to it. The well-regulated diabetic can, with few exceptions, participate in most activities and he meets with relatively little discrimination in job-seeking.[1] Is it necessary then for the social worker— whether in a medical setting or not—to be concerned about the implications of this handicap? The answer can be found by examining the illness more closely.

In diabetes, more than in any other chronic illness, there is a delicate interplay between the victim's emotional life and satisfactions and his ability to live with and control his condition. The requirements for adequate diabetic control can affect the person's attitude to himself and his interpersonal relationships. Much depends on the previously existing personality patterns of the individual and the interaction of his family life. Those persons who have made reasonably satisfactory adjustments find it easier

[1] A. H. Kantrow, M.D., "Employment Experiences of Juvenile Diabetics," *Diabetes*, Vol. 10 (1961), pp. 476–481. This article is a report on a survey of the employment experiences of the alumni of the camp for diabetic children in New York.

Reprinted from *The Social Worker*, Vol. 35 (February, 1967), pp. 6–10, by permission of the author and publisher.

to cope with diabetes, though even in the best of circumstances, there are periods of stress, anxiety and anger. For the person with problems, whether emotional or environmental, diabetes can be particularly upsetting and difficult.

Emotional Health and Control

An understanding of the interaction between emotional health and diabetic control, along with an understanding of some of the specific anxieties and problems encountered by the diabetic, should enable the social worker to assist him more skillfully.

There are varying degrees of diabetic severity. The older individual who develops diabetes generally has a milder form of the illness and his diabetes can be controlled through diet alone, or through diet and oral medication. In a person under forty years of age, diabetes is generally more severe, requires insulin therapy, and is often much more difficult to control.

Diabetes and Emotional Stress

While diabetes is generally considered to be an inherited condition, due to a metabolic defect, there is some indication that it can be precipitated by emotional stress. Some studies suggest that the onset of diabetes may have been preceded by a period of deprivation, particularly loss of emotional support, unconscious conflict and depression.[2] Obviously, in such situations, the individual is weakened in his ability to cope with the meaning of the diagnosis. The new diabetic may be shocked, frightened, and even have moments of panic. He may feel a sense of despair because he faces a lifelong incurable condition. The amount of technical information he must absorb about diet and insulin therapy can seem overwhelming, and he may have doubts about his ability to care for himself. Along with this great increase in anxiety can come feelings of inadequacy and insecurity as he is faced with the awareness of physical limitation, dependency on insulin and continuous medical supervision.

Parents of a diabetic child have many of the same reactions as the adult diabetic, and often have a great sense of guilt. Irrational feelings of having neglected their child, or of having passed on a hereditary defect are present in almost every instance. The parents of a diabetic child are often over-

[2] P. F. Slawson, M.D., W. K. Flynn, M.D., E. J. Kollar, M.D., "Psychological Factors Associated with the Onset of Diabetes Mellitus," *JAMA—Journal of the American Medical Association,* Vol. 185, No. 3 (1963), pp. 96–100. E. Weiss and O. W. English, *Psychosomatic Medicine, A Clinical Study of Psychophysiologic Reactions,* 3rd Edition 1957, pp. 334–335.

whelmed by the technical information given them. Parents, at such a time, need the opportunity to discuss their anxiety and receive supportive help in developing their strengths and capabilities.

Diabetes is controlled through a therapeutic regime consisting of a restricted diet, insulin injections, and regular exercise. Adequate rest and regularity in meals are important. As it is a condition which must be regulated on a day-to-day basis, diabetes must be controlled by the patient himself, or, in the case of a young child, by his parents. The doctor can determine the initial regulation, can advise, and can help in illness or emergency situations, but the diabetic himself is responsible for the actual treatment.

Emotional upsets, in addition to illness, will have a definite physiological effect, actually raising the blood sugar level, thereby adding to an already complicated job.[3] Diabetic coma and insulin reactions are two serious and immediate complications which can develop. In the former, the blood sugar level becomes too high, and the person loses consciousness after a period of time. In the latter, which can come on suddenly, the blood sugar level drops too low, and causes aberrant behaviour and, in the latter stages, results in unconsciousness. Both, if untreated, can lead to death.

Control Can Create Resentment

What meaning does this have for the diabetic individual and his family? The diabetic cannot "adjust" to his diabetes and forget about it. In order to control it effectively, he and his family must be constantly aware of and concerned about it. This situation can create resentment and irritation. The other members of the family find that, at times, their lives and social activities are limited by the diabetic's need to adhere to his regime. For children and adolescents this regime will add to already incipient feelings of being different. Diabetic women may have added concerns about their adequacy as it is difficult for them to carry pregnancies to completion. It is obvious that, even in the best of circumstances, there are going to periods of rebellion, frustration and resentment.

In a disturbed situation diabetes can add to an already charged atmosphere and be used by both the diabetic and his family in an attempt to solve neurotic conflicts. The diabetic regime can become the focus for arguments which usually reflect existing and more deep-rooted personality conflicts. The anger and frustration that all diabetics and their families feel will be exacerbated, added to more basic hostility, and reflected in destructive ways towards self and others. This can result in the diabetic's denial

[3] D. G. Prugh, "Psychophysiological Aspects of Inborn Errors of Metabolism," in H. I., V. F., and N. R. Lief (eds.), *The Psychological Basis of Medical Practice*, New York, Harper & Row, 1963, p. 421.

of the illness and in a lack of adequate concern, manifested in deliberate over-eating or neglect of insulin requirements. In this way the diabetic can control, and indirectly hurt, his family. As he becomes ill, he gains attention and sympathy but, at the same time, adds to his guilt feelings of being a burden. All of this can create a vicious cycle of anger, illness, guilt and depression. The immature, dependent diabetic may use his poorly controlled diabetes and resulting illness as a way of meeting his emotional needs.

Personality Patterns in Diabetes

Some observers say that dependent, passive behaviour is a frequent personality pattern in diabetes. Their views are summarized by Dr. David Hawkins:

> While a wide variety of individual personality patterns are seen in diabetes, clinicians have over and over commented on the frequency of marked passivity, masochism, extreme oral dependency, and frequent retreats into illness in these patients. Rosen and Lidz noted that the refractory diabetic patient "reacted to sibling rivalry by regressively seeking maternal attention by becoming helpless and demanding or negativistic rather than through more active measures." It is easy to see that this illness with its emphasis on diet would facilitate regression to whatever oral dependent behaviour was potentially present in the patient, and there is considerable evidence that in many individuals a passive dependent character structure antedated the onset of the clinical disease. Mirsky postulates that there is an inborn, metabolic problem from birth, even though signs and symptoms of the disease do not become manifest until later, and that this interferes with the development of a confident and mature outlook.[4]

Other observers emphasize that these diabetic personality patterns are the result of and not the cause of the disease. Doctors Philip Isenberg and Donald Barnett, in writing about the personality of the juvenile diabetic, say the following:

> What we have outlined above suggests that there are bound to be certain similarities in the group of diabetic children because of the traumatic effect of the onset of the disease on most families. The persistent vulnerabilities and character trends which have been studied and reported on are probably the consequence of the disease and not its cause. What has been reported is a certain suppression of emotions, a feeling of being oppressed by a frustrating outer world which forces the patients to subordinate themselves to its demands. As a group they feel somewhat restricted and have been shown to be less spon-

[4] D. Hawkins, M.D., "Emotions and Metabolic and Endocrine Disease," Lief, *op. cit.*, pp. 274–275.

taneous and free in the expression of their emotions and fantasies. Since therapy aims to control the disease by imposing restrictions on diet and requiring certain routines to be fulfilled many claim this tends to increase the feelings of being oppressed and frustrated.[5]

Insulin injections can carry implications or self-punishment or self-mutilation to the diabetic. If injections must be given by a member of the family, similar fears with consequent guilt can result for the nondiabetic. The strict regime may carry the implication of punishment and authority and may reactivate in the diabetic earlier unresolved conflicts.[6] Diet restriction may be linked in the individual's mind to a restriction of love or affection, with the result that he may, denying the seriousness of this for his illness, have periods of over-eating, even gorging himself.[7]

The marital partner, fearing that the diabetic may become totally dependent on him, and perhaps resenting the inevitable partial dependency, may become over-solicitous and concerned, thus accentuating the diabetic's sense of being handicapped. Insulin reactions can come on suddenly, even in the best-regulated diabetic. They can be embarrassing as well as dangerous and can result in the diabetic being at times dependent for life or death on his marital partner, family or occasional associates.

Reaction Manipulation

Reactions can be used by both the diabetic and the non-diabetic for control and manipulation. A beginning insulin reaction has some resemblance to an anxiety attack. There have been instances when a diabetic thought he was suffering from fairly frequent reactions but was actually suffering from anxiety (blood sugar levels were found to be normal or above normal).[8]

A case history reported in *Diabetes*, the journal of the American Diabetic Association, illustrates some of the interaction between neurotic disturbance and the control of diabetes.[9] A young woman diabetic was ensnared in a conflict between her parents and her husband. She was unable to decide whether to be the dependent child of her parents or develop a mature relationship with her husband. In spite of the fact that there were

[5] P. Isenberg, M.D., and D. M. Barnett, M.D., "Psychological Problems in Diabetes Mellitus," *The Medical Clinics of North America*, Vol. 49, No. 2 (1965), pp. 1127–1128.

[6] F. Upham, *A Dynamic Approach to Illness*, New York, Family Service Association of America, 1949, pp. 91–92.

[7] Lief, *op. cit.*, p. 420.

[8] E. Weiss and O. S. English, *op. cit.*, p. 342.

[9] G. L. Schless, M.D., and R. von Laveran-Stiebar, M.D., "Recurrent Episodes of Diabetic Acidosis Precipitated by Emotional Stress," *Diabetes*, Vol. 13, No. 4 (July-August, 1964), pp. 419–420.

frequent arguments and scenes between all members of the family, the presence of tension was denied.

This young woman was admitted to the hospital five times in one year in diabetic coma, always following a family argument. There was ample evidence that there was no neglect of insulin treatment or diet, and that the comas were her attempt to escape from her problem. She could retreat into the relative safety and neutrality of the hospital and at the same time receive attention and sympathy. Psychiatric help enabled both her and her family to develop some insight and alleviate the tension-producing situations. As a result her diabetes came under much better control.

Much has been written about the particular problems that are encountered in the family with a diabetic child and about the importance of seeing that the child's emotional growth is not blocked by the condition. There are some particular problems that may be encountered when diabetes develops in a family where there is already a disturbed parent-child or marital relationship. All parents have some resentment about the extra care and responsibility required by the diabetic child. However, in some instances, the child himself may be resented and rejected. Parents may show this by using the diabetic regime in a punitive way under the guise of achieving good control. Over-protection and over-anxiety can accentuate the child's sense of handicap and may be an expression of hostility. Parents may, by using the rationalization that the child must become independent, give the child too much responsibility for his diabetic control and then blame him when things go wrong. A history from the records of the Social Service Department of the Royal Alexandra Hospital, Edmonton, illustrates this latter point.

A diabetic child, aged eight years, was the third of four children. There was much conflict between the parents. The mother, a nervous tense woman, suffered from asthma. The father, quiet and passive, was somewhat aloof from the family situation. Neither parent understood diabetes adequately and neither was able to enforce the necessary discipline concerning diet and rest. The child was given a great deal of responsibility for his own diabetic care. When difficulties developed and he had to be hospitalized, he was blamed by his parents for this.

It would appear essential that the social worker be aware of the ramifications of diabetes in working with afflicted clients. Recognizing this the New York City Diabetic Association has set up a special counseling service for diabetics. This service not only works directly with diabetics, but also provides specialized information on diabetes to community agencies.[10]

While many diabetics appear to be able to cope successfully with their

[10] A. H. Kantrow, M.D., "A Vocational and Counselling Service for Diabetics," *Diabetes*, Vol. 12, No. 5 (1963), pp. 454–457.

condition, there are always a number who fail to do so and stumble through life with an increasing complex of physical and emotional problems. It is these people who are most likely to come to the attention of social agencies, and it is in working with them that a knowledge of the particular problems of diabetes is necessary.

EPILEPSY

CHAPTER 36

Social Work with Epileptic Patients

Larry L. Smith

It has been estimated that more than 4 million people in the United States have epilepsy.[1] Social workers who have counseled and dealt with patients who are epileptics can attest to the physical and psychosocial problems encountered by these individuals and their families. Ignorance, superstition, and misinformation prevailing among the public have "invested the term epilepsy with unwarranted fearful and distasteful connotations."[2] However, professionals who counsel epileptic patients must have an accurate and unprejudiced understanding of the illness if they are to help these patients and their families cope with the problems that attend it. Such an understanding should also be acquired by others who interact with these patients. The present article will therefore review many of the physical and psychosocial aspects of epilepsy and discuss how social workers can help epileptic patients and their families lead more productive lives.

Nature of the Disease

Epilepsy is not painful or disfiguring and does not shorten life. It has been defined as

> an intermittent disorder of the nervous system due presumably to a sudden, excessive, disorderly discharge of cerebral neurons [which] results in an almost

instantaneous disturbance of sensation, loss of consciousness, convulsive movement, or some combination thereof.[3]

Epilepsy may begin at any age and may affect both men and women. Epileptic seizures that occur before age 2 are generally related to developmental defects and birth injuries, whereas the cause of seizures that begin in the individual between the third and fifteenth years of life is unknown. Seizures occurring in the individual after age 25 are usually related to trauma or organic brain disease.[4] In a survey of nearly 2,000 patients with epilepsy, 51 percent of the patients reported having grand mal seizures, 8 percent petit mal, or minor, seizures, 1 percent psychomotor, or psychic, seizures, and the remaining 40 percent reported having two or even all three of these types of seizures.[5]

Grand mal seizures are the most common type of convulsion associated with epilepsy. They may begin with the individual's losing consciousness and uttering a cry. The back then becomes rigid, the muscles in the arms and legs stiffen, and the eyes roll upward. The arms and legs may make jerking movements, and there may be frothing at the mouth and wetting and soiling. Individuals experiencing these seizures may become pale or bluish in color and may bite their tongue or cheek as their jaw muscles clench. The seizures usually last for only a few minutes, and those who undergo them are exhausted and confused afterward and often fall into a deep sleep. Individuals usually have no memory of having undergone a grand mal seizure.

Petit mal seizures usually occur in children. These attacks are so brief that they are often overlooked, and many people experience them for years before their occurrence is noticed. After a brief loss of consciousness, the individual is able to continue with whatever he or she was doing before the onset of the seizure. Those undergoing such seizures seem to be daydreaming or staring momentarily, their arms may jerk slightly, and their eyelids may blink repeatedly. Petit mal seizures can occur in an individual many times each day and can eventually lead to grand mal attacks.

Psychomotor seizures are brief periods of clouded consciousness during which the individual may perform complicated movements. These movements may include walking, climbing, making chewing movements, and picking at or removing clothing worn. Unusual sensations such as strange tastes and odors are sometimes experienced at the beginning of a psychomotor attack, and the individual retains no memory of having experienced the seizure. Those undergoing such seizures may get up and walk about, may attempt to speak, and may resist or become violent when restrained.

Before they fall or lose consciousness, many patients experience sensations that warn them of the onset of a seizure. These warnings are called auras, and their appearance often enables the individual to find a safe place in which to prepare for the seizure and avoid injury. The most common aura is a sinking or ripping feeling in the stomach, but other auras include a tingling or numbness in the fingers or lips, a flashing light before the eyes, or a disagreeable taste or odor. A sensation of anxiety, tenseness, or fear may also constitute the aura of a seizure. Although an aura acts as a warning, it is actually the first part of the seizure and not a separate phenomenon.[6]

Treatment

Drugs called anticonvulsants are used to control seizures. However, no one drug controls every kind of seizure. Common anticonvulsants include Dilantin, Mysoline, Tegretol, and phenobarbital. All these drugs may have undesirable side effects, the most notable being the drowsiness and sluggishness caused by phenobarbital. Because anticonvulsants vary in their effects from one individual to another, an effective seizure control program for a patient is as individualized and specific as a prescription for a pair of eyeglasses.

Physicians usually begin treatment for epilepsy with one or two anticonvulsants they believe will control, with the least number of side effects, the type of seizure experienced by the patient. The dosage of these drugs may gradually be increased until the seizures are controlled or until the patient is taking as much medication as he or she can tolerate. In cases in which medication has been increased to the patient's level of tolerance and the seizures are still not completely under control, a third and perhaps even a fourth drug may be prescribed. In this way, new medications are added to the patient's regimen and dosages are adjusted over a period of time until the best possible effect has been reached in the opinion of both patient and physician.[7]

However, patients taking anticonvulsant drugs may still undergo seizures. If a patient experiences an aura, he or she may be able to find a safe place in which to have the seizure without falling or getting hurt. If the seizure occurs without warning, other people can help the patient in various ways. Injury can be prevented by cushioning the fall to the floor and by keeping the person from falling against sharp objects. Tight clothing should be loosened, especially at the neck, and saliva and froth should be wiped away from the mouth so that they are not inhaled. Before the jaw is clenched shut, a soft object too big to swallow should be inserted between the teeth to prevent the tongue and cheeks from being bitten. Because hard objects may damage the teeth, a folded handkerchief or a stick that is thickly wrapped with a cloth is best for this purpose. If the jaw is clenched, attempts should not be made to open it. Essentially, it is important not to restrain the body's movements during the seizure but to allow them to occur without the person or those nearby suffering injury. The application of strong restraint tends to make the person's movements more violent and can result in bone fractures and injuries to muscles and tendons.[8]

Accepting Epilepsy

Before patients can learn to cope with epilepsy, they and their families must accept the illness. That is often difficult for them to do in the face of the myths and superstitions that surround the disease. Some experts have even suggested that use of the term "epilepsy" be avoided because of the prevailing misunderstandings and distortions associated with it:

> The word "epilepsy," which in times past meant the "falling evil," has many unpleasant connotations, and although it is a useful medical term, probably it is best avoided in open discussions until the general public becomes more enlightened.[9]

These "unpleasant connotations" include suggestions of insanity, mental retardation, and possession by demons. The author believes that if the term "seizure disorder" were substituted for "epilepsy" on a widespread scale, patients and their families could avoid being associated with many of these implications and be spared some grief. However, this substitution of terms would be reduced to a question of semantics if the numerous distortions and untruths that are rife about epilepsy are not exposed to the general public.

One of the best ways in which social workers can help patients and their families accept the reality of epilepsy is through education. For example, each newly diagnosed patient at the University Medical Center in Salt Lake City, Utah, is given several brochures about epilepsy and is encouraged to read them with his or her family and to discuss any questions with their physician during their next visit. At that time the patient and family are introduced to their social worker, who discusses with them many of the psychosocial concerns experienced by other patients and the ways in which these concerns and problematic situations might be dealt with if they were to occur. The focus of the discussions with the physician and social worker is to instill in the patient and family the belief that epilepsy is an illness not unlike other medical disorders and that it can be controlled with the proper medication.

Myths and Fears

Social workers should be prepared to discuss many commonly held fears about epilepsy with patients and their families. Most of these fears are based on ageless myths, one of which states that epilepsy causes insanity and mental retardation. There is no evidence to suggest that this is the case. The persistence of such a belief may be attributable to the fact that brain injuries suffered in infancy have been known to cause both epilepsy and mental defects. Nevertheless, injury to the brain is only one of many possible causes of epilepsy. Electric shock, asphyxia, and high fever can also cause epileptic seizures. Social workers must help patients and families understand these facts and assure them that epileptic patients are not and will not become insane or retarded because of their seizures.

Another myth states that epilepsy is transmitted from one generation to another. However, hereditary factors play only a minor role in the occurrence of the disease, and the individual with epilepsy should not view his or her illness as a reason for not getting married or having children. The author has counseled a number of patients and families who have had this misconception about epilepsy, which was often fostered by relatives and friends who were ignorant or misinformed about the disease. Moreover, on more than one occasion he has counseled patients who have been rejected by friends because of epilepsy. In some instances, the discovery that the individual or another family member is epileptic has lead to broken engagements and annulled marriages.

It is important for social workers to help patients and their families understand that with proper medication epilepsy can in most instances be controlled without interfering with the individual's life-style and social functioning. Physicians, lawyers, plumbers, electricians, postal workers, and individuals in many other professions have had epilepsy and have continued to function. In short, patients can live happy and productive lives as long as they continue to take their medication on a regular basis.

Working with Children

Working with children who have epilepsy poses special problems for the social worker. To begin with, epilepsy is often difficult to diagnose in young children, for what may in fact be a petit mal seizure may be interpreted as the workings of a short attention span or an instance of momentary forgetfulness. Frequently, a child's illness is not diagnosed until a grand mal attack has occurred. Social workers dealing with parents who believe their child appears faint, confused, or distant should encourage them to consult with a physician as soon as possible. This is most important because obtaining an accurate diagnosis is the first step in coping with epilepsy.

Furthermore, it is generally difficult to explain to a child that he or she has epilepsy. Unlike adults, children are not always aware of their disheveled appearance following a seizure. It is also hard for them to imagine how confused and frightened some people become when witnessing an epileptic attack. They therefore have trouble understanding why their playmates might be friendly at one moment and frightened the next or why their friends might suddenly make fun of them or even push them away in fear. Being rejected by their peers in this way can be devastating for children and can lead to the development of serious emotional problems. Parents may also reject a child if they do not understand his or her illness and learn to cope with it.

Nevertheless, the parents of children who have epilepsy must help them gain an understanding of their illness. This may be difficult, depending on the age of the child. The author suggests that information about the disease be withheld from children until they are five years of age or are about to begin school. At this time, their parents should tell them they have a medical problem that sometimes causes them to be forgetful and even to black out. Although children are generally not able to recall having seizures, they often remember times during the day when they forgot what they were doing or became faint. Children who suffer from grand mal attacks can sometimes recall their disheveled appearance following a seizure and the embarrassment of soiling themselves.

Some parents can talk with their child about epilepsy with little or no difficulty. Others find the task distasteful and avoid it altogether. In many instances, social workers can help parents deal with this situation more productively by rehearsing with them what they should say to their child. The author has found that behavioral rehearsal of this kind helps alleviate the anxiety experienced by parents at the same time that it prepares them for some of the questions their child might ask. Above all, children need to be reassured that they are still loved and that their parents will do everything possible to help them with their medical problem. In addition, parents should stress to the child the importance of daily medication for the control of seizures and should reinforce in the child's mind that he or she is still worthwhile and can live a happy and productive life.

Dealing with the School

Children or young adults with epilepsy can suffer physical and emotional anguish if they undergo a seizure at school and those around them do not understand what is happening or how to help. The author believes it is wise for parents to tell school personnel about their child's illness and to meet with the principal and teaching staff before school begins. During this meeting, the parents should inform the staff of their child's medical problem and resolve any misunderstandings staff members might have about epilepsy. Dealing with the misconceptions people often have about the disease is an important part of the orientation program for new teachers in many school districts and is also included in the curricula of many universities that certify elementary and secondary school teachers. In addition, parents should clarify at this time what needs to be done if their child has a seizure while attending school. If a social worker is part of the school's staff, he or she can be an indispensable advocate for the child and provide principal and teaching staff with information and in-service training regarding epilepsy.

If the child has a seizure at school, the teacher and students in his or her class should already know what to do. This means that the teacher should talk to the students about epilepsy as soon as possible and tell them that some children in the school have epilepsy and may need their help. It is not necessary to identify these students by name, although the protective headgear worn by some children who are prone to seizures may require an explanation. In any event, the teacher should talk to the class about epilepsy as if it were any other medical problem. Role-playing with the students regarding what needs to be done if a child has a seizure is also helpful. For example, some students may assume the role of patient and may lay on the floor while others kneel around them and gently restrain them from rolling into desks, tables, chairs, and other hazardous objects.

If a child undergoes a seizure during class, it is important that the teacher review with the students what has occurred and how they can be more helpful next time. The teacher should also help them understand how the epileptic child may feel following an attack and discuss with them their responsibility to befriend and esteem the child regardless of his or her medical problem. This point is crucial if the child is to avoid serious emotional problems. The author believes that an educational program consisting of the elements just described should be followed by all elementary and secondary schools and all institutions of higher education. In those instances in which social workers are part of a school's staff, they can be instrumental in developing and implementing programs to deal with the problems that children with epilepsy encounter in school.

Working with the Family

Epilepsy can affect the lives of other family members besides the patient. For example, the parents of epileptic children frequently undergo severe emotional strain and must make significant adjustments in their attitudes and life-style because of their child's illness. The author has worked with a number of parents who tended to blame themselves for having had an epileptic child. Such individuals will meticulously review every phase of their lives in search of a clue as to why their child became ill. Sometimes one parent will blame the other, particularly if there is a history of epilepsy in that person's family. Other parents are embarrassed by their child's illness and worry about what other relatives and friends will think of them. The author has found that parents often react in this way because of the stigma associated with epilepsy. That is, after believing for years that epilepsy leads to insanity and mental retardation, these parents must reconsider their view of the disease and reconcile their feelings about it once they discover that their child is epileptic. This reconciliation is something their social worker must help them accomplish.

The brothers and sisters of children with epilepsy also experience similar problems. They are usually embarrassed by the illness and do not want the name of their family associated with it. The author has been told by some of these young people that other young men and women actually would not socialize with them because of the history of epilepsy in their family. The primary solution to these and other similar problems is education and open communication among the members of a family. Social workers should therefore encourage family members to learn as much as possible about epilepsy and to discuss their findings as individuals and as a family with the patient. The calling of a family council meeting by parents to clarify any misunderstandings or to discuss particularly difficult situations often has merit. However, if a family's problems persist, their social worker should encourage them to become involved in family counseling. Finally, patients' families also have a responsibility to share the information they obtain about epilepsy with relatives and friends. Only in this way will others learn the truth and become disabused about the disease.

Dealing with Society

Patients with epilepsy have to contend with certain prejudices and misconceptions that are prevalent in society about their illness. Although public education may someday help to alleviate or ameliorate problems stemming from these misconceptions, they are very much in existence at present. Employment, for example is one area in which epileptic patients may encounter difficulties, for they are faced with a dilemma whenever they look for a job. That is, if they tell their prospective employer they have epilepsy, they often will not be hired for that reason alone. On the other hand, they may withhold this information only to have their employer discover it anyway if their family physician is contacted as a reference or to obtain medical background information or if they have a seizure while at work. This kind of disclosure may result in their being fired.

Most patients deal with this problem by concealing their illness from a prospective employer and hoping that their medication will prevent them from having a seizure at work. The author believes that the decision of patients whether to tell their employer about their medical problem must be made by them alone. As a social worker, he helps them understand the advantages and limitations of each of these courses of action and then lets them decide what they want to do. If patients are refused employment or are fired because they are epileptic, however, he may suggest that they seek legal counsel or contact the local office of the American Civil Liberties Union.

In addition to having problems with employment, many patients with epilepsy find it difficult to obtain a driver's license. The laws of most states now specify that patients with a history of seizures can obtain a license to operate a motor vehicle only if they have been free of seizures for at least one year. Some states add the stipulation that such patients must be free of seizures without the aid of medication, whereas others grant licenses to patients who are taking anticonvulsant medication if their seizures have been controlled. Although these laws seem reasonable at first glance, many patients do not have the financial resources to see a physician regularly. Without regularly scheduled follow-up visits, however, it is impossible for a physician to certify that a patient has been free of seizures for at least one year. Indeed, the author has counseled many patients who could not obtain a driver's license because they did not have the money to see a physician on a regular basis. This situation leaves patients at a disadvantage because many jobs require the individual to use an automobile, either during or in order to get to work. For reasons such as these, the social work department at the University Medical Center in Salt Lake City initiated a program for obtaining funds from a number of charitable organizations in the community to enable many patients who could not afford medical care to receive it.

In short, epileptic patients and their families must struggle with a wide variety of social and emotional problems. Many of these problems are perpetuated needlessly because of widespread ignorance of the facts about epilepsy. One way in which truth about the disease can be disseminated is through public education. The Epilepsy Association of Utah has become involved in various educational efforts through the news media, public schools, and local service clubs and organizations. A number of patients, social workers, and volunteers from the foundation visit public schools throughout the state and tell students and teachers about epilepsy. They stress the following points during their presentation:

- Epilepsy does not cause insanity or mental retardation.
- Epilepsy is a medical problem not unlike diabetes or heart disease, and it can usually be controlled with the proper medication.
- People can help epileptic patients avoid serious injury during a seizure by following certain simple guidelines.
- Some of the world's greatest physicians, lawyers, scientists, and philosophers have had epilepsy and have lived remarkable lives despite the disease.

- Everyone has the responsibility to share the truth about epilepsy with family members and friends.

Conclusion

It will be difficult for many people to change the variety of false notions they have about epilepsy. For this reason, the Epilepsy Foundation of America has encouraged its local chapters to fight prejudice and discrimination through the courts and state legislatures. Largely as a result of these efforts, laws restricting whom patients with epilepsy can marry have been abolished, and employment practices and driving regulations in many states have been changed. A great deal more needs to be done in these areas, and the courts will probably be the scene of many important legal battles in the future.

Because of the many misconceptions that surround the term "epilepsy," patients who have this illness often suffer emotional as well as physical anguish. Social workers have the responsibility to teach patients, families, and the general public the truth about epilepsy and to fight for the rights of epileptic patients. In addition, they are responsible for acquiring those counseling skills that will help them work efffectively with patients and their families.

Notes and References

1. Eli S. Goldensohn and Howard S. Barrows, *Handbook for Patients* (New York: Ayerst Laboratories, 1974), p. 3.

2. Ibid.

3. Maxwell M. Wintrobe, ed., *Harrison's Principles of Internal Medicine* (6th ed.; New York: McGraw-Hill Book Co., 1971), p. 163.

4. David N. Holvey, ed., *The Merck Manual of Diagnosis and Therapy* (12th ed.; Rahway, N.J.: Merck Sharpe & Dohme Research Laboratories, 1972), p. 1280.

5. Wintrobe, op. cit., p. 164.

6. Goldensohn and Barrows, op. cit., pp. 4–6; and Wintrobe, op. cit., pp. 163–164.

7. Goldensohn and Barrows, op. cit., pp. 14–15.

8. Ibid., pp. 17–18.

9. Wintrobe, op. cit., p. 163.

GENETIC PROBLEMS

CHAPTER 37

Social Work with Genetic Problems

Sylvia Schild

The social work role with clients having genetic problems has been increasingly accepted in recent years. This acceptance, although often grudgingly given, stems partly from the rapid development of genetic counseling and the "concurrent growing awareness of its unique impact on the lives and aspirations of individuals and their families."[1] Geneticists and physicians in clinical genetics have been expressing concerns not only about the burgeoning demands of clients for genetic counseling but also about the quality and effectiveness of the services provided. Therefore, several exploratory research efforts have attempted to study the effect of genetic counseling on those receiving it.[2]

Genetic Counseling and Social Work

The researchers in a study at the University of Colorado Medical Center identified the following situations in which effective genetic counseling might be hindered and dissatisfaction with the counseling could result: (1) when the persons consulting the counselors strongly expected to be enlightened about what caused their problems and their expectations could not be met—which might happen, for example, if the etiology were undetermined, (2) when the genetic problem was only part of a whole complex of personal and interpersonal problems, (3) when the client requested genetic counseling solely to satisfy external pressures—explaining for instance, that "the doctor told me to come," (4) when clients had either strong preconceptions or unrealistic expectations of what genetic counseling could accomplish, and (5) when clients were unable to understand the risks of reoccurrence because these were stated mathematically in terms of probability.[3]

The researchers clearly specified a role for the social worker in follow-up interviews, which they defined as "an essential extension of genetic counseling services."[4] In their clinic, where psychosocial problems of the family were identified, these same researchers used social workers for evaluation, supportive counseling, and reinforcement and clarification of genetic information. In addition, social workers were responsible for referring clients to community resources and for guiding the liaison between the family and the genetic counseling clinic. The study stated: "Such a person [a social worker] is sensitive to potential problems involved in acceptance, denial, guilt, and other emotional responses which arise."[5]

As early as 1964, Tips and his associates had described similar functions for the social worker as a member of the clinical genetics team.[6] More recently Epstein, in arguing that it was essential to have a properly trained physician to do genetic counseling, pointed out that nonphysicians—whether geneticists with a Ph.D. degree, public health nurses, social workers, or genetic associates—also have a viable and valuable role in carrying out many tasks in the overall genetic counseling situation. These professionals, Epstein asserts, are not "genetic counselors" because this term is reserved for the "responsibility-taking medical geneticist-physician counselor" who provides genetic counseling.[7]

This limitation in the use of the term cannot be dismissed as simply a semantic issue. Clarification of roles and responsibilities is basic to understanding where nonphysicians fit into genetic situations. The author has long maintained that social workers do not do genetic counseling.[8] It is semantically confusing, therefore, to talk about social workers in genetic counseling although they do have an important place in the provision of genetic services.

It is estimated that about 98 percent of the people who could benefit from counseling about genetic problems are not seen by genetic counselors.[9] Thus the role of social workers with clients having genetic disorders includes genetic counseling but also extends beyond its range. Undoubtedly social workers encounter many more clients with genetic problems in other medical and health programs than they might see in genetic clinics such as facilities for the care of high-risk infants, pediatric, neurological, endocrine, or other specialty clinics, or kidney dialysis units. Other settings yield their fair share of clients with problems having genetic implications, such as family planning services, adoption and other child welfare agencies, public health programs, and welfare departments, which now serve many developmentally disabled clients. A significant number of clients served in a multiplicity of agencies and facilities for the mentally retarded also have genetic problems and concerns.

Regardless of the setting in which the social worker practices, the objectives of working with the client who has genetic concerns are the same. Invariably the major goal is to help the individual and the individual's family cope with the dislocations and disturbances occurring as a result of the genetic diagnosis. The worker also seeks to help the client get the maximum benefit from the medical treatment and from the management or rehabilitation procedures, and to further the client's positive adaptation to the presence of the genetic problem, thus enhancing the overall quality of life of both client and family.

How unique is social work practice that is related to genetics? The major contention of this article is that practice in this area is basically shaped by a deepened understanding of the characteristics of the genetic diagnosis and genetic counseling and of the impact that these aspects have on clients. Knowledge of the dynamics involved provides a basic reference for determining which individuals and families are most vulnerable and at high risk of being precipitated into a crisis predicament. The helping approaches most relevantly implied by this knowledge are ego-supportive and crisis interventive. Knowing what precipitates the crisis, understanding the meaning of the genetic diagnosis, and recognizing which situational and psychological tasks must be mastered for healthy adaptation and positive resolution of the crisis—these furnish the key to determining appropriate interventive strategies. As Meyer has clearly stated:

> Through improved knowledge, social workers can intervene in potential crisis situations, direct attention to populations-at-risk, specify those steps that enhance the ego-adaptive mechanisms of individuals caught in the pressure of crisis, and invent social supports that will encourage more accommodating and adaptable environments.[10]

Genetic Diagnosis

To better comprehend the nature of social work intervention in genetics, it is helpful to know what it is about a genetic diagnosis that evokes psychosocial stresses and dilemmas for identified patients and their families. It might be presumed that genetic counseling would provide the context within which most of the genetic questions and concerns would be satisfactorily addressed. However, the provision of genetic counseling has problematic aspects that may influence the psychological and social reactions and behavior of clients.

PERMANENCE

One characteristic of the genetic diagnosis is its permanence. A genetic diagnosis that is firmly established is, ipso facto, irreversible. It won't "go away" or "be cured," but is fixed; it is a permanent attribute of the individual. If there are physiological processes inherently or potentially threatening to normal physical health, growth, and development, then the chronic aspect characterizing genetic conditions comes into acute focus.

This chronic nature of the genetic problem may express itself as a threat at varying points in the life history of individuals and their families, for instance, in relation to significant events such as marriage or childbearing. Thus decision-making about crucial life tasks and aspirations may be affected by genetic concerns. The degree of the effect that chronicity has no doubt varies in direct proportion to the extent of the handicap, the severity of the disease or physical anomaly, and the burden of care involved. Even though a genetic defect may have had few if any unfavorable effects directly on a particular individual, the mere knowledge of possessing the defect (even if only as a carrier) may have had a subtle influence, which should not be overlooked, because it chronically presents problems at critical points in life.

FAMILY DIAGNOSIS

It is readily apparent that the genetic diagnosis frequently is a family diagnosis. Whenever inheritance is implicated, whether by transmission of autosomal dominant or recessive or X-linked genes, family members as well as the patient are automatically identified. The focus of attention necessarily shifts from being preoccupied solely with the needs of the presenting patient to dealing with the broader needs and concerns of the entire family. Problems about carrier status and the risk of reoccurrence become immediate and important.

PRECIPITATION OF CRISIS

A genetic diagnosis also has a propensity to precipitate a crisis. Many genetic disorders (for example, Huntington's Chorea, Marfans Syndrome, Tay-Sachs) are degenerative and result in an early death or a shortened life-span. A life-threatening diagnosis can easily propel family members into a crisis situation when individual and family integrity are challenged, when family aspirations (especially childbearing hopes) become questionable, and when psychological responses to impending loss are evoked. A genetic diagnosis may stimulate intense reactions not unlike the commonly reported patterns of response noted when a dignosis of mental retardation is made for a family member. In fact, many diagnostic problems seen in genetic clinics involve patients with developmental lags or mental impairment, who are seeking an etiologic explanation for the pathology.

Typically, crisis responses such as these arise as a result of the disruptive impact that the diagnosis has (1) on established values ("Is it morally right to have more children with the known risks?"); (2) on interpersonal relationships including the sexual relationship ("We must avoid pregnancy: your family has bad blood!"); and (3) on self-esteem and self-adequacy ("Look what I've done to my child!").

Less dramatic perhaps than crises due to internal factors are those externally produced. Adequate finances, resources for meeting medical demands, resources for preventing job interferences, facilities for proper nursing care, transportation, special training programs—if any or all of these are inaccessible, unavailable, or unsuitable, then a crisis may be precipitated. To the individual who is in crisis because of intrapsychic stresses, external support systems are as crucial to help in coping with a chronic-strain crisis as are a direct ego-supportive relationship and work with significant others.[11]

RISKS OF REOCCURRENCE

Most families who seek genetic counseling ask about the risk that the defect will reoccur in the reproduction of another child. If the concern is not expressed for the children that the parents themselves might bear, it is often related to the risks of reoccurrence for other children and for members of the extended family. Again, because of its very nature, a genetic diagnosis inherently identifies a threat in future childbearing—a threat that ranges from the low normal risk that holds for every pregnancy to a high one, such as a one-out-of-two chance or a 50 percent risk—and this potentially precipitates crisis. What may be a low risk to one person is a high one to another, and vice versa. It is important to understand what the diagnosis means to the person or persons affected. Such understanding helps the worker identify the particularly vulnerable ones who are at high risk of succumbing to crisis as well as facilitate resolutions to the crisis.

While it is imperative that individuals retain the right to determine their own course of action regarding reproduction—and while genetic counselors have justly held that the primary professional obligation is to provide correct information that will enhance clients' wisdom in decision-making—a strong case can be argued for helping clients check out the reality of their perceptions. This means that not only should clients be aware of the facts about the genetic disorder, but also that these facts should be considered against a framework of personal and family aspirations, the affective life of the significant persons involved, and interpersonal relationships, especially those of marital partners. Furthermore, with the help of a social worker who is knowledgeable in the field of genetics, the client should be able to move to a higher level of self-determination regarding reproduction. This self-determination would be based on the realities of the genetic disorder, the client's conscious understanding of personal realities (that is, the client's own perception and dynamic interpretation of the events), and the congruence or disparity between these two sets of realities.

COMPLEX PROCESSES

Characteristically, most genetic diagnoses involve highly complex biological processes. These processes often are beyond the client's and the family's level of scientific knowledge. Thus, there is a problem in explaining clearly the nature of the disorder and how it is inherited. There is limited and somewhat contradictory empirical evidence as to how much the clients who receive genetic counseling understand.[12] Research methodologies of the few studies that have been done are not comparable so that it is difficult to assess the findings with confidence. Indications strongly suggest that, in general, clients have a great deal of difficulty in comprehending the genetic information clearly unless it is clarified, interpreted, and reinforced in follow-up. The concept of normal probability is often distorted with misconceptions and confusion about the reproductive risks that may ensue. Suffice it to say that the genetic diagnosis, because of its own complexity, may cause misunderstandings and distortion of information. This indicates that it is important to have clear, articulate counseling; have a counselor who knows something about such factors as the client's intellect, education, and stability; and provide appropriate follow-up for reinforcement and clarification.

LABELING

Another potential source of problems is that genetic diagnosis, like any other diagnostic classification system, categorizes and labels a client; this is an inherent characteristic, understandably pertaining to the emphasis on the detection, prevention, and treatment of a pathological condition. Unfortunately, labeling also incorporates notions of difference or deviance, and it becomes subject to negative consequences when it is utilized to promote adverse social attitudes, behavior, or policies. Labeling, because it generalizes, can reinforce biased stereotypes and foster exaggerated fears and prejudices. On the other hand, to help individuals and their families come to terms with the impact that a genetic difference may have on their lives—and also to direct appropriate attention to the special needs of the diagnosed population—the social worker must deal realistically with various aspects of deviance.

Discussion

Genetic counseling is often provided to clients who are under great stress, coming as they usually do with problems of grave concern. Such counseling is frequently given to persons who have little knowledge and understanding of the complex biological processes involved and who understand only vaguely if at all the mathematical concepts of probability. Also, and most significantly, even when the diagnosis is confirmed, nothing more than academic information may be offered to the client by the physician or the genetic counselor. Little may be possible in the way of treatment or cure. A great burden is placed on the genetic counselor to provide anticipatory guidance balanced by considerable emotional support and encouragement. Because of the large number of clients who are seeking such help, there are necessarily great restrictions in what can be done because of limited time, energy, funding, and so on. Much of this burden can be shifted from the clinical geneticist to other disciplines. Social work is one discipline capable of furnishing the essential services.

ROLE AND FUNCTIONS OF SOCIAL WORKERS

Social workers can provide a range of services that have always fallen within the repertoire of activities that they render skillfully. These include obtaining social histories, doing preclinic orientation and assessments, making referrals, coordinating activities, and providing case management services. Specific knowledge regarding genetic problems can be obtained in a variety of ways long utilized by social workers whenever they have needed to acquire knowledge in their specific practice area—for example, in the field of mental retardation. The means they have used include on-the-job training, independent study, and participation in seminars, workshops, and formal courses of study.

In the area of genetics social workers can take responsibility for tasks related to the social dimensions of the genetic problem. The important elements required for carrying out these tasks are the skills and knowledge germane to all competent social work practice. When expertise in practice is coupled with a broad general understanding of fundamental genetic information and of the basic modes of transmitting inherited traits, the social worker can contribute, in addition to the tasks already mentioned, significant follow-up and supportive services that are not the same as those given in genetic clinics by genetic counselors and genetic advisors. Although there might be some overlap among the various professionals working together in genetic settings, social workers—given the opportunity—should be able to provide in a unique way the essential follow-up services that are the logical extension of genetic counseling.

SUPPORTIVE COUNSELING

One need is to provide supportive counseling for such problems as deterioration of the self-image, breakdown in communication, and deterioration of sexual relationships, all of which may occur as a result of the impact of the genetic diagnosis. As MacIntyre points out:

> In the unusually brief contact of genetic counseling which is primarily the giving of information, rarely is the counselor made fully aware of the presence or intensity of these kinds of feeling [despair, guilt, anger, inadequacy]. Many parents have indicated to me that during initial counseling there was no opportunity for them to express their feelings, and many of my physician colleagues, in referring patients for supportive counseling, have readily admitted a feeling of inadequacy, with respect to handling the kinds of complex emotional reactions which such cases present.[13]

MacIntyre makes a plea for specialized rehabilitative therapy carried out by therapists who are knowledgeable and also are familiar with the psychodynamics and the feelings of persons who have defective children. He further explains:

> The kind of rehabilitative therapy which I have discussed is not a part of genetic counseling per se. I can accept that, in so far as most genetic counselors have neither the time nor the training to deliver this type of extensive therapy, but to say that therefore we need not be sensitive to the existence and severity of the emotional problems described, that I cannot accept, for I believe that such sensitivity and concern is an extremely important part of effective genetic counseling....If there are serious, unsolved problems in our patients when we have completed genetic counseling, I believe we have the moral obligation to find help....[14]

MacIntyre, in addition, stresses the need to develop essential supportive service systems to provide this type of help and also the need to conduct research and train therapists who will provide supportive counseling.

The irony is that social workers are well equipped to provide just the kind of supportive counseling recommended. Yet somehow, it has been extremely difficult for MacIntyre and others in clinical genetics to see a role for social workers, perhaps because of (1) the myth that whoever deals with clients having genetic problems requires intensive grounding in scientific knowledge, (2) the ability of physicians to identify more readily with nurses and others in biological sciences, and (3) negative experiences or the lack of experiences with social workers. Responsibility for the current situation is not all one-sided. Social workers tend to shy away from acquiring scientific knowledge. They do not seem to articulate clearly and demonstrate visibly their professional viability in this area. Nor do they communicate convincingly to professionals in medical and scientific disciplines the scope and breadth of professional social work practice.

A CRISIS MODEL

Social workers could assume a role that might prove profitable and serve to reduce the distance between them and professionals of other disciplines. Out of their practice wisdom and experience, they might undertake the difficult tasks of conceptualizing the nature of the psychosocial problems that clients experience and sharing this knowledge with other disciplines.

The author has been attempting to formulate a crisis model for clients reacting to a genetic diagnosis—a model that delineates some of the psychological and situational tasks that clients must master for adequate crisis resolution and reduction. At the present time, five major psychological tasks have been identified:

- Reaffirming self worth
- Accepting the inherent limitations of the genetic diagnosis, which in turn involves accepting loss (for example, the loss related to bearing children with genetic defects)
- Reorganizing self-concepts and accepting a different body image
- Adjustment to the felt difference or aspect of deviance, including external coping with social stigma
- Mastering the role of person-having-a-genetic-defect or parent-of-a-genetically-defective-child in a way that does not contraindicate normal growth and personality development or inhibit healthy interpersonal relationships

Situational tasks that require mastery relate to such matters as these:

- Obtaining and carrying out appropriate treatment
- Obtaining specialized services and coping with agencies that will meet particular needs
- Coping with reactions and attitudes of significant others
- Altering life-style to accommodate to special needs and problems
- Insuring access to institutional programs of all kinds so that the basic needs that people have will be met at the same time that the special needs of the genetic situation are met

An understanding of these psychological and situational tasks facilitates the worker's abilities to help clients direct their energies constructively toward positive adaptation to the basic realities of the genetic diagnosis.

Social Workers in Genetic Programs

The actual employment of social workers in specialized genetic programs is limited at present. A survey conducted by the author in the fall of 1975 showed that only 73 social workers had been specifically hired in 15.4 percent of the genetic services programs in the United States; of these, 24 were employed part time.[15] However, 74 out of 133 genetic programs responding in the survey (or 78 percent) utilized social work services; these came primarily from hospital social work departments (71 percent of them) and regional center systems for developmental disabilities (26 percent). Services of social work graduate students were available in nine of the genetic programs.

When all the services provided are considered, regardless of the workers' source of employment, social workers performed a wide range of tasks for the genetic units. These included preclinic visits, pedigree history-taking, social histories and assessments, referrals to community resources, follow-up services (including casework and reinterpretation of genetic information), group work, coordination services, and research and educational activities. In the genetic programs employing social workers, at least 40 percent of the respondents reported tasks performed in the following categories: social histories, follow-up services, and preclinic visits. Referral to community agencies was reported by 72 percent of the respondents.

Although the direct involvement of social workers in genetic units seems limited, their actual contacts with clients who have genetic problems is vastly greater than is apparent on the surface. Another study is indicated to gather the necessary data about these contacts from social workers in hospitals, clinics, neighborhood health agencies, welfare and adoption agencies, and specialized settings for the developmentally disabled. This would be a step forward in determining and documenting the extent of social work involvement with genetic problems.

The fact that such a high proportion of the genetics programs surveyed made community referrals gives some support to the notion of wide social work involvement. It is apparent that, with the heightened publicity being given to genetic counseling and particularly to amniocentesis, more and more of the lay public is being sensitized to the area of genetics with resultant anxieties pertaining to family planning and reproduction. These concerns will no doubt be brought to social workers even if they themselves have not developed an awareness of the implications that genetic problems have for their profession. The wave of interest in genetics is so new that it is almost too soon to estimate the amount of social work engagement there might be in this area. It is to be noted that 29 percent of the survey respondents identified a need to have a social worker in the genetics program; the major deterrent was the familiar "lack of funding."

Summary

The generic utility of social work practice skills and knowledge applies to this field of practice as to any other. What is required is a delineation of the role that social workers are to take, a clear articulation of what they can do and do well, and their acquisition of the specific knowledge related to genetic problems that would provide the framework in which to practice social work in this area. From their practice experience, social workers in genetics are in a unique position to contribute important knowledge about their clients that would help to provide essential and needed services as well as guide social work intervention. The key role for social workers in genetics is the provision of supportive counseling to help clients deal with the social dimensions of their genetic problems. In other words, genetic social work focuses mainly on assisting clients with problems in living that are generated by a genetic diagnosis and that may be more problematic or distressing than the genetic defect itself.

Notes and References

1. Beverly De V. Reynolds, Mary H. Puck, and Arthur Anderson, "Genetic Counseling," *Clinical Genetics*, 5 (1974), p. 177.

2. *See*, for example, Reynolds et al., op. cit., pp. 177–187; Cedric O. Carter et al., "Genetic Clinic: A Follow-Up," *Lancet*, i (February 2, 1971), pp. 281–285; Claire O. Leonard, Gary A. Chase, and Barton Childs, "Genetic Counseling: A Consumers' View," *New England Journal of Medicine*, 287 (August 31, 1972), pp. 433–439.

3. Reynolds et al., op. cit., pp. 177–187.

4. Ibid., p. 178.

5. Ibid., p. 187.

6. Robert L. Tips et al., "The 'Whole Family' Concept in Clinical Genetics," *American Journal of Diseases of Children*, 107 (January 1964), pp. 67–114.

7. Charles J. Epstein, MD, "Who Should Do Genetic Counseling and Under What Circumstances?" *Contemporary Genetic Counseling: Birth Defects*, Original Article Series, Vol. 9, No. 4. (National Foundation—March of Dimes, April 1973), p. 43.

8. *See* Sylvia Schild, "Social Workers' Contribution to Genetic Counseling," *Social Casework*, 54 (July 1973), pp. 387–392; and Schild, "The Challenging Effort for Social Workers in Genetics," *Social Work*, 11 (April 1966), pp. 22–28.

9. William S. Sly, MD, "What is Genetic Counseling?" *Contemporary Genetic Counseling: Birth Defects*, Original Article Series, Vol. 9, No. 4 (National Foundation—March of Dimes, April 1973), p. 16.

10. Carol H. Meyer, "Introduction to Preventive Intervention: A Goal in Search of a Method," in Meyer, ed., *Preventive Intervention in Social Work* (Washington, D.C.: National Association of Social Workers, 1974), p. 7.

11. Sylvia Schild, "Counseling," in Richard Koch and James Dobson, eds., *The Multidisciplinary Approach to the Mentally Retarded Child and His Family* (New York: Brunner-Mazel, 1971).

12. *See*, for example, Reynolds et al., op. cit.; Carter et al., op. cit.; and Leonard et al., op. cit.

13. M. Neil MacIntyre, "The Need for Supportive Therapy for Members of a Family with a Defective Child." Unpublished lecture paper, School of Medicine, Case Western Reserve University, June 1975, p. 2.

14. Ibid., p. 4.

15. The survey questionnaire was mailed to the 234 genetic services listed in Daniel Bergsma, Henry Lynch, Robert T. Thomas, eds., *Birth Defects-Genetic Services; International Directory* (National Foundation—March of Dimes, March 1974). One hundred and thirty-three responses were analyzed, which approximates the number of units offering genetic counseling services. Many of the others were not applicable because they are primarily laboratory and research units.

HEMOPHILIA

CHAPTER 38

Some Psychosocial Problems in Hemophilia

Alfred H. Katz

Hemophilia is a congenital, chronic illness, about which relatively little is known although it affects some 40,000 persons in the United States.[1] The medical problems it presents are far better understood than are its psychosocial aspects. The latter have received little attention in this country except for an early paper by Cohen and Herrman and a fragmentary outline for psychiatric research by Poinsard.[2] This discussion is an attempt, based on some years of association with the problems of hemophiliacs, to sketch some of these psychosocial factors, since social workers may encounter persons with this illness in the course of their work.

Hemophilia is a hereditary ailment characterized by excessive bleeding. It is not yet subject to cure, but in the past two decades various therapeutic advances have been made in the direction of stopping or controlling hemorrhaging and in the management of some resultant problems. Genetically, hemophilia is the product of a sex-linked recessive gene which is transmitted by females, but which primarily affects males. It also occurs, but quite rarely, as a result of genetic mutation. In recent years a number of related "bleeding disorders" have been found, which are milder in

---

[1] Although the figures regarding the incidence and prevalence of hemophilia vary and are not definitive, this figure, given by Dr. Armand J. Quick of Marquette University, is the most commonly accepted estimate.

[2] Ethel Cohen and R. L. Herrman, "Social Adjustment of Six Patients with of Hemophilia," *Pediatrics*, Vol. III (1949), pp. 588–596. Paul Poinsard, M.D., "Psychiatric Aspects of Hemophilia," in *Hemophilia and Hemophiloid Diseases*, Brinkhous, ed., University of North Carolina Press, Chapel Hill, 1957.

Reprinted from *Social Caswork*, Vol. 40 (June, 1959), pp. 321–326, by permission of the author and America.

symptomatology than classical hemophilia, and which can be differentially diagnosed by refined laboratory procedures.

The severity of hemophilia varies from individual to individual although, generally speaking, severity remains comparatively stable among afflicted members of the same family. Some physicians (and patients) believe that there is a cyclical or seasonal variation in the onset and severity of bleeding episodes. Others believe that there is no such seasonal change, but that with maturation the affected individual learns to take better care of himself and is therefore less prone to situations where bleeding may be touched off.

With the introduction in the past twenty years of methods of banking blood, and particularly with the development of methods of processing human plasma through freezing or lyophilization, the treatment of hemorrhages has been greatly facilitated and the mortality rate among hemophiliacs has declined sharply. Owing to the volatility of the coagulative factor, the hemophiliac requires transfusions of blood or blood derivatives that have been freshly prepared, if the bleeding is to be stopped.

Although hemophilia is comparatively rare, it poses such severe problems of medical management and of psychosocial stress to the patient and his family that it must be considered a serious health problem for those affected and for the community. Not only does the moderately-to-severely affected individual have frequent, and at times almost uncontrollable, bleeding from external abrasions and sites, but even more serious forms of internal bleeding can occur from no apparent cause. Such bleeding episodes may be extremely painful, and often result in orthopedic problems. Hemophilic arthropathy, as it is termed, arises from such repeated bleedings into joint spaces. Orthopedic abnormalities and permanent damage to muscles and joints can occur from this type of bleeding. The approach of orthopedists and psychiatrists to appropriate measures of therapy and correction for such problems still varies considerably, and much of the therapeutic work that is being done is on an experimental basis.

Social Problems and Hemophilia

From this brief review of medical problems it can be understood that, both for patients and for their families, hemophilia reproduces many or most of the psychosocial problems of other forms of congenital chronic illness, but with some added special features. Prominent among the latter are the extreme feelings of distress, guilt, and self-reproach experienced by the parents of newly diagnosed sufferers, especially by the approximately 50 per cent who are unable to trace a history of hemophilia in their families, but who are suddenly confronted with a child bearing this ''hereditary taint,'' who forever after needs special care.

The protective care of the hemophilic infant and young child has to be extremely thorough to prevent the trauma that can result from normal childish exploration of the environment—crawling, body contact with furniture and floor, sharp-edged toys, and so forth. From a tender age the hemophilic infant must be protected from the more strenuous forms of physical contact with playmates and play objects; at the same time normal curiosity, growth, and socialization have to be fostered through stimulation by other means. *Thus the most general and pervasive psychosocial problem for these parents is to give their child physical protection and, at the same time, avoid making him overdependent and eventually a psychological invalid.* This all-pervading problem imposes tremendous burdens on the self-restraint and psychological maturity of the parents, siblings, and others in the hemophiliac's immediate environment. When he reaches school age, these problems are aggravated. The necessity of reaching a viable balance, of treading the narrow line between physical protection and psychological overprotection now involves teachers, playmates, and others in the child's environment.

The possibility of danger to the child is aggravated by the fact that frequently the young hemophiliac offers no external physical signs of his condition and thus appears to other children to be completely normal. Perhaps because of the difficulty of limiting the child's physical activity at this time, the school years are often the period of most frequent occurrence of hemorrhagic episodes. It is common for hemophiliacs to miss many weeks of the school term as a result of requiring rest and immobilization after, or between, periods of hemorrhage. Repeated bleeding can also lead to weakness and anaemia, with their effects on vitality and energy levels. The loss of time in school involves not only possible academic retardation and its important emotional concomitants, but the equally important loss of contacts with other children, of the socializing effects of play, and of the maturational benefits of social activity within a peer group.

It is also clear that if a hemophilic child is born into a family in which other male children are not affected by the disease, he tends to pre-empt major attention in the family, and there is a consequent withdrawal of attention from siblings.

Among the urgent and continuous pressures confronting the parents of a hemophilic child are the threat of being called upon at any moment to secure emergency medical attention for a hemorrhage; the consequent necessity of staying close to sources of such care; and the cost of such attention, not only in relation to the services of a physician, but particularly in relation to the replacement of blood or blood derivatives that may be used in transfusions. On the latter score, in some parts of the United States the American Red Cross does supply blood or blood products for hemophiliacs without requiring replacement by the individual user. In other localities the voluntary organization of hemophiliacs—The Hemophilia

Foundation—may assume the responsibility and sometimes can cover the emergent needs of a particular family. Since, however, a hemophiliac may require as many as fifteen to twenty pints of whole blood to meet the exigencies of a single episode—and in the course of a year may require as many as one or two hundred pints of blood—this voluntary organization is usually overwhelmed and cannot meet all the requests. Thus, the drain on the finances and the energies of afflicted families is enormous. In those localities where blood or blood derivatives have to be purchased, the minimum cost to the family is $10 or $12 per unit, exclusive of administration fees. Therefore, the financial drains are constant, chronic, and severe; and these drains have important psychosocial consequences in increasing intrafamilial tensions and in promoting shame, withdrawal, and social isolation tendencies.

Other medical costs result from the frequent hospitalizations that are necessary for hemophiliacs. Although many of these families have hospital insurance, it is not at all uncommon that a hemophiliac will require repeated hospitalizations every few weeks and thus exhaust within a short time the coverage by hospital insurance for the whole year. In some states, Crippled Children's programs may carry a portion of the cost of hospitalization, but eligibility for such aid is frequently defined by the state only in relation to the performance of corrective orthopedic procedures and is not available for the simpler procedure of treating a bleeding episode and its sequelae.

Such other emergent costs as those for transportation, ambulances, appliances and braces for those orthopedically afflicted, and special fees of medical consultants are all constant accompaniments of this condition.

As indicated above, the area of schooling and vocational preparation is a critical one for the hemophilic child. In this regard, parents require much help, counseling, and support in order to understand the importance of maintaining the child's independence, autonomy, and self-reliance insofar as possible, and to handle the child appropriately.

Problems of Adults

One of the striking observations regarding the hemophiliacs with whom I had contact was of the number of young adults in the group who lacked a stable occupation. When referrals of young men who were mild or even moderate sufferers were accepted by the State Division of Vocational Rehabilitation, the possibilities of their becoming self-maintaining were found to be excellent. However, this resource was little known and not widely utilized by the families of sufferers. It was my experience that social service assistance is rarely sought by or extended to adult patients in hospitals or attending clinics. The hospital social services for hemophiliacs tend to concentrate efforts on the problems of young children, their eligibility for assistance under Crippled Children's programs, and other such tangible services as camp arrangements, which are helpful and which carry a good deal of meaning for parents.

What has been found lacking, however, has been an approach to the hemophiliac through a program of counseling and advisement that would start at an early age, and that would tend to forestall the development of some of the special problems the hemophilic adolescents and young men encounter. The following case example illustrates some of these problems:

> Harry B, aged 26, a sufferer from classical hemophilia of moderate severity, had lived in a small suburban community of New York all his life. He was a handsome young man, with no orthopedic involvements; yet he had been in and out of hospitals for years for treatment of hemorrhages and resultant internal complications. Harry was the only hemophiliac in a family of four sons. His father was a retired ship-building worker who received a pension. The three brothers—one younger and two older—worked at manual trades.
>
> Of apparently normal intellectual capacity, Harry had finished two years of high school after an elementary schooling that was irregular owing to his frequent illnesses. He was 19 when he decided that he felt awkward with the younger high school students and simply dropped out. He had had no jobs, but amused himself at home by watching television and playing records. He did not go out socially, but had one close friend, a young man who had taken an interest in him and had attempted to arrange blood donations for him.
>
> Harry played the piano and spoke of wanting to become a musician. He wanted to study at a school where he could learn to make transcriptions for jazz orchestras. He could not, however, afford to attend such a school, and did not know whether, after taking such training, he would be able to get a job in this field.
>
> Harry verbalized his interest in such vocational planning, but had not followed through on suggestions that were made to him of discussing the plan with the State Vocational Rehabilitation Division. This failure to follow through seemed to be a characteristically apathetic approach to his own situation.

It is clear that casework help to Harry and his parents would have had to begin when Harry was much younger if realistic vocational counseling and referral were to take place. In extending casework help to his parents, the caseworker would have had to take into account the special medical and psychological problems experienced by the hemophiliac during various phases of his development. To be helpful, the caseworker would have had to be aware of the very special frustrations and anxieties that both Harry and his parents had encountered. As this case reveals, the caseworker must be particularly aware of the problems associated with the hemophiliac's adolescence. In addition to the maturational stresses of normal adolescence, the hemophiliac experiences growing awareness that he is afflicted with a chronic disease, one that has multiple implications for marriage and parenthood roles and for the highly valued role of worker in our culture.

The adolescent hemophiliac thus may call into question his own adequacy in relation to most of the important adjustment indices in the adult orld. Unless he is helped to explore and understand the ramifications of these feelings and reactions by means of a professional relationship, he can easily lose his way, and, like Harry B, retreat into a chronic passive dependency which is not realistically related to his actual medical condition. I found particularly noteworthy the number of such apparently "lost," passively dependent, apathetic, and depressed personalities encountered among young adult hemophiliacs. That I also encountered a relatively small number of comparatively active and outgoing individuals, who had made what seemed to be a good adjustment to their illness and disability, should also be stated. In perhaps a majority of cases there were problems of overdependency and passivity. It should be possible for many hemophiliacs, through skilled casework help, to achieve a better adjustment that will involve coming to terms with limitations in relation to their image of themselves, their possibilities of becoming vocationally active, and their problems of social life.

A readily acceptable focus for such casework help to adolescents and young men would seem to be the area of vocational planning. The possible range of occupations that can be followed by the hemophiliac is limited by several factors: (1) the innate capacities of the individual; (2) the severity and frequency of occurrence of disabling episodes; (3) the presence and degree of correction of orthopedic defect; and (4) the attitudes of potential employers. Within a framework of such limitations, hemophiliacs have been able to function in the professions, in education, small businesses, and clerical occupations. Generally speaking, severe physical exertion is not advised, although one encounters hemophiliacs who are laborers, bus and truck drivers, machinists, and workers in other active trades. Awareness of the many vocational possibilities open to him and of available community resources for helping him secure employment in one of them can be decidedly therapeutic for the young hemophiliac, even without exploration of deeper, underlying feelings.

The problems of social life are also acute for the young adult who suffers from his constant awareness of the implications of his condition for marriage and parenthood. Awareness of such problems frequently imposes a pattern of withdrawal from group or individual relationships, which in turn intensifies his feelings of loneliness, isolation, and depression. Through simple encouragement, some young men have been helped to try, and have found considerable support from, planned participation in social and recreational activities with other handicapped or non-handicapped persons.

Problems of Female Relatives

One of the most serious areas of conflict is that experienced by the female members of a hemophilic family. Their conflict arises from the fact that they may be carriers of the defective gene, although they are not personally affected by the illness. Genetic data indicate that there is a fifty per cent chance that the daughter of a male hemophiliac will be a carrier of the defective gene. There is a fifty per cent chance that a male child born to a carrier will be a hemophiliac. *All* the daughters of a female carrier of the gene are themselves carriers. Thus, in the well-known instance of Queen Victoria, who was a hemophilic carrier, all her daughters were carriers; they married into the royal houses of Spain, Germany, and Russia, where, among their male children, several hemophiliacs were subsequently found.

There is at present no reliable test which indicates whether or not the daughter of a hemophilic male is herself a carrier of the defective gene.* Researchers are continuing to try to develop such a test but so far without success. In view of this, the psychological situation of the potential carrier is understandable. Attitudes range from shame, and the impulse to conceal the possible hereditary defect, to withdrawal from social contacts and extreme depression. It has been found that the daughters can be helped through professional or lay sources to face realistically the alternatives that confront them. Some daughters of hemophiliacs, for example, have been ready to take a chance on marriage and motherhood; they may rationalize their actions by the belief that, first of all, they have a "fifty-fifty" chance of having a healthy son; or that the care of a hemophilic child is not such a tremendous burden and is to be preferred to childlessness; or they may be convinced that the improvements in therapy developed over recent years, and the prospects of current research, give promise of more effective control or even a cure. Some women have sought to adopt children rather than to risk a perpetuation of the defective gene. Adoption has been arranged, to the writer's knowledge, in several instances, both within and outside the structure of social agency services. It is of interest to note that among hemophilic families known to me, there are several with two or more affected sons, and that such multiple-sufferer families are found in religious groups that do not have prohibitions against birth control practices.

Editor's Note: This article was published in 1959 and does not include recent developments in this research.

Therapeutic Aspects of Help
to Hemophiliacs

Like other groups of the specially disadvantaged and handicapped, hemophiliacs and their families can draw great strength from group associations. In those communities where the voluntary agency concerned with their problems exists, these families have been able to work out generally superior arrangements for blood procurement, medical services, and special schooling. The less tangible advantages of participation in such "self-help" groups are also worth stating. Among these are: (1) overcoming the sense of isolation and overwhelming distress, frequently experienced by parents as a first reaction to the diagnosis of hemophilia; (2) provision of accurate information regarding problems of medical management, child care, blood procurement, and so forth; (3) socialization through contacts and exchange of experience with other families who can contribute to knowledge about developmental phases and problems that can be anticipated; (4) provision of organized or informal opportunities to discuss the parents' fears, frustrations, and satisfactions arising from the particular difficulties of caring for a hemophilic child; (5) opportunity to discuss broader and longer-range problems that can be anticipated on behalf of the child so that planning can be done; (6) possibility of securing through group action better facilities of a therapeutic and educational nature for their children; (7) cathartic effects of such personal participation, which helps to relieve anxieties by channeling them into constructive outlets.

As stressed in the foregoing, it seems to me that casework services are extremely important for both parents and patients, to help forestall and minimize some of the problems that have been described in this article. Such assistance can help to define and resolve for the parents some of the major feelings that may inhibit their handling their child in a way that combines necessary physical protectiveness with maximum psychological self-reliance. Early establishment of a relationship with a caseworker enables the hemophilic youngster to express his own perceptions, fears, anxieties, and wishes about himself, that for one reason or another cannot find adequate expression in his family group. Vocational planning can and should be instituted early in order to assist the hemophiliac to "capitalize his losses" by turning to academic or quiet hobbies, to make up for the fact that he cannot be an active participant in body contact athletics and rough games. Early counseling is particularly imperative for the individual who does not have the intellectual endowment suitable for pursuing academic courses of study, in order to steer him to an appropriate and consistently pursued course of preparation leading toward ultimate employment.

The older adolescent and the young adult need constant encouragement and opportunity to discuss their personal problems and reactions in other than the emotion-fraught home situation. One way social workers can also help in this area is by arranging special opportunities for group participation in existing social agencies, community centers, and informal clubs. Posing these problems and needs, however, does not answer the question of who in the community, that is to say, what professional group, will take responsibility on behalf of such patients. From my experience with hemophiliacs, I should estimate that not more than twenty per cent of the afflicted families in a large city have had contacts with social agencies. Although individual situations must be dealt with individually, it is apparent that once the definite diagnosis of hemophilia is made, the resultant psychosocial, educational, vocational, and other social problems of a patient and his family are numerous, diverse, long-continuing, and almost uniformly present. It would seem of great benefit, then, to have centers established for information, referral to appropriate resources, and, if possible, direct casework and related services—such as group counseling—that would utilize specific knowledge of the condition and its effects. The hemophilia associations are not yet strong enough nor do they have financial resources sufficient to provide such services, although they recognize the necessity for them. It would thus seem that in this, as in other fields of chronic illness, the community is in need of a new type of casework service, one that offers comprehensive information and knowledge of resources appropriate to meeting the needs of the chronically ill, along with some direct services of both a casework and a group character. The challenge of meeting the needs of the hemophilic patient and his family is a persistent and urgent one for social workers in all settings.

KIDNEY DISEASE

CHAPTER 39

Impact of Kidney Disease on Patient, Family, and Society

Kathleen M. Hickey

The National Kidney Foundation estimates that over seven million Americans now suffer disease of the kidney. More than 125,000 people in the United States die from kidney disease each year. If transplantable kidneys were available, seven thousand of these persons could be saved.

The long periods of chronic illness, repeated hospitalizations, and the overwhelming amount of stress placed on patients and families have implications for social work. It is the purpose of this article to provide information about kidney disease and methods of treatment and to point out some of the social problems in order that social workers might be better prepared to assist clients with kidney disease. The material in this article is drawn from experience at the Kidney Transplant Service of the University of Minnesota Hospitals, a teaching facility of 826 beds, with 125,000 outpatient visits each year. The Kidney Unit has 25 hospital beds and 220 patients attending the Transplant Out-Patient Clinic.

The person who is faced with the loss of kidney function manifests a state of crisis. Permanent kidney failure formerly resulted in death; choices today are limited to implantation of another person's kidney, kidney dialysis, or death. Two methods of treatment offer a chance for life—hemodialysis (use of artificial kidney machine) and kidney transplantation.

Reprinted from *Social Casework*, Vol. 53 (July, 1972), pp. 391–398, by permission of the author and the Family Service Association of America.

Hemodialysis has shown itself to be a feasible means of prolonging the lives of people with permanent kidney failure. The treatment procedure involves implantation of tubes (cannulas) into the arm or leg of a patient. The cannulas are inserted into the artery and vein and are connected by a shunt that lets the blood flow from one cannula to the other between treatments. When a patient comes in for treatments, the cannulas are connected to tubes leading to the artificial kidney machine that removes the impurities from the blood. The patient must spend several hours lying in bed attached to the machine, as a dialysis may take from four to twelve hours and is required two or three times a week.

Kidney transplantation, which involves grafting of an organ from one individual to another of the same species (homograft), has now advanced to the stage in which it is the treatment of choice for persons with permanent renal failure. Successful transplantation removes the patient from the "sick role"; dialysis does not. He feels better, sources of stress are lessened, and he is able to assume a functioning role. The aim of transplantation is to restore the individual to a normal functioning life.

Physicians have intensified research and study on kidney transplantation as a method of treatment for several reasons. (1) Deaths were numerous among young people; (2) kidney transplantation is technically the easiest method to perform; and (3) the kidney is the only vital paired organ of which a human being can lose one and still survive well. Also, if the body does reject the new kidney, the patient can be maintained on the artificial kidney machine. It is anticipated that improved immuno-suppressive drug therapy, organ preservation, and more accurate tissue typing will, within the next few years, greatly reduce rejection reactions and increase the chances of longer life.

The University of Minnesota Hospitals has a liberal admission policy. Although a patient must meet certain medical criteria, social and economic factors do not play roles in a patient's acceptance. Patients also do not have to be state residents. Those rejected by other centers and those with disease or complications, such as diabetes, are accepted. Because of these factors, social problems are perhaps more prevalent and severe.

In 1971, eighty patients received kidney transplants; of this number, sixty-three were adults, and seventeen were children under sixteen years of age. Of the group, thirty-four received cadaver (deceased, nonrelated donor) transplants. All the children and twenty-nine of the sixty-three adults received kidneys from blood-related donors. When a patient receives a kidney of a related donor, his chances for survival with a functioning kidney are much greater.

Surgical illness is a "human experience" and produces new adaptations that may or may not be pathological. The dramatic character of transplantation surgery diverts attention from social problems inherent in the medical procedures, such as failure of the operation to meet expectations of the patient and family, disruption of family equilibrium, and investment of public funds to meet these costs. Renal failure and transplantation precipitate a crisis that may be defined differently by the patient and family. The crisis situation may mobilize or it may incapacitate them.

The discussion that follows will be based on the experiences of the social worker assigned to the Kidney Transplant Unit. The social worker assists the staff by obtaining detailed information in the form of social histories concerned with the impact of the disease on the patient and his family. The major functions of the social worker are to help the patient face his current environment and work through his feelings, fears, and attitudes and to help him strive toward a realistic adjustment and plan for his future life after discharge. The social worker explores the interaction and dynamics of members of a family—their attitudes, ways of communicating, and patterns of coping. Adherence to the patterns of a past life is not always indicative of the future but may identify specific problem areas. The focus is on helping families retain their integrity and functions.

The social work role varies with each patient. It consists of (1) helping the individual to understand the extensive treatment plan, (2) counseling with the patient and family in working out acceptance of the medical problem and methods of modifying some of its aspects by exploring ways for more satisfying relationships, (3) assessing readiness for acceptance of help from community and similar resources, (4) acting as a resource person and liaison with community agencies, (5) providing casework services to assist the patient and family, and (6) offering public education.

In order to coordinate information to assist the physician so that the patient can receive maximum benefit of treatment at University Hospitals, the "Hospital Team Conference" was initiated and is concerned with a comprehensive program for total care. The team attempts to alleviate forces that interfere with the patient's ability to receive and accept medical care. There is also considerable interaction and intense involvement among patients and between patients and staff. Social systems that characterize hierarchy among the patients are evident. Codes and rules are established, and patients redefine these roles and set up new expectations and responsibilities of which the staff must be aware in order to meet the needs. A therapeutic environment is encouraged by the staff through team conferences, physical therapy, occupational therapy, and diversional activities.

The Chronically Ill Patient and Hemodialysis

Hemodialysis prolongs the life of patients by the use of the "artificial kidney." Patients unable to receive a kidney transplant, those awaiting a cadaver donor, and patients who have had rejected transplants are maintained on dialysis. The treatment procedure can return a patient to a reasonably normal existence but presents some physical side effects and psychological complications. Although hemodialysis alleviates the uremic syndrome and the patient generally feels better, there are diet restrictions, problems with blood pressure, feelings of weakness, impotence, periodic hospitalizations, and shunt complications (clotting), any of which may prevent participation in living activities. Most patients experience some degree of apprehension before dialysis and tend to become most anxious at the beginning and end of the treatment when the shunt is disengaged or when technical difficulties arise. Attention span is often short, and it has been noted that some patients defend themselves against their anxiety by intellectualization or through sleep. Dialysis can be a frightening experience as a patient is able to observe his blood leaving and returning to his body. He may experience various degrees of fantasies and distorted body imagery, and he may view himself as not wholly human. The dialysis technician and nurse, who are particularly close to the patient, must deal realistically with the patient's anxieties concerning the machine. After dialysis, temporary weakness and nausea from salt and water loss is present; this weakness is often accompanied by lethargy.

Thus, hemodialysis does not completely alleviate difficulties of renal failure, and patients may be faced with a future of chronic illness. Patients, however, may function adequately in the "sick role." The passive dependent person probably will make an adjustment to dialysis but may have difficulties in long-term adjustment after a successful transplant. Patients on dialysis are also placed in a dependent situation and may never accept the shunt as an integral part of themselves. The cannula is a constant reminder of their condition and dependence on the dialyzer. A state of mental depression is not uncommon and follows the general grieving sequence of stages. At first patients tend to use denial; then they go through a period of grief and mourning, followed by anger and frustration, which may give way to depression or regression. Then constructive attempts are made to adjust to the illness and treatment plans. (A temporary depressive phase is also noted immediately following transplant.)

It is not uncommon for the patient on dialysis to violate a dietary or fluid restriction. Patients are carefully taught about permitted and forbidden food and its significance in relation to their illness and life. Nevertheless, patients frequently refuse to eat designated foods, request foods they know they are not allowed, or eat in the hospital canteen. Food can assume great importance for the patient under stress. The traditional methods for relieving anxiety and tension, other than food, are often not permitted for the dialysis patient. He may be advised to stop smoking or restrict alcoholic and fluid intake. He may not be allowed lengthy trips or participation in rigorous activity. These prohibitions may result in hostile feelings, and the patient may attempt to use his diet to control his situation, seek gratification, and release his stress. Another form of behavior that might be interpreted as an act of resentment, denial of illness, or desire for self-harm is the patient's neglecting to take care of his shunt.

Long-term dialysis requires sacrifices on the part of the patient and his family because of the special requirements and frequent trips to the hospital for dialysis. The patient and family members may resent this intrusion on family life and display open hostility and guilt, often directed at the staff. The patient's self-image and role can change greatly during this period.

The time of dialysis (day or night) and the distance to the center are important factors in the patient's total rehabilitation and his ability to be gainfully employed or perform household duties. Thus, chronic hemodialysis has a profound psychological impact on the patient and his family.

The Transplant Patient and His Family

The transplant patient must plan to remain under medical supervision for an indefinite length of time. The prospect of transplantation presents freedom from pain and provides an opportunity to engage in meaningful activity. Conflict may arise between the patient and family. The patient may feel more threatened by new independency in assuming the "healthy role" than by facing death. The choice of a kidney donor requires family decisions that can produce a high degree of stress. This decision-making crisis in kidney transplantation is unique; all the members of the family know that one could be saved by the sacrifice of another. The act of donation may be inconsistent with other life patterns and may not follow a rational decision-making process. Man is used to identifying with a model, and the lack of norms and customs to use as guidelines would appear to cause a great amount of tension and stress. The patient knows that if he receives a kidney from a family member, his chances for survival are twice as good as they would be from a cadaver kidney. Reactions to receiving a cadaver kidney have been studied extensively; however, from observation, attitudes vary from curiosity about the person who donated and how his death occurred to indifference and relief that the patient does not have to be concerned about family responsibilities or obligations to the donor. Some relatives reveal a sense of grief about the inability of the family members to contribute toward saving the patient's life. The attitude regarding the donated cadaver organ seems to differ between recipient families and donor families, the latter probably viewing donation as a gift and sacrifice.

The length of the interval between the first knowledge that a transplant is needed and the time of the surgery influences psychological attitudes. The patient exhibits various degrees of psychological decompensation pertaining to the donated kidney, based on intrafamilial relationships and personality makeup. Particularly if the recipient is an adult, he will look beyond his immediate family for a potential donor. Role obligations for family members (siblings, aunts, or other close relatives) are unclear in our culture with the possible exception of parents' donation to children. Parents who donate seem to feel that their donation is not so spectacular or extraordinary but something natural to do for their child. Siblings appear unclear about this obligation to donate a kidney. Realistically, the donation of a kidney would cause the donor discomfort, loss of work time, and a small risk of kidney loss for himself later in life. Some families are subjected to many pressures, and the decision to donate a kidney may be a very stressful process. Many of the patients do not approach the entire family but request another member to do so, and this member may play a key role in the recruiting of donors. The patient usually has a good idea if a family member will not volunteer because of ambivalent family relationships; he accepts this fact and is satisfied to wait for a cadaver donor. However, in less close relationships, decision-making can be very difficult. Studies are currently being conducted by Dr. Roberta Simmons of the Sociology Department at the University of Minnesota on the nature of this crisis, focusing on the extended family and on the relative who does not donate a kidney. It has been observed that some relative donors, however, may question their responsibility for the recipient's life; likewise, the recipient may feel threatened in taking the kidney. There is also some indication of feelings of greatness versus hypochondrism on the part of the recipient and donor. In general, donors postoperatively display pride and increased self-esteem and handle their emotions and physical discomfort well.

Patients, both adult and child, become quite sophisticated and knowledgeable about their medical conditions. The patient takes an active part in his treatment program and is able to understand and speak the medical terminology. He learns about the detailed functions of the kidney and about the complex medications and their purposes. "Dialysis and transplantation" are explained thoroughly to him. The kidney disease patient understands his medical diagnosis and prognosis and the reasons for this renal failure in more detail than do most chronically ill patients. The medications given after transplant are essential for the life of the new kidney and the patient's life. The patient knows this and must accept the medications, which may produce observable side effects and impose psychological implications. The first year post-transplant is probably most crucial; problems such as rejection of the organ will most likely occur during this time period. Thus, even after discharge from the hospital, patients often must be readmitted for rejection episodes. This threat, which continues to cause work and home disruptions, adds to the patient's fears.

The high level of emotional involvement in regard to the donation and possible rejection of the new kidney may arouse great anxiety, grief, and disruption of family equilibrium. Rejection of a transplanted kidney produces changes in relationships and a breakdown in defenses. Changes in roles in the patient's total life situation may be consequences of chronic illness or kidney rejection. Successful transplantation, however, also may produce new life situations and adaptations that do not automatically insure total social and psychological rehabilitation.

The changes in total life situation and attitudes of the transplant recipient may, for example, influence women to change their attitudes in regard to childbearing as against adoption of a child. Marital and sexual relations that have been altered drastically because of the patient's uremic condition during dialysis treatment may make the post-transplant adjustments difficult. Employment retraining may be indicated. Conflicts or problems existing prior to transplantation, on the other hand, may be resolved following a successful transplant.

Teen-agers who receive a transplant have special problems. Absences from school, loss of friends, and conflicts in regard to sex and dating appear to be common. The adolescent is apt to find his body image and identity more of a problem than he can handle.

The social problems a child with kidney disease faces differ from those of the adult. His lack of knowledge and immaturity make the medical treatment plan less well understood and more frightening. Often the child's personality is formed during lengthy and recurrent hospitalizations. The parents' fears and concerns and the limitations of the illness influence the child's development.

Children frequently identify very strongly with a kidney that has been received from a parent donor. For example, a thirteen-year-old boy who received a kidney from his father stated, "I have the only kidney for a boy my age that flew forty missions over Germany."

The parents of a child who has a successful kidney transplant must learn a whole set of new adjustments. Their general concerns and overprotection must be modified to enhance the child's normal development. Siblings who have had competitive feelings and resentment because of special favors and privileges accorded the ill child may add to the difficult readjustment of parents and patient. At times, even the marriage itself must be rebuilt and the entire family relationships recast, requiring assessment, time, and work. Most families need the services of a caseworker during this process.

The social workers in hospitals need to be sensitive to the reactions of patients and relatives so that they can provide guidance and support when needed. During the patient's hospital course, he usually seeks out other patients and compares progress. Strong friendships may form, offering each other a great deal of support. On the other hand, inaccurate information is often exchanged. Relatives, too, may misinterpret another patient's medical status and assume that the same fate is in store for their relative. When a patient becomes acutely ill or dies, the other patients generally become agitated, withdrawn, and depressed; feeling tones are easily picked up and transferred one to another and should be discussed. Because of the critical nature of the illness, the social worker must be able to understand and recognize his own feelings about death and have substantial medical knowledge so that he can empathize with and relate to all patients' families.

Financial Costs and Community Responsibility

The cost of medical care for kidney transplant patients ranges from $10,000 to $80,000. The average cost at the University Hospitals is approximately $16,000 for total inpatient care exclusive of professional fees. Chronic dialysis treatment may amount to between $5,000 to $15,000 on a yearly basis, whereas it is hoped that transplantation is a one-time expense. Eventually, these costs will decrease because of shorter hospital stays and medical advances. The principal sources of financial help at the present time are private insurance, federal research grants, and public welfare programs. Thus, the financial costs entailed by chronic hemodialysis and transplantation impose a problem for the patient, his family, and society. Loss of economic, social, or personal status can become a serious problem and can greatly affect the patient's adjustments and capacity to function. Economic variables directly influence family attitudes as do those of culture, religion, sex, age, and length of illness.

The middle-class patient, who may have insurance coverage and a fairly adequate and stable salary prior to hospitalization, may be required, when his insurance coverage is less than his expenses, to apply for welfare assistance—a plan difficult for many to accept. Furthermore, because they own property and have financial assets, many are ineligible for public assistance until legal income requirements are met. The tragedy is compounded for farm patients who are faced with the necessity of selling their land and sacrificing their livelihood and financial independence. For patients residing outside the metropolitan area, there is the additional financial strain of transportation and maintenance costs. Most welfare departments and communities are not able to authorize funds to meet these expenses.

Major financing for the medical expenses of these patients comes from public funds under Title XIX of the Social Security Act. The provisions of the act make it possible to provide complete care for these patients. However, state plans, the interpretation of the act, and procedures by local community agencies impose limitations that create difficulties. The large amount of money required to provide medical care for patients who have severe renal disease, moreover, may be more than a community considers justifiable for one individual. The alternatives are for those in medical practice to refine technical methods to reduce costs and for the federal government to grant financial assistance to institutions involved in development of new methods of medical care. Kidney disease is a major community health problem and thus has serious implications for every community whose social agencies cannot offer constuctive services to help these patients.

Among men and women under twenty-five, kidney diseases are the second highest cause of work loss in the United States today. From age twenty-five on, these kidney-related diseases are the fourth highest cause of work loss. The Kidney Foundation, the only major voluntary agency relating itself to the total problem, states that one of every twenty-five persons in any community suffers from some form of kidney disease. Thus, in order for the patient to receive maximum benefit from medical care, his financial, social, and psychological needs must also be met by the community and society.

Employment

Generally, when the patient who has had a successful kidney transplant is ready for discharge from the hospital, he has no vocational restrictions imposed upon him. Ideally, the patient can return to his former job. Realistically, however, his former job may not be available. The prolonged treatment and hospitalization, the financial costs, complexity of medications, periodic checkups at the hospital, and drastic changes in the patient's life situation may have interfered with work performance and resulted in loss of his job. Overprotection is often manifested by family members; it impedes the patient's return to work and independency and interferes with his rehabilitation. Patients, too, fear that harm may come to the new kidney if they engage in strenuous work or extracurricular school activities. Because the majority of patients receive Social Security Disability or county assistance, it is difficult for them to relinquish this aid until they are secure in a new job. Employers hesitate to hire persons who receive Social Security Disability. Many employers do not understand the nature of kidney transplants and do not wish to risk employing someone who might be readmitted to a hospital at any time. Thus, patients may be rejected because they have received an organ transplant. The primary reason generally given is the restrictions imposed by insurance and union policies of large companies.

Physical side effects produced by medication, such as cushioned face, may also prevent patients from seeking the type of employment they want or from resuming past activities. Family relationships and support are important in determining the patient's successful rehabilitation and his return to a level of activity that is equal to, or surpasses, the level prior to the onset of kidney disease.

Vocational rehabilitation and counseling services should be enlisted prior to the patient's discharge from the hospital. Studies focused on defining "rehabilitation" and "adjustment" pretransplant and posttransplant would be useful with the recognition that definitions vary. The mere fact that a person has returned to work following transplantation does not automatically conclude that he is "rehabilitated." The quality of the individual's functioning must be explored. When the gainful employment he has returned to is satisfying to him and to his needs, employment can be used as an indicative factor of rehabilitation.

Moral and Ethical Aspects of Transplantation

Transplantation of human organs is a new era in medical history. The availability of new surgical techniques that prolong and save the lives of thousands of individuals makes it necessary to examine current beliefs concerning the use of organs from the bodies of other people. There are fears within the population regarding the donation of organs, as evidenced by the customs and the mass media. The value of the body, fear of mutilation, sickness, and future health are all considerations and should be correlated with religious beliefs, socioeconomic status, sex, age, race, and culture.

The development of living organ banks is an attempt to institutionalize societal fears. The signing of a donor card may represent a wholesome impersonal aspect, although it is questionable whether people view this action realistically or view it as socially desirable. In the past it has been thought that people who sign cards donating vital organs to a medical center to be used for others are from the better educated, higher socioeconomic groups and view this act as humanitarian. Recent studies, however, indicate that people in the lower socioeconomic groups also wish to make a donation of parts of their body—possibly as a contribution to society or from religious motivation.

The use of organs from the body of a healthy, functioning individual raises moral questions. The extent to which one individual may impose on another is an ethical consideration. The rights of people to safeguard their own bodies can never be denied. In some of these instances the moral and family pressures on donors impose obligations that deny this right.

Another ethical aspect of the procurement of organs involves the purchase of organs for transplants when immunological techniques are perfected. More organs would then be available on a case-negotiation basis. Because American culture is based on paying for what one receives, this action might not be disturbing to the population. If purchase of organs were authorized, the use of family and cadaver donors would be less of a necessity. However, purchase of organs raises the difficulty of determining price. A high price for organs would certainly discriminate against the poor. The selling of organs might also be interpreted as a partially suicidal gesture. Through laws, it is likely that attitudes and customs regarding transplantation and donation may change, and donation may come to be viewed as a social obligation rather than as a gift or sacrifice.

At the University of Minnesota Hospitals the criteria used for selection of people to receive a renal transplant or to be maintained by hemodialysis are based primarily on medical decisions. As yet, the quality of life the patient will be able to lead or the contributions he can make cannot be determined or defined without enlisting value judgments. Transplantation provides a "potential" life with a new organ. The moral issue is, "Are we doing what we are supposed to do?" Focusing on the quality of life and on transplantation and developing ways of improving present situations are needed.

Other questions raised pertaining to the moral and ethical aspects of transplantation might include the high costs of maintaining dialysis and transplant units of equipment and of training of specialized personnel. People undoubtedly will question the future of transplantation and the possible creation of genetic pools. There are also ambiguities concerning whether to view transplantation as research or treatment, thereby affecting the cost-benefit ratio.

Technical problems of transplantation are now being surmounted and the risk of death reduced. Perhaps we should also look at what technology has not accomplished. Technology may change or eliminate some of the forementioned problems. For example, selection criteria may never have to be defined if the use of mechanical or animal organs replaces the use of human organs in transplantation.

Kidney transplants are successful and are becoming a socially approved procedure. Society lags behind the technological aspects of transplantation, and we must prepare ourselves to meet the psychological and social needs imposed by transplantation in order for these members of society to return to a functional life. The social worker, who has direct contact with the patients, staff, and community agencies, has a professional obligation to transmit accurate information to the public and inform agencies of the needs of certain groups of people in an attempt to establish new resources or change existing attitudes and conceptions.

Conclusions

Social factors are being recognized as important components of kidney disease. Extreme importance is attached to the period following acute illness when the patient regains his health. The patient's attitudes toward kidney disease range from acceptance, resentment, and feelings of inadequacy to withdrawal and exclusiveness. Attitudes of the family members can result in increased dependency, overprotection, and unwanted sympathy. The patient who returns to the community sometimes needs complete economic and social rehabilitation, or he may undergo only relatively minor adjustments. The psychological manifestations are manifold, especially in patients and families when transplantation has failed. The threat or fear of rejection and the high degree of emotional involvement can prevent the patient from resuming his normal life.

In describing some instances of family conflict, decision making, stress, and the impact of kidney disease on the patient, on his family, and on our society, is not intended to imply that the information presented is valid for all potential transplant candidates. In many instances, dialysis, donation, and transplantation run a fairly smooth course and only minimal amounts of rehabilitation are required in order for the patient to resume a fully functioning life.

A program of early social evaluation in the course of the illness should be designed to detect patients whose defenses and coping patterns seem ineffective. The degree of personality disintegration that may accompany organ transplantation has made it evident to medical personnel that a more comprehensive program must be developed to meet the total needs of these patients.

This is a new era in medical history, which offers an opportunity for health to thousands of people with kidney disease. The social worker has an essential contribution to make to the total treatment plan. The new developments present a challenge to social workers to use their skill and knowledge to assist patients to obtain the greatest benefits from medical care and to participate in the healthful living that new treatments promise.

MULTIPLE SCLEROSIS

CHAPTER 40

Group Work Intervention with a Multiple Sclerosis Population

Gary John Welch and
Kathleen Steven

For several decades we have seen the development of parallel movements in group rehabilitation care: a professional care approach utilizing techniques of counseling and psychotherapy, and a self-help approach. While there is a wealth of information available concerning the theory and practice of group methods to promote personal and interpersonal change (e.g., Cartwright & Zander, 1968; Ohlsen, 1970; Shaffer & Galinsky, 1974; Yalom, 1975), little attention has been focused on the use of group methods to meet the specific needs of disabled individuals. The nature of the self-help process has likewise been discussed at length (e.g., Grosz, 1972, 1973; Hurvib, 1970; Jacques, 1972; Jacques & Perry, 1974; Katz, 1965, 1967, 1970; Mowrer, 1972; Reisman, 1965; Wechsler, 1960; Wright, 1971; Yalom, 1970), but there has been little attempt to provide a bridge between the professional care and self-help models.

In the current study the two approaches are combined in that a self-help organization for individuals with Multiple Sclerosis requested professional guidance in the supervision of a therapy group for its members. The intervention program described below was developed in response to that request. The organization's leadership had identified the problem areas among group members: self-imposed social isolation, negative self-image,

Reprinted from *Social Work with Groups*, Vol. 2, No. 3 (1979), pp. 221-234, with permission of the Haworth Press.

and stressed family relationships. The intervention program was formulated within the context of the organization and its operating philosophy, that of self-help and mutual aid.

Prior to discussing the group members and the intervention setting, it is important to discuss how the term 'self-help group' is being employed in the current study. Tracy and Gussow (1976) note that there are two basic types of self-help groups: groups that are truly mutual-help associations (e.g., Emphysema Anonymous, Mending Hearts, Reach to Recovery, A.A.) and groups that are more foundation-oriented with the emphasis on promoting biomedical research, fund raising, public education, and legislation (e.g., The National Heart Association, American Diabetes Association, The Muscular Dystrophy Association). The self-help group in the current study is of the first type of self-help group. The organization was not affiliated with the National Multiple Sclerosis organization and was therefore dependent on local support for funding and operational assistance.

The core members of the treatment group included nine Multiple Sclerosis victims (five female, four male). Three individuals were chair bound and six were to some extent ambulatory. Ages ranged from mid-20s to late 40s. In addition to the regular group members, parents, spouses, and other interested parties attended intermittently. The average group attendance was 15 individuals. The setting for the group was the self-help organization's small offices. The meeting area was cramped and attendance was often limited due to lack of space.

In addition to the problem areas identified by the organization's leader, mentioned above, the professionals identified deficits in the areas of self-management skills and assertiveness as major problem areas for Multiple Sclerosis victims. Multiple Sclerosis is rarely fatal, but is usually a progressively disabling disease. It is one of the most common organic diseases affecting the nervous system and disables primarily by interfering with motor activities. Multiple Sclerosis almost invariably strikes individuals between the ages of 20 and 40. As there is no known cure for Multiple Sclerosis, individuals are left to reconcile themselves to the illness and learn to cope with its numerous and varied effects. The intervention program described below combines cognitive restructuring, modeling and behavior rehearsal, homework assignments, the presentation of didactic material, and group process in an attempt to overcome the deficits identified above.

Method

Group sessions were conducted weekly for 10 weeks, two hours per meeting, with each successive session devoted to a new topic. Topics were either leader or group member generated. The specific format of individual sessions varied depending upon content and purpose; however, a general procedure was followed weekly.

Each session began with a 30 to 45 minute didactic introduction to the content area under consideration. Content was presented by group leaders, guest speakers, or group participants. Identified were common dilemmas in the content areas, factors potentially influencing individual adjustment, and new ways of coping with the experience of a progressive debilitating disease. After the content was presented, the remainder of the group time was devoted to group discussion, problem-solving, modeling, and role rehearsal. As an example of didactic content and homework assignments an outline of weeks four and five is presented in Table 40–1 (p. 466).

INTERVENTION PROCEDURES

Group Process. Attention is given below to the intervention procedures implemented in the treatment program. The procedures are outlined and presented as if somehow operating in a state of mutual exclusion. This is due to the limits of written expression and for the benefit of clarity. In practice there is interaction among the intervention approaches in that affective, cognitive, and behavioral functioning are interrelated and the timing of several intervention procedures coincide.

In addition to the specific intervention procedures discussed below, a major variable influencing outcome may be labelled group process. The following discussion is an attempt to identify some aspects of group process (e.g., the catalytic effect, vicarious learning, and social reinforcement) which are assumed to have contributed to treatment outcomes. First a catalytic effect was observed in the group as individual participants began to share experiences. Consistent with previous research (Jourard, 1971; Kangas, 1971) participant response to self-disclosure was self-disclosure, the consequence of which was the realization of similarity. The sense of being faced with the possibility or certainty of some degree of permanent disability precipitated serious emotional reactions which demanded basic psychological readjustments. Participants realized their commonality with others who, like themselves, were confronted with the pervasive changes and accommodations inherent in attempting such major readjustments. Exposure to other individuals who had coped or were successfully coping with such adjustments functioned to provide positive adaptive models to several group members. For example, a sense of community developed as group members began to verbalize their feelings of alienation and isolation (frequently self-imposed). As specific personal experiences of embarrassment of rejection were shared, members became aware of their similarities and were able to focus their energies on constructive problem-solving.

Second, the Multiple Sclerosis group, with its problem-solving focus

TABLE 40-1.   A Two Week Sample Outline of Group Meeting Content and Homework Assignments

Week 4

Content Areas:

1. A physical therapist discussed and demonstrated a program of exercises for M.S. patients. The exercises were tailored to the needs of specific members.
2. There was a discussion of how to incorporate appropriate exercises into individual group members' daily routine.
3. Participants presented the previous week's homework assignments.

Homework Assignment:

Each group member was asked to select two or three of the exercises appropriate for his/her specific condition and incorporate them into their daily routine. He/she was to record (mentally note, write down, or have someone else record) the exercise, when and how often it was performed, and to list any noticeable effects or problems.

Week 5

Content Areas:

1. Discussion and review of last week's homework assignment.
2. A didactic presentation was given on various relaxation techniques using imagery, diaphragmatic breathing, and self-hypnosis as a possible means of pain and anxiety control.
3. Group practice of several specific exercises was undertaken, and was followed by a discussion of their potential usefulness for individual group members.

Homework Assignment:

1. Each group was asked to select one of the relaxation exercises and apply it when he/she became aware of the onset of anxiety, tension, or pain. Group members were asked to record the results of both their ability to recognize the onset of the above and the impact of relaxation.
2. An ongoing concern of group members was the lack of public acceptance of M.S. victims and the resulting lack of recognition and support for their organization. As a result of this concern, individuals with particular abilities were given individual homework assignments to facilitate the group goal of greater public acceptance and support (e.g., one individual volunteered to write a short speech which could be presented by group members to civic and religious organizations; others agreed to contact individuals in the media in an effort to educate the public regarding the organization).

and extensive discussion time, was designed to promote vicarious learning. Many group participants maintained strong negative self-evaluations based on changed physical abilities and possible wide mood swings that can accompany Multiple Sclerosis. Personal disclosure by participants who were attempting to continue to live meaningful and full lives offered constructive ways of viewing self in relation to the disease process. The value of attempting to capitalize upon changed physical and non-physical capacities was strongly emphasized. These alternatives were important in motivating participants to take steps in their own behalf. The intervention program was structured so as to provide group members with responsibilities which focused on their capabilities rather than disabilities. Additionally, group members' efforts directly benefited the individual, the group, or the self-help organization which provided direct reinforcement for effort expended. For example, two group members, no longer able to actively practice their professions, wrote newspaper articles intended to provide the public with a more accurate compassionate picture of the Multiple Sclerosis patient. Each of their articles was published in a local newspaper.

Third, participants, as well as group leaders, functioned as social reinforcers for other participants. The group was structured to allow each participant numerous opportunities to receive the attention of others. There were frequent expressions of peer understanding and support. Such expressions were of particular value to Multiple Sclerosis patients engaged in comprehensive change and concommitant self-doubt. The homework assignments were designed and implemented to accomplish these objectives. Time was allotted in each group meeting for individual presentations of the assignment and for group response. For example, in the eighth week group members had been asked to use specific assertive communication skills in an interaction with an authority figure (viz., V.A. or social security personnel, landlords, physician). The following week, each group member shared his experience and received feedback from the group. Feedback included support for attempts to complete the assignment, suggestions as to alternative approaches, and recognition for "success."

Cognitive Restructuring. Though the adjustment problem presented by Multiple Sclerosis can be severe, many participants exacerbate their situation with irrational, catastrophizing beliefs. A number of authors (e.g., Beck, 1970; Ellis, 1962; Goldfried, Decenteceo, & Weinberg, 1974; Kelly, 1955; Meichenbaum, 1974) have developed therapeutic procedures based on the assumption that behavioral and psychological change can be brought about by modifying an individual's assumptions and expectations about the world around him and his consequent internal verbalizations. The concepts "expectancy" and "assumption" can be translated into what is generally known by experimental investigators as cognitive set. The treatment goals of cognitive restructuring involve the alteration of negative cognitive set, irrational assumptions, and internal verbalizations.

The group leaders employed a modified version of Goldfried and Goldfried's (1975) systematic guidelines for cognitive restructuring. The steps followed included: (1) presenting a rationale; (2) presenting a method for identifying irrational assumptions; (3) self-intervention; and (4) creative problem-solving.

As a framework for cognitive restructuring, the authors utilized Ellis' (1962) Rational-Emotive Therapy (RET). Rational-Emotive Therapy was selected for its practical straightforwardness and its demonstrated efficacy in a number of controlled outcome studies (DiLoreto, 1971; Meichenbaum, 1972; Meichenbaum, Gilmore, & Fedoravicius, 1971; Trexler & Karst, 1972). A short introductory lecture was provided outlining RET's A-B-C method of viewing human psychological functioning and its disturbances. Starting with C (the upsetting emotional consequence, perhaps feelings of worthlessness, anxiety, or depression), and moving to A (the activating experience), group members were shown that between A and C there is the intervening variable which Ellis labels B (the individual's belief system). The belief system may be rational or irrational, but either case provides the basis for the connection between A and C through internal dialogue.

The method for training participants to the identification of irrational assumptions was based upon an analysis of Ellis' (1962) typical irrational beliefs. Understanding these tenets of rational judgement was considered requisite for corrective mediation and resulting behavior change. Group discussion and homework assignments were used to facilitate understanding. Homework involved participants in an attempt to apply the appropriate "rational point" to a current adjustment problem through the device of writing a short essay in which irrational cognitions were actively refuted. (For several Multiple Sclerosis group members it was not possible to write and an alternate assignment involving tape recording the essay was substituted.)

After the groundwork was laid and group members began to understand how irrational internal dialogues precipitated emotional disturbance, the participant could use his emotional reactions as "cues" to consider the question: "What am I telling myself about the situation that might be irrational?" As with any new skill there was an initial period of awkwardness and a pervasive sense of artificiality. With continued practice, however, the new response pattern of rational self-appraisal became habituated.

There are adjustment difficulties which required more than a rational self-appraisal. To be optimally effective as an intervention technique, cognitive restructuring was combined with the emission of specific behaviors which were incompatible with the irrational belief system. In this treatment program, group members were required to emit behaviors which were incompatible with their sense of isolation, negative self-image, and sense of powerlessness over self and environment (refer to Table 40-1). Some situations required the development of creative solutions to actual problems. In addressing these situations, the current authors adapted a technique employing four sequential steps to provide a learning experience in creative problem-solving. The procedure discussed below was first suggested by Roosa (1973) for application to family therapy. The steps include: (1) the statement of a problem situation in clear, unambiguous language; (2) the suggestion of possible options for solution of the problem; (3) an analysis of possible consequences for each solution; and (4) the simulation of the skills required to put the solution into action. Step 4 was employed only if a skill deficit was evident. These four steps were applied by the group to organizational problems which were of major concern to group members; that is, the lack of effective public relations and lack of funding.

Although the acquisition of problem-solving skills was programmed into the homework assignments, the usefulness of the procedures was occasionally demonstrated in the meetings themselves. A case in point is a disagreement over household responsibilities which erupted between two married group members. The leaders modeled the application of problem-solving skills to a "real" problem. Group members contributed by suggesting possible options and discussing possible consequences of the various options.

Modeling and Behavior Rehearsal. As problems were specified and desirable courses of action identified, participants frequently communicated an inability to perform actions leading to problem solution. To facilitate the participants' incorporation of the desired behavioral action/response, specified behaviors were modeled by the authors assuming the role of the participant whose problem was under consideration. That participant assumed the role of interactor while remaining group members either played significant others in the situation or observed the interaction.

The modeling role playing situation was repeated two or three times. Then the roles were switched to allow the participant an opportunity to begin practicing the desired behavior. As the participant became comfortable with the behavior, other group participants were enlisted in the role of responder. With the instruction of the group leaders, responders presented successively greater demands of skill incorporation on behalf of the participant. This procedure reinforced the participant in his skill development, shaped the participant into more sophisticated skill performance, and supported generalization of the skill.

After completion of behavior rehearsal the participants discussed the anticipated consequences of the newly incorporated skill. Group members provided further reinforcement to the participant in training through positive verbal feedback and encouragement to try the skill in vivo. For example group members rehearsed various ways of responding to others' perceived negative response (e.g., avoidance, rejection, ridicule) to their illness. Individuals would report to the group their efforts to practice these responses in vivo. These attempts would frequently stimulate others to initiate their own efforts.

Homework Assignments. While skill development and practice are legitimately accomplished in the group, the goal of intervention is the performance of the behavior in its natural context. The promotion of behavior transfer and generalization was accomplished through homework assignments. This procedure has been found to be most efficacious with educational and skill building treatment approaches in which the individual practices new behaviors and attitudes (Shelton & Ackerman, 1974). Consistent with Rose (1974, p. 103) the homework assignments were designed and implemented as follows:

1. Assignments were highly specific. Participants were aware of the exact actions/responses to be displayed, the conditions under which the behaviors were to be performed, and the appropriate alternatives should the appropriate condition fail to occur.

2. Assignments were realistic and supportive of reasonable change. The probability of success was high, and yet the assignments were challenging.

3. Participants made a verbal commitment in the presence of peers to attempt performance of the assignment.

4. Participants reported to the group their attempts to carry out the assignment. Monitoring of the change effort by the group provided an opportunity for positive reinforcement for trying to implement the behavior. This procedure provided an opportunity to evaluate the behavioral response against the reality of natural circumstances. The outcome of such an evaluation at times led to slight modification of the behavioral response. Although modifications were not great, occasionally a reinitiation of behavior rehearsal was indicated. Thus, reporting to the group was an effective way to gain corrective input.

Results and Discussion

The Multiple Sclerosis group combining the self-help model with professional supervision was evaluated based on client satisfaction, and completion of homework assignments. Client satisfaction was assessed in the last group meeting during which individual group members were asked to rate the value of the group to them personally along several dimensions from the value of group homework assignments to participant evaluation of group size. As Table 40-2 indicates, all group members highly rated the value of the group experience along all dimensions.

TABLE 40–2.   Client Evaluation of Program Usefulness

Areas Evaluated	Rating By Group Members*					Number Partici-pants
	Not at all Helpful	Not Very Helpful	Neutral	Helpful	Very Help-ful	
1. Group Homework Assignments				44%	56%	9
2. Individual Homework Assignments			11%	33%	56%	9
3. The Use of Co-leaders					100%	9
4. The Use of Non-M.S. Leaders				22%	67%	8
5. Presentations by Guest Speakers				11%	89%	9
6. Presentations by Group Members				33%	67%	9
7. Meeting Format				11%	89%	9
8. Involvement of Family Members in Group Activities			22%	33%	44%	9
9. Contributions (input) of Group Leaders				11%	89%	9
10. Contributions (input) of Group Members				11%	89%	9
11. The Size of the Group in Relation to:						
a. Your willingness to self-disclosure		11%	22%	22%	33%	8
b. Your ability to have input		11%		78%	11%	9

* Each group member rated the usefulness of each component of the intervention program. The results indicate the percentage of group members who rated the experience in a particular category.

Due to the nature of the group, which was an attempt to combine self-help concepts with the technical expertise of trained therapists, client satisfaction is regarded as the most relevant outcome measure employed. Group members established individual goals, suggested and occasionally provided content, and were generally responsible for the group experience. Under these conditions their satisfaction is of primary importance. The therapist-led self-help group operated on the ideas that both group members and therapist were equal partners in the change effort, and that the value of a particular therapist to the group was a function of the results of therapeutic procedures employed.

Completion of homework assignments was selected as a less subjective outcome measure as it was in keeping with the nature of the self-help group that members be actively involved in the process of change for themselves and other group members. Each week group members were given a common homework assignment. Occasionally individual group members were given specific homework assignments in keeping with individual objectives, interests, or capabilities. Combining group and individual assignments, 27 homework assignments were given. Of these, 23, or 85%, of the homework assignments were completed. This result suggests the group was successful in motivating self-help activity.

In addition to the above, several preliminary conclusions have been reached regarding maximizing the efficacy of the professionally guided self-help group approach to intervention with the Multiple Sclerosis population. The opinions expressed here are based upon observation of one group and must, therefore, be regarded as tentative. These early conclusions regarding treatment methodology may function as guidelines for other practitioners contemplating such treatment groups. Furthermore, until such time as data derived from controlled experimental studies is available, the following observations may be of heuristic value.

Problem-solving Focus.   Pervasive change is inherent in the process of Multiple Sclerosis. Such change results in problem-solving which is either haphazard or planful, active or passive. With large, time-limited groups it is desirable to train participants in individual problem-solving. Through the problem-solving orientation, the group functioned to provide services to its members. Information regarding social outlets was shared, a network for exchanging self-care information was established, and creative ways of coping with loneliness and uncommitted time were developed. The group created a vital social/interpersonal network for solving special problems.

As specific problems were considered in the group, the expectation was established that most problems are manageable. It was determined from participants through self-report (verbal feedback) that the cognitive restructuring generalized from the exercises in group problem-solving to individual problem-solving outside the group.

Heterogeneous Versus Homogeneous Grouping. The Multiple Sclerosis group was heterogeneous in terms of participant age, time since onset of the disease, and major adjustment problem area. Heterogeneous grouping enabled participants to view problems of Multiple Sclerosis as they might emerge over time and provided exposure to long-term problem-solving. The homogeneity of the group was emphasized through designing the program around several topical areas of adjustment that allowed participants to confront specific problems with others in similar situations. The advantages of heterogeneity and homogeneity were thus combined to serve the objectives of the program.

Use of Co-leaders. While a co-leader is not essential, participants indicated their preference for co-leaders. The presence of two leaders facilitated more specific problem focus and enabled the provision of more individualized attention. Furthermore, there was benefit from the diversity of experience and expertise of each leader.

Group Versus Individual Treatment. For the Multiple Sclerosis victim, the group offers several advantages over individual treatment. First, the group described was designed to emphasize vicarious learning through the provisions of extensive group discussion time. Second, the benefits of peer understanding and support, characteristic of many treatment groups, are particularly valuable to individuals engaged in comprehensive change and concommitant self-doubt that are typical of one in the process of adjusting to Multiple Sclerosis. Third, the group served to motivate individual participants toward productive and regenerative change. As participants report successful resolution of problems, motivation toward individual change was enhanced. Finally, the group facilitated the development of a viable social/interpersonal network for the participants.

References

BECK, A. Cognitive therapy: Nature and relation to behavior therapy. *Behavior Therapy*, 1970, *1*, 184–200.

BECK, D. F., & JONES, M. A. Progress on family problems: A nationwide study of clients and counselors' view on family agency services. *Family Service Association Census Report*, 1970.

CARTWRIGHT, D., & ZANDER, A. *Group dynamics: Research and theory.* New York: Harper and Row, 1968.

DILORETO, A. O. *Comparative psychotherapy: An experimental analysis.* Chicago: Aldine-Atherton, 1971.

ELLIS, A. *Reason and emotion in psychotherapy,* New York: Lyle Stuart, 1962.

GOLDFRIED, M. R., DECENTACEO, E. T., & WEINBERG, L. Systematic rational restructuring as a self-control technique. *Behavior Therapy*, 1974, 5, 247–254.

GOLDFRIED, M. R., & GOLDFRIED, A. P. Cognitive change methods. In F. Kanfer & A. Goldstein (Eds), *Helping people change*. New York: Pergamon Press Inc., 1975.

GROSZ, H. J. *Recovery, Inc., survey: A preliminary report*. Chicago: Recovery, Inc., May 1972.

GROSZ, H. J. *Recovery, Inc., survey: Second report*. Chicago: Recovery, Inc., 1973.

HURVITZ, N. Peer self-help psychotherapy groups and the implications for psychotherapy. *Psychotherapy: Theory, research, and practice*, 1970, 7(1),41–49.

JACQUES, M. E. Rehabilitation counseling and support personnel. *Rehabilitation Counseling Bulletin*, 1972, 15 (3), 160–171.

JACQUES, M. E., & PERRY, J. W. Education in the health and helping professions: Philosophic context, multi-disciplinary team models and cultural components. In J. Hamburg (Ed.), *Review of allied health education*, vol. I. Lexington, Ky: University Press of Kentucky, 1974.

JOURARD, S. M. *Self disclosure: An experimental analysis of the transparent self*. New York: John Wiley and Sons, 1971.

KANGAS, J. A. Group members' self-disclosure. *Comparative Group Studies*, 1971, 2, 65–70.

KATZ, A. Application of self-help concepts in current social welfare. *Social Work*, 1965, 10 (3), 68–74.

KATZ, A. Self-help organizations and volunteer participation in social welfare. *Social Work*, 1970, 15 (1), 51–60.

KATZ, A. Self-help in rehabilitation: Some theoretical aspects. *Rehabilitation Literature*, 1967, 28 (1) 10–11, 30.

KELLY, G. A. *The psychology of personal constructs*. New York: Norton, 1955.

MEICHENBAUM, D. H. *Cognitive behavior modification*. Morristown, N.J.: General Learning Press, 1974.

MEICHENBAUM, D. H. Cognitive modification of test anxious college students. *Journal of Consulting and Clinical Psychology*, 1972, 39, 370–380.

MEICHENBAUM, D. H., GILMORE, J. B., & FEDORAVICIUS, A. Group insight versus desensitization in treating speech anxiety. *Journal of Consulting and Clinical Psychology*, 1971, 36, 410–421.

MOWRER, O. H. Integrity groups: Basic principles and objectives. *Counseling Psychologist*, 1972, 3 (2), 7–33.

OHLEEN, M. *Group counseling*. New York: Holt, Rinehart, and Winston, 1970.

REISSMAN, F. The "helper" therapy principle. *Social Work*, 1965, 10 (2) 27–32.

ROOSA, J. B. *Situation, options, consequences, simulation: A technique for teaching social interaction*. Paper presented at the annual meeting of the American Psychological Association, Montreal, Canada, 1973.

ROSE, S. D. A behavioral approach to the treatment of parents. In J. Thomas (Ed.), *Behavior modification procedure: A sourcebook*. Chicago, Illinois: Aldine Publishing Co., 1974.

SHAFFER, J., & GALINSKY, M. D. *Models of group therapy and sensitivity training.* Englewood Cliffs, N.J.: Prentice-Hall, 1974.

SHELTON, J. L., & ACKERMAN, J. M. *Homework in counseling and psychotherapy.* Springfield, Illinois: Charles C. Thomas, 1974.

TRACY, G., & GUSSOW, Z. Self-help health groups: A grass roots response to a need for services. *Journal of Applied Behavioral Science,* 1976, *12* (3), 381–397.

TREXLER, L. D., & KARST, T. O. Rational-emotive therapy, placebo, and no- treatment effects on public speaking anxiety. *Journal of Abnormal Psychology,* 1972, *79,* 60–67.

WECHSLER, H. The self-help organization in the mental health field. Recovery, Inc., A case study. *Journal of Nervous and Mental Disorders,* 1960, *130* (4), 297–314.

WRIGHT, M. E. Self-help groups in the rehabilitation enterprise. *Psychological Aspects of Disability,* 1971, *18* (1) 43–45.

YALOM, I. *The theory and practice of group psychotherapy.* New York: Basic Books, 1970.

YALOM, I. *The theory and practice of group psychotherapy.* New York: Basic Books, 1975.

NEUROLOGICAL DISEASES

CHAPTER 41

Patients with Progressive Neurological Diseases

Gladys Lambert

Unlike the patient with an acute but transient illness, the patient with a progressive neurological disease is faced with an incurable, debilitating illness that may eventually lead to total physical dependency and a shortened life span. The long, slow course of the disease causes overpowering anxiety in both the patient and his family, especially in those instances where other family members have had the same disease or where the patient knows other persons with the same diagnosis whose condition is more advanced than his. The dread of, and then the horror of, being unable to walk, feed oneself, get out of bed, and take care of one's toilet needs has been graphically described by articulate patients.[1] As the patient becomes increasingly helpless and disabled, he and his family are called upon to make new and difficult emotional adjustments that frequently require social work intervention.

Progressive neurological diseases, which affect the brain and spinal cord, are primarily of unknown etiology. They vary in onset from early childhood and middle age to the later years of life. Multiple sclerosis, Parkinson's disease, and Huntington's chorea, a hereditary disease, are common in this group. Although symptoms vary with each disease, some fairly typical ones include involuntary irregular movements of the face, head, and hands; transient paralysis and weakness of extremities; instability of gait; and numbness and loss of sensation in various parts of the body.

[1] Georgia Travis, *Chronic Disease and Disability* (Berkeley, Calif.: University of California Press, 1966), pp. 111–12.

Reprinted from *Social Casework*, Vol. 55 (March, 1974), pp. 154–159, by permission of the author and the Family Service Association of America.

Basic Considerations

The patient with a progressive neurological disease is confronted not only with the normal stresses of living but with the additional problems and limitations inherent in his illness. The adjustment he makes depends to a large extent on his previous level of social functioning, the nature of the illness and its meaning to him, the existence of significant others who rally around him and are available to help, and his access to concrete resources. These factors, when applied to the patient, can provide the social worker with psychosocial diagnostic clues to the patient's coping potential and can serve as the basis for formulation of a treatment goal and plan.

The patient with a satisfactory life adjustment prior to illness is more likely to cope adequately than a person whose previous adjustment has been poor or at best marginal. In evaluating the pre-illness level of social functioning, consideration should be given to the nature of the patient's previous family and social relationships and the extent to which these have been sustained and positive. His performance in such roles as spouse, parent, and worker provides clues about previous adjustment.

The physical limitations of a progressive neurological disease invariably interfere with the patient's performance of his previous role responsibilities. In our culture the husband carries primary responsibility for providing the family income. When he is the patient, the family is threatened with a loss or reduction of income and frequently a lower standard of living. For many men, the role of provider is a source of both status and deep personal satisfaction. Having to relinquish this role can result in a loss of self-esteem, a feeling of inadequacy, and an accompanying depression. Such reactions are culturally reinforced by the value our society places on productivity, self-reliance, and physical strength, particularly for men.

The patient who is a wife and mother may find it increasingly difficult to handle responsibilities attached to these roles. If she is the mother of an infant or young child, she may be unable to lift him or otherwise minister to his physical needs. Housework may become increasingly difficult. However, the reaction of each patient to these limitations will depend on the meaning they hold for him. Jeanette R. Oppenheimer points out that some individuals and families gain new satisfactions in the patient role because it serves to meet long-existing but previously unfulfilled needs. For many patients, however, the reverse is true. In his role as a patient, the individual may expect to be considered helpless and deserving of sympathy and tender care; he may anticipate that others in the family will take on protective functions and attitudes. These actions and attitudes, however, do not always come spontaneously from family members, who are charged with his care while simultaneously being affected by his abdication of his customary role. They may resent the onerous duties placed on them and the patient's release from his own duties.[2]

The patient's ability to cope can be greatly influenced by the support and encouragement of friends and family. If the patient is married and has relatives who can share some of the responsibilities of the overburdened spouse, the adverse repercussions of the illness on the marital relationship are often less excessive. However, the too-ready response by the family to the patient in his new role may create further problems for him as he experiences the loss of a role that had deep meaning; he may feel no longer needed or valued.[3] When there are no family or friends, or the relationship is extremely poor, the patient may rely heavily on the social worker for help in coping with the problems confronting him.

The availability of resources in the community can alleviate some of the more concrete problems facing the patient and his family and allow time for long-range planning. These resources may include various programs—frequently financed through medical insurance and local welfare departments—that provide for physical care of the patient at home and care of young children in the family. Although such programs exist in many communities throughout the country and render valuable help, they do not adequately meet the needs of the patient with a progressive disease because the help offered tends to be time-limited whereas the patient's needs often are not. Commercial programs which do not have this built-in limitation are usually prohibitive in cost for most middle-income families. In addition to the need for long-term home care services, community respite programs would be invaluable in offering temporary physical and emotional relief for families from care-taking responsibilities. Unfortunately, many communities have not yet addressed themselves to the long-term needs of this patient group.

Sometimes the problem faced by the patient and his family is not a lack of access to concrete resources but rather a reluctance to accept what is available. Applying for social security disability benefits and other forms of assistance may symbolically represent an admission of disability and dependency which neither the patient nor his family is yet ready to face.

Treatment Implications

The social worker in a medical setting is in a particularly good vantage point to intervene and help the patient and his family begin to cope with emotional and social aspects of a progressive neurological disease and pre-

---

[2] Jeanette R. Oppenheimer, Use of Crisis Intervention in Casework with Cancer Patient and His Family, *Social Work*, 12: 48 (April 1967).

[3] Ibid.

vent family dysfunction. Because the patient frequently visits a clinic or hospital for treatment of his illness, he is accessible to the worker. For some persons it may be less threatening to accept help with psychosocial problems in a setting which has medical treatment as its primary function.

If the patient and his family are to be helped to cope with a progressive neurological disease, it is important that the social worker not be overwhelmed by the disease process itself and that he keep the medical diagnosis in its proper perspective. The diagnosis should be viewed as a source of clues to the possible areas in which the patient and his family may need help.

In treating the patient, it is essential that the social worker provide opportunity for him to express and clarify feelings about his illness. Those in his immediate environment, his family and friends, often feel threatened by such expression and may overtly and covertly prevent him from doing so. The expression of feelings can liberate emotional energy needed to cope with the changes and limitations in his life and lessen his need to displace anger and frustration onto family and the medical team. Irving N. Berlin notes that he has known a number of seriously handicapped neurological patients for whom the continued opportunity to express their feelings about their handicap, without an attendant show of anxiety, helplessness, and hopelessness from the therapist, has helped them to focus their attention on the realities imposed by their handicaps and to proceed to do what they could to earn their own livings, to be productive, and thus to be more satisfied with themselves and happier despite severe and incapacitating handicaps.[4]

Since the patient's feelings are never completely resolved and often need to be dealt with during various stages in the progression of the illness, it is extremely important for the worker to be aware of his own feelings about the illness and to bring these under conscious control. Unless he is able to do so, he will be less prepared to help the patient with his feelings.

The patient's use of denial in coping with his illness, particularly when it is first diagnosed and during its early stage of progression, is fairly common and has been much discussed in the literature.[5] Denial can serve a useful purpose and should not be questioned unless it interferes with the patient's treatment and makes it impossible for him to handle reality problems precipitated by his medical condition. The use of denial is a signal that the patient is not yet emotionally able to face his illness and all of its implications for him and his family. Each patient has his own timetable for acceptance.

[4] Irving N. Berlin, A Review of Some Elements of Neurology: Part II, *Journal of Social Casework*, 37: 493–500 (December 1956).

[5] Harry S. Abram, Psychological Responses to Illness and Hospitalization, *Psychosomatics*, 10: 218–23 (July–August 1969).

Case Illustrations

The following case summary illustrates early intervention of the social worker, initiated to help a patient with multiple sclerosis express and clarify feelings about his disability and begin to cope with his situation.

Multiple sclerosis generally afflicts the patient during the most productive years of his life, between the ages of twenty and forty. The fatty substance called myelin, which acts as a protective covering for the nerve fibers of the spinal cord and brain, disintegrates, thereby blocking and distorting nerve impulses which control speech, vision, movement, and balance. Although early symptoms may disappear, over the years they reappear in more severe forms, resulting in paralysis and often urinary and bowel incontinence.

Mr. B, aged thirty-four, married and father of five children aged seven years to twenty-one months, was referred to the hospital social worker by his physician because of Mr. B's concern about his family's income during his hospitalization. He was hospitalized following the onset of blurred vision and paralysis of limbs. The tentative diagnosis of multiple sclerosis was confirmed. Nine years earlier, he had experienced transient visual difficulty and at that time there was conflicting medical opinion as to whether he had multiple sclerosis. Mrs. B, a full-time housewife and former registered nurse, was expecting their sixth child. Two years earlier, when Mr. B accepted a research position with a pharmaceutical company, they had moved into a new community, leaving behind relatives and friends.

Mr. B was an intelligent, capable young man who took pride in his role as husband and provider for his family. Mrs. B derived gratification from her role of wife and mother. In the marital relationship, she appeared maternal and more dominant, with no desire to work outside the home.

The worker saw Mr. and Mrs. B during and after hospitalization to help him adjust to his illness and its repercussions on their life. There was periodic consultation with Mr. B's physician and the nursing staff regarding his medical condition, prognosis, extent of impairment, and capabilities. This information was essential to the worker in helping the B family plan realistically for the future. Mr. and Mrs. B were given the opportunity to express their feelings about Mr. B's illness. Mr. B reacted to his diagnosis with depression and a verbalized fear of becoming dependent on "public charity." He expressed disapproval of disabled people he had known who lacked initiative and expected others to take care of their needs. Such feelings reflected his own conflict and anxiety about dependency.

After leaving the hospital, Mr. B returned to work for approximately eight weeks. However, a subsequent exacerbation of his condition, resulting in further weakness of limbs and unsteady gait, made it impossible for him to continue working. Although eligible for veteran's and social security benefits, he initially denounced each as charity and was only able to accept these sources of income when a representative of the Veterans' Administration pointed out that he should consider the needs of his family. The social worker recognizing Mr. B's need to deny his dependency needs, supported his rationalization that he had decided to accept help only because of his concern about the needs of his family. The family was able to manage on a reduced income chiefly as a result of their ability to economize.

Mrs. B, faced with her husband's illness as well as her pregnancy, avoided discussion of her own dependency needs. Because of her nursing background and experience, she understood a great deal about Mr. B's illness. Although she generally used strong intellectual defenses, she expressed a sense of loss and anger toward Mr. B for permanently depriving her of some aspects of companionship which he had not fully gratified previously. She recalled her own fondness for dancing and her attempts to prod him into dancing with her. Now, because of his condition, there was little possibility that he would ever be able to dance.

Looking ahead to the future, Mrs. B expressed the philosophy of enjoying to the fullest each day spent with her family. She used casework help to handle reality problems resulting from Mr. B's illness. The worker responded at the level Mrs. B sought and gave her advice and guidance about procedures and requirements for social security benefits and temporary public assistance. Mrs. B expressed a sense of shame in having to accept the latter and needed an opportunity to discuss her feelings and receive support from the worker before proceeding with the application.

In anticipation of Mrs. B's confinement, the worker helped her to consider various alternatives for the care of the children, and she was able to ask a relative to help. Following Mr. B's discharge from the hospital, both partners experienced some difficulty adjusting to his presence at home all day. The noise of the children distressed him and he expressed his feeling that his wife was not strict enough with the children. She complained that he was underfoot frequently and began to explore possible outside activities which would take Mr. B out of the home for a portion of the day, since he was ambulatory with the aid of a cane. Mrs. B, who had a retarded brother, suggested Mr. B volunteer his services at a local center offering day care activities for retarded children. Mr. B became enthusiastic about the volunteer experience, and the worker encouraged him to discuss his role at the center, supported his involvement, and gave recognition for his contribution to the children at the center who needed his interest and help. When Mr. B again saw himself as a productive person and when his self-esteem increased, the couple's relationship also improved.

As this case illustrates, a progressive neurological disease has emotional implications, not only for the patient but for his family as well. Sometimes it is not until the patient develops residual impairments that the full implications of the illness become an emotional reality. Since all relationships contain some ambivalence, the negative, resentful feelings of the patient's spouse and other family members are bound to increase as the patient becomes increasingly helpless and dependent on their care. Because they recognize that the patient is not responsible for his condition, they often feel guilty about these feelings; they then may become rejecting or depressed and overprotective of the patient. By helping family members express their ambivalent feelings without responding in a judgmental way, the social worker can help them cope with their responsibilities in a way which is constructive for family and patient.

The patient's increasing helplessness may upset the previously established balance in the marital relationship. A frequent area of difficulty is the change in the patient's ability to meet the needs of his spouse. Highly vulnerable are those marriages in which the ill spouse had played a protective nurturing role toward a highly dependent spouse. The increasingly disabled spouse may also be unable to meet the sexual needs of his partner or to fulfill his own. The nature of the couple's companionship frequently undergoes a change. Some previously shared social and recreational activities may need to be modified or curtailed and other substitutes found.

The following case illustrates the role of the social worker in sustaining a couple during the acute and terminal stages of the wife's progressive illness and prolonged hospitalization.

Mrs. R, a thirty-one-year-old married woman, mother of six children ranging in age from twelve years to seventeen months, was hospitalized because of a severe exacerbation of multiple sclerosis. She was unable to walk or sit upright in a wheelchair. She could not feed, bathe, or dress herself and was incontinent. Mrs. R's condition had been originally diagnosed shortly after the birth of her youngest child. Since then she had been hospitalized for brief periods but had been able to resume her normal activities as wife and mother.

She was referred for help to the hospital social worker by a staff nurse because of the concern Mrs. R expressed regarding care and supervision of her children. Mr. R, a construction worker, had been at home recovering from a back injury but was now ready to return to work.

This was the second marriage for both Mr. and Mrs. R, whose first marriages had ended in divorce. The present marriage had been plagued by long-standing differences over disciplining the children, especially the three older ones who were born during Mrs. R's first marriage. She was extremely protective of them and saw Mr. R as too strict and rigid. The two children of Mr. R's first marriage lived with his ex-wife in another state. Despite this area of tension in their relationship, they had positive feelings for each other. They shared common goals, had middle-class aspirations, and were buying their own home.

The social worker explored with them various alternatives for the care and supervision of the children and helped obtain a homemaker from the county department of social services. Later, the three children of Mrs. R's first marriage went to stay with their parental grandmother who lived nearby. When the homemaker was placed in the family, Mr. R returned to work. The worker maintained periodic contact with the county department of social services throughout the seven months of Mrs. R's hospitalization. There was a sharing of information regarding her condition and the family's adjustment to the homemaker.

Mr. R, a rather passive dependent man, had relied on his wife to make decisions regarding the family, and he continued to do so, with her acquiescence. To the worker, he showed considerable sorrow over her illness and he expressed his dependency on his wife by complaining about the lack of comfort and care when the house was run by the homemaker. The worker recognized his longing to have Mrs. R recover and return home to him.

Mrs. R, an intelligent, determined woman, displaced her anxiety about her illness onto continuing anxiety about the children. Under the increasing stress of her condition, complicated by a pulmonary embolism, she became quite paranoid for several weeks. She suspected her husband of poisoning her, transmitting a venereal disease to her, and seducing her ten-year-old daughter. There was no evidence to substantiate these suspicions, which subsided once her condition improved.

There was a change in social workers when, after three months of hospitalization in the neurology division, Mrs. R was transferred to the rehabilitation unit. Although Mrs. R's illness resumed a downhill course with a poor prognosis, she was able to spend some weekends at home with her family. Before the weekend visits began, the worker visited the home to evaluate its adequacy and determine the kind of equipment Mrs. R would need.

Both partners continued to use denial and to express hope in coping with Mrs. R's poor prognosis. They formulated plans for their future together in anticipation of her recovery and return home. Mrs. R continued to focus on the needs of her children. She was concerned about the academic performance of the eight-year-old daughter of her first marriage who was in a classroom for emotionally disturbed children. The worker conferred with the school personnel and shared pertinent information about Mrs. R's condition, interpreting the needs of the family.

The worker consulted frequently with members of the rehabilitation team regarding the changes in Mrs. R's physical condition. Because there was no improvement in her ability to function, the worker began to help Mr. R to consider the chronic care needs of his wife. Because of his dependency on Mrs. R and because he saw placement as essentially an unloving act, he was insistent on taking her home when discharged. However, as her condition further deteriorated, the focus shifted to helping him face the imminent loss of his wife.

After Mrs. R's death, Mr. R came to see the worker and talked about his wife's death and the plans he had made for the care of the children, following consultation with the county department of social services. The children of Mrs. R's first marriage were to remain with their paternal grandmother. Two children of his marriage to Mrs. R were to live with his mother in another state and the remaining son, a first-grade pupil, would continue to live with him. He had arranged to have his cousin supervise the child while he worked.

Summary

Because of the difficulties which patients with progressive neurological diseases and their families must face, they often need the help of a caseworker periodically during the course of the disease. The worker can help the family to cope with the members' ambivalent feelings about the patient while helping the patient to clarify his feelings and maintain a sense of self-worth and dignity. This task is exceedingly challenging in a society that places a high premium on self-reliance and productivity.

ORGAN LOSS

CHAPTER 42

Organ Loss, Grieving, and Itching

Kemal Elberlik

Body Image

A teacher once asked his students where they would choose to have a third eye if it were possible to have one. Some replied that a third eye in the center of the occipital region would be useful because with it they could see the back of the body. Some favored placing it in the abdomen or in the stomach to permit a view of the inside of the body.

One, however, said that having a third eye on the tip of the index finger would be ideal; he pointed out that then he could point it in any direction he wanted, and could see inside and back of his body and objects in the environment, and could touch most of the things he could see and see what he was unable to touch. All the students were eager to see the parts of the body invisible to them in ordinary circumstances, and they all expressed a need to know the total body. Optic experience is important in acquainting us with the nature of the external world and our relationship to it, and it also plays a dominant role in the creation of the body image.

Schilder[1] speaks of the body image as being, in simple terms, the picture of one's own body that each of us has formed in his own mind, and he stresses the special contribution of the senses of sight and touch in determining what that picture will be. But we also experience movement, both fine and gross, with the body and within it, and the kinesthetic gives further dimension to the self. Thus a *third eye* on the index finger would be a prime refinement of the individual's ability to know his environment

Reprinted with permission from the *American Journal of Psychotherapy*, Vol. 34, No. 4 (October 1980), pp. 523–533.

and his self, action and touch giving final shape to the bodily self as it appears to him and as he believes that others perceive it.

The effect of body image on the emotions can be illustrated at one extreme by children so effectively "pretending" to be giants that they suddenly become unwontedly "brave" on the playground; and at another extreme by the sensibility of the orchestral conductor Giulini, who says of music, "Until I feel it in my physical body I cannot conduct it." It follows that when the body is damaged and a new, flawed body image must be acknowledged, emotional and behavioral alteration can be expected, although it may be manifested so subtly as to require careful clinical scrutiny.

Niederland[2] suggests that an early body defect tends to leave an aura of unresolved conflict because of its concrete nature, its permanence, and its cathectic significance. Greenacre's[3] work supplements this view; she talks about a primitive "body disintegration anxiety" in serious disturbances of the early body image, and proposes that defective development of the body image contributes significantly to the establishment of fetishism.

Volkan[4] refers to the importance of the mother's role in the crystallization of the child's image of his own body. The mother's perception of a child's physical deformity may persist long after the deformity has been corrected, and may thus be conveyed to the child in the interaction of the mother-child unit. The mother of a child with a body defect can further traumatize her child if the mother-child unit functions poorly and she overstimulates the child's body or attempts to perform physiotherapeutic or orthopedic maneuvers.[5]

The evaluation of the body image is important in facilitating and completing the process of separation-individuation. Separation begins with the discovery of a world beyond the mother-me, and is activated by the beginning crystallization of body boundaries during the symbiotic period and thereafter. Growing intrapsychic awareness of separation, and the continuing practice of differentiation promote the formation of appropriate representations of self and object essential to the development of the ego.

The infant assimilates aspects of the key persons in his environment as his ego and superego by introjecting and incorporating them, then depersonalizing these introjects and identifying with them. They become part of his self. Early separation is dealt with by introjection-identification. Since humans change greatly from birth to adulthood to old age, body image is not constant.[6] Nonetheless, the effect of early experiences of separation-individuation and psychosexual development upon the body image—and even to a certain extent upon the physical body itself—is evident.

The early body image begins with contribution from all of the senses, and from all available emotional resources. The construction of the early self-representation is accomplished through the first autonomous ego functions, i.e. sensation and perception, both of which are strongly influenced by libidinal as well as aggressive drive derivatives. The infant soon becomes able to connect sensation with the appropriate body part, and is early engrossed in enjoyment of feedback mechanisms as he obtains gratification from touching and being touched. Those parts of the body accessible to his searching hands will take on unique importance for him, and as he makes contact with them and with objects in the environment, introjection and identification come into play in the determination of the postural model.

The discovery of erotic zones, and the ability to eroticize, play a significant part in the investment in the body. Those body parts that can easily be reached by the hands come to have a psychological meaning that does not pertain to parts that are out of sight and out of reach. At different stages of early development different areas of the body have different values and carry differential loads of emotional reference. Such progression from one bodily focus to another is recognized in our reference to the oral, anal, and phallic stages and their corresponding types of personality. Early experience and the degree of identification shape the perception of any given body part as good or bad,[7] pleasing or repulsive, clean or dirty, loved or disliked; and such attitudes and values help to determine what the body image will be.

ORGAN LOSS

It is self-evident that the individual's reaction to organ loss will substantially depend on what the significance of the lost organ has been to him, both realistically as a functional body part and unconsciously as a symbol. Nevertheless, one must anticipate emotional reaction to a physical change in the body, whether gradual or sudden, and this is much like the loss of a key figure whose disappearance alters the individual's immediate environment; although mediated by the nuclear personality, this reaction is likely to involve acute anxiety and grief, even among the so-called well-adjusted, and the physician who fails to appreciate his patient's emotional distress in such circumstances is falling short of meeting his patient's needs.

It is now clear that unless there are complications, the process of mourning goes through predictable phases.[8-10] After an acute phase, well described by Lindemann,[11] the "work of mourning"[12] takes place. There is shock and denial, then anger, then a search to regain the lost object, and disorganization, which, in the absence of complications, gives way to new organization that includes both inner and outer adaptation to the loss. Freud[12] indicated that this process is likely to take two years.

Such manifestations—the progress through different phases—may also appear in "established pathological grief,"[13] and extreme ambivalence and conflict concerning separation and union are present, and an introject and "linking objects" are established. Of course, if the patient disruptively identifies with the lost object, he presents a clinical picture of depression, as Freud[12] has established.

The loss of a key person is often expressed as a physical loss: "When my husband died it was as though an arm or a leg had been torn from my body." In the ensuing inevitable mourning and depression the mourner may express a sense of painful emptiness in the chest or epigastrium when the reality of the loss penetrates the consciousness. It is interesting that in a single study of grieving Parkes[14] observed a group of widows with a group of amputees. All of these subjects had suffered severe loss, and half of them experienced the same reactions, being numb at first, and then showing a strong tendency to deny the loss. Fifty-two percent of the amputees and 62 percent of the widows said they could not believe what had happened.

Then came anxiety and distress, often severe and readily evoked by any reminder of the loss. Fifty-nine percent of the amputees and 72 percent of the widows said they made a conscious effort to avoid thinking of or being reminded of their loss. At last the pangs diminished, and the subjects began to surrender hope of getting back what they had lost. They felt depressed and apathetic. Even a year after the loss, 63 percent of the amputees and 76 percent of the widows still felt disinclined to think of the future, but there were signs of improvement and reorganization, and a redirection of feelings and behavior finally took place.

The reaction to either kind of loss was seen to have two aspects: a feeling of external loss, and a feeling of internal change. External loss elicits separation anxiety and grief, separation anxiety being the principal emotion to arise after any major loss for which one is not fully prepared. Parkes's patients who had lost limbs exhibited grief in much the same way as those who had lost important others; the typical dream of the bereaved dealt with seeing the dead person alive again, and 38 percent of the amputees dreamed of the restoration of the lost limb.

Volkan's[15] work with "established pathological mourning" indicates, however, that this is only half the story, since the typical dream of seeing the dead alive also includes elements that indicate the wish to "kill" him, as it were, in order to end the process of mourning. Similarly, it can be said that the person who has lost a part of his body wants to have it back, but at the same time wants, under the influence of the reality principle, to "lose" it in order to finish his mourning process. The individual coming to terms with loss will experience sadness before his new model has developed to the point at which he seeks out and relates in a satisfactory way to new external objects. And the process may not move toward a satisfactory outcome, but be exaggerated, delayed, or distorted.

Parkes's study points to the existence of phantom husbands as well as phantom limbs. The persistence of either may do no harm, but there are other residues of the old working models that need to be replaced or modified in such a way that they contribute to affective functioning rather than intefering with it.

Case Reports

CASE 1

The problem of the first patient I will present in this connection was far less obvious than an amputated limb. Bill was a 31-year-old, well developed and well nourished white man who disavowed any major emotional problem but spoke of having had bad blackouts and being unable to work, to concentrate, or to keep up any continuing relationships. He spoke also of shunning any intellectual or emotional involvement, feeling strange about his body, and being curious as to why he had so little interest in life. He had gone several times to the emergency room because of fainting, disorientation, and vomiting, and he continued to suffer from heartburn, headache, and occasional *itching* all over his body. He reported having had chest surgery in the recent past. I then learned from his physician that Bill had been a patient in his hometown hospital on several occasions, complaining of abdominal and chest pains. Although his physician had diagnosed musculoskeletal chest pain and panic reactions, the crucial disclosure was that Bill had Klinefelter's syndrome. Questions of a possible vascular origin of his headaches and hysterical personality had been raised during hospitalizations a year or two before I saw him.

He had been married for ten years, and although his marriage had had its stormy moments, there had been no recent turmoil. The couple was untroubled about the absence of children; indeed, the wife herself had been told by a gynecologist that she was unable to have a child. The revelation that Bill's "chest surgery" had been done for the correction of gynecomastia, with mammectomy on both breasts, led to an account of his attempts to accommodate to the effects of Klinefelter's syndrome on both his functioning and his body image.

Bill told me that after puberty he was very restless, and constantly acted out in an effort to demonstrate his masculinity. He always sought work in jobs available only to strong, masculine men, in which physical strength (power) was required. He dated heavily, drank a great deal, and was often engaged in physical combat of some kind. His first hospitalization took place when he had a problem with one knee. The physical examination made at that time disclosed not only an infectious process in his right knee, but gynecomastia and bilateral hypoplasia. He had always felt concern about the overgrowth of his breasts, but this was the first time he had had to face a medical verdict concerning his condition. It took six years for him to make up his mind to submit to a mammectomy. Surgery for hiatal hernia was performed soon after this, and was followed by several more operations to correct postsurgical complications on the chest.

He had exhibited hysterical physical symptoms for two years, wandering pains and itching foremost among them. Psychological tests given at this time pointed to the possibility of feelings of inadequacy and difficulties in interpersonal relationships. His defensive style was effective only in a very limited way, and the prospect of his being able to deal effectively with periods of increased life stress was poor. He was suffering from a continuing need to act out on account of his complex sexual identities, and he was unable to deal adequately with the reorganization of body image after his chest surgery. His history of acting out during his postpubertal stage was related to his genetic characteristics and his gynecomastia.

His inability to form a cohesive body image or stable identity was an important factor in his inadequate coping with his mammectomy, which affected both his physical and emotional equilibrium. His postoperative complications and emotional disorientation continued as an accompaniment to ego impairment. He could not deal with the change in his body, and expressed his frustration and anger by blaming the surgeon and the complicated surgery he had performed. His hysterical behavior and acting out actually related to the fragility of his nuclear identity. Denial and anger were the affective roots of his pathological reaction to the loss of the already delicate balance between body and self-image. His wandering pains and *itching* were probably attempts to reorient himself and to work through toward the formation of a new body image, which in turn might be expected to foster a stable identity. The inability to form the necessary new body image brings with it the threat of disintegration, and Bill's great anxiety and mild depersonalization and anger reflected his frustration over his incapacity. Any realistic orientation to his bodily state was unfortunately being blocked by his denial, anger, and extreme frustration.

CASE 2

Joe was a 46-year-old white man who was unemployed and divorced. His chief complaint was insomnia, headache, and spells of *itching*, mostly on the upper extremities and the face. He was also depressed. When 13 years old, he had sustained a fractured pelvis and rupture of the bladder in a truck accident. His injuries had led to 30 hospital stays, and several operations, both major and minor. Complications in his urinary tract had finally been corrected by major surgery two years before he came to our attention. An artificial ureter and the construction of an artificial orifice in the perineal area made it necessary for him to sit down to urinate, and to devote considerable time to cleaning himself in the absence of adequate sphincter control. He could seldom go for more than a few hours without urinating. He had abdominal and gastrointestinal disturbances, and a large inoperable inguinal hernia for the discomfort of which he wore a brace.

Joe had married at 20. At that time his physical condition was adequate, and he and his wife had three children. When the corrective surgery for the urinary tract became necessary a few years after his marriage he became impotent, and his wife left him on that account when he was 33 years old. After her departure he lived with his mother and a bachelor brother, who died four years before we saw Joe. His mother died during the following year, and he was unable to work after her death, moving in with an older brother and his wife with whom he continued to live, doing their domestic work and driving them to their places of employment. He became responsible for all of the household tasks that usually fall to a woman's lot, and gradually dropped all other interests and contacts, occupying himself altogether with the feminine role. He was passive-dependent and very fragile. Although he expressed hopelessness, he denied any suicidal ideation, and had no history of attempted suicide.

The losses he had suffered were major; although he still had a penis it was not functional, and he had to accomodate to the artifical urinary tract and orifice in the perineal area. In addition, he was obliged to function in the role of a helping mother, and to reorganize his body image to take into account not only physical alteration but also the disturbance in and alteration of gender role.

Joe's losses—the loss of sexual function resulting from several ureter dilations and the final surgical construction of a new orifice, and the death of his mother—threatened his identity and his feelings of integrity. He was unable to make any real effort to return to his active role, but accepted a passive posture, continuing to be a housekeeper instead. From time to time his pain would become acute and his constant itching intolerable; his distress led him to visit the emergency room often. His frequent touching suggested the "eye on the index finger," since it served many purposes and activated the integration possible after mutilation. He had to keep the orifice of the ureter clean, and he became obsessed with this process, feeling the need to touch the orifice more often than was necessary. This constant need to touch reflected the need to know the new opening of his body, and was also a replacement of his need to see it. Although his penis was not functional, it was still physically present.

Joe's constant preoccupation with his dead mother minimized the affective reality of the loss of a functioning penis. His unresolved grief for her combined with his grief for what had been lost to him through the mutilation of his body. He had recurrent dreams of going fishing with his mother, although in reality they had never fished together; the lost penis seemed to be symbolically displaced by the fish they caught in the dreams. His denial of the loss of sexual integrity and his earlier physical image was displaced and extended in the concomitant mourning process.

The constant itching of Joe's face was a kind of testing related to his gender identity as it involved touching and seeing his beard and his features. It was necessary for him to test and assimilate these visual and tactile perceptions of his physical self. Itching and pain were important in supporting the redistribution and reintegration of what had been his in the past and what was still available to him. They were essential to the formation of a new image for the present and the future. He kept hoping for some quick benefit from medication, and I saw him only six times. Dependent on his brother and sister-in-law, he kept using denial, somatization, and passivity as major defenses in his unresolved grieving for his losses.

CASE 3

Tom was a 69-year-old black man with bilateral amputation of the legs below the knee. He had suffered from diabetes mellitus since 1951, and was an inpatient when I saw him. He had lost his left leg from gangrene in 1974, and his right in 1975, but was under regular treatment that included careful management of his diet. At the time he was hospitalized because of severe depression and isolation—several months after the second surgical procedure—he was living with his son but was unable to care for himself or to function adequately. He recalled having suffered severely from phantom-limb pain for some time, and being disturbed by occasional itching in the stump and upper extremities.

His wife had died in 1954, leaving him with two children whom he cared for and educated. After his son moved out of their home in 1976 Tom tried to commit suicide. He lived alone after that, dependent on outside help because of his inability to care for himself. A year later he made a second suicide attempt and was taken to the hospital with severe depression. After treatment there he went to live with his son and daughter-in-law, but was taken to the State Hospital in 1978 in a depressed state.

When I saw him he was totally amnesic, negative, and uncooperative, but after regular contact with him was established he became communicative, although his hopelessness never abated. He had no place to go, and on the basis of past rejection feared being rejected again. His amnesia about his operations, etc., continued. He could remember the pain of his phantom limbs and his trouble with itching, but not his attempts at suicide, the events of his hospitalization, or other experiences of that period. I saw him for only a short time in the hospital since he rejected therapeutic contact. He refused to consider a prosthesis.

Tom had undergone what were surely drastic organ losses, but he was suffering also from the rejection by his children, during the time of his incomplete recovery from the grief of his amputation. So he continued in a state of delayed and unresolved grief, with marked hopelessness and helplessness. His behavior continued to be passive-aggressive, and his negativistic attitude continued to reflect the impulse to self-destruction that had been exhibited in his two attempts at suicide. The total physical structure is important for total and effective functioning. Injuries, illness, and the loss of an organ often disturb emotional balance.

Discussion

All three of the patients described suffered from some degree of alteration in their relationships with others, and exhibited denial, displaced anger, dread of dependence on others, phantom phenomena, a loss of social and professional orientation, and marked regression, all of which closely parallel the symptoms (fixation) of complicated pathological grief reactions, and relate to major organ losses in these cases. The *itching* and wandering pains, characteristic and persistent symptoms, were the dominant psychophysiological reactions, and will be examined from the point of view of bringing back or giving up the lost parts in the psychodynamics of established pathological mourning.

The phenomenon of the phantom member is described by Kolb[16] as usually disappearing within two years, but it seems probable that the inability to reorganize the body image after the phantom disappears lasts much longer than is supposed. Jarvis[17] and Simmel[18] found the phantom manifested chiefly in sensations of itching; and Hoffman[19] reports a phantom eye that manifested itself in itching of the brow. Kolb indicates that pain in a phantom member, or in the area of physical disturbance, may serve as symbolic expression of anxiety over the loss of a member and the threat to dependency needs that the issue has brought about. He postulates also that the phantom may express sadomasochistic identification with a depressive equivalent, as is seen in the second and third cases described here.

The ability to exert voluntary control of a member's movement is an important factor in the construction—and reconstruction—of the body image. Löfgren[20] notes that the normal autonomous motility of the penis is in itself anxiety provoking. The mouth and the anus are genetically highly erogenous zones in their developmental period, and before long they become part of the voluntary system, whereas the penis does not.

Moreover, because it is anatomically less firmly attached than most other parts of the body, it is not surprising that fantasies about its possible loss occur. The rarity of a phantom penis, the organ's peculiar sensitivity to touch, and the changes it undergoes in puberty support the conclusion that one cause of castration anxiety is its failure to become a securely anchored part of the body ego. The second patient I described, who had a penis without function, never developed a phantom penis but manifested persistent and overwhelming castration anxiety as well as depression.

In an article on organ transplants and their relation to body image and psychosis, Castelnuovo-Tedesco[21] noted that recent experience with organ transplantation has contributed to our understanding of the phenomenon of body image, particularly to the concept one has of the arrangements within the body. He goes on to say that life-saving operations that remove some diseased body part seem to restrict or limit the body image; the patient, having experienced a loss, is often depressed. Many have a tendency to retain the lost member or organ in fantasy, as is evidenced by the phantom phenomenon.

The life-extending surgery of transplantation, however, enlarges the body image. Something has been added, and the patient must make room for it so that something previously exterior to the self can be felt as included within the ego. This investigator feels that body image is maintained by a rather fluid process that is strongly influenced by—and that in turn influences—the level of ego integration, including the degree of regression present at any given time. The first case here demonstrates acute anxiety and mild depersonalization as signs of marked regression and extreme ambivalence.

The individual whose completeness of body image is disturbed by a sudden physical change or loss of function faces a situation that is without precedent in his experience. After some time he may be successful in reconstructing a new body image by reactivating all perceptive systems and continuing to reintegrate and reorganize his feelings and attitudes. The reorientation to the new situation with what remains constitutes an attempt to accept a new image. However, pain or physical irritation will change the postural model of the body, and whatever area of the body has been attacked or mutilated can become the focus of the self and the object of attention not only for the sufferer but for those in the environment as well. Such a powerful concentration of internal and external emotion when centered in that part of the body is overloaded with the early integrated emotional experiences, and these will activate and mobilize early unresolved conflicts and fantasies. Such regression may disturb the successful orientation to the loss, and cause impairment of the ego. The restoration of satisfactory function depends psychologically on the resolution of the early unresolved experiences and their presently existing sequelae. Constructive medical care on a continuing base is often the determinant of successful physical and psychophysiological reorientation.

ITCHING AND SCRATCHING

As noted, all three of the cases described exhibited itching. It seems that itching and/or scratching, accompanied by phantom phenomena or wandering pain, become the core of experimentation in the restructuring of the mental image of the body. Itching makes for restlessness, and it is painful. Scratching may comfort the surface of the body, but dealing with an irritated part of the body by scratching it can activate sadomasochistic tendencies. According to Musaph[22] many people scratch without actually having an itch. Scratching may be simply a motor discharge of such emotional tension as might appear in someone embarrassed or lost in concentration. In some cases scratching can produce itching.

The element of pleasure in such a largely unconscious movement is evident. Some people develop a way of scratching that produces sensations of mild pain that they enjoy; this might be compared to masturbation. In this connection the element of skin eroticism should be considered. Itching and scratching may provide dermal erotic gratification. Each phase of infantile sexuality can give dermal eroticism its special color. Thus itching can be a sign of repressed anxiety, repressed rage, or repressed sexuality. Certainly we cannot ascribe to any one single psychological meaning all occurrences of itching, particularly since it may indeed be symptomatic of some physical illness.

Nonetheless, the emotional libidinal exchange involved in ministering to the body's needs by ''scratching where it itches'' contributes to the knowledge of the total body. In each of the cases described here, wandering pain and itching appeared in other parts of the body than those from which a member had been lost. The total body image must be reconstructed by rechecking what remains. Optical and tactile perceptions, along with motility, are the most important elements in such reconstructive attempt, and the grieving is a normal emotional process in reconstruction after internal loss.

It is interesting to note how common it is for the geriatric patient to complain of itching, which, however much it may be due to the dryness of aging skin, is also evidence of the need to recheck the boundaries of a body that is undergoing profound alteration from the body image to which the aged person was so long accustomed. The old can tolerate no further loss; what remains to them must be constantly checked. Their limited control of voluntary movement and their dread of further loss make it necessary to monitor what is still there, and touching can very well be a sign of the power of the body image to galvanize the individual's resources.

Summary

Three cases in which the patients had to modify their body images because of surgical change are described. In their postsurgical period all gave evidence of undergoing complicated mourning. This article examines itching and scratching manifested in all three from the point of view of its contribution to the patient's exploration of his new body image.

References

1. SCHILDER, F. *The Image and Appearance of the Human Body*. International Universities Press, New York, 1950.
2. NIEDERLAND, W. C. Narcissistic Ego Impairments in Patients With Early Physical Malformations. *Psychoanal. Study Child*, Vol. XX, 1965, 518–34.
3. GREENACRE, P. Certain Relationships between Fetishism and the Faulty Development of the Body Image. (1953) In *Emotional Growth*, International Universities Press, New York, 1971, pp. 9–30.

4. VOLKAN, V. D. *Primitive Internalized Object Relations*. International Universities Press, New York, 1976.

5. FREUD, A. The Role of Bodily Illness in the Mental Life of Children. In *The Writings of Anna Freud*, Vol. 4, International Universities Press, New York, 1952, pp. 260–79.

6. ABSE, D. W. *Hysteria and Related Mental States*. Williams and Wilkins, Baltimore, 1966.

7. SCHOENBERG, B. and CARR, A. Loss of External Organs: Limb Amputation, Mastectomy and Disfiguration. In *Loss and Grief: Psychological Management in Medical Practice*. Columbia University Press, New York, 1970.

8. HARTMANN, H. *Ego Psychology and the Problem of Adaptation*. International Universities Press, New York, 1939.

9. BOWLBY, J. Process of Mourning. *Int. J. Psycho-Anal.* 42:317, 1961.

10. POLLOCK, G. Mourning and Adaptation. *Int. J. Psycho-Anal.* 42:341, 1961.

11. LINDEMANN, E. Symptomatology and Management of Acute Grief. *Am. J. Psychiatry* 101:141, 1944.

12. FREUD, S. *Mourning and Melancholia*. (1917). Standard Edition, Vol. XIV, London, Hogarth Press, pp. 237–58, 1957.

13. VOLKAN, V. D. Death, Divorce and the Physician. In *Marital and Sexual Counseling in Medical Practice*. 2nd ed. Abse, D. W., Nash, E. M. and Louden, L. M. R., Eds. Harper and Row, New York, 1974.

14. PARKES, C. M. Components of the Reactions to Loss of a Limb, Spouse or Home. *J. Psychosom. Res.*, 16:313, 1972.

15. VOLKAN, V. D. Typical Findings in Pathological Grief. *Psychiat. Q.*, 44:231, 1970.

16. KOLB, L. D. Disturbance of the Body Image. In *American Handbook of Psychiatry*, 2nd ed., Arieti, S. E., Ed. Basic Books, New York, 1975.

17. JARVIS, J. H. Post-Mastectomy Breast Phantoms. *J. Nerv. Ment. Dis.*, 144:266, 1967.

18. SIMMEL, M. L. Phantom, Phantom Pains and Denial. *Am. J. Psychother.*, 13:603, 1959.

19. HOFFMAN, J. Facial Phantom Phenomenon. *J. Nerv. Ment. Dis.*, 122:143, 1955.

20. LÖFGREN, B. Castration Anxiety and the Body Ego. *Int. J. Psycho-Anal.*, 49:408, 1968.

21. CASTELNUEVO-TEDESCO, P. Organ Transplant, Body Image, Psychosis, *Psychoanal. Q.*, 42:349, 1973.

22. MUSAPH, H. Psychodynamics in Itching States. *Int. J. Psycho-Anal.*, 49:336, 1968.

PAIN

CHAPTER 43

Family-oriented Treatment of Chronic Pain

Alletta Jervey Hudgens

The medical field is beginning to experiment with family-oriented treatment and with integrating systems theory and learning theory into traditional treatment programs. This paper describes the outcome of a short-term, family-centered, behavioral approach to chronic pain at the University of Minnesota Hospitals. Family members were taught operant conditioning techniques which rewarded non-pain oriented behavior in the patient.

Twenty-four patients and their families completed the Pain Treatment Program in 1974 and 1975. The paper reports their level of functioning before and after the program and the work with the family system during treatment. The goals of treatment included improving family relationships, regaining occupational roles, eliminating prescription pain medication, increasing tolerance for selected exercises, and reducing use of the health care system. By treating the total family, 75% of the patients and families were able to lead normally active and satisfactory lives again.

Health care practitioners are coming to realize that even chronic pain can be understood and treated within a family system perspective. If the family operates as a system to enlarge or to maintain a pain problem, then the family needs to be treated to bring the pain problem under control. As a result, programs have been developed which integrate a family-oriented and behavioral treatment program for chronic pain.

The family-oriented pain treatment program discussed in this paper

Reprinted from the *Journal of Marital and Family Therapy*, Vol. 5, No. 4 (October, 1979), pp. 67–77. Copyright 1979 American Association for Marriage and Family Therapy. Reprinted by permission of the Association and the author.

497

involved 24 patient-families completing the treatment program in 1974 and 1975, in the Physical Medicine and Rehabilitation Service at the University of Minnesota Hospitals. A detailed description of the clinical treatment program process has been published elsewhere (Anderson, et al. 1977; Hudgens, 1978). The program is modeled after one at the University of Washington at Seattle (Fordyce, 1976).

Understanding Chronic Pain: A Social Learning Approach

Pain normally serves as a warning signal that something in the body's system is not right. However, when pain persists more than four to six months and becomes chronic, it is useful to consider the possibility that the pain may have come under the influence of powerful learning or operant mechanisms (Skinner, 1953). Pain responses or signals, such as moaning, grimacing, limping, and complaining, which occur over a long period of time, can become systematically followed by favorable consequences (positive reinforcement) in the family and surrounding environment (Fordyce, 1976). For example, a patient might get more attention from family members, be able to avoid work, or obtain financial compensation.

Pain that began as a physiological response can later be experienced as a learned response or a mixture of the two. When healthy behavior (patient does not demonstrate pain) is not reinforced or rewarded, or when healthy behavior is followed by unpleasant consequences, it is even more likely that the pain behavior will be maintained or even be increased.

According to social learning theory, if pain behavior is learned it can also be unlearned. Using an operant conditioning approach, new behaviors that indicate activity and health can be consistently and systematically rewarded and pain behaviors ignored. As a result, new behaviors can be taught which can provide a more satisfactory life for the pain patient and family. There is precedent for the effectiveness of behavioral systems therapy for families (Olson, 1976).

Family Systems and Chronic pain

The systems model views the family as a complex unit of interacting personalities and forces. When pain enters a family it is a powerful force that often controls the structure, the actions, and reactions of family members. Pain can effect sweeping changes in family roles, realign subsystems within the family, and isolate family members from each other and from outside influences. Consequent anger and guilt can change a normally functioning family into a frustrated, rigid, and unhappy group of people.

To bring about a change in such a family there must be a change in the entire system. The family system seeks balance, and a change in the patient alone will result in efforts by the rest of the members to return the system to its prior way of operating, with pain as the controlling force.

This paper will demonstrate the importance of a supportive family unit, and of working with the entire family to bring about behavioral changes that will result in satisfactory functioning for the family system.

Description of Patients and Families

SELECTION CRITERIA

General criteria for admission to the program were the following:

1. There was at least one "significant other" who had sufficient contact with the patient to constitute a social system for effective support and change, and who was willing to work with the program.
2. The patient and family understood the program and wished to undertake it.
3. There were significant, identifiable behaviors associated with the pain, and considered modifiable by the staff.
4. There were identifiable reinforcers for healthy behaviors.
5. All other treatment methods had been unsuccessful or were not feasible.
6. Chemical dependence was not a primary problem.
7. The patient was not suffering from overt or underlying schizophrenia which might have affected his/her ability to benefit from the program.
8. There was no pending litigation in regard to the pain problem.

In the two years of this study, 86 patients (50 women and 36 men) were evaluated for admission to the program. Using the aforementioned criteria, 29 (33%) were accepted in the program. Three of these chose not to undergo treatment, and two who entered dropped out before completing treatment. Thus, the final group in this study (N=24) consisted of 18 women and six men who completed the program.

Other demographic data are as follows: Age ranged from 23 to 72, the mean age being 46. There was one black female patient, the rest were white. Nineteen (79%) of the patients were married, four were widowed, and one was single. Fifteen (65%) of the patients had some high school education, eight (33%) had some college education, and one patient had a graduate degree. Seventeen patients (71%) came from large families of four or more children. As to socioeconomic status, eight patient-families were professional or managerial, four were clerical or sales, nine were laborers, and

TABLE 43-1.   Problem Areas and Improvement for 24 Pain Patients and
Families *

Problem Area	No. of Families With Problem Before Treatment	No. of Families Improved After Treatment
Patient very dependent on spouse or significant other	18	18 (100%)
Indirect communications	18	11 (61%)
Narrow social contacts	16	13 (81%)
Inability to handle anger appropriately	15	13 (87%)
Sexual conflicts	11	7 (64%)
Power struggle between spouses	10	7 (70%)
Spouse of patient had difficulty expressing warmth and affection	10	7 (70%)
Spouse of patient openly resentful of patient's illness	10	8 (80%)
Conflict over male-female roles	7	5 (71%)
At least one child in the family had adjustment problems (stealing, bowel control, setting fires)	6	4 (67%)
Large debt due to pain problem	6	5 (83%)**

* The number of problem areas was not the same for all families. Families had an average of five problems each
** No more debt added and plans underway to reduce former debt.

three were farmers. This assumes that the seventeen housewives identified with their husband's socioeconomic status.

The social histories given by the patients revealed a number of factors present in patients' childhood homes. Ten reported harsh, demanding, or distant parents. Seven had lost one or both parents in childhood. This raises the question whether pain patients may show a significant lack of healthy, emotionally giving parent figures in early life.

In seven cases, the patient had experienced a significant amount of illness as a child, and in another seven cases one parent had been chronically ill or disabled. Merskey and Spear (1967) and Tuohy (1972) noted that pain patients frequently have an immediate family member who was injured or severely physically disabled.

Table 43-1 lists problems observed in the families by staff during counseling and in other family interactions. Each family had two or three problem areas and the most common problems were high patient dependency, indirect communications, narrow social contacts, and difficulty handling anger. The number of families who experienced sexual conflicts might be an underestimate because pain patients often deny sexual functioning problems. The narrowing of social life occurred in 60% of the families.

Initial Diagnostic Assessment

MEDICAL DIAGNOSIS

In the group of 24 patients studied, nineteen (79%) experienced lower back pain. Of these nineteen patients, five had additional pain in other body areas. There were two patients with upper back and neck pain, two patients with headaches, and one with perineal pain after prostatectomy. Patients had an average of 2.5 surgeries each. All had been unable to work, to be satisfactorily active, or to function adequately in social relationships for an average of four years.

Sixteen (two thirds) of the group had a significant problem with overdosing on pain medications, and half of these (N=8) currently or formerly had severe problems with chemical dependency.

MINNESOTA MULTIPHASIC PERSONALITY INVENTORY

The mean MMPI profiles for the group appear similar to those found by Sternbach (1974). The "conversion V," or neurotic triad, with elevations on hypochondriasis, depression, and hysteria (scales 1,2,3) as shown in Figures 43–1,2,3, generally reflects the tendency to preoccupation with bodily functions and complaints. Clinicians familiar with the scales commonly note repression and denial as defenses against anxiety and depression. The majority of the sample refused to consider any psychological explanation for their pain, although some were able to do so after the pain behavior lessened in treatment, and they could function more adequately.

There was not any distinctive personality type associated with chronic pain patients. The patients did tend to be hysteroid (scale 3) or naive, self-centered, and immature in their communications with their surrounding

FIGURE 43–1. Composite MMPI profile of 6 male patients who showed significant long-term improvement in the Pain Treatment Program

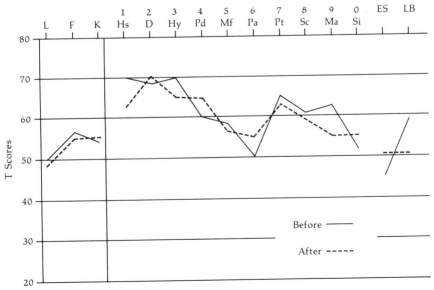

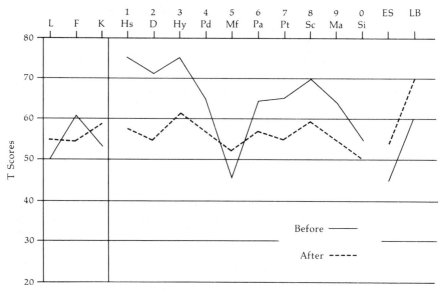

FIGURE 43–2.   Composite MMPI profile of 12 female patients who showed significant long-term improvement in the Pain Treatment Program

FIGURE 43–3.   Composite MMPI profile of 6 female patients who did not achieve significant long-term improvement in the Pain Treatment Program

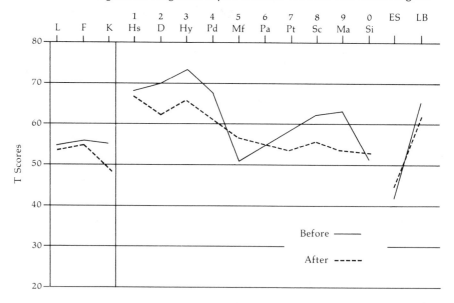

social system. One group of ten patients (42%) were very demanding of themselves and allowed themselves little or no pleasure, which was reflected by a high score on compulsivity (scale 7).

Curiously, life histories tend to show that most chronic pain patients functioned adequately before they had pain problems (Sternbach, 1974). It appears likely that the pain produces the neuroticism and the increased awareness of physical symptoms that we see in them.

ASSESSING REINFORCEMENT OF PAIN

In assessing the function and reinforcement of pain, staff observations were gathered from charts and conference notes. They included present behavior related to former behavioral patterns, satisfactions, and problems as described by patients and families.

In all cases pain functioned to obtain medical attention. Likewise, medical treatment, surgery, and the administration of pain medications often reinforced and maintained pain behavior.

Most patients appeared to have several functions for pain in their lives. The most common one, controlling/manipulating others, was observed in half the patient-families (N=12). An equal number of patients (N=11) seemed to use pain to justify dependency. Other functions observed included earning rest, avoiding sex, gaining attention, punishing others, controlling anger, and avoiding close relationships.

TABLE 43-2.   Reinforcers for Pain Behavior

	No. of Families
Attention from others	16*
Spouse gives negative attention (fusses about inactivity or intake of pain medications)	9
Financial gain for disability	9
Others take over duties	7
Community mores sanction social discussion about pain and medical problems	6

* Family members used an average of two reinforcers for pain behavior in the patient.

Goals and Plan of the Family-oriented Program

Goals for treatment for the 24 patient-families in this study were to increase family interactions around issues other than pain, to improve family relationships, to regain occupational roles, to eliminate the use of prescription pain medication, to increase tolerance for selected exercises, and to reduce use of the health care system.

Since pain was treated as learned behavior, the pain behaviors were the initial focus of treatment. The aim was to decrease specific pain behaviors and increase healthy behaviors. The inpatient program lasted seven to nine weeks, followed in most cases by an outpatient program of one to five weeks.

One major goal was to change family interactions so that the patient did not use pain in communication and interaction with others. The social worker and family developed a contract to help the family focus on specific objectives to be pursued with the patient.

Each family had at least one "significant other," usually the spouse of the patient, who came into the hospital two or three times a week for an hour to work with the social worker in retraining to ignore pain related behavior and to reinforce health related behavior of the patient. Later in the program joint interviews with the patient and spouse, and then with the entire family, served to examine and to treat problems, such as maintaining well behaviors, in the transition to the home environment. [This aspect of the problem has been discussed in detail elsewhere (Hudgens, 1978).]

While the social worker worked with the entire family, other hospital staff members worked with the patient in the hospital. Again, all pain behaviors were consistently and systematically ignored and well behaviors reinforced. Occupational therapy and physical therapy helped to slowly strengthen muscles weakened by pain and disuse. Pain medications were given on a time contingent basis and slowly reduced to zero. Work activities were introduced. Work evaluation and counseling psychology often were involved in helping the patient plan to resume meaningful activity, paid or unpaid, upon returning home. The patient kept daily graphs of exercise and activity progress for him/herself and others to see. This helped the patient and others to see him/herself as a responsible, adequate, functioning person.

The rehabilitation setting, which emphasized increased physical activity and visible, attainable goals, played a critical role in family motivation and expectations. Patients and their families were assured that the rehabilitation team believed the pain was real and treatable, regardless of the etiology of the pain problem. Staff emphasized that the program was not designed to eliminate pain, but to change behavior in order to more effectively cope with pain.

Methods and Design

This paper describes changes in the 24 patients and family members before and after treatment. A social history was obtained from the patient and family, staff observation, family interviews, physical examination, medical records, and the Minnesota Multiphasic Personality Inventory. Reports of the community physician also contributed to the data base.

There were six variables that measured success in the program. Family relationships were measured relative to the problems listed in Table 43-1, and measurement was effected through self-report of the patient and other family members and observed behavior reported by staff and family members. Occupational role improvement was measured in the same way. Personality changes were measured by the MMPI. Activity level was assessed by changes in exercises prescribed for patients, and by reports of patients and family regarding activity outside the hospital setting. Medication intake was measured by the staff-monitored and recorded medication program. Use of the health care system was measured by interactions with the hospital staff and by the quantity and nature of contacts with the family's community physicians, reported by the family and the physicians.

Follow-up data were obtained six months to two years later in personal interviews for twelve patient-families, by telephone interviews for eight others, and by letters or second-hand reports for four patient-families.

Effectiveness of the Program at Discharge

IMPROVEMENT IN FAMILY RELATIONSHIPS

Changes in the family system were often dramatic. An eight-year-old child, seeing her patient-mother walk for the first time without crutches, rushed into her arms with reinforcing hugs. A man unable to work for five years returned to his former job as a construction worker and regained his former role as a laborer and family provider. A grandmother, who had used pain to gain sympathy and resentful attention from her grown children, renewed her role as the "best cook in the family" and enjoyed visits from her grandchildren and family once again.

Table 43-1 gives the percentage of families for which problem areas significantly improved after treatment. These figures were obtained from chart notes regarding observations of behavior by staff and from self-report of patients and families.

In addition to these improvements in previously assessed problem areas, three-fourths ($N = 18$) of the families reported a significant increase in recreation and leisure time spent within the family circle and in visiting friends and relatives.

Other individual patient gains had a positive effect on the satisfaction with family life reported by their families. Almost two-thirds of the patients reported a more optimistic and happy outlook on life ($N = 17$), feeling more in control of their lives (N=7), and having a more positive self- concept (N=16). Over half the group (N=14) also demonstrated more assertive behavior.

IMPROVEMENT IN OCCUPATIONAL ROLES

The most frequently observed and reported occupational improvement was the patient's return to some type of useful work, paid or unpaid, that was satisfactory for the patient and family. At the time of discharge this was true for 83% (N=20) of the patient-families. Home-making was the most common undertaking for fourteen patients; six returned to full-time paid employment. Of these same twenty patients, six began education or retraining programs, and three found volunteer work.

MMPI CHANGES

As illustrated in Figures 43–1,2, and 3, post-treatment MMPI profiles tended to drop into a normal range, especially for the women. There was a dramatic drop in the neurotic triad (scales 1,2,3) for the women, indicating less concern with bodily functioning, less depression, and fewer hysteroid characteristics. Since the scales retain the "conversion V" pattern, one would still expect the patients to dwell on physical functioning under stress. There was less dependence (lower scale 3) and less anxiety (lower scale 7). The drop in scales 3,7, and 9 together reflect a reduction in anxiety and agitation. Ego strength (ES scale) increased, indicating greater feelings of self worth.

The profiles of the men showed that they did not change as much as the women. They had fewer bodily complaints (scale 1) and denied less (scale 3), but male depression scores (scale 2) were a bit higher after treatment, indicating their morale had not changed. This might be explained by the following. In our society it is highly valued for men to have paid employment. Employment for former back patient males is not easily attainable, and therefore work was not available as a reinforcer immediately after treatment. In comparison, almost every woman in the sample was a housewife who could return immediately to what she and society considered a productive life over which she had more control.

ACTIVITY LEVEL AND EXERCISE TOLERANCE

At the time of discharge, each patient demonstrated an activity level normal for his/her age and sex. Patients reported that weekends at home were quite different from before treatment; the patient and family lived a normally active life, interacting and enjoying each other without reference to pain or other physical complaints.

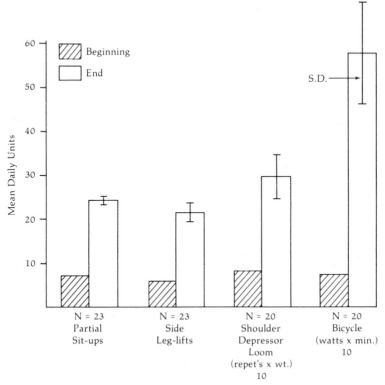

FIGURE 43-4. Changes in the four most common exercises during the treatment program

Exercise tolerance rose considerably, as shown in Figure 43-4, which compares the beginning and end of the inpatient treatment for the four more often prescribed treatment activities. At the time of discharge, each patient was given an exercise program to continue daily for the rest of their lives.

MEDICATION INTAKE

Chronic pain patients relied heavily on pain medications, and overdosing was common. The use of medication differed widely in number, type, and frequency. Only one of the twenty-four patients took no medication before the program. As a group, they were using forty different types of medication. Eighty-three percent (N = 20) were on some type of pain medication, and 75% (N = 18) of this group were taking narcotic analgesics. During the course of the program, the amount of medication given was reduced until, by the last two weeks of the program, all patients had no pain medication. The increases in activity level and exercise tolerance, despite the elimination of all pain medications, supported the program assumption that an operant conditioning approach can effectively reduce dependence on drugs.

USE OF THE HEALTH CARE SYSTEM

During the treatment period, staff worked with the patient's community physician to continue the well behavior reinforcement program, insuring the maintenance of appropriate well behavior after treatment. This was an extension of a systems approach to the community system which interacts with the family system. At discharge, 20 (83%) of the patients and families were using the health care system appropriately.

Follow-Up Evaluation

At the time of the follow-up six months to two years after treatment, eighteen (75%) of the patient-families had maintained their gains as demonstrated in continuing satisfactory family relationships and occupational roles, continued exercise and activity, absence of prescription pain medication, and normal use of the health care system.

Six women did not maintain these gains. The most salient feature of this group was the lack of a strong social support system. Three were widows living alone. Two lived with spouses who did not consistently reinforce well behavior and ignore ill behavior. Only one of these six women had an adequate support system.

Differences on the MMPI were also obvious between the women who continued to do well six months to two years after the program and those women who did not maintain their gains. In comparing the women who did well (Figure 43-2) with those who did not (Figure 43-3), one observes that the former were initially more passive-aggressive and manipulative (the 4, 5, 6 "V") than the latter women who appeared more depressed. It may be that women who show a dramatic neurotic triad and complain more might more easily learn different coping methods than depressed women.

Social Factors in Success and Failure

A strong support system seems to be the most salient factor in the long-term successful functioning of the patient-family. Sternbach (1974) noted that married patients with family support did better in a pain treatment program. He found that in a strong supportive family, the prognosis for constructive adjustment to pain was better. Strengths included mature caring for each other, a satisfactory marriage, flexibility, and the ability to use help in readjustment. Where outside resources were also available, prognosis was even better. Friends and relatives who were open to change and who were basically mature strengthened the family support system. Community opportunities for increased social contacts and supportive services were also helpful.

The willingness of the spouse or "significant other" to modify his/her behavior toward the patient was one criterion used in acceptance to the program. Two-thirds (N = 16) of the families demonstrated this by their understanding and acceptance of the program and by showing evidence of concern for the patient and desire to help. In the eight families where the families did *not* modify their behavior, half the patients did not succeed in maintaining treatment gains six months or more after the program. Three of these four were widows living alone, so that their families were tangential to the living environment. Only one widow in the program succeeded, and her "significant other" was a 20-year-old son who still lived with her part time. The four patients who succeeded in keeping their gains despite the inability of the family to modify behavior exhibited at least one of the following factors: unusual strength in assertiveness and independence, illness of the spouse enabling the former patient to feel needed, and the return of one patient to a desired job.

The problems of middle age appear important in chronic pain development and management. The median age of the sample was 44. Older men and women facing the crisis of middle age might use pain as a reaction to numerous frustrations: children leaving home, a couple's inability to deal with increased time with each other, facing unachieved dreams and improbable hopes. A study cited in Soulairac (1968) of 430 patients with somatic pains for which the clinician found no physiological evidence, observed a preponderance of patients between the ages of 30 and 50.

A look at the large group of housewives (N = 17) in this sample is instructive. Skolnick (1973) noted that more married women than single women were bothered by physical pains and ailments. In a study by Pratt (1973), two-thirds of the mind-affecting drugs prescribed were to women.

The importance of returning to useful work, whether paid or unpaid, was seen in the lasting results in a family system. In the United States, usefulness and productivity are important values. If these values are strong in a family, the feasibility of useful work as a target goal in pain treatment should be considered in undertaking such an expensive and difficult program.

A number of interesting questions could be researched in the future. Do family structure and function influence the emergence of pain as a health problem? How does a family's belief about illness and its treatment affect the development and treatment of pain problems? What factors enable a family to manage pain constructively without intervention?

Conclusion

Of those family factors that predict success in an operant conditioning program, two factors appear to be important. Every patient-family in this sample who remained well demonstrated at least one of these features: 1) the family with whom the patient lived was supportive and amenable to retraining, 2) the patient was able to learn assertiveness and to develop control over his/her own environment. Community agency support often helped to reinforce family strengths, though in no instance could it replace family support.

It also appears that maintaining gains in the long run occurred more often where the families attended to and improved their skills in communication, such as awareness and expression of feelings, when they learned appropriate, assertive behaviors.

In summary, this study demonstrated the importance of treating the whole family in changing the management of the chronic pain of one member within the family system. Patients with a closely interacting and supportive family system that cooperated in learning to manage pain constructively maintained their gains after a retraining program, whereas those patients without a participating and cooperating, supportive family system did not maintain their gains. It is also important to enlarge the system approach to include in the treatment plan such resources as physicians, ministers, employers, and relatives interacting with the patient and family.

References

ANDERSON, T. P., COLE, T. M., GULLICKSON, G., HUDGENS, A., ROBERTS, A. H. "Behavior Modification of Chronic Pain: A Treatment Program by a Multidisciplinary Team," *Clinical Orthopedics*, Nov.–Dec., 1977, *129*, 96–100.

FORDYCE, W. E. *Behavioral Methods for Chronic Pain and Illness*. St. Louis, Mo.: C. V. Mosby Co., 1976.

HUDGENS, ALLETTA, "The Social Worker's Role in a Behavioral Management Approach to Chronic Pain," *Social Work in Health Care*, Winter, 1978, 3, 149–157.

MERSKEY, H., and SPEAR, F. G. *Pain: Psychological and Psychiatric Aspects:* London: Bailliere, Windall and Cassell, 1967.

OLSON, D. *Treating Relationships*. Lake Mills, Iowa: Graphic Publishing Co., 1976.

PRATT, L. "The Significance of Family in Medication," *Journal of Comparative Social Studies*, 1973, *1*, 13–31.

SKINNER, B.F. *Science and Human Behavior*. New York: Macmillan Company, 1953.

RETARDATION

CHAPTER 44

New Directions for Work with Parents of Retarded Children

Enola K. Proctor

Recent advances in the fields of special education and behavioral psychology are paving the way for more innovative social work with parents of retarded children. With new expectations of improvement and equipped with new methods, social work can now move beyond its traditional, often limited emphases to help parents facilitate their children's development. This article, after briefly reviewing some traditional emphases, will explore the unique contribution that social workers can make and some methods which can be employed toward that end.

Traditional Emphases

A common entry point for social workers is the time of diagnosis of retardation, when parents are emotionally upset and their child's prognosis may seem irreversibly hopeless. Accordingly, professional literature has thoroughly documented parents' emotional states and needs. Accounts are presented of parents' experiencing emotions of grief, sorrow, shock, depression, anger, guilt, and self-pity,[1] and responding by rejecting initial

---

[1] Pauline Cohen, The Impact of the Handicapped Child on the Family, SOCIAL CASEWORK, 43:137–42 (March 1962); Ada Kozier, Casework with Parents of Children Born with Severe Brain Defects, SOCIAL CASEWORK, 38:183–89 (March 1957); Arthur Mandelbaum, The Group Process in Helping Parents of Retarded Children, *Children*, 14:227–32 (November–December 1967); Ann Murphy, Siegfried Pueschel, and Jane Schneider, Group Work with Parents of Children with Down's Syndrome, SOCIAL CASEWORK, 54:114–19 (February 1973); Simon Olshansky, Chronic Sorrow: A Response to Having a Mentally Defective Child, SOCIAL CASEWORK, 43:191–94 (April 1962).

Reprinted from *Social Casework*, Vol. 57 (April, 1976), pp. 259–264, with permission of the author and the Family Service Association of America.

diagnoses, seeking other medical opinions, and searching for a cause of retardation.[2]

This same literature identifies as goals of intervention helping parents to accept the diagnosis, to deal with the accompanying emotions, and to learn to view their child as having a limited potential.[3] Toward these ends, workers have been limited to those methods of support, clarification, and facilitation of the exploration of feelings that are employed in individual casework or group work practice.[4]

Helen Beck suggests that the development of professional practice has been hampered by a "seeming lack of promise of returns from work in the field of retardation."[5] To social work practice and theory, retardation has not seemed very amenable to treatment,[6] and professional involvement has seemed unpromising. Social work practice and theory, then, may not have moved far beyond issues related to diagnosis, and may reflect a view of retardation as an irreversible, relatively static condition to which acceptance and at times resignation seem the only possible responses.

This view, held for so long and perhaps still prevalent in practice, should be examined in light of current evidence. The assumed irreversibility of the seemingly hopeless condition of retardation is now being challenged by the discovery of ways, some small and some large and dramatic, to reverse the irreversible. Although shock and frustration may still accompany a diagnosis of retardation, the child, the parents, and the professionals can move ahead to deal with issues of growth and development. Technologies in special education and behavioral psychology are being employed to produce advances of a range, degree, and rate that professionals had not previously thought possible due to limitations assumed inherent in retardation. Improvements in level of intellectual functioning and self-help, language, motor, and social skills are now, however, increasingly viewed as possible for even the severely retarded.[7] As management of these symptoms is demonstrated, a contemporary view re-

---

[2] Cohen, The Impact of the Handicapped Child, p. 137; Murphy, Pueschel, and Schneider, Group Work with Parents of Children with Down's Syndrome, p. 114.

[3] Kozier, Casework with Parents of Children Born with Severe Brain Defects, pp. 183–89; Arthur Mandelbaum and Mary E. Wheeler, The Meaning of a Defective Child to Parents, SOCIAL CASEWORK, 41:360–67 (July 1960); Helen Perlman, Help to Parents of the Mentally Retarded Child: A Diagnostic Focus, in Social Work and Mental Retardation, ed. Meyer Schreiber (New York: John Day Company, 1970), pp. 346–65.

[4] Helen Beck, Counseling Parents of Retarded Children, Children, 6:225–30 (1959); Kozier, Casework with Parents of Children Born with Severe Brain Defects, p. 185; Murphy et al., Group Work with Parents, p. 117; Mandelbaum, The Group Process in Helping Parents of Retarded Children, p. 231.

[5] Beck, Social Services to the Mentally Retarded (Springfield, Ill.: Charles C. Thomas Co., 1969), p. 101.

[6] Ibid.

[7] William Gardner, Behavior Modification in Mental Retardation (Chicago: Aldine Publishing Co., 1971), p. 22.

gards retardation as a dynamic rather than a static condition, one amenable to modification and improvement through casework, counseling, education, and training.[8]

But these advances are usually provided by other specialists, such as teachers and behavioral psychologists. Where are social workers? Have they reflected the dramatic progress that has occurred in special education, and found promise in this field? What implications for social workers, particularly working in conjunction with parents, are raised by advances in child training? Perhaps social workers must embark on a new course—a course marked by knowledge of current behavior change methodologies, new attitudes toward retardation, and new skills to be made available as training for parents.

Need for New Directions

The need for new directions in social work was clarified for the author recently when introducing a rapid toilet training program[9] to the parents of an eleven-year-old, "moderately" retarded boy. The child, who was living at home and was enrolled in a special education school, met the behavioral entry criteria for the toilet training program, and school personnel were convinced of his suitability for the training. The parents, however, did not believe that their son could profit from the training. Ten years before, they had been advised by a social worker to recognize that their son would never attain certain skills, among them toilet training. They had "accepted" the fact of his retardation and resigned themselves to his limitations. Staff, however, proceeded with the program, focusing on the child's toileting habits and the parents' attitudes of resignation as equally important targets for change. Although the boy learned to initiate proper toileting behaviors at school, he was less successful at home. The parents expressed, at times explicitly, their conviction that the social worker of ten years ago was correct in predicting their son's limitations.

The experience of these parents, unfortunately not unique, makes obvious an important fact: attitudes of resignation, perhaps realistic ten years ago, are both unrealistic and detrimental today. Resignation is unrealistic because advances in knowledge and training methodology expand at such a rate that we can never state with certainty that a child will not surpass a given level of development. Resignation is, in addition, detrimental because negative attitudes may actually prevent a child from reaching his full

---

[8] Michael Begab, Some Basic Principles as a Guide to More Effective Social Services, in *Sourcebook on Mental Retardation for Schools of Social Work*, ed. Meyer Schreiber and Stephanie Barnhardt (New York: Selected Academic Reading, 1967), p. 1–4.

[9] Nathan Azrin and Richard Foxx, A Rapid Method of Toilet Training the Institutionalized Retarded, *Journal of Applied Behavioral Analysis*, 4:89–99 (Summer 1971).

potential. Charles Pascal observes that when adults define and treat a child as if he is retarded, the behaviors which will be attended to by those around him are behaviors which are expected, namely those compatible with the concept of retardation.[10] Research with mothers of retarded children reveals a tendency for those who describe and view their children as defective to see the child as an infant and to respond by overstructuring the child's environment.[11] Workers' biases or stereotypes, too, may result in self-fulfilling prophecies if their expectations of poor outcomes cause them to feel discouraged about intervention.[12] Negative attitudes in workers and parents may, therefore, result in the retarded child's remaining or becoming less active, less competent, and less self-sufficient than he might otherwise become.[13] Accordingly, acceptance and resignation to limits can no longer be accepted as appropriate goals of casework treatment.[14] and workers must take care that negative attitudes, in parents or in themselves, are not engendered or reinforced, even inadvertently, by sympathetic counseling. Social work's tradition of concern for families of the retarded can be channeled in some new directions.

Proposed New Directions

This article proposes two emphases for future social work practice with parents of the retarded: First, that social workers themselves must adopt and then instill in parents new, healthier expectations toward the retarded; second, that beyond the realm of attitudes, social workers can help equip parents with more effective skills for working with their children.

If expectations are realistic, attitudes toward work with the retarded can remain positive and not become negated by frustration and failure. Although learning may be slow and occur in small increments, retarded children can learn, and those around them must expect achievement. Thus the attention of professionals and parents should be focused neither on

---

[10] Charles Pascal, Application of Behavior Modification by Parents for Treatment of a Brain Damaged Child, in *Adaptive Learning: Behavior Modification with Children,* ed. Beatrice Ashem and Ernest Poser (New York: Pergamon Press, 1973), pp. 299–309.

[11] Sue Seitz and Robert Holkenga, Modeling as a Training Tool for Retarded Children and their Parents, *Mental Retardation,* 12:28–30 (April 1974); Shlomo A. Sharlin and Norman A. Polansky, The Process of Infantilization, *American Journal of Orthopsychiatry,* 42:92–102 (January 1972).

[12] Jean Gottman and Samuel Leiblum, *How to do Psychotherapy and how to Evaluate it* (New York: Holt, Rinehart and Winston, 1974), p. 21.

[13] Seitz and Holkenga, Modeling as a Training Tool, p. 28; Sharlin and Polansky, The Process of Infantilization, p. 93.

[14] Edward Fuller and Kieth Kieth, The Social Work Role in Institutions: A Critical Assessment, *Mental Retardation,* 12:61 (June 1974).

upper limits to a child's achievement nor, impatiently, on global learning tasks.

The fostering of positive yet realistic expectations, then, might begin with a reexamination and modification of the attitudes of social workers. Professionals' attitudes are explicitly and implicitly transmitted to parents and affect the quality of services delivered;[15] these attitudes should reflect current progress in the field of special education.

Social workers can then help instill in parents realistically positive expectations toward their children in several ways. First, parents should be encouraged to expect their child to learn only *one skill or behavior at a time.* Such a focus is realistic because it delimits learning to manageable proportions, yet positively identifies a goal to be achieved. Second, parents can be assisted in assessing their child's readiness to learn the identified target skill. Realistically, a child's learning can only proceed on the basis of existing skills; yet assurance that a child has achieved skills prerequisite to a new task is evidence for optimism. Third, parents should be assisted in identifying and ordering the component substeps of the task to be achieved. Progress will occur in small increments; these increments should therefore be the focus of parents' attention and positive expectations. By directing parents' sense of frustration, provide a focus for expectations, and contribute to a realistic foundation for confidence that the child can achieve.

Positive expectations of achievement can serve as a basis for a second focus of social work with parents of the retarded, which is the provision of more effective skills for working with their children. Exclusive attention to parents' attitudes and feelings has been recognized as minimal treatment,[16] particularly in light of growing evidence that workers can help equip parents with new ways of responding to their children.[17] In day-to-day tasks, parents can help maximize their children's self-sufficiency[18] and workers can help prepare them to do so. Parents assume a role of teacher to their children, and social workers assume a role of consultant or trainer to parents.[19] These roles present several advantages. Parents are usually the first to encounter and have to deal with problematic behavior, and they

[15] Begab, Some Basic Principles, p. 3.

[16] Norman A. Polansky, Donald R. Boone, Christine DeSaix, and Shlomo A. Sharlin, Pseudostoicism in Mothers of the Retarded, SOCIAL CASEWORK, 52:643–50 (December 1971).

[17] Benjamin Moore and Jan Bailey, Social Punishment in the Modification of a Pre-School Child's Autistic like Behavior with a Mother as Therapist, *Journal of Applied Behavioral Analysis,* 6:497–507 (Fall 1973): Joel Ray, The Family Training Center: An Experiment in Normalization, *Mental Retardation,* 12:12–13 (February 1974).

[18] Polansky et al., Pseudostoicism, p. 643; Luke Watson and Joan Bassinger, Parent Training Technology: A Potential Service Delivery System, *Mental Retardation,* 12:3–10 (October 1974).

[19] Roland G. Tharp and Rolf J. Wetzel, *Behavior Modification in the Natural Environment* (New York, Academic Press, 1969), p. 206.

can facilitate the transfer of learning from school or treatment to home.[20] In addition, parents of retarded children can gain a great deal of satisfaction from contributing to their child's achievement.[21]

Parental assistance has frequently been employed by social workers to help eliminate problem behavior in their children. However, in the field of retardation, perhaps uniquely, parents can help their children to acquire adaptive behavior, particularly self-help and social skills. Tasks which parents may help teach in day-to-day activities include language acquisition, play behavior, toilet training, dressing skills, feeding skills, attention focusing, and imitation.[22] To guide parents in developing these behaviors in their children, social workers need not become expert speech therapists, psychologists, or special educators. However, familiarity with learning processes may be required. Social workers may then fulfill their unique and most important role: translating the processes of child education to parents and helping them to generalize these processes within new contexts. In addition to specific adaptive skills, social workers working with parents may also focus on more general problems of behavior management, such as discipline issues or parent-child communication. Skills imparted in counseling may then be individualized and applied in a variety of situations which may later arise in the home.

Methods of Parent Counseling

Social workers may draw on a variety of methods to help provide parents with skills for working with their children. Selection of a method involves consideration of parents' needs, and strengths, the problem or task facing the child, and practical considerations of time and economy with respect

[20] Sheldon Rose, Ronal Parson, Betty Jarman, and Carol Hethlenthal, Group Training of Parents as Behavioral Modifiers of Their Own Mentally Retarded Children (unpublished paper, The University of Wisconsin at Madison, 1972); Rose, Group Training of Parents as Behavior Modifiers, *Social Work*, 19:156–62 (March 1974).

[21] Sandra B. McPherson and Cyrille R. Samuels, Teaching Behavioral Methods to Parents, SOCIAL CASEWORK, 52:148–53 (March 1971).

[22] V. L. Baldwin and H. D. Fredericks, eds., *Isn't It Time He Outgrew This? Or a Training Program for Parents of Retarded Children* (Springfield, Ill.: Charles C. Thomas, Publisher, 1973); Eric Marsh and Leif Terdal, Modifications of Mother-Child Interaction, *Mental Retardation*, 11:44–49 (October 1973); Baldwin and Fredericks, *Isn't it Time*, Kathleen Jeffords, Leslie Danzig, and Kathleen Fitzgibbons, Group Training of Parents as Behavioral Modifiers of their own Mentally Retarded Children, unpublished paper, The University of Wisconsin, 1971; Baldwin and Fredericks, *Isn't it Time*, William Butterfield and Ronal Parson, Modeling and Shaping by Parents to Develop Chewing Behavior in their Retarded Child, *Journal of Behavior Therapies and Experimental Psychiatry*, 4:285–87 (December 1973); Jeffords, Danzig, and Fitzgibbons, Group Training of Parents, p. 6; Sebastian Santostefano and Stayton Stayton, Training the Pre-School Retarded Child in Focusing Attention: A Program for Parents, *American Journal of Orthopsychiatry*, 37:732–43 (July 1967); and J. Richard Metz, Conditioning Generalized Imitation in Autistic Children, *Journal of Experimental Child Psychology*, 2:389–99 (December 1965).

to the worker's total responsibility. Any one of the methods to be reviewed below may be employed individually or in groups. Individual counseling may be preferable with the child who is acquiring or modifying a unique behavior or when the parent needs individual attention and assurance from the worker. Groups, however, are advantageous and economical if several parents or children have similar abilities and problems. In groups, parents can learn from each other, encourage each other, and offer acceptable suggestions and examples. The parent who shares the "teaching" role can learn and gain self-confidence. For socially isolated parents, the group may be the only audience with whom to share achievements and the only source of encouragement and support.

DIDACTIC COUNSELING

With a didactic approach, the worker assumes the role of teacher, passing on to parents skills in behavior management.[23] Programmed texts, designed to teach parents principles of behavior change, and the exercises for application are increasingly used by social workers,[24] especially in group treatment. A number of texts are available and applicable to parents on a variety of educational levels.[25] To individualize this approach and for specific skill training, such as toilet training, feeding skills, and attention focusing, the worker may find it useful to write his own material. Text material has two major advantages: procedures and behavior sequencing are clearly presented and may be referred to repeatedly by parents, and application and generalization to situations occurring at home are encouraged, often through "homework" assignments.

MODELING

A second technique effective in parent counseling is modeling, wherein the worker, teacher, or other parent demonstrates correct interaction with a child. Simple advice is seldom sufficient to add skills to a parent's repertoire of behaviors and often leaves parents wondering exactly what they are supposed to do once they are home. Modeling is especially effective when the desired behavior in the child occurs infrequently or when the desired response is new to the parent.[26] The thoroughness of modeling

---

[23] McPherson and Samuels, Teaching Behavioral Methods, p. 148

[24] Rose, A Behavioral Approach to the Group Treatment of Parents, *Social Work*, 14:21–29 (July 1969).

[25] Baldwin and Fredericks, *Isn't it Time*; Wesley Becker, *Parents are Teachers* (Champaign, Ill.: Research Press, 1967); Gerald Patterson and M. Elizabeth Gullion, *Living with Children: New Methods for Parents and Teachers* (Champaign, Ill.: Research Press, 1968).

[26] Stephen Johnson and Richard Brown, Producing Behavior Changes in Parents of Disturbed Children, *Journal of Child Psychology and Psychiatry*, 10:107–21 (October 1969).

can serve to increase the parent's confidence in knowing what can be done, and then doing it. Seeing is believing.

REHEARSAL

A third effective method of parent training is rehearsal, in which the parent performs, evaluates, and repeatedly practices the responses he is to perform at home with his child.[27] The role of the worker, in addition to modeling, is to support, to encourage, and to praise the parent's performance. This method has the advantages of showing the parent not only that his child can perform a new task, but that, in addition, the parent is being instrumental in helping the child, thus demonstrating to the worker an understanding of the desired behavior and appropriate response to the child.

VIDEOTAPE

For workers with access to videotape equipment, the small investment of time required to learn to use the equipment can produce enormous benefits. In counseling with parents, videotape has at least two advantages: Once on tape, exact model presentation of desired interaction with children can be presented to numbers of parents any time it is needed; specialized personnel, such as a speech therapist, need not be present each time parents meet to learn more about language acquisition. Videotape may be used to provide parents with immediate replay of their filmed interactions with their child; mistakes can be quickly identified and the positive reinforcement of successes can be presented. One father, when viewing the filmed replay of his successful management of lunchtime feeding of his usually troublesome daughter, exclaimed that he would not have believed that he had been so successful without seeing it himself. The replay presented powerful reinforcement, while enabling him to closely examine his successful response to his daughter.

Any method selected for a particular time and task must be augmented by the worker's demonstration of respect for and support of the parent. Counseling should be made relevant to the needs of the parent and child. A clear definition of procedures and goals can serve to minimize parents' anxiety[28] and maximize the likelihood of parents' successes. And, most important, demonstration of concern and conviction that the parent can be successful must come clearly and frequently. Efforts at behavior management and skill acquisition require considerable investment of parents' time and energy. Frequent phone calls can be effective communica-

[27] Rose, A Behavioral Approach, p. 27.
[28] Ibid., p. 29.

tors of the worker's support. That support, in combination with innovative counseling methods, offers to parents of the retarded child positive expectations and specific skills for dealing with a situation for which social workers have too long offered only understanding.

While psychologists and special educators have particular expertise at developing change modalities for retarded children, social workers are uniquely prepared to encourage, train, and support parents in the vital application of day-to-day expectations and guidance.

CHAPTER 45

An Eclectic Approach to Group Work with the Mentally Retarded

Phyllis Laterza

Working with the developmentally disabled young adult, in a group work setting, requires a treatment model which is both flexible and diversified. Enhancement of each individual's potential through role learning within the group suggests that methodology be adaptable to individual learning pace and interest, while at the same time remaining congruent with overall group work purpose. To achieve this balance, the group worker must combine a variety of group work models in his practice. Further, he must creatively extract from each model interventions and techniques which will facilitate the process of socialization to adult roles and assist the individual in developing interpersonal relationships.

The Agency Role

The agency setting plays a significant role in implementing a creative treatment approach. While practice incorporates generic strategies and innovative techniques, program design must provide structure and group purpose if it is to support the socialization process. The Agency* offering the program to be discussed here is a non-profit, voluntary agency which has been able to implement an innovative approach to group practice with the mentally retarded. One program within the agency setting is the Evening Adjustment Center. This program is designed to serve the needs of

*The Young Adult Institute Workshops, Inc.

Reprinted from *Social Work with Groups*, Vol. 2, No. 3 (1979), pp. 235–246, with permission of the Haworth Press.

those individuals whose IQ falls within the moderate, mild, and borderline range. Often these individuals have had early childhood experiences which did not provide for optimal socialization. Some have spent their formative years in institutions, while others have remained at home in a sheltered family environment. In both situations they have been isolated from the mainstream of everyday community life.

The program design at this agency also provides for a wide range of structured learning experiences in small groups, each focusing on a specific area of concern to the young adult. Each client participates on a weekly basis in a group on goal planning, career development, social skills, independent living skills, and self-awareness. The techniques and levels of intervention used in practice with these groups of young people struggling to achieve adulthood despite their handicap will be elaborated throughout this paper.

The Socialization Process

The small group experience serves as a preparatory stage where the individual can experiment, try out new roles, and develop a sense of self-awareness and achievement. Elizabeth McBroom (1976) emphasizes the importance of the group approach to the process of socialization when she points out:

> The very terms of socialization theory suggest that group work is usually the method of choice: the social interaction aspects of personal change are enriched and accelerated in the group as a socializing environment. The goal of social competence assumes functioning in a group rather than in isolated activities.[1]

Group Interaction

McBroom (1976) suggests that the central dynamic in her group work model, "Socialization Through Small Groups," is "member to member helping."[2] When mutual aid is central to group purpose, then it follows that the methodology must provide for group interaction. The task of the group worker is to redirect communication between group members.

Often the mentally retarded experience difficulty in expressing their opinions, feelings, and attitudes in an assertive manner. They frequently direct their conversation toward the group worker, even when referring to, or about, someone in the group. There is also a tendency to look toward the leader, limiting eye contact and interaction to a one-to-one encounter. Intervention here should focus on helping the individual establish contact with other group members, by asking him to redirect his flow of conversation to the other group member involved or to the entire group if he is making a generalized statement.

When written here, this sounds rather simplistic; in practice, this is not the case. For example:

> In an actual group situation where a fishbowl exercise was used to promote self-assertion, cooperation and observation skills, Betty was asked to direct her feelings and observations to Paula, the other group member she had been assigned to observe. It became more difficult for Betty to express herself, as she spoke from the "I" position and looked directly at Paula.

As group interaction increases, opportunities for growth and change expand. Individuals begin to own their feelings and take responsibility for them. Experiencing this sense of separateness is extremely beneficial for this client population who often have limited ego boundaries. Frequently, their adult object relations are characterized by symbiotic attachments to an over-involved parental figure. Becoming aware of "self" as separate from "other" assists in promoting individuation and facilitates adult role behavior.

Group interaction can also act to assist an individual in experiencing himself through another. This type of member interaction can enrich self-awareness as it provides a new frame of reference for self-understanding. Interactions can result in conflict or harmony. In either case, the potential for a learning experience is increased as members interact.

The group worker might intervene if it is felt that an individual is unable to integrate positive feedback. He can summarize and explore the feelings between members in an attempt to seek closure. For example:

> Paula had received positive feedback from Betty on her leadership abilities. This interaction had the potential of increasing Paula's self-confidence, especially since she was not working and experiencing a loss of self-esteem. Yet Paula's response indicated a discount of her actual abilities. "I was only trying to help," she responded. After summarizing the interaction, the worker asked, "Do you see yourself as a leader?" Paula's response was again hesitant and ambivalent. "Sort of," she said. Again the worker attempted to promote interaction and mutual aid by asking Paula to look at her peers and ask for feedback. Each member was able to point out past achievements Paula had made. With this support, she was then able to share with the group other experiences and achievements in which she had demonstrated leadership skills.

Catherine Chilman (1971) sums up the importance of social interaction in enriching the socialization process when she states:

> One of the basic aspects of the entire life process is that of an increasing differentiation and growing complexity of the self both in reference to and within

the self, and in reference to attitudes, perceptions, feelings and behaviors toward others.[3]

Action-oriented Group Work

In an attempt to bring about behavior change and increase social competence the group worker can use an action-oriented approach to learning. Interventions aimed at enlightening and developing insight often fall short of desired goals, for the mentally retarded may not be able to conceptualize an abstract idea. However, when the same information is presented in such a way that the individual can become directly involved in "doing" rather than "talking," he becomes an active participant in the change process.

Helen Northen (1969) emphasizes the importance of "doing" when she refers to it as "achievement of competence in action." She suggests that:

> If a person is confronted with situations and tasks which can be mastered, the resulting feelings of success may strengthen the ego and make possible further success.[4]

With the mentally retarded self-esteem and self-image are especially low and their sense of identity is often obscure. In their complex developmental struggle they may have been unable to master the tasks necessary for adult role behavior. A group work approach which involves participation in the here and now can help to bring about a more positive self-concept.

Action-oriented group work can also provide a source for immediate gratification. The retarded often have a low frustration and tolerance level with behavior patterns characterized by passive dependent attitudes. Experiencing immediate success not only brings about gratification, but it can also act to motivate and stimulate interest. At times, the group worker can assume a teaching role while using an action-oriented approach. For example, in the fishbowl exercise previously illustrated,

> ...all members were assigned tasks which involved their continued participation throughout the first half of the group process. Half of the group members were involved in problem-solving (they were instructed to purchase as a group $200.00 worth of merchandise from a shopping catalog). The other half were instructed to observe. The group worker spent time alone with the observers and provided specific instructions on what behaviors they might look for (e.g., listening skills, cooperation, leadership abilities, non-verbal behavior, etc.). The members in the inner circle completed the task while the observers recorded their behavior. When the problem-solving task was completed the observers then completed their task by providing feedback on individual behaviors.

As this case illustration suggests, growth and change can occur by having group members participate in action-oriented work. As these individuals experience themselves succeeding, they gain a sense of accomplishment as they assume adult role behavior. In this particular illustration, they had an opportunity to experience competency in decision-making, listening, observing, and acting autonomously while carrying out their tasks. Their tasks included writing, reading, speaking, keeping records, shopping, and planning, all of which are necessary for adult role enactment. At the same time, the group approach to socialization provided peer feedback which acted to reinforce the accomplishment. The group worker can play an instrumental role in teaching and demonstrating a specific task, and can also offer support as the group members experiment with various roles.

Modeling

The use of modeling techniques in working with the retarded can also influence change. Modeling provides a clear, concrete learning experience which the retarded adult is capable of assimilating into his knowledge base.

The group worker can begin by helping members clarify their problem-solving situations. At this point, individuals can frequently determine appropriate alternatives to pursue. Difficulty often arises in following through on a determined course of action. Often alternatives involve confronting other people in their environment. Here the retarded lack skills in assertion. The use of role playing can be instrumental in helping the individual rehearse his anticipated course of action. When an individual is hesitant or unwilling to attempt a role play, modeling can be used by the group worker to provide an example of assertive behavior. Once the individual has observed the worker take on his role, he can usually incorporate some of the skills and then rehearse using role play in the group situation. This type of intervention permits the worker to use himself as part of the change process, and offers the group member a new frame of reference for behavior. Whenever possible the group worker should utilize other group members who are capable of performing a modeling technique, as this stimulates member to member helping.

Behavior Contracts

Contracts are especially suitable for this population as they provide structure and a viable answer to the question, "How will I change a particular behavior?"

Behavior contracts should: (1) be created by the client with the support and guidance from the worker; (2) be brief, clear, and specific; (3) be focused on one area for change; (4) be positively oriented (behavior changes should be written stating what the client will do rather than what he should not do); (5) be signed by the client and the group worker.

Behavior contracts exist within and as a part of group life. Group members can also play a role in assisting the individual in forming and maintaining a behavior contract. Through the process of group interaction, individuals are often confronted by their peers with behaviors which are undesirable and inappropriate to overall group purpose.

Glasser and Garvin (1976) demonstrate the relationship of behavior contracts to group process when they point out:

> ...problematic behavior is generated, maintained and changed through interaction between the client and those individuals and institutions in his environment.[5]

When individuals make re-decisions within the group process that suggest the use of a behavior contract, the group worker can actively promote group interaction by supporting the individual in asking for feedback from his peers on alternative modes of action. As behavior contracts are often familiar to the retarded they can frequently offer each other valuable and appropriate knowledge based on their own past experiences. Again, this strengthens mutual aid.

Once a contract is made, the group worker can enlist the support of all the group members in helping the individual maintain his contract. Often they can learn how to provide positive reinforcement by modeling the group working and being encouraged to do so. Eventually the group members will be able to act independently. This type of peer help reinforces independence, a vital component of socialization. The following case illustration demonstrates this process:

> Mary often had difficulty in assuming adult role behaviors on structured social outings with the group (e.g., she would fall asleep on subways, lag a block behind the group, and become infantile in speech and mannerisms when attention was not focused on her). Her friendly and outgoing personality often made it possible for her to manipulate other group members into rescuing her from situations she was capable of resolving herself. Group members eventually became frustrated by her dependency needs and confronted her with her adult responsibilities. The group worker intervened by helping the members explore how their roles were reinforcing the unwanted situation. As the group members gained awareness they confronted Mary and refused to rescue her. At the same time they were very supportive and acceptant of wanting her along on trips. Faced with this change, Mary decided to form a behavior contract outlining what she wanted from the

social outings (her goal) and what adult behaviors would be most enhancing to achieve this goal. The contract provided structure while the group members provided maintenance and support.

The Use of Transactional Analysis

Transactional Analysis, originally theorized by Eric Berne (1961), provides an additional model for developmental growth, and is especially suitable for group work method. Robert Goulding (1972) describes Berne's early findings as he suggests:

> ...we became aware of the fact that each of our patients was actually three people, and that their behavior and feelings changed...depending on which ego state was in control. One moment we were watching a frightened child, the next moment we were listening to a stern parent...and then we were listening to a rational problem solving adult; and we began to realize that our patients characteristically assumed one of these three identities, i.e., Parent, Child or Adult...[6]

Since its inception, T.A. theory has expanded to include the diagnostic understanding of an individual's injunctions, games, rackets, and life decision, and how these factors unfold to determine a life script which the individual then follows.

What makes T.A. especially suitable for use in treatment of the mentally retarded is its flexibility and easy comprehension. While the group worker may need a more complex knowledge base of psychoanalytic and T.A. theory to make an accurate diagnosis of scripting and subsequent treatment interventions, this abstract conceptualization is not mandatory for the group member to make gains in his developmental growth.

The mentally retarded can be taught some of the basic tenets of the theory and learn to apply them in their own life experiences. For example, group members can learn the three ego states (Parent-Adult-Child) and the characteristics of each, and further, can learn to identify when they are exhibiting behavior from a particular state. They can then use this awareness in their transactions with other group members and gain additional insight into their own behaviors. Hopefully, they can later apply these skills to situations outside of the group experience.

This T.A. knowledge base can provide the retarded with an internal sense of power and control over their own behaviors. As they learn to identify the ego states and the transactions they are involved in, they can also decide from an adult position to change transactions which produce conflict for them. This is especially growth-oriented as behavior changes which take place are the result of an internal decision rather than pressures from the external environment.

T.A. also helps the individual to develop adult thinking. It is not unusual for the retarded to be infantilized by their parents, professionals, and the community. As the retarded begin to use their Adult ego state, they are better able to find alternatives and make independent decisions.

T.A. is also useful for group work situations which involve problem-solving work. Members can step into their Child ego state to express their feelings, their Parent ego state to offer support and guidance to each other, and their Adult ego state to gather information, conceive of alternatives, and then jointly make decisions that will insure their common needs.

T.A. theory and practice is compatible with traditional social group work models. For example, Helen Northen (1976), in her model "Psycho-social Practice in Small Groups," shares some commonalities with the T.A. approach. A major focus for change in Northen's model is social interaction. In T.A. terminology interaction takes place through transactions.

Northen sums up the factors influencing social interaction when she states:

> The basis of social interaction is human communication...communication consists of the verbal explicit, and the intentional messages between people; it is also consists of the nonverbal processes by which persons influence one another...As members of a group exchange feelings and thoughts or participate in activities there is a reciprocal and cyclical influence of members upon each other.[7]

In T.A., transactions provide a conceptual basis for all social interaction and can be viewed as one target for change. In a group process where emphasis is placed on member interaction to promote change, a T.A. knowledge base can greatly enhance communication skills.

Incorporating the Systems Approach

The external social forces affecting the retarded's developmental growth are multilateral. William Schwartz (1976), in his "Mediating Model" for group work intervention, suggests that the social work function "directs itself not to the individual or to the social, but to the relationship between the two."[8]

The group worker attempting to bring about change through the small group process must also look beyond this level of intervention and actively engage himself with all the participants in his client's system. Handicapped individuals often find themselves engaged in several professional relationships simultaneously. The network of services and the social institutions involved may be quite diversified.

For example, readying himself for the competitive job market usually brings the individual in contact with state agencies responsible for financial sponsorship in job training. The vocational training itself generally means attendance in a workshop setting. Often he resides in a hostel with its own professional staff. Remediation needs may bring him in contact with educational institutions. His handicap may also make him eligible for income maintenance and here he is generally involved with state and federal agencies. His family relationship is still another factor in his overall functioning.

Mediating this complex system, even for the average citizen, can prove overwhelming and unsatisfactory in terms of coordinating an effort which is fruitful. Yet, coordination of these services is mandatory not only in ensuring change, but in stabilizing the developmental gains the individual is able to acquire. As Schwartz (1976) points out:

> In any complex system, however, and particularly one in which great power exists and is unequally distributed, a force is needed to guard the symbiotic strivings and keep the interaction alive when each party is tempted to dismiss the other as unreachable.[9]

The group worker, providing services to a client on a regular weekly basis, is in an excellent position to assume this mediating role. Focusing on coordination of services, the group worker can invite all the participants to meet and jointly share their knowledge of the client. In this way, the client's strengths and weaknesses can be used to plan future interventions. This also suggests that a treatment plan will be a more viable one, as it will reflect the external conditions affecting the individual's socialization process. The client taking part in these meetings can also benefit from hearing his achievements verbalized. This group assessment can also provide him with a reference point to set realistic and reachable goals.

All of the interventions discussed here have the common goal of providing opportunities for role learning not available in the social network. The early socialization of the mentally retarded is often characterized by isolation inside an institution or in a sheltered home environment. The norms, values, and roles learned are limited to the attitudes expressed by significant others in their immediate surroundings. Through the small group process resocialization is taking place. These individuals are learning "selfhood and self-realization through social connectedness."[10]

If role learning is to have a growth directed goal it must remain flexible rather than conforming. Through the process of socialization the individual must also become knowledgeable in effectively changing his environment to meet his needs.[11] The group worker's interventions must be realistic in terms of attainable goals, while supporting individual strengths and encouraging creativity.

References

1. McBroom, E. Socialization through small groups. In R. W. Roberts & H. Northen (Eds.), *Theories of social work with groups.* New York: Columbia University Press, 1976, p. 299.
2. Ibid, p. 292.

3. Chilman, C. Socialization and interpersonal change. *Encyclopedia of social work,* 1971, 2, 1295.

4. Northen, H. *Social work with groups.* New York: Columbia University Press, 1969, p. 77.

5. Glasser, P. H., & Garnin, C. D. An organizational model. In R. W. Roberts & H. Northen (Eds.) *Theories of social work with groups.* New York: Columbia University Press, 1976, p. 88.

6. Goulding, R. New directions in Transactional Analysis: Creating an environment for redecision and change. In C. J. Sager & H. S. Kaplan (Eds.), *Progress in group and family therapy.* New York: Brunner/Mazel Publishers, 1972, pp. 105–106.

7. Northen, H. Psychosocial practice in small groups. In R. W. Roberts & H. Northen (Eds.), *Theories of social work with groups.* New York: Columbia University Press, 1976, p. 127–128.

8. Schwartz, W. Between client and system: The mediating function. In R. W. Roberts & H. Northen (Eds.), *Theories of social work with groups.* New York: Columbia University Press, 1976, p. 183.

9. Ibid, p. 183.

10. McBroom, E. Socialization through small groups, 1976, p. 272.

11. Hartford, M. Socialization methods in social work practice. *Encyclopedia of social work,* 1971, 2, 1311.

Bibliography

BERNE, ERIC. *Transactional analysis in psychotherapy.* New York: Ballantine Books, 1961.

BERNE, ERIC. *Beyond games and scripts.* New York: Ballantine Books, 1976.

JAMES, MURIEL, & JONEWARD, DOROTHY, *Born to win.* New York: New American Library, 1978.

NORTHEN, HELEN. *Social work with groups.* New York: Columbia University Press, 1969.

ROBERTS, ROBERT, & NORTHEN, HELEN, eds. *Theories of social work with groups.* New York: Columbia University Press, 1976.

SAGER, CLIFFORD, & KAPLAN, HELEN SINGER, eds. *Progress in group and family therapy.* New York: Brunner/Mazel Publishers, 1972.

WOLPE, J. *The practice of behavior therapy.* New York: Pergamon Press, Inc., 1969.

SICKLE-CELL ANEMIA

CHAPTER 46

Psychosocial Aspects
of Sickle-Cell Anemia
in Adolescents

*Shirley Conyard, Muthuswamy Krishnamurthy,
and Harvey Dosik*

Sickle-cell anemia is a chronic hereditary, hemolytic anemia found in descendants of Africans, Italians, Greeks, and others from the area near the Mediterranean Sea. In the United States, it is found most commonly in Blacks, occurring in about one of four hundred births of Black babies.[1] An estimated fifty thousand Blacks in the United States alone have sickle-cell anemia.[2] This disease is not a new problem. The basic clinical conditions were observed as early as 1910 by James B. Herrick, a physician, in the bloodstream of a Black West Indian student.[3]

Sickle cells are elongated red blood cells with sharp double points, giving the cell a crescent shape rather than the round, disc shape of normal red blood cells. The cells resemble the narrow, curved blade of a sickle used to cut grass; hence the name, sickle-cell anemia. Sickle-cell anemia is characterized by a chronic hemolytic anemia, that is, a deficiency of red blood cells due to their excessive destruction, and intermittent crises of variable frequency and severity involving fever and pains in bones, joints, and abdomen. In addition, there is an increased incidence of bacterial infection. A multiplicity of symptoms may occur with gradual involvement of many tissues and organ systems, for example, splenic congestion and a somewhat enlarged liver. Life expectancy is reduced; many sufferers succumb in infancy or early childhood, and most do not survive their fourth decade. The clinical picture is quite varied, however. Some patients remain relatively asymptomatic for many years, whereas others become severely disabled or die at an early age.[4]

Although some features of the disease may be seen at any age—for example, anemia, painful crises, and bone infarcts—others occur characteristically in certain age groups. For example, clinical manifestations are generally first noted between 6 months and 2 years of age. The most common problems present in this age group and throughout childhood are infections and dactylitis, that is, joint pains, swelling, and limited motion. In adolescents and young adults, leg ulcers, aseptic necrosis of the femoral head, and retinal lesions are usually seen.[5]

In the past, treatment has been supportive and limited to the symptoms, only attempting to alleviate pain or combat infections as they occur, since there is no treatment of the disease itself. For example, when pain is severe or if vomiting and dehydration supervenes, hospitalization is necessary. Fluids are then given intravenously along with analgesic drugs such as codeine or meperidine. A variety of intravenous fluids such as electrolyte solutions, dextrose, dextran, and plasma have reportedly been effective in alleviating pain, presumably through their ability to mobilize trapped sickle cells. However, severe pain may persist for days or even weeks in some cases despite these measures.[6] This treatment produces little or no side effects.

However, the physical aspects of sickle-cell anemia constitute only one facet of the health problem. Sickle-cell anemia also causes severe social and emotional problems. The normal adolescent is characterized psychologically as attempting to achieve emancipation from their parents and increasing independence.[7] However, Whitten and Fischoff described the chronically ill adolescent as afraid to be an autonomous individual, withdrawn from relationships, having limited aspirations and poor self-esteem, feeling depressed, helpless and fearful, and preoccupied with death.[8] Singler described chronically ill patients as fearful, nonverbal, bolated, and having damaged self-esteem.[9] Whitten and Fischoff postulate the existence of similar emotional and social problems in patients with sickle-cell anemia, but this has never been documented.[10] With this in mind, the authors investigated the behavior patterns of twenty-one adolescents with sickle-cell anemia to see whether they resembled the patterns found with other chronic diseases.

Evaluation of Adolescent Patients

In 1972, with the aid of funding from the National Institutes of Health and the National Heart and Lung Institute, a comprehensive sickle-cell clinic was established at the Jewish Hospital and Medical Center of Brooklyn,

New York. A social worker was assigned to study the emotional problems of persons suffering from sickle-cell anemia and to carry out emotional rehabilitation when it was needed.

The social worker evaluated a total of twenty-one adolescents, nine males aged 14 to 19 and twelve females aged 13 to 19. All the adolescents in the study were in school, and all came from the same social and economic background, that is, they lived in ghetto areas and came from low-income, one-parent families with three or more siblings. Table 46-1 describes the composition of the group, according to age, sex, and type of hemoglobinopathy.

There are two types of sickle-cell anemia of differing severity. Individuals with SS hemoglobin have inherited sickling hemoglobin (S) from both parents. Individuals with SC hemoglobin have inherited sickling hemoglobin (S) from one parent and a different type, crystallizing hemoglobin (C), from the other parent. Hemoglobin SS disease and hemoglobin SC disease are both characterized by a chronic hemolytic anemia. However, the clinical manifestation from intravascular occlusion and vaso-occlusion is generally less severe in those with SC disease than in those with SS disease. The incidence of bacterial infections is also much less in individuals with SC disease, but they have a greater frequency of aseptic necrosis of the femoral head, retinal infarcts, and renal papillary necrosis.[11]

Each patient and his or her family were seen by the social worker in the clinic and on admission to the hospital to evaluate the patient's needs, to assist in discharge planning, to provide casework treatment, and to serve as liaison between the patients and other helping agents such as nurses and physicians. To further assess the patients' emotional and social problems, the study also included evaluations by the patients' parents and their schoolteachers. Each patient was rated good, fair, or poor on the following criteria: leadership, mental response and/or communication, relationship with peers, relationship with teachers, adjustment to school, participation in school activities, independence, reaction to suggestions and criticisms, responsibility, reaction to own illness, neatness, and attendance record (other than for acute illness). Each evaluator was unaware of the others' ratings. The evaluations of the parents and the schoolteachers for each patient concurred with the worker's findings. The results were compiled

TABLE 46-1.   Patients Studied, According to Sex and Hemoglobinopathy

HEMOGLOBINOPATHY	MALE	FEMALE	TOTAL
SS	6	9	15
SC	3	3	6
Total	9	12	21

TABLE 46-2. Results of Evaluation of Adolescents with Sickle-Cell Disease

NUMBER OF SUBJECTS

| | SS DISEASE | | | | | | SC DISEASE | | | | | |
| | Male | | | Female | | | Male | | | Female | | |
CRITERIA	GOOD	FAIR	POOR	GOOD	FAIR	POOR	GOOD	FAIR	POOR	GOOD	FAIR	POOR
Leadership			6	1	3	5			3		2	1
Mental response and/or communication		2	4		3	5		2	1		2	1
Relationship with peers		1	5	1	0	8			3		3	1
Relationship with teachers		1	5	4	4	1	1	1	1		1	2
Adjustment to school		2	4	3	2	4		3			1	2
Participation in school activities				1	1	8	1					
Independence		1	6	1	1	7	1	1	3		1	2
Reaction to suggestions and constructive criticisms		4	2		4	5		2	1		2	1
Responsibility	3		6	3	2	4		1	2		1	2
Reaction to own illness	2		4	1	4	4	2	1	2		1	2
Neatness	3		3	6	2	1	2	1		2	1	
Attendance record		2	4	4	1	4	1	2		1	2	

at the end of the study by averaging the ratings of all three evaluators, and these results are shown in Table 46-2.

Psychosocial Problems of Patients

Patients in the study showed a high degree of isolation, dependence, fear of illness, and withdrawal from normal relationships with peers in school and their family members. Other emotional problems included poor self-image, depression, anxiety, nonverbalization, and preoccupation with death. All the patients showed an overall poor performance on the criteria, although the females fared better than the males in certain areas such as responsibility, adjustment to school, leadership, and neatness. The sex variation shown in this study is probably due to natural maturation, since girls mature earlier than boys, and to social environment, since girls are encouraged early to develop their skills.[12] There appeared to be little or no difference in performance between patients with SS disease and patients with SC disease.

The study confirmed the hypothesis that the psychosocial aspects of sickle-cell disease resemble those of other chronic illnesses. However, this psychosocial profile does not have the same cultural, social, and environmental impact on patients with other chronic diseases that it has on patients with sickle-cell anemia. First, sickle-cell anemia is primarily a disease of Black people. Second, most information concerning sickle-cell anemia is presented in negative terms, for example, that people with the disease have short life spans, are unable to work, should not have children, and should not take part in activities such as sports. Third, parents who have children with the disease experience feelings of guilt. Finally, professional people in the medical and social sciences have inadequate training or background to deal comfortably with the problems of counseling and medical treatment of the sickle-cell patient. In other words, patients, parents, and medical professionals all experience a feeling of hopelessness. Hope is offered by society to patients with other chronic diseases but not to sickle-cell patients.

Task-oriented Group

The study unmasked many emotional and social problems experienced by sickle-cell patients. Since there is no effective medical treatment for relatively asymptomatic patients with uncomplicated sickle-cell anemia, the authors believe that these individuals would benefit greatly from counseling.[13] In the past, individual casework was utilized to meet the patients' severe emotional and social needs and to enable them to grow emotionally.

However, this method tended to compound patients' feelings of uniqueness and did not provide them with the experience of peer relationship and peer socialization. It also fostered the patients' dependence, which at times would shift from the parents to the social worker. The authors felt that a group approach would be a successful alternative method of treatment, and initiated a pilot study to test this hypothesis.

By design, the group was a closed, task-oriented group. "Task-oriented" is defined here as putting into practice the concerns of the group as expressed in its discussions through the carrying out of assigned tasks. The group's aims were to build on the strengths and knowledge that the adolescent patients already had in order to reduce anxiety, enhance social functioning, achieve self-fulfillment, and if possible, resocialize the patients emotionally so that they could enter the "normal" mainstream of life. The authors believed this could be accomplished by freeing each patient from the myths and misconceptions he or she held about the illness.

Scheduled meetings were held once a week for 1½ hours from September 1973 until May 1975. The interviewing and evaluating of the adolescents chosen for the group have already been described. The six patients selected from among the twenty-one in the study had been rated fair and poor on all the variables in the evaluation. They were also chosen because they showed a positive interest in improving themselves and agreed to take part in group counseling. The group was made up of three males and three females ranging in age from 13½ to 15. Four of the group members had SS disease, the other two had SC. The group attendance was very good, no more than one member ever being absent at one time. Member participation was one of the group's most important features, since the social worker was trying to develop peer-group identity and group cohesiveness to create free-flowing group communications and participation.

Role of the Social Worker

To begin with, the social worker had to remove all barriers that would keep patients from attending the group meetings, such as problems with carfare or fear of traveling alone. During the group process, the social worker acted as a catalyst, creating stimuli for group interaction. Initially, the social worker led the sessions, giving some guidance, arranging for the various group tasks, and choosing some of the topics for discussion. Other topics for discussion were chosen by the group. As time passed, the social worker's role developed into that of an observer, except for explaining medical data, intervening for the protection of a group member, or restructuring the sessions when the group strayed from the topic of that session.

The group discussions focused on two types of problems experienced by the members: medical problems and social problems. Discussions of medical problems dealt with (1) members' knowledge about sickle-cell anemia; (2) their ability to handle themselves during crises and when asymptomatic; (3) members' growth and development, including delay in development, sex characteristics, and physical growth; and (4) feelings about having the disease, including fears and myths concerning early death and feelings about physical activities, being alone, and traveling alone. Topics relating to social problems included the following: (1) adjustment to school, for example, fear of being ill in school, difficulty in keeping up with homework, absences, and relationships with peers and teachers; (2) members' feelings about themselves as persons, in particular about their uniqueness and handicap, and about being stigmatized or socially outcast; (3) effects on social life caused by the illness, including feelings of embarrassment and rejection, relationships with peers and family members, blaming of parents for the illness, and feelings of guilt toward healthy siblings, who often had to wait for parents' attention while it was focused on the patient; and (4) members' perception on the future in relation to college, marriage, and children.

Tasks

For the first twelve weeks the group members were still apprehensive about exposing and sharing their feelings with each other, which limited group interaction. Not until discussions were accompanied by performance of tasks did the members begin to function as a group.

The first task was a project for the entire group—organizing a party for the entire population of the sickle-cell clinic. It was carried out quite successfully with some help from the social worker. Besides creating a few inflated egos, this task provided the group with three very important factors, namely, group interaction or free-flowing communication, interest in the group, and motivation to carry out other tasks.

Next, the entire group went on a field trip, and each member was supposed to bring a friend. This task was difficult and created a lot of anxiety because it called for the members to share themselves with people other than those in the group. Once their anxiety was worked through, the second task was carried out over and over again on other field trips and outings. The group went to such places as museums, libraries, plays, baseball and football games, the United Nations, colleges, parks, zoos, and several restaurants. As a result, the group members began to form independent peer relationships. Through these group outings, the members learned how to travel by themselves, and their minds and eyes were opened to aspects of life other than those in front of their house or just up the block.

The third task involved removing the adolescents from classes for the handicapped in school and also having them participate in gym classes if their physician approved. This task began to work away at the fears and myths surrounding physical activity and the feeling of physical handicaps. It also made each group member aware of his or her limitations and began to build positive coping mechanisms. Parents and teachers reported that the adolescents became more outgoing and experienced no ill effects from participating in gym and being placed in regular classes.

The next task was designed to test the progress made during the group sessions that dealt with independence and ego strength in relation to sociability. After this discussion, the group members began to search for something of interest to take on as an independent project. Among the female members, one began music lessons, the second took dance lessons, and the third became vice-president of a handicapped group in her neighborhood. One male joined the Salvation Army band and a second got a part-time job. The third male, whose emotional growth lagged behind the other members, felt that he needed more time before selecting an outside activity.

The fifth group task was to attend a normal "sleepaway" camp. The members participated in all camp activities, including learning how to swim. No one became ill, and all members stayed for two weeks. The group members were given excellent ratings by the counselors at the camp, leadership, relationships with other campers and counselors, participation in camp activities, independence, reaction to their handicap, temperament, and responsibility.

For their final task, all group members, except the one who was lagging behind, obtained summer jobs. Their employers found them to be good workers, and they have worked every summer thereafter.

Discussion

The major emotional factors describing the characteristics of sickle-cell patients were depression, feelings of helplessness, fear, poor self-esteem, and poor self-concept.[14] Treatment of these problems involved participation in the task-oriented group, which gave the adolescents the opportunity to verbalize their feelings, receive constructive education, and actually test themselves in situations that they most feared. It also helped them to move toward what may be termed "social responsiveness," or taking part in normal social activities and responsibilities. As Parsons stated, the sick person is exempt from normal social responsibilities.[15]

The first two tasks, giving a party and going on outings with a friend, were important because they put each member into a position of exposing him- or herself. These tasks covered a wide range of the group members' fears, such as communicating, that is, relating to another person; carrying out tasks; forming peer relationships with group members, schoolmates, or neighbors; and, most of all, being accepted. All adolescents need to feel they have some acceptance by their peers and will withdraw from social relationships if they feel acceptance does not exist.[16] The success of the first two tasks helped the group members to gain some self-esteem and confidence in their ability to carry out a specified task and succeed. Members were motivated to take on the third task which challenged their limitations and imperfections.

This task, participating in normal classes, enabled the group to continue with the last three tasks by reinforcing confidence in themselves and boosting their self-esteem. At this point, they began to enjoy life, going to school, and relating to their peers. Their attitude at home and school improved. Adolescents with sickle-cell anemia may place themselves in a stressful situation to prove that they are like other adolescents if they are not allowed to prove their capabilities in planned supervised activities, such as the ones provided by this task.[17]

The final three tasks can be described as emancipating and future-oriented tasks. These allowed the group members to begin experiencing a certain amount of independence and to start reaching for self-fulfillment. Most of all, these tasks helped the group members to become a part of society, enhancing their sociability and developing their talents, from camping to earning money. To sum up, all six tasks helped the individuals in the group to reach more of an emotional and social balance, hence, "normalcy."

Summary

The task-oriented group method used in this study was more successful than individual casework or a discussion group. The tasks that the group members were asked to do required them to modify certain patterns of social behavior, demanded taking of risks, and clearly spelled out the behaviors to be undertaken. In making a commitment to carry out the tasks, each member recognized that he or she had to make a choice between action and inaction. By acting, each individual was saying, "This is what I am willing to try to achieve," thus beginning immediate action to solve his or her problem.[18] This advantage is not present in the individual casework method, where socialization and interaction with peers are limited. Similarly, a discussion group with no action will often leave the members with their problems unresolved.

The ideal number of participants for a group is not clear. The group described contained six members, enough for an adequate amount of interaction, but not so many that members would be neglected. The two-year period of interaction provided enough time to research and discuss topics and to find social resources for group tasks. This period enabled the group to develop better feelings about and understanding of themselves and their illness. It enabled the authors to gain a better understanding of the psychosocial makeup of adolescents with sickle-cell anemia. This successful group approach to adolescents with sickle-cell anemia should lead others to try a similar approach and to apply it to groups of children and adults as well.

Notes and References

1. *Sickle Cell Counseling: A Committee's Study and Recommendations* (Los Angeles: Los Angeles County Department of Health Services, Chronic Disease Control Division, Community Health Services, March 1973), p. 8.

2. Marion Barnhart, Raymond L. Henry, and Jeanne Lusher, *Sickle Cell* (Kalamazoo, Mich.: Upjohn Co., 1974), p. 7.

3. *See* Stanley H. Smith, "The Sociopsychological Aspects of Sickle Cell Anemia," *First International Conference on the Mental Health Aspects of Sickle Cell Anemia* (Rockville, Md.: U.S. Department of Health, Education & Welfare, 1974).

4. Barnhart, Henry, and Lusher, op. cit., 36.

5. Ibid., pp. 36–37.

6. Ibid., p. 86.

7. H. Thornburg and D. Ershel, "Behavior and Values: Consistency or Inconsistency," *Adolescence*, 8 (Winter 1973), pp. 513–520.

8. Charles Whitten and Joseph Fischoff, "Psychosocial Effects of Sickle Cell Disease," *Archives of Internal Medicine*, 133 (April 1974), pp. 681–689.

9. Judith R. Singler, "Group Work with Hospitalized Stroke Patients," *Social Casework*, 56 (June 1975), pp. 348–354.

10. Whitten and Fischoff, op. cit.

11. Barnhart, Henry, and Lusher, op. cit.

12. R. G. Wiggins, "Difference in Self-Perception of Ninth Grade Boys and Girls," *Adolescence*, 7 (Winter 1973), pp. 491–496.

13. William J. Williams et al., *Hematology* (New York: McGraw-Hill Book Co., 1972), p. 421.

14. Ibid.; Talcott Parsons, *Social System* (New York: Free Press of Glencoe, 1951); and Santosh Kumar et al., "Anxiety, Self-Concept and Personal and Social Adjustments in Children with Sickle Cell Anemia," *Journal of Pediatrics*, 88 (May 1976), pp. 859–863.

15. Parsons, op. cit., p. 23.

16. Whitten and Fischoff, op. cit.

17. William R. Montgomery, ''Psychosocial Aspects of Sickle Cell Anemia,'' *First International Conference on the Mental Health Aspects of Sickle Cell Anemia,* pp. 31–39.

18. *See* William J. Reid and Laura Epstein, *Task-Centered Casework* (New York: Columbia University Press, 1972), p. 147.

STROKE PATIENTS

CHAPTER 47

Group Work with Hospitalized Stroke Patients

Judith R. Singler

Each year in the United States, thousands of persons suffer cerebrovascular accidents—strokes. Many of these persons require hospitalization for extensive rehabilitation therapy, including physical, occupational, and speech therapies. For some, the reward for weeks of physical and emotional toil is a return home to family and friends; for others, the long hours of struggle lead to a nursing or rest home; still others find themselves confined indefinitely, perhaps permanently, to hospitals for the chronically ill.

To meet the needs of severely handicapped patients, social workers have long utilized casework skills. In 1961, Esther White described the difficulties of casework in the early stages of illness, noting that patients (in her experience, adult polio patients hospitalized for six to twelve months) were often nonverbal with staff and family, as well as with other patients, in areas that related to their illness.[1] She ascribed this lack to a dual fear on the part of the patient: a fear of antagonizing staff by negative comments and a fear of confirming in their own minds what they feared most about the illness. Other writers[2] have noted the reactions of patients to

---

[1] Esther White, The Body Image Concept in Rehabilitating Severely Handicapped Patients, *Social Work*, 6:51–58 (July 1961).

[2] See, for example, Samuel B. Kutash, *The Application of Therapeutic Procedures to the Disabled*, Office of Vocational Rehabilitation Services Series, No. 343 (Washington, D.C.: U.S. Department of Health, Education, and Welfare, 1956), pp. 10–14; and Shirley London, Group Work in Limited Therapy Situations, in *Social Work with Groups: Selected Papers from the National Conference on Social Welfare* (New York: National Association of Social Workers, 1959), pp. 41–51.

Reprinted from *Social Casework*, Vol. 56 (June, 1975), pp. 348–354, with permission of the author and the Family Service Association of America.

catastrophic illnesses, citing anxiety and depression, as well as the damage to the individual's self-esteem, all of which combine to isolate him from people around him. Thus isolated, the patient may feel his condition is unique, so that others, especially those who are well, are unable to understand his predicament and are unable to help him. For this type of patient, casework early in his hospitalization may have limited value.

An alternative method of treatment is, of course, the group. Use of group work in this situation offers several benefits, perhaps the most significant of which was stated by Gisela Konopka: "Human beings cannot stand alone. The group is not just one aspect of human life, but it is life blood itself because it represents the belonging to humanity."[3] Thus, for the stroke patient, separated from much of his former world, the group becomes a potential vehicle of return to self, to others.

Youville Hospital is a private, nonprofit, 305-bed rehabilitation and chronic disease hospital in Cambridge, Massachusetts, receiving patients from the greater Boston area. In 1971, it was decided by the social service department of the hospital to initiate a discussion group for rehabilitation patients who had suffered cerebrovascular accidents. The writer was involved from its inception in December 1971 to December 1972. There were sixty-five beds on two wards devoted to patients admitted specifically for rehabilitation. Each patient and his family were seen on admission by a social worker, who remained on the case throughout the patient's hospital stay, acting as liaison between patient, family, and the hospital, providing direct casework treatment when needed, assisting in discharge planning, and providing staff consultation when indicated.

Group Structure

By design, the group was open-ended and had an open membership system. Its aims were to provide support for members, to reduce anxiety, and to promote increased self-acceptance. Any hemiparetic or hemiplegic patient (that is, one who had suffered partial or total paralysis on one side of his body) who was able to speak and be understood by others, as well as to comprehend others, was invited to attend. Each was on the rehabilitation program for one week prior to attending his first group meeting. This plan allowed the patient to acclimate himself. Meetings were held once weekly for one hour, apart from the regular therapy schedule. New members were expected to attend three sessions as a part of their total rehabilitation program; after that, the decision to continue was up to the individual.

[3] Gisela Konopka, *Group Work in the Institution* (New York: Association Press, 1972), p. 22.

Members ranged in age from thirty-two to eighty-eight for women and from forty-one to seventy-nine for men. The actual number of patients attending any one meeting varied from three to twelve. The total number of patients served in the first thirteen months of the program was sixty-one; of this group, fifty-nine had suffered strokes. There was no maximum on the number of sessions an individual could attend, but membership ceased on discharge from the hospital. In practice, attendance ranged from three to seventeen sessions.

With new patients joining and older members leaving almost weekly, the group membership was quite fluid. This open membership system was given careful consideration before the group was begun. The continuous admission and discharge procedures of the hospital favored such a system, because every stroke patient had an opportunity to join the group. The system was recognized as having limitations, most obviously that of stunting potential group movement, as well as the difficulty of obtaining group cohesion. It should be noted, however, that primary consideration was not the development of an intense group identity but individual growth through the group process. Aware of the fluctuating stroke patient population within the hospital and variable lengths of patient hospitalization and encouraged by the success of a like-structured group in reducing isolation and depression among parents of handicapped children,[4] the writer began an open-ended group for stroke patients and other hemiparetic or hemiplegic patients.

Role of the Social Worker

The role of the social worker in the position of group leader was, as noted by Hans S. Falck,[5] to act as a catalyst to the members, to provide stimulus and some guidance to their interaction, and to answer questions on hospital policy or other objective or technical matters. The worker was also the planner of the meetings, arranging for the room and for refreshments. In practice, the worker initially led the meetings, beginning the discussions and choosing topics for discussion. In time, the members began to introduce their own concerns, seeking responses not from the worker, but from each other. At this point, the worker saw her role become that of an observer, watching for any adverse reactions on the part of any mem-

[4] Ann Murphy, Siegfried Pueschel, and Jane Schneider, Group Work with Parents of Children with Down's Syndrome, SOCIAL CASEWORK, 54:114–19 (February 1973).

[5] Hans S. Falck, The Use of Groups in the Practice of Social Work, SOCIAL CASEWORK, 44:63–67 (February 1963).

ber, and occasionally intervening to return the members to the topic of that session.

Content of the Meetings

A working pattern arbitrarily established by the worker in the initial meetings received support from the members and continued for over a year. This pattern provided each member with the opportunity, at his first meeting, to tell the circumstances of his stroke. No one declined to do so. Each member could begin to express himself in the group and, more important, to answer what seemed to be a need for such a recitation, seen commonly in these patients in this early, self-centered stage of adjustment. It also provided the opportunity for the members who had been in the group longer to disassociate themselves to see the problems that others were experiencing.

Discussion among members can be divided into several areas: (1) gathering of information about strokes, the hospital, and therapy; (2) sharing of experiences and feelings; and (3) identification of fears and problems. In all of these areas, the members tended to support one another and to test their perceptions of themselves against the others. Gathering of information often overlapped with the sharing of experiences, providing insight for both patients and worker.

Two men were discussing the difficulties of putting on a brace, then shoes, and, finally, a T-shirt. Mr. C recounted, very humorously, a tale of how he had one day become hopelessly entangled in his shirt, requiring a nurse to extricate him. Mr. K, who had been quietly listening to the entire exchange, suddenly uttered a great sigh of relief, stating, "I thought I had to be the only one who couldn't get a shirt on right." He added that he had not mentioned it before, even to his therapist, because he was so embarrassed by his failure. Now obviously relieved, he went on to emphasize that for him such items as his inability to wind a watch, scratch his shoulder, and comb his hair were more discouraging than his loss of ambulation. Mr. C agreed. "It's just one more thing we have to depend on someone else for. The big things are much easier to take. These little things, they are really hard."

Here a man's self-esteem, battered down by his inability to perform what had once been an elementary task, was boosted by the knowledge that he was not alone in this difficulty. Embarrassed by his failure and perceiving this problem as unique to himself, he had not mentioned it and, thus, had created a situation which further isolated him from others. The additional activities he mentioned were quickly picked up by another member as relating to personal independence, an insight which provoked considerable discussion.

Members, especially when first attending, appeared to gain considerable satisfaction from sharing their own experiences. Indeed, they would often seem to vie with one another, each wanting to tell a tale of greater frustration or greater success. An obvious expression of their self-centered state, such a recitation also seemed to enable many individuals to begin to identify both strengths and weaknesses and, in some measure, to begin to come to grips with them. It is interesting to note that as each patient began to adjust to his own disability and to accept himself as he had become, a move away from this competition could be seen, with members more frequently commenting on the progress or successes of others. One patient put it this way: "At first all you can see is what you can't do, but after a bit, you find yourself doing some new things. After that worries seem less, and you can look at other people and at the rest of the world again."

Group Support

Although physical disabilities are the ones most apparent to other persons, for the stroke patient himself heightened emotionalism is often a frustratingly incapacitating feature of his disability.

> Mrs. G., attending for the first time, told the others of her experience in suffering the stroke. While doing so, she began to sob uncontrollably, tried to apologize, but only cried even more. Mrs. M and Mrs. K immediately came to her support, both with tears in their eyes. Mrs. M explained that a tendency toward crying "just seems to be a part of the total effect of a stroke, as if the mind just can't believe what has happened to the body."

In the early weeks of the group, the writer pointed out to members, in response to questions, the fact of heightened emotionalism's often accompanying a cerebrovascular accident. The members quickly learned to explain this fact to each other, thus helping to allay the anxiety of their fellow patients, while gaining some mastery over the mysteries of their own conditions.

Just as they shared their successes and helped each other to cope with some of the frustrations of living with handicaps, the members also slowly began to confront the negative attitudes, feelings, and experiences of some members. This process began with a single member's wondering aloud if the others ever became depressed, noting that he was very discouraged about his minimal progress. Others agreed that they had felt the same way at times, suggested activities for leisure time to avoid thinking only of one's own problems, and emphasized that it was important to find someone to talk with about these feelings. Gradually, they began to see the group as the "someone" who would listen. Once this realization occurred, a solution for the problems voiced became less crucial; the sharing of the feeling was the important factor, with longer-participating members most often providing advice and guidance for the newer members. In the weeks after this step, members began to bring up regularly such questions of feelings and attitudes.

Their greatest challenge as a group came in a session that brought into the open perhaps their greatest fears.

> Mr. F, usually amiable and jovial, suddenly blurted out, "The work isn't really worth anything when you have nothing to live for. There's no sense in going through all this if things aren't going to change. Me, I have nothing to live for. I might as well die." The others appeared stunned and sat silently staring at the table. Mrs. P., an eighty-eight-year-old widow, tried to support him, saying she, too, had felt this way. The response from Mr. F was an angry, "But you can walk: I can't even pull up my pants. And I don't even have a mind: I'm of no use to anyone anymore." Others tried to respond but were overwhelmed by the intensity of Mr. F's remarks. Finally, Mrs. P tried again. "You seem to be comparing yourself to the past, to the way you used to be. I think that we have to go day by day, not remembering the past too much or worrying about the future. And you can be useful—even just by talking or listening you can help someone else." By this time some of the others had recovered sufficiently to voice added support, emphasizing that activities were secondary to being alive. Others added that they, too, often wanted to give up, that daily therapy often seemed futile. Mr. F gradually relaxed and tearfully thanked the others for helping him, adding that he "just had to get it out into the open" and expressing relief that the others shared his feelings.

In this manner, members gradually began to confront themselves and each other with the reality of their handicaps. Sharing their successes had been easy for most of them and had, in some cases, enabled them to avoid consideration of their own failures. Mr. F, in the meeting described above, brought out what probably had occurred to all of them at some time. They could not provide a solution for his lack of progress in therapy or for the severity of his stroke, but they could and did listen and voice support. The recitation had a visibly cathartic effect on Mr. F. The isolation he had felt was revealed as a self-imposed burden. In addition, his directness had forced others to confront their own situations and to examine their own feelings.

> Mrs. M. was depressed and tearful over her slow progress in therapy. Others had tried to comfort her and share their similar feelings. Finally, Mr. R, began speaking

loudly and rapidly to avoid her interruptions. "Look lady, quit feeling so sorry for yourself. All of us are going through the same thing. You can do more than I can do. You have enough guts to pick yourself up right now and face your situation and begin to adjust. We can't do it all for you. We'll all help each other, but we have to learn to help ourselves, too. And if you or I will never walk again, well, we had just better learn to face it instead of making ourselves and everyone else miserable wishing for something that we will never have."

These two incidents also illustrate a prime benefit of this type of membership pattern: the development of a nurturing and supportive role for the older members, through which they could guide, chastise, praise, and empathize with the newer members. Such comments, far from being rejected even when harsh, were almost always well received by the group members.

Confronting Fears

In the early weeks of group life, the members dealt largely with such concrete matters as techniques learned in therapy, circumstances of their own strokes, hospital policies, and shared experiences of weekend visits home. In these weeks, the group included two patients who were hemiparetic as a result of externally caused injuries rather than strokes. Because their handicaps were in large measure the same, they were included in the group. However, an occurrence at one meeting in the third month of the group points up an important difference in their respective adjustment patterns.

Mr. O, who had suffered a rather mild stroke, hesitantly asked if he could "talk about something no one seems to ever mention. I was afraid to ask my doctor ... but what are the chances of any of us having another stroke?" Everyone looked to the worker for an answer, and she referred the question back to the group itself. Several members commented that they had not asked their doctors because they thought it "would just be more bad news." Two members, however, the nonstroke hemiparetics, were puzzled by this attitude, saying, "If it happens, it happens, but you can't worry about it." The remaining members sought a response from the worker, who answered in very general terms about the various causes of strokes and means of protecting oneself beforehand and mentioned the importance of discussing this query thoroughly with their own physicians. The group became very subdued, and several comments were made on the difficulty of continuing in therapy with such a threat over their heads. This discussion went on for some time, until the two hemiparetic patients again blurted out their disagreement with this attitude. The stroke patients were quiet, almost embarrassed by their earlier comments. Mr. O said, "I guess if you haven't had a stroke you can't really know what it is like. I just don't know if I could bear to start all over again with hospitals and therapy. It would be too much to ask of a person."

In subsequent meetings, this fear of a second stroke was brought up repeatedly. At times, the members discussed it at length; at other times, they simply alluded to it. It became obvious to the writer that this fear of another stroke underlay much of the members' conversation while in the group and, thus, perhaps some of their behavior. This fear was an area of concern which the nonstroke hemiparetics did not share, and they found it difficult to relate to the profound, very visible effect its mention had on the others. As in the incident above, their inability to comprehend this reaction in those who had suffered a stroke caused the other patients to become embarrassed and concerned over these very honest feelings. Because of the important role this fear seemed to play in the lives of these patients, the writer decided to restrict the group thereafter to persons who had suffered a stroke.

Another cause of anxiety for these patients was concern over acceptance by the nonhospital world. From the early days of hospitalization, when a patient's image of himself was so dependent on the staff, a bond was formed. This bond gave support and encouragement that was felt and recognized by these patients when they approached discharge, became increasingly anxious about how the "outside world" would receive them. White, in writing on the rehabilitation of the severely handicapped, saw the hospital as a microcosm, reflecting attitudes of the community and preparing the patients for posthospital adjustments.[6] The patients in the stroke group, however, discerned a definite distinction between the attitudes of the hospital staff and those of individuals in the community. They felt that the understanding and supportive attitudes of the staff would not be found after their discharge, and all were concerned about this problem. The open membership system greatly facilitated the intense quizzing of members who went home for weekends about the reactions of people to their presence in stores, churches, parks, and other public places. The interpersonal relations in the hospital as well as in the group had made the difference in their movement toward acceptance of their limitations, and they despaired of finding such relationships in the community.

Complaints

Members tended at times to voice complaints about such things as hospital policies, food, ward difficulties, and nursing or therapy procedures. These

---

[6] White, The Body Image Concept.

complaints usually occurred in cycles, most often when the group members were in periods of little progress in therapy. Such occurrences may be viewed as a means of venting frustration incurred in their necessarily regimented lives. Anxieties concerning discharge and weekend visits were also vented here, as well as the periodic irritations of daily life. What is important is that the group provided, for both patients and staff, a setting in which anger and frustration could be freely voiced, with little risk of offending anyone. Patients were vividly aware of their dependence on the staff and were often reluctant to voice complaints directly to them. Hence, the group provided a useful vehicle for them.

Discussion

The major purpose of the meetings was to provide a means of regular and continuing support for persons who had suffered a stroke. The members accomplished this aim in discussion of their fears and anxieties and in the sharing of experiences both in and out of the hospital. Initially, patients were depressed and discouraged, still bound and isolated by the initial terror of suffering the stroke, yet also fearful of what the future would hold. As each patient recounted the circumstances of his stroke to the others, he gained his first measure of group support. That feelings of depression and anger, as well as joy over improvement, were voiced illustrates the value of the group in providing an opportunity for the members to test their new images of themselves in a comfortable setting. In addition, the regular influx of new members provided an input of opinions and attitudes which were an added source of material for discussion.

The most readily observable effect of the open-ended membership system was the development of an almost parentally supportive spirit among the members. A newer member, often just beginning to realize the extent of his impairment, was frequently jolted by the information given him by the others. The myth of a miracle cure was dispelled and replaced with the hard reality of the work of therapy. It was not uncommon to find this same member several weeks later coming to the aid of a newer patient, struggling to cope with the same frustrations that had earlier perplexed and dismayed him. The satisfaction individuals gained from these exchanges should be viewed in the light of an often-voiced fear—that of becoming useless. The fact that, while gaining in the understanding of their own conditions, members were apt to achieve a measure of utility should not be underestimated.

This method of membership rotation did have limitations. The primary difficulty involved the depth of discussion. During periods when several new members entered simultaneously, much of the group time was spent in the introductory stage. In general, the longer-term members were more concerned over specific problems in their adjustment and wanted to discuss these with the other members. With new members entering weekly, this effort was hampered. In view of this fact, the membership system might be modified by allowing new members to join at established intervals, perhaps once every three or four weeks. This change would permit the advantage of developing support but would limit the problem of frequent repetition and thus allow more time for discussion of substantive issues of concern to the longer-participating members.

The anticipated problem in group cohesion was of less importance than expected, especially after the restriction of the group to stroke patients. Apparently, the fact of the stroke provided a bond of its own, with a strength that overcame some of the difficulties of the membership rotation.

Conclusions

The open-ended group of hemiplegic and hemiparetic patients discussed here presents a viable alternative to the time-limited group, especially in settings where individuals remain for an extensive and indeterminate period of time. Meeting weekly, the group became a vehicle for the discussion of fears, frustrations, and practical concerns for the future. Although all hemiplegics shared certain practical adjustment problems, those who had suffered a stroke were found to have such a strong and specific fear of its recurrence that the decision was made to limit the group to stroke patients.

This membership pattern found a special benefit in the development of a nurturing, protective system in which the more experienced members aided the newer members in their initial adjustment stages. The results included a decrease in individual isolation as evidenced by increasing interest in others and simultaneous gains in self-esteem and personal satisfaction.

TRANSPLANT

CHAPTER 48

Treating Families of Bone Marrow Recipients and Donors

Marie Cohen, Irene Goldenberg, and Herbert Goldenberg

A recent dramatic medical breakthrough in the treatment of acute leukemia and aplastic anemia involves replacing the patient's bone marrow with fresh marrow of a matching type from a donor, typically a close relative. Because the technique is fraught with numerous physical dangers, the UCLA Bone Marrow Transplant Center, one of six such centers in the United States, utilizes the skills of oncologists, radiologists, microbiologists, immunologists and in the case of children, pediatricians. The need for social work and psychological services is increasingly recognized.

This paper is directed specifically at the team management of these disorders, and by implication, of a wide variety of serious, threatening, or terminal illnesses. Few human experiences are filled with such suffering and anguish to both family and hospital staff as those involved with malignancies, especially when the patient is a child and there is the imminent threat of a premature separation and an unfulfilled life (Ablin, Binger, Stein, Kushner, Zoger and Mikkelson, 1971). Nevertheless, with few exceptions (Lansky, 1974; Spinetta, 1974), little attention has as yet been directed at the potential usefulness of social-psychological interventions on an oncology ward. In this paper, we intend to describe a crisis-focused

Reprinted from the *Journal of Marriage and Family Counseling*, Vol. 3, No. 4 (October, 1977), pp. 45–52. Copyright 1977 American Association for Marriage and Family Therapy. Reprinted by permission of the Association and the authors.

family therapy approach involving the patient and his or her family, to offer several relevant case histories from among the ten families already seen, and to draw some conclusions regarding the best utilization of a physician-therapist team concept for families where one member is terminally ill.

History of the Problem

The general literature on death and dying, once a taboo subject, has burgeoned in the last two decades (Feifel, 1959; Fulton, 1965; Kübler-Ross, 1969). Attitudes toward the prospects of one's own death, unspoken fantasies that it can be resisted and cajoled, the reliance on denial of the inevitable, and coming to terms with the process and finality of death have all been investigated (Weisman, 1972).

Fear, anger, depression, resentment, even relief, are common responses to receiving a fatal diagnosis (Kübler-Ross, 1969). Hamburg (1974) has outlined a common sequence of responses in family members who must learn to cope with such news; guilt; self-blame (perhaps if the diagnosis had been made earlier, the chances of successful treatment would increase); hope (perhaps a curative miracle drug will be discovered in time to save the person's life). As the disease progresses, as hope diminishes, relatives live on a day-to-day basis, wishing for one more remission of symptoms before death. Finally, there is a resignation to the inevitable outcome, in preparation for the eventual loss.

While hospital personnel—doctors and nurses—are trained in the technical aspects of dealing with a patient's illness, they receive little training regarding the disclosure of an impending death, or even how to approach the subject with the patient and his/her family members (Glaser and Strauss, 1965). Dying is a temporal process, as much a social phenomenon as a biological one. That is, death of a family member takes place over a period of time and calls for a series of social readjustments. Death expectations are a key determinant in how others (family, hospital staff) act during the dying process (Glaser and Strauss, 1968). It is our contention that an approach to the entire family experiencing this crisis may facilitate the necessary, if painful, readjustments to death in one of its members.

The Bone Marrow Transplant

Both leukemia and aplastic anemia are ordinarily fatal diseases of the bone marrow, the blood-forming organs. In the former, frequently referred to as cancer of the blood, there is an abnormal proliferation of white blood cells. In the case of the latter, there is a defective production of red and white blood cells and platelets. Three types of medical intervention are possible: drug therapy, radiation therapy, and bone marrow transplant. Unfortunately, each has certain potential deleterious effects. For example, to be effective against leukemia cells, drug therapy must be of such high dosages that bone marrow may be destroyed in the process. A similar consequence may result from high doses of radiation therapy. A third possibility is to use these powerful therapeutic agents and then give the patient new marrow cells through a bone marrow transplant from a compatible donor.

The medical procedure is a drastic one, calling for the complete suppression of his or her bone marrow. After matching for genetic factors through tissue typing, the marrow recipient receives the new marrow from a closely-matched sibling and then receives continual supportive blood transfusions from other family members. If successful, the patient is rescued from death for an undetermined period of time; in rare cases this extension of life may be the length of the patient's normal life span.

A Family-focused Crisis

Family members inevitably are participants in every phase of the patient's treatment. Frequently, they must interrupt their employment and home routines, sometimes for several weeks, in order to relocate in an unfamiliar city (in this case Los Angeles). Once there, donors must devote most of their days to traveling between their hotel room, the patient's room, and the Red Cross cell separating machine. The patient must spend six to eight weeks or more on "reverse isolation" while undergoing this medical procedure. He or she is kept in a private room and is severely restricted in contact with the outside world. Those few family members who are permitted to visit must wear caps, gowns, masks, and gloves. Since the patient must be kept immune to infection, no intimate physical contact is possible.

Several severe psychological stresses must be coped with by the patient in this isolated-bed "life island": inhibition of motor activity, loss of intimacy with loved ones, dependency on others, physical and social isolation, separation from family and, finally, confrontation with the severity of the illness. (Köhle, Simons, Weidlich, Dietrich and Durner, 1971). The parent who is a patient cannot have contact with his or her children because the children might introduce infections which could be fatal since the parent has no functioning immune response or body defense. This has severe intra-psychic and interpersonal repercussions, not merely for the patient, but for the entire family unit.

Each participating family member is in a highly stressful situation. In particular, the bone marrow donor's commitment is usually intense and extremely personalized ("flesh of my flesh, bone of the bone"). All members experience a disruption of family life as well as share in the fantasy that somehow their loved one will be saved from imminent death.

To date, the transplant procedure has extended lives from one to eleven months, with a mean thus far of seven months. One patient apparently has returned to normal health.

The Role of Family Therapy

While major attention of necessity is directed at those medical procedures that are life-supporting, there is also an important role for psychotherapeutic intervention. Lansky (1974), focusing on childhood leukemia, points out how patient management becomes more complex with some of the newer medical treatments which prolong remissions. Such remissions frequently allow the parents to stop grieving, deny to themselves that their child is fatally ill, perhaps even become elated; unfortunately, such hopes are short-lived and sooner or later they must be reoriented to reality. While Lansky notes typical family disruptions—fathers spend increasing amounts of time away from home, siblings develop adjustment problems, the family is deserted by friends, relatives and neighbors who themselves fear death—he advocates crisis-oriented individual sessions with disturbed members. On the other hand, Ablin et al. (1971) describe family conferences with the hospital staff that parents later rated as highly significant in helping them cope with the crisis of discovering their child's diagnosis of leukemia and his/her eventual death. Such conferences are essentially supportive as well as informative regarding etiology, therapy and prognosis.

We have followed a family crisis model in such situations because we assume that all the family members function in the shadow of their loved one's death, although commonly they deny and repress affect in their daily behavior, feelings and attitudes. Typically, the family dysfunction is blamed on the disease rather than the maladaptive family response to the crisis brought on by the patient's life-threatening illness.

One purpose of the family therapeutic approach (Goldenberg and Goldenberg, 1975) is to ease the psychological impact of the severe medical procedures on all concerned. Frequently, the crisis may exacerbate previous underlying pathological interactions among family members, and these must be recognized and resolved. All must help in coming to terms with the possible impending death of the patient, while still maintaining hope. The family therapist must help frightened, confused, distrustful relatives to mobilize their existing coping mechanisms and learn new, more adaptive ones appropriate to the immediate crisis situation. The family must work through together the issues of forthcoming separation and loss, overcoming the wish to avoid or deny the inevitable. This is complicated by the magical fantasies of the physician, the psychotherapist, and the family, each of whom needs or wants to believe death can be forestalled.

Some Family Case Histories

Disequilibrium in both family structure and function are inevitable consequences of the illness, hospitalization, and bone marrow transplant. For example, a 12-year-old girl is forced to assume the role of homemaker and surrogate mother to her four-year-old sister in the absence of her mother, hospitalized for months at a time with acute myelogenous leukemia. At the same time she becomes a confidante of her lonely, uncertain, 26-year-old stepfather. Another adolescent, a 13-year-old boy, living alone with his divorced mother, must take on the role of a substitute husband when she falls ill with leukemia. Despite the circumstances, she clearly is delighted, as is he, with his new-found adult status. Such role changes among family members are typical and in most cases need not necessarily prove maladaptive in the long run. In most cases we have seen, shifts in function are appropriate, provided that the child's psychological and social development are not stunted and provided, too, that he or she does not become the sole keeper of the family's sudden burdens.

The following case study illustrates such shifts in roles within the family:

> In Tom G.'s family, the family caretaker role was adopted by the 16-year-old sister, Dee, who also was the marrow donor for Tom, an 18-year-old, black adolescent who had marrow aplasia. Their father, physically disabled, held little status in the family, was generally devalued by all family members. Mrs. G., an anxious, hypertensive person, had been married and divorced several times prior to her current marriage. Dependent and insecure, she openly stated that her children would have to take care of her during this family crisis. Ordinarily the therapist, one of the authors, would have attempted to block this abandonment of "normal" role functioning. However, in this family and under these circumstances it appeared as though Dee could assume a great deal of the emotional support functions for her mother, her two brothers, and herself. She also appeared able to ask for additional support when she needed to be less "grown up." The therapist thus gave her encouragement to pursue this new role.

The continuing experience with families of transplant candidates has taught the hospital staff some diagnostic indices of "elasticity" in family functioning. It is helpful to know if the family can identify those members who emerged as leaders and followers in prior family crises. A family can profit from interventions if they have insight into their prior functioning. It is also often profitable for families to become aware of how in the past they may have scapegoated a member as being solely responsible for their problems. The following case illustrates how scapegoating and denial are common strategies for avoiding confronting the painful truth of a family crisis situation, while presenting to the world a picture of a fraudulently warm family atmosphere:

The S. family came to UCLA Hospital from a neighboring state in order to get a bone marrow transplant for Carol, age 16, their eldest daughter. She had been diagnosed as suffering from acute myelogenous leukemia four months earlier, and her condition had been refractory to all other therapeutic intervention. Carol was accompanied by her parents and three younger siblings. The family described themselves as warm and close, the proof being their leaving for California as soon as they heard that Carol had been accepted for the transplant procedure. They down-played their lack of financial and social resources in the new city, denied that Mr. S.'s unemployment of four months' duration was a strain on him and them. They were here to do all they could for Carol.

The cracks in this warm and supportive family veneer first appeared when they had to sign for Carol's transplant. The informed consent form clearly mentions the possibility of the patient's death. Though everyone continued to support their desire for the transplant, Mr. S. began appearing at the hospital drunk, and his wife began losing weight rapidly while denying that her husband's behavior or anything else bothered her.

In family therapy sessions, Carol expressed her feeling that she was the sole cause of her family's "new" problems, and admitted that she felt her death would bring relief to the family, feeling she had been an emotional and financial burden on them since the time of the original diagnosis. Her brother and sister were finally able to voice the forbidden expressions of resentment toward Carol for becoming ill and causing their travels to this strange city with no friends. They held her responsible for their parents' fights, daddy's drinking, and their missing graduation day at school.

Family therapy was directed first at uncovering the many deeply held but largely unexpressed feelings experienced by each of the family members—feelings of grief, depression, caring and hostility. As these previously forbidden feelings were expressed, the therapist was able to reassure all the family that such reactions were common in attempting to deal with a possible impending death. Each member learned to accept his or her own ambivalence toward Carol's condition—a combination of positive love and concern along with negative feelings of resentment and irritation. Finally, the therapist helped them, collectively, to accept the leukemia as a family crisis that required an allied family effort to cope with satisfactorily.

Coping Strategies

Coping effectively involves far more than self-protection from stress. The adaptive person (or family) must approach the situation with plans, calculate risks and opportunities, seek information to prepare for probable difficulties and keep all possible options open (Hamburg, 1974). Typical for families of bone marrow recipients and donors is this sequence: denial; acceptance of the diagnosis but not the prognosis; acceptance of the prognosis.

To be effective, family therapy must be tailored to the point in this sequence which reflects the family's current set of attitudes and expectations. For example, the therapeutic approach differs widely if the patient is newly admitted to the hospital or admitted for the last time because death is imminent. Similarly, whether the patient is to receive an immediate transplant or such a decision may be postponed may have an impact on the course and thrust of family therapy. Finally, of course, the degree of physical illness and patient availability influences the form and content of the psychotherapeutic intervention.

Typically, all concerned first attempt to cope with the reality of impending death through denial; they wish to screen it out of awareness or reverse it. Family behavior during this phase may be characterized by hostility toward physicians or other staff and refusal to accept or understand the diagnosis. At this point, usually following hospital admission, the social worker is likely to focus on concrete problems such as family finances and living arrangements and not on the patient's possible death.

Osgood (1964) has suggested that physicians adopt a psychotherapeutic stance, providing the entire family with a full explanation of the disease and its treatment, removal of unwarranted fears or guilt feelings, and above all, helping to instill a thread of hope and comfort that somebody cares. To preserve hope, Osgood even offers the initial possibility that the diagnosis is incorrect and that a cure may be found in time. However, in our experiences, one consequence of Osgood's last suggestion is that all involved (physician, therapist, family members) will in all probability have to relinquish that hope fairly soon. Hospital personnel in particular must do so with each succeeding patient, so that cynicism and hope need to be carefully balanced.

During the second phase, the patient and his/her family come to accept the reality of cancer, while still denying its implied terminal prognosis. Not uncommonly, physicians may unconsciously foster the fantasies of family members concerning the patient's life expectancy. Frequently, this may be an attempt on the physician's part to diminish his/her own personal distress regarding the loss of the patient through death and one's helplessness to reverse its inevitability. However, if the physician refuses to deal with the medical reality, the family does too. The family may resist accepting the prognosis if they see the physician resisting it. The task for the family therapist during this second phase is often to become the insistent bearer of reality which, in effect, means the bearer of bad news.

In the third and final phase, hopefully, the patient, family, and staff arrive at a realistic acceptance of the medical reality and its inevitable outcome. If death occurs before both the family and staff have worked through this separation process, there may be serious consequences for all concerned. The family will be set back in its efforts to restructure, remobilize, and return once again to the real world. Staff, still grieving, will find it difficult to take on new patients with similar prognoses.

The Family Therapist: Role and Conflict

We have seen that in the general therapeutic process with dying patients, the position of the therapist as both part of the family and separate from it is imperative for effective intervention. This phenomenon is one of the most delicate therapeutic problems in working with oncology patients. The therapist must be empathetic with the patient who is being blamed and rejected. At the same time, he or she must be on guard against being caught up in, and thus aiding and abetting, the family's *mythification of death:* the process in which the incipient pain of separation and loss is denied, and in which it is expected that the dying person will deny his experience in order to spare others a confrontation with their own mortality (Pattison, 1975).

One conflict necessarily faced by all therapists dealing with oncology patients is the therapist's feelings and attitudes regarding his/her own ultimate death. Another is how not to succumb to the family's (or one's own) wish that the therapist be omniscient and omnipotent.

The family therapist stands for a degree of reasoned intervention in an environment which appears arbitrarily to give and take lives by magical means. The patients cannot do without the physician and are out of control in their physical functioning. They psychotherapist intervenes to strengthen the existing psychological coping mechanisms of the patient and his/her family members. He/she moves into the family's system and assists the family in using its own coping mechanisms for support. Such direct interventions are designed to help family members and support them as individuals even if that means they may have to recognize their end as a family unit due to a member's imminent death. The therapist has to function in the "family unit" within the hospital ward, supporting individuals and the system itself to allow the unit once again to take on a new member-patient.

Finally, the therapist must recognize the primary physician's need for a delicate balance of hope and reality orientation. The therapist helps to guide the physician toward the acceptance of the loss of a patient by helping the physician to reject the magical omnipotence with which the family invests him and which turns into inevitable rage at the death of the patient.

References

ABLIN, A. R., BINGER, C. M., STEIN, R. C., KUSHNER, J. H., ZOGER, S., & MIKKELSON, C. A conference with the family of a leukemic child. *American Journal of Diseases of Children*, 1971, *122*, 362–364.

FEIFEL, H. (Ed.) *The meaning of death.* New York: McGraw-Hill, 1959.

FULTON, R. (Ed.) *Death and identity.* New York: Wiley, 1965.

GLASER, B. G., & STRAUSS, A. L. *Awareness of dying.* Chicago: Aldine, 1965.

GLASER, B. G., & STRAUSS, A. L. *Time for dying.* Chicago: Aldine, 1968.

GOLDENBERG, I., & GOLDENBERG, H. A family approach to psychological services. *American Journal of Psychoanalysis*, 1975, *35*, 317–328.

HAMBURG, D. A. Coping behavior in life-threatening circumstances. *Psychotherapy and Psychosomatics*, 1974, *23*, 13–26.

KÖHLE, K., SIMONS, C., WEIDLICH, S., DIETRICH, M., & DURNER, A. Psychological aspects in the treatment of leukemia patients in the isolated-bed system 'life island.' *Psychotherapy and Psychosomatics*, 1971, *19*, 85–91.

KÜBLER-ROSS, E. *On death and dying.* New York: Macmillan, 1969.

LANSKY, S. B. Childhood leukemia: The child psychiatrist as a member of the oncology team. *Journal of the American Academy of Child Psychiatry*, 1974, *13*, 499–508.

OSGOOD, E. E. Treatment of chronic leukemias. *Journal of Nuclear Medicine*, 1964, *5*, 139–153.

PATTISON, E. *The fatal myth of death in the family.* Presented at the American Psychiatric Association's 128th Annual Meeting, May 5, 1975.

SPINETTA, J. J. The dying child's awareness of death: A review. *Psychological Bulletin*, 1974, *81*, 256–260.

WEISMAN, A. D. *On dying and denying.* New York: Behavioral Publications, 1972.

PART IV

Sociocultural Factors

Interest in the sociocultural aspects of client functioning as a necessary ingredient of the diagnostic process continues to be of import and concern within the social work literature. Important and influential as this emphasis has been on practice attitudes and understanding, the amount of material written by social workers concerning direct practice implications of these data has not been remarkable, at least not if the professional literature is used as an indicator. The need to do more has been frequently stressed; the results have been uneven. This is the smallest section in the book and the one for which the fewest articles were located.

Obviously social work is just beyond the beginning point in translating the importance of these dimensions into generalized therapeutic considerations. Clearly certain topics are emphasized more than others. This itself is probably a reflection of the sociocultural climate in which we live and practice.

It is evident that the articles in this section point out more gaps in the literature than do those in the other sections. Nevertheless, they do reflect a trend toward increased development of this dimension in our practice. The area where we seem to have the most difficulty in applying these sociocultural factors is in treatment. We take them into account in assessments but as yet do not make rich use of them in what we do with clients. For example, this is the only section of the book that does not contain any specifically group treatment article. This is surprising.

It would seem that some of the diagnostic dimensions of sociocultural factors would be particularly available to group approaches. If, for example, the Kluckhohns' work on value orientations is considered, especially the dimension of "relational value orientation," it could be hypothesized that collaterally oriented persons would be expected to involve themselves more easily and presumably more effectively in group treatment than individually oriented clients. Also one would expect that a

561

client who had a strong value orientation that emphasized the family and the extended family would be particularly well suited for family therapy. To date, this has not been discussed in the literature.

Certainly the component of this topic on which we have focused the greatest attention is ethnic and racial differences. The vast majority of articles located for this section addressed various aspects of black-white reality, with a secondary emphasis on poverty.

Whether correctly or not, we have focused our writings on specific groups rather than efforts at general theory building. Thus, in the search for this edition many more articles dealing with additional ethnic groups were found than in the previous search. It is clear from each writer's work that there is more conviction about the nature and impact of differences than about the possibility of general theory. Each author stresses that the group about which he or she is writing is so different from any others that there can be little to learn to apply to other groups. Each new group requires a new assessment, diagnosis, and treatment.

Thus we must await further experience with focused emphasis before we can move to some general considerations of ethnicity as a variable in diagnosis and treatment. Some beginning writing was found that did address the question of ethnicity as a generic variable.

The importance and significance of class factors as a diagnostic variable have been given less attention in the literature than ethnic factors. Of the articles addressed to this variable, more attention has been given to lower-class clients than other classes. This is to be expected, since this segment of society has long been presumed to be the special interest of social workers.

Most articles dealing with the lower class emphasized the imprecision of this category. Within the term is included a wide range of problems, persons, forms of behavior, and differences. There is a tendency in the articles to give most attention to the multiproblem and severely economically deprived families living in submarginal conditions. Implied in this is the erroneous idea that membership in the lower class presumes the need for treatment.

Florence Hollis acknowledges the usefulness of social class as a diagnostic variable and the necessity of modification of treatment emphasis rather than distinct methods in formulating treatment plans. She also stresses the lack of precision of the variable and the danger of letting it become a stereotype. Authors emphasize the necessity to understand the impact of the clients' milieu on their functioning to avoid seeing psychopathology rather than reaction to stresses and conflicts in the life situation, and to diagnose and treat individually rather than by generality. Orcutt's article moves the conceptualizing of work with lower-class families forward.

Important as it is to understand lower class clients, it continues to be essential for the development of practice theory that we examine other segments of the class structure. We are still uncomfortable in declaring our interest in and commitment to clients from other segments of the socioeconomic continuum. We seem to have overreacted to some of the criticisms about our failure to meet the needs of the poor and thus not conceptually focused on non-lower-class clients. Some progress in this area can be seen, and two articles relating to other than lower-class clients are included.

Obviously, the range of clients receiving social work treatment is widening to include all facets of society. It would be helpful to the whole profession if our colleagues would make more available their experiences with clients from different classes. Private practitioners could make an important contribution here, as they frequently treat clients from parts of society not always found in the regular clientele of agencies.

Personal and group values are dimensions that have received particular attention in recent years. To date, work in this area has indicated some interesting leads for practice, which must be given further attention. Some correlation between values and interview content has been demonstrated as well as value differences between workers and clients.

Clearly, in our society there are clients who are in stress as a result of value conflicts or in value transition and are turning to us for help with this stress. We are now more comfortable with the concept that values are an important component of the client–worker situation and that some difficulties in the relationship formerly seen as transference and related resistance phenomena can be caused by value differences. There is still much to be done in this area, with more experience and more practice-based research required to help clarify the therapeutic significance of values.

Status and role are two further areas of the client's sociocultural profile to which further attention in our literature is required. Some work has been done on the impact of the professional status and both the implicit and explicit authority components of it. More is needed. From the viewpoint of role, we know that in contemporary society many clients are involved in some aspect of role change—sometimes recognized and sometimes not. At times such periods of transition can be a growth experience for persons; others can be the source of crisis. We undoubtedly have developed some expertise in this area that should be more widely discussed in the clinical periodical literature.

One final concept that has not been significantly evident in the literature is the importance of a client's religious identity as a component of treatment or indeed as a source of stress. This too is a facet of the sociocultural makeup of a person, but one with which we seem to be uncomfortable. We have developed significant components of our service delivery systems along sectarian lines but, interestingly, have not given much attention in our own literature to the way this facet of the client's or worker's psychosocial profile can be an asset to treatment or, indeed, a source of conflict and stress. In this edition one article is included on one problematic area of religion in our society, that of cults.

CONCLUSION

It is clear that extensive and interesting gains have been made in the profession regarding the incorporation of social science concepts into practice. It is equally clear that much still remains to be done to to translate our interest in and appreciation of these concepts into operational case-directed activities. Some dimensions of a sociocultural nature have not been fully explored, as mentioned above. The search for theoretical concepts that can help us more effectively develop and apply a profile of treatment techniques most applicable to the individuality of the client and his sociocultural situation can be observed in all the contributions but needs to be further emphasized.

ETHNICITY

CHAPTER 49

African-American Clients: Clinical Practice Issues

Darielle L. Jones

Culture—the knowledge, art, beliefs, and customs transmitted among a group of individuals—has long been recognized as a significant determinant of the behavior and values of members of an ethnic group. However, social scientists and clinicians tend to use the norms of the Anglo-European society or culture in assessing the attitudes and behavior of people of various cultural backgrounds. This approach is ethnocentric because the underlying assumption is that Anglo-European culture is superior and is the absolute norm against which one evaluates all other cultures and their members. In fact, however, Anglo-European culture is simply one of many different cultures, all of which are of equal integrity.

The African-American client has been a victim of this ethnocentric approach. (In this article the term "African-American" will be used interchangeably with the more commonly known term "Black.") The author contends that it is essential to use an African-American cultural framework in evaluating African-American clients. This article examines the differences between using the two frames of reference to illustrate how the Anglo-European framework tends to result in an inappropriate, inaccurate, and often negative evaluation of the African-American client, while the African-American framework tends to clarify the functionality of certain behavior of the African-American client. With this perspective, the behavior may be viewed, then, not only as appropriate but as a strategy for coping with or conquering stresses—an asset.

Anglo-European Framework

First, the author will examine use of the Anglo-European framework, illustrations of which are helpful in pointing out inappropriate and detrimental consequences for African-Americans. For example, the term,
"culturally deprived," coined in the 1960s by the dominant society in reference to low-income African-Americans and other nonwhite ethnic
groups, represents a total denial of the existence or value of African-American culture. It is an ethnocentric assessment because it equates culture
with dominant white culture and is detrimental to African-Americans because it implies that nothing is of value in African-American culture. Because their culture is worthless, it seems to say, African-Americans are
worthless.

The second illustration centers on an analysis offered by a psychiatrist,
the author's professor in a course on adolescence taken in a school of social
work. The professor suggested that African initiation rites of male circumcision at puberty represent the elders' expression of hostility toward adolescent members of their tribe. Hence, the rites are viewed as sadistic.
However, if one recognizes the traditional African value placed on the endurance of the male for the survival of the family and tribe, then an alternate and more accurate interpretation is that male circumcision during
puberty rites is preparation for the stamina that is necessary in manhood.
Mbiti elaborates,

> The physical pain which the (African) children are encouraged to endure is
> the beginning of training them for difficulties and sufferings of later life. En-
> durance of physical and emotional pain is a great virtue among Akamba peo-
> ple, as indeed it is among other Africans, since life in Africa is surrounded by
> much pain from one source or another.[1]

The third illustration concerns the statement that Columbus discovered America (in 1492). Since both Indian and Black people lived in America prior to the coming of Columbus, he was obviously not the
"Discoverer" of this land.[2] He was simply the first European to make this
discovery. To credit Columbus as the "Discoverer" is to say that the world
consists only of Europeans. It is an egocentric as well as ethnocentric distortion and exemplifies how distortions can become institutionalized into
routine, unquestionable "truths."

Clark also addressed the distinction between Black culture viewed from
an Anglo-European framework—what he refers to as the "Study of
Blacks"—and Black culture viewed from a Black framework—"Black Studies." He illustrates the differential analysis that results when applying the
two frameworks toward a definition of problems in the Black community.
For example, the expression, "alienation and isolation from middle-class
white institutions" (study of Blacks) is contrasted with the expression,

''experiences of exploitation with white middle-class institutions, and the failure of school officials to accord recognition and respect to Black culture'' (Black studies).[3] The former views the problem as deviant behavior on the part of Blacks, the latter as the racism that permeates the dominant society's institutions. It is evident from these examples that a distorted diagnosis is the probable result of evaluating the African-American client from the Anglo-European cultural perspective.

African-American Framework

Some African-American social scientists and clinicians, in recognizing such distortions, have identified various behavioral patterns of Blacks within the frameworks of traditional African society and African-American culture. Ladner, in her study of Black womanhood, discusses the fact that childhood among African-Americans is distinguishable in several aspects from childhood among whites. The majority of Black children have never been able to have a ''protected, carefree, and nonresponsible'' childhood.[4] Black parents are unable to provide protection and comfort for their children as a result of the discriminatory practices of the dominant society. The need for a parent to deal openly with this fact with his or her young child tends to raise the relationship between them to a more mature level. This relationship becomes the means by which the parent prepares his or her child for survival in a hostile world.

The Black child must confront reality not only in terms of race but also in terms of various illegal, amoral, or violent events that may occur in his or her environment. Ladner noted that one of the consequences of these community influences is the development of an emotional precocity among Black girls that often exceeds their chronological years.[5] In the course of her study, Ladner also noted the remarkable ability of many Black children to handle stressful situations. Therefore, she concluded that as a result of their exposure to harsh conditions, these children develop a great deal of strength and adaptability which enables them to adjust to and cope with the world—hence, to survive.[6]

The frame of reference provided by Ladner's observations also can be used to assess the role expectation, within the Black community, of older siblings caring for younger siblings. This practice represents a functional adaptation of families in which both parents or a single parent must work. In the author's opinion, meeting this responsibility often can lead to the early maturation of the Black adolescent. This view conflicts with that of the white clinician who generally has interpreted this pattern as destructive to the maturational development of the Black adolescent. Although it is evident in some cases that maturational development of the Black adolescent has been limited by this kind of responsibility, it is also true in many instances that it has provided an opportunity for further growth and maturation. The extent to which an adolescent can master a task can serve as an additional source of self-esteem.

The role expectation the Black community holds of the Black adolescent caring for younger siblings and performing household chores is not confined to the female. This practice reflects the existence of the flexibility of roles between males and females in the Black community. Hill has identified this as one of five characteristics, viewed as strengths, of the Black family. The other include strong kinship bonds, high achievement orientation, strong work orientation, and strong religious orientation.[7] These characteristics are discussed as follows.

Strong kinship bonds and the extended family are directly traceable to traditional African culture, which valued the collective group above the individual.[8] The important influence on family maintenance and development of grandmothers, aunts, uncles, grandfathers, and cousins cannot be overestimated. Documentation shows that quasi-kin relationships, in which genetically unrelated people are informally adopted by another family, were pervasive during the period of slavery in the United States.[9] This phenomenon continues to exist today in Black communities. African-Americans often make reference to "play" brothers, sisters, aunts, and so on, who may not reside in the same household but who are considered a part of the family because of close emotional rapport. In addition, many African-Americans informally adopt children in their community. Contrary to the popular belief that large numbers of Black children remain in adoption agencies because they are unwanted by the Black community, the number of Black children informally adopted or absorbed into Black homes, as of 1972, outranked those legally adopted by a ratio of 10 to 1.[10] The Black community absorbs more nonrelated children than any other ethnic group in this country.[11]

As an illustration of the high achievement orientation of low-income Black families, Hill notes that a majority of low-income Black parents aspire to a college education for their children.[12] He notes further that an overwhelming majority of Black college students come from lower- and working-class families.[13] This suggests that these children not only internalize the educational aspirations of their parents but actively pursue the realization of these goals.

The fourth strength of Black families, as identified by Hill, is a strong emphasis on work and ambition—what he terms strong work orientation. As one example of this, data are cited which indicate that 60 percent of the Black poor work as compared with about 50 percent of the white poor.[14] In addition, Hill notes the historically powerful role of the Black church as a mechanism for survival and advancement of Black people. The extensive and traditional involvement of Black families in the Black church—termed strong religious orientation—is the final strength identified by Hill.

Another distinct cultural phenomenon identified by African-American social scientists is the African-American concept of time. Among Black people, it is known as CPT (colored people's time), which is later than the scheduled time. Nobles traces CPT to the traditional African concept of time.[15] Time, in the African framework, is phenomenal rather than mathematical. That is, in the traditional African sense, time is not a precise mathematical entity around which an event is developed but rather a flexible notion that is determined by when the event (phenomenon) occurs. For example, a party is scheduled to begin at 9 P.M. Most likely, the Anglo-European host would feel that around 9 "it's time" for the party, People of African descent would not be expecting anyone at 9 and would feel that "it's time" for the party whenever guests arrive. Nobles has aptly suggested that a more appropriate enunciation of CPT is "communal potential time."[16]

Finally, White suggests that Blacks have a great tolerance for conflict, stress, ambiguity, and ambivalence.[17] He refers to the facility Blacks have for handling situations whose meanings in Anglo-European and African-American cultures differ and thus seem contradictory to whites. He cites an illustration involving a white psychologist who had difficulty assimilating a Black nationalist's attendance at a storefront church meeting, a Black nationalist rally, and a bar, all in one evening. White notes that what appeared to be logical contradictions to the psychologist were all related and consistent on an emotional level to the Black person.

Diagnostic Implications

In discussing African-American behavior, attitudes, and values from an African-American framework, it is apparent that the assessment of the Black clinician may be at variance with that of the white clinician. The disparity is likely to be even greater when the white clinician's assessment takes no account of the systems approach to behavioral analysis. The systems approach is an essential tool in formulating diagnoses and treatment plans, since it identifies the various impinging settings (or systems) in which the client interacts or is acted upon and integrates this into the assessment of the individual. In the case of the African-American client, this assessment must include the Black community as well as the larger dominant society. Billingsley has made effective use of this in his work on the Black family.[18] The following subsections will examine some of the more common diagnostic distortions encountered in relation to the African-American client.

POOR IMPULSE CONTROL

African-Americans are often labeled erroneously as having poor impulse control or an inability to postpone gratification. This assessment is applied to a variety of behaviors, which may range from verbal or physical violence to a refusal to wait until tomorrow for an emergency welfare check. Poor impulse control, in this author's definition, is the relative inability to control or deny emotional urges that, when gratified, result in destructive or antisocial consequences. That is, no one would refer to people making plans on the spur of the moment to have a picnic as having poor impulse control.

It is important to talk in terms of *relative* inability as one considers the context in which poor impulse control is alleged to have occurred. That is, the measurement of self-control must be assessed in relation to the degree of provocation. In making such a diagnosis, what most white clinicians fail to consider is the extent to which stimuli operating in the life of the average urban Black constantly test his or her ability for self-control. This factor is as crucial to assessing self-control as the extent of danger is to the assessment of bravery. It is also why medals for bravery go to soldiers on the battlefield and not to those on the sheltered bases.

If one considers the compounding frustrations and stresses of waiting in clinics all day for health care that may or may not be affordable, waiting in department of social service centers all day and perhaps the following day for assistance with basic needs (food and shelter), waiting for months or years for housing repairs, living in a community where one's personal safety is constantly at risk, witnessing one's children graduate from high school without being able to read, and so on, *then*, one might justifiably conclude that the African-American demonstrates a remarkable degree of impulse control. A systems diagram of the client helps to identify institutions (both formal and informal) with which the client interacts. (See Figure 49–1.) Most of these institutions, both within and without the community, are sources of stress, largely due to bureaucracy, inefficiency, and built-in design for failure. (Those institutions termed "without" are primarily controlled by the dominant society but may or may not be located within the community physically.)

RAGE

Although in recent years, the ramifications of oppression have been expounded so frequently that the tendency is to view them as clichés, they are nonetheless daily realities in the lives of most African-Americans. And there is no question that the environment provokes an overwhelming rage that is repressed, displaced, sublimated, internalized, and vented. The venting of rage may often appear inappropriate if considered only in relation to the immediately precipitating event. However, provocations in the life of the average African-American are long-standing and cumulative. Therefore, although the immediate provocation may be minor, when it is seen in light of myriad other precipitating events, the combination may

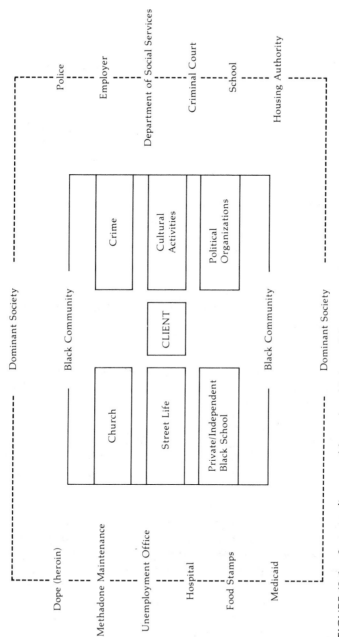

FIGURE 49-1. Systems diagram of formal and informal institutions

result in the release of pent-up anger. This is a form of displacement. From this broader perspective, the client's response in many instances does not appear inappropriate. For example:

> An African-American nurse threatened to physically harm an emergency room clerk who was indifferent to the former's verbal inquiries as to why her sister, while disoriented from a car accident, was allowed to walk to X-ray unescorted.

If one considers this event alone, then the assessment might well be that the nurse had poor impulse control. However, if one also considers that the nurse previously had been witness to various other occasions in the emergency room when she felt medical practices were careless and possibly even life endangering, then her behavior appears appropriate not only in terms of her *total* experience with the emergency room but in terms of her desire to arouse some interest in her concern for her sister's safety.

Another example may help broaden this perspective by demonstrating that the displacement of accumulated rage may sometimes be a function of the client's perception of the likelihood of repercussions. This process necessarily involves a great deal of selective self-control, which may operate on an unconscious level. For example:

> A student bringing clothes to a friend in detention is treated in a hostile manner by the attendant, also Black (but viewed as a tool of the dominant society), who screens the clothes. Although enraged by this hostile display of pseudoauthoritativeness, she avoided any confrontation for fear that it might result in revocation of her visiting privileges. However, days later, she vented her anger verbally for the slightest provocation by a white student, whose perceived ability to effect negative consequences was minimal.

This process of expressing rage at an object in direct relation to the perceived consequences that the object can bring to bear may account for workers of lower status—that is, hospital clerks rather than physicians, correction officers and other inmates rather than wardens—often bearing the brunt of clients' rages. It may also be reflected in the extent of Black-on-Black homicides in which rage is displaced and immediately precipitating events may be minor. It is as though the defenses that inhibit the expression of rage are immobilized to a lesser degree with a similarly or relatively powerless person than with a person viewed as more powerful. Further study is indicated to determine whether this represents some form of unconscious recognition of the lesser value of Black life, objectively in society, and subjectively, in terms of the client's own possible negative self-concept. However, it appears that the factor of accessibility alone is insufficient to explain this phenomenon.

A final element that contributes to the seeming inappropriateness of verbal and physical expressions of rage is that in our increasingly bureaucratic society, rage is often provoked by systems and institutions that fail to meet the needs of clients. Since it is difficult to express rage at an intangible, the people who represent the system become the recipients of clients' rage, even though the former may have no control over the system itself.

It is imperative that clinicians (1) translate the effects of system-client interaction into intra- and interpersonal terms, and (2) incorporate these dynamics in their psychosocial assessment of the client. In this manner, the assessment will reflect a broader understanding of both psychological and social determinants of the client's functioning.

CONCRETE VERSUS ABSTRACT THOUGHT

Concrete thought is preoccupied with the specific and actual in one's environment as opposed to the symbolic, theoretical, or generalized. It represents the antithesis of abstraction. The term "concrete" is often used as a pejorative characterization of the thought processes of African-Americans. Among white clinicians, it is used as an indicator of deficiencies in intelligence and mental health.

In her personal and professional experience, the author has noted a tendency for the masses of African-Americans to be concrete in their thinking, by which she means they focus primarily on the pragmatic and basic realities of their existence. This does not exclude the ability for abstract thinking but reflects a functional preference based on the demands of the life space in which they live. Furthermore, it would appear that this is an appropriate measure which demonstrates that a client is in touch with his or her reality. For example, for a working man of marginal income to contemplate a possible analogy that food is to table as flowers are to $\underline{?}$ when he is not sure he will be able to provide food for his family at all, would, in the author's judgment, illustrate a thought disorder. He would not be in touch with the reality of his situation. On the contrary, he should be thinking concretely about food as escape from hunger and about what actions he can take to obtain it. Abstraction, in this case as in some other instances, may represent a form of denial and escapism. Taken to an extreme, it may fail to have any meaning.

The value placed by the dominant society on abstract thought as superior to concrete thought represents exactly that—a value judgment. It is the author's contention that both processes are equally valuable and appropriate, given various circumstances. The author further contends that although African-Americans may be more inclined to think in concrete or pragmatic terms because of an environment that makes the achievement of survival needs an ongoing preoccupation, African-Americans are able to and do utilize abstract thought at times when they chose to do so. Jazz, a Black art form, is one such example of this. The pervasiveness of religious beliefs among Africans and African-Americans is another.

Intelligence tests, often a source of denigrating the intelligence of Black youngsters, represent an artificial and imposed "environment" in which abstract thinking is required. A colleague of the author demonstrated how easily one might fail to respond as desired if the mind set required is not indicated. For example, a Black adolescent was asked the meaning of "people who live in glass houses shouldn't throw stones." Her response was because the glass might break. My colleague confided that upon first reaction, she found the adolescent's answer reasonable. However, noting the psychologist's evaluation of this response as concrete and as evidence of the adolescent's primitive thinking, my colleague then considered the phrase "people who live in glass houses..." in terms of the more abstract meaning—those who are vulnerable to attack about their own frailties should not attack others about their shortcomings.

The choice of one answer or the other is determined by one's priorities and the awareness of which mind set one is being asked to use. For the person whose life is beset by constant struggle for basic needs, priority in focus is more likely to be concrete, that is, the house will be damaged or destroyed. The person whose life-style is generally free from such worries may tend to use mental energy to ponder life on a more abstract level and therefore will interpret the proverb more readily in terms of its abstract meaning. Neither person is necessarily precluded from either ability. However, each might require previous information regarding the mind set sought (abstract or concrete) in order to provide the response that his or her counterpart would be likely to give. That is, just as Blacks may not do well on an intelligence test devised by white psychologists, whites would not be likely to perform well on an intelligence test devised by Black psychologists because of differences in cultural values, expectations, and experiences. However, neither test would be a reliable indicator of intelligence. The dominant society might be more aware of this if the intelligence of white children was always being tested and measured in terms of the cultural experiences of Black children, with the result that the white children received deficient scores and were labeled inferior in intelligence. Nonetheless, clinicians have a responsibility to recognize the effect these cultural biases have on their assessment of intelligence, mental health, or any other variable of a minority group.

SUSPICION/PARANOIA

For the African-American, suspicion and even some paranoia—that is, feeling that efforts to oppress and suppress are the result of an organized network—are a healthy adaptation to the reality of a largely hostile environment. As Ladner points out. "The negative experiences which Blacks have encountered in this society have fostered and perpetuated within them [Blacks] suspicion and hostility."[19]

Viewed within the context of the overall environment, suspicion and paranoia represent survival instincts. This behavior is particularly evident and appropriate in relation to systems and individuals working within them. It is important that the clinician not *assume* that suspicion and paranoia exhibited in his or her interaction with the client is characteristic of the client's social interactions. It is common practice to assume that the client-therapist relationship reflects the client's interaction within the community. This assumption underlies the concept of transference. It negates, however, the client's perception of the clinician as part of a system or institution that the former may view as hostile or oppressive.

DEPENDENCE/INFANTILISM

The environmental factor often overlooked in diagnosing the African-American client as dependent or infantile relates again to how the client perceives (1) the clinician and, (2) the clinician's likelihood of providing assistance. African-American clients are forced to develop creative strategies in their bid for survival. One strategy may be to present themselves as dependent and helpless, reasoning that they are more likely to enlist the assistance of the clinician if they act in this manner rather than if they present themselves as capable of managing or coping. Social workers are more likely to be targets of this strategy simply because they are in a better position than other clinicians to gain access to various community resources. Various institutional practices foster and reinforce this strategy. For example, a working mother of two children with a net annual income of $4,300 is financially ineligible for Medicaid.[20] Because of income and family size, this family can be considered part of the working poor. Medical care is frequently beyond their means, and their feeling of frustration about the lack of assistance available to them as people who struggle to support themselves, contrasted with the assistance given to those who are totally dependent, is often vented on the hospital social worker. Furthermore, they conclude that one must be helpless or totally without resources to get assistance.

Wesson has noted the dual character presented by Blacks as they adopt one posture in negotiating within the dominant society and another within the Black community.[21] The origins of this behavior can be traced to the days of slavery in this country when Black people often presented themselves to whites as happy-go-lucky, childlike, and servile. The feigned posture of infantilism and subservience was part of a strategy to manipulate slave owners and lull them into a false sense of security, thereby forestalling physical cruelty to slaves. In reality, Blacks were often plotting to revolt, escape, or poison slave owners.

TREATMENT IMPLICATIONS

Various aspects of African-American culture may provide support and resources for the Black client. An awareness of these factors is useful in formulating and carrying out treatment plans. For example, knowledge of the extended family can be helpful to the clinician in handling intrafamilial conflict with an adolescent who may want to or be coerced to leave home. The extended family may provide an alternative resource to maternity homes and foster care agencies and may also provide the client with the reassurance of dealing with people who are familiar to her and have a more personal interest in her well-being.

The following two case situations also illustrate how knowledge of African-American culture can be instrumental to effective treatment:

Mrs. X, a Black woman in her fifties, was seen in the hospital social service department one month after the death of her husband from a prolonged illness. She described feelings of numbness and an inability to cry since his death. She was fearful that this would lead to a "breakdown," as she felt it had some years before when her mother died from a similar illness. She recalled that many months after her mother's death she had become so anxious and unable to sleep that she sought psychiatric help and was then told that she had not worked through her grief.

The author suggested that Mrs. X listen to some of her gospel music records at home, as a part of the supportive therapy. This suggestion was based on the author's awareness of the stirring emotional and cathartic qualities of gospel music within the African-American culture. This proved to be an effective tool in helping to initiate the grief process in Mrs. X, who, as a result of listening to this music, was able to cry and begin to get in touch with her sadness and feelings of loss.

The second example follows:

Miss H, a 22-year-old single Black woman, whose childhood was characterized by trauma and neglect by an alcoholic mother, nonetheless displayed considerable strength in her parenting of three children. However, this capability was severely tested when one of her newborn twins died from sudden infant death syndrome at home.

In addition to supportive therapy offered by the worker, attempts were made to enlist supportive contact from the Black Muslim Temple. This course of action was based on the clinician's awareness of (1) the strength

Miss H obtained from her faith in this religion and its tenets, despite the fact that she had not joined the Temple officially and (2) the cohesiveness and community outreach characteristic of the Black Muslim organization at that time. The organization's contact with Miss H during this crisis proved to be an asset.

Conclusion

This article has demonstrated, by drawing on the author's personal and professional experiences as well as on the literature, that ethnocentricity has biased and distorted the white clinician's perception, assessment, and treatment of the client representative of the masses of African-Americans. Implicitly, the Black clinician who has had little contact or identification with his or her people also may be guilty of clinical practices based on the values, attitudes, and behavior of the dominant Anglo-European society. As a result, clinicians usually perceive the behavior of the African-American client in a negative way and often regard it as psychopathologic. However, when African-American clients are assessed within the framework of their culture and community as well as in their community's relationship to the larger society, it is often possible to ascertain the function of some of the behavior, which makes the behavior constructive and appropriate. This does not preclude the recognition of psychopathology among African-Americans but seeks to sort out and eliminate some of the behaviors and processes that have been labeled erroneously as psychopathology because of ethnocentric biases of mental health professionals.

The systems approach, which incorporates the effects of client-system interaction into the diagnostic formulation, is a complementary tool toward this end. Diagnoses made by clinicians about Black clients will tend to change as their knowledge of African-American behavior is expanded. Courses of treatment traditionally recommended may in turn be altered and expanded as an increased awareness of African-American culture increases the number of techniques and resources at the disposal of the clinician.

Notes and References

1. John Mbiti, *African Religions and Philosophy* (Garden City, N.Y.: Doubleday & Co., 1970), p. 161.
2. Ivan Van Sertima, *They Came Before Columbus* (New York: Random House, 1976).
3. Cedric Clark, ''Black Studies or the Study of Black People,'' in Reginald Jones, ed., *Black Psychology* (New York: Harper & Row, 1972), p. 13.

4. Joyce Ladner, *Tomorrow's Tomorrow: The Black Woman* (Garden City, N.Y.: Doubleday & Co., 1971), p. 57.

5. Ibid., p. 62.

6. Ibid., p. 65.

7. Robert Hill, *The Strengths of the Black Family* (New York: Emerson Hall Publishers, 1971).

8. Mbiti, op. cit., p. 141.

9. Herbert Gutman, *The Black Family in Slavery and Freedom, 1750–1925* (New York: Pantheon Books, 1976), pp. 217–229.

10. Maye H. Grant, "Perspective on Adoption: Black into White," *Black World*, 22 (November 1972), p. 68.

11. Ibid.

12. Hill, op. cit., p. 30.

13. Ibid.

14. Ibid., p. 9.

15. Wade Nobles, "African Philosophy: Foundations for Black Psychology," in Jones, op. cit., p. 30.

16. Ibid., p. 31.

17. Joseph White, "Toward a Black Psychology," in Jones, op. cit., p. 46.

18. Andrew Billingsley, *Black Families in White America* (Englewood Cliffs, N.J.: Prentice-Hall, 1968).

19. Ladner, op. cit., p. 75.

20. *New York State Medicaid Pamphlet*, Publication No. 1006 (rev. ed.; Albany: New York State Department of Social Services, 1975), p. 6.

21. K. Alan Wesson, "The Black Man's Burden: The White Clinician," *Black Scholar*, 6 (July–August 1975), p. 15.

CHAPTER 50

A Black and White Approach to the Problem of Racism

Esther Fibush and BeAlva Turnquest

The basic commitment of casework is a dual one—to both the social and the psychological approaches to human problems. Because of this commitment, "a diagnosis of an individual's unhappiness ... cannot ignore a diagnosis of the sickness of society and what it is doing to the person's life."[1] There can be no doubt that white racism qualifies as major social pathology in the United States. Its significance to the lives of its black victims has been powerfully documented, and there is increasing recognition of its contribution to the problems of other minority groups.[2]

From the environmental standpoint, racism is expressed in political, socioeconomic, and cultural institutions that enable the dominant white group to promote its own material interests at the expense of other groups. From the psychological standpoint, it is expressed in a number of related attitudes whereby white individuals attempt to promote their own psychic security through an assumed superiority to members of other groups. Racism is thus not only a means by which white people maintain a very real environmental advantage but also a mechanism for attempting to maintain a psychological advantage.[3]

[1] Bertha C. Reynolds, The Social Casework of an Uncharted Journey, *Social Work*, 9: 16 (October 1964).

[2] Documentation exists in great variety, dating back to abolition days. A notable recent addition to the literature is William H. Grier and Price M. Cobbs, *Black Rage* (New York: Basic Books, 1968).

[3] The concept of racism used here is formulated from several sources. It rests in a general way on Gordon W. Allport, *The Nature of Prejudice* (Cambridge, Mass.: Addison-Wesley, 1954). It is also influenced by Stokely Carmichael and Charles V. Hamilton, *Black Power: The Politics of Liberation in America* (New York: Vintage Books, 1967); and by Whitney M. Young, Jr., *Beyond Racism* (New York: McGraw-Hill, 1969).

Reprinted from *Social Casework*, Vol. 51 (October, 1970), pp. 459–466, by permission of the authors and the Family Service Association of America.

Racist attitudes in individuals both arise from and contribute to racist institutions. In the treatment situation, the caseworker sees the ways in which the social pathology is interwoven with individual psychopathology. Although psychological racism takes a variety of forms and serves a variety of purposes, depending on both the social and the individual dynamics involved, it always includes the assertion of an assumed superiority on the basis of race. Identification with one's own racial group does not in itself constitute racism. Racism arises when racial identity is seen and used as a mark of superiority or inferiority inherent in a person by reason of his racial group membership. Racism ranges from overt white supremacist attitudes to various covert attitudes, including unconscious fantasies about imagined racial characteristics.

Institutionalized racism is a flagrant wrong and must be eliminated through social and political action. Casework treatment is in no way a substitute for such change, nor is the caseworker excused from participating in advocacy or activism when these are indicated. In his daily practice, however, the caseworker remains primarily a therapist and a clinician. In this capacity he conducts with the client, white or black, a search for mental health that rejects the concept of superiority or inferiority on the basis of color.

There have been numerous studies of the social and psychological factors associated with prejudice in white people.[4] There has also been some discussion of the impact of racism on the treatment of white patients by black therapists.[5] The scarcity of literature by white caseworkers on the subject of white racist clients suggests that there has been avoidance, denial, or repression of a painful subject. Caseworkers have concentrated a great deal of attention on the black victims of racism. It seems high time that more attention be given its white carriers.

Clinical Study

This article is the outcome of a collaborative exploration into white racism by a black caseworker and a white caseworker. Its purpose was to understand the ways in which racism plays a part in the client's problems or

---

[4] See T. W. Adorno et al., *The Authoritarian Personality* (New York: Harper & Brothers, 1950); George Simpson and J. Milton Yinger, *Racial and Cultural Minorities: An Analysis of Prejudice and Discrimination* (New York: Harper & Brothers, 1958); and Bruno Bettelheim and Morris Janowitz, *Social Change and Prejudice* (New York: Free Press of Glencoe, 1964).

[5] See Leonard C. Simmons, "Crow Jim": Implications for Social Work, *Social Work*, 8: 24–30 (July 1963); and Andrew E. Curry, The Negro Worker and the White Client: A Commentary on the Treatment Relationship, *Social Casework*, 45: 131–36 (March 1964). From the standpoint of psychoanalytic psychotherapy, see interview with Dr. William H. Grier, A Negro Therapist Discusses Treating the White Patient, *Roche Report: Frontiers of Clinical Psychiatry*, 4: 5, 11 (March 15, 1967).

defense against problems, in the interaction between client and case-worker, and in the caseworker's attitude toward the client. It was believed that the black-white relationship is a significant factor in casework treatment and might be used as an important tool in the treatment of white racist clients.[6]

The setting was a family service agency in a west coast urban community that has presently a minority population of 40 percent and a "minority" school population of approximately 70 percent. Although the agency continues to serve a substantial number of white middle-class clients, a survey conducted in February 1969 showed that minority clients constituted 44 percent of all clients seen, and that 22 percent of agency clients had incomes below the $4,000 "poverty" level, with another 32 percent at incomes below $7,000. It is an agency that has no present access to funds for financial assistance or to any other direct means of altering the environmental reality for economically deprived clients. It must, therefore, count heavily on what can be accomplished by casework alone.

Clients who come to a family agency are not representative of the population at large. They are a highly selected group—in large measure a self-selected one. They see themselves in need of a kind of help that their image of the family agency suggests will be offered them. Within this client population there are few white clients who express extreme racist attitudes, just as there are few black clients who express extreme hostility toward whites—this situation is doubtless a factor of the self-selection involved. Of this client population, a number of cases were examined from the standpoint of racism as a treatment consideration; some of them were chosen as case examples.[7]

Attention was given not only to the case material but also to the case-workers' reaction to it and to their reaction to each other in the course of their discussion. Discussion was deliberately free-flowing, to encourage the expression of personal as well as professional reactions. There was a conscious effort to recognize factors related to racism wherever they were found—in client or caseworker, black or white—and to trace them to their psychological and social sources.

It became clear very quickly that there would be no simplistic application of either sociological or psychological concepts, that each case had its unique configuration of factors from both sources, and that the case-worker's interpretation might in itself be a stereotype of psychoanalytic, sociological, or personal derivation. Discussion between caseworkers provided a check on each other's assumptions, with the black worker speak-

---

[6] Curry, The Negro Worker and the White Client, p. 135.

[7] For the sake of simplicity, examples presented in this study are all of individual treatment cases. Both workers also carried cases in family group therapy and in joint marital counseling in which racism was a factor. The black worker also was conducting group therapy with two racially mixed groups in which, of course, racist attitudes played some part.

ing from the standpoint of a black life experience and the white worker from that of a white life experience.

As a working hypothesis for this study, racism in the white client was defined as a defense mechanism indicative of the individual's failure to achieve a sense of identity as a human being of dignity and worth. It was seen as being used primarily in defense against anxiety-provoking feelings of inferiority or inadequacy, shame or guilt. It was thought also to exist in a latent state, coming to conscious awareness or overt expression when other, more habitual modes of defense were threatened.

This definition of racism was adopted for purposes of casework treatment and may or may not have wider application. It represents primarily an effort to find a more therapeutic approach to racism in white clients than just to deplore it.

Some Case Examples

There were many white clients with whom the subject of race did not seem to need discussion. Some of these clients were obviously so engrossed in other problems in their lives that it would have been inappropriate to introduce the subject. Others had already begun to come to grips with the problem of racism and were actively combating it in some way, so that discussion would have been superfluous. A few white clients brought up the subject of race with the black worker; there were others, however, with whom the caseworker felt an undercurrent of feeling that suggested that the matter of color be brought into the open.

The purpose in discussing the subject was primarily to free the treatment situation from unnecessary anger and guilt arising from avoidance or denial of the difference in color. It was found that whenever it was possible to discuss the black-white confrontation with a white client (whenever, that is, the subject was not too threatening to the client), the discussion proved to be ego-strengthening. Not only did it free emotional energy for the pursuit of treatment, but it often enabled the client to grapple with other, more realistically threatening situations in his life. The need for such discussion did not arise with the white caseworker, but it was felt that the coincidental advantage of the opportunity to explore and help the client understand the meaning of a special kind of emotional encounter was thereby lost.

The person-to-person encounter between black worker and white client means different things to different clients. For some it is so highly charged emotionally that the worker's blackness becomes a paramount factor in treatment. Such was the case with Miss G.

Miss G was a young white woman who was described by the white intake worker as attractive and articulate, with a problem involving the excessive use of fantasy but with no apparent difficulty entering into a casework relationship. Miss G was assigned to the black worker, who immediately noticed that Miss G was acting out some fantasied role in the casework setting just as she did in her real life situation. During the first treatment hour, the black worker felt that her blackness was interfering in some way, but she did not feel sure enough of this appraisal to bring it up during the session. Miss G canceled her second appointment.

In the next session, Miss G plunged into a discussion of her feelings about black people, her surprise at the worker's being black, and her fear that she might inadvertently say something offensive to the worker. Exploring these remarks, the worker found that some of Miss G's feelings were attributable to her lack of contact with black people and her considerable contact with white people who spoke of black people in a derogatory way. Surprisingly, in this area Miss G had not made use of fantasy, and exploration of the subject of black-white relationships proved to be her first venture into a search for authenticity.

In this instance, the black-white encounter precipitated the client into a "real" relationship in which she had to grapple honestly with authentic feelings, thus bypassing the habitual defense system and laying the groundwork for the development of healthy ego-functioning.

There are some white clients who appear to have such deep feelings of empathy with black people that one would expect to find them actively engaged in combating racism. When in fact they are not so engaged, the black caseworker might well suspect an effort at ingratiation. This is not always the case, however, as exemplified by Mrs. T.

Mrs. T's problem was her inability to take action. She suffered from anxiety about her own aggression and was unable to assert herself or even to express her feelings in most situations. This was especially true in her marriage, and it was the marriage that was the focus of casework treatment. As Mrs. T gained insight into her problem, she was delighted to find herself openly and freely expressing disagreement on racial issues with her covertly and sometimes overtly racist acquaintances.

At the other extreme, there are white clients who show evidence of deep feelings of anger and hatred toward black people, yet can accept psychological help from a black caseworker.

Mr. S came to the agency reluctantly at the urging of a relative. He was entertaining ideas of suicide and had, over a period of several months, almost starved himself to death. His depression had been precipitated when his wife of many years had left him for another man. Mr. S told of the many plans he had in mind to kill this man. There was something about the way Mr. S talked that prompted the worker to ask if the "other man" had been black. Mr. S confirmed this and added that he had to admit it was this fact that prompted such murderous feelings.

Having been helped to bring this emotionally fraught matter into the open, Mr. S was able to continue the interview in a more spontaneous way. Because the black caseworker had reacted to him with positive subjective feelings, a rapport was established that enabled Mr. S to recognize his need for treatment and made it possible for him to follow through on the worker's referral to a clinic. One might speculate that the black worker's ability to accept Mr. S's racist feelings provided relief from his immobilizing anger and guilt, freeing him from his obsessive murderous fantasies sufficiently to seek the psychiatric treatment he needed.

The white client may initially have a greater feeling of safety with a black caseworker than with a white worker. Ironically, this sense of trust arises in part from the inferior position imposed upon the black person in a white-dominated society. Moreover, because the black worker may seem at so great a social distance from the realities of his own life, the white client may experience an additional feeling of safety. As treatment progresses, however, there may be development of regressive transference with all its hostile negative elements.

Mrs. L was divorced from her husband but continued to cling to him through a variety of manipulative maneuvers that indicated a severe dependency problem. She was assigned to a white worker and responded to supportive treatment by making some progress toward more independent functioning. The basic problem went untouched, however, and when the white worker left the agency, Mrs. L felt she needed to continue. She asked to be assigned to the black worker who had seen her at intake. This worker had initially had a negative reaction to Mrs. L although Mrs. L had not at that time expressed any racist attitudes.

When the black worker shifted from a simple supportive role to a focus on the intense dependency needs, the negative transference came to the fore, and with it all the previously concealed racist attitudes. Exploration of these feelings indicated that Mrs. L had fastened onto those stereotypes of black people that most reflected her own character problem: dependency, efforts to win acceptance by ingratiating behavior, and various other aspects of childlike or impulse-indulging action. The black worker had intuitively reacted at intake to a defense mechanism in Mrs. L that touched directly on the problems and adaptive techniques developed by black people in a racist society and on Mrs. L's unconscious racist feelings. It became clear that Mrs. L was attempting to deal with ego-dystonic traits by means of projection onto a scapegoat.

The black worker must find some way of handling his own feelings about racist material for the therapeutic benefit of the client.

As the negative transference emerged, Mrs. L's derogatory remarks about black people became more and more difficult to tolerate. The fact that Mrs. L tried to resolve her guilt by seeing her black caseworker as the one exception to the stereotypes served only to "add insult to injury." Mrs. L was not ready for an interpretation of the stereotypes as a projection of her own problems, and the worker feared that any attempt at such an interpretation would be an acting out of her own anger at Mrs. L and therefore destructive to the client.

Discussing the countertransference problem with her white colleague, the worker realized that her attempt to suppress her own anger at racist remarks was unrealistic, despite her awareness of the underlying psychological problems that prompted them. She therefore decided to talk with Mrs. L about her anger.

Mrs. L's reaction was surprise. Recognizing that the worker did indeed feel anger and that such anger was a natural response by a black person to racist remarks, Mrs. L could see that she tended to be unaware of other people's feelings in all her relationships. This was a problem she was ready to work on. Treatment could then proceed on the basis of Mrs. L's insight into her interaction with people in her real-life situations, and the development of further negative transference and countertransference was avoided.

If treatment can accomplish its purpose without special attention to racist attitudes, there is some possibility that the client's racist attitude may simply drop away as he no longer needs it.

Miss J was illegitimately pregnant. Her problems involved conflict with her mother, anger at rejection by her father, and inability to compete successfully with her more demanding siblings for the limited emotional and material supplies in the family. She was from a white, low-income, working-class family that often had to seek help from "the welfare" and that habitually used racist sentiments to deny their own feelings of inferiority and inadequacy. She was able to function well at work but was in danger of losing her job when her pregnancy became known. Miss J quite freely expressed occasional racist opinions.

The white worker ignored these expressions, concentrating on helping Miss J make a plan for leave of absence from work, adoption placement for the baby, and a program for additional education. The crucial factor was to bypass "welfare" in the process, thus effectively separating Miss J from the family pattern of recourse to a kind of help that she felt degrading and humiliating. As Miss J worked her way up the status scale, her self-esteem grew, she no longer needed to feel superior by means of racist attitudes, and she began associating on equal and friendly terms with black colleagues and acquaintances.

Judging from the limited evidence obtained, Miss J's use of racism may have been superficial, primarily a status factor. She had sufficient ego-strength so that when a few doors were opened for her, she could satisfy her need for upward mobility and was then able to adopt a value system appropriate to her more secure environmental situation. One might speculate that because she had not been using racism as a basic personality support, she might have given up her racist attitudes more quickly with a black worker who symbolized the middle-class values toward which she was striving.

There is an occasional instance of a white client for whom racism is not merely a defense mechanism but the very ground on which he stands.

> Mr. R came to the agency because he disapproved of his daughter's association with "hippies," a group of white liberal high school students who were tutoring black children in a ghetto area. Mr. R, at fifty-eight, was essentially a defeated person, separated from his wife and alienated from his children, struggling to maintain upper middle-class status among more successful business and professional men within his own reference group. He not only disapproved of his daughter's being in direct contact with black people, whom he saw in every way as inferior, but also of her having close social contact with "gentiles" for fear she might marry outside her faith. Mr. R's sense of personal failure was so great, both emotionally and socioeconomically, that he had retreated into a fantastically narrow concept of his own "in-group" and viewed all outsiders as dangerous threats to what little security he could feel within his self-imposed ghetto.

Mr. R was himself the victim of one variety of racism and the carrier of another. His "identification with the aggressor" had become for him a necessity of life. The white worker decided not to attempt any confrontation with him; whether or not the confrontation implicit in a black caseworker's presence in a counseling capacity might have been more therapeutic for him is questionable. Fortunately, it was clear from Mr. R's report that his daughter had sufficient ego-strength to pursue her own purposes despite her father's objections.

From the standpoint of casework treatment, the matter of racism seemed to be a peripheral factor with Miss J and a central one with Mr. R. In neither instance did the casework relationship itself provide the opportunity for a direct therapeutic encounter. The significant factor from the standpoint of treatment, however, was that the casework relationship could proceed successfully where racist stereotypes were not an essential defense mechanism, as with Miss J, but was entirely blocked where racism constituted a major character defense, as with Mr. R. This finding suggests that the ways in which racists attitudes are used in the defense system may provide an important diagnostic and prognostic clue for treatment.

The treatment possibilities are ordinarily not so easily evaluated, however, because racism is likely to be but one component of a complicated network of defense mechanisms within the personality structure. When it is difficult to assess the significance of racist attitudes to the total treatment picture, the white worker may be confronted with his own conflicts in regard to racism. He may wish to disassociate himself immediately from the client's attitudes, but if he does so, he risks the possibility that the client will feel rejected or attacked and will drop out of treatment. If he disregards the racism, he must be able to handle his own sense of participation in racist guilt so that his own emotional reactions will not block treatment.

Because racist attitudes often provide a defense against awareness of anxiety, such attitudes may contribute to the resistance that arises during the course of treatment and must be dealt with in some way. Dealing with these attitudes will be double difficult when racism is ego-syntonic to the client, not only because it contributes to his psychic comfort but also because it corresponds to his perception of a real-life situation. If the white caseworker attempts to deal with racist stereotypes as an incorrect perception of reality, the client may experience this attempt as an attack on his cognitive functions; the matter could then easily degenerate into an "argument" that encouraged the client in intellectualization and rationalization.

It may be necessary for the caseworker to remind himself that the primary purpose of casework treatment is not to attack the defense mechanisms as such, but to strengthen the client's ego capacity sufficiently so that he no longer has need of destructive or self-destructive defenses. It is the ego that perceives reality and that provides the means for dealing with the life situations so as to maximize the attainment of satisfaction. The ego also, however, erects defenses against the awareness of painful emotions and thus blocks its perception of some very significant inner realities; in the pursuit of physic comfort, the ego often handicaps itself in performing its own basic task. The caseworker must therefore be prepared to enlist the ego in an exploration of inner emotional factors as well as of outer reality circumstances.

> Mrs. M came to the agency about her son, age seven, who was soiling. On exploring the social situation, it became apparent that Mrs. M needed supplemental financial assistance and was probably eligible for Aid to Families with Dependent Children (AFDC). She was unwilling to apply, stating that the welfare department favored "Negroes," and indicated her feelings about black people by a facial expression that suggested she was smelling something unpleasant.
>
> The white worker commented on her statement and was able to help Mrs. M decide to make an AFDC application. She did not comment on the facial expression because her own reaction to it was so intensely negative. It was obvious, however, that the facial expression was a nonverbal clue to the meaning of the child's symptom. It later became apparent that Mrs. M's background of economic and emotional deprivation had produced in her a self-hatred that her son was acting out, and that her feelings about black people were actually her feelings about herself.
>
> The worker focused on the reality problem of financial need without also exploring the psychological implications of the nonverbal communication. Having failed to come to grips in the initial encounter with the racist attitude, the

worker's guilt mounted, and when Mrs. M again made a racist statement, the caseworker expressed direct disagreement. By that time, regressive transference elements were operating, and Mrs. M ostensibly accepted the disagreement without objection. She then became involved in a sadomasochistic relationship with a man of minority group identification, acting out her problem instead of trying to understand and deal with it in therapy. Ego-oriented casework provided no direct access to the unconscious factors involved, the opportunity for using the racist material to reach a deeper level of emotion was gone, and the case was eventually closed without any real progress having been made.

The case of Mrs. M exemplifies the dilemma for the white caseworker. Had the racist attitude been picked up immediately, the caseworker would have found it extremely difficult to use it in some constructive way. An immediate response would have had the advantage, however, of eliciting a "real" rather than a "transference" reaction from the client, and thus might have prevented the client's acting out later in treatment. By the time this study was undertaken, the damage had already been done, and it was too late to test the proposition that discussion with a black colleague might be the most useful kind of consultation for such a problem.

In handling his own feelings about racism, the white worker is often a novice. The black worker has the painful advantage of having had to cope with his reactions to racist attitudes all his life. The problem of dealing with racist defense mechanisms therapeutically requires all the understanding and creativity that black and white workers together can bring to it. Even so, it is possible that the treatment of choice for certain racist clients would be group therapy in a racially mixed group, in which the client could face the irrationality of his racist attitudes without direct confrontation with a caseworker.

Conclusion

Judging from the clients studied, racist attitudes in clients must be viewed as an important casework consideration, both from the standpoint of diagnosis and of treatment. The evidence suggests that the presence of a black caseworker sometimes represents a therapeutic encounter in itself. There is also some indication that confrontation by a black worker taps a deeper emotional level with some white clients than is available in ego-oriented treatment with a white caseworker, indicating that the racial composition of a staff has direct bearing on the effectiveness of its treatment program. This evidence does not, however, excuse the white caseworker from facing his own problems in working with racist clients—and perhaps, in some instances, disqualifying himself.

It would also seem that while black people necessarily suffer from the white assumption of superiority, white people do not necessarily gain a corresponding advantage in psychic security (despite their very real advantage from the exploitation of racist institutions). Racist defense mechanisms do not promote, at least in white applicants for casework help, a viable sense of self-esteem, and may indeed be a diagnostic clue indicative of failure in some important ego task. There seems to be considerable reason for caseworkers to shift some of their attention at this time from the black victims of racism to its white carriers. The carriers of the disease may in fact be sicker than its victims.

Where there is sickness in society, everyone is in need of healing—the carrier as well as the victim, the caseworker as well as the client. The first and basic task is to make whatever changes are necessary to bring the society from sickness to health. The caseworker who deals with the individual client, family, or small group is obviously not contributing much to this larger task. Nevertheless, in his daily practice, he may be doing something to limit the spread of the disease.

During the course of this study, both caseworkers realized that any conclusions they might hope to reach would be less important than their growing sense of security in talking together about a subject that is as emotionally charged for caseworkers as for clients. What had started primarily as an intellectual enterprise became an emotional experience in which they were able to share openly and honestly their feelings about black-white relationships. Both became convinced that without such emotional communication between black and white staff members, casework practice will take on its own sterile and intellectualized stereotypes, with both black and white clients.

Caseworkers may read all the "right" books, say all the "right" things, and participate in all the "right" causes, but if black and white do not share their feeling as well as their thinking, they will remain handicapped in achieving their goals. In view of the experience of one such venture, it would appear that when black and white caseworkers talk together freely, the black-white relationship becomes a source of strength and security that has a direct carry-over to work with all clients, black and white.

Intellectually speaking, this study represents only a tentative and preliminary effort to understand and deal with the problem of racism in the treatment situation. Emotionally speaking, however, the implications could be as vast as was James Baldwin's vision in *The Fire Next Time*:

> If we—and now I mean the relatively conscious whites and the relatively conscious blacks, who must, like lovers, insist on, or create, the consciousness of the others—do not falter in our duty now, we may be able, handful that we are, to end the racial nightmare, and achieve our country, and change the history of the world....[8]

[8] James Baldwin, *The Fire Next Time* (New York: Dial Press, 1963), p. 119.

CHAPTER 51

American Indians: Working with Individuals and Groups

E. Daniel Edwards and Margie E. Edwards

There are approximately one million American Indians living in the continental Unites States today.[1] The 1970 census reported that about 80 percent of all American Indians claim to be members of some 250 tribes.[2] In addition, there are an almost equal number of native Alaskan groups located throughout Alaska.[3] Each of these tribes is unique. Many of them continue to maintain their own tribal languages, values, customs, religions, and leadership systems.[4]

The Place of the Group in American Indian Culture

Historically, American Indians developed societies with well-defined roles, responsibilities, government and economic systems, recreational and leisure styles, religious rites and ceremonies, and social behavior in which group involvement, support, and consensus played major roles. Their social, economic, and political traditions reflect a strong emphasis on group involvement and decision making.

Group solidarity was achieved in a number of ways. Many "work" assignments were combined with recreational and leisure activities. El-

[1] Jamake Highwater, *Fodor's Indian America* (New York: David McKay, 1975), p. 61.

[2] Mary Ellen Ayers, "Counseling the American Indian." *Occupational Outlook Quarterly* (Washington, D.C.: U.S. Department of Labor, Spring 1977), p. 24.

[3] Ibid.

[4] Ibid.

Reprinted from *Social Casework*, Vol. 61 (October, 1980), pp. 498–506, by permission of the author and the Family Service Association of America.

derly American Indians taught the younger people crafts, narrated myths, gave moral talks, and in other ways instructed the young.[5]

Some tribes utilized "potlatches" to achieve group solidarity. These gatherings were held to bestow titles or other honors, to conduct family rites, to show mourning, to announce a new chief, to save face, and to demonstrate power and wealth. All members of the family group presenting the potlatch participated in the preparation and actual event, which would last for several days and feature huge amounts of food, dancing and singing, and the giving of many gifts.

Group consensus was valued by most Indian tribes. Many meetings, discussions, and "powwows" were lengthy because American Indians strove for group consensus, not majority rule, in their decision-making processes that would affect the majority of Indian people. Each individual's opinion was heard and weighed in arriving at decisions affecting the group. Although group consensus was highly valued, so was the Indian's appreciation for each person as an individual. Most tribes respected the individual and allowed each person a great deal of freedom and autonomy, particularly in those areas that would have more repercussions for the individual than for the group as a whole. However, Indian values were repeatedly reinforced. The individual was well acquainted with those values and roles that reinforced group closeness. They were also well aware of areas in which individual decision making was allowed.

Cultural Strengths and Weaknesses

Culturally, American Indians enjoy many group activities. They are energetic, fun-loving people who enjoy sports, games,[6] music, crafts, participation in ceremonies, and a variety of other small and large group recreational and cultural activities. Hospitality, generosity, good humor, and good sportsmanship are values that have been emphasized in their group activities. Self-discipline, self-control, and self-development were emphasized through play. Feelings of pleasure and enjoyment were shared by participants and spectators.[7]

Since the time of Christopher Columbus, many detrimental cultural changes have been imposed on the American Indian people. In 1890, after the massacre of the Sioux at Wounded Knee, South Dakota, all Indians recognized as such by the federal government were relocated on reser-

---

[5] Clark Wissler, *Indians of the United States* (New York: Anchor Books, 1966), p. 274.

[6] Stewart Cullen, *Games of the North American Indians* (New York: Dover Publications, 1975).

[7] Brad Steiger, *Medicine Talks: A Guide to Walking in Balance and Surviving on the Earth Mother* (New York: Doubleday, 1975), p. 67.

vations.[8] This disruption of Indian culture, combined with subsequent attempts at forced assimilation, broken treaties, and unfulfilled promises has contributed greatly to the Indian's distrust of Anglos and subsequent poor relationships. Because of these events, American Indians may require a substantial time commitment before they develop professional relationships with non-Indian social workers.

The diversification of American Indian tribes and individuals may also contribute toward blocking of group cohesion. Historically, some tribal groups have competed against one another, and there are carry-overs of past events to present-day relationships that may negatively affect group involvement. Many different lifestyles and philosophies exist among American Indians today, which sometimes lead to feelings of diviseness.

Stereotypes and Myths

A number of stereotypes and myths persist regarding American Indians, many of which are incorrect or short-sighted. Examples of these stereotypes include: Indians are oil-rich, lazy, drunken, unproductive, good with their hands but not with their heads, on the government dole, stoic, long-suffering, warlike, blood-thirsty, debauched, barbaric, unemotional, aloof, and with little hope for the future. Other stereotypes view Indians as proud, controlled, reserved, honest, sharing, and self-sufficient.

American Indians are as individualistic as members of any other group. These stereotypes, however, cannot help but influence their feelings toward themselves as well as their perceptions of the non-Indian's attitude toward the Indian. The National Congress of American Indians felt so strongly about the image of American Indians that they began a national public relations campaign in 1969 to create a "new and true picture" of American Indians that would portray important values and result in an improvement of the Indians' image to Indians and non-Indians alike.[9]

Relationships in Cross-racial Situations

DEALINGS WITH AUTHORITY

The historical treatment of America Indians provides some basis for their suspiciousness of Anglo people in "authority" roles. On occasion, Indian clients have been "promised" results that were not obtained, or

[8] Sar A. Levitan and William B. Johnston, *Indian Giving: Federal Programs for Native Americans* (Baltimore: Johns Hopkins University, 1975), p. 7.

[9] Howard M. Bahr, Bruce A. Chadwick, and Robert C. Day, eds., *Native Americans Today: Sociological Perspectives* (New York: Harper and Row, 1972), pp. 48–49, 524.

they may have misunderstood the procedures, "promises," or role of the professional person. These misunderstandings may lead to suspiciousness, mistrust, and reluctance to become involved with other professionals.

Social workers should move slowly, identify problems and procedures clearly, make commitments regarding situations in which they have control, follow through consistently, and use client strengths appropriately in order to help develop feelings of trust and establish professional relationships. For example, an eight-year-old girl was returned from foster care to the care of her mother. A month later, the girl ran away. Her mother located her, spoke with her firmly, and told her that she was wanted and needed and was never to run away again. The daughter complied. The social worker praised the mother for the strength she had shown in locating her daughter and setting the limits for her daughter's behavior.

In working with an American Indian client, the social worker should assume an appropriate authoritarian position that permits the client to assume as much responsibility as possible for his or her activities, discussions, and decision making.

SOCIOCULTURAL EXPECTATIONS

Indians have been taught to value themselves, their families, clans, and tribes, and to adhere to values that are revered by their various tribal groups. When working with these clients, social workers should consider the values of each specific tribe.

As social workers learn about the specific Indian tribal group with which they are working, they will be more able to discuss tribal matters, cultural customs, and current areas of concern to the group. This understanding will facilitate a more successful intervention.

It is important for social workers to understand that Indian values are interwoven throughout their culture, lifestyle, religion, and daily activities. In many Indian tribal groups tribal values are reinforced through the use of ceremonies. When ceremonies are held, it is important for family members to participate, even if participation requires traveling long distances or giving up other commitments.

Non-Indian social workers should expect that it will take time before they are trusted and accepted by the Indian people with whom they work. The sometimes rapid turnover of social work staff has contributed to the wariness with which American Indians approach relationships with a new social worker. Social workers can expect that it will take three to six months before they are accepted by the people in traditional Indian communities.

In the "not too distant past," all social workers working with American Indians have been non-Indian. In recent years, a number of professional and paraprofessional American Indian people have been employed to work with Indians. Regardless of the ethnic background, Indian clients will individually and collectively assess the expertise and commitment of any helping person before relationships will develop.

Introspection is often difficult for Indians. Self-evaluations may also be difficult for students involved in professional training programs. Indians reared in the traditional ways of their tribes may have difficulty talking about themselves. Indian tradition dictates that Indians do not exaggerate their abilities or use their own name or the word "I" excessively. Traditionally, Indian people are expected to know their strengths but not to exaggerate them; they are to exhibit confidence, but not flaunt their skills. An Indian client may bring another person with them to an interview so that they will have someone there who can speak on their behalf.

American Indians believe that people should be able to understand one another; it is not necessary to explain one's feelings or problems in detail. The Indian client therefore, often expects the professional person to be able to understand without the client having to voice concerns in detail.

Many American Indians have learned to relate to new situations by being passive. The pace of the interview must be geared to motivate clients to respond more as an interview progresses. Social workers should strive to feel comfortable in periods of silence, to listen, hear, understand, and respond as an American Indian would as important considerations are discussed. One technique that is helpful in building a relationship with American Indians is helping clients resolve tangible problems. Economic needs, employment referrals, health care, school-related problems, housing, and other tangible needs often bring clients to a social service agency. Helping an Indian client obtain the services desired facilitates the development of a relationship that may continue in subsequent contacts or allow the client to return for services in the future.

LANGUAGE PROBLEMS

Most American Indians are bilingual; however, some Indians, particularly older ones, may not speak English very well or at all. A social worker must assess the client's communication skills and respond appropriately.

Because the bilingual client's vocabulary in English may be limited, verbal messages may be misinterpreted. It is not uncommon for American Indians to ask how long they "have to come" to see a social worker, when what they are really asking is "will this experience be long enough and important enough for me to risk getting involved?" It is also common for young people to ask repeatedly when groups will be held, will they be allowed to attend, and so on. This constant questioning of others about events is a result of past experiences in which many enjoyable activities were cancelled or discontinued. They fear that this enjoyable experience may also not continue. Social workers need to clarify the purposes for social work intervention and the time commitment, and help clients develop positive therapeutic relationships at an appropriate pace.

Clients may also not understand what is being proposed in the case of a group experience. On one occasion, several group members were participating in a group activity collecting pine cones in the nearby mountains. They also went to the local park to add more to their collection. Several group members then asked if they could also go to the cemetery to find more pine cones. One group member did not know what a "cemetery" was; she came from a very traditional Indian family who had a great deal of respect for dead people. Upon entering the cemetery, she became very frightened. Had the group worker told her the group was planning to go to a "graveyard" instead of a "cemetery," the girl would have understood the terminology used and would have been in a better position to express her feelings about this experience.

With some bilingual clients, it is necessary to explain problems that the English-speaking social worker can express in English with one or two words. In some Indian languages there is not a word that means "retarded" or "developmentally disabled." Some words that are closely related are entirely different. For example, one Indian mother was very frightened when she asked. "You don't mean my child is crazy, do you?" when the social worker had tried to explain that her child had some learning problems and would probably be classified as an educably retarded youngster. It therefore requires a great deal of time to work with bilingual clients where language barriers are present.

Using Culture-Specific Techniques

Because of the vast number of individual tribal groups, it is important for the individual and cultural values of each American Indian, individually and as a group, to be considered in social work intervention. Efforts should be directed toward helping clients understand the social work intervention process. It is also important to consider modifying procedures when it would be beneficial to the client.

Sometimes Indian clients' problems are related to someone close who has recently died. In the interview process, when a topic directly relates to the deceased, it is wise to use a term such as sister, brother, father, and so on, other than the person's given name because it is a violation of tradition to use the dead person's name. Moreover, if the social worker feels that he or she may not have the expertise to handle the above topic, a suggestion could be made to involve the skills of a medicine man, should the client desire.

When helping clients solve problems, a social worker may use role-playing techniques that reflect the here-and-now within the client's culture. The clan system may be utilized to support or implement change. For example, if a male Indian is having problems with his in-laws, and his culture does not allow him to speak directly to his mother-in-law, role playing the use of other clan members as intermediary sources could be helpful.

Eye contact may sometimes cause uneasiness with an Indian client. The worker should develop a technique of looking elsewhere when interviewing or develop an activity or game where worker and client can talk without constant eye contact.

It is important for workers to understand when Indian clients may be experiencing conflicts related to their cultural values. For example, one young adult Indian male had a difficult time identifying goals for his future. It was very difficult for him to verbalize these frustrations when working with a social worker because he had been taught by a very traditional father that "any Indian 'worth his salt' was to handle all of his problems on his own." It was important for the social worker to verbalize this conflict between the client's own personal frustrations and the expectations of his culture. After discussing these verbally, the young man was able to look at his options and plan for his future. However, at the end of the interview he showed evidence of being embarrassed. During the subsequent interview, he was very quiet. The social worker once again verbalized the conflict and identified for the young man the ways in which he was assuming responsibility for himself; the worker also provided feedback that indicated he saw the young man as a valuable, worthwhile, strong, capable person. This feedback was important to the self-esteem of the client. The client terminated shortly after this interview, but would return for counseling on a limited basis.

The setting in which the social work services are provided is important to the success of the treatment. Some young people who have been reared on Indian reservations will be more verbal and responsive in outdoor settings, where the atmosphere is similar to their home environment. Adults may also prefer to work with the social worker on the porch or in an outdoor patio area.

The use of humor, particularly as it relates to being teased and teasing one another about incidents related to everyday living, can help set a positive atmosphere for the Indian client. Indian people tease and use humor as an indication of acceptance and comfort. If social workers can make fun of themselves and the things they do, Indian people often read this as an indication of the social worker's comfort in the experience also.

It is important for social workers to assess the uniqueness of each client, whether the client is seeing the worker as an individual or as a member of a group. In dealing with the Indian client, however, it is also important to assess the degree of affiliation and identification with traditional Indian culture, the conflicts that exist between minority and majority culture values, the willingness to risk, and the real issues with which the Indian client desires help.

A consistency of appointments with clients should be maintained, and appointments should not be broken, unless absolutely necessary. Sessions should be held regularly, even if some members are missing. Clients should be given time to warm up to the counseling or group situation, time to think through matters being discussed and possible alternatives, and time to unwind in terminating the sessions.

When a client does not keep an appointment, the worker should make an effort to contact the client to let the client know that he or she was missed, then the appointment should be rescheduled. The worker should avoid imposing any feelings of guilt on the client. Clients should understand what they can expect from the social worker and what the social worker will expect from them. Once the relationship has been developed, it is important to identify goals and to partialize the assignments to be accomplished. Short-range goals often help clients see that something of worth is being accomplished.

Relationships with Indian clients take time. Workers must avoid overestimating a relationship initially. Even though a relationship is developing, and the client's goals are being worked on, the Indian person may still desire distance in the relationship.

Social workers must not underestimate the relationship at termination. Many American Indians develop close working relationships with professional people, both individually and in groups, and may wish to continue the relationship, even though it is necessary to terminate. Clients may become physically ill, avoid final sessions, develop other problems, or negate the benefit of the services they have received. They may, however, respond with appreciation and identification of areas of personal growth.

Because of the Indian's belief in the value of individuality, some of them will consider it inappropriate to discuss the problems of other members of their families in meetings with social workers.[10] Social workers can be helpful by expressing and understanding of this value and the conflict it may cause. The value of individuality also dictates to some Indians that they must resolve individual problems on their own. In such situations, social workers should identify their role as a "sounding board" and help Indian clients develop their own plans for working through the conflicts involved.

---

[10] Ronald G. Lewis and Man Keung Ho, "Social Work with Native Americans," *Social Work* 20 (September 1975): 380–81.

Intervention Strategies and Skills with Groups

The value that American Indians place on consensus can readily be used in forming the basis of group work practice.[11] When working with clients in groups, solutions to problems should take into consideration the Indian client's cultural traditions and values. These cultural resources may be seen by the clients as valuable and appropriate resources to use in other times of stress as well.

Working with Indians in task groups may require a long-term investment. Individual citizens and elected or appointed tribal representatives often seek to be involved in decisions that will affect Indian people as a group. Consensus for community activities and programs is still valued by some American Indian tribes.

One of the roles of a professional worker in task groups is to interpret and clarify policies for committees, suggest viable alternatives, help identify leadership and potential leadership among American Indian people, see that programs and policies are enacted at a suitable pace, and support appropriately American Indians who assume leadership roles on policy-making boards and committees. These procedures may be time-consuming, but they will result in more effective policy decisions. For example, one task group assignment on an Indian reservation involved several months of work to establish a boys' home. Members of the Indian community were actively involved in all aspects of this project, from initial planning to implementation. When the home was established, it was accomplished with the support, interest, and sanction of the community.

It is important that practitioners working with groups of American Indians become acquainted with resources available in the community. Once relationships are established, referrals for other community services can be a part of the group experience. The interest and support of the worker and other group members may motivate some participants to seek assistance from other agencies.

Groups led by more than one leader have been a successful technique, especially with groups of children, adolescents, married couples, and families. Co-leaders provide support for one another as well as gain greater insight and awareness into the problems and strengths of group members.

Providing positive reinforcement for clients is particularly important. In the initial stages of a group's development, it may be more appropriate to provide positive reinforcement on an individual basis. Being praised in front of other group members in the initial stages of a group's development may often be embarrassing and culturally inappropriate in working with groups of American Indians. When group cohesiveness is developed,

---

[11] Charles E. Farris and Lorene S. Farris, "Indian Children: The Struggle for Survival," *Social Work* 21 (September 1976): 388.

group members may appropriately provide positive support to one another.

Treatment methods with American Indians experiencing alcoholism problems should be task-centered. Social workers should continue to reach out to Indian clients with understanding and sensitivity. Specific tangible goals should be identified for Indian clients that can realistically be achieved.

Family group sessions with Indian families may involve participation from extended family members, members of the clan, and others. These sessions may need to be informal in nature and require longer periods of time to develop relationships and to achieve desired goals. The work accomplished, however, will be with the knowledge and support of a large number of significant people.

YOUTH GROUPS

The wide diversification of American Indians lends itself to considerably creativity in programming for Indian groups. Activity groups are especially enjoyed by Indian youths. These groups have been helpful in boarding school settings, because they provide group members with an opportunity to discuss mutual interests and concerns, to develop talents and skills, to enjoy experiences in the community, to develop leadership skills, to discuss future goals and plans, and to enjoy the association of one another.

Leadership groups with young Indians have been particularly successful. These groups are designed to help group members practice and develop their leadership skills and share their group experiences with others.

Special interest groups may also be developed to meet specific needs of Indian young people. A group may focus on participation in outdoor activities such as hiking, mountain climbing, hunting, or fishing. Other groups may develop special interests such as American Indian dancing, beading, or making dance costumes. A cooking group, where youths learn to cook traditional Indian foods, could provide an appropriate outlet for young people.

Community or school project groups can be developed for Indian youths to choose their own projects. They may ask to have the local gym remain open one night per week. They may develop a volleyball program at the gymnasium or Indian center. Another project may seek to have the school library open one night per week with special help available to Indian students to help them with homework assignments, school papers, or special projects. For example, one young Indian leadership group planned and decorated a float for their high school's homecoming parade. Other Indian classmates were somewhat apprehensive about participating in building or riding on the float until they saw the finished product, which was so attractive that several young Indian people volunteered to ride on the float.

Groups that help to make Indian young people aware of community resources are helpful. Group members could visit employment centers, job service centers, businesses that hire young people for on-the-job training, technical colleges, junior colleges, and four-year colleges. It is important for young Indian people to talk with older Indians who are actively involved in employment, training, or educational programs as they visit various sites.

Groups which focus on increasing positive feelings about one's "Indianness" could also be helpful. The University of Utah's American Indian Social Work Career Training Program staff recently conducted a group experiment with American Indian girls.[12] Group members participated in a number of discussions and activities that were related to traditional and modern-day American Indian activities, including dancing, singing, beading, crafts, foods, and games. Discussions related to historical, cultural, and present-day concerns of American Indians. Everyone involved perceived this group as a positive experience. The use of experimental groups such as this have been successful with Indian young people, who seem to enjoy participating in innovative group experiences.

GROUPS FOR THE ELDERLY

Groups for the elderly have been particularly well received. They enjoy participating in crafts and cultural activities specific to their own cultural group and to other tribes as well as doing modern-day crafts that originate in the dominant culture. Excursions of both long and short duration are motivating group activities. Some Indian aged groups have planned fundraising events to provide financial assistance for such excursions. They enjoy sports activities, including bowling and golf. Dinners and special events where food is served are also very popular among American Indian aged. American Indian elderly have keen senses of humor; they enjoy participating in groups, and enjoy one another's company. They tend to be willing to risk and involve themselves in new activities.

WHAT THE WORKER CAN DO

Groups can be organized around clear purposes and goals. Group members should actively participate in the formulation and modification

---

[12] E. Daniel Edwards et al., "Enhancing Self-Concept and Identification with 'Indianness' of American Indian Girls," *Social Work with Groups* 1 (Fall 1978): 309–18.

of these goals. Programming for group sessions should tie in directly and specifically to individual and group goals.

An effective group programming method is that of "unit programming." Group workers and members agree to focus on the attainment of two or three goals over a period of four to ten group sessions. These goals may include self-image improvement, development of communication or problem-solving skills, developing better relationships with peers, understanding racial and cultural differences and similarities, or achieving skills in American Indian activities. The repetition involved in unit programming is reinforcing and facilitates the attainment of goals.

Group members should be encouraged to use their new skills in their relationships with people outside of the group. Assignments should be given to group members to assist them to achieve their goals. Assignments should be discussed at each group session with continued encouragement or modification as necessary.

For example, Sharon, a teenage girl who did not have many friends, was given two tickets to a weekend movie at her boarding school. Sharon agreed that she would take a friend with her. The following week Sharon returned to see the group worker with the two movie tickets. Sharon said that she had wanted to go to the movie, but was reluctant to ask a friend to go with her. The assignment was restated for the coming weekend. The next week the group worker met Sharon and the friend who had gone with her to the movie. This "beginning friendship" was then generalized to others at the boarding school.

A group worker should use the communication patterns that are evident in the group. For example, one group of adolescent girls was particularly artistic. The group worker asked each of the girls to draw a picture of something that was causing them some concern or difficulty either at school, home, or with their friends. Every group member willingly participated in this activity. This exercise helped many of the quieter group members to discuss their concerns more freely.

Group workers should reserve time after each group session for group members who would like to stay and talk individually or in subgroups with the worker. A flexible time period for group sessions also allows group members to bring up areas of concern when they are ready to do so. It is not unusual for Indian group members to bring up problems at the end of a group session; this is most often not an avoidance technique.

For example, a young adult alcoholism group was meeting to reinforce the maintenance of their sobriety. After an involved group discussion, one group member indicated that she had a concern that she wanted to share with the group. She then proceeded to discuss a "dry drunk" incident (an experience where a recovering alcoholic has all the symptoms and reactions commonly associated with heavy drinking, when no drinking has occurred). She was very troubled by this experience. The group helped to identify the incident, shared similar experiences, and offered understanding and possible alternatives for ways of handling future episodes. She was most relieved, and expressed her appreciation to the group.

Group workers have alternative methods to offer as many services as possible to clients, thus allowing them choices. The more choices which can be made available to American Indians, the better the opportunities for success. Social work services may be offered to clients individually, with their friends or acquaintances, in subgroups, small groups, leadership groups, or special project groups.

Implications for Education and Practice

Social work education should undertake to prepare American Indians and non-Indians to practice with people from both cultures. Students should be prepared to practice social work with individuals, groups, and communities in a generalist approach. Social work techniques that have the most potential for work with Indians should be emphasized in innovative and creative approaches.

Practicum opportunities should be made available for Indians in agencies serving Indians exclusively, agencies serving non-Indians exclusively, and agencies serving both Indians and non-Indians. All students should have opportunities for choice in terms of their practicum placements and an opportunity to work with clients from a variety of ethnic cultures. Practicum instruction should be highly professional. American Indian professional faculty and consultants should be available in both the academic and practicum settings.

Students should be encouraged to invest themselves in an ongoing learning process. This process should encourage students to develop an interest in continuous learning that will better enable them to meet the unique needs of special populations throughout their social work careers.

Students should gain expertise with several group techniques and how they may be combined and integrated to provide the best possible services for American Indians. Students should acquire both activity skills (including American Indian cultural activities) and discussion approaches to meet the needs of each client and group more effectively. Students should also strive for greater self-awareness and understanding of themselves and their professional roles.

Specific American Indian content should be integrated into the curriculum in such a way as to provide a knowledge base to enhance social work practice with Indians. This knowledge base should include historical, cultural, and present-day concerns. Students should understand that minority people participate within two cultures—the majority culture and their own minority culture—and they must understand the concerns and strengths utilized by American Indians as they negotiate relationships within both the majority and their minority cultures.

CHAPTER 52

Social Work with Asian Americans

Man Keung Ho

Asian Americans are one of the most neglected minorities in America.[1] Unlike the blacks, Chicanos, and recently the American Indians, Asian Americans have tried to maintain their social structure with a minimum of visible conflict with the host society. Historically, the have accepted much prejudice and discrimination without voicing strong protests.[2] Their cultural heritage as Asians, historical experiences in a discriminatory society, and their unique problems and concerns are relatively unknown to other Americans.

In fact, Asian Americans frequently have been described as "the most silent minority," "the quiet Americans," or "the model minority." Pei-Ngor Chen attributes such a misconception to two significant factors: the general public's tendency to stereotype ethnic groups and Asian tendencies to hide the "darker side" of their culture, as well as other cultural values militating against self-assertion and open expression of thoughts and feelings to outsiders.[3] It is unfortunate that the prevalent belief that Asian Americans are somehow immune to the effects of white discrimination has served to mask a multitude of problems, such as poverty, unemployment, physical and mental illness, educational deficiencies, and social service inadequacy and unavailability. Problems of Asian Americans

---

[1] The definition of an Asian American remains necessarily broad and flexible—it has traditionally included the Chinese and Japanese, and more recently the Filipino, Korean, and South Sea Islanders, especially from Guam and Samoa.

[2] Roger Daniels and Harry H. L. Kitano, *American Racism: Exploration of the Nature of Prejudice* (Englewood Cliffs, N. J.: Prentice-Hall, 1970); Gail DeVals and Karen Abbott, The Chinese Family in San Francisco, unpublished master's thesis, University of California, Berkeley, 1966; Samuel M. Lyman, *The Asian in the West* (Reno, Nev.: University of Nevada, 1970).

[3] See Pei-Ngor Chen, The Chinese Community in Los Angeles, SOCIAL CASEWORK, 51:10 (December 1970).

Reprinted from *Social Casework*, Vol. 57 (March, 1976), pp. 195–201, by permission of the author and the Family Service Association of America.

and their experiences resulting from white American discrimination have been discussed elsewhere.[4] This article focuses on the indigenous cultural influences operating among Asian Americans and social work intervention with this unique ethnic group.

Salient Cultural Values

FILIAL PIETY

At the beginning of the mid-nineteenth century, the lure of the Mountain of Gold, intensified by social upheavals and natural disasters in many of the Asian countries, began drawing the excess populations of Asia to the Americas. These Asian immigrants brought with them the cultural trappings of a rigid social order in which they generally occupied the lowest position. Among the fundamental beliefs of Asian society were the doctrines of filial piety and an unquestioning respect for and deference to authority. Thus, the individual was expected to comply with familial and social authority, to the point of sacrificing his own desires and ambitions.

PARENT–CHILD INTERACTION

Clearly defined roles of dominance and deference based on paternalism virtually preclude any discussion and debate in a traditional Asian family. The role of the parent is to define the law; the duty of the child is to listen and obey. Communication flows one way, from parent to child. Directive messages predominate, and exchanges are generally brief and perfunctory. Constantly battered by prohibitions and orders, the Asian child begins to see himself as an obeyer rather than a director. The second generation of Asian American families no doubt has altered considerably this traditional family structure, but the configuration of the traditional parent-child interaction is basically unchanged.[5]

SELF–CONTROL

Asians generally are taught to respect all elders and to enhance the family name by outstanding achievement in some aspect of life, such as academic or occupational success. Conversely, an individual learns quickly

[4] See Ford H. Kuramoto, What Do Asians Want? An Examination of Issues in Social Work Education, *Journal of Education for Social Work*, 7:3 (Fall 1971); Harry L. Kitano, ed., *Asians in America* (New York: Council on Social Work Education, 1971); Ronald A. Kimmigh, Ethnic Aspects of Schizophrenia in Hawaii, *Psychiatry*, 23:4 (1960): Pei-Ngor Chen, Samoans in California, *Social Work*, 18:2 (March 1972).

[5] Edwin O. Reischauer and John K. Fairbank, *East Asia: The Great Tradition* (Boston: Houghton Mifflin, 1960), p. 33.

that dysfunctional behavior such as juvenile delinquency, unemployment, or mental illness, reflects upon the entire family. If he feels his behavior might disrupt family harmony, he is expected to restrain himself. Indeed, Asian culture values highly self-control and the inhibition of strong feelings.[6]

SHAME AS A BEHAVIORAL INFLUENCE

Seen from an Asian American point of view, individualism, with its emphasis on aggressive competition with those of any status, conflicts totally with traditional Asian respect for authority and filial piety toward parents and ancestors. Violation of that tradition almost inevitably leads to family tension and possible disruption. It is understandable, therefore, that if the Asian American is unable to acquiesce to the teachings and commands of family elders, he will suffer a sense of guilt and shame which colors his behavior, not only in his home but in his total society as well.

MIDDLE POSITION VIRTUE

In the training of children. Asian parents emphasize a social norm that cultivates the virtues of the middle position, in which an individual should feel neither haughty nor unworthy. In pursuing this norm, both the child and his peer group are held responsible for his actions. For example, a teacher, in talking to the misbehaving child about a given incident, will at the same time involve the entire class, making the child's destructive behavior a class problem that needs correcting for the sake of the group.

AWARENESS OF SOCIAL MILIEU

An Asian's consciousness of the welfare of the group also is related to his acute awareness of his social milieu, characterized by social and economic limitations and immobility. Thus, he becomes highly sensitive to the opinions of his peers and allows the social nexus to define his thoughts, feelings, and actions. In the interest of social solidarity, he subordinates himself to the group, suppressing and restraining any disruptive emotions and opinions. Moreover, an Asian American's compliance with social norms, which provides him with social esteem and self-respect, is so fundamental that even differences in wealth and social status are considered no excuse for deviation.

FATALISM

Fatalism, a calm acceptance of one's situation, also pervades the Asian American culture. Constantly buffeted by nature and by political upheaval

[6] See Karen A. Abbott, *Harmony and Individualism* (Taipei: Oriental Cultural Service, 1970).

over which he clearly had no control, the original Asian immigrant adopted a philosophical detachment and resignation that allowed him to accept what he perceived to be his fate with equanimity. Instead of trying to ascertain underlying meanings in events, the Asian met life pragmatically. He became adept at making the most of existing situations rather than attempting to understand and control his environment to create his own opportunities. It is unfortunate that this adaptability, the very factor that contributed to his original success in America, would later become a serious handicap; his continuing silence could only let him fall further behind the alien American culture that encouraged, and indeed demanded, aggressiveness and outspoken individualism.

INCONSPICUOUSNESS

Experiences with segments of American society which were racist further convinced the Asian immigrant of the need and value of silence and inconspicuousness. Fear of attracting attention was particularly acute among the thousands of immigrants who had come to America illegally to circumvent genocidal immigration laws designed to decimate the Asian American colonies by preventing formation of new ones and denying replacement members to established ones. If caught, these immigrants had little hope of justice; the California Supreme Court ruled in 1855 that their testimony was inadmissible as evidence.[7] Fear and distrust still linger today among the descendants of these immigrants. It is understandable why Asians are extremely reluctant to turn to governmental agencies for aid, even in cases of dire need.

Implications for Social Work Practice

In view of the potential suspicion and feelings of guilt and shame of the Asian American client who needs social services, initial social worker contacts with him require unique skills and a high level of sensitivity. Considering the Asian American client as an individual who may react differently to conflicts, and considering intra- and intercultural group differences, the worker should never let stereotypes cause him to assume knowledge of the client's needs and reactions without first consulting with him.[8] Instead, an open-minded attitude usually will be a key to opening up the client to reveal and discuss his problems. The following example illustrates this point:

[7] Lyman, *The Asian in the West.*

[8] See Man K. Ho, Cross-Cultural Career Counseling, *Vocational Guidance Quarterly*, 21:3 (March 1973).

The behavior of Mrs. C's son has recently been out of control. Mrs. C is a widow, an immigrant from a small village of Hong Kong, where the uncle usually assumes the role of disciplinarian when the father is absent. Without implying that Mrs. C should discipline her son, the worker simply asked her what solution she would suggest so that she would not continuously need to worry about her son's behavior. Upon realizing the unavailability of the uncle's assistance, Mrs. C suggested that she had to assume the disciplinarian role herself, for she could no longer endure the misery of continuously seeing her son disgracing her deceased husband.

An Asian American client who seeks social services is risking possible family rejection and ostracism from his own cultural group. A social worker, therefore, should ensure the confidentiality of his service. Moreover, he should capitalize on the opportunity to point out to the client the kind of strength which he possesses in seeking help and rehabilitation, and to assure him this action is congruent with keeping up his family's good name.

Being aware of an Asian American's expectation of clear role definition and pragmatic approach to problem solving, the worker can reduce client suspicion and resistance if, during the first interview, he openly relates to him the agency's services and functions, and the kind of assistance that he can expect. Further, he should be explicit in discussing his work relationship with the client, who is unaccustomed to functioning with ambiguity. Since generally it takes a great deal of change and effort for an Asian American client to become a social service recipient, the worker should not engage him prematurely in ambitious long-term services and goals. Instead, short-term service with concrete results usually is needed, at least during their first contacts. Then, through witnessing the tangible success of the worker's effort, the client can establish more trust and confidence, and engage in possible long-term services and goals. The social worker should be aware that the majority of Asian American interpersonal problems center upon family conflict and cultural marginality. As a result, treatment service which focuses on exploration of self-identity and fulfillment of self-esteem will have less meaning to the client and may actually enhance guilt feelings derived from his inability to subordinate his own desire to live harmoniously with his parents and peers.

Mr. B is a second-generation Korean high school student who experiences difficulty in getting along with his immigrant parents who violently object to his long hair. A worker's efforts in helping him to see that his need for wearing long hair has to do with his self-identity caused him to become more depressed and silent as he began to realize that he was satisfying his self-concept at his parents' expense. He withdrew from service after the first agency visit, clearly without having successfully resolved his conflict with his parents.

In view of Asian American client reluctance to admit to problems, suspicion concerning the use of social services, and frequent handicaps in the use of the English language, it is doubtful that the current practice of utilizing confrontative techniques and approaches (such as transactional analysis and Gestalt techniques) can produce effective results in working with this client group. Instead, a directive approach, with emphasis on humanistic attitudes and concrete service, seems to work more effectively.

Work with Families and Groups

Since admission of problems is seen as a lack of self-control, determination, and willpower, and as a family defect, open sharing of problems in a group is intolerable for most Asian American clients. Therefore, it is doubtful that the active intervention of a single worker who employs the traditional techniques of treating the family as a unit can be effective, because clients will feel that family problems and conflicts should be resolved within the family circle.

USING A MODIFIED GROUP APPROACH

Group work practice which conforms to the nuclear family and the extended family structure, however, can produce positive results.[9] The following example demonstrates the involvement of nonparental relatives, within the extended family structure, to achieve a modified group approach to disciplining children.

> Mr. and Mrs. T, a Samoan couple, had a great deal of difficulty in keeping their children from playing in the street. They would punish the children severely by locking them in the closet for a period of twenty-four hours if they were caught. Mrs. M, a relative of the family, discussed the situation with a social worker friend. The worker asked her to arrange a time when the T family could come to her house for tea. After the worker became acquainted with the Ts, he casually brought up the difficulty of rearing children in a strange land. The Ts became very anxious and turned to the worker for advice. The worker in turn referred them to Mrs. M, who revealed that her success in disciplining her children primarily consisted of discussing the situation with them. Times and ways had changed drastically since she was a child, and she was not sure the old way of disciplining was the best, she added.

[9] See Man K. Ho, Outreaching Approach to Counseling with Foreign Students, *Journal of College Student Personnel*, 15: 1 (January 1974); Chen C. Chang, Experiences with Group Psychotherapy in Taiwan, *International Journal of Group Psychotherapy*, 22:2 (April 1972).

A family treatment team consisting of a male, a female, and a child worker also can be effective in working with Asian families, as the following experience indicates:

L. C., an American-born Chinese and a junior high school student, experienced a great many learning difficulties. He habitually skipped school, and, as a result, was unaware of his homework assignments. Both of his parents were passive individuals who were confused by and ashamed of their son's behavior. Also, they were having severe marital problems and were striving to present a facade, pretending their marriage was on solid ground and that it had nothing to do with their son's failing in school.

L. C. was aware of his parents' problems and defensiveness, and took advantage of their vulnerability by indulging himself whenever he pleased. A family treatment team consisting of one male and one female therapist was quite successful in helping the parents to gain some insights into their problems and to communicate more openly and fully; attempts to resolve their son's school problem, however, were met with continuous resistance, especially from L. C. himself, who accused the treatment team of conspiring with his parents against him. With the permission of the family, a child worker, actually the same age as L. C. and a personal friend of the male therapist, was introduced as an additional member of the treatment team. When L. C. repeatedly blamed his parents' marital problems for his own problems, the child worker pointed out that his skipping school was a sign of "copping out" and that continuation of this activity would only bring him failure. "We all have problems, but we have ourselves to blame if we do not live up to our share of responsibilities," added the child worker. The child worker's intervention gradually lessened the guilt feelings of the parents, who later were able to better assume the limiting role in dealing with their son.

For treatment groups to produce therapeutic results, members are expected to confront each other openly from time to time. Such aggressive behavior, however, is looked upon as rude by Asian Americans, who are taught to respect and not to openly challenge others' views. Free participation and exchange of opinions in a group also contradict Asian values of humility and modesty.[10] "Don't be a showoff or engage in any behavior that smacks of being a braggart," is a common Asian admonition, and it is directly responsible for assigning Asian Americans silent-member roles in a group. The following dialogue explains why an Asian American prefers nonverbal participation in a group.

Mr. O was a thoughtful and resourceful member of the group, although he never volunteered his opinion without the worker's encouragement. The rest of the

[10] Royal Morales, The Filipino-Americans and Samoans, paper presented at the Los Angeles County Department of Public Social Services Executive Orientation, Affirmative Action Program, Los Angeles, California, August 17, 1970.

group members valued and listened to what he had to say. When Mr. O was asked for the reasons behind his frequent silences, he said that it is better to be quiet than to ramble on and say nothing or say something that is not well thought out; the talkative person is essentially an attention-seeking, narcissistic individual; besides, the more one talks, the more chance one would have of making mistakes by saying the wrong thing.

Group interaction requiring members to compete with each other will further alienate Asian Americans, who do not wish to be singled out as winners or as losers, both of whom are considered deviants from the Asian cultural norm. Instead, Asian American group members usually welcome participation in a group atmosphere that allows them the opportunity to share problems and help each other with them. The concept of mutual aid and reciprocity is so humanistic and so fundamental to Asian culture that group members operating in this fashion are no longer conscious of the cultural inhibitions and defenses previously prohibiting social worker intervention with their problems. Worker skill in leading a reciprocal group of Asian Americans is demonstrated in the following report:

> Long silences, which are usually indicative of group resistance, had plagued a group of Asian Americans. After one such silence, the worker commented that because he did not feel comfortable with the silence, he imagined the members generally felt the same way. He asked the members to identify what was happening so that more could be accomplished within the time allocated for group interaction. One member immediately said that he no longer could afford to waste time sitting in a group in which the members did nothing but stare at each other. He asked the worker if he could share with the group the reason behind his silence. Would that, he added, be answering the worker's concern? The worker thanked him and said that the members' input was most needed for the group to head in the direction that was most beneficial to all members.

A worker's application of reciprocal models or any other humanistic techniques in working with Asian Americans in groups should capitalize on the authority invested in him as a professional and as an agency representative.[11] Instead of letting the group be self-directive, the worker needs to be more assertive and structured, particularly in the beginning stages of group interaction. As the group becomes more cohesive and members become more supportive, the role of the worker should be less directive, because the true value of group process and the dynamics of the group as a whole should be able to flourish without worker manipulation. But worker inability to provide preliminary structure to the group will only

---

[11] For detailed description of reciprocal group work model, see William Schwartz, Toward a Strategy of Group Work Practice, *Social Service Review*, 36:8 (September 1962); Alan F. Klein, *Effective Groupwork: An Introduction to Principle and Method* (New York: Association Press, 1972).

enhance group member anxiety and ambiguity, unwelcome to Asian American clients.

Work with Asian Americans in the Community

Asian American avoidance in dealing with conflict presents a great handicap to the community worker who employs conflict as a means for effecting social change and community development. Therefore, it is imperative that the community worker never present himself to the Asian American community as an antagonist or troublemaker. Instead, he should exercise his sincerity to impress upon them his concern and real caring for their welfare. The worker will also find that he can win support from the community if he initiates programs that are small in dimension and sure of success. Since betterment of social milieu and concern for fellowmen is an accepted element of Asian doctrine and cultural consciousness, a community worker may use this element as a leverage point to mobilize collective effort in community action. The following case illustrates this point.

> At a meeting with residents who were concerned with the cleanliness and health problems of a Filipino neighborhood, the worker solicited the group's help by pointing out that, regardless of who was at fault for littering the neighborhood, the Filipinos usually were blamed. The area was identified as a Filipino neighborhood, and its physical appearance would not allow the Filipinos to deny that they were contributing to the problems. After a prolonged and heated discussion, the group finally realized that individual as well as collective efforts were needed to change the image of the neighborhood. By changing the image of the neighborhood the group felt that each member could "save face." The collective effort to "save face" was directly responsible for a cleaner and more sanitary neighborhood.

Cooperating with Community Leaders

A community worker should be cognizant of the power vested within the established group and family associations in the Asian community. Due to Asian American cultural tradition and social and economic immobility, leaders in Asian American communities tend to have a long history of occupying high positions, and they are usually sensitive to potential threats to their status and interests. Obviously, in working for social change it is essential that this power group, already accepted by the community, not be forgotten or bypassed. Even if the community worker is of Asian American descent, it is essential that he establish positive work relationships with and capitalize on the resources possessed by indigenous leaders: if not, he will only discover later that early winning of the leaders' support, rather than alienation, would have been a shorter route to the same goals.[12] An Asian American community will rarely be persuaded by a stranger to make any social change. The change would be too much opposed to tradition and attempts at bringing it about would create uncertainty and negative reactions, all of which could be avoided by involving the community's leaders at the outset in the change efforts.

Conclusions and Implications

The term "Asian American" encompasses many ethnic groups, each with intragroup differences; different individuals within each subgroup may react differently to certain conflict or crisis situations. Therefore, it is impossible for a social worker always to know exactly how to react to an Asian American client. As a result, it is necessary that the worker be willing to plead ignorance when necessary, to listen more carefully, to be less ready to come to conclusions, and to be more open to having his presuppositions corrected by the client. That is, he must want to know what the situation is and must be receptive to being taught.[13] Such an unassuming humanistic attitude is the key to working with Asian Americans.

Additionally, working effectively with the Asian American requires more than merely understanding his cultural background, his American experience, and his present problems. Most importantly, the worker needs to respect him as an individual first, and as an Asian American second. A worker who assumes that traditional Asian society is "primitive" and Western self-directed society is "modern" will be less likely to respect the Asian American as an individual. Respecting an Asian American as a worthy person with cultural differences simply means recognition of the fact that "yellow is not white and white is not right."[14]

Finally, recognizing the fact that yellow is not white has many other important implications, the most obvious being that social work practice knowledge based on white culture is inadequate when applied to Asian Americans. It also implies that there is a need for social work education to incorporate Asiatic culture content in its current curriculum. For Asian American social problems to be effectively ameliorated, there is a need to educate more Asian American social workers and to provide inservice training to agency staff who are currently working with Asian Americans.

---

[12] Chen, The Chinese Community in Los Angeles, p. 597.

[13] Alfred Kadushin, The Racial Factor in the Interview, Social Work, 7:92 (May 1972).

[14] Kuramoto, What Do Asians Want? p. 12.

CHAPTER 53

Initial Contacts with Mexican-American Families

Ignacio Aguilar

Schools of social work have, for the most part, been oblivious to the need for adapting methods of practice to minority groups. Rather they teach practice derived from a generic method that is dictated primarily by the majority. Yet much social work practice is carried out in the United States with minority groups and, too often, social workers apply it by a blanket method supposedly effective with all people.

Each minority group has its own problems and personality—derived from long-existing cultural and moral values, language, patterns of behavior, socioeconomic conditions, ethnic background, and many other factors. Social work practice in a minority community shows that besides the variations that must be made in the generic method to suit individuals, certain adaptations should be made in applying social work methods to the specific minority group.

During ten years' experience in a California community made up mainly of Mexican-Americans, the author learned from the people in the community how to adapt some of the key concepts and techniques of social work to the needs and the life-style of Mexican-Americans and how to avoid some common obstacles to the development of goodwill.

This article briefly outlines different cultural values and patterns of behavior—and barriers to assimilation in an alien society—which the social worker should consider in making initial contacts with Mexican-American families. How social work method was adapted in this initial contact phase in order to provide effective counseling is illustrated by a case example of work with a family in the author's community.

Reprinted from *Social Work*, Vol. 17, No. 3 (May, 1972), pp. 66–70, with permission of the author and the National Association of Social Workers.

Initial Contact

There is no doubt that one of the most important and difficult processes in social work is the beginning phase, that is, starting to work with a client. Green and Maloney describe this phase as one in which

> ... emotional interaction takes place. The worker focuses on an emotional engagement with a purpose, explores the possibilities of person(s), agency and worker finding a realistic *common purpose*. On the other hand, the client(s) naturally and rightly questions moving into a relationship with the worker.[1]

Since the first encounter determines the dynamics of the relationship and the kind and quality of the interaction between worker and client, a correct start is vital.

Awareness of differences, an understanding of why the differences exist, and experience in dealing with people of the specific minority group—all these are important to the social worker in establishing feelings of friendliness and confidence from the outset. Without them, a worker can unknowingly arouse antagonism or cause the client to withdraw in fear or confusion.

Patterns of Living

The social worker in a Mexican-American community finds that his ways of work are strongly influenced by the people's patterns of living, which differ in many respects from those of people having a Protestant Anglo-Saxon background. Consideration of concepts, attitudes, and patterns of behavior that are likely to have a marked effect on the beginning stages of social work method can help to assure that vital correct start.

The Leisurely Opening. When Mexican-Americans meet to negotiate or arrange affairs, the first step is to set the climate or *ambiente*. A preliminary period of warm, informal, personal conversation precedes the discussion of the concerns that brought them together. Jumping into the middle of serious and controversial affairs—as many persons in the United States are inclined to do—seems confusing and even discourteous to most Mexican-Americans.

Language. Language is, of course, one of the main problems in working with non-English-speaking people. How can a social worker help people if he cannot communicate with them? How can a common purpose be es-

---

[1] Rose Green and Sara Maloney, "Characteristics of Movement in Phases of the Social Work Relationship." Unpublished paper, University of Southern California, Los Angeles, 1963 (Mimeographed.)

tablished if that purpose cannot be discussed? How can a worker start where his clients are and proceed at a pace comfortable to them when he cannot even start at all? Obviously, for any social worker in a Spanish-speaking community, fluency in the language is a tremendous asset and for those dealing directly with clients it is a necessity—both for communicating and establishing rapport.

Attitude Toward the Law.   Having to deal with the law is considered shameful by the average Mexican-American family, and the family members are disinclined to accept it as a common practice. The social worker needs to reassure his clients that dealing with the law offers them an honorable way of protecting their interests and legal rights. He will also have to explain their relation to such persons as probation officers and the police and tell them about legal services available to them. Knowledge of the basic elements of the Mexican system of law, as well as the system in the United States, will enable him to interpret these subjects more intelligibly to his clients.

Influence of Religion.   Religion plays an important role in the Mexican-American home and shapes the lives of the entire family. As Heller notes:

> Some observers have reported that the church continues to exercise a strong influence in the Mexican-American community. For example, Broom and Shevky contend that "the church is the principal agency of cultural conservatism for Mexicans in the United States and reinforces the separateness of the group." They specify that they have in mind not only the parish organization of the Catholic Church but also the Protestant Missions "with their functional sectarian attributes." There seems to be little doubt that the "religious factor" (to use Professor Lenski's phrase) plays an important role in the rate of acculturation of Mexican Americans.[2]

Role of the Male.   The concept of the male in society and in the family is important to the understanding of the person of Mexican ancestry. It is not only a concept of philosophy, it is a way of life, quite different from the "American way of life." Paz describes the *macho* concept as follows:

> The ideal manliness is never to "crack", never to back down.... Our masculine integrity is as much endangered by kindness as it is by hostility. Any opening in our defenses is a lessening of our manliness.... The Mexican macho—the male—is a hermetic being, closed up in himself, capable of guarding both himself and whatever has been confided to him.[3]

[2] Celia S. Heller, *Mexican American Youth: Forgotten Youth at the Crossroads* (New York: Random House, 1966), p. 19.

[3] Octavio Paz, *The Labyrinth of Solitude*, Lysander Kamp, trans. (New York: Grove Press, 1962), pp. 29–31.

The traditional role of the husband and father in the Mexican-American family is explained by Heller, as follows:

> According to the traditional norms the husband is regarded as the authoritarian and patriarchal figure who is both the head and the master of the family, and the mother as the affectional figure in the family.[4]

The Extended Family.   To Mexican-Americans the extended family is of great significance in their pattern of living; they take it for granted that in time of trouble they can always count on the family to help out. Again quoting Heller:

> Not only in size, but also in organization the Mexican-American family displays an unusual persistence of traditional forms. It continues to be an extended type of family with strong ties spread through a number of generations in a large web of kinships. These ties impose obligations of mutual aid, respect and affection.[5]

Barriers to Cooperation

The social worker dealing with Mexican-Americans may well find that there are certain obstacles to be overcome before he can gain his clients' confidence and they can work together smoothly and effectively in endeavoring to solve problems. These obstacles may involve attitudes of other people with whom the Mexican-Americans associate or they may be related primarily to the clients' own attitudes.

Prejudice.   Unfortunately, in many sections of the United States Mexican-Americans—especially the families of poor and unskilled workers—are likely to encounter prejudice. This can occur within the community at large, can reach out to the children in school, and can even be found among persons in the helping professions.

Unfriendly or antagonistic feelings conveyed by insensitive people in positions of authority hinder the progress of such families in becoming assimilated and assuming responsibility. These families with limited financial resources and limited knowledge of English are likely to become the target of prejudiced individuals reluctant to help those who do not fit readily into the mold of middle-class American society. Too often, help is not offered at all. Or it may be offered in such a way that acceptance requires departure from familiar behavioral patterns. Indeed, prejudice in its purest and ugliest manifestations becomes one of the most common prob-

[4] Heller, op. cit., p. 34.
[5] *Ibid.*, p. 34.

lems the minorities face in their encounters with helping professionals. It can also be one of the social worker's greatest obstacles to building confidence.

The Strange System.   It is hard for the parents in a Mexican-American family to understand the "system" with which they have to deal as they endeavor to cope with their problems. It becomes in their minds a kind of hydra-headed creature, with authorities cropping up from all sides to make demands upon them and press in on their privacy. Yet these families have to learn how to deal with the system if they are to become active partners in the process of being helped. They have to learn how to exercise their rights and to assert their self-worth and esteem as human beings in a society they do not understand. As Hollis notes:

> This emphasis upon the innate worth of the individual is an extremely important, fundamental characteristic of casework. It is the ingredient that makes it possible to establish the relationship of trust that is so essential to effective treatment. From it grow the two essential characteristics of the caseworker's attitude toward his client: acceptance and belief in self-determination.[6]

For truly effective social work practice with minority groups, the social worker must learn as well as the client. Much more needs to be done in the way of teaching the uniqueness of the cultures of these groups to social workers and others in the helping professions if they are to provide worthwhile assistance to those who need the most help.

The following case illustration presents only the beginning stages in working with a typical family in a Mexican-American community in California. With further involvement, all other orthodox social work methods had to be modified somewhat in order to help the family fully.

CASE ILLUSTRATION

Family X is made up of the parents and three children: a girl 6 years old and two boys, aged 7 and 16. Mr. and Mrs. X were legally married at one time, but because of serious marital problems and pressures from Mrs. X's family were divorced three years ago. However, they managed to resolve their problems and came together again; the church never considered them divorced. The family lives in a small house in the back of a large empty lot that has not been taken care of properly. Weeds have taken over the majority of the land, so that they conceal the house.

   The probation department referred Family X to the community center because neither the father nor the mother were able to communicate in English. The probation officer explained that this family needed counseling and also

[6] Florence Hollis, *Casework: Psychosocial Therapy* (New York: Random House, 1964), p. 12.

"someone who could speak their language." The parents were unable to control their 16-year-old son, Freddy, who had been placed on probation for running away from home regularly.

Mrs. X had been told to call the center for an appointment. This might have been sufficient to start the helping process for an Anglo-Saxon Protestant family; for a Mexican-American family it was not. Not only was it difficult for the family to overcome the shame of having to deal with the law, but Mr. X—who made all the decisions—had been disregarded by the probation officer. It was decided that establishing contact was up to the center, on the assumption that this would be difficult or impossible for Mrs. X.

ESTABLISHING CONTACT

The director of the community center called Mrs. X, identifying himself in Spanish as a social worker who knew that her son had been in some trouble, and explained that the center was a voluntary not a governmental agency. It was suggested that Mrs. X ask her husband if he could come with her to the center. She agreed to do so and to call back later in the evening when her husband came home from work, adding, "It is good to talk to someone who can speak Spanish." The fact that Mrs. X had been asked to consult her husband about a conference for the two of them put her in a situation in which she did not have to decide on her own. Her husband was now involved in the decision-making.

A few days later Mr. and Mrs. X came to the center for the interview. True to Latin custom, the first hour was leisurely, the talk mainly about familiar things that they could comfortably share with the worker. Conversation centered about Mexico, where they had lived until about two years before. They shared information about their respective families and mentioned how difficult it was for them to get used to the American way of life. Here they had no close relatives nearby to whom they could turn when problems arose. It was disconcerting for them to have to bother people outside the family.

ALIEN SURROUNDINGS

It was no wonder that Mr. and Mrs. X were having a hard time, not only with their son, but with the society surrounding them, which was completely alien to them and highly threatening to their way of life. In their own little house at the end of the big lot, hidden by the growing weeds, they had found an island isolated from the outside world—up to the time that their son had gotten into trouble. But then they had to face the world, and it was difficult to understand and more difficult to be understood.

They were not pressed to talk about their son's situation in detail. They decided to come back the following day to talk about this problem after the probation officer had come to see them.

The purposes in mind for this first interview were accomplished: to meet Mr. and Mrs. X personally and to establish a comfortable relationship that would lead to a partnership once they were able to share their problems with the social worker. The next step would be to share a common purpose, in this case, helping Freddy.

Mr. X was included in the helping process from the beginning. Had he been left out, it would have meant that Mrs. X was assuming an improper role, that Mr. X was being put down by her, and that his role as head of the household plus his *macho* role were being jeopardized.

The following day Mr. and Mrs. X came a little late to the meeting and were reluctant to talk about their conference with the probation officer. Mr. X just kept silent, looking down. Mrs. X, red-eyed, finally said, "I am very ashamed. You should have heard what the probation officer said about us. He blamed us for all the troubles with Freddy and said that if we were not able to speak English we should go back to Mexico. Perhaps worst of all, our daughter heard all of this because she had to translate for us."

It was suggested that they arrange to meet the probation officer the next time at the center; there the social worker could translate for them and make the necessary interpretations. Thus the harmful effect of the probation officer's prejudices against them would be minimized. Mr. and Mrs. X were assured that they had certain legal and moral rights that had to be respected—among them the right to be treated as human beings. Major differences between the systems of law in the United States and Mexico were explained, as were the functions of the probation department and the role of its officers.

Mr. and Mrs. X then seemed somewhat relieved and looked less tense and fearful. Mrs. X thanked the social worker and, looking at her husband, said: "We are not ignorant and dumb. We just did not understand anything about what was happening."

This family is not unusual. Nor are its problems. Many families in minority communities are facing problems like these every day. The situations can be far more critical when compounded by illness and poverty. Preparing the social worker in advance to serve such families effectively—rather than leaving it up to him to learn on the job from the community—offers a challenge to the schools of social work.

CHAPTER 54

Interdisciplinary Approach in Work with Vietnamese Refugees

Daniel S. Sanders

The refugee problem, an increasing feature of the twentieth century, is a challenge to the conscience of nations and the world community. There have been different interpretations of the term refugee but the notion of an individual voting with his or her feet in the quest for freedom is a recurrent theme. The feature of voting with one's feet, is for the refugee, by no means a planned, orderly process. It is often a crisis situation, involving intense psychological and emotional conflicts, confusion and threat to personal life. A refugee in this sense who is uprooted from his or her home, has crossed a frontier, and seeks protection and sustenance from a government or authority other than his own.[1] Interestingly, in today's world, in some situations individuals may find themselves as refugees even in their own countries, especially in situations of protracted civil wars and secession of territory.

The Vietnamese Refugee Situation in the United States

The sudden influx of Vietnamese refugees uprooted from their culture and society and airlifted to the United States posed serious problems and challenged the ingenuity of all those who attempted to work with them in a helping role. However, to a nation consisting largely of immigrant and refugee people from diverse ethnic and cultural backgrounds—who came seeking freedom, hope, and opportunity to build new lives—the problems

Reprinted from *International Social Work*, Vol. 21, No. 4 (1978), pp. 10-15, by permission of the author and the publisher.

faced by Vietnamese refugees should not be insurmountable. An important feature of the Vietnamese human drama, the situation of being uprooted from Vietnamese culture and society, is the speed with which it unfolded.[2] In the initial phase, over 130,000 Vietnamese suffered through the same ordeal at a pace hitherto unprecedented. The recent Cuban migration was perhaps larger but it was spread over a longer period of time.

The rapidity with which the Vietnamese refugees with a markedly different race and culture entering American society for the first time in such a large number compounded the problems usually associated with refugee resettlement.[3] The culture shock experienced by people who spoke another language and who represented a non-western society is perhaps not comparable to anything encountered previously in refugee resettlement work. Their experiences were even more traumatic due to the fact that the initial contacts that they had an arrival were very often with the military and the immigration officials. To some extent the ordeal of processing on arrival and the bizarre series of steps taken were inevitable. Individuals had to submit themselves to photography for ID cards, people had to be finger printed for the first time in their lives, and they had to be issued meal cards and accommodated in temporary camps until satisfactory arrangements could be made for sponsorship. But would it have helped more if social workers, clergy, counselors, language specialists, health educators and others had access to the refugees from the outset? The position taken in this paper is that an interdisciplinary approach in work with refugees from the outset contributes more to effective refugee settlement.

The Significance of an Interdisciplinary Approach

Given the complexity of the refugee situation and the need for support services and resources in a number of areas such as health, education, social work, employment and legal services to mention only a few, the interdisciplinary approach of collaborative efforts on the part of several professionals crossing boundary lines to make a concerted attack on refugee problems becomes a vital necessity. It is an important consideration in both short-term and long-term efforts to deal with the refugee situation.

The interdisciplinary approach seems particularly useful in exploring new and difficult problem areas, in working with people of diverse racial and cultural backgrounds and in devising effective solutions to the many complex problems faced by refugees uprooted from their traditional society and exposed, as in the case of the Vietnamese refugees, to radically different cultural and socio-economic conditions. In discussing the interdisciplinary approach it should be pointed out that the mere arrangement of diverse professionals working side by side in their specific areas of expertise in refugee work does not necessarily constitute an interdisciplinary approach. There is need for much more drawing from each other's professional knowledge and skills in a collaborative effort to develop new strategies and solutions as necessary.

Professional workers in the human services area—including social workers—when confronted with complex problems related to special groups such as immigrants and refugees, are more likely to question some of the assumptions underlying traditional approaches to solving problems, to changing existing policies, and to devising new approaches and techniques in solving such problems.[4] The interdisciplinary approach seems particularly helpful when there is the need to effect institutional and policy changes in areas such as education, immigration and employment with a view to meeting the special needs of refugees. Educators, social workers, employment counselors, and lawyers could, for example, collectively utilize their resources and skills and exert pressure to open up the opportunity structure for refugees in areas such as education, vocational training, professional development, and employment.

In the field of child welfare, specifically adoption, for example, the collective efforts and resources of several professional groups was called for in Hawaii in effecting a change in adoption laws of the State to meet the needs of refugee orphan children from Vietnam. Initially the new parents of Vietnamese orphans in Hawaii were given guardianship by the Family Court but legal adoptions were not possible due to missing information on children's background and parentage. As a result of the collaborative efforts of concerned professional and citizen groups, a bill was passed by the State Legislature and signed into law by the governor, which introduced the necessary flexibility to meet the needs of refugee orphan children and paved the way for their full adoption. According to the bill if a child entered the United States under "extraordinary circumstances ... by reason of which ... the existence, identity and whereabouts of the child's parents, is not reasonably ascertainable ..."[5] then the consent of the child's biological parents is not necessary for the child's adoption. The only condition specified is that there should be a year's waiting period before adoption. This change in adoption laws to meet an obvious human situation was effected without too much delay due to the collective effort of interested professional groups and individuals.

Interdisciplinary collaboration should be a feature at different levels of intervention in the effort to resettle refugees. In addition to collaboration at the policy, planning and programme development level, it is also vital in the actual delivery of services, in providing the necessary psychological, emotional and social supports to the refugee child, for example, in the school setting or to the adult who needs vocational training to find his place in the world of work. It is highly desirable that interdisciplinary consultation and collaboration is provided from the very outset in refugee work. In a sense the success of the refugee settlement process is influenced by the nature of the initial contacts, the experiences in evacuation, in re-location, in camps and in the kind of early support services made available to the refugees. As the two-person study team from the National Institute of Mental Health pointed out, the quality of the refugees' initial contacts most likely influence their perceptions of the new environment and creates either a positive or negative disposition toward satisfactory adjustment in the future.[6] It is vital, therefore, that from the inception of a refugee pro-gramme there are professionals such as language specialists, teachers, so-cial workers, anthropologists, doctors, psychiatrists and public health specialists, who along with military and immigration officials, are involved in plans for refugee evacuation and resettlement to make the programme as humane and effective as possible by drawing on their combined knowl-edge, skills and experience.

The interdisciplinary approach in work with refugees becomes even more important when the language and cultural differences such as those encountered in work with Vietnamese refugees are taken into considera-tion. The social worker would be in a better position to work out a plan of action with the refugees for their betterment, whether at the individual and family level or at the community and institutional policy level, if there is the opportunity to collaborate as necessary with a language specialist, anthropologist, educator, and health specialist, to mention only a few.

The development of a plan of action to support the Vietnamese refugee family may necessitate interviewing Vietnamese refugees who could be reached only through the language specialist; the plan may necessitate tak-ing note of the cultural traditions and beliefs among Vietnamese people which the anthropologist may help to understand more fully; additionally, specific aspects of the overall plan may involve skills in family planning techniques with which the health specialist may be most competent to deal. Given the refugees' experiences of language difficulty, culture shock, feel-ings of anxiety and conflict between deeply held value preferences and beliefs of the past and the newer values and cultural patterns to which they are exposed on arrival, the interdisciplinary approach of different professionals working collaboratively across boundaries, taking note of cultural differences, value conflicts and preferences in providing help seems vital.

Social workers come into contact with refugees in both the immediate and long-term efforts to resettle them. In both types of efforts the situation of cultural differences between the worker and the refugees, and between the refugees and the host society become key considerations. The social worker should be alert and sensitive to cultural predispositions, differ-ences in value positions and the reality of value conflicts in interactions and efforts to help refugees. Efforts should be made to identify both strengths and limitations in the value preferences, family patterns and tra-ditions of the refugees, to go beyond the disposition to look for problems merely because of the cultural differences, and to avoid the tendency to stress individual adjustment to the neglect of environmental change.[7]

Social workers' experience with immigrant groups indicates that there are social and economic pressures which stand in the way of accepting the "stranger" as an equal, especially if his or her racial and cultural background seems different.[8] This may well be operative in the case of the refugees—despite the initial sympathy and concern—especially if their language and culture patterns are very different. In the case of the Vietnamese refugees, for example, the fact that they arrived in such large numbers at a time when the country was experiencing an economic recession with obvious impact on the employment situation may have contributed to some mixed feelings and resentment on the part of the general population. This might be more so due to their cultural and racial difference and their "strangeness."

Social workers need to address themselves to this situation realistically and with sufficient self insight and understanding as to their own possibly ambivalent feelings. First of all the tendency to stereotype the refugee's culture should be avoided at all costs. The practitioner should also be alert to the possibility of labeling the behaviour pattern of the refugee as pathological when in point of fact it may be, in the context of the refugee's culture, positive adaptive behaviour aimed at reducing anxiety and helping to cope with the problem. It is also necessary to recognize the fact that social workers themselves—no matter how hard they may attempt to deny this—may at times share in the prejudices and resentments of the population toward immigrants and refugees.[9] An honest acknowledgement of this possibility and an openness to learn from the seemingly strange culture of the refugee may be the starting point of an effective helping role.

This is not to deny the serious conflicts and problems that individuals and families from another culture are likely to experience when they are uprooted from their society and are exposed to new sets of norms, traditions and culture patterns. They may experience a condition of "anomie" where there is at least temporarily a lack of certainty about norms and values, and doubts expressed about the legitimacy of their earlier rules of conduct.[10] The social worker could with integrity and good judgment help the refugees to become comfortable with new norms and adapt, to the extent necessary, to differing cultural practices and traditions. In this process of facilitating adaptation, the social worker should be sensitive to possible pressures in the new environment that may contribute in some instances to the refugees throwing overboard deep seated elements of their culture that are positive and vital to their cultural identity. Alternatively, the refugees may in the face of undue threat to deeply held cultural values and practices react very defensively and negatively. Changes in cultural patterns, attitudes, and practices would inevitably mean pain and conflict for the refugees and the social worker's role in facilitating the positive changes necessary for effective functioning in the new cultural environment cannot be minimized.

Considerations in Future Refugee Work

In discussing considerations in future refugee work it will be helpful to draw from the lessons of the current experience in work with Vietnamese refugees and to explore some critical questions. How effective are immediate crisis-oriented interdisciplinary efforts in work with refugees? How are conflicts and tensions between immediate and long-range concerns among professionals with diverse orientations resolved? What is the potential for long-term interdisciplinary collaboration in refugee work? These and other questions need to be explored.

In refugee work the vital necessity for immediate action to respond to the crisis situation cannot be overstressed. The extent of human suffering and confusion demand prompt attention. Crisis-oriented interdisciplinary efforts could make an important contribution in meeting the immediate needs of the refugees. But it is necessary to develop a long-term plan of action and resettlement, even as crisis-oriented efforts are under way. There are bound to be tensions and conflicts between professionals of different orientations as refugee operations make conscious efforts to move from the initial phase of rescue efforts and treatment, to long-term considerations such as education, professional reaccreditation, employment and housing. The medical personnel whose contribution in the crisis phase is crucial have a significant contribution to make in developing long-term resettlement efforts as well. It is important that doctors, nurses, educators, social workers, employment counselors and housing specialists function as colleagues in a combined effort. Interdisciplinary effort whether long-term or short-term should be based on collegial relations and team effort. No one discipline profession should dominate the programme efforts.

As mentioned earlier, the interdisciplinary team effort in work with refugees becomes vital when there are language and cultural differences that are likely to be encountered in work with refugees. The social worker is in a better position, given his or her educational preparation and experience of work with people in a helping role, to develop an effective plan of action involving the refugees themselves, to understand their likely value conflicts and to avoid the tendency to stereotype their behavior patterns, if there is the opportunity to collaborate as necessary, for example, with the language specialist, the educator or the anthropologist.

Another important factor in future efforts at refugee work is the development of well coordinated short- and long-term plans, involving public and voluntary agencies. A concerted approach especially at the national level involving both governmental and voluntary agencies with policies and programmes designed to have a positive impact cannot be minimized. Similarly, at the state level, state agencies such as the Department of Education, the Department of Public Welfare, the Department of Health, and interested voluntary agencies should be involved from the very outset in collaborative efforts to resettle the refugees.

It is noteworthy that voluntary agencies have continued to play a key role in the humane and effective resettlement of refugees. The goal of helping refugees to become productive and contributing members of society cannot be pursued effectively without voluntary agency support increasingly in the future. It is also necessary to harness the support of other special groups such as mass media, citizen groups, and especially the refugees themselves in efforts to help them to take their rightful place in the new society. For a basic consideration in the success of the effort to help refugees become productive and contributing members of society is their acceptance by the general population and a deeper and more sustained understanding of the refugee's predicament by the public.

Notes

1. Elfin Rees, "The Refugee Problem: Joint Responsibility", *The Annals*, May 1960, Vol. 329, p. 17.

2. C. J. McNaspy, "The New Faces at Fort Chaffee", *America*, Feb. 1976, Vol. 134, No. 5, p. 96.

3. See U.S. Senate, Committee on the Judiciary. *Indo-China Evacuation and Refugee Problems—Part IV* (Staff report, 94th congress, 1st session) (Washington, D.C.: U.S. Government Printing Office, 1975).

4. Juliet Cheetham. *Social Work With Immigrants* (Boston: Routledge & Kegan Paul, 1962), p. 172.

5. "War's Children, One Year Later", *Honolulu Star Bulletin*, April 27, 1976.

6. "Warning Sounded on Rise in Refugee Culture Shock", *Honolulu Star Bulletin*, July 18, 1975.

7. Daniel S. Sanders, "Dynamics of Ethnic and Cultural Pluralism: Implications for Social Work Education and Curriculum Innovation", *Journal of Education for Social Work*, Vol. II, No. 3, 1975, p. 98.

8. Juliet Cheetham. *Social Work With Immigrants*, p. 3.

9. *Ibid.*, p. 12.

10. *Ibid.*, p. 84.

SOCIOECONOMIC CLASS

CHAPTER 55

Casework and Social Class

Florence Hollis

Students of social-class phenomena have observed that many persons follow a life style that is characteristic of the particular socioeconomic class to which they belong. If this observation is valid, caseworkers should attempt to answer two questions. To what extent are differences in life style of major importance for casework among people of different socioeconomic classes? The second question goes further and can be stated more specifically: To what extent is it true that a person who is impoverished needs a kind of casework that is basically different from the kind needed by a person who has an adequate income? Before presenting some of the data available that may help us to find answers to these questions, I should like to call to mind the concern that social workers—family caseworkers, in particular—have traditionally shown for low income and impoverished families and to emphasize the fact that service to these families continues to be a responsibility of family service agencies.

A Long-held Commitment

The wave of concern now being felt in this country for those who are not sharing in our general prosperity, who are underfed, shabbily clothed, and poorly housed, is reminiscent of the spirit of the early and middle 1930's, when a cure was sought in social reforms that were primarily economic in nature. Social workers viewed the mass unemployment of those years chiefly as the result of failures in the economy. We constantly fought the

Reprinted from *Social Casework*, Vol. 46 (October, 1965), pp. 463–471, by permission of the author and the Family Service Association of America.

opinion so often expressed by comfortably employed and employing citizens that "people are too lazy to work"; and we sought to show that, except for a small minority who were socially disturbed, the phsycially fit unemployed would gladly return to work as soon as work became available. Moreover, we were insistent that, until work was available, adequate financial assistance had to be provided so that families could live in decency. The validity of our point of view was amply sustained by the events of the late thirties and the war years, when public assistance rolls shrank to a small fraction of their former size and thousands of persons, previously classified as completely unemployable, again became wage-earners.

Today we are again aroused by the problem of poverty, as automation, migration, lack of education, and other factors combine to prevent full employment of our potential labor force. More jobs there must be; but the new jobs will be different from the old ones, and workers must be provided with the skills needed to fill them. The school drop-out is the symbol of the new concern, associated as it is with delinquency and unemployability, rooted as it is in conditions that are derived from the very fact of poverty itself.

Obviously social work is not a complete answer to the problem of unemployment. Overcoming this social ill will require the efforts of many disciplines, but social work does have work to do with the individuals who have been victimized by joblessness. Although personal problems are not a major *cause* of unemployment, they often are the end *result* of the social deprivations and pressures brought about by the poverty created by unemployment. Once these poverty-induced problems have become imbedded in the individual, employment alone can no longer cure them.

Within the social work sphere, casework carries the major responsibility for direct work with individuals and families grappling with the day-by-day realities of life without an adequate income. Dealing as it does with both the individual environment and the individual personality, casework alleviates some of the pressure of poverty, on the one hand; on the other hand, it attempts to undo, or to help the individual overcome, the damage his personality has suffered from years, or even a lifetime, of grinding and humiliating deprivation.

This obligation to the victims of poverty has been recognized by casework ever since its beginnings. But despite the widespread recognition among the casework leaders of the thirties of the need for casework services in public assistance,[1] in most states relatively little emphasis was subsequently placed upon the training of graduate caseworkers for the public assistance field. This was in contrast to the situation in child welfare, where the Children's Bureau had long been able to give leadership to the devel-

[1] Elizabeth H. Dexter, "Has Casework a Place in the Administration of Public Relief?" *The Family*, Vol. XVI, July, 1935, pp. 132–37; Rosemary Reynolds, "Do We Still Believe Case Work Is Needed in a Public Relief Agency?" *The Family*, Vol. XIX, October, 1938, pp. 171–77.

opment of adequately trained personnel. Today the aspirations of the public welfare workers of the early thirties are about to become a reality. The current push for the expansion of income-maintenance programs on an insurance instead of a "needs" basis and for the long-needed simplification of eligibility procedures will increase the opportunities for providing casework service under public auspices and so increase the demand for professional skill in working with low-income families.

Family caseworkers in voluntary agencies are also deeply engaged in serving low-income families. In the past thirty years casework service to middle-income clients has greatly expanded. Its value to persons above the poverty line has been demonstrated, and caseworkers have developed a methodology particularly relevant to problems of personal and interpersonal adjustment. But the family agency's extension of its service to middle-income clients by no means signifies that it has abandoned casework with low-income families or work with practical problems. Problems of personal and interpersonal adjustment are not a monopoly of middle- and upper-income clients. The poor have psychological problems too! Although family agencies vary in the socioeconomic make-up of their caseloads, a survey made up by the Family Service Association of America showed that, in 1960, 72 per cent of the clients interviewed and 67 per cent of those who had five or more interviews were in the lower or lower-middle class. The lowest socioeconomic class (the group which approximated the population designated as Class V in the August Hollingshead two-factor index of social position) accounted for 43 per cent of all clients interviewed and 37 per cent of those who had five interviews or more.[2] Clearly, the family agency is deeply involved in serving the economically deprived.

Confusions About Class Differences

Turning now to the question concerning social class differences in life style and their significance for casework, I should like to comment on some of the confusions inherent in this subject. The first confusion is the result of lumping together—as if they were all the same—multiproblem families, hard-to-reach families, and impoverished families. Although there is considerable overlapping of these groups, they are by no means identical. Reports of the St. Paul study of multiproblem families indicate that more than 25 per cent were above the public assistance income level and that 53 per cent functioned above the marginal level in economic practices. Furthermore, 64 per cent functioned above the marginal level in their relationship

[2] Dorothy Fahs Beck, *Patterns in Use of Family Agency Service,* Family Service Association of America, New York, 1962, p. 26, supplemented by a memorandum, August, 1964.

with the worker.[3] Similarly, many low-income families are not multiproblem families, nor are they all hard to reach. Countless low-income families can use casework service, once it is made available to them, with no more difficulty than can financially secure families. Their problems are augmented by their poverty and consequent pressing, practical problems, but they are not *necessarily* hard to reach.

The second confusion about the matter of class differences arises when low-income families are erroneously viewed as a homogeneous cultural group. It is easy to recognize that within this group are found many older persons and families, reduced to poverty by illness or óther misfortune, who really belong to the middle class by virtue of their educational level and their previous employment. After these segments are eliminated, however, the term "culture of poverty" is sometimes used to refer to the ways of life of clients whose incomes approximate the level of public assistance or are even less—and many non-public-assistance families fall in this group—who have not finished high school, who are able to do only unskilled work, and who are, often, members of "female-based" families.

It is frequently claimed that persons in this latter type of low-income family tend to lack motivation for self-improvement, to feel that their lives are controlled by fate rather than by their own efforts, to prefer present to future gratification, and, therefore, to be uninterested in long-time planning. They are supposed to be "expressive" in the sense of acting out feelings and emotional needs rather than controlling them, to have a poor time sense, to project the blame for their troubles on external forces, to be unable to express feelings in language or to comprehend abstractions, to have no belief in the value of talking as a way of solving problems or straightening out feelings, and so to be inaccessible to what is called "traditional casework."

In actual fact, how much homogeneity is there in this low-income, poorly educated, vocationally unskilled group? In it can be found first- and second-generation families from many ethnic backgrounds; old American families—white, Negro, and Puerto Rican—who have recently migrated to the city from rural areas; and families that have lived in the same general area for three or more generations. These families also vary widely in religious affiliation, in family structure, and in education. The educational gap between the illiterate or barely literate individual and the high-school dropout is surely as great as that between the high-school graduate and the holder of a graduate degree.

And to what cultural influences will these different kinds of low-income families be exposed? All will be influenced to some degree by the

[3] Ludwig L. Geismar and Beverly Ayres, *Families in Trouble*, Family Centered Project, Greater St. Paul Community Chest and Councils, St. Paul, Minnesota, 1958, p. 48; Ludwig L. Geismar and Beverly Ayres, *Patterns of Change in Problem Families*, Family Centered Project, Greater St. Paul Community Chest and Councils, St. Paul, Minnesota, 1959, p. 39.

dominant middle-class culture. They will be influenced by the values and customs of the blue-collar working class of which they are a part. They will be influenced by the values and customs of their parental families if these differ from their own culture and by the values and customs of any subgroup that they themselves may comprise.[4] Robert Merton, Lloyd Ohlin, and Richard Cloward hold very persuasively that a significant portion of juvenile delinquency in low-income families is caused by one aspect of this fact—that is, by the conflict between the high aspirations youngsters have assimilated from middle-class culture and the meager opportunities available to them for realizing these aspirations. There is every reason to believe that many, many low-income, poorly educated individuals do not share a common "culture of poverty." Hylan Lewis and Camille Jeffers stress the diversity found among lower-class individuals in the Child Rearing Study in Washington, D.C.[5] In the Stirling County study it was found that there was "more diversity than consensus ... and ... a tendency ... toward isolated behavior and unpredictability."[6] Richard Slobodin says of Upton Square, "individuality and idiosyncrasies of character flourished there as they do not at present in conformist middle-class society."[7] In work with low-income families we must steer clear of any tendency to stereotype. Stereotyping can lead to undue discouragement, unwillingness to perservere, the offering of even less service than the client can use, and even abandonment of the willingness to try to help at all.

The Effects of Persistent Poverty

At the same time that we resist the temptation to stereotype, we should be alert to any data that can add to our understanding of either the personalities of low-income persons or the situations by which they are con-

[4] For similar points of view, see William L. Yancey, *The Culture of Poverty: Not So Much Parsimony*, a paper based on research sponsored by the National Institute of Mental Health, Grant No. MH-09189 (unpublished); Jerome Cohen, "Social Work and the Culture of Poverty," *Social Work*, Vol. IX, January, 1964, pp. 3–11.

[5] Hylan Lewis, "Culture, Class and the Behavior of Low-Income Families," a paper given at the Conference on Lower Class Culture, New York, N.Y., June 27–29, 1963, sponsored by the Health and Welfare Council of the National Capital Area, Washington, D.C. (unpublished); Hylan Lewis, "Child-Rearing Practices Among Low-Income Families," *Casework Papers, 1961*, Family Service Association of America, New York, 1961, pp. 79–92; Camille Jeffers, "Living Poor," a report for restricted circulation, Child Rearing Study, Health and Welfare Council of the National Capital Area, Washington, D.C. (unpublished).

[6] Charles C. Hughes and others, *People of Cove and Woodlot*, "Stirling County Study of Psychiatric Disorder and Sociocultural Environment," Vol. II, Basic Books, New York, 1960, pp. 394–95, cited by Lewis, "Culture, Class and the Behavior of Low-Income Families," *op. cit.*

[7] Richard Slobodin, " 'Upton Square': A Field Report and Commentary," Child Rearing Study, Health and Welfare Council of the National Capital Area, Washington, D.C., 1960, p. 13, cited by Lewis, "Culture, Class and the Behavior of Low-Income Families," *op. cit.*

fronted. Material based upon participant observation is particularly valuable when combined with psychological understanding. Caseworkers are beginning to join sociologists in studies of extremely deprived families. Louise Bandler, in her report of the South End Family Program in Boston, describes work done with thirteen extremely deprived Skid Row families.[8] The mothers in these families were virtually children, competing with their own offspring as if they were siblings; their households were completely disorganized; the parents were so inarticulate that they literally did not have words for their emotions, or knowledge of abstraction, or even such fundamental knowledge as why a baby cries.

The workers in this program found that they could visit these clients without an invitation and that if they returned regularly, chatted in a neighborly fashion, and offered help with practical problems when they could, they would be allowed to stay. They might then have the chance to demonstrate that a baby stops crying more quickly if someone feeds him, changes his diaper, turns him over, or picks him up than if he is yelled at or hit. Gradually the workers learned that even these little-girl mothers wanted to do better by their children than they themselves had been done by; that the mother yelled at the baby and hit him partly because she actually did not know why he was crying or what else to do and partly because the crying made her feel so bad—so inadequate in the care she was giving her child.

Both experience and study show that long-time poverty results not only in actual deprivation of food, inadequate and shabby clothing, crowded and run-down housing but also in illness or at least depleted energy, a strong sense of inferiority or lack of self-esteem, and often a great sensitivity to criticism, even though this sensitivity may be overlaid by defensive hostility, denial, and projection. The client who is the victim of persistent poverty is often discouraged to the point of being chronically depressed. He almost surely has underlying resentment, anger, and disbelief that the caseworker—a well-dressed, healthy, well-educated member of the middle class—can respect him or be relied upon to help him. Motivation and aspiration are often not absent; but disappointment after disappointment and frustration after frustration may have forced him to bury his hopes for himself—if not for his children—so that he will no longer be vulnerable to so much pain. Jeffers has observed a cycle in the aspiration level of low-income families: the unrealistically high goals of early life are replaced by discouragement, embitterment, and apathy, except for the hope that the children will succeed where the parents have failed.[9]

---

[8] Louise S. Bandler, "Casework with Multiproblem Families," *Social Work Practice, 1964*, Columbia University Press, New York, 1964, pp. 158–71.

[9] Jeffers, *op. cit.*

Oversimplifications Concerning Poverty

Much has been made in recent years of the failure of the middle-class worker to understand the ways of the lower-class family. The implication has been that caseworkers seek to impose their own middle-class values and goals inappropriately on the lower-class client. Perhaps the sheer size of the problem of helping these families and our frustrations at the slow progress we have made have led us to do some scapegoating of our own. Perhaps we have created an easy victim by accusing the middle-class worker of imposing his values on lower-class clients. If this does, in fact, occur, it is indeed an error. But an even greater error is the more subtle one of failing to see the aspirations and motivations—the craving for liking, respect, and help—that may lie beneath the client's hostile, couldn't-care-less, touch-me-not exterior. (We should remember, too, the months of hard work that sometimes are required to overcome the resistance of the economically secure client.)

Guilt, too, can be underestimated or not perceived because we are accustomed to look for certain behavioral signs more common to the middle class. Deborah Shapiro's preliminary study of illegitimacy among girls of different classes and racial backgrounds indicates that both the parents and the children in low-income Negro families share in the general cultural disapproval of bearing children out of wedlock.[10] The sense of alienation, or anomie, so often cited as prevalent in low-income groups may well be due, in part, to the real lack of group-accepted, internalized norms of conduct that make the individual's behavior predictable to himself so that, in a sense, he knows himself as a stable entity. But it may also be a reflection of his lack of self-esteem—a lack induced partly by the attitudes of others and partly by his own dissatisfaction with his inability to achieve the goals he has set for himself.

It must always be kept firmly in mind that a family's life style is influenced not only by the amount of its income but also by its ethnic background and religious affiliation, the educational level of its members, its place of residence (urban or rural), and—perhaps more than any other factor—family structure. The fatherless, or "female-based," family—or, to put it another way, the family in which the father's relationship is tenuous—is found so frequently in the low-income group that our observations of the behavior that appears to be characteristic of this type of family structure often color our conclusions in regard to the total group. (It is estimated that this type of family makes up about 40 per cent of the lowest income group.) Much of the behavior of adolescent boys in these families seems traceable to the effort of the growing boy to escape the domination of his

[10] Deborah Shapiro, *Social Distance and Illegitimacy: A Report of a Pilot Study,* Columbia University School of Social Work, New York, 1965.

mother by identifying with an exaggeratedly aggressive and tough ideal of masculinity. The significance of this factor of family structure and behavior, as contrasted with economic differences, was highlighted in a recent study of twenty adolescent boys who were making a poor adjustment to school despite their having superior intelligence. Richmond Holder and Edliff Schwaab found that these boys had been cared for in early life by parent substitutes; their mothers were dominant in the home but preoccupied with affairs outside the home; they had too little contact with their fathers; they had a negative feeling toward education, a sense of futility and indifference toward their own future work, a lack of motivation, a desire for success by magical means, a poor self-image, an orientation to pleasure-seeking, and a lack of impulse control.[11] Without doubt these boys would have been school dropouts had they not been the children of *wealthy* parents suffering from an overdose of *affluence*.

The Old and the New

Having answered the first question by citing a number of characteristics commonly found in persons who have been subjected to poverty over a long period of time—but which are by no means absent in other strata of society—we can now turn to the second question. To what extent do such differences as do exist point to the need for a different kind of casework for people from different classes? Those who feel strongly that casework with low-income families is different often speak of "traditional casework" and characterize it as a form of psychotherapy designed for verbal, well-motivated, middle-class neurotics. To anyone truly knowledgeable about modern casework, this description has a curiously nostalgic but hollow ring. Where, oh where, has the middle-class neurotic gone! It is true that the middle-class client does not find the office interview by appointment the same kind of obstacle to getting help that the low-income client may find it. But is the ceremony of an office interview the essence of casework? As a matter of fact, it is only in the child guidance clinic, the mental hygiene clinic, and the family service agency that private interviewing rooms are the prevailing mode. Even in these agencies, much that proved so disconcerting about the home interview of a few years ago is no longer so troublesome, as the use of joint and family interviews has increased. As one of my students put it, "Why should it be harder for the caseworker to listen to the turned-on television set of the resisting, home-visited client than to the weekly intellectualizing of the resisting, office-appointment

[11] Richmond Holder and Edliff H. Schwaab, "The Impact of Affluence on the Personality Functioning of Adolescent Boys in Treatment," a paper delivered at the Annual Meeting of the American Orthopsychiatric Association, New York, March, 17–20, 1965 (unpublished).

client?'' Resistance may take different forms in different classes, but it certainly is not unknown in work with economically secure people.

Earlier in this article reference was made to certain characteristics of casework practice with the low-income family—the use of the home visit, the worker's persistence in visiting even when the family seems to be resistive, the need to overcome the client's initial distrust partly by ''doing for him'' rather than relying wholly on the verbal handling of the resistance. Practical problems certainly play a larger part in work with disadvantaged families than they do in casework with those who are economically secure. There is a greater need for actual demonstration and for giving information. The importance of the worker's maintaining an accepting, noncritical attitude in order to overcome the client's lack of self-esteem and lessen his inner feelings of guilt and unworthiness cannot be overestimated. The worker must refrain from counterattack when the client's hostility bursts through and must avoid challenging the client's defenses except under special circumstances, for example, with certain types of acting-out delinquents. Over and over again the literature stresses the critical importance of these familiar components of casework practice in work with the low-income family.

A few ingenious new techniques and new combinations of familiar procedures have been devised recently. Rachel Levine has reported the worker's use of games, arts, and crafts during the home visit as a means of observing the family members' behavior patterns and of teaching, by demonstration, less destructive and hostile ways in which they can relate to one another, the use of words instead of acting out to settle differences, and so on.[12] Frank Riessman advocates role-playing and other game-like devices and suggests the use of ''helper therapy'' as is now done by Alcoholics Anonymous and similar organizations.[13] Indigenous homemakers and home teachers have been used as an adjunct to the treatment process at Mobilization for Youth in New York City. This organization has also established neighborhood service centers through which emergency help can be given and from which referrals for more sustained service are sometimes made. Riessman also recommends that service be available in the evenings and during week ends.

Another facet of casework with the low-income client, which is frequently mentioned in the literature, is the importance of accepting him for service at the point of crisis. Waiting lists are particularly inappropriate for this group. Moreover, the likelihood that the client will be reached and held in treatment is thought to be significantly greater when he is assigned directly to the worker who will be responsible for the case. A change of

[12] Rachel A. Levine, ''Treatment in the Home,'' *Social Work*, Vol. IX, January, 1964, 19–28.

[13] Frank Riessman, *New Models for a Treatment Approach to Low Income Clients*, Mobilization for Youth, New York, March, 1963)unpublished).

workers after the first interview should be avoided. It is widely recognized that what Riessman has called "anticipatory socialization" will usually be necessary: the client will have to be gradually aided to understand how talking can help, that there is something he can do about his own situation, and that the worker has no magic but that by their talking together ways can be found to make life somewhat better. This process is often equally necessary with the middle-class client!

Much has been made of the difficulty of the worker's finding the right words to use with the low-income client, particularly in the discussion of feelings. There are, of course, some clients with whom this is truly a problem. Most workers report, however, that if they use simple, everyday English, they have no difficulty. Intellectualization and the use of technical language is helpful with neither lower-class nor middle-class families.

How Basic Are the Treatment Modifications?

In the foregoing discussion we have been noting certain techniques and styles of working that seem to be particularly useful in the casework treatment of low-income families. Do these techniques and styles constitute a brand of casework that is entirely different from the "standard brand"? Or are they only relatively minor variations? In discussing this question of methodology, I should like to refer to my own recently developed classification of casework procedures.[14] In this classification distinction is first made between direct work with the client himself and work in the environment on the client's behalf. Direct work with the client is then subdivided into six major sets of procedures, the first four of which also apply to environmental work:

1. Sustaining procedures in which the worker shows interest in the client and acceptance of him, and, by making reassuring comments, tries to increase his self-confidence or decrease his anxiety
2. Procedures of direct influence in which suggestions, advice, and sometimes admonition are given in an effort to guide the client's behavior
3. Exploration and ventilation

The next three types of procedures deal with communications involving three types of reflective consideration:

4. That pertaining to current person-situation interaction
5. That pertaining to the dynamics of response patterns and tendencies

[14] Florence Hollis, *Casework: A Psychosocial Therapy*, Random House, New York, 1964, Chapters IV, V, VI, and VII.

6. That pertaining to early life factors of developmental significance to present ways of functioning

Indirect work—that is, casework with others on the client's behalf—makes use of the first four of these sets of procedures and an additional one, the mobilizing of resources.

Practically everything the worker does in the traditional casework treatment process can be classified under one of these headings. Different client problems and different personality diagnoses call for various blendings of these procedures and various emphases. If this classification is applied to casework with low-income families, what do we find?

First, we certainly find that environmental treatment—indirect work—is of very great importance. Here the worker must exercise resourcefulness, persistence, and ingenuity; he must be skillful in working with other social agencies and knowledgeable about both agency and nonagency resources. He must often work with other persons on the client's behalf; and though the contact may be of short duration, an interview with such a person calls for skill in all the procedures used in direct work with the client, with the exception of dynamic and developmental understanding. Furthermore, legwork as well as telephone work is essential. Over and over again it has been demonstrated that the initial building of the relationship with the client in the economically hard-pressed group is greatly facilitated by skillful environmental work. Be it noted, however, that environmental work is also of great importance with children and older people and with many seriously disturbed clients with or without a good income.

In direct work with the client, it seems quite clear that the client of low income with little education usually needs a large measure of *sustainment*—comparable, in fact, to the amount needed by the depressed or extremely anxious or guilty client in the better educated, economically comfortable group. The need for sustainment has been stressed over and over again in the material produced by workers who have been concentrating on casework with the low-income client. He is often highly distrustful of the caseworker, and if his self-esteem is low and his fear of criticism pronounced, he will need a very large measure of the expression of interest and concern, of respect for him and his abilities, and of the worker's desire to help him.

Much of the literature also emphasizes that this client more often needs *suggestions and advice* than do others. To a degree this may be true, but the worker must carefully assess whether or not a particular client really does need this approach. The low-income client is often quite capable of thinking about himself and his situation if the worker sticks close to the realities of life and to the client's true concerns, and if he uses words that are simple and expressive. If the client does, indeed, need suggestions and advice, the worker must be sure that his standing with the client is on firm enough ground to make his advice acceptable—to say nothing of the fact that it must be advice well attuned to the client's values and circumstances.

Exploration may sometimes proceed at a slower pace than with the more verbal, better-educated client. But once the low-income client's confidence has been established, he is likely to speak freely, particularly of feelings of anger and frustration, sometimes directed against the worker himself. The worker's acceptance and understanding of these feelings, combined with his continued interest in the client and his nonretaliation, will go a long way toward establishing a firm relationship.

As with the middle-class client, when the low-income client is able to think things through for himself, it is preferable that he do so. Simplicity of language and slowness of thought should not be mistaken for incapacity. As with most clients, whatever their income, in reflective discussion the emphasis will often be on understanding practical problems, understanding other members of the family, and foreseeing the outcome or effect of the client's own ways of acting and handling things rather than on intrapsychic understanding. The client's learning to see reality clearly, and thinking of what to do about it, often occupy the major part of his interview time. In this process, the worker may have to take more initiative in giving information, explaining, and demonstrating than would be necessary with the better-educated client.

In the worker's use of demonstration his clarity about what is to be conveyed and his careful judgment about the right time for transmitting it effectively to the client are based on the same knowledge that underlies his use of the verbal procedures through which the client is led to greater understanding in other forms of reflective consideration. Moreover, it should by no means be assumed that the low-income client does not need to, and is unable to, understand his own feelings; the way in which he responds to the environment; and those happenings in his daily life that touch off his feelings. Poor education is not synonymous with low intelligence, and simple ways can be found to express fairly complicated ideas if the worker has enough ingenuity to devise them.

It is probable that the caseworker makes less use of procedures designed to encourage reflective consideration of dynamic factors in the personality and factors of developmental significance when the client has had little education, but these procedures are not entirely ruled out. As a matter of fact, contrary to popular impressions, caseworkers make relatively little use of these procedures, even with the middle-class client. Some of the doubts expressed about the appropriateness of "traditional casework" for low-income families reflect a gross misunderstanding of the nature of present-day casework treatment; it should not be confused with psychoanalytic psychotherapy, which is practiced by psychiatrists. Casework is noted as much for its emphasis on environmental and supportive work as for its techniques of clarification and experiential treatment. In all its various procedures special emphasis is given to the value of a warm, accepting relationship as both a supportive and a corrective experience for the client. The caseworker's attempts to effect personality change are limited to specific modifications of the client's ego or superego that can be brought about through an understanding of conscious and preconscious content, through a corrective relationship, and, under certain circumstances, through environmental changes. Casework does not attempt to effect a basic reorganization of the client's personality through his gaining insight into deeply buried experiences. The emphasis of present-day casework is on helping people to deal with their immediate problems, to understand others better, and, when appropriate, to bring about limited but highly important changes in their ways of functioning and, therefore, in their personalities. For many low-income people these are by no means impossible goals.

Summary

There are, indeed, differences between casework with the average low-income, poorly-educated client and casework with the average middle-income, well-educated client. But these are differences in specific techniques and in emphases rather than in basic casework *method*. Work with impoverished families involves the use of all the procedures valued in work with more advantaged groups. In addition, it requires the use of certain innovations or modifications of traditional techniques—for example, demonstration and role-playing, which have heretofore been used chiefly in work with children and with borderline or recovering schizophrenics.

In trying to understand clients of low income, we must beware of the stereotype. They differ from one another fully as much as do clients in the middle class. At the same time, we must be sensitive to the effects of grinding deprivation, of poor education, of being devalued in a status-minded society, and often of growing up in a fatherless family in a neighborhood where opportunities for crime abound and opportunities for reaching the goals to which their membership in American society leads them to aspire are very, very scarce.

We must also guard against depriving these clients of the opportunity of receiving adequate casework help by our holding stereotyped and erroneous preconceptions about their limitations. The caseworker trying to help impoverished families needs not only all the skill in both diagnosis and treatment that he needs in work with other types of families but also great ingenuity, resourcefulness, flexibility, and patience. Above everything else—as the work of Overton, Henry, Wiltse, Fantl, Cloward, Riessman, Bandler, and many others has amply demonstrated—he needs to have faith in the possibility that the client is capable of change and a deep desire to help him do so.

Acknowledgments

I should like to acknowledge the contributions of three students—Rosalyn Lowenstein, Alice Schmacher, and Mary E. Woods—to the content of this paper. Their term papers were of distinct value for both information and ideas.

CHAPTER 56

Family Treatment of Poverty Level Families

Ben A. Orcutt

Poverty is both an objective and subjective phenomenon. Objectively, there is too little income to provide adequately for basic needs. Subjectively, the inability to meet needs and expectations is shrouded with emotion and may be felt differentially, depending on life-style and exposure to affluence. The increase in modern technology, wide availability of goods, and powerful advertising serve to stimulate the desires and expectations of people; however, those who are chronically poor may be so enmeshed in a struggle for survival that hope and expectations become blunted.

Poverty is currently measured by a poverty index centered around the economy food plan developed by the United States Department of Agriculture, and reflected in changes in costs of living. The Bureau of the Census,[1] in 1975, identified as poverty level: an income of $5,038 or less for a family of four for the year 1974. Regardless of how poverty is measured, however, it has a depressing and erosive effect on individuals and families.

It is reported that 25.5 million Americans are living on submarginal incomes.[2] Of those persons sixty-five years old and over, about 4.3 million (22 percent) were below the low income level. In addition, statistics reveal that 12.6 million persons below the poverty level were living in families headed by a male and there were 5.5 million related children under eighteen years of age in these families. Further, 7.8 million persons were living

[1] U.S. Bureau of the Census, *Statistical Abstract of the United States*, 96th (Washington, D.C.: U.S. Government Printing Office, 1975), p. 399.

[2] U.S. Bureau of the Census, Characteristics of the Low Income Population, 1971, *Current Population Reports*, no. 86 (Washington, D.C.: U.S. Government Printing Office, 1972), pp. 4–30.

Reprinted from *Social Casework*, Vol. 58 (February, 1977), pp. 92–100, by permission of the author and the Family Service Association of America.

below the poverty level in families with a female head, in which there were 4.8 million related children under eighteen years of age. It is clear from these statistics, that a great number of submarginal families have a male head, which suggests relatively intact, but struggling families.

This article describes the poor family with multiple deficits in relational processes in which socioenvironmental conditions are so impoverished that interaction at the market place is limited. It is important to emphasize that all poor people do not have social, psychological, or relationship problems, but being poor greatly increases one's vulnerability. Florence Hollis warns of the fallacy of lumping together the so-called multiproblem, hard-to-reach and impoverished families.[3] Although there may be overlapping problems, many low-income families are not multiproblem or hard to reach. It seems advantageous to identify poor families who may be poorly functioning in many areas of their lives as those with multiple deficits. It is this author's intent to underscore the need for social work concern with these families, who experience multiple concomitant deficits; problems, of poor and crowded housing, health problems, relationship difficulties, family break-downs, delinquency, addictions, and so forth. All of these problems mean pain and frustration for the individual, the family, and the larger society.

Helen Harris Perlman writes dramatically of experience with poor people in the Washington Heights and the Harlem areas of New York City, where she learned the lesson

> that a long repeated experience of being dead-poor, disadvantaged, stigma-tized, closed off from the common good, a chronic experience of deficits of means, resources, opportunities or social recognition, will cut down the hu-man spirit, constrict its capacities, dwarf or debilitate its drives. I became ag-onizingly aware of how details of everyday living may add up to a massive, overwhelming sense of defeat, frustration, and anger, and of how, then, to maintain social relationships and carry daily tasks, all the energies of the ego must be used chiefly to cover over, hold back, defend, protect. Yet even in this squalid jungle there were here and there those persons, young or old, whose thrust and ability and determination to beat the devil—to study, to help the kids look forward to a better day, to hold on to a job and "make it"—leaped forth as affirmations of life and hope.[4]

Perlman is cautioning that the conscious strivings and energies of the ego must be reached for in the human being. It is imperative that the family and the environmental strengths be supported for change.

In the multiple deficit families, structural organization may be char-

---

[3] Florence Hollis, Casework and Social Class, in *Differential Diagnosis and Treatment in Social Work*, rev. ed., Francis J. Turner, ed. (New York: The Free Press, 1976), pp. 552–64.

[4] Helen Harris Perlman, *Perspectives in Social Casework* (Philadelphia: Temple University Press, 1971), p. xviii.

acteristically loose, inefficient or conflictual, and dependency generationally perpetuated. The parent as the primary agent of socialization may have never learned cognitively or affectively what he needs to teach or to be a parent to children. Inadequate learning and self-image tend to be generationally perpetuated. Ivan Boszormenyi-Nagy and Geraldine Spark emphasize that children can be used as an arena to rebalance the parent's own unfair exploitation; underlying abusive behavior toward their children may be unresolved individual and marital conflicts, which derive from negative loyalty ties to the family of origin.[5] Shirley Jenkins' research also notes the pain and despondency of the neglectful parent when his child needs to be placed.[6] Evidence is mounting that direct intervention must be multifaceted in order to serve families undergoing multiple stresses.

All foci of the social work practice system—social policy, planning, organization, and the direct services to individuals, families, and groups—must be utilized to alter poor environmental conditions and to foster the growth potential of these families. This article is focused, however, on four major propositions important to the task of mobilizing direct social services efficiently to aid this target population. First, a major effort must be made by social agency systems to reach the multiple deficit, dysfunctional family in need. Second, intervention must address the transmission of generationally perpetuated problems. Third, intervention strategies must be carried out in combinations to include four foci: the individual, the nuclear family, the family of origin, and the representatives of the interlocking community agencies. This step requires individual and conjoint sessions with a coordinated plan of action identified and participated in by the clients and the interlocking agencies with which they are linked. The final suggestion involves planned follow-up of treatment with accountability for service located with a central agency to provide an open door in the event of future insurmountable stress.

Danuta Mostwin's model of short-term multidimensional family intervention covers many of these aspects in its unique approach to dealing with the stress and magnitude of family difficulties in individual and family sessions that may include the additional participation of other agency workers.[7] This idea can be further expanded through agency commitment, organization of service patterns, a combination of individual and family group strategies, and maintenance of a followup and open-door policy.

---

[5] Ivan Boszormenyi-Nagy and Geraldine Spark, *Invisible Loyalties* (New York: Harper & Row, 1973), p. 300.

[6] Shirley Jenkins, *Filial Deprivation and Foster Care* (New York: Columbia University Press, 1972).

[7] Danuta Mostwin, Social Work Interventions with Families in Crisis of Change, *Social Thought*, 2:81–99, (Winter 1976) and Mostwin, Multidemensional Model of Working with the Family, SOCIAL CASEWORK, 55:209–15 (April 1974).

Outreach to Families

In regard to proposition one, a concerted, organized pattern of identifying and reaching vulnerable families that enables and stimulates their mutual participation in a change process will be acceptable to them and is required for any substantial change. The unit of attention must be the family as it transacts with the systems of its environmental space.

Families who are alienated from the larger community and have become locked into a lifestyle fraught with poor tolerance of frustration, weak controls of rage or sexuality, self-defeating relationships, who have parents functioning as siblings, and who are prone to acute crises in their lives, pose special problems for growing children. The White House Conference of 1970 reported that in 1968, approximately 10 percent of the fifty million school age children had moderate to severe emotional problems.[8] This statistic does not imply that all of these children came primarily from families of lower socioeconomic status, but the magnitude of the problem deserves attention. The family must be viewed systemically, with its transaction to all linking systems assessed, for interventions to enhance the restorative exchanges with the environment for the individual and family.

Virginia Satir points out that it may well be that the family system is the primary means by which individual internal dynamics are developed. From Satir's observations of families where there are symptoms or problems, the rules of the family system do not totally fit the growth needs of its members in relation to survival, intimacy, productivity, and making sense and order, for all of the family members who are parts of the system.[9] Salvador Minuchin and Lynn Hoffman, as well as others, graphically describe the structural dysfunctioning in the family, which may or may not be multiple deficit, of cross-generational coalitions that tend to maintain, detour, or perpetuate marital conflicts, or that prevent normal growth and separation.[10] The emphasis in family intervention is on restructuring boundaries, shifting and delineating role tasks, and dealing with the dynamics of the relationship system that lock in the scapegoated or problem member. Actions are stimulated that will maximize family competence and self-confidence with the expectation that structural and relationship changes, supported by environmental changes, will indeed move the family to a new and more functional equilibrium.

Changes in family functioning are complex, especially when there is a

---

[8] James K. Whittaker, Causes of Childhood Disorders: New Findings, *Social Work*, 21:91–96 (March 1976).

[9] Virginia Satir, Symptomatology: A Family Production, in *Theory and Practice of Family Psychiatry*, ed. John G. Howells (New York: Brunner/Mazel, 1971), pp. 663–64.

[10] Salvador Minuchin, *Family and Family Therapy* (Cambridge: Harvard University Press, 1974); and Lynn Hoffman, Enmeshment and the Too Richly Cross-Joined System, *Family Process*, 14:457–68 (December 1975).

parental life pattern of self-defeating behavior with few positive environmental resources, nurturance, and stimulation. Motivation and hope can be difficult to achieve. Intervention must be massive to unleash family adaptive forces for change. Althouh social work must serve families from all segments of society, the social worker must emphasize innovative direct services to help the impoverished who suffer multiple deficits, especially in their environment and in their interpersonal relationships. Advocacy and negotiation of environmental resources and services to reduce the frustration and deprivation must be as high on the helping scale as the intrafamilial, interpersonal relationship dimension. The social worker must reach out to link the family with every possible systemic input that can transmit new energy, knowledge, information, and emotional relatedness into the family system.

Attuned to the impact of environmental transactions, Ross V. Speck and Carolyn Attneave, through social network intervention, use the massive, relational environment for nurturing, growth, and healing.[11] They report network intervention in which as many as fifty friends and relatives of a patient may be assembled for intensive sessions of discussion, interaction, and psychodynamic exploration. In these sessions the difficulties experienced by the patient and his family are discussed and dramatized within the larger network, which itself goes through several distinct stages and where successful changes may occur.

Second-Generation Problems

The second proposition concerns the finding that dysfunctional families tend to reflect transmission of problematic behavior and adaptive patterns originating in their families of origin. The relationships over three generations must be assessed and the intervention processes must include the three generations.

Murray Bowen asserts that a certain amount of immaturity can be absorbed by the family system and that large quantities may be bound by serious dysfunction in one family member. The family projection process focuses on a certain child or children and may leave others relatively uninvolved. Bowen notes, however, that there are other families where the quantity of immaturity is so great, that there is maximum marital conflict, severe dysfunction in one spouse, maximum involvement of children, conflict with families of origin, and still free-floating immaturity. The mechanisms that operate outside the nuclear family ego mass are important in determining the course and intensity of the process within the nuclear family. When there is a significant degree of ego fusion, there is also a bor-

[11] Ross V. Speck and Carolyn Attneave, *Family Networks* (New York: Pantheon Press, 1973).

rowing and sharing of ego strength between the nuclear family and the family of origin.[12]

Boszormenyi-Nagy and Spark postulate that the major connecting tie between the generations is that of loyalty based on indebtedness and reciprocity.[13] Loyalty ties and the forms of expression may be a functional or a dysfunctional force connecting the generations. The person remains deeply committed to the repayment of benefits received; the struggle for all adults is to balance the old relationship with the new and to continuously integrate the relationships with one's early significant figures with the involvement and commitment to current family relationships.

Of the voluminous literature describing multiple deficit, loosely organized, low-income families, none is so poignant with regard to generational immaturities as the descriptions of Louise Bandler on the North Point Family Project in Boston.[14] The parents' immaturity and inability to exercise even minimal skills in maintenance of daily routines in the home, in care and discipline of children, and in interaction with the outside community were striking. It was common for one-parent mothers to parentify the older child, assume a sibling position, and reflect the deep unmet dependency needs that stemmed from their own parental deprivation. Bandler speaks of the mothers' relationship to and nurturing of their children as being so affected by their own pressing needs that they could not distinguish them from the needs of their children, even when their children's needs were urgent. When the parent's own affective development and learning has been greatly impaired by a depriving social environment and parental failure of dependable, consistent, nurturing objects, it is predictable that immaturity will abound with deep dependency needs, feelings of resentment, anger, inadequacy, and low self-esteem. The needs and loyalties in the conflictual family relationships diminish family strengths for coping and must be addressed.

Combination of Intervention Strategies

The third proposition, to repeat, states that intervention targeted to the family unit must be a combination of sessions with the individual, conjoint nuclear family and family of origin, and community agencies. These four foci must be balanced in regard to the use of a modality that can address itself to: (1) the parent's and child's individual need for nurturance and growth; (2) the family systems' communication, structural, and role defi-

---

[12] Murray Bowen, The Use of Family Theory in Clinical Practice, in *Changing Families*, ed. Jay Haley (New York: Grune & Stratton, 1971), pp. 177–78.

[13] Boszormenyi-Nagy and Spark, *Invisible Loyalties*, pp. 216–24.

[14] Louise Bandler, Family Functioning: A Psychosocial Perspective, in *The Drifters*, ed. Eleanor Pavenstedt (Boston: Little, Brown and Co., 1967), pp. 225–53.

cits and the scapegoating mechanisms that have become patterned or supportive of myths and collusions within the family; (3) the inclusion of the family of origin to deal with destructive patterns or loyalties that are transmitted and to strengthen whatever positives that can be enlisted for growth; and (4) the conjoint meeting of the linking agencies and family to weave a massive, coordinated effort toward new goals and change. The coordinated agency sessions with the family are of the highest importance, for the family system then becomes more thoroughly integrated in a positive way with linking services and social resource systems. Hypothetically, if the individual and family sessions are agreed upon to be carried primarily by the social worker in the residential treatment center where the child is placed, the child welfare, probation, or related agencies involved would also plan together in family sessions a course of action that supports the major goals. When the child can be returned from residential treatment to the home, new plans for continuation and followup should emerge, depending on the case situation. In this example, the responsibility and accountability would be carried by one agency—the residential treatment center—for the major treatment role with the collaboration and additional service input of linking agencies. As growth and change occur, the collaborating agencies should continue with the family to locate the central responsibility of the helping service.

Need for Followup

High risk families require followup at intervals and a central resource for help when stresses become insurmountable. Too often their ties to the agency have not been strong enough to stimulate their reapplying for help in times of stress and they lose the gains they had made. The four steps outlined above should substantially improve the family's social functioning and their capacity to anticipate and deal with stress, reducing the self-generated crises that bring the families to agencies at the time of stress and that allow a dropping out when the crisis subsides.

It has been observed that seriously impaired families do not always use a crisis approach effectively. For example, Naomi Golan suggests that:

> While they manifest the overt symptoms of urgency, disordered affect, disorganized behavior, and ineffectual coping, closer examination shows that underneath the superficial appearance, the basic character structure reveals severe and chronic ego depletion and damage. The crisis appearance involved is not a reaction to the original hazardous event, but a maladaptive attempt to ward off underlying personality disturbance or even psychosis. While such persons, often classified as borderline personalities or character disorders, may need help in emergencies, they do not seem to be able to engage in the crisis res-

olution work involved in learning from earlier experiences and in developing more adaptive patterns.[15]

With coordinated and masive input, learning can occur that will make possible some shifts in the social functioning of immature families.

In such families, a family service agency might well be the central agency among the collaborating agencies which maintains the open door for help and periodic followup, especially when there are growing children. Margarat B. Bailey's findings in the Alcoholism Inter-Agency Training Project conducted by the staff of the Alcoholism Programs of the Community Council of Greater New York reported that regardless of whether the alcoholic was referred to a special agency such as an alcoholism clinic, to a mental health clinic, or to another service, it was imperative for the family agency making the referral to retain the locus of treatment.[16] Otherwise, the sensitive alcoholic tended to fall through the cracks between the services. This situation is quite analogous to the multiple deficit family or a severely impaired family.

With the overburdened staff of social service agencies, including the correctional, mental health and medical facilities, is there sufficient time for the suggested followup, collaboration, and location of central responsibility? In the long run, it would be more economical for resources to be used massively and in a coordinated way during periods of stress. Depending on the needs of the family, substantial improvement in the family system equilibrium could be predicted with this kind of consistent help and strengthening of their coping powers to handle their predicament when threatened.

It has been more than twenty years since the Report of the Family Centered Project of St. Paul, Minnesota.[17] It reported that 6 percent of the city families accounted for 77 percent of its public assistance, 51 percent of its health services, and 56 percent of its adjustment services in mental health, corrections, and casework. The striking fact was that many of these families were known to a range of agencies during chronic periods of crisis, but coordination in agency services and resources was not sufficiently integrated to insure improvement in the family system's equilibrium. Today, families are still divided among agencies without sufficient attention to the transactional processes within the family, the agencies, and the social environment that could be coordinated for change.

---

[15] Naomi Golan, Crisis Theory, in *Social Work Treatment*, ed. Francis J. Turner (New York: The Free Press, 1974), p. 442.

[16] Margaret B. Bailey, *Alcoholism and Family Casework* (New York: New York City Affiliate, National Council on Alcoholism, 1974), p. 189.

[17] Alice Overton, Katherine H. Tinker and Associates, *Casework Notebook Family Centered Project* (St. Paul, Minn.: Greater St. Paul Community Chest and Councils, 1957).

Illustration of Need for Intervention

The following case illustration highlights the need for the strategies indicated—focus on a family unit with a growth-inducing individual relationship, conjoint sessions of the nuclear family with the family of origin, and the agency service network. Formed groups could also be used as appropriate. Exemplified in the following is the fact that coordinated efforts with clients can bring change in a family in which there is severe psychological damage and where overt rage and child abuse are generationally perpetuated.

James, an eight-year-old, white, Catholic boy of lower socioeconomic advantage was referred for residential placement because his mother was considered emotionally disturbed and unable to handle him.[18] James ran away from home taking his younger brother, Jerry, aged five, with him. James frequently set fires in the home and in the community. He was also enuretic and his school attendance was poor.

Mrs. A, James's mother, was a twenty-eight-year old divorcée who received an Aid to Families with Dependent Children grant. She resided with her younger son, Jerry, in a five-room apartment in the central city. James was born out of wedlock when Mrs. A was seventeen. His father disappeared before his birth and his whereabouts were unknown. Mrs. A's mother would not permit her to keep the child so that she was forced to relinquish James to foster placement, where he spent the first twenty-one months of his life. She later married and while pregnant with her second son, Jerry, she was able to regain possession of James. She was separated from her husband soon after the birth of Jerry and eventually divorced him, because he was serving a sentence in the penitentiary. Since her divorce, she had dated several men and just prior to James's placement in residential care she was jilted in an affair of several months' duration.

James was placed in residential treatment to provide him with a consistent environment of warmth, acceptance, and discipline. Initially, he had great difficulty adjusting to the environment: disrupting his class by manipulating fights between others and running away from school, his cottage, and the treatment center. When his mother and brother visited him, he would go into wild temper tantrums when it was time for them to leave, and the early visits precipitated his running away.

Initially, it was extremely difficult to engage James in regular treatment sessions; he was hostile, resentful, and frightened. His home environment included inconsistent, abusive, and seductive mothering coupled with neglect. His punishment for misbehavior was severe and cruel. For example, following a fire-set-

[18] The author is grateful to Thomas J. Ciallelo, student at Columbia University School of Social Work, New York, New York, for the case illustration.

ting episode, Mrs. A would punish him—first, by holding an extinguished hot match against his hand; second, by burning him with a lighted match, and third, by holding his hands over a lighted stove. One time he was badly injured.

Mrs. A readily admitted that she had tormented James with a knife, urging him to stab himself to prove that he was a man. When he had failed to do so, she dressed him in girls' clothing to make fun of him. This act was a frequent punishment which she had used when James argued or disagreed with her. When questioned, she seemed unable to grasp the potential danger of her act, with its psychological implications.

On another occasion, it was reported that because James forgot to remind her to turn off the gas when cooking and the food burned, she knocked him unconscious. When he came to, she did allow him to lie down and rest for several hours. Mrs. A admitted to beating him severely and said that at times she thought she might kill him.

In contrast to her loss of control when enraged, Mrs. A spoke in loving terms of her children and openly demonstrated affection for James on her visits to the treatment center. She said she missed him very much, that he would often sleep with her, and that they were a great comfort to one another. She brought him gifts and books, showed pride in his reading ability, and encouraged his education. She also brought construction toys, which he liked.

The disturbed mother-child relations described here bear close relationship to the mother-grandmother relationship and to the larger family constellation in which Mrs. A was reared and continued to be actively involved. Mrs. E, Mrs. A's mother, also lived in the central city with her fourth husband and two teen-age sons. One of these sons was Mrs. A's natural brother and the one person in the family for whom she felt some closeness. He was a narcotics addict.

Mrs. E's treatment of Mrs. A as a young girl bore similarity to Mrs. A's treatment of James. For example, Mrs. E had disciplined Mrs. A for wearing a short skirt to school by forcing her to strip naked and sit on the steps in the hall outside their tenement apartment for other tenants to observe. In relating this incident, Mrs. A said, "No wonder I started to act like a whore; she made me feel like one."

Mrs. A spoke of having tried suicide several times. She had seen several psychiatrists and was once hospitalized. She had also been seen intermittently at an outpatient psychiatric clinic in the city. Its records indicated that she had been placed in a parochial children's home at age six after stabbing her father and attempting to kill her mother. She had also received psychiatric treatment at age nine, age fifteen through seventeen, and again as a young adult in the city hospital. Mrs. A related details of attacking her husband with a knife for intimating that she behaved like her mother.

Mrs. A and her family of origin have a history of impulsive violent outbursts and fights. However, their ambivalence and distorted loyalties compel them to seek out one another repeatedly. At the time of one of these violent episodes, a family life space session was held on the spot to evaluate the situation. During the session, which was full of arguing and shouting, a pattern emerged of the belittling and scapegoating of Mrs. A by her own family.

From the above material, it can be observed that three generations of disturbed family relationships are characterized by inadequate nurturance and weak control of rage. As communication with Mrs. A's own family was characterized by harsh violence, inconsistency, and ambivalence, so she related to her own children. In the early sessions she appeared to be a rebellious adolescent and at the same time was in strong competition with her mother for possession and control of her own children. Her relationships with men were marked by abandonment, disappointment, and failure. Her role as healthy mother-father for her two children has been distorted and generational boundaries crossed as she alternately seduced and aggressively rejected her son James. However, because she had been the scapegoat in her family of origin, James, who was split off from the family in infancy and represented her bad self, came to serve the same role within the nuclear family.

Over the years, attempts were made by various agencies to help Mrs. A but no consistent change was noted. She reached out by attending a few individual therapy sessions at a local mental health clinic, but then would discontinue. A homemaker was once sent by the bureau of child welfare to assist with care of the home and children, to teach her more consistent methods in child rearing, and to free her to utilize her skills as keypunch operator. She was unable to follow through. The evidence was clear that while the grandmother openly encouraged these interventions on her daughter's behalf, she also undermined their success with interference and criticism. There was no purposeful plan to work with the family of origin. In addition, Mrs. A's caseworker at the bureau of child welfare reported being so overloaded with cases that she could not adequately support and assist her in her efforts.

The worker described Mrs. A clinically as having a severe borderline disorder. Individual interventive sessions, where Jerry was generally present, attempted to strengthen her grasp of reality situations and anticipation of consequences and to increase impulse control through learning and identification in a dependable relationship and through active tasks and limits so as to experience achievement and to relieve stress. It was hoped that order and routine in the home could be accomplished. These sessions were laborious and trying in the beginning as Mrs. A lashed into tirades blaming her mother and step-father for interference in her life and in the care of her children. She condemned the bureau of child welfare worker for failing to maintain contact with her or to assist her with care of Jerry or job placement; she blamed the residential treatment center for giving her double messages and keeping James away from her. At the same time, Jerry would run wildly about the house grabbing food from the table, smashing toys, and hitting at the worker. Mrs. A would attempt to reprimand him verbally, but when this procedure failed she would hit him and threaten him with punishment "by you know what!" without clarifying what she meant. She would seem to restrain herself from harsh discipline during the interview as the worker utilized the situation to discuss dealing with Jerry and his multiple health problems. Mrs. A. talked of taking him to the hospital but criticized the doctors for incompetence and lack of action. She blamed the bureau of child welfare worker for not helping her follow through with the out-patient clinic appointments for him. In due course, however, her anger and projections began to subside as she worked in individual sessions with the young male social worker. Gradually she began to accept some responsibility for her own actions.

As the work progressed and the worker checked the validity of her claims against the bureau of child welfare and the mental health clinic, he arranged with Mrs. A to have an interagency meeting for the purpose of clarifying their assistance on her behalf and for Jerry. Problem-solving also included the issue of home visits for James.

The worker helped Mrs. A to expand her understanding of James's needs as they toured together the campus of the center and visited James's teachers, child-care staff, religious instructor, and other involved personnel so that she, as a parent, could get first-hand reports on his adjustment and progress.

On one such occasion, she returned to her individual session and began to speak of her current personal problems with her family of origin. She became very emotional and tearful and began to consider why James had had to be placed; however, in the beginning she was not able to connect the consequences to her own behavior. She could only see James as the problem (running away and setting fires) and being interfered with by her mother.

Confrontation to help her begin to see her own responsibility brought further tears, evasion, and an attack on the worker and the institution for giving her a run-around and keeping her from her son. However, her worker moved to a more supportive approach; he communicated his belief that she sincerely loved James, that James had expressed love for her, but that James was very frightened of her.

She responded thoughtfully that she believed James feared her because at times, when she was in a bad mood or was extremely nervous, she had punished him too severely for not obeying her. She quickly added that she had recently changed her method of punishment from physical beatings to having him kneel on the floor with his arms outstretched, as she had been punished by a teacher in her youth. This discussion was the first time that she could consider alternate methods of punishment and consequences and could begin to use concrete suggestions. Later, she brought out that she thought James's fearfulness was also connected with his witnessing much physical violence between herself and her mother and her ex-husband.

Once Mrs. A had made the above disclosures and shared these insights, she was helped to draw further connections between her severe treatment as a child and her present handling of her own children. Family treatment sessions with Mrs. A, her children, and her family of origin were not held. However, the destructive intergenerational ties, modeling, and scapegoating can be seen. Conjoint sessions could increase their ability to detach and reduce the destructive hostile-dependent indebtedness. Any strengths and family supports could then be more easily mobilized.

Individual sessions were equally important with James. The worker tried to meet James at his emotional level by using play in the treatment sessions and to interact with him at his cottage setting. In play James was initially cautious in inviting the worker to join in his games and creative activities. He enjoyed immersing his hands in globs of brown paint and smearing them over paper. He seemed to look for disapproval. When his paintings began to take form, the worker noticed that he chose bright red, black, and gray. He was intense and aggressive in his painting. Verbalization of such feelings as anger and fear by the worker brought responses associated with blood, monsters, and fires.

Often he enjoyed punching a toy clown in a very aggressive way. He asked whether the clown inside the toy was being hurt when he hit him. He questioned whether a person would be hurt if a picture of someone he disliked were pasted on the toy clown's face and he hit it. He stated he did not really want to hurt anyone, even if he did dislike them. To alleviate this confusion between reality and fantasied thoughts, the worker began to help him separate his fantasies and feelings from actions. In the course of one session when punching the toy clown, James said that he wished that it were his mother and little brother.

This discussion occurred at the time of a heightened controversy over his home visits. He spoke of a recurrent dream which he had had at home and which had reappeared. The dream involved the stabbing and killing of his mother and brother. Observing his fear and disturbance, the worker explained that many people have similar dreams or nightmares and that they usually follow feelings of anger at being punished unjustly that cannot be expressed to people they love or depend upon. He seemed somewhat relieved by the explanation, and it marked the beginning of their talks to straighten out his disturbing fears and feelings. It served to connect these with his experiences at home.

The interagency meetings inspired Mrs. A to obtain further help at the mental health center. She later began to work part time to supplement her Aid to Families with Dependent Children check and took the initiative to arrange for an appropriate sitter and health care for Jerry. She was helped to be more active in age-appropriate activities and to achieve some skill and success toward enhancing her strengths and the ability to regulate and control herself.

Social work practice that is family system oriented and coordinates the treatment among the significant interlocking systems with followup and centralization of responsibility will vastly improve the outcome with the high-risk and vulnerable poor family that has been locked into a generationally perpetuated destructive lifestyle.

CHAPTER 57

Family Therapy and the Black Middle Class: A Neglected Area of Study

Dennis A. Bagarozzi

When reviewing the family therapy literature, one is struck by the dearth of empirical work which deals specifically with the treatment of Black middle class families. The purpose of this article, therefore, is to focus on some of the factors which the author believes have contributed to the current state of affairs, to offer some conceptual guidelines for working with these families, and to address some unresolved issues concerning the treatment of Black families by White clinicians.

The term Black middle class family is used herein to describe families which are: (a) economically secure, (b) conjugally stable, and (c) upwardly mobile.

In such families, either one or both spouses is steadily employed and household economics fall substantially above the poverty level. These families value stable and enduring conjugal relationships and strive to achieve this ideal. The dominant orientation is one of upward mobility, achievement, and assimilation into the opportunity structure of the larger White society.[1]

Why a Neglected Area of Study?

False notions seem to be held by many clinicians and laymen alike that they already possess valid and reliable information concerning Black mid-

Reprinted from the *Journal of Marital and Family Therapy*, Vol. 6, No. 2 (April, 1980), pp. 159–166. Copyright 1980 American Association for Marriage and Family Therapy. Reprinted by permission of the Association and the author.

dle class family structure and functioning. These erroneous beliefs often take the form of stereotypes such as: the Black matriarchy, the pervasiveness of one-parent households, illegitimacy within the Black community as a whole, and the overall instability of Black marriages. These stereotypes have been perpetuated, in part, by inaccurate generalizations drawn from early works of pioneering researchers who investigated *lower class* Black families (e.g., Moynihan, 1965; Rainwater, 1966). These misconceptions still persist, however, despite the Civil Rights movement of the 60s and the emergence of a larger middle class.

There have been relatively few qualitative investigations of the Black middle class family. Those that are available (e.g., Frazier, 1966; Scanzoni, 1971), however, offer the clinician few insights into the internal dynamics of these families which can be used for clinical intervention. The White therapist, therefore, has little to draw on for assistance in his/her work with such families. If one does not have Black colleagues with whom to confer, or if one's supervisors are White, the therapist might be tempted to apply the little that has been written about treating the lower class Black family to his/her work with the Black middle class.

Since no empirical data are available, the White clinician's main source of guidance derives from therapists' personal accounts and anecdotal reports. For example, Zuk's (1971) clinical experiences with Black lower class families and Jewish middle class families has led him to make the following generalizations: (a) Jewish families are likely to talk more in family therapy and to be more self-disclosing than Black families, (b) Jewish families find the prospect of extended family treatment to be appealing; Black families tend to fear long-term contact, (c) Jewish families are verbally facile; Black families are slow to express themselves in words, are distrustful, and maintain distance from the therapist, (d) Jewish families are easiest to engage in treatment; Black families are the most difficult, and (e) Jewish families are good therapy risks. Blacks are not.

The acceptance of Zuk's (1971) account as if it reported empirical findings rather than as personal experience which may not be generalizable to the Black community as a whole may interfere with the qualitative practice of family therapy in the Black community. Recently, in contrast to Zuk's idea, Sattler (1977) has proposed that family therapy may be particularly relevant for lower class Black clients because it tends to be action-oriented, short-term and to focus on changing concrete behaviors rather than developing insight.

In order to counteract some of the stereotypes and clarify some misconceptions, reference will be made to the latest sociological research concerning the Black middle class. These findings will be discussed in terms of family systems concepts. By doing this, it is hoped that some general guidelines for family intervention can be developed.

A Family Systems Perspective

The systems paradigm (Haley, 1959, 1976; Jackson, 1957) appears to be an appropriate framework for conceptualizing Black family processes because it seems to transcend ethnic, racial, and socioeconomic boundaries and offers specific guidelines for analyzing how a particular family functions. The Black middle class family will be discussed below in terms of a number of central concepts of systems theory.

SYSTEMS GOALS

Lederer and Jackson (1968) emphasized that humans are goal-directed, and the goals that individuals strive to achieve are strongly influenced by cultural norms. For the majority of Americans, a stable, monogamous marriage is a goal to be attained. In this respect, Black middle class families do not differ from their White counterparts (Billingsley, 1968). Black middle class parents have been found to share similar goals and expectations for their children with White middle class parents (Berger and Simon, 1974). Scanzoni (1971) found that most Black middle class children whom he studied experienced their parents as giving them more than adequate preparation for marriage and family life, had stressed educational attainment to achieve upward mobility, and aided them in achieving these goals through financial and emotional support and modeling.

BARRIERS TO GOAL ATTAINMENT

While their basic goals do not differ significantly from their White counterparts, Black middle class families find their attainment more difficult because of discrimination and prejudice which is inherent in many social, cultural, and economic institutions in the United States. These barriers to goal attainment contribute to the Black client's reluctance to seek help from White clinicians in private practice, in social agencies, and in mental health facilities which are seen as supportive of the same social system which erected those barriers (McAdoo, 1976). Such attitudes may explain to some extent why Blacks have been found to drop out of therapy earlier and more frequently than Whites do (Raynes & Warren, 1971; Sue, McKinney, Allen & Hall, 1974).

Discrimination also affects the internal dynamics of Black families. Scanzoni (1971) found that the more economic-status rewards a husband supplies to his wife, the more she sees him as meeting her expressive needs, and the less likely she is to resent him. Since middle class Blacks tend to use Whites as reference points for education, income, and job status, inequities in social advancement and financial reward allocation become salient and the resentment which results may cause Black wives to become dissatisfied with their spouses' consumption potential. If the wife reacts to this disappointment with annoyance, there is a good possibility that the hostility will be reciprocated (Patterson and Hops, 1972). Such treatment by the wife will tend to compound the already existing resentment and frustration that the husband experiences because he has been denied access to the opportunity structure. As a result, he may displace his negative feelings on to his wife. The escalating cycle of mutual coercion may work to undermine the types of successful marital exchanges and bargains which are believed to take place in White middle class families. This explanation has been offered as one possible reason for the greater dissolution of marriages among higher status Black families than among comparable White couples (Scanzoni, 1971).

TRANSACTIONAL PATTERNS AND SYSTEMS BOUNDARIES

It is impossible to understand Black family functioning unless one views the Black family in the context of the Black community in which it lives and the dominant White society from which it has been excluded. Because the Black community has been set apart from White society, informational barriers have been erected between the two groups. When such barriers exist, coalitions inevitably form between members in each of the segregated groups (Haley, 1976). As a result, many Black families have become intimately involved with subsystem groups within the Black community like church groups and kinship groups. Stack (1974) has described how kinship ties and extended family problems may become an integral part of family life. The Black family system, therefore, is one which is relatively more open to influences outside of the nuclear family than is the White middle class family unit. Adult children, relatives, friends, and children of extended family members often are cared for and periodically may become part of a family unit (Stack, 1974). Such permeability of boundaries makes the family more susceptible to inputs from other systems within the Black community. This continual flow of new information necessitates frequent structural changes and adjustments in family members' role relationships.

POWER IN THE BLACK MIDDLE CLASS FAMILY

Sociologists noted that Black middle class spouses tend to share power in a more egalitarian fashion than do White middle class spouses (Jackson, 1973). These findings have important clinical implications. For example, if a spouses's power to influence the conjugal decision-making process is derived from his/her ability to dispense or withhold resources (Scanzoni, 1971), it follows that egalitarian relationships will develop more often in those marriages where both spouses possess approximately equal amounts of reward power. Some clinicians (Bagarozzi & Wodarski, 1977, 1978) suggest that when power is shared equally in this manner, the probability of successful conflict resolution is greater than when large discrepancies exist. It also has been postulated that behavioral contracting will be most effective when resource power is shared equally between spouses (Rappaport & Harrell, 1972).

THE NATURE OF SYSTEMS DEVELOPMENT: HOMEOSTASIS AND MORPHOGENESIS

The growth, development, and ultimate viability of any living system depends upon its ability to utilize positive feedback, to change organizational structures and interactional patterns, to meet changing internal demands and external pressures, and to set new and more complex goals. In addition to these morphogenic processes, families also must be able to use negative feedback in order to maintain certain levels of homeostasis which provide order, predictability and stability. Young (1969) has described four possible ways in which Black family systems might function while preparing their children to live in a White controlled society. They might: (a) lack any clear plan except to attempt to meet crises as they arise, (b) physically remove themselves from any stresses caused by the majority groups, (c) willfully maintain externally imposed or self-imposed segregation, or (d) attempt to remove major barriers to assimilation into the opportunity structure.

There is mounting evidence (Scanzoni, 1971) which shows that Black middle class families have elected to function according to the latter principle of removing barriers to assimilation. From my perspective, this course of action probably will prove to be most beneficial for Black middle class family development since it requires the family to function in a manner which closely approximates those systems described as morphogenic and viable (Wertheim, 1973). While the first three alternatives might allow the family to maintain the status quo or to continue its existence unhampered, they do not allow for continued growth and development.

DIFFERENCES BETWEEN BLACK AND WHITE MIDDLE CLASS FAMILIES

It is important to recognize that there are a number of differences between Black and White middle class families even though they are similar in a number of ways. For example:

1. The stages of the family life cycle proposed by some sociologists (Rodgers, 1972) may not be as clearly defined in the Black community as they are believed to be in the White middle class. For example: in the Black community, children (of relatives who cannot care for them, or grand-

children born to a teenage unwed daughter or a divorced son or daughter who is working and not available for parenting) still may be entering the household at what is normatively considered to be the launching phase (Deitrich, 1976). In the White community, this phase usually is concerned with the spouses' attempts to readjust to each other and their new roles after their children's departure.

2. While Black family boundaries may be more open to outside influences (McAdoo, 1976, 1978), they may be more rigidly closed to inputs which come from the White community (Grier & Cobbs, 1979).

3. The more egalitarian power structure among the Black middle class also affects husband and wife roles. For example, there are fewer sex-linked roles and tasks among the Black middle class than there are for Whites (Dietrich, 1976). This may stem from the fact that more Black wives are employed than are White wives (Scanzoni, 1971).

Black Families and White Therapists

While this article was being written, I was unable to locate any empirical work which addressed the issue of racial differences between therapists and family members and the effects these differences might have on the outcome of family therapy. A definitive statement about the interaction of these factors, therefore, cannot be made at this time. Some initial work in the field of individual psychotherapy has been conducted, however, which may shed some light on this issue. A number of individuals have postulated that inherent difficulties arise whenever White therapists encounter Black clients (Phillips, 1961), and that sociocultural and racial biases held by White clinicians make rapport between therapist and client extremely difficult (Vontress, 1972). Some limited support for racial stereotyping has been found (Waite, 1968).

In a comprehensive analysis of empirical studies, Sattler (1977) found that Blacks do prefer same-race therapists over White therapists, but that competent White professionals are preferred to less competent Black professionals. He also found that the therapist's style and technique are more important factors in affecting Black client's choices than is the therapist's race. Preference for therapists was found to be related to the client's temperament, with highly dogmatic Black students preferring same-race practitioners. Middle class Blacks tended to have similar attitudes and expectations toward therapy and its potential outcome as did middle class Whites.

Sattler (1977) found that results from analogue studies and actual therapy sessions point to the same conclusion: Black clients do benefit from therapeutic services offered by White clinicians, but the lack of research on therapy conducted by Black clinicians makes it impossible to evaluate whether Black therapists are more effective with Black clients than are White therapists. Studies of non-clinical interviews have found White interviewers to be as effective with Black clients as Black interviewers (Ewing, 1974). Based upon his review, Sattler (1977) believes that when White therapists are empathic, experienced with Black clients, and use techniques that meet their clients' needs, they are likely to be especially effective with them.

It becomes obvious that a clear statement about the effects of racial differences and outcome in individual psychotherapy cannot be made at this time. Although the findings outlined above are meager, they represent an effort to investigate a sensitive and essential component of the psychotherapeutic process. It is hoped that future investigations will provide some insights into the effects that a therapist's race might have on his/her ability to intervene across racial lines, to cross family systems' boundaries, to establish a therapeutic alliance, to enter into a family's interaction process, and to effect positive changes within family systems. These findings also should alert professionals, educators, and clinical supervisors to aspects of training and therapy which heretofore have been neglected; that is (a) how the therapist's racial attitudes, prejudices, expectations, and perceptions influence his/her work with families of different racial groups, (b) to what extent our contemporary models of family process and family therapy reflect a White middle class ethnocentrism, and (c) whether ignorance of a client's background and differences in language usage and communication style are barriers to rapport between racially different therapists and family members.

Clinical Implications

1. While Black middle class Americans are more similar to their White counterparts than they are to lower class Blacks, they still should be considered an ethnic subsociety which is bound together by a common definition and treatment by the dominant White society (Billingsley, 1968). The anger which results from such treatment, therefore, must be dealt with in the therapy process (Halpern, 1970). Helping family members recognize and deal with this anger may prove to be an essential component of treatment, especially when the therapist is White. Once these feelings are confronted, the therapist can begin to help family members use them in more constructive and self-actualizing ways.

One may wonder whether the therapist should become an active agent of social change, or whether he/she should merely support Black clients in their struggle to make better use of their capacities and potentials. The answer seems to rest with the individual therapist. Sattler (1977) has suggested a dual role: (a) to help clients recognize the sources of their difficulties and (b) to restructure society by eliminating those forces which perpetuate discrimination and limit individual achievement. The family therapist has an additional task. He/she must help family members become aware of how anger at societal injustices may be displaced and acted out within the family context. He/she also should help families determine how much of their difficulties stem from the effects of discrimination and how much they result from personal dysfunctional behavioral styles, faulty communications patterns, unverbalized expectations or coercive interpersonal behavior change attempts.

2. The therapist should be aware of the possible influences on family processes of kinship and community groups. McAdoo (1976) has described how interference from extended family members may create marital difficulties when family members are unable to say "no" to unreasonable demands made by their kin and relatives. He suggests that the clinician should help the clients to differentiate from their extended family and to develop healthy boundaries between families. To achieve these goals, he suggests seeing the family member and his/her kin in separate sessions. Once family boundaries have been negotiated, the therapist can work to repair or develop new boundaries within the nuclear family.

The clinician might find it advisable to view Black family systems in terms of the social networks in which they exist (Speck & Attneave, 1973), rather than as isolated nuclear families which are more characteristic of the White middle class. Kinship groups also can be used by the therapist as support systems. For example, grandparents may be used as parental surrogates who can provide nurturance and acceptance for an abused or scapegoated child.

3. Since many Black middle class families have egalitarian family structures, behavioral contracting may prove useful (Patterson & Hops, 1972; Rappaport & Harrell, 1972).

Conclusion

Within any family, there exists a dynamic interplay and continual transaction among three cultures: (a) the family culture, with its own rules, myths, and secrets, (b) the culture of the ethnic or racial group of which the family may be part, and (c) the broader culture of the society. Understanding this interplay and how the family may use its subculture and that of the dominant society to maintain a homeostatic balance may be an important part of the assessment and diagnostic process. In order to effect change, the therapist first must be permitted to enter the family system. Understanding the ethnic and social subculture may facilitate this process. Once the therapist has gained admittance, confronting racial and ethnic differences may help the therapist gain acceptance. Eventually, however, attempts will be made by the family to neutralize the therapist's change efforts by making him/her a member of the system who is invested in maintaining the status quo. Perhaps this is when the family will use racial and ethnic differences to resist change. Metacommunicating about this process may be necessary if treatment is to proceed and change is to be brought about. The efficacy of such an approach, however, awaits empirical verification.

In this article, I have attempted to treat a topic which has been neglected in the family therapy literature, to highlight where research might be conducted, and to offer some tentative suggestions for understanding and working with Black middle class families. It is hoped that this article will draw attention to the need for qualitative research in this important area of study.

References

BAGAROZZI, D. A. & WODARSKI, J. S. A social exchange typology of conjugal relationships and conflict development. *Journal of Marriage and Family Counseling*, 1977, *3*, 53–60.

BAGAROZZI, D. A. & WODARSKI, J. S. Behavioral treatment of marital discord. *Clinical Social Work Journal*, 1978, *6*, 135–154.

BERGER, A. & SIMON, W. Black families and the Moynihan report: A research evaluation. *Social Problems*, 1974, *22*, 145–161.

BILLINGSLEY, A. *Black families in White America*. Englewood Cliffs, N.J.: Prentice-Hall, 1968.

DIETRICH, K. T. A critical reaction to sociological research on Black families. Unpublished paper. Texas Agricultural Experiment Station, Texas A&M University, 1976.

EWING, T. M. Racial similarity of client and counselor and client satisfaction with counseling. *Journal of Counseling Psychology*, 1974, *21*, 446–449.

FRAZIER, F. F. *The Negro family in the United States*. Chicago, IL: The University of Chicago Press, 1966.

GRIER, W. W. & COBBS, P. M. *Black rage*. New York: Bantam Books, 1969.

HALEY, J. *Problem solving therapy*. San Francisco: Jossey-Bass, 1976.

HALEY, J. The family of the schizophrenic: A model system. *American Journal of Nervous and Mental Disorders*, 1959, *129*, 357–374.

HALPERN, F. Psychotherapy in the rural south. *Journal of Contemporary Psychotherapy*, 1970, *2*, 67–74.

JACKSON, D. D. The question of family homeostasis. *Psychiatric Quarterly Supplement*, 1957, *31*, Part 1, 79–90.

JACKSON, J. J. Family organization and ideology. In K. S. Miller & R. M. Dreger (Eds.), *Comparative studies of Blacks and Whites in the United States*. New York: Seminar Press, 1973.

LEDEREV, W. & JACKSON, D. D. *The mirages of marriage.* New York: W. W. Norton, 1968.

McADOO, H. R. The impact of extended family variables upon the upward mobility of Black families. Unpublished paper, Families Research Project, 1978.

McADOO, J. L. Family therapy in the Black community. Unpublished paper presented at the American Orthopsychiatric Association, 1976.

MOYNIHAN, D. P. *The Negro family: The case for national action.* Washington: Department of Labor, 1965.

PATTERSON, G. R. & HOPS, H. Coercion, a game for two: Intervention techniques for marital conflict. In R. C. Ulrich & P. Mountjoy (Eds.), *The experimental analysis of social behavior.* New York: Appleton-Century-Crofts, 1972.

PHILLIPS, W. B. Role of the counselor in the guidance of Negro students. *Harvard Educational Review,* 1961, *31,* 324–326.

RAINWATER, L. Crucible of identity: The Negro lower class family. *Deadalus,* 1966, *95,* 172–216.

RAPPAPORT, A. & HARRELL, J. A behavioral exchange model for marital counseling. *Family Coordinator,* 1972, *21,* 203–212.

RAYNES, A. E. & WARREN, G. Some distinguishing features of patients failing to attend a psychiatric clinic after referral. *American Journal of Orthopsychiatry,* 1971, *41,* 581–588.

RODGERS, R. *Family interaction and transaction: The developmental approach.* Englewood Cliffs, N.J.: Prentice-Hall, 1972.

SATTLER, J. The effects of therapist-client racial similarity. In A. Gurman (Ed.), *Effective psychotherapy.* Pergamon, 1977.

SCANZONI, J. H. *Opportunity and the family.* New York: The Free Press, 1970.

SCANZONI, J. H. *The Black family in modern society.* Boston: Allyn and Bacon, 1971.

SPECK, R. V. & ATTNEAVE, C. L. *Family networks.* New York: Pantheon, 1973.

STACK, C. B. *All our kin: Strategies for survival in a Black community.* New York: Harper and Row, 1974.

STUART, R. B. An operant interpersonal program for couples. In D. H. Olson (Ed.), *Treating relationships.* Lake Mills: Graphic Publishing, 1976.

SUE, S., McKINNEY, H., ALLEN, D. & HALL, J. Delivery of community mental health services to Black and White clients. *Journal of Consulting and Clinical Psychology,* 1974, *42,* 794–801.

VONTRESS, E. E. The Black militant as counselor. *Personnel and Guidance Journal,* 1972, *50,* 576–580.

WAITE, R. R. The Negro patient and clinical theory. *Journal of Consulting and Clinical Psychology,* 1968, *32,* 427–433.

WERTHEIM, E. S. Family unit therapy. The science and typology of family systems. *Family Process,* 1973, *12,* 361–376.

YOUNG, D. R. The socialization of minority peoples. In D. A. Goslin (Ed.), *Handbook of socialization theory and research.* Chicago: Rand McNally, 1969.

ZUK, G. H. *Family therapy: A triadic-based approach.* New York: Behavioral Publications, 1971.

Note

1. For a fuller and more complete description of the Black middle class family, the reader is referred to J. H. Scanzoni, *The Black family in modern society* (Boston: Allyn and Bacon, 1971).

CHAPTER 58

Social Work with the Wealthy

Elizabeth Herman McKamy

Social work education and practice equip social workers to deal with people who are primarily disadvantaged by their economic, social or cultural backgrounds, and secondarily disadvantaged by intrapsychic or physical handicaps. Psychosocial studies underline the fact that social workers are trained to consider not only a client's psychopathology, ego strengths, and immediate family situation, but also to evaluate these as assets and liabilities relating to capacity for *minimal* functioning within the community's socioeconomic framework.

Although a substantial number of social workers are recognized as competent psychotherapists and psychoanalysts, the deepest root of their identity is grounded in orientation toward alleviating poor people's distress. Gordon Hamilton, Annette Garrett, Helen Harris Perlman, Charlotte Towle, and others have illustrated the systems and conditions of human suffering of those who lack the basic resources for an equal position in society. Many social workers, along with some of their first clients, moved on: but the generic identity of social workers as helpers of the poor remains.

Oriented as he is toward helping the poor, how does the social worker approach work with the wealthy? Even though most people are adversely affected by a troubled world economy today, a small segment of the population regards money as no obstacle in searching for and obtaining psychiatric care. Characterized not only by affluence, the wealthy patient and his family often have an impressive heritage of achievement. Dysfunction arises frequently from an acute or chronic psychodynamic conflict, rather

Reprinted from *Social Casework,* Vol. 57 (April, 1976), pp. 254–258, by permission of the author and the Family Service Association of America.

than from social or economic stress impinging on a weak psychological structure.

In a traditional public or voluntary institution the multiproblem family might manifest social, economic, or educational malfunction in conjunction with psychiatric problems. Conversely, multiproblem families in private settings are usually characterized by a complexity of psychodynamic breakdowns and few, if any, social, economic, or educational ones. Whatever purity of approach this fact may afford, it nonetheless demands that the social worker reassess some of the basic assumptions of his task.

The Social Worker's Role

As part of his role at The C. F. Menninger Memorial Hospital, the social worker usually functions as liaison between hospital and family. As a member of the patient's treatment team, the social worker is the primary interpreter of the history and current situation of the family for the team. While this information helps the team to better understand the patient, it also facilitates clearer insight into countertransference phenomena as they develop. Based on an overall understanding, the team recommends individual psychotherapy, group psychotherapy, family therapy as adjuncts to the patient's milieu treatment program. The social worker communicates the team's concept of the problems and its recommendations to the family.

Whether intensive family therapy or planned periodic visits are recommended during the course of hospitalization, the family is encouraged to become involved. Some families are amenable from the beginning to their own active participation in the process; others are resistant.

Affluence and successful management in business and social spheres characterize many of the families with whom the staff work. Such families are accustomed to and adept at controlling their environment. They rarely experience situations where their own resources are not sufficient to solve their problems. In fact, such people seldom find themselves having to ask for help. The social worker, popularly thought of as a helper of the socially and economically distressed, finds himself in an unusual position.

He needs to defend himself and his professional task in an arena which is somewhat alien both to him and to his clients; he is not used to working with people of wealth and power, and his clients are unused to asking for help. Treatment difficulties arise involving families with means because of long-established patterns of resistance to placing themselves in a position seemingly controlled by others. The social worker too may experience conflicts in relating to people whom society may deem more capable and influential than he.

Wealth as Power

"You get what you pay for" is a maxim to which our culture has given credence. Despite progress in social security and public and voluntary health and child-care services, the belief is still espoused that the more an individual pays, the higher the quality of service he gets. Accordingly, one might expect that where direct party payment for service prevails, there is also a greater demand for achievement and performance. The rich are people who do not have to knock on doors, deal with secretaries, or with middlemen of any kind. Indeed, they are people who can put pressure on the hospital administration regarding anything that is done or not done to the designated patient. Such pressure, filtered down to the clinician, can be a stimulus for excellence on the job, or it can be experienced as a constraint.

Although most hospitals support their workers in clinical decisions, whether they meet, or fail to meet, the immediate approval of the patient and his family, there still remains an atmosphere of concern: the call of the board member who attempts to persuade through threat if an acquaintance is not given the treatment that he or his family dictates; the angry removal by a family of its member who is a well-known writer; the elopement of a patient of national renown, as a consequence of disagreement with staff; the threat made to a hospital that a much-needed grant will be withheld if existing policy within, for example, the social work discipline is not altered to accommodate what an individual family feels are its particular needs at a given time.

Powerful, educated, wealthy families are accustomed to direct access and management over what they have bought. They are used to controlling business and, as they see it, payment for private hospitalization is not unlike an investment in a business. In not offering a precise prospectus, however, the psychiatric hospital business often stimulates anxiety in families and the concomitant impulse to want to dictate and control through familiar patterns, for example, demand and litigation. Currently, health services and practitioners are particularly sensitive to suggestions of or hints at litigation. A hospital may be known to support its employees in their clinical decisions, but the concern for legal consequence to the institution and the individual employee still exists. Such concern is a significant influence—for better or worse. Sometimes the accessibility of resources and information to families, coupled with direct party payment for service, facilitates communication and cooperation with the treatment team. At other times, however, the very assets that allow these people to choose "the best" can make delivery of "the best," as clinically determined, a tenuous and difficult task.

Rich or poor, most families defend themselves against the recognition that they, as well as the patient, are part of the problem. Pain, confusion, and fear of change are orchestrated in almost any troubled family into a complexity of defenses that resist intervention. At the time when hospitalization of the patient has become necessary, most families would prefer, consciously or unconsciously, that the problem, namely the patient, be treated and that they, the family, support such treatment but remain essentially outside of it.

Visits, encouragement, and assuming responsibility for things the patient can not do are among the many ways a family can help its sick member while he is in the hospital. Most often, though, when deep understanding and change of personality are the goals of treatment, families have to become more intensively and purposefully involved.

Resistances of the Wealthy

The wealthy sometimes present resistances to more active therapeutic involvement that are different from those of other kinds of families in other kinds of settings. "We're functioning just fine" is often heard from families of the patients treated in our hospital. Frequently, such a statement is difficult to confront.

> Father, for example, may be operating at full capacity as a corporation lawyer while at the same time involving himself in a home and social life replete with every sign of success. Mother, with children grown beyond school age, may have returned to her earlier career as a drama reviewer for the city newspaper. She explains that this job has always allowed her a flexibility of hours so that she can maintain her home as the first priority in her responsibilities. The patient's oldest sibling may have just married, while another enters his second year of college. All members of the family, including the designated patient, state that the only problem is the patient's illness.
>
> As the patient, who had seriously attempted suicide shortly after beginning college, gains confidence in his treatment staff, he evidences in his behavior anxieties about separation from the family that showed up initially in psychological testing. He has always feared leaving his parents because he sensed from an early age that there were deep marital problems that might emerge were he to move away from home. Crazy as these fears may be, this seventeen-year-old's suicide attempt might lend sufficient evidence of trouble in the family to induce the treatment team to recommend family therapy along with the hospitalization of the patient.

Involving the Family in the Therapy

By the time hospitalization is necessary, chronically ill patients and their families are often veterans of years of psychiatric care. A high level of general education and sophistication, coupled with multifaceted and often un-successful experience with doctors, psychologists, psychiatrists, and so forth, can form an impressive defensive structure. Some of these families and patients use diagnostic jargon with ease. They are skilled at antici-pating interventions and interpretations. Moreover, they can intellectually acknowledge an understanding that they may not truly feel. They can take the therapist's seat literally and figuratively.

A physician father, for example, may insist that continuing to medicate his daughter is his effort to be helpful and expedient in the treatment proc-ess. A mother may defend herself against recognizing the family problems that are stirred up by her daily calls to her son. She explains that her psy-choanalyst at home is encouraging a closer relationship between herself and her children. An entire family can lucidly explain the dynamics of fam-ily life as they relate to the patient's illness. They can even try to convince the social worker that this understanding is more than enough homework for them to think about while the patient is in the hospital.

Splitting away from the central focus of family treatment by intellec-tualization and bringing in auxiliary supports and other specialists can present formidable resistance to intervention by the social worker. Al-though putting forth parallel interpretations and offering alternative con-crete supports to the family can be useful some of the time, more often the social worker finds that sharing his experience of the family process in action is the most effective means of engaging them in a working alliance.

"We'll support anything you do" is a position taken by some families. Years of struggle and pain with a chronically ill relative have brought them over the threshold of frustration into hopelessness. Such families have come to feel that all they can offer their sick member is protracted financial security in a private hospital. In such a setting they hope that the patient will have the maximum of physical comfort while they themselves find a long-desired peace of mind. These families may experience difficulty in translating their passive despair into a sense of personal purpose in a treat-ment process. The unremitting illness of the patient has come to seem like an unremitting affront to the family's ability to cope and care. The very hope that the social worker communicates in his effort to engage the family can easily be taken by them as a further insult to their capacity to be good parents or caring people.

Difficulties in Establishing a Working Alliance with the Family

In a state hospital, the proposition of unlimited financial backing for any treatment approach would be unlikely and fairly extraneous to the admin-istrative system. In a private hospital, however, where the treatment teams feel constrained at times by the presence and power of families, there can be a temptation to collude with a carte blanche proposal that full responsibility for the patient be left in the treatment team's hands, thus excluding the family from the therapeutic task.

The very fact that the family's wish to reject the patient seems so blatant can stimulate in the team a counter wish to reject them; allowing the family to remove itself entirely from the arena of treatment. Yet, when the goal is to help facilitate an integration of the patient's past in a way that will enable him to function autonomously as an adult in the future, it is almost always advisable that the family be accessible to work with the treatment staff. In the ongoing process with such families, the social workers often have to deal with their own frustrations, anger, and temptation to assume a "better" parental role that by its nature might have them reenact the same pathological patterns that the patient and his family experienced among themselves.

In work with less advantaged people, a social worker is usually able to help a family see that there are areas of dysfunction within the overall structure of their lives. Financial difficulties are common concerns, as are frustrations about underachievement in school or community. An asset in establishing a working alliance with socially or economically disadvantaged families is the social worker's often-given position as role model. When the social worker is viewed by the family as someone who has achieved an admirable level of professional, economic, and social success, the family may feel that at least some learning may take place from their contact with him.

With wealthy, successful families whose apparent level of functioning is at the apex of our social structure, it can be more difficult to establish this necessary working alliance. The social worker may find himself relying more on symptomatology revealed in the process of a family meeting than in the factual information shared. There may be fewer nonverbal assets to rely on in his initial work with these people. There is less likelihood of the social worker being taken from the start as a role model in the classical sense. Moreover, with the affluent family comes the additional demand for the social worker to be in touch with his own feelings about assuming an authoritative position with people whose lifestyle connotes a formidable authority in its own right.

Countertransference

Most of those who work in a psychiatric setting—psychiatrists, nurses, psychologists, activities therapists, aides, social workers—are from lower to upper middle-class backgrounds, and have grown up with the injunction that in order to achieve or maintain a comfortable income for themselves they have to work. Most people on the staff of a private hospital do not come from backgrounds of wealth. Therefore, at the risk of being simplistic, one might say that the presnt achievements of the individual members of a hospital staff are based on individual resourcefulness and effort, and the staff members' future financial and social prospects are, relatively speaking, somewhat limited.

Most social workers bring with them to their jobs a professional image as it was originally hewn out of their predecessors' exclusive work with the poor. Like his colleagues, the individual social worker has to consider countertransference that may be stimulated by his contact with patients. He may envy and resent the wealthy. Furthermore, he may find difficulties in being assertive enough, or difficulties in being too assertive in trying to counter a tendency to appease. In a psychosocial paradigm, prominent patients and their families may well represent parental figures to the social worker. And, similarly, a recovered patient may threaten as yet another powerful figure in the social worker's environment. In fact, enabling the privileged patient to achieve, or regain, his potential level of functioning might well mean helping him to *exceed* the social worker within the socio-economic framework of society.

Finding ease with the fact that one's patients and their families might, out of the context of their current distress, far outdistance one along the continuum of success that exists in our culture is a sobering thought. Yet this difference in status militates against the social worker's efforts only insofar as he is unaware of its importance.

In working with wealthy patients and their families, the social worker must exert care to maintain a sensitive and strong self-image. He may need to take extra pains to strengthen his professional identity while realistically accepting both his assets and limitations. Armed with such insights into both his personal and professional background, he can formulate realistic goals and keep a sense of perspective. Only then can he effectively manage his job, especially the tasks centering around work with wealthy patients and their families.

The treatment of people of means may be limited by their wealth just as treatment of the poor may be limited by their poverty. Nevertheless, along with the unique difficulties that such caseloads present, there exist some equally unique assets. Wealthy patients and their families can, by and large, afford a treatment program individually determined on the basis of their needs. If indicated, families can travel for scheduled appointments, as many do at The C. F. Menninger Memorial Hospital. Or they can pay for adjunctive treatment at home. Most of the people worked with are verbal and can become motivated toward a goal they think worthwhile. They are resourceful and can focus their energies over an extended period of time if it is necessary. Many of them have generations of security and comfort behind them, and can therefore envision regaining an overall peaceful existence which to less privileged people might be a Utopia unknown.

When these assets can be channeled into a therapeutic alliance, the rewards for all are considerable. Such an alliance, as a prerequisite for meaningful treatment, evolves from a sensitivity to the social worker's personal and professional feelings, awareness of the fears, anxieties, and defenses of the patients, and an acceptance of the unique strengths that each patient and his family, no matter how wealthy, bring to the private hospital setting.

VALUES

CHAPTER 59

Effect of Value Reevaluation on Current Practice

Francis J. Turner

Over the past two years, the writer has become increasingly aware of a group of clients whose psychosocial stress has originated from two related yet separate phenomena—a personal reevaluation of values and ethics and a recurrence of previously dormant superego concerns. This article examines these two phenomena and offers some knowledge and practice implications of their occurrence. It includes some case illustrations, theoretical comments, implications for learning, and diagnostic and management observations.

It is no surprise that persons in our society are experiencing value and ethical difficulties during a period of rapidly changing value and ethical systems at all levels of society. What is noteworthy is that persons are turning to social work professionals for help in dealing with such problems. This trend is significant in relation to the tradition in which the client's values were considered as a therapeutic no-man's-land and the therapist's values as something to be kept private and rarely shared with the client. Whether social workers adhered to these taboos is, of course, a moot question.

This tradition is now changing. Individuals, groups, and families are turning to us for help with stress in psychosocial functioning directly related to value and ethical conflicts that are sometimes recognized, sometimes not. These clients are diagnostically within the range of normal functioning, yet still in need of skilled help. Such requests require that

Reprinted from *Social Casework*, Vol. 56 (May, 1975), pp. 285–291, by permission of the Family Service Association of America.

social work professionals respond in an understanding and helpful way and give this content more consideration.

It should not be surprising that a challenge to one's ethical position or a commitment to change one's value position would have implications for the superego component of personality, especially if the approach to practice is from a developmental base. Each person brings to new situations his whole developmental history, including superego development. These pasts influence how we are affected by or affect out present. But we also know that this is not a one-way influence; new experiences and perceptions can shift, alter, diminish, or increase the extent to which our pasts influence the present and, in turn, alter the way we will function in the future.

It is because these two phenomena—one society-wide and current and the other individual and past-related—can reciprocally influence each other that their simultaneous occurrence becomes of interest and importance therapeutically. Four types of situations that the writer has observed and which are related to this topic are described in the case illustrations below.

Case Illustrations

First, there is the client who initially appears in a mild or moderately severe crisis situation resulting from a shift in life view, the effects of which are only partially recognized and understood.

Mr. M is an intelligent, successful businessman of forty-five, who experienced a mild crisis reaction that he related to a recent upset in his marriage. This upset had resulted in diminished effective functioning in most life areas, including his business. His sales had dropped off drastically, and he was facing the possibility of losing his position. It was soon evident that his stress was more broadly based than the difficulty with his marriage; he was, in fact, in a process of reevaluating his whole view of life, his commitment to his marriage, and his aspirations.

In brief, he was striving to move from a rigid view of life and duty to a more open one in which self-fulfillment was the goal. This upheaval had reactivated some of his earlier ambivalent feelings toward his father, a man who had high standards and expectations of him that he rarely could meet. These feelings became transferred both to his boss and to the therapist and showed in his wanting to please and to hurt. Only after some of this material was clarified and he began to recognize both his present shifting perceptions and commitments and the strings on him from the past was he able to begin to function in his accustomed self-fulfilling, socially responsible manner and to reexamine his commitment to his marriage.

A second type of client in a value dilemma is the individual who recognizes that he has altered his self-concept along with his perception of desirable behavior and responsibility; the problem that moves him to seek help stems from his inability to follow through on the implications of his value shifts.

Mrs. J is a twenty-five-year-old woman of above-average intelligence, married to a successful, upwardly mobile man whom she met while both were in the armed forces. She had felt abandoned by her husband and unfulfilled in her role as mother of three. To counter these feelings, she began taking university courses at night and became involved in a women's discussion group. She was significantly influenced by the campus climate and the content of some of her courses and decided to pursue a full university career along with her responsibilities as wife and mother. Although her husband concurred with this plan and encouraged her, the decision evoked a wave of anxiety and marked ambivalence that confused her husband and put severe strains on the marriage. In individual and joint interviews with her and her husband, it quickly became apparent that her decision had evoked both the spectre of her dead father—a controlling, demanding man who viewed women as being second- best—and her feelings about her highly critical, dependent mother, who was still alive. Several stormy interviews took place in which some of the components of the unresolved emancipation from parental demands and expectations were worked through and their influence on her present goals clarified. Following this stage, Mrs. J began to follow through on her decisions and resumed effective functioning as wife and mother.

A third form of value-related problems concerns marital situations where support for the altered life view is not present and where the stress comes from the lack of such support. This problem appears to be the situation in an increasing number of marriages in which there have been several years of a reasonably stable, apparently healthy relationship of essentially mature spouses. Nevertheless, under the influence of recent societal trends, conflict emerges as one or both partners begin to change attitudes toward broad life objectives, role perceptions, or moral stances related to sexual conduct within or outside the marriage. Examples are the man who decides to leave a secure job after several years in order to establish his own business or the woman who wishes for a new career outside the home. In these cases, the conflicts that emerge frequently evoke the same superego immaturities identified earlier.[1]

The fourth cluster of problems in this area is similar to some traditional family problems but with a new dimension. These cases involve value and ethical shifts that have taken place differentially in various family subsystems. Customarily, social workers have seen these from the viewpoint of

[1] Elizabeth Bott, Urban Families: The Norms of Conjugal Roles, in *The Psychosocial Interior of the Family*, ed. Gerald Handell (London: George Allen & Unwin, 1968), pp. 141-58.

the parent-system and sibling-system dyad, but currently other kinds of subsystem splits seem to be taking place. Usually social workers have viewed them as normal maturational emancipation struggles and have understood the superego components of the child's struggle. What has not been given sufficient attention is the real value-based struggle. The latter situation is considered here: a situation where there has been a value shift in some component of the family that results in new stress. One example involved a changed perception of the acceptability of parents' arranging an abortion for a fifteen-year-old daughter.

> Mr. and Mrs. N had long been a stable, socially conscious couple with strong church ties. In recent years, Mrs. N had begun to question some of her long-held moral views, and it was concerning the decision on the daughter's abortion that the couple realized how far apart they had grown in their perceptions of acceptable behavior. This differential perception on the part of the parents created additional conflict for the girl who was struggling with her own emerging system of morality. This issue was never resolved for the family, and the daughter eventually left home following the abortion. Mr. and Mrs. N's marriage suffered a serious blow. After several months, they began to make some progress in reestablishing a functioning system with themselves and their other children.

No doubt there are other clusterings of cases.[2] The four categories above identify some situations in which the persons involved have histories of adequate functioning and mastery of many life situations but have met unmanageable difficulties in psychosocial functioning because they, significant others, or significant institutions have altered or questioned earlier-held positions on values, ethics, or responsibilities. In seeking to resolve these attitudinal changes, they have also found themselves struggling with issues stemming from their own maturational histories. To fully assist these clients, it is necessary to understand both their superego functioning and current social value changes.

Background on the Superego

In the 1923 article "The Ego and the Id," Sigmund Freud redescribed the personality structure in a manner that gave proper emphasis to the superego.[3] Important as this reconceptualization was, professionals have tended to direct more emphasis and interest to the censoring, restricting, inhibiting components of the superego than to some of its more positive

---

[2] Eric J. Cleveland and William D. Longaker, Neurotic Patterns in the Family, in *The Psychosocial Interior of the Family*, ed. Handell, pp. 159–85.

[3] Sigmund Freud, The Ego and the Id, in *The Standard Edition of the Complete Psychological Works of Sigmund Freud*, ed. James Strachey (London: Hogarth Press, 1961), 9: 19–39.

components. The fact that the process of superego development affects the person's attitudes to himself, his perceived esteem or lack of it, and his attitudes to authority persons, initially parents and parent-like authorities but ultimately all authorities, has been understressed.

The superego goal for the maturing person is the development of a psychic structure that fosters the establishment of norms, attitudes, and identities in a way that is increasingly autonomous. This stance permits an individual throughout life to set his own life rules and attitudes and to select the societal systems by which he will be influenced, rather than be directed with little autonomy.[4]

It has been generally accepted that by early adulthood a person has developed a functioning and generally stable superego and a self-image reasonably well accommodated to the significant others and systems within which he functions. Apart from some gradual maturing and realignment of life views as identified in the last three of Erik H. Erikson's eight stages, professionals have presumed that there would be little change in a person's ethical stance, although it was understood that other components of self-image and self-attitudes would change.[5]

Values and Ethics

We no longer live in a social system where values are stable in individuals, family systems, ethnic groupings, or larger political or religious systems. Both ethical and value systems are in flux for many individuals and groups. By *ethics* is meant those consciously adhered to, explicit or implicit, codes of behavior that govern the lives of individuals and groups. Values are those less obvious and less conscious pragmatically oriented preferential choices, almost automatic in operation, that assist individuals to develop patterns of selection from the vast array of daily decisions and choices. The latter are more accurately called value orientations. Although ethics and values or value orientations are separate but related concepts, they do tend to be combined in the general term *values*.

From the ethical aspect, there are many individuals who have drastically altered their long-held convictions about such things as duties to one's country and to one's neighbors, be they old or young, born or unborn. Questions of when one is or is not a human person, when one is or is not alive or dead, are now clearly topics for dispute.

In the area of value orientations, there are interesting and rapid shifts. From a North American society that probably in Florence R. Kluckhohn's

---

[4] Eunice F. Allen, Psychoanalytic Theory, in *Social Work Treatment*, ed. Francis J. Turner (New York: The Free Press, 1974), pp. 19–41.

[5] Erik H. Erikson, *Childhood and Society* (New York: W. W. Norton & Co., 1950), pp. 219–34.

scheme had a predominant first-level orientation to the future, to doing, to individuality, and to man over nature, significant components of society have shifted to a present, being, collateral, man-with-nature orientation.[6] Thus, many persons who had thought their moral and value development had been completed are having to face a new developmental challenge, obviously with differing degrees of success.

Both ethical and value shifts have taken place within the social work profession that must be acknowledged in current practice. Ethically, social workers have had to come to terms with the same questions as society or at least come to terms with their unanswered dilemmas. From a value orientation perspective, there have also been some shifts that are influencing practice styles. The increased interest in present-oriented, here-and-now, short-term therapeutic engagements, the value placed on experiential kinds of therapy, the heavy involvement in groups, and the expanded interest in communities and community action and in environmental and ecological issues all reflect value orientation shifts and reorderings from an individualistic, long-term, future-oriented, insight-based, problem-solving approach.

These comments about value orientations should not be viewed as definitive, but only as indicators of this much-discussed and well-identified social phenomenon. Of more relevance to this article is a brief consideration of what social work has already learned from this development and what implications are emerging for practice.

Implications for Knowledge

One thing we all have learned is that ethical and value systems are not as stable and unchanging as social workers had thought. Whether or not historians or philosophers held this view, practitioners have tended to view moral codes and value systems of themselves and their clients as generally fixed, once professional and personal maturity was achieved. Many social workers have been surprised at the ability of persons to make dramatic and fundamental shifts in standards and behavior, a further example of the ongoing learning about one's ability to change and mature. People are highly flexible and adaptable.

Social workers have also learned that the ability to adjust to new norms and values is not as age-related as had been thought. Some of the most flexible persons, in regard to values, observed in recent years have been old, and some of the most restricted and value-constricted have been among the young. It is misleading to overstress the positive results because

[6] Florence R. Kluckhohn and Fred S. Strodtbeck, *Variations in Value Orientations* (Evanston, Ill.: Row Peterson & Co., 1961).

it is also evident that many personal and social problems arise from these identified changes—problems of both a primary and secondary form. The term *primary* refers to the problems of those individuals for whom value changes produce internal stress and uncertainty that can approach or reach crisis situations. The term *secondary problems* covers those situations that emerge as a result of internal value changes—that is, the effects of the changes on significant others in a person's life, such as parents, spouse, or children.

A further component of value-related problems is their frequent connection to a person's developmental history. Many persons, in the process of working through alterations of formerly held standards, experience a resurgence of developmental gaps and painful experiences. As professionals have learned from crisis work, earlier unsolved issues frequently are reawakened under stress, and such reexperiencing presents to the client and the alert therapist an opportunity to work on them. This opportunity is the so-called second-chance aspect of crisis work.

Because value issues and superego development and functioning are closely related, some unfinished components of superego development can be dealt with in these situations. Because of the high possibility of current-based, value-related contents evoking emotions and material from the past, therapists must be sensitive to the effect of such transferred feelings, especially with negative components.

The above material becomes further complicated in working with adolescents and the family. The struggle for the adolescent to face parental standards and to accept, reject, or modify them in making them his own is sufficiently difficult at any time. It becomes even more crisis prone when the parents are in conflict, transition, or confusion in this area. This kind of situation sets up a reciprocating form of influence which puts further stress and confusion on both the parents and the adolescent, thus exacerbating the superego struggle. If, in addition to this parent-sibling value struggle, a therapist is struggling with his own value conflict or dilemma, the potential for therapeutic confusion is vast.

Superego development is closely related to one's psychosexual development and the formation of attitudes toward acceptable or nonacceptable conduct. However, the sphere of sexual attitudes, beliefs, and practices is one of the areas most influenced currently by societal value shifts. Thus, as persons are influenced by changing societal sexual values, they may reexperience earlier superego conflicts that would complicate the resolution of value issues in this area.

Diagnostic and Management Implications

From the viewpoint of diagnosis, the above information suggests that it is important for social workers to be alert to the possibility of value dilemmas as a key source of conflict or stress in their clients. At times, these conflicts will be obvious, but this source of stress may not be apparent to the client and can be overlooked or misunderstood by both client and worker. Implied in this description is the necessity to focus more attention than has been common on the value and ethical orientation of clients, particularly when there is a likelihood of these life areas' being in transition, either in the client or in his life space. The worker must also consider the risk of being overenthusiastic about the possibility of value dilemmas and developing a tendency to see them where they do not exist. We do not have sufficient data about the prevalence of this type of situation. However, as a general diagnostic stance, it is better to be aware of the possibility of various presenting situations than to be surprised by their occurrence.

The necessity of anticipating the appearance of revived unfinished developmental material in situations where value shifts are in progress has been described. In such instances, professionals must be interested in developmental history and alert to developmental clues available from current functioning. Indicators of the intensity, consistency, and appropriateness of superego functioning can be derived from such factors as the client's attitudes toward his aggressive and sexual impulses, his attitudes to authority figures, and, most important, his level and profile of self-esteem. When there are concerns of more than a minor nature in these areas accompanying reactions to value matters, the likelihood of intrapsychic, historically based therapeutic complications is high.

From a case management viewpoint, several observations can be suggested. Assuming that both current value stress and earlier-based reactions are present, there are at least three choices open. One would involve focusing only on the present value material, assuming that its resolution would reestablish an adequate level of functioning without having to reexamine earlier material. A second stance would include focusing primarily on developmental material, with the rationale that helping the client resolve unfinished material from the past would free him to deal objectively with the present. The third perspective would involve attempting to find a balance between the two sources of strain and to seek for growth-enabling resolution of both areas. Although the writer's preference is for the latter approach, the decision must be made on the experiences of the individual situation and the theoretical stance of the therapist.

In working with clients in these situations, one of the crucial responsibilities of the therapist is to be aware of his own value dilemmas and value shifts and the extent to which such developments may have reactivated developmental scars that could, in turn, influence his perceptions and reactions to the client-worker relationship. If there is adequate awareness of therapist involvement in the relationship, careful attention must be given to the probable presence of transferred feelings. They will be significant if earlier parent-child conflicts on standards and values are active. Because of the importance of such early experiences, there is the risk of moving too quickly into potentially negative material; the therapist may become the recipient of these negative feelings before the relationship is sufficiently strong to tolerate them. Frequently, discussions of values and moral standards take on a rational, discursive, philosophical format and appear present-oriented, with the result that the affective component and reactions are unperceived or misunderstood.

In situations where the client is struggling to evaluate and to understand, the writer has found it helpful to share personal value concerns and dilemmas. This step seems to help some clients appreciate that the struggle is more widespread than his own and to obtain a more reality-based perception of the worker. It is also useful in helping the client to begin to understand the new demand of current psychosocial functioning—learning to live comfortably with uncertainty and change. Professionals clearly underserve their clients if they convey to them, either overtly or implicitly, certainties in these areas that they do not have or that others do not have. However, when therapists have arrived at value solutions and have found ways of resolving uncertainties, they can be helpful in sharing this success with clients. Clients do expect professionals to share their knowledge and views and the benefits of their experience as a way of answering their own questions. The risks of overusing authority are known, but failure can also result from not sharing knowledge and experience.

When professionals are involved in helping clients explore and struggle with value-related issues, much of the interview content will consist of "reflective thinking," the D material of Florence Hollis's outline.[7] This type of procedure leads the client to reflect upon a range of components of his significant environments and the nature of his responses to them. In these cases, the client should be helped to reflect on both the conceptual and attitudinal component of values and to look at their influence on himself and others. Although the focus will tend to be present-oriented, there will be some reflective consideration of the past and its influence on the present. Support will be needed, especially as the client struggles to risk new ideas or new actions. These are situations in which clients individually and jointly need information, new ideas, and the opportunity to reflect, discuss, and share. Because of this tendency, working with groups of parents, for example, with similar related concerns and value dilemmas can be rewarding to the professionals and helpful to the group members.

Implied in the need for discovery and discourse is the need to look for resources not ordinarily used, such as colleagues from the disciplines of theology and philosophy. Many persons in our society need direct contact with theologians and philosophers in a consultative role to struggle with

[7] Florence Hollis, *Casework: A Psychosocial Therapy* (New York: Random House, 1972), pp. 109–24.

moral, personal, and familial value dilemmas. Related to the possible need for information as well as an enabling and corrective experience, the possibility of clients' having mistaken or incorrect views and perceptions of significant others and systems in their lives can not be ignored. Of particular concern are persons who believe they have cut themselves off from significant groups—for example, church or family membership—because of their perceived violation of rules or norms. There has been a dramatic reevaluation of some moral and ethical positions in many societal systems that can accommodate a much wider range of viewpoints and practices than in an earlier day. Tremendous relief and comfort can be available to persons from friends, families, and systems when they find acceptance in lieu of expected rejection.

Another component of work with this kind of client is the question of the length of involvement. There are clients in this category for whom the present emphasis on short-term treatment is both adequate and the treatment of choice. However, factors are emerging to indicate that some identified value-based cases will require a much longer period of treatment, especially in situations where the value issues have revived significant earlier superego material that has to be reassessed. Often, these persons can be helped initially on a short-term basis, especially if a crisis has developed, but they will be underserved if the professionals involved do not offer the opportunity to build on the crisis through some further maturational progress of which they are capable. In this kind of situation, where a form of personal reevaluation and recommitment to the future based on the freedom gained in value shifts is taking place, probably four to six months of contact will be required.

The kinds of situations discussed in this article represent a range of therapeutic opportunities for which several current thought systems offer rich resources. Initially, the developmental and superego concepts are best understood and managed from an ego-psychological framework. Existential thinking is important to fully appreciate the questions of purpose and authenticity that value questions can raise. Crisis theory is necessary to understand the normalcy yet the wide-ranging effects of high-stress situations and their reopening of earlier life episodes. Crisis theory gives some clear indicators of the skills helpful to bring about growth-producing solutions. Finally, role theroy is useful both for the therapist and the client to sort out changes in role perceptions and role enactment that result from alterations in ethics and values.

To responsibly understand and aid in such cases, a reexamination and use of social work's traditional knowledge of superego development and functioning, linked to current views on treatment, will provide social work professionals with the necessary knowledge and skill. Some research efforts should be made to clarify the extent and parameters of these cases and to experiment with alternate approaches.

RELIGION

CHAPTER 60

Religious Cults, the Individual and the Family

Lita Linzer Schwartz and Florence W. Kaslow

In the late 1960's "hippies" and "flower children" ostensibly "dropped out" of a society filled with an unpopular war, poverty, racism, and materialism. In the 1970's, young adults have turned instead to a variety of religious cults that similarly present individuals with the opportunity to separate from their families, renounce the larger society and find a sense of belonging and of purpose in a visible and demarcated subculture. The counter culture of the 1960's featured drugs, sex and radical philosphy (Roszak, 1968); today's cults are drugless, ascetic, asexual, and politically more conservative. Although parents were disturbed and upset when their children became part of the "Haight-Ashbury" scene or drug oriented communes elsewhere, they knew that the choice was deliberate and hopefully only represented a transitional phase. That is often not the situation in the case of membership in today's pseudo-religious, expansion-minded cults.

An additional source of contemporary parental distress is the fact that becoming a cult[1] member involves a religious conversion; and acceptance of the new religion then frequently demands a complete rejection of the family as well as of its values, traditions and sanctions, while perhaps affording the opportunity the young adult seeks to rebel and escape to what *seems like a viable alternative to the family*. It may therefore represent initially a declaration of (personal) independence. The cults offer members a milieu

Reprinted from the *Journal of Marital and Family Therapy*, Vol. 5, No. 2 (April, 1979), pp. 15–26. Copyright 1979 American Association for Marriage and Family Therapy. Reprinted by permission of the Association and the authors.

in which to negate the technology, education, science and rationality which are so highly respected, even venerated, by their parents, and to replace these with learning acquired through spiritual devotion and mysticism. (Daner, 1976, p. VI)

Parents whose children embrace the cults have asked, "How could any religion that as its first consideration tries to break the biological and psychological bond between child and parents be good? How can they pose as Christians, when they reject one of the commandments that underpins the Judeo-Christian philosophy: 'Honor thy father and thy mother.'" (Adler, 1978). Therein lies the lure and strength of the cults' approach—a demand for complete fidelity and allegiance to their mission which provides a sense of meaning in life and a purpose for living for a confused, existentially adrift young person away from the influence of his or her parents which could dilute the intensity of the involvement.

Cult membership thus affects the family and the individual in ways more basic and destructive than earlier modes of withdrawal from the family orbit. Joining a cult is seen as a total and permanent commitment, whereas parents could at least hope that being a "hippie" was a temporary phase for their children. Cult membership becomes inextricably linked with the opportunity to help save the world by assisting "the Messiah" (Singer, 1979, p. 82) and who can defect from such a grandiose mission?

The Cult phenomenon has catapulted onto the national scene in the past decade. One reads with a mystified horror about the Manson gang in California and the mass suicide at Jonestown, Guyana. One sees young sari-wearing, head-shaven members of the Hare Krishna playing pitiful instruments, chanting and peddling literature on city sidewalks, or clean faced, wholesome looking Moonies selling candy or pretzels on corners to "raise money for my Church." Several descriptive and expository books have been written about the cults, but little has appeared in the professional literature which attempts to (1) analyze the dynamics of the families from which cult members come, (2) determine the common factors in the personality profiles of the recruits, (3) look at how the cults accomplish the conversions, (4) assess the impact of the cult experience and of either deprogramming or voluntary exodus from the movement, (5) the treatment interventions that might prove or have proven efficacious with troubled individuals and families who have become entangled with the cults.

Therefore, this article attempts to fill this gap by providing a concise overview of the main premises and features which appear central in one kind of cult, those which recruit from the upper-middle and upper class college student population. (We are speaking mostly about cults similar to the Unification Church [Moonies], Hare Krishna, Church of Scientology, the Jesus Movement and Alamo Christian Foundation). Further, it attempts to delineate and explicate, based on perusal of the existing literature, on clinical observations gleaned in treating ex-cultists, and on semi-structured in-person interviews with former cult members, their relatives, and with therapists and clergymen who have treated them once they have left the cult, some of the key ingredients that led to vulnerability and something about treatment strategies that seem to prove helpful.

This material is intended to provide tentative hypotheses about the young people who have become ensnared by the growing cult phenomenon that appears to entail brain-washing and extreme personality conversions, euphemistically called "snapping" because of the apparent instantaneous quality of the change. (Conway and Siegelman, 1978). It is further intended to stimulate dialogue among family therapists and hard research by clinicians so that we will be better able to comprehend the cults, their appeal and impact—perhaps to prevent some young people from joining and certainly to more knowledgeably and effectively treat those who have re-entered the larger society and their families when they seek our "healing" services.

Individual and Family Dynamics as Precursors to Cult Vulnerability

In the United States, adolescence is often a protracted period of personal limbo and turmoil. School, which teenagers often find irrelevant and boring, fills their days. Their relationships with their parents, though possibly under-girded with affection, suffer frequently from mutual misunderstandings tinged with resentment and recriminations of non-appreciation, the expectation of adolescent rebellion, and inter-generational conflict over values and life styles. The search for personal, individual identity and independence ascribed to this life stage (Erikson, 1968) is in conflict with the realities of the psychological and economic dependence they have on their parents and with their need for belonging, affiliation and reciprocal loyalties (Nagy and Spark, 1973). Idealism, with concomitant anger at parental hypocrisy, real or exaggerated, and at the ills and injustices that exist in our society, is a dominant value in the late teens and early twenties. Social disorganization and political chicanery further contribute to feelings of alienation and disillusionment.

One's failure to individuate and achieve a strong sense of separate identity, and at the same time, the inability to reduce the feeling of loneliness, is a serious hazard in a complex society. The resulting unpredictable behavior, rapid mood swings, role confusion and identity diffusion, described so clearly by Erikson (1950), parallels the general profile that appears in the literature about the young people successfully recruited by the cults and proselytization movements. According to published descriptions (JCRC Report, 1976; Daner, 1976) they evidence:

1. Willingness to accept a leader as a major source of authority and arbiter on acceptable behavior to whom they become extremely devoted
2. A disturbed time perspective
3. Use of a group identity to reduce the sense of personal "incompleteness"
4. Acceptance of a rigid belief system that results in clannishness and intolerance of non-believers
5. A confusion of values
6. A search for a prescribed and structured daily routine

The emerging young adult, usually from an upper middle-class background, rejects the obvious materialism surrounding him, and attempts to disassociate himself from the ambition, narcissistic pursuits, and superficial concerns that appear to consume his parents' lives. At the same time, the youth seems to sense a serious deficit within the family, an absence of ethical/moral/spiritual values in actual practice and the lack of a raison d'etre.

There is ample evidence to demonstrate that parents who are leaders in community affairs, ostensible or real subscribers to religious values, and who genuinely try to be "good" parents may also be afflicted with rebellious children, as are non-leaders and negligent parents. A few examples should suffice to make the point. In 19th century Alsace, the brothers Ratisbonne, sons of the lay leader of the Jewish community, not only were converted to Catholicism, but founded a religious order (Congregation of Notre Dame de Sion), the mission of which was to educate and convert Jewish children. (Isser, 1978). In Britain's royal family, Edward VIII was the ultimate rebel in rejecting not only his parents' values, but a kingdom. Closer to home, public officials have children who are arrested in connection with drug sales or possession, and psychotherapists have children who evidence severe "behavior problems" in school. The publicity, sometimes notoriety, that accompanies these events heightens the feelings of guilt, hurt, resentment, shame and anger felt by the parents. These "negative" emotions, which provoke anguish and turmoil, are also in conflict with the affection that parents hold, or claim to, for their errant children.

What kinds of underlying dynamics have been observed in families whose children must yank themselves away from the bonds of family ties so forcefully as to be vulnerable to the pull of a cult? Some patterns we have observed follow. In some cases, seemingly exemplary parents hold out a model of perfection that their children are unable to fulfill; in other situations the closeness much admired by friends is a pseudo-mutual one (Wynne, 1958) or an expression of an overly enmeshed family (Minuchin, 1967).

The extreme dependency evidenced by many of those who accept the recruiter's bait and become embroiled in the cult, further substantiates the supposition that they grew up in quite enmeshed families. Vickers (1977) notes that earlier periods in history were characterized by the high value placed on *responsibility*—to family and community. Such responsibility *to others* is a hallmark of the enmeshed family. Today's culture, however, values personal *autonomy* more than responsibility. Because these two values conflict, children from enmeshed families experience a real bind in trying to survive in an autonomy-valuing world. This may be why they are so susceptible to giving up autonomy in favor of an even more confining/enmeshing group that they can be responsible to for all their behavior. It will tell them exactly what to do, when and how.

Another dynamic which appears clinically is that contradictory communications from "good" parents have been internalized—"we love you tremendously *but* we resent your continuing needs and demands and want time alone—(to follow our own inclinations)—so you must go to camp, boarding school and/or far away to college." All of this is communicated at the meta-level; at the manifest level it is expressed as "camp is the best possible way for you to spend the summer, and therefore, we are sending you away because we love you and want you to have the best."... Often few rules of behavior have been incorporated since external structure was missing. Frequently, the father, who is upwardly mobile and determined to become successful, is away from home, working long hours to support his family or for personal aggrandizement, or playing golf to "make contacts" to enhance his career. Thus, the presence and influence of the father as a male authority figure has been minimal. (As might be anticipated, those non-vulnerable young adults we have talked to, taught, or treated, indicated strong, sometimes domineering, fathers whose expectations about acceptable behavior were quite clear. The strength of the father-child relationship appears to be a critical factor in the vulnerability/non-vulnerability of youth to cult recruitment. Those who have had a reasonably satisfying ongoing relationship with a strong father do not need to become part of an organization headed by an omniscient and omnipotent father figure.

In addition to the individuation and rebelliousness of adolescence, and the searching by this group for a strong father-person as a source of guidance and wisdom, other conditions usually are present to increase vulnerability in the young adult. Cult recruiters tend to look for the "loners," the disillusioned or floundering ones and those who are depressed. (Stoner and Park, 1977; Patrick, 1976). Other likely recruits are those who are confused by rapidly changing values, perhaps between keeping virginity and succumbing to peer and libidinal pressures to become involved sexually, and who therefore seek external authoritative answers to resolve their inner conflicts in preference to having to make their own difficult choices. Or, some of the vulnerable are extremely anxious about the responsibilities of adulthood and welcome the cocoon of perennial childhood offered by the cults (Rice, 1976). As indicated earlier, many have been reared in permissive homes and crave more structure and direction.

In the case of converts to the Jesus movement, it has been suggested that many of them (97% in one sample) have simply moved from *drug addiction to a different sort of dependency* (Simmonds, 1977). This last adaptive response is a more voluntary one, however, than most of those being stressed here, and may even be viewed by some parents as less harmful than drug addiction. (JCRC Report, 1976, p. 11) Nevertheless, the possibility is raised that involuntary converts may also be "addictive personalites," highly anxious, low in self-confidence (Peele and Brodsky, 1975), and dependent on external persons or organizations for answers to their personal and existential questions. As noted in the introductory comparison of youth and sub-culture in the 1960's and 1970's, the surface differences do not totally mask the basic similarities of meeting affiliation and dependency needs, providing an alternative family to the one from which the rebellious young person is trying to individuate and/or escape, and a way of asserting one's uniqueness.

Salzman, in an intriguing article on "Types of Religious Conversions" (1966), discusses several cases, principally those he calls "regressive" conversions. In discussing one treatment case involving a Protestant who planned to convert to Catholicism and to become a monk in an ascetic order, he writes:

> Shortly before he began therapy he detailed his plans for conversion in a long letter to his family which was full of both subtle and direct hostility, directed primarily at his father. His family had always been quite antagonistic to the Catholic Church; *thus his plans represented a double blow to them since he proposed both joining the Church they disapproved of, and removing himself forever from contact with them.** (pp. 16–17)

The parallel to those joining the cults should be apparent, although in the case chronicled by Salzman, the proposed conversion is clearly voluntary, whereas in the cults it is not.

Recruitment and Conversion

Cult recruiters are trained to look for the apparently friendless and "lost." They offer a gentle, supportive affection, followed usually by an invitation to join the recruiter for dinner at the latter's home. Here, the friends of the recruiter make the lonely one feel that he is part of their circle—warmly welcomed, the center of their loving attention. The evening's discussion focuses on the group's efforts to help those who are disadvantaged, to rid society of its ills, and perhaps to save the world from destruction. Religion

*Italics inserted by current authors.

is rarely mentioned, although it is obvious in the case of the Hare Krishna movement. At the end of the evening, the "recruit," who has been accorded seemingly *unconditional acceptance*, is invited to return for a weekend or longer. If he does so, he is again greeted with warmth and, in addition, is constantly surrounded by his new friends. The activities of singing, listening to lectures, communal eating and work activities, and prayer are again "low-key," but very enticing and gratifying, and verge on the hypnotic. The astute leaders fill every moment so that the newcomer has little time to think about what he is experiencing (Lofland, 1977; Adler, 1978; Stoner and Parke, 1977; Weisen, 1977a).

The technique used is the classic method of thought reform or coercive persuasion. This requires continuous supervision and indoctrination in a fully controlled environment. Such an environment often takes the form of a retreat in a setting isolated from telephones and other normal communication channels; every escape route is blocked. Simultaneously, the victim is *"robbed of the usual social supports of his beliefs and values;... he is subjected to a massive pressure to conform to a new, unanimous society ..."* (Holt, 1964, p. 296). Isolated from the familiar and surrounded with a smothering blanket of "love," based on a well devised strategy called "love bombing" (JCRC Report, 1976), the recruit feels guilty if he rejects the messages being given him. As this "visit" continues, the group focuses on the recruit's weaknesses, assaulting aspects of his previous identity, and applying the principles of behavioral reinforcement systematically. Ties to family members, former associations, and personal standards must be destroyed if resistance to the new ideology is to be overcome. Sincerity and enthusiasm for the movement and *its* ideology must be generated and positively reinforced in order to gain the youth's total commitment. In this process, a new identity is created. The conversion to the cult is complete when the individual himself sets out to proselytize others. (Schwartz and Isser, 1978; Salzman, 1966). As Hacker, a forensic psychiatrist, pointed out in discussing terrorists and crusaders, modern conversion techniques are "novel in that they produce not merely consent but inner conviction" (Hacker, 1976).

Holt's description of the features of the educational phase of the thought reform process, which appears in a chapter entitled, *"Forcible indoctrination and personality change"* (1964, pp. 295–298) is indeed chilling. He indicates that:

1. Thought reform is prolonged;—it goes on for months or years.
2. It is conducted continuously around the clock (also Singer, 1979).
3. It occurs in a completely controlled environment—no contrary information is available.
4. It utilizes social aspects of environmental control: "on the one hand,... (he is) robbed of the usual social supports of his beliefs

and values; on the other, he is subjected to a massive pressure to conform to a new unanimous society ..." (p. 296).

5. Thought reform is personalized.
6. There is a lack of privacy.
7. There is an assault upon previous identity.
8. There is systematic application of rewards and punishments.
9. Sincerity and enthusiasm are demanded—"total emotional commitment to the new idea" (p. 297) is mandatory.
10. All sources of resistance to the new ideology are exhausted—fostering "symbolic death of the old personality" (p. 297).
11. "Thought reform demands that its victims be active in reforming others" (p. 297)—proselytizing.
12. Synthesis and reconstruction—birth of a new identity.

It is not surprising that the group of cults under consideration here share in common the following characteristics and that they utilize many of the techniques elucidated by Holt to indoctrinate and convert.

1. A charismatic leader
2. Demand total submission to an overriding male authority (father-God figure)
3. Engage in conversion to their rigid belief system that perceives all non-believers (non-members) as the enemy
4. Demand complete commitment to the cult group as one's family and a negation of ties to the family of origin
5. A communal life style
6. Restrict communications with non-members—except for—
7. Active recruitment efforts
8. Physiologic deprivation (of food, rest, health care)
9. Fund raising for the leader and cult community, ranging from selling various items to surrender of all of one's assets

We have frequently been asked how these cults differ from close knit, ethnocentric religious groups such as the Mormons, Amish and Orthodox Jews. Despite some resemblances, key fundamental differences include that the family as a whole is encouraged to be active in the church and to be concerned for one another, that deprivation of adequate nutrition, sleep and health care are not sanctioned, one is expected to have personal belongings and a family place of residence, and privacy is accorded to all.

Impact on the Family

The negative impact on the family of this involvement with the cults is greater than the usual reaction to youthful alienation because of the way in which it occurs. There is a perception of entrapment, of uninformed consent, of cunning recruitment efforts, that is very frightening. There is also the parents' realization that at some deep, unconscious level their offspring has moved very far away from them emotionally, rejecting them and their heritage—and this is extremely painful. The rejection may well have been a two way process. Efforts to reestablish contact may stir up the young person's fears of again becoming overly dependent or attached and the parent's fears of battling anew. Parents also realize it may be extremely difficult to break through to the individual's pre-cult behaviors when he is surrounded constantly by members of his new, potent, replacement "family." Attempts by the family of origin, when contact is re-established, if this is possible, to reason with the youth may only result in driving him "underground" within the cult; that is, the cult may relocate the member and make his whereabouts impossible to trace. Deceptive answers from cult leaders such as "we do not know where your son is" are not uncommon. Apart from efforts to kidnap and "deprogram"[3] the young adult, efforts presently floundering in a legal quagmire, (ACLU, 1977), and which may also prove deleterious to the young person's mental health since they are usually carried out against his wishes (JCRC Report, 1976, pp. 35–36), what happens within the family when one of the young adult children is "lost" in this way?

Any number of emotional reactions occur, depending upon the individual personalities, interrelationships, and undercurrents present in a given family unit. Shock and bewilderment—"How and why did this happen to *us*?"—are initial responses. Following this, parents may be overwhelmed by a sense of failure and guilt, in that they were not supportive of or involved enough with their child, or they were too permissive and overly involved, or did not provide him with sufficient ego-strength and sense of self to resist the beckoning persuasion of the cult. They may be very hostile to the straying child, feeling that the episode is deliberately directed against them by an ungrateful, disloyal, and retaliatory child. They may be furious at the cult and its deceptive recruiting tactics and at the government for allowing such pseudo-religious groups to operate, protecting them under provisions of freedom of religion and granting them tax exempt status. Often they feel devastated, helpless, hopeless, with nowhere to turn. The family's sudden and continuing sense of loss and unresolved grief is sometimes analogous to that felt by families who have experienced the death of a child. They may blame each other for the child's abandonment of all they consider of value, thus precipitating a marital crisis.

Note that throughout, most parents view the individual in question as a child, not *as* an adult, and therefore as not ready to make his own decisions. This may not be totally in error. Holt (1964) and other investigators have indicated that part of the thought reform process involves reducing the individual to child-like dependence. It seems that such regression is essential so that transformation of a person's cognitive processes and personality organization can occur. Conway and Siegelman (1978) label this phenomenon of seemingly sudden, drastic personality change *snapping*; this word encapsulates the moment at which the person takes on a new identity, adheres to the cult's articles of faith totally, believes in the omnipotence of the cult's spiritual leader, is willing to proselytize for the movement and in many cults—sees non-believers as "being with Satan". Also, as to their being children, if they were more mature, autonomous and self-directing—they would not be vulnerable to the seduction of the cults which require submergence, even destruction, of one's uniqueness and independence.

There may also, of course, by physical consequences for parents in the form of a heart attack or severe psychosomatic reactions—uncontrollable crying, self punishment, or irrational outbursts. Younger siblings may be bewildered, frightened, hostile, or extremely anxious. The parents may also become concerned about the possible influence of the cult convert on these younger siblings as cults encourage members to actively recruit their brothers and sisters. Inter-generational conflicts may erupt. In short, the very fabric of the family is threatened (Weisen, 1977b) by a bigger, richer, more powerful, alternative family. Clearly therapeutic intervention is often needed to help family members cope with this crisis in their midst.

Therapeutic Intervention

The mental health professions have been accused of not assuming leadership in attempting to understand the appeal of cults, the myriad problems enmeshment in them evokes for the member and his family, in helping bereaved parents deal with the family crisis, or in treating de-programmed ex-cultists (Conway and Siegelman, 1978). Many therapists have remained remote from the cult scene, not attempting to become knowledgeable about this new phenomenon. Although some groups of therapists have held program meetings on the topic, this has tended to be the exception for professional organizations. Only now are papers and panels on the cults slowly beginning to appear on conference programs. There is a dearth of literature on the topic in the professional journals—which seems to confirm the accusation of non-concern and involvement. Numerous well respected therapists have told us that there is nothing special one needs to know to treat this population since cult membership is only a new manifestation of adolescent rebellion and should be handled as such; thus missing the added dimensions wrought from such a total experience and the accompanying traumatic personality and life style changes.

When parents of a young cultist turn to their churches, communal agencies, or private therapists for help, they rarely find anyone who is conversant with the many facets of this complex problem (Levine and Slater, 1976). In an excellent comprehensive report on "The Challenge of the Cults," a special study committee of the Jewish Community Relations Council of Greater Philadelphia (1976, pp. 47–78), came up with specific recommendations regarding *Help for Parents* which we have paraphrased and expanded considerably with the intent of making them valid for many communities and religious groups. Parents who learn that their child is in a cult need to know where to get information, advice, and aid. They need factually correct data about what cults are and particularly about the specific cult that has indoctrinated their own child (Singer, 1979). They need to know what their options are in terms of responding to this situation, that is, what has worked for other parents who have been confronted with a similar problem and what the legal ramifications of different options are likely to be. The assistance they require will probably include legal, psychological, social, and possibly financial aid. More specifically:

1. There is a need for a central clearinghouse in each community through which parents can make their initial contact with the agencies and/or individuals who may be able to help them. Family Service Agencies and Community Mental Health Centers are good possibilities and may designate several staff members who have (or are willing to acquire) special expertise on the subject.

2. The availability of an agency as a central clearinghouse should be publicized widely. Special mailings might go to clergy, educators, college counselors, therapists, family physicians and others who are likely to have the first contact with a distraught parent so that these people will know where to refer them.

3. Community agencies and religious institutions should develop a cooperative network for the provision of services to parents of cult members so that the factual material accumulated can be disseminated to all helping professionals for use with parents, thus giving them a solid data base upon which to evaluate the options being considered.

4. Provision of *group counseling* for parents of cult members is a sound and desirable practice. They seem to need a special support system of others who are experiencing the same plight, share their consternation, can candidly discuss feelings and together explore ways to cope and actions to take.

5. Many of the family's difficulties that seem to have exacerbated the susceptibility of a young person to the lure of the cults stem from long-standing problems and uncertainties that parents have about their effectiveness as parents. Programs such as standard Parent Effectiveness Training might be appropriate to help group members develop better parenting skills, thereby diminishing the vulnerability of their younger children. Or

in a parents' support or therapy group, their self blame and guilt can be a focal point; once this is reduced and the reality of their child's involvement confronted head on, they may be enabled to pick up the threads of their own shattered lives and begin to plan more effectively for next steps regarding the family's missing member specifically and their overall functioning more generally.

6. Therapists who are consulted by parents should be cognizant of the legal issues that surround what is called "kidnapping" one's own child back—at least enough to recommend that the parents contact an attorney knowledgeable about this topic, and about the legal decisions in earlier pertinent cases. They should also be well informed about the pros and cons of deprogramming and the possible long-lasting effects of one's having been a committed cult member—malnutrition, other diseases since medical care is negligible, a sense of loss and isolation when the close-knit cult support group is unavailable if one has been snatched away from it unwillingly, confusion about the two very different realms in which one has lived, residual thought disorders, guilt and shame over their earlier responsiveness to the cult, listlessness and a lack of purpose, and sometimes a frantic zeal to help "save" and deprogram others.

Life After the Cult and Treatment Considerations

Many young people who are involuntarily deprogrammed, and some who voluntarily leave the cults and rejoin their own families, seek professional help during the re-entry and readjustment phase. We believe it is incumbent upon therapists who are called upon to treat this population that they have an understanding of the cult phenomenon and what it means to join one, to live within its habitat and share the cult life style, to leave it and to be reunited with one's nuclear family. Some ex-cult members report they were told that deprogrammers "are of Satan", that if they leave the cults they are "doomed to be invaded by Satan", and that many other horrors will befall them—intimidating and traumatic pronouncements indeed.

The impact of such an experience is staggering on all family members. There is likely to be a mixture of many conflicted feelings—parental joy that their offspring is home, tempered by anger or confusion over the original renunciation of them. The ex-cultist may be partially relieved to be back in the outside world and wondering how he got "hooked", he may be fearful of punishment by the cult for his defection, he may experience periods of "floating" and altered states of consciousness, or he may yearn to return to an "Ashram" or other cult residence and resent his parents' latest interference in his life. Frequently a profound depression is experienced. Because of the complexities of these situations, the fragility of the family relationships, the fears and hurts that have been sustained—each case should be carefully evaluated and the treatment of choice recommended.

We have come to the conclusion that since one's family background and relationships appear to contribute to one's vulnerability to the cult's invitation to join as well as to one's leaving of the cult, family involvement in the treatment is often essential for lasting progress to be made and for family members to attain a better understanding of one another, respect for each other's differences, needs and goals. Thus, all members of the family unit should be involved in treatment. If the intensity of the conflict between parents and ex-cult member is extremely high, it is quite probable that concurrent treatment is more feasible, at least at the beginning, so that the ex-cult member has a caring, "tuned-in" therapist all to himself, who may represent, as the cult did, an authority source and ego ideal outside of the family, but this time one who does not demand total loyalty and renunciation of the parents. In this way, each of the parties can separately receive all the attention and concern and have a private time to ventilate feelings and clarify thoughts. If each voices some desire for a rapproachment, then it is likely they can be seen concurrently by the same therapist. However, if the antagonism is still acute and mistrust rampant, it is advisable that they see different therapists who can collaborate without violating confidentiality. Where, during the initial family evaluation session(s), it appears everyone is interested in working on the problems together, then conjoint family therapy constitutes the most efficacious treatment strategy.

It is important to try to comprehend the function the young adult's joining of the cult served for the family system. Was this already a scapegoated member being extruded, was he diverting attention from an about to erupt parental war in order to save his mother and father's marriage; or was he perhaps designated to lead the family on a quest for spiritual fulfillment? An adequate mapping of the family's genogram and understanding of their equilibrating mechanisms and structure is essential in helping them toward greater awareness of their needs and transactions as they strive toward wholeness and health. The former cult member often suffers something akin to withdrawal symptoms during the period following his exodus, and one of these is the loss of a sense of group belonging and the feeling of identity and mission this provides. Thus, it is often advisable to involve the young person in a therapy group with other ex-cult members who are facing similar dilemmas and with whom he can sympathize, share, identify, and seek solutions. Such an involvement in group therapy can occur during the same time that the person participates in family therapy so that healthy peer group ties are fostered which replace those that may have been abruptly terminated. Often the ex-cult member feels alien to his pre-cult friends and needs to establish new meaningful friendships; the therapy group provides a transitional place to do this. Regardless which treatment modality is selected, it is crucial that the therapist be clear about his own views on the cults, be able to articulate his ideas if asked what he really thinks, and that these are consistent with the ethical values and philosophy that undergird his therapeutic practice. An optimistic outlook is important; to convey pessimism is to exacerbate the despair deep within the patients. They yearn to know if they will ever again function effectively as independent, competent individuals not prone to floating and thought dissociations.

In some instances, the young adult should not move back into his parents' home, yet to live alone would be to heighten the pervasive sense of isolation. Perhaps mental health professionals might be instrumental in collaborating with other public spirited citizens in seeing that attractive, high quality, small group residences are developed in which ex-cult members can reside with a sense of both camaraderie and privacy; of belonging and independence; of mutual concern and individual responsibility; residences that offer group therapy and wholesome group activities and are staffed by "house parents" who can provide necessary, but not intrusive, nurturance and guidance.

Since many of the ex-cult members gravitate into pseudo-religious cults, one can assume some of the attraction is related to a spiritual-religious quest. Thus, the healing process might well need to minister also to the individual's unmet spiritual needs. A communique from Rabbi Gerald Wolpe (1978) speaks cogently to this point:

> I have met enough cultists and former cult members to realize that therapy has to take the religious phenomenon into consideration. It may be a "culte de moi" but these children are speaking in religious and pseudo-religious terms. The vocabulary is quite clear, and in many cases, thoroughly traditional. If that vocabulary is misunderstood or ignored, then therapeutic activity is doomed from the very beginning ... From time to time, I deal with families of both Jewish and Christian persuasion who have to adjust to a returning former cultist ... Much of the strain deals with the inability of the family to accept the fact that there is a serious spiritual vacuum in the ... family values. The cultic member is caught between his sense of love and loyalty to the family to which he wants to return [including the knowledge that he has caused pain to others] and his sense of déjà vu in a spiritually bereft home. Many of the youngsters have said to me after some weeks at home, "nothing has changed; they are the same and they just don't understand that they are hypocrites." In a significant cross identification [transference]*, they will make the same accusation towards their therapist accusing him/her of "secularism", a position that they hold in great disdain. They contrast the definite value position of their former cult] setting with the ambivalence of a technique (therapy) that seems to urge a vague adjustment.

*Bracketed words inserted by authors.

In no way is my reaction to be construed as a crusade for using clergymen as therapists; they (most of them) are not trained in that direction ... However, as it is recommended that clergymen learn therapeutic techniques and values in order to become more conversant with their utilization and to recognize their own limitations, so it is imperative for therapists ... to recognize the essential key of the spiritual element in this process and problem.

Given the above, any therapist treating ex-cultists and/or their families must have a great depth and breadth of knowledge and skill to draw upon, the flexibility to use an appropriate combination of treatment modalities—individual, group and family, as well as to collaborate with religious leaders and pastoral counselors, to help make special living arrangements, to construct support systems and perhaps to help move the young person back into college or toward a fulfilling job.

Summary

In this article we have tried, in bold strokes, to paint a collage regarding those who become cult members and the ramifications of their involvement on their entire family.

Although the cults do not publish membership statistics, they jointly claim millions of members. The Unification Church (Moonies) alone officially claims 30,000 members in the United States (JCRC Report, 1976, p. 15). Thus, since a sizeable number of young people and their families are involved and will continue to be affected by this phenomenon which has traumatic reverberations for those affected, it is incumbent upon therapists to learn about, try to make sense of, and be ready to treat this population and to contribute to the body of literature on this subject. We believe concurrent or conjoint family therapy usually constitutes the treatment of choice and that whenever feasible, group therapy should be used as an adjunct to family therapy for the ex-cult member. This is a fertile field for basic and applied research; one we dare not ignore if we believe in doctrines of free will, personal responsibility, individuality, autonomy, physical and mental health, and self actualization.

References

ADLER, W. Rescuing David from the Moonies, *Esquire*, (June 6), 1978, *89*, (10), 23–30.

AMERICAN CIVIL LIBERTIES UNION, *Civil Liberties*, Sept. 1977.

CONWAY, F. & SIEGELMAN, J. *Snapping: American's Epidemic of Sudden Personality Change*, Philadelphia: J. B. Lippincott, 1978.

DANER, F. J. *The American Children of Krsna*, New York: Holt, Rinehart and Winston, 1976.

ERIKSON, E. H. *Childhood and Society*, New York: W. W. Norton, 1950.

ERIKSON, E. H. Identity: *Youth and Crisis*, New York: W. W. Norton, 1968.

HACKER, F. J. *Crusaders, Criminals, Crazies: Terror and Terrorism in our Time*, New York: W. W. Norton, 1976. (particularly chapter on "Rape of the Mind")

HOLT, R. R. "Forcible indoctrination and personality change". In P. Worschel and D. Byrne, (Eds.) *Personality Change*, New York: John Wiley, 1964, 289–318.

ISSER, N. The Mallet affair: Case study of a scandal. Unpublished manuscript, 1978.

Jewish Community Relations Council of Greater Philadelphia Committee Report, *The Challenge of the Cults*, Philadelphia: JCRC, 1976.

LEVINE, S. V. and SLATER, N. E. Youth and contemporary religious movements: psychosocial findings. *Canadian Psychiatric Association Journal*, 1976, *21*, 211–420.

LOFLAND, J. *Doomsday Cult*, (enlarged ed.), New York: Irvington Publishers, 1977.

MINUCHIN, S., MONTALVO, BRAULIO, *et al. Families of the Slums*, New York: Basic Books, 1967.

NAGY, I. B. and SPARK, G. *Invisible Loyalties*, New York: Harper and Row, 1973.

PATRICK, T. (With T. Dulack), *Let Our Children Go*, New York: E. P. Dutton, 1976.

PEELE, S. and BRODSKY, A. *Love and Addiction*, New York: Taplinger Publishing, 1975.

RICE, B. Messiah from Korea: Honor thy Father Moon. *Psychology Today*, Jan. 1976, *9*, (8), 36–47.

ROSZAK, T. *The Making of a Counter Culture*, New York: Anchor Books, 1968.

SALZMAN, L. Types of religious conversion, *Pastoral Psychology*, 1966, *17*, (8), 8–20; 66.

SCHWARTZ, L. L. Cults and the vulnerability of Jewish youth, *Jewish Education*, 1978, *46*, (2), 23–26; 42.

SCHWARTZ, L. L., and ISSER, N. "A note on involuntary techniques". *Jewish Social Studies*, 1979, in press.

SIMMONDS, R. B. Conversion or addiction. *American Behavioral Scientist*, 1977, *20*, 909–924.

SINGER, M. T. Coming out of the cults, *Psychology Today*, Jan. 1979, 72–82.

STONER, C. and PARKE, J. A. *All Gods Children: Salvation or Slavery?* Radnor, Pa.: Chilton Book Co., 1977.

VICKERS, G. The weakness of western culture, *Futures*, 1977, *9*.

WIESEN, I. Inside Alamo, *Jewish Press*, Sept. 2, 1977 (a).

WIESEN, I. Mind Control, *Jewish Press*, Sept. 9, 1977 (b).

WOLPE, RABBI G. Private communication, Nov. 1978.

WYNNE, L. C. *et al.* Pseudomutuality in the family relations of schizophrenics, *Psychiatry*, 1958, *21*, 205–220.

Notes

1. Cult is used herein to denote a group of people who submit to the authority of a self-proclaimed (and often charismatic) religious leader, and who are united by a rigid set of "sacred" beliefs and attitudes shaped by that leader, and who, as a result, tend to be estranged from reality and their fellow humans (after Salzman, 1966).

2. He is used in the generic, literary sense and not intended to have any sexist. political connotation.

3. Deprogrammers like Ted Patrick employ many of the same "thought reform" techniques as do cult leaders—restricted environment, sleep deprivation, positive reinforcement for desired changes in behavior—but for a more socially acceptable end. One must question here if the ends therefore justify the means. It is also important to note the similarity to Skinnerian behavior modification approaches and to techniques used by est and at marathon sessions at growth centers.

PART V

Presenting Problems

In this section of the book each of the articles selected deals with a discrete area of social work intervention. They are not presented as a comprehensive overview of the full range of problems met in social work practice. Rather, they serve as examples of how problem, or identified need, is an important component of the diagnostic process.

This section did not appear in the first edition, although some consideration was given to including a section like this. The decision not to include it was based on the perception that requests for service, as discussed here, were of a different conceptual order from those qualities of personality constituting a client's psychosocial identity considered in the first four parts.

Further thought led to the conclusion that its absence could be interpreted as implying that the four prior sections represent the essential variables in diagnosis, and the request for service is secondary. This would in turn imply that variations in modality, method, or technique altered only in relation to the former and not the latter. These articles belie this concept. It is evidently not any more valid than the other extreme, which would hold that the request for service or the identified problem was the essential independent variable upon which the choice of modality or technique depended.

The idea of problem, as distinct from the client's biopsychosocial identity, is an essential concept for our profession. It is also an elusive term, because the focus of our professional attention is directed to several components or subsystems of a client's significant social system rather than a single one. Problem indeed is important, but of greater importance is person with problem.

We know that we have resisted identifying the sole object of our professional activity as personality change lest we be seen as attempting to pattern ourselves too closely on the example of other professions. Yet we know that much of our direct work with clients does aim at altering patterns and indeed structures of personality. We have equally avoided identifying our activities as being directed only to behavioral change. At times we have attempted to claim our unique focus to be the social problems of clients, that vast area of people's interactions with others and with situations. But only by semantic "legerdemain" can we exclude from any concept of social work the altering of personality functioning and behavioral change. Dr. Bill Reid has made a major contribution to the understanding of problem in his development of task-centered practice.*

In the last edition the difficulty in conceptualizing the concept of problem and separating it from the other four sections was raised. It is evident that an argument could be made that some of the topics included in this section might just as well have been put into another section. For example divorce could be considered under developmental stages, enuresis under physical disorders, and school phobias with psychosocial problems. But they do not quite fit, and hence the section entitled "Presenting Problems."

An examination of the articles in the previous edition led to the conclusion that two characteristics separated these articles from the other sections. These were "normative considerations," and "fortuitous events." Further thought, influenced by the addition of other topics, suggests that this group of articles can be better divided into four types of problems, with some of the topics having characteristics of more than one category.

The first grouping of problems could be called "interpersonal." These deal with situations that arise out of interpersonal relationships where a role change has resulted. Here would be included the topics of unmarried parents, step-parenting, and divorce. The second group of articles relates to situations that are considered by a significant component of society as undesirable or as variations from the expected or the desired. This heading could be called "normative problems." From this perspective the articles on suicide, school phobia, anomie, and abortion would be grouped.

A third grouping of articles relates to desired or sought for "changes in physical functioning." Here would be included the material on vasectomy, obesity, and enuresis.

Lastly, there are the articles that last time were referred to as fortuitious events, but on further consideration all have an aspect of "assault" to them either by natural events or by the actions of others. The articles on rape, incest, natural disasters, and family abuse cluster here.

The development of classification systems is not an end in itself. For the practitioner they are useful if they lead to a clearer perception of general problem areas, needs for service, or patterning of intervention that

*William J. Reid, Task-Centered System (New York: Columbia University Press, 1978).

help make us more sensitive to the understanding of commonalities in situations and thus more efficient in responding to need.

I am not sufficiently convinced that the fourfold division of presenting problems is as yet useful in helping to develop effective practice theory. Hence the articles are not divided into separate categories but rather are listed alphabetically. The authors of the various articles for the most part did not write from a conceptual position of problem theory. Rather they were attempting to give their understanding and management of a particular situation met in practice. Further work obviously is needed to see if there are commonalities in dealing with particular kinds of problems.

It is not being suggested that the articles reflect the entire range of specific problems dealt with in current practice. The list does reflect the range of problems being addressed in the professional literature of the profession and probably has a bias in it related to current societal interests. For example among the articles located for possible inclusion were a large number of rape and other forms of assault. There was an equally large number on divorce, separation, and remarriage, while for some topics only single articles were found.

The fact that there are patterns in writing in which some topics are given more attention than others is not necessarily a bad thing. It is the way knowledge develops. What is of equal importance, though, is that the existence of popular topics does not exclude either the addressing of other topics or, more importantly, the search for a theoretical construct that links diagnostic and interventive strategies across groups of problems.

It is evident from the literature that one of the most dramatic changes in current practice is the growing comfort in an approach to practice that is built on diversity. That is, as new or difficult problems are addressed, the challenge for the practitioner is what can I put together to respond effectively to this situation from the range of theories, services, techniques, methodologies, and resources.

How this diversity enriches the scope of our practice is particularly evident in Part V. For example, behavior modification has given us new approaches to the age-old scourge of enuresis. Sociological theory helps us understand and manage the changing roles faced by the step-parent. Existentialism gives us both a basis to recognize the prevalence of the suffering caused by anomie and a viewpoint with which to confront it. Finally, crisis theory permits us to understand the impersonal kind of disaster, such as a train wreck, and the highly personalized disaster, such as a rape episode.

In the article on school phobia can be seen another component of our multitheory trend. Here the authors identify varying theoretical implications of school phobia but point out that there is a growing consensus about the management implications. In the article on the unmarried mother we find

Strean encouraging us not to abandon earlier theoretical perceptions but to expand and enrich them in light of further understanding.

We have been less than dramatic in our literature from the viewpoint of generalizing as a step to theory-building. Even though we have a strong tradition of "problem-solving" approach to practice, the literature still reflects a strong tendency to view problems as discrete entitites rather than as contributing to an expansion of problem-solving theory.

It is hoped that within the next few years we can progress in making use of the full range of systems available in current practice to develop a more general understanding of what specific interventive and therapeutic steps are appropriate to different situations and different clusters of situations. In the meantime it may be necessary to continue to address individual problems separately as demonstrated by these articles, until we build a richer literature on the diagnostic and treatment implications of the presenting problem.

ABORTION

CHAPTER 61

Social Work Service to Abortion Patients

Alice Ullmann

On July 1, 1970, abortions were legalized in New York State. In the following fifteen months about 200,000 abortions were performed in New York City. Although this demand on services apparently presented no particular problem to the health care facilities in the city, debates about abortion continue among the health professions, religious groups, and the general public. In the face of much public discussion, it is pertinent to ask how the women who are undergoing abortions are affected. What are the psychological implications of having an abortion? Why do women make that decision? Do they need help in coping with their decision?

Background

Review of the literature about the implications of abortion does not provide a definitive point of view about psychological conflict regarding abortion or psychological sequelae. Psychologically oriented studies are rare and often deal with the psychiatrist's dilemma in recommending therapeutic abortion. Experience with legal abortion in this country is not yet extensive enough to have produced studies; those from other countries are not always pertinent, in view of cultural differences.

Some years ago, Helene Deutsch wrote of the legal and religious influences in the field of abortion over the centuries and pointed out that it is likely that there have been even deeper psychological motivations against

Reprinted from *Social Casework,* Vol. 53 (October, 1972), pp. 481–487, by permission of the author and the Family Service Association of America.

abortion. These motivations, she suggested, are connected with the instinct of self-preservation and the urge to motherhood. She also noted that there must be ambivalence, in that the pregnancy is rejected even though becoming pregnant represented a wish fulfillment. Abortion, some women feel, destroys something in themselves. Deutsch further reported that, during menopausal depressions, some women who have had abortions express self-accusation—but more recent thinking indicates that this may represent a vehicle for depression rather than its cause. She also described a change in the relationship between the man and the woman after abortion. Since Deutsch's work was published in 1945, it may well reflect the mores of that period.[1]

Mary Calderone has also cautioned about the psychological effect of abortions.[2] Most literature, however, does not support these suggestions. In fact the consensus appears to be that "legal abortion can be performed without fear of severe psychic harm to the woman."[3] Liberalization of abortion laws doubtlessly reflects this opinion, and recent polls of physicians and psychiatrists have shown large majorities in favor of legalizing abortion.[4] It is generally agreed that a woman's reaction to abortion is determined by her general psychological state. However, certain psychological symptoms, it is reported, do appear. One of these is guilt, sometimes as a reaction to the clinical procedure, sometimes as a result of the punitive attitude of those caring for the patient. The guilt may be mild or severe. This guilt and the rarity of severe depression are well described by George S. Walter in his review of the literature.[5] The Kinsey group reported that abortion did not effect subsequent sexual behavior of women.[6]

Edward Senay describes women applying for abortion as a population in crisis.[7] In his clinical experience, there were many instances of insomnia, somatic complaints, anxiety, and suicidal ideation, as well as an intense preoccupation with the problem of ending the unwanted pregnancy. This report reflects experience with psychiatric indications for abortion. One might argue that the women who no longer require pyschiatric evaluations, and can obtain legal abortions based on the decision between patient and physician, are not under as much psychological stress. A Scandinavian study shows that the majority of women who have undergone legal

[1] Helene Deutsch, The Psychology of Women, vol. 2: Motherhood (New York: Grune and Stratton, 1945).

[2] Mary Calderone, ed., Abortion in the United States (New York: Harper & Row, 1968).

[3] George S. Walter, Psychologic and Emotional Consequences of Elective Abortion, Obstetrics and Gynecology, 36: 482–91 (September 1970).

[4] Eric Pfeiffer, Psychiatric Indications or Psychiatric Justification of Therapeutic Abortion?, Archives of General Psychiatry, 23: 402–07 (November 1970).

[5] Walter, Psychologic Consequences of Abortion.

[6] Paul H. Gebhard et al., Pregnancy, Birth and Abortion (New York: Harper & Row, 1958).

[7] Edward C. Senay, Therapeutic Abortion—Clinical Aspects, Archives of General Psychiatry, 23: 408–15 (November 1970).

abortions do not suffer major psychological sequelae.[8] However, it is not known how many women who ask for abortion have preexisting psychological problems which may be exacerbated by the procedure. Senay speaks of this high-risk group and describes a mourning process that almost invariably takes place and can affect a woman in different ways, depending on preexisting psychological status.[9] He reports, also, that specific questioning of the patients will elicit reports of guilt, depression, and anxiety. *American Journal of Public Health* of March 1971 contains a number of articles about abortion. In one of these, Henry P. David asks for research in psychosocial factors in abortion.[10] He maintains that more should be known about psychosocial implications now that more and more states are liberalizing their abortion laws.

Planning a Service

Prior to 1970 the social workers at New York Hospital—a large voluntary, university hospital in New York City—were involved in obtaining psychiatric recommendations for women seeking abortion. These requests originally came at the rate of about one a week, but in the period immediately before July 1970, there were about five a week. Experience with these patients had shown that they reflected the psychological adjustment of almost any patient group. That is, some women were under greater stress than others, some had histories or evidenced symptoms of varying degrees of psychological disorders, some, although under stress, showed general emotional stability. The problems involved in obtaining an abortion on psychiatric grounds caused all of them some stress.

Supporters of legal abortion claim that the procedure is a simple one and often describe it as less traumatic than a tonsillectomy. Experience of the social work staff in interviewing the patients mentioned above, however, showed that the majority of patients had psychological difficulties in making the decision to have the abortion. This group of patients served to make it clear that the women requesting abortion after July 1970 would be under stress of varying degree and that every effort should be made to provide a social work service.[11]

When the new law came into effect, New York Hospital set aside a

[8] Martin Ekblad, Induced Abortion on Psychiatric Grounds: A Follow-up Study of 479 Women, *Acta Psychiatrica et Neurologica Scandinavica*, suppl. 99 (1955), p. 1.

[9] Senay, Therapeutic Abortion.

[10] Henry P. David, Abortion: Public Health Concerns and Needed Psychosocial Research, *American Journal of Public Health*, 61: 510–17 (March 1971).

[11] The writer is grateful to the obstetrical and gynecological unit of the Department of Social Work in the New York Hospital for aiding in data collection and providing the patient service, and to Miss Margaret Mushinski for her assistance in preparing the statistical report.

thirty-bed clinical ward for private and service abortion patients separating them from obstetrical and gynecological patients. The service patients were seen in the clinic first and admitted to the hospital within a few days. Private patients were not seen in the hospital prior to admission.

The social workers turned their attention to the service patients who could be seen prior to admission. Because of the amount of time involved, individual interviews to find problem situations were not feasible. The decision to see patients in groups, therefore, was a logical means of handling the situation. The group session would provide education about the abortion procedure and family-planning methods and had the added benefit of the interest and support of the nursing staff who eventually became coleaders of the groups.

Further rationale for the establishment of the groups was to allow for the expression of conflict regarding the abortion and to help the patient deal with possible adverse family, religious, and social class attitudes. Group censures may cause feelings of isolation as well as guilt and anxiety in the prospect abortion patient who often has to face the procedure alone. Peer groups would offer the patient the opportunity to share her feelings with others in a similar situation. They might support the patient in the decision-making process. The goal of the groups was therefore threefold: (1) to help the patients share and express feelings of conflict within the group, (2) to help members of the group support each other, and (3) to provide education about abortion and medical procedures and to clear up mistaken ideas about abortion and family planning. It was also hoped that the group process would help to identify those women with significant psychosocial problems or stress so that further help could be offered to those patients.

THE PATIENTS

Prospective patients were asked to join the group for a discussion with the social worker, but joining the group was not compulsory. The group meetings took place after every clinic session, and each group met once.

From September 1, 1970, to February 26, 1971, 598 patients were seen in groups, an average of five in each session. This total represented roughly 75 percent of all abortion patients who came to the clinic. Most of those women who did not attend a group session gave as a reason that they wanted to get home. This applied particularly to those coming from out of town. Some who did not wish to join a group explained that they felt they had nothing to discuss, no questions to ask. Each patient coming into a group was asked to complete a small card containing questions of area of residence, age, marital status, race, religion, occupation, source of support, how the patient heard about the service, what birth control methods had been used, and why the patient was seeking an abortion. There were no refusals to fill out the cards although a few patients omitted some items and eighteen patients did not give reasons for seeking the abortion.

As shown in Table 61-1, 60 percent of the patients came from New York City, 5 percent from New York State, and 33 percent from states other than New York. The largest percentage of patients (40 percent) were between the ages of twenty and twenty-four. One-third of the patients were married. Single women comprised 46 percent of the patients, and the remaining 21 percent were divorced, separated, or widowed. The patients were primarily white (68 percent), and the largest percentage of the women were Catholic (47 percent). Almost a third were housewives, a little more than a fifth were employed as clerical or sales personnel, and skilled workers and students were almost equally represented (13 percent and 14 percent, respectively). More than one-half (55 percent) had completed high school, almost a quarter (23 percent) had only an elementary education,

TABLE 61-1.   Percentage Distribution of Respondents' Characteristics

Characteristics	Percentage of respondents	Characteristics	Percentage of respondents
Age		*Marital status*	
Under 19	15	Single	46
20–24	40	Married	33
25–29	24	Separated	14
30–34	12	Divorced	6
35–39	7	Widowed	1
40+	2	Unknown	[a]
Race		*Occupation*	
White	68	Housewife	32
Black	26	Clerical, sales	21
Other	5	Student	14
Unknown	1	Skilled	13
Religion		Professional, managers	10
Catholic	47	Unknown	7
Protestant	34	Unskilled	3
Jewish	4	*Area of residence*	
Other	10	New York City	60
None	3	New York State	5
Unknown	2	Other states	33
Education		Unknown	2
Elementary	23	*Means of support*	
High school	55	Self	38
College	16	Husband	26
College+	2	Public assistance	21
Unknown	4	Parents	11
		Other	3
		Unknown	1

[a] Less than one percent
N = 598

and almost a fifth (18 percent) had attended college. The majority of the patients were self-supporting; 21 percent were receiving public assistance.

Table 61–2 shows that one-quarter of the patients had used the pill for birth control, and 46 percent had used no birth control at all. Table 61–3 reflects the reasons given for seeking an abortion; the women were given the opportunity to cite more than one reason. Lack of sufficient money was the reason given by the largest percentage of women (43 percent). Being unmarried was cited by 37 percent, even though actually 46 percent

TABLE 61–2.   Methods of Contraception

METHODS	PERCENTAGE OF RESPONDENTS
None	46
Pill	25
Foam	10
Diaphragm	6
Rhythm	6
Coil	5
Condom	3
Other	2
Jelly	1
Average number of methods per patient[a]	1.1

N = 598

[a] Totals amount to more than 100 percent because there were multiple responses. Percentages were calculated from the number of respondents, not the number of responses.

TABLE 61–3.   Reasons for Abortion

REASONS	PERCENTAGE OF RESPONDENTS
Money	43
Not married	37
Not ready	31
Work/school	30
Too many children	20
Other	8
Not husband's child	5
Unknown	3
Average number of reasons per patient[a]	1.8

N = 598

[a] Totals amount to more than 100 percent because there were multiple responses. Percentages were calculated from the number of respondents, not the number of responses.

were single. This fact is more significant when *single* is considered to include divorced, separated, and widowed, in which case the percentage of unmarried women is actually 67. It is not clear what was meant by the response, *not ready*, but it was included because earlier experience with abortion patients had shown this to be a reason frequently cited. It appears to include a combination of such reasons as lack of money, desire to space children, and general unpreparedness. The work/school category usually represented school for high school students and work for the older women, although there were some women interested in continuing education.

THE GROUPS

When examining the content of the group discussions, the characteristics of the women should be borne in mind. It is possible that women of different ethnic and educational backgrounds would have other concerns about abortion.

Six social workers participated in the program. A nurse clinician acted as coleader to insure that the educational and clinical aspects of abortion could be handled effectively. One of the leaders usually began the meeting with a statement that being admitted for an abortion has caused many women some degree of social and emotional stress and that hospital personnel wanted them to have the opportunity to discuss their questions and concerns. This comment usually brought out requests for information about the abortion procedures, but it appeared that these questions could not be handled through a purely educational approach. Questions about the procedure included who exactly would do the procedure and what the length of anesthesia would be. The questions also reflected fear of the procedure and its aftereffects. For instance, the question of subsequent sterility came up quite often. For many women this would be their first hospitalization, and they wanted to know what it was like to be in a hospital, whether they would be separated from the obstetrical patients, and when they could be visited. They needed education and information, but more than this they were asking for reassurance that the procedure was not harmful.

It was necessary to encourage the group members to express their conflicts on some occasions, but most of the women were very ready to talk about their underlying feelings. The question of guilt came up at every session. It appeared that although abortion had been legalized, it was still felt by many of these patients to be an illegal procedure. Apparently, in this situation, the change in law has come before the change in heart. Religious issues came up very rarely so that the guilt expressed or implied was usually not based on religious conflict. There was discussion about "killing the baby," fear that society would judge them, stress on secrecy, expression of guilt about becoming pregnant and undergoing an unnatural procedure. Often group members tended to appeal to the leaders for alleviation of their guilt. The leaders found that what helped the group most was to receive this reassurance from each other, and they guided the group to talk to each other rather than to the leaders.

It seemed very clear that the majority of women were ambivalent. They described how they suppressed their motherly feelings, which they said they possessed but did not want at this time. They said they did not want to think of the fetus as a baby. There was regret by some that while pregnancy should be a wonderful experience, they could not go through with it now. Many wanted quick admission so that the fetus would not have a chance of becoming "too real."

A frequent topic of discussion was the attitude of the clinic personnel. The women complained they were being talked at, treated like numbers rather than people, and kept waiting too long. They felt the professional staff condemned them. On further discussion it appeared that these reactions had much to do with how the patients felt about themselves; however, the attitude of personnel was a problem at times and certainly bears further exploration. Some patients expressed much anger on such subjects as racism, fathers of the babies, and promiscuous women; again it appeared that some of this feeling was projection of their own anxiety and ambivalence.

Feelings of isolation was also apparent, although the records show that very few patients actually went through planning for the abortion alone. In the groups, however, many patients regretted not being able to discuss their problems with their families. Many out-of-town patients described what it was like to come to New York and to the hospital without family or peer support. Even those who had discussed their plans with families and friends felt that ultimately the decision and experience were personal ones which others could share only to a limited extent.

In some groups, patients talked about their backgrounds and families, their other children, about being or not being married, and about birth control and family-planning. Some blamed birth control device failures, but many admitted to ignorance of birth control methods. This fact is interesting because it was not an educationally deprived group. Knowledge about birth control is apparently not related to education. One might, or course, question the motivation of these women to become pregnant but the group discussions did not deal with this question. The women spoke about their jobs and how to handle job absence. Usually they found someone in the group who had similar experiences and others who had opinions and feelings about these subjects.

Joint leadership was a problem at times. It did provide for nurses and social workers to cooperate in a service to patients and gave them an opportunity to work together. In general, the nurses tended to lean toward more active participation; they taught, guided, and reassured. The social workers tended to encourage the group members to talk to each other and derive help and support from each other. Nurses and social workers met to discuss these differences in approach, but they remained a problem. The nurses were a definite asset in providing information and education about the abortion procedures. However, as the social workers became more familiar with the information, it was not as important to have the nurse handle the educational aspects.

Discussion

No attempt was made at a formal evaluation of the group meetings. A number of patients mentioned during their subsequent hospital stay that they had found the meeting personally helpful and reassuring in relation to staff attitudes. The social work staff felt that the sessions gave patients an opportunity to discuss their questions and concerns with professional staff and with group members having similar experiences. The contact resulted in mutual support and relief of tension. Further evaluation of the group experience would have to be based on study and control groups.

Approximately one patient in every three groups was seen individually subsequent to the group sessions. Some of these patients sought individual service; in other cases the social worker, having identified a disturbed patient during a session, would speak with her afterward, offering help. Service was given most often in relation to ambivalence about the abortion and less frequently in relation to concrete problems such as housing, absence from work, or financial questions. The group sessions were therefore of some help in individual case-finding.

Another area requiring further study and observation is the attitude toward abortion of the professional personnel, who are bound to have some personal conflicts and to be affected both consciously and unconsciously by positive or negative public attitudes. It is quite likely that physicians and nurses—both trained to save lives—find abortion a difficult subject to deal with and have conflict about participating in the procedure. Patients seem to be quickly aware of this feeling. Although social workers are less involved in the actual abortion procedure, they are also likely to have their own conflicts. Another question one might ask is whether men and women have different attitudes about abortion. It would be useful, also, to analyze the contribution of the group leaders and to evaluate the group process in general.

The greatest amount of work, however, needs to be done in the whole area of the nature of emotional conflicts in patients undergoing abortions and the presence or absence of psychological sequelae. For instance, do all women suffer some emotional conflict or ambivalence, and if so, do they all need professional help? Is abortion today a procedure acceptable to most women as a way of limiting family size? Is seeking an abortion symptomatic of other psychological conflict, and does it take place in the presence of other psychological problems? To obtain answers to these questions it would be necessary to conduct personal interviews including follow-up after the abortion.

Summary

This article has examined some of the literature about the psychological aspects of abortion. The 598 patients who came to a large voluntary hospital in New York City and were seen in group-counseling sessions were described, and such subjects as use of birth control and reasons for abortion were considered. The content of the group discussions were examined in an attempt to determine if a need was being met. There was no formal evaluation of the effect of the groups, but it appeared that useful information about abortion was given, that group members expressed their ambivalent feelings, and that they felt that they had derived some benefit from the group experience.

ABUSED CHILDREN

CHAPTER 62

A Model of Therapy with Abusive and Neglectful Families

Susan J. Wells

Family therapy has remained an undeveloped aspect of treatment with abusive and neglectful families. This may be because much of family intervention is based on verbal interaction, and abusive or neglectful families are often not amenable to "talking treatment." Nevertheless, family therapy may be a viable treatment modality in protective services. Issues such as communication through behavior, individual and familial isolation, misperceptions of other family members, blaming one another, or denial of a problem are indications for intervention with the family as a whole.

The problem, then, is how to adapt a talking treatment to this clientele. Polansky has worked for years on developing the concept of verbal accessibility, or "the readiness of the client to communicate in speech, and to permit others to communicate with him, about his most important attitudes."[1] Polansky has used it with neglectful mothers on an individual basis as an assessment tool, indicator of treatability, and guide for intervention.[2] Verbal accessibility might also be applied to work with families in a similar manner. The aspects of verbal accessibility that relate to interpersonal interactions and the communication patterns of abusive and neglectful families will be examined in this article and integrated to form a model for practice.

Verbal Accessibility

Polansky describes verbal accessibility as "relative between persons and within a given person." This concept has to do with what Polansky terms "determinant attitudes"—attitudes "whose change seems most likely to bring about strong changes in other related attitudes."[3] Readiness to communicate about determinant attitudes is a product of the situation, the moment, and interpersonal interaction. Verbal accessibility has been operationalized by a global scale that is designed to measure the client's willingness to "talk meaningfully about feelings." The scale's range consists of the following six points:

> (1) Spontaneous verbalization; (2) Spontaneous with the caseworker's explicit encouragement; (3) Responsive, equal give and take with the caseworker; (4) Receptive, little give, lots of take; (5) Unresponsive, complete lack of response despite explicit encouragement; (6) Avoidance or evasion of verbal expression.[4]

This scale can be applied in one interview or over several contacts and has demonstrated construct validity and interrater reliability in work with individuals. Although the scale calls for rating of "spontaneous verbalization," it is important to remember that it refers to verbalization of "determinant attitudes," which may be translated into "feelings." The quantity of talk is not as important as the quality. That is, what is significant is the client's ability to speak meaningfully and "stand behind" his or her words rather than to spout mere verbiage.[5]

In the article "Verbal Accessibility in the Treatment of Child Neglect," Polansky et al. propose several possible etiologies of low verbal accessibility. There may be a lack of intellectual capacity or psychological immaturity, which are structural deficiencies, or there may be dynamic problems such as neuroses. In *Ego Psychology and Communication*, Polansky builds a theoretical framework for verbal accessibility from an integration of social theories, ego psychology, and cognitive learning theories. He draws from a wide range of theorists, including Kurt Lewin, Hellmuth Kaiser, Lev Semenovich Vygotsky, and others.[6] The explication that follows is drawn from Polansky's book and is chiefly concerned with structural deficiencies.

Verbal accessibility is a function of the personality. It is stable over time and in varying social situations and is predictable from other knowledge about a person. It is also responsive to contextual factors.

Individual verbal accessibility develops in the system of family interactions. The development of thought and speech occurs together in several stages. After mastering some use of speech, the child uses it out loud in connection with thinking through activities and subsequently begins to internalize his or her thoughts. For an adult, thought determines language, and a person's facility with language may, in turn, determine the development of thought. It follows that if a child is discouraged by any means in the use of language, his or her cognitive growth will also be limited. The resulting difficulty in thinking abstractly would impair the adult's ability to differentiate shades of feelings and would limit his or her capacity for problem-solving, thinking logically, and conceptualizing patterns of behavior or experience.

Polansky supports this with a study involving Appalachian mothers receiving Aid to Families with Dependent Children.[7] Low verbal accessibility in these women was highly correlated with the mothers' immaturity, limitations in cognitive skills, inability to see themselves as separate from but related to other members of the family, and what Polansky termed "primitive feelings of loneliness." Moreover, low verbal accessibility was also related to mothers' past problems in educational achievement, dating, and occupational adjustment.

From this understanding of verbal expression and capacity for coping, the reason for effectiveness of "talking treatment" becomes apparent. With a client who is verbally accessible, the worker uses the client's verbal expression to help him or her "learn to talk in rational, abstract and problem-solving ways."[8] The client develops a capacity to think in these ways, and this eventually becomes a part of his or her coping mechanisms. In conventional modes of treatment, then, verbal accessibility is a necessary prerequisite for intervention.

Family Communication

Scherz describes communication within the family as

> the channel through which the rules and roles, processes of identification and differentiation, management of tasks, conflicts and resolutions ..., in short the business of life is conducted.[9]

The family is a system in constant interaction with its environment and whose members are continually communicating with one another. The family has a history, a structure, and patterns of communication that are determined by unspoken rules and roles. This communication may also be characterized by a degree of verbal accessibility. Recalling that verbal accessibility is a product of the moment, the situation, and interpersonal interaction, this readiness to communicate can also be considered a group or family phenomenon.

Although they credit varying theoretical frameworks, Satir, Minuchin et al., and Polansky all write about communication in the service of developing one's own individuality in the family or group, the need for many people to deny what Satir termed their own or other's "different-ness," and individuals' use of communication to this end.[10] On the individual level, differentiation from others may be denied because of lack of self-esteem or fears of separation. Polansky, writing about groups, hypothesizes that environmental stress may also lead to the need for "fusion," or denial of separateness. Whatever its source, such denial of separateness could result in group norms that limit verbalization of individual attitudes, recognition of interpersonal differences, and expression of nuances of feelings. These norms would be passed on to the young, and the group atmosphere would be characterized by pressures toward uniformity (especially in attitudes and feelings), the use of a restrictive linguistic code, and relative verbal inaccessibility.

It would follow that individual needs or environmental issues may interact with patterns of verbal and nonverbal expression, resulting in a "family style." Minuchin et al. note that this family style has affective, behavioral, cognitive, and communicational properties. It would also include family verbal accessibility.

Multiproblem Families

The incidence of abuse and neglect has been associated with poverty, discrimination, the parents' own history of having been abused or neglected, and family disorganization. This discussion will focus on some of the cross-class characteristics of abusive and neglectful parents and the resulting family patterns of communication. Multiproblem and abusive and neglectful families are considered together in the discussion because of the premise that the key to understanding families is understanding their interaction with one another and their environment. Whether they came to the worker's attention as a result of juvenile delinquency or reported abuse is not as important as assessing the changing their ways of interacting with one another and the world. The findings of the studies discussed in this section indicate that, regardless of how they are labeled, these families have similar patterns of communication.

Thus, although there are differences in functioning among abusive and neglectful families, some similar underlying dynamics seem to exist. Several commonly recognized but not necessarily universal traits of parents in these families are impulsiveness (or, conversely, apathy), immaturity, poor self-image, underlying rage or feelings of desolation, concrete thinking, and inability to meet one another's overwhelming needs. These patterns may result in the parents' turning to their children for gratification and expecting more from the children than they are capable of giving. As the parental needs envelop the children, familial patterns of interaction are created.[11]

In work with multiproblem families, some of whom were violent, Rosenthal and associates observed two extremes in family functioning.[12]

One extreme involved families that exhibited "inertia, feelings of futility, feelings that they were no good, and had no control over their fates," and the other consisted of those that were involved "in constant activity which often included antisocial acts." These authors saw the former group as "depressed in affect, content and [often exhibiting] motor retardation." The second group lacked impulse control, but once their activity stopped, they also seemed depressed. The authors, therefore, saw the needs and dysfunctions of both groups as essentially similar.

Other studies and clinical observations found similar patterns of family functioning. For example, Minuchin et al. discuss "enmeshment" and "disengagement," and Polansky et al. distinguish "impulse-ridden" and "apathetic-futile" mothers.[13] Although Polansky et al. distinguish five types of neglectful mothers, these two are outstanding for their ongoing nature and existence outside of psychosis or mental retardation. Minuchin et al. described the style of communication in multiproblem families as one in which people do not listen or respond to one another, gain attention by yelling, do not resolve conflicts or develop themes, have a limited emotional range, and are not able to elaborate on questions or gather information. They also described two extremes in patterns of communication. At one end, the family is highly active and emotions are volatile, and at the other extreme members are apathetic and seem oblivious to one another. Positive feelings are rarely expressed in the latter group, and behavioral injunctions such as "don't" are common.[14]

In a study of patterns of interactions in middle-class professional families, Riskin and Faunce identified similar dynamics.[15] Using a scale that measured clarity, commitment, agreement, disagreement, intensity of affect, continuity of topics, quality of relationships, and interruptions, as well as which other family members each person spoke to, they were able to classify five different patterns of family interaction ranging from normal to multiproblem. Two of the five patterns, designated as "multiproblem" and "child-labeled problems," showed strong similarities to patterns of disorganized families from lower socioeconomic groups. The multiproblem families had three or more labeled problems such as neurosis, marital problems, or psychosomatic illness. The child-labeled families had problems that only related to the children, for example, acting out or underachieving.

Although incidence of abuse and neglect was not part of this study, certain findings were strikingly similar to those of Minuchin et al. and Rosenthal et al., namely, that families studied were either prone to violence or apathetic. The "multiproblem" families had great potential for explosive behavior. They were the most unclear, had the most topic changes, were highest on injunctions such as "behave yourself," sought or shared little information, experienced a lack of support in relationships, and felt a high amount of attack. These families had a high degree of interaction between children and minimal interaction between parents. They took part in power struggles without resolving them and seemed like a collection of isolated people talking past each other. The families with child-labeled problems were seen as "low-keyed, sullen, argumentative, non-cooperative, muted … [and slightly] … depressive … [with] hints of underlying power struggles."[16] They expressed little affect and much disagreement. These families were the second highest on behavioral injunctions, had fragmented conversations, and had "bland" or "neutral" relationships.

The consistency in the findings of several studies conducted that included families with a variety of class characteristics indicates the existence of distinctive patterns of communication in families that tend toward violence or have a high potential for abuse or neglect. Applying the construct of family verbal accessibility, one may interpret the patterns of interaction as defenses against a hostile environment or feelings of "primitive loneliness." These feelings result in family norms that perpetuate inability to differentiate shades of feeling, to "stand behind one's words," and to allow for individuation of family members. Conversely, in an unrelated study of patterns of family interactions, Mishler and Waxler found that "normal" or "unlabeled" families were more consistently open and direct in expressing their feelings to one another.[17]

Thus, one facet of assessing a family would be to determine its relative degree of verbal accessibility. Such an assessment might then be seen as a way to determine "treatability"—the capacity or willingness of the family to engage in the process of change.

Family Therapy

Abusive and neglectful families typically "act out their lives," do not value talking in problem-solving, are not introspective, and expect help to be in the form of advice or concrete goods.[18] Needless to say, especially in the case of low-income families, some intervention will be more concerned with trying to affect the environment. The point here, however, is to examine ways to intervene in the families' patterns of communication.

The major difficulty in adapting conventional therapies to such families has been the requirement for some verbal facility and ability to conceptualize on the part of the family members, for example, to be able to perceive and discuss patterns of interaction. For this purpose, the concept of verbal accessibility may be a helpful addition to the worker's assessment. The application of this concept to the family as a whole has not been previously proposed and is therefore untested. However, this author would suggest that families are more or less verbally accessible and that family verbal accessibility would be helpful in planning appropriate treatment.

It may be possible not only to look at a family's pattern of interaction as Riskin and Faunce did in their study of middle-class families, but also to evaluate the family's spontaneity of expressions of affect in interactions with the worker. This would involve using the global scale for verbal accessibility and scoring the readiness of the family as a unit to talk about feelings with each other and the worker. The score, ranging from 1 (spontaneity) to 6 (avoidance), would reflect the total interaction between the family and worker, not the verbal accessibility of individual members. Since the scale is intended for use with individuals, its use with a small group such as the family is a subject for further study to see if it would, in fact, measure the readiness of the family as a whole to engage in the change process. Although thus applied, the scale would not be useful as a measure of individual coping abilities, it might very well prove to be a way of measuring family style as discussed earlier. For example, it might correlate with a family's communication rules, encouragement of differentiation, and so on. Because the scale is a measure of the quality of verbalization, not quantity, it would be an invaluable tool for the worker in assessment and intervention.

With a family that has a low degree of verbal accessibility, the treatment goal, of necessity, must be to increase verbal accessibility. In work with individuals, Polansky sees the goal not only as a means to involve the client in ongoing treatment but also as treatment itself. The relationship between verbal accessibility and coping abilities suggests that enhancement of one will aid in the development of the other.

Intervention

Protective intervention often involves the use of authority, such as the court system, to ensure the safety of the child. Work with the family as a whole can be used in conjunction with such methods. Family therapy may be appropriate during arranged visits between a child in care and the family, or it may effectively prevent the need for placement.

The overall goals for work with multiproblem families are to enable the parents to have more satisfying lives so that they can better cope with child rearing and to enhance the quality of interaction between parents and child.[19] Specific goals may include enhancing parents' self-image, increasing the family's capacity for enjoyment, aiding in self-differentiation, and strengthening parental and marital roles. These aims are accomplished by developing family members' abilities to identify problems and to offer alternative ways to resolve them.

The dynamics of abusive and neglectful families suggest that their family communication will often be nonverbal. Family-oriented intervention has certain possible advantages in work with such families: there is less pressure on the individual to perform verbally, and there is less focus on individual inadequacies—a point on which parents in these families are particularly sensitive.

Intervention with families that are low in verbal accessibility (a score of 4 or more on the global scale) should be action oriented. The lower the score, the more time and effort must go into simple, concrete activity with the family. Polansky outlined techniques that have been found to enhance verbal accessibility with individuals and that are equally applicable in family situations. These include encouraging conversation, no matter what the topic; beginning with topics that are concrete, external, and superficial; building a noncritical, accepting atmosphere; aiding the client in naming feelings; attending to every opportunity for discussion of key issues; dealing with cultural or familial injunctions against discussing personal matters; maintaining absolute honesty; and developing and maintaining one's own verbal accessibility.[20] Within the context of these techniques, the worker can develop a variety of action-oriented interventions.

In work with groups of children who were verbally inaccessible, Ganter, Yeakel, and Polansky found that structuring, limit-setting, and controls were helpful.[21] In work with families, these techniques might also be used to intervene in both their activities and verbal communication. The children in the study accepted the controls only temporarily at first but were gradually able to control their own behavior. Initially, choices of play activities were limited to decrease confusion and the level of excitability, but they were then gradually widened to give the children an opportunity to develop their own problem-solving abilities. Additional techniques included noting "momentary experiences of success," avoiding open competition, and limiting their own expectations of performance. The workers consistently labeled actions verbally and helped the group members begin to do the same. They also intervened in disruptions to describe the situation verbally and to "talk it out." The workers also found the audio recorder to be a useful tool that is more readily available than videotape and two-way mirrors. They used it to interject clarifications and comments while recording the children's streams of talk. Listening to the recordings of their emotional outbursts accompanied by a calm, clarifying commentary was helpful to the children. In encouraging the use of the recorder, a worker reasoned with one child that "he did not know what he thought until he heard what he said" and that "if he did not know what he thought, he could not know what he was doing."[22]

In work with low-income multiproblem families, Levine combined concrete services with activities such as arts and crafts or simple games.[23] One of her co-workers used a tool chest to repair toys and household items in visits with a family. Levine usually introduced the activity, such as working with clay, to the children and talked with the whole family while she worked. Initially the parents hung back on the periphery, but eventually they joined in. Often, the parents could be involved in the context of demonstrating how one might play with the children. These activities became the vehicle through which problems were introduced and conflicts resolved. Levine proposed that families, just as children, could experience success, learn how to have fun, and learn problem-solving through play. Other excellent opportunities for intervention may be organized around food, a basic socializer; learning to negotiate community services; and simply getting out of the house.

Play at first may be parallel—that is, people may play in the same place at the same time but not together. The type of activity chosen will be indicated by the assessment. More active families would find play with some movement more congruent with their life-style, whereas it would be difficult to engage an apathetic family in a very active undertaking. The worker should also be careful not to choose pursuits that eliminate opportunities to talk. Nonverbal communication is important, but it has limits when it is the only communication. The goal is to increase talking skills, and the chosen means must reflect this.

As a family's verbal accessibility increases, other activity-oriented interventions that rely more on verbal skills may be introduced. For example, role-playing gives the family members a chance to experience relationships from new perspectives, and family sculpting gives them an opportunity to arrange the family as they see it, using the other members as clay and placing them physically in different positions. At this point, talking as a problem-solving method should be emphasized more heavily. Some ways of doing this would be stating rules for communication (for example, insisting on feedback), pointing out different levels of messages, formulating problems and alternatives verbally, and partializing problems. As with other forms of treatment, there is no hard and fast rule about moving from one level of intervention to another. Progress will develop gradually as the family is ready.

Rosenthal and associates found that engaging the family was the most crucial and difficult stage of family treatment. Two common problems were continuous resistance in the form of blaming one another and stormy verbal or physical fights. After the workers recovered from the shock of such violence, however, intervening in chaos was often easier than intervening with more passive families. Sheer perseverence of the worker, combined with a consistent nonblaming attitude and a clear definition of the problem, was most helpful in engaging the family. These authors note that home visits are an absolute necessity, as does Levine.[24] A team approach was helpful to avoid being overwhelmed by the family's difficulties. As with other forms of treatment of abuse and neglect, the family approach requires involvement over time. This may mean a minimum of a year and possibly more.

An important facet of developing verbal accessibility in clients is the worker's own verbal accessibility. Clients' responsiveness often depends on their perceptions of the worker as willing and able to help. This not only calls for good will on the part of the worker, but also for skilled intervention. The development of such skills is not an easy task. Feelings of frustration, helplessness, and anger often seem overwhelming. Support from co-workers and supervisors as well as from the agency's staff development program is essential for the worker to maintain a high level of functioning.

Indications for Treatment

Rosenthal and associates found that some indications for family therapy with multiproblem families were cohesiveness; widely shared pathological patterns that were destructive to the self-esteem and functioning of the members; and an underlying, shared depressive quality.[25] As used by these authors, cohesiveness refers to strong boundaries around the family unit, tying the members together in a dysfunctional system. Verbal inaccessibility also seems to be a primary indication for family intervention. Scherz sees it as a treatment of choice in a chaotic family, where order must be introduced and individuals cannot face personal problems. Family intervention is also indicated when individuals have great needs for dependence but cannot trust in a one-to-one relationship or when they are too rivalrous to permit any one person to have his or her own worker.[26]

Contraindications for family therapy include evidence of an "irreversible trend towards disintegration and breakup of the family" or the self-centeredness of one client to the extent that he or she cannot participate in joint interviews.[27] If the family has a need to involve the therapist as a primary member of the family so that the therapist loses his or her separate identity or if one member needs to have the therapist all to him- or herself, family therapy will fail. If the parents cannot act as parents, it is better to see them without the children or to provide them with additional, individual support while still working with the family.

The use of verbal accessibility as a tool for assessment and an indication for intervention has been successful in one-to-one interactions with adults and in work with groups of children. Verbal accessibility is a construct that also lends itself conceptually and pragmatically to work with families. Accurate understanding of a family's readiness to communicate in words about members' most important thoughts and feelings could be crucial in designing the most effective plan for helping and for gaining initial entry into the family process.

Notes and References

1. Norman A. Polansky, *Ego Psychology and Communication: Theory for the Interview* (Chicago: Aldine Publishing Co., 1971), p. 182.

2. Norman A. Polansky et al., "Verbal Accessibility in the Treatment of Child Neglect," *Child Welfare*, 50 (June 1971), pp. 349–356; Polansky, Christine DeSaix, and Shlomo Sharlin, *Child Neglect: Understanding and Reaching the Parent* (New York: Child Welfare League of America, 1972); Polansky, Robert D. Borgman, and DeSaix, *Roots of Futility* (San Francisco: Jossey-Bass, 1972).

3. Polansky, *Ego Psychology and Communication*, pp. 187 and 191.

4. Polansky et al., op. cit., p. 351.

5. Polansky, *Ego Psychology and Communication*, p. 216; and Norman A. Polansky, "On the Interjudge and Interobserver Reliabilities of Verbal Accessibility, Apathy-Futility, Impulsivity and Involvement Indices, etc., Incorporating Judges Ratings: Interparental Resemblances, Also," Unpublished research memorandum, School of Social Work, university of Georgia, Athens, December 1, 1977.

6. Polansky et al., op. cit., p. 352; and Polansky, *Ego Psychology and Communication*.

7. Polansky, *Ego Psychology and Communication*, pp. 217–219.

8. Ibid., pp. 198–199.

9. Frances Scherz, "Theory and Practice of Family Therapy," in Robert W. Roberts and Robert H. Nee, *Theories of Social Casework* (Chicago: University of Chicago Press, 1970), p. 235.

10. Virginia Satir, *Conjoint Family Therapy* (Palo Alto, Calif.: Science and Behavior Books, 1967); Salvador Minuchin et al., *Families of the Slums: An Exploration of Their Structure and Treatment* (New York: Basic Books, 1967); and Polansky, *Ego Psychology and Communication*.

11. Ray E. Helfer and Henry C. Kempe, eds., *Child Abuse and Neglect: The Family and Community* (Cambridge, Mass.: Ballinger Publishing Co., 1976); and Polansky, DeSaix, and Sharlin, op. cit., pp. 11–19.

12. Perihan Aral Rosenthal et al., "Family Therapy with Multi-problem, Multi-children Families in a Court Setting," *Journal of the American Academy of Child Psychiatry*, 13 (1974), pp. 126–142.

13. Minuchin et al., op. cit., p. 217; and Polansky et al., op. cit.

14. Minuchin et al., op. cit., p. 201; and Salvador Minuchin, "Conflict-Resolution Family Therapy," in Jay Haley, ed., *Changing Families* (New York: Grune & Stratton, 1971), p. 149.

15. Jules Riskin and Elaine E. Faunce, "Family Interaction Scales," in Paul Watzlawick and John Weakland, eds., *The Interactional View* (New York: W. W. Norton & Co., 1977), pp. 101–127.

16. Ibid.

17. Elliot G. Mishler and Nancy E. Waxler, *Interaction in Families: An Experimental Study of Family Processes and Schizophrenia* (New York: John Wiley & Sons, 1968), p. 219.

18. Minuchin et al., op. cit., p. 36.

19. Rosenthal et al., op. cit.: Polansky, *Ego Psychology and Communication;* and Helfer and Kempe, op. cit.

20. Polansky et al., op. cit., pp. 354–356.

21. Grace Ganter, Margaret Yeakel, and Norman A. Polansky, *Retrieval from Limbo* (New York: Child Welfare League of America, 1967).

22. Ibid., p. 70.

23. Rachel A. Levine, "Treatment in the Home," in Eileen Younghusband, ed., *Casework with Families and Children* (Chicago: University of Chicago Press, 1965), pp. 115–129.

24. Rosenthal et al., op. cit.: and Levine, op. cit.

25. Rosenthal et al., op. cit., p. 128.

26. Frances H. Scherz, "Multiple-Client Interviewing: Treatment Implications," *Social Casework,* 42 (March 1962), pp. 120–125; and Frances Lomas Feldman and Frances Sherz, *Family Social Welfare: Helping Troubled Families* (New York: Atherton Press, 1967), p. 259.

27. Nathan Ackerman, "Family Psychotherapy," *Encyclopedia of Mental Health,* Vol. 2 (New York: Franklin Watts, 1963), pp. 612–632, as cited in Joan W. Stein, *The Family as a Unit of Study and Treatment* (Regional Rehabilitation Research Institute, University of Washington School of Social Work, 1969), p. 80; and Joanne Geist and Norman Gerber, "Joint Interviewing: A Treatment Technique with Marital Partners," *Social Casework,* 41 (February 1960), pp. 76–83.

ANOMIE

CHAPTER 63

Existential Psychotherapy and the Problem of Anomie

Donald F. Krill

A characteristic of the present age is the increasing freedom of people from traditional ties and associated systems of mores, folkways, and religious disciplines, coupled with the fact that instead of flowering in their new-found freedom a large share have become muddled, confused, highly anxious, and self-driving, and in general resort to ways of "escaping their freedom."[1] Such modern maladies as alcoholism, increased divorce rates, overuse and experimental use of drugs, and the general entertainment and recreation manias have been linked with this desperate flight or search (which one it is depending, perhaps, on the person).

In 1962 Pollak presented several ideas related to this issue:

> Strangely enough, the clients who represent the greatest challenge to social work and a wider community at the present time do not suffer from the scars of submission to the reality principle. They suffer from the ineffectivenss of having retained the pleasure principle as a guide of living. They lead a life of normlessness conceptualized by Merton as anomie.... With people who are victims of anomie we have no theory of helping and tradition of success. The culture of social work here is faced with the challenge of becoming a rearing and binding, superego demanding profession rather than of being a liberating one.... Here social workers will have to come to terms with a phenomena of normlessness which makes liberating or improving efforts miss the mark.[2]

[1] Erich Fromm, *Escape from Freedom* (New York: Holt, Rinehart & Winston, 1941).

[2] Otto Pollak, "Social Determinants of Family Behavior." Paper presented at the Mid-Continent Regional Institute, National Association of Social Workers, Kansas City, Mo., April 1962, p. 6.

Reprinted from *Social Work*, Vol. 14, No. 2 (April, 1969), pp. 33–49, with permission of the author and the National Association of Social Workers.

Many respond to this problem by talking all the more vehemently of the need for increased services in education, welfare, and mental health, but while there is truth in this they miss the central point that is being proclaimed by the existentialists: People have lost contact with many basic human realities that they must accept and understand if they are to have a sense of personal direction or meaning in their lives. One need only look at present-day common behavior patterns and voiced attitudes to see this. With regard to the concept of human love, closeness, and intimacy, it can be seen that marital disappointments are commonly dealt with by divorce, adultery, alcoholism, increased work (the notion that more money or prestige will change the marriage), and individualized social circles that allow two near-strangers to remain together under the same roof "for the sake of the children." The concept of death is often dealt with by avoidance of it as a fact with implicit meaning for present conduct or weak hopes for some scientific "deep- freeze" solution, and of course by the whole ridiculous ritual of the funeral parlors.

Efforts of the Church

The illusion behind such maneuvers is the widely held belief that one can manipulate and control life in such a way as to bring oneself happiness, security, and freedom from suffering. This idea has been nourished throughout this century by utopian hopes stemming from scientific rationalism. The effort has backfired insofar as men have become increasingly estranged from many realities of the human condition. These attitudes have at the same time considerably weakened the position of the church, which in the past had been the fount for people's sense of direction and meaning and the support for their capacity to endure hardship. Needless to say, the church, especially since the Reformation, has had its part in nurturing the very hopes in scientific rationalism that have weakened its influence. Now the church itself is struggling for a new language and new means with which to express its fundamental ideas, knowing that people have been alienated and disillusioned and have come to feel indifferent toward traditional presentations of beliefs and truths.[3]

The church, as mentioned, has always concerned itself with the conflicts, ideas, feelings, and behavior that make up the state of mind called anomie. Presumably, the church should have important contributions to make to the psychiatric and social work professions in their efforts to cope with this problem. An interesting development in society has been furthered by those serious students of or searchers after a religion that refuses

---

[3] This is the basic conflict in the "Honest to God" debate. *See* John A. T. Robinson, *Honest to God* (Philadelphia: Westminster Press, 1963); and David L. Edwards, *The Honest to God Debate* (Philadelphia: Westminster Press, 1963).

to return to Sunday school fantasies, hopes, rituals, and platitudes. The new religious vitality is one that seeks a sense of direction and unity in the intimacy of direct experience with this world of tasks, suffering, and possibilities. The forerunners of this surge were such religious existentialist thinkers as Dostoevsky, Kierkegaard, Berdyaev, Bergson, Jaspers, Marcel, Maritain, Tillich, Niebuhr, Barth, and Buber. This is the true religious revival and has nothing to do with increased church attendance, faith healing, and the renewed interest in Gospel singing. A profound movement toward unity among the world's religions is in progress and this includes a strong effort toward a unity between religion and science as well.

A similar movement has occurred apart from the church, yet seems related to the same precipitating conditions and personal needs. This has expressed itself in the arts and literature and theoretically in the avid interest of many in existential philosophy and Zen Buddhism—two areas of modern thought representing West and East that are remarkably similar in their concern for the discovery of meaning in the direct, immediate experience of life as one lives it.

The existentialist movement in the fields of psychiatry and psychology may well provide a body of knowledge that is highly valuable and useful in our quest for some answers to the problem of anomie. Existentialism is a philosophy derived from man's immediate experience of the world in which he lives—a confrontation with the realities of the human condition and the establishment of a personalized meaning from them. As a philosophy of daily experience it should be capable of speaking meaningfully about ideas that can be grasped by the unsophisticated, much as a novel does.

Pollak's words (". . . becoming a rearing and binding, superego demanding profession") are provocative to the ears of social workers who have identified their goals, along psychoanalytic lines, to be in marked contrast with his suggestion. There is the ring here of paternalism, authoritarianism, and a judgmental attitude. But let us look at what the church has attempted to accomplish over its many centuries of existence and what this may have to say to us through the modern views of existentialism.

The church has always attempted to deal with the sufferings of people by providing them with a sense of meaning that transcends their own self-derived, suffering-based feelings of futility about life. Religious people have found courage to endure through acceptance of what is considered to be divine revelation. The fundamental services of religion to an individual are the provision of guidance in his way of living and the experience of union with an ultimate reality that relates him to others and all that exists through the transcendent power in which he believes. Religious dogmas, orders, sects, rituals, sermons, discussion groups, sacraments, social action, study, prayer, and meditation are some of the varied efforts to accomplish these two basic services. This variety of approaches reflects the church's efforts to serve people of varying capacities and levels of motivation and understanding. The mental health movement faces a similar problem.

Psychiatry cannot be equated with religion, for the sphere of divine revelation and speculation on the mystery of transcendence is beyond the scope and capacity of scientific methods. But the human need for guidance in the management of one's life and the experience of unity through relatedness to others outside oneself are certainly within its realm. It is here that the existentialist movement has attempted to relate a philosophy of life to mankind's problems by focusing, as the church has done, on guidance and relatedness. This is why the existentialist movement is most commonly characterized as stressing meaning in life and authenticity in relationships.

Existentialism Versus Anomie

Elsewhere the writer defined the concern of existentialism as "meaningful living through self-encounter in the situation at hand despite a world of apparent futility."[4] Essentially, this means that one derives or helps another derive an attitude and direction toward life by becoming increasingly aware of life as he lives it and what this living entails. It is for this reason that the problem of anomie—of aimless, futile, normless lives—can be constructively related to by existentialist thought.

The process of growth in existentialism emphasizes the following reality concepts: increasing awareness of self-deceptions that attempt to define the self as fixed and secure; confrontation with the knowledge of personal freedom and its accompanying responsibilities; discovery of meaning in one's sufferings that actually helps establish a direction in life; realization of the necessity of dialogue or intimacy that nurtures change, courage, and self-assertion; and finally a decision for continued commitment that prizes freedom above attachment to childhood strivings and self-deceptions. This commitment is characterized by responsive action in the world of tasks, duties, and possibilities, in contrast to narcissism and self-pity.[5]

Let us contrast this with patterns of thought and behavior implicit in the state of mind labeled anomie. The characteristic of normlessness mentioned by Pollak is a result of several attitudes about oneself and also oneself in relation to others and the world in general. These attitudes are anti-existential in content because of the nature of the implicit beliefs and assumptions about freedom, responsibility, suffering, authenticity, love, and commitment. The sources of these attitudes are many and have been

---

[4] Donald F. Krill, "Existentialism: A Philosophy for Our Current Revolutions," *Social Service Review*, Vol. 40, No. 3 (September 1966), p. 291.

[5] *Ibid.* This entire article is a development of these ideas.

ably described by such social critics as Erich Fromm, Allen Wheelis, Colin Wilson, David Riesman, and William Whyte.

Anomie is derived from a Greek word meaning "lack of law." As a sociological concept it describes the breakdown or failure of those forces (standards, sanctions, norms, rules, values) that ordinarily bind people together in some organized social whole. This social whole is characterized by a sense of duty and obligation of people toward one another that preserves organization. There are different degrees of anomie and it may take several forms, outlined by Cohen as "confrontation by a situation for which there are no relevant rules, vagueness or ambiguity of the relevant rules, or lack of consensus on which rules are relevant and in the interpretation of rules."[6]

Tiryakian states:

> To liberate the individual from all social constraint, adds Durkheim, is to abandon him to his unlimited wants, to demoralize him and to lead him to despair. What the individual should feel, more acutely than ever before, is the need for moral rules.[7]

He suggests that what is latent in the writings of Durkheim that differentiates the notions of solidarity and anomie are societal analogues of what the existentialist terms an individual's "authentic" and "unauthentic" existence.

Anomic Man

The existentialists have enriched our understanding of "anomic man" in both fictional and philosophical descriptions of the "unauthentic man," the man of "bad faith," and "alienated man." These assessments demonstrate that the anomic state of mind and attitude are not to be limited to delinquent, sociopathic, multiply deprived individuals but apply to an ever increasing number of people at all levels of present-day society. Attitudes typical of anomic man will now be examined.

There is a sense of aimless drifting, or at times being helplessly driven, both of which relate to one's sense of impotence and personal insignificance. One considers oneself as being fixed in place either by tradition, heredity, social position, or psychological and social determinism. One has been formed, or perhaps victimized, by the powers that be or by those that were before.

---

[6] Albert K. Cohen, "The Study of Social Disorganization and Deviant Behavior," in Robert K. Merton, Leonard Brown, and Leonard S. Cottrell, Jr., eds., *Sociology Today: Problems and Prospects* (New York: Basic Books, 1959), p. 481.

[7] Edward A. Tiryakian, *Sociologism and Existentialism* (Englewood Cliffs, N.J.: Prentice-Hall, 1962), p. 31.

Paradoxically, along with this sense of missing personal freedom and hence diminished responsibility there is an increased expectation that one's surrounding environment should change in such a way as to bring one increased comfort, protection, and happiness. The experience of suffering is therefore often felt to be unfair, and bitterness as well as envy arises toward others in more fortunate circumstances. Quick and easy solutions are sought to manipulate the environment in order to reduce any personal pain and bring about a state of pleasure or comfort. The variety of efforts is vast and extends from pills and television to infidelity and alcoholism.

A Mexican-American leader recently defended his people, who are accused of filling the jails and reformatories of the Southwest, with this interesting observation:

> When a Mexican kid is brought before the judge he is usually honest in admitting he committed the crime and ready to accept whatever consequences come—leaving his future to God. When an Anglo is in the same situation, he'll do anything possible to avoid a charge of guilty to get out of being punished.[8]

One's sense of self as a feeling, thinking, changing person is replaced by a notion of self as dependent on support from outside. One plays roles or "markets oneself" in such a way as to manipulate others to view one in a specific way that meets one's needs. Relationships are characterized by superficiality, calculation, and "game-playing." Other props used are the identification of self with groups, such as religious, political, or professional, or with slogans and characteristics of models found in society and given acceptance or even acclaim, such as "the good Joe, the hustler, the smart operator, the playboy, the status seeker...."[9] When such supports are challenged or threatened, one is prepared to fight righteously and defend his self-identity to the bitter end.

What is apparent in this entire description is that one hides one's inner self both from others and from one's own sensitive judgement. There is an ongoing effort to gratify needs by actions and manipulations and a fleeing from being alone with oneself. Such exercises as meditation and self-examination become foreign, or if adopted are used with magical, naïve expectations that usually end in disappointment. Intuition and spontaneity tend to be lost or warped.[10] The simple joys to be found in the beauty and mystery of life and responsive participation in the ongoing order of things are rare. One feels alienated from other people, the world,

[8] Rudolph Gonzales, lecture-discussion given to the Child Psychiatry Department of the University of Colorado Medical Center, Denver, November 1966.

[9] A comprehensive elaboration of these "models" is found in Henry Winthrop, "American National Character and the Existentialist Posture," *Journal of Existentialism*, Vol. 6, No. 24 (Summer 1966), pp. 405–419.

[10] This theme is fully developed in Franz E. Winkler, MD, *Man, The Bridge Between Two Worlds* (New York: Harper & Bros., 1960).

and oneself, yet hides this fundamental panic beneath desperate efforts to grasp, contain, and fortify a sense of identity, false as it is.

Advantages of Existential Psychotherapy

This description of attitudes and behavior is not a presentation of symptoms, but rather a way of life—an anti-existentialist way of living—that has developed to significant proportions in our age. Because anomie can be considered to be an attitude toward life, existential psychotherapy has a unique advantage over many other forms of psychotherapy. The outstanding difference does not lie in techniques or methods, for the existential approach may occur with insight, crisis-oriented, family, group, or supportive therapies. It may be directive, nondirective, or analytical. The uniqueness of existential psychotherapy is that it attempts a philosophical reorientation through the use of therapy content and behavior. There is a process of challenge, re-education, and reconstruction of the patient's basic way of viewing himself, his relation to others, and the world at large.

The mental health professional performing the therapy (hereafter called the therapist) holds to a number of existential philosophical premises based on his perception and understanding of reality. The experiences that are lived through in therapy are utilized to demonstrate and highlight the philosophical implications of those realities apparent in these experiences. Soon experiences take on new meanings for patients, who are helped to rethink and redevelop their own outlook on life in a fresh manner.

It is true that the patient takes on certain values and philosophical attitudes of the therapist. This occurs in any form of psychotherapy to a certain degree. What is important here is that the therapist knowingly permits this. He has in mind certain existential realities within his philosophical frame of reference that he wants the patient to see, understand, and accept if he is to overcome his problems. The goal in this approach is not insight into early traumas, reassurance, catharsis, or enabling the patient to grow in a nondirective atmosphere. It may include any or all of these, but the goal itself is a philosophical re-education through direct experience.

The relation between anomie and emotional illness must also be understood. Each can exist without the presence of the other; however, in our present society both occur simultaneously and are interrelated in a vast and growing number of cases. The attitudes of anomie actually predispose the person to emotional illness.

The general view among existentialists of the development of emotional disorders stresses the following factors. Two human needs are considered most fundamental: (1) to be loved and to experience a sense of unity with what is other than oneself and (2) to grow through ongoing creative and responsive change. These are interrelated inasmuch as the mature person, at the moment he is authentically creative by responding to the tasks and opportunities of the world about him, is also experiencing a sense of unity by feeling needed or being a vital and unique part of his own specific area of the world (life space).

A child needs the trust and confidence of his parents to develop as a loving and creative person. As he discovers certain creative or loving expressions to be unacceptable to his parents, he experiences the threat of loss of love. With this goes the fear of a disintegration of his sense of self, for one's early identity is dependent on approval and acceptance by one's parents. This fear of parental rejection is equal to the adult fear of death, for the meanings are precisely the same. To live, to preserve some sense of self, a person willingly gives up or hides those aspects of personality that would produce rejection and adapts himself to what he believes his parents want from him, thus making himself acceptable and of worth. This pattern of self-conformity to a necessitated image in childhood continues into adulthood; one relates to others as if it were still necessary to uphold the same image in order to be acceptable and loved.

What is apparent here are the elements of calculated choice of behavior initially and ongoing manipulative efforts to maintain for others a set image of oneself. Trouble results from the fact that manipulative behavior fosters distance rather than love and intimacy in relationships, and also the clinging effort to maintain and express only specific aspects of the self results in frustration of free and creative growth. The two fundamental needs become endangered and the result is symptoms that cry out distress and a need for help. Guilt and anxiety are often seen to be reality based. Anxiety may be experienced when a person realizes that he could act in a spontaneous and creative way that would express his true, responsive self in a situation, yet to do so would endanger the image he feels he must preserve to be acceptable to others and himself. Guilt may occur when he chooses behavior that preserves his own childhood-based image at the expense of a growth possibility. Genuine open communication and sincere efforts of self-examination actually threaten the image that one wishes to maintain and are thus avoided.

Treatment Goals

Anomie encourages a pattern that leads to emotional disturbance insofar as it emphasizes a helpless, weak, predetermined notion of oneself as lacking freedom and responsibility; a manipulative view of human relationships that nourishes superficiality, deceit, and distance; and an avoidance of pain as one tries with various self-deceptions to resist the meaning of guilt and anxiety in order to hide from what is real within oneself. The causes of anomie are sociological and historical, but the existence of anomie is itself an important contribution to mental illness. When anomie is a part of the emotional problem, it should be dealt with and the issue of treatment then becomes partly philosophical in nature.

The specific treatment goals for existential psychotherapy are essentially philosophical achievements in terms of a patient's coming to grips with those aspects of reality that will produce a significant change in his view of life and his relation to it. The five goals that would appear most important are these:

1. Aiding the process of disillusionment
2. Confronting freedom
3. Discovering meaning in suffering
4. Realizing the necessity of dialogue
5. Accepting the way of commitment

Therapeutic techniques familiarize the patient with these goals, or realities, both by educational guidance and direct experience, much as the church directed its people toward spiritual growth. The balance of this paper will present methods by which these goals may be achieved. Emphasis will not be on an analytical or long-term insight-oriented psychotherapy from the existential framework, but rather on techniques useful for casework, group work, and reality-oriented psychotherapy.[11]

The description of therapy may seem somewhat disjointed, since the author's intention is to develop an over-all sense of direction for therapy rather than a complete system applicable to all clients. There is, of course, the question of which people would most benefit from this approach.

This same question must now honestly be asked about psychoanalytic psychotherapy. Studies of its results with many clients who seemed appropriate middle-class candidates for therapy as well as of persons in low-income groups have clearly indicated its gross ineffectiveness. It has had its successes too, but such studies raise radical questions about whether it is the most useful approach for our age. The entire community psychiatry movement is a vivid response to doubts about traditional methods and efforts toward new, creative approaches.

To what group of clients does Pollak refer when he speaks of "victims of anomie?"[12] Is there a difference between this group and those people who manifest anomic symptoms as a result of depressive conflict? Existential psychotherapy is not being suggested here as a cure-all, nor is it possible to say with assurance exactly what sorts of persons will benefit from it, any more than psychoanalytic practitioners can comfortably state this. May and Frankl have both expressed the view that the existential approach

[11] Two recent books illustrating the existential-analytical view are Avery D. Weisman, MD, *The Existential Core of Psychoanalysis* (Boston: Little, Brown & Co., 1965); and J. F. T. Bugental, *The Search for Authenticity* (New York: Holt, Rinehart & Winston, 1965).

[12] *Op. cit.*

is more attuned to the problems of our age.[13] Fromm, sharing many of the existential concerns about the plight of modern man, has challenged the psychoanalytic approach on this same basis.[14] The reality-oriented psychotherapists (including Glasser, Ellis, Mowrer, and O'Connell) utilize techniques that are closely aligned with the existential treatment goals mentioned, and have worked successfully with neurotics, psychotics, and sociopaths. As early as 1933 Jung made the following relevant comments:

> A psycho-neurosis must be understood as the suffering of a human being who has not discovered what life means to him.... Among all my patients in the second half of life—that is to say, over thirty-five—there has not been one whose problem in the last resort was not that of finding a religious outlook on life.... This of course has nothing whatever to do with a particular creed or membership of a church.... Today this eruption of destructive forces has already taken place, and man suffers from it in spirit.... That is why we psychotherapists must occupy ourselves with problems which, strictly speaking, belong to the theologian. But we cannot leave these questions for theology to answer; the urgent, psychic needs of suffering people confront us with them day after day.[15]

Aiding the Process of Disillusionment

The major task with this goal is gradually to reveal to the patient the reality that the very way he goes about thinking of himself and relating to other people defeats his purpose. His efforts at self-assurance and manipulation of those to whom he wishes to be close are marked with inconsistencies and self-deceptions that result in alienation and the limited expression of his potentialities. Habit patterns are revealed to him that consistently distort reality in his daily living. This process is anxiety provoking, of course, and requires the accompanying nurture of the therapeutic relationship.

The therapist must be well trained and experienced in the knowledge and operation of self-deception. Perhaps his most direct acquaintance with this is to have undergone psychoanalysis or psychotherapy himself. A corresponding discipline occurs in those religious orders that require intense self-examination by priests, monks, and the like in a search for personal truth. It is perhaps unfortunate that modern Protestant seminaries have for the most part replaced such personal struggle and discipline with rational teaching of history and theory.

[13] Rollo May, ed., *Existential Psychology* (New York: Random House, 1961), p. 21. Viktor Frankl, *The Doctor and the Soul* (New York: Alfred A. Knopf, 1955), pp. 3–26.

[14] Erich Fromm, D. T. Suzuki, and Richard Demartino, *Zen Buddhism and Psychoanalysis* (New York: Evergreen Publishing Co., 1963), pp. 135–136.

[15] C. G. Jung, *Modern Man in Search of a Soul* (New York: Harcourt, Brace & Co., 1933), pp. 225, 229, and 241.

A therapist aims initially at understanding the specific, unique patterns his client uses in viewing and relating to his world of tasks and relationships and his sense of self-adequacy. It is often important to develop some historical picture of the client to identify the presence of early patterns that still carry over into his present life adjustment. The existence of these patterns is also identified in the way the patient relates to the therapist. Because of the therapist's ability to maintain himself as a free, authentic person in the therapeutic relationship, he fails to be manipulated by the client's habitual efforts, although his interest and understanding remain solid and intact. As a free person, the therapist has no egotistical investment in curing or failing to cure the client. He offers reality, with himself as a therapeutic agent, but the client must always realize that the choice between change and growth on the one hand and flight toward the security of habitual patterns on the other is his own.

This process of challenging a person's manner of viewing his problem (as well as his general life conduct) can be illustrated in part by the techniques used with an open-ended therapy group for alcoholics conducted by the author. An alcoholic who wishes to join the group is told quite directly at the beginning how his problem will be viewed. This is done in a brief individual orientation session with the therapist. The prospective group member is told that alcoholics usually drink for a specific reason and that reason has to do with feelings that are difficult to bear without the aid of alcohol. Such feelings result from the way he sees himself and also the manner in which he relates to those with whom he wishes to have a close relationship. To benefit from therapy he must abstain from alcohol so that he can experience the feelings behind his drinking and talk about them in the group. By being as open and honest as possible, the group can help him come to an understanding of his problems and change them, so that the suffering caused by inner feelings can be managed better or diminished. It is emphasized that alcoholics can be helped in different ways, but if the client wants group therapy he must accept this notion of the helping process.

In the course of therapy he will usually find opposition to his personal view of his problems. Such ideas as the alcoholic's being born this way, having an incurable disease, or being inherently weak or hopelessly dependent are simply not accepted by the group. What is stressed instead is that the alcoholic never learned appropriate and workable means of expressing and meeting his needs. The manipulative ritual with his spouse is a good example. The cycle of drinking, fighting, threatening separation, confessing failure and appealing for another chance during the hangover period, and the final acceptance by the martyred wife provide several elements of closeness. There is an exchange of feelings, including anger, hurt, despair, contrition, forgiveness, and refound hope. But the closeness is short lived and must be repeated because it fails to deal with the genuine daily relationship struggles between the marital partners.

During therapy it becomes increasingly apparent to the alcoholic that his efforts to control interactions with other group members are related to the specific view he has of himself as a person, which he feels obliged to maintain. Yet this image and his strivings to maintain it are the sources of both his failure at intimacy and his inability to satisfy his needs, as well as an infringement on his ability to think and express himself in new ways.

The following Zen story illustrates how a monk's view of others stemmed from his own self-image. A perceptive friend disillusions his self-complacency.

> Following a heavy rain, two Zen monks were walking together along a muddy road. They came upon a dismayed young maiden in a quandary about how she might cross the road without soiling her low-hanging silk kimono. "Come on, girl," said one monk as he lifted her in his arms and carried her across. The two monks resumed their journey without a word to each other. Finally, at a temple at which they were lodging that evening the second monk could no longer restrain himself: "We monks don't go near females, especially not young and lovely ones. It is dangerous. Why did you do that?" The first monk whimsically replied, "I left the girl there. Are you still carrying her?"[16]

Confronting Freedom

In therapy the process of disillusionment dwells on the negative side of personality wherein values, attitudes, judgments, and behavior are revealed to be colored by childhood assumptions. This view of self is counterbalanced by an increasing awareness of the adult part of oneself, which is characterized by the freedom and responsibility available to a person in his daily functioning. Some basic ideas about the nature of the self and its capacity for freedom are stressed.

The self is never a fixed, closed, totally predetermined form; it is only a person's own fears and self-deceptions that make him think this is the case. Everyone is considered to be responsible in accordance with his age. Each is also a completely unique person unlike anyone who ever was or ever will be. His adult self is in a constant process of change and growth. The process of growth requires the ongoing assertion of freedom—the capacity to transcend what one has been before. A person chooses his future direction and utilizes his past knowledge and experiences as he relates to the present, deciding what is to emerge in him. He alone is responsible for his aspirations and whether he strives to fulfill them.

The person comes to see that while he is possessed by childhood striv-

---

[16] Paul Reps, *Zen Flesh, Zen Bones* (Garden City, N.Y.: Anchor Books, Doubleday & Co., 1961), p. 18.

ings that seem to inhibit and interfere with his desired growth, this need not be accepted fatalistically. He chose these patterns as a child because of circumstances that at that time seemed to necessitate them. But as an adult he possesses the same freedom to choose differently and, because he is an adult, the circumstances are no longer the same. It is only his fear that seems to make them so. He can manage new reality-based judgments of situations and how he will respond to them. A certain detachment from identified childhood strivings will be required, and the resulting sense of uncertainty will be painful, yet as a human being he does possess the freedom to accomplish change. His sense of direction will arise entirely from his own unique assessment of the duties, responsibilities, and inner promptings in his daily life. A responsive relatedness to what is going on about him helps him respond to the adult needs and potential within him.

Therapy is partly the teaching of a basic skill: how one may choose a response that is different from the one prompted by identified childhood strivings and their accompanying feelings. It encourages a developing sensitivity to meaning and reality in the confronting therapeutic situation. The client is repeatedly faced with the fact that he does have some choice in the matter at hand, and many of his rationalizations to the contrary are based on his fear and need to maintain old props for security. Therapy, then, does not emphasize the nature of his early bondage that must be relived and changed through the handling of transference manifestations, nor is it viewed as a complete remaking of a person's basic character. Instead, it helps the client to identify actual reality-based choices in the present situation and find satisfaction by asserting himself as a free being.[17] Consistent with the emphasis on the client's capacity to choose freely and decide his own direction from what lies within himself is the therapist's willingness to allow him to accept or reject therapeutic interpretations or suggestions. The therapist is not an authority on the specific manner in which a client is to choose and live his life, although he is an authority on the basic elements of the human condition and what this means with regard to the development of emotional disorders and the way toward growth and change.

A client's direct experience of his freedom to rise above the powerful negative driving forces in his daily life is a crucial therapeutic happening. Helping him to recognize choices he had hidden from himself is one way of accomplishing this. There may be many other ways that to date have not been explored and attempted in a sufficiently significant fashion.[18]

[17] A detailed description of this technique is found in Richard L. Sutherland, "Choosing—As Therapeutic Aim, Method and Philosophy," *Journal of Existential Psychiatry*, Vol. 2, No. 8 (Spring 1962), pp. 371–392.

[18] One method utilizing casework techniques was described in Gerald K. Rubin, "Helping a Clinic Patient Modify Self-destructive Thinking," *Social Work*, Vol. 7, No. 1 (January 1962), pp. 76–80.

The logotherapy of Frankl includes a number of such examples. He sometimes utilizes humor and exaggeration of notions based on a client's neurotic assumptions about his own helpless condition. His aim is always to enable the client to acquire a new perspective on his symptoms and his own nature so that he does not continue to identify his total self with his neurotic symptoms, compulsions, or feelings. He also may suggest that a patient imagine himself to be twenty years older and review his present situation from that vantage point. The patient is able to identify instances in which more desirable choices might have been made by him "back then," and by so doing grasps the importance of the unique opportunity facing him at the present moment.[19]

Kondo, writing on "Zen in Psychotherapy" suggests as an adjunct to therapy the use of sitting meditation, which provides the patient with an experience of "single-mindedness"—an intuitive sense of the unity of body and mind that can enable him to detach himself from old childhood strivings bidding for present control.[20] The exercises of Gestalt psychology are aimed at a similar accomplishment.[21]

Another unique approach is Japan's *Morita* therapy. This is a therapy for hospitalized patients that is related to the philosophy of Zen Buddhism, which itself has many similarities to existentialism. Upon being hospitalized, a patient is placed in solitary confinement for the first several days, with only himself and his thoughts for company. He is asked to maintain a diary from the day of admission. Gradually he is permitted simple work activities and limited contact with a therapist. His range of contacts and tasks is slowly broadened and he begins to experience a sense of satisfaction in performing minor functions and relating to something other than himself. The nature of his problem is interpreted to him by the therapist, who has studied his diary. This interpretation has nothing to do with early trauma or deep insight into childhood relationships. Rather, it is aimed at emphasizing the foolishness and futility of the self-preoccupied existence the patient maintained until his hospitalization. It is further directed at arousing a sense of humility and genuine acceptance of his daily life circumstances as being not only bearable but an intrinsic vehicle for meaning and satisfaction, if he would only perform the tasks required of him instead of brooding over his unhappy lot in life. This treatment approach is continued until the patient is discharged from the hospital in anywhere from one to two months.

What is important in these approaches is the patient's developing awareness of a different aspect of himself—that part of him is beyond the

---

[19] Viktor Frankl, *The Doctor and the Soul* (New York: Alfred A. Knopf, 1957).

[20] Akihisa Kondo, "Zen in Psychotherapy: The Virtue of Sitting," *Chicago Review*, Vol. 12, No. 2 (Summer 1958).

[21] *See* Frederick S. Perls, Ralph F. Hefferline, and Paul Goodman, *Gestalt Therapy* (New York: Julian Press, 1951).

control of childhood striving and compulsive feelings. This aspect of self can manage a perspective over his total self and situation and thereby direct his choices in new ways. This part of him is also adult, creative, and—most important—real. There are lessons to be learned here from the novelists and film-makers who depict men and women discovering new and critical perspectives of their lives. Dickens' *A Christmas Carol* is a classic example, as is Dostoevsky's *Crime and Punishment*. The same theme occurs in Bergman's film *Wild Strawberries* and Fellini's *8½*. In *La Strada* Fellini presents a delightful vignette in which the feeble-minded heroine of the film is confronted by the clown–high-wire artist in a moment of utter despair. He laughs at her troubled face and tells her how foolish it is to feel her life is completely meaningless. He picks up a pebble and tells her that even this serves some purpose—that if it did not, then there would be no purpose in the entire star-strewn heavens. This statement at this particular time resulted in a profound change in the young woman.

The root of one's hope and sense of dignity lies within the preservation of belief in one's freedom, as well as its assertion over and against the forces that seem determined to defeat one. This is quite apparent in the thinking of many alcoholics involved in the therapy group mentioned earlier. The commitment to abstinence from alcohol emphasized by Alcoholics Anonymous reflects the same idea. One alcoholic who has been ''dry'' for five years put it this way: ''My choice is to drink again and face complete hopelessness or else to refuse alcohol and stand at least a fighting chance for happiness sometime.'' Here is commitment that accepts suffering and frustration without a guarantee of bliss. What is rewarding is the free and ongoing act of refusing to use alcohol as an escape.

As mentioned, in group therapy the notions about the alcoholic being some predetermined, unchangeable kind of being are challenged. It is important that group members sense the personal belief of the therapist in their capacity for freedom. The therapist must always go beyond the role of a sympathetic nursemaid to the ''hopelessly sick and downtrodden.''

A technique similar to some of Frankl's ideas was used effectively with this group. It had to do with handling the frustrations of one member as his assertive efforts at communication in the group continually failed. He could state his ideas openly until someone disagreed and requested that he clarify something. Then he experienced a blocking of thought that resulted in his having to back down. Next he would withdraw emotionally from the group and feel increasingly depressed at being overpowered by his own anxiety. It was pointed out that he had identified an important pattern within himself. While it was true that he could not control the rising feelings of anxiety and subsequent blocking, he did have control over how he reacted to this. On the one hand, he could give himself up to the notion that he was impotent and helpless and withdraw from any further efforts. On the other hand, he could strive to maintain attention to the continuing group discussion, so that when his anxiety subsided somewhat he could again assert any ideas he might have on some aspect of the discussion. When he was later able to do this, it was emphasized that he was not allowing the feelings to control him, but could find satisfaction in remaining the assertive kind of person he wanted to be in the group.

Repeated assertion that two parts of an individual can be identified—that which strives for new ways of thought, expression, and action and that which is fearful of this because of certain false assumptions about self and others based on childhood experiences—has been found to be quite meaningful to the group. The question that follows is: "Which of these two parts rules in you?"

Discovering Meaning in Suffering

The central theme in the writings of Dostoevsky and Kazantzakis is that suffering is an inherent part of life and one's growth as a person is dependent on acceptance of and being willing to grapple with this suffering. This same thesis must form a crucial part of psychotherapy. The therapeutic stance is that one can learn from one's suffering, but to do so one must bring it out into the open where it can be faced.

A client will seldom be thrown by the frightening and guilt-ridden aspect of himself if the therapist is not. The therapist must be willing to share the client's sufferings by simply being there, as Rogers emphasizes.[22] His acceptance and deep understanding of this suffering can be conveyed by avoidance of reassurance or easy solutions. He may occasionally reveal examples of his own or another's personal struggles, to emphasize that suffering is a shared human condition.[23] Therapeutic techniques are often used to help a person endure his suffering instead of becoming embittered by it or clinging to weak notions of how it may someday be replaced by pleasure and comfort.

In the group of alcoholics described, an important part of the discussion content is learning to read the underlying meanings in what a person presents. These may be expressions or descriptions of guilt, anxiety, anger, depression, somatic illnesses, or acting-out behavior. Essentially, it is some

[22] Carl Rogers, "Becoming a Person," in Simon Doniger, ed., *Healing: Human and Divine* (New York: Association Press, 1957), p. 61.

[23] This openness by the therapist is described in Sidney M. Jourard, *The Transparent Self* (Princeton, N.J.: D. Van Nostrand Co., 1964), pp. 39–65. O. Hobart Mowrer also emphasizes such openness in his integrity therapy. A critique of his over-all approach is made by Donald F. Krill in "Psychoanalysis, Mowrer and the Existentialists," *Pastoral Psychology*, Vol. 16 (October 1965), pp. 27–36.

feeling or behavior that has troubled a person about himself. The group's effort, then, is to examine the factors surrounding the occurrence in order to discover its meaning. Perhaps the person's response was not only natural, but could be considered mature. On the other hand, it may reveal an important aspect of a person's problematic life pattern. Guilt may reveal the inhibition of growth potential in a situation or behavior that is seen as being in conflict with what the person feels he could or should be doing. Anxiety may indicate that he has the potential to behave in a significantly different way but fears the consequences of so doing. Anger is often seen to be a way of blaming others for what are really one's own shortcomings. These concepts of common meanings associated with varying kinds of feelings soon become useful tools for group members to apply to themselves as well as to one another in subsequent meetings.

For example, a relatively new member of the group, 37 years old, commented that he was operating at "low gear" and could see no reason for this other than what he had once been told by a psychiatrist—that he must constantly punish himself because his parents had always been critical of him. Another group member inquired when the depression had become more apparent to him. The onset was pinned down to the previous Saturday night when he had wanted to go to a movie with his wife, who had encouraged him to go alone since she wanted to do her hair that evening. He had accepted this and gone alone. Further questioning by the group led him to see his disappointment and annoyance and his failure to let his wife know what he was feeling. Because he was afraid to show his own needs to her he had avoided any effort either toward changing her decision or attaining a closer understanding with her. The result was loneliness, resentment, and guilt over his own passivity. This incident revealed a pattern in their marital relationship related to his own fear of being hurt if he exposed a dependency need.

Then there is the type of suffering that either must be endured for a long time—perhaps for life—or else evaded by drinking: loneliness and a sense of emptiness, often accompanied by bitterness and envy. The person may have no friends or spouse, or a spouse who resists all efforts at a more intimate relationship. Perhaps the alcoholic, despite his efforts, finds himself unable to be more open and direct even within the therapy group. Here the only creative effort possible may be the continued endurance of suffering. It is natural to envy those whose upbringing, capacities, and circumstances have resulted in a far easier adaptation to life. Yet to endure suffering can still be meaningful. For some it will be a gesture of faith that relates them to a divine force or power. For others it will be a way of remaining true to the human condition—refusing false havens. For still others it will be a means of relating to the fraternity of alcoholics, who often find courage and hope in the continued sobriety of their brothers.

Suffering is a human reality not to be seen as a meaningless, chaotic disruption of a person's life. There is no pleasure principle norm that says to suffer is to be out of kilter with life. The opposite is the case—to live is to accept suffering. Its acceptance depends on some understanding of its hidden meaning—often seeing it as a guide toward potential growth. Suffering gives direction to one's freedom.

Realizing the Necessity of Dialogue

All that has been said with regard to disillusionment, freedom, and suffering would be no more than empty thoughts without the nourishment of dialogue. Creative growth and change are seldom intellectual decisions activated by willpower alone. The supportive sense of intimacy and relatedness involved here does not apply only to the therapeutic relationship. As mentioned, it may be an experience of unity with a deity, with fellow alcoholics, or with the human condition.

What must take place in the dialogue of therapy is revelation by the client of what is unique within himself, to which the therapist responds with interest, concern, acceptance, and validation of the client's feelings about himself. This does not, of course, mean continuing approval, but the willingness of the therapist to grasp and understand what is being revealed, even in the throes of disagreement. Increasing directness and openness of communication are therefore necessary. Also required is the lessening of manipulative efforts to control the relationship. There is a risk in allowing another person to respond to one freely. When a person ceases his efforts to control another's image of him, he often experiences a feeling of extreme panic, for his sense of self seems to be at the mercy of another's unknown response. Yet true dialogue requires this, and one of the most significant accomplishments in therapy is for two persons to be authentic and free in relation to one another. This, of course, requires that the therapist reveal himself as a human being with feelings, thoughts, and spontaneity.[24] The client must come to see himself as co-equal with the therapist by virtue of his humanity, and the therapist, to encourage this, must be adept at avoiding the client's efforts to control him.

The capacities both to trust and verbalize are inseparable from such dialogue. Clients will therefore vary in their ability to relate in the way described, and the therapist must carefully assess the modifiability of the client. For some people an effort to change meaningful relationships will be the goal sought. For others a more open dialogue with the therapist

---

[24] The concept of therapeutic openness and authenticity is well developed in Helen E. Durkin, *The Group in Depth* (New York: International Universities Press, 1964), sect. 2, pp. 249–276.

alone will be the only effort to implement this necessary aspect of the human condition.[25]

Group and family therapy are excellent proving grounds for examining methods of communication and the reason for failures of dialogue. In the group of alcoholics again, from time to time the specific ingredients of dialogue are structured. There is the initiator and the listener. Courage is often required to initiate a problem, for the response of others is uncertain. Courage is again needed by the listener in his attempt to develop the picture the initiator has begun through sincere curiosity. Responses such as advice-giving, early intellectual interpretations, and silence are frequently identified as defenses against a closer involvement with the initiator's problem. Genuine interest and an effort to understand more deeply may lead the listener to disagree with or challenge the initiator, with the accompanying threat of conflict. It may also lead the initiator to expect to receive a satisfactory solution to his problem from the listener, which the listener is fearful he may not be able to produce. On the other hand, the initiator may feel obliged to accept a listener's advice—even though he is doubtful of its applicability—and be silent in an effort to avoid conflict and the risk of displeasing others in their efforts to be of help.

The fears mentioned in efforts at dialogue can often be clarified in such a way that an individual will see and experience the fact that his very maneuvers to preserve a specific self-image negate the possibility of closeness. To become aware of this is also to realize the self-destructive aspects of one's manipulation of others. One may be more secure through feeling one has control of another person, but for genuine love and closeness to occur, the other must be allowed freedom of response. A gesture of love from another whom one feels one has successfully manipulated can be little more than emotional masturbation. One's own growth and knowledge of oneself is also dependent on the free assessment of others whose view is naturally different in some respects from one's own. To resist another's free opinion is to close off an opportunity for personal growth.

Accepting the Way of Commitment

The way of commitment refers to a loyalty to those realities of the human condition one has discovered to be true and meaningful for oneself. The basis for a new philosophy is found in the realization of the nature and pattern of certain childhood strivings and a disillusionment with some previous way of achieving self-security; recognition that there is a part of one-

[25] A differentiation of therapy goals in accord with categories of client modifiability is described in Donald F. Krill, "A Framework for Determining Client Modifiability," *Social Casework*, Vol. 49, No. 10 (December 1968), pp. 602–611.

self that is adult, free, and spontaneous; the finding of ongoing direction and a sense of meaning in one's sufferings; and finally through experiencing some possibility of genuine, sincere intimacy with another. As members of the described group of alcoholics stay on in therapy, these reality factors often become part of their lives as is manifested in the framework within which they use therapy sessions and relate to one another's problems. Gradually they have integrated elements of a new life-style.

It is helpful to think in terms of a model of the committed and authentic person as representing the ideal result of an acceptance of the existential realities described in this paper. While such a model would not be an expectation for all patients, it does add clarity and direction to our thinking. The characteristics are the opposite of those describing the state of anomie. One's sense of self is not seen as fixed, determined, or able to be constructed and secured by some set of achievements that prove one adequate because others finally recognize and applaud one. Rather, one's sense of self, as a narcissistic ego, is laughed at for its foolish and self-defeating strivings. Humor—as the capacity to laugh at oneself—is a natural characteristic. The self is seen now as having an ongoing relation to the world, constantly changing as new situations arise, forever being tapped by new possibilities, suspicious of the self-satisfaction that can lead to rigidity. The self as the center of attention and fortification increasingly is lost and replaced by a more avid interest in others, the tasks of one's daily life, and the beauty and wonder of the world about us. As the young English friend of Zorba the Greek said of him, "Zorba sees everything every day as if for the first time."[26] As one disciplines oneself away from self-clinging and delusional attachments to childhood strivings, a creative spontaneity unfolds that is invested in many aspects of one's life—not focused in one isolated area of achievement.

This new state of self is similar to the mindlessness and nothingness in Zen Buddhism, meaning that the mind operates freely without attachment. The inflow of intuitive response with this state of mindlessness is illustrated in a Zen tale of a young man who wanted to learn the art of swordsmanship and apprenticed himself to a master swordsman. He was, however, disappointed when he was refused permission even to hold a sword, but instead had to prepare his master's meals and perform various chores. As the student went about these chores he was periodically assaulted by his master, who would suddenly appear and hit him with a stick. The student was told to defend himself, but every time he prepared for an assault from one direction, it would come from another. Finally, in utter confusion and helplessness, he gave up his hyperalertness. It was only then that he could intuitively sense the direction of the next attack

---

[26] Nikos Kazantzakis, *Zorba the Greek* (New York: Simon & Schuster, 1959), p. 51.

and defend himself adequately. This is a practice of discipline in certain forms of personal combat in Japan even today.

This turnabout way of viewing the self is also the essence of true religious conversion. In religious terms, the self becomes detached from the idols of past devotion and is related now to the will of God, viewing the tasks and relationships of daily life as calling forth a response from oneself that in turn accomplishes a sense of divine unity in the act of free, open, and giving relatedness.

Buber describes this turnabout experience as a change from a reacting "I-it" relation to the world to a responding "I-Thou" relation. Instead of using people in one's environment as objects to support and gratify a self-image, one "enters into relation with the other," whatever form this might take, and such a contact is characterized by awe, respect, care, and creative response.[27] Tillich speaks of this experience as discovering the "courage to be" as a result of experiencing oneself as "being grasped by the power of Being itself." As one feels that one's most ego-gratifying strivings are illusory and false, one also has a sense of being affirmed as worthy and acceptable in spite of the fact that such acceptance has not been earned by the energy expended in these false strivings. The acceptance of this affirmative experience allows one to carry out one's daily tasks with a lessened need for the old security striving. One's "acceptance of being accepted" is seen to be a reunion with the transcendent power of Being that gives meaning to life.[28]

A nonreligious discussion of this same theme is found in Frankl's logotherapy, which is designed to arouse an awareness of the "task character of life." This concept is developed by using the realities of the patient's everyday life. Considering such factors as family background, the nature of time, awareness of death, ever changing circumstances, and ever changing personality, the therapist emphasizes that every person is singular, is unique. Not only will there never be another like him but even the exact circumstances of a momentary situation will never again be precisely the same, so that each decision possesses uniqueness. He is free to respond to the moment at hand, and when he grasps the tremendous sense of responsibility that goes with his uniqueness (which he bears sole responsibility for shaping), then his daily tasks take on a special meaning never before experienced. When he has truly reached this stage, he loses his self-preoccupation in a new sense of responsible relatedness to daily happenings. This might be labeled a new form of self-concern, but the essential difference is that the direction is outward—giving, doing, creat-

[27] The best critique of Buber's thought is found in Maurice S. Friedman, *Martin Buber: The Life of Dialogue* (New York: Harper & Bros. 1959).

[28] Paul Tillich, *The Courage To Be* (New Haven: Yale University Press, 1952).

ing, and enduring—rather than inwardly striving, securing, protecting, and possessing.

A significant portion of Frankl's logotherapeutic technique is designed to enlighten a patient about the kinds of values or possibilities that seem to await realization or actualization in his concrete life circumstance. Values are seen to be creative, experiential, and attitudinal in nature and vary, of course, with the patient. Creative values may refer to work tasks or even to those that may be artistic or athletic. Experiential values have to do with enjoyment of the world about one and this includes the closeness of an interaction in personal relationships. Attitudinal values are those that can be realized as one accepts and endures suffering that is unavoidable or unchangeable. From this perspective, it is apparent that some values can be identified as real and meaningful for any patient, regardless of the nature of his limits and circumstances.[29]

Mowrer and Glasser state that the key factor in therapy is helping a patient identify for himself clearly how he believes he ought to behave—what values seem important to him personally. He can then identify how his actual decisions and behavior are at odds with the way he wants to be. The necessity of changed behavior is stressed, regardless of the feelings involved, in order to bring about the person's increased acceptance of himself as worthy and hence as acceptable to others. Self-pity and self-preoccupation are replaced by identification of one's value and by commitment.[30]

Conclusion

The problem of anomie should be seen as a way of life in itself that must be countered by philosophical efforts that become meaningful through the process of psychotherapy. Existentialism is an especially useful philosophical base because it draws its central themes from man's immediate experience of his life. Its emphases on disillusionment, freedom, suffering, authentic relationships, and commitment deal directly with their opposites, which are characteristics of anomie. Existentialism should not be considered a completed philosophical system, but rather a series of emphasized realities that can be adapted to other forms of philosophy and religious belief, depending on the background and thought of the individual therapist.

A danger in the misuse of psychoanalytic thought is the reduction of man to primitive animal drives. Notions of chaos and determinism prevail

[29] Frankl, op. cit.

[30] O. Hobart Mowrer, The Crisis in Psychiatry and Religion (Princeton, N.J.: D. Van Nostrand Co., 1961); William Glasser, Reality Therapy: A New Approach to Psychiatry (New York: Harper & Row, 1965).

in this attitude about man's nature, and the resulting pleasure principle goal for people is simply insufficient for those experiencing anomie. The process, common among many psychoanalytically oriented therapists, of classifying and categorizing symptoms and behavioral expressions according to a system based on the primacy of animal drives accentuates this very problem. This process is viewed as "scientific" because it is wholly materialistic, but it is not scientific at all. The belief in the primacy of animal drives is as much a faith as the assumptions espoused in existentialism and other humanistic psychologies.

For the existentialists, man's biological drives are important and must be understood, but they do not fully explain man's nature. As a matter of fact, emphasis on the primacy of instinctual drives is a way of viewing human beings at their minimum level of functioning rather than their maximum level. At this maximum level man has freedom, the power to transcend his egotistical strivings, courage to venture, and a capacity to endure. The spirit is available to men, but they must sometimes seek it out to become aware of its existence. Kazantzakis, in *The Last Temptation of Christ*, expressed the nature of this spirit by proclaiming man as the being who gives wings to matter.

Freud was reported to have said to Binswanger, the existentialist psychoanalyst: "Yes, the spirit is everything.... Mankind has always known that it possesses spirit; I had to show it that there are also instincts."[31] Freud's contribution has been immense and he responded honestly and courageously to what he viewed as the problems of his society. But the repression of sexuality, with its resulting neuroses, is not the most common problem in our modern society of *Playboy*, the Hollywood love goddesses, and birth control. To reestablish meaning and direction in people's lives there is a need in the psychotherapeutic method for philosophical guidance and value education. By leaving this up to the church a therapist is being blind to the essential function of therapy for anomic man. This presents an identity problem for many therapists who have long been fond of criticizing and belittling the church, for now, as therapists, they are called on to serve patients in the very way in which for centuries the church has attempted to serve them.

[31] Ludwig Binswanger, *Sigmund Freud: Reminiscenses of a Friendship* (New York: Grune & Stratton, 1957), p. 81.

DISASTER

CHAPTER 64

Train Crash: Social Work and Disaster Services

Leona Grossman

In a fast-moving, technological society it is to be expected that the unpredictabilities in nature as well as human fallibility will continue to result in periodic catastrophes. What science may have accomplished in mastery over the natural environment seems to be balanced out by what its sophisticated technology has confounded.

However horrendous it may seem, the possibility of danger and disaster is indigenous to today's world. Two emerging issues are involved in all such happenings: how to cope and how to prevent. The focus on prevention has received by far the greater emphasis in its concern with such matters of technological safety as prevention of mine casualties, safety devices in factories, railroads, airplanes, and so forth. Investigations into responsibility and the possibility of legal reprisal act as powerful control agents. A fair amount of research has been conducted on natural disasters that have claimed large numbers of lives. It is only recently, however, that serious attention has been given to the human perspective: the intricate processes people use to cope with disasters, which have now been identified as "disaster behavior."

Several case studies and theoretical analyses of disasters have appeared in the literature of disciplines other than social work.[1] In the past

[1] *See,* for example, A. F. C. Wallace, *Tornado in Worcester: An Exploratory Study of Individuals and Community Behavior in an Extreme Situation,* "Disaster Study No. 3" (Washington, D.C.: National Academy of Sciences–National Research Council, 1965); George H. Grosser, Henry Wechsler, and Milton Greenblatt, eds., *The Threat of Impending Disaster: Contributions to the Psychology of Stress* (Cambridge, Mass.: The M.I.T. Press, 1964); R. R. Dynes, *Organized Behavior in Disaster* (Lexington, Mass.: D. C. Heath & Co., 1970); R. I. Leopold and H. Dillon, "Psycho-Anatomy of Disaster: Long-Term Study of Post-Traumatic Neuroses in Survivors of a Marine Explosion," *American Journal of Psychiatry,* 119 (April 1963), pp. 913–921.

Reprinted from *Social Work,* Vol. 18, No. 5 (September, 1973), pp. 38–44, with permission of the National Association of Social Workers.

ten years, however, the subject has been dealt with only rarely in social work journals.[2] Although written accounts of such incidents usually contain some skew, they still have pragmatic value. Since disasters evoke strong, instantaneous emotional responses, research of the "hard-fact" variety is a bit more difficult.

The Study of Disasters

The literature on behavior in extreme situations can be divided into three general categories: popular and journalistic accounts, official reports, and scientific or professional studies. Popular accounts generally reach a wide audience and convey their message with dramatic impact and strong human appeal, though their scientific usefulness may be limited.[3] Official reports constitute more technical accounts that are frequently found in organizational journals, annual reports, or trade magazines. These are usually pragmatic. Scientific literature is varied and can be subdivided into scholarly studies and professional studies. Thus far, the scholarly studies have been descriptive and usually noninterpretive.[4] Professional studies "employ the concepts, categories of observation, and research techniques of the disciplines they represent," and are usually specific studies dealing with specific variables.[5]

Several scientific studies of behavior in extreme situations are of value in developing generalizations. Those that deal with situations of specific stress offer some possibilities for constructing a "disaster theory."[6]

Behavioral scientists have not been drawn to research on disasters. This may be because they tend to view such extreme events as isolated incidents, without observing the patterns they follow, or because these events do not lend themselves to control by scientific procedures.[7]

Only within the last decade have a few efforts been made to institute systematically controlled studies of disasters. Many of the larger universities have developed research projects with funding from the National

[2] Herbert Blaufarb and Jules Levine, "Crisis Intervention in an Earthquake," *Social Work*, 17 (July 1972), pp. 16–19; Richard I. Shader and Alice J. Schwartz, "Management of Reactions to Disaster," *Social Work*, 11 (April 1966), pp. 99–104.

[3] John R. Hersey, *Hiroshima* (New York: Alfred A. Knopf, 1964).

[4] J. E. Thompson, *The Rise and Fall of the Maya Civilization*, (Norman, Okla.: University of Oklahoma Press, 1954).

[5] Wallace, op. cit.

[6] *See*, for example, Irving L. Janis, *Air War and Emotional Stress* (New York: McGraw Hill Book Co., 1951); A. H. Leighton, "Psychological Factors in Major Disasters," *Medical Projects Reports* (Rochester, N.Y.: University of Rochester, 1951); Bruno Bettelheim, "Individual and Mass Behavior in Extreme Situations," *Journal of Abnormal and Social Psychology*, 38 (October 1943), pp. 417–452; R. A. Lucas, *Men in Crisis* (New York: Basic Books, 1969).

[7] Wallace, op. cit., pp. 14–17.

Academy of Sciences–National Research Council. These studies have been essentially sociological, initially stimulated, perhaps, by the possibility of nuclear attack.

In 1963 the Disaster Research Center at Ohio State University was instituted and has since conducted field work at approximately seventy-three disaster sites. These studies have concentrated on various aspects of community organization in disaster situations.[8]

Theory

All definitions of disaster include the idea of a destructive force, nonhumanly or humanly induced, that strikes without warning and has a widely disruptive impact on normal functioning. Disasters harbor the potential for widespread public upset. In organizing one's thinking about disasters, it is possible to draw upon concepts from several areas of knowledge. There is a large body of material on psychological responses to situations of severe stress.[9] Such studies have revolved around specific situations that attempt to formalize the range of individual responses and evaluate the adaptive and nonadaptive aspects. Related to this are the many and varied analyses of panic behavior that focus on the instinct to flee in critical situations.[10]

Wallace formulated the concept of a "disaster syndrome" that is usually manifested by aimless wandering, stunned or dazed responses, extreme passivity or suggestibility, sleep disturbance, irritability, somatic distresses restlessness, and isolation.[11] Recently this concept has been refined and elaborated into a "post-stress syndrome."[12] In his well-known studies of reactions to the Coconut Grove fire in a Boston nightclub in 1942, Lindemann has connected many of these reactions to the more fundamental processes of bereavement, mourning, and grief.[13]

All these pieces of theory or sets of generalizations fit, at least in part, into reactions to disasters and offer possible explanations for the range of observable behavior. They are drawn from psychological and social psy-

---

[8] Dynes, op. cit., pp. 10–14.

[9] *See* Grosser et al., op. cit.; Irving L. Janis, *Psychological Stress* (New York: John Wiley & Sons, 1958); Henry Krystal, ed., *Massive Psychic Trauma* (New York: International Universities Press, 1969).

[10] Duane P. Schultz, *Panic Behavior: Discussion and Readings* (New York: Random House, 1964).

[11] Wallace, op. cit.

[12] H. C. Archibald and R. D. Tuddenham, "Persistent Stress Reactions after Combat," *AMA Archives of General Psychiatry,* 12 (May 1965), pp. 475–481.

[13] Erich Lindemann, "Symptomatology and Management of Acute Grief," *American Journal of Psychiatry,* 101 (September 1944), pp. 141–148.

chological theory and are usually based on empirical evidence taken from a number of incidents.

A particularly interesting structural and more sociological framework for understanding the natural history of a disaster has been developed by Powell and Rayner.[14] They divide a disaster into seven sequential phases: warning, threat, impact, inventory, rescue, remedy, and recovery, and attribute specific variables to each phase. All seven of these phases need not occur in each disaster. Some, like the Chicago transit crash to be described, start with impact, omitting the phases of warning and threat.

More important, continued study must be made of treatment following a disaster. The reality of a threat to survival and the urgency of immediate rescue have naturally tended to overshadow the covert psychological wounds. These might not immediately express themselves in behavior, but might become embedded in mental functioning and have disturbing residual effects. Some of the recent professional literature on death and mourning has an important relevance.[15] Studies have emphasized the effectiveness of encouraging survivors to talk about their experiences and emotions.[16]

Analysis

The intent of this paper is to discuss and analyze only one part of the total event, that concerning the participation of social workers and their interactions with the victims' friends and relatives. It is not often that one witnesses in such dramatic form the basic application of professional values and skills. Unusual as well is the opportunity to observe collective behavior at this level of emotional intensity and stress.

The article will deal with the participation of a social work staff, some of whom were personally involved while others were more removed and could observe the processes unfold with more perspective. This can be considered a natural history of a disaster, with attempts to analyze selected aspects, speculate on meanings, and hopefully, arrive at a few generalizations. It is particularly valuable, because it offers an unsimulated field experience. Through collective input and corrections by members of the staff and people of other disciplines, the usual pitfalls of bias have been

[14] J. W. Powell and J. Rayner, *Progress Notes: Disaster Investigations, July 1, 1951–June 30, 1952.* (Washington, D.C.: Chemical Corps Medical Laboratories, Army Chemical Center, 1952).

[15] Elisabeth Kübler-Ross, *On Death and Dying* (New York: Macmillan Co., 1970).

[16] S. E. Perry, E. Silber, and D. A. Block, *The Child and His Family in Disaster: A Study of the 1953 Vicksburg Tornado,* "Disaster Study No. 5" (Washington, D.C.: National Academy of Sciences–National Research Council, 1956); Archibald and Tuddenham, op. cit.

kept to a minimum. The analysis was undertaken immediately following the events in order to reduce the distortion of retrospect.[17]

This undoubtedly would have been a more valid analysis had a team of uninvolved researchers been able to study the situation with complete objectivity. Several disaster rescue centers that are now studying the problems seriously have made this recommendation. Perhaps this is something that the field of social work should consider in relation to its own professional interests and range of experiences.

Train Crash

On October 30, 1972, a crash on a local Chicago railroad claimed the lives of forty-five passengers and left more than three hundred persons injured. The catastrophe occurred at 7:27 A.M. on a Monday, when passengers were on their way to work. These were able-bodied, young to middle-aged workers, going about their beginning-of-the-week routine. Disaster struck with no warning.

The impact was immediate and critical. Certainly on the part of the victims there was no thought that such an event could conceivably take place. Most of these commuters had been using this transit system for some time. Although the possibility of casualties in daily living exists, the majority of people are not normally preoccupied with such a likelihood. In this era of escalating stress, the only plausible attitude is to maintain a realistic vigilance for the possibility of crisis. This has some implications for mental health in our present society. It makes added demands on the adaptive capacities of individuals, organizations, and communities.

In this situation, the time of the accident and the fact that it occurred at a train depot situated between two hospitals were among the more fortunate factors in the tragedy. In fact, one of the hospitals, the Michael Reese Hospital and Medical Center, had just completed and rehearsed its disaster plan so that it could immediately mobilize and institute a significant rescue operation. The fire and police departments were also prepared to join the hospital in meeting the immediate challenge. Without these factors the list of deceased might have been significantly longer.

Impact

Although the literature on disasters discusses impact in terms of those who are direct victims of the disaster, the definition needs to be enlarged to include other people also acutely involved. Extreme events such as this

[17] The staff met as a group several times immediately following this event. They talked among themselves, checking out their reactions and feelings. After a little while, when they were somewhat removed from the emotional impact of that particular day, they were able to evaluate and conceptualize their experiences.

one have multiple impact points. One was the impact on family members and friends who, on hearing of the incident, rushed to the scene. This group of people under severe stress remained in communication with the social work staff throughout that eventful day. They came in droves and were directed to the lobby and lounge of the nurses' residence. The initial effect was total chaos.

A second point of impact was on the staff of social workers at Michael Reese Hospital, most of whom did not know of the accident until their arrival that morning. Faced with this challenge, the staff quickly recovered from the initial shock and confusion and, joining the throngs in the nurses' residence, organized themselves into a functioning subsystem.

Morale was high and the staff reacted instantaneously to each task, accepting requests from whoever issued them and attempting to suppress any uncontrollable anxiety. The initial mobilization of forces rapidly assumed a structure in which roles were covertly defined and rational leadership emerged. It was this spirit of cohesiveness that provided the stability required by the fragmented subsystem of relatives and friends. This supports the generalization that "high group morale and cohesiveness will generally minimize the disaster effects of impact."[18] At the termination of the impact phase, the two subsystems (professional and lay) were moving in complementary fashion, each gaining strength from the other. Urgent needs for comfort and help demanded the support and total involvement of the social work staff and in the end neutralized the mechanisms that usually separate professionals from clients.

The staff had to deal with its own set of interpersonal reactions before it could function as an organic whole. Following the initial shock and immediate immersion, there was some recoil, some jockeying for power or status. There was competition for social credits, measured by the number of relatives and friends who looked to them for help. Staff members later reported having been pushed aside by their colleagues and experiencing momentary anger. But such feelings were not reinforced because of the urgency of other needs. The situation itself determined the structure that finally emerged. Each staff member discovered some satisfying level of usefulness, accepted the leadership of others, and developed effective modes of nonverbal communication through symbols and cues. These were important, since time did not always permit speech.

Inventory and Rescue

For the purposes of this analysis these two phases, which Powell and Rayner's model separates, can be combined. One phase flowed into the other. In the inventory phase, survivors began to feel concern for others and to reach out helpfully. At the point of rescue, outside professionals, other

---

[18] Shader and Schwartz, op. cit., p. 101.

hospital staff, nearby service departments, members of the clergy, and volunteer workers moved in to offer further support. As family and relatives engaged in their desperate search for survivors, the professionals were there to inform, guide, and offer hope and comfort.

Great reliance was put on the steady dissemination of information. Lists of the injured and dead were relayed continuously to the social work staff from the hospital's public relations department. Social workers, supported by members of the clergy, acted as the major informers.

The waiting population proved to be admirably controlled. Family members clung together and comforted one another. Strangers sat side by side, locked in their personal thoughts, not speaking but observant of others' reactions. A few people attached themselves to members of the staff, returning periodically for news. They seemed patient when reassured that someone was personally concerned about them. Volunteers stayed with people who seemed lost and confused, or who wanted to talk or cry. Some needed physical comfort such as someone to hold their hand or pat their shoulder. Even staff needed this from each other. The function of touching is frequently underestimated and even frowned upon in a professional relationship, but in this case the taboo was lifted. In essence, the staff responded in a totally human way and the overall effects were appropriate. Food played an important part in the role of comforting. The hospital had supplied generous amounts of coffee and sandwiches for all staff and visitors.

As the day wore on, the tension mounted and families began to search for information with increased anxiety. Their relentless questioning might easily have overtaxed an already fatigued staff who remained, nonetheless, remarkably patient. As it became clear that the remaining groups might have to face the news of a death, the level of staff empathy increased. Relatives and friends were encouraged to express their fears, to cry, and to talk endlessly. Efforts to sustain hope continued; other hospitals were contacted in a further search for more complete information. The increased activity was again used to suppress the mounting anxiety and concern.

A final handful of families had to be directed to the morgue to identify relatives. This tragic episode was handled by one of the priests. Emotional responses were extreme—one Mexican woman experienced an "ataque," others wept or screamed. Families turned to one another in their sorrow; professionals seemed locked out, or chose to remove themselves.

Aftermath

"An experience of extreme danger is not over once the danger is past, even for those who survive it intact. Something has intruded into their emotional life which requires some time to assimilate.''[19] This was relevant to all who experienced the Chicago disaster.

Despite the exhaustion of most staff members after this experience there was, nevertheless, a feeling of having accomplished something and of having extended oneself fully to others. But there were also the disquieting feelings of having observed and empathized with severe loss and grief. In practically each staff member, this aroused repressed memories of past personal loss, and responses ranged from emotional outbursts to attempts at denial. Staff meetings, informal discussions, and group meetings with patients held over a period of several weeks eventually helped to reconcile the arduous events of that day.

A joint decision was made to help those survivors interested in working out their mourning and grief. All those with whom staff members had worked and those who had been treated in the emergency room were notified. Although attendance was small, these follow-up meetings proved meaningful for those who came. Several persons attended a few times, others just once. The groups were composed of survivors, relatives, and staff members.

Analysis of the process in these groups revealed some similarities to ordinary reactions of shock or mourning. To begin with, survivors tended to ruminate over the precise details of the crash in an attempt to work through their own preoccupations. The less verbal members appeared to be listening intently, as if vicariously going through the experience. Most persons seemed to recall minutely what had been happening just before the crash. Many had superstitious reasons for why they survived while others were killed. Some wondered about their decision that day not to ride in their usual car, which was subsequently demolished.

Several who came away shaken but not badly injured struggled with reactions of moral censorship in the belief that they should have done more to help others. They were disappointed in themselves, because their immediate response had been to flee from danger rather than turn back to help. One young woman had not even allowed herself to face this truth until well into the meeting. Then, after listening to others, she was able to say what was truly troubling her and evidently had motivated her to attend. Her belief in herself as a helpful person had been shattered by her flight reaction. She prefaced this disclosure by unconsciously citing what appeared to be an irrelevant account of how she had offered shelter and food to a stranger the night before the accident. The comparison between this incident and her behavior at the accident indicated how confused she felt about herself as a "good" person. Some discussion about the range of panic reactions helped to put her feeling of self-worth together again, although she will probably be haunted with this for some time.

[19] Martha Wolfenstein, *Disaster: A Psychological Essay* (Glencoe, Ill.: Free Press, 1957), p. 135.

The somatic effects of the accident were fairly consistent: headaches, sleep disturbances, startle reactions, and gastric distresses. One survivor experienced immediate amnesia and could not recall how he had escaped without injury from the car that had been demolished and had claimed the highest number of casualties. The method in which he might have escaped worried him and he strained to put together the pieces of his memory. Another survivor had developed a tremor in one hand. Others were grappling with phobias of one kind or another, and practically all the victims were afraid to board the train again.

Survivors discovered that talking to each other had a cathartic effect and as such was a vital part of recovery. They uniformly felt that not even close family members could fully understand and empathize with their experience. Those few relatives who did accompany survivors to the sessions gained a better understanding. In some situations we could almost see the walls that separated relatives and survivors break down and could sense the change of attitude. In one situation the mother of a daughter who had been injured in the crash accompanied the young woman to some of the sessions. She expressed irritation and guilt for not having "been with my daugher in time of need." Through this irrational reaction the staff gained insight into the relationship of overdependency that existed between the two. This experience underscored the importance of working through feelings with close relatives as well as survivors, since guilt reactions are prevalent in both groups. In this case the group discussion helped the participants recognize and accept these emotions while pointing out their irrationality.

In several instances, the emotional reactions to this event were linked to past experiences either real or vicarious. A few of the men had had army experiences and this disaster touched off feelings of horror, fear, shame, disgust, or guilt. Having mutually shared these past experiences, certain of them were able to form bonds and to support each other's feelings. On the other hand, there was the occasional tendency to deprecate and embarrass others for not being "more courageous." These reactions came from persons who used them to hide their own feelings of inadequacy. Depression and sudden outbursts of anger of the "why me" variety were constantly present.

The social work staff were totally involved in these group sessions. Because they themselves had experienced a wide range of emotions they were able to relate with empathy and reflect more openly upon their reactions. This made each group session an existential "experience." Growth in insight, and closer relationships with one another were some of the positive gains from this intense involvement.

Efforts were made to reach out to the families of the deceased. Although each overture seemed to be appreciated, the bereaved families were not interested in talking with each other. They sought the intimacy of family or the comfort of religion, but they seemed to have no immediate wish for contact with strangers.

There remained one more group of survivors—patients who had been seriously enough injured to require hospitalization. This coincided with the traditional role of hospital social work. These patients had the same urgent need to talk of the accident in detail and compare impressions. The feelings of grief and anger felt by those close to them needed attention as well. In one extreme situation there seemed to be a pathological denial of the severity of the survivor's condition, but this was attributed to a preexisting disturbed relationship.

Conclusions

This experience provided verification of some assumptions concerning the behavior of people in stressful situations. Under serious threat, most adults are oriented toward mutual helpfulness rather than toward destructiveness or panic, especially if consolidated leadership is provided to create models for positive action. Even under extreme conditions, behavior can be fundamentally adaptive and orderly. For this to happen, a social structure that permits mutual caring and helpful involvement must exist. In its commitment to the survivors, the social work staff offered such a model. Because of the pressures of daily routine, it is frequently possible to lose sight of these cardinal professional values.

Personal experience, especially of a highly emotional kind, provides significant opportunities for growth through self-reflection and feedback. In this situation members of the staff revealed qualities that had never before surfaced. This produced increased mutual respect. The total experience reconfirmed the effectiveness of the social work role in crisis intervention, in which action as well as a high level of empathy and respect for human dignity are major priorities.

DIVORCE

CHAPTER 65

Divorce: Problems, Goals, and Growth Facilitation

Dory Krongelb Beatrice

The rapidly increasing divorce rate in the United States indicates that divorce is a phenomenon widespread enough to affect most individuals either directly or indirectly. Accordingly, people going through divorce are increasingly represented in social work caseloads. This article will first present what divorcing persons are saying about their complex situations and the many problems they face. A framework for significant goals in divorce work will follow. Divorce groups, which attempt to develop support systems and to facilitate movement toward significant goals in the divorce process, will then be discussed as a way to resolve some of these problems.

Problems of Divorcing Persons

One of the most difficult problems faced by divorcing persons is that of identity crisis.[1] They often feel that the entire structure of their lives has fallen apart, leaving them empty, worthless, and with nothing to offer. Loneliness can be overwhelming, as can loss of a sense of purpose. This may be especially true of the long-married wife and mother whose identity revolved completely around her marriage, family, and her role and status as a homemaker. With that gone, she wonders, "Who am I?"

[1] Reva S. Wiseman, "Crisis Theory and the Process of Divorce," *Social Casework* 56 (April 1975): 205–12.

Reprinted from *Social Casework*, Vol. 60 (March, 1979), p. 157–165, by permission of the author and the Family Service Association of America.

Economics is another major problem area. Vocational identity may be part of this, especially for the homemaker who feels a financial and/or emotional need to work outside the home after a divorce.[2] In such a case, "marketability," or the development of needed work skills, needs to be assessed.[3] This process may be blocked by inexperience, low self-esteem, reality issues such as child care, guilt over childrens' emotional needs, and so on. E. E. LeMasters found that, although households headed by women make up only about 10 percent of all United States households, they constitute about 25 percent of families in the poverty group in American society.[4] Another study of divorce and poverty found that "a family headed by a female is more than twice as likely to be poor and stay poor as one led by a male—28 percent versus 12 percent.... Divorced women who are heads of families are worse off financially than any other family leaders and much more likely to live below the poverty line."[5]

In addition to the realistic problems of dividing up the economic assets of a two-parent household, property battles become overloaded by the emotions involved, in which the objects of the battle serve as symbols of the emotional pain the contestants are feeling. This is also true in the case of custody battles. As the divorcing couple becomes involved with lawyers, the legal ramifications of their decision may become an additional source of confusion and bewilderment. Much has been written in the way of critique of the way the legal profession currently interacts with divorce clients: lawyers are trained to defend their clients' interests and attack those of the spouse; they are not trained in family and marital dynamics, and so on.[6] The result is that lawyers often unwittingly contribute to escalating the marital conflict, rather than to aiding in its resolution.

ROLE CONFLICTS

Another area of difficulty and confusion for the single parent may be in dealing with role conflicts and role shifts. The single parent wonders, "Should I try to be both mother and father to my children?" In many cases the responsibilities of the now-absent spouse's role falls upon the remaining present parent to absorb. When this is so, conflicting parent roles may be overwhelming to the present parent. For example, parents may need to work and be away from their children because of financial necessity; yet they feel this is a time when their childrens' needs for them is especially

[2] Ibid., p. 210.

[3] Kenneth Kressel and Morton Deutsch, "Divorce Therapy: An In-Depth Survey of Therapists' Views," *Family Process* 16 (December 1977): 413–43.

[4] E. E. LeMasters, *Parents in Modern America* (Homewood, Ill.: Dorsey Press, 1970).

[5] "A Surprising Profile of America's Poor," *U.S. News and World Report*, 8 (November 1976), pp. 57–58.

[6] Kressel and Deutsch, "Divorce Therapy," p. 425.

great. The parent feels overwhelmed by the many demands on him or her and may feel totally helpless and inadequate to meet them.[7] There may be strong feelings of needing to compensate to the children for the divorce, with guilt then adding to the demands of the situation. A related problem is how, in the face of so many real demands from others, can they get something emotionally for themselves; where is the single parent's emotional replenishment going to come from?

An encouraging development in the area of overwhelming single-parent responsibilities is that "an increasing number of men who have been separated or divorced from their wives ... have consciously chosen to remain fully involved in their children's upbringing and to assume increased responsibility for taking care of them."[8] There is also a trend among family therapists to work with the entire family after a divorce in order to ensure continuing constructive involvement of both parents in the child's life.[9]

While single parents try to juggle shifting roles, they must also deal with the reactions and attitudes of others. Many divorcing people have had the experience of suddenly finding themselves dropped from past friendships and relationships, just at a time when they feel most in need of others. In spite of the increasing acceptance of divorce in our society, many vestiges of stigma remain which label divorced people as deviants, misfits, failures, or threats to intact marriages. Consequently, divorced people may internalize these perceptions and see themselves the same way.

EFFECTS ON THE CHILDREN

The sense of failure may be especially intense in relation to one's children. Divorcing parents wonder if they are doing irrevocable damage to their childrens' development by ending their marriage, and they have many questions about how best to handle and help their children through this difficult period. Sometimes the trauma to the parent is such that it is difficult to have enough energy left over to deal effectively with the children. Many dysfunctional parent-child patterns may appear during this period. In a study of young boys and their mothers, Kay Tooley found that "women raising children alone after divorce often find their new sociopsychological world frightening and unmanageable. Perceiving this, their

---

[7] Kay Tooley, "Antisocial Behavior and Social Alienation Post Divorce: The 'Man of the House' and His Mother," *American Journal of Orthopsychiatry* 46 (January 1976): 33–42.

[8] Harry Finkelstein Keshet and Kristine M. Rosenthal, "Fathering After Marital Separation," *Social Work* 23 (January 1978): 11–18.

[9] David Weisfeld and Martin S. Laser, "Divorced Parents in Family Therapy in a Residential Treatment Setting," *Family Process* 16 (June 1977): 229–36; and Janice Goldman and James Coane. "Family Therapy After the Divorce: Developing a Strategy," *Family Process* 16 (September 1977): 357–62.

young sons may undertake a counterphobic defense of themselves and their mothers, manifested as antisocial behavior."[10]

Another common problem is acting out by the parents of all their unfinished feelings about their ex-spouses through the children. Parents may unwittingly use the children as weapons against the ex-spouse: "Conflicts leading to divorce persist afterward and the child can remain a pawn in parental maneuvers after the divorce as well as before."[11] Joan B. Kelly and Judith S. Wallerstein found that strong wishes for the parents' reconciliation persisted in a third of their sample of early latency age boys, and that these fantasies were "either being kept alive by the openly expressed wishes of a parent, or the parent-child relationship had deteriorated to such an extent that the child perceived reconciliation as his only hope."[12]

Loyalty conflicts are often exacerbated by parental interaction.[13] Many single parents engage in role reversal and look to the child as a substitute spouse, searching for the love, companionship, and protection that are lacking in their lives. Very distraught parents may imply that the divorce is the children's fault, thus adding to the feelings of responsibility, guilt, and rejection that the children may already have. Or they may inappropriately displace all of their anger, frustration, fear, and helplessness onto the children.

EFFECTS ON ABSENT PARENTS

Whereas custodial parents may at times feel resentful and overwhelmed by all the responsibilities of their new situation, absent parents have another set of problems. They may be kept away from the children by an extremely hostile situation surrounding attempts to see them. The roles of the former spouses who continue relationships with their children are often plagued by ambiguity and confusion on all sides. The new relationships with the children lack a clear-cut definition. A tremendous sense of loss at the separation from the children is experienced. No longer in the house, the absent spouse (usually the father) is, in effect, stripped of most of his former authority; he feels doomed to frustration as he tries to influence and shape the children's lives the way he had hoped. Guilt and anxiety are intense: "The anxiety they experienced was made up of many components and involved fear of losing their relationship with their chil-

[10] Tooley, "Antisocial Behavior," p. 33.

[11] Jack C. Westman, "Effect of Divorce on a Child's Personality Development," *Medical Aspects of Human Sexuality* 6 (January 1972): 38–55.

[12] Joan B. Kelly and Judith S. Wallerstein, "The Effects of Parental Divorce: Experiences of the Child in Early Latency," *American Journal of Orthopsychiatry* 46 (January 1976): 20–32.

[13] Ibid., p. 29.

dren, of losing their status within the family as a source of self-definition, of being criticized by their ex-spouse, of being rejected by their children, and of losing their roots and the structure and continuity of family life."[14] Fear of inadequacy as a single parent is also strong.

NEW RELATIONSHIPS

Another major problem area for newly single people develops as they venture out into the world of the opposite sex. The central conflict here is likely to be independence versus intimacy. They may long for the closeness, companionship, sex, and shared responsibilities of an intimate relationship, yet they are enjoying their newfound freedom and have many fears of vulnerability based on the dissolution of the marriage. In the areas of dating and sexuality, new singles often experience a resurgence of unresolved adolescent conflicts, and this self-perceived regression can be quite demoralizing. Low self-esteem is likely to add to one's fears of new relationships. Yet, "there is a real need to explore further interpersonal and sexual potentials ... the need to experiment sexually at this time is of vital importance to many divorcing persons."[15] New relationships may also create unexpected reactions in the children than can bewilder the parents.

Significant Goals in Divorce Work

In the course of working with divorcing people, it is necessary to erect a general framework of significant goals. Reaching these objectives, in addition to clients' individual goals, are critical if one is going to successfully negotiate the divorce experience and be able to grow through it.

GRIEF WORK: DEALING WITH LOSS

One of the most crucial aspects of finding autonomy and growth out of this crisis situation is the person's ability to fully accept and mourn the loss of the mate, to say good-bye to the spouse, the marriage, and whatever other losses are experienced. The absent parent is dealing not only with the loss of spouse, but of the children, too.

Grieving must be done, yet is often blocked, both from within and from sources outside the individual. Society has no ceremony for mourning the loss of a spouse through divorce, in contrast to the funeral and rituals surrounding death. This leaves the divorced person very much alone in a labyrinth of confusion, anger, despair, sadness, and fear. In addition,

---

[14] Keshet and Rosenthal, "Fathering After Marital Separation," p. 12.
[15] Wiseman, "Crisis Theory and Divorce," p. 210.

intense ambivalence is often a feature of this time. "Grief work must be done with great thoroughness or there will remain the danger of constantly living in the presence of the open casket of a dead marriage."[16] Newly single people often need to say good-bye not only to their former spouse, but to an entire past. When people are able to deal with divorce in a "growthful" way, they will be faced with the prospect of change in life-style, responsibilities, freedoms, relationships, in their children and themselves. In order to become ready for these pervasive changes, they must be able to come to terms with, and let go of, the past.

It is important to communicate to clients an atmosphere that is permissive to feelings so that they will internalize this permission and allow themselves to grieve. Therapists need to be familiar with the grief process[17] and how it relates to divorce, so that they can facilitate mourning and help bring it to completion.[18] They need to help clients allow their anger, depression, confusion, fear, and sadness, and help this develop into eventual acceptance of the loss, with reintegration and growth. Therapists need to help clients express their pain and their hopes, their resentments and appreciations of their former mate, what they miss, and what they enjoy in their new life. Therapists need to help remove the blocks and let all this happen.

> For example, when Mr. and Mrs. Y sought marriage counseling, Mrs. Y stated that she wanted a divorce after twenty-one years of marriage. Exploration revealed that she felt strongly about ending the marriage, but had agreed to marriage counseling in the hope that it would soften the impact on her husband, who had initially talked about suicide if she left him. He entered counseling in the hope that they could heal the marriage. As it became more and more clear that Mrs. Y did not want to invest any more in the marriage, Mr. Y continued to insist that things were improving, and to deny the ending of the marriage. Mrs. Y, feeling more and more frustrated at her inability to get through to Mr. Y, resorted to the passive-aggressive means of having him find her in bed with another man. This speedily brought the marriage to an end. Mr. Y soon entered a divorce group (Mrs. Y left the state) and spent several sessions ventilating his anger at his wife's lover. The group and leaders confronted him on his wife's responsibility for the situation also. As he gradually began to allow himself to feel anger toward her, he was able to break through his denial and move through grieving. He was soon able to let go of the marriage and reinvest his energies in other relationships, which offered him more than his marriage had for a long time. Eventually, he even became grateful for the divorce. He found more vitality in his own life and in more satisfying relationships.

[16] Ibid., p. 206.

[17] Elisabeth Kübler-Ross, *On Death and Dying* (New York: Macmillan Co., 1969).

[18] Wiseman, "Crisis Theory and Divorce," pp. 205–12.

DEVELOPMENT OF SUPPORT SYSTEMS

One of the critical needs during and after a divorce is for an authentic and workable support system. Loneliness and isolation are often intense problems for the divorcing individual, and the development of meaningful relationships is important to combat these.

This can be a fruitful time to help clients reassess their relationships in general and what they want to give to and get from them in the future. It can be a time to discover that independence and intimacy are not mutually exclusive, but that one can build a relationship on one's own terms. It can be a time to choose new friends who are nurturant and reject those who are toxic. For example, in working with women who took a submissive role in their marriages, it was discovered in the course of divorce work that they also reproduced this role in many of their relationships. As they began to place a higher priority on their own needs, to increase their self-esteem, and to become more assertive, they were able to either change some of those relationships or leave them for healthier ones.

This is a time to encourage clients to broaden the range of their relationships with others, to find satisfaction in the company of several or many people rather than channel all of their companionship needs into marriage. Close friends become important and same-sex relationships deepen. This can be a time to explore one's sexuality and, perhaps, nonsexual intimacy with the opposite sex.

The other aspect of developing a support system is that of developing *self*-support. This often seems nearly unattainable to the person emerging from the marriage with crushed self-esteem, yet it can be developed. The self-supporting person will convert loneliness into solitude, taking pleasure in a certain amount of aloneness. Therapists can help clients discover how to activate their own capabilities and resources and take responsibility for their own fulfillment in order to experience growth out of pain and loss. Therapists also need to help clients work through their feelings of failure and inadequacy, which may be intense. Without resolution of these feelings, self-esteem will be greatly damaged. The issue of self-support is closely related to the third task, that of developing autonomy.

DEVELOPMENT OF AUTONOMY

Successful divorce work also involves developing a sense of autonomy and new self-identity as a whole—in divorcing persons, the ability to see themselves as growing human beings in their own right. This can be most difficult for people who married before developing their own identity in the first place, perhaps having sought to find themselves through their spouse or their marriage. "Divorce forces the individual to take up the work of individuation once more without the illusory support of the marriage."[19] Suddenly finding oneself alone in the search for identity can be a frightening and lonely experience, but it also offers tremendous potential for growth. The search involves separating one's identity from familiar roles as wife and mother, breadwinner and father, and sorting out one's own uniqueness as an individual. Therapists need to help clients ask themselves what *their* feelings, needs, resentments, capacities, limitations, thoughts are. They need to help clients get in touch with and accept undiscovered or suppressed aspects of themselves, thus becoming more whole.

This is a particularly potent time to reevaluate one's male or female identity, and to develop qualities that will round out and enrich the overall personality. For example, Harry Finkelstein Keshet and Kristine M. Rosenthal found than single fathers had a very difficult time relating to their children's emotionality at first. However, "to maintain the emotional attachment between himself and his children, a father must develop a sensitivity to them." He must face their dependency, their feelings of powerlessness, their emotions, and their irrationality, as well "as elements that he himself had to suppress during his own childhood as he acquired the veneer of masculinity.... As an adult he has an opportunity to resolve them for himself in new and better ways."[20] The female has this opportunity to develop her stereotypically "masculine" traits—aggressiveness, strength, competence, and independence, as well as her career interests. Reva S. Wiseman has delineated four areas of identity—personal, vocational, social, and sexual—that can be reworked during this time.[21] In general, therapists also need to help clients take responsibility for their own lives, based on their sense of individuality, autonomy, self-support, and relatedness to the world.

REEVALUATION OF THE MARITAL RELATIONSHIP

Another important component of divorce work is reevaluation of the marriage. Therapists need to help clients sort out what happened in the marriage. How did it come to be dissolved? What were the strengths and weaknesses of the relationship? What was each partner's contribution to the problems? What led them to choose this person as a mate originally? What vestiges of their relationships with their parents were brought into

[19] Goldman and Coane, "Family Therapy After the Divorce," p. 362.
[20] Keshet and Rosenthal, "Fathering After Marital Separation," p. 18.
[21] Wiseman, "Crisis Theory and Divorce," pp. 209–10.

the marriage; how did these affect the marriage? What have they learned from this experience? What will they do differently in the future? It is important for divorcing persons to gain some insight into the unconscious conflicts and distortions that led to the choice of mate, and to gain an appreciation of their contribution to the dysfunctional patterns in the old marriage. "A one-sided view of the marital breakdown was taken as *prima facie* evidence that something far short of an optimal divorce had been achieved."[22] Therapists are all familiar with the person who leaves an unhappy marriage, only to quickly enter another relationship with similar dysfunctional patterns. Those with long-standing patterns of pathological mate-selection will need the most help here.

An example of following a dysfunctional pattern is Mrs. S, who sought therapy after the break-up of a second marriage. In both her first and second marriages she had become a battered wife, yet had wanted both marriages to continue, and blamed herself completely for their dissolution. Her history revealed, predictably, a childhood in which she had been frequently beaten by her father. She grew up assuming that she must have done *something* to deserve this treatment, and that it was all her fault. She also had learned to associate affection and attention with abuse. Thus, she sought the same type of relationship in her marriages, highly motivated by crippling guilt and a need for punishment. When one husband left her, she again felt it was her fault and she proceeded, unconsciously, to seek and find exactly the same situation in a second marriage.

The reevaluation process is designed to break up this sort of pattern, and to get people moving in a more satisfying direction. Ms. H, who sought therapy during a separation from her husband, is someone who may be able to break past patterns. She was ambivalent about divorce, feeling the marital relationship had grown empty, but fearing another poor choice of mate. As her original choice of her husband was explored, some understanding of some of the unconscious reasons for it were gained. She had been extremely angry at her mother and had chosen the only boyfriend that her mother disapproved of as a passive-aggressive maneuver. Also, she had seen her father as a weak man who submitted to her mother's domination. Ms. H. had tended at first to choose men who were also submissive so that she could dominate them as her mother did her father; but the man she chose to marry was quite domineering himself and filled the more assertive role she had wanted her father to fill.

Because Ms. H's therapy is currently at this stage, the outcome cannot be presented here. However, it is quite likely that, as Ms. H gains these insights, she will be able to make a freer and healthier choice of men in the future.

---

[22] Kressel and Deutsch, "Divorce Therapy," p. 422.

COPING WITH REALITY DEMANDS

As always, therapists need to start where the client is, and some clients may be too overwhelmed with reality problems to have any energy available for grief work, reevaluation, or identity development. To make peace with the demands of reality, such as employment, money, housing, child care, child management, and so on is crucial. If not peace, at least peaceful coexistence can be hoped for. In their fascination with the intrapsychic and interpersonal dynamics of clients, therapists should not underestimate the force with which these practical problems impinge on clients, especially bearing in mind the facts and statistics cited earlier regarding divorce and poverty. Social workers, by virtue of orientation and training, should be especially sensitive to these problems, know the community resources well, and make appropriate referrals. This is where the utilization of other agencies such as social services, legal aid facilities, vocational counseling, and so on may be appropriate.

Therapists can help solve some of these reality problems, teaching problem-solving techniques in the process. They can assist clients with tackling one thing at a time, building successes bit by bit, so that their self-esteem, independence, and capacity to cope and grow are increased in the process. What will emerge from these processes are people who are coping with the demands of reality, have reevaluated the marriage and assimilated the divorce, have developed a clearer evolving positive sense of themselves as unique individuals, and are developing caring and authentic relationships with others.

The Divorce Group

Increasingly, the divorce group is being used as a vehicle to assist those who are in the process of divorce with their many problems, some of which have been outlined above. Such groups are usually time-limited (optimally about twelve to sixteen weeks), designed that way to communicate the idea that what most of the members are experiencing is an adjustment reaction, with improvement likely over a relatively short period of time. Those who are dealing with more chronic emotional difficulties in addition to divorce may benefit from such a group, but will often need to go on for further individual or group therapy. In the divorce group that is described here, membership is closed after the first or second meeting so that relationships can develop and deepen.

FORMAT AND MATERIALS

The group is loosely structured in format, with some structured materials being used at the beginning to facilitate interaction and help members discover common areas of concern. Examples of materials used include brief, relevant magazine articles, and a sentence completion questionnaire developed for the group with open-ended statements such as: "Some of my strongest needs now are for ..."; "When I'm feeling lonely, I ..."; and "Since my marriage broke up, my children ..." Pregroup interviews are used with all members, and individual goals are established.

One of the original assumptions in starting this type of group was that a variety of group members, at different stages of dealing with a common core of difficulties, would have a lot to offer each other, and this has proved to be true. The people who have solved some of the problems of divorce provide tangible evidence to the others that it can be done, that one can grow through the crisis. This approach affirms their growing sense of independence and competence as they discover that they can help themselves and each other, rather than feeding into a sense of dependence on professional experts. A sense of "normalcy" of an adjustment reaction to divorce also develops, as opposed to people believing they are "going crazy" because they feel depressed, angry, confused, and so on.

AVOIDING SEXUAL STEREOTYPES

It is extremely important to recruit and include both men and women for the group. Many people emerged from their marriage with inaccurate stereotypes of the opposite sex based on their former spouses; developing emotional intimacy through the group with other members of the opposite sex who are different from their ex-spouse is an important corrective process. For example, in one session several women began expressing anger about their ex-spouse's neglect of the children and failure to send child support payments. This soon grew into a general expression that "Men are no good." However, the input of the male members of the group about *their* feelings about their children, which was quite different from what the women had experienced, had a corrective impact and helped the women put their feelings back onto a personal rather than global plane.

As was previously mentioned, one of the major goals of divorce work is to develop a workable and authentic support system. The value of simple support in a client population that is experiencing loss, isolation, and loneliness should not be underestimated. "The companionship of other formerly marrieds of the same and opposite sex becomes an important form of support to the divorcing person and is a positive force in helping to work through the divorce process."[23] Members experience universality in discovering that they share the same problems, fears, and worries as many others in their situation. They find understanding, acceptance, and vali-

---

[23] Wiseman, "Crisis Theory and Divorce," p. 211.

dation of their emerging identities; thus feelings of the stigma of divorce are also lessened. Members value the honesty, emotional intimacy, and self-disclosure possible in this setting as compared to other social situations. A lasting support network may grow from the group and should be encouraged by the leader. Supportive confrontation usually develops, with a tone of "I recognize what you're doing because I've done it myself."

FACILITATING GROWTH THROUGH ACCEPTANCE AND GROUP SUPPORT

Self-esteem increases with support, validation, and acceptance, but is also aided by the discovery of the capacity to help others through their pain. Many found the emotional replenishment lacking in their lives coming from the group.

Some of these effects are illustrated by the example of Mr. J, who was having a very difficult time preparing to divorce his wife of twenty-one years. He joined the divorce group for support, and for preparation to face the difficulties and pleasures that might await him. He was highly ambivalent and fearful about the divorce. He was especially concerned about how others, especially his children, would react to him, and about his isolation in a world of married friends. He also expressed a strong sense of emptiness and loss—the disillusionment of feeling that the goals he had struggled with for years had come to nought. He had never felt satisfied.

He entered the group with great anxiety. He listened to others share their problems and their successes, and he expressed his fears. He gradually began to feel that it was up to him to grow from the divorce. He began to tell others about the divorce, and found acceptance and support among his (grown) children and friends. Self-esteem began to increase. The divorce became final, and he felt relief. He found he could talk things over with his wife as they never could before, but both felt increasingly certain they had made the right decision. They began to evaluate what had gone wrong, to learn from it, and to move off in different directions. This freed him to experiment with different aspects of his personality, and to strengthen his sense of identity and autonomy. Through supportive confrontation in the group, he learned how he had tried to control others, and he began giving that up. In its stead, he discovered more control over his *own* life. He also began, with the help of the group, to examine his overly strong superego and to allow more of his own wishes and needs to surface. He began appearing more relaxed and gave up taking tranquilizers. He stopped feeling overly responsible for and the need to control others, and became more responsible for his own wants and needs. He was able to discover an inner sense of direction. Finally he reported, "I feel more satisfied than I ever have before."

FEELING WHOLE AGAIN

In another example, discussion focused on how people had dealt with a common reaction to divorce, that of feeling like half a person with nothing much to offer others. Several people had found help by getting out with others, meeting people, and getting involved in satisfying activities. But Ms. E raised the question of whether such things could emotionally replace the marital relationship, or if this remained an empty place in people. There were varied reactions, with several members saying that such activities helped them feel better about themselves and made them less lonely, but did not fill the gap. Others said they struggled with this by focusing on their own growth and fulfillment rather than looking for others to fill them up.

The central theme that tends to develop (with leader facilitation) is that of the two sides of the divorce coin—pain coupled with growth. Many feel tremendous losses and deprivations, but are gradually able to discover new freedoms and opportunities. Although it is, of course, important for the leader to be accepting of the pain and trauma involved for divorcing persons, it is also crucial that he or she explore and support the tremendous growth potential of this crisis.

Summary

This article has sought to share the author's findings and observations from working with divorcing individuals. The central issues faced in divorce are seen as problems of identity crisis, loneliness, economics, vocational identity, legal issues, role conflicts and shifts, need for emotional replenishment, loss of support system, sense of failure, parenting (both of the present and absent parent), intimacy, and sexuality.

An understanding of the problems of divorce leads to a formulation of the principal goals in divorce work: movement through grief work, development of support systems, development of autonomy and identity, reevaluation of the marriage, and coping with the demands of reality.

The use of groups of divorcing individuals has been very helpful in developing support systems and in facilitating movement toward the other significant goals in the divorce process. Clients are able to utilize such groups to maximize the growth potential of the crisis of divorce.

ENURESIS

CHAPTER 66

The Conditioning Treatment of Childhood Enuresis

R. T. T. Morgan and G. C. Young

Enuresis, or bedwetting, is one of the most widespread disorders of childhood, and is a problem frequently encountered by most social workers. It is a source of embarrassment to the sufferer, often invoking ridicule or punishment, and can place an intolerable burden upon intrafamilial relationships—especially in those large families living in overcrowded conditions, where several children may wet the bed. For the majority of enuretics, to be a bedwetter carries adverse emotional consequences, and many exhibit some degree of reactive disturbance. Even where this is not apparently the case, enuresis imposes a limit on the child's choice of activities; few enuretics can happily go camping or to stay with friends. In residential establishments, the daily wash of bed-linen is unpleasant and onerous. Because of its widespread, offensive, embarrassing and potentially disturbing nature, the problem of the management and cure of enuresis should be of concern to any caseworker or residential worker involved with an enuretic child; all too often both natural parents and houseparents are forced into a fatalistic acceptance of, and accommodation to, enuresis as an inevitable correlate of child upbringing. It is the purpose of the present paper to suggest that this need not be so, and to describe a rational and well-validated approach to the cure of enuresis, which deserves careful consideration for the benefit of the child sufferer.

Much confusion and many theories exist regarding the aetiology and treatment of enuresis; the literature is extensive and the folk-lore rich. Confusion is enlarged by the use of enuresis as a paradigmatic battle-

Reprinted from *British Journal of Social Work*, Vol. 2 (Winter, 1972), pp. 503–509, by permission of the authors and the Association.

ground between conflicting schools of psychological opinion which present mutually exclusive interpretations of this particular disorder. What is urgently required by the social worker confronted with an enuretic child is a relatively simple and well-substantiated form of treatment which offers a high probability of permanent cure without producing harmful side effects.

Consideration of enuresis in terms of a learning deficiency has led to the development of conditioning techniques as a treatment of enuresis. Learning theory postulates that bladder control may be regarded as learned behavior, and enuresis as a failure to acquire or maintain appropriate learned responses. According to the Yerkes–Dodson principle (Eysenck, 1960), the efficiency of learning is affected by drive level, very low or very high levels of drive leading to less effective learning as opposed to some intermediate level which is optimal. This optimal intermediate level of drive varies according to task complexity, and is lower for more complex learning tasks. Application of this principle to the learning of urinary continence suggests three major variables affecting the ability to any particular child to acquire bladder control; (1) the optimal level of drive for a task of a given complexity, (2) the degree of complexity represented to the child by the task of acquiring bladder control, and (3) the level of drive induced by the environment. There are individual differences in the ease with which children acquire control of bladder function, as there are in learning to swim or riding a bicycle, and environmental stresses, whether general or specifically related to toilet training, may affect one child more than another. During the third year of life there seems to exist a 'sensitive period' for the learning of continence, during which the child's sensitivity to appropriate learning situations is most acute. Stresses and anxieties during this period may produce over-optimal levels of drive which act to the detriment of learning and render the child enuretic (Young, 1965b; 1969; MacKeith, 1968; 1972). In the case of the 'secondary' enuretic, who loses bladder control after an appreciable period of normal continence, the learned pattern of control is disrupted by the intrusion of some new anxiety-provoking stimulus, such as disturbances in the family or problems at school. Because appropriate learning is less likely to take place outside the sensitive period, transient stress during the third year of life may produce the lifelong, or 'primary' enuretic, and secondary enuresis may persist even when its provoking stress has disappeared.

Conditioning treatment is based on the assumption that whatever influences may have led to a failure or breakdown of learning, appropriate learning may best be effected by maximizing the impact of the learning situation. The simplification of the learning situation also serves to reduce the decremental effects of whatever over-optimal drive may still be present, by reducing task complexity and thus raising the optimal level of drive according to the Yerkes-Dodson principle.

Treatment itself involves the use at home of a simple commercially produced 'enuresis alarm' (Young, 1965a; Turner, Young and Rachman, 1970).*

The alarm provides a powerful auditory stimulus in the form of a loud buzzer which is activated as urine makes electrical contact between a pair of gauze mats beneath the sleeping child. The alarm, when triggered, is switched off by the child, who then completes urination in the toilet. The alarm thus conditions in the child the two separate responses of awakening and of the inhibition of micturition, both in competition with the response of reflex urination to the stimulus of a full bladder. These responses, repeatedly evoked, eventually supercede that of reflex urination, the learned inhibitory effect of bladder stimulation tending to raise the general tone of the bladder muscle (the detrusor) so that the child not only awakes to urinate, but can eventually sleep for the entire night without either wetting or waking.

It is essential that the alarm is used properly and consistently, and that its use is adequately demonstrated. A high level of interest and involvement on the part of a social worker or houseparent is vital to the success of the treatment. It is necessary to maintain a simple record of wet and dry nights throughout treatment. Some children are punished for wet beds and some parents express the opinion that the child is 'lazy'—it is necessary to counter attitudes likely to increase the child's stress in a situation in which over-optimal drive may already be present. Furthermore, certain management practices such as fluid restriction and 'lifting', which are detrimental to conditioning treatment, should be discouraged. Indeed, it is quite likely that regularly lifting a child may train him to need to urinate at a certain time of night.

The success of conditioning treatment in practice has been well demonstrated. Young (1969) lists 19 clinical studies of such treatment in which the percentage success rate ranged from 63% to 100%. Two carefully conducted studies have found conditioning to be significantly superior to psychotherapy in the treatment of enuresis (Werry and Cohrssen, 1965; De Leon and Mandell, 1966).

The conditioning treatment described above is not new, the first suggestion of such treatment occurring in a paper written by Nye in 1830 (Glicklich, 1951). The therapeutic effects of a signal used to alert nurses to wet beds were accidentally discovered by Pfaundler in 1904, and have been continuously studied ever since. However, the use of conditioning treatment for enuresis has yet to find wide acceptance among social workers and those entrusted with the residential care of children.

Until very recently, it was justifiable to question the efficacy of treating

---

*Such as the 'Eastleigh', manufactured and supplied by N. H. Eastwood & Son, Ltd., 48 Eversley Park Road, London, N.21.

enuresis in the manner described, on the grounds that regardless of patient or treatment variables, approximately one in three children could be expected to relapse to wetting once again following initial cure (Young and Morgan, 1972a). Although not affecting the initial success of conditioning in arresting enuresis, such a relapse rate posed a serious question regarding the long-term usefulness of the treatment. Recently, however, a technique has been developed capable of producing dramatic reduction in relapse by strengthening the pattern of relevant learned responses beyond the level necessary to effect initial arrest of wetting. Known as 'overlearning', the technique requires the child to continue to use an enuresis alarm while drinking up to two pints of fluid in the last hour before retiring, once an initial success criterion of fourteen consecutive dry nights has been achieved (Young and Morgan, 1972b).

Perhaps one of the major reasons for the presently limited acceptance of conditioning treatment by social workers is that, not conversant with such conceptualizations of enuresis, many have permitted certain common and popular assumptions to escape rigorous question. The concept of enuresis as a somatic expression of emotional disturbance is thus traditionally accepted without question. Indeed it is often assumed that the coexistence of enuresis and disturbed behavior in the same child demonstrates a causal relation between the two. Such inference is in contradiction of the research findings of Tapia et al. (1960), who found that disturbed children are not especially prone to enuresis, nor enuretics particularly prone to disturbance, and of Baker (1969), who found neither projective personality tests nor assessment of adjustment by psychologists to distinguish enuretics from non-enuretics. The finding that the *persistence* of enuresis relates to familial inadequacies and family disruption, the problem persisting longest where family pathology is most severe (Stein and Susser, 1967), tends to support the view that environmental stresses rather than innate personality disorders are responsible for interference with the normal process of acquisition of bladder control. It is logical to assume that in such circumstances, emotional disturbance and enuresis may coexist, but as quite separate responses to the same external environmental influences. It is thus also logical to give treatment for enuresis as a separate entity, even where it occurs in a context of multiple problems.

A frequent objection to the direct, or 'symtomatic', treatment of enuresis by conditioning techniques is that the elimination of enuresis by these methods may lead to harmful consequences for the child's emotional adjustment. The specific predictions made by opponents of conditioning techniques are that, since a disturbed child is assumed to require an expressive symptom, a substitute symptom will emerge following the removal of enuresis; and that by removing enuresis, disturbance will be increased. Investigation of these predictions has found them to be unsupported. Baker (1969), investigating the 'symptom substitution' prediction, found no supporting evidence in his study of conditioning treatment and its consequences. Most clinicians testify to *improvement* in emotional adjustment following relief from enuresis (Yates, 1970; Young, 1965a). There need, therefore, be little concern that conditioning treatment may do harm to any child.

The above predictions derive from the common assumption that enuresis is a symptomatic expression of deep emotional disturbance, rather than a learning deficit, and that the child thus 'needs' and must not be deprived of his bedwetting. Therapy is directed instead at the inferred disturbance. The behavioral view, however, asserts that enuresis is a useless and troublesome habit from which appropriate training can provide relief. It is unnecessary to assume that because a child cannot control his bladder function, he must 'need' to be unable to do so, and to proceed to 'interpret' the feelings he is presumed to be expressing in somatic form.

Various forms of interpretation of a child's inability to control the act of micturition in the accepted manner have provided a wide variety of possible 'meanings'. One of the most common is the theory of regression, which states that enuresis, being similar to infantile incontinence, represents the attempted return of the older child undergoing stress to the presumed security of infancy. The enuretic may thus be saying, by wetting the bed, 'I will take the privileges of a baby, which you deny me' (Fenichel, 1946). A second range of interpretation is based upon the assertion that urination is equivalent to a sexual act. Fenichel thus regards enuresis as frequently a masturbation-equivalent; although the expected replacement of enuresis by mature forms of sexual gratification at puberty is not found in the age/incidence curves for enuresis (Jones, 1960). As a conversion symptom (i.e. a somatic expression of inner conflict or disorder), enuresis may, writes Fenichel, often be regarded as a 'discharge instrument of the Oedipus impulses'. Such theorists frequently interpret enuresis as an aggressive act—or, where this seems inappropriate, an act of passive submission. Thus enuresis in girls is seen as an active assumption of the male sexual role through fear of males as destructive aggressors—while in boys it is considered to represent assumption of a passive female role through fear of destruction by women consequent upon playing a male sexual role (Gerard, 1937; Fenichel, 1946). Ferenczi (1925) actually produced enuresis in a number of normally continent persons, by suggesting retention of urine to test a professed potency in the inhibition of micturition and thus apparently 'exhausting' the urinary musclature. This procedure was explained as serving to 'unmask a tendency to enuresis with which the patient had been quite unfamiliar and which threw light on important parts of his early infantile history' (Ferenczi, 1925).

It is maintained that when such interpretations of enuresis are rejected as unnecessary elaborations of a learning failure, the removal of enuresis (by conditioning techniques) is superficial; and cannot represent 'real' cure.

However, no more elaborate criterion for the cure of enuresis seems necessary, than that bedwetting should be eliminated without harmful side effects; it is difficult to imagine what further 'cure' is required when a formerly wet child is no longer enuretic, and is better adjusted than before. It is questionable to withhold from any child the chance of relief from wet beds, unless conditioning treatment were proven to be either ineffective or harmful. The infant learns bladder control, and learning failure can be countered by the more effective training afforded by an enuresis alarm.

Apart from lack of information and attitudes of reserve, many are deterred from the use of conditioning treatment by the practical problems involved. When an alarm is used in the home situation, parental cooperation is vital, and may well require a high level of supervision by a caseworker. Parents, siblings (and even patients) who sabotage treatment to avoid disturbed nights will not achieve success; cooperation must be secured before treatment is introduced and should be maintained throughout its duration. The presence of overcrowding and multiple occupation present additional problems, and it may be necessary to arrange for a separate bed in cases where an enuretic shares a bed with another member of the family.

It should prove possible in residential establishments to arrange medical screening for possible organic pathology, and the appropriate supervision of treatment could be undertaken by the staff. Older children can assume virtually full responsibility for the conduct of treatment. Young children and those slow to awaken to the alarm will require a staff member to assist, to ensure that the child awakes and to change the wet sheets before resetting the apparatus. Treatment naturally places a burden upon child-care staff, just as it does upon parents, but treatment forms an essential part of caring for an enuretic child.

Conditioning treatment of enuresis, when properly and consistently carried out and followed by a period of overlearning therapy, thus carries great promise of effective and stable cure without harmful side effects. As such it demands careful consideration by all having professional contact with enuretic children.

References

1. BAKER, B. L. (1969) "Symptom Treatment and Symptom Substitution in Enuresis," *J. Abnorm. Psychol.*, 74, 42–49.
2. DE LEON, G. and MANDELL, W. (1966) "A Comparison of Conditioning and Psychotherapy in the Treatment of Functional Enuresis," *J. Clin. Psychol.*, 22, 326–30.
3. EYSENCK, H. J. (1960) *Handbook of Abnormal Psychology*, Pitman, London.

4. FENICHEL, O. (1946) *The Psychoanalytic Theory of Neurosis*, Routledge & Kegan Paul, London.

5. FERENCZI, S. (1925) "Psycho-analysis of Sexual Habits," *Int. J. Psychoanal.*, 6, 372–404.

6. GERARD, M. W. (1937) "Child Analysis as a Technique in the Investigation of Mental Mechanisms: Illustrated by a Study of Enuresis," *Am. J. Psychiat.*, 94, 653–68.

7. GLICKLICH, L. B. (1951) "An Historical Account of Enuresis," *Pediatrics*, 8, 859–76.

8. JONES, H. G. (1960) "The Behavioral Treatment of Enuresis Nocturna," *in Behavior Therapy and the Neuroses* (Ed. H. J. Eysenck), pp. 377–403, Pergamon, Oxford.

9. MacKEITH, R. C. (1968) "A Frequent Factor in the Origins of Primary Nocturnal Enuresis: Anxiety in the Third Year of Life," *Develop. Med. Child Neurol.*, 10, 465–70.

10. MacKEITH, R. C. (1972) "Is Maturation Delay a Frequent Factor in the Origins of Primary Nocturnal Enuresis?" *Develop. Med. Child Neurol.*, 14, 217–23.

11. STEIN, Z. A. and SUSSER, M. (1967) "The Social Dimensions of a Symptom. A Sociomedical Study of Enuresis," *Soc. Sci. & Med.* 1, 183–201.

12. TAPIA, F., JEKEL, J. and DOMKE, H. R. (1960) "Enuresis: An Emotional Symptom?" *J. Nerv. Ment. Dis.*, 130, 61–6.

13. TURNER, R. K., YOUNG, G. C. and RACHMAN, S. (1970) "Treatment of Nocturnal Enuresis by Conditioning Techniques," *Behav. Res. & Therapy*, 8, 367–81.

14. WERRY, J. S. and COHRSSEN, J. (1965) "Enuresis—an Etiologic and Therapeutic Study," *J. Pediat.* 67, 423–31.

15. YATES, A. J. (1970) *Behavior Therapy*, John Wiley, New York, Ch. 5.

16. YOUNG, G. C. (1956a) "Conditioning Treatment of Enuresis," *Dev. Med. Child Neurol.*, 7, 557–62.

17. YOUNG, G. C. (1956b) "The Aetiology of Enuresis in Terms of Learning Theory," *Med. Offr.*, 113, 19–22.

18. YOUNG, G. C. (1969) "The Problem of Enuresis," *Br. J. Hosp. Med.*, 2, 628–32.

19. YOUNG, G. C. and MORGAN, R. T. T. (1972a) *Analysis of Factors Associated with the Extinction of a Conditioned Response. Behav. Res. & Therapy.* In press.

20. YOUNG, G. C. and MORGAN, R. T. T. (1972b) "Overlearning in the Conditioning Treatment of Enuresis," *Behav. Res. & Therapy*, 10, 147–51.

INCEST

CHAPTER 67

Family Dynamics of Incest: A New Perspective

Christine A. Dietz and John L. Craft

Sexual abuse of children is the least reported category of criminal activity in proportion to its occurrence, and only one-quarter of these incidents are committed by strangers.[1] It is estimated that 100,000 children are sexually abused each year.[2] Yet, until recently, the discussion of incest has been a greater taboo than its practice. As a result, knowledge about incest is scanty and limited to a few articles in the professional literature. Most of these articles consist of case study reports or generalizations based on a small number of cases that do not yield reliable data on the incidence of incest or on the characteristics of the individuals and families involved.

Little is offered in the way of objective data on incest and a good deal of speculation takes place. Social workers involved in the identification and treatment of incest in families must rely on their own opinions and attitudes and those conveyed in the literature as a basis for their intervention. This may result in inadequate, misdirected, or unsympathetic treatment of family members.

A prevalent attitude presented in the literature is that the mother of the incest victim is the true abuser in the family, engineering the entire incestuous relationship or perpetuating it through her unconscious consent. One purpose of the study reported here was to explore the role of the mother in incestuous families, as perceived by protective services

[1] Vincent De Francis, *Protecting the Child Victim of Sex Crimes Committed by Adults* (Denver: American Humane Association, 1969).

[2] Ibid.

Reprinted from *Social Casework*, Vol. 61 (December, 1980), pp. 602–609, by permission of the author and the Family Service Association of America.

workers, and to examine the attitudes of these workers toward the typical mother. A related purpose was to determine whether parallels and possible connections between incest and wife abuse exist, in the hope that this may stimulate further research into the total pattern of violence in incestuous families.

Review of the Literature

Most incest victims are female. Vincent De Francis reports that girls outnumber boys ten to one as victims of sexual abuse.[3] The precise incidence of father-daughter incest is unknown; however, most authors agree that it represents a considerable portion of sexual child abuse. Ida U. Nakashima and Gloria E. Zakus state that it is the most frequently reported form of sexual abuse.[4]

FAMILY PATTERNS

Incest is typically seen as an isolated phenomenon rather than as part of a pattern of family violence and conflict. Yvonne M. Tormes, in a 1968 study, found that thirteen out of twenty incestuous fathers were physically violent to their wives and other members of their families, as well as sexually abusive to their daughters.[5] This study is frequently cited by other authors, but the issue of the father's physical violence and its effects on other members of the family, particularly the mother, is not addressed. Only one other study since 1968 appears to have addressed this issue directly; Diane H. Browning and Bonny Boatman found that a majority of the incestuous fathers were physically violent to other family members as well.[6]

The relationship between incest, the sex-role configuration of the family, and the cultural influences supporting these sex roles are also not taken into account. The typical incestuous family is patriarchal; the father is the authoritarian head of the household. He may underscore his authority with physical violence, drink heavily, and be unduly restrictive of his daughter's social life.[7] Tormes also reports an "affectionate" type of father (seven

[3] Vincent De Francis, *Plain Talk About Child Abuse* (Denver: American Humane Association, 1972).

[4] Ida U. Nakashima and Gloria E. Zakus, "Incest: Review and Clinical Experience," *Pediatrics* 60 (November 1977): 696.

[5] Yvonne M. Tormes, *Child Victims of Incest* (Denver: American Humane Association, 1972).

[6] Diane H. Browning and Bonny Boatman, "Incest: Children at Risk," *American Journal of Psychiatry* 134 (January 1977): 69.

[7] See, for example, Tormes, *Child Victims*; Browning and Boatman, "Children at Risk"; De Francis, *Protecting the Child Victim*; and Narcyz Lukianowicz, "Incest: Paternal Incest," *British Journal of Psychiatry* 120 (1972): 301.

out of twenty cases) who does not use force or threats in sexual relationships with his daughter, but who is careful to obtain her consent, either through "tenderness" and concern, or bribes of money or gifts.[8] Mothers in these families are generally viewed as passive, dependent and submissive, chronically depressed, overburdened, and unable to protect their daughters or exert a restraining influence on their husbands. They are described as unloving and rejecting, as sexually frigid, as aware of the incest and perpetuating the abuse or colluding in it, as pushing their daughters into the maternal role, as failing to offer emotional support to their daughters or failing to report the incident, and as blaming the child for the occurrence of incest.[9] According to the literature, then, the real abuser in an incestuous family is the mother. By frustrating her husband sexually, failing to support her daughter emotionally, or foisting her maternal duties and responsibilities onto her daughter, she engineers the incestuous relationship.

In reviewing the literature, however, one is also struck by the parallels between this kind of family and one in which wife abuse occurs. One such similarity is the connection between heavy drinking and abuse; another is the sex-role configuration of the families. Both kinds of abusive families are typically patriarchal, with dominant husbands and submissive wives.[10] These similarities suggest that there may well be wife abuse in incestuous families, a suggestion that is supported by Tormes and Browning and Boatman.[11] If this is the case, it casts an entirely different light on the mother's behavior in incestuous families. Further investigation of these similarities is clearly warranted.

Daughters in these families are also influenced by the patriarchal family structure. Their personalities appear to be as passive as those of their mother's. Tormes[12] suggests that the daughter imitates the mother's behavior in response to the father's domination and abuse. Some authors have suggested that the victims accept the incest, or even seduce their

---

[8] Tormes, Child Victims.

[9] See, for example, ibid.; Bruno M. Cormier, Miriam Kennedy, and Jadwiga Sangouriz, "Psychodynamics of Father-Daughter Incest," Canadian Psychiatric Association Journal 7 (October 1962): 203; Lukianowicz, "Paternal Incest"; De Francis, Protecting the Child Victim; Harold I. Eist and Adeline U. Mandel, "Family Treatment of Ongoing Incest Behavior," Family Process 7(September 1968): 216; Pavel Machotka, Frank S. Pitman, III, and Kalman Flomenhaft, "Incest as a Family Affair," Family Process 6 (March 1967): 98; Jean Benward and Judianne Densen- Gerber, "Incest as a Causative Factor in Anti-Social Behavior: An Exploratory Study," Contemporary Drug Problems 4 (Fall 1975): 322; and Ruth B. Weeks, "The Sexually Exploited Child," Southern Medical Journal 69 (July 1976): 848.

[10] For information on wife abuse, see John P. Flynn, "Recent Findings Related to Wife Abuse," Social Casework 58 (January 1977): 13; Margaret Ball, "Issues of Violence in Family Casework," Social Casework 58 (January 1977): 3; and Beverly B. Nichols, "The Abused Wife Problem," Social Casework 57 (January 1976): 27.

[11] Tormes, Child Victims; and Browning and Boatman, "Children at Risk."

[12] Tormes, Child Victims.

fathers into such relationships.[13] However, several studies describe acting-out on the part of the victim (that is, running away from home, prostitution, drug abuse, delinquency) and emotional problems such as guilt, depression, and low self-esteem, which call into question the extent of the daughter's passive acceptance of incest as well as the assumption that incest is not emotionally damaging to the victim. Whether or not the daughter overtly resists the sexual relationship with her father, the resulting emotional and behavioral problems demonstrate her emotional resistance and her awareness that this kind of relationship is not socially acceptable. As for the victim's so-called "seductivity," her passive and submissive character at home suggests that she would lack the assertiveness necessary to "seduce" her father, as well as the emotional strengths to resist his advances.

The physical violence of many of the fathers, or the subtle pressures of the "affectionate" fathers described by Tormes, leave the victim with no effective means to resist her father's advances.[14] Physical injury may also result, although, as with wife abuse, this is not a primary focus of the literature. In 11 percent of the sexual abuse cases reported by De Francis physical abuse was also noted.[15] However, although other authors briefly discuss medical indications of sexual abuse, discussion of physical injury through incest, the connection between physical and sexual abuse, and the long-term effects on the child are largely lacking in the literature.

Faced with a lack of demographic and descriptive data, social workers must rely primarily on their own beliefs and attitudes in treatment of incestuous families. These attitudes are formed during their training as well as by the literature. The literature is not only based on limited statistical data, but may also reflect the ideological orientation of the authors, including their opinions about incest, women, or the ideal family. These viewpoints cannot be objectively supported and may be detrimental to the client.

The Study

To investigate the existence of detrimental attitudes among workers in contact with incestuous families, a survey was conducted to determine whether protective service workers believe: (1) that families in which incest occurs also experience other forms of family conflict, particularly spouse abuse

[13] See Nakashima and Zakus, "Review and Clinical Experiences"; Cormier, "Psychodynamics of Incest"; Richard M. Sarles, "Incest," *Pediatric Clinics of North America* 22 (August 1975): 633; Renee S. T. Brant and Veronica B. Tisza, "The Sexually Misused Child," *American Journal of Orthopsychiatry* 47 (January 1977): 80.

[14] Tormes, *Child Victims.*

[15] De Francis, *Protecting the Child Victim.*

and physical child abuse; (2) that mothers of incest victims condone the incestuous relationship, and that mothers are as responsible as their husbands for its occurrence; and (3) that they are inadequately prepared to work with families in which incest has occurred.

METHODS

Protective service workers in the Iowa Department of Social Services were surveyed, because these workers would be the most likely to encounter incest cases. A three-part questionnaire was developed and mailed to 200 of these workers throughout the state.

The first part of the questionnaire sought demographic and descriptive information based on the respondents' best estimates of their agencies' clients. Information requested included characteristics of the family and its individual members, such as employment of the parents, income levels, area of residence, and personality characteristics. A question regarding the number of cases seen yearly in each of the counties was also included. The final questions in this part concerned the frequency of suspected wife abuse, husband abuse, and physical child abuse in the families.

The second part of the questionnaire was designed to elicit information about referral sources, the kinds of services provided by the agencies, and the legal disposition of the cases. This information is not included in the present report.

In the third part, respondents were asked to indicate their degree of agreement with a list of statements about incestuous families and the training or preparation they had received for working with this kind of family.

FINDINGS

The typical incestuous family seen by Iowa Department of Social Services protective services workers has four to six members. They are in a low to low-middle income bracket; 77 percent of the clients earn below $10,000 yearly, and 66 percent live in small communities of less than 10,000 residents. However, although they are not usually geographically isolated, 81 percent of the workers believe that the families have a worse than average relationship to their community. The father is most often the breadwinner and authority figure in the family, and 44 percent of the workers believe that he underscores his authority with physical violence. However, despite his position in the family, his self-esteem is low, and 55 percent believe that the father has a drinking problem. Seventy-four percent of the respondents stated that the wife works at home as a homemaker, 41 percent saw her as passive and submissive to her husband's authority, 67 percent stated that she has a low self-image, and 49 percent that she is depressed. The marital relationship is poor, and the majority of the respondents stated that the mother does not seek professional help, either for her daughter, with whom she does not have a strong relationship, or for herself. According to 78 percent of the workers, the mother is likely to be a victim of abuse by her husband. The daughter shares her mother's passive and submissive traits, but is seriously upset by the incestuous relationship, resulting in emotional or behavioral problems of some sort. She is not socially adept and has poor relationships with her peers. All of these findings parallel the literature.

Physical Abuse in Incestuous Families.   According to a large proportion of the workers surveyed (80 percent), when incest occurs in a family, some other form of abuse is also likely to be going on. Furthermore, this abuse is most often perpetrated by the father on his wife or daughter, or on both simultaneously. When physical violence is cited as a characteristic of any family member, the majority identify it with fathers. Seventy-eight percent of the respondents *suspect* wife abuse "occasionally" or "frequently" in the incestuous families with whom they work, while 76 percent *suspect* physical child abuse. The response to the same question regarding husband abuse was the reverse, 70 percent "seldom" or "never" *suspect* this form of abuse.

Cross-tabulations reveal a significant relationship between wife abuse and physical child abuse, but no relationships between either wife abuse or physical child abuse and husband abuse were found. In other words, wife abuse and physical child abuse are more likely to be found in the same families than either of these types of abuse and husband abuse. In addition, 53 percent of the workers stated that the victim is frequently physically injured by the incestuous abuse. These results support the conjecture that some fathers in incestuous families underscore their authority by physical abuse of their wives and physical and sexual abuse of their daughters.

Looking at the overall pattern of abuse in the family in this way should absolve the mother of charges of "unconscious consent," in many cases by virtue of her own victimization. One indication of this so-called consent has been the mothers' failure to report incest. Literature on wife abuse frequently addresses the issue of the wives' failure to report their physically abusive spouses or to leave the relationship. Many reasons are given for this, all of which could apply equally well to mothers of incest victims: fear of violent physical retaliation by their husbands, lack of safe refuges for themselves and their children, unwillingness or shame at admitting abuse to outsiders, and lack of financial or emotional resources to provide for themselves and their children. Tormes lists other reasons that mothers may fail to report incest, including an inability to believe that her husband is capable of incest, lack of confidence in help from public agencies, and fear of involvement with the law.[16]

To these inhibiting factors, Burgess[17] adds yet another: the mother's divided loyalty between her husband and her child. These mothers enact the traditional maternal role and seek their primary satisfaction within the home, although their influence there may be minimized by their husbands. For these women, loyalty to one's spouse is likely to be among the traditional values embraced. How, then, does she deal with a situation in which this traditional value conflicts with another, equally sacred value: The duty to protect one's child? The traditionally passive, submissive woman is not prepared for the assertive behavior required to report her husband for incest. If she is physically abused and emotionally battered as well, she is quite likely to be unable to take steps to protect either her daughter or herself from abuse, let alone handle the added strain of reporting her husband and facing the financial, emotional, and legal problems that could result from his conviction. To make the decision to leave an abusive husband is to make a crucial life decision at a time when a woman is physically and emotionally at her weakest.[18] This is doubly true for the woman whose loyalty is divided between her husband and her child. Many mothers, passive already, may react to this dilemma by further passivity and inactivity, not because they reject their daughters, but because of fear and a lack of emotional strength to deal with the consequences of reporting incest. To accuse such women of "colluding" in incest, or "pushing" their daughters into the maternal role, results in "blaming the victim" in this double-bind situation.

The findings also suggest that the daughter learns to tolerate abuse from the example of her mother and emulates her passivity and submissiveness to her father. In addition, the issue of protection of both mother and daughter from the violence of the father is raised, an issue that may be at odds with the traditional social work value of preservation of the family. A paradoxical finding of this study was that although most of the workers believed that the father should not be incarcerated, a majority indicated that he should be removed from the home. It is not clear, however, as to where the father should be removed.

Mothers' Unconscious Consent and Shared Responsibility.   The hypotheses that workers believe that mothers condone the incestuous relationship and that they believe that the mother shares equal responsibility for its occurrence were confirmed by the data. Respondents believed that the mother gives

---

[16] Tormes, *Child Victims.*

[17] Ann Wolbert Burgess, "Divided Loyalty in Incest Cases," in *Sexual Assault of Children and Adolescents,* ed. Ann Wolbert Burgess et al. (Lexington, Mass.: Lexington Books, 1978).

[18] Kristy Kissell, Coordinator, Aid and Alternatives to Victims of Spouse Abuse, Iowa City, Iowa, personal communication.

her unconscious consent to incest (87 percent) and that she is equally responsible for its occurrence (65 percent). Seventy-nine percent agreed that she does not seek professional help for her daughter. This is consistent with the literature.

Workers' agreement with the latter statements were cross-tabulated with other factors (reading books or other professional literature, worker training, wife abuse, physical violence, and the number of incest cases seen by the agency) to identify factors contributing to the formation of these attitudes. A moderate relationship was found between reading professional literature about incest and the belief in the mother's unconscious consent to incest, although a stronger relationship was found between such reading and the belief that mothers are equally as responsible as fathers for the occurrence of incest. Interestingly, belief in unconscious consent or equal responsibility does not appear to be affected by the belief that wife abuse or physical child abuse may occur in these families, nor does it appear to be related to the number of incest cases seen. Cross-tabulations of these variables yielded no significant results. Thus, the incest literature appears to be a stronger factor in the formation of these beliefs than the evidence presented by the workers' experiences with clients and their families.

Worker's Lack of Training.   Iowa protective services workers generally believe that their skills and training for working with incestuous families are inadequate (76 percent). This is in spite of the fact that a large minority (44 percent) have received some sort of specialized training in working with incestuous families, such as workshops, short courses, or in-service training, and 79 percent have sought out and read books and articles in professional journals to increase their understanding. Most of them (86 percent) believe that working with incestuous families is especially problematic, and 95 percent believe that they need more information, training, and skills to help these families.

DISCUSSION

Believing that the mother unconsciously consents to incest may be interpreted as an effort to resolve cognitive dissonance within the worker.[19] According to Festinger, cognitive dissonance is created when two cognitions, knowledges about the world, do not fit together. Cognitive dissonance is unpleasant and gives rise to efforts to reduce it, usually by distorting reality.

The child protective service worker is subjected daily to cognitive dis-

[19] Leon Festinger, *A Theory of Cognitive Dissonance* (New York: Harper and Row, 1957); and Leon Festinger, *Conflict, Decision, and Dissonance* (Stanford, Calif.: Stanford University Press, 1964).

sonance. Called upon to take strong action to prevent sexual abuse, the worker may be able to do little to meet this goal. Treatment of the entire family within the home could potentially result in further incidents of sexual abuse. Removal of the father from the home may create even worse problems, such as dissolution of the family. Short of incarceration, it is never clear as to where the father should be removed. Faced with this conflict, the child protective service worker frequently either delays acting or takes no action at all. If there is a subsequent occurrence of sexual abuse, the worker is faced with additional dissonance. The worker's view of him or herself as effective and capable is dissonant with the repetition of sexual abuse of the client. Believing that the child's mother is ultimately to blame can help the worker to resolve this dissonance. And attributing the consent to the mother's "unconscious" removes the necessity of directly blaming the mother for her consent. Thus, there is nothing the worker could have done to prevent repeated abuse.

A large majority of workers were found to *suspect* that wife abuse is coexistant with incest. At the very least, suspicion of wife abuse should suggest to a worker that a mother may have legitimate fears for her physical safety which make it unlikely that she is able to protect her daughter from incest, either by reporting the incident, if she is aware of it, or by seeking professional help. It certainly does not automatically imply that she would push her daughter into an incestuous relationship, or give her consent to such a relationship. It is difficult to conceive how being a possible victim of physical abuse oneself makes one equally responsible with the abuser for the sexual abuse of one's child. On the other hand, how can "unconscious consent" or "equal responsibility" be determined? Does the belief in these factors result in a self-fulfilling prophecy or a selective attention mode of dissonance reduction? If a worker believes that unconscious consent to incest is frequently given by mothers of victims, will he or she not look for "signs" of such consent in his or her clients, possibly inferring the existence of such consent from ambiguous evidence? For example, one medical journal states that "we see mothers only too happy to turn over the burdensome sexual role to the daughters, and to this end mothers take jobs that require them to be absent from the home in the late afternoon and evening hours."[20] It seems quite likely that reading such statements (which abound in the literature) could lead a worker to view a mother's afternoon or evening work hours as an indication of her consent to incest. In addition, the idea that the mother finds her sexual role "burdensome" reflects the Victorian idea that women find sex repugnant and are only too happy to escape from their "duty" to their husbands. The statement further suggests that mothers willingly sacrifice their daughters to incestuous relationships in order to avoid sex, a vastly different inter-

---

[20] Weeks, "Sexually Exploited Child."

pretation than viewing the mother herself as a possible victim of abuse. From statements of this kind it becomes clear that biased views of women continue to be passed on to workers through the professional literature, and that workers tend to cling to such biases even when presented with evidence to the contrary.

Conclusions

One of the most important findings of this study involved workers' feelings toward working with incest. The workers indicated their dissatisfaction with their training regarding incest, a feeling that working with incest was particularly problematic for them, and a heavy reliance on professional literature for information regarding incest. Few articles on incest were found in social work journals during the review of the literature for this research. These two observations make it clear that the profession needs to address the issue of incest more clearly and directly through professional literature, through training programs and workshops, and through professional education.

Because books and journal articles are such an important source of information on incest for most protective services workers, they should be reviewed carefully for adequacy of information and unintended bias. That such bias exists is attested to by the workers' acceptance of the idea of the mother's unconscious consent to incest, in the face of evidence of her possible victimization as well. When evidence of such consent is found in the mother's work outside the home or in her reluctance to have sex with her husband, we end up by "blaming the victim" of abuse and holding her responsible for the abusive behavior of her husband. Although it is clear that mothers have the responsibility of protecting their daughters, their inability to do so should not be construed as willingness to victimize their daughters. At the same time, this attitude obscures the dilemma the mother faces, caught between two socially prescribed roles: supporter of her husband and supporter/protector of her daughter. To point an accusing finger at a woman caught in such a dilemma is inconsistent with social work values of respect for the individual and nondiscriminatory treatment. Given the fact that workers believe that incest is prevalent today, failure to take these considerations into account can result in inadequate or misdirected service to a sizeable number of families.

There were marked similarities between the profiles of incestuous families generated by the workers and profiles of families involved in wife abuse in the literature. There are several implications of this finding. First, more than one form of abuse should be suspected when abusive patterns are present. Failure to be aware of this possibility has resulted in the "blaming the victim" approach discussed above. Second, further research is needed to complete the picture of abusive families. Such research, taking the entire family pattern of abuse into account, may significantly increase our understanding of the causes and nature of all types of family violence.

Implications for Professional Education

Schools of social work should incorporate information about rape, incest, and spouse abuse into their curricula, because these are issues that affect every woman in our society in some way. At the same time, examination of the patriarchal structure of our society and the sex-role stereotyping that continues through the media and the educational system could help eliminate some of the sexist approaches that have been taken with victims of these crimes. Examination and elimination of the social causes of the individual problems of clients is a part of the heritage of social workers that is too often forgotten. Inclusion of women's issues in all aspects of the social work curriculum, particularly core courses, is a step toward this goal.

Another equally important addition to social work curricula is the issue of violence. The media, the educational system, and other social institutions legitimate violence as a problem-solving method and encourage competitiveness and physical dominance as opposed to cooperation and egalitarian values. Inclusion of content on the causes, nature, and effects of violence, as well as discussion of alternatives, can be useful to social workers both in their individual practice and in their roles as responsible citizens. Social workers have a responsibility to re-educate violent families and to help counteract the support they receive from other social institutions for their violent behavior.

Another effective method of training workers is in-service training. Workshops on domestic violence and incest should be offered periodically by county departments. In addition to the content discussed above, a review of crisis intervention techniques, the legal and social aspects of abuse, the problems faced by victims in extricating themselves from abusive situations, the attitudes and fears held by workers toward incest, violence, and members of incestuous families, the worker frustrations in working with such families, commonly held myths about incest, and a review of community resources for victims and their families should all be included. In addition, role playing and group discussion of difficult cases or problems frequently encountered by workers (such as confronting an incestuous father) could be helpful to workers. Such training sessions would clearly require a large investment of time; however, given the high incidence of incest and the frustrations faced by workers, such an investment is clearly warranted.

In addition to professional education, it is the responsibility of every social worker to examine his or her personal biases or lack of information and to attempt to correct the effects of these in individual professional practice. Research shows that social workers take this responsibility seriously, as indicated by their efforts to seek out professional literature and additional training to increase their understanding of incest. It then becomes the duty of social work educators, trainers, researchers, and writers to gather and provide the necessary information and understanding for these workers.

OBESITY

CHAPTER 68

Obesity Treatment:
Research and Application

Kay M. Stevenson

The Problem

The problem of treating obesity in those who are more than 20 pounds (9.1 kg) overweight according to actuarial standards (the definition of obesity in this paper) is one of growing concern to health professionals. Long before obesity is identified clearly as a medical risk, a person may suffer from the social stigma of being overweight (Sash, 1977). The importance of the psychosocial aspects in weight reduction and maintenance programs is receiving more and more attention. However, a broad range of medical and psychosocial interventions has failed to produce a classification schema indicating the treatment(s) of choice for any given individual or group of patients. Practitioners may experience great frustration that few of those seeking assistance in losing or maintaining weight loss reach their goals.

Although obesity represents a health and social problem of major significance in this country, there has been relatively little research to determine causes or to evaluate the effectiveness of alternative treatment approaches to either short-term weight reduction or long-term maintenance. Howard and Bray (1977) suggest three reasons for the dearth of studies regarding this problem. One is that the study of obesity and its treatment is not fashionable. Few, if any, institutes are devoted solely to its investigation. Second, the topic is complex and often seems unamenable to controlled research. Causes appear to be numerous but are not clearly defined. Perhaps of greatest importance to social workers is the

Reprinted from *Social Work in Health Care*, Vol. 4, No. 2 (1978), pp. 165–178, with permission of the Haworth Press.

frequent problem that interventions result in minimal or no weight loss and fail to ensure long-term weight maintenance. Interventions of choice, based on evaluation of effectiveness, have not been adequately indicated for the treatment of obesity.

Physical and Social Considerations

Evidence that obesity is correlated with increased medical risk has not been demonstrated with consistency. However, in a study conducted by Strata, Zuliani, Caronna, Magnati, Pugnoli, and Tirelli (1977), obesity was implicated as a major contributing factor in the development of diabetes, atherosclerosis, hypertension, arthritis, and other disabling diseases. In another study (Berchtold, Berger, Greiser, Dohse, Irmscher, Gries, & Zimmermann, 1977), cardiovascular risk factors were investigated. It was found that the most frequent risk factor was hypertension (71%), followed by glucose intolerance (49%). Only 12% of the subjects were without risk factors. The prevalence of risk factors increased with age and amount overweight. It was concluded that those with gross obesity were at high risk of coronary disease.

Obesity may be defined as one of the conditions identified within the broad classification of social diseases in technological societies. Treatment effectiveness has proved limited, at best. In a long-term study by Dalla Volta, Benedetti, Dagnini, Dalla Volta, and Zerbini (1962), satisfactory results were found in only 30% of the cases, partial success was reported in another 30%, and insufficient or no results were found in 40%. Strata et al. (1977) believe that these disappointing results are due to ''many socioeconomic, environmental, and psychological factors which hinder the execution of therapy, to the lack of compliance by the patient, and to the paucity of specialized centers for treatment'' (p. 200).

Obesity has been associated with a major predisposition to trauma and premature death, to impaired physical and psychological efficiency, to reduced work productivity, and to disrupted social and sexual relationships (Strata et al., 1977). The skilled intervention of a range of human services professionals is required not only for treatment of those presently obese persons but also for prevention and education about this increasing health and social problem.

Population Characteristics

The literature reports a number of characteristics that may distinguish the obese person. These characteristics may be broadly classified as (a) social/environmental or (b) behavioral.

Social/environmental factors include a higher responsiveness to external cues (Pudel & Oetting, 1977; Rodin, Bray, Atkinson, Dahms, Greenway, Hamilton, & Molitch, 1977), lack of realistic anticipated rate of weight loss (Ford, Scorgie, & Munro, 1977), and a negative relationship between obesity and social class (Dodd, Stalling, & Bedell, 1977). It should also be noted that there is a significant attrition rate among patients who enter treatment for obesity (Bray, 1976; Ley, Bradshaw, Kincey, Couper-Smartt, & Wilson, 1974; Seaton & Rose, 1965). Furthermore, Rodin et al. (1977) reported that persons believing that they, rather than fate or circumstances, were responsible for things that happened to them—high internal locus of control (Rotter, 1966)—lost weight at a significantly faster rate than those who were low on this factor. Seaton and Rose (1965) found that patients who had a disease to which obesity was relevant (e.g., diabetes) did better than those who did not have such a disease.

In a survey of a number of experiments made over 6 years, it was found that those subjects who were presently obese, and also those who were defined as latently obese, were characterized by a greater responsiveness to environmental cues to trigger eating than were nonobese persons (Pudel & Oetting, 1977). Rodin et al. (1977) also found that those who were less responsive to external cues were most successful in losing weight in an outpatient obesity clinic program.

In a study of 235 females in four comparison groups, each participant was asked to state her anticipated rate of weight loss for each week or month of dieting after the initial weeks of the program. The groups compared were: (a) those enrolling in a commercial program for the first time; (b) those already attending the same program; (c) those attending hospital-based weight reduction clinics; and (d) those reenrolling in a commercial program. It was found that only 27% of those attending programs for the first time had realistic anticipated rates of weight loss, "while 60% of those reenrolling and 90% of those currently attending slimming clubs were realistic in their expectations" (Ford et al., 1977, p. 239). Those who were most in excess of their ideal weight were least realistic.

Yet a third social environmental factor to be examined is the relationship between social class and obesity. As might be anticipated, Dodd et al. (1977) found a negative correlation between obesity and social class ($p < .001$).

Behavioral characteristics that have been studied and reported include: (a) rate of eating; (b) amount of food selected; and (c) time of food shopping. Pudel and Oetting (1977) and Stunkard and Kaplan (1977) found that obese persons consume more food per minute than do the nonobese. Pudel and Oetting (1977) suggested that this behavior appears to be related to stress and is a learned, rather than a biological, response. They found this reaction to be more frequent in females than in males.

A second behavior that appears to distinguish the obese from the nonobese is the amount of food taken. Although they found no agreement about a particular "obese eating type," Stunkard and Kaplan (1977) noted that, in a review of 13 studies, obese persons typically chose more food than did nonobese persons.

Following a study referred to in Stuart and Davis (1972) which reported that obese women who shopped before dinner purchased 19.7% more than those who shopped after dinner, the authors of the study encouraged people to shop after meal hours. However, Dodd et al. (1977) reported that when obese and nonobese females were compared in their buying habits, *both* groups consistently bought more prior to meals ($p < .001$), regardless of social class or meal hour. Males displayed similar tendencies, although the differences were not significant.

Implications for Treatment

Several implications for treatment of the obese may be stated from these findings. Because the obese person appears to be influenced significantly by external cues, it may be appropriate to concentrate on manipulation of the environment in treatment programs. Rodin et al. (1977) found not only that successful weight loss was related to social conformity and desire for social acceptance but also that success was not related to self-esteem. Such findings may be of importance in choice of focus for intervention.

Ford et al.'s (1977) findings that few women are realistic, at least initially, in anticipating their weight loss while dieting, suggest the need to reinforce realistic expectations during the course of a treatment program. Dodd et al.'s (1977) report of a negative relationship between obesity and social class suggests that the target population at greatest risk and in greatest need may be those least able to afford the costs of weight reduction programs. Strategies for providing services to this group require attention; the needs and characteristics of the low socioeconomic population merit further investigation.

The typically reported high attrition rates in weight reduction programs and the lack of maintained weight loss indicate that treatment approaches may be failing to identify and provide adequate and/or appropriate motivation for the patient's continued efforts. Perhaps lack of motivation is related to the unrealistic expectations of many persons who seek treatment. Appropriate goals may need to be stated clearly and re-evaluated regularly throughout the program.

The importance of locus of control is a concept familiar to many social work practitioners. Those persons who believe that their obesity is due to poor eating habits and feel they are responsible for their own problem and its resolution have been most successful in initial and sustained weight loss (Rodin et al., 1977). Such evidence may point to interventions stressing internal locus of control and active confrontation of patients who attribute their obesity to external causes. Decreasing sensitivity to external cues might enter into such intervention strategies.

Because patients who have diseases related to obesity tend to lose weight more successfully, a treatment approach that presents hard data on risks of obesity in the development of particular disease entities might be indicated as a preventive measure. The impact of such a strategy has received no attention in the literature reviewed.

A variety of weight reduction programs do include strategies for behavioral change. Patients are encouraged to slow their rate of eating by such methods as consciously chewing more slowly and putting their cutlery down between bites. Such techniques appear to be an appropriate response to the research on the rate of eating among the obese. Treatment programs may also attempt to reduce the amount of food taken by insisting that the person eat only at certain times in a certain location, and that servings be measured. Patients may be urged to food shop only after meals as part of the intervention strategy.

Treatment Settings and Personnel

Four settings predominate as locations for weight reduction programs. The first, based on the assumption that obesity, like alcoholism, is a self-induced condition due to overeating, has led to the development of nonprofit *self-help* groups. Literature on such groups is scarce, both in description and effectiveness. Trémolières (1975) reports that in France, a group of 15 to 20 obese persons, aged 17 to 75 years, consulted a physician, weighed in regularly, and provided support to each other to continue weight loss and maintenance efforts, following an Alcoholics Anonymous model.

The commencement of self-help groups led to the creation of *commercial* programs for weight reduction. Stunkard (1972) studied 22 chapters of TOPS, the oldest and largest commercial enterprise for weight reduction. He found that using a criterion for success of 20 pounds (9.1 kg) or more, the success rate was 10% in the least and 62% in the most effective chapter.

Outpatient obesity clinics provide a third alternative setting for weight reduction programs. A review of the literature reveals little information about the nature of these programs or indications of effectiveness when compared to other program settings.

The fourth typical setting for weight reduction programs is that of *inpatient* treatment in hospitals. Patients, under the care of physicians, receive a range of interventions, including restricted or starvation diets, oral treatments, and/or surgery. Though hospital social workers may be involved in the treatment of obese inpatients, the literature does not discuss the impact of social work intervention in such programs.

However, in a randomized double-blind trial, it was found that patients assigned to physicians did no better as a group than those assigned to nonphysicians in a 9-week outpatient treatment program (Atkinson, Greenway, Bray, Dahms, Molitch, Hamilton, & Rodin, 1977). These findings support the view that nonphysicians may be effective in treating the obese patient. In a 10- to 18-year follow-up of overweight patients (Craddock, 1977), frequent consultations with patients proved to be a significant aspect in the success of reduced weight maintenance. These findings may have implications for social work intervention with obese patients.

Treatment Approaches

Though they may overlap in theory and execution, three treatment approaches that predominate in the literature may be arbitrarily designated as (a) insight therapy, (b) cognitive treatment, and (c) behavioral intervention. The majority of weight reduction programs appear to be executed in group treatment. Psychotherapy to develop insight is practiced with individuals with some frequency; cognitive and behavioral techniques are more typically utilized in group settings, according to the literature.

The underlying assumption of insight therapy is that obesity due to overeating may be attributed to psychic abnormalities (Alexander & Flagg, 1965; Bruch, 1973). Although Richardson (1947) reports success in individual psychotherapy, the effectiveness of such a report is difficult to assess due to lack of appropriate control studies (Chlouverakis, 1977). Practitioners who endorse this approach purport that the effort to develop insight may be the treatment of choice when weight loss is not occurring and a change in attitude is indicated before progress can be made. Bruch (1957) states, "For many people overeating and being big is a balancing factor in their adjustment to life. Ineffective as it is, it represents the best form of adaptation that such people have been able to make" (p. 13). For these persons, the recognition that alternative adjustment patterns are available to them may be requisite to developing the motivation to lose weight. It should be noted that in a controlled study comparing four treatments approaches in group settings, all three experimental groups did better than the untreated group. Although the behavior modification group showed the most improvement immediately following treatment, the insight psychotherapeutic group was the only group of the four that did not show gains within 8 weeks after completion of the program (Wollersheim, 1970). These findings support the view that insight therapy may have the most significant long-lasting effect of the treatment approaches tested.

The cognitive approach maintains that the principal determinant of emotions, motives, and behaviors is the individual's thinking. In other words, thinking shapes behavior (Turner, 1974). Mahoney (1975), a notable cognitive theorist, contends that some of the basic assumptions underlying the behavioral approach have remained unexamined. His data suggest that cognitive factors (beliefs) may exert a stronger influence on food consumption than some of the behavior change techniques typically used.

Dunkel and Glaros (1978) hypothesized that subjects taught self-instructional skills (cognitive approach) would be more successful in losing weight than those taught only stimulus control skills (behavioral technique). Self-instructional treatment consisted of teaching the subject to "talk" covertly to him/herself in managing hunger, desire to eat, and fatigue and boredom associated with physical exercise. They found that a *combination* of self-instructional and stimulus control treatment was more effective than the stimulus control treatment alone. The self-instructional treatment *alone* was more effective than the placebo control treatment. Continuing weight loss was occurring 7 weeks following completion of treatment for those in the combined and self-instructional groups. It may be concluded that the self-instructional component appears to be an effective aspect in continuing weight loss both in treatment and at time of follow-up almost 2 months after completion of treatment.

Behavioral therapy has shown notable short-term success as a treatment approach with selected populations (Harris, 1969; Stuart & Davis, 1972). In this approach, obesity is perceived as a consequence of observable habits that contribute to excessive caloric intake and inadequate energy expenditure (Chlouverakis, 1977). Aversion therapy, associating the thought of food with an unpleasant event, has proved relatively unsuccessful, perhaps because the source of discomfort associated with the aversion is insignificant when compared with the pleasure of eating (Stuart & Davis, 1972).

Another behavioral approach, that of operant treatment, focuses only on increasing or diminishing existing behaviors. "The patient is asked to eat in one room and in only one place in that room; to engage in no other activitiy while eating; to avoid the purchase of high calorie foods; to make small portions of food appear as large as possible; to slow the pace of eating by interposing a delay after the start of the meal and to keep diet, exercise and weight records" (Chlouverakis, 1977, p. 10). Bellack (1975) found a combination of antecedent stimulus control procedures, accompanied by a variety of contingency management techniques, to be an effective approach in treatment.

Though the treatment efforts utilizing operant techniques suffer from the attrition experienced in all weight reduction programs, some of the outcome results, nevertheless, have been impressive. However, a review of studies in which behavioral techniques have been used reveals several important problems: (a) the lack of long-term effects of treatment (i.e., Wollersheim, 1970); (b) high dropout rates (Stuart & Davis, 1972); and (c) variable success during treatment (Sloan, Tobias, Stapell, Twisstto, & Beagle, 1976).

Implications of Research

In the absence of a comprehensive classification schema of characteristics of the obese population, treatment approaches, and their selective effectiveness in a variety of settings with a broad range of health care personnnel delivering services, a number of questions appear salient for the social worker's consideration in treatment-related issues:

1. Is the chosen treatment amenable to universal application, or is it appropriate only in specific circumstances for selected populations or subjects?
2. If the treatment is applicable to specified groups only, what are the relevant characteristics that distinguish that group for a particular treatment approach?
3. How durable are the results of a treatment approach?
4. To what extent is the success of a novel treatment approach due to the enthusiasm and dedication of staff whose energy may not accurately reflect the validity of the approach itself? (Chlouverakis, 1977).

One Program: Trym Gym

The program to be described has not been evaluated for effectiveness. It is being reported for the following reasons: (a) it combines a number of the approaches reported in the literature; (b) it relies heavily on social work intervention in its service delivery; and (c) other than those assuming a medical model, there are few descriptions of obesity treatment programs, providing a basis for discussion, comparison, and subsequent evaluation.

Trym Gym, a 10-week weight reduction course, is built on four basic assumptions:

1. It is assumed that, in contrast to some treatments for the acutely ill, effective intervention with the obese requires active participation on the part of the subject.
2. It is believed that the goal of the health care team in treatment is to influence the obese person in accepting major changes in life patterns.
3. The health care team teaches (explicitly and implicitly) that weight

regulation requires long-term maintenance and continued attention to attitudes and behaviors.

4. There is an underlying assumption that effective treatment requires continuity—not only within the treatment team and program but also with respect to the recipient of services and his/her family and relevant community support systems (Aiken, 1976).

Trym Gym is housed in the Ambulatory Care Centre, Health Sciences Building, University of Calgary, in Calgary, Alberta, Canada. Calgary is a rapidly growing city of over 500,000, including a significant population of Americans. The university setting for the program encourages the perception that the experience is to be seen as educational and instructive. Classes are held in a small conference room equipped with a circular table, a blackboard, a one-way mirror, and audiovisual equipment. A second conference room is used for weekly weigh-in procedures. The exercise component of the program is held in the gymnasium of the nearby Nursing Students' Residence where locker rooms are available for both men and women.

The course is offered three times per year. Each participant pays a fee of $30 to cover basic costs. Classes meet 1 hour per week, followed by an hour of exercise. There is a 2nd hour of exercise on another weekday. It is seen as an integral component of the program. Two times of day are available to participants: a morning class and exercise program for homemakers, and an evening course for employed persons. Class size ranges from 8 or 10 to 20 persons. Ideal size is considered to be 12 to 15.

Comparison of the morning and evening groups on certain characteristics provides for interesting speculation about program focus and effectiveness. Both groups are typically Caucasian, varying in socioeconomic status from lower middle to upper middle class. The morning group is exclusively for women; the evening group usually includes three or more men. Age ranges from early adolescence to late 50s, with the modal age falling between 25 and 40. A basic criterion for admission to the program is a minimum of 20 pounds (9.1 kg) to lose; physicians' reports must be submitted, indicating that the person is able to participate in the rigorous exercise program. Although both morning and evening programs suffer from some attrition, the morning group usually has a higher dropout rate. The evening typically reports greater overall weight losses than the morning group.

The program staff consists of a nurse-practitioner (team coordinator), a dietitian, a physiotherapist, and two social workers. The social workers are final-year BSW students, completing a 3-month block practicum at the Ambulatory Care Centre. They are under direct supervision of a clinical instructor from the faculty of social welfare, University of Calgary. The supervisor, who also acts as senior social work consultant to the program, may attend weekly team conferences and observe the students either in class sessions or via a one-way mirror. The instructor and the team coordinator both contract with the student to provide supervision and instruction.

Team responsibilities are delineated clearly. The nurse-practitioner screens prospective participants, completes an intake interview, obtains baseline diet and exercise data, and monitors results of the required medical examinations. She coordinates weekly team meetings, participates in class discussions, and monitors individual and group progress throughout the 10 weeks. She also assumes responsibility for follow-up.

The dietitian aids each participant in constructing a weekly diet, monitors food intake on weekly records, lectures, and leads group discussion on topics of individual and family diet planning, grocery shopping, and entertaining. She attends team meetings and class sessions, participating in group discussions as appropriate.

The physiotherapist leads the 2 hours per week of exercise for the class. She teaches exercises that can be done in other environments and provides individual consultations to participants with physical limitations. She attends weekly team meetings.

The social workers, with the nurse-practitioner, provide continuity and ongoing feedback to participants. Because of the broad scope of the social work role in the program, two social workers are assigned to each class. At the time of intake, the participant may be seen by both the nurse and the social worker. Social history taken includes questions regarding the nature of family dynamics, identification of problem eating patterns, alcohol consumption, baseline physical and recreational activities, and previous weight loss efforts. Expectations of loss are discussed. Participants are encouraged to work toward an average loss of 2 pounds (.9 kg) per week. Anticipated variations from week to week are explained. At the time of intake, the person is asked to take baseline data on present eating behaviors for 1 week prior to the commencement of the course.

The social workers weigh in each group member at the beginning of every class and briefly discuss progress or lack of it with the person. This procedure is seen as significant in affording an opportunity to provide both support and confrontation at a time when the person is impacted by the consequences of his/her efforts.

The social workers give two class lecture/discussions: one on emotional factors related to successful weight loss, and one on behavioral management. After experimentation with a variety of formats, it has been concluded that the presentation about emotions and motivation is basic to all further course content, and has therefore been instituted as the first topic for class discussion.

For 5 to 10 minutes at the beginning of each class, the social workers introduce a new behavior to be practiced during the week, such as: eating in one room, in one place in the room; putting cutlery down between bites;

and shopping only after meals. Questions are entertained, and the success of the previous week's behavior is discussed.

At each class, social workers are responsible for providing leadership, direction, and focus to group discussions. The usual format is a 20-minute lecture, followed by 40 minutes of group discussion. Intervention includes: identifying individual dysfunctional patterns that contribute to overeating; group problem-solving to select more functional alternatives; support and confrontation.

Following the 1-hour class, social workers typically escort the group to the gym and participate in the hour of exercise. They also participate in the 2nd weekly hour of exercise. The purpose for this involvement is three-fold: (a) it provides an informal, somewhat relaxed environment for further discussion between the social worker and individual group members; (b) it offers a model for participants; and (c) it encourages social workers to adopt regular exercise as an integral part of their weekly schedules. The benefits of locker room discussions have been noted as a fortuitous spin-off of social work participation in exercise sessions.

Additionally, the social workers telephone any participants who miss one or more weekly sessions. Problems or resistances are discussed. If indicated, the social worker suggests further individual assessment and may refer a participant for individual, couple, or family counseling from the social work unit in the Ambulatory Care Centre. Due to easy access and open communication with the social work unit, referral may be rapid and minimally stressful for the client. He/she is familiar with the setting and may meet the therapist at the time of classes or exercise sessions. Though controlled study of the impact of this immediate weekly follow-up and rapid referral has not been completed, team members believe that this procedure has reduced the attrition rate from the program.

Social workers also attend the 1-hour weekly team meetings at which individual participants' or team members' problems are discussed, team interactions reviewed, planning completed, and progress monitored for subsequent discussion with the class. The total time required of a social worker to participate in one class (morning or evening) is approximately 6 to 10 hours per week: 1 hour per class, 2 for exercises, 1 for team meetings, and the remainder for telephoning absentees and for individual assessments. Planning time for lectures and debriefing following group discussions constitutes an additional time commitment.

Topics for the 10 lecture/discussions vary from one course to another, depending upon the interests and characteristics of a given group. A typical course outline is shown in Table 68–1.

Following completion of the course, participants are encouraged to continue regular attendance of exercise sessions. There is no size limit to these sessions and no additional cost to the individual. For 6 months after completion of the program, the nurse-practitioner requests that members return for monthly weigh-ins. Subsequently, members are asked to return

TABLE 68-1.   Topics for Lecture/Discussion

Week	Topic	Team Member
1	"Emotional and Motivational Factors in Weight Loss"	Social worker
2	"Planning Your Diet"	Dietician
3	"The Importance of Physical Recreation in Your Life-style"	Physiotherapist
4	"Setting up a Behavior Program that You Can Live With"	Social worker
5	"Entertaining; Cooking for a Family"	Dietician
6	"Medical Risks of Obesity"	Guest Physician
7	"Eating Out"	Dietician
8	Open discussion (usually about problems with family related to losing weight)	All team members
9	"Slimming Styles and Makeup to Enhance Your New Image"	Guest Beautician
10	Course evaluation	All team members

for weigh-ins at 1 year, 18 months, and 2 years. Though members are telephoned for this follow-up, few participants return.

This program attempts to address the individual needs of the participant. Individual interventions during the program typically seek to increase insight and motivate the person to develop a perception of internal locus of control. Although some social workers have introduced transactional analysis concepts, Gestalt exercises, and systematic desensitization as specialized techniques, the basic treatment remains primarily cognitive and behavioral in orientation.

Some 10-week sessions have been more successful than others. Typically, there is at least a minimal group weight loss. For some groups, the loss is substantial. Although this program has not been rigorously examined and evaluated, a subjective measure of its success may be indicated by the following observations: (a) the program does not advertise, yet courses are routinely filled early; (b) physicians from the Ambulatory Care Centre refer their obese patients to the program; and (c) most participants are referred by previous program recipients. Although these observations are indicators of satisfaction rather than effectiveness in weight reduction outcomes, it may cautiously be assumed that a probable relationship exists between the two factors.

Discussion

Miller and Hersen (1975) suggest that the acceptance of untested treatment methods for obesity reflects frustration with the disparity between the cogent need of many people and the lack of hard data on the nature of the problem, the population at risk, and effective approaches to care. Health practitioners working with the obese require substantial data on the social, emotional, attitudinal, cognitive, environmental, and physiological factors associated with successful treatment. Furthermore, long-term treatment effects are yet to be demonstrated with any rigor.

Further study relevant to social work intervention might include: (a) direct observation of behaviors to determine dysfunctional patterns; (b) theory building to compile and share knowledge applicable to a variety of addictive, problematic life patterns, including obesity; (c) research on the interrelationship between obesity and other addictive behaviors, such as smoking and excessive alcohol consumption; and (d) integration of physiological, psychosocial, and behavioral characteristics of the problem and impact of alternative treatment approaches (Miller & Hersen, 1975).

The implications of obesity for the health and welfare of the populations in developed countries are considerable. Prevention, education, and treatment require major life-style changes for many individuals. Social work intervention can play a significant role in providing such services. Practitioners may also assume the important responsibility of contributing to the developing body of knowledge about the problem for both the obese and the potentially obese.

References

AIKEN, L. Chronic illness and responsive ambulatory care. In D. Mechanic (Ed.), *The growth of bureaucratic medicine.* New York: John Wiley & Sons, 1976.

ALEXANDER, F., & FLAGG, G. The psychosomatic approach. In B. Wolman (Ed.), *Handbook of clinical psychology.* New York: McGraw-Hill, 1965.

ATKINSON, R., GREENWAY, F., BRAY, G., DAHMS, W., MOLITCH, M., HAMILTON, K., & RODIN, J. Treatment of obesity: Comparison of physician and non-physician therapists using placebo and anorectic drugs in a double-blind trial. *International Journal of Obesity.* 1977, 1(2).

BELLACK, A. Behavior therapy for weight reduction. *Addictive Behaviors,* 1975, 1(1).

BERCHTOLD, P., BERGER, M., GREISER, E., DOHSE, M., IRMSCHER, K., GRIES, F., & ZIMMERMANN, H. Cardiovascular risk factors in gross obesity. *International Journal of Obesity,* 1977, 1(3).

BRAY, G. *The obese patient.* Philadelphia: W. B. Saunders, 1976.

BRUCH, H. *The importance of overweight.* New York: Norton, 1957.

BRUCH, H. *Eating disorders.* New York: Basic Books, 1973.

CHLOUVERAKIS, C. Dietary and medical treatments of obesity: An evaluative review. *Addictive Behaviors,* 1977, 1(1).

CRADDOCK, D. The free diet: 150 cases personally followed-up after 10 to 18 years. *International Journal of Obesity,* 1977, 1(1).

DALLA VOLTA, A., BENEDETTI, A., DAGNINI, G., DALLA VOLTA, S., & ZERBINI, E. *The obesity clinic.* Rome: Pozzi, 1962.

DODD, D., STALLING, R. & BEDELL, J. Grocery purchases as a function of obesity and assumed food deprivation. *Interventional Journal of Obesity,* 1977, 1(1).

DUNKEL, L., & GLAROS, A. Comparison of self-instructional and stimulus control treatments for obesity. *Cognitive Therapy and Research,* 1978, 2(1).

FORD, M., SCORGIE, R., & MUNRO, J. Anticipated rate of weight loss during dieting. *International Journal of obesity,* 1977, 1(3).

HARRIS, M. Self-directed program for weight control: A pilot study. *Journal of Abnormal Psychology,* 1969, 74.

HOWARD, A., & BRAY, G. (Eds.) The age of obesity. *International Journal of Obesity,* 1977 1(1).

LEY, P., BRADSHAW, P., KINCEY, J., COUPER-SMARTT, J., & WILSON, M. Psychological variables in the control of obesity. In W. Burland, P. Samuel, & J. Yudkin (Eds.), *Obesity symposium.* Servier Research Institute. Edinburgh: Churchill Livingstone, 1974.

MAHONEY, M. The obese eating style: Bites, beliefs, and behavior modification. *Addictive Behaviors,* 1975, 1(1).

MILLER, P., & HERSEN, M. (Eds.) Editorial: Research on addictive behaviors: Current needs *Addictive Behaviors,* 1975, 1(1).

PUDEL, V., & OETTING, M. Eating in the laboratory: Behavioral aspects of the positive energy balance. *International Journal of Obesity,* 1977, 1(4).

RICHARDSON, H. Psychotherapy of the obese patient. *New York Journal of Medicine,* 1947, 47.

RODIN, J., BRAY, G., ATKINSON, R., DAHMS, W., GREENWAY, F., HAMILTON, K., & MOLITCH, M. Predictors of successful weight loss in an outpatient obesity clinic. *International Journal of Obesity,* 1977, 1(1).

ROTTER, J. Generalized expectancies for internal vs. external control of re-inforcement. *Psychological Monographs,* 1966, 80.

SASH, S. Why is the treatment of obesity a failure in modern society? *International Journal of Obesity,* 1977, 1(3).

SEATON, D., & ROSE, K. Defaulters from a weight reduction clinic. *Journal of Chronic Diseases,* 1965, 18.

SLOAN, C., TOBIAS, D., STAPELL, C., TWISSTTO, M., & BEAGLE, W. A weight control program for students using diet and behavior therapy. *Journal of the American Dietetic Association,* 1976, 68,(5).

STRATA, A., ZULIANI, U., CARONNA, S., MAGNATI, G., PUGNOLI, C., & TIRELLI, F. Epidemiological aspects and social importance of obesity. *International Journal of Obesity,* 1977, 1(2).

STUART, R., & DAVIS, B. *Slim chance in a fat world: Behavioral control of obesity.* Champaign, Ill.: Research Press, 1972.

STUNKARD, A. The success of TOPS, a self-help group. *Postgraduate Medicine,* 1972, 51.

STUNKARD, A., & KAPLAN, D. Eating in public places: A review of reports of the direct observation of eating behavior. *International Journal of Obesity,* 1977, 1(1).

TRÉMOLIERÈS, C. [An obesity club]. *Cahiers de Nutrition et de Diététique*, 1975, *10*(1).

TURNER, F. (Ed.) *Social work treatment: Interlocking theoretical approaches.* New York: Free Press, 1974.

WOLLERSHEIM, J. Effectiveness of group therapy based upon learning principles in the treatment of overweight women. *Journal of Abnormal Psychology*, 1970, *76.*

RAPE

CHAPTER 69

Rape Trauma Syndrome

Ann Wolbert Burgess and
Lynda Lytle Holmstrom

Rape affects the lives of thousands of women each year. The Uniform Crime Reports from the Federal Bureau of Investigation indicated a 121-percent increase in reported cases of rape between 1960 and 1970. In 1970, over 37,000 cases were reported in the United States (1). A District of Columbia task force studying the problem in the capital area stated that rape was the fastest growing crime of violence there (2).

The literature on sexual offenses, including rape, is voluminous (3–5), but it has overlooked the victim. There is little information on the physical and psychological effects of rape, the therapeutic management of the victim, and the provisions for protection of the victim from further psychological insult (6–9).

In response to the problem of rape in the greater Boston area, the Victim Counseling Program was designed as a collaborative effort between Boston College School of Nursing and Boston City Hospital to provide 24–hour crisis intervention to rape victims and to study the problems the victim experiences as a result of being sexually assaulted.

The purpose of this paper is to report the immediate and long-term effects of rape as described by the victim.

Reprinted from *American Journal of Psychiatry*, Vol. 131 (1974), pp. 981–986. Copyright 1974, the American Psychiatric Association.

Method

STUDY POPULATION

The study population consisted of all persons who entered the emergency ward of Boston City Hospital during the one-year period July 20, 1972, through July 19, 1973, with the complaint of having been raped. The resulting sample was made up of 146 patients: 109 adult women, 34 female children, and 3 male children.

We divided these 146 patients into three main categories: (1) victims of forcible rape (either completed or attempted rape, usually the former); (2) victims in situations to which they were an accessory due to their inability to consent; and (3) victims of sexually stressful situations—sexual encounters to which they had initially consented but that went beyond their expectations and ability to control.

The rape trauma syndrome delineated in this paper was derived from an analysis of the symptoms of the 92 adult women in our sample who were victims of forcible rape. Future reports will analyze the problems of the other victims. Although not directly included in this paper, supplementary data were also gathered from 14 patients referred to the Victim Counseling Program by other agencies and from consultation calls from other clinicians working with rape victims.

A major research advantage in the location of the project at Boston City Hospital was the fact that it provided a heterogeneous sample of victims. Disparate social classes were included in the victim population. Ethnic groups included fairly equal numbers of black and white women, plus a smaller number of Oriental, Indian, and Spanish-speaking women. In regard to work status, the victims were career women, housewives, college students, and women on welfare. The age span was 17 to 73 years; the group included single, married, divorced, separated, and widowed women as well as women living with men by consensual agreement (see Table 69–1). A variety of occupations were represented, such as schoolteacher, business manager, researcher, assembly line worker, secretary, housekeeper, cocktail waitress, and health worker. There were victims with no children, women pregnant up to the eighth month, postpartum mothers, and women with anywhere from 1 to 10 children. The women ranged in physical attractiveness from very pretty to very plain; they were dressed in styles ranging from high fashion to hippie clothes.

INTERVIEW METHOD

The counselors (the coauthors of this paper) were telephoned when a rape victim was admitted to the emergency department of Boston City Hospital; we arrived at the hospital within 30 minutes. We interviewed all

TABLE 69-1.   Distribution of Marital Status by Age (N = 92)

MARITAL STATUS	Age (in Years)				
	17–20	21–29	30–39	40–49	50–73
Single	29	25	0	2	1
Married	2	1	2	2	0
Divorced, separated, or widowed	2	6	7	2	2
Living with a man by consensual agreement	4	5	0	0	0

the victims admitted during the one-year period regardless of time of day or night. Follow-up was conducted by use of telephone counseling or home visits. This method of study provided an 85-percent rate of direct follow-up. An additional 5 percent of the victims were followed indirectly through their families or reports by the police or other service agencies who knew them. Detailed notes of the interviews, telephone calls, and visits were then analyzed in terms of the symptoms reported as well as changes in thoughts, feelings, and behavior. We accompanied those victims who pressed charges to court and took detailed notes of all court proceedings and recorded the victims' reactions to this process (10, 11). Contact with the families and other members of the victims' social network was part of the assessment and follow-up procedure.

Manifestations of Rape Trauma Syndrome

Rape trauma syndrome is the acute phase and long-term reorganization process that occurs as a result of forcible rape or attempted forcible rape. This syndrome of behavioral, somatic, and psychological reactions is an acute stress reaction to a life-threatening situation.

Forcible rape is defined in this paper as the carnal knowledge of a woman by an assailant by force and against her will. The important point is that rape is not primarily a sexual act. On the contrary, our data and those of researchers studying rapists suggest that rape is primarily an act of violence with sex as the weapon (5). Thus it is not surprising than the victim experiences a syndrome with specific symptomatology as a result of the attack made upon her.

The syndrome is usually a two-phase reaction. The first is the acute phase. This is the period in which there is a great deal of disorganization in the woman's lifestyle as a result of the rape. Physical symptoms are especially noticeable, and one prominent feeling noted is fear. The second phase begins when the woman begins to reorganize her lifestyle. Although the time of onset varies from victim to victim, the second phase often begins about two to three weeks after the attack. Motor activity changes and nightmares and phobias are especially likely during this phase.

The medical regimen for the rape victim involves the prescription of antipregnancy and antivenereal disease medication after the physical and gynecological examination. The procedure usually includes prescribing 25 to 50 mg. of diethylstilbestrol a day for five days to protect against pregnancy and 4.8 million units of aqueous procaine penicillin intramuscularly to protect against venereal disease. Symptoms reported by the patient need to be distinguished as either side effects of the medication or conditions resulting from the sexual assault.

The Acute Phase Disorganization

IMPACT REACTIONS

In the immediate hours following the rape, the woman may experience an extremely wide range of emotions. The impact of the rape may be so severe that feelings of shock or disbelief are expressed. When interviewed within a few hours of the rape, the women in this study mainly showed two emotional styles (12): the expressed style, in which feelings of fear, anger, and anxiety were shown through such behavior as crying, sobbing, smiling, restlessness, and tenseness; and the controlled style, in which feelings were masked or hidden and a calm, composed, or subdued affect was seen. A fairly equal number of women showed each style.

SOMATIC REACTIONS

During the first several weeks following a rape many of the acute somatic manifestations described below were evident.

1. *Physical Trauma.* This included general soreness and bruising from the physical attack in various parts of the body such as the throat, neck, breasts, thighs, legs, and arms. Irritation and trauma to the throat were especially a problem for those women forced to have oral sex.

2. *Skeletal Muscle Tension.* Tension headaches and fatigue, as well as sleep pattern disturbances, were common symptoms. Women were either not able to sleep or would fall asleep only to wake and not be able to go back to sleep. Women who had been suddenly awakened from sleep by the assailant frequently found that they would wake each night at the time the attack had occurred. The victim might cry or scream out in her sleep. Victims also described experiencing a startle reaction—they become edgy and jumpy over minor incidents.

3. *Gastrointestinal Irritability.* Women might complain of stomach pains.

The appetite might be affected, and the victim might state that she did not eat, food had no taste, or she felt nauseated from the antipregnancy medication. Victims described feeling nauseated just thinking of the rape.

4. *Genitourinary Disturbance.*   Gynecological symptoms such as vaginal discharge, itching, a burning sensation on urination, and generalized pain were common. A number of women developed chronic vaginal infections following the rape. Rectal bleeding and pain were reported by women who had been forced to have anal sex.

EMOTIONAL REACTIONS

Victims expressed a wide gamut of feelings as they began to deal with the aftereffects of the rape. These feelings ranged from fear, humiliation, and embarrassment to anger, revenge, and self-blame. Fear of physical violence and death was the primary feeling described. Victims stated that it was not the rape that was so upsetting as much as the feeling that they would be killed as a result of the assault. One woman stated: "I am really mad. My life is disrupted; every part of it upset. And I have to be grateful I wasn't killed. I thought he would murder me."

Self-blame was another reaction women described—partly because of their socialization to the attitude of "blame the victim." For example, one young woman had entered her apartment building one afternoon after shopping. As she stopped to take her keys from her purse, she was assaulted in the hallway by a man who then forced his way into her apartment. She fought against him to the point of taking his knife and using it against him and in the process was quite severely beaten, bruised, and raped. Later she said:

> I keep wondering maybe if I had done something different when I first saw him that it wouldn't have happened—neither he nor I would be in trouble. Maybe it was my fault. See, that's where I get when I think about it. My father always said that whatever a man did to a woman, she provoked it.

The Long-Term Process: Reorganization

All victims in our sample experienced disorganization in their life-style following the rape; their presence at the emergency ward of the hospital was testimony to that fact. Various factors affected their coping behavior regarding the trauma, i.e., ego strength, social network support, and the way people treated them as victims. This coping and reorganization process began at different times for the individual victims.

Victims did not all experience the same symptoms in the same sequence. What was consistent was that they did experience an acute phase

TABLE 69-2.   Severity of Symptoms During Reorganization Process by Age
(N = 92)*

	Age (in Years)				
SEVERITY OF SYMPTOMS	17–20	21–29	30–39	40–49	50–73
No symptoms: no symptoms reported and symptoms denied when asked about a specific area	7	4	2	0	0
Mild symptoms: minor discomfort with the symptom reported: ability to talk about discomfort and feeling of control over symptom present	12	16	0	2	1
Moderate to severe symptoms: distressing symptoms such as phobic reactions described: ability to function but disturbance in lifestyle present	12	5	1	1	2
Compounded symptoms: symptoms directly related to the rape plus reactivation of symptoms connected with a previously existing condition such as heavy drinking or drug use	7	5	3	3	0
No data available	0	5	4	0	0

* At time of telephone follow-up.

of disorganization; many also experienced mild to moderate symptoms in the reorganization process, as Table 69-2 indicates. Very few victims reported no symptoms. The number of victims over age 30 was small, but the data at least suggest that they might have been more prone to compounded reactions than the younger age groups.

MOTOR ACTIVITY

The long-term effects of the rape generally consisted of an increase in motor activity, especially through changing residence. The move, in order to ensure safety and to facilitate the victim's ability to function in a normal style, was very common. Forty-four of the 92 victims changed residences within a relatively short period of time after the rape. There was also a strong need to get away, and some women took trips to other states or countries.

Changing one's telephone number was a common reaction. It was often changed to an unlisted number. The woman might do this as a precautionary measure or as the result of threatening or obscene telephone calls. The victim was haunted by the fear that the assailant knew where she was and would come back for her.

Another common response was to turn for support to family members not normally seen daily. Forty-eight women made special trips home, which often meant traveling to another city. In most cases, the victim told her parents what had happened, but occasionally the victim contacted her parents for support and did not explain why she was suddenly interested in talking with them or being with them. Twenty-five women turned to close friends for support. Thus 73 of the 92 women had some social network support to which they turned.

NIGHTMARES

Dreams and nightmares could be very upsetting. Twenty-nine of the victims spontaneously described frightening dreams, as illustrated in the following statement.

> I had a terrifying nightmare and shook for two days. I was at work and there was this maniac killer in the store. He killed two of the salesgirls by slitting their throats. I'd gone to set the time clock and when I came back the two girls were dead. I thought I was next. I had to go home. On the way I ran into two girls I knew. We were walking along and we ran into the maniac killer and he was the man who attacked me—he looked like the man. One of the girls held back and said, "No—I'm staying here." I said I knew him and was going to fight him. At this point I woke with the terrible fear of impending doom and fright. I knew the knife part was real because it was the same knife the man held to my throat.

Women reported two types of dreams. One is similar to the above example where the victim wishes to do something but then wakes before acting. As time progressed, the second type occurred: the dream material changed somewhat, and frequently the victim reported mastery in the dream—being able to fight off the assailant. A young woman reported the following dream one month following her rape.

> I had a knife and I was with the guy and I went to stab him and the knife bent. I did it again and he started bleeding and he died. Then I walked away laughing with the knife in my hand.

This dream woke the victim up; she was crying so hard that her mother came in to see what was wrong. The girl stated that in her waking hours she never cries.

TRAUMATOPHOBIA

Sandor Rado coined the term "traumatophobia" to define the phobic reaction to a traumatic situation (13). We saw this phenomenon, which Rado described in war victims, in the rape victim. The phobia develops as a defensive reaction to the circumstances of the rape. The following were the most common phobic reactions among our sample.

Fear of Indoors. This occurred in women who had been attacked while sleeping in their beds. As one victim stated, "I feel better outside. I can see what is coming. I feel trapped inside. My fear is being inside, not outside."

Fear of Outdoors.   This occurred in women who had been attacked outside of their homes. These women felt safe inside but would walk outside only with the protection of another person or only when necessary. As one victim stated, "It is sheer terror for every step I take. I can't wait to get to the safety of my own place."

Fear of Being Alone.   Almost all victims reported fears of being alone after the rape. Often the victim had been attacked while alone, when no one could come to her rescue. One victim said: "I can't stand being alone. I hear every little noise—the windows creaking. I am a bundle of nerves."

Fear of Crowds.   Many victims were quite apprehensive when they had to be in crowds or ride on public transportation. One 41-year-old victim said:

> I'm still nervous from this, when people come too close—like when I have to go through the trolley station and the crowds are bad. When I am in crowds I get the bad thoughts. I will look over at a guy and if he looks really weird, I will hope something bad will happen to him.

Fear of People Behind Them.   Some victims reported being fearful of people walking behind them. This was often common if the woman had been approached suddenly from behind. One victim said:

> I can't stand to have someone behind me. When I feel someone is behind me, my heart starts pounding. Last week I turned on a guy that was walking in back of me and waited till he walked by. I just couldn't stand it.

Sexual Fears.   Many women experienced a crisis in their sexual life as a result of the rape. Their normal sexual style had been disrupted. For the women who had had no prior sexual activity, the incident was especially upsetting. For the victims who were sexually active, the fear increased when they were confronted by their husband or boyfriend with resuming sexual relations. One victim said:

> My boyfriend thought it [the rape] might give me a negative feeling to sex and he wanted to be sure it didn't. That night as soon as we were back to the apartment he wanted to make love. I didn't want sex, especially that night.... He also admitted he wanted to know if he could make love to me or if he would be repulsed by me and unable to.

This victim and her boyfriend had considerable difficulty resuming many aspects of their relationship besides the sexual part. Many women were unable to resume a normal sexual style during the acute phase and persisted with the difficulty. One victim reported, five months after the assault, "There are times I get hysterical with my boyfriend. I don't want him near me; I get panicked. Sex is OK, but I still feel like screaming."

Clinical Implications

MANAGEMENT OF RAPE TRAUMA SYNDROME

There are several basic assumptions underlying the model of crisis intervention that we used in counseling the rape victim.

1. The rape represented a crisis in that the woman's style of life was disrupted.
2. The victim was regarded as a "normal" woman who had been functioning adequately prior to the crisis situation.
3. Crisis counseling was the treatment model of choice to return the woman to her previous level of functioning as quickly as possible. The crisis conseling was issue-oriented treatment. Previous problems were not a priority for discussion; in no way was the counseling considered psychotherapy. When other issues of major concern that indicated another treatment model were identified by the victim, referrals were offered if the woman so requested.
4. We took an active role in initiating therapeutic contact as opposed to more traditional methods where the patient is expected to be the initiator. We went to the hospital to see the victim and then contacted her later by telephone.

MANAGEMENT OF COMPOUNDED REACTION

There were some victims who had either a past or current history of physical, psychiatric, or social difficulties along with the rape trauma syndrome. A minority of the women in our sample were representative of this group. It became quite clear that these women needed more than crisis counseling. For this group, who were known to other therapists, physicians, or agencies, we assumed a secondary position. Support was provided for the rape incident, especially if the woman pressed charges against the assailant, but the counselor worked closely with the other agencies. It was noted that this group developed additional symptoms such as depression, psychotic behavior, psychosomatic disorders, suicidal behavior, and acting-out behavior associated with alcoholism, drug use, and sexual activity.

MANAGEMENT OF SILENT RAPE REACTION

Since a significant proportion of women still do not report a rape, clinicians should be alert to a syndrome that we call the silent reaction to rape. This reaction occurs in the victim who has not told anyone of the rape, who has not settled her feelings and reactions on the issue, and who is carrying a tremendous psychological burden.

Evidence of such a syndrome became apparent to us as a result of life history data. A number of the women in our sample stated that they had been raped or molested at a previous time, often when they were children or adolescents. Often these women had not told anyone of the rape and had just kept the burden within themselves. The current rape reactivated their reaction to the prior experience. It became clear that because they had not talked about the previous rape, the syndrome had continued to develop, and these women had carried unresolved issues with them for years. They would talk as much of the previous rape as they did of the current situation.

A diagnosis of this syndrome should be considered when the clinician observes any of the following symptoms during an evaluation interview.

1. Increasing signs of anxiety as the interview progresses, such as long periods of silence, blocking of associations, minor stuttering, and physical distress.
2. The patient reports sudden marked irritability or actual avoidance of relationships with men or marked change in sexual behavior.
3. History of sudden onset of phobic reactions and fear of being alone, going outside, or being inside alone.
4. Persistent loss of self-confidence and self-esteem, an attitude of self-blame, paranoid feelings, or dreams of violence and/or nightmares.

Clinicians who suspect that the patient was raped in the past should be sure to include questions relevant to the woman's sexual behavior in the evaluation interview and to ask if anyone has ever attempted to assault her. Such questions may release considerable pent-up material relevant to forced sexual activity.

Discussion

The crisis that results when a woman has been sexually assaulted is in the service of self-preservation. The victims in our sample felt that living was better than dying and that was the choice which had to be made. The victims' reactions to the impending threat to their lives is the nucleus around which an adaptive pattern may be noted.

The coping behavior of individuals to life-threatening situations has been documented in the work of such writers as Grinker and Spiegel (14), Lindemann (15), Kübler-Ross (16), and Hamburg (17). Kübler-Ross wrote of the process patients go through to come to terms with the fact of dying. Hamburg wrote of the resourcefulness of patients in facing catastrophic news and discussed a variety of implicit strategies by which patients face threats to life. This broad sequence of the acute phase, group support, and the long-run resolution described by these authors is compatible with the psychological work rape victims must do over time.

The majority of our rape victims were able to reorganize their lifestyle after the acute symptom phase, stay alert to possible threats to their lifestyle, and focus upon protecting themselves from further insult. This latter action was difficult because the world was perceived as a traumatic environment after the assault. As one victim said, "On the exterior I am OK, but inside [I feel] every man is the rapist."

The rape victim was able to maintain a certain equilibrium. In no case did the victim show ego disintegration, bizarre behavior, or self-destructive behavior during the acute phase. As indicated, there were a few victims who did regress to a previous level of impaired functioning four to six weeks following the assault.

With the increasing reports of rape, this is not a private syndrome. It should be a societal concern, and its treatment should be a public charge. Professionals will be called upon increasingly to assist the rape victim in the acute and long-term reorganization processes.

References

1 Federal Bureau of Investigation: *Uniform Crime Reports for the United States.* Washington, DC, U.S. Department of Justice, 1970.

2 *Report of District of Columbia Task Force on Rape.* Washington, DC, District of Columbia City Council, 1973, p 7 (processed).

3 AMIR, M. *Patterns of Forcible Rape.* Chicago, University of Chicago Press, 1971.

4 MACDONALD, J. *Rape: Offenders and their Victims.* Springfield, Ill., Charles C. Thomas, 1971.

5 COHEN, M., GAROFALO, R., BOUCHER, R. et al. "The Psychology of Rapists." *Seminars in Psychiatry* 3:307–327, 1971.

6 SUTHERLAND, S., SCHERL, D. "Patterns of Response Among Victims of Rape." *Am. J. Orthopsychiatry* 40:503–511, 1970.

7 HAYMAN, C., LANZA, C. "Sexual Assault on Women and Girls." *Am. J. Obstet. Gynecol.* 109:408–486, 1971.

8 HALLECK, S. "The Physician's Role in Management of Victims of Sex Offenders." *J.A.M.A.* 180:273–278, 1962.

9 FACTOR, M. "A Woman's Psychological Reaction to Attempted Rape." *Psychoanal. Q.* 23:243–244, 1954.

10 HOLMSTROM, L. L., BURGESS, A. W. "Rape: the Victim Goes on Trial." Read at the 68th annual meeting of the American Sociological Association, New York, N.Y., Aug. 27–30, 1973.

11 HOLMSTROM, L. L., BURGESS, A. W. "Rape: the Victim and the Criminal Justice System." Read at the First International Symposium on Victimology, Jerusalem, Sept. 2–6, 1973.

12 BURGESS, A. W., HOLMSTROM, L. L. "The Rape Victim in the Emergency Ward." *Am. J. Nursing* 73:1741–1745, 1973.

13 RADO, S. "Pathodynamics and Treatment of Traumatic War Neurosis (Traumatophobia)." *Psychosom. Med.* 4:362–368, 1948.

14 GRINKER, R. R., SPIEGEL, J. P. *Men Under Stress.* Philadelphia, Blakiston, 1945.

15 LINDEMANN, E. "Symptomatology and Management of Acute Grief." *Am. J. Psychiatry* 101:141–148, 1944.

16 KÜBLER-ROSS, E. "On Death and Dying." *J.A.M.A.* 221:174–179, 1972.

17 HAMBURG, D. "A Perspective on Coping Behavior." *Arch. Gen. Psychiatry* 17:277–284, 1967.

SCHOOL PHOBIA

CHAPTER 70

Steps in the Return to School of Children with School Phobia

Elisabeth Lassers, Robert Nordan, and Sheila Bladholm

Children with school phobia present a difficult problem that is very upsetting to the child, his family, the community, and the therapist. Suddenly, for little or no apparent reason, the child refuses to go to school. He insists on staying home and may complain of aches and pains. When his parents urge him to go to school, he may cry, perspire, become pale, and show other signs of severe panic that are relieved only when his parents finally allow him to stay home. The longer he stays home, the harder it becomes to send him to school, and he soon develops "school phobia."

A great deal had been written about school phobia, and many views have been expressed about the dynamics and treatment of the problem. The most thorough reviews of the literature with extensive bibliographies are those of Esther Marine (1–3) and Kahn and Nursten, (4, 5). In spite of the great divergency of opinion, most authors agree that the child's early return to school is of prime importance, and the focus in this paper is on the appropriate steps before, during, and after returning the child to school (6–18). While most therapists probably use these steps to some extent, we feel that it is relevant to look at them more specifically, to relate them to the casual mention of their use in the literature, and to draw on our own experiences for particular illustrations.

Reprinted from *American Journal of Psychiatry*, Vol. 130 (1973), pp. 265–268. Copyright 1973, the American Psychiatric Association.

School Phobia

The term "school phobia" needs to be differentiated from truancy and simple school withdrawal. A "truant" is a child who is absent from school without either his parents' or the school's permission. Other children may be kept home for some reason by the parents, and this may be termed "school withdrawal." Both problems are social in nature. The child with school phobia, on the other hand, may *want* to go to school but *cannot* and becomes acutely anxious even at the thought of leaving home. To some extent, "school phobia" is a misleading term, in that it is usually symptomatic of another problem–the tie between parents and child and the resulting conflicts (4).

Most authors suggest that the basic difficulty is a mutual hostile-dependent relationship between mother and child or, much less frequently, between father and child (7-9, 19-25). While the parents overtly urge the child to go to school, they give nonverbal cues interpreted by the child as suggesting that he stay home (6-9, 21, 26-31). When these children are in school, they frequently fear that death or injury will occur to a family member, most likely as a result of their fear that their hostile wishes might come true (8, 9, 13, 15, 16, 23-25, 27, 29, 32-37). The child feels an urgent need to go home, then, to make sure that his "beloved one" is still alive and well. Frequently, there is a precipitating event, such as a death or illness in the family, or the child's own illness (8, 9, 11, 16, 21-23, 38, 39). After this acute precipitating event has passed, the child will then refuse to return to school.

Returning the Child to School

The treatment of school phobia has caused considerable controversy in the literature, with approaches ranging from psychoanalytic therapy (11, 32) and "analytic first aid" (15) to child guidance approaches, conditioning (33), and other rapid treatment methods (10). An early controversy dealt with how quickly to return the child to school; although there are still some authors who feel that an early return to school may interfere with intensive therapy (24, 40), most authors cited in this paper believe that rapid return to school is essential, though they may differ over the method of therapy to be used after the child has been returned to school. Our own experience confirms this belief.

There are several reasons for returning the child quickly. The children who do go back seem to improve rapidly, while those who remain at home become increasingly anxious, so that it becomes more and more difficult to return them to school at a later date. Since a large part of the problem seems to be the mother's difficulty in letting the child go, the successful experience of his being back in school permits both the parent and the child to function in a more usual way; if anxiety continues to be a problem, it can be dealt with in psychotherapy.

How can early return to school be accomplished? In our work, we have found that several steps are necessary which must be initiated as quickly as possible. These steps are set forth below, along with illustrative case reports.

STEP I: PHYSICAL EXAMINATION

Obviously, if the child has a real physical illness that keeps him out of school, lack of attendance cannot be called "school phobia." The first step, then, in dealing with a child who is staying home because of physical complaints is to determine whether there is an organic basis for his condition. It should be kept in mind, however, that physical symptoms, mostly minor and chronic, such as headaches, gastrointestinal upsets, or mild respiratory symptoms may be used by the child and his family as an excuse to keep him out of school, thus masking a real school phobia.

STEP II: PSYCHIATRIC EVALUATION

The next step is to rule out an incipient psychosis or other serious pathology, since school avoidance in such cases is usually seen as a secondary symptom rather than as a primary problem. The therapist should conduct an interview with parents and child and then determine the seriousness of the difficulties.

Case 1. Charles was hospitalized at age 13 for "chest pains" but was discharged soon after when examination revealed no organic cause for his complaints. Four months later he was brought to the Child Psychiatry Clinic because he had refused to return to school after his discharge. Charles was spending most of this time in his room, though he slept very little and had frightening nightmares; he was also fearful of members of other races and nationalities and fantasied attacks both upon them and upon members of his family. Charles was anxious, had delusions of grandeur and persecution, and had tenuous reality testing. School avoidance was thus a symptom of psychotic decompensation; immediate hospitalization was recommended.

The second purpose of the diagnostic interview with the child and his parents is to determine the individual and family dynamics involved and the precipitating event that resulted in school phobia. While certain relationships and problems might be expected, they are not always present in every case and, even when found, their expression can vary widely.

Case 2. Randy, a six-and-a-half-year-old black boy, was referred to the clinic after he had been out of school for nearly a year. When he first started kindergarten, he cried and the teacher suggested that he stay home until the following year. The next September, he had a successful first day at school, but on the second day he was hit by a car and suffered a broken leg. After being in the hospital in traction for three weeks and at home in a hip spica cast for seven weeks, he had sufficiently recovered to return to school, but he refused.

Randy came from a severely disorganized ghetto family. He was the eighth of 11 children, and his parents were divorced when he was three and a half years old. His maternal grandmother, to whom his mother was very close, had died when his mother was pregnant with Randy. The mother herself had a history of depression and suicidal attempts. Her tenth child was born two months before Randy was to start first grade, and she was pregnant with her 11th at the time of the interview. Randy's older sister, who had taken a mothering role toward him, had also been pregnant at the time he started kindergarten.

While Randy was not able to verbalize his problems easily, his play fully revealed his concerns. While in the hospital he had been quite lonely, and he was still angry that his mother had not visited him. He knew that his mother was expecting another child and feared that he would again be left alone. Past desertions—by his father, by his mother during other pregnancies, by his sister during hers—all contributed to his anger and his fear of being abandoned once again. The anger could not be expressed, however, since he still needed his mother, and it is likely that he felt that he must stay home to make sure that his mother had not been destroyed by the destructive fantasies he had about her. Randy was still concerned about the injury to his leg, with unresolved castration fears.

Randy's mother was overwhelmed by her own problems and those of her family. Though she was irritated by Randy's demands and clinging behavior, she also worried about him and "loved" him while he was ill and at home. It may be that he was a "special" child to her, since she was pregnant with him when her own mother had died and he had provided comfort to her then; but at the same time, she may have had strong feelings of rejection for him. Whatever the reason, her dependence upon him and her communication of these concerns to him did not promote his easy return to school.

STEP III: FINDING A THERAPEUTIC ALLY

One of the most important steps in returning the phobic child to school is to find one or more persons who can function as a source of strength. This can be someone in the family or someone outside—a teacher, a minister, or even a family friend. This person acts as a kind of aide to the therapist—someone who is more often present and more available to the family on a day-to-day basis, and who can act both as an agent of external control and as a support to parents and child.

Case 3. In the case of Sally, an eight-year-old girl, the family physician provided the extra support that was needed to get her back in schoool. It was he who had initially referred her to the clinic, since his own examinations and those of several other physicians indicated that there was no physical basis for the child's complaints, and it was his insistence that finally brought the family to the clinic. Sally's complaints of headaches and nightmares began when the family had moved just before school started; this had been the fifth such move in five years, and Sally had recently asked when the family would be moving again. Her mother had been hospitalized four times since Sally was born; the last hospitalization, for a hysterectomy, occurred when Sally was six and precipitated a depression in the mother that she "hid" from the children. Sally had one older sister who was said to be "bad," but who received more of the parents' approval since they prized her independent behavior.

Assessment of the case was made in close collaboration with the referring physician, who then informed Sally's mother of the findings. She put up immediate resistance to accepting Sally's problems as being emotional, indicating that Sally had had a reaction to a penicillin shot, which had kept her home for two weeks, but the doctor assured her that the "reaction" was simply the result of Sally's hyperventilation. He reiterated that he had found no physical problems in his examination and told the mother that she could best help the girl by standing firm and insisting that Sally go to school.

Although the mother agreed to the plan, the doctor felt she was not convinced; but when the social worker checked with the mother a few days later, Sally was in school. The mother admitted that forcing a "sick" child to go to school made her feel guilty, but she was determined to follow her doctor's advice and to keep Sally in class. She asked for help in finding a local agency that would provide therapy for the girl, but later, when she was recontacted, the mother indicated that the family had not followed up on the referral since Sally was still in school and things were going well.

STEP IV: THE INTERPRETIVE INTERVIEW

Once the therapist has established that the child is not physically ill or seriously disturbed, has some understanding of the dynamics of the case, and has identified someone who can provide extra support, an interpretive interview is needed to discusss the problems with the family and to set up the expectation that the child can return to school immediately. The therapist should confirm that nothing is physically wrong with the child and indicate that the child is truant unless he goes back to school at once. He should show his willingness to help the family and child find ways to make his return to school easier. If the precipitating cause is obvious, it should be discussed, and fears ("Will I be a bad mother if I make him go to school?") should be dealt with sympathetically. The therapist should be understanding but firm in his resolution that the child return to school, suggesting that the only alternatives are a truancy petition or hospitalization in a psychiatric unit that has classroom facilities. A mild tranquilizer may be prescribed for a few days to alleviate some of the renewed anxiety over the return to school.

STEP V: PLANNING

The therapist, the family, and the school should draw up plans for returning the child to class and set a date in the near future. If at all possible, a face-to-face meeting should be held so that a plan can be worked out among all those involved. In some cases, it may seem advisable to return the child gradually, through a kind of "deconditioning" process, letting him return home after part of the day or permitting him to retire to the principal's office from time to time. In other cases, a complete return may be desirable so that the child has no "outs."

> Case 4. The school not only took an active part in planning the return of Jenny, age nine, but was also a source of strength for the family. Just before a minor illness that kept her out of school, Jenny's grades had begun to drop, and later, looking back, the parents realized that the change occurred after her father lost a finger in an accident at work. Jenny began to complain of sore throats and was even hospitalized with tonsillitis; she could not return to school. A crisis was reached two months later when Jenny set two fires within two days.
>
> At the interpretive interview with the parents, it was suggested that Jenny be returned to school immediately, the next day if at all possible. The mother's ambivalent feelings came out at once—she did not want to be a "bad mother" by sending a sick child to school, nor did she want her daughter to miss so much school. With support, she was able to get Jenny off to school the following morning, but Jenny used one of her previous symptoms to foil the plan. She vomited and was sent home. Again the mother, teacher, and principal were contacted, and it was agreed that Jenny would stay in school, even if she did vomit. Jenny tried to find a way home again and was successful: she vomited down the front of her dress. At last, when a final plan of sending extra changes of clothes to school was worked out, Jenny settled down and did not remain out of school any longer.

STEP VI: SUPPORT

Jenny's case and some of the others discussed show the importance of the therapist's continuing involvement in guiding and supporting the family as it made the critical adjustment of returning the child to school. Phone calls were made, office visits were arranged, and, in some cases, home and school visits were necessary. Sometimes drug therapy was necessary, usually for a limited time. Whatever the need, the therapist should make himself available so that he can provide the help and support that both parents and child need to make the return to school successful.

STEP VII: FOLLOW-UP

At the time that the child returns to school (successfully, one hopes) he, his parents, and the school should understand that the therapist will be checking at regular intervals to determine his progress. To the family, this says that the therapist is interested and still available; to the school, it indicates the therapist's willingness to continue to be involved and to provide consultation whenever the teacher or principal needs it. In the cases described here, some contact has been maintained; at last report, all the children except Randy were still in school and coping adequately.

STEP VIII: PSYCHOTHERAPY

Ideally, follow-up would be only one aspect of a total therapeutic plan but, although psychotherapy was offered all the families mentioned above, non accepted. Once the child was back in class and free of overt physical symptoms, the overall anxiety level was apparently reduced enough that further therapy was rejected. Although we have little information concerning the later development and adjustment of the children, neither they nor their siblings have returned to the clinic with the same or other symptoms.

Discussion

School phobia frequently appears as a symptom in response to a subtle, often ambivalent, message from the mother or another family member that life is insecure and the child had better stay at home. Staying at home then leads to a vicious circle of withdrawal from the growth- promoting stimulation of learning and peer relations, further regression and withdrawal, increasing embroilment in a hostile-dependent relationship with parents, more intense anxiety, and more extreme school rejection.

At the same time, in moments of healthier ego functioning, both parents and child know that the child should be in school and, at some point, they reach out for help. If he acts quickly, the therapist can strengthen this functioning through his own authoritative support and the temporary reliance on family members, school personnel, or someone else outside the family in order to work out a plan for the child's immediate return to school. Then, with some of the anxiety of both parents and child relieved, and the message clearly stated that the child must return to school, he can usually go back to class. Once there, the child can use the accomplishment for further growth and the symptoms usually do not reappear (12).

Although the return to school puts an end to the secondary gain of staying at home and induces growth, it does not solve the family's basic problems, for which further therapy may be needed. Unfortunately, in the cases described here, the families were not ready for treatment. It could be argued that they might have been better motivated for further treatment if they had been denied relief of the symptom, but this would be risky since school phobia itself is so crippling and becomes harder to treat the longer the child's return to school is put off.

Conclusions

This paper has focused on the specific steps we have found useful in returning the school-phobic child to school as soon as possible. The first step is to rule out any organic reasons for the symptoms through a physical examination and then to determine the dynamics of the situation through a psychiatric examination. Next the therapist should search for a therapeutic ally, someone who can support the family on a day-to-day basis through the period of crisis. With these steps accomplished, an interpretive interview can be held with the family and the expectation should be set up that the child can return to school immediately. A plan is devised in cooperation with school personnel and, during the critical first days after the child's return, frequent support is given by the therapist. Follow-up contact is made and, if possible, the family is involved in psychotherapy.

References

1. MARINE, E. "School Refusal: Review of the Literature," *Social Service Review* 42:464–478, 1968.

2. MARINE, E. "School Refusal Treatment in Two Agencies: a Follow- up Study of Intervention by a Child Guidance Center and an Attendance and Counseling Division of a School System." Ph.D. dissertation, University of Pittsburgh, 1966.

3. MARINE, E. "School Refusal: Who Should Intervene? (diagnostic and treatment categories)." *J. Sch. Psychol.* 7:63–70, 1969.

4. KAHN, J. H., NURSTEN, J. P. *Unwillingly to School: School Phobia or School Refusal–a Medico-Social Problem*, 2nd ed. New York, Pergamon Press, 1968, pp. 1–19, 227, 271.

5. KAHN, J. H., NURSTEN, J. P. "School Refusal: a Comprehensive View of School Phobia and Other Failures of School Attendance." *Am. J. Orthopsychiatry* 32:707–718, 1962.

6. COHEN, N. J., LEONARD, M. F. "Early Pediatric Management of Acute School Avoidance," in *Modern Perspectives in Child Development*. Edited by Solnit, A., Provence, S., New York, International Universities Press, 1963, pp. 419–441.

7. EISENBERG, L. "School Phobia: a Study in the Communication of Anxiety." *Am. J. Psychiatry* 114:712–718, 1958.

8. ESTES, H. R., HAYLETT, C. H., JOHNSON, A. M. "Separation Anxiety." *Am. J. Psychotherapy* 10:682–695, 1956.

9. FUTTERMAN, E. H., HOFFMAN, I. "Transient School Phobia in a Leukemic Child." *J. Am. Acad. Child Psychiatry* 9:477–494, 1970.

10. KENNEDY, W. "School Phobia: Rapid Treatment of Fifty Cases." *J. Abnorm. Psychol.* 70:285–289, 1965.

11. KLEIN, I. "The Reluctance to Go To School." *Psychoanal. Study Child.* 1:263–279, 1945.

12. LEVENTHAL, T. WEINBERGER, G., STANDER, R. et al. "Therapeutic Strategies with School Phobics," *Am. J. Orthopsychiatry* 37:64–70, 1967.

13. MILLAR, T. P. "The Child Who Refuses to Attend School." *Am. J. Psychiatry* 118:398–404, 1961.

14. REGER, R. "A School Phobia in an Obese Girl." *J. Clin. Psychol.* 18:356–357, 1962.

15. SPERLING, M. "Analytic First Aid in School Phobias." *Psychoanal. Q.* 30:504–518, 1961.

16. SUTTENFIELD, V. "School Phobia: a Study of Five Cases." *Am. J. Orthopsychiatry* 24:368–380, 1954.

17. WARNECKE, R. "School Phobia and its Treatment." *Br J. Med. Psychol.* 37:71–79, 1964.

18. WARREN, W. "Acute Neurotic Breakdown in Children with Refusal to Go to School," *Arch. Dis. Child.* 23:266–272, 1948.

19. COLM, H. N. "Phobias in Children." *Psychoanal. Rev.* 40:65–84. 1959.

20. COOLIDGE, J. C., HAHN, P. B., PECK, A. L. "School Phobia: Neurotic Crisis or Way of Life?" *Am. J. Orthopsychiatry* 27:296–309, 1957.

21. DAVIDSON, S. "School Phobia as a Manifestation of Family Disturbance: Its Structure and Treatment." *J. Child Psychol. Psychiatry* 1:270–287, 1961.

22. JARVIS, V. "Countertransference in the Management of School Phobia." *Psychoanal. Q.* 33:411–419, 1964.

23. JOHNSON, A. M., FALSTEIN, E. I., SZUREK, S. A. et al. "School Phobia." *Am. J. Orthopsychiatry* 11:702–711, 1941.

24. WALDFOGEL, S., COOLIDGE, J. C., HAHN, P. B. "The Development, Meaning and Management of School Phobia." *Am. J. Orthopsychiatry* 27:754–780, 1957.

25. WALDFOGEL, S., TESSMAN, E. HAHN, P. B. "Learning Problems: a Program for Early Intervention in School Phobia." *Am. J. Orthopsychiatry* 29:324–332, 1959.

26. EISENBERG, L. "School Phobia: Diagnosis, Genesis and Clinical Management," *Pediatr. Clin. North Am.* 5:645–666, 1958.

27. GLASER, K. "Problems in School Attendance." *Pediatrics* 23:371–383, 1959.

28. MALMQUIST, C. P. "School Phobia: a Problem in Family Neurosis." *J. Am. Acad. Child Psychiatry* 4:293–319, 1965.

29. RADIN, S. S. "Psychodynamic Aspects of School Phobia." *Compr. Psychiatry* 8:119–128, 1967.

30. RODRIGUEZ, A., RODRIGUEZ, M., EISENBERG, L. "The Outcome of School Phobia: a Follow-up Study based on 41 Cases." *Am. J. Psychiatry* 116:540–544, 1959.

31. SPERLING, M. "School Phobias: Classification, Dynamics and Treatment." *Psychoanal. Study Child.* 22:375–401, 1967.

32. BROADWIN, I. T. "A Contribution to the Study of Truancy," *Am. J. Orthopsychiatry* 2:253–259, 1932.

33. GARVEY, W. P., HEGRENES, J. R. "Desensitization Techniques in the Treatment of School Phobia." *Am. J. Orthopsychiatry* 36:147–152, 1966.

34. HERSOV, L. A. "Refusal to Go to School." *J. Child Psychol. Psychiatry* 1:137–145, 1960.

35. MESSNER, A. A. "Family Treatment of a School Phobic Child." *Arch. Gen. Psychiatry* 11:548–555, 1964.

36. PAPPENHEIM, E., SWEENY, ,M. "Separation Anxiety in Mother and Child." *Psychoanal. Study Child.* 7:95–114, 1952.

37. SPERLING, M. "Mucous Colitis Associated with Phobias." *Psychoanal. Q.* 19:318–326, 1950.

38. COOLIDGE, J. C., TESSMAN, E., WALDFOGEL, S. et al. "Patterns of Aggression in School Phobia." *Psychoanal. Study Child.* 17:319–333, 1962.

39. LEVENTHAL, T., SILLS, M. "Self-image in School Phobia." *Am. J. Orthopsychiatry* 34:685–695, 1964.

40. GREENBAUM, R. S. "Treatment of School Phobias: Theory and Practice." *Am. J. Psychother.* 18:616–634, 1964.

STEPPARENTING

CHAPTER 71

Working with Stepfamilies: Principles of Practice

Harriette C. Johnson

Despite the prevalence today of families that include stepparents and stepchildren, relationships among the members of stepfamilies have received relatively limited attention in the professional literature. The preponderance of books that have appeared on stepfamilies have either been "how to do it" manuals or anecdotal accounts.[1] Accurate statistics of the number of adults and children who have become related through remarriage have not been compiled. It has been well documented, however, that a large and increasing number of marriages end in divorce, that many of these marriages have produced children, and that the majority of divorces are followed by the remarriage of one or both partners.[2] Estimates of the number of stepfamilies in this country range up to fifteen million or more.[3]

Social workers frequently encounter stepfamilies in a variety of settings. Although every family has features that are idiosyncratic, several characteristics of stepfamilies are inherent in the institution of the stepfamily itself. Each of these phenomena is described in all or most of the existing works on the subject. Nevertheless, practitioners sometimes fail to recognize these situation-generated dynamics for what they are and instead interpret them as being indicative of "family pathology."

This article will attempt to cull from the literature the common characteristics of stepfamily relationships. It is intended to provide a framework for understanding these relationships that will be useful to practitioners in both counseling and noncounseling situations. To understand the origins of the characteristics commonly seen in stepfamilies, it is first necessary to explore the sociological and historical contexts in which the present-day phenomenon of remarriage involving children has developed.

Sociological Context

Stepfamilies have alternately been referred to as "reconstituted," "blended," and "synergistic" families. All these designations imply that the stepfamily is a variation of the nuclear family unit. Furthermore, they convey the connotation that it is a deviant, aberrant, or second- class form of the "real" family, which consists of biological parents and their children.

The stigma and negative associations attached to stepfamilies derive from two cultural traditions: first, the "wicked stepmother" image from archaic fairy-tale representations of the family reconstituted after the death of one parent: and second, the image of the contemporary stepfamily that is most often the aftermath of divorce, not widowhood. Consider the ugly pictures of the jealous stepmother and the tarnished divorcée: add the philandering husband who abandons his family for a home-wrecking temptress; and round out the myth with an image of the innocent victims–that is, the children–who must endure years of pain and suffering because of their parents' behavior. No wonder the resulting composite is the unsavory, less- than-whole, "reconstituted" family. In this scenario, parents are the objects of blame, children are the objects of pity, and some stigma attaches to all family members.

The existing literature on stepfamilies emphasizes the analysis of the stepfamily as a psychological phenomenon separate from its environmental context. With the exception of Duberman, who has examined the stepfamily from a sociological perspective, too little attention has been directed to the sociological and economic origins of the stepfamily.[4] Stresses and tensions endemic to stepfamily relationships have their roots in social conditions arising from economic change and culturally conditioned beliefs and expectations. The tendency to overlook these origins may result, in social work practice, in a worker's making a "case" out of a stepfamily–that is, in the worker's looking for pathology and then applying a medical therapeutic model to treat it. Unfortunately, such an approach tends to reinforce the feeling experienced by members of the stepfamilies that they are failures in human relations by virtue of being part of a stepfamily.

The fact that millions of stepfamilies are now in existence should suggest that there are forces exterior to families and individuals that create conditions favorable to divorce and remarriage. An examination of the historical and economic antecedents of the present situation supports this thesis.

Historical Antecedents

It is well known that prevailing family arrangements in the United States have changed.[5] A shift has taken place away from a predominance of large extended-family groups that included biological parents and children, grandparents, aunts, uncles, and cousins toward the ascendance of the nuclear family, consisting of father and mother and their biological children. The nuclear family, in turn, has given way to a variety of alternatives. These include one-parent families, stepfamilies created by the remarriage of one or both parents, families based on common-law arrangements, communal living, the intermittent presence of sexual partners of single parents raising children alone, and joint parenting by homosexual unmarried parents.

The causes for the disintegration of the extended family are well known. Prominent among these is the geographic dislocation of workers required by industrial capitalist production.[6] Young breadwinners have had to take jobs at varying distances from their families of origin. Families with young children have thus been separated from the emotional and physical support formerly supplied by relatives and have had to fend for themselves in the area of child rearing. Some young couples fortunate enough to stay in one place for a number of years form new extended families with neighbors and friends. Others fail to do so because of cultural and attitudinal differences between themselves and those living in close proximity to them. Still others never stay in one place long enough to develop surrogate family relationships with nonrelatives.

The increasing frequency of breakdown of the nuclear family is a predictable sequel to the disintegration of the extended family. Aspects of modern urban living that have contributed to the deterioration of the nuclear family include the opportunity for women to become self-supporting; the emotional upheaval caused by frequent work-related geographical moves; the insecurities engendered by the vagaries of the job market; the weakening of social norms prohibiting separation, divorce, and sex outside marriage; the isolation of young mothers from other adults in the daily work of child rearing and homemaking; and the unalleviated burden of responsibility for the care of children experienced by parents because of the absence of extended-family structures.

In general, people whose nuclear families have been broken up by some combination of stressful conditions seek to reconstitute familial living arrangements in one of the alternative modes previously described. Despite the fact that a large minority of the total population now lives in one or another of these alternative arrangements, the notion of the nuclear family as the "real" family is still in ascendance. Other life-styles are still regarded by the mainstream of American society–including many people who assume these life-styles–as deviant or inferior substitutes. These factors and the historical and cultural antecedents of the present situation just described should be kept in mind when specific characteristics of stepfamily relationships are considered.

Common Characteristics

Some or all of the aspects and characteristics about to be outlined are present in every situation in which a single parent acquires a new mate. These are observable whether the family members are living together or are in contact with each other through visits. Although the intensity of feeling related to these aspects is likely to be greater when stepparents and stepchildren live together on a full-time basis than when children and adults see one another on visits, it should be remembered that these factors are present to some degree in all stepfamily relationships.

COMPLEXITY

When a single parent remarries, his or her new spouse may be a single addition to the family, may bring children into the family as visitors, or may bring children into the family unit consisting of those who live together. When two people who are already parents remarry, both new spouses may add children to their full-time or part-time ménage. The greater the number of newly acquired family members, the greater the complexity of the relationships with which family members must cope. Stepfamilies are characterized by multifaceted relationships involving a variety of people whose roles are in flux. Each relationship carries with it a set of expectations and a question of delineation of turf. "Turf" refers to the boundaries outlining the rights, privileges, and possessions of each individual, and these boundaries may be physical or psychological. As the number of adults and children added to the family constellation increases arithmetically, the number of relationships increases at an exponential rate.[7]

Each individual in the family must find some way of relating to each other individual. Even though a stepparent and the natural parent of the same sex may never see one another, they must relate to each other in regard to expectations and turf. In terms of expectations, what is the natural parent expected to do vis-à-vis the children, and what is the stepparent of the same sex expected to do? In regard to turf, what rights and privileges does each have?

When people who are already parents remarry, a new type of extended family comes into being. Unlike members of the traditional extended family, however, members of stepfamilies have not lived in close proximity with each other for years. They are likely to have different life-styles and values. This factor, combined with the number of diverse relationships with which family members must cope, contributes to the high degree of complexity found in reconstituted families.

VARIABILITY

Unlike children in the original nuclear family, stepchildren do not start their life with a stepparent but instead are introduced to him or her at some point during the course of their development. This introduction may take place at any age and under a variety of different conditions. Differences between the situations of individual stepfamilies are the outgrowth of a large number of variables having to do with the children, the natural parents, and stepparent, and external environmental conditions. Variables relating to the children include the following: age of the children at the time of the parent's remarriage, degree of attachment to the absent parent, length of time since loss of the absent parent through death or divorce, degree of continuing involvement with the absent parent, degree of attachment to and need for the natural parent in the home, number of siblings and stepsiblings with whom to compete or share activities, special needs related to health or disability, personal charm and attractiveness, and extent of need for parenting from the stepparent.

Variables relating to the natural parents include the following: amount of time and energy available for the children, degree of emotional investment in the children relative to involvement in other aspects of life, degree of stress being experienced in life, extent of antagonism toward the exspouse, ability to manage the home, physical and mental well-being, and expectations concerning what one is entitled to get out of life. Level of expectation is an important factor because high expectations are likely to be accompanied by stress when they are not fulfilled. Last, the following variables relate to the stepparent: whether he or she has raised children, amount of previous experience with children, extent of need to assume a parenting role with the stepchild, extent of emotional investment in nonfamily activities such as career or avocational interests, willingness to share the spouse with the children (which is related to the individual's expectations about what he or she should be getting and what the children should be getting), previous experience and comfort with family living, and presence of own children who need time and attention.

As a general rule, the degree of solidarity that develops in the reconstituted family is likely to be a function of the interplay of the variables described. For example, a stepmother who is deeply involved in her work may get along well with stepchildren with whom she is living and who receive a good deal of attention from both their natural parents. Because of her emotional investment elsewhere, she may not be intrusive in the lives of the children. However, the same woman might clash with her spouse and stepchildren if the natural mother of the children were uninvolved with them. Under such circumstances her husband might look to her to assume a major mothering role, and her stepchildren might crave attention and affection from her.

UNCLEAR EXPECTATIONS

Parents, stepparents, and children all have expectations about the proper behavior for themselves vis-à-vis every other family member. In addition, they have expectations about what feelings are proper for them to experience toward every other member, as well as expectations about the proper behavior and feelings for every other member in regard to themselves. Frequently, however, these notions are not clearly thought out or formulated, let alone articulated. Since society does not have a tradition of behavioral codes and norms to pass on to new members of stepfamilies, these individuals are caught in a confusing state of not knowing exactly what they are supposed to do and what they are supposed to feel. Is a stepmother some version of a mother? If so, is one supposed to have feelings toward a stepmother that are similar to what one feels toward a mother? Is a stepsibling an unrelated peer or friend with a set of parents different from one's own? Or a new rival for one's own parent? Is one supposed to feel the same way about one's stepchildren as one's own children? Are adults supposed to love other people's children in general? Or only their own? Or should they feel love for their own and for the children of their new spouse? Such questions illustrate a central characteristic of stepfamily relationships that can be classified under the heading of "role confusion."

Discomfort arises from the uncertainty and ambiguity inherent in stepfamily relationships because of a lack of societal prescriptions. In addition, problems arise from discrepancies between what one thinks one ought to do and to feel and what one actually does and feels. Similar disparities exist with respect to the expected and actual behaviors and feelings of other family members toward oneself.

A common but fallacious belief often held by people who became part of a stepfamily is that they are supposed to love each other.[8] Realistically, however, there is no more reason to love a stepparent or a stepchild than there is to love an in-law. Although positive feeling may develop over a period of years, intense positive feeling such as that which often exists between parents and children is unlikely to occur, unless the children are very young at the time of remarriage and the stepparent assumes a primary parenting role. Thus, a major task to be undertaken in work with stepfamilies is the clarification and formulation of the expectations of each family member with respect to himself or herself and the other family members.

LOSSES AND GAINS

The realignment of family arrangements often results in gains for some individuals and losses for others. For example, the new wife of a divorced man gains a portion of his time, income, and affectionate feelings, which were formerly the exclusive province of his children. Conversely, when stepchildren enter the home, the new spouse loses privacy and time alone with his or her mate. Since realignments invariably result in some trade-offs, there will be winners and losers in the family. It is to be hoped that each member who experiences some loss will also derive some compensating gain; however, this is not always the case.

Having less time than before with a parent or having to share a parent's affection with an outsider constitutes a substantial loss, and as such it is a realistic basis for anger and hostility. Having to relinquish privacy in one's own home in order to take in someone else's children is also a realistic basis for hostility. These losses are often a built-in component of life in a stepfamily. They are real and need to be openly acknowledged as such. This can be done by statements like these: "I know my getting married again and living in Jane's home is hard on you. But it's better for me. I was lonely by myself."

QUESTIONS OF TURF

Questions concerning turf or territory are closely related to the issue of competition. Turf can be physical ("This is my house–what right do you have to live here?") or emotional ("My Daddy belongs to me, not you"). Each family member coming from his or her previous family intrudes on the turf of the others. Just as a new spouse intrudes on the stepchildren's turf ("Sundays with Dad are mine; you're horning in"), the children in turn intrude on that of the spouse ("I have a right to be alone with my husband once in a while"). Finally, stepsiblings intrude on each other ("Why do I have to share my toys with you?").

DIFFERENCES IN LIFE–STYLE

People with different life-styles are often thrust on one another when a remarriage takes place. The new additions to the family are not chosen by the family as a group but by the adult who is acquiring a mate. This is so even when the stated purpose of the remarriage is to "find a mother (or a father) for the children." The acquisition of stepparents or stepchildren can be likened to the acquisition of an in-law.

Conflicts stemming from differences in preexisting life-styles arise within stepfamilies in relation to various aspects of living. These include the following areas:

- Discipline: Who should enforce it, how should it be enforced, and when?
- Eating habits: Does the family eat together or separately in front of the tv?
- Division of labor: Whose responsibility is it to cook, clean, do the laundry, get the car fixed, and attend parent-teacher conferences?
- Attitudes toward sex: Should family members see each other undressed? Should teenage children engage in sex?
- Use of alcohol and drugs: Is such use acceptable for parents? For children? To what extent?
- Attitudes toward obligations: How important is it to pay bills, get to appointments, turn in homework, or call to let other family members know where you are?
- Manners: What behavior should be considered impolite?
- Household rules: What rules govern using the phone or keeping curfews?
- Expression of hostility, aggression, or disagreement: How much is acceptable?

In working with reconstituted families, the practitioner should undertake an analysis of the life-styles of the preexisting families. The items just listed should be systematically examined to identify sources of conflict that may exist without the awareness of family members.

BENEFITS

Families with whom social workers come in contact are usually experiencing some kind of distress. Stepfamilies in which positive elements outweigh problems or tensions are therefore infrequently seen in social work practice. There are, however, several benefits that can accrue from remarriage. The worker and family members should try to identify benefits that already exist. In addition, potential benefits should be explored so that they can be developed. These include the following:

1. Relief from the constant physical and emotional burdens of child care. Couples can sometimes be alone for weekends while children visit their other parent. Respite from caring for children may be easier for remarried couples to obtain than for some couples who have never been divorced.
2. Children can often form relationships of friendship and solidarity with stepsiblings on the basis of common, shared experiences.
3. Children who have been raised in an atmosphere of strife prior to a divorce frequently have the opportunity to see a parent and stepparent live harmoniously.

4. Parents who are emotionally satisfied have more to give their children than parents who are lonely or frustrated from being single.

5. Children may expand their circle of friendly, interested adults—that is, develop new extended families—by acquiring new relatives such as stepgrandparents.

Practice Principles

Although every family's situation represents a unique configuration of variables, the commonality of certain features of stepfamilies suggests some practice principles that may be useful. To begin, a social worker who encounters tensions in a stepfamily needs an understanding and knowledge of the sociological and economic bases for the breakup of nuclear families and remarriage. As already indicated, the worker lacking such an awareness is likely to see pathology and treat sickness. The starting point for assessment and intervention planning should be the exploration of common factors such as unformulated role expectations, not an analysis of idiosyncratic pathologies.

In addition to individual and family counseling, various kinds of groups should be used whenever possible. Separate groups for children and parents as well as intergenerational groups are desirable. Groups can be used to educate families about the common aspects of their situation, to break down isolation and feelings of being stigmatized, and to develop a vehicle for self-help. However, one difficulty that may be encountered in forming a group is the inability to find families that are sufficiently similar. Differences of social class should be minimized whenever possible when planning the formation of a group. In addition, consideration should be given to organizing mutual self- help groups similar to Parents Without Partners. These might be called Parents With New Partners, Kids With New Parents, or Second-Time-Around Families.

When counseling is used with a particular family, the mix of individual, joint, and family interviews arranged will depend on the worker's assessment of the family's needs. Since different situations require different arrangements, no general prescriptions can be made. Nevertheless, a structured approach to family assessment may aid the worker and the family in identifying significant dynamics. Written questionnaires may be given to family members, asking them to spell out their concepts of their own and others' roles; their own and others' turf; their assessment of the benefits and losses they have experienced with respect to time, money, and affection; and their own life-style as compared with that of other family members. The process of writing answers for the questionnaire may help family members formulate and clarify their expectations. It may also help both family and worker identify areas of conflict that may not be immediately apparent during an interview.

Some relationships between stepparents and stepchildren are characterized primarily by competition. In such cases, neither the stepchild nor the stepparent involved has an emotional need for anything the other has to offer; the adult and child have few or no common interests; and they either have no personal liking for each other or may feel active animosity. Under these conditions, it is best to give up the pretense that a family exists now or is going to exist in the near future. The reality is that everyone is marking time until the child grows up, and the most viable strategy is for the stepchild and stepparent to spend as little time together as possible. The natural parent should work out a separate relationship with each. Lack of positive feeling should be recognized as unfortunate but understandable under the circumstances involved.

However, when active dislike is present between child and stepparent, it is imperative that the natural parent assume most of the parenting responsibility, particularly the unpleasant tasks of disciplining or punishing. Unloved and unwanted stepparents are not legitimate in the eyes of stepchildren. Abdication by the natural parent in this kind of situation adds fuel to an already burning fire and leaves both child and stepparent feeling angry and abandoned.

As already indicated, work with stepfamilies should always include an exploration of the positive aspects of the situation. When family members fail to see any benefits to themselves in a situation, the worker should help them explore any actual as well as potential benefits that might be developed. Finally, outside supports and resources should be sought out and whenever possible used to the fullest to alleviate stress and promote solidarity.

Summary

Although most of the literature on stepfamilies is anecdotal and descriptive, certain characteristics of such families are noted with great frequency in many of the existing works. The most common of these include a high degree of complexity and variability; unexpressed or unformulated role expectations; competition for resources of time, money, and affection, often attended by losses and gains for family members; conflicts related to turf; and differences in life-styles. Certain benefits derived from membership in a reconstituted family have also been noted.

Several principles for practice have been suggested. A fundamental principle is that the practitioner's overall approach should be based on an awareness of the economic and sociological context of divorce and remarriage. This is of great importance. Undue attention to family "pathology" reinforces the belief of family members that the stresses and tensions they experience are due to personal inadequacies. In general, then, the starting point for assessment and intervention planning should be the exploration of those dynamics inherent in the institution of the stepfamily.

Notes and References

1. *See,* for example, Ruth Roosevelt and Jeannette Lofas, *Living in Step* (New York: McGraw-Hill Book Co., 1975); June Noble and William Noble, *How to Live With Other People's Children* (New York: Hawthorn Books, 1977); Jean Rosenbaum and Veryl Rosenbaum, *Stepparenting* (Corte Madera, Calif.: Chandler and Sharp Publishers, 1977); and Davidyne Mayleas, *Rewedded Bliss* (New York: Basic Books, 1979).
2. Mayleas, op. cit.
3. Lucile Duberman, *The Reconstituted Family: A Study of Remarried Couples and Their Children* (Chicago: Nelson-Hall Publishers, 1975).
4. Ibid.
5. Harold L. Wilensky and Charles N. Lebeaux, *Industrial Society and Social Welfare* (New York: Russell Sage Foundation, 1958), pp. 67–83.
6. Ibid.
7. A nuclear family with three children contains five people, ten relationships (the parents' relationship with each other, each parent's relationship with each child, and each child's relationship with every other child), and five areas of turf. When a stepparent without children is added to a three-child nuclear family following divorce, the number of relationships increases to fifteen. When the children's other natural parent also remarries, the number of relationships increases to twenty. (This count does not include a relationship between the new spouses of the original natural parents.) Should one stepparent have two children of his or her own, the number of relationships and sets of expectations jumps to thirty-seven. Add a new baby to the reconstituted family, and forty-six relationships are involved. Should both stepparents have children of their own, the number of relationships and sets of expectations can easily approach one hundred, even in a relatively small family.
8. *See,* for example, Gerda L. Schulman, "Myths that Intrude on the Adaptation of the Stepfamily," *Social Casework,* 53 (March 1972), pp. 131–139.

SUICIDE

CHAPTER 72

Suicide: Answering the Cry for Help

David J. Klugman, Robert E. Litman, and Carl I. Wold

Suicide, which accounts for at least 20,000 deaths per year in the United States, ranks among the first ten causes of adult deaths in this country.[1] In addition to completed suicides, there are numerous suicide attempts and threats. It has been estimated that each year in the United States about half a million people are affected by a range of suicidal crises, making it a major public health problem.[2]

The purpose of this paper is to examine some characteristics of suicidal individuals and to discuss evaluation and treatment approaches and the need for consultation when suicidal crises arise. The professional activity described took place at the Los Angeles Suicide Prevention Center.[3]

[1] Sam M. Heilig and David J. Klugman, "The Social Worker in a Suicide Prevention Center," *Social Work Practice, 1963* (New York: Columbia University Press, 1963).

[2] Normal L. Farberow and Edwin S. Schneidman, eds., *The Cry For Help* (New York: McGraw-Hill Book Co., 1961). *See also* Louis I. Dublin, *Suicide: A Sociological and Statistical Study* (New York: Ronald Press, 1963).

[3] Robert E. Litman, MD, Edwin S. Schneidman, and Norman L. Farberow, "Los Angeles Suicide Prevention Center," *American Journal of Psychiatry*, Vol. 117, No. 12 (June 1961), pp. 1083–1087. The Suicide Prevention Center has been supported by grants from the National Institute of Mental Health, administered through the University of Southern California School of Medicine.

Reprinted from *Social Work*, Vol. 10, No. 4 (October, 1965), pp. 43–50, with permission of the authors and the National Association of Social Workers.

Reaction to Crisis

A striking aspect of suicidal people is that they do not form a homogeneous group. They come from a broad spectrum of different life situations and are not seen as similar in personality. Some are stable people with roots in family and community life, while others lead unstable lives, riddled with failure in all their interpersonal dealings. All these people, however, share in common the condition of being in a serious life crisis. They are no longer able to sweep their feelings under the rug of indifference and denial. They must face their feelings of hopelessness, helplessness, and dependency. Most commonly their symptoms are those of a severe depressive syndrome–sleep disorder, appetite loss, and psychomotor retardation. Often there are disorganized activity states with exaggerated tension, perturbation, and pan-anxiety.

The crisis may or may not be related to specific life stresses. Such events as a divorce or the death of a loved one, financial loss, or sudden legal involvements may trigger suicidal concerns. In a number of suicidal people, however, there is no discernible precipitating stress. Rather, there seems to have been a slow, steady loss of the ability to function adaptively. With these people there is an erosion process under way such that their roots in life are gradually pulled loose. Relatives, friends, lawyers, helping people, and agencies become alienated and unable to help.

In a suicidal crisis there is a radical change in the person's view of himself and his relationships with others. This often shows itself as an increase in stereotyped perceptions, i.e., it is difficult for people in a suicidal crisis to generate new ideas, feelings, or plans without help from others. A suicidal person is often severely constricted in thinking about his problems. He has so little perspective that the past seems forgotten and the future is unimaginable. His view of the present is rigidly confined to a small number of alternative behaviors of which suicide is one. The following case illustrates this point.

Mr. A, a 38-year-old married man, was referred to the center because of suicidal threats. He had been employed as an aircraft mechanic on the same job for twelve years and had led a quiet, stable life until his wife of ten years had left him in order to be free to see other men. They were not divorced and neither of them wanted to effect a complete separation. Periodically Mrs. A returned to him, contrite about having left, and each time he welcomed her return. However, his disgust with himself and unconscious anger toward her grew as the returns and separations continued. It was noted that he was acutely agitated and depressed, had lost weight, slept very little, and had suffered acute psychological distress. He was about to give up his job, which in the past had provided major satisfactions for him. His conception of his situation was that he could not continue to live with his wife on the present basis but he could not give her up. He loved

her and she loved him, but she was now confused and hurting him unintentionally. He hoped that, magically, the situation would prove to be a bizarre mistake,
a sort of nightmare. Yet, because of his unbearable anxiety, he could no longer
wait for this resolution. He was aware of wanting to kill Mrs. A and he was acutely
aware of wanting to kill himself.

Mr. A had lost his ability to see himself clearly. The crisis he had entered
distorted his view of who he was, where he had been, and what might happen
in the future. Nothing satisfied him anymore, nor could he achieve satisfactions.
He admitted to feeling helpless and without hope, powerless to change–killing
himself seemed the only solution. The center's staff openly disagreed with his
conclusion of hopelessness, and he was told that because of his depression his
view of himself and his situation was distorted in such a way that realistic alternatives were not available to him. Staff expressed concern about him, pointed
up his need for help, and advised him that there was a good chance that with
professional aid he could regain healthy perspectives. The offer of help was accepted eagerly and he began working on a plan for his recovery. He was seen
briefly each day for a few days, until he entered regular outpatient psychotherapy
at another agency.

Ambivalence about Dying

This case raises another important characteristic of suicidal people. They
are intensely ambivalent about dying.[4] If someone really intended to die,
would he tell others about it who would try to prevent his death? Such
communications may cast doubts on the sincerity of the suicidal person.
Combined with one's own anxieties about helping a suicidal person, these
attitudes impede the helping process. The result is that some suicidal people are not taken seriously, which can tip the balance dangerously toward
suicide.

An appreciation of the ambivalent state of the suicidal person helps to
make sense of behavior that otherwise appears insincere. During such a
crisis, there is an admixture of conflicting feelings. In nearly all cases, regardless of obvious attempts to manipulate other people or dramatic bids
for emotional response from others, there are genuine wishes to die and
to be rid of tension, pain, or confusion. These death-seeking feelings range
from well-thought-out plans to impulsive, erratic outbursts that would be
lethal only through a combination of adverse chance factors.

Often the mixed motives include rescue fantasies as well as wishes to
die. The suicidal person is looking for a rescuer to serve as an alter ego at
a time when his own ego functions are severely impaired. Some of these

[4] Edwin S. Schneidman and Norman L. Farberow, eds., *Clues to Suicide* (New York: McGraw-
Hill Book Co., 1957), chap. 11; and Robert E. Litman, MD, "Emergency Response to Potential
Suicide," *Journal of the Michigan State Medical Society*, Vol. 62, No. 1 (January 1963), pp. 68–72.

rescue wishes are realistic, but many are magical in character; both types influence the demands made on the rescue person. Thus Mr. A recognized realistically that he was unable to resolve his dilemma without help, that he was weakened, and that his suicidal feelings served to communicate this to the center's staff. Unrealistically and magically, he hoped the center would make a sudden change in the present relationship between him and his wife. He wished only for his wife to love and care for him by meeting all his needs. He saw the helping person as an all-powerful figure who entered his life to make sweeping changes for the better.

Finally, to appreciate better the ambivalence associated with suicide the rescuer should guard against basing his feelings and actions primarily on the content of the suicidal person's communications. He may hear: "Leave me alone; I don't want your help," from a person crying out loudly for help. Someone who desperately wants to go to a hospital and be taken care of will say: "I'd rather die before going to the hospital." These statements demonstrate vividly the ambivalence about being helped. This ambivalence is especially acute in the case of suicidal men. Approximately twice as many men as women kill themselves. Although a man may feel emotionally incapacitated, he cannot bear to know that others may recognize this.

Helpful Techniques

Just as there are differences in the personality characteristics of suicidal persons, so are there differences in the degree of suicidal risk, which usually falls into one of three broad categories: mild, moderate, or high. An important part of the work at the Los Angeles Suicide Prevention Center has been to evaluate the degree of suicidal risk of patients referred and then to recommend appropriate treatment modalities. Generally, mild-risk patients can be treated optimally at social work or family service agencies, moderate-risk patients at outpatient psychiatric clinics, and high-risk patients in psychiatric hospitals. The purpose of this section is to describe some helpful evaluative and treatment techniques developed at the center.

TELEPHONE CONTACTS

Ninety-five percent of initial patient contacts begin on the telephone; the rest are walk-ins. These calls range from emergencies to situations of little or no suicidal risk; regardless of initial impression, however, every call is treated seriously. As a defensive or testing maneuver the caller will often begin in a joking or hostile way. Unless this is accepted and understood for what it is (a defense against feelings of inadequacy), the caller may not go on to reveal his real suicidal feelings and an important therapeutic opportunity may be lost.

The initial telephone call is regarded as extremely important.[5] Sometimes it is the center's only contact. Great care is therefore accorded to it. Usually from twenty to forty minutes are spent carefully evaluating the situation, trying to form a positive relationship by moving into the situation rather than away from it. Staff want the caller to learn quickly that they are interested, they wish to help him, and improvement is possible regardless of how desperate he feels. Above all, staff try to instill a feeling of hope, pointing out, for example, that the center has helped many people with similar problems or that together some new alternative way of dealing with his problem may be found.

Specifically, the job on the telephone is to get information, to evaluate the situation—especially the suicidal potential—and to recommend a course of action. This is all done concomitantly and questions are woven in whenever possible at appropriate moments. The aim is to give the caller a therapeutic experience; staff avoid asking for information in a formal, routine way. They do ask for identifying information and request the caller to discuss any current stress he is under. Further, they ask if there is any past suicidal behavior and any history of medical or psychiatric treatment. If there is a "significant other" in the patient's life, his name and telephone number, which can be of crucial importance in an emergency, are requested. Staff talk about suicidal feelings and thoughts openly, having learned that this relieves some of the anxiety the patient feels. Evasiveness or secretiveness about suicidal feelings increase his anxiety and the danger of a suicidal act.

OFFICE INTERVIEWS

In the office staff are able to do a more intensive evaluation of a patient's suicidal potentiality. The following are taken into account: the amount of stress he is under, the symptoms that disturb him, suicidal plan or feelings (in detail), his financial and interpersonal resources, and, finally, his character—that is, whether he had a history of stability or of chronic disorganization and instability. This is usually done in one interview but may be extended to two or more office visits. Staff's attitude throughout is one of interest, encouragement, hope for the patient, and optimism about the eventual outcome. At the conclusion of the interview the patient is asked to complete a shortened form of the Minnesota Mul-

[5] Robert E. Litman, MD, Norman L. Farberow, Edwin S. Schneidman, Sam M. Heilig, and Jan A. Kramer, "Suicide-Prevention Telephone Service," *Journal of the American Medical Association*, Vol. 192, No. 1 (April 5, 1965), pp. 21–25.

tiphasic Personality Inventory, a psychological test consisting of a series of 479 true or false questions, which usually takes about an hour to complete. Selected patients are asked aditionally to fill out a social history form or other research materials. An important aspect of the psychological testing and completion of forms is that it forces the patient to think of himself–past, present, and future–which helps to re-establish his identity in his own mind, a valuable therapeutic assist to anyone in a suicidal crisis.

If there is a spouse or a significant other in the patient's life, that person is asked to come in with him. Often this person is the patient's most valuable resource and it is therefore desirable for him to participate in helping the patient to get through the critical period and then to follow up with recommendations made by the center. The following is an example of work in the office with a middle-aged depressed man.

Mr. R, a 50-year-old married man, was referred by his physician because of severe depression and overt threats of suicide. His son, a 27-year-old police officer, had committed suicide two weeks previously by shooting himself in the temple with his service revolver. He left no note and the motives for his death remained a mystery. Mr. R, who had been depressed before this incident, now felt anxious, tense, unable to concentrate, and nearing exhaustion. He thought of death frequently and expressed a desire to follow in his son's footsteps by shooting himself.

Mr. R. was employed as an equipment maintenance worker, and had been with the same company for twenty-one years. He was a steady worker but he had no hobbies or social life. He and his wife had been married for thirty years, had raised a family, and Mrs. R was now working in order to help with expenses. She was a thin, tense individual who strove to be a good wife but had become more of a mother to her husband. She was sexually frigid.

Mr. R was the sixth of a family of ten children. His father was an alcholic who abused the family. Because of the difficult times, Mr. R quit school after the eighth grade. He became a sporadic alcoholic and at such times was ugly and abusive; he was beaten up on several occasions. He continued to drink after his marriage, but stopped thirteen years ago and has not had a drink since. Mrs. R reported that during the years he drank he was able to shout and express his hostility, but after he stopped he apparently had no satisfactory way of expressing his angry feelings and had become more and more depressed.

Mr. R was treated at the center with psychotherapy and antidepressant medication, and his wife was asked to come in for supportive therapy. His depression and suicidal thinking did not abate, and it was concluded that hospitalization would be necessary. When Mr. R was told, he refused to submit to this and threatened to do away with himself first. After careful evaluation of the risk involved, staff decided to continue to see him as an outpatient, but with a focus on the need for hospitalization. After two more weeks of concentrated effort with him, the center enabled Mr. R to accept its recommendation and enter a psychiatric hospital. In the hospital he responded well to a series of electroshock treatments, dropped his suicidal ideation, and was then able to return to work.

Mr. R was rated a high suicide risk based on his age and sex, high stress, depression, and suicidal preoccupation. The center's decision to try to treat him at first as an outpatient was based in part on the stability of his work and married life and the fact that he had never had a previous try at outpatient psychiatric treatment.

Mr. R is representative of many suicidal persons seen at the center. Under the brunt of some overwhelming life stress, they begin to experience distressing physical or mental symptoms that sharply heighten their discomfort. If in addition they happen to be emotionally constricted or immobilized with respect to some potentially constructive relief-bringing action, they may develop a severe depression, fears of becoming mentally ill, or extreme tension and anxiety. Under these conditions of near-intolerable affect, they begin to consider suicide as a relief or escape from their tensions and confusions or as a final resolution of their problems. This is a most critical time for these patients, a time when they are likely to request help. With help available and with someone responding appropriately, the suicidal risk usually subsides within a short period of time.

Suicidal Crisis Consultations

One of the special features of emergency psychotherapy at the Los Angeles Suicide Prevention Center is the emphasis placed by the staff on frequent consultations. These are informal case discussions conducted in a spirit of rapid communication, mutual support, and teamwork, often leading to continuous collaboration by several therapists. The purpose of this section is to describe this type of consultation as a specific therapeutic device for counteracting certain serious technical problems often associated with suicidal crises. Among these are the prevailing sense of urgency and responsibility, the required personal and emotional involvement by the therapist, and the contagious quality of the patient's panic and pessimism.

The stresses may induce problem reactions in the therapist. Among these are overwhelming affects such as anxiety, anger, or hopelessness, constriction of thought, impulsive actions, or complete immobilization. Frequent informal consultations tend to prevent panic and build up the therapist's self- confidence. Fears of overlooking vital points are allayed. Consultations encourage imaginative solutions to problems and help the therapists preserve their feelings of personal identity and sense of humor even though they participate sympathetically in many frustrating interpersonal transactions.

REASONS FOR CONSULTATIONS

Cases that are unusual, associated with legal complications, bring the clinic into conflict with other community agencies, or involve a high suicide risk should have consultations. In evaluating high suicide danger for the patient, probably the best single indicator is the therapist's awareness of his own anxiety. Therapists feel some anxiety at some point with nearly every case. Failure to experience anxiety while interacting with a suicidal person, whether owing to poor imagination or excessively strong defenses against anxiety, disqualifies a therapist for work in the center. Therapists learn various strategies and techniques for dealing with suicidal persons and, by taking appropriate actions, keep their anxiety at levels suitable for effective work.

The consultation is probably the most usual device for constructively handling anxiety in the therapist, who should be alert enough to recognize when he needs help. For instance, when a therapeutic interaction has such impact on the therapist that his reactions spill over into his private life he needs a consultation quickly.

The therapist's anxiety may be focused in one or more of several possible areas. He may be having difficulty in understanding, evaluating, or diagnosing the personality or reactions of the patient and his relatives. "Do these symptoms mean schizophrenia?" "He says he still enjoys sexual relations. Does this contradict the possibility of suicide?" "Do you think his wife can be trusted to keep an eye on him over the weekend?"

Many problems involve decisions about direct action. "Must he go to the hospital immediately or can hospitalization wait a day or two?" "How can I get her to come to the clinic?" "To which psychiatric agency should this patient be referred?"

Sometimes the therapist feels he is in over his depth. "Whenever I talk to this patient she seems to get worse!" "I'm afraid to let her leave the office because she might hurt her baby!" "Have you ever heard of someone who liked to kill stray cats?" "This man hired a woman to tie him up and choke him into unconsciousness!"

SPIRIT

The spirit of the consultation, which has been derived historically from the original approach of the center's staff to patients, is probably more important than the content. In the first phase of the center, patients were selected one at a time and studied carefully by a team consisting of a psychiatrist, psychologist, and psychiatric social worker. The patient was nominally the responsibility of the psychiatrist but, in practice, whichever member of the team came to have the longest and most intense relationship with the patient took over the practical responsibility for the therapeutic contact and was referred to as the therapist of record. In later years, as the case load increased, the practice of team collaboration on each case could not be maintained nor was it necessary. Consultations continue the spirit of collaboration. Both the therapist and consultant are members of a team and are responsible for the patient's welfare.

There is a great difference between supervision and consultation. The act of supervising is essentially the direction and critical evaluation of instruction as, for instance, in a school or teaching clinic. To supervise is to inspect with authority. To consult is to confer together, to take counsel, to interact and consider, and to give advice leading to action.

The formal case conference is designed to stimulate the entire staff, to formulate research problems, and to continue the education of all, but often adds extra problems, extra speculations, and extra possibilities for the therapist to consider. By contrast, the informal consultation aims to clarify the problem, reach a decision, and motivate toward action.

The center feels strongly that the consultant must share in the responsibility for the outcome of the case and must feel personally involved in the consultation as the therapist must feel personally involved with the patient. One of the most important functions of the consultant is to point out situations when it is time for the therapist to let the patient go. Sometimes correct tactics require the consultant to take the patient over from the original therapist and become the patient's new therapist.

The consultation should start with a statement by the therapist of the reasons he feels anxious and his idea of the goal of the consultation. For example:

> The problem is that this girl is 17 and a minor, so I don't see how we can keep on seeing her here, without consent from her parents. But she won't tell us her family name or address, and she says she will break off with us and commit suicide if we try to find out.

> I'm afraid this man will not follow our recommendations for more psychotherapy. How can we keep him motivated for treatment now that he has come out of his depression?

> Here is a 50-year-old man, pretty much alone and friendless. The only thing that keeps him going is work, but he is very depressed now and I have to decide whether to insist that he go immediately to the hospital.

The therapist should then give a brief case report. The consultant listens to make sure that nothing vital has been omitted and tries to visualize the circumstances of the problem and imagine possible solutions. Finally, a course of action is determined. In the first example, it was decided that the adolescent patient would be seen for a few more interviews and that her parents would be involved as staff's relationship with her strengthened and she could better accept this necessity. In the second example, it was decided to bring the patient's wife to the clinic, acquaint her with the problem of insufficient motivation in her husband, and try to use her to increase his motivation. In the last example, it was decided to see the patient daily as an outpatient for a while in the hope that he would improve. If he did not improve, he would be sent to the hospital.

Emergency consultations are characterized by a lack of formal structure. They may take place in offices, halls, or at lunch. They may involve two or more staff people of the same or different disciplines. For example, the psychiatrist asked a psychiatric social worker where to refer a patient who only spoke Hungarian (the International Institute, a casework agency for foreign-speaking, was suggested). A clinical psychologist asked a social worker to call a patient's brother to check on additional information about the husband who had left her. In relating the case history, he realized that several important aspects were still unclear to him. A social worker talked for an hour with a discouraged starlet who was going to take an overdose of pills. Next morning he received a letter of gratitude and a nude picture, as well as a promise to come in for an interview. Naturally, he requested some consultation with his colleagues before proceeding with the therapy. The following case was presented by a social worker to the chief psychiatrist for consultation.

Mr. C, a 32-year-old steel worker, was threatening to commit suicide in reaction to a divorce action by his wife. The referral was initiated by the wife's employer and she joined him on the telephone. No one knew of Mr. C's present whereabouts but he had been trying to reach his wife at her place of work for the past two days, threatening suicide. The wife was afraid of him because of his previous violence and did not want to see him. She and her employer wondered if they could get him to contact the center by some sort of trick. The social worker expressed great concern about Mr. C, who sounded to him like the kind of person who was capable of acting on his impulses and of committing suicide in this context.

The consultant felt the situation was serious and suggested that an appointment be given the wife. Mrs. C was advised that the next time Mr. C called her place of employment he should be told she was going to the center and should be given the center's number to call. Mr. C did call, was referred to the center, and after a long conversation came into the office. The social worker interviewed him and then asked the consultant to talk with him also.

Mr. C was a muscular ex-fighter, former captain of his high school football team, who had always earned a good living as a steel worker but had had bad luck with his two marriages. He was not an alcoholic or chronically unstable, but one received the impression that he was impulsive and had perhaps too many fights—there may have been a trace of brain damage. It was known that he had taken a large overdose of sleeping tablets two weeks before, for which he had been hospitalized, but he had demanded his release from the hospital. He found it hard to put things into words and could not explain exactly why he felt compelled to commit suicide. He felt that he would have to do something if he did not get to see his wife; that something would be to kill himself.

Two things were picked up by the social worker and the consultant: (1) The patient felt warmly toward his mother and father in another city and was concerned about the effect of his suicide on them. (2) His suicide threat represented a need for some sort of action. The possibility of substitute action was emphasized with him. After consultation and discussion, it was decided that Mr. C would return to his home town. A long-distance telephone call was made to his parents and his father took a plane to come and meet him.

It can be seen from this case that at each point where doubt existed the consultation helped resolve the indecision so that the participants could move toward further action and resolution of the problem.

Summary

In order to facilitate recognition of suicidal persons the following common characteristics are noted: (1) an objective and/or subjective breakdown in coping abilities accompanied by feelings of collapse and helplessness, (2) severely constricted perceptions of themselves and their difficulties, (3) acute ambivalence about dying and living and receiving help. Various techniques have been developed at the Los Angeles Suicide Prevention Center for evaluating suicide risk and recommending appropriate action. These techniques have the effect of interrupting death thoughts and suggesting action directed toward continued living. Therapists work under special stress owing to the prevailing sense of urgency and great responsibility, the required personal involvement, and the contagious quality of the patient's panic and pessimism. Frequent informal consultations are mandatory as a technical device to maintain the therapists' morale and keep anxiety at an optimal level. These informal case discussions are conducted in a spirit of rapid communication, mutual support, and collaborative teamwork.

THE UNMARRIED MOTHER

CHAPTER 73

Reconsiderations in Casework Treatment of the Unmarried Mother

Herbert S. Strean

An historical overview of social work's philosophy about and orientation to the unmarried mother yields several sequential trends. Until the early 1920's virtually the sole concern of the social agency was the unmarried mother's infant and help to the mother herself was rarely considered. As dynamic psychiatry made its inroads and began to influence social work's thinking and activity, the unmarried mother began to be appreciated in her own right and the purposiveness of her behavior was pondered. With the fairly recent advent of ego psychology and the social sciences, the unmarried mother's complete role network–her relationships to various subsystems, e.g., ethnic group, kinship ties, and so on–has become part of the caseworker's psychosocial diagnosis and enriched his treatment plan for her and her child.[1]

Concomitant with the impact of sociology, anthropology, and social psychology on social work has been the intensification of the profession's sense of social responsibility.[2] The cluster of economic, social, psychological, and health variables that are now seen as impinging on the unmar-

---

[1] *See* Jane K. Goldsmith, "The Unmarried Mother's Search for Standards," *Social Casework*, Vol. 48, No. 2 (February 1957), pp. 69–73; and Vera Shlakman, "Unmarried Parenthood: An Approach to Social Policy," *Social Casework*, Vol. 47, No. 8 (October 1966), pp. 494–502.

[2] Herbert H. Aptekar, "Education for Social Responsibility," *Journal of Education for Social Work*, Vol. 2, No. 2 (Fall 1966), pp. 5–11.

Reprinted from *Social Work*, Vol. 13, No. 4 (October, 1968), pp. 91–100, with permission of the author and the National Association of Social Workers.

ried, and health variables that are now seen as impinging on the unmarried mother have pointed to a more pressing need for the provision of community resources.[3] While the social planner and policy-maker have presented valid arguments reiterating that effective casework alone cannot be considered the complete answer to the unmarried mother's plight,[4] as Perlman has pointed out, casework is not dead and individualized services will probably always be necessary for some people even if optimum provision of resources could be achieved.[5]

It is incumbent on caseworkers not only to locate where they may legitimately offer their expertise in helping the unmarried mother, but constantly to scrutinize their method and avoid the danger to which Kadushin has pointed, namely, the acceptance of traditional practices in lieu of tested theory.[6] It is the purpose of this paper to evaluate some of the conventional diagnostic hypotheses and classical treatment plans that have evolved in casework with the unmarried mother; certain modifications in casework interventions will be proposed that may more accurately meet certain of the unmarried mother's maturational needs and more expediently enhance certain aspects of her psychosocial functioning.

Review of the Literature

Analysis of the past two decades of social work literature reveals that periodicals in the field have been replete with data on the unmarried mother. Most of the articles have aimed at sensitizing social workers to the subtleties and intricacies of the unmarried mother's personality and/or enriching interventions for her. Virtually every paper or book has begun with the axiom that a multitude of factors contribute to a young woman's becoming pregnant out of wedlock.

Until recently, the search for causes has utilized the metapsychological framework of psychoanalysis and the theme pervading most of the literature in the 1940's and '50's was that the unmarried mother had a conflicted relationship with her own mother and was improperly nurtured at early levels of development. In addition to being the recipient of fragmented mothering, she was seen as having often experienced her father

---

[3] Martin Wright, "Comprehensive Services for Adolescent Unwed Mothers," *Children*, Vol. 13, No. 5 (September–October 1966), pp. 171–176.

[4] *See* Aptekar, *op. cit.*

[5] Helen Harris Perlman, "Casework Is Dead," *Social Casework*, Vol. 48, No. 1 (January 1967), pp. 22–25.

[6] Alfred Kadushin, "The Knowledge Base of Social Work," in Alfred J. Kahn, ed., *Issues in American Social Work* (New York: Columbia University Press, 1959), pp. 39–79.

as withdrawn and cold.[7] Common to most of these young women has been an alleged narcissistic character structure, i.e., the girls have been described as extremely preoccupied with their own infantile wishes, which they have had to discharge impulsively. The baby she conceived has frequently been considered to be narcissistic extension of the unmarried mother and her wish to mother the baby seen as similar to psychologically mothering herself.[8]

The level of ego development of most of these girls has been viewed as "infantile" or "primitive." "They also feel very deprived or depraved."[9] According to most authors, they have not developed mature methods of resolving conflicts and are so self-absorbed that they cannot love others.[10] The young woman has often reported a feeling of being an "ugly duckling" most of her life and conceiving a baby has been in part an attempt to make restitution for her own defects.[11]

The unmarried mother as observed by most psychoanalytically and social work-oriented professionals appears to manifest severe superego lacunae and therefore has been considered delinquent in internalizing societal norms and standards. Not having witnessed in her own home the positive values inherent in a wholesome husband-wife or parent-child relationship, she has been declared incapable of setting standards for her own behavior.[12] Often she has come to the social agency during her fourth or fifth month of pregnancy, seeking specific services; she has tended to withdraw from contact when a plan for the baby has been concluded. Few have taken kindly to the idea of regular casework sessions and if the client has appeared well motivated for continuing treatment, she has been viewed as suspect. The unmarried mother has frequently been described as resistant, defensive, and unresponsive to treatment, usually demanding immediate pragmatic solutions and becoming angry if these are not forthcoming.[13]

The treatment of choice for unmarried mothers has been an ongoing relationship with a female caseworker. Often deserted by the putative

[7] See A. Ferdinand Bonan, "Psychoanalytic Implications in Treating Unmarried Mothers with Narcissistic Character Structures," Social Casework, Vol. 44, No. 6 (June 1963), pp. 323–330; and Joseph E. Lifschutz, Theodosia B. Stewart, and Ada M. Harrison, "Psychiatric Consultation in the Public Assistance Agency," Social Casework, Vol. 39, No. 1 (January 1958), pp. 3–8.

[8] Bonan, op cit.; Jane G. Judge, "Casework with the Unmarried Mother in a Family Agency," Social Casework, Vol. 32, No. 1 (January 1951), pp. 7–14.

[9] Bonan, op. cit.

[10] Lifschutz, Stewart, and Harrison, op. cit.

[11] Judge, op. cit.

[12] Goldsmith, op. cit.

[13] Rose Bernstein, "The Maternal Role in the Treatment of Unmarried Mothers," Social Work, Vol. 8, No. 1 (January 1963), pp. 58–65; and Bernstein, "Are We Still Stereotyping the Unmarried Mother?" Social Work, Vol. 5, No. 3 (July 1960), pp. 22–28.

father and having experienced emotional abandonment by her own mother, the client allegedly needs "a motherly person who will serve as a refuge during a time of stress."[14] A woman caseworker, it has been concluded, can most appropriately serve as "a healthy object for identification, making it possible [for the client] to accept herself as a woman."[15] Since four out of five unmarried mothers who come to a social agency give the baby up for adoption, it has been alleged that for the mother to give her baby to a woman caseworker is like "making up" with her own mother and thus finalizing a bad experience.[16] (Of the unmarried mothers who do not come to agencies, many do not give their babies up for adoption; of this group, most—especially young Negro women—turn the baby over to their own mothers.)[17]

During the last several years the social work field–as reflected in its literature–has slightly altered its focus on the ummarried mother. Instead of concentrating almost exclusively on the client's psychological motives and internal dynamics, the field has been more preoccupied with unmarried motherhood as a social problem, shown more concern for the culture and subculture in which the young woman resides, considered the significant others in her environment, and been quite sensitive to the social values impinging on her.[18] The Negro unmarried mother in particular has received much consideration; she has been reported to be more indifferent and less sensitive to the stigma of illegitimacy because of a greater tolerance of it in her subculture.[19] Although frequently turning over the care of her child to her own mother, the Negro unmarried mother is nonetheless ascribed "an exceptional maternal capacity" and a sexually fertile constitution.[20]

Although the increments to social work's knowledge of the unmarried mother have been substantial and despite valiant attempts on the part of many skilled workers to involve the client in a meaningful casework relationship, as Friedman stated recently, "We are still powerless to alter the script."[21] These clients frequently remain resistant to social work intervention, in many cases seek service but not understanding, usually do not continue treatment after the baby is born, and it has not been uncommon

---

[14] Peter Blos, *On Adolescence* (New York: Free Press, 1961), pp. 27–28.

[15] Lifschutz, Stewart, and Harrison, *op. cit.*, p. 50.

[16] Helen L. Friedman, "The Mother-Daughter Relationship: Its Potential in Treatment of Young Unwed Mothers," *Social Casework*, Vol. 47, No. 8 (October 1966), pp. 502–507.

[17] Wright, *op. cit.*

[18] *Ibid.*; Shlakman, *op. cit.*; and Sidney Furie, "Birth Control and the Lower-Class Unmarried Mother," *Social Work*, Vol. 11, No. 1 (January 1966), pp. 42–49.

[19] Bernstein, "The Maternal Role in the Treatment of Unmarried Mothers," and "Are We Still Stereotyping the Unmarried Mother?"

[20] Bernstein, "The Maternal Role in the Treatment of Unmarried Mothers."

[21] *Op. cit.*

for them to repeat the same experience that brought them to the agency in the first place.[22]

Revised Diagnosis

Re-examination of the literature reported and experimentation in a few selected agencies in the New York and New Jersey area have led to a revised diagnostic picture of the modal unmarried mother. The treatment plan that has evolved in light of this enriched understanding will be presented both theoretically and by case illustrations.

During the year 1966–67 the writer was permitted to read the case records and/or discuss with the caseworker involved procedures utilized in the treatment of fifteen unmarried mothers seen in four different public and private agencies. Seven of these cases were treated either exclusively by a male worker or by a male conjointly with a female caseworker. The remainder were all seen by female workers and served as a control group for this modest pilot study.

Although this study involved a small number of cases and lacked many of the requirements of a rigorous experimental design, our findings prompted us, nevertheless, to question the traditional view of the unmarried mother, namely, that the answer to the riddle of her behavior resides to a large extent in her relationship to her own mother. Careful review and analysis of many cases illustrated in the literature and of those in treatment at the agencies that the researchers selected at random to visit induced us to hypothesize that the aforementioned conventional view regarding the etiology of the unmarried mother's dynamics provides too narrow a focus and results in a premature closure of her dynamic picture as well as of the casework plan for her.

It appears necessary in light of this study to reconsider seriously the entire family gestalt to which the unmarried mother relates. More often than not, the client is not merely caught in the web of an ambivalent, cold mother-daughter relationship, but frequently has been a pawn in a tempestuous marital relationship. More than occasionally, her birth has stimulated much rivalry between her parents, with the mother clinging to her and the father behaving quite seductively. It is frequently the father's seductiveness that has overstimulated her immature ego and aroused powerful sexual fantasies with which she has found it extremely difficult to cope. As a result, it is not uncommon to find in the histories of unmarried mothers strong prudishness, puritanical attitudes, and other forms of reaction formation defensiveness.[23]

[22] Frances H. Scherz, "'Taking Sides' in the Unmarried Mother's Conflict," *Social Casework*, Vol. 28, No. 2 (February 1947), pp. 57–60.
[23] Bonan, *op. cit.*

As the power struggle between the girl's parents mounts and she attempts to deal with her divided loyalties, identifying for a time with her mother and then for another period with her father, the potential unmarried mother gradually finds it more and more difficult to fuse and integrate maternal and paternal introjects. She is never quite certain whether she is male or female, and is almost incessantly flirting with each possibility. As adolescence approaches and the need "to prove" herself assumes even more important dimensions, sexual promiscuity becomes one avenue by which to reassure herself of her tenuous femininity.[24]

Quite frequently the girl's parents have separated or become divorced, with the father leaving the home altogether. His absence activates Oedipal and incestuous longings, but because of the girl's recognition of her mother's angry and vitriolic feelings toward her husband, she has to repress and suppress her attachment to her father; she cannot discuss her distress with her mother because of the latter's bias. It is perhaps being left alone with a mother who the young girl feels has deprived her of a father that may account in great measure for what has been referred to as a "pathological and ambivalent mother- daughter relationship." Possibly it is the father's withdrawal that may arouse in the client the self-image of being ugly, "deprived and depraved"—deprived not so much of pregential and pre-Oedipal love from a mother, but of Oedipal contact with a father; depraved not so much because of a poor maternal object with whom to identify, but because she has been overwhelmed with sexual fantasies and can no longer cathect them in the direction of her sexually exciting but unavailable father. Schmideberg has pointed out: "Many girls became promiscuous during wartime because their fathers were away."[25]

Unwed Mother's Mother

The author does not wish to negate the tremendous influence of the mother in the unmarried mother's development, but rather to appreciate the mother even more—she is not merely an ambivalent object but a figure who enacts many roles and who is relating to many significant others in the client's environment. All of her interactions and transactions are witnessed by her daughter and affect the latter's self-image and attitude toward the world.

In attempting to comprehend more thoroughly the unmarried mother's own mother, many life histories of the latter were studied. It was found that frequently the mother was recapitulating her own life story with her

[24] Blos, *op. cit.*

[25] Melitta Schmideberg, "Psychiatric-Social Factors in Young Unmarried Mothers," *Social Casework,* Vol. 32, No. 1 (January 1951), pp. 3–7.

daughter. Often the victim herself of cold, withdrawn, and punitive fathering, she appeared to arrange to live vicariously through her daughter as the latter subtly but sexually interacted with her father. However, out of jealousy and competition with her daughter, who was achieving what she could not, the mother threw roadblocks into the very dyad that she herself had initiated. This does make her an ambivalent object for identification. However, the ambivalent feelings that the unmarried mother feels toward her own mother are nurtured by her fantasies toward her father, which she cannot share with her mother but must rather keep hidden from her. It is these forbidden and secretive sexual impulses toward the father that are often acted out in a clandestine affair; because they are forbidden, they are expressed in a way that will bring punishment.

What should be emphasized is that the girl's resentment toward her mother arose not so much because the latter failed to nurture her properly at early developmental levels, but because the mother has distorted heterosexual attitudes that can only intensify the young girl's conflict. Also of tremendous importance are the client's conflicting feelings toward her father, whom she fantasies as a sexual partner but fears as too engulfing. She is contemptuous of her father because he has not responded maturely as a husband to his wife. If he had been a responsible husband, the girl reasons, then he would have been free enough to relate to his daughter as a growing girl rather than primarily as a sexual object. He had become simultaneously too attractive and too dangerous to his daughter and her developing ego cannot withstand the excruciating dilemma. Therefore, the baby that the unmarried mother conceives is not only the baby that she wishes to be, but often is the fantasied outcome of incest. Is it any wonder that after the product of incest has been born the client does not want to face her mother figure, the caseworker? Her incestuous guilt is too overwhelming, so that at best she turns the baby over to the mother figure to whom she feels it rightfully belongs, and leaves!

In the majority of cases reviewed it was found that when the father withdrew, the mother-daughter relationship, although desired as a refuge by the daughter, became a battleground with both mother and daughter appearing as two immature girls. The mother was seen by her daughter as unable to provide sexual guidance or advice about men or to cater to her maturing sexual interest and questions. Therefore, it has tentatively been concluded that when the young woman appears infantile, demanding, and hyperdependent in her early casework interviews, this occurs not so much because of a fixation at primitive and infantile levels, but as a regression to earlier modes of satisfaction because present conflicts are too overwhelming and the current environment is not sufficiently supportive.

Most of the mothers studied viewed their teen-age daughters as a potpourri of unintegrated conflicts and impulses with whom a relationship was too burdensome. In several cases the mother herself often turned to sexual affairs as a refuge, frequently looking for "fatherly-type men." As one mother, speaking on her daughter's behalf as well as her own, said: "Neither of us had a good father so we thought we were 'punks' as girls. Getting a guy to 'knock us up' somehow tells us that at least for a while we're O.K." However, because the self-hating impulse has remained active throughout, these women frequently chose men who left them or, if they remained, became insensitive and infantile father figures.

The absence of the father altogether or the presence of a father who deprives his daughter of the satisfactions of being a girl (and not just a sexual object) seems to appear where unmarried motherhood occurs most frequently, namely, among lower socioeconomic Negro families. The girl during the course of her development has usually had some relationships with older men that have frequently been tantalizing, but the consistent unavailability of a mature father figure is ubiquitous. Certainly the host of attendant economic and other social variables inherent in the Negro constellation should not or cannot be minimized; it is, nonetheless, a virtual truism that unmarried motherhood is prevalent in circumstances in which the father is unavailable.[26]

While the importance of the father in a girl's psychosocial development has in general been relatively undefined and the effects of paternal deprivation largely unspecified, we are beginning to become sensitized to the uniquely paternal contributions necessary for a girl's development as she shifts from primary to secondary dependency. As Forrest has pointed out, for a female to be fulfilled as a person and a woman, the father's presence from infancy through childhood, girlhood, and adolescence aids and abets psychological growth.[27]

How Help Is Offered

Because it has been tentatively hypothesized that part of the etiology of the unmarried mother's difficulty is the absence of mature fathering, that the quest for "pre-Oedipal mothering" on her part stems more from a regression to old modes of functioning than from a fixation, and that the client's mother is so flooded with anxiety of her own that renders her incapable of meeting her daughter's maturational needs–especially the need to see her mother function in mature heterosexual relationships–it is proposed that casework intervention must seek to meet these unmet needs.

Is it not possible that the way the unmarried mother experiences casework help as it is presently structured for her may recapitulate the ugly

[26] Wright, *op. cit.*

[27] Tess Forrest, "Paternal Roots of Female Character Development," *Contemporary Psychoanalysis*, Vol. 3, No. 1 (Fall 1966), pp. 21–31.

experiences that brought her to the agency in the first place? More than nine times out of ten she is confronted by a female worker who initially wishes to "understand" her rather than immediately give her tangibles, such as advice and information about the baby's delivery and the external factors attending it. What the client usually wants from the caseworker initially, namely, informative advice, is what her mother could not give her. When her initial requests are subjected to study rather than immediately met, she does become "demanding and hostile." If the hostility is not seen as a defensive response to the hurt and anguish the client is feeling because no one cares about her, the kind of power struggle that transpired with her own mother might ensue with the caseworker.

Another feature of the way help is offered to the unmarried mother that repeats past traumas is the absence of a man in the treatment plan. Occasionally the putative father is interviewed if available and sometimes the client's own father is approached, but most social agencies working with unmarried mothers, especially group residences, have a completely female atmosphere. While the less traditional agencies and more modern caseworkers have inaugurated casework plans that include the few men in the girl's life (and with good results), it is the author's finding that this is more the exception than the rule.[28] When a male worker, trained or untrained, becomes part of the treatment plan and if in addition signficant men in the girl's environment are sought out, the casework experience for the unmarried mother comes closer to meeting her psychosocial deprivations. Because, according to the writer's data, the most fundamental lacuna in the unmarried mother's ego development has been the lack of men and women working together in her behalf, it is this latter experience, if planfully utilized as part of work with her, that can improve the casework results appreciably.

Suggested Treatment Model

In several cases by plan and in some cases by accident the following structured approach has been found to be most beneficial in casework treatment of the unmarried mother:

1. Because the unmarried mother comes to an agency in a state of crisis and panic that has been precipitated by her illegitimate pregnancy and frequently exacerbated by her mother's anxiety, her father's withdrawal, and the putative father's emotional and often physical isolation, she will inevitably conduct herself in a regressed, infantile, and demanding manner. The female caseworker, rather than making interpretations about the

---

[28] Francis L. Feldman and Francis H. Scherz, *Family Social Welfare: Helping Troubled Families* (New York: Atherton Press, 1967), p. 386.

client's behavior or asking questions in an attempt to clarify her motives, should try to answer her questions immediately. Initially, information should not be provided about agency practice and policy unless the client asks for this; rather, she should be given information that *she wants for herself.* As the client is "given to" in terms of what she wants, the worker is gradually experienced as the nurturing mother who has her psychological daughter's best interests in mind and is genuinely relating to them.

2. With the caseworker's demonstration of concern about matters pertaining to the client's physical care–who the doctor will be, diet, medical prescriptions, appropriate exercises, details of the delivery, and so on–the client usually begins to become more interested in the worker as a person. As a result, she begins to share with the worker the experiences that brought her to the agency, her confusion regarding sexual matters, and her debilitating experiences with her parents. She often comes up with a statment or question that disguises, yet implies, a cry for help as if casework treatment were to begin only now (although contacts have transpired for several weeks). The wish for help is usually couched in statements about her poor self-image and her desire to be rid of it. As the caseworker relates to the client's formulation of her own problems and concerns, the idea of treatment or counseling can be discussed meaningfully and nondefensively by both worker and client.

3. At this stage a male worker should be introduced to the client for counseling. The rationale for this proposal should be explained to the client as follows: "I agree that your relationships with men have caused you a lot of difficulty. I think, therefore, that it would be helpful for you if you had a male caseworker. As you learn to get along with him, I'm quite sure that you'll be able to get along with many other men in the future."

The client initially interprets this proposal to mean that the female caseworker will be "dropping out of the picture." The caseworker should explain: "On the contrary, I'll be around whenever you need me. You are still concerned about doctors, nurses, hospital visits, and the like, and I'm here to help you with these concerns." Invariably, after two or three interviews the client's response is euphoric and ecstatic: "You mean I'll have you both. That's great!"

4. The opportunity to work with a male worker and not lose the female worker offers the client the opportune situation of which she has been deprived. Given a nonseductive male and a mother figure who is genuinely concerned increases the self-image positively, mobilizes previously intact ego functions, and frequently enables the client to reflect genuinely on herself and her interaction with her environment, present and past.

5. The triadic relationship continues after the birth of the infant and as long as the client needs it. In addition, if the girl's father, mother, or the baby's putative father can be part of the treatment plan, the client feels far from alone but instead enjoys "all the attention I am getting."

6. From time to time, and dictated by the client's needs and requests, both male and female workers see her together. The rationale for this maneuver is explained as follows: "We want you to have the opportunity really to experience a man and a woman working together in your behalf."

Experimentation has been done not only with trained workers but with untrained workers as well. Given appropriate supervision, it has been found that persons with only undergraduate education can adapt to the cited approach, provided it is well structured in advance so that salient client responses can be anticipated and appropriate interventions timed accordingly. The six steps enumerated appear to offer the client an emotionally corrective experience with an unambivalent mother figure and a nonseductive father figure. The treatment is designed to meet the developmental needs of the unmarried mother–to feed her when she needs emotional nourishment, to educate her when she needs information and knowledge, and to offer her fatherly admiration and maternal tenderness when these are required.

Case Illustrations

Miss A, a young Negro woman of 31, had five illegitimate pregnancies. Living in a housing project and on welfare, she was frequently drunk, often depressed, and managed her home and children with extremely limited care and discipline. The management of the project sent a female case aide—an untrained worker—to "see what could be done" before processing an eviction.

The worker found Miss A's house extremely untidy, her children poorly cared for, and Miss A in the third month of her sixth pregnancy. The case aide told Miss A that the management of the project had suggested that she be seen, but before the worker could finish her opening remarks, the client bellowed: "Oh, they want to throw me out because they don't like the way I keep the house!" The worker looked around and said calmly: "I'm sure things are very difficult for you. You must have it very rough." The client spent the next half hour talking about how her children were a burden to her, that meeting their physical needs was impossible, how difficult it was to make ends meet financially, and that the only pleasure she got once in a while was "a little sex and a little drink." The worker remarked that she could understand how sex and drinking could be her only pleasures but wondered if there was anything that she, the worker, could do to bring her some pleasure. Miss A pointed to the children's clothes and her poor furniture, and mentioned that she had limited time for herself. The worker immediately responded: "I'll get in touch with a few places and people and see what can be done."

The worker did get in touch with the department of welfare and other agencies in the community in order to supply Miss A with some of the tangibles she requested. Therefore, with some physical needs met—clothes for the children and mother, mattresses and beds, and a volunteer for some babysitting—the client began, in her second interview, to talk about her current pregnancy and previous ones as well. She said that she knew "damn well that I don't appeal to men" and that all of her sexual affairs turned out to be one-night stands. When the worker took note of the client's feelings of depreciation vis-à-vis men, and said: "You think that the only reason men would have anything to do with you is to go to bed, don't you?" Miss A tearfully reported how she remembered as a little girl wishing that a boy friend of her mother's who intermittently visited the house "could be my father." She then spent some time talking about her wish for a father who "would have really cared about me" but how her mother "just didn't meet up with a good man to live with."

As Miss A continued to talk about her feelings of deprivation in her heterosexual relationships, the worker gradually introduced the subject of a male worker, who was part of the same social service department of the housing project. Miss A did not ask for any explanation of the entrance of the male worker into the situation but seemed to sense the rationale behind the introduction and merely said: "Great!"

In contrast to the manner in which Miss A usually cared for the house, the male worker at his first interview found it to be extremely tidy and the children and Miss A well groomed. This held true at subsequent visits. While Miss A continued to see the female worker about plans for the baby and dealt with the situation quite responsibly, with the male worker she talked about the possibility of working, which he encouraged. Through his efforts, Miss A took a job in the postoffice, did excellent work there (enough to receive part of a maternity leave with pay), and talked with both of her workers about the new "but different" men in her life who "seem to respect me."

While a case situation like Miss A's will remain open for some time and Miss A will see both workers intermittently, at one interview she explained the modifications in her life by saying: "I got a good mommy and daddy—that's all you need to feel good!"

Miss L, a 19-year-old Jewish girl, came to a family agency during her fourth month of pregnancy. Referred by a physician, she blurted out in her first intake interview: "I want to give up my baby for adoption." The female caseworker immediately responded: "Then I think you've come to the right place. That's our business here; maybe we can help you!" The client, a little surprised, said: "Good, I thought you'd want to ask me a bunch of personal questions!" The worker responded: "Oh, I thought you'd want to ask me a bunch of questions!" The client stated that she did, and asked many pertinent questions about hospital delivery, seeing the baby, nurses, residence, and so on, all of which the worker answered directly, truthfully, and factually. Miss L gladly initiated a second appointment with the same worker, and on leaving said: "Enjoyed it!"

Miss L arrived on time for her second appointment and within a few minutes volunteered without prompting the details of her pregnancy and of previous relationships with young men. She was able to say: "I know I've used sex to make me feel adequate. I guess I've wondered most of my life how much of a female I am!" When the intake worker asked her how she accounted for her "feeling of inadequacy," Miss L described her relationships with her parents. According to her, her mother was extremely concerned with her own appearance and "always squabbled with my father." Her father was described as a "sensitive and passionate man," who "used to tickle me a lot." Further references to Miss L's father led the worker to help her focus on the highly stimulating experiences with him and the longings she felt for him when her parents separated when she was 16. On her own, Miss L dated her sexual acting out with her father's leaving home.

Miss L participated actively in the intake interviews and eventually requested treatment. She was assigned a male worker to whom she eagerly remarked in the first interview: "I need to see a man counselor so that I can get along with men better." Rather quickly she attempted to initiate a mutually seductive relationship with the worker. When he pointed this out to her, she experienced it as a rejection, saying quite pitifully: "No men like me," and recalled relationships with young men in which she felt abandonment and rejection. The worker responded: "Just because it wouldn't be good for treatment for me to have sex with you doesn't mean I want to leave you!" The treatment became quite challenging for Miss L at this point. She found it difficult to believe that a man could like her and yet not go to bed with her. Here the worker was able to say: "If we weren't more interested in seeing you get help it might be fun," thus demonstrating to her that a father figure could have sexual feelings but could control them.

Miss L continued her treatment after the baby was born. The worker was able to involve both of her parents in the delivery and adoption proceedings. Interestingly, Miss L's father asked for treatment himself and was referred for private psychotherapy. The female worker Miss L saw at intake was utilized at strategic times during the process—once when Miss L wanted information about gynecological matters and another time when Miss L was thinking about attending a college that was the worker's alma mater.

Miss L visited both workers after she left the community and went away to college. Eventually she became interested in a career in social work.

Summary and Conclusion

Examination of the social work literature on the unmarried mother and investigation of cases in selected agencies led to the conclusion that the dynamic formulations that have placed the prime etiological factor in the mother-daughter relationship required modification and further elaboration. While the importance of pre-Oedipal nurturing in the mother-daughter relationship should not be discounted in the study, diagnosis, or treatment of the unmarried mother, it was proposed that the client must be viewed within her total family constellation. Important, therefore, is the unmarried mother's perception of her parents' interaction as well as her unique relationship to her father.

De-emphasized in the literature has been the importance of the father's contribution to the unmarried mother's sexual difficulties. His seductiveness and eventual withdrawal were seen as prime factors in the development of the girl's difficulties. The question was raised as to whether the prevalence of unmarried motherhood in certain subcultures may be due, in part, to a high incidence of absence of the father.

A structured treatment plan involving male and female workers who would offer the unmarried mother a corrective emotional experience was presented along with case illustrations.

VASECTOMY

CHAPTER 74

Implications of Vasectomy
for Social Work Practice

Sarah F. Hafemann and Catherine S. Chilman

It has been estimated that over three million living Americans have had a vasectomy,[1] and the popularity of this procedure as a method of contraception has been growing in recent years. It is important that social workers become well informed on this subject so that they may more effectively carry out their various roles as counselors, educators, and social planners. However, little information has appeared in the professional social work journals about vasectomy and its effects. This article presents an overview of medical, social, and psychological research. Popular attitudes as reflected in the popular press are also surveyed, and some implications for social work practice are suggested.

Medical Aspects of Vasectomy

Vasectomy is a simple, safe surgical procedure performed to sterilize the male. It consists of cutting or blocking the tube (vas or vas deferens) through which sperm pass to the penis. As a method of male sterilization, vasectomy has been widely performed since the 1930s;[2] and today throughout the world it is the most commonly performed operation on the adult male.[3]

[1] Gilbert Kasirsky, *Vasectomy, Manhood and Sex* (New York: Springer, 1972), p. 17.

[2] W. S. Haynes, Vasectomy, *Medical Journal of Australia*, 20: 1045–48 (May 1967).

[3] Stanwood S. Schmidt, Vasectomy: Indications, Technic, and Reversibility, *Fertility and Sterility*, 19: 192–96 (March–April 1968).

Reprinted from *Social Casework*, Vol. 55 (June, 1974), pp. 343–351, by permission of the authors and the Family Service Association of America.

Physicians vary widely in the qualifications they demand of patients requesting a vasectomy for sterilization. Some doctors perform the operation with no evaluation of the patient's life situation or personality. Others may require a stable family unit, minimum ages for husband and wife, at least two children including at least one son, a personal interview, the consent of both husband and wife, a psychiatric evaluation, and a consultation with another physician.[4]

There may or may not be a physician-required waiting period before the actual operation. Most vasectomies are performed in the doctor's office under local anesthetic. The patient prepares himself at home by bathing and shaving the scrotal area. Then, in the office, the area is cleansed with antiseptic and the doctor manipulates the vas to separate it from other tissues so that it is positioned immediately under the skin. Local anesthetic is then injected into the skin and around the vas. The manipulation and injection are the only parts of the procedure that may be uncomfortable. After the anesthetic has taken effect, an incision of three-quarters to one inch is made on one side of the scrotum and a segment of the vas is lifted out.

Early methods involved cutting the vas and tying it to itself with the two ends pointing in opposite directions.[5] A more recent development includes the use of small tantalum clips to close off the vas.[6] There has been considerable criticism of the earlier method because it seems to lead to a greater chance of the formation of sperm granuloma (small nodules appearing around the cut end of the vas where sperm cells may be escaping) and eventual recanalization (forming of a new channel between the closed ends of the vas).[7] After the vas has been closed off, only a few stiches are required to close the incision in the scrotum. After one side has been completed, the procedure is performed on the other. Some physicians prescribe a sedative or tranquilizer for the patient to take before the operation. Any pain after the anesthetic wears off can usually be managed by aspirin and codeine.

After the operation, the patient should wear a scrotal supporter to prevent strain on the wound. Most men can go back to work the day after the operation, and many vasectomies are scheduled for Friday mornings so the patient will have a weekend in which to recuperate. Intercourse may be resumed one to ten days after the operation.

---

[4] Harold Lear, Vasectomy—A Note of Concern, *Journal of the American Medical Association*, 219: 1206–07 (February 28, 1972); and D. M. Potts and G. I. M. Swyer, Effectiveness and Risks of Birth-control Methods, *British Medical Bulletin*, 26: 26–32 (January 1970).

[5] Kasirsky, *Vasectomy, Manhood and Sex*, p. 52.

[6] William M. Moss, A Sutureless Technic for Bilateral Partial Vasectomy, *Fertility and Sterility*, 23: 33–37 (January 1972).

[7] Stanwood S. Schmidt, Vasectomy, *Journal of the American Medical Association*, 206: 522 (April 19, 1971); and Donald J. Dodds, Reanastomosis of the Vas Deferens, *Journal of the American Medical Association*, 220: 1498 (June 12, 1972).

It is crucial to realize that sterility does not result immediately. Even though no new spermatozoa will be released, there will be mature sperm remaining in the male's reproductive tract. For this reason, sperm counts must be made before other contraceptive measures can be safely abandoned. Samples are obtained either by masturbation or the use of a condom during intercourse. There has been continuing debate whether the samples should be requested after a certain amount of time or after a certain number of ejaculations. Research has shown that approximately 68 percent of any remaining sperm is ejaculated at each emission.[8] The suggestion has been made that the first sperm count be made after ten ejaculations instead of waiting twelve to sixteen weeks after the operation.[9]

The operation is considered to be extremely safe in terms of mortality and is also the most effective method of birth control, with a failure rate of .15 pregnancies per year per 100 couples; this rate is slightly lower than that for tubal ligation and considerably lower than for any other contraceptive method.[10]

As far as morbidity rates for vasectomy are concerned, there is great variation depending on interpretation by the patient or the doctor.[11] The most common immediate complications of vasectomy are infection, bruising, and pain. All three can be kept to a minimum by careful surgical technique.[12] Study has shown that these problems are bothersome to only a small proportion of vasectomy patients. At present, the most significant long-range complication appears to be formation of spermatic granulomas which may occur in the epididymis or at the cut end of the vas any time after vasectomy. These may become painful and require surgical removal.

Perhaps the most disconcerting complication of vasectomy is spontaneous recanalization of the vas, with the possibility of a resultant impregnation. The risk of this happening is about one-half to one precent.[13] Some doctors feel that what actually may happen is simple failure to maintain other contraceptive measures until sterility is finally achieved, but others disagree with this viewpoint.[14]

Possible long-term effects of vasectomy on the hormonal balance have also been investigated. Of major importance is the fact that the production

---

[8] Matthew Freund et al., Disappearance Rate of Spermatozoa from the Ejaculate Following Vasectomy, *Fertility and Sterility*, 20: 163–70 (January–February 1969).

[9] Schmidt, Vasectomy, p. 522.

[10] Joseph E. Davis, Vasectomy, *American Journal of Nursing*, 72: 509–13 (March 1972).

[11] Davis, Vasectomy, p. 509.

[12] Stanwood S. Schmidt, Technics and Complications of Elective Vasectomy: The Role of Spermatic Granuloma in Spontaneous Recanalization, *Fertility and Sterility*, 17: 467–81 (July–August 1966).

[13] Davis, Vasectomy, p. 511.

[14] C. D. Muller, Consideration of Sterilization Vasectomy, *Northwest Medicine*, 54: 1,427–30 (December 1955).

of sperm is not affected by vasectomy.[15] Not only do sperm continue to be produced, but also testosterone, the male sex hormone.[16]

There is a sizable body of medical literature available on the subject of reanastomosis (the surgical reversal of sterility due to vasectomy). This operation is extremely difficult to perform and the success rate tends to be low.[17]

With restoration of fertility so difficult, it has been proposed that men could protect themselves against the need to have the operation reversed by freezing some of their sperm and placing it in a sperm bank in case another child were wanted at a later date. Although the techniques of sperm banking have been developed, there has been little research on patient demand for this service.

Medical opinion has given greater acceptance to vasectomy in recent years. In 1968, the American Medical Association examined the reasons doctors cited for not performing vasectomies—legal or religious considerations and concern for psychiatric trauma. This editorial concluded that vasectomy for reason of contraception alone should be available to couples who did not display psychiatric contraindications.[18]

Psychological Aspects of Vasectomy

Any couple's experience with vasectomy is complex, with many factors influencing their response to this method of birth control. The research on the psychological aspects of vasectomy reflects the difficulty of studying such subjective phenomena. Much of the work has been colored by the individual bias of the investigator. The relative lack of valid and reliable studies in this area has been a serious omission in the literature of medicine and the behavioral sciences. Work already done can start to answer some of the questions related to vasectomy but a great deal more research is needed.

The medical literature includes several studies reported by doctors who have done vasectomies in their private practices. For the most part, the studies show overwhelming approval of the operation on the part of the patients. These studies, however, have many shortcomings. Usually only

[15] R. S. Grewal and M. S. Sachan, Changes in Testicle After Vasectomy: An Experimental Study, *International Surgery*, 49: 460–62 (May 1968).

[16] Raymond G. Bunge, Plasma Testisterone Levels in Man Before and After Vasectomy, *Investigative Urology*, 10:9 (July 1972).

[17] David Rosenbloom, Reversal of Sterility Due to Vasectomy, *Fertility and Sterility*, 7: 540–45 (November–December 1956).

[18] Voluntary Male Sterility, *Journal of the American Medical Association*, 204: 821–22 (May 27, 1968).

surface questions are asked, such as "How would you rate your enjoyment of sexual intercourse since the operation?" and "Would you have the operation if you had it to do all over again?"[19] Characteristically, these studies are conducted over a short period of time, usually six months to a year after the operation. Often the questionnaires do not include open-ended questions but only a checklist for the respondent to complete. It is further reported that many men do not go to their regular family physician for this operation and therefore are not as likely to return to the doctor who performed the actual surgery if difficulties arise.[20]

The studies undertaken by psychiatrists and psychologists specifically to investigate psychosexual results of vasectomy also tend to be unsatisfactory. One of the difficulties is the bias introduced by Freudian theory. Freud's teachings regarding the Oedipal complex and castration anxiety predispose many researchers to expect pathology to result from vasectomy and thus to direct their investigations toward possible pathological outcomes. Many of these studies are further weakened by the use of very small samples, with the heightened possibility of sampling error. Adequate control groups were not set up in a number of investigations. As with the doctors' studies discussed above, many of these studies have not been conducted over a sufficient length of time.

In addition to the methodological difficulties with much of the published research, a new problem has been introduced in our understanding of this aspect of vasectomy. The rapid increase in the number of men undergoing this surgery and the seeming acceptance of this method of birth control may drastically alter many psychological and social effects of male sterilization. As vasectomy becomes increasingly accepted throughout society, the lessened negative cultural sanctions may make the vasectomized male feel less deviant or defensive. Earlier studies that revealed temporary adverse social-psychological effects for some males might yield fewer negative findings if they were carried out today.

The best-known and most careful research in this area was undertaken by David A. Rodgers and Frederick J. Ziegler. Their first article reports on a group of forty-eight California males who underwent vasectomy. Preoperative tests showed that this sample was "much more representative of the stable, productive, successful group in the culture than either the emotionally disturbed or the economically and socially improvident group" and they appeared to be "motivated primarily by rational considerations and were relatively free of neurotic concerns about the consequences of

[19] Pauline Jackson et al., A Male Sterilization Clinic, *British Medical Journal*, 4: 295–97 (October 31, 1970).

[20] Elzena Barnes and Glenna B. Johnson, Effects of Vasectomy on Marriage Relationships: A Descriptive Analysis of 26 Cases Seen in Marriage Counseling by Family Service-Travelers Aid, Des Moines, Iowa, 1964 (unpublished).

the operation.''[21] A follow-up study of thirty-five of these men between one and two years postoperatively found that although they expressed almost unanimous satisfaction with the operation, the Minnesota Multiphasic Personality Inventory (MMPI) scores indicated evidence of increased psychological disturbance for some of them. The authors suggested that preoperative hypochondriasis or concern over masculinity may be predictive of difficulties following vasectomy.[22]

Rodgers and Ziegler continued their work with a larger study involving forty-two couples who chose vasectomy and thirty-nine couples who chose ovulation suppression pills as their method of birth control. Two subgroups of twenty-two couples each—closely matched in terms of age, early sexual history, education, and income—were also studied. Initial testing and interviews were conducted, and follow-up testing and psychiatric interviews were conducted, two years later. When the vasectomy group was compared to the pill group, the first was found to do more poorly, on the average, in the areas of sexual and psychiatric adjustment and marital satisfaction. Some of the vasectomized men emphasized masculine role behavior which called for modifications in their wife's behavior and in the marriage itself. ''We thus infer that the vasectomy husbands are more vulnerable to the threats of the typical husband-wife rivalries than they were preoperatively.''[23] In a later discussion of these findings, the authors suggest that the vasectomized men tended to avoid behavior that might call into question either their manliness or the appropriateness of the operation. In so doing they showed an increase in culturally approved masculine behavior, along with a decrease in the kind of behavioral flexibility that would be most conducive to a happy personal life and comfortable marriage.[24]

Despite research evidence of poorer average psychological functioning, the vasectomy group expressed satisfaction with the operation and tended to blame other events for changes in their personal or marital lives. The study further reported that the vasectomy couples felt that the preoperative interview was quite useful in reducing or eliminating confusion about the operation. The postoperative interview was also reported by some to have improved understanding and communication between hus-

---

[21] David A. Rodgers et al., Sociopsychological Characteristics of Patients Obtaining Vasectomies from urologists, *Marriage and Family Living*, 25: 335 (August 1963).

[22] David A. Rodgers et al., A Longitudinal Study of the Psycho-Social Effects of Vasectomy, *Journal of Marriage and the Family*, 27: 59–64 (February 1965).

[23] Frederick J. Ziegler, David A Rodgers, and Sali Ann Kriegsman, Effect of Vasectomy on Psychological Functioning, *Psychosomatic Medicine*, 28: 62 (January-February 1966).

[24] David A. Rodgers, Frederick J. Ziegler,, and Nissim Levy, Prevaling Cultural Attitudes About Vasectomy: A Possible Explanation of Postoperative Psychological Response, *Psychosomatic Medicine*, 29: 367–75 (July–August 1967).

band and wife. The authors suggest that such discussion may attenuate the potential traumatic impact of vasectomy.

In attempting to identify the causes of the poorer adjustment of the vasectomy group, a study of prevailing cultural attitudes about vasectomy was undertaken in the mid-1960s. Projective tests were given to a group of seventeen couples of a Protestant church group and 127 undergraduate psychology students to determine their attitudes toward couples using oral contraceptives or vasectomy. The couple using vasectomy was seen in a less favorable light by both groups, but there was no consistent characteristic ascribed to the vasectomy couple. According to the authors, a major problem about this form of contraception for the vasectomized male is the nonspecificity of the negative cultural judgment. Thus, the judgment "could never be completely disconfirmed [sic]."[25]

In a follow-up study, the researchers noted a return to virtual similarity between the oral contraceptive and vasectomy groups over four years' time. Differences in scores on the MMPI and the California Psychological Inventory decreased for both groups of husbands and wives. The investigators expressed some surprise that, in light of some of the earlier studies, they did not find more sizable long-range changes in the psychological functioning of the vasectomy couples. Although the sample was too small to develop predictive capability adequately, it appears that the earlier impression that hypochondriacal men or men insecure about their masculinity are unsuited to vasectomy was not validated four years postoperatively. The investigators also stressed that the extensive contact with the study team which provided opportunities to ventilate and discuss areas of concern may have prevented some adverse reactions.[26] It should be recalled, however, that Ziegler and his colleagues studied only a small group of couples, that these people were generally middle-class and economically secure, and that extensive counseling may well have been a factor in mitigating possible negative after-effects. So far as we now know, the ultimate effects of vasectomy on personal and marital adjustments are not likely to be different from those associated with use of oral contraceptives.

The task of investigating the psychological ramifications of vasectomy is not yet complete, but several old wives' tales may have been disproved. Research findings show that, in all likelihood, vasectomy does not cure sexual problems. Although release from the fear of an unwanted pregnancy may increase a couple's pleasure in lovemaking, a vasectomy apparently does not cure frigidity, impotence, or premature ejaculation. Vasectomy seems not to increase or decrease infidelity, divorce, or sepa-

---

[25] Ibid., p. 373.

[26] Frederick J. Ziegler, David A. Rodgers, and Robert J. Prentiss, Psychological Response to Vasectomy, *Archives of General Psychiatry*, 21: 46–54 (July 1969).

ration.[27] It also does not appear that men are pressured to have vasectomies by overbearing wives.

Changing Public Attitudes

It has been suggested that cultural attitudes influence men's adjustment after vasectomy. An examination of the popular press, from 1960 to the present, provides ample evidence of a shift in public opinion about sterilization.

Throughout the early 1960s, vasectomy gained in popularity. In the five-year period of 1959–1964, the incidence of vasectomy doubled. Attitudes changed slowly, however; even in the mid-1960s "to most Americans there [was] something peculiarly disturbing about the words 'abortion' and 'sterilization.' They [were] uncomfortable words, not exactly obscene but not polite either."[28] Advocates of voluntary stterilization did not propagandize so much as they simply attempted to break down prejudices.

The spectacular increase in vasectomy began in 1967 with the first warnings from British doctors of the possibility of blood clots forming as a result of taking birth control pills. The number of vasectomies has doubled every year since then. Several other factors were also responsible: the 1965 Supreme Court ruling in *Griswold* v. *Connecticut* which expanded the right of privacy to include birth control; the 1968 decision by Planned Parenthood–World Population to include voluntary sterilization in its program; and the decisions of the United States Department of Health, Education, and Welfare and the Blue Cross-Blue Shield to approve payments for voluntary sterilization. The decline of American puritanism and the growing concern about the problems of overpopulation also influenced the rising popular acceptance of sterilization. A crucial step in the changing of public opinion was the gradual conversion of the medical profession. In 1968, an editorial in the *Journal of the American Medical Association* declared vasectomy to be "safe, quick, effective and legal" and took doctors to task for not performing the operation in the absence of certain contraindications.[29]

The 1970 Senate hearing on the safety of the birth control pill stimulated a further surge of interest in vasectomy. Articles describing vasectomy and discussing its tremendous gain in popularity appeared in numerous popular magazines. The information contained in these articles

[27] D. A. Rodgers and Frederick J. Ziegler, Changes in Sexual Behavior Consequent to Use of Noncoital Procedures of Contraception, *Psychosomatic Medicine*, 30: 495–505 (September–October 1968).

[28] Walter Goodman, Abortion and Sterilization: The Search for Answers, *Redbook*, October 1965, pp. 70–71.

[29] Voluntary Male Sterility, p. 822.

appeared to be medically accurate; it was stressed that vasectomy is not castration and does not alter sex drive or performance. Husbands who had had vasectomies were portrayed as intelligent, considerate, and assured of their manhood.

The 1970 National Fertility Studies reported:

> By 1970 sterilization was the first choice of contracepting [sic] couples where the wife was 30–44 years old (25 percent, as against 21 percent for the pill); and among couples of all ages intending no more children, sterilization was second only to the pill.[30]

These data reflect practices antedating the Senate hearings on possible adverse side effects of the birth control pill. Statistics obtained today would probably show an even higher use of sterilization.

Female sterilization is more prevalent among blacks than whites and is used by 21 percent of the fertile black couples who desire no more children versus 18 percent for whites. However, vasectomy is nine times more prevalent among whites than blacks. Blacks and low-income people may be reluctant to seek vasectomies because of misinformation about the consequences of the operation. Vasectomy, as opposed to tubal ligation, is most acceptable to low-parity white couples with above-average education and income. Fears of genocide are frequently expressed by some black males. In general, cultural innovations tend to be picked up first by urban people at higher socioeconomic levels.

The pendulum has now begun to swing away from a wholesale endorsement of vasectomy. Concern has been expressed that vasectomy may become a fad. William A. Nolen has urged that couples consider in advance all aspects of vasectomy, including fears regarding the operation, its nearirreversibility, the possibility of divorce or death of spouse or of children, and assumptions that the operation would, of itself, solve marital problems.[31] The issue of formation of sperm antibodies in the vasectomized male has signaled the beginning of a reappraisal of the safety of the operation. Additional medical research addressed to this problem has not yet made its way into the popular press.

At present there are still many couples who have completed their families or have chosen to forego parenthood completely but have not chosen a permanent method of birth control. The incidence of vasectomy is likely to increase as more of these couples learn what vasectomy involves, talk to friends or relatives who have had the operation, and become concerned about the possible deficiencies of other birth control methods.

---

[30] Harriet B. Presser and Larry L. Bumpass, The Acceptability of Contraceptive Sterilization. Among U.S. Couples: 1970, *Family Planning Perspectives*, 6: 18–26 (October 1972).

[31] William A. Nolen, Vasectomy: A Cautionary Note, *McCall's*, June 1972, p. 60.

Implications for Social Work Practice

Although not exhaustive, the social and psychological research on vasectomy can provide important leads for social workers. The implications of the available research touch on the areas of prevasectomy screening and postoperative follow-up, marital discord after vasectomy, pregnancy after vasectomy, and the desire for reversal of sterilization.

These implications might well apply to social workers in such activities as program-planning and program development, education, and counseling. They may also apply to social workers in a variety of settings: medical, family service, marriage counseling, family life education, and so on. As literature reviewed in this article suggests, vasectomy involves more than a medical procedure. Social workers, as well as physicians and other human service professionals, have important contributions to make. The social worker involved in such a team approach will require additional training beyond the basic understanding of human sexuality and birth control that all social workers should possess. The training necessary for social workers who frequently work with couples and individuals who may be considering vasectomy should include advanced understanding of vasectomy and alternative contraceptive methods and techniques, including the experience of observing a vasectomy operation; effective counseling and therapy skills; and, finally, a clear and continuing awareness of one's bias and values and those of any sponsoring agency. Implications for counseling and education include consideration of factors related to both prevasectomy decision-making and postoperative adjustments.

Social and psychological prevasectomy screening should probably be conducted in a joint interview with both partners, preferably by a male-female interview team unless special circumstances indicate other approaches. To rule out possible undue influence of one spouse by the other, each should also be interviewed separately. The counselor should explore the reasons both the male and his spouse have for seeking a vasectomy as well as their related attitudes, feelings, and understandings. Before the vasectomy, the couple should be encouraged to consider how their decision might be affected by divorce or death of a spouse or the illness or death of their children, if they have any. Alternatives of adoption and sperm-banking should be explained realistically. (At present, frozen sperm does not seem to last indefinitely, and adoptable children are becoming less available.) Couples should be discouraged from thinking of the surgical reversal of vasectomy as a possibility, since the chance of restoration of fertility is so low. The final decision should be left until the couple have been fully informed, have achieved a clear understanding of the possible complications, and have examined their feelings regarding future changes in their life situation. The social worker should be clear that the couple also have thorough knowledge of alternative birth control measures.

No scale has yet been devised to predict which couples may regret vasectomy or have related social or psychological problems. Contraindications to vasectomy include such factors as impulsiveness, high levels of related anxiety on the part of either partner, hopes that a vasectomy will improve the marital relationship, or a decision based on an overzealous commitment to population control or women's liberation ideology. Social workers should not be too quick, however, to reject couples who manifest some degree of anxiety, insecurity, or difficulty in their relationship, because (1) any surgery is likely to be accompanied by some anxiety; (2) no intimate relationship is completely free of problems; and (3) no individual is completely free of sex-role confusion or insecurity.

In their contributions to the formulation of administrative policy, as well as in their handling of screening interviews, social workers will need to be aware of their own biases about vasectomies for certain couples, for example, very young or childless couples. A possible result of a too-rigid policy regarding acceptance or exclusion is that many couples would seek the operation from physicians who have no screening procedures at all and no provision for follow-up. Policies can be flexible if the couple are provided the opportunity to discuss fully their expectations and anxieties, if the couple have adequate knowledge of vasectomy and of alternative methods of contraception, and if they appear to be comfortable and firm in their decision.

Ideally, every couple who choose vasectomy as a method of birth control should be encouraged to come in for a postoperative interview at the time of the second sperm count. This interview would allow for discussion and clarification of any anxieties or problems that have arisen or may be foreseen. If pre- and postoperative interviews with a knowledgeable and skilled counselor like a social worker become common, it is possible that the rate of postoperative complications might decline.

According to the available research evidence, these postoperative problems involve sexual dysfunction, pregnancy, and a desire for reanastomosis. Sexual dysfunction after vasectomy is usually of psychological origin. For example, if the fear of pregnancy is used by a couple to restrict their sexual activities, a vasectomy eliminates their rationale. With this limit removed, they may find that one or both of them may not wish to engage in more frequent intercourse for a variety of reasons. Skilled marriage counseling may help the couple resolve problems in this area.

According to available evidence, the likelihood of pregnancy following vasectomy is very small. Spontaneous reanastomosis occurs rarely. If the male has received laboratory confirmation of his sterility, the chance of viable sperm remaining in his reproductive tract is also minimal. In the rare case that pregnancy does occur after vasectomy, it may be accompanied by suspicion of the wife's infidelity or the wife's fear that she is suspect. Skilled social workers may be helpful in these cases.

Ill-advised physicians have frequently let the couple work such problems out by themselves; social workers should not ignore such problems and can perform a useful function. A first step is a repeat sperm count to assess the possibility of a reanastomosis. The question of abortion may also be raised. Social pressure on the couple may be great if family and friends have been informed that a vasectomy had been obtained. Some couples may not wish to have a sperm count and will assume that the pregnancy resulted from spontaneous reanastomosis, rather than confront directly the question of infidelity.

Inevitably, some couples will change their minds about vasectomy and will request reanastomosis. The social worker should not hold out bright promise to these people. Vasectomy must be considered as permanent. Because possibility of surgical correction of vasectomy is so slight and because the surgery is so much more complex than the original vasectomy, it may be more fruitful to explore the significance of the reemergent desire for children and the acceptability of substituting other goals or satisfactions. In the case of the death of a child, the desire for another child may be a manifestation of grief and a sense of loss which, with help, can be accepted without the need to restore fertility. In cases of remarriage after divorce or the death of a spouse, the desire to cement the marriage may be expressed by other means than conceiving a child. If a couple's economic or emotional situation has changed and they feel themselves able to care for additional children, adoption or foster care may be suggested.

Most social workers will see problems related to vasectomy in the context of problems within the marriage and family. Ziegler and fellow researchers have suggested that vasectomy may produce changes in the husband's and wife's behavior that may increase marital tension.[32] These changes reflect a polarization of male and female behavior as a result of the male's trying to prove that his masculinity is not impaired. Recent changes in public opinion that give greater social approval to vasectomy may have reduced the likelihood of this possible effect. Social workers should check for increased sex-role rigidity in couples who experience increased marital tension after vasectomy. Techniques useful in marital and family counseling are apt to be appropriate here.

Within the society as a whole and in their roles as program planners and educators, social workers can contribute to policies that provide freedom of individual decision-making regarding vasectomies and access to high-quality related services for people at all income levels. Recent court cases have affirmed the right of a woman to be sterilized at her own request.[33] There has not been a comparable decision on vasectomy. It is desirable that freedom and rights in this area be scrupulously maintained.

[32] Ziegler, Rodgers, and Kriegsman, Effect of Vasectomy on Psychological Functioning, p. 62.
[33] Vivian Cadden, Very Private Decision, *Good Housekeeping*, May 1972, p. 85.

As in many other areas, it is important that social workers not project their own values or bias on their clients. Properly informed, they can join with other professionals in educating the public about vasectomy and in assuring that adequate related services, including counseling, are made available to all persons who desire them.

Index